Hugo Münsterberg's Psychology and Law

American Psychology-Law Society Series

Books in the Series

Emergency Department Treatment of the Psychiatric Patient
Susan Stefan

The Psychology of the Supreme Court
Lawrence S. Wrightsman

Proving the Unprovable
Christopher Slobogin

Adolescents, Media, and the Law
Roger J. R. Levesque

Oral Arguments Before the Supreme Court
Lawrence S. Wrightsman

God in the Courtroom
Brian H. Bornstein and Monica K. Miller

Expert Testimony on the Psychology of Eyewitness Identification
Edited by Brian L. Cutler

The Psychology of Judicial Decision-Making
Edited by David Klein and Gregory Mitchell

The Miranda Ruling: Its Past, Present, and Future
Lawrence S. Wrightsman and Mary L. Pitman

Juveniles at Risk: A Plea for Preventive Justice
Christopher Slobogin and Mark R. Fondacaro

The Ethics of Total Confinement
Bruce A. Arrigo, Heather Y. Bersot, and Brian G. Sellers

International Human Rights and Mental Disability Law
Michael L. Perlin

Applying Social Science to Reduce Violent Offending
Edited by Joel Dvoskin, Jennifer L. Skeem, Raymond W. Novaco, and Kevin S. Douglas

Children Who Resist Postseparation Parental Contact
Barbara Jo Fidler, Nicholas Bala, and Michael A. Saini

Trauma, Stress, and Wellbeing in the Legal System
Edited by Monica K. Miller and Brian H. Bornstein

Psychology, Law, and the Wellbeing of Children
Edited by Monica K. Miller, Jared C. Chamberlain, and Twila Wingrove

Murder in the Courtroom: The Cognitive Neuroscience of Extreme Violent Behavior
Brigitte Vallabhajosula

Rational Suicide, Irrational Laws: Examining Current Approaches to Suicide in Policy and Law
Susan Stefan

International Perspectives on Violence Risk Assessment
Edited by Jay P. Singh, Stål Bjørkly, and Seena Fazel

Adolescence, Privacy, and the Law: A Developmental Science Perspective
Roger J. R. Levesque

The Ethical Practice of Forensic Psychology
Gianni Pirelli, Robert A. Beattey, and Patricia A. Zapf

The Jury Under Fire: Myth, Controversy, and Reform
Brian H. Bornstein and Edie Greene

The Science and Law of School Segregation and Diversity
Roger J. R. Levesque

Criminal Juries in the 21st Century: Contemporary Issues, Psychological Science, and the Law
Edited by Cynthia J. Najdowski and Margaret C. Stevenson

The Behavioral Science of Firearms
Gianni Pirelli, Hayley Wechsler, and Robert J. Cramer

A System of Pleas
Edited by Vanessa A. Edkins and Allison D. Redlich

Hugo Münsterberg's Psychology and Law

A Historical and Contemporary Assessment

Brian H. Bornstein

and

Jeffrey S. Neuschatz

OXFORD
UNIVERSITY PRESS

OXFORD
UNIVERSITY PRESS

Oxford University Press is a department of the University of Oxford. It furthers the University's objective of excellence in research, scholarship, and education by publishing worldwide. Oxford is a registered trade mark of Oxford University Press in the UK and certain other countries.

Published in the United States of America by Oxford University Press
198 Madison Avenue, New York, NY 10016, United States of America.

CIP data is on file at the Library of Congress
ISBN 978–0–19–069634–4

9 8 7 6 5 4 3 2 1

Printed by Marquis, Canada

In memory of Jere Link, who taught me to appreciate several things that contributed to the making of this book: German history and culture, a well-made manhattan, and the life of the mind.

—BB

I dedicate this book to Rita Neuschatz and Jimmy D. Reed for their unconditional love and support. A better mother and father-in-law I could not ask for.

—JN

Contents

Series Foreword

This book series is sponsored by the American Psychology-Law Society (AP-LS; www.ap-ls.org). AP-LS is an interdisciplinary organization devoted to scholarship, practice, and public service in psychology and law. Its goals include advancing the contributions of psychology to the understanding of law and legal institutions through basic and applied research; promoting the education of psychologists in matters of law and the education of legal personnel in matters of psychology; and informing the psychological and legal communities and the general public of current research, educational, and service activities in the field of psychology and law. AP-LS membership includes psychologists from the academic, research, and clinical practice communities as well as members of the legal community. Research and practice are represented in both the civil and criminal legal arenas. AP-LS has chosen Oxford University Press as a strategic partner because of its commitment to scholarship, quality, and the international dissemination of ideas. These strengths will help AP-LS reach its goal of educating the psychology and legal professions and the general public about important developments in psychology and law. The focus of the book series reflects the diversity of the field of psychology and law, as we will publish books on a broad range of topics.

In the latest book in the series, *Hugo Münsterberg's Psychology and Law: A Historical and Contemporary Assessment*, Brian Bornstein and Jeffrey Neuschatz have authored a book that is as interesting as it is instructive. Replicating the structure of Münsterberg's original text, *On the Witness*

Stand (1908), Bornstein and Neuschatz take the reader chapter by chapter through each of Münsterberg's essays, providing a summary of each and the conclusions reached by Münsterberg as well as a description of the current state of the science for the topic of focus. The summary of Münsterberg's work, interwoven with a contemporary analysis of the issues, provides readers with both a historical as well as a contemporary understanding of issues relevant to psychology and law.

Bornstein and Neuschatz begin with a brief overview of Münsterberg and his contributions and then move into a replication of *On the Witness Stand*, starting with an introduction, and then moving into chapters on illusions, the memory of the witness, the detection of crime, the traces of emotions, untrue confessions, suggestions in court, hypnotism and crime, and the prevention of crime, with each chapter presenting a compelling historical and contemporary analysis. The icing on the cake is the final chapter by Bornstein and Neuschatz, which summarizes what Münsterberg got right, what he missed, and what we're missing now.

Hugo Münsterberg's Psychology and Law: A Historical and Contemporary Assessment presents a comprehensive and detailed analysis of issues addressed by Münsterberg in 1908 and that remain relevant today. Scholars, researchers, policymakers, and practitioners will find this book a compelling and informative overview of the history and current state of psychology and law.

Patricia A. Zapf
Series Editor

Acknowledgments

Many books have a long gestation period, but this one's was longer than most. In one sense, it has been building since Hugo Münsterberg published *On the Witness Stand* in 1908. In another, more realistic sense, it has been percolating for roughly 13 years. Around 2005, Steve Penrod shared with one of us (Brian) an early book on psychology and law by G. F. Arnold, which was published 2 years before Münsterberg's book. In 2007 Brian and Steve presented a paper analyzing Arnold's view of the field, and comparing it to Münsterberg's, at a conference—entitled *Off* the Witness Stand—hosted by the John Jay College of Criminal Justice in honor of the upcoming centennial of Münsterberg's book (Bornstein & Penrod, 2008). The conference inspired Brian, in collaboration with Chris Meissner, to propose a special issue on Münsterberg to the journal *Applied Cognitive Psychology*. The special issue appeared the following year as "Basic and Applied Issues in Eyewitness Research: A Münsterberg Centennial Retrospective" (Bornstein & Meissner, 2008). The conversations with Steve and Chris, and the papers from the conference and special issue, made two things very clear: first, although Münsterberg was generally regarded as the founder of psychology and law, his specific contributions to the field had become somewhat neglected over time; and second, there were a lot more efforts being made, by many more scientists, in early attempts to apply psychology to legal issues than just those of Hugo Münsterberg.

The time therefore seemed ripe for a book offering a historical and contemporary reappraisal of Münsterberg's psycholegal work. The idea morphed through several iterations until Jeff's coming on board as coauthor lent the project renewed energy and focus, and led eventually to the present volume. This final incarnation has benefited from those early conversations and collaborative efforts with Steve Penrod and Chris Meissner. Other colleagues have contributed to the book as well, in ways small and large. We received helpful feedback and suggestions on some of the chapters from Jonathan Golding and Monica Miller; assistance preparing the references from Danielle DeLoach, Megan Hillgartner, Baylee Jenkins, and Alexis LeGrand; and a keen proofreading eye from Ginger Neuschatz, Preston Mote, and Kylie Key. Brian benefited from time off from some of his usual teaching responsibilities at the University of Nebraska–Lincoln while working on the book. In addition, this material is based upon work Brian completed while serving at the National Science Foundation. Any opinions, findings, and conclusions or recommendations expressed in this material are those of the authors and do not necessarily reflect the views of the National Science Foundation. Any mistakes that remain are, of course, the authors' responsibility.

We are grateful to Patty Zapf, editor of the AP-LS book series; Sarah Harrington, editor for Oxford University Press; and the rest of the production team at Oxford. The AP-LS book series is an enormous contribution to the field, and we are honored to be a part of it. The series is in very good hands with Patty and Sarah, and we greatly value their support of this project. Moreover, we think the existence of the series, and the breadth of topics that it covers, would make Hugo Münsterberg very pleased and proud.

Writing this book has been a lot of fun, but it has also been demanding at times. It would have been much less fun, and much more demanding, without the love and support of our families. We cannot express enough our thanks to Melissa Bornstein, Lillian Bornstein, and Christie Emler, and to Ginger and Daniel Neuschatz, for their patience and understanding.

Finally, we dedicate this book to some very important people in our lives. Brian dedicates it to Jere Link, a dear friend who passed away about a year before the book's completion. Jere loved Germany, where we met in 1985, and he knew seemingly everything about its history and culture. He was incredibly generous with that knowledge (and his opinions!), and my thinking about a vast array of topics—history, literature, music, religion, letter writing, and bourbon cocktails, among many others—benefited greatly from his tutelage over the years. His impact on my intellectual development was more than I can say or repay, and I regret that I never thanked him for it. Fortunately, like all good teachers, he didn't do it for the recognition. Lieber Freund, how much I wish we could talk about Hugo Münsterberg over a manhattan or two, while listening to "Der Rosenkavalier."

Jeff dedicates the book to his mother, Rita Neuschatz, and his father-in-law, Jimmy D. Reed. Both provided support and encouragement throughout the project and frequently kept me motivated and on task. My mother has assumed this role throughout my whole life. I can't say enough to repay them for their love and kindness.

Hugo Münsterberg's Psychology and Law

1

Overview

Not the quiet work of the scientist's cell, but a far reaching public activity, the organization of the realms of politics and Kultur, the transference of scientific knowledge and methods to the demands of practical life. . . . But at the same time he was an investigator of penetrating sharpness, with a power of presentation marked by genius . . .

—from "Hugo Münsterberg: In Memoriam" (Stern, 1917, p. 186)

Credit: History and Art Collection / Alamy Stock Photo

Every field or school within psychology has one or more individuals who are acknowledged as "founders" or critical early figures: Watson for behaviorism, Freud for psychoanalysis, Piaget for developmental psychology, Lewin for social psychology. Arguably, the search for these founding fathers is simplistic and even misguided—the various schools, movements, and subdisciplines, like scientific psychology itself, arose more from the zeitgeist than from the efforts of a single, larger-than-life individual (Hunt, 2007). For example, Freud's predecessors and contemporaries who conducted and published very similar research included Adler, Breuer, Charcot, Janet, and Jung; Watson's work shared much in common with earlier and contemporaneous research conducted by Angell, Dewey, Pavlov, Thorndike, and Twitmyer. The reasons why one person becomes most closely associated with the development of a field, while others are lost to the mists of history, are complex, and they may have as much to do with luck and force of personality as with the work's intellectual merit or broader impact. This is not to detract from the key figures' contributions, which have stood the test of time, but merely to acknowledge that they were, to a very real extent, products of their times as well. Nonetheless, certain individuals stand out as unusually influential in a field's origins.

Among this group, a few select individuals have the distinction of contributing to the origin of multiple fields. One such figure is Hugo Münsterberg, who is widely regarded as one of, if not *the*, key figure in the development of both legal/forensic and industrial-organizational psychology.[1] For example, one textbook on the history of psychology (Lawson, Graham, & Baker, 2007) states that "Münsterberg was an early founder of forensic psychology" (p. 207) and that "Münsterberg may be considered America's first industrial psychologist" (p. 209). Münsterberg is unique for other reasons as well: He was a very public and controversial figure (this also applies to some other founders, such as Watson and Freud), and whereas many of the founders' ideas have fallen out of favor in mainstream academic psychology (e.g., Watson's radical behaviorism, Freud's psychoanalysis), many of the ideas and research approaches expounded by Münsterberg continue to thrive. Indeed, contemporary law-psychology is still grappling, by and large, with the same issues raised by Münsterberg in his seminal book *On the Witness Stand: Essays on Psychology and Crime* (1908; see Bornstein & Meissner, 2008).

An inspection of Münsterberg's book shows that it is still extremely topical and relevant. The book's title notwithstanding, it deals with a variety of topics in addition to witness (particularly eyewitness) testimony. More specifically, it addresses issues that are still hotly debated among psychologists, lawyers, and judges, such as the reliability of hypnosis, eyewitness suggestibility, false confessions, and criminal responsibility. The core topics—eyewitness testimony and confessions—are particularly important because of their role

---

[1] Another "double threat" is Lightner Witmer, whom many identify as the founder of both clinical and school psychology (Lawson, Graham, & Baker, 2007).

in wrongful convictions, as demonstrated by the recent spate of DNA exonerations. These topics have each been the subject of a "white paper" by the American Psychology-Law Society, reviewing the empirical research and discussing the implications for the criminal justice system (Kassin et al., 2010; Wells et al., 1998). Thus, despite being over 100 years old, Münsterberg's work still has major policy implications. However, the book itself is not widely circulated, and much modern psycholegal scholarship fails to acknowledge the debt it owes him.[2]

The purpose of the present volume is twofold: first, to summarize the chapters and conclusions of *On the Witness Stand*, making Münsterberg's insights available to a new generation of scholars and students; and second, to present the "state of the science" on the very issues that Münsterberg raises. Thus, the book provides a historical perspective, as well as a contemporary, comprehensive review of topics that are central to the discipline of psychology and law. In essence, each chapter asks, "What have we learned about this topic in the 110 years since Münsterberg first wrote about it? Has subsequent research shown him to be right or wrong?" The succeeding chapters will answer these questions by adopting a structure that parallels *On the Witness Stand*; each chapter will summarize the content of Münsterberg's corresponding chapter, interleaved with a contemporary assessment of the topic.

To introduce (or reintroduce) Münsterberg to modern readers, the remainder of this overview chapter includes a brief biography of Münsterberg and a summary of his research contributions. We then situate *On the Witness Stand* within the context of other contemporaneous work that addressed legal issues. The chapter also introduces considerations that are important to a reassessment of Münsterberg's work, such as evolving empirical and publishing practices in psychology and some of the divergent approaches within the field, such as basic versus applied approaches and clinical versus experimental psychology in legal contexts.

Hugo Münsterberg: A Biographical Sketch

Hugo Münsterberg was born on June 1, 1863, the son of a lumber merchant, and raised in Danzig, Germany, "the Venice of the North" (Münsterberg, 1917). Although his family was Jewish, Münsterberg converted to Lutheranism after his father died in 1880 (his mother had died when he was 11). The conversion was motivated by expediency more than by faith; Jews in Germany faced anti-Semitism and professional obstacles, especially in academia (Hale, 1980). He went to the University of Leipzig to study medicine but was diverted by a course offered by Wilhelm Wundt, whose experimental

[2] Electronic versions of *On the Witness Stand* are available, and Forgotten Books reprinted it in 2015 (available on amazon.com).

laboratory at Leipzig, formally opened in 1879, is generally regarded as the world's first formal psychology laboratory (others, such as William James and Wundt himself, previously conducted psychological research without the auspices of institutional recognition). Münsterberg joined Wundt's laboratory—working alongside James McKeen Cattell, among others—and earned his PhD in physiological psychology from Leipzig in 1885; he subsequently obtained his MD from the University of Heidelberg.

Münsterberg took a position at the University of Freiburg, where he was a private docent and subsequently "professor extraordinarius" of philosophy.[3] The latter position came with a stipend for laboratory expenses; his initial laboratory at Freiburg was in his own house and paid for with his own funds (Hale, 1980; Spillmann & Spillmann, 1993). He taught courses on philosophy, psychology, and education and quickly began drawing students from Germany and abroad (Spillmann & Spillmann, 1993). His first student to complete a PhD was Edmund Delabarre, an American who had studied previously with James (Münsterberg, 1917; Simon, 1996).

While a student at Leipzig and later on his own at Freiburg, Münsterberg often clashed with Wundt, the dominant (and domineering) figure in German psychology, and he chafed under Wundt's narrow conceptualization of the field. Experimental psychology also had only a marginal position at most German universities (Hale, 1980). Thus, in 1892, when James invited Münsterberg to replace him, for a 3-year term, as director of the psychology laboratory at Harvard, with its associated prestige and higher salary ($3,000/year), Münsterberg took a leave of absence from Freiburg to accept the position, which was within the Division of Philosophy. James and Münsterberg had met in 1889 at the First International Congress of Psychology in Paris, and they stayed in touch. James, who had his own issues with Wundt's approach to psychology, was very impressed with Münsterberg's work, which he cited in his *Principles of Psychology* (James, 1890; see Landy, 1992), and he was concerned that Harvard had fallen behind in the new science. Münsterberg took the position despite a somewhat low opinion of America, which he thought of at the time as "a land where no other interest but the hunt for the dollar is known and where humbug and corruption flourish" (Münsterberg, 1917, p. 36). He did not expect the move to be permanent, but merely "a kind of scientific expedition to the New World" and a romantic adventure for him and his wife (Münsterberg, 1917, p. 36). Münsterberg and James became close when they vacationed together in Switzerland in between Münsterberg's

[3] Although the title of "extraordinary professor" sounds impressive, it is the modern-day equivalent of an untenured assistant professor—someone without the responsibilities of an "ordinary" full professor. As a private docent, Münsterberg was somewhere between a private tutor and a lecturer, without a salary, and compensated from fees that students paid to attend his lectures (Hale, 1980; Landy, 1992). In a posthumous unfinished autobiography, he refers to himself as an assistant professor at the time (Münsterberg, 1917).

accepting the offer and traveling to the United States (James was on sabbatical in Europe at the time; Münsterberg, 1917).

Münsterberg enjoyed the intellectual ferment of Harvard and Boston society. He had an immediate impact at Harvard, where he established and ran a modern, complex facility with 40 rooms. The laboratory was organized on the German model; it had electricity, a machine shop, and equipment for various kinds of research, especially physiological, introspection, reaction time, and sensation and perception experiments (Hale, 1980; Landy, 1992; Popplestone & McPherson, 1994). Like many researchers of the day, Münsterberg had to create his own research tools, in the absence of standard, commercially available equipment. For example, he designed a chronoscope—known as the "Amerika" or Münsterberg chronoscope—that measured in units of .01 of a second (Popplestone & McPherson, 1994). Not even 30 years old when he first came to the United States, his initial stay at Harvard "was enormously successful" (Landy, 1992, p. 789)—in addition to establishing one of the best labs in the country, he published steadily, demonstrated mental tests at the 1893 World's Fair in Chicago, and was invited to be one of the 31 charter members of the American Psychological Association (APA) and one of only two non-Americans (with Cornell's Edward Titchener, an Englishman, the other). His courses were popular and had high enrollment; in his first year he co-taught introductory psychology (officially listed as Philosophy 2) with James before teaching it on his own in later years (Hale, 1980).

Nonetheless, he was uncomfortable in the United States, partly because of the language; he had learned Greek, Latin, and French as a schoolboy, as well as a little Arabic, but he did not study English until he was at Leipzig (Münsterberg, 1917). He could read English but did not speak or understand it well before coming to the United States (Hale, 1980). Shortly after arriving at Harvard, he sought (as he did for the remainder of his life) a full professor (Ordinarius) position at a prestigious German university, and he had only taken a leave of absence from Freiburg in the first place. In 1895, he took a leave of absence from Harvard and returned to his former position as Professor Extraordinarius at the University of Freiburg, bringing several of his American students with him (Spillmann & Spillmann, 1993). He was replaced at Harvard temporarily by Delabarre, who by then was teaching at Brown University (Simon, 1996).

Unable to obtain a more favorable position in Germany or a neighboring German-speaking country—a desirable position at the University of Zürich fell through, possibly due to anti-Semitism, and Freiburg declined to promote him—he gave up his German professorship and came back to Harvard in 1897. Despite losing interest in experimental work by this time, he renewed his direction of the laboratory and was elected Philosophy Division chair in 1900, a position he held until 1906 (Hale, 1980; Landy, 1992). Although he was occasionally tempted to return to Germany—especially when offered the philosophy chair at the University of Königsberg once held by Immanuel Kant (Münsterberg, 1917)—he spent the rest of his career at Harvard. He and his family made regular personal trips to Germany, and he spent a year from 1910 to 1911 as a visiting exchange professor at the University of Berlin. He described that year, in which "the emperor and all official Berlin" attended his opening address and he oversaw the creation of a new Amerika-Institut to facilitate cross-cultural exchange and understanding, as "the crowning year of my life" (Münsterberg, 1917, p. 46). Thus, although he never became fully Americanized or lost his deep sense of Germanness, Münsterberg eventually adapted reasonably well to his adopted home.

As described in the following sections, Münsterberg's scholarly interests expanded continually during his time at Harvard, a period in which the philosophy department was taking on an increasingly psychological flavor. He supervised a large number of graduate students, who spoke warmly of his mentoring and generosity (Hale, 1980). Many of his students went on to make significant contributions to psychology in their own right, including Floyd and Gordon Allport, Harold Burtt, Edwin Holt, William Marston, Sidney Pressey, Edward Tolman, and Robert Yerkes (Landy, 1992). Unlike nearly all of his contemporaries, Münsterberg also worked with and encouraged women students and hired them as his laboratory assistants (Lawson et al., 2007; Thorne & Henley, 2005). For example, after working with Mary Whiton Calkins, who was auditing classes at Harvard and participating in research, he petitioned Harvard to admit her as an official PhD candidate. Münsterberg wrote: "With regard to her ability, I may say that she is the strongest student of all who have worked in the laboratory in these three years. . . . The Harvard Ph.D. attached to the name of Mary W. Calkins would mean not only a well deserved honor for her, but above all an honor for the philosophical department of Harvard University" (Furumoto, 1980, p. 62). After Harvard refused to admit her, Münsterberg and several other faculty (including William James) held an unauthorized PhD examination for Calkins, which she passed. Despite never receiving her degree and experiencing discrimination throughout her career, Calkins had a long and distinguished career, which included being the first woman elected president of the APA in 1905 (Lawson et al., 2007).[4]

His support of Calkins and other women students notwithstanding, Münsterberg was hardly a feminist by today's standards. For example, he believed that many of the problems in American society could be traced to the decay of the family, especially traditional gender roles. He supported

---

[4] In 1902, Harvard approved a recommendation that Calkins, along with three other women who had done graduate work at Harvard but were ineligible for a Harvard PhD because of their gender, be awarded a PhD from Radcliffe College. Alone among the candidates, Calkins declined. Shortly before her death in 1930, a number of prominent Harvard psychology graduates—including Robert Woodworth, Robert Yerkes, and Edward Thorndike—again petitioned Harvard to award Calkins the PhD, but Harvard again refused (Lawson et al., 2007). Against this backdrop of widespread gender discrimination, Münsterberg's support of Calkins and other women students is particularly noteworthy.

education for women, but mainly to make them better wives, and not to make them independent or train them for careers (Hale, 1980). He believed that most women could not handle the rigors of advanced study anyway (i.e., Calkins was an exception). He even objected to the predominance of women schoolteachers, who were poor role models for young boys (Hale, 1980). Münsterberg wrote about "the intemperance of women," in which he criticized women for their hypocrisy in leading the prohibition movement while being intemperate in other aspects of their own behavior, such as spending money frivolously (Münsterberg, 1910a). He could also be paternalistic, as in discussing sex education. For example, "a thorough study indicates clearly that the girl who falls [into a life of prostitution] is not pushed passively into her misery" (Münsterberg, 1914a, p. 21). Rather, she knows too much about sex and lacks the moral fiber to resist temptation. These examples show that Münsterberg was, in most respects, a typical man of his class and generation.

His stature at Harvard, as well as his efforts to popularize and apply psychology (see later), made Münsterberg a leader not only in the field of psychology—he served as the seventh president of the APA in 1898—but something of a public intellectual. He was also president of the American Philosophical Association (1908–1909) and frequently sought out for his opinion on scientific and policy matters.[5] These activities, along with his scholarly and popular writings, made him "perhaps the best-known psychologist in America in the early part of the 20th century" (Thorne & Henley, 2005, p. 267). As further evidence of the high esteem in which he was generally held, he helped organize the International Congress of Arts and Sciences in St. Louis in 1904, was on the Nobel Prize nominating committee in physiology and medicine in 1906, and served on several editorial boards (Landy, 1992).

His attitudes toward and relationship with his adopted country were somewhat paradoxical. Despite never feeling quite at home in the United States, Münsterberg endeavored throughout his life to strengthen relations between Germany and the United States and to enhance their mutual understanding; German Americans were the country's largest minority at the time. He wrote frequently on American culture and customs from a German and psychological perspective, for both German and American audiences (e.g., Münsterberg, 1901, 1910a, 1913a). He was founding director of the Amerika-Institut in Berlin, which he envisioned as part of a larger "Auslands-Institut" (Foreign Institute), and he advocated the adoption of American higher education practices in German institutions (Stern, 1917). In general, "Münsterberg came to see his position at Harvard as that of a semiofficial ambassador from Germany to American academia" (Hale, 1980, p. 88).

[5] Holding the presidency of both the American Psychological and Philosophical Associations is an impressive achievement, but it was not that uncommon in the late 19th and early 20th centuries. Others to wear both hats include George Ladd, John Dewey, William James, and Mary Whiton Calkins.

Yet he also used his status as a prominent academician to share his views on controversial issues of the day, such as prohibition and America's entry into World War I, both of which he opposed. He opposed prohibition because he believed that moderate consumption of alcohol could yield social benefits, especially among industrial workers, such as increased efficiency (Hale, 1980; Münsterberg, 1913c)—albeit not when consumed at work. His position on alcohol was, arguably, not entirely disinterested; in exchange for his writings on the subject, wealthy German American brewers donated to some of his pet projects, such as Harvard's Germanic Museum (Hale, 1980). The rationale underlying his position on the war was simpler and less empirically driven; as a German, even after many years in the United States, he supported the fatherland, although he claimed it was more than that. He advocated nationalism as a general principle, which on a macro level contributed to historical progress and international relations, and on a micro level had an invigorating effect on the individual (Hale, 1980). His fervent support of Germany leading up to and during World War I (Münsterberg, 1914d, 1915b) led him to begin "a spiritual war against the traditional English sentiment at Harvard" (Stern, 1917, p. 186).[6]

Münsterberg seemed at times to be a provocateur who enjoyed a degree of notoriety—his principal biographer calls him "a publicist" (Hale, 1980, p. 3), and Sporer (2006, p. i) refers to him as "a market crier"—and his positions on these issues were not always popular. Combined with a personal style that many found pompous and condescending, the man himself became increasingly unpopular. His pro-German stance, as the events that precipitated World War I and the war itself unfolded, brought him condemnation and ridicule. He attempted to explain the war in terms of a fundamental historic conflict between the Teutonic ideal of thought and the Slavic ideal of feeling (Hale, 1980). At best he was seen as a naïve apologist for German militarism and imperialism (e.g., Powys, 1914); at worst he was suspected of being a German spy, even by some government figures, such as Robert Lansing, President Woodrow Wilson's Secretary of State (Hale, 1980). He meddled in politics, befriending the German ambassador to the United States and arranging for him to receive an honorary degree from Harvard. He communicated regularly with German and American government officials, even meeting and corresponding directly with Theodore Roosevelt, William Taft, and Woodrow Wilson, and he claimed to have influence over German Americans in electoral politics (Hale, 1980; Moskowitz, 1977).

These activities led to his losing many friends and his eventual ostracism. In a letter to his German colleague William Stern, he wrote: "Of course almost all of my old relations are severed, especially here in Boston. Most of my friends here no longer recognize me; I have been thrown out of clubs and put out of academies. All their rage has concentrated upon me. But we hold

[6] Münsterberg dedicated his first book-length defense of German actions around the time of World War I "to all lovers of fair play" (Münsterberg, 1914d); he dedicated the sequel "to my brothers" (Münsterberg, 1915b).

out" (Stern, 1917, p. 187). In Münsterberg's case, he held out against hate mail, death threats, and calls for his removal from the Harvard faculty, deportation, or internment. The president of Harvard, Charles Eliot, rebuked him on multiple occasions (Thorne & Henley, 2005). Thus, the last few years of his life were difficult, to say the least. It is no exaggeration to conclude that "At the time of his death . . . Münsterberg was an object of public scorn and was well on the way to professional ostracism" (Landy, 1992, p. 787).

He had not been back to Germany since 1912. He had planned to go with his family in the summer of 1914, but he was forced to postpone the trip when his daughter developed scarlet fever, and the outbreak of war that autumn postponed it permanently, to his great dismay. On December 16, 1916, Münsterberg suffered a fatal stroke, an event he feared as his health declined over the previous few years, while delivering a lecture at Radcliffe College. Harvard cancelled classes in his honor. His posthumous autobiography ends with the plaintive plea, "When shall I see my fatherland again" (Münsterberg, 1917, p. 48). World War I was responsible not only for his inability to travel to Germany in his later years, but also, to some extent, for the subsequent decline in his reputation. Within just a few years of his death, he had largely faded from the scene, due in large part to his perceived anti-Americanism—ironic, given his steady efforts to increase understanding between Germany and the United States—and his controversial, arguably publicity-seeking and self-aggrandizing personality (Landy, 1992). He continues to be mentioned in textbooks as an important historical figure, but little attention is paid to his scientific efforts. The scant appreciation of Münsterberg nowadays is unfortunate, as he made invaluable contributions to forensic psychology, among other psychological subdisciplines, and many of the issues he raised continue to resonate today.

Münsterberg's Work

Law-Psychology Pioneer

Münsterberg's contributions to the nascent field of forensic psychology were both scientific and professional. From a scientific perspective, "*On the Witness Stand* (1908) was a tour de force in articulating a behavioral research agenda in forensics" (Landy, 1992, p. 792). As the remainder of the present volume explicates, Münsterberg's book—which contains the bulk of his writing on the subject—addresses a large number of the topics that continue to occupy psycholegal researchers, such as eyewitness memory, suggestibility, false confessions, lie detection, and criminal responsibility (he did not, of course, cover absolutely everything; see Chapter 11 on "What Münsterberg Missed").

His first forensic work was done in a private capacity, when a defense attorney in Chicago asked him to review the records of Richard Ivens, a client who had been convicted of murder after confessing and later retracting his confession (Benjamin & Baker, 2004; Hale, 1980). J. Sanderson Christison, a local physician/criminologist/author who was involved in the case, believed that the confession had been induced by hypnotic suggestion and asked Münsterberg to review the case. In Münsterberg's opinion, the interrogation that led to the confession was suspicious, and the man was intellectually disabled; he concluded that he was very likely innocent. Münsterberg's letter was released to the press, which angered the judge, who accused him of meddling after the fact. In the end, Münsterberg's intervention had no effect—the man was hanged. Münsterberg subsequently published a series of popular articles on psychology and law in magazines like *McClure's* and *Metropolitan*; these articles, which addressed problems with confessions, eyewitness testimony, detecting deception, and other issues, became the best-selling *On the Witness Stand* (Moskowitz, 1977). We examine their contemporary relevance in the following chapters of the present volume.

Münsterberg wrote little about psychology and law apart from *On the Witness Stand*, although he did include a chapter on "legal psychology" in his textbook on applied psychology (Münsterberg, 1914c), and a chapter of his 1914 book *Psychology and Social Sanity* (Münsterberg, 1914b) was devoted to "The Mind of the Juryman."[7] Münsterberg begins this chapter by acknowledging the pervasive myth—then as now—that juries are irrational and capricious (Bornstein & Greene, 2017): "Every lawyer knows some good stories about some wild juries he has known, which made him shiver and doubt whether a dozen laymen ever can see a legal point. But every newspaper reader, too, remembers an abundance of cases in which the decision of the jury startled him by its absurdity" (Münsterberg, 1914b, p. 181). However, he goes on to extol the jury's importance in administering commonsense justice (cf. Finkel, 1995): "Better to have some statutes riddled by the illogical verdicts than legal decisions severed from the sense of justice which is living in the soul of the nation" (p. 182). Münsterberg touches on a number of topics that continue to be prominent in research on jury decision making: jury selection ("A jury of artisans and farmers understands and looks into a mass of neutral material as well as a jury of bankers and doctors," p. 184); group dynamics in jury deliberation ("The mass consciousness is not an adding up, a mere summation, of the individual minds, but the creation of something entirely new," p. 185); and jury simulation methodology ("We must therefore artificially create a situation which brings into action the judgment, the discussion, and the vote, but if we are loyal to the idea of experimenting we must keep the experiment free from all those features of a real jury deliberation which have nothing to do with the mental action itself," p. 188).

Ultimately, Münsterberg (1914b, p. 183) concludes that juries get it right most of the time and that "the social significance of the jury system ought not

---

[7] The chapter was an expanded version of an article he published the previous year in *The Century* (Münsterberg, 1913d).

to be guided by the few stray cases in which the emotional response obscures the truth." Regrettably, he argues that juries' relatively high level of performance holds only for juries composed of men. He bases this stance on the results of the main experiment described in the chapter, in which he had groups of men (Harvard students) and groups of women (advanced women students) view a series of trials in which he presented them with two cards covered with white paper dots. The cards had a varying number of dots, which were of various sizes and arranged in different patterns. Participants' task was to judge whether the upper card on each trial contained more, fewer, or the same number of dots as the lower card. Participants made individual judgments (first by writing them down, then by a show of hands); discussed the matter for 5 minutes, attempting to arrive at unanimity; voted again; deliberated for 5 more minutes; and voted a third time. Deliberation improved the votes of male groups from 52% to 78% correct, whereas female groups started and ended at 45% correct. Münsterberg assures the reader that the difference on the initial ballot is trivial, and that "I had no prejudice in favour of or against women as members of the jury . . . I was only anxious to clear up the facts" (Münsterberg, 1914b, p. 195).

Münsterberg's facts, especially the 78% versus 45% difference on the final ballot, led him to conclude that because "[t]he woman remains loyal to her instinctive opinion" (Münsterberg, 1914b, p. 198), she is less susceptible to reason, and deliberation would be less effective. Although he professes not to pass judgment, he can only conclude that in the interests of justice, women should not serve on juries: "Hence we have no right to say that the one type of mind is in general better than the other. We may say only that they are different, and that this difference makes the men fit and the women unfit for the particular task which society requires from the jurymen" (p. 198). Indeed, "the psychologist has every reason to be satisfied with the jury system as long as the women are kept out of it" (p. 202).

Münsterberg's statements regarding women jurors likely seem appalling to modern readers, and we have no desire to defend them. Rather, as we will do in the succeeding chapters, each of which analyzes a specific topic covered in *On the Witness Stand*, we situate it within its historical context while providing a contemporary reappraisal. Münsterberg wrote at a time when the women's suffrage movement in the United States was in full force. Women had served on juries in several (mostly Western) states and territories at least since 1870, but those jurisdictions were the exception (Vidmar & Hans, 2007). The Nineteenth Amendment, giving women the right to vote, was ratified in 1920, only 6 years after publication of *Psychology and Social Sanity*, and even that did not automatically give women the right to serve on juries. They continued to be ineligible in some states and could claim an automatic exemption in others. The US Supreme Court did not rule that excluding or automatically exempting women from jury service was unconstitutional until the 1970s (*Duren v. Missouri*, 1979; *Taylor v. Louisiana*, 1975; see, generally, Vidmar & Hans, 2007). It seems likely that the issue of women jurors was prominent at the time, and that Münsterberg was weighing in on it, as he did on so many other issues.

With respect to the accuracy of Münsterberg's conclusion regarding juror gender, more recent empirical research shows that the relationship between jurors' gender and their trial judgments and behavior is complex. Male and female jurors reach comparable verdicts in many, if not most, kinds of cases. However, women are relatively more likely to side with the prosecution or a civil plaintiff in cases involving child or sexual assault victims, with plaintiffs in sexual harassment claims, and with capital defendants (Bornstein & Greene, 2017; Devine, 2012). Less research has been conducted on the relationship between gender and juror behavior during deliberation, but that which has been done shows that women are less likely to be chosen as foreperson, participate less, and both see themselves and are perceived by other jurors as less persuasive (Devine, 2012). Although Münsterberg may have been wrong about the existence of gender differences in terms of women or men reaching "better" decisions, he was clearly right in calling attention to the subtle yet reliable differences in how male and female jurors make decisions—both individually and as members of deliberating groups—at trial.

From a professional perspective, Münsterberg made two important contributions to the field of psychology and law: first, he consulted with attorneys on psychological issues relevant to their cases. As in the Ivens case, this work was not without controversy. For example, on assignment for *McClure's* magazine, he attended the 1907 Idaho trial of "Big Bill" Haywood, a labor activist, and three other union leaders. They were on trial for conspiring to kill Frank Steunenberg, a former Idaho governor, and the current governor invited Münsterberg to attend the trial as a scientific investigator (Moskowitz, 1977). Because of the victim's high profile and the volatility of the labor and socialist movements in early 20th-century America, the case garnered a great deal of media and popular interest, with public demonstrations in support of Haywood in most major American cities (Hale, 1980).

The key witness in Haywood's trial was Harry Orchard, who had confessed to planting the bomb that killed Steunenberg and who implicated Haywood. After observing Orchard's final, 30-minute testimony and administering nearly 100 tests (e.g., word association) to him in his cell to ascertain his truthfulness, Münsterberg concluded that Orchard was telling the truth and Haywood was guilty—which he let slip to a reporter on the train back to Massachusetts (Hale, 1980). Even though Münsterberg's opinion was widely reported before the jury reached a verdict, Haywood (represented by Clarence Darrow) was acquitted. For his part, Münsterberg was harshly criticized for grandstanding and interfering with the legal process. Münsterberg did not testify to his conclusions in court, and when he eventually published his account of the trial, he backtracked slightly, saying only that Orchard genuinely *believed* he was telling the truth; Münsterberg could not say what the actual facts were. Nonetheless, his examination of Orchard spurred subsequent work on deception detection (see Chapter 5). Additionally, his assessment of Orchard and statements about the results of his examination were similar to what a modern-day consultant or expert witness might do.

Although it took some years for this sort of work to become accepted by the legal system, trial consulting is now a well-entrenched component of the law-psychology discipline (e.g., Wiener & Bornstein, 2011), and psychological expert testimony—at least on many topics—is widely accepted and on some topics virtually required (e.g., competency determinations). It is unclear whether Münsterberg ever actually testified as an expert witness, but he consulted on other cases and planned to testify in at least one case where his testimony was ultimately not needed (Weiss & Xuan, 2015). Thus, modern-day trial consultants and eyewitness experts owe Münsterberg a debt of gratitude.

Münsterberg's second contribution to law-psychology as a profession was his strong advocacy for psychology's relevance to public policy and the courts. As described in Chapter 2, his advocacy was not particularly tactful; nor was it received well, and to some degree, tension between the fields of psychology and law still exists. Nevertheless, the relationship is considerably more amicable now than it was in the past, and it is growing friendlier all the time (Monahan & Walker, 2011). To the extent that judges, legislators, and other policymakers are now receptive to psychological and other social scientific research, Münsterberg is one of the individuals we have to thank.

Major Nonforensic Contributions

A significant challenge in summarizing Münsterberg's career, in spite of its relative brevity, is trying to find an area of psychology to which he did *not* contribute. He conducted laboratory research on sensation and perception (e.g., optical illusions, for which he coined the term "pseudoptics"), the will, consciousness, individual differences, and experimental methods. He published on all of these topics, as well as on philosophy and social commentary, in both German and English. It is difficult to compile a comprehensive bibliography of his work, but he published at least 20 books and numerous articles in both scientific journals and the popular press, and he also edited four volumes of *Harvard Psychological Studies* (Hale, 1980; Landy, 1992; Moskowitz, 1977).[8]

During his lifetime, Münsterberg was, and continues to be, at least as well known for his efforts to apply psychological research to business and industry as for his forensic work (Moskowitz, 1977). According to Hale (1980, p. 148), "[n]o questions in applied psychology, in fact, attracted him more than those of industrial organization and efficiency." His major works in the industrial-organizational (I/O) domain were *Psychology and Industrial Efficiency* (Münsterberg, 1913b), which was a bestseller (Benjamin & Baker, 2004), and *Business Psychology* (Münsterberg, 1915a). In these books, he covered vocational guidance, advertising, personnel selection and management, mental

[8] The frontispiece of his final psychological book, *The Photoplay: A Psychological Study* (1916/1970), lists 24 books under the heading "Books by Hugo Münsterberg." Only a few of the entries appear to be translations or German and English editions that cover much of the same material.

testing, workforce efficiency, and motivation, among other topics. He was a strong proponent of testing as an element of personnel selection and evaluation, and just as he had in the legal arena, he consulted with practitioners. He developed job-specific tests for a number of different occupations (e.g., telephone operator, trolley car operator, ship captain). He then collected data to validate the effectiveness of the tests. These examples illustrate his commitment to using psychology for the betterment of life, which he referred to as "psychotechnik." Psychotechnik was a forerunner of fields like ergonomics and human factors (Thorne & Henley, 2005), but to Münsterberg the term encompassed a broader philosophy of social engineering—using psychology to shape a better society. In that sense it has something in common with Watson's behaviorism (Hale, 1980).

In addition to conducting applied research, Münsterberg strove to legitimize the field. He organized an official program in applied psychology at Harvard, taught a course in applied psychology at the University of Berlin in 1910–1911, and published books on the topic: *Grundzüge der Psychotechnik* (*Principles of Psychotechnics*; Münsterberg, 1914a) and *Psychology General and Applied* (Münsterberg, 1914c). He also recommended, unsuccessfully, to both Kaiser Wilhelm II and President Woodrow Wilson that they establish independent government research bureaus in applied and industrial psychology (Hale, 1980).

There are many parallels between Münsterberg's efforts to apply psychology to law and to business. In both areas, he did private consultation as well as more standard academic research; in both areas, he produced scholarly and popular accounts; and in both areas, he arguably receives more credit than he deserves. For example, as with forensic psychology, the extent to which Münsterberg was the sole, or even the first or most significant, "founder" of I/O psychology is highly debatable (Kuna, 1978). Other psychologists, such as Walter Dill Scott, Harry Hollingworth, and even John Watson were applying psychology to business and commercial matters (e.g., advertising, training) at the same time if not sooner. Much of Münsterberg's recognition in both forensic and I/O psychology, and his wearing of the "founder" mantle, comes from his being in the right place at the right time: an authoritative Harvard University expert at a time when American businesses and the courts were rapidly expanding and becoming interested in science. In addition, people took what Münsterberg, one of the most visible and prolific psychologists in the country, had to say seriously.

Given his positive attitude toward applying psychology in the courts and in the workplace, it is perhaps unsurprising that Münsterberg also supported applying it in other contexts where he played a less central role himself than he did in forensic and I/O psychology. In fact, there seems to be no domain to which he was unwilling to apply it; he was "the first all-round applied psychologist in America" (Anastasi, 1964, p. 4). For example, he was one of the first psychologists to see the discipline's relevance to the nascent fields of clinical psychology, paranormal psychology, and media psychology.

Münsterberg treated patients in both Germany and the United States—having a medical degree, there would have been no barrier to his doing so—and experimented with various interventions. He took patients only if they posed interesting scientific questions, and he never accepted a fee (Lawson et al., 2007; Moskowitz, 1977). He generally explained mental illness in medical/physiological terms or as a mismatch between the environment and the person (Landy, 1992; Moskowitz, 1977). Consistent with his work on suggestibility in memory (see Chapter 8), he sometimes employed hypnosis and emphasized the power of therapeutic suggestion—that is, directly telling patients that they should expect to get better (Lawson et al., 2007). His work on hypnosis therefore had a therapeutic as well as a theoretical flavor to it (Münsterberg, 1909b; Münsterberg et al., 1910; see also Chapter 9, this volume), and he reported success in treating a wide range of problems (Moskowitz, 1977; Münsterberg, 1909b). His clinical work was not without its failures and risks, however—one paranoid patient threatened him with a gun (Moskowitz, 1977). His interest in psychotherapy and hypnosis notwithstanding, Münsterberg was opposed to psychoanalysis and had reservations about the notion of the unconscious (Landy, 1992). He also warned against lay intrusion into the field of psychotherapy and felt that it should be practiced only by those trained in medicine (Münsterberg, 1909b).

In the late 19th and early 20th centuries, paranormal phenomena like spiritualism and clairvoyance were extremely popular, and not only among practitioners and gullible laypeople. Psychical research—largely, but not entirely, focused on debunking claims of paranormal phenomena—was a significant element in the fledgling science of psychology; among others, William James considered himself a psychical researcher, believed it should be a part of mainstream psychology, championed the work of spiritualists, and regularly attended séances himself (Benjamin & Baker, 2004; Sommer, 2012). Münsterberg and several of his contemporaries in the United States (e.g., Hall, Titchener, Cattell, and Jastrow), in contrast, viewed research on psychical phenomena "as a threat to rationality and the scientific and social order" (Sommer, 2012, pp. 24–25). In their opinion, psychical research delegitimized psychology as a science.

Münsterberg (1899, 1913c, 1914b) argued that rather than conflating psychology and parapsychology, psychological research methods could, and should, be used to study and explain supposedly supernatural phenomena in scientific terms, such as hypnotism, hysteria, hypersensitivity to sensory cues, and dissociation. He applied this approach on multiple occasions. For example, he examined Beulah Miller, a 10-year-old Rhode Island girl with purported telepathic powers (Münsterberg, 1913c; see also Münsterberg, 1914a). Beulah could supposedly "read in the mind of anyone present anything of which he is thinking," read words on a blackboard with her back turned, and guess what a visitor had in his pocket (Münsterberg, 1913c, p. 16). While documenting her much better-than-chance performance (e.g., at guessing a card he had drawn from a deck), Münsterberg proposed that it resulted not from mind reading but from her ability to pick up, subconsciously, very subtle cues in the other person's behavior. He tested his hypothesis by having her attempt to read someone's mind while blindfolded or without her mother or sister present and aware of the correct answer. He even likened her to the horse Clever Hans, with her family members fulfilling the role of von Osten.

Münsterberg's most celebrated episode of psychic defrocking involved an Italian medium named Eusapia Palladino. Palladino's performances, which involved levitation, telekinesis, and materialization of human forms, gained her fame and admirers in her native Naples. James and a number of other scientists concluded that her supernormal abilities were genuine. When she traveled to the United States in 1909 for an American tour and to be investigated by scientists, Münsterberg attended two sittings, in which he exposed her as a fraudulent cheat (Münsterberg, 1910b; reprinted in Münsterberg, 1910a). A man had sneaked into the room and covertly positioned himself between Palladino and a table she sought to have her controlling spirit (named John) lift up, while observers controlled her hands and feet (there is some dispute about whether the man was Münsterberg's assistant or simply another guest at the sitting; Sommer, 2012). The man caught her, causing her to scream, after "she had simply freed her foot from her shoe and with an athletic backward movement of the leg was reaching out and fishing with her toes for . . . the table" (Münsterberg, 1910a, pp. 142–143). Although Münsterberg consequently pronounced her a fraud, he suggested that like Beulah Miller, she might not be responsible; rather, he believed that she suffered from hysteria and was not conscious of her actions.[9] The spiritualists got their revenge shortly after Münsterberg's death. In the ultimate posthumous insult, a medium in Boston reported a message from him saying, "Spirit return is a truth" (Hale, 1980, p. 183).

In Münsterberg's final scholarly book (Münsterberg, 1916/1970), he applied psychology to the then-new medium of moving pictures—as he referred to it in the book's title, "the photoplay."[10] The work covers the mental processes involved in attending to and perceiving pictures on the screen, perceiving depth and apparent movement (including a discussion of Wertheimer's recent studies of the phi phenomenon), forming impressions and associations to the material, and responding to various cinematic techniques (e.g., rapid scene shifts, close-ups). He also describes the role of imagination and suggestion, as well as the importance of feelings and emotions (e.g., sympathy)—both those displayed by the actors and the ones elicited in the viewer. Ever the philosopher as well as the psychologist, he includes sections on "the esthetics of the photoplay," in which he addresses such subjects as the purpose of art—not

[9] James dismissed Münsterberg's exposure of Palladino as "a buffoon article, as if written by a bagman" (Sommer, 2012, p. 32) and believed that it showed "his genius for self-advertisement and superficiality. Mendacity too!" (Sommer, 2012, p. 33).

[10] According to Moskowitz (1977), Münsterberg became a film buff after a play based on *On the Witness Stand*—"The Third Degree," by Charles Klein—was turned into a successful film.

merely to imitate nature, but "to transform the world so that it becomes a thing of beauty" (p. 144) and the relative merits of live theater versus film. His conclusion, that film is a unique aesthetic medium in its own right and not just a poor imitation of theater, was tarnished somewhat by rumors that he received payment from the cinema industry (Hale, 1980).

In related magazine articles, Münsterberg presents these same ideas to a lay audience, while also addressing the questions of why movies exert their appeal and the risks and benefits of their being viewed by impressionable young minds (Langdale, 2002). He argues that movies can be educational, but they can also model immoral behavior, and the rapid presentation of images "accustoms the mind to haste and superficiality" (Langdale, 2002, p. 194). Ultimately, Münsterberg reaches the same conclusion regarding the psychologist's proper role in the film world as he does in the legal domain and other real-world contexts—namely, psychologists have much to add. In an article published in *Cosmopolitan*, he states: "The time seems ripe for [the physicist's] scientific brother, the psychologist, to enter the field and to lead the photoplay to those wonders which its progress has begun to suggest since the leaders dared to leave the paths of mere theatrical performance. The more psychology enters into the sphere of the moving pictures, the more they will be worthy of an independent place in the world of true art and become really a means of cultural education to young and old" (Langdale, 2002, p. 182).

Ironically, although Münsterberg is clearly a pioneer in the field of applied psychology, he came to an appreciation of psychology's practical applications only gradually. He was initially quite critical of efforts to apply psychology to fields like business and education (Benjamin, 2006), calling the rush to psychology for answers to practical questions "psychologism" (Hale, 1980). In part, this illustrated his view, which was not uncommon, that the democratization of science posed a threat to academic control of the discipline (Hale, 1980). Münsterberg was especially critical of attempts to use psychology to improve the educational system, such as the child study movement (e.g., Münsterberg, 1898). He wrote, "Our laboratory work cannot teach you anything which is of direct use to you in your work as teachers; and if you are not good teachers it may even do you harm, as it may confuse you and inhibit your normal teacher's instincts" (Münsterberg, 1898, p. 166). The response to Münsterberg's article was divided and loud. Some of the feedback was positive, but many of Münsterberg's psychology colleagues disagreed with his dismissal of applied psychology. A large number of prominent psychologists, such as Cattell, Thorndike, Witmer, Titchener, Dewey, and Hall, published critical responses to Münsterberg's article (Benjamin, 2006).

Münsterberg eventually changed his tune with respect to applied psychology in general and educational psychology in particular. As the aforementioned examples illustrate, he became a leading proponent and practitioner of applied psychology, although he continued to maintain that teachers should not apply psychology in the classroom themselves; rather, schools should bring in psychologists to do it for them (Hale, 1980). Benjamin (2006) argues that

Münsterberg's "transformation" resulted mainly from his need for attention, the public's growing interest in scientific applications, and Münsterberg's own recognition of the applicability of psychology. The change was likely gradual, and one could argue that his willingness to adapt his stance in response to mounting evidence is to his credit. He even published a book on the psychology of pedagogy, *Psychology and the Teacher* (Münsterberg, 1909a), in which he claimed that he was not recanting his previous statements but that the field had simply caught up, to the point where it now had something (albeit still relatively little) to offer (Benjamin, 2006; Moskowitz, 1977).

In appealing for psychology's relevance to real-world problems, he often overreached. Even his friend and admirer William Stern (1917), while eulogizing Münsterberg as "an investigator of penetrating sharpness, with a power of presentation marked by genius" (p. 186), acknowledged that "It is true that often he showed more boldness and power to image future possibilities than he did cautious technical knowledge" (p. 188). His advocacy of applied psychology, and the resistance to it on the part of most academic psychologists and the public, contributed to Münsterberg's fall from grace in the years following his death (Landy, 1992). The current prominence of psychological applications across a great many domains and applied psychology's acceptance both within the profession and by the larger public provide posthumous vindication of Münsterberg's approach to the field.

Münsterberg in Historical Context

Like the other psychological schools and subdisciplines mentioned at the beginning of the chapter, forensic psychology was not created by Münsterberg out of whole cloth. Rather, similar work was being conducted at roughly the same time within both psychology and related disciplines. To gain a full appreciation of Münsterberg's contributions, it is necessary to situate his work within this larger historical context.

Psychology and Its Sister Social Sciences

Like psychology, other social sciences had a significant philosophical history dating back centuries, before adopting a more empirical form along the lines of their current manifestation. Yet as with psychology, a systematic approach to the discipline, as well as widespread use of the terms themselves, did not really begin until the 19th century. Sociology, for example, coalesced into a scientific discipline through the efforts of figures like Auguste Comte (1798–1857) and Émile Durkheim (1858–1917) in France, Max Weber (1864–1920) in Germany, and Herbert Spencer (1820–1903) in England (Barnes, 1948; Maus, 1962). Other parallels between sociology and psychology include a leading role in the early years by German scholars (Barnes, 1948) and, following the world wars in the 20th century, tension and divergence between European (especially German) and American approaches (Maus, 1962). Some of the same figures were even influential in both disciplines; for example, Wundt's theory of folk psychology encompassed central sociological topics like myth and religion, culture, social organization, and social evolution (Goldenweiser, 1948).

From a subject matter perspective, criminology is probably the social science most closely related to psychology and law. Much of the early criminological research dealt with the origins of crime at both the individual (e.g., Cesare Lombroso's [1876/2006; 1899/1911] emphasis on biological factors) and group levels (e.g., le Bon's [1896] theory of crowd behavior). Le Bon even devoted a chapter of his book on crowds to criminal juries, inasmuch as juries, as a group of individuals, are a type of heterogeneous crowd. On the one hand, his impression of juries is not very positive: "Like all crowds, juries are very strongly impressed by sentimental considerations, and very slightly by argument" (p. 168); and "[j]uries, like all crowds, are profoundly impressed by prestige" (p. 169). On the other hand, he concludes that "I do not perceive a single case in which, wrongly accused of a crime, I should not prefer to have to deal with a jury rather than with magistrates. I should have some chance that my innocence would be recognized by the former and not the slightest chance that it would be admitted by the latter" (pp. 173–174). This work clearly foreshadows later research on jury sympathy and judge-jury differences, such as the classic study by Kalven and Zeisel (1966). Although le Bon's description of juries is conceptual and anecdotal, Sporer (1982) describes an empirical comparison of judges to lay jurors conducted by Kobler in 1914. Other early criminological research, such as that done by Lombroso and a number of his Italian contemporaries, was also highly quantitative (Crawford, 1948).

Several criminologists and jurists of Münsterberg's era were interested in eyewitness testimony, as well as criminal psychology. Legal scholars, of course, have recognized the fallibility of eyewitness testimony for centuries and used their assumptions about eyewitness memory—often in the absence of empirical support—to devise rules of evidence (Sporer, 1982). Several early 20th-century legal treatises included psychological assumptions about eyewitness behavior and, in some of them, experimental evidence (e.g., Gross, 1897/1918; see, generally, Slesinger & Pilpel, 1929). Recommendations on properly conducting eyewitness lineups date back at least to the 1830s (Sporer, 1982).

Münsterberg's Law-Psychology Contemporaries

Just as scientists in other disciplines were interested in legal issues, so were a number of Münsterberg's psychology peers. Among psychologists, perhaps the preeminent psycholegal research topic was eyewitness memory, or as it was commonly referred to at the time, the psychology of testimony. This was true not only for those conducting primarily experimental research, like Münsterberg, but also for figures better known for their work in other areas, like Alfred Binet and Sigmund Freud. Binet briefly addressed the forensic implications of suggestibility in his 1900 book *La Suggestibilité* and subsequently called for a "science du témoignage" (science of testimony; Binet, 1905), a proposal echoed by Claparède (1906). Freud (1901/1960, pp. 147–148) applied motivated forgetting to eyewitness testimony in *The Psychopathology of Everyday Life*, writing "it seems to me that [motivated forgetting] has still not yet been sufficiently strongly emphasized in assessing testimony in courts of law [footnote omitted], where the process of putting a witness on oath is clearly expected to have much too great a purifying influence on the play of his psychical forces."

The bulk of this research was conducted in Germany, meaning that Münsterberg almost certainly would have been familiar with it. In addition to studying involuntary eyewitness errors (i.e., omissions, distortions, intrusions), these researchers also addressed intentional distortions of testimony (i.e., lying; Sporer, 2006). William Stern and Otto Lipmann founded a journal devoted to eyewitness memory, *Beiträge zur Psychologie der Aussage* (*Contributions to the Psychology of Testimony*) in 1903, which was expanded and renamed the *Zeitschrift für angewandte Psychologie und psychologische Sammelforschung* in 1907 (*Journal for Applied Psychology*, which is still a leading German journal but now focuses exclusively on I/O psychology; Sporer, 2006, 2008; Whipple, 1909).[11] Sporer (1982, 2008) makes a creditable case that Stern, not Münsterberg, is the figure most responsible for legitimizing eyewitness testimony in particular, and applied psychology in general, as areas of study. In addition to founding an eyewitness journal, Stern conducted extensive research on eyewitness testimony, including such topics as individual differences (especially age) and means of improving eyewitness testimony. He also coined the term "applied psychology" and founded an institute for applied psychology. Importantly, he advocated an interdisciplinary approach, which inspired experimental research on the topic by a large number of "psychologists, physicians, psychiatrists, pedagogues and even jurists" (Sporer, 1982, p. 329). This work established a sizeable knowledge base by the 1920s and led to some of the earliest instances of policy reform efforts and expert testimony on eyewitness issues (Sporer, 1982, 2006). "For example, already in 1905/06 Stern demanded the use of a lineup as opposed to a mere showup" (Sporer, 2008, p. 743), a recommendation that rings as true today as it did then (see, e.g., Neuschatz et al., 2016).

Although the majority of early eyewitness work was conducted in Europe and published in languages other than English, there was some awareness of the topic in the United States. Beard (1878) and Cattell (1895) both addressed the accuracy of eyewitness testimony many years before Münsterberg published *On the Witness Stand*. For example, Beard (1878, p. 59) observed: "Equally important in its bearings on the scientific study of testimony is the recognition of the fact that memory is far more untrustworthy than has been commonly supposed." He supported this statement with the results of experiments he

---

[11] Sporer (1982) comments that "Aussage," although frequently translated as "testimony," is a broader term more akin to "verbal report." Hence, it encompasses verbal reproductions of memory in numerous contexts and not just forensic settings.

conducted using the "Russian game" (nowadays known more commonly as the telephone game), in which participants try to repeat a story to one another in sequence. As Beard found, the stories do not agree well and contain a number of omission and commission errors. Eyewitness error was also discussed within the context of paranormal occurrences (i.e., a witness to a purportedly supernatural event might simply have misperceived or misremembered it; Hodgson & Davey, 1887).

Moreover, work being done outside the United States was disseminated to American audiences fairly quickly, most notably in a series of articles that Guy Montrose Whipple, of Cornell University and later the University of Illinois, published in *Psychological Bulletin* between 1909 and 1917 (Whipple, 1909, 1910b, 1912, 1913, 1914a, 1915, 1917). In these articles, Whipple provided more-or-less annual summaries of the latest eyewitness research. In the first article in the series (Whipple, 1909), entitled "The Observer as Reporter: A Survey of the 'Psychology of Testimony,'" he focuses on the importance of various methodological and statistical choices in conducting eyewitness research, such as the type of stimulus (e.g., pictures or an event), exposure time, retention interval, form of report (e.g., narrative statement or "interrogatory"), and type of question (e.g., leading vs. nonleading). He summarizes recent findings by Binet, Stern, and others. Interestingly, he pays considerable attention to the work of Marie Borst, one of the few women researchers of the day. Borst was a Swiss schoolteacher and student of Stern who was one of the first to use female participants in her studies (Meares, 2016).

Subsequent articles by Whipple cover eyewitness research being done in Germany, France, Bohemia/Czechoslovakia, Belgium, Italy, Austria, Switzerland, England, the Netherlands, and the United States (specifically Münsterberg's work). Wigmore (1909; discussed at greater length in Chapter 2) mentions research in Russia, India, and Chile. Whipple also describes early instances of expert testimony on eyewitness reliability in some of these same countries (Whipple, 1912, 1913). For example, in a Belgian murder trial a researcher named Varendonck provided expert testimony for the defense on the unreliability of child eyewitnesses. The jury acquitted the defendant, leading Whipple (1912, p. 268) to conclude that "[t]he psychology of testimony has, therefore, found its way formally into the court room and saved a man's life." Sporer (1982) describes similar cases where psychological experts addressed eyewitness reliability in the late 1800s and early 1900s. These historical reviews offer conclusive evidence that Münsterberg was one among many; by World War I, eyewitness memory was a vibrant research field with practitioners all over the world.

Key Considerations

Sciences evolve. This is true in many respects, ranging from subject matter and methodology to training and professionalization. A contemporary reappraisal of a historical work like *On the Witness Stand* requires a consideration of some of these changes. Two that are especially relevant to an understanding of Münsterberg's work are evolving standards of publication and research, and tensions within psychology: between basic and applied approaches and between clinical and nonclinical work.

Evolving Conventions in Scientific Publishing and Research

A close inspection of Münsterberg's book highlights, for the modern reader, how empirical practices and scholarly writing have changed over the years. He supports his ideas with experimental evidence, demonstrations, and anecdotal observation. But he sometimes describes an experiment without saying who conducted it, and other times he mentions a name without citing a specific source. Conventions for making scholarly attributions have changed.

The standards for conducting and publishing research in psychology have evolved over the years. Prior to the advent of institutional review boards (developed in response to several problematic biomedical and behavioral research studies in the mid-20th century) and the codification of APA style (first promulgated in 1929), there was enormous variability in research methods and reporting. To judge by today's standards, early psychologists tended to be less diligent when attributing the source of their ideas and less thorough when describing their methodology. Charges of plagiarism did occasionally occur (Benjamin, 2006), and Münsterberg himself was accused of falsifying his results (Hale, 1980). Data analysis might or might not include rudimentary descriptive statistics, and it rarely included inferential statistics. Yet even by his era's prevailing standards, Münsterberg was lax in terms of attribution and data analysis (Landy, 1992).

Just as important as *what* early psychologists published is *how* they published. Few journals existed at the time, especially in English: the *American Journal of Psychology* was founded in 1887, the *Pedagogical Seminary* (currently the *Journal of Genetic Psychology: Research and Theory on Human Development*) in 1891, *Psychological Review* in 1894, the *British Journal of Psychology* and *Psychological Bulletin* in 1904, *Journal of Applied Psychology* (the American version) in 1917, and the *International Journal of Psychoanalysis* in 1920. Accordingly, leading scholars were just as likely, if not more likely, to publish monographs as journal articles. Indeed, the bulk of Münsterberg's more scholarly publications—at least once he began writing in English—were in book form, which would be an anomaly for a psychological researcher today.

Moreover, leading psychologists wrote for popular as well as scientific audiences, though none perhaps as extensively as Münsterberg. John Watson contributed to *Harper's*, *McCall's*, and *Cosmopolitan* magazines (Bigelow & Morris, 2001), and Münsterberg published hundreds of articles in popular media like *Atlantic Monthly*, *Harper's*, *McClure's*, the *New York Times*, the *Boston Globe*, and the *Metropolitan* (Landy, 1992). According to Landy, for a period of time he was in the *New York Times* an average of once a month. In part, his tendency to write for popular outlets later in his career reflected his sensitivity to criticism of early efforts to write more serious scientific work in English (Hale, 1980; Landy, 1992). It likely also reflects the efforts by psychologists of the era to introduce laypeople to their relatively new discipline.

Standards for conducting research have changed as well. Some of the studies and demonstrations conducted by Münsterberg and other psychologists at the turn of the 20th century would be difficult, if not impossible, to conduct in the early 21st century. In *On the Witness Stand*, Münsterberg describes one staged crime, covered in greater detail in Chapter 4, that involved gunshots in a classroom. He presents a similar staged crime, involving gunshots and a clown, done at a meeting of a scientific association. The witnesses to that incident were "made up of jurists, psychologists, and physicians, all, therefore, men well trained in careful observation" (p. 51). Despite their training, of the 40 witnesses, only one omitted less than 20% of the facts, and 34 of 40 made errors of commission (i.e., they made statements that were false). Overall, a majority of witnesses made errors of omission or commission on about half of what they had seen. Such "dramatic experiments" were apparently not at all unusual at the time; Münsterberg (p. 53) says they "have recently become the fashion and almost a sport."

Today, when institutional review boards (IRBs) closely regulate human subjects research, it is hard to imagine being able to conduct a dramatic experiment like the ones described by Münsterberg. Restrictions on human subjects research have existed for centuries, but early policies tended to be local, limited in scope, and focused on biomedical, as opposed to behavioral, research (Schneider, 2005). In 1900, Münsterberg's own Prussian Ministry of Religious and Medical Affairs promulgated an informed consent requirement for nontherapeutic medical intervention, after a syphilis immunization study led to several subjects contracting the disease (Schneider, 2005). However, serious attention to research ethics did not occur until after World War II, when abuses perpetrated by Nazi researchers came to light. The Nuremberg war crimes trials led to the creation of the Nuremberg Code, which provided the first clear standards for human subjects research (Moon & Khin-Maung-Gyi, 2009). Explicit guidelines developed gradually in the United States, with the creation of modern IRBs resulting from the World Medical Association's Declaration of Helsinki in 1964 (and subsequently revised), several memoranda issued by the US Public Health Service in the late 1960s/early 1970s, and the National Research Act of 1974. The Act, which was largely a direct response to ethically questionable biomedical and behavioral research, such as the Tuskegee Syphilis and Stanford Prison studies, created the National Commission for the Protection of Human Subjects of Biomedical and Behavioral Research. The Commission issued the well-known Belmont Report in 1979. IRBs continue to evolve (Moon & Khin-Maung-Gyi, 2009), but their basic scope and practices have been fairly well established since the Belmont Report. With their emphasis on informed consent, individual rights, and the risk-benefit ratio, live demonstrations involving crimes for the purposes of eyewitness research would be much harder to conduct.

Nonetheless, some eyewitness researchers have managed to conduct staged crimes even in the IRB era (see Memon, Mastroberardino, & Fraser, 2008). For example, Buckhout (1974; hence conducted before the National Research Act and Belmont Report) staged a mock assault, in which a student attacked a professor, on a college campus in front of 141 unsuspecting witnesses (for more detail on Buckhout's study, see Chapter 4). More often, staged events are nonviolent crimes, like theft (e.g., Lindsay, Wells, & Rumpel, 1981), or interactions without any criminal activity whatsoever (e.g., Bornstein & Zickafoose, 1999). These deviations from naturalistic witnessing situations, though understandable from an ethical and logistical perspective, raise questions about the external validity of the research (Chapter 4 covers these methodological issues in more depth).

Many Psychologies

Although psychology as a scientific, data-driven enterprise has existed since the mid- to late nineteenth century, a consensus about what constitutes "psychology," in either subject matter or methodology, has not. It may be tempting to view psychology's grappling with its relationship to other disciplines (e.g., its sister social sciences, neuroscience) and the proper number and makeup of its own subdisciplines (e.g., clinical, cognitive, developmental, social, etc.) as being of recent vintage; however, these issues have been part of the field as long as there has been a field. Two overlapping areas of dissension that have particularly bedeviled the field, and that are of great relevance to psychology and law, are conflicts between basic and applied psychology, as well as between clinical and nonclinical psychology.[12]

The basic-applied distinction refers to research that emphasizes fundamental psychological theory in well-controlled laboratory settings or that seeks primarily to answer practical questions in naturalistic settings. Münsterberg lived and worked at a time when tensions between basic and applied researchers in the United States ran high. Most of the founders (in 1892) of the APA were academics who not only performed laboratory research themselves but eschewed research in less controlled settings as unscientific (Hunt, 2007). Despite their efforts to keep psychology a laboratory science, change came rapidly, thanks mainly to World War I and social forces like industrialization

[12] The clinical-nonclinical contrast is often characterized as "clinical-experimental" or "clinical-laboratory." Such distinctions, while a convenient shorthand, are spurious, insofar as much clinical research is experimental (e.g., randomly assigning mentally ill participants to receive different therapeutic interventions), and laboratory research can use clinical populations (e.g., memory comparisons involving depressed vs. nondepressed participants). We therefore opt to distinguish between clinical and nonclinical approaches.

and compulsory education. Opportunities for applying psychological methods and theories abounded, especially in clinical and industrial settings. As more and more psychologists, like Münsterberg, began working in applied settings, the hard-core experimentalists became increasingly disenchanted and periodically attempted to split off and form their own professional organizations—ones devoted to basic research (Cautin, 2009). Yet they were swimming against the tide—a 1920 survey of APA members, who constituted practically all the psychologists in the country, showed that slightly more than half could be classified as applied (as opposed to "pure") psychologists (Terman, 1921).

It is, of course, possible for research to be both basic and applied, but most research takes one approach or the other, and the field of psychology and law is no exception (Bornstein & Meissner, 2008). Within the domain of eyewitness testimony, for example, there are regular debates about the extent to which basic research findings generalize to applied settings and whether the empirical knowledge base is sufficient to implement procedural reforms in practice (e.g., Clark, 2012; Malpass et al., 2008; McQuiston-Surrett, Malpass, & Tredoux, 2006). The tradeoffs between basic and applied research are important to discuss in any psychological domain; they are arguably especially important in psychology and law, where empirical findings can influence policies with a dramatic effect on people's lives.

In its purest form, the basic-applied distinction refers especially to where the research is being conducted (i.e., lab vs. real-world setting), with implications for the sorts of questions that are being asked and methods being used. Beyond that, many psychologists working in real-world settings do not conduct research themselves but apply psychology by providing services to clients. As Münsterberg demonstrated in his own work, the areas in which these consumers of psychological research operate are extremely diverse, but the largest number are those seeking treatment for some sort of mental illness or condition. Hence, clinical practitioners have come to dominate professional psychology, at least in the United States, and today the most prominent aspect of psychology is clinical practice. Indeed, this is what most laypeople think about when they think about "psychology."

As with the conflict between basic and applied psychology, current tensions between clinical and nonclinical psychology date back to Münsterberg's day and the early years of the APA (Cautin, 2009). Key figures like Wundt, Titchener, and Freud viewed the treatment of persons with mental illness as more properly within the purview of psychiatry or neurology, rather than psychology (though Freud did support the training of lay analysts, an effort thwarted primarily by American psychoanalysts; Gay, 1988). The growing influence of practitioners within APA led many nonclinicians, most of whom were academic psychologists, to view APA as a guild. It was a major factor in the founding of the Psychonomic Society in 1959 and the American Psychological Society (now the Association for Psychological Science) in 1988 (Cautin, 2009; Dewsbury & Bolles, 1995).

Within law-psychology specifically, clinical and nonclinical work are both currently thriving. Leading journals in the field publish research on a variety of clinical and nonclinical topics (Reed, Dellapaolera, Thimsen, & Bornstein, 2018), and the discipline's professional organizations (e.g., the American Psychology-Law Society) contain large numbers of both academics and practitioners. As described earlier, Münsterberg conducted psychotherapy himself in furtherance of his research aims. He evaluated persons involved in the criminal justice system and wrote about the causes of criminal behavior and criminal responsibility (see Chapter 10). In bringing together general nonclinical research and individualized assessments, he "was an early example of the scientist-professional model that was adopted widely in psychology in the 1950s and was known as the Boulder Model for training clinical psychologists" (Lawson et al., 2007, p. 125). Although Münsterberg lacked formal training in clinical psychology (none existed), by virtue of his medical training he was adept at clinical practice. His dual training made him a good role model for psychologists practicing more than 100 years later.

Conclusions

There is no definitive answer to the question of how influential a figure Hugo Münsterberg was, or whether he deserves to be considered *the*, or even *a*, founder of forensic psychology or applied psychology more broadly. It might be an oversimplification to identify any single individual as *the founder* of just about any discipline or subdiscipline, but Münsterberg clearly deserves to be on a short list of *founders* for both forensic and I/O psychology. He was a public intellectual and a scholar of impressive accomplishments, but he also lived at a time when interest in psychology, in both academia and applied settings, was burgeoning. Thus, the extent to which he "had precipitated the flood rather than merely ridden its crest" is unclear (Hale, 1980, p. 184). Nevertheless, a closer inspection of *On the Witness Stand*, his seminal work in forensic psychology, shows that he was incredibly prescient. As the remainder of the present volume illustrates, the fundamental psychological processes that he identified underlying such phenomena as suggestibility, confessions, deception, and criminality are still relevant. They are intensively researched in psychological research and addressed in legal opinions and policy decisions. Münsterberg also did much for the development of professional psychology in the United States, by combining basic experimental and applied approaches to psychology; clinical, nonclinical, and consulting endeavors; diverse research methods; and scholarly and mainstream publications. Hugo Münsterberg anticipated developments that would come to define psychology in the 20th century and that continue today. We can still learn a great deal from his work, as we endeavor to show in the remainder of the book.

2

Introduction

The lawyer alone is obdurate.

—Münsterberg, *On the Witness Stand* (1908, p. 10)

In his introductory chapter to *On the Witness Stand* (1908), Münsterberg gives a very brief and selective summary of the history of experimental psychology and how it arose from the disciplines of philosophy, physiology, and physics. He describes how experimental methods went from studying only "some little facts in the periphery of mental life—borderland facts between mind and body" to "the study of memory and the connection of ideas, then of attention and of imagination, of space perception and time sense; slowly they became directed to the problems of feeling and emotion, of impulse and volition, of imitation and reasoning. . . . It may be said that there is now hardly a corner of mental life into which experimental psychology has not thrown its searchlight" (pp. 6–7).

That would be a remarkable statement to make in 2018, let alone in 1908. He then observes: "It may seem strange that this whole wonderful development should have gone on in complete detachment from the problems of practical life . . . [I]t seems astonishing that no path led from the seclusion of the psychological workshop to the market-place of the world" (p. 7). Consistent with his other writings (e.g., Münsterberg, 1898; see Chapter 1), he is cautious about rushing too soon to apply laboratory research to real-world contexts, before it has acquired a solid foundation, and he gives the example of educational psychology as a cautionary tale.[1] "But now experimental psychology

[1] The size and scope of the empirical foundation that is necessary before one can comfortably generalize from laboratory research to real-world contexts

has reached a stage at which it seems natural and sound to give attention also to its possible service for the practical needs of life" (p. 8).

Although Münsterberg acknowledges that psychology's history was relatively short when he wrote *On the Witness Stand*, in his opinion the field had matured enough for practical fields to benefit from psychological research—the most obvious ones, in his opinion, being education, medicine, art, economics, and law. Practitioners in all of these fields, and even politicians, military officers, and ministers, "are ready to see that certain chapters of Applied Psychology are sources of help and strength for them. The lawyer alone is obdurate" (p. 10). Not only lawyers have failed to sit up and take notice of psychology; judges and jurors likewise "are sure that they do not need the experimental psychologist" (p. 10). Why is the lawyer so obdurate? Münsterberg does not really say, other than commenting that "[t]hey go on thinking that their legal instinct and their common sense supplies them with all that is needed and somewhat more" (p. 11). After introducing this theme in the introductory chapter, Münsterberg makes similar inflammatory comments throughout the book, such as that "while the alienist is always a welcome guest in the court room, the psychologist is still a stranger there" (p. 46).[2]

In a sense, Münsterberg's entire book is an indictment of the legal profession for neglecting psychology—an indictment that did not go unanswered. The most influential response—partly because of the identity of the writer, and partly because of the quality of the critique—was by John Henry Wigmore (1909). Wigmore was one of the best-known legal scholars in the United States (Doyle, 2005); at the time he was dean of the Northwestern University Law School and had recently published his multivolume *A Treatise on the Anglo-American System of Evidence in Trials at Common Law* (Wigmore, 1904). The *Treatise*, commonly known as *Wigmore on Evidence*, is a defining (and many would say definitive) work in the law of evidence. It is still in print after going through numerous editions and has been revised and updated by contemporary scholars (the most recent iteration comprises five volumes; Leonard et al., 2015). Thus, any criticism of *On the Witness Stand* by Wigmore was sure to be noticed. As described in the previous chapter, Münsterberg was quite well known in the United States when the book was published; but Wigmore was at least as well known, and—given Münsterberg's penchant for sensationalism and his political views—Wigmore was almost certainly more highly respected in academic and legal circles.

The first section of the present chapter covers Wigmore's criticisms of Münsterberg in depth. The next section of the chapter provides a brief historical sketch of the field of law-psychology as it developed over the 70 years

---

is a question of continuing concern to legal psychology (see, e.g., Clark, 2012; Malpass et al., 2008; Wixted, Mickes, & Fisher, 2018).

[2] An alienist is an outmoded term for a psychiatrist.

or so following the Münsterberg-Wigmore contretemps, up until the mid-1970s. By that time the field had become reasonably well established through the creation of professional organizations (e.g., the American Psychology-Law Society) and scholarly journals, as well as the emergence of trial consulting as a way for psychologists and other social scientists to make practical application of their knowledge to the legal system.

The development of law-psychology as a field of scholarly inquiry is inextricable from the courts' use (or lack thereof) of psychological research on legal topics. The issue was at the heart of Münsterberg's and Wigmore's disagreement, and more than 100 years later, it is still one of the more prominent issues in the field. The third and final section of the chapter discusses the relationship between the disciplines of psychology and law and identifies the courts' major concerns with psychological research, with a particular emphasis on those related to research methodology (e.g., external and ecological validity). Wigmore (1909) was one of the first to raise these methodological and other substantive concerns, but they are recurrent themes in research on eyewitness memory and other psycholegal topics (Chapter 4 covers this issue in greater depth).

Wigmore's Response

Münsterberg Sued for Libel!

Wigmore's (1909) response to Münsterberg, published in the *Illinois Law Review*, is not a typical law review article by any stretch of the imagination, apart from the number of footnotes (107). It is a satirical piece, structured as a mock trial for libel in the case of *Cokestone v. Münsterberg.*[3] Wigmore describes the defendant as "a professor of psychology in the faculty of arts and sciences of the Ancient and Honorable University of Cambridge, Bay State" (p. 399). The lawsuit was filed in the Superior Court of Wundt County on April 1, 1908, and the trial was held in Windyville (Illiana) on April 1, 1909, before Judge Solon Wiseman. "The plaintiffs were represented by Mr. Simplicissimus Tyro as counsel. The defendant's counsel were the celebrated Mr. R.E. Search, assisted by Mr. Si Kist and Mr. X. Perry Ment" (p. 401). The

[3] "Mock trial" is a very fitting term, as Wigmore mocks Münsterberg mercilessly in the article. For example, he describes Münsterberg as delivering addresses on "The Psychology of the Waste-basket" and "Studies in Domestic Psy-collar-gy; No. 11, the Psychology of the Collar-Button." The name of the lead plaintiff appears to be a tribute to Sir Edward Coke (1552–1634), a prominent British jurist during the Elizabethan and Jacobean eras whose writings and judicial decisions influenced the American Bill of Rights. Coke was renowned for his defense of the common law system. The plaintiffs included unnamed "other" members of the bar.

courtroom was packed, in anticipation of "the forceful and witty epigrams of the popular psychologist" (p. 401).

According to the complaint, the defendant's book, *On the Witness Stand*, contained "certain assertions erroneous, incorrect, and untrue, concerning the said plaintiffs, in their capacity as members of the bar" (p. 399). Wigmore provided numerous examples of the defendant's libelous statements (there was no shortage of fodder) and listed his false assertions in detail:

> That there existed certain exact and precise experimental and psychological methods of ascertaining and measuring the testimonial certitude of witnesses and the guilty consciousness of accused persons;
>
> That these methods were superior to those hitherto in use in American Courts;
>
> That these methods were fully accepted and indorsed [*sic*] by psychologists in general as applicable to American judicial practice;
>
> That these methods and their legal applicability had long been publicly made known by psychologists in printed scientific journals and treatises;
>
> That such journals and treatises were accessible to the members of the legal profession in general in the United States;
>
> That the information therein contained had either been offered by psychologists to the legal profession for its practical use and had been rejected, or had been totally ignored by the said profession;
>
> That such rejection and such ignorance constituted a gross neglect of professional and civic duty by the members of the said profession, including the plaintiffs; and
>
> That such neglect of duty had been so long continued and so obstinate that there remained for the psychologists no remedy but to invoke public opinion to coerce the profession to perform its duty by using the said methods;
>
> All of which assertions, by reason of their incorrectness, had caused much ridicule, dislike and contempt, by means of which the said plaintiffs had been greatly injured in their said good names, to their damage, for which they asked the sum of one dollar compensation. (p. 401)

The plaintiffs sought only nominal damages because their true objective "was to vindicate the honor and the intelligence of the profession to which they belonged" (p. 404). In his defense, Münsterberg—the only witness—maintained that his assertions were true. The questioning focused on two issues: whether "exact methods of experimental psychology [were] available and valuable for practical use in trials" (p. 404) and whether those methods "could be actually now used and relied on in trials as being superior to the methods hitherto in use" (p. 405). The bulk of the article then consists of a lengthy Q&A between Mr. Tyro, the plaintiffs' attorney, and Münsterberg. In the course of his testimony, Münsterberg was forced to admit, among other things, that much of the empirical knowledge was not widely available, being published in languages other than English or not widely distributed; that it was not American judges' responsibility to introduce psychological (or any other) expert testimony; that leading English-language psychological conferences, treatises, and journals did not mention the discipline's legal applications; that Münsterberg himself "gave not a single citation of any journal or treatise to help the lawyers to the study of the subject, much less took the trouble to prepare . . . a bibliography" (p. 411); that many psychologists viewed the research as very preliminary, especially when it came to relying on it in expert testimony; that many judicial opinions displayed a solid grasp of psychological principles; and that abstract empirical findings had limited applicability to individual cases.

In his closing argument to the jury, Mr. Tyro advocated a "friendly and energetic alliance of psychology and law, in the noble cause of justice" (p. 432). Yet he also, in what would have been especially galling to a real-life, proud German defendant like Münsterberg, quoted Goethe in support of his argument: "There are two things of which a man cannot be careful enough: of obstinacy, if he confines himself to one line of thought; of incompetency, if he goes beyond it" (p. 432). The jury, of which Mr. Demos was elected foreman, apparently agreed that Münsterberg was both obstinate and incompetent; without retiring to deliberate, it announced "after a few moments' whispering, . . . 'We find for the plaintiffs, with damages of one dollar'" (p. 433). The judge agreed with the verdict but had a final word for the plaintiffs, who "ought not to . . . take such a verdict without understanding how narrow had been their escape. They owed their escape merely to the circumstance that the defendant had applied the right epithets to the wrong charges" (p. 433). Specifically, in focusing on the legal profession's obduracy with respect to eyewitness testimony, Münsterberg had not criticized them for their ignorance of criminology, which was the subject of his final chapter on the prevention of crime (see Chapter 10). Judge Wiseman chastised the legal profession in Münsterberg's stead for failing to take advantage of the increasingly well-established field of criminological research, and he put in a plug for the upcoming National Conference on Criminal Law and Criminology (American Institute of Criminal Law and Criminology, 1910).[4]

The entire article is, simply put, a brilliant piece of satire, still entertaining more than 100 years after its publication; and like any satire, it is one-sided to the target's detriment. Nonetheless, it is noteworthy in several additional respects. First, it repeats commonplace objections to expert testimony on eyewitness memory, namely, that the factors affecting eyewitness performance are general knowledge, already known to jurors and judges,

[4] The conference was organized, not coincidentally, by Wigmore himself, in celebration of Northwestern Law School's 50th anniversary.

and that general research findings lack applicability to individual witnesses in real cases. Despite the increasing admissibility of eyewitness expert testimony, these objections are still widespread (Benton et al., 2007). Second, it shows that contrary to Münsterberg's claims, some lawyers—John Henry Wigmore, at least—were extremely familiar with psychology and related social sciences. Unlike Münsterberg, who "gave not a single citation of any journal or treatise" (p. 411), Wigmore included an appendix with a bibliography of 127 "articles and treatises to 1907 inclusive, relating to the experimental psychology of testimony" (p. 435), written in several different languages. The bibliography contains work by such prominent psychologists as Stern, Wertheimer, Galton, Cattell, Binet, Jung, and Freud, as well as a number of lesser-known researchers. Wigmore even showed his belief in psychology's value by conducting demonstrations on eyewitness memory in the classroom (Doyle, 2005). And third, Wigmore's logic is compelling: At the time Münsterberg wrote *On the Witness Stand*, there had been some, but not yet a great deal, of research on eyewitness testimony; and access to much of the contemporary research likely would have been severely limited, even for well-educated attorneys who spoke and read multiple languages.[5]

Importantly, and as the remainder of the present volume will show, Wigmore's logic is no longer applicable. Eyewitness research has become so voluminous that a review of the field can scarcely be contained in a single volume (see, e.g., Lindsay et al., 2007; Toglia et al., 2007); the majority of eyewitness researchers, with some exceptions, are now perfectly comfortable encouraging the courts to admit expert testimony on eyewitness behavior (e.g., Cutler, 2009); and access to scholarly research is considerably easier in the early 21st century than it was in the early 20th century. Nonetheless, Wigmore's criticisms contributed greatly to a quiescence period for the field of psychology and law, as described later (see "Psychology and Law: A Brief History").

Aftermath

Münsterberg's work garnered other harsh reviews, such as one with the colorful title "Yellow Psychology" (Moore, 1907), in which the author complained about Münsterberg's presumption in telling judges how to go about their business, especially when what he was saying was a matter of common sense.[6] Never one to shy away from a fight—or additional publicity—Münsterberg (1907, p. 145) responded, facetiously apologizing that "I had indeed not known that the jurists of the land were so excellently versed in psychological

[5] The situation might have been different, of course, if Münsterberg had written during the age of the Internet, open-access journals, and Google Translate.

[6] Moore (1907) was responding not to *On the Witness Stand* but to an earlier article on eyewitness testimony, published in *McClure's*, that Münsterberg incorporated into the later book.

knowledge." Wigmore's detailed reply to Münsterberg, demonstrating such a good grasp of the psychological literature, suggests that he—and likely other jurists as well—was not at all opposed to applying psychology to the legal system; rather, he was opposed to the cavalier way in which Münsterberg proposed to do so, his blanket statements, and his tone. Wigmore's article was so scathing that, in conjunction with Münsterberg's growing disrepute toward the end of his life (see Chapter 1), it effectively quelled the incipient law-psychology movement for a number of years.

Münsterberg was not the only one to observe the courts' reluctance to avail themselves of the findings of psychological research. According to Whipple (1909, p. 155), "the [experimental] method has been criticized, particularly by jurists, on the ground of over-simplification, general artificiality and consequent non-applicability to the problems of real life—criticism which is, I think, entirely intelligible, however incorrect." In stating that the situation appeared to be better in Germany than the United States, he made an unambiguous reference to the Münsterberg-Moore/Wigmore dispute: "so far as I know the epithet 'yellow psychologist' has not been applied as yet to any German investigator, as it has been to a well-known psychologist in this country" (Whipple, 1909, p. 155). Curiously, 5 years later Whipple commended Wigmore for incorporating psychological facts and principles in the latter's book *The Principles of Judicial Proof*—once in passing (Whipple, 1914a) and once in a full-length review (Whipple, 1914b). He concluded his review by stating that "as a psychologist keenly interested in the application of psychological experiment to legal problems, [this reviewer] has read this work with the greatest satisfaction and profit" (Whipple, 1914b, p. 317). Whether this reflected a change of heart on Whipple's or Wigmore's part, or simply an independent review of a distinct work, is unclear; but it is worth noting that Whipple (1914b) reviewed the book for the *Journal of Criminal Law and Criminology*, which Wigmore founded (in 1910) while dean of Northwestern, and of which Whipple was an associate editor.

Münsterberg, and by association psychological research on eyewitness memory, continued to be held in rather low esteem by the legal community for quite some time. For example, in 1935 Cairns referred to *On the Witness Stand* as a "rash and presumptuous little book" (cited in Ogloff, 2000, p. 458). Doyle (2005) likened Münsterberg's efforts to those of a general who "launched ill-prepared troops in a premature frontal assault across badly chosen ground and into the teeth of a strongly defended position," bringing about "a legendary interdisciplinary Armageddon" (pp. 9–10). Nonetheless, there were sporadic efforts to apply psychological theories and methods to legal questions.

Psychology and Law: A Brief History

Chapter 1 reviewed research on eyewitness testimony being conducted in the late 19th and early 20th centuries in a number of countries, as well as related work in sociology and criminology. Within psychology, other psycholegal topics were also being addressed, and psychology and law as a distinct discipline was beginning to coalesce. A significant challenge in describing the field's history is operationalizing "psychology and law," as many psychologists investigate topics with legal implications, just as many legal scholars explore topics with psychological implications.[7] This operationalization problem is nothing new. In 1929, Slesinger and Pilpel compiled one of the earliest bibliographies of the field, consisting of 164 entries written from psychiatric, sociological, legal, and psychological perspectives.[8] They observed that "From the mass of titles selected for this bibliography and the equally large mass left out of it, it would be difficult to define legal psychology" (p. 678). It has not become any easier to define in the years since, as the mass of titles and topics continues to expand. Following Tapp (1976, p. 360), we focus on "those efforts that were explicitly psychology-and-law directed in terms of the design of the endeavor (experiment) or the discussion of the results."

One such effort actually predated Münsterberg's work. Two years *before* the publication of *On the Witness Stand*, George Frederick Arnold, a British civil servant and judge working in India, published *Psychology Applied to Legal Evidence and Other Constructions of Law* (Arnold, 1906; see Bornstein & Penrod, 2008). Arnold's work covered many of the same topics as Münsterberg's, such as perception, memory, suggestibility, hypnotism, responsibility/sanity, and emotion. In some ways, however, Arnold's work was more expansive than *On the Witness Stand* (Bornstein & Penrod, 2008). For example, it was more grounded in legal theory and processes; provided a broad overview of the cognitive processes of attention, association, and memory; and applied psychology to key legal constructs like the reasonable person standard, causation, and intent. Arnold was deeply familiar with the psychology of the day; although he gravitated toward the more philosophically inclined psychologists (or psychologically inclined philosophers), such as Berkeley, Bain, Stout, and James, he also included important early experimentalists like Wundt, Binet, and Ribot. In the second edition (1913), he added Münsterberg, whose law-psychology book had appeared in the interim. Arnold's work received only minimal notice from contemporary psychologists (Bornstein & Penrod, 2008). Whipple (1914a, p. 248) wrote that it "can scarcely be said to reflect or embody any of the recent experimental work, as its author apologizes for the inability to read German." Although Arnold was largely ignored by the psychological community, Wigmore (1909) included Arnold's book in his Appendix.

---

7 A related challenge is what to call the field and its practitioners. For a thoughtful discussion of nomenclature, see Ogloff (2000).

8 Slesinger and Pilpel (1929) included Münsterberg and Wigmore but acknowledged that their bibliography, which concentrated on works from the late 1920s, was necessarily incomplete. For "older literature" (p. 692), they referred readers to summaries by Whipple, Stern, and others.

The next book devoted entirely to psychology and law, of which we are aware, was Brown's (1926) *Legal Psychology: Psychology Applied to the Trial of Cases, to Crime and Its Treatment, and to Mental States and Processes*, followed a few years later by Harold Burtt's *Legal Psychology* (1931). Burtt trained with Münsterberg at Harvard (Grisso, 2018), and his volume, even more than Münsterberg's or Arnold's, resembles a modern-day law-psychology textbook. The table of contents includes chapters on errors in sensation and perception, memory, suggestion and hypnotism, problems of the jury and judge, confessions, deception detection, the "mentally disordered" and "mentally defective," predelinquency, punishment, and education and crime prevention (it also includes a chapter on eugenics). In the preface, Burtt states that his initial impetus for writing the book was to have a text for a university course in the subject, presumably at Ohio State University, where he was on the faculty. "Subsequently, however, the conviction has developed that there was a much larger field for such a work among the members of the legal profession" (Burtt, 1931, p. vii). He explicitly strove to strike a balance between what would benefit lawyers and what would contribute to psychology students' learning, in the hope that "the reader will come to appreciate the importance of the objective, painstaking scientific approach to problems of legal psychology" (p. viii). As evidence that legal psychology was becoming an accepted part of the discipline, William Marston—another one of Münsterberg's Harvard students—became the first "Professor of Legal Psychology" at American University in 1922 (Grisso, 2018; Heilbrun, Grisso, & Goldstein, 2009).

Increasingly, psychologists began turning their attention to legal questions. Wilhelm Wundt (1918) even devoted the ninth volume of his "folk psychology" to the law. Importantly, Wundt's discussion of law was more a psychological explanation of legal concepts like justice than an application of experimental psychology to legal research questions (Jakob, 1992). A purist like Wundt would not have believed that it was feasible, or desirable, to study a complex system like the law in a rigorous experimental fashion (Hunt, 2007). Fortunately, that did not prevent others at the time from attempting to do so. For example, Whipple (1915) described a comparison by Kobler (1914) of lay versus professional judges—they reached similar results, but both showed evidence of simplification and distortion. This work foreshadowed more recent research on lay adjudicators (e.g., Hans et al., 2017).

Other early work on lay adjudicators was conducted by Weld, who examined the decisions of both individual jurors (Weld & Roff, 1938) and deliberating juries (Weld & Danzig, 1940). For instance, in an unusually naturalistic jury simulation, Weld and Danzig conducted a live moot civil trial before an all-male jury, an all-female jury, and a mixed-gender jury. Mock jurors, who were students, rated their own verdict leaning at 18 different stages of the trial (e.g., after direct and cross-examination of each witness) and then deliberated for 30 minutes. Three findings are particularly noteworthy. First, although "the jurors did not reach decisions through a logical analysis of the case . . . the juries as a whole were well aware of the important issues in the case" (p. 534), and their judgments throughout the trial tracked the orientation of the evidence. Second, there were no gender differences, which stands in stark contrast to the much less realistic deliberation study conducted by Münsterberg (see Chapter 1). And third, deliberation did little to change jurors' predeliberation leanings (see Devine et al., 2001).

Lawyers were also beginning to turn their attention to psychology, in works targeting legal audiences like *Psychology for the Lawyer* (McCarty, 1929), *Law and the Lawyers* (Robinson, 1935), *Law and the Social Sciences* (Cairns, 1935), and *Law and Learning Theory: A Study in Legal Control* (Moore & Callahan, 1943; see, generally, Ogloff, 2000). Law schools began incorporating social science into their curricula, and law schools were hiring psychologists and other social scientists to be on their faculties as early as the late 1920s (Ogloff, Tomkins, & Bersoff, 1996). According to Monahan (2018), Donald Slesinger was the first non-JD psychologist to be full-time faculty at an American law school (hired by Yale Law School in 1927).

Although these attempts to unite the two disciplines doubtlessly kept the flame alive, in the decades following *On the Witness Stand* there was really no concerted effort to forge a new and interdisciplinary field. Grisso (2018, p. 6) refers to the period from 1930 to 1960 as "the dormant era." According to Tapp (1976, p. 361), "[t]he scattered attempts during the 1920s, 1930s, 1940s, and 1950s by psychologists or lawyers . . . reflected little progress in the rapprochement between psychology and law . . . Not until the late 1960s and early 1970s was the exchange between psychologists and lawyers on matters of justice and law anything more than sparse and sporadic." Up until that point, "the development of the law and psychology movement . . . occurred more by chance than by planning" (Ogloff, 2000, p. 458). The key question is, what changed? Perhaps the volume of research had simply reached a critical mass, a tipping point; or perhaps, as Tapp argues, larger societal changes (e.g., modernization, social unrest, rising rates of crime and violence, a growing awareness of individuals' and institutions' rights and responsibilities) tipped the balance. Ogloff et al. (1996) point to the advent of clinical/professional psychology in the years following World War II, creating a demand for forensic assessment, and the use of psychological research in prominent court cases (e.g., *Brown v. Board of Education of Topeka*, 1954), as other instrumental factors. Regardless, by roughly 50 years ago, psychology and law had crystalized as a more-or-less coherent discipline.

These developments contributed to what is perhaps the most significant development—the founding of the American Psychology-Law Society (AP-LS) in 1969, along with the Society's inaugural conference in 1974 and the initial publication in 1977 of both its flagship journal, *Law and Human Behavior*, and a book series.[9] AP-LS began informally in 1968, when a handful

---

[9] As the present volume is part of the AP-LS book series, we hope readers will forgive the shameless plug.

of like-minded psychologists found one another at the annual American Psychological Association convention in San Francisco (Fulero, 1999; Grisso, 1991). The organization's constitution and bylaws were ratified in 1969; the constitution "announced the Society's intentions to promote the psychological study of law, to influence legislation and public policy, and to promote the effective use of psychology in the legal process" (Grisso, 1991, pp. 216–217). The initial focus was mainly on clinical/forensic practice and communicating psychology in the courtroom (i.e., expert testimony), with a minor element of basic research as well (Fulero, 1999). These goals and focus are all highly compatible with Münsterberg's statements in the first chapter of *On the Witness Stand*.

This same period, of the late 1960s/early 1970s, saw the creation of interdisciplinary law-psychology academic programs (the University of Nebraska–Lincoln created the first one in 1974), law-psychology university courses at both the undergraduate and graduate levels, educational materials to be used in those courses, and additional journals (e.g., *Law and Society Review* in 1966, *Criminal Justice and Behavior* in 1974) (see, generally, Bornstein, Wiener, & Maeder, 2008; Fulero, 1999; Ogloff et al., 1996; Tapp, 1976). More traditional journals in psychology also published special issues on the new field (e.g., *Journal of Personality and Social Psychology* and *Professional Psychology* both published special issues on psychology and law in 1978; Fulero, 1999). Organizations with an overlapping mission, such as the Law and Society Association (founded in 1964) and American Academy of Forensic Psychology (founded in 1978), were also holding meetings, publishing journals, nurturing law-and-social-science research and professional practice, and supporting training programs. Extramural funding opportunities increased with the formation of the National Science Foundation's Law and Social Sciences Program in 1971. It is probably an exaggeration to say that by the mid-1970s law-psychology had "arrived," considering that work in the discipline had been going on, in one way or another, for 70 years or more, and that it continues to evolve. Nonetheless, professional organizations, scientific journals, and specialized training programs are all important benchmarks for a discipline and clear indications that it has become established (Cautin, 2009; Hunt, 2007). No doubt Münsterberg would have been pleased, even if he were also dumbfounded that it took so long.

Psychology *and* Law, or Psychology *Versus* Law?

A recurrent question in the field of law-psychology is how well the two disciplines coordinate their efforts. Of course, they have different goals and procedures, so it would be unrealistic ever to expect perfect alignment. As Tapp (1976, p. 398) observed, "the intertwining of psychology and law, like science and justice, is a difficult orchestration." Nonetheless, there are many instances where they can work together so that one can benefit the other, as in establishing policies governing the rights and responsibilities of persons with mental illness, evaluating psychologically vulnerable populations involved in court proceedings, or determining the circumstances under which eyewitnesses are likely to be more/less accurate. A growing awareness that the law can serve as a healing agent—or at least as an institution less likely to cause harm—has informed, for example, the therapeutic jurisprudence movement (Wexler & Winick, 1996). The question, then, is how much social sciences like psychology can work in concert with the courts, and how much they are at odds with one another.

Law and social sciences, including psychology, take very different epistemological approaches, and the threads of the two disciplines have come together and diverged over the years, with an overall trend toward increasing collaboration (Monahan & Walker, 2018). According to Monahan and Walker, social science in law originated in the "jurisprudential revolution" that took place in the late 19th and early 20th centuries. Although Monahan and Walker focus on American jurisprudence, related developments were occurring in other countries (Jakob, 1992; Shaboltas, 2017). This jurisprudential revolution involved a transition from a classical, heavily rationalist and deductive jurisprudence that believed every case had a single, correct legal solution, to a more realistic, inductive approach that took the social context into account (Monahan & Walker, 2018). The newer approach went hand in hand with the sociological jurisprudence movement, which emphasized the use of empirical data to understand the social contexts in which law operated (Ogloff et al., 1996). Not coincidentally, the transition was accompanied by the change in legal education from an apprenticeship to a university-based model (Ogloff, 2000; Ogloff et al., 1996), as well as a growing desire on the part of many jurists and policymakers to use law as a means of reforming social policy (Monahan & Walker, 2018), akin to the goals of therapeutic jurisprudence (Wexler & Winick, 1996). Also not coincidentally, this was the same period during which Münsterberg was active and psychology and its sister sciences were achieving scientific legitimacy. In exhorting the courts to rely more heavily on psychological research, Münsterberg was, to a considerable extent, merely tapping into the zeitgeist. The vehemence of Wigmore's response suggests that Münsterberg overshot his mark, but in calling for the courts to rely on social scientific evidence in the early 20th century, he was not completely out in left field.

The closest connection between psychology and law presently is in the area of forensic psychology, which includes both clinical/professional psychology (e.g., risk assessment and treatment of offenders) and experimental psychology (e.g., social, cognitive, and developmental psychological research on legally relevant issues). Some of the experimental research directly addresses legal questions (e.g., the effect of allowing jurors to take notes on their evidence comprehension, verdicts, and overall satisfaction with jury service), whereas other experimental research speaks more indirectly to issues that arise in the civil or criminal justice system (e.g., investigation of the factors affecting eyewitness memory). Psychologists and other mental health professionals (e.g., psychiatrists, social workers) work in the legal system in a great variety of capacities, most of which involve the clinical assessment and treatment of individuals for various purposes or the provision of expert knowledge (see, generally, Melton et al., 2007; Skeem, Douglas, & Lilienfeld, 2009). Psychologists share their expertise in numerous ways: as expert witnesses appointed by judges, testifying before legislative bodies, or retained by private parties; and as trial consultants working with attorneys. Psychological research can be, and has been, used to determine facts or provide context in specific cases, to make law, and to assist attorneys in litigation. Thus, as Münsterberg anticipated, psychology and law come into frequent contact.

However, because they differ fundamentally in both their substance and their method, tensions continue to arise. Much of this tension derives from a reliance on different methods: Law is primarily deductive, meaning that it emphasizes the application of general principles to individual cases, whereas psychology, like all sciences, is primarily inductive, emphasizing the use of data from individual cases to formulate or test general principles. This distinction can create problems in determining the relevance of general background research, of the sort often relied on by expert witnesses, to individual cases. For example, several years ago one of us testified as an expert witness for the defense in a case of attempted homicide. The crime involved a drive-by shooting, in which the victim saw the assailant approach, lean out of his car, and fire a gun at him. At a pretrial admissibility (*Daubert*) hearing, the expert testified about research showing the detrimental effects on eyewitness accuracy of arousal, weapon focus, and limited exposure. On cross-examination, the prosecutor quite rightly asked, "Did you examine this witness? Do you know that he experienced a high degree of arousal or focused his attention on the perpetrator's weapon? Do you know how long he actually spent looking at the perpetrator's face during the encounter?" The answers, as is typical for this sort of expert testimony, were "no, no, and no." The prosecutor then argued—as Wigmore (1909) and many others have done since—that the research, while seemingly perfectly legitimate, was not relevant to the case at hand. This reasoning is common in eyewitness cases and not an infrequent reason for excluding eyewitness expert testimony at trial (Benton at al., 2007). The judge in this particular case excluded the testimony on grounds that the effect of these factors on eyewitness memory was a matter of common sense—another common rationale for excluding eyewitness expert testimony (Benton et al., 2007).

In addition, law is deferential to authority and precedent, whereas science is skeptical toward authority and precedent. Given the centrality of empirical data in science, it is essential that the methods used to gather and analyze the data be sound (e.g., reliable and valid). Following in the tradition of Wigmore, courts have often been critical of psychological research on the grounds of validity, questioning the extent to which the research truly measures what it purports to measure.

The aspects of validity to which courts most frequently refer—either explicitly or implicitly—are external and ecological validity. External validity refers to generalizability—that is, whether a study's conclusions apply beyond the study sample—whereas ecological validity refers to whether the study's procedures are an accurate representation of the real-world context under investigation (e.g., using a lineup task that closely mirrors the way lineups are actually conducted by law enforcement). Higher ecological validity generally translates to higher external validity, but the two are not necessarily linked. It is therefore a mistake to dismiss a study just because it is low in ecological validity; yet courts do that routinely, often assuming that because a study is low in verisimilitude, the results would not generalize (Bornstein & McCabe, 2005). Research that has addressed the issue of ecological validity in psycholegal research, however, has found little in the way of consistent differences (Bornstein & McCabe, 2005; Penrod & Bornstein, 2007). Because of ethical and practical constraints, questions of interest sometimes cannot be studied easily, or even at all, in their natural setting (e.g., the effect of traumatic events on memory; certain variations in trial procedures). Moreover, enhancing a study's ecological and external validity can come at the cost of diminishing its internal validity (i.e., whether a study's methods justify the inferences that can be drawn, within the circumstances of the particular study itself).

There is no easy solution to the problem of balancing the different types of validity. Some evidence exists that courts are becoming more savvy about social scientific evidence (Monahan & Walker, 2018), due partly to the increasing frequency with which they encounter it and efforts to refine the admissibility criteria for scientific evidence (Faigman et al., 2014), as well as to efforts to make legal scholarship more data-driven, like the empirical legal studies movement (e.g., Ho & Kramer, 2013). With respect to eyewitness testimony in particular, most jurisdictions now allow expert testimony and/or specialized jury instructions on the issue, at least under some circumstances (Benton et al., 2007; *State v. Henderson*, 2011). Although the legal system is still, in some respects, resistant to psychological research (e.g., Doyle, 2005; Monahan & Walker, 2018), the field of psychology and law has made enormous legal inroads in the last 110 years. Münsterberg's lament may still ring true in certain courtrooms, but law and social science are much less adversarial than they were when Wigmore penned his response to Münsterberg. Psychology and law are more likely to work together now than in opposition.

Conclusions

Münsterberg was very explicit about what the law could gain from psychology, but he largely ignored what psychology could gain from the law. Psychology has much to offer the law, but for psycholegal research to matter, it must be legally informed and willing to take the concerns of legal practitioners and policymakers seriously (Ogloff, 2000). The one-sided nature of Münsterberg's view of the law-psychology relationship likely contributed to the initial rejection by the legal community of his appeal to the courts that they should take more notice of psychological research. Fortunately, the field has evolved tremendously in the 110 years since he wrote *On the Witness Stand*. After a period of mostly sporadic interaction, psychology and law—especially in the United States, but also elsewhere—came together for good in the late 1960s and early 1970s. Much of this is due to the creation of the American Psychology-Law Society and related organizational efforts, but social forces also played a large part. Despite the substantive and methodological differences between psychology and law, they are in many ways a natural fit. The law needs good psychological and other social scientific research and expertise, and psychology must take legal considerations into account when providing services to clients and when devising research that applies fundamental psychological principles to legal and policy questions.

How best to do that remains something of an open question. In some respects, Münsterberg was a strong advocate of ecological validity, as in encouraging the use of field studies with naïve witnesses (see Chapter 4). Yet at other times he evinced a willingness to extrapolate from a relatively meager database of less-than-naturalistic studies. Perhaps, as raised in the previous chapter, that reflected his publicity- and confrontation-seeking nature. Whatever the reason or reasons for this inconsistency, it arguably did the field of psychology and law no favors. Fortunately, although Wigmore (1909) and others were highly critical of *On the Witness Stand*, they shared a belief that psychology had enormous potential to aid the justice system. There is still a degree of resistance among judges and policymakers to psychological research—especially in certain courts and on certain topics—but for the most part they are a good deal more receptive to psychological science than they were a century ago.

3

Illusions

But do we really all perceive the same thing, and does it have the same meaning to us in our immediated absorption of the surrounding world? Is the court sufficiently aware of the great differences between men's perceptions, and does the court take sufficient trouble to examine the capacities and habits with which the witness moves through the world which he believes he observes?

—Münsterberg, *On the Witness Stand* (pp. 18–19)

In his "Illusions" chapter, Münsterberg discusses how people perceive the world and, more specifically, how people who witness the same events can give widely different accounts. To introduce the chapter, Münsterberg gives examples of court cases that illustrate this point. The first case he mentions involves an automobile accident. One witness under oath testified the road was dry and dusty and the automobile was going slowly. By contrast, another witness indicated that it had rained, was muddy, and the car was traveling at a very high rate of speed. The two witnesses also gave very different accounts as to how many people were on the street. Münsterberg indicates that neither witness had any reason to be disingenuous: "Both witnesses were highly respectable gentlemen, neither of whom had the slightest interest in changing the facts as he remembered them" (p. 15).

Münsterberg goes on to refute what he considers to be the conventional wisdom about perception: "It is generally taken for granted that we all perceive our surroundings uniformly" (p. 18). As the car accident example illustrates, this is not always the case. He maintains that courts, to their downfall, do not rely on psychologists to help ferret out differences in psychological issues: "Legal theorists have even proudly boasted of the fact that the judges always found their way without psychological advice, and yet the records of such cases, for instance, in railroad damages, quickly show that the psychological inspirations of the bench are often directly the opposite of demonstrable facts" (p. 19).

For the remainder of the chapter, Münsterberg discusses a series of experiments that would be considered little more than classroom demonstrations, rather than rigorously controlled laboratory experiments, by today's standards. His demonstrations reveal how people witnessing the same event may have quite disparate memories of that event. For example, he mentions a demonstration that he did in class whereby his students were required to answer a series of questions regarding things that were shown or heard in the class. Münsterberg showed the class a white piece of cardboard with 50 black spots on it. The spots were placed in a haphazard manner, and the board was displayed for 5 seconds. The students' task was to determine how many spots were on it. Their estimates ranged from 25 to 200. Münsterberg repeated the experiment with 20 spots on the cardboard. The pattern of results was unchanged: The estimates were still quite variable, ranging from 10 to 70. Münsterberg indicated that the subjects were "highly trained, careful observers, whose attention was concentrated on the material, and who had full time for quiet scrutiny" (p. 21). Münsterberg gives no credence to the suggestion that students were not working diligently and answering honestly: ". . . and the hundreds of answers which I received showed clearly that everyone had done his[1] best" (p. 21).

As he continues, Münsterberg describes a number of cases and experiments that illustrate the vagaries and unreliability of human perception and memory, showing that multiple witnesses often perceive the same event quite differently—producing what he refers to as "illusions." He relates these illusions to expectancies, suggestibility, and individual differences, and he complains that courts are too quick to accept confident witnesses' statements at face value. These phenomena have all been investigated extensively in the eyewitness literature. Because suggestibility is covered in a separate chapter (Chapter 8), this chapter will focus on other related phenomena, such as unconscious transference, change blindness, and inattention blindness.

In addition to these memory errors, we will also discuss how witnesses can be confident in their memories even when they are inaccurate. The confidence–accuracy (CA) relationship has been one of the most controversial and complex aspects of eyewitness memory, as the strength of the relationship varies depending on a number of individual and situational characteristics, as well as methodological and analytic choices (Leippe & Eisenstadt, 2007; Wixted et al., 2015). Although the CA relationship is stronger in some circumstances than in others, it is relatively weak in the circumstances corresponding to most crimes, and it is weaker than most people think (Bornstein & Greene, 2017; Leippe & Eisenstadt, 2007). Furthermore,

---

[1] There were only men at Harvard during the time Münsterberg was teaching there.

even though laypersons expect confidence to be a reliable predictor of accuracy (Benton et al., 2007; Bornstein & Greene, 2017), confidence can be influenced by postidentification events (e.g., feedback; Lampinen, Neuschatz, & Cling, 2012; Steblay, Wells, & Douglass, 2014). Thus, the supposed reliability of confidence in predicting eyewitness accuracy is another "illusion."

Unconscious Transference

Houts (1956) described a case of memory illusion or misidentification wherein a ticket agent had been robbed and subsequently identified an innocent person as the culprit. The man wrongly identified by the ticket agent had been an occasional customer. The witness identified the innocent bystander because he remembered having previously encountered him but was unable to recall the context of their interaction. A similar case in 1983 led to Lenell Geter's receiving a life sentence for a series of robberies. Eight months into his sentence, he was released when new evidence revealed that a different man had committed the crimes. Shortly after the robberies, the key eyewitness was shown a lineup in which Geter was pictured. The witness indicated that the suspect was not in the lineup. Several months later the witness was shown a new lineup that contained four new photos and Geter. This time the witness wrongly identified Geter as the culprit. The witness had mistakenly associated a feeling of familiarity with Geter's photograph with the crime and had forgotten that the picture was shown in the first lineup. Today, researchers refer to this type of error as the bystander effect or unconscious transference.[2]

Unconscious transference occurs when an eyewitness misidentifies an innocent bystander as the culprit because of a previous encounter with that bystander which occurred in another context. The witness is unable to remember the specific context in which the bystander was encountered and incorrectly attributes the sense of familiarity to the crime (Buckhout, 1974; Loftus, 1976); thus, the bystander is incorrectly identified as the culprit. Read and colleagues (1990) defined the phenomenon as the mistaken shift of one person's identity to another person who had been previously encountered in another context.

Unconscious transference is fairly common in legal proceedings and has been mentioned in at least two US Supreme Court decisions (*Stovall v. Denno*, 1967; *United States v. Wade*, 1967). A survey of experts in both 1989 (Kassin, Ellsworth, & Smith, 1989) and 2001 (Kassin, Tubb, Hosch, & Memon, 2001) reported that 84% (1989 data) and 81% (2001 data) of the sample believed that the laboratory data on unconscious transference were

---

[2] Legal scholar Glanville Williams (1955) introduced the term *unconscious transference*.

reliable, and when these experts were asked more specifically about whether these results were reliable enough to testify in court, 67% (1989) and 66% (2001) of the sample indicated that they were.

In the first known study on unconscious transference, Buckhout (1974) had students witness a staged assault on a professor. Seven weeks after the crime, students were asked to identify the attacker from a lineup that contained the culprit, a bystander who was present at the crime scene, and four never-before-seen fillers (i.e., people who were not present in the staged crime). Forty percent of the students correctly identified the culprit. Of the 60% who identified someone other than the culprit, 41% incorrectly identified the bystander. This may seem like a very high rate of false bystander identifications. Unfortunately, the author did not include a control condition wherein participants did not see the bystander, so it is difficult to know whether the bystander misidentification percentage was significantly different from what would be expected by chance alone. The bystander might simply have been an unusually good foil for some unknown reason.

In order to ensure that the bystander effects reported by Buckout (1974) were not due to the similarity in appearance of the bystander and culprit, Loftus (1976) varied the bystander and culprit. Loftus had college students listen to an audiotaped crime while simultaneously viewing photographs that corresponded to people in the story. Three days later, participants were presented with either a target-present (TP) or target-absent (TA) lineup and asked to make an identification of the culprit who had committed the crime. The TP array contained four unfamiliar faces and the culprit. The TA lineup was the same as the TP lineup except the culprit was replaced with an incidental character in the story or innocent bystander. When the culprit was present in the lineup, Loftus found that he was correctly identified 84% of the time. In the TA condition, 76% were misidentified, and 60% of those were mistaken bystander identifications.

Although Loftus's (1976) study demonstrated that a higher rate of bystander identifications compared to other lineup fillers was not due to the similarity in appearance, she was unable to distinguish whether participants actually were able to recall the circumstances or context of their encounter with the bystander. Presenting only facial photos means participants were not exposed to any behavioral or contextual information associated with any of the story characters. It is possible that these contextual cues could aid retrieval and eliminate the effect. In fact, a key explanation of unconscious transference is that it is easier for a witness to recall a face than the context in which the face was encountered. One theory suggests that unconscious transference occurs because the bystander is familiar but the context in which the person was encountered is forgotten and misattributed to the crime scene (see Ross, Ceci, Dunning, & Toglia, 1994).

Unconscious transference effects are obtained even when the participants are given explicit instructions to remember the faces that they witness for a future test (Brown, Deffenbacher, & Sturgill, 1977). In Brown et al.'s study, two confederates handed out testing materials at the beginning of a class. These confederates served as "culprits" or targets in the experiment. Class members were unaware that later they would be asked to identify these individuals, similar to how real eyewitnesses often would not know in advance that they would need to recall a face in the future. A few days after the initial viewing, participants were shown a matrix of 11 mugshots. The mugshots included a photograph of the confederate who had initially been seen handing out the test, as well as photographs of other people that had never been seen before by the class. Finally, in the third session, participants were presented with a live lineup. This lineup contained a target who had been seen both in person handing out exams and in a mugshot; the confederate who was only seen in person handing out exams; an individual who was seen only in a mugshot; and an individual who had not been seen before prior to the identification task. Participants were very accurate at identifying the person that was seen both handing out testing material and in the mugshot photos. Brown et al. also found support for unconscious transference, as participants were equally likely to identify (correctly) a person that they had encountered handing out tests but not in the mugshots as they were to identify (falsely) an individual that they had seen only in a mugshot. Brown et al. replicated these results with intentional instructions that informed participants to attend to the faces they saw for an upcoming test. These results point out the risk, or the illusion, of familiarity that can be created from viewing mugshots, a phenomenon that is referred to as the mugshot exposure effect (see Deffenbacher, Bornstein, & Penrod, 2006; Goodsell, Gronlund, & Neuschatz, 2009).

The harmful effect of previous exposure to a person is not relegated to mugshot exposure and has been replicated across numerous memory paradigms. For example, Heinz and Pezdek (2001) examined the extent to which presenting witnesses with an initial TA lineup affects their subsequent lineup accuracy. Participants were shown a photograph of a culprit. A week later, participants were asked to make an identification from one of two intervening TA lineups. One of these lineups contained a designated suspect that served as the innocent suspect, whereas the other lineup did not contain this specific suspect. Participants returned to the laboratory 2 days later and were asked to make a final identification from one of three lineups: a lineup containing both the culprit and the innocent suspect, a lineup containing only the culprit, or a lineup containing only the innocent suspect. The results revealed that familiarity mattered. Correct identifications were highest when participants were presented with a culprit-only lineup, and false identifications were highest when participants who had seen the innocent suspect in the intervening lineup saw the innocent-suspect-only version of the lineup at the final identification test.

Since the initial demonstrations of unconscious transference, subsequent research has attempted to identify the boundary conditions of the effect and understand the mechanisms that govern it. Read et al. (1990), in a series of five experiments, attempted to produce the unconscious transference effect;

however, the effect was observed only in Experiment 5. In Experiments 1–4, the culprit approached store clerks in a shopping mall and asked them for 20 quarters in exchange for a $5 bill. Clerks that were in the transference condition were also exposed to a bystander, who approached the clerks and asked if the clerks had seen his wife and child. Clerks who were in the control condition were never exposed to the bystander. The clerks were then presented with a lineup containing the bystander and four unfamiliar foils. The clerks in the transference condition were less likely to misidentify the bystander than clerks who had been in the control condition. The clerks in the transference condition indicated that they remembered the interaction with the bystander and did not misidentify him in the lineup.

In Experiment 5, Read et al. (1990) staged an event where an electrician, who served as the culprit, interrupted a class to fix an electrical problem. Prior to this event, the students in the transference condition had also been exposed to another individual, the bystander, who handed out exam materials to the class as they took their seats. Control group participants were never exposed to the bystander. Two weeks later, all participants were presented with a lineup containing either the bystander or the culprit, plus four other unfamiliar foils. Participants were asked to identify the individual who had come to fix the electrical problem. Read et al. found that participants in the transference condition were twice as likely to misidentify the innocent bystander as were participants in the control condition. In addition to this, 23% of the participants in the transference condition indicated that they had seen the bystander in another context as well as the scene of the crime.

On the basis of these studies, Read et al. (1990) argued that unconscious transference is unlikely to occur in real criminal proceedings. That is, in conditions which closely resemble what happens in real crime situations, like Experiments 1–4, unconscious transference was not found. Furthermore, Read et al. concluded that if witnesses do recognize a bystander, they will also remember the context in which they encountered the bystander and reject the bystander as the culprit.

The conclusions of Read et al. (1990), whether one accepts them or not, raise two very provocative questions: Why does unconscious transference occur? Does the witness really believe that the bystander was the actual culprit? There are several possible explanations as to why a witness may confuse a bystander for the culprit. First, a witness may actually believe that the bystander and culprit are the same person. That is, a witness may have no conscious recollection of the bystander until the witness encounters him or her in the lineup and choose the bystander based on a feeling of familiarity, as in Heinz and Pezdek's (2001) study and the case of the ticket booth agent mentioned earlier. This is referred to as the automatic processing account because memory of the bystander is formed automatically. A similar account was offered by Ross et al. (1994), in which they referred to it as "memory blending" or "conscious inference" because the memory of the bystander and culprit get merged together, and the witness believes that the culprit and the bystander are the same person. Second, there is the source monitoring approach based on the work of Johnson and colleagues (see Johnson, Hashtroudi, & Lindsay, 1993). This account assumes that a witness is aware that the bystander and the culprit are two separate people, but at the identification, they confuse *where* they encountered each and wrongfully decide the bystander was the culprit.

In a series of experiments, Ross et al. (1994) tested these three accounts of unconscious transference. In the first study, participants viewed one of two mock crime videos. In one version, participants saw a video of a female teacher's day spent playing with and reading to children. At the end, she is shown leaving her wallet on a table in the cafeteria, where a male culprit steals money from the wallet. In this first (control) video, the only adults were the female victim and the male culprit. However, in the second (transference) video, an additional male actor is seen reading to the children. When asked to make an identification, participants who had been in the transference condition were approximately three times more likely to identify the innocent suspect (the male reading to the children) than those in the control condition. Furthermore, follow-up questions revealed that the majority of the participants in the transference condition believed the person seen reading to the children and the person who stole the money to be the same person. Given that participants were able to recall the context in which they believed they had encountered the suspect, this study suggests that automatic processing is unlikely to be the theoretical mechanism behind these misidentifications.

Following Experiment 1, the authors used studies 2 through 4 to clarify the underlying explanation for these identifications. In Experiment 2, the authors were completely able to eliminate the difference in mistaken innocent suspect identifications between the transference and control conditions by informing participants in the transference condition that the male seen reading to the children was not the same person who later stole the money. The authors concluded that this makes it unlikely that the unconscious transference errors were occurring due to deliberate source monitoring errors, because when participants realized that there were two separate individuals, the rate of innocent suspect identifications significantly decreased and no longer differed from that of the control condition.

Finally, Experiments 3 and 4 attempted to identify the stage in memory where these errors originate. In Experiment 3, there were two transference conditions that differed in terms of when participants were asked if they had seen the culprit at any other time in the film. One group was asked this question before the lineup, and the second was asked after making an identification from the lineup. The authors hypothesized that should conscious inference occur at encoding, there should be no differences between the responses of the two transference groups. Conversely, if conscious inference occurs due to the lineup identification procedure, participants should make unconscious transference errors when asked about the context only after viewing the lineup. The results showed that there was no difference in participants' responses, thereby suggesting that these errors are occurring at the time of encoding. The authors provided further evidence for this account in Experiment 4, where participants were asked to pause the crime tape any time they believed they had seen the male character twice. Again, participants in the transference condition indicated they believed the innocent suspect and the culprit to be the same person by stopping the tape when they saw the robber. Taken as a whole, these data suggest that unconscious transference is a fairly robust phenomenon, but the mechanism(s) that mediate the effect are not yet well understood.

In summary, unconscious transference is a reliable effect that can have deleterious consequences for eyewitness identification. It is one of the perceptual or memory errors, what Münsterberg would call an illusion, that can fool an eyewitness into believing that an innocent bystander was the culprit. As noted by Read et al. (1990), although the effect seems to be reliable, the boundary conditions are not well known. It stands to reason that the effect would be greater in magnitude as the original memory trace fades or becomes weaker, because the original memory trace will be harder to access and compare to the memory test (or identification test in this case; see Loftus [2005] for a discussion of discrepancy detection in eyewitness memory). In addition, the theoretical underpinnings of the effect have remained difficult to discover. Whatever the mechanism, we agree with the conclusions of Read et al. (1990) that the more conditions of real crimes are not conducive to accurate memory, the more conducive they are to memory errors or illusions such as unconscious transference.

Change and Inattention Blindness

Closely related to unconscious transference are the phenomena of change blindness and inattention blindness. Change blindness is the inability to detect major changes in the perceptual environment (Rensink, O'Regan, & Clark, 1997; Simons & Levin, 1997). If one experimenter leaves the room and a second experimenter returns, failure to notice that there were two experimenters would be an example of change blindness. Inattention blindness is the failure to notice objects in a visual scene. An example of inattention blindness would be the failure of a police officer to notice a gun on the passenger's seat during a routine traffic stop. As will be discussed later, Simons and Schlosser (2017) used this scenario in their inattention blindness study. Inattention blindness differs from change blindness in that it is a failure to notice an object (or person) altogether as opposed to failing to notice that an object (or person) has changed. Change blindness and inattention blindness represent the type of perceptual illusions that Münsterberg is referring to in *On the Witness Stand*.

Change Blindness

As mentioned earlier, change blindness is the failure to notice changes, sometimes major changes, in the visual scene (Rensink et al., 1997). It is important to note that these changes are above the threshold of human visual capacity, which means that they are easily detectable by the unaided human eye. Although it seems change blindness likely occurs often and would have eyewitness implications, there has not been a lot of research on the topic as it applies to eyewitness memory.

Of particular importance to eyewitness memory, a number of studies have demonstrated that participants do not notice an identity change in a scene. One of the earliest studies involving identity change (Levin & Simons, 1997) required that observers view a video clip of an actor getting up to answer a telephone call. In the video, a change of camera angle occurs simultaneously with the change of identity, so the person seen answering the phone is a different actor. One-third of the participants failed to notice that change, even though there were considerable differences between the two actors' appearances. Levin and Simons argued that participants' inability to detect the change could not be due to inattention, as the actions that were illustrated were central to the event.

One of the first examinations of change blindness in the context of face perception was conducted by Humphreys, Hodsoll, and Campbell (2005). Humphreys et al. used the "flicker" paradigm in which the original and altered stimuli are separated by blank displays and repeatedly shown until the participant notices the change (Rensink, O'Regan, & Clark, 1997). Researchers typically measure how long it takes participants to notice the change. Humphreys et al. used the flicker methodology to show participants four women (two were Indian women and two were White). The results were analogous to cross-race identification findings in which people are more accurate at identifying people from the same race as opposed to a different race (Bornstein, Laub, Meissner, & Susa, 2013; Meissner & Brigham, 2001). That is, Indian participants were quicker to notice the change in the Indian faces, and White participants were quicker to notice the change in White faces.

In their classic change blindness study, Levin, Simons, Angelone, and Chabris (2002) incorporated a lineup identification task into their procedure. In this study participants were recruited to participate in an experimental study in exchange for candy (yes, candy). While participants were filling out the consent form, the experimenter, under the guise of getting more experimental materials, ducked behind a counter and was replaced by another similarly dressed experimenter. The second experimenter continued the conversation with the participant as if nothing had changed. Only 5 of the 20 participants, or 25%, noticed that there were two experimenters. The experimenter later found that 6 of the participants, just prior to participating in the experiment, had been at a meeting in which a change blindness study was discussed. Only two of those participants noticed the change. In Experiment 2, Levin et al. added a lineup identification task to the change blindness procedure. For both experimenters, the authors created two separate four-person TP lineups. There were four separate lineups with different fillers for each lineup. The task was to pick out the first experimenter they encountered. Those who noticed the change had more correct identifications than those who did not notice the change. Furthermore, those who missed the change correctly identified the experimenter 26% of the time, which is at chance level (chance with a four-person lineup would be 25%).

Change blindness was utilized in a more traditional eyewitness paradigm by Davies and Hine (2007). They were interested in exploring whether the common factor mediating face processing and identity change is a poor initial representation of the person involved, and whether variables that influence eyewitness identification should also influence change blindness and vice versa. Prior to watching a video that included the identity change of the burglar, participants were either provided with instructions that let them know their memory would be tested later (intentional) or were not provided instructions (incidental). After the video, participants were asked if they noticed anything about the burglar, and they were asked to pick the burglar out of a lineup that contained both burglars from the video and four fillers. Overall, participants noticed the identity change 39% of the time. Participants who noticed the change performed better on the lineup task than those who did not notice the change. Of the 31 participants who noted the change, 29 selected at least one of the burglars out of the lineup, and 20 identified both burglars. In contrast, of those who did not notice the change ($n = 49$), not one identified both burglars. A separate study by Davis, Loftus, Vanous, and Cucciare (2008) also found that failure to detect an actor change led to worse lineup identification performance. More specifically, they found that participants who failed to detect the change were significantly more likely to misidentify someone from a TA lineup.

One problem with change blindness studies in the eyewitness identification field is that the lineups do not conform to standard lineup practice (Fitzgerald, Oriet, & Price, 2016). The lineups include both actors in a single lineup (Davies & Hine, 2007; Davis et al., 2008) or too few lineup choices (Levin et al., 2002). Either issue is unlikely to happen in real-world lineups, making generalization to the real world problematic. Fitzgerald et al. identified and addressed this issue by having participants complete a six-person lineup containing either the culprit or the innocent bystander. In this study, participants watched a video of a person entering a building and then saw another individual commit a crime. Overall lineup accuracy was higher for people who detected the change than those who did not. More specifically, in the group viewing TA lineups, people who detected the change were more likely to correctly reject the lineup than people who did not notice the change. For the TP lineup, participants who noticed the change were somewhat more likely to choose the culprit than those who did not notice the change, but this difference was not significant. Thus, the literature on change blindness, albeit sparse, consistently shows that change blindness harms identification performance.

Inattention Blindness

As mentioned earlier, inattention blindness is the failure to notice an object in the visual scene. Consider, for example, a Colgate advertising campaign for dental floss that was launched in Brazil but was widely disseminated in the United States on social media sites such as Pinterest and Reddit (see Figure 3.1). This campaign used inattention blindness to demonstrate how people would not notice missing or additional body parts in a photograph: If the person pictured had something in his teeth, then people may not see his right ear is missing (see Nudd, 2012).

Probably the most famous demonstration of inattention blindness is the Simons and Chabris (1999) gorilla study. In this study, participants saw people in white and black shirts playing with a basketball, and the participants' task was to count how many passes were made by the white-shirted players. Black-shirted players never handled the ball. During the video, a person wearing a gorilla costume walked into the middle of the group, beat her chest, and walked out of the scene. The gorilla was in the scene for a total of 5 seconds and, as can be seen in Figure 3.2, the gorilla is quite apparent. However, 46%, or nearly half of the participants, failed to notice the gorilla. Although we think it is relevant to eyewitness memory, inattention blindness has not been

Figure 3.1. Inattention blindness example in Colgate advertising campaign.

Figure 3.2. Example of inattention blindness (from Simons & Chabris, 1999).

widely studied as it applies to psycholegal issues. In fact, we know of only two studies that attempt to bridge this gap: Simons and Schlosser (2017) applied it to police officers in a simulated traffic stop, and Clifasefi, Takarangi, and Bergman (2006) applied it to intoxicated participants.

Simons and Schlosser (2017) were interested in whether inattention blindness would be attenuated if the object was a threat to the observer. To test this, they had police academy trainees and police officers engage in a simulated traffic stop. During the stop, a gun was located in full view on the passenger's side dashboard. The driver was instructed to act cooperative, agitated, or hostile to the police officer. Presumably, the more hostile the driver, the more of a threat the gun would be. Regardless of the driver's interaction style or degree of hostility, the results revealed inattention blindness: 58% of the trainees and 33% of the police officers failed to notice the gun. This study demonstrates that inattention blindness can occur in naturalistic situations that are threatening.

Clifasefi et al. (2006) conducted a modified version of Simons and Chabris's (1999) gorilla study. Participants in this study were given alcohol or a nonalcoholic placebo, and members of both groups were made to believe they were or were not drinking alcohol. As was the case in the original study, the participants' task was to count basketball passes of the white-shirted players, while during the video the person in the gorilla suit entered for 5 seconds. Only a third of the participants noted the gorilla, and inattention blindness was exacerbated by alcohol consumption. Participants were brought to a blood alcohol concentration level of only .04, which is half the legal limit for driving in all 50 states. The participants who drank alcohol noticed the gorilla just 18% of the time, whereas the sober witnesses noticed her 46% of the time. The authors suggest that these findings have implications for the testimony and reliability of intoxicated witnesses, whose performance is worse than sober witnesses in several other respects as well (see Chapter 8).

One explanation of inattention bias is that participants are engaged in and attending to the primary task to the exclusion of other activities that may be going on in the environment (Chabris, Weinberger, Fontaine, & Simons, 2011). Chabris et al. had participants observe a person jogging and either count how many times he touched his head during the run (high load condition) or just watch him run without counting (low load condition). Along the route, a fist fight breaks out between two other confederates. At the end of the run, participants were asked if they noticed the fight. Almost all of the participants in the noncounting conditions noticed the fight (72%), whereas fewer than half of the counters (42%) noticed the fight. Thus, the greater one's cognitive resources are tapped, the harder it is to notice changes in the environment. It is easy to see how this theory would relate to eyewitness identification. To the extent that a witness is occupied on another task such as driving or talking on the phone, it would be more difficult to notice changes that occur in the environment and the failure to notice the change could subsequently harm eyewitness memory or eyewitness identification.

Confidence

Eyewitness confidence is one of the most studied areas of psychology and law (Roediger, Wixted, & DeSoto, 2012). Eyewitness researchers have generally described the CA relationship as a weak to moderate relationship (see Neuschatz & Cutler, 2008). This is counterintuitive, as it seems logical that witnesses who display high confidence would be more accurate in their identification decisions. In fact, other research domains, such as general and text-based knowledge, show a strong positive correlation between confidence and accuracy (Stephenson, 1984; Stephenson, Clark, & Wade, 1986). For this reason, we consider the CA relationship to be an illusion similar to what Münsterberg discusses in his chapter. As is the case with unconscious transference and change blindness, highly confident but inaccurate witnesses can mislead jurors (Bornstein & Greene, 2017; Cutler, Penrod, & Stuve, 1988; Wells & Quinlivan, 2009), a point that Münsterberg realized 100 years ago: "And no subjective feeling of certainty can be an objective criterion for the desired truth" (p. 49). However, the eyewitness research community's thinking regarding the CA correlation for identification is changing and becoming less mysterious or illusory—albeit more complicated and nuanced.

General Findings and Measurement Issues

As mentioned, the CA relationship in other memory domains is quite strong (Krug, 2007). Researchers who have examined memory for general knowledge have found a strong CA relationship (Barclay & Wellman, 1986; Perfect, 2004; Schneider & Laurion, 1993). For example, Stephenson et al. (1986) examined the relationship between levels of subjective confidence and the recall of details after reading text and found a strong CA relationship. Similar results have been replicated with expert bridge players (Keren, 1987). However, novice bridge players were not as well calibrated with their confidence judgments. As Krug (2007) points out, this suggests that one theory about the poor CA relationship in eyewitness memory may involve the experience of the rememberer. According to this theory, participants tend to demonstrate better CA relationships for memory of general and text-based knowledge than for eyewitness events because they are better able to use past experiences when assessing memory strengths and weaknesses (Hollins & Perfect, 1997; Juslin, 1994; Perfect, Hollins, & Hunt, 2000). This is more difficult with eyewitness events, as most people, thankfully, have little past experience in this situation and no basis on which to gauge the strength of their memory.

Confidence is one of the most persuasive elements in determining whether a witness will testify and whether the witness will be believed by a jury (Cutler, Dexter, & Penrod, 1990). The Thomas Doswell case is an illustrative one (see the Innocence Project for a more in-depth description of the Doswell case, https://www.innocenceproject.org/cases/thomas-doswell/). In 1986, a woman was attacked as she entered work in a Pittsburgh hospital. The culprit followed the victim into the hospital and raped her. On the day of the crime, the victim was shown a photographic lineup in which Doswell's, and only Doswell's, photo was marked with a capital "R." It was later discovered the "R" on a photo indicated that person had been charged with rape. The victim in Thomas Doswell's case testified, "This is the man or it is his twin brother," and rated her certainty at 10 out of 10 (Garrett, 2011, p. 63). Despite her confidence in the recollection, the victim's immediate description of her attacker was actually dissimilar to Doswell and included that he had a full beard, which Doswell did not have when he was picked up by police just 3 hours after the crime. Doswell was exonerated after serving 19 years in prison. In a similar case, the victim in Donald Wayne Good's trial recalled being so sure her attacker was present in the lineup that merely viewing his photo caused her to become emotionally and physically impaired. DNA evidence later exculpated Good. In each of these cases, and many others, the eyewitnesses were convincingly confident in their decisions when they testified in court, and they later recalled that they always had been confident. Yet, when examining the cases more closely, Garrett (2011) found that the initial confidence reported at the time of the identification was not high (or initially a filler had been selected, or the lineup had been rejected). Rather, the confidence of these witnesses had inflated over time due to a variety of factors (e.g., postidentification feedback, suggestion, multiple exposures).

Laboratory research has also documented the influence of eyewitness confidence on jurors' perception of eyewitnesses. Cutler, Penrod, and Stuve (1988) asked mock jurors to use their knowledge about eyewitness testimony to make judgments about the culpability of a defendant in a criminal trial and about the likelihood that the identification was correct. Of all the eyewitness variables manipulated, witness confidence was the only reliable predictor of juror perceptions, revealing that when a witness was highly confident in an identification, participant jurors returned more guilty verdicts and rated the likelihood of the identification being correct as greater. The level of confidence expressed during questioning is also highly persuasive to jurors (Krug, 2007). Jurors view eyewitnesses as more credible when their level of confidence is high during questioning and give disproportionate weight to confidence in making their verdict decisions (Cutler, Dexter, & Penrod, 1990).

The problem of confident and therefore, persuasive, yet unreliable, eyewitnesses has led some US states to modify their pattern of jury instructions regarding eyewitness identification procedures. In Massachusetts, instructions were adapted from New Jersey's 2012 reforms (in the wake of *State v. Henderson*, 2011) to include the warning that the confidence level expressed by a witness does not necessarily equal accuracy, especially when the level of confidence has changed from its first evidenced recording (Supreme Judicial Court Study Group on Eyewitness Evidence: Report and Recommendations to the Justices, 2013). Georgia has modified its jury instructions several times to reflect evolving attitudes regarding eyewitness confidence. One of the most aggressive changes came in 2000, when the Georgia Supreme Court deemed expert testimony regarding the general weakness of the CA correlation admissible, but only when the court deemed it appropriate, and not for every case involving eyewitness testimony (*Jones v. State*, 2000). More recently, Georgia's instructions were revisited yet again, and this time the instructions eliminated the permissibility of confidence as a factor for jurors to consider, stating "We can no longer endorse an instruction authorizing jurors to consider the witness's certainty in his/her identification as a factor to be used in deciding the reliability of that identification" (*Brodes v. State*, 2005).

There are two primary statistical methods used to assess the CA relationship: the point-biserial correlation and the calibration curve. Most eyewitness researchers have historically employed the point-biserial correlation, but calibration curves have increasingly been used recently (Bornstein & Zickafoose, 1999; Brewer & Wells, 2006; Juslin, Olsson, & Winman, 1996; Palmer et al., 2013; Wixted et al., 2015). These statistics assess the absolute (calibration curves) or relative (point-biserial) monitoring of the relationship between confidence and accuracy. Absolute monitoring focuses on how over- or underconfident a person is relative to his or her accuracy (Wixted et al., 2015). Thus, a person who indicates he is 90% confident in his answers, but is accurate on only 60% of those answers, is 30% overconfident. Relative monitoring, on the other hand, signals whether the person is more or less confident in one answer as opposed to another. Wixted et al. (2015) argue that absolute monitoring, specifically calibration curves, allow psycholegal researchers to answer questions that are crucial from a legal perspective: How accurate are eyewitnesses that are (for example) 90% confident? Krug (2007) argued that researchers should use both measures to evaluate the CA relationship because absolute and relative monitoring measure different aspects of the CA relationship. We agree with Krug (2007) that a more complete understanding of the CA relationship will be gained by considering both absolute and relative monitoring methods.

Another way to conceive of the CA relationship is as a within/between hybrid correlation (see Roediger et al., 2012). With regard to the CA correlation, within-participants variation refers to whether participants are more accurate when they are more confident than when they are less confident; between-participants variation refers to whether more confident participants are more accurate than less confident participants. Roediger et al. argue that when the CA relationship is based on one item and one confidence rating, it is often a hybrid within/between correlation. This scenario is typical in eyewitness research, as well as in real crime situations, where participants or witnesses generally view one culprit and make a single confidence judgement based on the likelihood they identified the correct person. This approach can be useful for courts of law that need to assess the accuracy of an eyewitness to a single event with one culprit (see Roediger et al., 2012), and to determine whether a witness with relatively high confidence is more likely to be correct than a witness with relatively low confidence.

However, the point–biserial correlation may not always be the best measure of the CA correlation. Correlations between confidence and accuracy using the point–biserial correlation were once the norm in eyewitness studies (see Krug, 2007; Roediger et al., 2012). A point–biserial correlation is the same as a Pearson's product moment correlation except one of the independent variables is dichotomous (accurate or inaccurate). For example, in a study conducted by Cutler, Penrod, and Martens (1987), 165 students watched a videotaped enactment of a robbery and later attempted to identify the thief from videotaped lineups. Various aspects of the viewing conditions and lineup were manipulated. In all conditions, participants rated their confidence in the accuracy of their identifications immediately following their decisions. Across all conditions, the correlation between confidence and accuracy was significant but interpreted as being relatively weak in magnitude ($r = .20$; $p < .05$). The correlation between confidence and identification accuracy has been the subject of several meta-analyses over the years (Bothwell, Deffenbacher, & Brigham, 1987; Cutler & Penrod, 1989; Deffenbacher, 1980; Shapiro & Penrod, 1986; Sporer et al., 1995; Wells & Murray, 1984), which have generally reported weak-to-moderate CA correlations in lineup identification tasks. For example, Wells and Murray reported a CA correlation of less than .07 for lineups, and Neuschatz et al. (2016) found even smaller correlations for both lineups and showups.

Sporer et al. (1995) conducted one of the most comprehensive meta-analyses on the CA relationship. Their analysis included 30 studies and over 4,000 witnesses. The average correlation across studies was .27, higher than what has typically been reported but in line with the .20 reported by Cutler et al. (1987). However, Sporer et al. argued that it might be more forensically relevant to examine only those people who chose from the lineup, or whom they referred to as "choosers," because choosers are more likely to appear as witnesses in court. The CA correlation was significantly higher among witnesses who made positive identifications (r = .41) than among witnesses who rejected their lineups (r = .12). Sporer et al. argued that this correlation was strong enough to advise the legal system that confidence is a valid, albeit imperfect, measure of witness accuracy. Nevertheless, even given moderate to higher CA correlations, researchers still have argued that the relationship between confidence and accuracy is small. Wells and Quinlivan (2009) argued that informing jurors that there is a relationship between confidence and accuracy is misleading and could lead to wrongful convictions if jurors are persuaded by the confidence of the eyewitness.

Confidence calibration is a more appropriate measure of the relationship between confidence and accuracy (Juslin et al., 1996). Juslin et al. demonstrated that point–biserial correlations ranging from 0, no correlation, to 1, perfect correlation, could exhibit perfect calibration. In other words, low point–biserial correlations do not necessarily imply a poor CA relationship. Rather, the true magnitude of the relationship between confidence and accuracy is revealed by calibration curves. Moreover, these results are consistent with theoretical decision-making models (e.g., signal detection theory) that predict a strong relationship between confidence and accuracy in a variety of judgment domains (Bothwell et al., 1987; Brewer, Weber, & Semmler, 2007).

Juslin et al. (1996) conducted the typical eyewitness experiment, although they used police officers as participants. The police officers watched a mock crime video and then completed a lineup identification task that was either TP or TA. Participants' calibration was very good, especially for the most confident participants (who are the ones most likely to testify).

CA relationship using calibration remains intact even in more naturalistic studies. In Palmer et al. (2013), potential participants were approached in public places and asked to view a confederate for either 5 or 90 seconds. Participants made an identification either immediately or 2 weeks after the encounter. Once again, participants were well calibrated, and once again calibration was nearly perfect at the highest levels of confidence. This was true for both the short and long retention intervals.

The strong CA relationship holds when different types of identification tasks (simultaneous lineups, sequential lineups, and showups) are compared with calibration (Neuschatz et al., 2016; see Figure 3.3). In a large meta-analysis including over 8,000 participants, Neuschatz et al. evaluated the

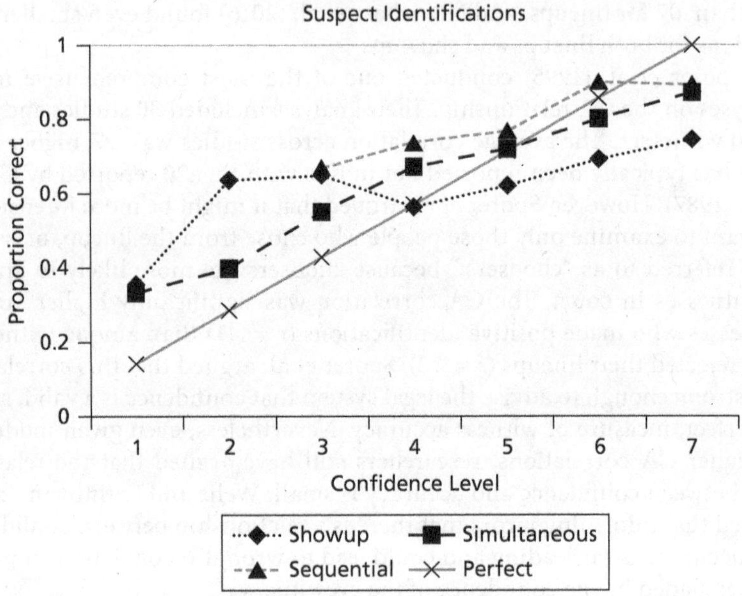

Figure 3.3. Confidence calibration curves for suspect identifications comparing simultaneous lineups, sequential lineups, and showups (from Neuschatz et al., 2016).

CA correlation using point–biserial correlations and calibration curves for suspect identifications. The results for the calibration curves largely replicated the findings of Palmer et al. (2013); the conditions that led to the most accurate responding were also the best calibrated. That is, participants in the simultaneous and sequential lineups were more accurate and better calibrated than the showup participants. However, participants in all three identification procedures were well calibrated, especially at the highest levels of confidence. Participants were less well calibrated at the lower levels of confidence, especially for showups. In sum, when calibration is used with the most forensically relevant witnesses, those who identify a suspect with high confidence are, generally, highly accurate.

The strong CA relationship also seems to hold for witnesses from actual police lineups. Two studies by Behrman (Behrman & Davey, 2001; Behrman & Richards, 2005) investigated the relationship between lineup identification decisions and eyewitness confidence in actual criminal investigations (we discuss other aspects of these studies in Chapter 4). It is impossible to create calibration curves for real cases because the guilt of the suspect is unknown. One can, however, look at the relationship between confidence and identification in cases where there is, or is not, a high probability that the suspect was the culprit, which is what Behrman and Davey did. In their archival analysis, cases were examined that contained strong corroborating evidence that the suspect committed the crime (i.e., a confession or other physical evidence). Confidence was assessed on a 2-point scale ("unsure" vs. "sure"). Taking suspect identifications from the strong-evidence lineups as correct and filler IDs as incorrect, they found that the proportion correct for low-confidence witnesses was .47 (7 out of 13 "unsure" witnesses picked the suspect), whereas the proportion correct for high-confidence witnesses was .92 (11 out of 12 "sure" witnesses picked the suspect). Wixted et al. (2015) showed very similar results for a recent field study by Wells (2014) involving 349 lineups administered by the Houston Police Department.

There seems to be a contradiction between the laboratory findings of a strong CA relationship, when appropriately measured, and the many real-life false identifications—as evidenced by the DNA exonerations—that are made with high confidence. There may be two explanations for this finding. First, as suggested by Garrett (2011), many of these identifications were originally made with lower confidence and then confidence increased by the time the witness took the stand. Thus, the CA relationship may be intact at the time of the identification, which would be consistent with the experimental data (see Wixted & Wells, 2017).

An alternative explanation for the discrepancy between the laboratory and the real-world CA relationship may be due to the different conditions that exist in the laboratory and the real world (National Research Council, 2014; Wells, Smalarz, & Smith, 2015; Wixted & Wells, 2017). Wells and colleagues suggested that the CA relationship is strong, and confidence is a good predictor of accuracy, if the identification occurs under pristine conditions—that is, fair lineups, double-blind lineup administration, and immediate confident assessment. Similarly, Deffenbacher's (1980) optimality hypothesis, in which he stated that the degree of the CA relationship for eyewitness events depends on how optimal the viewing conditions are, maintains that the more optimal the conditions (e.g., good lighting, long exposure, no stress), the stronger the confidence calibration (see also Bothwell et al., 1987). The problem is that pristine identification procedures and optimal viewing conditions occur in the laboratory but are infrequent in the real world, which reduces the real-world CA relationship relative to the lab. One such variable that depresses the CA relationship in the real world is postidentification feedback.

Postidentification Feedback

Postidentification feedback is one of the most widely cited and studied of the factors that influence confidence without influencing accuracy (see Douglass & Smalarz, 2019; Douglass & Steblay, 2006; Quinlivan, et al., 2009; Steblay et al., 2014; Wells & Quinlivan, 2009). Postidentification feedback refers to any statement made to the witness by the administrator or any other source of information (e.g., the witness discovering that the suspect has been arrested or being asked to testify at the suspect's trial) that likely conveys to the witness the accuracy of the identification choice. In the original study of this effect, Wells and Bradfield (1998) had participants watch a video clip from a security camera and make an identification from a TA lineup. Following the identification, some of the participants were told that they had made an accurate selection ("Good, you identified the suspect"), whereas others were given no feedback. Participants who were given confirming feedback subsequently reported that they paid more attention to the perpetrator, were more confident in their identification, and had a clearer view of the perpetrator compared to participants who were not given feedback. The fact that participants' confidence was increased even though they were inaccurate demonstrates how postidentification feedback can distort the CA relationship.

Confirming feedback makes witnesses feel more confident regardless of the accuracy of their identification, and as discussed previously, confidence is persuasive to jurors. Of course, if an eyewitness makes an inaccurate identification, then jurors are relying on bad indices of witness accuracy—which could be high confidence or something else—and as a result could be wrongfully convicting innocent suspects. This possibility was confirmed by Douglass, Neuschatz, Imrich, and Wilkinson (2010), who showed mock jurors testimony of participant eyewitnesses who either were given confirming feedback or not. Eyewitnesses who received confirming feedback were rated as more accurate, and the mock jurors were more likely to convict based on that testimony relative to those jurors who saw the eyewitness but did not receive feedback. Smalarz and Wells (2014) found similar results.

In summary, there are several conclusions that can be derived from the CA literature. First, confidence is malleable and can be affected by factors unrelated to the memory of an event, such as postidentification feedback. This explains why people can have confidently held, detailed memories that are inaccurate—what Münsterberg would refer to as an illusion. Second, confidence and accuracy can be highly correlated under some circumstances. As expressed by Wixted and Wells (2017), when an identification procedure is appropriately conducted (i.e., good fillers, unbiased instructions, double-blind administration) and confidence is recorded immediately after the identification, then a witness's confidence and accuracy are quite well calibrated. In other words, under these circumstances, confidence can be a good index of accuracy.

Conclusions

Münsterberg's ideas about perceptual and memory illusions are consistent with the generally accepted theory of reconstructive memory (e.g., Neisser, 1967). The basic idea is that memory is frequently changing and updating to accommodate new information. A memory, once formed, is not set in stone or preserved as a pristine picture. The information that we encode is incomplete and disorganized; thus, it requires us to fill in the gaps with what we know about how the world operates. For example, one may ask himself if he called his brother on his birthday, and he may think that he must have, otherwise his mother would have called and reprimanded him. Unfortunately, the memory gaps can be filled in with information that is correct or incorrect. This may happen unbeknownst to the rememberer and explains why people can have memories that are richly detailed but inaccurate, or what Münsterberg would call illusions.

We think that this theory of memory also explains the other phenomena that we discussed in this chapter, such as change blindness and inattention blindness. Attention and memory are severely limited resources, so much information is not noticed or retained. In other words, memory and perception, as amazing as they are much of the time, are notoriously imperfect; this imperfection can lead to memory errors, which can be quite consequential, and even downright catastrophic, in forensic contexts.

4

The Memory of the Witness

> *The most essential condition remained, of course, always the complete naïveté of the witnesses, as the slightest suspicion on their part would destroy the value of the experiment.*
>
> —Münsterberg, *On the Witness Stand* (p. 51)

In this chapter, Münsterberg illustrates the sorts of errors to which eyewitness memory is susceptible by describing several experiments conducted in naturalistic settings (e.g., staged crimes). It is worth quoting the most entertaining example at length, as a way of illustrating the differences between the sorts of experiments that were feasible then versus now.

> A few years ago a painful scene occurred in Berlin, in the University Seminary of Professor von Liszt, the famous criminologist. The Professor had spoken about a book. One of the older students suddenly shouts, "I wanted to throw light on the matter from the standpoint of Christian morality!" Another student throws in, "I cannot stand that!" The first starts up, exclaiming, "You have insulted me!" The second clenches his fist and cries, "If you say another word—" The first draws a revolver. The second rushes madly upon him. The Professor steps between them and, as he grasps the man's arm, the revolver goes off. General uproar. In that moment Professor Liszt secures order and asks a part of the students to write an exact account of all that happened. The whole had been a comedy, carefully planned and rehearsed by the three actors for the purpose of studying the exactitude of observation and recollection. Those who did not write the report at once were, part of them, asked to write it the next day

> or a week later; and others had to depose their observations under cross-examination. The whole objective performance was cut up into fourteen little parts which referred partly to actions, partly to words. As mistakes there were counted the omissions, the wrong additions and the alterations. (pp. 49–50)

Von Liszt's experiment is interesting on many levels, not least of which is the clear absence of any legal or ethical considerations by either von Liszt or Münsterberg (the experiment was apparently suggested to von Liszt by Stern; see Sporer, 2008). Many contemporary eyewitness researchers would be appalled by Münsterberg's referring to it as a "comedy" and would shudder to think what injuries might have resulted to those in the room.[1] In this and other experiments described in the chapter, he explains how observers' memories are erroneous due to several factors, such as the passage of time, emotion, individual differences, expectations, and postevent suggestion. He emphasizes the importance of doing field studies as opposed to laboratory experiments, as did some of his contemporaries: Stern (1904/2000) also called attention to the value of using staged events—which he called the "realistic method"—as opposed to the "picture method."

Notwithstanding the ethical concerns raised by von Liszt's experiment, it illustrates many of the methodological considerations that are central to conducting eyewitness research: the selection of independent variables, such as the retention interval and whether witnesses provide a free report or do so under cross-examination; which aspects of the event to focus on, such as speech versus actions (and in other studies, person identification); and the decision about how to measure performance, in terms of omissions, additions, and alterations. Finally, of course, there is the overriding issue of whether the witnesses know they are participants in an experiment—that is, whether they are what we might call "naïve" witnesses or are merely simulating the role of witnesses.[2] We refer to the latter as "aware" witnesses, because

---

[1] Consider, for example, the current debate over whether guns should be allowed on college campuses. As of August 2017, 11 states (Arkansas, Colorado, Georgia, Idaho, Kansas, Mississippi, Oregon, Tennessee, Texas, Utah, and Wisconsin) had laws permitting concealed carry of guns on postsecondary campuses—some with restrictions as to who or where. Other states ban concealed weapons on campus, and still others leave it up to individual institutions. See, for example, http://theconversation.com/more-states-are-allowing-guns-on-college-campuses-81791; http://www.ncsl.org/research/education/guns-on-campus-overview.aspx.

[2] Paralleling the jury decision-making literature, it is tempting to refer to witnesses who know they are not observing a genuine event, but are merely doing so for research purposes, as "mock witnesses" (on mock jury research, see Bornstein, 2017a; Bornstein et al., 2017). However, the "mock witness" paradigm has taken on a very specific meaning in the eyewitness literature, namely, a procedure for evaluating lineup fairness. In a mock witness study, persons who did not witness the crime are provided with an actual witness's description of

they are aware that the event is a simulation and that they are participating in a research study. The issue is an important one because it speaks to external validity. If aware witnesses differ from naïve witnesses in meaningful ways, then the results of research on the former might not generalize to the sorts of real-world witnesses that are of forensic interest (though research on aware witnesses might still be valuable when developing theories of how memory works in general). In the present chapter, we compare the conclusions from studies of naïve and aware witnesses to explore whether witness naïveté is a possible moderator—such moderating effects speak directly to the question of whether Münsterberg's advice about naïve witnesses still applies today. Such a comparison necessarily entails a consideration of the various research paradigms used to study naïve eyewitnesses.

Münsterberg's chapter also covers different types of memory, especially those corresponding to different sensory modalities (he also discusses individual differences and vividness, which figure prominently in contemporary research on suggestibility and false memories; these topics are treated more extensively in Chapter 8). Münsterberg's discussion of different sensory modalities raises the question of "earwitness" versus "eyewitness" memory. Courts tend to treat identification witnesses comparably regardless of witnessing modality, yet there are important differences (Laub, Wylie, & Bornstein, 2013; Yarmey, 2007). Following our discussion of eyewitness research methodology, this chapter will review research on earwitness versus eyewitness memory.[3]

Eyewitness Research Methodology: Naïve Versus Aware Witnesses

Contemporary eyewitness researchers have, until recently, largely ignored Münsterberg's advice to study naïve witnesses. Rather, they have tended to favor well-controlled laboratory studies. Laboratory participants are not necessarily aware—for example, they might think they are doing a study unrelated to eyewitness memory (see later discussion of staged crime studies)—but most of the time, participants in an eyewitness experiment know they are part of an eyewitness experiment. This approach has yielded a

the perpetrator and then make a lineup identification; if they are more likely to choose the suspect than chance, then the lineup is biased against the suspect (Doob & Kirshenbaum, 1973; Malpass, Tredoux, & McQuiston-Surrett, 2007). To avoid confusion, we therefore refer to "naïve" versus "aware" witnesses rather than to mock witnesses.

[3] A final topic that Münsterberg touches on in this chapter is déjà vu, which can be thought of as another kind of illusion involving a misplaced sense of familiarity (see Chapter 3). Although déjà vu is subjectively compelling, the topic has not been heavily researched (Gerrans, 2014).

wealth of useful data, but it has also been criticized as lacking relevance to real-world phenomena (Flowe, Finklea, & Ebbesen, 2009; Lane & Meissner, 2008; Malpass et al., 2008). The apparent "generalizability gap" has also been used by courts to dismiss experimental psychological research (Benton et al., 2007; Monahan & Walker, 2018), despite little evidence showing that methodological variables, such as correspondence to real crimes, alter empirical conclusions (Penrod & Bornstein, 2007).

Naïve Versus Aware Witnesses: What Differs?

Eyewitness research, as a field, has paid some attention to the matter of naïve versus aware witnesses (e.g., Murray & Wells, 1982; Shapiro & Penrod, 1986; Yarmey, 2004). However, this research largely begs the question of how, exactly, the two situations differ. Table 4.1 illustrates some of the ways in which naïve and aware witnesses likely differ, in both encoding and retrieval processes. At encoding, one situation or the other might lead to greater attention and deeper processing. However, this could go either way. On the one

Table 4.1 Possible Differences Between Naïve and Aware Witnesses at Encoding and Retrieval

Encoding Processes	Would Increase
Genuine crime more interesting	Naïve accuracy
Genuine crime more distracting, poses threats to well-being	Aware accuracy
Need to remember real crime for later investigation	Naïve accuracy
Experimental participants explicitly told or implicitly expect memory test	Aware accuracy
Genuine crime produces stronger, and possibly different kinds of, emotional response	Varies
Retrieval Processes	
Lineup/interview with police more engaging	Naïve accuracy
Lineup/interview with police more stressful	Aware accuracy
Concern about letting guilty party go free	Naïve choosing
Concern about false identification	Aware choosing
Genuine lineup creates pressure/obligation to choose	Naïve choosing
Genuine lineup means witness might have to testify	Aware choosing
Fear of reprisal	Varies

Note. If the entry under "Would Increase" is "varies," then the effect could go in either direction, depending on additional factors (see accompanying text for explanation). Increased accuracy is always positive, but increased choosing is not necessarily a desirable outcome; it leads to a higher hit rate when the suspect is the perpetrator, but to a higher false identification rate when the suspect is innocent.

hand, believing one is observing a genuine (as opposed to a simulated) crime could be associated with greater interest, and hence deeper processing, especially if the simulated event is part of a boring course requirement; on the other hand, witnessing a genuine crime—especially if it involves a threat to one's own safety—could be associated with poorer encoding. Consider, for example, how closely one can attend to a murder scene displayed on a screen *inside* a movie theater versus the same scene occurring on the street *outside* the theater. The latter situation presumably has many distractions, paramount among which are concern for one's own and for the genuine (as opposed to the cinematic) victim's well-being.

Even more subtly, believing one is witnessing a real versus a simulated crime could lead witnesses to attend to different aspects of the event without affecting their overall attention level or degree of processing. Relatedly, there might be differences in intentional versus incidental encoding—again, in either direction. Knowingly witnessing an actual crime could make a witness aware of the need to remember the event for later testing (i.e., intentional encoding), but witnesses do not always know that they are witnessing an actual crime and hence do not consciously process the information with the aim of remembering it later (i.e., incidental encoding). For example, a witness might think that she is watching someone innocently pick up her own laptop computer from a table, only to learn later that it was a theft. Conversely, experimental participants are often told at the outset that their memory will be tested, and they might expect a memory test even if they are not explicitly told that one is forthcoming. All of these factors—attention, level of processing, intentionality—could contribute to differences in witnesses' overall motivation, producing cascading effects on their cognitive processes.

Naïve and aware witnesses are also likely to differ in the intensity and type of their emotional response. As every theater- or moviegoer knows—and as Münsterberg (1916/1970) himself recognized—"make-believe" events witnessed in a theater or one's own living room are entirely capable of eliciting intense emotional reactions. Yet it stands to reason that witnessing a violent crime on screen or on stage, knowing that the actors are not really being hurt and one's own well-being is not in jeopardy, causes less intense emotions than witnessing the same crime in reality. Negative emotional arousal generally has harmful effects on eyewitness memory, but the effects are complex and vary depending on how arousal is measured and what aspects of performance are being measured (e.g., recall of central vs. peripheral details; see, generally, Bornstein & Robicheaux, 2009; Deffenbacher, Bornstein, Penrod, & McGorty, 2004). Moreover, the type of negative emotion produced—fear, anger, or disgust—likely differs, and these various emotional states are associated with different kinds of cognitive processing (Tiedens & Linton, 2001). At an even more subtle level, it is possible that the same type and intensity of emotion differ in important ways depending on whether they are "real" or experienced vicariously.

Similar differences could occur at retrieval: When giving a report to police or making an identification, naïve and aware witnesses likely vary in their motivation, attention/processing (both quantity and quality), and affect (both quantity and quality). Interacting with law enforcement officers in the aftermath of a crime, as opposed to being questioned by research psychologists, could be stressful in and of itself (Bornstein, Hullman, & Miller, 2013; Krix et al., 2016). In addition—and possibly affecting their motivation, attention, and affect—naïve witnesses could worry about fear of reprisal, what happens if their behavior sends an innocent person to prison or lets a guilty person go free, or whether they will ultimately have to testify at trial (Murray & Wells, 1982). They might also feel more pressure or obligation to make a positive identification (Eisen, Smith, Olaguez, & Skerritt-Perta, 2017). Some of these factors would motivate naïve witnesses to be more likely to make an identification than aware witnesses (e.g., worry about letting a bad guy go free, pressure to choose), whereas others would motivative them to be less likely to make an identification (e.g., worry about a false identification, desire not to testify). Still others could move the response criterion either way: Fear of reprisal might motivate a witness to make an identification (i.e., "I need to make sure he gets locked up so he doesn't come after me") or to avoid making an identification (i.e., "I need to stay out of this so he doesn't want to come after me"). Whether shifting to a more conservative or more liberal response criterion is "desirable" depends, of course, on whether the perpetrator is actually in the lineup. Thus, there are many ways in which naïve and aware witnesses differ, and a number of possible mechanisms could underlie these potential differences.

Despite (or perhaps because of) these differences, it is very difficult to compare naïve and aware witnesses directly. That would require exposing the two kinds of witnesses to the same event, leading some to believe it was a real event while informing others that it was a simulation. Although not impossible, it would be challenging to create or capture an event that is equally plausible from either perspective; moreover, as the von Liszt example amply illustrates, leading participants to believe they are witnessing a real event when they are not raises a host of ethical complications (the converse—leading participants to believe a real event is being staged for research purposes—is probably simply untenable). It is more feasible to investigate these effects indirectly, by examining the effect of variables presumably correlated with awareness, such as type of encoding or whether one is witnessing a crime or a neutral scene.

To circumvent these problems, several techniques provide data that permit inferences about the correspondence between naïve and aware witnesses. First, meta-analysis can either examine studies of awareness-relevant variables directly or analyze them as potential moderators of the effect of other system or estimator variables (i.e., variables under the control of the legal system vs. those that are not controllable but that nonetheless predict eyewitness performance). Second, studies of naïve witnesses alone can be examined for their agreement with the results of laboratory studies. Several research paradigms for studying naïve witnesses exist: archival studies, case studies, and staged crimes or field studies in which the unwitting witnesses were really research participants (e.g., Mecklenburg, 2006; Valentine, Pickering, & Darling, 2003; Wells, Steblay, & Dysart, 2015; Wixted, Mickes, Dunn, Clark, & Wells, 2016). We discuss these approaches to studying naïve witnesses following a review of studies that assess—directly or indirectly—whether methodological variables like witness awareness moderate the effects of other variables.

Direct Comparisons of Witness Awareness

In a rare attempt to examine the question directly, Yarmey (2004) had a female research confederate approach individuals (witnesses) in public places and speak to them for approximately 15 seconds; witnesses either were or were not told that it was for purposes of a research study and that they should remember what she looked like, making them aware or naïve witnesses (in Yarmey's terminology, the witnesses were "prepared" or "not prepared"). The experiment also varied the duration of the retention interval (2 minutes vs. 4 hours), the target's disguise (with or without a baseball cap and sunglasses), and the presence of context reinstatement instructions prior to the memory test, which involved both a recall test for the target's appearance and a lineup identification task (target present [TP] or target absent [TA]). There were several noteworthy findings: First, witness preparation improved recall but not identification. Second, identification performance was moderately accurate overall: 49% for the TP lineup and 62% for the TA lineup. And third, contrary to other research (e.g., Deffenbacher, Bornstein, McGorty, & Penrod, 2008; Krafka & Penrod, 1985), target disguise, retention interval, and retrieval instructions had no effect on identification.

Other studies have found, like Yarmey (2004), that being aware of a forthcoming memory test facilitates better recall (Sporer, 1996) but not better identification (Cutler et al., 1987; Shapiro & Penrod, 1986). One explanation for the discrepancy could be the well-documented finding that verbal recall and face recognition draw upon fundamentally different cognitive and neurological processes (Neath & Surprenant, 2015), which helps to explain the "elusive and generally weak" relationship between eyewitnesses' event recall and their identification ability (Meissner, Sporer, & Schooler, 2007, p. 21; see also Meissner, Sporer, & Susa, 2008). Many variables affect recall and recognition differently (Neath & Surprenant, 2015), and participant awareness could simply be another one of them. However, as described next, other approaches to investigating awareness effects yield roughly comparable findings for recall and recognition.

Murray and Wells (1982) observed that most staged crime studies disclose the experimental nature of the undertaking to witnesses after the event but before their memory is tested. Essentially, witnesses are told something like "We staged that event for experimental purposes; now let's see how good your memory is." Real witnesses, in contrast, believe they are witnesses, and not research participants, all the way through. In our terminology, participants in most staged crime studies go from "naïve" to "aware" in the midst of the experiment. Murray and Wells pointed out that there are practical (as well as ethical) reasons making it difficult to maintain the deception all the way through the memory task. Nonetheless, aware witnesses—even when they are naïve at the time of encoding and become aware only at the time of retrieval—might differ from naïve witnesses in terms of their affect or motivation, producing potential consequences in terms of their performance.

To address this issue, Murray and Wells (1982) staged a crime, in which a thief disconnected and stole a video game, in front of unsuspecting participant witnesses (university students). Following the crime, all participants were told that a theft had occurred and that the experimenter was calling Campus Security. Before a confederate, dressed as a uniformed policeman, arrived to administer the lineup, half of the witnesses were told the following: "There was no real theft. The theft you saw was staged by us. We'll explain later, but for now we want you to continue to behave the same way you would have behaved if we hadn't told you that the theft was staged. The Campus Security person will be arriving soon, and he's also one of us" (Murray & Wells, 1982, p. 46). The other half of participants were not given this information (Murray and Wells referred to these participants as "uninformed"; they would be "naïve" in our terminology). The researchers also manipulated the perpetrator's presence in the lineup (i.e., TA vs. TP) and the physical similarity of the nonsuspect lineup members to the perpetrator (high vs. low).

Witness awareness exerted little effect overall. It had no effect on participants' decisions (identifying the suspect, identifying a foil, or rejecting the lineup) in the TA lineup. In the TP lineup, naïve witnesses were significantly more likely to choose a foil and marginally less likely to identify the perpetrator. The confidence–accuracy (CA) correlation was also stronger for aware than for naïve participants. Thus, the pattern of results was largely the same regardless of witness awareness; moreover, to the extent that there were differences, witnesses in more naturalistic circumstances (i.e., naïve witnesses) did worse—they made more false (foil) identifications and marginally fewer suspect identifications in TP lineups, and their subjective confidence was a poorer predictor of their lineup accuracy.

Eisen and colleagues (2017) conducted three similar experiments but used single-person showups rather than lineups. As in the Murray and Wells (1982) study, after participants witnessed a theft (of a laptop) and before taking part in the identification task, half were told that the theft was staged for research purposes and viewed a showup administered by the experimenter ("lab" or "aware" participants, to use our terminology); the other half were not debriefed until after viewing a showup administered by a police officer ("field" or "naïve" participants). Naïve participants were 2.5–4.6 times more likely (depending on the experiment) to make a positive identification than aware participants, in both TA and TP showups. The difference reflected a criterion shift, such that naïve participants were simply more likely to identify the suspect as the thief. The effect was even more pronounced after removing field/naïve participants who suspected the procedures were staged.

Overall, although few studies have compared eyewitness awareness directly, they suggest that more naturalistic witnessing conditions—that is, those akin to what naïve witnesses experience—do not enhance eyewitness performance. Compared to aware witnesses, naïve witnesses recall less information (Yarmey, 2004), and their identification performance is at best the same (Murray & Wells, 1982; Yarmey, 2004) and at worst inferior (Eisen et al., 2017). Evidence of a criterion shift (Eisen et al., 2017), which raises the hit rate while also increasing the risk of false identifications, supports the importance of investigating motivational differences between naïve and aware witnesses.

Meta-analysis: Indirect Comparisons of Witness Awareness

Considering how much research has been conducted on eyewitness memory, it should not be surprising that it has also been extensively meta-analyzed. Early meta-analyses covered large swaths of the field (e.g., Shapiro & Penrod, 1986), but as the field has grown, more recent meta-analyses have mostly focused on one or a handful of variables at a time (for a partial review, see Penrod & Bornstein, 2007). These meta-analyses afford an opportunity to examine the effect of witness awareness indirectly, as many, but not all, of them included variables related to witness awareness, or some other aspect of verisimilitude, as either main effects or possible moderators.

For example, Shapiro and Penrod (1986) examined several variables that might reasonably distinguish naïve and aware witnesses: expectation of a future identification test, type/depth of encoding, and exposure duration. The applicability to witness awareness lies in the assumption that in the real world, most witnesses will not expect a future identification test and will tend to have relatively poor encoding and relatively brief exposure to the culprit. Expecting one's memory to be tested affected neither correct nor false identifications; however, both encoding—whether manipulated by encoding instructions or degree of elaboration—and exposure influenced performance, such that deeper encoding and longer exposure time were both associated with better performance, especially in terms of correct identifications. These effects of encoding processes and exposure duration were confirmed in a more recent meta-analysis conducted by Bornstein and colleagues (2012).

Shapiro and Penrod (1986) also conducted a study-characteristics analysis, in which they explored possible patterns of relationships between variables and performance across studies, rather than meta-analyzing variables manipulated within studies. Variables that typically covary between naïve and aware witnesses, such as attention and knowledge of the identification task, accounted for a significant portion of the variation in identification performance. Factors that tend to go along with being an aware witness, such as paying closer attention, were associated with better performance, in terms of more hits, fewer false alarms, and better discrimination between old and new faces (*d′*; see also Penrod & Bornstein, 2007).

Several focused eyewitness meta-analyses have also included variables relevant to the naïve-aware distinction as possible moderators. For the most part, these variables have failed to moderate effects of the primary variables of interest. For example, the sequential-versus-simultaneous lineup advantage in terms of fewer false identifications in TA lineups is the same for live versus video presentation, long versus brief exposure to the culprit, and long versus short retention intervals (Steblay, Dysart, & Wells, 2011; this study updated a previous meta-analysis by Steblay, Dysart, Fulero, & Lindsay, 2001). Where differences do exist, more realistic simulations tend to increase the magnitude of the variables' effects. For example, the cross-race effect is larger for relatively brief exposure durations (Meissner & Brigham, 2001), especially for White witnesses (Anthony, Copper, & Mullen, 1992); the weapon focus effect is stronger for relatively realistic, crime-like situations and for more threatening events (Fawcett, Russell, Peace, & Christie, 2013; Kocab & Sporer, 2016; Steblay, 1992); the effect of biased instructions is greater for live presentation than for photo displays (Steblay, 1997); and stress has a greater effect for staged crime than for nonstaged crime studies (Deffenbacher et al., 2004). Insofar as naïve witnesses, compared to aware witnesses, are more likely to have relatively brief exposure to the culprit and to view a live, realistic event, then they are more susceptible than aware witnesses to the effects of these various system and estimator variables. Although there are exceptions to this rule—for example, Steblay (1997) found that biased instructions exerted a smaller effect when witnesses to a staged event remained naïve throughout the lineup task than when they were debriefed before the lineup—for the most part, system and estimator variables produce effects at least as large in circumstances that characterize naïve witnesses as in circumstances that typify aware witnesses. Penrod and Bornstein (2007) concluded that "when the effects of substantive variables vary across different research methodologies, they are larger for more realistic procedures" (p. 550) and "[i]f anything, much eyewitness research *underestimates* the magnitude of effects" (p. 551, emphasis in original).

Most of the studies summarized here dealt with person identification rather than event recall. A number of studies have compared the effectiveness of different techniques, some of which were developed based on psychological principles, for interviewing eyewitnesses in the field (Fisher & Schreiber, 2007). Several of these studies have also included moderators relevant to the naïve-aware witness distinction.

Probably the best known of the evidence-based interview protocols is the Cognitive Interview (CI), developed originally by Fisher and Geiselman (1992; for review, see Fisher & Schreiber, 2007; Köhnken, Milne, Memon, & Bull, 1999; Memon, Meissner, & Fraser, 2010). The CI is based on fundamental principles of memory encoding and retrieval, such as context reinstatement and remembering from a variety of perspectives (Fisher & Geiselman, 1992). Compared to standard police interviewing techniques, the CI consistently and substantially increases recall of correct details, along with a small increase in errors (Memon et al., 2010; some of these studies, especially those with children, have used an enhanced or modified version of the CI). It benefits diverse populations, improving recall in elderly witnesses (Memon et al., 2010); child witnesses, though to less of an extent than in adults (Memon et al., 2010); and both adults (Clarke, Prescott, & Milne, 2013) and children with intellectual disabilities (Milne, Sharman, Powell, & Mead, 2013).

In their meta-analysis of the CI, Memon et al. (2010) included several moderator variables relevant to the methodological questions covered in the present chapter: retention interval, event presentation medium (live/staged vs. video/slide/narrative), and event type (crime/accident vs. neutral scenario). The effect of these variables was mixed, depending on the dependent measure (correct, incorrect, or confabulated details). The advantage of the CI decreased with longer retention intervals, in terms of eliciting fewer correct and more confabulated details; crime or accident scenarios produced smaller effect sizes for correct details than more neutral events; and presentation medium failed to moderate the CI's effect in any respect. Importantly, even when there was a difference, the CI still exerted a substantial positive effect on recall of correct details in the more naturalistic conditions (*d*'s > 1.0 in the longest retention interval and crime/accident scenario conditions). Overall, then, the effect of the intervention held across these methodological variations, although it abated to some extent under more naturalistic conditions.

Studies of Naïve Eyewitnesses

Another means of addressing the impact of witness awareness is to study naïve eyewitnesses in naturalistic settings and ask whether their memory performance is comparable to that of eyewitnesses in laboratory experiments. Researchers have studied naïve eyewitnesses using three main approaches: archival studies, case studies, and staged crime or field studies. Archival studies involve a post-hoc analysis of existing data from actual police lineups or interviews, usually from a substantial number of cases; case studies involve a more intensive analysis of a smaller number of cases, often with the collection of additional data (e.g., researcher interviews of witnesses); and staged crime and field studies involve original data collection from naïve persons who have witnessed a staged or unstaged crime, for which some element of system (e.g., lineup administration) or estimator (e.g., race of the target) variables is typically manipulated. There is a degree of overlap among these methodologies—for example, archival data can be categorized after the fact in a manner that makes them somewhat comparable to a priori field studies (Steblay, 2018)—yet the taxonomy is a useful way to begin thinking about the pros and cons of different research methods, and the ways in which their results might both converge with one another and correspond to laboratory findings.

Archival Studies

Archival studies involve an analysis of case files, including witness statements or lineup identifications, obtained from police and/or prosecutors. These studies provide rich, real-world data, but they are limited by the difficulty—and often the impossibility—of corroborating accuracy (Memon et al., 2008; Steblay, 2018). However, two factors make archival studies informative. First, although it is virtually impossible to determine whether a given lineup suspect is truly guilty, it is easy to determine that some lineup members—those who are known innocent foils—are truly innocent. Thus, foil identifications in archival studies are clearly errors. Second, "ground truth," in terms of whether the suspect was truly guilty or the witness's verbal report was correct, can often be estimated by the strength of other evidence, such as a confession, other witnesses' reports or identifications, or surveillance video footage. These corroborating sources are often absent and are themselves unreliable (see, e.g., Chapter 7 on false confessions), but they are strongly suggestive of eyewitness accuracy in the field. These studies therefore provide valuable information about the frequency with which eyewitnesses make positive suspect identifications and the factors that predict whether identifications are more or less likely.

Several studies of actual eyewitness identifications, in both the United Kingdom (Horry, Memon, Wright, & Milne, 2012; Slater, 1994; Valentine et al., 2003; Wright & McDaid, 1996) and the United States (Behrman & Davey, 2001; Wells et al., 2015), have found that roughly one-quarter to one-third of positive identifications are of foils known to be innocent (for review, see Bornstein, 2017b; Lampinen et al., 2012). One study in Scotland found a real-world foil identification rate as high as 42% (Memon et al., 2011). In one respect, foil identifications are a case of "no harm, no foul"—that is, an innocent foil suffers no negative consequences. In another respect, however, they are highly problematic. If we accept the premise that some suspects are, like lineup foils, actually innocent, then those innocent suspects are just as likely as foils to be victims of false identifications. Indeed, they are almost certainly *more* likely, inasmuch as they are likely to resemble the true perpetrator more closely than the foils resemble the perpetrator in many cases. Thus, the true false identification rate—factoring in mistaken suspect identifications—is going to be higher than one in three. Moreover, the false identification rate does not account for misses—cases in which the perpetrator is in the lineup, but the witness fails to pick him out.

Suspect identifications occur more often under some circumstances than others (Bornstein, 2017). For example, identification (i.e., choosing) rates are higher for adult witnesses who are bystanders, as opposed to victims; are relatively young; are close in age to or of the same race as the suspect; have a relatively long exposure to the culprit or a relatively brief retention interval; view a one-person showup, as opposed to a lineup; and make fast decisions with high confidence (Behrman & Davey, 2001; Behrman & Richards, 2005; Horry et al., 2012; Memon et al., 2011; Tollestrup, Turtle, & Yuille, 1994; Valentine et al., 2003). Child witnesses (Memon et al., 2011) and witnesses who give a detailed description of the culprit are also more likely to choose the suspect (Valentine et al., 2003). Although some of these variables, such as age (Fitzgerald & Price, 2015), retention interval (Deffenbacher et al., 2008), exposure time (Bornstein et al., 2012), own- versus other-race identification (Meissner & Brigham, 2001), and confidence (Wixted et al., 2015, 2018), do predict identification accuracy, they do so imperfectly and often in a nonlinear fashion (e.g., Deffenbacher et al., 2008; Fitzgerald & Price, 2015). Moreover, other of these variables—for example, showups (Neuschatz et al., 2016) and amount of descriptive detail (Meissner et al., 2007, 2008)—are poor predictors of accuracy. Witnesses' descriptions of perpetrators tend to be fairly impoverished—one study found that only sex, height, general appearance/race, skin color, age, and head covering were mentioned by over 50% of robbery witnesses—but the information they do provide is reasonably accurate (van Koppen & Lochun, 1997; see, generally, Meissner et al., 2007; Sporer, 1996).

With regard to the amount of incriminating evidence—another way of estimating a suspect's presumptive guilt—the findings are mixed. Behrman and Davey (2001) found fairly constant levels of suspect identifications as a function of evidence strength, but Tollestrup and colleagues (1994) found that witnesses were more likely to identify suspects against whom there was relatively strong evidence. Summarizing across these archival studies, the literature suggests that to some extent, factors that predict positive suspect identifications and those that predict accurate identifications mostly go hand in hand; however, the literature also shows that certain factors unrelated to greater accuracy also predict positive identifications, and—perhaps most troubling—large numbers of lineup identifications are demonstrably erroneous. Overall, then, the results of archival studies are largely consistent with the results of laboratory experiments of eyewitness memory.

Case Studies

Case studies differ from archival studies in that they focus on witnesses to one or a handful of crimes, rather than a large database of crimes, and the researchers interview the witnesses instead of relying entirely on law enforcement records. Thus, the analysis is necessarily narrower and based on a smaller sample size, but it can also be deeper. For example, Yuille and Cutshall (1986) interviewed 13 witnesses to a shooting incident. The crime involved the robbery of a gun store, after which the store owner pursued the robber and a shoot-out took place on the street, killing the robber and wounding the store owner. Witnesses, who viewed the incident from different places along the street, were initially interviewed by police, most of them at the scene; they subsequently provided a free account and answered specific questions in a 45–90-minute interview with the researchers, 4–5 months after the event. Yuille and Cutshall categorized information as action details, person descriptions (e.g., age, height, clothing, etc.), or object descriptions, and they determined accuracy by comparing witnesses' statements to police, public safety, autopsy, and medical reports, as well as to statements by other witnesses, and they inspected the scene of the crime themselves. The amount of detail provided by witnesses in both police and research interviews varied widely, but they tended to emphasize action details in both interviews. Of the information that witnesses provided, their accuracy exceeded 70% across both interviews and across all of the detail categories, though it was higher for action details and object descriptions than for person descriptions. There was no relationship between witnesses' self-reported stress level at the time of the crime and their accuracy.

Subsequent case studies have found largely comparable results—namely, that eyewitnesses are more likely to remember some kinds of information than other kinds; that their accuracy for what they do remember is reasonably good, with accuracy rates for many, if not most, kinds of information exceeding 70% and even 80%, even several months after the crime; and that their level of stress/negative emotion is unrelated to accuracy (Christianson & Hübinette, 1993; Odinot, Wolters, & van Koppen, 2009). At first glance, these conclusions seem to be at odds with the preponderance of experimental research on eyewitnesses, which has generally emphasized the unreliability of eyewitness performance and the adverse effects of stress. The apparent discrepancy can be explained, at least in part, by calling attention to several important distinctions: the amount remembered versus the accuracy of what is remembered; different performance metrics (e.g., person identification vs. event recall, recall for different aspects of the event, etc.); witnesses' varied roles in the event (e.g., victim vs. bystander); the relatively small sample size in case studies and the challenges involved in controlling for extraneous factors and verifying what really happened; the complex relationship between emotion and memory (e.g., for central vs. peripheral details); and the difficulty in estimating one's emotional state long after an event as opposed to "in the moment." Nevertheless, these case studies show that eyewitness performance can be quite good in some respects and in some circumstances; they offer a caution against the simplistic conclusion that eyewitness memory is inherently unreliable.

Staged Crimes/Field Studies

A handful of enterprising researchers have staged events in the field or the lab in order to measure witnesses' memory for the event, and others have been able to implement experimental manipulations with police in the field. These studies are extremely difficult to conduct, for a variety of reasons: access to police officers and real witnesses, ethical considerations, difficulty using true random assignment and avoiding confounds, and challenges in determining accuracy and preserving records (see, generally, Steblay, 2012; 2018; Wells, 2008). Because of these obstacles, there are fewer staged crime and field studies in the eyewitness corpus than we, as a field, might prefer; nonetheless, there have been a number of good exemplars since the Münsterberg era.

Staged crime studies underwent something of a renaissance in the 1970s and 1980s (Memon et al., 2008). In one of the earliest of these efforts, Buckhout (1974; see Chapter 1) took a page from von Liszt's book and staged several crimes in classrooms on campus (e.g., an assault, a purse snatching). For example, in one study a student "attacked" a professor, after which Buckhout took sworn statements from the 141 witnesses. He then asked the unsuspecting witnesses to identify the perpetrator from a six-person TP lineup 7 weeks later. Different lineup conditions varied the presence/absence of instruction bias (the biased instructions led witnesses to believe the guilty party was in the lineup) and the presence/absence of photospread bias (in the biased photospread, the perpetrator had a distinctive expression and his picture was positioned at an angle).

Witnesses' descriptions of the incident and the perpetrator's appearance had numerous inaccuracies; mean total accuracy was only 25% of the maximum score possible. On the lineup, only 40% correctly identified the perpetrator; many of those who made errors, including the "victim," chose an innocent bystander instead (see discussion of unconscious transference in Chapter 3). Even with biased instructions and a biased photospread, which should lead to the highest accuracy rate in a TP lineup, only 61% of witnesses made a correct identification (the 7-week retention interval doubtlessly contributed to the overall low level of performance; 7 weeks is unusually long for a research study, but not out of the ordinary in real criminal investigations, where it can take a while for police to locate a suspect and/or witnesses).

General Findings

Because these studies involve deception—participants are unaware that they are participating in a research study until after the study has been completed—the sorts of events in staged crime studies are usually a good deal more limited, and more routine, than they were in von Liszt's and Münsterberg's (and even in Buckhout's) day. Many staged crime studies have been conducted not so much with the goal of understanding eyewitnesses' memory processes, per se, as for purposes of studying how observers evaluate eyewitnesses. In these two-stage studies, one group of participants first witnesses a staged crime and subsequently attempts to recall details of the event and/or make an identification. In the second stage, another group of participants observes the witnesses to the staged crime—either live or, more often, on video—as they make their report or identification. The Stage 2 participants then evaluate the eyewitnesses and predict whether they were accurate or not. To produce varying numbers of accurate and inaccurate witnesses, the researchers sometimes vary elements of the witnessing conditions during Stage 1.

Results from the first stage of these prediction studies, which involve naïve witnesses, generally confirm the findings from studies of aware witnesses (for review, see Bornstein & Greene, 2017; Boyce et al, 2007). For example, in one of the earliest such studies, Lindsay et al. (1981) had participants witness a staged theft, in which a confederate stole a calculator from the cubicle where the participant was waiting for the experimenter to return. Different stimulus conditions varied exposure time to the thief and whether the thief disguised his facial features: 12 seconds exposure to a thief wearing a knit cap that covered part of his ears and all of his hair; 12 seconds exposure to a thief wearing a cap that covered part of his hair; or 20 seconds exposure to a capless thief. Identification accuracy in a subsequent lineup was 33%, 50%, and 74% in the three conditions, respectively (they deleted from these calculations participants who made no identification or were not willing to be cross-examined on what happened). Although 12–20 seconds is not terribly long in an absolute sense, it is a relatively long time to be exposed to one other person in a small cubicle, and likely as much time as many eyewitnesses have to view criminals. The Lindsay et al. scenario also contained better viewing conditions than many real-world crimes (e.g., distance, lighting, etc.). It is therefore striking that between one-quarter and two-thirds of participants made inaccurate identifications in these circumstances. Other staged-crime studies have shown similar levels of performance, using both TP and TA lineups (e.g., Lindsay, Wells, & O'Connor, 1989; Wells & Lindsay, 1983).

In many cases, the events are not crimes of any sort but are, rather, an encounter that participants attempt to remember afterward. Nevertheless, these studies are a unique and creative way of studying the memory of witnesses who are involved in a genuine event yet unaware that their memory is going to be tested. For example, Platz and Hosch (1988; see also Hosch & Platz, 1984) had experimental confederates interact with convenience store clerks; the confederate was White, Black, or Mexican American; the race/ethnicity of the clerks varied naturally as well. The interactions, which lasted 3–4 minutes, insured that the clerks looked at the confederates by having the confederates adhere to a set script, such as asking for a pack of cigarettes, paying for the purchase with pennies, and then asking for directions. Two hours later, a different confederate conducted a TP lineup. There were two noteworthy findings: first, the clerks' performance was mediocre overall, with a correct identification rate of only 44.2%; second, all three groups of clerks were better at identifying customers of their own race/ethnicity than of other race/ethnicities, corroborating the cross-race effect (or own-race bias) that has been demonstrated extensively in laboratory research (Meissner & Brigham, 2001; Wilson, Bernstein, & Hugenberg, 2016). Correct identification rates in the own-race conditions were 53.2%, 53.6%, and 63.6%, for White, Mexican American, and Black participants, respectively; the comparable figures for other-race identifications were 37.2%, 30.4%, and 50.0%. Wright, Boyd, and Tredoux (2001) also found the cross-race effect in naturalistic field conditions.

Penrod and Bornstein (2007) meta-analyzed the results of the Platz and Hosch (1988) study in conjunction with three other field studies (Brigham, Maass, Snyder, & Spaulding, 1982; Krafka & Penrod, 1985; Pigott, Brigham, & Bothwell, 1990). Although the studies varied in terms of the nature of the event, the independent variables, and the sample (e.g., convenience store clerks, bank tellers), eyewitnesses' lineup performance was quite similar across studies. In TP lineups, the correct identification rate ranged from 34% to 48%, and foil identifications ranged from 14% to 45% (unweighted averages of 42% and 32%, respectively). For the two studies using TA lineups, the false identification rates were 34% (Krafka & Penrod, 1985) and 37.5% (Pigott et al., 1990). Thus, eyewitnesses in the field in this set of studies made large numbers of errors, just as do eyewitnesses in the lab. Perhaps more important, the field studies generally showed that system and estimator variables operate similarly in the two contexts. In addition to demonstrating the cross-race effect (Brigham et al., 1982; Platz & Hosch, 1988), witnesses in both the field and the lab were more accurate when the context of the encounter was reinstated than when it was not (Krafka & Penrod, 1985).

Other staged crime and field studies have largely replicated these two main findings: first, that error rates are substantial; and second, that factors affecting (or predicting) eyewitness performance in the laboratory function similarly in the field. For example, field studies have found that witnesses who make fast decisions are more accurate than witnesses who make slow decisions (Key et al., 2017; Sauerland & Sporer, 2009); eyewitnesses tend to overestimate the duration of an encounter (Yarmey, 1993); they make more false identifications when given biased instructions (Malpass & Devine, 1981) or under the influence of alcohol (Dysart, Lindsay, McDonald, & Wicke, 2002); they favor center lineup locations in a photo-array over edges and corners, and top-row locations over bottom-row locations (Palmer, Sauer, & Holt, 2017); high levels of stress have an adverse impact on eyewitness identification (Morgan et al., 2004; Valentine & Mesout, 2009); and young child witnesses perform worse on lineups and recall measures than older children and adults (Brigham, van Verst, & Bothwell, 1986), and they are also more suggestible (Leichtmann & Ceci, 1995).[4] In all of these studies, which varied widely in their methodological characteristics, error rates of all types—foil identifications and false rejections in TP lineups, and foil identifications and false identifications (of an innocent suspect) in TA lineups—were substantial,

[4] Not all well-documented laboratory findings have been replicated in the field. For example, in the field study described earlier by Yarmey (2004), there was no effect of disguise (target with or without a baseball cap and sunglasses), retention interval (2 minutes v. 4 hours), or retrieval instructions (with or without context reinstatement) on lineup identification, although disguise and retention interval did affect recall of the target's appearance.

with overall error rates typically in the neighborhood of 30%–50% (varying both across studies and across conditions within studies).

Field Studies of Interviewing

Although the bulk of eyewitness interviewing research has been conducted in laboratory settings, it has also been studied in the field (Fisher & Schreiber, 2007; Memon et al., 2010). In one of the earliest such tests (Fisher, Geiselman, & Amador, 1989), police detectives recorded their interviews with crime victims and witnesses. There were two crucial comparisons: the interviews of detectives before versus after training in use of the CI, and the interviews of trained versus untrained detectives. The pre-post comparison showed a 47% increase in the amount of information elicited after CI training, and the trained-untrained comparison showed a 63% difference in favor of the CI-trained detectives. These differences were not due to the cognitive interviews simply taking longer. Moreover, despite the difficulty of verifying what actually happened in the field, corroboration rates were equivalent pre- and posttraining; in other words, CI training increased the amount of information elicited from witnesses without diminishing its accuracy.

More recently, Gabbert, Hope, and Fisher have developed the Self-Administered Interview (SAI), modeled on the CI, for use with witnesses when limited police resources do not allow for an immediate interview conducted by a law enforcement professional (Gabbert, Hope, & Fisher, 2009; Hope, Gabbert, & Fisher, 2011). Several laboratory studies have demonstrated that the SAI increases eyewitnesses' information output relative to free recall, in terms of eliciting more correct and incorrect details; overall accuracy of the two techniques is roughly the same (e.g., Gawrylowicz, Memon, & Scoboria, 2014). The SAI is beneficial outside the laboratory as well, improving memory (compared to free recall) for a staged crime (theft of a cell phone) witnessed under stressful conditions (Krix et al., 2016).

Special Cases

Two of the more controversial topics in the eyewitness identification literature in recent years are lineup presentation method (i.e., simultaneous vs. sequential) and the nature of the CA relationship. Both topics have been addressed in field studies. Although sequential lineups are becoming increasingly popular as a matter of policy (Clark, 2012; Malpass, 2006), not all eyewitness researchers are convinced that they are superior to simultaneous lineups (e.g., Malpass, 2006; McQuiston-Surrett et al., 2006; Wixted, Mickes, et al., 2016). Overall, research comparing sequential and simultaneous lineups shows a reduction in false identifications with sequential lineups (Steblay et al., 2001, 2011); however, this body of research has been criticized for having empirical and theoretical gaps (e.g., Malpass et al., 2008), and the reduction in false identifications of the innocent is offset by a (smaller) reduction in correct identifications of the guilty (Clark, 2012).

Several field studies comparing sequential and simultaneous lineups have been conducted, in a number of American jurisdictions and also abroad (Sucic, Tokic, & Ivesic, 2015), often in conjunction with blind administration. Unfortunately, they do little to clarify the picture. Depending on the particular study, this work has found a simultaneous advantage in terms of fewer known-innocent filler and more suspect identifications (Mecklenburg, 2006); a simultaneous advantage in terms of fewer identifications of suspects likely to be innocent (Amendola & Wixted, 2015; Wixted, Mickes, et al., 2016); a sequential advantage in terms of fewer known-innocent filler identifications (Klobuchar, Steblay, & Caligiuri, 2006; Wells et al., 2015); and no advantage for either procedure in any respect (Sucic et al., 2015).[5] Interpretation of the studies has been complicated further by methodological concerns. For example, the Illinois field study (Mecklenburg, 2006) has been criticized for confounding lineup presentation method with blind administration and containing other methodological flaws (Schacter et al., 2008; Steblay, 2011; Wells, 2008).

As described in Chapter 3, skepticism toward eyewitness confidence dates back to Münsterberg himself, and confidence's limited predictive value is important, given that both courts and laypeople (e.g., jurors) place considerable weight upon it (Bornstein, 2017; Bornstein & Greene, 2017; Leippe & Eisenstadt, 2007). "Poor" is, of course, a relative and subjective term, and along with this general assessment, research dating back 30 years or more has shown that confidence reliably predicts eyewitness accuracy better under some conditions than others (see Chapter 3). The extreme variability of the CA relationship, along with the diversity of ways for measuring it, makes it hard to compare the results of laboratory and field studies in this respect; nonetheless, we can examine whether the variables that affect the magnitude of the relationship operate similarly in the two contexts. Taken by itself, confidence is at best a moderately significant predictor of eyewitness accuracy in field studies measuring both identification (Klobuchar et al., 2006; Palmer et al., 2013; Sauer, Brewer, Zweck, & Weber, 2010; Sauerland & Sporer, 2009; Sucic et al., 2015; Yarmey, 2004) and recall (Odinot et al., 2009; Yarmey, 1993). For example, Sauerland and Sporer (2009) had experimental confederates (targets) engage pedestrians in conversation for 15–60 seconds. Thirty seconds later, an interviewer approached the participant and conducted a TP or TA lineup; participants estimated their confidence on an 11-point scale (0%–100%). Accurate participants were significantly more confident than inaccurate participants, but the mean confidence for the two groups was not

[5] The Klobuchar et al. (2006) field study did not manipulate lineup presentation method; rather, all lineups were double-blind, sequential lineups. They reached their conclusions by comparing the results to field studies using simultaneous lineups and laboratory research using both sequential and simultaneous lineups.

all that divergent: 67.8% versus 52.7%. However, the predictive value of confidence was greater for choosers than for nonchoosers and, among choosers, when high confidence coincided with making a relatively fast identification. Other field studies have obtained similar patterns (e.g., Palmer et al., 2013; Sauer et al., 2010; Wixted, Mickes, et al., 2016). Thus, in both staged-crime and field studies, conditions that promote a strong CA relationship in the laboratory do so among naïve witnesses as well (Wixted et al., 2018; Wixted & Wells, 2017), although there is some variability depending on how the CA relationship is measured (Palmer et al., 2013).

Witnessing Modality

The very name of the phenomenon in question—*eyewitness* memory—implies a specific sensory modality. This seems obvious, and we tend to take it for granted, but it bears reflection. Eyewitness memory necessarily means memory for stimuli that witnesses have *seen*. But of course, witnesses do more than see; they also hear, smell, taste, and touch. The cognitive processes involved in remembering information processed via these different sensory modalities are similar in some respects yet different in others. As Münsterberg observes, "There are different types of memory, which in a very crude and superficial classification might be grouped as visual, acoustical, and motor types" (p. 61). He goes on to discuss witnessing modality primarily in terms of differences both between and, even more so, within individuals; that is, a witness "may be asked what he has seen, what he has heard, what he as [*sic*] spoken, how he has acted, and yet even a most superficial test might show that the mechanism of his memory would be excellent for one of these four groups of questions and utterly useless for the others, however solemnly he might keep his oath" (p. 62). One can readily imagine a situation where a witness's memory for motor actions, smell, or taste would be relevant to a case (e.g., "What did the allegedly spiked drink taste like?"); however, insofar as humans are primarily a visual and auditory species, after *eye*witnessing, the sensory modality that most often takes on forensic relevance is *ear*witnessing.

Eyewitness and earwitness memory are conflated to a significant degree. In witnessing a crime, as in most other naturally occurring situations, we process visual and auditory information concurrently. For example, we hear what the mugger is saying while we see him point his gun at us. Consequently, interviewers of eyewitnesses question them about what they heard along with what they saw, and research on event recall tends not to distinguish between the two.[6] A cleaner distinction, albeit still not a perfect one, can be

[6] There are exceptions. As described earlier in the chapter, some research distinguishes, for example, between recall for different aspects of an event, such as action details versus person and object descriptions (see, e.g., Yuille & Cutshall,

made when it comes to identification decisions—that is, in comparing witnesses who make visual versus auditory identifications. Many crimes involve perpetrators who are heard but not seen: the identity thief who obtains private information over the phone, the kidnapper who demands a ransom by phone, the bank robber wearing a mask, the rapist who assaults his victim in the dark, the sight-impaired victim or bystander, and so on. Conversely, some perpetrators are seen but not heard: the assailant seen down the block or through a car window, the bank robber who silently passes the teller a note. To our knowledge, comprehensive data on the incidence of crimes with predominantly visual versus auditory cues do not exist; the former are certainly more common, but the latter are far from infrequent. Thus, a fair amount of research has investigated how well witnesses can make auditory identifications overall, as well as the kinds of system and estimator variables that affect their performance (Yarmey, 2007). We review that research shortly, after first providing a brief overview of how the courts treat earwitness evidence.

The Law of Earwitness Testimony

American courts make little distinction between witnesses as a function of sensory modality; rather, they tend to apply standards developed for appraising eyewitness reliability, such as the *Biggers* criteria (*Neil v. Biggers*, 1972; reaffirmed in *Manson v. Brathwaite*, 1977), when assessing earwitness reliability (Laub et al., 2013). In determining whether a suggestive identification procedure violated a defendant's right to due process, these criteria take into account the witness's opportunity to view the criminal at the time of the crime, the witness's degree of attention, the accuracy of the witness's prior description of the criminal, the witness's level of certainty, and the amount of time between the crime and the identification (*Neil v. Biggers*, 1972; see Wells & Quinlivan, 2009). As described in the following section, relying on the same jurisprudence when making decisions about earwitness and eyewitness testimony is problematic because processes of auditory and visual memory—especially in terms of voice versus face identification—differ in important ways (the *Biggers* criteria are problematic even when applied only to eyewitness identification; Wells & Quinlivan, 2009).

Courts' failure to make much of a distinction between earwitness and eyewitness testimony means that, as with eyewitness testimony (Benton et al., 2007), courts are highly variable in their treatment of this kind of evidence. To establish the parameters of earwitness testimony jurisprudence, Laub and colleagues (2013) analyzed appellate court decisions in 226 earwitness cases from a variety of jurisdictions (predominantly US states and federal courts). Nearly all courts held that voice identifications were admissible;

1986). Although this research shows that some kinds of event details are remembered better or worse than others, it is not quite the same as comparing memory for different sensory modalities.

they were deemed inadmissible in only 5% of cases, and roughly half of those exclusions were on procedural grounds, rather than scientific concerns about the reliability of the evidence.[7]

When a voice identification occurred under suggestive circumstances, courts conducted a *Biggers*-like analysis, using the aforementioned *Biggers* or related criteria, to determine whether the suggestive procedures rendered the voice identification so unreliable as to create a substantial likelihood of misidentification. Suggestive procedures included using a small number of voices (as few as one) in the lineup; not matching lineup members on voice quality; allowing the witness to see (and not merely hear) the suspect; and referring to the suspect in a voice lineup by the same number as in a prior visual lineup, in which the witness made a positive identification. Weighing the totality of the circumstances, all 30 courts that considered the question ruled the identification admissible in spite of the suggestive procedures (Laub et al., 2013). Thus, courts are quite deferential to voice identification evidence, just as they are toward visual identification evidence.

Part of the courts' deference toward voice identification evidence might reflect a reliance on safeguards to assist jurors in weighing it properly, especially when the voice lineup was suggestive. Indeed, a number of courts in the Laub et al. (2013) sample addressed the use of safeguards. The most common safeguard discussed was cross-examination; many courts justified allowing questionable identifications because attorneys could cross-examine the earwitness. All of the courts that discussed cross-examination admitted the voice identification. However, other safeguards, such as special cautionary instructions and expert testimony, were raised much less frequently, each appearing in fewer than 5% of the cases. Moreover, special instructions and expert testimony on earwitness testimony were both held inadmissible more often than they were allowed.

Courts' reluctance to use safeguards besides cross-examination in earwitness cases is unfortunate because such safeguards could help educate the jury. Jurors find earwitness testimony persuasive (van Wallandael, Surace, Hall Parsons, & Brown, 1994). Although they know less about earwitness than about eyewitness memory (Philippon, Cherryman, Bull, & Vrij, 2007; Read & Desmarais, 2009), they rely on the two kinds of evidence to about the same degree (Laub, Kimbrough, & Bornstein, 2016; McAllister, Dale, & Keay, 1993). This is obviously less than ideal if, as the literature suggests, earwitnesses are less accurate than eyewitnesses. Certain safeguards, especially expert testimony and closing arguments containing information on the factors that affect identification accuracy, can sensitize jurors to aspects of earwitness testimony that make it more versus less reliable (Laub et al., 2016).[8]

[7] The admissibility rate for visual identifications is likely comparably high, though Laub et al. (2013) did not make a direct comparison.

[8] Laub et al. (2016) also included a jury instruction safeguard; this condition did not make participants more sensitive to the earwitness testimony.

This is an argument in favor of greater incorporation of these safeguards in trials with earwitness evidence.

Earwitness Identification: An Empirical Summary

As Münsterberg was aware, auditory and visual identification invoke fundamentally different psychological processes, making them very difficult to compare directly. Nonetheless, the general consensus is that overall, eyewitnesses are superior to earwitnesses in terms of their identification accuracy (Yarmey, 1995, 2007). One explanation for this difference is that faces—especially unfamiliar faces—are usually processed for later recognition, whereas speech is normally processed for comprehension (Cook & Wilding, 1997).

In a superficial sense, variables affect eyewitness and earwitness performance similarly. For example, earwitness identification performance is affected negatively by disguise (Orchard & Yarmey, 1995), lack of familiarity with the target (Yarmey, Yarmey, Yarmey, & Parliament, 2001), relatively brief exposure times (Cook & Wilding, 1997; Orchard & Yarmey, 1995), and relatively long retention intervals (Clifford, 1983; Clifford, Rathborn, & Bull, 1981). All of these variables likewise affect the accuracy of eyewitness identifications (Laub et al., 2016). And as with eyewitness memory, the relationship between earwitness accuracy and confidence in the identification tends to be modest but is highly variable depending on a number of system and estimator variables (Yarmey, 2007). Thus, there are many parallels across the two domains.

On closer inspection, however, there are important differences (Laub et al., 2013). Memory for voices fades more rapidly than memory for faces, meaning that the forgetting function varies between the two modalities (i.e., the shape of a curve charting performance as a function of delay differs for auditory versus visual identification); voices can be disguised more readily and in different ways than facial appearance (e.g., volume, accent, speech rate, and articulation vs. hair length/style, facial hair, and eyeglasses); voices are subject to larger within-person variation over stimulus sampling than faces (i.e., one's voice will vary more widely on separate occasions than one's face). Postevent information also has a greater effect on earwitness than on eyewitness recall (McAllister, Bregman, & Lipscomb, 1988).

Finally, although some of the system variables that are relevant in visual lineups also arise in constructing auditory lineups, such as the number of lineup members, the best method of selecting fillers, the use of a double-blind lineup, and whether the lineup should be presented live or via a prerecorded medium (i.e., photoarray/videotape or audiotape), auditory lineups also introduce several unique system variables. These include deciding what each lineup member should say (e.g., the same utterance as that spoken during the crime, or something else), how long the lineup utterance should be, the tone of voice in which it should be spoken (e.g., if the voice was yelling during the crime, should it be yelling during the lineup?), and whether the speaker should be visible to the witness. Moreover, the system variable that has probably garnered the most attention recently in eyewitness lineups—namely, sequential versus simultaneous presentation—is utterly meaningless in the earwitness context, where lineups must necessarily be sequential (though it is fun to imagine the chaos that would ensue with a voice lineup in which all the lineup members spoke simultaneously).[9]

Because of the difficulty in extrapolating from eyewitness to earwitness performance, guidelines recommending best practices for working with identification witnesses—conducting interviews as well as identifications—have been largely silent when it comes to earwitnesses (e.g., National Research Council, 2014; Technical Working Group on Eyewitness Evidence, 1999; Wells et al., 1998). Yarmey (2007) sought to fill this gap by proposing 16 recommendations for working with earwitnesses, especially in terms of administering voice lineups. Some of the recommendations roughly parallel widely recommended eyewitness lineup procedures, such as conducting the lineup as soon as possible, including five foils along with the suspect, selecting foils who match the witness's description of the perpetrator's voice, using unbiased instructions (i.e., instructing witnesses that the perpetrator may or may not be present), using lineups rather than showups, and obtaining a prompt confidence judgment. Other recommendations are more earwitness-specific: using tape recordings rather than live presentation; using tapes even when the voice was originally heard over the telephone; and having lineup members avoid words or phrases spoken during commission of the crime, speak in the same tone of voice as the perpetrator, and provide a 10–15-minute spontaneous speech sample from which a 30–60-second excerpt should be used for the lineup. We are unaware of any jurisdictions that have implemented Yarmey's very sensible recommendations or evaluated their effectiveness. Despite his admonishment that "prosecutors and trial judges should be very cautious in trying and hearing cases based solely on speaker identification evidence" (Yarmey, 2007, p. 128), courts' general receptivity to earwitness identification evidence, as described earlier, means that they continue to run a substantial risk of wrongful convictions in earwitness cases.

Conclusions

The field of eyewitness research encompasses diverse methodologies. Laboratory research predominates, but it is complemented by numerous exemplars of meta-analyses, archival research, case studies, staged crimes, and field studies. Although the findings from various research paradigms do not converge perfectly, by and large they are comparable. Eyewitnesses make

9 Thanks to Evelyn Maeder for making this suggestion.

many errors in the field as well as in the laboratory, in terms of both recall and person identification. Moreover, factors that affect performance in one paradigm tend to exert similar effects in other paradigms, and studies directly or indirectly comparing naïve and aware witnesses show few consistent differences, except for a tendency for aware witnesses to perform better in some respects. There is also some evidence of a disconnect in the effects of verisimilitude on event recall, as opposed to person identification. With respect to person identification, factors related to awareness or ecological validity tend to have no effect or, where there are differences, to produce stronger effects in more naturalistic conditions. The picture is less clear with regard to recall: The CI is a less beneficial interview technique—though still advantageous, compared to a standard police interview—as conditions become more naturalistic; and case studies show that eyewitnesses can be quite accurate in *what* they recall, albeit limited in how much they recall.

This pattern of findings suggests three conclusions. First, "laboratory measures can have some external validity" (Memon et al., 2008, p. 844)—that is, they are generalizable to real-world situations. Second, laboratory experiments—where participants are more likely than witnesses in the field to realize that they are part of an experiment where their memory will be tested—likely provide a high-end estimate of witnesses' overall accuracy level, at least in terms of person identification. And third, we cannot simply assume that recognition and recall processes will operate similarly in eyewitnesses.

Does this mean we should feel confident about foregoing more naturalistic eyewitness research altogether, even if only for identifications, and just rely on laboratory experiments? Not at all. Even if the research community were to become comfortable generalizing from laboratory findings to the real world, courts have demonstrated abundantly that they are not (Benton et al., 2007; Monahan & Walker, 2018). Thus, more naturalistic research methods are valuable in making the case for evidence-based reform. In addition, it is impossible to know whether laboratory findings generalize unless analogous research is conducted using nonlaboratory techniques, thereby providing a basis for comparison. This is especially important as new research questions emerge. Finally, study-space analysis has demonstrated that much experimental eyewitness research is constrained by a paucity of methodological variation (Malpass et al., 2008; Memon et al., 2010), meaning that it sometimes does a relatively poor job of capturing the rich variety of ways that eyewitnesses, and those who interact with them (e.g., police), really function in the field. For these reasons, a breadth of empirical approaches, including relatively naturalistic methods like field studies, should always have a place in eyewitness researchers' armamentarium.

One solution—recommended many years ago by Murray and Wells (1982) but rarely implemented—is to proceed in stages, using controlled laboratory procedures and aware witnesses to document effects initially, and then proceeding to more naturalistic studies with naïve witnesses. As they suggest, "once a variable has been found to be robust and reliable with the informed [aware] procedure there should be an attempt to validate it further with an uninformed [naïve] procedure. In this way we can use a relatively safe and effective paradigm to weed out the most promising variables" (Murray & Wells, 1982, p. 52).

Münsterberg's preference for staged crime and field studies notwithstanding, every method has something to offer, and the diversity of research methods is one of the things that makes eyewitness research so lively and interesting. In the words of one leading eyewitness researcher, "Eyewitness research presents opportunities for the full circle of the scientific method, from the laboratory to the field and back again. An interesting phenomenon is shaped into a laboratory research question; meta-analysis synthesizes laboratory results; laboratory principles are strategically tested in the field; theory is enriched as the reasons underlying a phenomenon are clarified; new questions emerge" (Steblay, 2012, p. 824).

5

The Detection of Crime

The more complex the machinery of our social life, the easier it seems to cover the traces of crime and to hide the outrage by lies and deception. Under these circumstances, it is surprising and seems unjustifiable that lawyers and laymen alike should have given any attention, so far, to the methods of measurement of association which experimental psychology has developed in recent years.

—Münsterberg, *On the Witness Stand* (p. 76)

As the title states, Münsterberg devotes this chapter to identifying criminals and, more specifically, to how to detect deception. The oldest method for ferreting out criminal facts is torture, as evidenced by the chapter's opening line: "As old as the history of crime is the history of cruelties exercised, in the service of justice, for the discovery of criminal facts" (p. 73). Although Münsterberg acknowledges that torture as a means of interrogation may have, at one time, been common practice, he doubts that it ever yielded reliable results. "At all times, innocent men have been accused by the tortured ones, crimes which were never committed have been confessed, infamous lies have been invented, to satisfy the demands of the torturers" (pp. 74–75). Münsterberg writes that the laboratory offers a better, more reliable way of detecting deception and criminal facts: "In the laboratory we are not confined to the chance material which daily life offers; we can prepare and control the situation" (p. 79). In lieu of torture, police should rely on what Münsterberg refers to as "inner associations." In his opinion, these associations are much harder to disguise, and the methodology allows for a trained psychologist to detect deception easily.

When he uses the term "inner associations," Münsterberg is referring to the notion that ideas and concepts are connected or associated together because they are experienced in close temporal or spatial proximity. When one idea comes to mind, the associated idea or memory may also be retrieved.

"Of course, everyone knows that our memory ideas link themselves with our impressions—that a face reminds us of a name, or a name of a face; that one word calls another to mind; that even smell or taste may wake in us manifold associations" (p. 77). Münsterberg believes, based on the work of Jung, that these associations can be employed to detect deception and crime. The basic experimental situation that Münsterberg refers to involves reading a list of 100 or so words to the suspected deceiver and requiring the person to say, as fast as he can, the first word that comes to mind. The list of words will contain mostly common or benign words that serve as control or baseline items, as well as what Münsterberg refers to as "dangerous" words. Dangerous words are words that are in some way related to the forbidden act. The list of words should be presented several times. Münsterberg writes that the innocent person will consent to such an experiment because he has nothing to hide, and the guilty person will also consent because he wants to appear as though he has nothing to hide. According to Münsterberg, this simple experiment will reveal guilty knowledge in three ways.

The first way the association method will reveal the guilty person is through a kind of priming. In the chapter, Münsterberg uses the example of a woman who is slain in her room, with a yellow canary next to her body. The suspected party will be wary of words related to the crime or dangerous words such as "bird." Considering the guilty person will be on alert for such words, there may not be any discernible reaction to the words. However, the word should bring to mind, according to Münsterberg, all the gruesome details of the crime. Those with guilty knowledge may reveal themselves two or three words later when asked for the first color that comes to mind, and they respond "yellow." Münsterberg would argue the guilty person would respond "yellow" only because of the connection of the yellow canary with the murder. Thus, the deception may not be revealed until several words after the dangerous word in the experiment.

The second way the association will reveal the deception is through changes in the associations that occur over repeated presentations of the list. Typically, when there is no deception, associations will remain the same over repeated trials: "If it was 'house'–'window' first, then it will probably be 'house'–'window' again. But a number of associations have been changed, and a careful analysis will show that these are first of all the suspicious ones" (p. 85). It is Münsterberg's contention that words associated with the act will give rise to ever-changing associations, but neutral words will bring to mind only the same unchanged association. Thus, the changes in responses over repeated trials will happen only for words related to the crime, and these changes will reveal the deception. Reaction time is the final way in which the guilty or deceptive person will be revealed. "A word which stirs emotional memories will show an association-time twice or three times as long as a commonplace idea" (p. 86).

As support for his arguments, Münsterberg writes about one of Jung's clinical cases in which an elderly man suspected his 18-year-old nephew of stealing his money. Jung asked the younger man to come in for a general evaluation during which Jung administered the association test. Jung prepared a list of 100 associations as part of a general medical exam. As part of the association test, there were 37 "dangerous" words included in the 100. The dangerous words referred to objects in the room from which the money was taken or to the punishment for crime. The test results revealed, according to Münsterberg, that the younger man was in fact stealing the money. For example, the average reaction time to neutral words was 1.6 seconds, whereas the reaction times to the words "burglar" and "jail" were 4.6 and 4.2 seconds, respectively. According to Münsterberg, the reaction times to some dangerous words were depressed, but in many cases, there was also a delay in the reaction time to the next neutral word that followed the dangerous word. As reported by Münsterberg, the nephew initially denied any wrongdoing but when confronted with the results of the association test, the boy capitulated and admitted his crimes. In Münsterberg's words, "The brutalities of the third degree would hardly have yielded such a complete result, nor the technicalities of the legal evidence, either" (p. 90). Somewhat uncharacteristically, Münsterberg fails to consider the possibility that confronting the nephew with this supposedly scientific proof of guilt might have elicited a false confession (see Chapter 7).

Although the association test may seem unreliable as a measure of deception detection to modern researchers, the rationale for such a test is sound and remains the basis for many modern-day lie detection techniques. The basic idea is that there are discernible differences between truth tellers and liars in terms of their reactions to crime-related items, in this case, words. This is the same rationale as that of the Guilty Knowledge Test or, as it has come to be known, the Concealed Information Test (CIT). Briefly, the assumption is that there will be different physiological responses to crime-related items versus non-crime-related items when the person has guilty knowledge.

Throughout the chapter, Münsterberg also writes about the effect of response latency or reaction time as a way of detecting crime: "In this way, during the last twenty years, there has developed an exact and subtle study of mental associations, and through such very careful observation of the time-differences between associations a deep insight has been won into the whole mental mechanism. The slightest changes of our psychical connections can be discovered and traced by these slight variations of time, which are, of course, entirely unnoticeable so long as no exact measurements are introduced" (pp. 81–82). Researchers interested in studying the mind have been using reaction time to learn about mental events since before psychology was an established science. In fact, in the 1800s, Donders (1868/1969) used a simple reaction time procedure to measure how long it took to make a decision. In the simple reaction time condition, he asked participants to hit a button as soon as the light appeared. He compared this to a choice reaction time task condition in which participants had to determine if the light was illuminated at one or two locations. It was Donders's hypothesis that the amount of time to make a decision equaled the reaction time from the choice reaction time condition minus the reaction time from the simple reaction time condition. Donders's contributions are very important, not only because his was one of the first psychological experiments, but also because he demonstrated that mental events could be studied with observable data in carefully controlled experiments. From the beginning of the 20th century, researchers have conducted experiments or empirical tests that examined the relationship between confidence and speed of response (i.e., reaction time) on sensory judgment and memorial accuracy (Dallenbach, 1913; Henmon, 1911; Peirce & Jastrow, 1884). In fact, Dallenbach (1913) was interested in variables that affected the reliability of eyewitness memory, and his work was based on Münsterberg's ideas outlined in *On the Witness Stand*.

In the sections that follow, we first review the research on reaction time as a measure of lie detection. We then summarize new lie detection procedures that take advantage of brain scanning (event-related potentials or ERP) and brain imaging (functional magnetic resonance imaging or fMRI). Then, following the spirit of Münsterberg's chapter, we review research on effective ways to detect deception. These involve different interviewing techniques such as imposing greater cognitive load, asking unexpected questions, and requiring the story to be told in reverse chronological order. The final section of the chapter continues with Münsterberg's theory of employing reaction time to detect crime and reviews how reaction time has been applied to determining eyewitness identification accuracy.

Reaction Time and Deception Detection

Although response latencies have a long history in experimental psychology, their use in deception research has been sporadic. Jung's Association Reaction Method was one of the earliest attempts to use reaction time to detect deception. Russian researcher Alexander Luria (1928, as cited in Trovillo, 1939) also compared the time it took crime suspects to generate associations to crime-related and crime-unrelated words. Luria observed longer reaction times and greater variability for guilty suspects, which he interpreted as validation for his method of detecting criminals. Other researchers have tried without success to replicate Luria's findings (Marston, 1920). After the failure to replicate Luria's initial findings, reaction time as a measure of deception or crime detection lost favor, and there was a hiatus in the research until the 1990s (see Suchotzki et al., 2017).

According to Verschuere, Suchotzki, and Debey (2015), in the 1990s, several computerized tasks were developed that employed reaction time to detect deception. Verschuere et al. argued that these methods originated from paradigms in cognitive psychology and were adapted for deception research. These cognitive paradigms include, but are not limited to, the lexical decision task (Locker & Pratarelli, 1997), Stroop task (Gronau, Ben-Shakhar, &

Cohen, 2005), oddball task (Seymour, Seifert, Shafto, & Mosmann, 2000), and Implicit Association Test (Sartori et al., 2008). Of these cognitive paradigms with reaction time as the principal measure, two that have shown the greatest success in differentiating truth tellers and liars are the oddball task and the Autobiographical Implicit Association Task (aIAT).

Reaction Time-Concealed Information Test (Oddball Task)

The Reaction Time Concealed Information Test (RT-CIT), or oddball task, is used in many deception detection studies (Verschuere et al., 2015). The Concealed Information Test (CIT) is used to ascertain whether a person recognizes crime-relevant information that would be known only to someone who committed the crime or was a co-conspirator. In the standard CIT, the examiner presents several items to an examinee, but only one item pertains to the crime. The test items are carefully chosen so that the crime-relevant and non-crime-relevant items are indistinguishable for innocent examinees. Items are presented in blocks and repeated several times in different orders within each block. During the interview, physiological responses (e.g., ERPs) to the items are recorded. If the physiological responses do not differ between crime-related and non-crime-related items, the examiner infers that the examinee is telling the truth. In contrast, if the responses differ between the crime-related and non-crime-related items, it is an indication that the examinee is being deceptive or has guilty knowledge pertaining to the crime. The CIT has been validated by laboratory studies that have demonstrated its effectiveness and reliability in detecting deception (for review, see Ben-Shakhar & Elaad, 2003). The field studies with the CIT have been less successful at detecting deception (Ben-Shakhar, 2012; Matsuda, Nittono, & Allen, 2012). As the name suggests, the primary measure of deception with the RT-CIT is reaction time, rather than physiological measures, and the key comparison is how quickly the examinee responds to crime-related and non-crime-related items. Deception is indicated by differences in response times to crime- and non-crime-related items.

Many studies have used the RT-CIT in conjunction with ERPs. As a result, the reaction time data have not always been the main dependent measure and many times go unreported (see Verschuere et al., 2015). However, in the studies that have reported reaction times, the results are exceptional. For example, Allen, Iacono, and Danielson (1992) required participants to hide the fact that they had learned target words prior to the task. The reaction time measure was nearly perfect in classifying who was or was not concealing information. As pointed out by Verschuere et al. (2015), the problem with these ERP studies is that it is unclear if the results would generalize to situations in which the RT-CIT is used without ERP.

Seymour et al. (2000) investigated whether impressive reaction time effects for lie detection would still occur without concurrent ERP measurements. To that end, they had participants memorize a list of code words as a part of a mock espionage task. It was a speeded reaction time task, meaning participants had to respond within a specified time limit. The results of three experiments replicated the impressively high sensitivity levels found with ERP studies (see Allen et al., 1992). The RT-CIT, without concurrent ERP measures, works equally well when applied to faces as to words (Seymour & Kerlin, 2008). These latter two results confirm that the RT-CIT is effective as a stand-alone procedure and that it is effective with complex stimuli.

The RT-CIT has even been adapted for use with a mock crime paradigm (Visu-Petra, Miclea, & Visu-Petra, 2012). Visu-Petra et al. (2012) had student participants in the guilty condition steal a CD containing exam questions from a backpack, whereas innocent participants had no knowledge of the theft. During the RT-CIT examination, all participants were asked to respond as quickly as they could to a set of pictures that they had recently memorized. They pressed "yes" if the picture was in the study list and "no" if the item was not studied. The "no" items included crime-related pictures like a backpack. In contrast to innocent participants, guilty participants responded more slowly and made more errors with the crime-related pictures. As was the case with words and faces, the RT-CIT discriminated the guilty from the innocent participants at a very high rate.

Reaction time–based measures of deception detection are not only effective, but they are more accurate or at least as accurate as other, more typical, polygraph techniques (we discuss the validity of polygraphs at length in Chapter 6). Verschuere, Crombez, Degrootte, and Rosseel (2010) directly compared the RT-based tests and polygraph tests within a single session. The RT test was more accurate at detecting deception than the polygraph test, exceeding the detection efficiency of the autonomic nervous system measures (e.g., skin conductance). Similarly, Visu-Petra, Bus, and Miclea (2011) used a mock crime scenario to compare the RT-CIT to the more commonly used CIT with physiological measures paradigm. The detection of concealed information was very good for both assessment techniques and revealed that the two methods had similar detection accuracy rates (Visu-Petra et al., 2011). These results confirmed the validity of the RT-based test and indicated that its discriminative power is similar to the CIT when used with traditional physiological measures such as skin conductance.

Despite these impressive validity and accuracy estimates, neither the CIT nor the RT-CIT has been applied extensively in real-world forensic settings (Nahari & Ben-Shakhar, 2011).[1] Several explanations have been offered to explain why the CIT or RT-CIT has not been more widely adopted. Chief among these explanations is the lack of external validity for the RT-CIT

[1] For a review of current limitations of the CIT, see Ben-Shakar (2012); Matsuda et al. (2012).

studies. Simply put, the contrived laboratory setting in which these measures are tested may not generalize to the real world. Indeed, it is difficult to argue that college students in an experiment are similarly motivated to avoid detection as are persons detained by the police who are trying to avoid being arrested. Realistic mock crime studies with varied populations and tasks that include incidental encoding of crime-related information are needed before this deception measure will enjoy widespread use in the field.[2]

In addition to the lack of external validity, there is some concern that countermeasures can be more easily employed with reaction time as opposed to other autonomic responses. Reaction time, unlike other autonomic responses such as skin conductance, can be internally or voluntarily controlled. This means that reaction times can be intentionally sped up or slowed down, which would jeopardize the validity of the test. Furthermore, there is no guarantee that examinees in real-world settings would follow the critical instruction to respond as quickly and accurately as possible.

The Autobiographical Implicit Association Task

The Implicit Association Task (IAT) was developed as an indirect measure of attitudes (Greenwald, McGhee, & Schwartz, 1998). It consists of many blocks that employ different rules for categorizing words. For example, when trying to assess one's attitude toward abortion, words may have to be sorted first into good versus bad, and then on the next block they may have to be sorted into pro-choice versus pro-life. In the third block, a right key press may be required for words that are good and pro-life, and a left key press for words that are bad and pro-choice. In the fourth block, the response options are switched, so that a left key press is used for words that are good and pro-life, and a right key press is used for words that are bad and pro-choice. On the fifth block, good is paired with pro-choice and bad with pro-life. The primary assumption is that ease of pairing provides a measure of association strength. Faster pairing in the third block (pro-life, good) than in the fifth block (pro-choice, good) is taken as an implicit preference for the pro-life position.

The IAT was applied to lie detection by Sartori et al. (2008), who employed a series of "I" statements—hence the Autobiographical Implicit Association Task (aIAT). In the aIAT, true and false statements are presented as contrasting facts to assess the ease of pairing. For example, a true fact (I own a home) or a false fact (I live in an apartment) might be paired with contrasting statements (I robbed a liquor store vs. I did not rob a liquor store). Sentences are presented individually and in random order. Participants are instructed to classify them as quickly as possible. Easier or faster pairing of innocent statements (I did not rob a liquor store) with the true statement (I own a home)

---

[2] These criticisms, which speak to the work's ecological and external validity, are similar to those leveled against much experimental eyewitness research and that are reviewed in the previous chapter.

is taken as an indication of truth, and faster pairing of guilty statements (I robbed a liquor store) with the false statement (I live in an apartment) is thought to indicate deception.

Sartori et al. (2008) tested the validity of the aIAT in a series of six experiments using different populations (students and community volunteers who were professed drug addicts) and materials (where one spent her last holiday, whether one's driver's license had been suspended for drunk driving, what drugs one has used, and so forth). In Experiment 2, participants were randomly assigned to steal a CD (guilty condition) or read about a mock crime involving stealing the CD (innocent condition). The classification accuracy of the aIAT was very high in all six experiments, one of which was independently replicated (Verschuere, Prati, & De Houwer, 2009).

The results from the aIAT are certainly impressive and encouraging. As pointed out by Verschuere et al. (2015), one of the greatest advantages of the aIAT is its flexibility, as it can be used with almost any materials. In fact, it has been used to detect motives to lie as well as the lies themselves. Agosta, Pezzoli, and Sartori (2013) asked participants to reveal actual lies they told and why they lied. With the aIAT, the authors found that not only could they successfully detect lies, but they could also use the test to reveal the reasons for telling those lies. The adaptation demonstrates the flexibility of the test. However, the aIAT relies on reaction time and, as such, suffers from some of the same maladies as the RT-CIT—namely, reaction time can be consciously controlled, so the test could, potentially, be fooled by a conscientious liar.

Suchotzki et al. (2017) conducted a large-scale meta-analysis of reaction time–based lie detection techniques. The meta-analysis included 114 computerized reaction time studies (n = 3,095). The authors included only computerized reaction time studies because face-to-face interviews do not allow the precision in measurement that is required for reaction time–based tests (see Verschuere et al., 2015).[3] The reaction time tests that met the inclusion requirements were the RT-CIT, the aIAT, the Sheffield Lie Test, and the Differential Deception Paradigm. Of the 114 studies, 34 used the RT-CIT, 9 used the aIAT, 55 used the Sheffield Lie Test, and 16 used the Differential Deception Paradigm or some variant of it. The Sheffield Lie Test requires participants either to lie or to tell the truth about a set of stimuli based on a predetermined cue. For example, the cue may be color, and the participants would be instructed to respond truthfully if the question is in blue and to lie if the question is in red. In this test, an individual participant lies and tells

[3] A person holding a stopwatch does not provide the resolution and reliability that is needed to adequately measure reaction time for deception detection. Furthermore, reaction time measurement requires averaging over a series of trials, and it would be very hard for a person with a stopwatch to be consistent in the measurements over repeated questions. At the very least, the person would be much less consistent than a computer, which will not get tired or distracted.

the truth about the same stimuli over repeated trials (Spence et al., 2001). The crucial contrast is between responses to the same items on truth and lie trials. Reaction times to all responses are recorded. In the Differential Deception Paradigm, participants are cued to tell the truth about one set of stimuli and to lie about another set (Furedy, Davis, & Gurevich, 1988). Unlike the Sheffield Lie Test, the crucial contrast is between responses to different stimuli.

The results of the meta-analysis revealed a significant reaction time effect. More specifically, the overall average for difference between lying and telling the truth was 112 ms, with lying taking longer than truth telling. The Sheffield Lie Test had a lying-truth difference of 179 ms, which was the widest separation on any of the tests. The differences in reaction time on the other three tests were 49 ms, 149 ms, and 106 ms for the RT-CIT, aIAT, and Differential Deception Paradigm, respectively. In addition to the overall effect, the authors examined some important variables that may moderate the reaction time results, such as the type of instructions and motivation to deceive. With regard to the type of instructions, the authors found that the reaction time difference for lying and telling the truth did not vary based on whether participants were told to respond as fast as they could or if they were not given any instructions on how fast to respond. The motivation to deceive did reduce the effect; however, the reaction time difference between lying and telling the truth was still significant. This is an important result, as one of the criticisms of deception detection research is that the motivation to avoid getting caught lying is much less for college students than it would be for people in the real world who are trying to avoid legal consequences.

The authors also examined the effect of countermeasures. In this context, countermeasures refer to intentional actions that would allow the person's deceptions to go undetected. For example, trying to respond more slowly to crime-related facts in reaction time–based detection tasks would be a countermeasure. There were 17 studies, with a total of 384 participants, where countermeasures were employed. The reaction time measures were not susceptible to countermeasures, as there was no significant moderating effect when participants were instructed to use countermeasures.

Measures Based on Brain Activity and Imagery

As technology has progressed, so has polygraph equipment and, as a result, the research on lie detection. Recently, lie detection researchers have begun measuring brain activity directly (ERPs) and taking images of the brain (fMRI). The advantages of ERPs and fMRI are that measures can be taken in real time and the tests are less susceptible to countermeasures, or so it was originally thought.

Event-Related Potentials

ERPs are voltage changes in the brain in response to specific events or stimuli. ERPs are usually measured with small electrodes, which are attached to the head and record electrical activity in the brain. Each electrode measures activity from groups of neurons that are thought to fire together. The electrical activity is recorded as the participant is presented with different events or stimuli. In the case of lie detection, the ERPs are measured in response to different questions that are thought to be indicative of truth telling or deception. ERPs have been frequently used with the CIT in lie detection experiments (see Iacono, 2015). In this case, the brain activity for the crime-related question would be compared to the activity for control questions or questions unrelated to the crime.

Iacono (2015) argued that ERPs provide several advantages over other autonomic nervous system responses that have been used more often in lie detection research, such as galvanic skin response and respiration.[4] According to Iacono, the most promising brain wave–based CIT test involves recording of the P300 wave. The wave is so named because it has a peak at 300 ms when simple stimuli are presented; however, the peak occurs later when complex stimuli are presented (Iacono, 2015). The P300 is particularly well suited for use with CIT because it is sensitive to the frequency of stimulus presentation and it varies with strength of recognition (Johnson, Pfefferbaum, & Kopell, 1985). With the CIT, crime-related questions are presented less frequently than non-crime-related questions. Thus, when the P300 wave is used in conjunction with the CIT for innocent people, there should not be a well-defined P300 for any items because none of the items should be recognized. However, if a person does recognize the crime-related questions, indicating deceit, then there should be a distinct P300 wave, but there should not be a discernible wave for control or unfamiliar questions.

A study by Rosenfeld and colleagues (1988) was one of the first to use the P300 wave in conjunction with the CIT to detect deception. Participants pretended to steal one item from a box containing 10 items. The crime-related item is referred to as the probe item, and the other 9 items are "irrelevant" items. During the testing phase, participants were repeatedly presented[5] with the names of all 10 items in the box and were instructed to say "no" to all items (including the "stolen" item), thereby indicating that none of the items was familiar to them. In addition to the 10 items from the box, there was one irrelevant item or "target" to which they were instructed to say "yes." This was done in order to ensure that they were paying attention. Because the

[4] Galvanic skin response is a change in the heat and electricity that passes through the skin via nerves and sweat.

[5] In ERP studies, items are usually presented repeatedly because ERPs are small in magnitude and may be obscured in a single trial, so responses are averaged over repeated trials of the same stimulus (see Rosenfeld, 2011).

participant is presented with three types of stimuli (probes, irrelevant items, and target items), this is known as the three-stimulus protocol or 3SP. For 9 of the 10 participants, Rosenfeld found a distinct P300 wave for the item that participants were instructed to steal but not for the other items in the box. There was also a distinct P300 wave for the probe item. Since the original work, Rosenfeld and colleagues have published over two dozen papers replicating and extending the findings, including an examination of countermeasures (see Rosenfeld, 2018).

It was thought that the P300-CIT was immune to countermeasures because the stimuli were presented so rapidly, the response involved neurological activity, and it happened in mere milliseconds (see Ben-Shakhar & Elaad, 2002, Rosenfeld, Ben-Shakhar, & Ganis, 2012). Although it would be nice if the test were immune to countermeasures, it turns out that these claims are exaggerated and the test can easily be tricked. As mentioned earlier, making a unique response to a test probe will produce a P300 wave (Rosenfeld et al., 1988); therefore, it ought to be possible for the examinee to make a unique covert response (e.g., toe tap, eye blink, and so forth) to irrelevant stimuli and elicit a discernible P300 wave. This would obscure the difference between the probe item and the irrelevant item and, thereby, eliminate the discriminative value of the test (see Rosenfeld, 2018; Rosenfeld, Soskins, Bush, & Ryan, 2004).

Compromising the test with a simple response is, in fact, simple to do. Rosenfeld et al. (2004) demonstrated that countermeasures could be effective when used to confound the P300-CIT. The authors utilized a mock crime scenario with six details selected as target probes (crime-related details), 24 details defined as irrelevant items, and 6 other details defined as irrelevant probes. The task was to make the same response to all items except the six irrelevant probes, which required a different response. Participants were randomly assigned to three groups: innocent, countermeasure, or no countermeasure-simply guilty. The countermeasure group was instructed to make a covert act (e.g., pressing the left forefinger on the left leg, wiggling the big toe, and so forth) when they were presented with irrelevant stimuli from a particular category (e.g., animals). The no countermeasure–simply guilty group was instructed not to perform countermeasures. The P300-CIT outcomes in terms of diagnosing guilt were 82% in the no countermeasure–simply guilty group as opposed to 18% in the countermeasure group (the rate was 9% for the innocent group). These results were replicated in a similar experiment by Mertens and Allen (2008). Unlike what was originally thought, these studies have shown that deception detection tests based on P300 amplitude as a recognition index may be readily defeated with simple countermeasures that can be easily learned and applied.

Countermeasures pose a serious challenge to the effectiveness of the P300-CIT. As a result, Rosenfeld and colleagues (Meixner et al., 2013; Rosenfeld & Labkovsky, 2010) started examining ways to combat the countermeasures. Rosenfeld and Labkovsky (2010) discovered a previously unknown

ERP component termed P900. The P900 wave occurs 850 to 900 ms after stimulus offset. In this study, participants were instructed to engage in covert countermeasures for two of four irrelevant stimuli. More specifically, participants were asked to make an extra mental response—"imagine your last name"—when those stimuli were presented. The P900 was apparent only for irrelevant stimuli that were not countered. The P900 was not evident for the probe or irrelevant countered stimuli. Rosenfeld and colleagues (Labkovsky & Rosenfeld, 2012; Meixner et al., 2013) have replicated these initial findings, further indicating that P900 may provide evidence of deception as well as attempts to evade detection through countermeasures.

Functional Magnetic Resonance Imaging

Anyone who has had a sports-related or back injury is familiar with MRI and fMRI. fMRI is a technique for mapping and measuring brain activity. fMRI takes advantage of the fact that blood flow increases to areas of the brain that are active and maps the blood oxygenation level-dependent (BOLD) signal. Blood contains iron, which has magnetic properties. Thus, if a magnetic field is presented to the brain, the iron molecules line up like magnets. fMRI indicates the presence or absence of brain activity because the blood in more active areas of the brain loses some of its oxygen, making the molecules more magnetic and, as a result, more responsive to magnetic fields.

The typical fMRI designs and most of the available lie detection studies center on the comparison between BOLD responses for two or more conditions. For example, maps of the BOLD signal recorded while a participant is lying can be contrasted with maps recorded when the participant is telling the truth or not responding. Inferences about the neural correlates of deception are then based on the overlap or differences in the BOLD maps during the lying and truthful states.

In typical fMRI lie detection experiments, participants are asked to answer truthfully to some questions and lie in response to others. The BOLD contrast between the two conditions (i.e., the pattern of BOLD signals detected when the participant is lying minus the pattern of BOLD signals detected when the participant is being truthful) is thought to reveal brain regions where activation is correlated with lying. Through the use of this paradigm, researchers have determined that the parietal-frontal areas are significantly more active when the individual is lying (see Rusconi & Mitchener-Nissen, 2013). This has been interpreted to mean that lying requires more effort than telling the truth. There is also evidence that the limbic system is more active during lying when more ecologically valid stimuli are used (Hakun et al., 2009). The limbic system is associated with emotional responding. Thus, lying may take more effort and be more emotionally taxing than telling the truth. (In fact, it seems that way when the authors try to deceive their wives about presents they may or may not have bought them for the holidays.)

A study by Langleben et al. (2005) was one of the first to use fMRI for lie detection in conjunction with a modified version of the CIT. In this study, participants were presented with several types of playing cards: lie cards, truth cards, and distractor cards. Participants were instructed to lie about possessing "lie" cards and to tell the truth about possessing "truth" cards. For distractor cards, participants were instructed to be honest about not having any of these cards. The results showed that certain parts of the brain were active when the participants were lying that were not active when they were telling the truth. More specifically, the lateral prefrontal cortex and the medial superior prefrontal cortex were more active during deception than truth telling. The authors developed a mathematical model based on these regions to distinguish deception from truth telling. The final model had an accuracy rate of 76.5%. Sensitivity and specificity were also high, at 68.8% and 83.7%, respectively. In this case, accuracy is how well the model discriminates truthful from deceptive cases. Accuracy is often the average of sensitivity (correctly classifying deceptive cases as deceptive) and specificity (correctly classifying truthful cases as truthful). Several researchers using fMRI procedures have found similarly high accuracy rates (see Ganis, 2015 for a review).

In fact, Ganis and colleagues (2011) reported perfect accuracy (100%). Ganis et al. (2011) also used a modified version of the CIT where participants lied about their birth date while being presented with a series of irrelevant dates. The actual birth date engaged several areas of the brain that were not active when irrelevant dates were presented. Ganis et al. found that the lateral prefrontal area could be used to classify truth and deceptive trials with 100% accuracy. As was the case with the Langleben et al. (2005) study, the prefrontal area of the brain seems to be active when people are deceptive, but there is less activity in this region when people are telling the truth.

Most fMRI lie detection studies will not provide 100% accuracy; however, the accuracy rate from these studies is still very high. Ganis (2015) found that all the previously published studies ($n = 10$) that quantified detection accuracy from fMRI had an average accuracy rate of 82%. The average specificity and sensitivity were 84% and 81%, respectively. Although the accuracy rate may seem high, Ganis points out that this is not much higher than the accuracy rate with traditional polygraph studies conducted in the laboratory (82%).

Similar to the polygraph, fMRI deception detection procedures have had a difficult time penetrating the legal system and gaining admissibility in the courtroom. Polygraph testing in the judicial system has been subject to ongoing concerns about the reliability and the generalizability of the findings to real-world settings (Stern, 2002; polygraphs are discussed in greater detail in the following chapter). These same concerns exist for neuroimaging means of lie detection.

The accuracy of fMRI lie detection, like polygraph tests, is quite impressive; however, it is unclear if or how this accuracy translates to applied settings. In other words, what counts as high accuracy in the laboratory might not be adequate for forensic situations. The fact that the fMRI lie detection procedures overall have an average accuracy rate of 82% may not be meaningful to the court when a particular individual fails or passes the test. As mentioned earlier, the accuracy of the test is the average of the sensitivity and the specificity of the test. However, the probability of a true positive result also depends on the base rate or the frequency of lying, which is unknown in the general population.

Not only are there reliability issues, but there are also concerns about the verisimilitude of the laboratory procedures relative to the real world. It is hard to imagine a situation that is less like the real world than laboratory lie detection studies. For the most part, the fMRI studies are conducted on college students who are not facing any repercussions if they are caught lying and who have little motivation to avoid being caught. This population is probably not very similar to the criminal population, so it is unclear if the findings would generalize to the population of criminal offenders. Furthermore, because students have nothing to lose if they are caught lying, they are likely considerably less motivated to confound the test, which also calls into question the generalizability of the results.

These issues came to the forefront in *United States v. Semrau* (2011). Semrau was accused of Medicare fraud and sought to introduce an fMRI lie detection expert in his defense. This individual, who was a noted expert and pioneer in the field of fMRI lie detection, testified that the defendant was truthful when he denied committing fraud. Due to various issues, there were three separate fMRI scans conducted on the defendant. The first and third sessions were negative for deception, whereas the second was positive. However, Semrau complained of fatigue during the second test, and the questions that were asked were complicated and difficult to understand. These issues were corrected during the third test, and Semrau was once again found to be truthful. The judge in the evidentiary hearing ruled against admitting the expert testimony at trial. The judge's opinion focused on the ecological validity issues, specifically the motivation of the students as opposed to real-world defendants and the fact that college students may not be representative of the population. Furthermore, the court opined that getting students to lie in the laboratory may be more indicative of task compliance than lying (see Langleben & Moriarty, 2013, for a more extensive review of the case). In addition, three separate scans with inconsistent results really make one question the validity of the test. Semrau was not successful in his appeal. The appellate court affirmed the trial judge's opinion that there is no known error rate in the real world, and it is unclear how the laboratory error rate generalizes to real-world situations (*United States v. Semrau*, 2012).

Effective Ways to Detect Deception

Considering the crux of this chapter is about detecting deceit and crime, it seems appropriate to explore ways to maximize the detection of deception. In the next chapter (Chapter 6), we mention some of the ways in which people err in trying to detect deceit. They include overreliance on verbal and nonverbal cues that are not indicative of lying, overconfidence in one's ability to detect deceit, the facts that the behavioral cues to lying are very hard to detect and that lies are often embedded in truthful accounts, and not taking into account that some people are better liars than others. In this section, we discuss some strategies one may want to avoid when trying to detect deception and ways in which one might overcome these errors in order to increase or maximize one's chances of successfully detecting deception. We also review some techniques that are more efficacious than others in revealing lies.

Vrij, Granhag, and Porter (2010) wrote an excellent review on how to avoid being deceived, and we review some of that work here. The first recommendation made by Vrij et al. is to avoid relying on cues, verbal or nonverbal, that are not correlated with lying and to pay more attention to cues that are indicative of deceit. This sounds obvious and easy, but it requires people to ignore the commonly held myths about liars, such as that they avoid eye movements or have a tendency to fidget (see "Global Deception Research Team," 2006; Vrij, 2008). It may require some effort and training for people to ignore spurious cues to deception in favor of more diagnostic cues, and unfortunately, this training has shown very mixed results.

According to Vrij, Mann, Leal, Vernham, and Vaughan (2016), the typical training procedures involve watching or listening to video- or audiotaped interviews of several people telling truth or lies. Typically, participants are asked to pay attention to or focus on particular cues and ignore others. Other studies use a procedure in which participants are told which behaviors are and are not diagnostic of lying before watching or listening to the interviewees. Finally, there is a feedback procedure in which participants are given feedback as to their judgments on truth and deceit. In all of these procedures, the trained participants are compared to a control group which receives no training.

As mentioned earlier, studies have been unable to prove that training universally improves lie detection. Training can even harm performance. For example, Kassin and Fong (1999) trained college students in the Inbau interviewing technique (Inbau et al., 2001). The Inbau technique is a common, and arguably the most common, interrogation technique taught to police. It is a nine-step interrogation procedure that is thought to lead to reliable confessions and, as such, should allow the interrogator to determine when the examinee is lying. Kassin and Fong found that participants trained in this method actually were worse at detecting deception than their untrained counterparts. Studies conducted on police have also found that training hampers lie detection relative to no training (Vrij, 1994; Vrij & Graham, 1997).

In contrast, many other training studies with college students have revealed that trained observers are better able to detect liars than are the nontrained controls. This is true regardless of the training procedure (Frank & Feeley, 2003; Vrij et al., 2016). However, the gains in deception detection for trained participants tend to be small in magnitude. This suggests that there are limitations on the extent to which training can improve lie detection. It is worth noting that these training programs may not reflect the true potential of training as a lie detection aid. In the studies that have found small improvements, the training programs were typically very brief, lasting no more than 15 minutes. There is some evidence that longer, more extensive training would be more beneficial to lie detection (Porter, Woodworth, & Birt, 2000; Porter et al., 2010). For example, Porter and colleagues have employed training programs of 2 days (Porter et al., 2000) and 2 hours (Porter et al., 2010), and their participants demonstrated much greater success in lie detection than what is typically found in training studies.

Another mistake to be avoided when trying to detect deceit is what has been referred to as the "Othello error" (Ekman, 1997, 2001; Vrij, Granhag, & Porter, 2010). In Shakespeare's play, the titular character accuses his wife, Desdemona, of being unfaithful. Desdemona, realizing that she cannot prove her innocence, reacts with an emotional outburst, which Othello misinterprets as evidence of her guilt. With regard to deception, interviewers must avoid Othello's mistake and not interpret nervous or emotional behavior as indicators of guilt. It is quite plausible that truth tellers would be scared or nervous as a result of being accused of wrongdoing. Furthermore, they may fear that there will be negative consequences if they are not believed. The point is that an emotional response is not diagnostic of deception, so deception detectors should avoid relying on emotional behavior (see Bond & DePaulo, 2006, 2008). This may be especially true in high-stakes situations where cognitive biases are likely to be more prominent (Porter & ten Brinke, 2009).

Although catching liars is no easy task and we have noted some pitfalls to avoid, there are also strategies and interviewing techniques that can improve deception detection (Vrij, 2004; Vrij, Granhag, & Porter, 2010). More specifically, Vrij et al. recommend imposing a greater cognitive load, asking unanticipated questions, asking the interviewee to tell the story in reverse chronological order, and requiring the interviewee to maintain eye contact during the interview. All of these techniques attempt to exacerbate the small differences that exist between liars and truth tellers, so the differences are more readily detectable.

One approach to catching liars involves trying to increase the differences in the verbal and nonverbal cues between liars and truth tellers. Although some differences do exist in verbal and nonverbal behaviors, these tend to be small or subtle differences and, as such, they are difficult to detect (see Vrij et al., 2010). Rather than relying on these small differences, researchers have examined interviewing strategies that make these differences more apparent and, therefore, more detectable. The two strategies that we review here are imposing cognitive load and the strategic question approach.

Imposing cognitive load takes advantage of the fact that lying is more cognitively taxing than telling the truth (Vrij, 2008a), and it takes longer to produce lies (Suchotzki et al., 2017). It simply takes more time and effort to fabricate a story than it does to tell the truth. Once you have fabricated the story, you have to remember the fabricated details so that you do not contradict what you have said. In addition to remembering the fictitious details, one must make sure not to reveal any actual, true details that are evidence of guilt. However, one must reveal enough true details in order to look credible and must more closely monitor behavior so that it does not seem as though one is lying. In other words, a liar does not want to give off nonverbal cues that indicate lying. All of this requires cognitive resources and monitoring. Thus, the idea behind imposing cognitive load is that, at some point, people who are lying will exhaust their cognitive resources and reveal their deception (Vrij, Fisher, Mann, & Leal, 2006).

Another way of putting it is that truth telling and lying require different processes. Truth telling involves retrieving and reconstructing a past experience. Lying, on the other hand, requires the creation of a new story. However, not just any story will do. The fabricated story must be plausible, and it must not contradict itself. When no personal memories or scripts are available for lie construction, the working memories of liars will be heavily burdened, reducing the capacity for speech production (Sporer & Schwandt, 2006, 2007). Liars must also monitor listeners for signs of suspiciousness. All of this will tax the liar's cognitive resources more than the truth teller's.

The temporal order in which the story is told is one way to increase cognitive load and magnify the cues to deception. More specifically, asking for the story to be told in reverse order increases cognitive load because telling stories in reverse chronological order runs counter to the typical sequential way in which we retell stories. It also disrupts schema-driven and reconstruction processes that aid retrieval (Geiselman & Callot, 1990). Vrij, Mann, Fisher, Leal, Milne, and Bull (2008) had liars and truth tellers retell their stories either chronologically or in reverse chronological order. Observers identified more cues for deceit when the stories were told in the reverse order. More important, participants who watched the reverse-order group had an easier time distinguishing truth from lies than control participants who heard the stories in the proper temporal order. In the control condition, only 42% of lies were correctly classified, whereas in the reverse-order condition, 60% of lies were correctly identified. It is worth noting that liars could defend against this strategy by rehearsing the story in reverse chronological order. However, we believe it would take a very savvy deceiver to be aware of this paradigm and to formulate ways to confound the test in the real world.

Cognitive load can also be increased through the type of questions that are asked, what Vrij, Granhag, and Porter (2010) refer to as the *strategic questioning* technique through unanticipated questions. It has been repeatedly demonstrated in the literature that people who are deceptive rehearse their answers, which creates an opportunity for interviewers to trip them up and detect their deception. The rehearsal can be effective only if the deceiver has accurately anticipated the interviewer's questions. To the extent that they have not adequately anticipated what they will be asked or if there are questions they did not anticipate, then deceivers can be tripped up and caught.

Vrij and colleagues (2009) empirically tested the unexpected question approach to deception detection. In this study, Vrij et al. interviewed liars and truth tellers about having lunch together. In reality, they did have lunch together, but liars were instructed to convince the interviewer that they did not. All pairs were given the opportunity to prepare for the interview together. The interviewer asked an opening question that the participants had anticipated (e.g., What did you do in the restaurant?) and unanticipated questions relating to spatial (e.g., Who were the closest diners to you?) and temporal (e.g., Who finished the food first, you or your friend?) aspects of the event. Finally, they were asked to draw a picture of the restaurant's dining area. Based on the anticipated questions, lying and truth telling pairs could not be classified above chance. However, based on the unanticipated questions, liars and truth tellers could be correctly classified 80% of the time.

Another way to increase cognitive load is to instruct the interviewee to maintain eye contact. Typically, people look away from the person to whom they are telling a story because maintaining eye contact is distracting (Doherty-Sneedon & Phelps, 2005). Vrij, Mann, Leal, and Fisher (2010) instructed some truth tellers and liars to maintain eye contact with the interviewer while retelling stories, whereas other truth tellers and liars were given no instructions regarding eye contact. As is typically done in deception research, the interview was videotaped and shown to observers. Imposing cognitive load through maintaining eye contact made the cues to deceit more apparent to observers and made those observers more accurate in discriminating lies from truths.

In summary, there are several ways in which people can reliably detect deception. In line with Münsterberg's idea, reaction time is an effective way to catch liars, as are brain scanning and imaging techniques. These techniques may have high accuracy in the laboratory but have not caught on in forensic settings. This may be due to the lack of verisimilitude between the laboratory and real-world settings. In addition, college students, who are the sample for most studies, may not be representative of the real-world population and, therefore, the results may not generalize to the real world. In light of these issues, researchers have also explored different interviewing techniques, such as imposing cognitive load and strategic questioning, that show promise in terms of catching liars. However, with all of these techniques, more research is needed with different populations and more ecologically valid procedures before they should be adopted in real-world forensic settings.

Response Latency and Eyewitness Identification

Response latency has been used, not only to detect deception, but also to determine the accuracy of an eyewitness's identification. Recently, reaction time or response latency has emerged as a promising marker of eyewitness identification accuracy. Response latency in eyewitness research is defined as the time it takes for the eyewitness to make a decision about the identity of the perpetrator (i.e., from a lineup). Researchers consistently have shown that there is a negative relationship between response latency and identification accuracy. More specifically, accurate identification decisions are associated with shorter response latencies than are incorrect decisions (Dunning & Stern, 1994; Key et al., 2017; Smith, Lindsay, & Pryke, 2000; Smith, Lindsay, Pryke, & Dysart, 2001). Reaction time first caught on as a mainstream variable of choice for eyewitness researchers with the work of Sporer (1992, 1993).

Sporer (1992, 1994) suggested that the negative relationship between response latency and accuracy is a result of the search process. He proposed that participants engage in a sequential search, regardless of whether it is a simultaneous or sequential lineup, wherein each member of the lineup is compared to an image of the culprit in the eyewitness's memory. When the image of the culprit is encountered in the lineup, a decision can be made very quickly because the culprit should have many features that overlap with the image in memory. In contrast, fillers, or members of the lineup who are not the culprit, will have, on average, fewer features that overlap with the image of the culprit, which will necessitate more deliberation and take the participant more time to accept or reject the lineup. Once a positive choice is made, the task is ended and there is no need to examine the other lineup members. As a result of the sequential comparison process, there is a negative relationship between response latency and accurate eyewitness decisions (i.e., faster responses for correct decisions). The negative relationship only holds when witnesses make a lineup choice. This finding can still be explained by the sequential matching process. Positive decisions allow the witness to stop the search, and all lineup members do not then need to be evaluated, whereas lineup rejections (i.e., not picking a member of the lineup) require that all lineup members be evaluated, so on average the search process should be quicker when there is a positive response (Smith et al., 2000; Sporer, 1992, 1994).

An alternative theoretical explanation for the negative relationship between response latency and accuracy posits different types of processing for the correct and incorrect identification decisions (Dunning & Perretta, 2002; Dunning & Stern, 1994). Dunning and Stern argued that accurate eyewitness judgments are automatic, fast, and unconscious decisions, whereas inaccurate judgments are deliberative, slow, and conscious decisions. Therefore, the differential processing leads to the negative statistical relationship between response latency and accurate identifications.

To test these ideas, Dunning and Stern (1994) analyzed the lineup identifications of 368 witnesses and found that accurate witnesses were likely to use an automatic, recognition-based strategy, whereas those who were incorrect relied on a deliberative, process-of-elimination strategy. Furthermore, witnesses making an automatic decision were likely to say that the nonchosen lineup photos had no effect on their decision and that their memories had a greater impact on their decision than did the other photographs. Deliberative choosers stated the opposite. To clarify, automatic choosers compare their memory of the perpetrator to the lineup photos and focus on the photo only if it matches their memory for the perpetrator. This is very similar to the absolute judgment strategy proposed by Lindsay and Wells (1985). Deliberative choosers compare each lineup photo to the others and choose the photo that most closely matches their memory of the perpetrator. They then compare their memory of the perpetrator to the most similar lineup member and indicate whether that person is the perpetrator. This mirrors Lindsay and Wells's relative judgment strategy. Dunning and Stern also found that witnesses making an automatic decision responded faster than those making a deliberative decision. Consequently, not only are automatic choosers more accurate, but they choose faster than inaccurate witnesses who use a deliberative decision-making strategy. This is intuitive because accurate witnesses who can quickly eliminate incorrect choices from the lineup make their decisions faster than those who consider each lineup member; therefore, accurate witnesses should choose faster than inaccurate ones. It is important to note that Dunning and Stern asked only those witnesses who made a positive identification about their decision-making strategies; thus, the researchers could not assess the decision-making strategies of nonchoosers.

Knowing that accurate witnesses choose more quickly than inaccurate ones is helpful, but this knowledge may not be enough to prevent wrongful convictions of innocent suspects. Rather, it may be more beneficial to establish a time boundary for correct identifications, such that any witnesses choosing after this time boundary are deemed inaccurate and not allowed to testify. Dunning and Perretta (2002) were the first to establish an optimum time boundary, based on response latency, for identifying accurate witnesses using lineups. They posited that this time boundary should consistently identify decisions with a high probability of being correct. In addition, the boundary should be consistent across all viewing conditions and stimuli, as automatic decisions should not be affected by changes in the decision context (Dunning & Stern, 1994). Dunning and Perretta conducted time boundary analyses for four data sets by computing the proportion of correct identifications made before and after several time boundaries, then conducting chi-square analyses to determine which time boundary was superior. They found an optimal time boundary of 10–12 seconds; specifically, this boundary was most reliable for distinguishing between accurate and inaccurate witnesses. Participants who made an identification within this time range were accurate almost 90% of the time, whereas those who chose after this time range were accurate approximately 50% of the time. The authors offered a caveat that not all witnesses choosing outside of this range are inaccurate, and these results should be replicated across a wide variety of variables before being generally accepted as a standard for determining which witnesses are correct.

These data provided boundary conditions that could be tested in several ways. In an attempt to test the 10–12-second rule, Weber et al. (2004) conducted a meta-analysis on the data of 3,213 participants involved in response latency-accuracy research as applied to eyewitness identifications. They confirmed the finding that inaccurate choosers had slower response latencies than accurate choosers. Unlike Dunning and Perretta (2002), however, Weber et al. failed to find one optimum time boundary that reliably postdicted accuracy across stimuli and data sets. Additionally, Dunning and Perretta reported that 90% of witnesses choosing before 10 seconds were accurate; Weber and colleagues found that only one study out of eight yielded a proportion of accurate responding greater than 80% when witnesses chose before 10 seconds. Subsequently, they concluded that the 10–12-second rule does not reliably distinguish between false and correct identifications and should not be adopted by the legal system.

Clearly, there is a need to consider other factors that could affect the time boundary. In concurrence with this supposition, Brewer, Caon, Todd, and Weber (2006) also evaluated the 10–12-second rule established by Dunning and Perretta (2002). In addition, the authors tested the competing predictions of the automatic-deliberative account and recognition memory models of information accumulation (Van Zandt, 2000) and diffusion processes (Ratcliff, 1978). These recognition memory models suggest that a decision is made when the evidence accumulated by an individual reaches a criterion level. As the ability to discriminate between stimuli (in this case, lineup photos) decreases, the decision takes longer. This is predicted to occur for both correct and incorrect decisions, meaning that the optimum time boundary is likely to be variable. Consistent with this account, Brewer and colleagues found that the optimum time boundary was later in conditions where slower decisions were made on average, indicating that the optimum time boundary should be variable across different conditions. This is contrary to the automatic-deliberative account of decision making. Rather, the findings of this study support the recognition memory models cited earlier. They also found an optimum time boundary ranging from 5 to 36 seconds, depending on age of the sample, lineup structure, and stimuli, indicating that the 10–12-second rule is not resistant to changes in decision context.

In summary, two findings emerge from the studies that have employed reaction time measures to determine the accuracy of eyewitness identification. First, it is clear that accurate positive lineup decisions are made faster than inaccurate decisions. Second, there is no clear time boundary that can be used to classify eyewitnesses definitively and accurately. In fact, the boundary, as indicated by Brewer et al. (2006) and Key et al. (2017), appears to vary with stimuli and lineup procedures. This latter finding is unfortunate, as it seems to indicate that reaction time, at least in an absolute sense, will be a less useful measure in forensic settings with regard to the accuracy of identifications.

Conclusions

Münsterberg's ideas about detecting crime are consistent with modern-day research on deception detection. Granted, the association test may not be a reliable way to detect guilty knowledge, but the idea of using reaction time to catch liars is an evolving literature, as emphasized by the recent meta-analysis by Suchotzki et al. (2017), which found lying to be more cognitively demanding than telling the truth and, consequently, that it takes longer to tell lies. This conclusion is similar to Münsterberg's ideas about how association tests reveal deception. Neurological measures (e.g., ERPs, fMRI) also show potential in detecting deception.

In addition to detecting deception, modern-day researchers have taken reaction time measures and applied them to the study of eyewitness identification. Several researchers (e.g., Dunning & Stern, 1994, Key et al., 2017, Sporer, 1992, 1993) have confirmed that accurate eyewitnesses respond faster than inaccurate eyewitnesses. Reaction time measures, as indicated by Münsterberg, have enormous value in both the laboratory and the field; once again, Münsterberg's writing seems to foreshadow these important issues. The challenge for psycholegal researchers is how to exploit these findings when dealing with actual suspects and eyewitnesses.

6

The Traces of Emotions

Yes, the hidden feeling betrays itself often against the will of the best comedian in life. It may be easy to suppress intentionally the conspicuous movements by which we usually accentuate the emotions. It is not necessary to become wild with anger and to collapse in sorrow, we may even inhibit laughter and tears, and a New Englander will never behave like a Southern Italian. But the lips and hands and arms and legs, which are under our control, are never the only witness to the drama which goes on inside—if they keep silent, others will speak.

—Münsterberg, *On the Witness Stand* (pp. 113–114)

Anyone who has ever watched the World Series of Poker on television knows what a "tell" is. A tell in the parlance of poker is a cue or indicator that can signal one's strategy to the opponents. Poker players work very hard to disguise or cover their emotions and behavioral responses during a game. Some players go so far as to wear sunglasses to cover their eyes when they are playing. Why do they do this? They do it because poker players believe that subtle cues can reveal their hand to their opponents and that these little cues can mean the difference between winning and losing. If you can figure out your opponent's tells, these behavioral or physiological cues can be employed to ascertain when he or she is bluffing, and this information can in turn be used to beat your opponent. According to Münsterberg, people have physiological, behavioral, and emotional responses when they are hiding something or are emotionally attached to some object. A trained psychologist could easily uncover these cues and, in Münsterberg's view, this makes the scientist useful for the legal system.

In Chapter 6, Münsterberg discusses what he refers to as "trace emotions." By trace emotions, Münsterberg is referring to what he describes in the opening quote: the underlying emotional, physiological, and behavioral responses elicited by lying or hiding information. Münsterberg argues that the police methods of detecting these underlying traces are crude and subject to confirmation bias. "There cannot be justice if we base our judgment on the detective's claim that a man blushed or trembled or was breathing heavily. It would hardly be better than those superstitious decisions of early times" (p. 116). As an alternative, Münsterberg offers scientific inquiry as an unbiased way of detecting these lingering trace emotions, or what he calls the hidden suggestions of consciousness.

Münsterberg goes on in the rest of the chapter to describe some experiments in which he demonstrates how science can detect trace emotions through arm movements, eye movements, respiration, heart rate, and skin conductance. Münsterberg starts with an experiment he conducted on himself in which he measured his arm movements and mood. In this experiment, he trained himself to move his hand, under normal conditions, 4 or 8 inches. Münsterberg conducted this experiment several hundred times over the course of a year, each time recording the distance and his mood. He found a relationship between his feelings and arm movements such that distinct sets of feelings were associated with particular variances of measurement. During periods of excitement, the movements became too long, and when depressed, the movements became too short. Münsterberg argues that this was the first demonstration of distinct sets of feelings manifested in behavior.

In the rest of the chapter he describes how eye gaze and other physiological reactions are also associated with different emotional states. For example, he describes how the eyes remain focused on an emotionally charged word after the head has been turned. By contrast, if the word has no emotional valence, then the eyes follow the head. In this way, the eyes reveal the emotional significance of the word or stimulus.

Münsterberg ends the chapter with some important and prescient points. First, he again argues that there is no doubt that experimental psychology is sufficiently equipped to assist the legal system. According to him, experimental psychology can objectively register and measure trace emotions. However, Münsterberg argues that science still cannot distinguish between the emotional states caused by a guilty conscience and the emotional excitement associated with being in a criminal proceeding. He concludes by suggesting that the usefulness of experimental psychology for the legal system may be confined to situations where information about a place, person, or thing needs to be extracted from a known suspect.

In the sections that follow, we start by discussing laypeople's and experts' beliefs about detecting the cues to deception. This is followed by a discussion of lie detection tests. More specifically, we review tests that use physiological measures like the Control Question and Guilty Knowledge tests. Then we review the current literature on verbal and nonverbal lie detection tests.

In the final sections, we ascertain whether experts agree that lie detection tests are reliable enough to be admissible in court, and we then conclude by reviewing state laws regarding the admissibility of lie detection tests in court.

Laypeople's and Experts' Stereotypes about Lying

As mentioned earlier, it is Münsterberg's contention that there are physiological markers associated with deception and emotional responding and that these markers could be reliably used to detect deception. Are there physiological markers associated with increased emotion? Undeniably, the answer is a resounding yes. When people become emotionally aroused, the autonomic nervous system kicks in, which triggers physiological responses such as increased blood pressure, quickening of the heart rate, and so on. Unfortunately, in contrast to Münsterberg's claim, these behaviors do not reliably predict deception (DePaulo et al., 2003). There are several reasons why that may be the case. One major reason is that it is nearly impossible to determine if the increase in arousal is due to deception or some other arousing stimuli (e.g., being interviewed by the police); that is, the physiological markers of arousal are nonspecific to deception. Another reason these physiological and behavioral markers are not correlated with deception is that people have incorrect beliefs about what behaviors are indicative of lying. Thus, they are often misled about when people are lying because they are using faulty indicators on which to make their judgments.

There are two ways in which researchers have typically attempted to assess people's beliefs regarding the cues to deception: surveys and experiments. With surveys people are usually given a list of behaviors (not making eye contact, sweating, fidgeting, and so forth), and they are asked to indicate which of these behaviors are indicative of deception. In the most common experimental method, participants are asked to watch videos of truth tellers and liars and rate the veracity of the people on the videos. In order to assess participants' beliefs after they judge the accuracy of the statement, they are asked to provide a rationale for their judgment. This allows the researcher to assess the participants' accuracy in their veracity judgment as well as to analyze their rationale for these judgments.

Survey research on laypeople's beliefs has typically been conducted on student populations as well as presumed expert deception detectors such as police officers and judges (Akehurst, Köhnken, Vrij, & Bull, 1996). Many of these studies actually compare the professionals to students and the results are fairly consistent across both groups (see Granhag & Vrij, 2005). In terms of physical behaviors, both students and police indicate that decreased eye contact and increased body movement are associated with deception. For example, Mann, Vrij, and Bull (2004) asked 99 British police officers how they knew someone was lying. The modal response reported by the officers was that liars avert their eyes. The second most frequent response was body movements. Similar findings came from an international research team called the Global Deception Team (2006). In this study, researchers from 58 countries asked 40 participants (20 males and 20 females) from their respective countries to answer the question, "How do you know when someone is lying?" The most frequently mentioned cue to deception was failure to maintain eye contact, which was mentioned by 64% of the participants and was the most frequently mentioned response for 51 of the 58 countries. In terms of verbal indicators, both groups agreed that truth tellers provide more detailed accounts and their stories are more consistent over time than those of liars. The research suggests that truth tellers do indeed provide more detail, but their stories are not more consistent over repeated tellings (Strömwall & Granhag, 2003).

The experimental approach provides a similar conclusion to the survey approach. In a study by Mann, Vrij, and Bull (2004), police officers were asked to detect deception from parts of videotaped interviews of actual suspects. After making their decisions, officers were asked to justify their choice by indicating which specific behaviors they relied on. The two most commonly reported behaviors were eye gaze and body movement (i.e., fidgeting).

Unfortunately, there is little to no empirical support for these participants' beliefs (Granhag & Vrij, 2005). In one of the most comprehensive meta-analyses to date, DePaulo et al. (2003) concluded that behavioral signs of deception are weak or inconsistent indicators at best. In fact, many of the behaviors laypeople associate with lying were not at all related to deception. For example, averting one's eyes was not correlated with deception (DePaulo et al., 2003). Similarly, Strömwall, Granhag, and Hartwig (2004) found that fidgeting, frequent posture shifts, and grooming were not indicative of lying.

Although police and laypeople have incorrect beliefs regarding what cues are indicative of lying, one group that seems to hold more accurate beliefs about the cues to deception are criminals. In this case, it may really take one to know one. There are only a handful of studies that have examined criminals' beliefs about deception, but the results are extremely interesting and bear mentioning (Granhag Andersson, Strömwall, & Hartwig, 2004; Vrij & Semin, 1996). For example, Granhag et al. surveyed college students, prison personnel, and prison inmates about which cues were indicative of deception. Unlike college students and police officers, the inmates were less likely to believe that fabricated statements were less consistent than truthful statements and thought that there would be no difference in body movements between truth tellers and liars.

Hartwig, Granhag, Strömwall, and Andersson (2004) also had college students and prison inmates judge the veracity of true and false statements. As is generally found, college students performed at a chance level, but inmates performed significantly above chance. When asked what they based their judgments on, the modal response from inmates was plausibility—that is to say, they thought that implausibility was associated with deception. By contrast, college students most often indicated consistency as the basis of their judgments. The research has shown that implausibility is indeed correlated with deception (DePaulo et al., 2003).

In summary, laypeople and professional lie catchers agree with Münsterberg that there are in fact tell-tale physiological and emotional cues to deception that can be detected. In fact, the leading police manual on interrogation practices (Inbau, Reid, Buckley, & Jayne, 2001) explicitly states that body movements and grooming gestures are reliable cues to deception. Two themes emerge from research on people's beliefs about cues to deception. First, laypersons and experts share similar beliefs that eye gaze and hand movements reflect deception. Second, these shared beliefs are misconceptions that lack empirical support (DePaulo et al., 2003). The other interesting pattern is that inmates have more accurate beliefs about the cues to deception and are better able to detect lies than trained professionals, police, or college students. The conclusions regarding inmates' beliefs need to be viewed cautiously because there are so few studies, but it seems to be a ripe avenue for future research.

People's expectations about lying give some insight as to why it is so difficult to detect liars; people rely on the cues that are misleading and not correlated with deception. Vrij, Granhag, and Porter (2010) reviewed several "pitfalls" or mistakes that people make when they try to detect deception. We briefly review some of those pitfalls. As is probably clear from the foregoing discussion, one of the biggest impediments to detecting liars is that detectors, both laypeople and police, rely on cues that are not correlated with lying. Unfortunately, there are no verbal or nonverbal cues that are uniquely related to deceit (see Depaulo et al., 2003). Furthermore, behavioral differences between truth tellers and liars are typically small, meaning they are difficult to detect (see Depaulo et al., 2003). As aptly put by Vrij et al. (2010), there is no Pinocchio test for detecting liars, which in turn makes detecting deception an inherently hard task.

Detecting liars is then made even more difficult, according to Vrij et al. (2010), by the facts that lies are often hidden in truths and liars are proficient at this kind of subterfuge. Often liars will tell true stories and only change specific but vital details. This may increase perceived credibility and make detection hard because most of the story is true. There is evidence that embedding lies within true statements is in fact what criminals often do (Hartwig, Granhag, & Strömwall, 2007; Vrij et al., 2010). In addition, some people simply are credible liars. There is very little research on what constitutes a good liar, but Vrij et al. speculate that good liars are likely to be people who do not find lying cognitively challenging, do not experience guilt or fear when lying, and are good actors.

Another pitfall or mistake relates to people's overconfidence in their ability to detect liars. People simply think they are better at detecting liars then they actually are, and this is true of people in professions that require them to detect liars as part of the job (Vrij et al., 2010). Research has consistently shown that police are no more accurate in their credibility judgments than less experienced controls, usually students, but they are more confident in their assessments (DePaulo & Pfeifer, 1986; Kassin, Meissner, & Norwick, 2005). This overconfidence is not unique to police officers, as it has also been seen with other professional groups such as FBI and CIA agents (Allwood & Granhag, 1999).

From an evolutionary standpoint, one would think that detecting liars should be something that people have become proficient at over time. It is vital to know when someone is deceiving or cheating you. Our general inability to detect deception is therefore surprising. Alas, as Virj et al. (2010) state, detecting liars is an inherently hard task, and it is made more difficult by our overconfidence and reliance on poor indicators of lying.

Detection Tests and Strategies

Physiological Lie Detectors

Lie detection devices have been around since ancient times (see Smith, 1969). For example, in 1000 BCE the Chinese had suspected liars chew rice powder and spit it out. If the masticated powder was dry, then the suspect was thought to be lying (Kleinmuntz & Szucko, 1984). Lombroso is credited with developing the first mechanical means of detecting lying (Barland, 1988). In 1895, Lombroso developed a machine that measured changes in blood volume in the arm. Increases in blood volume when questioned were thought to be indicative of deception.

The inventor of the modern polygraph test was Münsterberg's graduate student William Moulton Marston. As a graduate student at Harvard, Marston became interested in blood pressure when his wife said that when she got mad at him, she could feel her blood pressure rise (Lamb, 2001). During World War I, Marston thought his research and lie detector could be used to detect spies. Marston developed and tested the ideas laid out by Münsterberg in his chapter on trace emotions. Marston confirmed Münsterberg's theories by showing that blood pressure changes could be used to catch liars. In his research, he indicated that he was able to classify 96% of liars correctly (Marston, 1917). Marston's research on lie detection was a key issue in *Frye v. United States* (1923; see Weiss, Watson, & Xuan, 2014). Marston's testimony about his examination of the defendant, Frye, was excluded at trial; the appellate decision, affirming the trial court's ruling, established the well-known *Frye* (general acceptance) standard.[1]

[1] Desiring public recognition for his work—an ambition he might have acquired from his mentor Münsterberg—Marston subsequently volunteered to test Bruno Hauptmann, after Hauptmann requested a "truth test" following his conviction for kidnapping and killing the Lindbergh baby. The court declined the offer (Weiss et al., 2014). Weiss et al. argue that Marston's interest in deception

People throughout history have believed that lying is accompanied by measurable physiological and behavioral reactions. The polygraph was designed to measure these physiological changes and in turn detect liars. Lie detection tests can measure any conceivable physiological response, but common ones are blood pressure and heart rate. Many lie detection tests exist, but we restrict our discussion to the two most widely used: The Control Question Test (CQT) and the Guilty Knowledge Test (GKT) (Iacono, 2001).

Control Question Test

The Control Question Test (CQT) is just what the name implies; that is, the physiological responses to crime-relevant questions are compared to control questions. The relevant questions are directly related to the crime in question (e.g., "Were you at home the night your wife was assaulted?"). Control questions are loosely about the crime but designed to be vague enough that the suspect has to lie to avoid suspicion (e.g., "Have you ever physically hurt someone?"). The theory behind the CQT is that innocent suspects will show more arousal to control questions, because they are worried about sounding deceitful, than when they are telling the truth on relevant questions. Guilty suspects, on the other hand, should display the same pattern of physiological arousal on both relevant and control questions because they are lying on both types of questions.

There are two main ways in which the CQT has been tested: field studies and laboratory experiments. Both have their advantages and disadvantages. Typically, in field studies, actual polygraph results are evaluated by many experts. The problem with this approach is that there is no way to establish "ground truth." Researchers are forced to rely on case outcomes or confessions as a proxy for truth, and both measures are problematic. As will be discussed in Chapter 7, people confess for a variety of reasons other than that they actually committed the crime. And case outcomes, as we know from the Innocence Project and other organizations that catalogue wrongful convictions, are not a perfect measure of guilt.

In a typical laboratory experiment, participants are divided into two groups. Individuals in one group are taken to the study room and told to commit a crime (e.g., steal money out of a wallet), whereas individuals in the other group are merely asked to sit in the room for a time without engaging in a crime. The participants' task is to convince the interviewer that they are telling the truth and that they did not commit a forbidden act. The experimenter enjoys the advantage of knowing the truth (e.g., who stole and who did not), but the procedure lacks ecological validity, as there are no real consequences to getting caught in a lie. The students are not going to jail

detection influenced his decision to give Wonder Woman, a comic book character he created in his postacademic career, the Lasso of Truth.

if they are caught; on the contrary, they are not even getting docked their experimental remuneration. Thus, there is much less motivation to fool the examiner.

Regardless of how one feels about the underlying methodology, the accuracy of the test is surprisingly good, or at least better than one might expect given what we hear about polygraph tests in the media. According to Meijer and Verschuere's (2010) review, the CQT is extremely accurate. In this case and throughout this chapter, accuracy refers to detecting liars and correctly identifying truth tellers. Meijer and Verschuere analyzed four meta-analyses of laboratory studies which included 46 studies and 800 polygraph tests (400 guilty and 400 innocent examinees). Across the different studies, they estimated that the accuracy rate for detecting deceptive or guilty participants ranged from 78% to 82%, with only 7% to 8% of liars being falsely classified as truth tellers. The estimates for innocent participants being correctly classified ranged from 61% to 83%, whereas they were thought to be lying 10%–16% of the time. For field studies, the estimates for guilty suspects ranged from 84% to 89%, with a 1%–13% false-positive rate. Innocent suspects were accurately classified as telling the truth at estimates of 59%–75%, with a false-negative rate of 5%–29%.

Although the accuracy rate seems very high, the CQT has been criticized on several grounds. The most controversial aspect seems to be the notion that innocent suspects should show less physiological reactivity to relevant as opposed to control questions. This notion has been widely criticized on the grounds that there is no empirical or theoretical reason to suspect that relevant questions should elicit less arousal (Ben-Shakhar, 2008, Meijer & Verschuere, 2015). For example, being asked, "Were you at home the night your wife was assaulted," even for one who was not at home and is therefore innocent, could still be upsetting. In contrast, Raskin and Honts (2002) argued that a skilled polygrapher can create a supportive atmosphere that will reduce anxiety for relevant questions if the interviewee is not being deceptive. The problem with this explanation is clear: Accuracy of the test relies on the skill and expertise of the interviewer as opposed to the polygraph test itself.

Guilty Knowledge/Concealed Information Test

The Guilty Knowledge Test (GKT), or as it has come to be known the Concealed Information Test (CIT), was developed by Lykken (1959). Lykken was a staunch and outspoken critic of the CQT, and as a result he developed his own protocol for deception detection. The CIT requires the examiner to ask the suspect or interviewee a series of questions, all related to the crime. Each question has multiple answers that are asked seriatim (e.g., Was the victim stabbed in the (a) leg, (b) stomach, (c) throat, and (d) chest?). There is only one correct answer to each question, but the other alternatives are equally plausible. The police and the perpetrators presumably are the only ones who know the correct answer. Multiple physiological responses can be measured for all questions, but as originally designed by Lykken, the GKT only measured skin conductance.

The *orienting response* is the theoretical basis for the CIT (Ben-Shakhar & Elaad, 2003). The orienting response is a series of complex behavioral and emotional reactions to a novel stimulus or a change in stimulus. After repeated exposure, the stimulus is no longer novel and the orienting response is no longer exhibited, a process known as habituation. It was Lykken's (1959) contention that the correct answer or guilty knowledge will only elicit the orienting response from the guilty party. That is, a person with guilty knowledge of the crime will show increased reactivity to correct answers, whereas innocent people will display the same physiological reaction to all questions. After all, to an innocent person, all the alternatives are the same and none of them should carry any special significance or elicit increased reactivity.

One of the main advantages of the CIT is that the examiner has control over the false-positive rate (i.e., an indication that a truthful person is being deceptive; see Meijer & Verschuere, 2015). In the CIT the false positive means a stronger physiological reaction to the correct answer by chance. This would lead to a pattern of responding indicative of deception. In effect, this is a Type I error, indicating that a truthful person is lying. The examiner can control, and therefore reduce, this probability by increasing the number of questions and number of alternatives per question.

In terms of accuracy of deception detection, the CIT, similar to the CQT, is quite good. The CIT has been extensively studied since its conception. Ben-Shakhar and Furedy (1990) reviewed 10 laboratory studies. They found that across the 10 studies, liars were correctly detected 84% of the time and truth tellers were correctly classified 94% of the time. Elaad (1998) examined 15 studies and estimated the accuracy of the classification of liars and truth tellers to be 81% and 96%, respectively. In his review, Vrij (2000) estimated that the mean correct detection rates for guilty and innocent parties ranged from 78% to 86% and 94% to 99%, respectively (see also Ben-Shakhar & Furedy, 1990; National Research Council, 2003).

There have only been two field studies that have examined the CIT, and they have revealed similar results to laboratory studies with regard to innocent suspects, but they have had less success with guilty suspects (Elaad, 1990; Elaad, Ginton, & Jungman, 1992). Elaad et al. (1992) analyzed the real-life GKT tests of 40 liars and 40 truth tellers using only skin resistance as the physiological measure of deception. Ground truth was established by actual confessions from the suspect. As was the case with laboratory studies, the GKT was very accurate for innocent suspects, who were correctly classified 97% of the time. However, the real-life test had a more difficult time with guilty suspects, who were caught only 55.3% of the time. Elaad (1990) reported similar results in a separate field study, in which the rates for correctly catching liars and excluding truth tellers were 46.6% and 97.9%, respectively.

Although the CIT is very accurate, there seem to be several problems with the test that may give some insight as to why it is not more widely used. The effectiveness of the test is predicated on two factors: enough knowledge of the crime to generate questions (Ben-Shakhar & Elaad, 2003, Elaad, 1999) and, as was mentioned in the discussion of the field studies, the suspect must remember the details in order for orienting responses to be elicited (Meijer & Verschuere, 2015). With regard to number of questions, the police must have enough details to generate a sufficient number of questions and the perpetrator, but not the innocent suspect, must know those details. This may not occur often in real cases. Podlesney (2003; as cited in Meijer & Verchuere, 2015) reviewed over 700 cases in which the FBI used the CQT and found that only 7% contained enough information to meet both criteria of the CIT. Podlesney's findings need to be viewed cautiously because the FBI may have chosen to use the CQT as opposed to the CIT because the requisite information was not available. Thus, his findings may reflect a selection bias.

Elaad (1990) suggested the higher false-negative rate in real-life studies relative to the laboratory might be due to the longer retention interval in real-life crimes. The relatively long retention interval may have caused the guilty suspects to forget certain details about the crime and therefore fail to show the physiological response that would be expected if they were tested immediately. Several studies have varied the delay between the crime and the administration of the CIT and have found that the accuracy of the test is lower when there is a delay (Nahari & Ben Shakhar, 2011; Peth, Vossel, & Gamer, 2012). Elaad (1997) conducted a mock crime experiment with the CIT in which suspects were tested between 2 days and 1 week after the event. He found that many participants forgot almost 50% of the critical details. Given that many criminal interviews, unlike laboratory studies, occur days or weeks after the crime, these findings severely limit the use of the CIT in real-life cases. However, it should be noted that Meijer, Verschuere, and Ben Shakhar (2011) showed this effect may be confined to peripheral as opposed to central aspects of the crime—this makes sense, as peripheral details are more likely to be forgotten. It is also the case that the details of a crime may be better remembered than the events in an experiment.

The National Research Council (NRC, 2003) conducted a comprehensive analysis of polygraph research. The NRC had 14 leading scientists review the literature on polygraph testing, using strict inclusion criteria to be considered in their analyses. In order to be included, studies had to meet the following six standards: (1) sufficient documentation of the examination procedure to be replicated, (2) independently determined truth, (3) inclusion of both truthful and deceptive individuals, (4) sufficient inclusion of quantitative information to allow estimates of accuracy, (5) blind polygraph scoring with regard to truthfulness of the examinee, (6) and random assignment. Of the 194 studies they reviewed, only 50 laboratory studies and 7 field studies were found to meet all six inclusion criteria. Of these studies, 37 used the CQT and 13 the CIT.

The NRC committee assessed accuracy with Receiver Operating Characteristic curves (ROCs). More specifically, they plotted sensitivity (true positives, i.e., correctly detecting lying) on the x-axis and false positives (saying a truthful person is being deceptive) on the y-axis. Accuracy is expressed in area under the curve, which can range from 1 (perfect accuracy) to .5 (chance-level responding). They conducted these analyses for both laboratory and field studies. The overall accuracy for all laboratory studies was exceptionally good. The median accuracy was .86 with a range from .81 to .91. The accuracy of the field studies as measured by ROC was similar to the laboratory studies. With respect to the individual tests, CQT and CIT, the conclusions were not much different. The NRC analyzed 44 studies (37 laboratory and 7 field) that used the CQT. The area under the curve for the studies that used the CQT ranged from .85. to .89; for the 13 CIT studies that met the minimum criteria, the average area under the curve was .88.

In summary, the data clearly indicate that polygraph testing can discriminate truth from lies at rates much higher than chance. This conclusion follows from the meta-analyses and the NRC report (Meijer & Verschuere, 2010; Shakhar & Furedy, 1990; Vrij, 2000). Even with these impressive accuracy results, the NRC (2003) still expressed caution in the application and generalizability of these tests. They argued that accuracy of the lie detector is likely to be overestimated in the laboratory because most laboratory studies include naïve students who are not motivated to beat the test and are not trained in countermeasures. Countermeasures are behaviors that are designed to make deceptive answers appear truthful. They include relaxation techniques, producing pain before or during testing, as well as taking drugs or alcohol. There is evidence that some of these countermeasures do in fact fool the examiner (see Honts, Amato, & Gordon, 2001). This fact, coupled with the problem of establishing ground truth, led the NRC to be cautious about interpreting and applying the results from their review of polygraphs. It is this skepticism about polygraphs that has made it difficult for polygraph evidence to make its way into criminal courts. As described earlier, the precedent for the inadmissibility of polygraph evidence was established in *Frye v. United States* (1923). However, some courts have loosened this criterion and judge the admissibility on a case-by-case basis, as will be discussed later in the chapter.

Nonverbal Methods of Lie Detection

Nonverbal methods of detecting deception have been of interest since ancient times. The basic idea for nonverbal cues is that deception produces an emotional response that can be signaled behaviorally. To the extent that correct cues are known and identified, liars can be distinguished from truth tellers. According to Vrij, Mann, and Fisher (2006b), the only published protocol known to elicit behavioral responses as a means of detecting deception was developed by Inbau and colleagues (2001). It is known as the Behavioral

Analysis Interview (BAI). The BAI consists of asking nonthreatening and threatening questions. It consists of a standardized set of questions and is part of the Reid interrogation technique mentioned in Chapter 7. It assumes that liars are more uncomfortable than truth tellers and that this will be evident in their behavior. According to the rationale of the BAI, liars will demonstrate their deception by doing things like grooming their hair, averting their eyes, and shifting in their chair. In addition, the liars are thought to be more evasive in their verbal responses and less likely to be emphatic in their denial of committing the crime. Liars are also less likely to name other suspects or admit that a crime has taken place. They are thought to be less likely to identify other suspects because they cannot be sure the other suspects will not implicate them. Once it is determined that the suspects are being deceptive, they are then subjected to the Reid interrogation technique.

As mentioned earlier, the behavioral indices (e.g., fidgeting, grooming, crossing legs, averting the eyes) incorporated into the BAI have no empirical basis (DePaulo et al, 2003). There has been only one study that has supported the BAI and, not surprisingly, the authors were some of the same people that developed the BAI (Horvath, Jayne, & Buckley, 1994). Horvath et al. tested the BAI in a field study that used the real video interviews of 60 suspects in which the BAI was used. After inconclusive cases were eliminated, the accuracy rate of the technique was reported to be 86%. However, the limitation of this study, and the one that plagues all field studies in lie detection, is establishing the truth. In fact, Horvath et al. indicated that incontrovertible evidence for the truth could be established in only 2 of the 60 cases. When incontrovertible evidence was not available, the authors used confessions and systematic factual analysis. Systematic factual analysis involves looking at biographical information, opportunity, and motivation to determine if the suspect is lying. Both of these measures are fraught with problems. As noted in Chapter 7, people confess for a variety of reasons, which may or may not be related to whether they committed the crime. And the growing number of overturned false convictions speaks to issues associated with factual analysis as a measure of truth. Thus, without being able to establish the truth in 58 of 60 cases with any degree of certainty, it is impossible to interpret the results.

Laboratory results with the BAI have been a lot less encouraging than the Horvath et al. (1994) field study. For example, Kassin and Fong (1999) had undergraduates watch the first two of the four training tapes that make up the entire training seminar for the Reid interviewing technique. The first tape trains police on the analysis of verbal behavior (e.g., denials, use of first-person pronouns, evasiveness), and the second tape focuses on nonverbal cues to deception (e.g., grooming, eye contact). Following the training, trained and untrained participants were asked to rate the truthfulness of eight video interviews (four innocent suspects and four guilty suspects). There were two important findings. First, participants, regardless of training, were generally unable to distinguish truth tellers from liars. Second, and more surprising, the participants who were trained were less accurate and more confident than their untrained counterparts. The Reid training impaired performance! In support of these findings, Mann et al. (2004) found, in a study of real-life interviews, that the more police officers endorsed views based on the Reid technique, the less proficient they were at distinguishing truths from lies.

Vrij, Mann, and Fisher (2006a) also empirically tested the BAI with trained British police officers conducting the interviews. Participants were randomly assigned to be truth tellers or liars. Innocent participants just played a game, whereas guilty participants were told to take $10 from a wallet in the room. After the experimental task, all participants were told they were going to be interviewed by a police officer, and their job was to convince the officer that they did not take the money. The interviews were recorded and coded using the BAI coding scheme. The results were exactly the opposite of the predictions of the BAI; that is, truth tellers were judged to have exhibited more nervous behaviors than liars. Truth tellers were also judged to be more evasive than liars. Thus, according to the BAI, the truth tellers should be classified as liars and the liars should be considered forthright—the exact opposite pattern one would want from a deception detection inventory.

In summary, the use of nonverbal behavior as a way of detecting deception does not appear to be a viable avenue. Unfortunately, there is little to no empirical support for the idea that behavioral cues are diagnostic for detecting deception (Granhag & Vrij, 2005). In fact, studies of behavioral techniques for lie detection, like the Inbau et al. (2001) method, have repeatedly found that these techniques impair students' (Kassin & Fong, 1999) and police officers' (Mann et al., 2004) ability to distinguish truths from lies. It is unfortunate that most police manuals teach these methods, given that the behavioral cues can be misleading and cause innocent people to appear to be lying.

Verbal Lie Detectors

Although the idea of analyzing speech as a means of lie detection has a long history, the research on these verbal techniques has spiked in the last 50 years (Vrij, 2008). There are a number of speech detection techniques that have been shown to be reliable, but for the purposes of this chapter we will focus on the three that, according to Vrij (2015), are the most widely employed and/or researched: Speech Validity Analysis (SVA), Reality Monitoring Framework, and Scientific Content Analysis.

Speech Validity Analysis

SVA was specifically designed for use with children in child sexual abuse cases. SVA consists of four stages: case file analysis, semistructured interview, criterion-based content analysis (CBCA), and validity checklist. The first step is the case file analysis. The case file provides the interviewer with the players in the case as well as the facts that are and are not disputed. This should give the interviewer some insight as to what is alleged to have happened. Next is the interview, where, in the of case of child sexual abuse, the child provides his or her account of what happened. There are several procedures that are recommended for the interview, such as being familiar with the case and building rapport with the interviewee (Raskin & Esplin, 1991). It is recommended that the interview start with a free narrative where the child is given the opportunity to tell his or her account of what happened. Often interviewers are not provided enough information, so the free narrative can be followed with open-ended questions that encourage the respondent to provide more information.

All the interviews are recorded and transcribed for the CBCA. Trained judges then examine the interviews for the presence or absence of the 19 criteria of the CBCA. The basic idea is that the presence of these criteria is an indication of truth and the absence is indicative of deception. These criteria are divided into cognitive and motivational factors. Inclusions of cognitive factors are judged to be truthful because they are thought to be too hard to fabricate. For example, statements that are coherent, are not chronologically based, and include specific details are thought to be true. The motivational factor is based on the idea that truthful persons are less likely to be concerned with impression management. More specifically, they are less likely to be worried about appearing truthful because they *are* truthful. Thus, truthful people are more likely to admit to forgetting details, to correct themselves spontaneously, and to raise doubts about their own account. The final phase is the validity checklist, which takes into account that not all defendants and interviewees have the same cognitive capacity. Therefore, some defendants may display less of the criterion because of their age or limited cognitive abilities as opposed to being deceptive. The validity checklist takes this into account and helps the evaluator determine if any of the alternatives could explain the result.

The research on SVA has primarily been confined to laboratory studies and has generally examined the CBCA portion of the technique (it is not surprising that research has focused on accuracy, which is derived from the CBCA). Vrij (2008) summarized the 50 empirical studies that have used SVA. There were 20 instances in which the original research computed a CBCA score for truth tellers and liars. Typically, in these experiments, undergraduates are randomly assigned to tell the truth or lie. According to Vrij's (2008) analyses, the empirical results support the use of SVA as a reliable deception detection technique. In 80% of the studies in which the CBCA scores were available, truth tellers obtained significantly higher scores than liars. Vrij also found that, of the 19 questions on the CBCA, the question regarding the amount of details received the most support. In the 29 studies that reported the amount of detail, truth tellers gave more details than liars in all 29 of them. Vrij estimated the overall accuracy of the CBCA from 24 of the 50 studies to be around 71%. However, Vrij concluded that the results should be viewed cautiously, as there are important differences in using SVA in the laboratory and the real world that would likely affect the accuracy of the tool (see also Virj, 2005).

The problems with applying SVA to real-world cases are the same problems that affect almost all lie detection techniques. It is nearly impossible to establish ground truth, and there is no guarantee that people being interviewed by the police behave like students in an experiment. In fact, there are many reasons to believe that they will not behave the same way. In addition to these concerns, researchers have expressed doubt about the use of the validity checklist. More specifically, some factors that may affect responses on the CBCA, like suggestibility, are difficult to measure, and this may affect the accuracy of the test. In summary, the SVA can discriminate liars from truth tellers, but there are difficulties in applying the technique to real-world settings.

Reality Monitoring

In the reality monitoring framework (e.g., Johnson, Hashtroudi, & Lindsay, 1993; Johnson & Raye, 1981; Johnson, Raye, Mitchell, & Ankudowich, 2012), memory traces are viewed as a record of the cognitive processes and operations that are performed when one experiences an event. This record is thought to include, in varying degrees, information about the surface structure of the presented item, emotional responses to the item, and cognitive operations performed in generating or interpreting the item, as well as contextual and semantic details. The reality monitoring framework assumes that memories from different sources (e.g., imagined vs. experienced events) differ in their average qualitative characteristics. For instance, memory traces of real events are likely to include more perceptual details and fewer details about cognitive operations than are memories of internally generated or made-up events. Therefore, if real or true items come to mind, it is likely that many of the contextual, perceptual, and emotional details that were occurring at the time will also be included in the memory records. Conversely, the memory reports of imagined items will contain fewer of these qualitative details. It is important to note that erroneously believing an event occurred is different from knowing an event occurred and lying about its occurrence. Although the reality monitoring framework is typically applied to events that are imagined (rather than true), these qualitative differences in the memory record can be used to detect deception.

Vrij (2008) also summarized 10 deception detection studies that used the reality monitoring framework. He found that across these 10 studies, truth tellers were classified correctly, on average, 72% of the time, and liars were detected 66% of the time. Thus, the accuracy rates for the reality monitoring framework and SVA are very similar. As pointed out by Vrij (2008), because the reality monitoring approach is based on sound memory theory, it has wide appeal to researchers but is not used very much by practitioners. Furthermore, it has some restrictions on its use. This framework is less effective with children and memories from the distant past. Children may not differentiate fact from fantasy as well as adults, and their memory records may be less diagnostic of truth and lies (see Lindsay, 2002; Lindsay & Johnson 1987). Similarly, memories from the distant past may contain fewer details that can be used to distinguish actual memories from fabrications.

Scientific Content Analysis

Scientific Content Analysis (SCAN) was developed by Avinoam Sapir, a former Israeli police officer. It is used worldwide, including in the United States, Australia, United Kingdom, Mexico, and Qatar (Vrij, 2008). With this detection tool, individuals are required to write a detailed account of what occurred during the incident in question. They are instructed to write the narrative in such a way that a naïve person could understand what happened. This is similar to the way in which scientists write up their experimental procedures in journal articles. Once written, the narrative is analyzed by a trained SCAN expert on the basis of 12 SCAN criteria. As with the CBCA, it is thought that the presence of SCAN criteria is indicative of truth, and therefore these features are more likely to be present when a subject is being honest.

There is no agreed-upon list of criteria for SCAN, but some criteria do seem to occur repeatedly in the research literature and training manuals (for a complete list, see Vrij, 2015). Some examples include denial of allegations, social introductions, lack of conviction in memory, emotion, and out-of-sequence and extraneous information. According to SCAN theory, truthful people are more likely to deny the allegations and to introduce people socially into the narrative (e.g., My friend Brian and I went to the football game together). Deceptive people will be less likely to introduce specific people into the narrative (e.g., We all went to the football game together). Lack of conviction or memory, such as indicating that certain parts of the memory for the event are hazy or incomplete, is also an indication of deception. According to SCAN theory, truthful people are less likely to forget or leave out details. SCAN is also concerned with the structure of the narrative. It is thought that in a true statement the narrative should be structured such that the first 20% sets the context and leads up to the event, the proceeding 50% of the narrative is about the event, and the remaining 30% includes information about what happened after the event. Most of the criteria listed in SCAN are not based on scientific data and are in many instances at odds with scientific findings and theory. For example, we know of no data or empirical results that support the structure of the information breakdown as suggested in SCAN.

There is very little research on the validity of SCAN—only five studies according to Vrij (2015). Two of these studies are field studies and suffer from the limitations associated with all real-world studies of lie detection, namely that it is nearly impossible to determine ground truth. For example, in a study by Driscoll (1994), 30 suspects voluntarily gave statements before their polygraph tests, and these narratives were then examined by an expert. The expert was very accurate, as 73% of presumably truthful and 95% of presumably deceptive statements were classified correctly. However, once again ground truth was poorly established, so it is hard to know what the accuracy percentages actually mean.

A similar field study was conducted by Smith (2001) for the British Home Office. Smith, however, compared three levels of SCAN users with different experience to experienced detectives who were not trained in SCAN. Smith found slightly lower levels of accuracy than Driscoll (1994). There was, however, no difference in accuracy between the untrained detectives and all three SCAN-trained groups and, thus, there was no benefit of SCAN, per se (but see Armistead, 2011, for a different interpretation).

Nahari, Vrij, and Fisher (2012) conducted one of the few laboratory studies with SCAN. In this study, students were asked to write a narrative of a true or fabricated event. The narratives were analyzed with SCAN. The accuracy rates were not significantly different from chance. Other laboratory studies that have examined SCAN have not followed this method, so interpretation of the results is problematic. For example, Porter and Yuille (1996) evaluated only three of the 12 criteria, and participants gave oral statements that were later transcribed.

As noted by Vrij (2008), SCAN is widely used as an investigative tool in many countries. This is problematic, as the research on SCAN has lagged behind its popularity. There are a few studies examining the accuracy of the tool, and the ones that exist, with few exceptions, are riddled with methodological issues that make interpretation of the results difficult. In addition, the SCAN method is poorly defined, so the success of the method depends greatly on the examiners. Given the widespread use of SCAN, it is important for researchers to examine the efficacy of this deception detection tool carefully.

Cognitive Approach

Most recently, what has been called the *cognitive approach* to lie detection was developed. The basic idea was first acknowledged by Zuckerman, DePaulo, and Rosenthal (1981), who argued that lying is cognitively more taxing than telling the truth (see Chapter 5). The new and important element to this approach is that increased cognitive load associated with lying can be exploited by interviewers so that more cues to deception are revealed. More specifically, if lying is cognitively taxing, then adding to the cognitive load should leave fewer resources available for liars to cover or hide their deception.

As described in Chapter 5, two ways in which researchers have tried to increase the cognitive load are to have the interviewee tell the story backward or to ask unexpected questions. As the theory predicts, more cues to deception (i.e., fewer auditory details, more speech hesitations, and more leg movements) are apparent when liars tell their stories backward, as compared to truth tellers (Vrij et al., 2008), and liars have more difficulty answering unanticipated questions then do truth tellers (Leal, Vrij, Warmelink, Vernham, & Fisher, 2015). Although these techniques seem promising, they have not been universally embraced. For example, Vrij (2015) suggested that British police are reluctant to use this technique when interviewing suspects because it is an odd request in a naturalistic context.

There are several other cognitive approaches to lie detection, such as encouraging the interviewee to say more, the verifiability approach, and Strategic Use of Evidence (SUE). Encouraging the interviewee to say more is based on the idea that liars, when asked for more information, will provide less new information then truth tellers (Vrij, Hope, & Fisher, 2014). Conversely, the verifiability approach takes advantage of the fact that when liars do provide additional information, they tend to give details that cannot be substantiated. The goal of this strategy is for the interviewer to take advantage of liars' inclination to provide details because they think that more details are associated with truths; investigators can then trap them into providing details that can be verified (Nahari, Virj, & Fisher, 2014). SUE is based on the notion that liars are generally less forthcoming than truth tellers, and liars are more likely to use denials, such as denying that they were at a certain place (Granhag & Hartwig, 2008). Thus, when interviewers confront suspects with evidence that is true without revealing the interviewer knows that it is true, truth tellers' accounts become more consistent with the evidence than liars' accounts (Hartwig, Granhag, & Luke, 2014).

Are Lie Detection Techniques Reliable and Accepted in Court?

Considering the focus of Münsterberg's chapter on trace emotions (and, indeed, his entire book) is on how psychologists can inform the legal system, it is appropriate to review whether scientists and courts think that deception detection techniques should be admissible in court. This final section of the chapter applies the *Daubert* standard for expert testimony to a variety of (nonpolygraph) techniques, followed by a discussion of courts' holdings with respect to polygraphy.

Admissibility of Nonpolygraph Deception Detection Tools

Recently, Vrij and Fisher (2016) evaluated the legal admissibility of deception detection tools. They evaluated eight lie detection tools: Behavioral Analysis Interview (BAI), Comparison Question Test (CQT), Imposing Cognitive Load, Asking Unexpected Questions, Encouraging the Interviewee to Say

More, the Strategic Use of Evidence, the Verifiability Approach, and the Concealed Information Approach. Vrij and Fisher classified the first two as arousal-based tools and the latter six as cognitive-based tools (we reproduce part of their table in Table 6.1).

Vrij and Fisher used 10 criteria to evaluate the lie detection techniques. The first five were derived from the *Daubert* guidelines, which are the principal standard that US courts use to evaluate the admissibility of scientific evidence (*Daubert v. Merrell Dow Pharmaceuticals*, 1993). The *Daubert* test includes the following questions: Is the hypothesis testable, has the technique been scientifically tested, have the results of the test been peer reviewed and published, is there a known error rate, and is the theory on which the test is based generally accepted in the field?

According to Vrij and Fisher (2016), all lie detection techniques in Table 6.1 meet the first three criteria—that is, they have testable hypotheses, they all have been tested, and they have been peer reviewed. The number of peer review tests ranges from fewer than 5 for the BAI to more than 25 for both the CQT and the Concealed Information Test. The rest of the tools fall somewhere between 5 and 10 peer-reviewed published tests. With regard to criterion 4, there is no agreed-upon error rate for any of the eight tools from field studies. As mentioned earlier in the chapter, there are very few field studies, and the ones that exist are plagued with methodological issues. In terms of the laboratory studies, the error rate for the CQT and CIT is thought to be less than 20% (Vrij, 2008). The error rates for the other deception detection tools are less than 30% (Vrij, Fisher, & Blank, 2017).

Does the scientific community accept the principles on which these tools are based? This is one of the biggest criticisms the NRC (2003) had of polygraph testing. The NRC report deals almost exclusively with the CQT and CIT. The NRC committee goes as far as to say that the theory behind polygraph testing is not based on sound scientific theory—a viewpoint shared by others in the field (see Iacono, 2001). Vrij and Fisher (2016), however, argue that the CIT has been extensively tested and the principles on which it is based are generally accepted in the field. Vrij and Fisher also argue that the other tools have been developed more recently, so it is not yet known how they will be received by the scientific community.

Should any of these lie detection tools be admissible in court based on the *Daubert* criteria? There is no straightforward answer. Although judges who are gatekeepers of the evidence use the *Daubert* standard, it is unclear how they apply it. Does the scientific evidence need to pass all five criteria or just one or maybe three of the five? If we apply the strictest standard of requiring all scientific evidence to meet all five criteria set forth in *Daubert*, then none of the lie detection tools would be admissible. If we use the "general acceptance" standard, which is the *Frye* standard that *Daubert* replaced in most jurisdictions, then all but the BAI and CQT would be admissible. Vrij and Fisher (2016) suggest that all but the arousal-based test and imposing cognitive load are reliable enough to use in court.

Table 6.1 Overview of the Lie Detection Tools and Their Usefulness in Investigative Interviews

	Behavioral Analysis Interview (BAI)	Control/ Comparison Question Test (CQT)	Imposing Cognitive Load	Asking Unexpected Questions	Strategic Use of Evidence (SUE)	Concealed Information Test (CIT)
1) Is the scientific hypothesis testable?	Yes	Yes	Yes	Yes	Yes	Yes
2) Has the proposition been tested?	Yes	Yes	Yes	Yes	Yes	Yes
3) Has the technique been subjected to peer review and publication?	<5	>25	5–10	5–10	10–20	>25
4) Is there a known error rate?	No	<20%	Around 30%	Around 30%	No	<20%
5) Is the theory upon which the technique is based generally accepted in the scientific community?	No	No	No	Yes	Yes	Yes
6) Is the technique easy to incorporate in a typical information-gathering interview?	No	No	Yes	Yes	Yes	No

Note. The table addresses whether the particular lie detection tool satisfies the criterion posed (numbers 1 through 6) and, when applicable, the number of studies that have addressed the same.

Source: Modified from Vrij and Fisher (2016).

Admissibility of Polygraph Evidence in State and Federal Courts

The *Daubert* standard and Federal Rules of Evidence have shaped state and federal standards on the admissibility of polygraph evidence (most states have adopted *Daubert* and the Federal Rules of Evidence or something very similar). Among state courts, there are three primary categories regarding the admission of polygraph evidence: total exclusion, acceptance but only when the evidence is stipulated to by both parties, and acceptance even without the stipulation of both parties. New Mexico is the only state that falls into this last category (*State v. Bell,* 1977). In New Mexico, polygraph evidence is admissible if (1) there is evidence indicating the qualifications of the administrator; (2) there is testimony establishing the reliability of the procedure; and (3) there is testimony establishing the validity of the tests given to the relevant person. Most other states and the District of Columbia fall within the other two categories.

Twenty-seven states and the District of Columbia use a per se rule of exclusion for polygraph evidence. These states are as follows: Alaska, Colorado, Connecticut, Hawaii, Illinois, Kentucky, Maine, Maryland, Massachusetts, Minnesota, Mississippi, Missouri, Montana, Nebraska, New Hampshire, New York, North Carolina, Oklahoma, Oregon, Pennsylvania, Rhode Island, Tennessee, Texas, Vermont, Virginia, West Virginia, and Wisconsin. All of these states and the District of Columbia ban any use of polygraph evidence in court.

Seventeen states allow polygraph evidence when both parties stipulate to it in advance. Generally, this stipulation means that both parties agree to have the person of interest take a polygraph test and, regardless of outcome, the results are presented in court. However, the "losing side" is given the chance to cross-examine the expert who presents the polygraph results. The states that fall within this category are as follows: Alabama, Arizona, Arkansas, California, Delaware, Florida, Georgia, Idaho, Indiana, Iowa, Kansas, Nevada, New Jersey, South Dakota, Utah, Washington, and Wyoming. In addition to these states, two others allow stipulated polygraph results but only under certain circumstances. In North Dakota, stipulated polygraph results are admissible only in posttrial proceedings, and in Ohio the stipulated results are admissible only for corroboration or impeachment of evidence. There are three states that do not fall within the aforementioned categories of admissibility of polygraph evidence. Louisiana and Michigan allow polygraph evidence without the stipulation of both parties but only in posttrial proceedings. South Carolina, on the other hand, leaves the admissibility of polygraph evidence to the discretion of the trial judge.

Unlike the majority of state courts, most federal appellate courts do not have per se rules barring polygraph evidence. The two exceptions to this majority are the United States Court of Appeals for the District of Columbia

(*United States v. Skeens*, 1974) and the United States Court of Appeals for the Fourth Circuit (*United States v. Prince-Oyibo*, 2003). Beyond these two exceptions, federal appellate courts leave the admissibility of polygraph evidence to the discretion of the trial courts. However, such evidence is usually barred due to Rule 702 and/or Rule 403 of the Federal Rules of Evidence. Rule 702 deals with the admissibility of expert witnesses. This rule gives a specific criterion for determining if such testimony should be allowed in court: The testimony must be relevant and helpful, and its conclusions must be derived from scientific knowledge. Under Rule 702, polygraph evidence is often found inadmissible due to the lack of consensus within the scientific community on its accuracy. This lack of consensus brings into question whether polygraph evidence is truly derived from scientific knowledge. Rule 403 deals with the exclusion of evidence and states that evidence may be excluded if its probative value is outweighed by its chance of leading to unfair prejudice or misleading the jury. Polygraph evidence is often barred under Rule 403, as the results of a polygraph test have questionable probative value but are potentially very persuasive to jurors who do not understand the lack of consensus on the reliability of polygraph tests.

Conclusions

In conclusion, Münsterberg's thoughts on trace emotions are in line with the current literature with one, maybe large, exception. Münsterberg's thesis in the chapter is that trace emotions exist and that the scientific method can be used to uncover them. There is very little doubt that physiological and behavioral markers associated with deception exist. In fact, the NRC (2003) found that deception is discriminated from truth at levels significantly better than chance. As Münsterberg also correctly states, the police are not equipped to discriminate truth from lies. In fact, most recent studies suggest that laypeople and police are poor at detecting deception, and that police do not have an advantage in this regard (Granhag & Vrij, 2005). Laypeople as well as police base their truth judgments on behaviors that are not indicative of lying, such as eye gaze, grooming, fidgeting, and consistency within the story (DePaulo et al., 2003).

The fact that Münsterberg shared these stereotypes and believed that eye gaze and arm movements would reliably reveal hidden emotional traces and contents is the one place where his views are substantially at odds with the research. Münsterberg ends the chapter by suggesting that it will be difficult to distinguish between when the emotional arousal is caused by deception and when it is caused by simply being in an arousing situation. He realizes that physiological markers may be the same in both situations. This is a particularly important point and one that is still a source of concern today with the physiological measures of deception (Granhag & Vrij, 2005). Overall, in terms of trace emotions and lie detection, we would argue that Münsterberg's thoughts were mostly on the mark and ahead of his time. Many of his observations have been borne out by current research. That being said, lie detection is still looked on with considerable skepticism by the courts.

7

Untrue Confessions

Of course in a criminal procedure there cannot be any better evidence than a confession, provided that it is reliable and well proved.

—Münsterberg, *On the Witness Stand* (p. 143)

Münsterberg begins this chapter with the story of a murder case in Chicago for which he served as a consultant. The suspect in the case was convicted of murder and sentenced to death based on his confession, yet Münsterberg was convinced that the confession was false. The local newspapers were incredulous at the temerity of Münsterberg's opinion and attacked him with headlines such as "Harvard's Contempt of Court" and "Science Gone Crazy" (pp. 139–140). In this chapter, Münsterberg raises two important points that remain the subject of social science and psycholegal research today: People will falsely confess to crimes, and as demonstrated by the newspaper headlines, people reflexively believe confessions regardless of their veracity. In fact, Münsterberg notes how persuasive confessions are to juries: "The proof of the alibi seemed sufficient to some, but insufficient to others; most various facts allowed of different interpretation, but all hesitation had to be overcome by the one fundamental argument which excluded every doubt: there was a complete confession" (pp. 140–141). This statement not only identifies how persuasive confessions are to jurors, but it also indicates that a confession can trump other evidence such as an alibi. Once more, Münsterberg displays his prescience: False confessions, how confessions are interpreted by jurors, and how confessions can corrupt other evidence are all prominent themes in the literature today (see Kassin, 2015).

Münsterberg, as is evident in the epigraph, acknowledges that there can be no better evidence than a full confession but then speculates on why a person would falsely confess. He offers several reasons as to why someone might falsely confess, and he suggests that people might be coerced into a confession through threats and promises. "The essential argument, however, against the trustworthiness of confessions had a purely social origin: it referred to possible promises or threats by other members of the community" (p. 144). As an alternative, Münsterberg suggests that it may be an attempt to mitigate one's sentence by confessing to a lesser offense. He writes about a case in Vermont where two brothers, the Boorn brothers, confessed to killing their brother-in-law. "The evidence against the suspected appeared so overwhelming that they saw only one hope to save their lives—by turning the verdict, through their untrue confession, from murder to manslaughter" (p. 145).

Finally, Münsterberg indicates that people actually come to believe that their false confessions are true. "There can, indeed, hardly be a doubt that in some instances the confessing persons really believed themselves to be 'guilty'" (p. 146). Kassin (2015) has referred to the acceptance of a false confession as the truth by the confessor as a coerced compliant confession (more on this later in the chapter; see also Kassin & Wrightsman, 1985). Münsterberg continues along this theme and argues that once enough pressure has been brought to make the accused falsely confess, the accused will also contrive details to fit the story. As evidence for his point, Münsterberg gives the example of Ann Foster, who was accused of being a witch in Salem, Massachusetts, in 1692. Foster confessed that the devil came to her several times in the shape of a bird. She further confessed that she met with the witches of Salem, and they got on their "sticks" and went forth on a journey. Clearly, the accounts from the women of Salem cannot be true (if they are, then scientists need to rethink a number of phenomena). Although many of the women accused of witchcraft maintained their innocence, some admitted that they were witches and confabulated details to support their tales.

Münsterberg's supposition is supported, not only by historical accounts, but also by current psycholegal literature. Recently, Kassin (2015) argued that the details in the false confession which match the facts of the case are crucial to persuading the jury that the confession is true. The problem is that such matching details might not come simply from the (guilty) confessor's memory—they might be provided by the authorities, gleaned from the media or other third parties, or a lucky guess. For the rest of the chapter, Münsterberg writes about the way memory works to allow the confessor actually to believe his or her own (false) confession. Münsterberg's beliefs about memory are discussed in the chapters on memory illusions and suggestibility, so they will not be rehashed here. Instead, we provide a brief historical overview, followed by a review of the current literature on false confessions, including a discussion of people's beliefs about confessions, why some suspects falsely confess, our ability to detect false confessions, and the ways in which confessions can corrupt the evaluation of other evidence. The chapter concludes with an overview of jailhouse informant testimony, which is often referred to as a secondary confession. Secondary confessions are statements made by one person alleging that another person has admitted guilt to him or her.

Historical Overview

According to Wigmore (1970), the history of confession has gone through several distinct stages. In 16th- and 17th-century England, there were no exclusionary rules for confessions; they were accepted at face value and not questioned. In fact, the court had so much faith in the veracity of confessions that a confession precluded the need for a trial. Unsurprisingly, torture as a means of extracting confessions was commonplace, and the confessions these methods produced were accepted without question (Wigmore, 1970). This changed in the 19th century, when the judicial system became skeptical of confessions that were obtained through coercive methods. Finally, in the 20th century, US courts began evaluating the admissibility of confession evidence on a case-by-case basis. Prior to the 1950s, the court accepted that physical abuses such as restraints, prolonged physical discomfort, and beatings were coercive. For example, in the landmark case of *Brown v. Mississippi* (1936), the US Supreme Court readily accepted that beatings and threats of murder were coercive and unconstitutional. Gradually, the courts came to accept that coercion need not be physical, and that psychological threats and emotionally abusive tactics were just as coercive. In *Ashcraft v. Tennessee* (1944), there was no physical abuse, but the defendant was interrogated for 36 hours without reprieve. Once again, the Supreme Court ruled that the confession was not voluntary. In a similar finding, the Court ruled in 1964 that a confession was coerced because it was only obtained after the police repeatedly denied the accused's request for counsel (*Escobedo v. Illinois*, 1964). Not only were Escobedo's requests for council denied, but Escobedo's attorney went to the police and was repeatedly refused access to his client. Finally, in the landmark case *Miranda v. Arizona* (1966), the Court held that psychological threats are just as coercive as physical abuse. In addition, the Court made it imperative that the accused be made aware of the right to remain silent.

From all of these cases, voluntariness has emerged as the primary criterion for the admission of a confession. Did the suspect freely and voluntarily confess without any coercive elicitation from the interrogator? Neither case law nor psychological research provides a clear consensus on what constitutes coercion or voluntariness (Kaplan et al., 2019). The test of admissibility is whether the inducement precluded a free and rational choice and created a risk of false confession (see Kassin & Wrightsman, 1985).

The social scientific research has trailed behind Münsterberg and the courts. Although Münsterberg realized that people would falsely confess, it was not until almost 60 years later that the topic began to receive even a small amount of attention in the scientific literature. Bem (1966) had college students participate in what they thought was a lie detection experiment. Participants were presented with a list of words and asked to cross out specified words on the list. After the word list task, participants were trained to say true statements in the presence of a "truth light" and false statements in the presence of a "lie light." After the training, participants were required to state aloud that they previously had crossed out certain words and had not crossed out others. Half of these confessions were false, and each was made in the presence of one of the two lights. False confessions in the truth light produced more subsequent errors of recall and less confidence. Bem interpreted these results to mean that people's beliefs and attitudes could be manipulated by having the person engage in behavior that would endorse the attitude or belief. Thus, having participants make false confessions when the truth light was on led them to believe the confession was true. Shortly after Bem's article appeared, Zimbardo (1967) published an article that offered a social psychological perspective on the police interrogation process and detailed how it could lead to false confessions. In his review, Zimbardo indicated that police interrogations produce a similar situation to that of social influence studies. And the methods of social influence that are routinely employed can have a powerful effect on behavior, leading to social conformity or, in these cases, false confessions.

Around this time, Inbau and Reid (1962) published what was, at the time, and probably still is today, one of the leading manuals used to train police in the interrogation process. The manual endorses 16 strategies to induce a confession from a suspect. Kassin and colleagues (Kassin, 2014; Kassin & Wrightsman, 1985) condensed this stratagem into three major categories: minimization, maximization, and emotional appeal. Minimization is an attempt to indicate that the suspect may not be responsible for the crime due to extenuating circumstances such as self-defense or negligence. With the opposite approach, maximization, the interrogator exaggerates the seriousness of the crime, thereby implying that the consequences could be much worse (e.g., a longer prison term) if the suspect refuses to confess. Kassin and Wrightman suggested that using false evidence is another form of maximization. The false evidence ploy involves telling the suspect that incriminating evidence (e.g., fingerprints, DNA, eyewitnesses, and so forth) exists in an attempt to get the suspect to confess. The final category is an emotional appeal, in which the interrogator tries to persuade the suspect that confessing will make it easier on the suspect, the victim, the suspect's family, or the victim's family. One of the authors was consulted on a criminal case in which the interrogating officer used the emotional appeal strategy. The officer repeatedly told the suspect that if he did not confess she would have to search his grandmother's house, and she made sure to point out that it was very ungrateful of him to expose his elderly grandmother to the unnecessary stress when he could protect her by simply confessing.

The Inbau and Reid technique was employed by Wald and colleagues (1967) to classify the strategies used in 127 police interrogations in New Haven, Connecticut. Wald et al. not only observed the interrogations, but they also interviewed police officers and some suspects. Wald et al. observed that in 65% of the cases, officers employed one of the techniques outlined by

Inbau and Reid (1962). Furthermore, their observations revealed that a combination of emotional appeal and maximization was the most commonly used approach. More specifically, the police tended to overwhelm suspects with evidence of their guilt and then persuade them it would be easier on all involved if they just confessed.

About 20 years later, Kassin and Wrightsman (1985) came up with three psychologically distinct forms of false confessions: voluntary, coerced compliant, and coerced internalized. Voluntary, as the name implies, refers to a situation where a person falsely confesses to a crime without any external prompting or influence. Kassin and Wrightsman argued that this is the most inexplicable of all the types of false confession. Why would someone confess to a crime the person did not commit without any coaxing or elicitation from the authorities? However vexing this may be, there are scores of examples in which people falsely confess to a widely publicized crime.[1] Perhaps they confess to gain notoriety or to protect a loved one, but those explanations are merely speculative.

The other two types of false confessions are easier to understand, as they are products of coercion. A coerced compliant confession, as defined by Kassin and Wrightsman (1985), refers to a situation in which the interviewee gives a false confession in response to a coercive interrogation, even though the suspect knows that he or she is innocent. Kassin and Wrightsman suggested that many such confessions come as a result of torture and physical or psychological threats and are withdrawn during court proceedings. An illustrative example of this type involves Michael Crowe, who confessed to killing his younger sister, Stephanie (Tracy, 2003). In the late-night hours of January 20, 1998, Stephanie Crowe was murdered in her bedroom at her home in Escondido, California. Her older brother, Michael Crowe, became the main suspect because the crime scene suggested an inside job and Michael, then 14, was described as "distant and preoccupied upon learning about his sister's brutal murder." The police interviewed Michael several times without

---

[1] John Mark Karr provides an example of a voluntary spontaneous false confession. At the time of his confession, Karr was a 41-year-old elementary school teacher who falsely confessed to murdering JonBenét Ramsey. Ramsey was killed in her family home in Boulder, Colorado, at the age of 6. Karr claimed that he had drugged, sexually assaulted, and accidentally killed Ramsey. Autopsy reports conflicted with Karr's confession as there were no drugs found in Ramsey's body, and DNA found on her body did not match Karr's. Karr was eventually released from custody as authorities found Karr's account not credible and unsubstantiated by the physical evidence (Ferguson, 2015). In the famous Black Dahlia case in Los Angeles, as many as 50 people confessed to killing Elizabeth Short, otherwise known as Black Dahlia (Bray, 2006). Neither the Ramsey nor the Short murder was ever solved.

his parents' knowledge or an attorney present. On several occasions, the police erroneously told Michael that they had found physical evidence that incriminated him. The police even went so far as to tell him that he failed a fictitious polygraph machine which they referred to as a truth verification device. After an intense 6-hour interrogation, Michael confessed to killing his sister, providing no details and saying that he could not remember doing it. Police videotaped the interview; at times Michael is heard saying that he is only confessing to appease the police, but he was nevertheless arrested and charged with murdering his sister. In 1999, before the trial occurred, belated DNA testing on Stephanie's clothes found drops of blood that belonged to the actual murderer. In 2004, more than 6 years after the murder, Richard Tuite was convicted of voluntary manslaughter in the death of Stephanie Crowe. Incidentally, Tuite was detained and questioned on the night of the crime but was released after 20 minutes. Even with this conviction, it was not until 14 years after the crime that Michael Crowe was found factually innocent. Tuite was subsequently acquitted following a successful appeal and retrial; the case remains unsolved.

The final type of false confession is coerced internalized. A coerced internalized confession occurs when extreme interrogation methods are used, but unlike the coerced compliant confession, the suspect actually believes that he or she committed the crime. It is possible that the stress or fatigue of the interrogation could change the suspect's memory of the event, so the suspect truly comes to believe that he or she committed the crime. The case of Paul Ingram provides a good example of how people may believe their own false confessions. In 1988, his daughters, Ericka and Julie, accused Ingram of sexual abuse and satanic ritual abuse. His daughters started to remember the abuse at a retreat sponsored by Ingram's church, the Church of Living Water. His daughter Ericka claimed that the abuse was ongoing but had stopped when her father embraced Christianity. When questioned by his coworkers at the sheriff's office, Ingram acknowledged the allegations but had no explanation. Ingram was firm in his belief that his daughters were not liars. Ingram's coworker persuaded him to submit to questioning, which he did voluntarily and without the benefit of counsel. Throughout the interrogation, he kept insisting that he could not remember any of the things he was accused of doing. The detectives told him it was common for an abuser not to remember and that if he just started to confess anyway, the memories would return. Persuaded by his pastor and by his coworkers to visualize the events, Ingram came to remember the events and confessed to the crime. When his daughters' accounts were found to be physically impossible (e.g., the girls claimed they were raped over 800 times at satanic rituals and that Ingram performed abortions on them), the police simply asked Ingram to visualize and provide facts that were more consistent with physical realities. In 1989, Ingram sought unsuccessfully to withdraw his guilty plea. He was released in 2003 after spending over 13 years in jail (Wright, 1994)

False Confessions

A false confession is a false admission of guilt which is typically followed by details of the crime. Since the advent and use of DNA evidence, it has become easier to track the major causes of wrongful convictions. It is becoming clear, as Münsterberg alludes to in his chapter, that false confessions are a major cause of wrongful convictions. The Innocence Project (https://www.innocenceproject.org/) examines DNA exoneration cases and has found that in 350 exoneration cases, one in every four had a wrongful conviction due, in part, to a false confession. The Northwestern University School of Law: Center on Wrongful Convictions lists false confession evidence as the second most common cause of wrongful convictions in capital cases since the reinstatement of the death penalty in 1973 (Warden, 2004). If one considers jailhouse informant testimony as a form of confession, as we do (see later discussion), and combine it with primary confessions, then these two types of confessions have accounted for 65 of 111 (58%) wrongful convictions in capital cases. There are two important things to appreciate from these figures: First, there can be little doubt these numbers underestimate the actual number of wrongful convictions based on false confessions. Cases are included only when enough evidence still existed that convictions could be overturned, so it is reasonable to assume that this represents a small amount of the actual number of cases that involve false confessions. Second, and to Münsterberg's point, false confessions do occur, and they are a considerable problem for the judicial system and society. This is especially true considering that, in the vast majority of cases where there is a confession, the police stop the investigation. There is little reason for the investigation to continue after the suspect confesses and the police have the supposed culprit (see Drizin & Leo, 2004; Leo & Liu, 2009). What this means is that when there is a false confession, the actual criminal is still on the street to commit more crimes. In the sections that follow, we discuss how confessions are perceived by laypeople, why people falsely confess, whether false confessions can be distinguished from true admissions of guilt, and finally, what impact a false confession has on the rest of the criminal investigation.

Lay Opinion

In terms of potential jurors' beliefs about primary confession evidence, there have been a few surveys that provide this information (Chojnacki, Cicchini, & White, 2008; Costanzo, Shaked-Schroer, & Vinson, 2010; Henkel, Coffman, & Dailey, 2008; Kassin et al., 2005; Redlich, Summers, & Hoover, 2009). The survey data show that jurors have misconceptions about various legal issues, including false confessions and the abilities of trained police investigators, and are not always aware of important factors surrounding these issues (Costanzo et al., 2010; Henkel et al., 2008). For example, Henkel et al. (2008) found that people had a limited understanding of risk factors and interrogation practices that contribute to false confessions. In other surveys, only about 10% of survey participants admitted that the situational pressure of interrogation would result in their falsely confessing (Costanzo et al., 2010; Henkel et al., 2008), but in laboratory studies, 40%–43% of students falsely confessed to cheating on a test when the experimenter used harsh interrogation tactics and offered the students a deal (Rigoni & Meissner, 2008; Russano, Meissner, Narchet, & Kassin, 2005).

Leo and Liu (2009) surveyed 264 jury-eligible students from a large university in southern California. The authors were particularly interested in participants' perceptions of the coerciveness of interrogation techniques and the likelihood that these techniques could elicit true and false confessions. The authors found that psychological and other nonphysical forms of interrogation could be perceived as coercive. More specifically, respondents indicated that accusations and promises of leniency were slightly coercive, but that false evidence ploys were very coercive. Importantly, although respondents indicated that these techniques were coercive, they did not believe that these techniques were likely to elicit false confessions.

In a similar vein, Kassin and Sukel (1997) found that even when jurors recognized the confession was coerced via police pressure, they did not discount it when determining guilt. Jurors made the fundamental attribution error; they assumed that only guilty suspects would confess because they failed to account for situational pressures and could not imagine themselves ever being induced to falsely confess (Zimbardo, 2007). In another survey, Costanzo and colleagues (2010) found that mock jurors believed that police interrogators were better than ordinary people at identifying lies, whereas results from laboratory experiments reveal that police (and college students) perform at chance levels when determining the veracity of confessions (Kassin et al., 2005; see "Detecting False Confession," later).

Why Do People Falsely Confess?

Most people believe that suspects would confess only if they committed the crime and that it is rare for an innocent person to falsely confess (Henkel et al., 2008; Leo & Liu, 2009). Unfortunately, this belief is mistaken, as there have been many real-world and experimental examples demonstrating that people will readily offer a false confession. Kassin and Kiechel (1996), for example, found that people will falsely confess with a minimal amount of social pressure using the "computer crash" paradigm. In this paradigm, participants performed a typing task in which one participant read aloud a list of letters at either a fast or slow pace while a different participant typed those letters. Both participants were warned not to press the ALT-key because doing so would result in the computer crashing and the loss of all data. Unbeknownst to the participants, the computer program was designed to shut down automatically in the middle of the typing session, regardless of whether the ALT-key was actually pressed. Typing participants were led to believe that this malfunction occurred due to their accidentally pushing the ALT-key. When questioned, almost 70% of the participants in the study signed a confession admitting to pressing the ALT-key, even though they never actually hit the key. In addition, 28% of the participants internalized the confession. By internalizing the confession, participants actually believed that they had hit the key. Furthermore, 9% of the participants confabulated details. Participants not only confessed to pressing the ALT-key, but they also provided details of how they hit the ALT-key and caused the computer to crash. The social pressure during the experiment was minimal compared to the enormous amount of pressure that suspects must endure during an interrogation. If participants are willing to confess under minimal pressure, then one can easily imagine someone falsely confessing in a real-life interrogation.

Several follow-up studies have replicated and extended this effect (Horselenberg, Merckelbach, & Josephs, 2003; Horselenberg et al., 2006; Klaver, Lee, & Rose, 2008). Horselenberg et al. (2003) examined whether negative (monetary) consequences would reduce false confessions. Despite monetary penalties—participants who did not confess were paid $10, and those who confessed were told they would be paid only $2—the majority of the participants (82%) were willing to sign a false confession. Klaver et al. (2008) studied the effects of interrogation strategies (i.e., maximization or minimization) on false confession rates. For half of the participants, the interrogator emphasized the accidental nature of the prohibited act, suggesting the keyboard was extremely sensitive (minimization). The significant loss of data and the supervisor's irritation were emphasized during the other interrogations (maximization). The authors also manipulated the plausibility of the prohibited act by accusing students of hitting the ALT-key (plausible) or the ESC-key (implausible). More confessions were signed in the minimization condition than in the maximization condition (56% and 30%, respectively). Furthermore, when plausibility was low, confession rates dropped dramatically. The effect is even more pronounced with children, who tend to be more compliant and suggestible than adults (Candel, Merckelbach, Loyen, & Reyskens, 2005; Redlich & Goodman, 2003; see Chapter 8).

Using a novel digital editing paradigm, Nash and Wade (2009) replicated these results. Participants were led to believe that they were taking part in a gambling experiment which would require two experimental sessions to complete. When they returned for the second session, all participants were told that there was video evidence that they had cheated on the task (none actually cheated). Half were told only that the video existed, and the rest were shown a doctored video showing them cheating. The results were extraordinary, as nearly all participants signed the confession. Not only did they sign the confession, but the majority of participants (67% and 73% in Experiments 1 and 2, respectively) actually believed they had committed the false act. Under a minimal amount of pressure, the participants signed confessions and wrote details of how the false act occurred. The consequence for participants of not signing the confession was meeting with the supervisor to see whether they would lose the small payment of £6.00.

Although false confessions come from people from all walks of life, some populations are at greater risk than others. One factor associated with increased risk of false confessions is experience with the criminal justice system. It is counterintuitive, but the research suggests that persons with more experience with the criminal justice system and interrogations are more likely to falsely confess. Sigurdsson and Gudjonsson (1997, 2001) compared Icelandic inmates who had falsely confessed with those who did not. They found that self-reported false confessors had significantly more experience with the criminal justice system and a higher number of prison stays than inmates who did not report falsely confessing. In addition, these self-reported false confessors claimed to have been interrogated more than their tight-lipped counterparts. Thus, more experience with the criminal justice system and interrogations seems to lead to a higher risk for a false confession.

Two other groups that are overrepresented in the population of false confessors are juveniles and people with intellectual disabilities. Using the Kassin and Kiechel (1996) computer crash paradigm, Redlich and Goodman (2003) found that children aged 12–13 years and 15–16 years were more likely to falsely confess than adults (18–26 years old) when presented with false evidence. Grisso et al. (2003) examined children's and young adults' responses to hypothetical interrogations. The authors were specifically interested in whether the participants indicated that they would confess, deny the accusation, or remain silent. Consistent with Redlich and Goodman's results, participants between the ages of 11 and 15 were more likely to indicate that they would confess relative to older participants.

People with cognitive and mental disabilities are also overrepresented relative to the rest of the population in terms of false confessions (Drizin & Leo, 2004; Redlich, 2004). Redlich et al. (2009) surveyed 1,249 inmates with mental illness from six states about false confession and false guilty pleas. The authors found that self-reported false confession rates ranged from 9% to 28%. Consistent with Sigursdsson and Gudjonsson's (1997, 2001) findings, persons with more serious criminal histories were more likely to make false admissions as opposed to their counterparts with less involvement with the criminal justice system. Interestingly, Redlich et al. found that a major reason that self-reported confessors reported falsely confessing was that they thought they would be allowed to go home if they confessed. Juveniles and persons with diminished mental capacity may be at risk because they do not understand the interrogation process or have erroneous beliefs about how it may contribute to their false confession. Indeed, Rogers, Harrison, Hazelwood, and Sewell (2007) found that in a sample of defendants with mental disorders, most did not understand their Miranda rights. This finding, coupled with their expectation that confessing will expedite going home, suggests that they may not fully understand the interrogation process.

Detecting False Confessions

Of course, false confessions are problematic mainly if jurors and other legal stakeholders are unable to detect when a confession is false. Lassiter, Clark, Daniels, and Soinski (2004) elaborated on the computer crash paradigm and investigated potential jurors' perceptions of the false confessions. Lassiter et al. videotaped both true and false confessions from the participants involved in the ALT-key mishap. The videotaped confessions were then used as stimulus materials for a second experiment in which a separate set of participants rated the authenticity of the confessions by indicating whether they were true or false. The results suggested that participants accurately classified these confessions only at chance levels. As expected, participants were unable to detect whether the confessions were true or false, just as jurors were incapable of identifying false confessions during criminal trials in which an innocent defendant who confessed was falsely convicted (as evidenced by DNA exoneration data).

College students are not the only people who have difficulty differentiating between true and false confessions. Kassin et al. (2005) found that police officers (i.e., trained lie detectors) were as poor as college students when it came to detecting true and false confessions. Kassin et al. videotaped 10 prisoners giving both true and false confessions. The inmates confessed to the crime for which they were convicted (true confession) and for a crime that another inmate in the study committed (false confession). College students and police officers were asked to watch (or listen to) the video- or audiotaped confessions and determine whether the confessions were true or false. Police officers were no more accurate than college students in classifying the confessions. In fact, both groups' accuracy rates were not significantly different from chance.

False confessions are not only easy to obtain and difficult to detect, but they are also extremely persuasive to jurors. Kassin and Neumann (1997) investigated the power that a primary confession can have on jurors' decision making. Specifically, they investigated whether the presence of a primary confession would produce higher numbers of guilty verdicts than other forms of evidence (e.g., character, eyewitness, or a control condition with only circumstantial evidence). Participants received four trial transcripts of actual criminal cases (aggravated assault, first-degree murder, aggravated rape, and an automobile theft), each trial containing one of the kinds of evidence. The number of guilty verdicts for trials containing primary confession evidence was significantly higher than guilty verdicts for trials containing the other forms of evidence for all cases except theft. In a second experiment, the three types of evidence (confession, character, and eyewitness) were combined in the aggravated assault trial to investigate which evidence would be most persuasive. Consistent with Experiment 1, participants rated the primary confession evidence as the most incriminating. These two experiments demonstrate that potential jurors perceive primary confession evidence to be extremely persuasive.

Confession evidence is so persuasive that even when mock jurors in experiments realize that the confession was coerced, they continue to vote guilty at extremely high rates. Kassin and Sukel (1997) had participants evaluate trial transcripts containing a high-pressure confession (the suspect was in pain and the officer was brandishing a gun), a low-pressure confession (the suspect confessed during questioning while under mental and physical stress), or no confession. Kassin and Sukel found that when presented with a confession, mock jurors were more likely to deliver guilty verdicts relative to the no-confession control participants, regardless of the level of coercion under which the confession was obtained. Furthermore, participants in the high-pressure condition indicated that the confessions being involuntary did not affect their decision, and they still voted guilty more often than participants in the no-confession control group. Even when participants were able to detect that the confession was coerced, they were unable to make the correct legally prescribed decision and vote not guilty.

In a similar study with judges, Kassin and Wallace (2012) replicated these results. Judges were presented with trial summaries that had a confession and either strong or weak evidence. The confession was elicited via high pressure or low pressure, and there was also a no-confession control condition. The judges, unsurprisingly, were more likely to rate the confession as voluntary in the low-pressure condition than in the high-pressure condition. Furthermore, in the weak evidence condition, there was a significant increase in the conviction rate when there was a high-pressure confession relative to the no-confession control. As with the mock jurors in the Kassin and Sukel (1997) study, the judges were also influenced by a confession that was given involuntarily. This result speaks to the power and influence of confession evidence, as confessions determined to be involuntary still influenced the verdict decisions of judges.

What is it that makes confessions so persuasive and believable? Kassin (2015) has argued that there are two reasons: Statements against self-interests are reflexively believed, and the details in the confession are accurate in that they match the fact pattern for the crime. People are more likely to believe admissions of guilt as opposed to protestations of innocence. Levine, Kim, and Blair (2010) suggested that in the absence of a clear motive, most people will infer that the message or, in this case, confession is honest. Therefore, confessions are likely to be judged as true regardless of their actual veracity. Levine, Kim, and Blair had undergraduates judge true and false confessions and denials. As predicted, confessions were judged as honest more often than denials. The authors replicated these results with a sample of professional investigators. In addition, people believe that they would never confess to a crime they did not commit (Henkel et al., 2008; Leo & Liu, 2009). These two factors may explain why Münsterberg was treated so incredulously by the local newspapers when he suggested that the confession in the Chicago murder case was false.

The second reason for the believability and persuasiveness of confessions is that the false confession contains information that is accurate and that could only be known by the culprit. Garrett (2011) analyzed the trial transcripts from 38 cases of murder or rape with documented false confessions in which incontrovertible DNA evidence later exonerated all 38 defendants. Garrett (2011) offered the false conviction of Jeffrey Deskovic as an illustrative example. Deskovic was convicted of raping and murdering a 15-year-old classmate. Deskovic was interrogated by the police several times for many hours and divulged many details of the crime, including producing diagrams of the crime scene with information that was never released to the public. During his last interview, he indicated that he hit the girl with a Gatorade bottle, which the police were able to find at the crime scene, and which the police indicated under oath at trial that they found the day after Deskovic mentioned it. This fact was highlighted by the prosecution in closing arguments. Deskovic was convicted based on the false confession and the details associated with it. In 2000, the district attorney denied Deskovic's appeal for DNA testing. Six years later, a new district attorney authorized the DNA testing that exonerated Deskovic. Deskovic served 15 years before he was released in 2006.

Garrett's (2011) results are horrifying. In 36 of 38 cases (97%), the police indicated that the defendants reported specific details of the crime and details that could be known only by the culprit. It is unclear how innocent people were able to produce specific details of crimes in which they were not involved. One explanation may be that it was fed to them by police (i.e., false evidence ploys; see Perillo & Kassin, 2011). In fact, many investigators are trained in the Reid technique (Inbau & Reid, 1962), which includes the false evidence ploy as one of its tactics. The rationale behind this dubious tactic is that the interrogator will present fabricated inconvertible evidence of the suspect's guilt (e.g., DNA, fingerprints, etc.). It is legally permissible for law enforcement to engage in this type of deception (*Frazier v. Cupp*, 1969).

Forrest and colleagues (Forrest et al., 2012; Woody & Forrest, 2009; Woody, Forrest, & Yendra, 2013) examined the impact of false evidence ploys during an interrogation on jurors' decision making. The influence of fabricated evidence depended on the type of false evidence and veracity of the confessions (Forrest et al., 2012). Forrest et al. had participants read excerpts from real interrogations. The interrogations contained one of three types of false evidence ploys, and participants were later informed if the confession was true or false. The three types of false evidence ploys were *demeanor*, *testimonial*, and *scientific*. Demeanor false evidence ploys refer to a suspect's demeanor suggesting he was guilty. Testimonial false evidence ploys indicate that the police have evidence that placed the suspect at the crime scene. Scientific false evidence ploys suggest that there is forensic or scientific evidence that implicated the suspect. Participants rated the testimonial ploys as more coercive than the demeanor ploys; in addition, false evidence ploys were deemed more justified when the participants thought the confession was true. These findings are concerning considering that suspects are more likely to confess when confronted with false evidence (Perillo & Kassin, 2011).

Corrupting Influence of Confessions

Confessions not only influence jurors' guilt judgments; they also influence the perception of other forms of evidence by various legal actors. Kassin, Bogart, and Kerner (2012) examined DNA exoneration cases from the Innocence Project to ascertain whether cases that contained false confessions also contained other types of evidence errors. Consistent with the notion that confession corrupts other evidence, they found 78% of the false confession cases included other evidentiary errors. The most common error, which occurred in 68% of the cases, was faulty forensic evidence. In addition, many identification errors and false testimony from snitches were found, which occurred in 29% and 19% of the cases, respectively. One very interesting finding to note is that the false confession occurred before the other errors in two-thirds of the cases. As Kassin et al. (2012) point out, these results support the hypothesis that confessions influence other forms of evidence.

Researchers have found that primary confessions can influence polygraph examiners, handwriting evaluators, alibi witnesses, and eyewitnesses. Elaad, Ginton, and Ben-Shakhar (1994) had professional polygraph examiners score and assess polygraph records that were accompanied by statements that claimed either the examinee eventually confessed to the crime or that someone else confessed. The researchers found that the examiners, when presented with inconclusive polygraph records, correctly scored the records as being inconclusive a majority of the time. However, the examiners scored the records that were accompanied by a primary confession from the examinee significantly closer to the level indicating deception than the records accompanied by a primary confession from someone else. These findings suggest that even professionals are not exempt from the influence of contextual information in the form of a primary confession.

In a similar vein, Kukucka and Kassin (2014) presented participants with pairs of handwriting samples and asked them to evaluate the pairs for shared authorship both before and after receiving a case summary about an armed robbery. The case summary stated that one of the handwriting samples came from the perpetrator and the other sample came from the suspect in question. However, some participants read that the suspect confessed to the crime and then later recanted the confession, whereas other participants read that the suspect maintained his innocence throughout the interrogation. The researchers found that those in the confession condition significantly increased their rate of match judgments after being presented with the case summary, whereas those who did not read of a confession did not change their rate of match judgments.

Just as in the case that Münsterberg refers to, primary confessions also influence exculpatory evidence such as an alibi. Marion and colleagues (2016) investigated how alibi witnesses are influenced by an innocent suspect's confession. Participants were asked to corroborate the accurate alibi of a confederate, who had been in a testing room with the participant when money was stolen from a nearby office. After corroborating the alibi, the participants were presented with one of two versions of an incident report form, with Version One stating that the confederate confessed to stealing the money and later recanted, and Version Two stating that the confederate denied being involved in the theft. Of the participants who read of the confession, only 45% maintained their corroboration (compared to 95% who heard of the denial), and this number dropped even further, to 20%, among participants who were told that their corroboration might suggest they had made a deal with the confederate. These findings suggest that a confession not only can lead to the creation of more incriminating evidence, but it can also eliminate exculpatory evidence necessary for keeping innocent individuals from being wrongfully convicted.

A primary confession is so persuasive that it can even make eyewitnesses change their identification. In a study conducted by Hasel and Kassin (2009), participants witnessed a live mock crime in which a laptop was stolen. Afterward, the experimenter explained to the participants that the theft was part of a study on criminal investigations in which the experimenter would act as the detective and attempt to solve the crime. Participants were then presented with a photographic lineup that did not include the thief (a target-absent lineup) and were asked to identify the perpetrator and give a confidence rating for their identification decision. Two days later, participants returned to the laboratory and were told that the experimenter had reviewed all the eyewitness accounts and had interrogated a list of predetermined suspects. Among choosers (i.e., those who identified one of the members of the lineup as the perpetrator), the experimenter told some of the participants that the individual they identified from the lineup confessed during the interrogation; others were told that a particular suspect confessed, but it was not the individual they had identified. After receiving this information, participants gave another confidence rating for the identification they had made 2 days previously. Lastly, participants were presented with the same photographic lineup and were given the chance to reconsider their previous identification.

The researchers found an increase in identification confidence for the participants who were told the person they identified had confessed, whereas those who were told that another suspect confessed demonstrated a decrease in confidence. Additionally, when participants were given the chance to reconsider their identification, 60% of those who were told another suspect confessed changed their identification to identify the confessor (see Mote et al., 2018, for a replication).

Primary Confessions: Summary

It is clear from the DNA exoneration cases and laboratory studies that people will falsely confess, as Münsterberg indicated in his chapter. People will give a false confession when they are presented with minimal consequences (e.g., losing experimental credit) or when they are presented with false evidence. Adolescents and people with cognitive disabilities are at greater risk of falsely confessing than the rest of the population (Redlich et al., 2009). False confessions corrupt the processing and perception of other forms of evidence, even when that evidence is collected by forensic scientists or police (Kassin et al., 2012). Although false confessions seem to be relatively common, laypeople are unaware that they occur and do not believe that people would confess to crimes that they did not commit. Not only are false confessions common, comprising the major evidence in 15%–20% of DNA exoneration cases from the Innocence Project, but juries and judges find confessions extremely persuasive. They are persuaded by confessions even when they recognize that the confession was not voluntary.

Secondary Confessions

Primary confessions, like those discussed in the preceding section, are admissions by the suspect to law enforcement of committing a crime. Münsterberg omits reference to a different kind of confession, namely, jailhouse informant or criminal informant testimony. We refer to this testimony as a secondary confession (Key et al., 2018; Neuschatz et al., 2012; Wetmore, Neuschatz, & Gronlund, 2014). Secondary confessions are not direct admissions of guilt from a suspect to the authorities, but rather statements by a third party about another person's admission of guilt. A secondary confession, therefore, is a statement made by an individual who claims to have heard a suspect confess. Frequently, secondary confessions come from other inmates, also known as jailhouse informants or "snitches." A jailhouse informant is someone who, while in custody, allegedly receives one or more statements from an accused person, where the statements relate to offenses that occurred outside the custodial institution (see Neuschatz et al., 2012). Thus, there are two types of confessions: primary and secondary.

There is another distinction to consider with both primary and secondary confessions, and that is how the confession affects the confessor. In the case of a primary confession, the person making the confession is certainly harmed by the confession, as it is an admission of guilt to a legal authority. The accused may obtain a more favorable outcome than if he had not confessed but were still convicted, especially in terms of a more lenient sentence, but nonetheless there will be negative consequences for confessing. In the case of a secondary confession, the outcomes for the agent are all positive. Jailhouse informants receive enormous benefits, such as reduced jail time, money, and more privileges in jail, in exchange for their testimony (Los Angeles County Grand Jury, 1990; Natapoff, 2009; Sherrin, 1998).

Historical Overview of Secondary Confessions

The use of informants dates to at least the 4th century BCE, when the Athenian government relied upon informants to expose treasonous plots. Most likely the use of informants predates even this instance, stretching back to the beginning of organized government. As Bloom (2002) argues, governments require information about potential uprisings and challenges to their authority, and informants are one source of such information. Thus, informants and secondary confessions have a long and untrustworthy history.

Ancient civilizations employed informants primarily as sources of information about acts of treason. In ancient Athens, any person, regardless of station, could provide information regarding a past or upcoming treasonous act. The ancient Greek penal system punished treason with death, but it allowed those convicted of treason to receive a lesser penalty—banishment—in exchange for informing on other traitors. In 415 BCE, for example, some Athenians destroyed sacred pillars. Andicodes, one of the vandals, informed on one of his co-conspirators, his father, in exchange for banishment. His father, in turn, received a similar deal by informing on the other vandals (Bloom, 2002; Burckhardt, 1998).

Ancient Rome adopted a similar system for informants. They also rewarded common citizens for providing information about past or upcoming treasonous acts, and for otherwise assisting in rooting out treason. Perhaps the best-known case of this type of informant use is the story of Judas Iscariot (Bloom, 2002). One of the 12 Apostles, Judas is known as the one who betrayed Jesus (Matthew 10:4). According to biblical accounts, the Roman government wished to arrest Jesus, but they feared that a public arrest would lead to a riot by the large number of Jesus's followers and supporters. In order to avoid this outcome, the Romans enlisted the help of Judas to arrest Jesus in a private setting, at the Passover dinner. Judas led the Romans to the dinner and identified Jesus by giving him a kiss. For his help, Judas received 30 pieces of silver. Regretting his collusion with the Romans and his betrayal of Jesus, Judas later committed suicide (see Brown, 1994).[2]

---

[2] The example of Judas is similar to most secondary confession cases in many respects but different in others. Like most informants, he provided information to the authorities (i.e., Jesus's location and identity), and he received benefits (30 pieces of silver) for the information. However, it does not appear that he was charged with a crime himself or regarded as a co-conspirator, he was not in custody, and he did not relay a confession made to him by Jesus, the primary target of the authorities' interest. There are also questions about the extent to which he acted with free will. Thus, his case is somewhat unique, at least compared to the classic jailhouse informant situation.

Under the ancient system, anyone sentenced to death could increase his or her chances of survival by providing information to the government, regardless of the validity of the information. This is a common theme throughout the history of informant testimony: The penalty for fabricating evidence is no worse than the informant's existing punishment. Thus, there is no risk and only potential reward for fabricating information (see Bloom, 2002).

Medieval and Renaissance governments also commonly employed informers. These were people, not necessarily accused of a crime, who gave evidence against others in exchange for a reward. Under the law, citizens who provided information to the authorities regarding criminal activities were entitled to part of the fine that might be imposed upon the criminals. Abuses of this system were rampant. Consider, for example, the case of Jonathan Wild and his gang of thieves. In the late 17th century, Wild's gang made money by stealing goods and then returning the goods to collect the reward. Wild allegedly kept detailed records of his gang members' productivity and, once a member outlived his usefulness, Wild turned him in to the authorities for a reward (see Moore, 2004). Folklore has it that when a thief angered Wild, he would put an "X" next to the thief's name. A second "X," or "double cross," meant the end for the thief. This is purportedly the origin of the term "double cross."

In the early 19th century, police departments in both France and England became much more organized and effective. The informant system followed suit. In France, credit for such reform goes to Eugene Francois Vidocq (Briggs, Harrison, Meinnes, & Vincent 1996). While a young man, Vidocq caught the woman he loved cheating on him with a soldier. Vidocq savagely beat the soldier and was jailed for doing so. After several escapes and recaptures, Vidocq decided to turn his life around and offer his services to the police as an informant. Vidocq's offer was accepted, and he went to prison and began providing the police with information about criminal activities in France. After 21 months, authorities rewarded Vidocq for his efforts by releasing him from jail. Vidocq continued to use his contacts and knowledge of the criminal world to report criminal activities. Soon thereafter, Vidocq was appointed to lead the Parisian criminal investigation unit known as the Paris Sûreté and, during this time, he established a network of informants. In 1877, an English barrister named Howard Vincent, following the lead of Vidocq, organized the modern English informant system, creating a similar network of informants to help combat crime (Briggs et al., 1996).

The first known documented jailhouse informant case in the United States occurred in Manchester, Vermont, in 1819. Brothers Jesse and Stephen Boorn were accused of killing their brother-in-law, Russell Colvin. These are the same Boorn brothers that Münsterberg refers to in his chapter. The Boorn brothers had made no secret of their distaste for Colvin, and when Colvin turned up missing, suspicion fell upon the brothers. Jesse had the misfortune of sharing a jail cell with Silas Merill, a known and convicted forger. Merill testified that Jesse confessed to him. Based on Merill's testimony,

Jesse and Stephen were sentenced to death. As the story goes, however, they were saved from the gallows when Colvin turned up alive in New Jersey (McFarland, 1993).

The use of criminal informant testimony and secondary confessions is rampant and lucrative. A *USA Today* article (Heath, 2012) reported that since 2005, at least 48,895 federal convicts in the federal prison system—one of every eight—had their prison sentence reduced for helping government investigators. Furthermore, over the last 10 years, 11% or more of the people convicted for federal crimes had their sentence reduced in exchange for testimony. According to Heath, these figures underestimate the amount of cooperation that actually exists because these numbers take into account only cases in which the information regarding the cooperation was preserved in the court record and the prosecution found the information beneficial.

A 1990 report by a Los Angeles County grand jury entitled "Investigation of the Involvement of Jailhouse Informants in the Criminal Justice System in Los Angeles County" exposed a culture of utilizing and rewarding inmates who provided incriminating and often fabricated information about other inmates' purported confessions. For this comprehensive report, the grand jury interviewed 120 witnesses and reviewed thousands of documents, including court transcripts, internal memos, and district attorney files. It concluded that the typical jailhouse informant was someone who was incarcerated and facing a lengthy prison term, was highly motivated to gain favor with the authorities, did not have a commitment to the truth, was interested in serving his or her own interests, had previously testified for the prosecution, and wanted something in exchange for the testimony or help.

The Northwestern University School of Law's Center on Wrongful Convictions reviewed the cases of 111 persons released from death row between 1973 and 2004 after being exonerated and found false testimony from informants in more than 45% of those cases. This makes false testimony by informants the leading cause of wrongful convictions in capital cases in the United States. According to The Innocence Project, jailhouse informant testimony has contributed to more than 15% of wrongful convictions later overturned through DNA testing. In these cases, a statement from an informant with an incentive to testify tends to be the evidence that sealed the conviction.

Research on Secondary Confessions

The literature on secondary confessions is not as extensive as that on primary confessions, but it mirrors the findings that have been established in primary confession research. That is, with a small amount of social pressure, participants are willing to give false secondary confessions. Swanner, Beike, and Cole (2010) manipulated the computer crash paradigm described earlier in order to ascertain if a false secondary confession could be obtained for a minimal incentive. Like Kassin and Kiechel (1996), they assigned participants to the role of either reader or typist. Some of the readers were provided with false evidence that the typist had confessed to hitting the ALT-key, and some were provided with an incentive (extra experimental credit) to give evidence against the typist. Swanner et al. found that 79% of the readers were willing to sign a statement indicating that the typist had admitted to hitting the forbidden key and causing the program to crash. The admission rate was significantly higher for readers than for typists, of whom only 52% confessed (still an impressive number, in light of their probable innocence). Providing false evidence increased the confession signing rate for readers to nearly 100%. Thus, a minimal incentive (not having to come back for the second session and still receiving full class credit) sufficed to motivate the reader to inform against the typist. Just as the original paradigm indicated that primary confessions were common, similar results were found for secondary confessions.

One issue in Swanner et al.'s (2010) first experiment was that the authors had no idea if the secondary confessions were in fact false because the typist, who was a participant, could have hit the forbidden key. The researchers corrected this in Experiment 2 by having a confederate act as the typist so they knew that the confederate was not hitting the ALT-key. The results were unchanged, as an incentive affected the rate of secondary confessions only when the perpetrator denied hitting the ALT-key. Thus, the effect of an incentive is to increase false secondary confessions when the perpetrator denies committing the crime. This is the particular scenario in which a false secondary confession could be the most dangerous. When there is no primary confession or other concrete evidence, the prosecution is likely to rely on jailhouse informant testimony whether it is true or false in order to get a conviction.

Similar to primary confessions, not only will participants give false secondary confessions for a minimal incentive, but jurors find these false secondary confessions believable even if the informant has a motivation to fabricate the confession. For example, Neuschatz et al. (2008) investigated whether the source of the secondary confession or the incentive provided for the testimony would influence mock jurors' verdict rates. The secondary confession came from either a jailhouse informant, who received the confession information while incarcerated with the defendant; an accomplice witness, who was involved in the crime; or a community member (classmate), who indicated that the defendant confessed to him during a card game. The jailhouse informant or accomplice witness either did or did not receive an incentive (a 5-year jail sentence reduction) for testifying. These conditions were compared to a no-secondary-confession, no-incentive control condition. Overall, the secondary confession conditions provided significantly higher guilty verdicts, approximately 70%, whereas the control condition produced guilty verdicts of only 45%. The guilty verdicts did not differ as a function of whether an incentive was provided for the secondary confession testimony or the source of the secondary confession (jailhouse informant, accomplice witness, or community member), but they all differed from the control group.

The existence of a secondary confession led to an extremely high number of guilty verdicts, even when the informant was provided an incentive.

Neuschatz et al. (2008) used the fundamental attribution error to explain the null effect of informant incentive on jury decision making, hypothesizing that participants attributed to the jailhouse informant noble, internal reasons for testifying, such as feeling bad after viewing the families of the victims on television and then feeling the need to come forward with the information overheard from the defendant. This contrasts with attributing the informant's reason for testifying to the situational factor of an incentive. Yet, as the literature shows, the incentive could have been an extremely motivating force that was among the informant's main reasons for confessing (see Maeder & Pica, 2014).

Furthermore, secondary confessions are more influential than other forms of evidence. More specifically, Wetmore et al. (2014, Experiment 3) had mock jurors read four trial summaries (murder, rape, theft, assault) each containing only one key piece of evidence (secondary confession, primary confession, eyewitness, or no key evidence control) and asked them to make verdict decisions in each trial. The confession evidence, secondary or primary, provided the highest conviction rate, no matter which trial type featured it. The two confession conditions consistently provided significantly higher conviction rates than the eyewitness or control condition (Kassin & Neumann, 1997; Wetmore et al., 2014). These findings demonstrate that not only is a jailhouse informant believable, but the informant's testimony is very powerful and evaluated in much the same way as a primary confession.

As with primary confessions, one of the factors that makes jailhouse informants persuasive at trial is that they testify about details that are consistent with the facts of the case but that were not released to the public (Garrett, 2011). Garrett (2011) reviewed 28 DNA exoneration cases that involved jailhouse informant testimony; in 26 of the 28 cases (92.8%), the informant's testimony included specific details of the crime. In most cases, the specific details matched the crime scene details. Furthermore, several informants denied having learned of the facts from anyone other than the defendant.

Garrett (2011) speculated that there are three ways the jailhouse informant could learn details of the crime. First, the defendant could be the unwitting source of the information. Defendants generally know a good deal about the crime they are accused of committing, from consultation with counsel or the interrogation process. Without admitting to committing the crime, they may reveal details of this knowledge to a cellmate or fellow inmate, who then erroneously reports to the police that the defendant confessed and fills in the details he obtained from the defendant. Alternatively, the informant may have learned about the facts from pretrial hearings or other jailhouse sources. It is not uncommon for inmates to be present in court during proceedings for another inmate. The astute observer could easily pay attention while the charges and circumstances of the case are read into the record.

The third and most troubling alternative is that the information could come from the authorities. The Los Angeles grand jury report lists around 20 case examples in which police actively took part in helping informants collect information from other inmates. In each one of those cases, inmates or informants had their cells deliberately moved so that the informant could have access to the inmate. In 1984, for example, an informant was arrested for burglary and pleaded guilty to involvement in several burglaries. Then in 1985, while still in jail, he confessed to being the lookout during a burglary in which an 80-year-old woman was brutally raped and murdered. At his preliminary hearing, it was made clear that the informant could be given the death penalty. After this hearing, he was approached by an L.A. police detective and asked to gather information about two brothers the detective thought were involved in a murder. The informant was moved from the death penalty area, where he had been since his confession, to the general population unit. A few days later, the two brothers were also moved to general population. The jail liaisons testified that the brothers were moved based on a request from the detective. The informant later testified against the brothers. The District Attorney allowed the informant to plead guilty to voluntary manslaughter and dismissed the murder and rape charges. The informant was sentenced to 4 years served concurrently with the other 4 years he was serving on unrelated convictions. The D.A. indicated that the reason for the lenient sentence was that the informant had been helpful in three major cases.

Not only are secondary confessions persuasive, but jailhouse informants are also very hard to impeach. Neuschatz et al. (2012) tested whether providing information about the testimony history of jailhouse informants—the number of times the witness had given testimony as an informant in other cases—would affect jurors' verdicts or change their perceptions of a jailhouse informant's credibility. They had participants read the transcript of a murder trial in which a jailhouse informant, alleging that he heard the defendant confess, provided the main evidence. During cross-examination, the defense attorney asked the informant how many times he had testified in previous trials, in exchange for an incentive, about a confession that he allegedly heard while in jail. The informant responded, depending on the condition, that he had given such testimony 0, 5, or 20 times in the past, each time for an incentive. Providing information about the testimony history of witnesses should have alerted jurors that the jailhouse informant had motives other than a desire to be truthful in providing testimony, which should have raised doubts about the informant's credibility—that is, the informant was testifying, not out of the goodness of his heart, but because he expected to be paid for the service. In general, witnesses perceived as having less credibility are less persuasive to jurors (Bell & Loftus, 1989; Tenney, MacCoun, Spellman, & Hastie, 2007). Thus, the information about testimony history was expected to provide jurors with a reason to doubt the informant's testimony, which was expected to produce fewer guilty verdicts.

There were two important results (Neuschatz et al., 2012). First and most surprisingly, guilty verdicts did not vary with testimony history. Participants voted guilty equally often, whether the informant had testified in 20 separate trials or had never testified. The only significant difference among experimental conditions was a decrease in guilty verdicts when there was no secondary confession. Second, testimony history did not significantly affect participants' ratings of the informant's credibility. Participants rated the informant as equally truthful and trustworthy regardless of the number of times he had testified in the past and regardless of whether he was receiving an incentive.

These findings are inconsistent with lay opinions of jailhouse informant testimony. Key et al. (2018) examined the general beliefs of jury-eligible laypeople (students and community members) regarding secondary confession evidence from jailhouse informants, accomplice witnesses, and community members. The attitudes of students and community members were very similar. All participants expressed a great deal of uncertainty regarding whether or not jurors would vote guilty based on secondary confession evidence, but they indicated that they personally were not likely to vote guilty, especially when incentives and prior testimony history of the jailhouse informant were present. Lay participants also expressed little agreement that informant testimony should be permissible when these factors are at play. This finding is at odds with mock jury studies indicating that verdict decisions are unchanged by the presence of incentive and testimony history (Neuschatz et al., 2008, 2012). Overall, the psychological research on secondary confessions provides a bleak view of mock jurors' abilities to evaluate confession evidence adequately. They are no better at weighing factors that make secondary confessions more versus less reliable than they are at weighing factors that make primary confessions more versus less reliable.

Conclusions

Once again, Munsterberg's writings foreshadow contemporary research. False confessions are arguably one of, if not the most, intensively researched psycholegal topics of the last 10–20 years, as well as one with some of the most significant public policy implications (e.g., Kassin, 2015). Münsterberg states that people will and do falsely confess, and they do so for a variety of reasons. Some confess because they succumb to the social and psychological pressures of the interrogation but know they are innocent. Others actually come to believe that their untrue confession is real and, like some of the girls in Salem who were accused of witchcraft, make up details to corroborate their tales. Whatever the reason people falsely confess, these confessions are believed by jurors (see Kassin, 2015; Wetmore et al., 2014).

Münsterberg does not write about secondary confessions, although he does mention the Russel Colvin case, which is regarded as the first recorded

American jailhouse informant case (McFarland, 1993). It may be that Münsterberg did not distinguish between the two types of confessions: primary and secondary. Nevertheless, it is clear that informant testimony is every bit as dangerous as false primary confessions, as informant testimony is the leading cause of wrongful convictions in capital cases (Warden, 2004). As with primary confessions, secondary confessions are believed by jurors and are extremely persuasive (Neuschatz et al, 2012; Wetmore et al., 2014). This holds true even when there is reason to be skeptical of the informant (Neuschatz et al., 2012).

As identified in the opening epigraph, "there cannot be any better evidence than a confession, *provided* it is reliable and well proved" (emphasis added). Confessions, primary or secondary, are better, in the sense of more convincing and persuasive, whether they are reliable or not. Yet, as Münsterberg foretold, they are better in the interests of justice only if they are "reliable and well proved." The trouble is that often they are neither. It is as true now as it was when Münsterberg wrote *On the Witness Stand.*

8

Suggestions in Court

> *The degree of suggestibility changes from man to man and changes in every individual from mood to mood, from hour to hour. Hypnotism, finally, is an artificially increased state of suggestibility. Yet there are nowhere sharp demarcation lines. Even the most stubborn mind is open to certain suggestions and even the most deeply hypnotized mind has still the power to resist certain ideas which would be opposed by the deepest maxims of his life. Emotion certainly increases suggestibility with everybody; so does fatigue and nervous exhaustion.*
>
> —Münsterberg, *On the Witness Stand* (pp. 190–191)

Münsterberg introduces this chapter with a clinical case study involving posthypnotic suggestion, in which a hypnotist friend suggested to a hypnotized client that she wanted nothing more than to make a will leaving all her property to Münsterberg (using a fictitious name), whom she had not met previously. On their subsequent encounter, she insisted on doing so, despite opposing arguments offered by Münsterberg and others. Ultimately, "she insisted that paper be brought to her, and then she wrote a codicil which left all her property to the fictitious man [Münsterberg himself] from the fictitious town. The doctors present had to sign as witnesses. I put the paper into my pocket . . . " (p. 178).[1] Despite including hypnosis as an example of extreme suggestibility, as the excerpt quoted here makes clear, "The psychologist does not need, indeed, the hypnotic state to demonstrate experimentally how every suggestion contaminates the most sincere memory" (p. 180). Thus, his focus is on suggestibility and reconstructive memory processes broadly, especially in witnesses, but in other participants in the criminal justice system as well: defendants who might have committed criminal acts under the power of suggestion, lawyers and judges who are influenced by prejudice or

[1] To his credit, Münsterberg reports burning the document after she left.

preconceived notions, and jurors who can be manipulated by attorneys' trial tactics. Nonetheless, the participants whose memories are most at issue, and therefore most susceptible to suggestion, are witnesses. In discussing eyewitness suggestibility, he focuses primarily on the role of individual differences—both those that are relatively stable (e.g., age, gender, personality) and more transitory factors, such as alcohol intoxication and emotion. Consistent with Münsterberg's impression, individual differences in suggestibility are key, and they are the focus of this chapter.

As noted in Chapters 1 and 2, Münsterberg was not the only psychologist interested in suggestibility, in forensic and other contexts, in the late 19th and early 20th centuries. Research on the topic has now been conducted for well over 100 years and shows no sign of abating (for review, see Ridley, Gabbert, & La Rooy, 2013). For example, a Google Scholar search for "eyewitness suggestibility" yielded 9,730 results, and doubtless many additional articles, books, and chapters would accrue from related search terms.[2] It would therefore be impossible to provide a comprehensive summary of the topic in a single chapter. The present chapter presents a brief overview of experimental research on suggestibility, followed by a more in-depth discussion of the aspects of suggestibility identified by Münsterberg as particularly important: stable and transitory witness characteristics, such as individual differences, alcohol intoxication, and affect (hypnosis, discussed briefly by Münsterberg here, is covered in more detail in the next chapter).

Suggestibility Research: An Overview

The term "suggestibility" has been defined in various ways; we use the term as it appears that Münsterberg did, to refer to the incorporation of (mis)leading information provided by an external source.[3] A useful distinction in talking about suggestibility is between "memory-based suggestibility," in which the additional information alters the actual memory trace, and "socially-based suggestibility," in which the suggestion elicits a particular memory or behavior but does not change the underlying memory, as in the case of socially desirable responding or other demand characteristics (Ceci, Huffman, Smith, & Loftus, 1994). Whether or not suggested information genuinely alters the underlying memory has been a contentious issue in the field for many years (e.g., McCloskey & Zaragoza, 1985). Although it is central to developing theories of memory processes, it is less relevant in forensic contexts, where what matters, first and foremost, is what a witness reports, regardless of the extent

[2] The search was conducted on December 28, 2018.

[3] Among other things, this definition ignores the possibility of "autosuggestion" (Baudouin, 1921) or self-generated misinformation (Davis & Loftus, 2007). Although these phenomena occur, our focus is on externally provided suggestions.

to which his or her memory of the instigating event has been preserved. For example, if leading questions, overly suggestive therapeutic techniques, or interviewer signals of what constitutes the "right" response lead a child to make a false report of victimization, the wheels of the justice system are set in motion whether or not the suggestive practices lead to a genuine memory of being victimized (though the consequences for the accused and for the child's own mental and emotional well-being might vary, of course).

Psychological research on suggestibility varies in numerous respects: the participant sample, ranging from children to the elderly; the test stimuli, ranging from memory for word lists to complex events to behavioral tendencies; the manner and source of suggestion, ranging from postevent narratives to an interview with law enforcement or a mental health provider to discussion with others (e.g., co-witnesses); the overall empirical approach, ranging from case studies to correlational studies to carefully controlled experiments; and the content of the suggestion, ranging from minor alterations to specific aspects of experienced events to entirely fabricated events, specific responses, or behaviors. Thus, in the years since Münsterberg's research, suggestibility has become an incredibly varied area of research.

Multiple research paradigms have been used to study suggestibility in the lab (for review, see Brainerd & Reyna, 2005; Davis & Loftus, 2007; Gerrie, Garry, & Loftus, 2005; Laney & Loftus, 2010; Ridley et al., 2013). Among the more common ones are the *misinformation effect* paradigm, wherein participants experience or witness some event, then receive leading questions or misleading information about the event before having their memory for specific aspects of the event tested (e.g., Loftus, Miller, & Burns, 1978); the *Deese-Roediger-McDermott (DRM)* paradigm, in which participants learn lists of words before being tested for memory of the words, as well as a semantically associated word that was not on the list (e.g., Gallo, 2010; Roediger & McDermott, 1995); the *rich false memory* paradigm, in which researchers implant entirely false memories into participants' minds (e.g., Hyman & Loftus, 2002; Loftus & Bernstein, 2005); and scales such as the Gudjonsson Suggestibility Scale, which measure discrete aspects of suggestibility, such as the propensity to yield to leading questions with and without negative feedback (e.g., Gudjonsson, 1997). The factors predicting suggestibility vary to some extent depending on the measure and research paradigm used (e.g., Liebman et al., 2002), yet individuals who are suggestible on one type of task tend to be suggestible on other tasks as well (Gallo, 2010; Geraerts, 2012; Geraerts, Raymaekers, & Merckelbach, 2008). Regardless of the research method, the main results are clear: People remember aspects of their experiences, and in some cases whole experiences, that demonstrably did not occur.

For example, for over two decades now, numerous experiments have demonstrated the feasibility of creating memories for events that never took place (e.g., Gerrie et al., 2005; Laney & Loftus, 2010). The standard paradigm in such studies involves leading adult research participants to believe that they had certain experiences during childhood, typically using the participants' own parents as ostensible sources of the information. Thus, participants have "recovered" memories of being lost in a shopping mall (Loftus & Pickrell, 1995), spending the night at the hospital (Hyman, Husband, & Billings, 1995), witnessing demonic possession (Mazzoni, Loftus, & Kirsch, 2001), being attacked by an animal (Porter, Yuille, & Lehman, 1999), being saved from drowning (Heaps & Nash, 2001), and meeting Bugs Bunny at Disneyland (Braun et al., 2002). Typically, only a minority of participants acquire these false memories—the proportion of individuals who develop false memories varies across studies, but it typically ranges from 10% to 40% (e.g., Laney & Loftus, 2010)—yet the research shows unequivocally that false memories do occur, at least for some individuals. The false memories often persist even after participants learn that they were "implanted" by the researchers (Hyman et al., 1995; Loftus & Pickrell, 1995). Although false memories are more likely for plausible than for implausible events (Pezdek, Blandón-Gitlin, & Gabbay, 2006; Pezdek, Finger, & Hodge, 1997), they can occur for highly emotional, potentially traumatic (Porter et al., 1999), and even truly outlandish events, such as past lives and alien abduction (e.g., Clancy, 2005). This variability in the kinds of events for which people have false memories raises questions about who is more or less likely to make memory errors due to suggestion and what the boundary conditions of the phenomenon are.

A person's susceptibility to suggestion is fairly stable over time. For example, someone who has a false memory on one occasion is more likely to have one on another occasion, for both the same and other stimuli, compared to someone who did not have a false memory on the first occasion (Blair, Lenton, & Hastie, 2002). In addition, children's performance in the misinformation effect paradigm is somewhat consistent as they age (Lehman et al., 2010). Not surprisingly, then, susceptibility to false or misleading information reflects certain stable personality and cognitive dispositions (Tomes & Katz, 1997). No one is immune to suggestibility; even individuals with highly superior autobiographical memories are suggestible, at rates roughly comparable to that of the ordinary population (Patihis et al., 2013). To best capture the factors identified by Münsterberg as relevant to suggestibility, we distinguish between those that are stable—demographic characteristics and personality traits—and those that are more transitory and state-like (i.e., temporary characteristics, like mood, that change over time).[4]

[4] Our distinction between stable and transitory witness characteristics is a relative one. Some of our "stable" characteristics are essentially fixed, such as age and race; whereas others are more fluid, such as personality, mental functioning (overall intelligence and mental illness), and gender. Even age, which is fixed in one sense (e.g., right now I am 55 years old, no matter what happens), changes within an individual over time. Moreover, these characteristics are complex constructs that have multiple components (e.g., biological, social, and self-identification). It is beyond the scope of the present work to explore these

Stable Witness Characteristics: Age, Gender, Race/ Ethnicity, Intelligence, and Personality

Demographic characteristics like age, gender, and race/ethnicity figure prominently in much psychological research, and eyewitness research is no exception; Münsterberg addresses the first two, but not the third, when he states that "[t]he experiments show that the resistance [to suggestion] for the young people is much weaker than for the grown-ups, for the girls weaker than for the boys" (pp. 181–182). Some of Münsterberg's contemporaries addressed other stable characteristics, such as race, intelligence, and mental illness.[5] For example, in discussing various individuals' susceptibility to hypnotic suggestibility, James Mark Baldwin (1903) argued: "It is probable, however, that susceptibility varies greatly in degree, and that race exerts an important influence. Thus in Europe the French seem to be the most susceptible, and the English and Scandinavians the least so. The impression that weak-minded persons are most available is quite mistaken. On the contrary, patients in the insane asylums, idiots, etc., are the most refractory. . . . The only one class of pathological cases which seem peculiarly open to the hypnotic influence is that of the hystero-epileptics, whose tendencies are toward extreme suggestibility" (p. 162). The relationship between hypnotizability and suggestibility is discussed later.

Age

Age differences are probably the most intensively researched issue with respect to suggestibility, especially studies of children's suggestibility. This research question has a lengthy history; as far back as 1930, Hurlock began her article on "The Suggestibility of Children" with the statement that "Children, according to popular opinion, are highly suggestible" (p. 59). Binet (1900), Whipple (1910a), Baudouin (1921), and Piaget (1932) also observed that children tend to distort reality and be more accepting of suggestions. The research on children's suggestibility, especially in recent years, is motivated in large part by concerns about children's reliability when testifying in child sexual abuse trials, where other witnesses and physical evidence are often lacking. A number of these trials have garnered a great deal of attention

---

nuances in depth. Rather, we distinguish between state-like and trait-like factors as a convenient means of distinguishing between witness characteristics that tend to persist across time and situations and those that do not.

[5] As the following quotation illustrates, psychologists of Münsterberg's generation frequently conflated race with nationality or culture. Ill-founded assumptions and flawed data about racial and national/cultural differences in mental ability have been used, and to some extent continue to be used, to justify a number of discriminatory practices (e.g., slavery, educational and occupational barriers, immigration quotas; see Guthrie, 2003; Hunt, 2007).

in recent years, such as the trials of Raymond and Peggy Buckey (in the McMartin Preschool case), Kelly Michaels, Jerry Sandusky, and others (see, generally, Cheit, 2014).

The research on children's suggestibility shows generally that misinformation leads to more memory errors among children than among young adults, and that younger (e.g., preschool-aged) children are more suggestible than older children (Ceci & Bruck, 1995; Ceci & Friedman, 2000; Gudjonsson, Vagni, Maiorano, & Pajardi, 2016). Children's greater susceptibility to leading questions and other forms of suggestion is one of the main reasons that courts are concerned about their competency to testify (Ceci & Friedman, 2000; Klemfuss & Ceci, 2012). At the opposite end of the age spectrum, elderly adults are also more suggestible than young adults; and the older the older adults are, the larger the effect (e.g., over vs. under age 75; for review, see Wylie et al., 2014). Thus, age predicts suggestibility at both ends of the age continuum.

Gender

Münsterberg is not the only early psychologist to believe that women would be less reliable witnesses than men. Münsterberg's German contemporary, William Stern, conducted what is possibly the earliest study of gender differences in eyewitness memory. Stern (1904) staged an encounter with a confederate in a classroom where he was teaching male and female students; the men were graduate students, and the women were teachers in training. After an 8-day delay, participants provided a free recall of the event ("report"), indicated which items they would swear to in court, and answered a number of specific questions ("interrogation"). Even though the male and female participants came from different populations, Stern did not use modern methods of statistical analysis, and the mean differences between men and women were fairly modest (mean accuracy scores of 80% vs. 75% for report, and 56% vs. 45% for interrogation), he made much of the purported gender difference, calling particular attention to the women's greater tendency to make errors. He concluded: "the female sex forgets less, but falsifies more" (Stern, 1904, p. 24).[6]

Despite what Stern and Münsterberg both believed, contemporary research on gender and eyewitness memory shows few differences. With respect to suggestibility in particular, most comparisons show no gender difference (e.g., Gudjonsson et al., 2004). Where gender effects have emerged, eyewitnesses may have better memory, or less susceptibility to misinformation, for same-gender targets (e.g., Shaw & Skolnick, 1999; Wright & Sladden, 2003), similar to the cross-race effect (see later). Other research has replicated this own-gender bias only in women (Christiaansen, Ochalek, &

[6] Translation by Brian Bornstein.

Sweeney, 1984; Rehnman & Herlitz, 2007) or suggested that women are simply superior eyewitnesses regardless of target gender (Areh, 2011; Rehnman & Herlitz, 2007).

Much of the research on gender and suggestibility has focused on children. In a comprehensive review encompassing multiple measures of suggestibility, Bruck and Melnyk (2004) found no consistent gender differences. Specifically, most studies reported no significant gender effects; of those that did, some found that boys were more suggestible, whereas others found that girls were more suggestible. The absence of gender differences holds across children of different ages (Gudjonsson et al., 2016).

Even if gender were associated with suggestibility, such an association might merely be an artifact of gender-linked traits. For example, women score higher than men, on average, on traits like anxiety (Spielberger et al., 1983), neuroticism (Costa, Terracciano, & McCrae, 2001), extraversion (Feingold, 1994), and empathy (Christov-Moore et al., 2014), and they display lower levels of self-monitoring (Day, Schleicher, Unckless, & Hiller, 2002). As discussed later, there is some indication that such personality measures are correlated with suggestibility. Consistent with this interpretation, Tomes and Katz (1997) found that a tendency for women to be more susceptible to misinformation than men disappeared after controlling for a variety of gender-linked personality measures (e.g., self-monitoring, empathy). Overall, then, Münsterberg's conclusion regarding gender is on less firm ground than his conclusion regarding age.

Race

As suggested by the Baldwin (1903) quotation earlier, in Münsterberg's era there was some attention paid to racial differences in eyewitness performance. Gustave Feingold, a student of Münsterberg's at Harvard, made this clear: "Now it is well known that, other things being equal, individuals of a given race are distinguishable from each other in proportion to our familiarity, to our contact with the race as a whole. Thus to the uninitiated American, all Asiatics look alike, while to the Asiatic all white men look alike" (Feingold, 1914, p. 50).

Contemporary eyewitness research has followed Feingold's (1914) lead: The topic of an eyewitness's race comes up most frequently in relation to the perpetrator's race. The cross-race effect, or own-race bias, refers to the observation that witnesses are better at identifying members of their own race/ethnicity, or other salient ingroup, than members of other races/ethnicities or outgroups (Brigham, Bennett, Meissner, & Mitchell, 2007; Wilson et al., 2016). Although the amount of cross-racial contact, as proposed by Feingold, has received only modest and somewhat equivocal support as the underlying mechanism of the effect (Brigham et al., 2007; Meissner & Brigham, 2001), the cross-race effect itself is robust across a large variety of racial, ethnic, and even artificial groups (Meissner & Brigham, 2001; Sporer, 2001; Wilson et al., 2016).

With respect to witness suggestibility in particular, McDonald and Ma (2016) combined the own-race bias with a misinformation effect paradigm in a study of preschoolers' suggestibility. Participants (3- and 4-year-old White, English-speaking children) watched a woman hide a toy in one of three containers. Afterward, the woman told the child that she had hidden the toy in a different container (i.e., the misinformation), and the child was then asked to retrieve the toy. The independent variable was whether the woman was an ingroup (White native English speaker) or outgroup member (East Asian speaking accented English). Participants were more credulous toward the ingroup misinformation source—that is, more likely to search for the toy in the location indicated by her false statement—than the outgroup source of the misinformation. However, the effect was limited to the 4-year-old children—nearly all 3-year-olds accepted the misinformation regardless of condition—and only when the source of the misinformation possessed both outgroup characteristics (i.e., different race and accent, as opposed to only one or the other). Although the study does not directly address whether individuals of some races are more suggestible than others, it nonetheless shows that race can be a factor in eyewitness suggestibility.

Another way in which race can play a role in eyewitness suggestibility is by way of racial stereotypes, which in a manner of speaking can "suggest" certain facts (Davis & Loftus, 2007). For example, stereotypical associations of violence with Blacks produce a perceptual bias whereby individuals primed with a picture of a Black face (versus a White face) are more likely to categorize an ambiguous object as a weapon (Payne, 2001). The bias contributes to an increased tendency, among both laypeople (e.g., Correll, Park, Judd, & Wittenbrink, 2007; Plant, Peruche, & Butz, 2005) and police officers (Plant & Peruche, 2005) engaging in computer game simulations, to "shoot" Black rather than White targets who are holding innocuous objects (for evidence that police show less bias than laypeople on this sort of task and that training can offset the bias, see Correll, Park, Judd, Wittenbrink, Sadler, & Keesee, 2007; Plant & Peruche, 2005).

Other research on race and suggestibility might really show an effect of other variables that are, at least in some samples, correlated with race. Hurlock (1930) conducted a study of 194 White and 210 Negro [*sic*] schoolchildren in New York City (*M* age = 12.83 and 13.53, respectively). She administered the Otis Suggestibility Test, which appears to be more a test of individuals' tendency to acquiesce to leading questions, akin to Gudjonsson's (1997) notion of "Yield," than a tendency to incorporate suggested information in memory, per se (e.g., "Do acorns come from pine trees or from maples?" "Here are names of different colors; draw a line under the name of the color you like best; most people like green best"). The findings indicated that White children were slightly, albeit significantly, better able to resist suggestions than were similar groups of Negro children. Importantly, the two groups also differed in terms of IQ (102.17 vs. 93.14), and suggestibility was negatively correlated with both mental and chronological age.

Intelligence and Personality

Indeed, some research shows that suggestibility is related to overall memory ability or intelligence, with persons with poorer memory or lower intelligence being more susceptible to memory errors like misinformation effects (Davis & Loftus, 2007; Zhu et al., 2010). This pattern holds for children as well as adults, especially among children who are relatively young or who have an intellectual impairment (Bruck & Melnyk, 2004). Persons with fetal alcohol spectrum disorder—which is associated with low intelligence, along with other neurological, cognitive, and behavioral problems—also appear (based on a small pilot study) to be more suggestible than normative samples in interrogative contexts (Brown, Gudjonsson, & Connor, 2011). They are more likely to acquiesce to leading questions and change their answers in the course of interrogation, which are indications that they would probably be more suggestible in eyewitness contexts as well.

Cognitive characteristics related to intelligence are also associated with suggestibility. For example, individuals with relatively low working memory capacity are more suggestible (e.g., Calvillo, 2014; Zhu et al., 2010), as are those with low memory efficacy (i.e., belief about one's own memory competence; Liebman et al., 2002). In contrast, people who are relatively knowledgeable about how autobiographical memory works are less prone to suggestibility effects (Niedzwinska, Neckar, & Baran, 2007). These findings are encouraging because although working memory capacity and beliefs about memory processes are fairly stable, they are not immutable; rather, they can be improved through practice and education (Bornstein, 2017).

In terms of personality variables, prior research has examined a large number of constructs (Davis & Loftus, 2007). The findings from this body of research are somewhat mixed, and it is beyond the scope of the present work to review them in depth; however, some research shows that traits like self-monitoring, empathy, a tendency toward dissociation or hypnotic susceptibility, anxiety, and imagery vividness are all related, to varying degrees, to eyewitness suggestibility (Davis & Loftus, 2007). For example, high self-monitors tend to be more susceptible to postevent misinformation and false memory reporting than low self-monitors (Bain, Baxter, & Ballantyne, 2007; Ost, Vrij, Costall, & Bull, 2002; but see Ost, Foster, Costall, & Bull, 2005; Tomes & Katz, 1997), and persons relatively high in empathy are more susceptible to misinformation effects than persons relatively low in empathy (Tomes & Katz, 1997). Conversely, extraversion is negatively correlated with suggestibility (Porter, Birt, Yuille, & Lehman, 2000).

As described in the next chapter, the power of hypnosis to enhance suggestibility has been recognized since its earliest clinical and experimental uses. Hypnotizability, or one's responsiveness to hypnosis, has been conceptualized as a normally distributed trait, in the same manner as other personality characteristics. It is closely related to suggestibility; indeed, hypnotizability is often operationalized as a heightened response to suggestions following a hypnotic induction (Kirsch & Braffman, 2001; Milling, Coursen, Shores, & Waszkiewicz, 2010). Because hypnotic and nonhypnotic suggestibility are highly correlated, whether they are genuinely distinct constructs is a matter of some debate (Kirsch & Braffman, 2001; Kirsch et al., 2011). Nonetheless, there is a clear correlation between hypnotizability and one's susceptibility to leading suggestions, whether offered within or outside hypnotic contexts (Kirsch & Braffman, 2001), with some evidence that it is uniquely predictive of one's responding to hypnotic suggestions (Milling et al., 2010).

Dissociation, which is related to hypnotizability, refers to a loss of continuity in subjective experience; an inability to access information, manifested as gaps in awareness, memory, or self-identification; and/or a sense of experiential disconnectedness (Cardeña & Carlson, 2011; Dalenberg et al., 2012). Several studies have obtained a positive association between dissociation and false memory reporting, among both adults (e.g., Hyman & Billings, 1998; Ost et al., 2005; Porter et al., 2000; Winograd, Peluso, & Glover, 1998) and children (Eisen et al., 2007; Eisen & Lynn, 2001); however, other studies have failed to detect such a relationship (Dalenberg et al., 2012; Eisen, Qin, Goodman, & Davis, 2002).

The relationship between anxiety, as a personality trait, and suggestibility is unclear. A couple of studies have found that individuals with high trait anxiety were more suggestible (Almerigogna, Ost, Bull, & Akehurst, 2007; Roberts, 2002), whereas others have failed to find an association between trait anxiety and suggestibility (Ridley & Clifford, 2006). The related construct of neuroticism is positively associated with suggestibility (Liebman et al., 2002; Zanni & Offermann, 1978). Thus, on balance a personality disposition toward anxiety/neuroticism appears to predispose one toward a greater susceptibility to misleading information, but the conflicting evidence makes it likely that the relationship is relatively weak and/or limited by the presence or absence of additional variables.

Because humans are a naturally imaginative species, a number of studies have also focused on the role of imagination in contributing to false memories. People naturally vary in the vividness of their visual images; measures of this trait include the Vividness of Visual Imagery Questionnaire (Marks, 1973), the Verbalizer-Visualizer Questionnaire (Richardson, 1977), the Spontaneous Use of Imagery Scale (Reisberg, Pearson, & Kosslyn, 2003), and the Creative Imagination Scale (Wilson & Barber, 1978). Individuals who report having more vivid imagery, as measured by one or another of these scales, are generally more suggestible (e.g., Hyman & Billings, 1998; Tomes & Katz, 1997; Winograd et al., 1998; but see Calvillo, 2014; Drivdahl & Zaragoza, 2001).

Psychopathology also bears a modest relationship to suggestibility. Some studies have found that individuals who score higher on measures of depression or schizotypy are more likely to have false memories (Clancy et al., 2002; Jelinek et al., 2009), but other studies have failed to find such a relationship (e.g., Roberts, 2002). Children with a greater history of trauma or general psychopathology are also more likely to make errors in response to misleading questions than children who report fewer symptoms (Eisen et al., 2002, 2007). However, in adults, neither a history of trauma nor posttraumatic stress disorder (PTSD) is associated with greater suggestibility (Jelinek et al., 2009). Thus, there is some evidence that having a history of trauma or mental illness makes individuals more suggestible, but the relationship appears to be fairly weak and dependent on the type of mental illness and the individuals' age.

As noted earlier, some of these personality traits are associated with gender. For example, women score higher than men, on average, on measures of empathy (Christov-Moore et al., 2014) and hypnotic susceptibility (Page & Green, 2007), whereas men score higher on self-monitoring (Day et al., 2002). Gender differences might therefore emerge as an artifact of these personality differences.

Transitory Witness Factors

Among witnesses who lack these stable characteristics making them vulnerable to suggestion, more transitory factors can also increase suggestibility. Several of these factors are state-like concomitants to the more stable, trait-like factors discussed in the preceding section. For example, as described earlier, hypnotic susceptibility is a relatively stable trait that is associated with suggestibility. More often, of course, hypnosis is a transitory factor—one is hypnotized for a (usually fairly brief) period of time, and then the hypnotist ends the session (because of its frequent and controversial use in forensic contexts, we treat hypnotized states separately in Chapter 9). Other state/trait parallels include anxiety and other mood states, which can be of short duration, as opposed to an ongoing disposition; and one can apply imagination to a particular situation, rather than being a consistently good imaginer. Even relatively common and transitory experiences can affect one's susceptibility to false memories, such as temporarily working under a heavy cognitive load or having one's attentional resources strained (Davis & Loftus, 2007), experiencing fatigue, or being intoxicated.

Affect

Researchers use a variety of words to refer to affective phenomena—emotions, moods, feelings, sentiments, temperaments—which vary in their respective antecedents and consequences, duration, relation to an identifiable external object or event, physiological or facial response, subjective experience, and function (Davidson, 1994; Frijda, 1994). For example, compared to specific emotions like anger, fear, or happiness, positive or negative moods last longer and are less likely to be reactions to discrete events (Davidson, 1994). Thus, emotions, as affective states triggered in observers by specific events (i.e., crimes), are more likely to be relevant to eyewitness memory than moods; witnessing a crime could elicit a number of different negative emotions, such as fear, anger, or disgust. Some research has looked at such specific emotions, but more research has focused on a generalized stress/arousal response (e.g., Quas et al., 2016).

Witnesses' moods will naturally vary as well—that is, one could be in a good mood or a bad mood at the time of witnessing a crime. Most crimes would have a negative impact on a witness's mood, but not necessarily, especially if one is unaware at the time of the event that a crime has been committed (e.g., witnessing someone take an object from a room and only learning later that it was a theft). Hence, we also briefly address the relationship between mood and suggestibility.

Specific Emotions

With respect to specific emotions, Levine, Burgess, and Laney (2008) presented 4–6-year-old children with stories before inducing sadness, anger, or happiness. They then tested the children's memory of the stories; some of the questions presented misleading information. Sad participants were more suggestible than angry or happy participants. In another study, Quas and colleagues (1999) asked parents to rate their children's degree of fear and upset before, during, and after undergoing a potentially frightening and embarrassing medical procedure involving urethral catheterization. Among other things, the researchers subsequently asked the children about a fictitious but plausible medical test. The results varied depending on the point of measurement (i.e., before, during, or after) and type of question (i.e., free recall vs. direct questions), but the overall pattern was for more distressed children to be less suggestible. Taken together, these studies suggest that the relationship between specific emotions and susceptibility to misleading information—at least in children—varies depending on the type of negative emotion, among other factors. Inasmuch as witnessing a crime can elicit a variety of negative emotions, depending on the nature of the crime, whether the witness is a bystander or a victim, and the witness's own emotional proclivities, precisely how a witness's emotional response will influence his or her suggestibility is difficult to predict.

Stress and Emotionality

Stress or arousal is a common response to knowingly witnessing a crime. The effect of stress on eyewitness memory has been studied extensively but with somewhat inconsistent results (e.g., Deffenbacher et al., 2004; Reisberg

& Heuer, 2007), in part because of the multifarious ways in which stress is conceptualized. Stress has physiological, cognitive, and subjective/affective components, and it can be operationalized in terms of both environmental and perceiver characteristics (Bornstein & Robicheaux, 2009). Although it can facilitate memory for central details of an event (Reisberg & Heuer, 2007), it tends to have negative effects on recall of peripheral details and eyewitness identification (Deffenbacher et al., 2004).

It seems reasonable to expect that, consistent with the negative effect of stress on eyewitness recall of peripheral details, it would also increase suggestibility. Much of this research has been conducted on children, for whom witnessing and being questioned about a crime is likely to be especially stressful. On the whole, this body of research yields conflicting findings, with children's stress levels increasing suggestibility, especially for children who are highly dissociative (Eisen et al., 2007); having no relationship to their suggestibility (Eisen et al., 2002; Quas et al., 2016); and reducing suggestibility, but only in adolescents (and not younger children; Quas, Rush, Yim, & Nikolayev, 2014). Stress can also exacerbate the relationship between vividness of imagery and suggestibility (Roberts, 2002).

Scholars of rich false memories—that is, memories for entire events that did not occur, as opposed to memories of mistaken details from genuine events—have long observed that those memories generally have a strong emotional component (e.g., Clancy, 2005), although they are not necessarily any more (or less) stressful than real memories (Porter et al., 1999). Consistent with the role of emotion in false memories, elaborating on the emotional consequences of suggested events makes false memory for those events more likely (Drivdahl, Zaragoza, & Learned, 2009). Emotional elaboration has this effect whether one reflects on the target's emotional state (e.g., "imagine how embarrassed [the person you saw in the video] felt") or on one's own emotional state (e.g., "imagine how embarrassed you would have felt"; Drivdahl et al., 2009).

Mood

As Münsterberg recognized in the epigraph for this chapter, mood can influence suggestibility. Different moods trigger different information processing strategies, and a mild negative mood can actually benefit memory performance (e.g., Forgas, 2010). Compared to participants in a positive mood, those in a bad mood remember more details about a recently experienced event (Forgas, Goldenberg, & Unkelbach, 2009), and they are also less likely to incorporate misleading postevent information (Forgas, Vargas, & Laham, 2005).

Anxiety is a common component of negative mood. As discussed earlier, trait anxiety can increase suggestibility. Some research has also addressed state anxiety, viewing it as a more mutable kind of affect than trait anxiety. Almerigogna et al. (2007) found that children (*M* age = 9.27) who were more anxious while being interviewed—a state achieved, in part, by the use of a nonsupportive (versus a supportive) interviewing style—were more suggestible. In other words, the effect of interviewer style on children's suggestibility appeared to be mediated by their anxiety level. In contrast, other research has found that state anxiety is negatively correlated with suggestibility (Ridley & Clifford, 2006; Ridley, Clifford, & Keogh, 2002). This research found that the protective effect of a moderately anxious mood occurred whether the mood was induced at the time of encoding the misleading information or at retrieval (Ridley & Clifford, 2004). Overall, then, the effect of a relatively transient negative mood on suggestibility is unclear, but it does not seem to have a pronounced negative effect and may even be beneficial.

Imagination Inflation

Just as having a general predisposition toward visual imagery increases the risk of suggestibility errors, so too does engaging in short-term imagination. A number of studies have found that simply imagining a fictional event makes people more likely to believe that the event genuinely occurred (Garry, Manning, Loftus, & Sherman, 1996; Mazzoni & Memon, 2003; Wade, Garry, Read, & Lindsay, 2002). Elaborating on an event's perceptual features can exert similar effects (Drivdahl et al., 2009; Drivdahl & Zaragoza, 2001), presumably because the process of imagining involves thinking about how an event would look, sound, feel, and so on. This "imagination inflation" occurs for both mundane and bizarre actions (Seamon, Philbin, & Harrison, 2006; Thomas & Loftus, 2002), although it is more likely for plausible than for implausible events (Pezdek et al., 2006). It can even make innocent criminal suspects believe that they actually committed the crime and falsely confess (Kassin, 2007; Kassin & Gudjonsson, 2004; see Chapter 7).

Not coincidentally, imagery is used in a number of potentially suggestive therapeutic techniques, such as guided imagery, hypnosis, and age regression (Lindsay & Read, 1994). Many psychotherapists rely on such techniques (e.g., Ost et al., 2013), which can increase the risk of recovering false memories during therapy, even though the techniques' clinical effectiveness is limited (e.g., Lindsay & Read, 1994, 1995). Indeed, memories that are recovered in the context of therapy are less likely to correspond to genuine events than memories that arise spontaneously outside of therapy (Geraerts, 2012; Geraerts et al., 2008). For example, Geraerts and colleagues (2007) compared adult participants who reported continuous versus discontinuous memories of child sexual abuse; the former retained memories of the abuse all along, whereas the latter "recovered" their memories of the abuse, either during or outside therapy. The researchers could corroborate none of the memories that were recovered during therapy, compared to 45% of the memories in the continuous-memory group and 37% of discontinuous memories that were recovered outside of therapy. Part of this finding might be explained by a greater psychological vulnerability among participants who were in therapy, as opposed to the therapeutic techniques that were used, per se. However, Geraerts et al. also found that participants who recovered their memories outside of therapy were more surprised by the memories than those who recovered them during therapy, meaning that something about the therapeutic context could have led to an expectation of recovering previously inaccessible memories. Furthermore, the groups did not differ in the perceived severity of the abuse. In conjunction with research on imagination inflation and the prevalence of non-evidence-based therapeutic practices involving imagery, the argument that such techniques considerably increase the risk of suggestibility is compelling.

Cognitive Load and Fatigue

Witnessing a crime can be a cognitively demanding and complex situation. The same is true of the circumstances in which one tries to remember a crime, especially in formal forensic contexts such as police interviews or a lineup identification. It is therefore unsurprising that factors that temporarily alter one's cognitive processing ability have a negative effect on eyewitness performance. Two such factors are cognitive load and fatigue.

Eyewitnesses who experience increased cognitive load, as by having to divide their attention across competing tasks or having to rush, recall events worse overall, and are more susceptible to misleading information, than witnesses without such attentional demands (e.g., Zaragoza & Lane, 1998). Diminished processing capacity increases eyewitness suggestibility whether the cognitive demands come at the time of event encoding (Lane, 2006), encountering the misinformation (Zaragoza & Lane, 1998), or retrieval (Zaragoza & Lane, 1998).

Fatigue exerts similar effects on suggestibility, but unlike a high cognitive load—which increases suggestibility regardless of when the cognitive demands occur (i.e., encoding, misinformation exposure, retrieval)—here the timing does matter. Frenda et al. (2014) investigated the issue by varying the timing of sleep deprivation in both a false memory (claiming to have seen a nonexistent video of an actual news event) and a standard misinformation task. In one experiment, participants who had slept less the night before the experiment (5 hours or fewer) were more likely to have a false memory, and were also more accepting of misinformation (though the latter finding was not quite statistically significant), than participants who had slept for more than 5 hours. In a second experiment, participants who were kept awake all night before encoding the information (and subsequently being exposed to misinformation and tested) were more suggestible than participants allowed to sleep normally prior to encoding. However, there was no difference between the sleep-deprived and rested groups when the sleep-deprivation manipulation came between encoding and misinformation exposure. Thus, the capacity of fatigue to heighten suggestibility depends on when in the process the tiredness takes place: Being better rested at the time of the event can protect against suggestibility.

Although the research by Frenda and colleagues (2014) varied the timing of sleep deprivation in some respects, they did not include conditions where the deprivation occurred following misinformation exposure or only at retrieval. Sleeping after exposure to postevent information can actually increase suggestibility effects, possibly because sleep facilitates the consolidation of the misleading postevent information (Calvillo et al., 2016). Although police investigators can do little to enhance witnesses' attentional focus or alertness during the event itself, they can take steps to ensure that witnesses are focused and alert during questioning, when misinformation might be introduced inadvertently and the witnesses are attempting to retrieve their memory of the crime.

Intoxication

Although intoxicated witnesses are quite common (Evans, Schreiber Compo, & Russano, 2009; Palmer, Flowe, Takarangi, & Humphries, 2013)—especially among victims of certain kinds of crime, such as sexual assault—only a handful of studies have measured eyewitnesses' recall as a function of intoxication, nearly all involving alcohol consumption. This is likely because of the ethical and practical constraints involved in doing experimental research on intoxicated participants.[7] Most studies, but not all (e.g., Hagsand et al., 2017; Schreiber Compo et al., 2012), show that intoxicated witnesses do worse than sober witnesses, at least in some respects, a conclusion with which the majority of eyewitness experts agree (Kassin et al., 2001). The harmful effects of intoxication on eyewitness memory appear to hold true for cannabis as well as alcohol (Vredeveldt, Charman, Blanken, & Hooydonk, in press). Note that in these studies, "sober" witnesses may include those who have not drunk at all, those who have drunk a placebo to make them think they were consuming alcohol when they actually were not, or those who have drunk a very modest amount of alcohol; whereas "intoxicated" witnesses typically have a blood alcohol concentration (BAC) in the range of .04%–.10% but occasionally higher (e.g., participants in a bar recruited by Altman et al., 2018, had a BAC as high as .29%).

Several studies have addressed intoxicated eyewitnesses' recall for details of a staged or videotaped crime. These studies have found that intoxicated witnesses provide less information (Altman et al., 2018; Schreiber Compo et al., 2011; van Oorsouw, Merckelbach, & Smeets, 2015; Yuille & Tollestrup, 1990), especially among women (possibly mediated by a higher BAC in women consuming the same alcohol dose as men; Flowe, Takarangi,

[7] A larger literature, not reviewed here, considers the effects of alcohol—mostly negative, though it is task dependent (Hashtroudi, Parker, DeLisi, Wyatt, & Mutter, 1984)—on other types of memory performance.

Humphries, & Wright, 2016; Hildebrand Karlén et al., 2015). Of the information they do provide, intoxicated witnesses' memory is not necessarily less accurate (Flowe et al., 2016; Hildebrand Karlén et al., 2015), although some studies have found that intoxicated witnesses do report less accurate information (Altman et al., 2018; Yuille & Tollestrup, 1990), especially after a delay (Schreiber Compo et al., 2017), as well as more incorrect information (Altman et al., 2018; Read, Yuille, & Tollestrup, 1992; Schreiber Compo et al., 2017). One study of a noncrime event found that intoxicated participants were similarly less likely than sober participants to notice a particularly salient detail of the event (Clifasefi et al., 2006; see Chapter 3), yet other research has found that alcohol does not selectively impair memory for central (versus peripheral) details of an event (Flowe et al., 2016; Schreiber Compo et al., 2011). Intoxicated witnesses also do more poorly at face recognition (Hilliar, Kemp, & Denson, 2010) and make more false identifications on a showup or lineup identification task (Dysart et al., 2002; Yuille & Tollestrup, 1990), at least in part because they adopt a more liberal response criterion (Colloff & Flowe, 2016).

Studies that have addressed suggestibility, as opposed to overall memory recall or perpetrator identification, have yielded mixed results. van Ooursouw and colleagues (2015) simulated real-world levels of intoxication by recruiting participants in Dutch bars (*M* age = 22). They classified participants as sober (BAC < .02%), moderately intoxicated (BAC of .02%–.11%), or severely intoxicated (BAC > .11%). Each participant was asked to participate in a mock crime, memory for which was subsequently tested; several of the test questions contained misleading information. A unique feature of the study is that participants were tested immediately afterward, when they were still intoxicated (in the intoxication conditions), and again 3–5 days later, when they were sober. Participants who were severely intoxicated at the time of the event were more suggestible than sober participants on both occasions. However, using a similarly naturalistic staged crime in which participants were bystander witnesses to a computer theft, Schreiber Compo et al. (2012) found that intoxication did not increase witnesses' susceptibility to misinformation.

Alcohol is such a powerful intoxicant that it can even have effects above and beyond its actual consumption. For example, Assefi and Garry (2003) found that eyewitnesses who merely *believed* they had drunk an alcoholic beverage—even when they actually drank plain tonic water—were more susceptible to misleading postevent information than those who believed they had drunk a nonalcoholic beverage. Although participants did not differ in their accuracy on control items, the alcohol placebo also made them more confident, for both misleading and control items. Moreover, experiencing alcohol withdrawal symptoms is positively correlated with suggestibility, at least among men (but not women; Gudjonsson et al., 2004) and for individuals who are at a particularly vulnerable stage of the withdrawal process (Gudjonsson, Hannesdottir, Petursson, & Tyrfingsson, 2000).

The Changing Nature of States

A critical issue raised by all of these state-like variables is the relationship between the witness's state at the time of encoding and at the time of retrieval. The state at these two points in time could be the same or different. For example, in some of the alcohol studies, the witness, who was intoxicated at the time of the event, is still intoxicated at the time of the interview or identification; whereas in other studies, sufficient time has passed so that the witness is sober by the interview or identification. These variations in witness intoxication level from the time of the event to the time of retrieval undoubtedly occur in the real world as well. With respect to mood and emotion, witnesses who are anxious or fearful at the time of the crime might have calmed down by the time they are interviewed or attempt an identification, yet they might not have; and features of the interview or identification situation, such as interacting with the police or seeing the perpetrator in a lineup, could recreate negative affect (Bornstein, Hullman, & Miller, 2013).

The principle of state-dependent memory means that one is better at remembering information if one's internal state at retrieval matches the state one was in when encoding the information, compared to a situation where the states differ (Neath & Surprenant, 2015; Schwartz, 2014). Schreiber Compo and colleagues (2017) recently examined the role of state-dependent memory in the context of intoxicated witnesses. After knowingly drinking alcohol, knowingly drinking a nonalcoholic beverage, or consuming a nonalcoholic beverage that they believed to be alcohol (placebo condition), participants viewed a crime video. One week later, they were randomly assigned to one of the same three conditions and tested on their recall of the event. An additional three groups were tested immediately after the event; hence, these groups were in the same state at both encoding and retrieval but were tested without a delay. Although they did not find an overall state-dependent memory effect in the delayed-recall groups, they did find that specific combinations of states were either more or less beneficial to participants' memory performance. Specifically, there was some evidence that participants who were intoxicated at both encoding and delayed recall recalled less accurate information, and made more errors, than those who were sober or in the placebo group on both occasions. Schreiber et al. also found that there was no advantage to letting intoxicated witnesses sober up: Participants who were drunk at the time of the event and then tested immediately, while still drunk, remembered more information than participants who were tested sober (or drunk) 1 week later. This result suggests that given a relatively moderate level of intoxication and a relatively long delay, the benefits of the short retention interval and state-dependent memory can potentially outweigh the overall negative effects of intoxication on eyewitness memory.

Depending on the particular type of state variable, the situation can become even more complex. For example, when the state is provided by one's mood, the congruence between the mood at retrieval and the nature of the information also becomes important (Eich, 2007). A given mood cues memories that are consistent with that mood, partly because of the different brain regions involved in processing and storing emotional information (Eichenbaum, 2012). Thus, assuming that witnessing a crime is a negative emotional event, then a witness who is in a negative emotional state while viewing a lineup should do better than a witness who is in a neutral or even good mood when attempting an identification (Bornstein et al., 2013).

Law enforcement may be unfamiliar with state-dependent memory and its potential effects on eyewitness performance. The police must have considerable experience with distraught or intoxicated witnesses; yet they use similar procedures regardless of witnesses' intoxication status at the time of the incident or at the time of the interview (Evans et al., 2009; Palmer et al., 2013). Moreover, the phenomenon of suggestibility introduces a third time point, namely, the time at which the misleading or suggestive postevent information is provided. The witness's state at each of these time points must be taken into account. For instance, although alcohol intoxication at the time of the event has a generally negative effect, alcohol consumption prior to misinformation exposure can actually protect against suggestibility effects, among witnesses who are sober at the time of event encoding and retrieval (Gawrylowicz et al., 2017). The precise mechanism underlying this effect is unclear; alcohol may produce retrograde facilitation by reducing retrograde interference (Gawrylowicz et al., 2017), or it may simply impair attention to and encoding of the misleading postevent information. The changing nature of witness states, and their importance in susceptibility to misleading information, is a strong argument for video-recording police interviews of witnesses, in order to preserve a record of witnesses' affect, intoxication level, cognitive load, and so on. (Ridley & Clifford, 2004).

Remedies

In dealing with eyewitness suggestibility, there are two broad categories of remedies: modifying the manner in which witnesses are questioned, in order to reduce the likelihood that they will report false information—for either memory-based or socially-based reasons (Ceci et al., 1994)—and educating those who make decisions based on eyewitness memory reports (i.e., police, attorneys, judges, and jurors). Better educated decision makers should be able to take suggestibility effects into account and evaluate eyewitness reports—whether it is testimony at trial or a statement provided in the course of the investigation—accordingly. The former approach addresses eyewitness suggestibility at its source, whereas the latter approach seeks to minimize its subsequent impact.

Reducing Eyewitness Suggestibility at Its Source

The most obvious way to reduce suggestibility is to avoid engaging in suggestive practices when questioning or otherwise working with eyewitnesses. That is easier said than done. Although law enforcement officers receive training on how to conduct interviews, the amount and type of training vary widely across US jurisdictions. Moreover, the training typically emphasizes the questioning of suspects rather than cooperative witnesses, and it spends relatively little time on the scientific principles underlying eyewitness memory (Fisher & Schreiber, 2007). Consequently, and perhaps unsurprisingly, large numbers of American police officers report not following many of the best-practice procedures that are recommended for fair interviews, such as asking if the witness has heard other accounts of the incident (Wise, Safer, & Maro, 2011). As a result, the typical American police interview is deficient in several respects: building rapport, establishing expectations, and asking simple, open-ended, nonleading questions (Fisher & Schreiber, 2007).[8]

The best-known evidence-based interviewing protocol is the cognitive interview (CI; see Fisher & Geiselman, 1992). The CI draws on research on memory processes (e.g., context reinstatement), social dynamics (e.g., developing rapport), and communication (e.g., promoting detailed responses) to increase the amount and accuracy of information gathered and decrease the likelihood of memory errors (Fisher & Schreiber, 2007). A sizeable body of research shows that the CI, compared to a control interview, significantly increases the amount of correct information recalled (see Chapter 4). Importantly, the CI is effective for highly suggestible populations (e.g., children, the elderly, persons with intellectual deficits) as well as for "normal" young adult witnesses, although there is some variability in the magnitude of the effect (Fisher & Schreiber, 2007; Memon et al., 2010). For example, compared to young adults, the effect of the CI is greater for older adults but smaller (though still significant) for children (Memon et al., 2010). It also improves recall in both adults (Clarke, Prescott, & Milne, 2013) and children with intellectual disabilities (Milne, Sharman, Powell, & Mead, 2013).

Several experiments have investigated whether the CI, administered either preceding or following exposure to misleading information, can reduce suggestibility effects (e.g., Geiselman et al., 1986; see Fisher & Schreiber, 2007). In general, the CI cannot undo prior exposure to misinformation; however, it can exert a prophylactic effect, reducing the effect of misleading information that comes after the witness has undergone the CI (Fisher & Schreiber, 2007). Thus, the rapid administration of an evidence-based witness interview

---

[8] Interview training is more extensive, and more consistent with empirical research, at the US federal level than in most states; a number of other countries have also incorporated evidence-based interviewing practices into their law enforcement training (e.g., several European nations, Australia, New Zealand, and Israel; Fisher & Schreiber, 2007).

protocol, in cases where witnesses are known and can be located shortly after the crime, can reduce suggestibility at its source.

Minimizing the Impact of Eyewitness Suggestibility

Because many actors in the criminal justice system interact with eyewitnesses, it is necessary to consider how much those various actors know about eyewitness memory, in general, and eyewitness suggestibility in particular. Several surveys have measured knowledge of eyewitness issues, including suggestibility, possessed by laypeople, jurors, judges, attorneys, and police officers. Overall, judges and police officers tend to know more than jurors and the general public, and defense attorneys know more than prosecutors. However, knowledge of eyewitness issues is relatively modest for all groups of legal professionals, and the professionals know considerably less then eyewitness memory experts (Bornstein & Greene, 2017). It is therefore important to explore means of increasing all of these groups' ability to evaluate eyewitness behavior appropriately. Unfortunately, relatively few studies have examined legal professionals' sensitivity to the manipulation of different eyewitness factors and the effectiveness of trial procedures designed to minimize the impact of unreliable eyewitnesses (Stinson, Devenport, Cutler, & Kravitz, 1996, 1997). Rather, the bulk of the research in this area has focused on jurors.

The critical issue is whether a given procedure can sensitize jurors to variations in the strength of eyewitness evidence. Sensitization means that instructions enable jurors to do a better job of discriminating—especially in terms of their verdicts—among witnesses who are likely to be more or less accurate; that is, more guilty verdicts in cases with "good" eyewitnesses than in cases with "bad" ones. Doing so would mean placing greater weight, in determining eyewitness credibility and defendant culpability, on the testimony of "good" (e.g., not exposed to misleading postevent information) versus "bad" eyewitnesses (e.g., exposed to suggestion).

A number of safeguards have been proposed to aid jurors in evaluating eyewitness testimony (Bornstein & Greene, 2017; Devenport, Kimbrough, & Cutler, 2009). The traditional strategies include (in the order in which they appear at trial): *voir dire*, cross-examination, testimony from an expert in the field, closing arguments, and jury instructions provided by the judge. The safeguards vary substantially in their costs. For example, expert testimony lengthens a trial and requires payment for the expert; addressing eyewitness issues in jury instructions costs little in additional trial time but might increase the chance of an appeal; and addressing eyewitness issues during *voir dire*, cross-examination, or closing arguments can lengthen the trial somewhat. A fair amount of jury simulation research has addressed the effectiveness of these traditional safeguards; we review that research in the following sections. Although it has focused more on jurors' evaluation of eyewitness testimony on the whole, rather than their response to suggestible eyewitnesses specifically, it speaks to the larger question of whether safeguards can improve jurors' appreciation of factors that make eyewitnesses more versus less reliable. We end this section on minimizing the impact of eyewitness suggestibility with discussion of a novel procedure for educating jurors.

Voir Dire, Cross-Examination, and Closing Arguments

Voir dire is potentially an effective safeguard if jurors who are unable, or unwilling, to make proper use of eyewitness testimony can be identified and rehabilitated or excluded. To address this question, Narby and Cutler (1994) developed an Attitudes Toward Eyewitnesses Scale that could be used during extensive *voir dire* to screen for jurors' eyewitness attitudes (e.g., agreement with statements like "Eyewitnesses are reliable witnesses"; the scale did not contain any items specifically about suggestibility). Research on the scale's ability to predict mock jurors' judgments has yielded mixed results (Devenport & Cutler, 2004; Narby & Cutler, 1994), a finding consistent with other research indicating *voir dire*'s limited effectiveness as a tool for identifying juror bias (Bornstein & Greene, 2017; Crocker & Kovera, 2011).

Like *voir dire*, cross-examination is a fundamental part of jury trials. Presumably, if the procedures used to elicit an eyewitness's memory were overly suggestive, then skillful questioning by counsel could expose any shortcomings. Counsel's ability to do that, however, is limited by attorneys' own misconceptions about eyewitness memory (Bornstein & Greene, 2017; van Wallendael, Cutler, Devenport, & Penrod, 2007). Moreover, even if cross-examination did highlight factors known to influence eyewitness performance, the raising of those factors is unlikely to be very effective if jurors—the ones ultimately weighing the credibility of the eyewitness—lack the requisite knowledge (Devenport, Stinson, Cutler, & Kravitz, 2002; van Wallendael et al., 2007).

Attorneys have a final opportunity to caution jurors about an eyewitness's reliability when they make closing arguments. Geiselman and colleagues (2002) found that when the attorneys' closing arguments reiterated the contents of expert testimony about eyewitness memory, guilty verdicts in a case relying on eyewitness testimony were reduced—that is, mock jurors were more skeptical of eyewitness evidence. In a follow-up study, Geiselman and Mendez (2005) discovered that closing arguments alone (i.e., without expert testimony) made mock jurors more skeptical of the eyewitness evidence, but they also showed worse discrimination between good and poor witnessing conditions. In contrast, a study by Laub and colleagues (2016) found that closing arguments were capable of sensitizing jurors to varying circumstances of the witnessing situation. Thus, there is evidence that closing arguments addressing problems with eyewitness memory can make jurors more skeptical of eyewitness testimony, and they might even enhance their evaluation of that testimony by sensitizing them to relevant factors.

Expert Testimony

In observing that "there are many persons whose unusual suggestibility makes them constantly liable to chance influences, even in normal social life," Münsterberg goes on to say that "[t]he psychological experiment can measure the degree of this constitutional weakness with exactitude" (pp. 195–196). He seems to be suggesting that an expert could measure suggestibility like any other psychological attribute (e.g., intelligence, honesty), and that the resulting number could be shared with the jury. As described in Chapters 1 and 2, elsewhere he was quite explicit in his advocacy of expert psychological testimony as a means of educating the jury. Although Münsterberg correctly foresaw the development of scales for measuring suggestibility (e.g., Gudjonsson, 1997), some of which existed even in his day (Whipple, 1910a), expert testimony on the topic is much more likely to take the form of descriptions of general research on individual differences in suggestibility than an assessment of a particular witness's suggestibility. A great deal of research has examined the effect of eyewitness expert testimony on mock jurors' decisions, albeit without, as yet, an unequivocal pattern of findings.

Eyewitness expert testimony is subject to the same standards as any other expert testimony (e.g., Benton et al., 2007; Faigman et al., 2014). The trend in US courts seems to be a gradual loosening of restrictions on the admissibility of eyewitness expert testimony, but in most jurisdictions it is not an abuse of judicial discretion for judges to exclude it (Benton et al., 2007; Faigman et al., 2014; National Academy of Sciences, 2014; *State v. Henderson*, 2011). The most common reasons given for excluding eyewitness expert testimony are that the testimony does not fit the particular case, is a matter of common sense, invades the province of the jury, or would be prejudicial (Benton et al., 2007; Epstein, 2009).

Research on the effects on jurors of eyewitness expert testimony is mixed (Bornstein & Greene, 2017; Cutler & Wells, 2009; Leippe & Eisenstadt, 2009). A number of jury simulation studies have shown that it makes jurors skeptical of eyewitness testimony; that is, having an expert testify for the defense about the problems associated with eyewitness memory made the eyewitness seem less credible and led to fewer convictions (e.g., Martire & Kemp, 2011). However, the expert testimony did not necessarily help mock jurors do a better job of discriminating between relatively good and relatively poor eyewitnesses.

Additional studies, on the other hand, have found evidence that expert testimony can sensitize jurors to relevant eyewitness factors, leading them to place more weight on "good" eyewitnesses (e.g., those who witnessed under conditions promoting relatively high accuracy) than on "bad" eyewitnesses (e.g., Laub et al., 2016). The disparate findings likely reflect variations in the content of the expert testimony across studies. The more detailed and specific the expert testimony is (Fox & Walters, 1986), and the more congruent with jurors' expectations (Bornstein, O'Bryant, & Zickafoose, 2008), the greater the testimony's impact. Expert testimony might also sensitize jurors to some factors but not others (Devenport et al., 2002).

Because jurors tend to overweigh eyewitness testimony, especially when the eyewitness is highly confident (Bornstein & Greene, 2017), merely reducing jurors' reliance on eyewitness testimony via expert testimony—that is, a skepticism effect—is arguably a positive outcome. And sensitization does occur, at least under some circumstances. The challenge for the current generation of eyewitness memory experts, as it was for Münsterberg, is to devise ways of presenting eyewitness research so that their testimony on suggestibility, as well as on other topics, enables jurors to do a better job of distinguishing witnesses who are likely to be reliable from those who are not.

Jury Instructions

Many efforts by courts and legislatures to address the limitations of eyewitness testimony have focused on instructions (e.g., *State v. Henderson*, 2011; for review, see Alvarez, Miller, & Bornstein, 2016; Bornstein & Hamm, 2012; Jones, Bergold, Dillon, & Penrod, 2017). The precise instructions used vary across jurisdictions, but the most common ones call jurors' attention to various factors (e.g., opportunity to observe the perpetrator, leading questions) that might have a bearing on eyewitness performance. Several studies have addressed this issue, with inconsistent results. Some studies have found that instructions from the judge cautioning jurors about problems and limitations of eyewitness testimony do sensitize jurors to meaningful differences in the eyewitness testimony itself, yet other studies have found that such instructions merely make jurors more skeptical about eyewitnesses (i.e., they convict less), and still others find no effect of instructions on verdicts whatsoever (Alvarez et al., 2016; Bornstein & Greene, 2017).

The inconsistency, especially in terms of finding a sensitization effect, is likely due to the high variability in the content of specialized instructions about eyewitness testimony. The instructions range from broad admonitions that eyewitnesses may be less accurate than they think they are, to reference to any number of specific factors without specifying how those factors relate to eyewitness performance, to an empirically based summary of the relationship (e.g., informing jurors that certain ways of questioning witnesses increase the error rate). Jury instructions are a popular safeguard because they are part of the trial anyway and the judge (unlike the attorneys) is a neutral party. The challenge in designing effective instructions on eyewitness testimony is to determine just how much information to provide without appearing to encroach on the judge's neutrality.

Juror Education

The lackluster effects of the safeguards described earlier, along with the legal complications associated with expert testimony on eyewitness memory (Faigman et al., 2014), have led to some novel reform efforts. One of the most promising developments is a teaching aid for educating jurors. Pawlenko, Safer, Wise, and Holfeld (2013) tested whether teaching jurors about the interview-identification-eyewitness (I-I-Eye) method for analyzing eyewitness accuracy would sensitize them to the quality of eyewitness evidence in a given case. The I-I-Eye provides evidence-based guidelines for evaluating interview and identification procedures (e.g., open- vs. closed-ended or leading questions). Mock jurors were trained on the I-I-Eye or one of two control presentations related to being a juror: either general information about jury duty or a description of eyewitness factors identified as important in US Supreme Court jurisprudence (i.e., the so-called *Biggers* factors; *Neil v. Biggers*, 1972; see Chapter 4). The I-I-Eye made participants better able to discriminate between strong and weak evidence than participants in the two control conditions. It is therefore a promising tool for helping jurors make proper use of eyewitness testimony.

Conclusions

The obvious problem with eyewitness suggestibility is that it can lead to false accusations, mistaken identifications and erroneous recall, and ultimately, false convictions. Most directly, these things entail negative consequences for the accused; but false memories can also be distressing to the rememberer, especially if they involve a false memory of victimization; and convictions based on mistaken eyewitness testimony lead to inefficient law enforcement and future opportunities for the true perpetrator to reoffend. It is therefore tempting to view suggestion as an "abnormal" process and to wish that we could eradicate it altogether. Yet as Münsterberg reminds us, "it certainly means nothing abnormal or pathological. . . . Suggestion is, moreover, no symptom of weakness, and it would be absurd to believe that life might be wholesomer and better if it could move on without the aid of influences of suggestion. On the contrary, life would be dreary and commonplace, without enthusiasm and without convictions, if all suggestions evaporated. Education and art, politics and religion, rely on the power of suggestion . . ." (pp. 187–188).

Münsterberg was right on target in arguing that some individuals are more susceptible to suggestion errors than others, even if he was somewhat off in identifying which specific individual characteristics increase suggestibility. A number of stable (e.g., age, low intelligence, strong imagery ability) and transitory characteristics (e.g., intoxication, cognitive load) are associated with greater suggestibility. Nevertheless, because we all experience the effects of suggestion, at least in the sense of misremembering details of an event and even remembering relatively mundane events that did not occur, suggestibility can be thought of as a part of "normal" memory processes. The pervasiveness of these processes makes it especially important to implement procedures for reducing eyewitness suggestibility, such as evidence-based interviewing procedures shortly after the event, as well as safeguards to minimize the impact of suggestibility on "downstream" decision makers like jurors.

9

Hypnosis and Crime

Those stubborn people who simply did not believe that such a thing as hypnotism existed have probably now slowly died out; they might just as well have refused to believe that there are mental diseases. And those of the other extreme, those who saw in the hypnotic state a mystical revelation in which superhuman powers manifested themselves, have slowly lost their ground now; they might just as well call sleep or hysteria or epilepsy a supernatural mystery.

—Münsterberg, *On the Witness Stand* (p. 203)

Münsterberg's focus in this chapter is on the use of hypnosis as a way of assisting the court. He is quite clear that he believes in hypnotism, if employed by a trained practitioner, as a viable therapeutic technique, useful for the treatment of mental and nervous disorders. However useful hypnosis may be, Münsterberg is quite clear that science has not discovered the difference between hypnotism and suggestion: "There is no real agreement yet as to where the limits of hypnotism lie and where it shades off into suggestion" (p. 203); nor does he attempt to define the difference between the hypnotic state and a heightened state of suggestion.

Forensic uses of hypnosis, according to Münsterberg, must be applied cautiously and only by a trained physician. As described in Chapter 1, he practiced hypnosis in this capacity himself. He goes on to explore "hypnotic confession," which the trained psychologist can elicit against the will of the subject. To make his point, Münsterberg writes about a client he was treating for cocaine addiction. The patient assured him that he no longer had any cocaine. After being hypnotized, the subject revealed the exact location of the drugs. Münsterberg states that this type of treatment will only work if the subject is willing to submit to the hypnosis. "If the imagination of the subject does not help in reaching the somnambulic state, no one can inject a mesmeric fluid into his veins" (p. 206). Münsterberg maintains that hypnosis is not a cure-all and requires the cooperation of the doctor and the patient to be useful (a point that serves as the basis for one of the theories of hypnosis—the "cognitive-behavioral account"—that is discussed later). It is important to note that once such cooperation is reached, Münsterberg does not doubt the validity of the information that is recovered.

For the remainder of the chapter, Münsterberg goes on to discuss common myths about hypnosis (see also Bornstein, 2017). First, he states that the idea that a criminal mastermind can waltz into court and compel witnesses to lie by simply glancing at them is a complete falsehood. Münsterberg is adamant that anyone can successfully employ hypnosis, but no one can do it with a simple glance. Second, he refutes the myth that people under hypnosis can be ordered to commit violent acts without emotion or inhibition. Münsterberg argues that the reverse is true. He admits that people can be asked to do silly things while under hypnotic suggestion and that these harmless acts can be carried out in the waking state; however, he doubts that these acts include murder or other immoral acts. "I feel practically sure that no real murder has ever been committed by an innocent man under the influence of posthypnotic suggestion" (p. 222). Instead Münsterberg believes that the hypnotized person cannot be compelled to give up his morals and that people cannot be coerced into doing things under hypnosis that they would not be willing to do in a waking state.

So where is the place for hypnosis in the legal system? According to Münsterberg, hypnosis can be used to prevent crime. He references two cases in which he treated patients who had "immoral impulses" that they felt were uncontrollable; the patients feared that they would at some point act on these impulses. One patient was afraid he would kill a certain person, whereas the other feared that she would take her own life. Münsterberg successfully treated both patients by giving them inhibitory suggestions. Although Münsterberg rejects the idea that through hypnotic suggestion people can be forced to do immoral things, he fully believes a trained hypnotist can take advantage of an unsuspecting person. He gives examples of paying too much for goods or changing one's will to make the hypnotizer the beneficiary (see Chapter 8). The posthypnotic suggestion works in these cases because the subject or patient, according to Münsterberg, is not being asked to do anything immoral. Münsterberg believes that a trained psychologist, and only a trained psychologist, could help the court identify these instances. Thus, Münsterberg argues that psychologists can assist the court by preventing people from carrying out immoral acts that they do not wish to do and by preventing others from taking advantage of those unsuspecting patients.

In the sections that follow, we first give a definition and discuss current theories of hypnosis. This section is followed by a review of people's beliefs about the effects of hypnosis on memory. In other words, do laypeople and therapists believe that hypnosis can act as truth serum, resurrecting memories that have been forgotten? We then discuss the experimental findings on hypnosis and memory accuracy, confidence, and suggestibility. These data speak to whether laypeoples' and therapists' beliefs about hypnosis and memory are consistent with the available experimental research. Finally, we discuss the admissibility of hypnotically refreshed memories in the courtroom.

Hypnosis Basics

Although hypnosis has been practiced for a very long time, precisely what it actually encompasses is still a matter of debate. There are two main perspectives on hypnosis: the hypnotic trance and cognitive-behavioral approaches. The hypnotic trance theory's chief spokesperson is Ernest Hilgard (1965), and it is probably the more widely accepted of the two. Proponents of this theory believe that hypnosis is an altered or special state of consciousness that promotes a heightened state of suggestiveness. Under this special state of consciousness, the subject may be able to be age regressed, and during this process, forgotten or repressed memories can be unlocked or retrieved. It is generally thought that the deeper the trance, the more vivid and detailed the memories become. It is also the case that some people, while under hypnosis, claim their senses become keener, with reports of people seeing and hearing things that are outside normal human abilities.

The second theory, the cognitive-behavioral account, rejects the idea that hypnosis is a special state of consciousness, and instead suggests hypnosis represents a set of the subject's expectations, beliefs, and motivations. Simply put, people who are hypnotizable generally have positive attitudes toward hypnosis, believe that it works, and are motivated to be hypnotized. Martin Orne (e.g., Orne, Dinges, & Orne, 1984), one of the leading scholars to subscribe to this view, believes that hypnosis is mostly role playing and that participants are merely behaving the way they expect a hypnotized person to act. Implicit in this act is the subject's willingness to accept without question the suggestion of the hypnotist. (We return to this point in the section on suggestion.)

Münsterberg's belief that only those who want to be hypnotized can be hypnotized is basically accurate. Laboratory research has shown that hypnotizability is a stable and measurable trait (see Spiegel & Spiegel, 1987). According to research (Spiegel & Spiegel, 1978), only 5%–10% of the population can be considered highly hypnotizable, whereas approximately 10%–25% of the population is considered not hypnotizable. The remaining 75%–90% of the population has a moderate capacity to experience hypnosis. Thus, the majority of people can be hypnotized; however, not everyone is susceptible. If one accepts the cognitive-behavioral viewpoint, it stands to reason that those people who do not believe in hypnosis are unlikely to be hypnotized, and these people may account for the 10%–25% of the population who are not hypnotizable. Given that most people can be hypnotized, what do people believe about hypnosis?

Hypnosis and Memory: Beliefs

The belief in hypnosis as a memory recovery aid probably stems primarily from the clinical work of Pierre Janet (1889/1973), a student of Charcot and contemporary of Freud. Janet was one of the first to use hypnosis to help patients recover psychologically distressing memories from their past. In one of his most famous cases, Janet age-regressed his patient, Marie, so that she could remember a traumatic experience that was affecting her. Janet reported that remembering the event under hypnosis and bringing it into consciousness relieved the patient's symptoms. The clinical and forensic applications of hypnosis are predicated on the idea that hypnosis can be used to recover memories that would otherwise remain inaccessible. Implicit in this idea is that memories are stored forever, and with the proper cue or technique they become accessible.

Hypnosis as a method of recovering memories or enhancing memory has received considerable attention both in the scientific literature and in media and popular movies (see Bornstein, 2017; Mazzoni & Lynn, 2007). Some of this media attention, especially since the early 1990s, undoubtedly occurred as a result of the many patients recovering memories of childhood sexual assault during the course of therapy—many of which resulted in civil lawsuits or criminal charges. One such case involved Joan Borawick (*Borawick v. Shay*, 1994). Through hypnosis therapy, Borawick recovered memories of her aunt and uncle sexually assaulting her. These memories had remained dormant or inaccessible before the hypnotic therapy. Borawick testified, however, that her first repressed memory emerged while she was driving home from lunch one day, and shortly afterward, more memories of sexual abuse were recovered. The judge in the case excluded Borawick's testimony based on the hypnotist's lack of qualifications and the overall unreliability of the plaintiff's testimony. Although the court excluded the testimony in the Borawick case, it raises the possibility that had the hypnotist been more qualified, the court would have admitted the testimony. This ruling, by extension, gives credence to the idea that hypnosis is a reliable memory recovery technique if the hypnosis is conducted by a qualified practitioner, a point that is consistent with Münsterberg's views—though not with the treatment of hypnosis in all jurisdictions.

The belief that hypnosis can exhume forgotten memories remains prevalent, among both laypeople and professionals. Yapko (1994) conducted a survey of over 850 psychotherapists regarding their views on hypnosis and memory. Seventy-five percent of the respondents endorsed the statement that hypnosis allows patients to recall things that were not accessible without hypnosis accurately. A significant number of the therapists erroneously believed that memories obtained through hypnosis were more likely to be accurate, and that hypnosis can be used to recover accurate memories even from as far back as birth. Comparable rates of therapists endorsing hypnosis were reported by Poole, Lindsay, Memon, and Bull (1995) in their survey of licensed psychologists in the United States and Great Britain. Legault and Laurence (2007) reported similar results with a sample of Canadian therapists and social workers.

Laypeople hold similar beliefs about the effectiveness of hypnosis as a memory recovery tool. Johnson and Hauck (1999) evaluated the general public's beliefs and opinions about hypnosis and the source of those beliefs with a diverse sample consisting of undergraduate students, members of a social club, attendees of a women's spirituality conference, and members of a retirees' association. The results indicated that although the various sample groups obtained their information about hypnosis from different sources, their beliefs about hypnosis were remarkably consistent, and most respondents endorsed hypnosis as a form of therapy. Respondents also believed that hypnosis reduces the time needed to uncover issues that are the cause of a patient's problems.

In a more recent survey, Green and colleagues (2006) found that these beliefs are not culturally specific. Green et al.'s sample consisted of college students from Austria, Iran, Germany, and the United States. A total of 280 undergraduate students (70 from each country sampled) completed questionnaires assessing their opinions and beliefs about hypnosis. Although responses to some items varied by country, there was remarkable similarity across many items, suggesting that certain views and attitudes about hypnosis are not culturally specific. More important, on average 90% of the respondents agreed that hypnosis was a useful therapeutic technique to recover memories, a belief that did not vary with sample location (see Bornstein, 2017).

In fact, not only do many people believe that hypnosis is an effective memory recovery technique, but this belief is so pervasive that it can influence verdicts in criminal cases. For example, Wagstaff, Vella, and Perfect (1992) found that mock jurors were more likely to vote guilty when they were told that the evidence presented in the trial had been obtained through hypnosis; therefore, jurors gave greater credence to evidence that had been elicited through hypnosis because of the common, and possibly erroneous, belief that hypnosis is a reliable memory retrieval technique. For researchers, this is a troubling finding, given that research has shown the opposite to be the case. It is important to note that other researchers (e.g., Greene, Wilson, & Loftus, 1989) found that hypnotically retrieved memories were more persuasive than nonhypnotically refreshed memories that were retrieved after a week delay. However, nonhypnotically refreshed memories that were immediately retrieved were more persuasive than hypnotically refreshed memories.

In Münsterberg's time, most clinical practitioners, as well as the general population, viewed hypnosis as a reliable memory recovery technique. Since that time, this position has not been universally accepted. In fact, some established researchers, mostly in the United States, support the opposite position (Orne, 1979; Perry, 1997). Diamond (1980) went so far as to suggest that hypnotically refreshed memories are so unreliable and susceptible to suggestion that witnesses who have been hypnotized should not, under any circumstances, be allowed to testify in legal proceedings. Such skepticism concerning the efficacy of hypnosis as a memory recovery technique has continued to spread (Webert, 2003).

In summary, the fact that many clinical practitioners and laypeople share similar beliefs about the efficacy of hypnosis as a memory recovery technique has important implications for the legal system. If hypnosis is used to recover memory, and jurors believe that hypnotically refreshed memories are accurate, then jurors may be more likely to believe witnesses who have undergone hypnosis, such as in the Wagstaff et al. (1992) study. If these hypnotically refreshed memories are unreliable, then jurors could be misled by their confidence in the hypnotic memory recovery process.

Hypnosis and Memory: Empirical Findings

The research on forensic hypnosis has focused on three areas: accuracy of recall, confidence, and suggestibility. Most of the suggestibility research addresses whether hypnotized persons are more likely than nonhypnotized controls to incorporate suggested information into memory. A subset of the suggestibility literature looks at more extreme cases involving behavior—namely, whether hypnotized persons can be induced to commit crimes.

Recall Accuracy (Hypermnesia)

Generally, *hypermnesia* refers to increased recall over repeated testing (Payne, 1987), but more specifically, as it pertains to hypnosis, hypermnesia refers to increased recollection under hypnosis as opposed to the normal waking state. For example, True (1949), in his classic studies, claimed that adults who were hypnotized and age regressed to 4, 7, and 11 years old could remember the exact day of the week of their birthdays that year. Quite a feat indeed! However, Nash (1987) failed to replicate these findings with more methodologically sound experiments. In fact, Nash found no evidence that age regression increased recall accuracy.

Relinger (1984) reviewed the scientific literature on hypnotic hypermnesia. He divided the research into three types of studies involving (1) recall of nonmeaningful material, (2) recall of meaningful material, and (3) laboratory simulations of forensic situations. The results indicated that hypnosis consistently enhanced recall of meaningful material when measured in a free narrative format and that recall of nonsense material was generally not improved with hypnosis.

Consistent with Relinger's findings, Erdelyi (1994) also found that hypnosis increased recall for meaningful material (e.g., poetry, meaningful pictures). Erdelyi examined studies that were categorized according to the type of stimulus and memory tests. He found no hypnotic hypermnesic effect with recognition tests for nonmeaningful material (e.g., nonsense syllables, word lists). Erdelyi also suggested that the repeated retrieval effort and not hypnosis was responsible for hypermnesia; thus, repeated testing without hypnosis yields as much hypermnesia as with hypnosis. Other researchers have generally replicated these findings; hypnosis confers a memorial advantage for meaningful material (see Stager & Lundy, 1985) but not for meaningless material (see Salzberg & DePiano, 1980).

One thing that should be noted is that these studies have considered the total amount recalled, which tends to be a dubious measure of accuracy. Any measure of accuracy must consider the amount of correctly recalled material as well as the amount of incorrectly recalled material. In other words, is hypnosis increasing only accurate recall, or are increases in accurate recall accompanied by increases in recall of incorrect information? A memory enhancement technique is arguably not very effective if it increases recall of both accurate and inaccurate information. Ideally, any memory retrieval technique would increase only accurate information (see, e.g., discussion of the Cognitive Interview in Chapter 4). For hypnosis, this does not seem to be the case. Hypnosis lowers participants' threshold for responding and, consequently, they recall more information than nonhypnotized controls. However, the increase in accurate recall is offset by increases in recall errors. Thus, hypnosis leads to more information but does not result in more accurate recall (Erdelyi, 1994; Steblay & Bothwell, 1994). In fact, several studies have found that hypnosis produces more recall errors than nonhypnotic conditions (Kebbell & Wagstaff, 1997; Nogrady, McConkey, & Perry, 1985; Sheehan & Tilden, 1983). Contrary to popular belief, hypnosis is an effective mnemonic technique but one that comes with costs. The effects of hypnosis become even more dubious when considering people's extreme confidence in their hypnotically refreshed memories.

Confidence

Although hypnosis does not increase recall accuracy (when taking errors into account), it does increase confidence, and this increase occurs especially for incorrectly recalled items (Mazzoni & Lynn, 2007; Steblay & Bothwell, 1994). For example, Whitehouse, Dinges, Orne, and Orne (1988) examined hypnotic hypermnesia and confidence by first having participants with either high or low hypnotizability watch a brief film on poster making. After a delay, they completed two forced-recall tests. The first recall test was used as a baseline measure and no participants were hypnotized. During the second test, half of the participants were hypnotized. The authors employed a forced-recall test to control for response bias, and all participants were required to respond to each question even if they were guessing. Following each response, participants indicated how confident they were in the accuracy of their response.

Whitehouse et al. (1988) found no increase in the recall of accurate or inaccurate information for the hypnotized participants as compared to the nonhypnotized controls. There was, however, an increase in hypnotized participants' confidence ratings for incorrectly recalled items, and confidence inflation was greatest for highly hypnotizable participants. In addition, highly hypnotizable participants were significantly more confident in their guesses than were participants in the waking conditions.

Whitehouse et al.'s (1988) conclusions were confirmed in a meta-analytic study conducted by Steblay and Bothwell (1994). Steblay and Bothwell examined accuracy and confidence from laboratory studies that compared hypnotic and nonhypnotic recall. The meta-analysis included 24 studies and 38 tests of the hypothesis that hypnosis increased recall accuracy. Steblay and Bothwell found no benefit in recall from hypnosis. They did, however, find that hypnosis inflated confidence in recall accuracy. It should be noted, however, that the results for confidence are based on only nine studies, as not all the studies in the sample collected a confidence measure.

This *confidence inflation* effect, coupled with the recall accuracy findings, is problematic for proponents of the admissibility of hypnotically refreshed testimony. The data show that hypnosis does not increase accurate recall but does inflate confidence, and this finding is particularly strong for highly hypnotizable people. This is problematic for the legal system because confidence, at least when it comes to eyewitness identification (Wells & Quinlivan, 2009), is very persuasive to jurors. In fact, a highly confident eyewitness is one of the strongest and most persuasive types of evidence (see Bornstein & Greene, 2017; Cutler et al., 1988). Thus, hypnosis is dangerous in legal situations because of the potential to create a situation in which a highly hypnotizable witness will have high confidence in his or her erroneous memories and, thereby, be believed by the jury.

Suggestion

As described in the previous chapter, memory is highly susceptible to suggestion even in the absence of hypnosis. Although hypnosis does not increase accurate recall, it does increase suggestibility, or the willingness to accept and act on suggestions made by the hypnotizer. Braffman and Kirsch (1999) identified three factors that correlate highly with hypnotic suggestibility: imaginative suggestibility, motivation, and expectancies. Before examining each in turn, it is necessary to define relevant terminology. Many researchers have incorrectly used the terms "hypnotizability" and "hypnotic suggestibility" as though they were interchangeable (Kirsch et al., 2011). Hypnotizability is the change in suggestibility produced by hypnotic induction, as measured by differences in suggestibility for hypnotized and nonhypnotized participants. Hypnotic suggestibility is determined by responses to the *types* of suggestions commonly used in hypnosis (e.g., imagination) following a hypnotic induction.

Imaginative suggestibility is responsiveness to suggestions that can occur outside of the hypnotic context. Typically, hypnotic suggestions are imaginative suggestions that require the subject to "imagine a suggested state of affairs" (Kirsch & Braffman, 2001). It follows that an individual with a high level of imaginative suggestibility will therefore have a high level of hypnotic suggestibility, since both utilize the same type of suggestion (Braffman & Kirsch, 1999; Meyer & Lynn, 2011). In fact, "highly suggestible" would be a more accurate term than "highly hypnotizable" (Lynn, Laurence, & Kirsch, 2015), because most measures of hypnotizability actually assess responsiveness to hypnotic suggestions (Braffman & Kirsch, 1999; Kirsch et al., 2011).

How motivated an individual is to respond to suggestions is another critical determinant of hypnotic suggestibility, and a subject's motivation to behave in a way that supports the researcher's hypothesis—referred to as perceived demand characteristics—is of particular relevance to psychological experiments on hypnosis (Damaser et al., 2010; Orne, 1962). Often, participants are motivated to behave in a way consistent with these demands out of a desire to be a "good" participant. For instance, someone who believes that having feelings of involuntariness is the "correct" experience in hypnosis will behave in a way consistent with involuntariness during hypnosis in order to appear as a "good" patient or participant. Consequently, during hypnosis the person will actively use a variety of cognitive mechanisms to interpret the suggestions in a way that permits performing the suggestion and subjective demands (i.e., believing he or she did not control the movement) of the hypnotic suggestion (Barnier, Dienes, & Mitchell, 2008). Individual motivation will not always lead to enhanced responding, however. Motivations altered by boredom, frustration, poor rapport with the hypnotist, or desire to maintain an appearance of control can decrease hypnotic responding (Lynn & Rhue, 1991; Meyer & Lynn, 2011; Sheehan, Green, & Truesdale, 1992).

Expectations about what an individual will experience during hypnosis can strongly influence that individual's hypnotic suggestibility. These expectations, developed through life experiences, often define the hypnotic experience. Most individuals already have a preconceived notion about hypnosis, frequently rooted in movies, books, stories, and popular culture (see Bornstein, 2017; Green et al., 2006). These expectancies about hypnosis (true or not), like motivation, play a significant role in shaping the hypnotic experience.

An experience is defined as "hypnosis" during the induction. This labeling has several important consequences, the most important of which is the activation of all the expectations and beliefs an individual has regarding hypnosis (Wagstaff, 2009). These expectations function similarly to a self-fulfilling prophecy, in that the more someone expects a phenomenon to occur, the more likely it is to do so. Say that one of the college students from the study by Green and colleagues (2006) goes through a hypnotic induction. Because she already holds the expectancy that her memory will be enhanced, she is more likely to recall an early childhood memory after being given a hypnotic suggestion, even if that memory is false. In fact, research consistently reveals this pattern of prolific responding in instances of hypnotic recall (Erdelyi, 1994). This productivity is accompanied by a decrease in overall accuracy and an unfounded increase in confidence. Why is that? According to the response bias explanation, it is due to participants adopting a lowered or lax response criterion (Wagstaff, Wheatcroft, & Jones, 2011). In nonhypnotic situations, people more critically evaluate their responses and are less prone to dub a memory "real" if they are somewhat unsure of its authenticity. The expectation that hypnosis improves memory causes participants not only to report more memories, but also to have higher confidence in their accuracy simply because the memories were elicited during a hypnotic procedure. This is not to say that inaccurate memories are inevitable. Studies that use procedures which share features of a hypnotic induction (i.e., encouraging concentration, attention, and relaxation), like focused meditation, show better recall without the undesirable changes in accuracy or confidence (Wagstaff et al., 2004). Therefore, the expectations activated from an induction, and not the actual hypnosis, lead to increased hypnotic suggestibility.

The role induction plays in hypnosis is not limited only to previously held expectations. Equally important are suggestions made during an induction, which often redefine, emphasize, and develop specific expectations of the subject to increase hypnotic suggestibility. A hallmark of a good hypnotist is the use of language that encourages a state of relaxation (Wagstaff, 2009).

Hypnotists also increase hypnotic suggestibility by defining performance standards (Meyer & Lynn, 2011). The extent to which a performance standard is difficult to attain determines subsequent hypnotic suggestibility. Lynn, Vanderhoff, Shindler, and Stafford (2002) manipulated participants' performance standards, finding that when the experimenter defined hypnosis as entering a trance, as compared to simple cooperation with the hypnotist, participants exhibited correspondingly low and high levels of responsiveness. Additionally, McConkey (1986) found that people who are highly suggestible have easy-to-attain performance standards compared to people with low suggestibility.

Expectancies can be formed through explicit instructions or suggestions given by the hypnotist. By redefining beliefs about the "powers" of hypnosis, hypnotists can essentially prime individuals for specific hypnotic responses. For example, a hypnotist might state "hypnosis allows you to access memories as early as infancy," thereby suggesting to participants that not only can they expect to recall such memories, but through hypnosis, they would be capable of performing a task that they are normally incapable of doing. These suggestions provide an explanation for the occurrence of a particular hypnotic phenomenon, changing their expectations and increasing the likelihood that they will respond accordingly to later suggestions. Yet why do hypnotized participants report remembering things or doing things while under hypnosis that would normally be considered beyond their abilities?

One explanation is the *discrepancy detection principle*, which states that misleading information will likely bias people the most when they do not detect discrepancies between postevent information and memory for an original event (Hall, Loftus, & Tousignant, 1984). Applied to hypnosis, individuals are more apt to report pseudomemories for a hypnotically suggested event if the event could have conceivably occurred in real life and there is a reasonable explanation for why they did not previously remember it (Lynn, Matthews, & Barnes, 2009). A prime example of this is seen in pseudomemories developed during hypnotic age regression procedures. In a widely cited experiment, Spanos and colleagues (1999) gave participants a plausible explanation for why they would be able to access memories from the day after their birth. More specifically, they were told that they were high cognitive monitors, a condition that developed during the first days of birth from coordinated and practiced eye movements. Moreover, they were made to believe that they had experienced the event in question (having a mobile hanging above their crib). Two of the groups were submitted to age regression procedures, either hypnosis or "guided mnemonic restructuring."[1] Interestingly, 68 of the 78 participants who experienced age regression reported day-after-birth memories, with the nonhypnotic group reporting (95%, 37 of 39) more than the hypnotic group (79%, 31 of 39). The difference could be because the former group was told that while hypnosis only works with high hypnotizables, everyone could recall memories through guided mnemonic restructuring. This suggestion may have developed positive expectancies in participants by endorsing the belief that memory recall was likely, easy, accurate, and plausible, all of which led to increased hypnotic suggestibility.

In another experiment by Spanos, Menary, et al. (1991), participants incorporated the expectations expressed by the hypnotist into their past-life identity hypnotic reenactments. The "realness" participants assigned to the past-life identities also reflected suggestions communicated by the experimenter, with more participants assessing the identity as real when the experimenter defined the experience as real instead of imagined. It is apparent that expectations developed or encouraged by the hypnotist can have significant and immediate effects on hypnotic suggestibility.

Given how expectancies and motivations set the stage for hypnotic suggestibility, it is easy to forget the importance of individual differences in *non*hypnotic suggestibility (discussed at greater length in Chapter 8). In

[1] There was a no treatment control group that was not administered any memory-enhancing protocol, and this group was also not asked to produce any memories from early childhood. They were only asked if they had any dreams about infancy in the previous week (see Spanos et al., 1999, p. 207). Therefore, they were not included in the analyses of false memories.

fact, some studies did not find a significant relationship between induction and hypnotic responding, reporting instead that highly suggestive people respond similarly to both hypnotic and nonhypnotic imaginative suggestions (Braffman & Kirsch, 1999; Meyer & Lynn, 2011). This implies that inductions increase hypnotic suggestibility by making certain motivations and expectations more salient.

By first understanding how hypnosis influences suggestibility, we are then able to investigate the means of mitigating the unwanted effects of hypnosis, specifically, the increase in memory errors. The question, then, is whether there are ways to deter pseudomemories and improve overall accuracy. There has been moderate success in several experiments that manipulated motivations by either providing monetary incentives for discrimination between real and fake memories (Murrey, Cross, & Whipple, 1992) or changing perceived demand characteristics by implying the experiment was over (Barnier & McConkey, 1992). Other studies have reversed false memories by providing participants with an easy out (a "hidden observer"[2]) that allows them to account for reported pseudomemories while maintaining the expectations of the hypnotic context (Spanos et al., 1989; Spanos, Quigley, et al., 1991), although these findings have sometimes failed to replicate (Green, Lynn, & Malinoski, 1998).

In determining the likelihood of pseudomemories, Barnier and McConkey (1992) suggested that it is the level of hypnotizability that makes the difference. The fact that highly hypnotizable people are more susceptible to pseudomemories than those with lower hypnotizability may be due to the positive expectancies typically possessed by highly hypnotizable individuals (Lynn et al., 2009). A positive expectancy translates to a stronger conviction that they will respond hypnotically in some way, meaning they are more hypnotically suggestible. It follows that they would be more susceptible to developing pseudomemories following a hypnotic suggestion than people with negative response expectancies. Yet another reason for this phenomenon is that highly hypnotizable individuals are typically more committed to being a "good hypnotic subject" (Wagstaff et al., 2011). In Barnier and McConkey's (1992) experiment, only after the highly hypnotizable participants believed the study was over did their high rate of pseudomemories disappear. In other words, when the demand characteristics of the study were not applicable, the participants no longer aligned their behavior to fit that of a "good subject." Going a step further, this desire could be a symptom of the overarching

[2] Based on the work of Hilgard (1977), hypnosis researchers have employed a version of the hidden observer manipulation to help participants discriminate fact from fantasy such as the one used by Spanos et al. (1989). With the hidden observer, participants are told that deeply hypnotized people have a hidden part of the mind that is resistant to suggestion and if this hidden part is contacted by the hypnotist, then the hypnotized person will recall real memories (Spanos et al., 1989).

trait of social compliance. Indeed, several studies have reported that highly hypnotizable people are more susceptible to social influence (e.g., Spanos et al., 1989).

In one of the few studies that explored pseudomemories' resistance to cross-examination in court, Spanos et al. (1989) discovered that the number of misattributions, misidentifications in the lineup, and disavowals during cross-examination were related to the level of hypnotizability, not the use of hypnotic interrogation procedures. In keeping with experimental demand of acting as a good subject, the behavior of high hypnotizables changed depending on what the contextual demands for a good subject were. Initially, they might have made misattributions because they corresponded with the perceived demand to agree with information implied by the highly suggestive and leading questions; but when these demands changed during cross-examination, they were more inclined to change their previous answers. Additionally, high hypnotizables were much more likely to disavow their statements in the "hidden part" cross-examination than in the stringent cross-examination condition. In the stringent cross-examination condition, where participants were made to believe that a change of story would indicate dishonesty, they were less inclined to disavow their statements. Spanos et al. (1989) concluded that "variations in resistance to cross-examination are tied to participants' perceptions about how their disavowals are likely to be evaluated by significant others" (p. 288). Theoretically, then, by manipulating specific expectancies or motivations held by participants, pseudomemories can be reduced even for those most inclined to develop them.

Other researchers have looked at encouraging stringent monitoring and a conservative response criterion in the search for an effective way to reduce pseudomemories. According to the activation monitoring theory of false memories, higher rates of false memories persist when people do not monitor their responses in hypnosis because they assume hypnotically elicited memories will be accurate (Roediger, Watson, McDermott, & Gallo, 2001). If these beliefs were discounted through a negative suggestion about hypnosis, people may be disinclined to assume the memories are true, and false memory reports would decrease as a result of closer monitoring. Consistent with this theory, Dasse, Elkins, and Weaver (2015) determined that false memories are reduced in highly hypnotizable participants when monitoring is heightened and they are given a negative suggestion about their performance. Interestingly, a negative suggestion about performance reduced false memories more than a negative suggestion about hypnosis, supporting Spanos and colleagues' (1989) conclusion that targeting highly hypnotizable individuals' desire to be a "good subject" can be useful in managing false memories.

Understanding ways to safeguard against the development of pseudomemories in hypnosis is critically important when hypnotically refreshed memories are relied on in real-world settings. This is especially true with eyewitnesses, where the consequences of reporting false memories as accurate are notably detrimental, particularly when accompanied by a high level of confidence. Similar results may be seen in the related misinformation effect, which can also create false memories (see Chapter 8). Wagstaff et al. (2008) used the principles of response bias theory to reduce pseudomemories arising from the misinformation effect. Across two experiments, they found that providing both a warning about misleading information and a posthypnotic suggestion to discriminate between true and false information eliminated the misinformation effect. The misinformation effect disappeared, regardless of when the combination was administered (i.e., whether before or after participants first committed to inaccurate answers). In addition, the inflated confidence that is typically seen with hypnotically refreshed memories was absent. Once again, changing participants' expectations and demand characteristics mitigated the negative effects of hypnosis on memory.

It is clear that the popular belief that hypnosis inevitably leads to automatic and involuntary compliance with suggestions is not true. In actuality, people vary in their responsiveness to hypnotic suggestions as a function of many interacting variables, including nonhypnotic suggestibility, motivation, and expectancies. Hypnotic responsiveness is not caused by the hypnosis itself, but rather by expectations and motivations that are activated when a context is defined as hypnotic. Hypnotic suggestibility may be increased even more depending on what the hypnotist chooses to emphasize, define, or introduce throughout the induction and suggestion stages of hypnosis. The factors that hypnotists rely on to increase suggestibility are, conversely, the same ones that researchers manipulate in an effort to reduce the negative effects on memory attributed to hypnosis.

Crimes Committed by Hypnotized People

One particular concern about hypnosis, and one that Münsterberg himself addressed, was that an evil and skilled mesmerist could have an army of agents that would commit crimes. "One aspect offers itself at once: the hypnotised person may become the powerless instrument of the criminal will of the hypnotiser. He may press the trigger of the gun, may mix the poison into the food, may steal and forge, and yet the real responsible actor is not the one who commits the crime but the other one who is protected and who directed the deed by hypnotic suggestion" (pp. 219–220). Thus, agents under hypnotic control would commit all kinds of immoral acts, including murder, and would have no memory of the events in the waking state. Cinema fans may note the similarities between this hypothetical situation and the plot of *The Manchurian Candidate* (the 1962 original or 2004 remake; based on the 1959 novel by Richard Condon), wherein the main character serves as a brainwashed assassin who is a communist agent working in the United States. The Purple Man (a/k/a Kilgrave) also uses his hypnotic powers to control people, for criminal and other nefarious purposes, in the Jessica Jones comic books and television series. As far-fetched as it seems, the issue of hypnotic control has arisen in criminal cases in both the United States and Europe (see Laurence & Perry, 1983).

A pair of criminal cases from US history exemplify the complexities involved when hypnotic suggestion is employed as a criminal defense: *People v. Worthington* (1894) and *State v. Gray* (1895). In *Worthington*, a young woman (Worthington) was convicted of killing her second husband and sentenced to 25 years in jail. The woman appealed her case on the grounds that she was under the influence of hypnosis when she committed the act and was not in full command of her capacities. Trial records show that while the woman's first husband was abroad, she ran away with and married another man. When her original husband returned, he found Worthington and brought her back to the couple's home, where he ordered her to murder her second husband in order to preserve his honor as the first husband. Worthington acquiesced to his wishes and killed her second husband with a revolver supplied by the first. The court rejected her appeal, arguing that being told to do something was not the same as being hypnotized.

In contrast, in *State v. Gray* (1895) the court accepted that Thomas McDonald acted under the suggestion of his employer, Anderson Gray, when he committed murder. Gray, a wealthy farmer from Topeka, Kansas, hired McDonald as a farm hand. Gray quickly realized that he could exert control over McDonald through hypnosis, and, through hypnotic suggestion, Gray had McDonald murder a rival while Gray remained several miles away. McDonald confessed that he committed the murder while under the hypnotic influence of his employer. The court exonerated McDonald and convicted Gray. This marked the first American court case where the hypnotist was held responsible for a crime committed by someone under his or her hypnotic influence (see Figure 9.1).

In addition to these two American cases, one of the more famous and more recent cases of hypnotic coercion is that of Palle Hardrup, which took place in Denmark. In the 1940s, Hardrup committed two bank robberies in Copenhagen, where he shot and killed the bank tellers. At trial, Hardrup presented evidence that he was under the influence of hypnosis at the time of the robberies and was not in control of his actions. Hardrup was released, and his close friend and hypnotist was convicted. Interestingly, Hardrup was later committed to a mental institution, where he claimed that he was never hypnotized by his friend (Wagstaff, 2009). Despite the success of the defense in these cases, Perry (1997) reported that the number of cases in which hypnotic coercion is offered as a defense in the United States, and we suspect elsewhere as well, is very small.

Although the court rejected Worthington's defense, both McDonald and Hardrup were exonerated. Were the courts correct in their judgments of McDonald and Hardrup, that someone under the influence of hypnosis

THE HYPNOTIST MADE PRINCIPAL

His Subject Found Guiltless of Murder by a Kansas Court While He Bears the Penalty for the Crime.

TOPEKA, Kan., April 6.—The Supreme Court to-day rendered a decision in which hypnotism is recognized, both as a defense and as a ground for conviction of crime.

The case passed on came up from the Cowley County District Court. Thomas McDonald, without apparent provocation, shot and killed Thomas Patton near his home, in Winfield, May 5, 1894. He was arrested, charged with murder, and set up a defense that he was under the hypnotic influence of Anderson Gray, and was neither legally nor morally responsible for the deed. He was acquitted, and then Gray was put under arrest and tried for the murder. He was found guilty of murder in the first degree, notwithstanding the fact that he was not present when the crime was committed, the evidence for the State only going to show that he caused McDonald to commit the murder through hypnotic influence.

An appeal was taken to the Supreme Court, and, in an opinion rendered today, the ruling of the lower court was sustained.

The New York Times

Published: April 7, 1895

Figure 9.1. *New York Times* article reporting on the Kansas Supreme Court's decision to affirm *State v. Gray*.

can unwittingly be coerced into committing a crime? There has always been some debate as to whether a posthypnotic suggestion could be employed to induce a person to commit criminal or immoral acts at the behest of the hypnotist (see Laurence & Perry, 1983). In one of the earliest scientific treatments of the question, Levy (1955) acknowledged the debate but argued that the most reasonable position based on scientific study is that people can, in fact, be coerced into committing crimes through posthypnotic suggestion.

Levy's (1955) conclusion may seem odd; however, at the time he was writing, there were several laboratory demonstrations of hypnotized participants committing what normally would appear to that hypnotized participant (and others) as violent and/or immoral acts. For example, Wagstaff (2009) reported several demonstrations of hypnotized patients exposing themselves, throwing what they were led to believe was acid at an experimenter, committing minor thefts, and verbally berating others. In addition, Rowland (1939) and Young (1952) found that hypnotized participants would pick up what they believed to be a dangerous snake or throw acid at the experimenter while hypnotized but refused to do these things in the waking state. Due to the dramatic nature of these demonstrations, many researchers have questioned the ecological validity of the studies. More specifically, they have suggested that the deviant behavior occurred because the participants realized that they were in a contrived laboratory situation and they would not be responsible for their actions (e.g., Wagstaff, 2009). The studies, which involve inducing participants to act immorally or illegally, also raise ethical issues and would be very difficult to conduct under current ethical standards (see Chapter 1).

Orne and Evans (1965) tried to replicate the Rowland (1939) and Young (1952) studies using what is referred to as the simulator paradigm. In the simulator paradigm, nonhypnotizable participants, unbeknownst to the experimenter, are asked to feign being hypnotized and deceive the hypnotist/experimenter. They are, in effect, simulating hypnosis. In this study, there were 12 participants: six highly hypnotizable participants and six nonhypnotizable participants or simulators. Orne and Evans found that hypnotized participants and simulators were both willing to pick up a snake and throw acid at the experimenter when given a strong suggestion to do so. Given that there was no difference in the behavior exhibited between the groups, Orne posited that hypnosis was not required to compel people to engage in these immoral behaviors. The behavior is more a product of the participant's willingness to accept the suggestion of the experiment, or experimental demand, as opposed to hypnosis.

More recent evidence that hypnosis has no coercive effects was reported in a study by Wagstaff, Green, and Somers (1997). Wagstaff et al. hypothesized that people who had experienced hypnosis in the past, based on their experience with it, would know that there are no coercive effects of hypnosis. People who had no experience with hypnosis, on the other hand, would be more likely to believe in the coercive power of hypnosis. To test this hypothesis, Wagstaff et al. gave two groups, one with hypnosis experience and one without, a trial transcript in which the defendant testified that he was under hypnotic influence when he committed the crime and had done so against his will. The experimental task was to determine if the defendant was guilty. As predicted, many more of the people who had never been hypnotized were likely to find the defendant not guilty than were the participants who had experienced hypnosis. More specifically, many were willing to find him innocent in the group who had not been hypnotized. However, among the participants who had been hypnotized, not one was willing to find him innocent (i.e., none accepted the defense of automatism). This finding suggests that people who have been hypnotized realize, based on their experience, that people cannot be compelled to do things against their will when they are under hypnosis.

According to Orne, compliance has more to do with the degree of social pressure than hypnosis (Orne, 1972). Orne (1972) refers to Milgram's (1974) obedience studies as support for his position. In these studies, people were willing to give a harmful and potentially lethal shock to a confederate when instructed to do so by an experimenter. Although none of the participants were hypnotized, the majority still complied with the experimenter's instructions. In other words, it is more likely that obedience, rather than hypnosis, mediated the behavior of the participants in the Rowland (1939) and Young (1952) studies.

Similar to Orne (1972), Lynn and Rhue (1991) argued that, although involuntariness is a hallmark of hypnosis, hypnotic behavior (voluntary or involuntary) can be more easily explained by general cognitive and social mechanisms such as schemas, expectancies, agendas, hypnotizability, and situational demands. Viewed in this light, hypnotic behavior—up to and maybe even especially when it involves the commission of a crime—is not considered a loss of behavioral control but is, rather, goal-directed and strategic.

Admissibility of Hypnotically Induced Evidence in State and Federal Courts

When discussing the admissibility of hypnotically induced evidence in the United States, it is important to distinguish between testimony given by the criminal defendant and testimony given by the prosecution's witnesses. With regard to the defendant, the Supreme Court ruled in the landmark case *Rock v. Arkansas* (1987) that the state cannot invoke a per se rule of exclusion against a criminal defendant's testimony on the basis that it was hypnotically refreshed (Paterline, 2016). A per se exclusion rule would prohibit any memories retrieved during or after hypnosis from being introduced into evidence. The court stated that such a rule is a violation of the Fifth, Sixth, and Fourteenth Amendments, and that case-by-case evaluations must be made to determine if the hypnotically induced testimony is reliable enough to be given at trial. However, the court made it clear that this ruling applied only to criminal defendants testifying on their own behalf; therefore, the ruling did not bar per se rules of exclusion for witnesses who testify on behalf of the defense (Gill, 1989; see Scheflin & Frischhholz, 1999, for a comprehensive review of the history of forensic hypnosis).

Regarding the admissibility of testimony given by prosecution witnesses, state and federal courts that have addressed the issue have come to one of three conclusions: admissible, admissible contingent on predetermined guidelines having been met, or total inadmissibility (i.e., per se exclusion).

Five states and two federal circuits courts (7th and 9th Circuits; Louisiana, Maine, North Dakota, Tennessee, and Wyoming) have adopted the view that the jury should determine the credibility of the witness in light of the hypnosis.

Ten states (Colorado, Idaho, Kansas, Mississippi, New Jersey, Ohio, Oregon, South Dakota, Virginia, and Wisconsin) have adopted the view that testimony from prosecution witnesses retrieved through hypnosis can be admitted only if certain standards were adhered to during the hypnotic session (*People v. Romero*, 1987; *State v. Hurd*, 1981). The lead opinion on this topic is *State v. Hurd* (1981), where the New Jersey Supreme Court developed a series of guidelines that the hypnotist must follow for the testimony to be admissible: (1) Hypnosis should be conducted by a trained therapist, (2) the hypnotist should be independent of the prosecution, (3) information obtained prior to hypnosis should be recorded and retained, (4) the entire hypnosis session should be retained, and (5) only the hypnotist and subject should be present during the hypnosis. These standards, however, differ among jurisdictions, but all aim to reduce the chances of testimony being given if it was retrieved in overly suggestive sessions. In Oregon, a statute was passed that allowed hypnotically induced testimony to be given by both prosecution and defense witnesses, provided that the entire hypnotic session was recorded and the recording was made available to the opposing party (OR. REV. STAT. § 136.675, 1990).

The most common practice is to bar hypnotically refreshed memories altogether (Bartol & Bartol, 2006). In line with this standard, 22 states and one federal circuit court (5th Circuit; Alaska, Arizona, Arkansas, Connecticut, Delaware, Florida, Georgia, Hawaii, Illinois, Indiana, Iowa, Maryland, Massachusetts, Michigan, Minnesota, Missouri, Nebraska, New York, North Carolina, Pennsylvania, Utah, and Washington) find hypnotically induced testimony inadmissible. Likewise, the state of California passed a statute allowing for posthypnotic testimony to be admitted, contingent on the testimony's containing only information that was recalled prior to hypnosis.

In contrast, nine states and the District of Columbia have not reached a ruling on the admissibility of hypnotically induced testimony (Kentucky, Montana, Nevada, New Hampshire, New Mexico, Rhode Island, South Carolina, Vermont, and West Virginia). Additionally, several federal circuit courts (1st, 2nd, 4th, 6th, 8th, 10th, and 11th Circuits) have not ruled on the general admissibility of hypnotically induced testimony.[7] Likewise, the Third Circuit held that posthypnotic testimony was admissible because, in the specific case, the eyewitness's memory did not change after the hypnosis; however, the court did not give a general rule on admissibility.[8]

Lastly, lower courts in Alabama, Oklahoma, and Texas have ruled on the issue of hypnotically induced testimony, but their highest courts have not done so. The ruling in Alabama allows for this type of testimony, but only if the witness's posthypnotic identification was the same as it was prior to hypnosis. The ruling in Oklahoma, like the statute in California, allowed posthypnotic testimony if it contained only information recalled prior to hypnosis (*Harmon v. State*, 1985), whereas the ruling in Texas allowed for this type of testimony but only if the trial court deemed it reliable (*Zani v. State*, 1988).

Conclusions

Most of what Münsterberg says in this chapter is completely consistent with current thinking on hypnosis. First, he argues that hypnosis is an effective form of treatment. The empirical evidence suggests that hypnosis is indeed a very effective therapeutic technique for anxiety, obesity, phobias, and smoking cessation, to mention a few (see Kirsch, Montgomery, & Sapirstein, 1995). Münsterberg goes on to say that although hypnosis is an effective therapy technique, science cannot distinguish between hypnosis and nonhypnotic suggestion. This is a debate that continues today, as evinced by the two leading theories of hypnosis: the Hypnotic Trance and Cognitive-Behavioral views.

In addition, Münsterberg gives arguments refuting myths of hypnosis: the mesmerist controlling people with a glance and the hypnotist coercing people to commit evil acts. These, too, are in accord with current scientific thinking on hypnosis. The empirical evidence is clear that participants who commit immoral acts under hypnosis are doing so based on experimental demand as opposed to hypnotic suggestion. Orne and colleagues (e.g., Orne, 1972; Orne et al., 1984), as well as others, have successfully demonstrated that when appropriate experimental controls are followed, hypnotized participants do not engage in immoral acts. Furthermore, Münsterberg acknowledges that not all people can be hypnotized and that the patient must agree to be hypnotized. This is in accordance with empirical findings showing that 10%–25% of the population cannot be hypnotized (Spiegel & Spiegel, 1978).

Finally, Münsterberg addresses the ways in which hypnosis can assist the court, by explaining how a trained hypnotist could prevent crime by giving inhibitory suggestions regarding the criminal behavior. Münsterberg describes how he successfully administered a suggestion to a patient to prevent that patient from committing a violent act; however, a review of subsequent research revealed no evidence for hypnosis working in such a way (which is not to say that it couldn't work, merely that we could find no published research demonstrating it).

There is one glaring omission in Münsterberg's chapter, and that is a discussion of hypnosis as a memory recovery technique. He alludes to the topic in passing but never discusses it at length. From the chapter, one could surmise that Münsterberg believes that what is recovered during hypnosis is accurate, and he expresses confidence that hypnotically induced confessions are reliable. Significantly to the contrary, research abundantly shows that hypnosis increases the risk of false memories (for review, see Bornstein, 2017; Mazzoni & Lynn, 2007). The omission is surprising, considering how aware Münsterberg is of the potential for suggestion in general to introduce errors into memory reports (see Chapter 8). Of course, in his day the emphasis was very much on therapeutic uses of hypnosis. It is a shame that we cannot know what he would think of the accumulated research on hypnosis and memory (in)accuracy.

10

The Prevention of Crime

In short, it is not criminals that are "born," but men with poorly working minds.

—Münsterberg, *On the Witness Stand* (p. 241)

In the chapter "The Prevention of Crime," Münsterberg discusses the criminal mind and the role of psychologists in crime prevention. He begins the chapter with a story about a patient. The patient was a well-mannered, upstanding family man who went to the hospital after an accident. The patient was given a small amount of morphine each night to help him deal with pain and allow him to get a restful night's sleep. The patient became addicted to morphine and, as a result, lost his job and family.[1] Münsterberg used this example to make his major point in the chapter: The patient was not born with the addiction; it was created in the hospital. In other words, criminals are not born; they are made.

Münsterberg does not discount the role of genetics, however. In fact, his central thesis is that all people are born with impulses that may be desirable but are illegal or socially unacceptable. However, for a variety of reasons, the lawful person can resist or suppress these impulses, and it is only the person with some mental defect (i.e., being weak-willed, feeble-minded, etc.) who succumbs. Münsterberg believes that every idea gives rise to a counteridea: "The attractive impression gives the impulse to extend the arm, and the thought of danger gives the counterimpulse to withdraw the arm. The one tends to inhibit the other; the more vivid idea overpowers the weaker one; we do not grasp for the poisonous fruit, because the danger holds us back" (p. 237). For all humans, it is "a balancing of opposing forces" (p. 237) to hold

[1] The example shows that the current opioid crisis might differ in magnitude compared to previous generations, but perhaps not so much in kind.

in check those unlawful impulses, and criminals, according to Münsterberg, do not have the mental acuity or power to suppress the unlawful impulses. This definition is similar to the *Durham rule*, which states that a person is not guilty if the criminal act is a product of mental defect or disease (see *Durham v. United States*, 1954). As will be discussed later (in the section on "Criminal Responsibility"), the difficulty is in how to define mental defect or disease (see Finkel, 1995).

What, then, is the role of the psychologist in preventing these impulses from taking over and driving a person to criminality? According to Münsterberg, the role of the psychologist is to conduct experiments to discover the cues, triggers, or behaviors that allow these unacceptable impulses to overcome their counterimpulses. He argues that experiments, like reaction time studies, can be used to study what reinforces or inhibits these impulses. The same methods can be employed to study the effects of alcohol, bromides, caffeine, and so forth.

Finally, he discusses the influence of the environment as a way to prevent crime. "Everything which strengthens family life and works against its dissolution, everything which gives the touch of personal sympathy to the forlorn, helps towards the prevention of crime" (p. 262). Münsterberg's ideas about the importance of stability in the home and the environment foreshadow some of the most current thinking on how to prevent antisocial behavior.

Throughout the chapter, Münsterberg repeatedly states that criminals are "made, not born." Münsterberg is touching on a very important topic that scientists have debated for years, on the origins of criminality as well as pretty much everything else—a topic that is often referred to as the Nature versus Nurture debate. Is behavior the product of one's genetic makeup and related factors (Nature), or is it determined by the environment in which an individual develops (Nurture)? In terms of criminal behavior, are people genetically predisposed to be serial killers, rapists, or con-artists, or are they products of their environment? Over the last 10–15 years there has been an explosion of research on this topic as it relates to antisocial and criminal behavior. The surge in research is likely the result of technological advances that have made it easier to study genotypes and the brain than in the past. The bulk of this research is consistent with Münsterberg's point: Both genetic and environmental issues contribute to making a criminal, and which is more important, genes or the environment, is probably dependent on the individual. However, it is undeniable that both elements interact in determining behavior. For the remainder of the chapter, we consider the evolutionary perspective of criminal behavior, followed by the contributions of genetics, brain structures, and diet to antisocial behavior in general and to psychopathy in particular. We next discuss the importance of biological–environmental interactions, and the chapter concludes with a section on prevention of crime and forensic assessment.

Lombroso's Evolutionary Perspective

The Italian doctor Cesare Lombroso is credited as the father of modern criminology with the publication of his book *The Criminal Man* (Lombroso, 1876/2006), among other writings. Lombroso was an army doctor who became interested in the criminal mind while working in army lunatic asylums. In 1871, Lombroso was working as doctor and prison psychiatrist in a hospital for the criminally insane. During an autopsy of Giuseppe Villella, a notorious Calabrian thief and arsonist, Lombroso discovered that his subject had an indentation at the back of his skull, which he interpreted as a smaller cerebellum (the part of the brain that primarily regulates muscular activity). Lombroso concluded from this evidence, as well as that from other criminals he had studied, that some people were born with a propensity to offend and were savage throwbacks to early man. Lombroso's contribution to the field of criminology is undeniable, as he was one of the first to realize that crime and criminals could be studied scientifically.

Essentially, Lombroso believed that criminality was inherited and that criminals could be identified by physical defects that marked them as being atavistic or savage. The physical characteristics that marked criminals were thought to be from a more primitive stage of human evolution. For example, some of the physical markers identified were a large jaw, sloping forehead, and single palmar crease—all characteristics of early hominids like Neanderthals. According to Lombroso, different characteristics were associated with different patterns of criminal behavior. Manual dexterity and small, wandering eyes were the marks of the common thief, whereas murderers could be identified based on their glassy stares, bloodshot eyes, and big, hawk-like noses. Lombroso did not confine his studies to males; he was also interested in the female criminal. His measurements led him to conclude that female criminals were far more ruthless than their male counterparts. Female criminals tended to be lustful and immodest; they were shorter and more wrinkled, had darker hair, and smaller skulls than "normal" women. Lombroso's ideas dominated criminology in Europe in the late 19th and early 20th centuries.

The Genetic Basis of Crime

In his book *The Anatomy of Violence*, Adrain Raine (2013) relates the story of Jeffrey Landrigan. Landrigan never knew his biological father and was adopted at a young age. His adopted family provided a loving and supportive environment for Landrigan; however, he had brushes with the law beginning when he was 11. At age 20, he stabbed a friend to death outside the friend's trailer home. The two had been drinking, and Landrigan's friend had asked him to be the godfather of his child; for some reason, this request provoked Landrigan. After serving 7 years of a 21-year sentence, Landrigan escaped from prison and resurfaced in Arizona, where he met Chester Dyer, whom he later strangled with an electrical cord. Landrigan was convicted and sentenced to death. As Raine reports, another death row inmate told Landrigan about an inmate named Darrell Hill, whom he met when he was on death row in Arkansas. Hill turned out to be Landrigan's biological father. Hill, like Landrigan, killed two people and escaped from prison once. As if that were not enough to convince one of the genetic component of a predisposition for violence, Hill's father, Landrigan's biological grandfather, was also a criminal, who was shot to death by the police. Given that Landrigan never met his biological father or grandfather and was raised in a supportive family, the fact that he still followed in his ancestors' violent footsteps certainly suggests that there is a genetic basis for criminal behavior. However, to really understand this link, one has to examine adoption and twin studies, which allow for better experimental control than a single case study.

One way to explore the influence of genetics is to examine adoption studies. Adopted children are raised apart from their biological parents, giving researchers the opportunity to evaluate the effects of the environment on children who have biological parents with criminal records (experimental group) and those without (control group). The researcher can then evaluate the criminal history of adopted children to see if they are more like their biological or adopted parents.

In what must be one of the most comprehensive adoption studies, Mednick, Gabrielli, and Hutchings (1984) examined the criminal records of over 14,000 adopted children as well as the criminal records of their biological and adopted parents. The adoption records came from Denmark and occurred over a 20-year period (1927–1947). The authors defined criminal record based on number of criminal convictions. The results of the study definitively pointed out the genetic influence on crime. If there was no history of conviction for either the biological or adoptive parents, then the adopted children had a conviction rate of 13.5%. If the adopted parents had one conviction, then the conviction rate of adopted sons went up a little over 1 percentage point (14.7%). However, if the biological parents had at least one criminal conviction, the conviction rate spiked up to 20%, and if both sets of parents, adopted and biological, had a conviction, the conviction rate for adopted sons was about 24.5%. The authors also reported that even though the genetic influence of the biological parents ends at birth for adopted children, only biological parent criminality was significantly associated with increased convictions for the sons. As noted in the Landrigan case, there is clearly a genetic link; however, it is not the full story. Most adopted sons (84%) did not commit crimes, and an examination of the conviction rate of sons whose biological fathers had three or more convictions revealed that 75% had no criminal convictions. This finding indicates that having a biological predisposition toward criminality is far from deterministic.

Along with adoption studies, researchers have examined twins. About 2% of people are twins and of those, most are dizygotic or fraternal twins.

Fraternal twins occur when two separate zygotes develop in the womb at the same time. They are essentially as similar genetically as any sibling pair. Identical twins develop from the same zygote and, thus, are genetically equivalent but are much rarer and make up about 8% of all twins. Although twins are rare, they afford the opportunity to study the effects of genetics on behavior when the environment is held constant (or as constant as it can be). Researchers have employed twin studies to understand the effects of genes on many behaviors, including antisocial behavior (Baker, Burton, & Raine, 2002; Baker et al., 2007). Typically, in twin studies, the genetic contribution of a particular personality trait is determined by comparing the similarity of the trait in fraternal and identical twins—in other words, how similar identical twins are to each other relative to how similar fraternal twins are.

In a comprehensive twin study in southern California, Baker and colleagues (2002) recruited over 1,200 9-year-old twins to participate in a study on antisocial behavior. The researchers interviewed caregivers and teachers with a variety of measures all focused on antisocial behavior, such as questions asking whether the child skipped school, bullied other children, mistreated animals, or set fires. The results revealed that heritability, the amount of a trait that can be accounted for by genetics, was around .40 or .50 depending on where the measures came from—the teacher, parent, or child. This means that a little less than half of the variation in antisocial behavior was due to genetic variability. It is important to note that this also means that a little more than half of the variation in antisocial behavior is a product of the environment. These results have been replicated many times (see Moffitt, 2005, for a meta-analytic review).

Given the genetic component of criminal behavior, researchers have continually looked for the responsible gene(s). One such search led to the XYY syndrome (also known as Jacob's syndrome), a genetic condition in which a human male has an extra male (Y) chromosome, giving him a total of 47 chromosomes instead of the usual 46. This 47 XYY karyotype occurs roughly once in every 1,000 male births. From the time of this discovery, researchers have believed the extra Y chromosome to be the root of criminal behavior. This suggestion likely comes from the idea that the Y chromosome triggers the formation of male genitalia and the production of testosterone, and males are (in part thanks to testosterone) more aggressive than females; therefore, an extra Y chromosome would logically increase aggressiveness, which would lead to more criminal behavior.

To test this idea, Jacobs and colleagues (1965) conducted a study of inmates in a Scottish maximum-security hospital who were classified as dangerous, violent, and having criminal propensities. Jacobs et al. found that 1 in 28 had the XYY syndrome, which is much higher than what is found in the normal population (1 in 1,000). The researchers interpreted this to indicate that XYY syndrome may be the cause of antisocial behavior. Consistent with this thinking, Price and Whatmore (1967) reported a significant difference in the mean age of first criminal conviction for XYY males, age 13, compared with age 18 for their XY counterparts. In addition, the XYY group had a much higher number of convictions for crimes against property than XY males but a much lower number of convictions for crimes against persons. The families of the XYY males also reported a history of behavioral problems from early childhood. As Raine (2013) noted, these results and sensationalized media reports fueled a debate regarding the criminality and dangerousness of people with XYY syndrome.

However, the methodology of these early studies jeopardizes the interpretation of their results. The studies had small sample sizes and sample populations in which XYY syndrome men were more likely to be represented. For example, some of the earlier studies used relatively tall men rather than a random sample. Due to the extra Y chromosome, men with XYY syndrome tend to be taller than average, so this selection bias could have inflated the number of men in the study with XYY syndrome, which would skew the results and jeopardize the interpretations.

Witkin et al. (1976) debunked the myth of men with XYY syndrome being violent criminals. Using the comprehensive records of the Danish draft board, Witkin et al. screened a cohort of over 4,000 men, and 1 in 345 were identified as being XYY. This is higher than what is expected in the general population, but Witkin et al. chose to karyotype only the tallest men due to the cost of the testing (practicality often wins out in science!). This undoubtedly increased the percentage of XYY men that were identified. There were, however, some important results. First, XYY males were significantly more likely to be convicted of crimes than were controls. In fact, 42% of XYY males had criminal records, compared with only 9% of normal (XY) males. Witkin et al. reported, however, that the majority of these crimes were nonviolent, property crimes, such as vehicular offenses and shoplifting (see also Gotz, Johnstone, & Ratcliffe, 1999). More important, when only violent crimes were considered, there were no differences found between the XYY males and the controls in terms of criminal convictions. Second, both the mean IQ and educational attainment levels were significantly lower in the XYY group than in the control males, suggesting that any correlation between the XYY karyotype and criminality may be mediated by intellectual differences. Gotz et al. (1999) found similar results in a smaller longitudinal study in which XYY men (n = 16) were compared to XXY men (n = 13). These results run contrary to the notion that XYY males are simply more likely to be violent criminals.

Although Witkin et al. (1976) were able to dispel the myth that XYY men are prone to aggression, researchers have turned their focus to the gene that produces monoamine oxidase A (MAOA). MAOA is an enzyme in the brain that breaks down neurotransmitters such as noradrenaline, adrenaline, serotonin, and dopamine. These neurotransmitters are involved in impulse control, attention, and other cognitive functions. MAOA was first discovered when Brunner et al. (1993) genotyped a Dutch family that had been notorious for violence and crime. Brunner et al. found that the male offspring had a complete lack of the MAOA enzyme due to a genetic mutation of the MAOA gene. This finding has been supported by research on mice in which the MAOA gene has been removed (Shih et al., 1999). Shih et al. found that removing this gene in mice increased aggressive and violent behavior.

Although low levels of MAOA may automatically produce violent mice, human males require a push from the environment. The interaction between low levels of MAOA and the environment was noted in a study by Caspi et al. (2002), who found that males who had low levels of MAOA expression and were mistreated as children were more likely to develop antisocial behavior as adults than mistreated males with high levels of MAOA expression. Furthermore, maltreated children with low levels of MAOA had elevated levels of antisocial scores relative to children who were not mistreated with low levels of MAOA. In contrast, children with normal expression of MAOA displayed similar antisocial scores regardless of whether they were mistreated or not (Caspi et al., 2002).

A number of researchers and multiple studies have replicated the original findings of Caspi's team, demonstrating that the interaction between early exposure to abuse and low-activity MAOA increases the risk for antisocial behavior in men throughout their lifetime. Males with low expression of the MAOA gene are prone to criminal offending, conduct problems, and hostility. For example, Beaver and colleagues (Beaver, Boutwell, & Barnes, 2014; Beaver et al., 2013) linked low-activity MAOA with increased likelihood of males joining a gang and using a weapon in a fight. Similarly, Guo, Ou, Roettger, and Shih (2008) found that antisocial behaviors in male youth were associated with three genes: low-activity MAOA and two dopamine-related genes.

Once again, we come back to the question, are criminals born or made? The research is very clear that criminals are born *and* made. There is an interaction between one's genetic endowment and one's environment. The research demonstrates that male children with low expressions of MAOA, due to a genetic abnormality, are more likely to engage in antisocial and criminal behavior, but this appears to be the case only if they also come from bad environments or were mistreated as children (Beaver et al., 2013; Caspi et al., 2002; Guo et al., 2008). Other yet-to-be-discovered genetic markers might also play a part in predisposing individuals to violent/criminal behavior.

Brain Structures

Advances in brain imaging research are allowing unprecedented access to understanding the neurological roots of disorders such as psychopathy and antisocial behavior. Given the often-severe behaviors, such as violence and aggression, that correspond with such disorders, identifying factors that predispose psychopathy is particularly important.[2] Although functional and structural differences have been found in many areas of the brains of psychopathic versus nonpsychopathic individuals, most research has focused on two areas: the prefrontal cortex and the limbic system.

The Prefrontal Cortex

The prefrontal cortex is where higher level cognitive functions take place. Deficits in this region of the brain can have serious and wide-reaching implications, many of which are found in the behavior and characteristics of violent offenders, psychopaths, and antisocial individuals (Raine, 2013). Indeed, poor functioning in the prefrontal cortex is one of the most reliable correlates of violent behavior (Glenn & Raine, 2014; Yang & Raine, 2009). Researchers have put forth several hypotheses relating to prefrontal cortex function that account for this relationship. Perhaps the most well-known is the Somatic Marker Hypothesis (Damasio, 1994). Somatic markers are physiological responses such as increased heart rate, anxiety, and nausea that are associated with emotions. The hypothesis states that decisions are made through this association and are dependent upon whether the somatic marker is related to a reward or punishment (Damasio, 1994; Koenigs, 2012; Santana, 2016). Other theories suggest that the prefrontal cortex regulates and inhibits the amygdala (Koenigs, 2012) and plays a role in self-referential thought processes, which facilitate empathy, guilt, and embarrassment (Beer, John, Scabini, & Knight, 2006; Mitchell, Banaji, & Macrae, 2005). Prefrontal cortex dysfunction would thus inhibit those emotions.

Regardless of why, there is undeniably a relationship between prefrontal cortex dysfunction and violent behavior. In a meta-analysis of 43 brain imaging studies, Yang and Raine (2009) identified three subcomponents of the prefrontal cortex that exhibit abnormal functioning in violent individuals: the left dorsolateral prefrontal cortex (DLPFC), right anterior cingulate cortex, and right orbitofrontal cortex. The following sections will explore these prefrontal areas more closely.

Dorsolateral Prefrontal Cortex

The DLPFC is commonly thought of as being the "home" of executive functions such as planning, problem solving, self-regulation, cognitive flexibility, and modifying behavior in accordance with environmental feedback

[2] Psychopathy is characterized by a myriad of interpersonal, behavioral, and affective features (Dhingra & Boduszek, 2013). A person with psychopathy may be deceitful, charming, or impulsive; lack empathy; and show no remorse. Psychopathy is highly correlated with criminal and violent behavior (see Hare, Hart, & Harpur, 1991). Babiak and colleagues (2012) indicated that 15%–20% of the 2 million plus prisoners in the United States meet the clinical definition of psychopathy.

(Cummings & Miller, 2007; Fazio & Denney, 2015; Glenn & Raine, 2014; Yang & Raine, 2009). Dysfunction in the DLPFC could be related to impulsivity and poor behavioral control (Glenn & Raine, 2014; Yang & Raine, 2009). Performance on tests measuring executive functioning skills is consistently worse in psychopathic or antisocial individuals as compared to healthy control groups (Mercer, Selby, & McClung, 2005). One study found that executive functioning scores were related to both severity and frequency of violent offending; no such relationship was found for nonviolent offenses (Fazio & Denney, 2015; Hancock, Tapscott, & Hoaken, 2010). Poor performance by violent offenders was seen in measures related to impulsivity, concept formation, and self-monitoring. This supports Yang and Raine's (2009) hypothesis that reduced functioning in the left DLPFC is associated with poor behavioral control.

Anterior Cingulate Cortex

Located in the medial frontal cortex, the anterior cingulate cortex (ACC) plays a key role in motivation, reward and punishment, error detection, negative affect, and pain (Koenigs, 2012). Damage to the ACC has been shown to result in aggressive behavior (Devinsky, Morrell, & Vorgt, 1995), blunted affect and apathy (Koenigs, 2012; Tow & Whitty, 1953), and problems in emotion processing (Danckert et al., 2000; Hornak et al., 2003). Essentially, ACC dysfunction contributes to the poor decision making commonly found in antisocial individuals (Yang & Raine, 2009).

Ventral Prefrontal Cortex and Orbitofrontal Cortex

In general, the ventral region of the prefrontal cortex has received the most attention in the search for the neural basis of psychopathy and violence. This is unsurprising, given its role in emotion regulation (Meyer-Lindenberg et al., 2006), compassion (Toro et al., 2008), reward and punishment (Bjork, Chen, & Hommer, 2012; Rolls, 2000), response preservation (Ragozzino, 2007), fear conditioning (Birbaumer et al., 2005; Fairchild, Van Goozen, Stollery, & Goodyer, 2008), and social interactions (Rilling et al., 2007; Veit et al., 2010). Sufferers of a damaged ventral prefrontal cortex (vPFC) exhibit an absence of guilt, shame, or empathy (Barrash, Tranel, & Anderson, 2000; Koenigs, 2012) and low arousal to emotionally negative salient stimuli (Hare, Frazelle, & Cox, 1978; Patrick, Cuthbert, & Lang, 1994).

The vPFC includes the orbitofrontal cortex (OFC), which is involved in behaviors associated with appropriate social conduct (Fazio & Denney, 2015), particularly in restraining impulsive, emotional, affective, and violent behaviors (Hoskins, Roth, & Giancola, 2010). Damage to this area may cause poor judgment, impulsivity, and a lack of empathy, among other things (Cummings & Miller, 2007; Fazio & Denney, 2015). Individuals with lesions in the right OFC demonstrate inappropriate social behavior and impaired emotional processing and personality, whereas lesions in the left OFC are not associated with any abnormal social or interpersonal behaviors (Tranel, Bechara, & Denburg, 2002). Additionally, executive functioning skills in people with antisocial personality disorder are further diminished by orbitofrontal dysfunction (Brower & Price, 2001; Dolan & Park, 2002; Hoskins et al., 2010).

The Limbic System

In addition to the prefrontal cortex, deficits in the limbic system are prevalent in violent and psychopathic individuals, particularly in the amygdala and hippocampus, which relate to more primitive and instinctual processes such as emotion. Dysfunctions in these structures are a critical factor in neurological predispositions to violence or antisocial disorder.

Amygdala

The amygdala is considered the emotional center of the brain, involved in regulating emotions (Blumenfeld, 2002), empathy, fear conditioning (LaBar et al., 1998), and recognition of facial emotions (Blair, 2009). Studies of psychopaths show abnormal functioning in the amygdala compared to that of controls, including reduced activation in the amygdala during fear conditioning (Birbaumer et al., 2005) and when recognizing fear on others' faces (Marsh et al., 2008; White et al., 2012), consistent with the characteristic trait of low fear arousal in psychopaths (Tranel, Gullickson, Koch, & Adolphs, 2006). The amygdala also plays a key role in another aspect of psychopathy, namely the lack of empathy. In a 2013 study by Marsh et al., individuals were shown a photograph containing a pain-inducing injury and asked to imagine it happening to themselves or someone else. As expected, individuals with higher evidence of psychopathic traits exhibited lower activity in the amygdala.

Hippocampus

The hippocampus is involved in aspects of learning and memory as well as processing and interpreting social information (Raine, 2013). The interaction between the hippocampus and amygdala is particularly important in social and fear conditioning, and deficits in these structures have significant implications. Reduced functioning of the hippocampus has been found in violent offenders (Soderstrom et al., 2000) and psychopaths, many of whom exhibit poor fear conditioning (Hare et al., 1978). Criminal offenders and psychopaths exhibit underarousal to fearful stimuli, meaning they might never form the negative emotional experience that they would otherwise associate with a behavior, which would ultimately deter them from doing it again. For example, these individuals do not get anxious or sad when a parent scolds them for doing something wrong (dysfunctional amygdala), in part because they may not be able to register negative facial expressions or feel guilty (dysfunctional prefrontal cortex). Therefore, a punishment is not associated with that particular behavior and stored in the hippocampus, so they will not have a disincentive to repeat the socially unacceptable behavior. Raine explains this further, positing a "social push" hypothesis (Raine, 2002, 2013), which suggests that people who condition poorly (due in part to dysfunctional prefrontal cortex and limbic structures), even if they come from a good, healthy home, will not be socialized well into societal norms and will be more likely to develop antisocial tendencies. This is exactly what he found in children and violent offenders (Raine, Stoddard, Bihrle, & Buchsbaum, 1998).

Clearly, the interaction of these and other parts of the brain can explain many of the characteristics of psychopaths and violent individuals. However, another interaction may be just as important to look at: the different types of violence. Violence and aggression are commonly categorized into either affective or predatory actions (these categories are also called reactive/hostile or proactive/predatory, although they all essentially refer to the same thing). Affective violence is violence that is triggered by a perceived threat or autonomic arousal and is impulsive and emotional. Predatory violence is premeditated and often goal-driven (Fabian, 2010; Meloy, 2006). The two types of violence are associated with different brain structure functioning as well. Raine et al. (1998) separated brain scans into those of affective or predatory violent offenders. Although both groups had higher functioning in the subcortical limbic areas, only affective murderers had reduced functioning in some areas as well (especially in lower prefrontal glucose metabolism). The researchers theorized that whereas both groups have similar levels of aggressive impulses, the affective murderers are not able to control or plan their behavior because of their lower functioning prefrontal cortex (Raine et al., 1998). This is further supported by Broomhall (2005), who measured executive control skills in affective and predatory violent offenders. Affective offenders demonstrated markedly lower executive control performance than predatory offenders. Thus, the relationship between the frequency of violent offending and executive functioning found in Hancock et al.'s (2010) study could have been seen because the violent offenders included in the study were mostly affective. Lower prefrontal cortex functioning means they are less able to plan ahead and more likely to get caught and incarcerated.

In conclusion, evidence for a neurophysiological or neuropsychological basis for violence and psychopathy, both of which are associated with criminality, is abundant. Dysfunction in the prefrontal cortex and subcortical limbic structures contributes to the behavioral and cognitive aspects characteristic of psychopathy, including emotional deficits, impulsivity, poor decision making, and many more. Understanding structural and functional differences in these individuals can help aid diagnosis, treatment, and criminal proceedings.

Diet and Antisocial Behavior

The influence of diet on aggression and antisocial behavior has been investigated for more than 40 years (Hippchen, 1976). Most of the research has focused on blood sugar and cholesterol levels, the intake of micro-nutrients like iron and zinc, the intake of macro-nutrients like protein, and the intake of fatty acids like omega-3. More recently, meta-analyses have been conducted on these topics, and they have found that diet is correlated with antisocial behavior, irritability, and aggression (Benton, 2007; Gajos & Beaver, 2016). However, because there are a myriad of variables that influence both an individual's level of antisocial behavior and an individual's diet, it has been difficult to determine clear causal relationships. This complexity necessitates a discussion of the research on each area of nutrition as it relates to antisocial behavior.

One of the largest bodies of research has been conducted on sugar intake and blood sugar levels. In one of the early studies, Virkkunen et al. (1989) found a pattern of blood sugar change among Finnish violent offenders. Using the Glucose Tolerance Test (GTT), which assesses the rise and fall of blood glucose, the researchers found that violent offenders who committed crimes after being released had blood glucose levels that rose abnormally high and then fell abnormally low relative to nonrecidivistic violent offenders. Additionally, their glucose levels were very slow to recover. Similarly, Benton, Kumari, and Brain (1982) looked at blood sugar changes and aggressive tendencies among a sample of nondelinquent adults in Britain. They found that adults who had a rapid fall in blood glucose after the GTT were more likely to say that aggressive acts were justified and were more likely to include aggressive comments when presented with a frustrating situation. Overall, these studies show an association between low blood sugar and antisocial behavior.

Although these studies and others like them indicate a relationship between blood sugar levels and antisocial behavior, they are correlational and do not show clear causation. Linnoila and Virkkunen (1992) suggested that the relationship might be due to a third variable that causes both low blood sugar and antisocial behavior. The researchers hypothesized that this third variable may be serotonin levels, as low serotonin has been shown to be associated with both increased aggressive behavior and low blood sugar. However, a few studies have indicated a direct relationship between blood sugar and antisocial behavior.

Benton and Owens (1993) used an experimental paradigm in which male participants attempted to complete an impossible computer game. Half of the participants received a glucose drink to increase blood sugar, whereas the other half received a placebo drink. In the middle of the study, an attractive female experimenter told participants that their performance in the game was worse than most players. The researchers found that those in the glucose condition exhibited significantly less irritability in response to the experimenter's comment than those in the placebo condition. Overall, this study provides support for a direct causal relationship between blood sugar and antisocial behavior by implying that increased blood sugar significantly decreases antisocial behavior.

Similar to those studies on blood sugar levels, research has shown that cholesterol is associated with antisocial behavior (Golomb, Stattin, & Mednick, 2000; Hillbrand & Spitz, 1999). However, when discussing this association, it is important to distinguish between physical aggression and psychological aggression. Psychological aggression can be defined as feelings of anger and hostility, whereas physical aggression can be defined as behaving threateningly or causing physical harm. This distinction is necessary because the directionality of the association between cholesterol and these two forms of aggression differs. Among studies investigating psychological aggression and cholesterol levels, there is either no significant relationship (Rao, Carlson, & Rapport, 1991; Waldstein et al., 1993) or a small positive relationship (i.e., higher blood cholesterol levels are related to higher levels of psychological aggression; Fava et al., 1996). In contrast, studies investigating physical aggression and cholesterol levels have found a negative relationship between the two (i.e., lower cholesterol levels are related to higher levels of physical aggression; Buydens-Branchey, Branchey, Hudson, & Fergeson, 2000; Golomb et al., 2000), and this relationship has a stronger consensus within the literature than does the relationship between cholesterol and psychological aggression.

With regard to the relationship between cholesterol and physical aggression, Golomb et al. (2000) reviewed cholesterol measurements and police records from nearly 80,000 individuals in Sweden. The researchers found that those who had committed repeated acts of violence were significantly more likely to have lower cholesterol than those who did not have a history of repeated violence. Additionally, this finding held true even after the researchers matched the individuals on age, sex, alcohol use, and education level. Similarly, Buydens-Branchey et al. (2000) measured cholesterol and history of aggression among male psychiatric patients and found that patients who reported a history of violence had significantly lower blood cholesterol than those who did not report a history of violence.

In addition to these studies and others like them, some nonhuman primate studies have suggested a causal relationship between cholesterol and aggression (Kaplan, Fontenot, Manuck, & Muldon, 1996; Kaplan, Manuck, &

Shively, 1991). For example, Kaplan et al. (1996) used a within-subject design in which 23 monkeys were put on a high-cholesterol diet for 14 months and then were switched to a low-cholesterol diet for 20 months. During this time, the researchers measured the monkeys' behavior and their cholesterol levels. As expected, they found that the monkeys had lower cholesterol during the second phase and, during that time, the monkeys engaged in more frequent aggressive behavior.

Within the framework of diet and antisocial behavior, another area of research has explored the influence of the micro-nutrients zinc and iron and the macro-nutrient protein. Liu, Raine, Venables, and Mednick (2004) conducted a longitudinal study in which they measured 3-year-old children for signs of protein, zinc, and iron deficiencies and then measured their externalizing behavior (i.e., aggression, hyperactivity, and conduct disorder) at the ages of 8, 11, and 17. The researchers found that the children who had signs of nutrient deficiencies at age 3 had significantly higher rates of externalizing behavior across all three ages compared to the children who had no signs of deficiencies. Furthermore, the researchers found that sex and psychosocial adversity did not moderate the relationship; however, the children's cognitive ability did totally mediate the relationship at ages 8 and 11, such that the effect of nutritional status became nonsignificant when cognitive ability was entered as a covariate into their statistical analysis. This finding suggests that early childhood malnutrition leads to lower cognitive ability, which in turn leads to more aggressive behavior.

Further research in this area has suggested that micro-nutrients like iron and zinc may interact with other variables to influence antisocial behavior. Some researchers have found evidence that deficiencies in micro-nutrients and exposure to heavy metals (e.g., lead, mercury, manganese) can have a combined and worsening influence on aggression (Hubbs-Tait, Nation, Krebs, & Bellinger, 2005; Walsh, Isaacson, Rehman, & Hall, 1997). If this hypothesis is true, then the effects of heavy metal exposure (like a predilection for antisocial behavior) are exacerbated when a micro-nutrient deficiency is also present. For example, Walsh et al. (1997) monitored violent patients at an outpatient treatment center for 2 months and reported their level of aggression as well as the levels of zinc and copper in their blood. The researchers found that the violent patients had significantly higher copper-to-zinc ratios compared to a nonviolent control group. This finding lends support to the interaction hypothesis and suggests that micro-nutrient deficiencies coupled with heavy metal exposure can cause aggressive behavior.

In addition to blood sugar, cholesterol, and nutrients, omega-3 fatty acid deficiencies may also contribute to antisocial behavior. In a recent meta-analysis, Gajos and Beaver (2016) reviewed 40 studies, including 7,173 participants from 17 different countries. The studies included in the meta-analysis consisted of both intervention and observational studies. The researchers found strong support for a negative relationship between omega-3 consumption and aggressive behavior, indicating that increases in omega-3 led to decreases in aggression. For example, the meta-analysis included one study by Sorgi, Hallowell, Hutchins, and Sears (2007) who gave children with attention-deficit/hyperactivity disorder (ADHD) omega-3 supplements for 4 weeks until their levels reached those of the general population. Both before and after the supplement period, a psychiatrist reported on the children's aggressive behavior, and the results documented that instances of aggression significantly decreased after the children received the omega-3 supplements. Indeed, nearly all of the within-subject and between-subject studies in the meta-analysis revealed significant effects of omega-3 consumption. Likewise, a majority of the observational studies found an association between omega-3 and aggression, and the association was stronger for more severe forms of aggression. This meta-analysis and the studies it included indicate that increased omega-3 fatty acid consumption can decrease antisocial behavior, and that it may be more effective at combating serious aggression and violence than it is at combating lesser offenses.

In conclusion, the influence of diet on antisocial behavior has been investigated extensively, and the research indicates a significant relationship between the two. For example, increasing blood sugar and blood cholesterol decreases irritability and aggression (Benton & Owens, 1993; Kaplan et al., 1991). Additionally, iron, zinc, and protein deficiencies in young children are associated with antisocial behavior later in life (Liu et al., 2004). Research also suggests that deficiencies in iron and zinc may interact with heavy metal exposure (lead and mercury) and lead to worse antisocial behavior (Walsh et al., 1997). Lastly, increasing the intake of omega-3 fatty acids has been found to decrease aggression (Sorgi et al., 2007). Taken as a whole, this research shows the importance of proper nutrition in mitigating antisocial behavior. The implications of these diet studies are very interesting, as they suggest possibly dosing juvenile delinquents and criminals with sugar, vitamins, and omega-3. Later on in the chapter we review some of the results of studies testing this possibility (see "Intervention" section).

Biological and Environmental Interactions

Throughout the "Prevention of Crime" chapter, Münsterberg indicates that criminals are not born, they are made. Thus far, we have discussed the genetic and biological antecedents of antisocial behavior, and as Raine (2013) states, there is very little doubt that unfortunate genetic heritage, brain injury, and poor nutrition set the table for bad behavior as adults. However, genetic matter, brain injury, and nutrition are only part of the story; as alluded to by Münsterberg, and throughout this chapter, environment matters as well. In terms of antisocial behavior, criminality, and mental health, the environment matters *a lot*.

In his book *The Anatomy of Violence*, Raine (2013) gives an example of the importance of the environment from the Island of Mauritius. Mauritius is a small tropical island off the coast of Madagascar, and it was the location of a longitudinal study investigating children who were at risk for mental disorders. The study was initiated by Raine's mentor, Peter Venables, and taken over by Raine in 1987. The sample consisted of 1,797 3-year-olds from two towns on the island, Vacoas and Qautre Bornes. In this study, one of the factors of interest was heart rate, as a low resting heart rate is one of the correlates of aggression and antisocial behavior (see Ortiz & Raine, 2004). Heart rate also has the advantage of being easily measurable. One theory as to why low resting heart rate predicts aggression and antisocial behavior is that low levels of arousal represent a very unpleasant feeling, and those with a low resting heart rate are motivated to seek stimulation to increase arousal (i.e., heart rate) and thereby alleviate the unpleasant feelings associated with the low resting heart rate. The stimulation seeking can lead to engagement in aggressive or antisocial behavior (Ortiz & Raine, 2004).

In Mauritius, Raine discovered two children, a boy named Raj and a little girl named Joelle, who each had a very low resting heart rate and demonstrated fearlessness as 3-year-olds. Raj unfortunately turned out exactly as the experimental data predicted. According to Raine, he was fearless and people were frightened of him. He turned out to be a psychopath who showed no remorse or caution when scaring or hurting others. Joelle, on the other hand, sought out stimulation through discovery of new things. She became Miss Mauritius and lives a violence-free life. Raine (2013) speculates that Joelle may have been protected from the violent lifestyle because she was a woman, and women are raised and socialized differently from boys in terms of aggression. Whatever the reason, Raj and Joelle turned out differently, which underscores the fact that both environment and genetics are important in determining behavior.

Psychologists have known for a very long time that nearly all behavior is determined by the interaction between the environment and genetics. For example, in a seminal selective breeding study, Tryon (1940) bred rats to be "maze bright" or "maze dull." In other words, he selectively mated rats who made the fewest errors (maze bright) with each other and rats that made the most errors (maze dull) when learning to navigate a maze. Tryon then mated the most similar offspring for 21 generations, thereby successfully creating two strains of rats that were either good or poor maze learners. Cooper and Zubek (1958) placed rats from both strains in either a restricted environment (an empty cage with gray walls) or an enriched environment (a cage with designs on its walls and objects such as ramps, mirrors, swings, balls, slides, and tunnels placed inside). The rats that were raised in the impoverished environment made many errors when learning the maze, and this was true regardless of their origin group (maze bright or maze dull). The rats raised in the enriched environment made few errors. Given the manner in which these rats were bred, it seems clear that the changes in behavior were caused by the changes in environment. Cooper and Zubek argued that heredity and environment always interact to produce final behavior. However, can the behavior of rats selectively bred for several generations generalize to antisocial behavior in humans? The answer is a resounding "yes." Just like with animals, the interaction between the environment and genetics determines behavior, even with complex behaviors like violence and antisocial behavior.

Earlier in this chapter, the interaction of environment and genetics and its impact on behavior was examined through the findings of adoption studies and research on the MAOA gene. While reviewing the Mednick et al. (1984) adoption study, which highlighted the genetic influence on criminal convictions, we hinted that genetics were not the whole story. In another adoption study conducted on Swedish male adoptees, Cloninger, Sigvardsson, Bohman, and von Knorring (1982) found that when both biological parents (mother and father) had a criminal disposition and there was an environmental predisposition based on how they were raised, 40% of the adoptees committed criminal acts. When either the genetic or environmental predisposition was absent, only 12% (only genetic) or 7% (only environmental) engaged in criminal acts. Cloninger and Gottesman (1987) replicated these results with a female sample. It should be noted that the criminal rates were lower in the female study. With regard to the MAOA gene, Caspi et al. (2002) found that children with low levels of MAOA were more likely to develop antisocial behaviors if they were mistreated as children. This interaction has been replicated in many studies (e.g., Beaver et al., 2013, 2014; Guo et al., 2008).

In 2002, Raine published a comprehensive review of the environment-genetic interaction as it relates to antisocial behavior, criminal offending, and violence. One area that Raine identified as exemplifying the complex relationship between genetics and environment as they relate to antisocial behavior is complications that arise during pregnancy and birth, such as minor physical abnormalities (MPAs) and birth complications. Raine's findings in these areas illustrate the tremendous influence of the interaction between the environment and genetics on antisocial behavior.

MPAs (e.g., low-seated ears, furrowed tongue), according to Raine (2002), can be thought of as an indirect sign of some brain abnormality because they are thought to be markers for fetal neural maldevelopment. Along these lines, Kandel and Mednick (1991) assessed MPAs in 129 12-year-old boys and found that MPAs predicted violent offending at age 21. More germane to the present argument is that when the authors partitioned the sample into boys from stable homes and boys from unstable homes, MPAs predicted violence only in boys from unstable home environments. Brennan, Mednick, and Raine (1997) replicated this finding. They found that boys with MPAs and a history of family problems had unusually high rates of violent offending.

Along with MPAs, birth complications (e.g., forceps delivery, hypoxia, preeclampsia) have also been linked to antisocial behavior. Several studies have demonstrated that birth complications increase the risk of mental disorders, including conduct disorder and violence as an adult (Raine, 1993; Ratchford & Beaver, 2009). Birth complications are thought to contribute to brain and central nervous system issues, which are risk factors for antisocial behavior. Several studies have shown that birth complications interact with the environment to increase the risk of antisocial behavior (Raine, 2013). For example, Raine, Brennan, and Mednick (1994) found that birth complications, maternal rejection, unwanted pregnancy, and institutional care in the first year of life significantly predicted violent offending at 18 years old. The sample consisted of 4,269 males born in Copenhagen, and only 4% of the sample had both birth complications and maternal rejection. However, this relatively small percentage of the sample was responsible for 18% of violent crimes in the entire sample. Raine, Brennan, and Mednick (1997) followed up with the sample at age 34 and were able to replicate the biosocial interaction for violent but not nonviolent crimes. Similarly, Brennan and Mednick (1993) found that birth complications, coupled with parental mental illness, predicted violent offending.

It is clear from the anecdotal accounts, animal experiments, and correlational studies that behavior is a product of both one's genetic endowment and environmental conditions. Which factor is more important is less clear, but it likely changes depending on a host of other factors. One explanation for this pattern of results is Raine's (2002) *social push* hypothesis, alluded to earlier. Under this hypothesis, when a person is raised in a healthy, supportive environment and there is no environmental "push," then antisocial behavior is much less likely; when it does occur, it is best explained by biological factors. In contrast, the social environment may be more important when there are no biological risk factors present. Münsterberg argues that criminals are not born but made. It may be more accurate to say that criminal tendencies are born but environmental conditions will dictate whether these tendencies are expressed; that is, they provide the "push."

Prevention of Crime and Criminal Responsibility

Given that Münsterberg's chapter is entitled "The Prevention of Crime," we would be remiss if we did not address ways to prevent criminal behavior and the notion of criminal responsibility. These issues are large topics in their own right, so we situate our discussion within the context of the nature-nurture issues raised by Münsterberg. We first review research on early intervention as a means of treating antisocial behavior and thereby preventing crime, followed by a brief discussion of some of the tasks forensic psychologists perform in measuring the mental capacities of individuals charged with crimes.

Intervention

Antisocial behavior is generally now seen as a developmental disorder that begins in childhood, and conduct disorder as a child is one of the prerequisites for the diagnosis. Based on community surveys, the National Institute for Health and Clinical Excellence (2009) estimates that around 10% of children who display antisocial behavior develop antisocial personality disorder as adults. These estimates may be low, as many other people likely go undiagnosed or exhibit less extreme behavior and avoid clinical diagnosis. According to Scott, Briskman, and O'Connor (2014), organizations in the mental health field recommend early intervention as a promising avenue for the treatment of antisocial behavior. In fact, the US Surgeon General has called for studies on early intervention for antisocial behavior—before it leads to serious crime—and the National Institute for Health and Clinical Excellence (2009) has suggested that parental training could prevent later development of the antisocial behavior personality. As a treatment program, early intervention makes a good deal of sense, given the genetic–environmental interaction that we described earlier.

To date, there have been very few studies on the effectiveness of early intervention as a means of preventing crime; however, the few studies that have been conducted show promising and hopeful results. For example, Scott et al. (2014) conducted two follow-up studies on group parental training. One sample involved 120 clinic-referred 3- to 7-year-olds with severe antisocial behavior for which treatment was indicated; 93 of these individuals were reassessed between the ages of 10 and 17. The other sample comprised 109 high-risk 4–6-year-olds with elevated antisocial behavior who were selectively screened from the community; 90 of these were reassessed between ages 9 and 13. The parental training consisted of videotapes on parenting offered over 13–16 weeks. The videos covered play, praise and rewards, limit setting, and handling misbehavior. In each session, videotaped scenes of parents and children together were shown, depicting "right" and "wrong" ways of interacting with children under a variety of situations. In the sample for which treatment was indicated, the intervention resulted in some benefits for the children and parents. First, both elements of antisocial behavior—that is, antisocial behavior (assessed by a diagnostic interview) and antisocial character traits (assessed by a questionnaire)—were improved relative to the control group at the long-term follow-up assessment. In addition, the children's reading ability improved, and parents indicated that they felt more warmly toward their children. However, observation of parenting showed no differences in antisocial behavior between the treatment and control groups. Furthermore, teacher-rated and self-rated antisocial behaviors were unchanged. In the selective high-risk sample, early intervention was not associated with long-term improvement. Thus, the results of the training were somewhat mixed. Early intervention may prevent the development of antisocial personality and may improve academic performance with severely antisocial children for whom treatment is indicated. However, the same treatment with selective high-risk samples appears to be less effective.

Raine and colleagues (2001) assessed the effects of early enrichment and nutrition as a way of preventing schizotypal personality, conduct disorder, and criminal behavior. In this study, 83 children aged 3–5 years were assigned to a special enrichment program. The control group consisted of 355 children who experienced usual community conditions. The two groups were matched on temperamental, nutritional, cognitive, autonomic, and demographic variables. The enrichment program, which began at age 3, lasted 2 years and took place at specially constructed nursery schools. The program emphasized nutrition, health care, and physical exercise. The control sample attended the regular nursery school. The results of the enrichment program were dramatic: Children exposed to the enrichment program had lower scores for schizotypal personality and antisocial behavior at age 17 and for criminal behavior at age 23, relative to controls. The beneficial effects were most apparent in children who showed signs of malnutrition at age 3, particularly with respect to outcomes for antisocial behavior at ages 17 and 23.

It is clear that the most promising avenue to treatment for antisocial behavior and, by extension, later criminal activity, is early nutrition and early intervention. As described in the section on diet, children given omega-3 supplements showed a reduction in undesirable behavior. Furthermore, there are fewer violent crimes in countries in which people eat a lot of fish, a food rich in omega-3 (other cultural differences likely also contribute to this difference; see Raine, 2013). In addition to diet and nutrition, early intervention appears to benefit both parents and children, and the most encouraging early intervention programs include good nutrition as well as enrichment (Raine et al., 2001). The research on prevention of antisocial behavior is only in its infancy and will certainly mature over the years, but there seem to be some exciting and fruitful avenues to explore.

Competencies and Mental Capacities

Münsterberg is adamant that criminal behavior is made and not born. His statements are consistent with conventional thought: We all may have a propensity to commit crime, but whether that potential is realized is determined largely by the environment. However, whether these people should stand trial is another matter and is determined by their competency and their criminal responsibility. Once someone is arrested, there are several judgments and decisions that need to be made, and all have dire consequences for the accused. Competency refers to the present mental state of the accused at various stages (e.g., how well the person understands his or her Miranda rights, understands the trial process and decisions involved in the court proceedings, appreciates the nature of the sentence—especially when it involves execution—and whether he or she can communicate with counsel). Different standards are used for competency at different stages of the process (Melton et al., 2007); for exemplary purposes, we focus on competency to stand trial. Criminal responsibility refers to the person's mental state at the time the crime was committed. In other words, at the time the crime was committed, could the accused understand right from wrong? These two legal issues will determine if a person can stand trial and if the person is responsible for his or her criminal deeds.[3]

Competency to Stand Trial

Competency to stand trial (CST) refers to a person's mental ability to understand the trial proceedings and to communicate with his or her lawyer during trial preparation and at trial. Having a psychological disorder is not enough to be considered incompetent to stand trial (Bartol & Bartol, 2006). For example, many people have anxiety disorders or depression yet have the mental acuity to understand the trial process.

A substantial number of defendants are evaluated for competency each year in the United States. The estimates range from 50,000 (Skeem & Golding, 2001) to 60,000 (Bonnie & Grisso, 2000). Melton et al. (2007), in a survey of public defenders, estimated that 10%–15% of all criminal defendants, including those charged with felonies and misdemeanors, have issues related to their CST. It is estimated that even with all these competency evaluations, the overwhelming majority of defendants (80%) are found competent (Cochrane, Grisso, & Frederick, 2001).

As one might imagine, incompetent defendants typically have a long history of mental health and legal issues. A study by Steadman (1979) found, in a sample of 539 incompetent male defendants, that each had below average education and few job skills, as well as a long history of being moved back and forth between the legal and mental health systems. Hoge and colleagues (1997) compared persons in Virginia who had been declared incompetent and were receiving restoration treatment to people in custody awaiting trial and pretrial detainees receiving psychiatric treatment. Hoge et al. found that the three groups did not differ in terms of education or number of arrests, but the incompetent group did have a significantly longer history of prior psychiatric treatment. Clearly, the number of people who receive CST evaluation and the history of the people who are determined to be incompetent indicate that CST is a significant mental health and legal issue.

---

[3] Most research on competency deals with forensic assessment and the instruments constructed to help make that assessment. That discussion is beyond the scope of this chapter (see, generally, Melton et al., 2007), so instead we confine our discussion to a brief history of CST and the legal standard that is used to assess it.

The origination of CST can be traced back to the 17th century (Melton et al., 2007). Historically, as is the case today, defendants were required to enter a plea before trial. If the defendant refused to plead, the court had to decide if the refusal was due to obstinacy or by "visitation from God." Defendants who were determined to be obstinately mute were forced to endure *peine forte et dure*, a procedure in which increasingly heavy weights were placed on the defendant's chest until he pleaded or died. Defendants were spared this treatment if the refusal to plead was determined to be *mute ex visitatione Dei* (visitation of God). This latter category was originally reserved for those who were deaf and mute but was later extended to include the mentally ill. By the 18th century, the issue of CST became more of a general concern. In fact, in his famous commentaries, Blackstone held that competency of defendants was regarded as intrinsic to the fairness of a trial process (Blackstone, 1765/1979). Thus, the common law held that defendants who were mad should not be arraigned or undergo trial.

English-speaking courts have offered several justifications as to why defendants who are not mentally fit should be excluded from the trial process (Mossman et al., 2007). More specifically, a defendant who cannot communicate with his or her attorney may not have the capacity to pass on exculpatory information. In addition, if the courtroom is the site of a battle of wits between adversaries, then someone who is mentally unfit is at a distinct disadvantage in this arena. Finally, it is arguably inhumane to try someone who lacks the capacity or mental acuity to formulate his or her own defense.

The landmark case in the United States regarding CST is *Dusky v. United States* (see Mossman et al., 2007; it is striking to note that this case occurred in 1960, not so long ago). Milton Dusky was charged and convicted of unlawfully transporting a girl across state lines and raping her. He had two pretrial psychiatric evaluations. One diagnosed him with schizophrenic reactions of the chronic undifferentiated type. The second report (the one that was offered at trial) stated he could not assist counsel because of suspicious thoughts, including a belief that he was being framed. Even with both of these independent evaluations, the court found that Dusky was competent to stand trial. He was convicted of rape, and the Eighth Circuit Court of Appeals affirmed his conviction. The US Supreme Court reversed the appellate court's decision and held that the lower court's ruling that Dusky was oriented and could recall events was not sufficient to establish his competency to stand trial. Instead, the Court opined that the test for CST must determine whether the defendant has sufficient ability to consult with his lawyer with a reasonable degree of rational understanding, as well as a factual understanding of the proceedings against him. The Supreme Court remanded the case to the trial court to ascertain Dusky's present competency to stand trial and to retry him if he was found competent.

The Dusky standard makes several points clear about CST. First, the Court was clearly referring to the defendant's present mental status and not his status at the time of the crime. This is the main way in which CST differs from the determination of criminal responsibility. The Court indicated that the defendant must have a "reasonable" degree of understanding. It is impossible to know what a reasonable degree of understanding is, but it is certain that it is not a complete or perfect understanding. Finally, the Court made the same distinction that was made by English courts, in that CST refers to a defendant's capacity to communicate with his lawyer as opposed to his desire to do so. Thus, not wanting to talk to one's lawyer would not meet the CST standard (see Mossman et al., 2007).

Criminal Responsibility

Criminal responsibility, in relation to the insanity plea, is concerned with the offender's state of mind at the time the crime was committed. The law requires *mens rea*, or a guilty mind, to be established before someone can be convicted of a crime. Defendants may use other defenses to show that they are not responsible, such as self-defense and necessity. Self-defense refers to a situation in which the person commits a crime to protect himself or herself from harm. Necessity occurs when the crime is committed in an emergency situation in order to avoid more harm from occurring. For example, during a state of emergency, a person may break into a store and steal food and supplies for her starving family (a defense which did not, alas, help Jean Valjean—but then, he lived under a different legal system). The offender may not be responsible because the unlawful act could have saved lives. Unlike the insanity plea, in both the self-defense and necessity situations, the offender is aware that his or her act is illegal. The reverse is true for the insanity defense: At the time of the crime, the criminal defendant is not aware that the action is wrong. There is much less debate over either the self-defense or necessity defense as a counter to criminal responsibility, so we will concentrate on the insanity, or not guilty by reason of insanity (NGRI) defense.[4]

The most common test dates back to the mid-19th century English courts and is a variant of the wild beast test (Bartol & Bartol, 2006) According to this test, defendants are not responsible for their actions if they could not distinguish right from wrong at the time the act was committed. The right from wrong standard was changed to the irresistible impulse test, which was applied in the case of Daniel M'Naghten in 1843. This case set the standard for all subsequent jurisprudence on insanity in the United Kingdom and the United States. M'Naghten believed he was being persecuted by the English ruling party, the Tories, and the Prime Minister, Robert Peel, in particular. To end his persecution, M'Naghten traveled to London and attempted to assassinate Peel. There was no question as to whether M'Naghten fired the

---

[4] Several jurisdictions allow for a related, yet distinct, verdict of guilty but mentally ill (GBMI). Because NGRI is more common than GBMI and has a longer history, we limit our discussion to NGRI.

shots that killed Peel's secretary, Edward Drummond. However, the judge in the case halted the trial and instructed the jury to find M'Naghten not guilty. Due to M'Naghten's mental state, the judge believed he did not have the capacity to control his impulse and thus was not criminally responsible. After this decision, the English Courts re-examined the insanity test and adopted (or returned to) the right from wrong test that has become known as the M'Naghten test. It is interesting, and maybe ironic, to note that M'Naghten was not tried under the rule that bears his name and if he had been, he would likely have been found guilty. The M'Naghten test focuses on two elements: the culprit's being aware of what he or she was doing, and knowing right from wrong at the time of the act (see Bartol & Bartol, 2006).

M'Naghten is still the predominant test used in the United States. However, some jurisdictions have adopted other standards, such as the Durham rule or product test (Zapf, Green, & Rosenfeld, 2011). The Durham rule states that a defendant is not criminally responsible if he or she is suffering from mental disease or mental defect at the time of crime. This test focuses on the mental illness as opposed to the cognitive capacity to understand right from wrong, like in M'Naghten. The problem with the Durham rule is how to operationally define mental illness or mental disease (see Finkel, 1988). Münsterberg seems to favor the Durham rule when he says, "there are plenty of cases in which crime is committed from an irresistible impulse or from a total lack of inhibition or from other defects which exclude free self-determination . . . [I]n such cases we have clearly no longer any right to speak of crime; it is insanity" (p. 245). As discussed at the beginning of the chapter, he explains the failure to resist the criminal impulse in terms of the mind's inability to generate lawful counterideas.

It is nearly impossible to read about the insanity defense without coming across the case of John Hinckley, Jr. Public attention to the NGRI verdict was renewed in the wake of Hinckley's acquittal. In late March 1981, Hinckley shot President Ronald Reagan and three other men outside the Hilton Hotel in Washington, D.C. Reagan was leaving the hotel after giving a speech when Hinckley fired several shots at the president and his entourage. Reagan's press secretary, James Brady, was the most severely wounded—he was struck in the head. A bullet hit Reagan in his lung, just below the heart. A federal jury found Hinckley NGRI, which prompted Congress to modify the NGRI defense. Although there was considerable public outrage over Hinckley's acquittal, he was not released until September 2016, after more than 30 years of treatment and rehabilitation. Hinckley's lengthy detention is not unusual; on average, NGRI acquittees spend longer in secure facilities than do those convicted of comparable crimes (Bartol & Bartol, 2006).

In 1984, Congress passed the Insanity Defense Reform Act, which made several important modifications to the NGRI defense. Prior to the act, if the NGRI defense was initiated, the prosecution had to prove beyond a reasonable doubt that the defendant was sane. After the reform act, the burden of proof was shifted to the defense, and now the defense must show that the defendant could not appreciate the wrongfulness of the act due to mental defect or disease. Congress eliminated the volition prong of the defense, which means that as long as a defendant knows that the act is wrong, it does not matter whether he or she can control his or her actions; what matters is whether the behavior conforms to or violates the law. Thus, someone who comprehends that the act is wrong but cannot refrain from committing the act due to mental defect is no longer eligible for the insanity defense. In addition, experts are no longer allowed to give testimony regarding the mental state of the criminal at the time of the act; however, they are allowed to describe the behavior of the defendant and draw conclusions about any underlying mental disorder. Experts are not allowed to testify about the ultimate issue: the defendant's state of mind during the crime. Finally, courts have changed the wording of the verdict form so that now defendants must be found not guilty by *only* reason of insanity. The word "only" has been added to the original verdict form. The result of these modifications is that it is harder for the defendant to prove NGRI (Bartol & Bartol, 2006; Zapf et al., 2011).

Although many high-profile cases like Hinckley's have garnered a great deal of media attention, in actuality, it is a rarely invoked defense. It is estimated that the NGRI defense is raised in less than 1% of all felony cases (Golding, Skeem, Roesch, & Zapf, 1999). Contrary to popular perception, the NGRI defense is not used predominantly in capital cases. Silver, Cirincione, and Steadman (1994) found in a multistate study that only 14.3% of the cases using the insanity defense involved murder. With regard to success of the NGRI defense, the acquittal rate ranges from about 20% to 35%. For example, a study by Callahan, Steadman, McGreevy, and Robbins (1991) found, in an eight-state survey with 9,000 defendants who pleaded NGRI, that the acquittal rate was 25%. Other multistate surveys have reported similar acquittal rates (see Cirincione, Steadman, & McGreevy, 1995).

Conclusions

Once again, Münsterberg's thoughts are very close to the mark. Regarding criminal behavior, Münsterberg gives a nod to the work of Lombroso, suggesting his theories are interesting, but in the end, he rejects the claims because Lombroso discounts the role of society and the environment. It is not that Münsterberg does not realize that there is a genetic basis to criminal behavior. In fact, he cites a study of 127 boys from a school for delinquent children and indicates that of those 127 cases, 85 had parents who were alcoholics and 24 had parents who were "insane." Münsterberg goes on to say, "Not the criminal tendency was born with the poor children, but the insufficient capacity and resistance of the central nervous system; and this was their inheritance from abnormal and degenerate parents" (p. 243). This is almost exactly the point made by Raine (2013). Raine is more interested in the biological basis of antisocial behavior but is quick to point out that there is a biological–social interaction. Furthermore, the social push hypothesis explains the interaction. When the biological risk factors are not strongly present, the environment may be enough to "push" an individual to criminal and antisocial behaviors. Conversely, even when the environment is loving and supportive, as in the case of Jeffrey Landrigan (presented at the beginning of this chapter), biology may be too much to overcome.

But more to the point of the chapter: Can crime be prevented? This is still an open question; however, there are some promising avenues on the horizon. It appears that good nutrition and early intervention for parents and children are encouraging interventions (Raine et al., 2001). Nutrition can also play a significant role in preventing adolescent criminal behavior. The Gajos and Beaver (2016) meta-analysis revealed that increasing the amount of omega-3 fatty acids can decrease antisocial behavior and may be especially effective at combating relatively serious aggression and violence. Thus, modern-day psychologists and criminologists are picking up the gauntlet left by Münsterberg and using experimentation and science in their attempts to prevent violent crime.

11

What Münsterberg Got Right, What He Missed, and What We're Missing Now

Münsterberg was incredibly prescient in his view of what psychology could offer the law. Nonetheless, he neglected to include a number of topics that are currently of great concern to forensic psychologists, the criminal justice system, and policymakers. In this concluding chapter, we briefly summarize the major points on which subsequent research has proven him to be correct, discuss a number of issues that he neglected to consider, and look ahead to the future.

What Münsterberg Got Right

In Chapter 1, we stated that one of the book's central questions would be whether subsequent research has shown Münsterberg to be right or wrong. He got a remarkable number of things right:

- *Perception is malleable and prone to error ("illusions"), and confidence is no guarantee of accuracy.* Multiple witnesses can perceive the same event differently; they remember things that did not occur (false memory); they do not remember things that did occur, even when those happenings are highly salient (inattention and change blindness); they remember things that occurred in one context, time, or location as occurring elsewhere (unconscious transference); and they tend to be overconfident, though confidence can be predictive of accuracy under some, typically limited, circumstances (Wixted & Wells, 2017).

- *There are many ways to conduct eyewitness research, and each method has its pros and cons.* Münsterberg was a strong advocate for a naturalistic approach, such as staged crimes and field studies, in which witnesses are unaware that they are taking part in an experimental study. Although staged crimes and field studies are relatively rare in the modern-day corpus of eyewitness research, other data from the field, such as archival studies and case studies, are becoming more prevalent. Moreover, statistical techniques for combining large amounts of data (i.e., meta-analysis) can help allay concerns about drawing conclusions from limited data or from a narrow study space. Overall, the rich and varied methodologies used in eyewitness research can lend convergent validity to some of the findings; yet Münsterberg's call for more naturalistic studies, which is frequently echoed by the courts (Monahan & Walker, 2018), is something that contemporary researchers would do well to heed.
- *Psychological methods can be used to detect deception.* Münsterberg might have been overly sanguine about the effectiveness of such techniques: Most people, including legal professionals, are not much better than chance at detecting deception, at least in the absence of specialized training (e.g., Vrij, 2004), and they tend to rely on nondiagnostic, stereotypical behavioral cues (DePaulo et al., 2003). Moreover, this body of research suffers from methodological shortcomings (National Research Council, 2003) and can be criticized on legal grounds (Vrij & Fisher, 2016). Nevertheless, newer techniques for detecting deception, such as brain scans and reaction time, show promise (e.g., Suchotzki et al., 2017). The feasibility of using such techniques, which require some kind of specialized equipment, in the field is open to question, but they do support the basic principle that deception is detectable (of course, polygraphs require specialized equipment, and they are used routinely in the field, so perhaps it would not be so challenging after all).
- *False confessions are real, and real people confess falsely for a variety of reasons.* As with detecting deception, methods for detecting false confessions are not terribly effective, as most people, including legal professionals, are not very adept at telling true and false confessions apart (e.g., Kassin et al., 2005). This is partly the case because, as Münsterberg recognized, suspects sometimes come to believe that their false confessions are genuine (i.e., internalized false confessions). However, certain interrogation techniques, such as false-evidence ploys, do make false confessions more likely. Because confessions, whether true or false, are compelling and persuasive, it is important to adopt policies and practices that increase confessions' diagnosticity (i.e., practices that are more likely to elicit a true, instead of a false, confession; see Houston et al., 2014).

- *Eyewitnesses are suggestible, and some kinds of witnesses, and witnesses in some kinds of circumstances, are more suggestible than others.* Münsterberg identified some characteristics and circumstances as particularly problematic, such as age, affect, and hypnosis, but subsequent research has shown many other stable and transitory factors to increase or decrease suggestibility also. Importantly, Münsterberg pointed out that the power of suggestion is perfectly normal. It becomes problematic when individuals' memories are relied on in court after being subject to suggestive influences (see, e.g., Ridley et al., 2013).
- *Environmental influences are a key factor in producing criminal behavior.* Like early and contemporary criminologists, Münsterberg appreciated that in order to prevent crime, one must first understand what causes it. In emphasizing the importance of society and the environment, he did not totally discount the role of biological factors in predisposing persons to criminality, although he did regard Lombroso's heavily biological theory as too extreme. More recent research, while highlighting the contribution of biological factors (e.g., Raine, 2013), likewise takes as given the complex interplay of nature and nurture in producing criminal behavior.
- *Courts do not take full advantage of psychological research, and this neglect imperils the pursuit of justice.* This indictment of the legal system is, in a very real sense, Münsterberg's principal thesis. The courts have come a long way in this regard in the past 110 years; for example, psychological expert testimony is now commonplace, especially on clinical-forensic matters (Melton et al., 2007), and experimental research, such as that on eyewitness memory, has spurred important policy reforms (National Research Council, 2014). Even Wigmore would likely now concede that psychology has earned a seat at the table (if only the children's table). However, even though psychological research (and social science research in general) has made significant inroads, courts are often still reluctant to acknowledge its relevance to legal issues (Benton et al., 2007; Monahan & Walker, 2018). Moreover, most of the leading contributors to wrongful convictions—eyewitness errors, false confessions, and false informant testimony—are topics on which experimental psychology has a great deal to say. Despite a growing appreciation of the risks associated with these kinds of evidence, they continue to figure prominently in large numbers of wrongful convictions.

Thus, it is clear that by any reckoning, Münsterberg was incredibly prescient. If either of us had that kind of a hit rate a century from now, we (or our spirits) would be mightily pleased. Given what he got right, Münsterberg's legacy is secure.

What Münsterberg Missed

That is not to say that there were no misses—there were several. The heading of this section is probably a little bit unfair to Münsterberg. He did not pretend that *On the Witness Stand*—which he cobbled together from a series of magazine articles—was a comprehensive survey of psychology and law, or even of eyewitness testimony, the book's major focus. Moreover, one can hardly fault a seminal figure in a field for not seeing clearly where the field was going to go as it developed over the ensuing century. It would be like blaming Henry Ford for not foreseeing the advent of the electric car or Albert Einstein for not anticipating particle physics.[1] Or like expecting Babe Ruth to hit a home run every time at bat (Ruth hit a home run every 11.76 at bats, second on the all-time list behind Mark McGwire). The Ruth analogy is probably more apt than the Einstein or Ford comparison, for like Ruth, Münsterberg's strikeouts were prodigious—for example, his egregious contention that women were unfit to be jurors (see Chapter 1).

Despite the inherent unfairness of the question, in light of how psychology and law has developed over the past century (see Chapter 2), it is worth considering some of the topics that Münsterberg left out of his book. Some of these omissions, especially those dealing with eyewitness testimony, are surprising—one could argue that he *should* have covered them. Other core elements of modern-day psychology and law would have been harder for anyone working in the early 20th century, no matter how farsighted, to foresee. Thus, this section of the chapter has two parts: what Münsterberg (probably) should have included and what he (probably) could not reasonably have foreseen. Our coverage here is necessarily selective—we do not attempt to provide a comprehensive discussion of all the topics that Münsterberg left out of *On the Witness Stand*, as that would be a textbook in its own right, and psycholegal researchers are continually discovering new avenues of research.

What Münsterberg (Probably) Should Have Included

The legal actors to whom Münsterberg devotes the most space are eyewitnesses. He also discusses psychological processes in suspects, offenders, and third parties engaged in evaluating those actors (e.g., in detecting deception). However, he overlooks a number of important variables related to eyewitnesses, especially system variables (Wells, 1978). And he either pays only scant attention to, or completely ignores, other legal actors who make very consequential decisions that are influenced by the same sorts of heuristics and biases as those whom he does discuss.

[1] In the cases of Ford and Einstein, these examples illustrate how they were limited by the technology available at the time. As we describe later, this was true to an extent for Münsterberg, too.

System Versus Estimator Variables

Münsterberg focuses excessively, nearly exclusively, on estimator variables, especially witness characteristics. He ignores factors that have the potential to improve eyewitness performance in lineups and interviews. Considerable research has shown that certain procedures can elicit more information, more accurate information, and fewer errors (Lampinen et al., 2012; Wells, Memon, & Penrod, 2006). System and estimator variables are both important, insofar as they both relate to fundamental memory processes, and a better understanding of both categories of variables can help relevant third parties like police, judges, and jurors weigh eyewitness testimony properly. Nonetheless, system variables, by virtue of being amenable to manipulation by the legal system, have the added advantage of lending themselves directly to reform efforts. Most of these procedures do not "change" a witness's memory, per se, as the memory has already been formed at the time of encoding; rather, they can lead to superior retrieval.[2] Estimator variables, in contrast, cannot be altered in a manner to improve performance (with the possible exception of training those likely to witness crimes, like police, which the legal system does have under its control; such training has limited effectiveness; Paterson et al., 2017).

Accordingly, the bulk of eyewitness reform efforts have concentrated on system variables. Over the past 20 years, the eyewitness research community has promulgated recommendations for how to conduct eyewitness lineups and interviews to increase the amount of accurate information elicited and reduce errors (e.g., National Research Council, 2014; Technical Working Group on Eyewitness Evidence, 1999; Wells et al., 1998, 2006). The latest best-practice recommendations, issued by the National Research Council (2014) after an exhaustive review of the literature, include training law enforcement officers in eyewitness identification; using double-blind lineups and standardized instructions, including a statement that the perpetrator may or may not be in the lineup; documenting an immediate confidence judgment; and videotaping the identification procedure. Current U.S. Department of Justice guidelines (Yates, 2017) essentially adopt these recommendations, requiring—except in unusual circumstances—procedures like blind administration, unbiased instructions, an immediate self-reported confidence judgment, and documentation of the identification, preferably by video or audio recording.

Technological advances can be helpful in executing some of these recommendations. For example, computerized lineup administration can take the lineup administrator out of the equation, allowing for blind administration and minimizing or potentially even eliminating postidentification feedback. In addition, computer facial comparison algorithms can be used to

[2] Some procedures, such as postidentification feedback and postevent misinformation, do actually change the witness's memory.

select fillers that are similar to the suspect but not too similar, thereby maximizing identification accuracy (Bergold & Heaton, 2018). And advances in the affordability, usability, and portability of recording equipment naturally facilitate lineup documentation.

Other Legal Actors

Contemporary law-psychology has been regularly criticized for its narrow focus on only a subset of relevant topics, such as juror decision making and eyewitness testimony (e.g., Blumenthal, 2010; Wylie et al., 2018). Some evidence suggests that this criticism is exaggerated, or at least misplaced—law-psychology journals publish work on a wide variety of topics, though some journals are broader than others (Reed et al., 2018; Wylie et al., 2018). Nonetheless, some legal actors (e.g., eyewitnesses, jurors, offenders) have historically received, and continue to receive, more attention than others. Insofar as we (as a field) still fall into this trap, it is not surprising that Münsterberg did as well. A short list of legal actors who are susceptible to the same sorts of biases as those Münsterberg talks about with respect to eyewitnesses and suspects includes, but is not limited to, jurors, judges, attorneys, police, and parole officers.

Although Münsterberg included a chapter on jurors in a book published after *On the Witness Stand* (Münsterberg, 1914b; see Bornstein & Kleynhans, 2019), his own work on the topic was rudimentary by modern-day standards and reached the erroneous conclusion that women were unfit for jury service (see Chapter 1). Today, jury research is a core topic within law-psychology, comprising roughly 10%–20% of articles published in leading law-psychology journals (Reed et al., 2018; Wylie et al., 2018). Jury research has been criticized for having methodological limitations and for focusing on a relatively narrow subset of dispute resolution processes within the legal system—compared, for example, to plea bargains in criminal cases and negotiated settlements in civil cases, both of which occur much more frequently than jury trials. Yet even so, the jury's relevance to fundamental psychological processes (e.g., decision making, persuasion, hypothesis testing, group dynamics) and centrality to the American justice system mean that it is an area where psychology has much to offer the legal system (for review, see Bornstein & Greene, 2017; Kovera, 2017).

Judges resemble jurors in part of their job description—that is, they are factfinders in bench trials. Research on this aspect of judicial decision making demonstrates that they are largely susceptible to the same sorts of cognitive biases as jurors (e.g., Guthrie, Rachlinski, & Wistrich, 2001; Wistrich, Guthrie, & Rachlinski, 2005). Of course, judges do much more than that; for example, trial judges make important pretrial determinations (e.g., bail), issue evidentiary rulings, and sentence criminal defendants, and appellate judges interpret the law and make complicated legal determinations. Here also they may fall prey to common cognitive biases: They consider only limited factors in setting bail (Ebbesen & Konecni, 1975), possess limited understanding of key types of evidence like eyewitness testimony (Wise & Safer, 2004) and scientific evidence (Kovera & McAuliff, 2000), and are influenced by extralegal (as well as legal) factors in sentencing (Doerner & Demuth, 2010; Piquero & Davis, 2004). At the appellate level, their rulings reflect, to some extent, their attitudes and ideologies (Segal & Spaeth, 1993; Wrightsman, 2006). This is by no means to suggest that judges are poor at their jobs, merely that they are human. Münsterberg could have added to his indictment of the courts for ignoring psychological research findings the observation that courts' central figures, namely judges, themselves demonstrate all kinds of errors that can be explained in psychological terms.

Attorneys have less control over what goes on in court than judges, but a variety of fundamental psychological processes contribute to their behavior as well. For example, they have considerable say in whether a defendant pleads guilty, as well as, if the case does go to trial, how to structure a case and present it to the jury. These procedures raise issues related to social influence at the level of plea decision making (Henderson & Levett, 2018), and to story construction/interpretation (Pennington & Hastie, 1993) and persuasion at the trial level (McAuliff, Nemeth, Bornstein, & Penrod, 2003). Attorneys also rely on inaccurate psychological assumptions and are subject to bias when conducting voir dire (Crocker & Kovera, 2011) and dealing with eyewitnesses (Wise, Pawlenko, Safer, & Meyer, 2009). And because prosecutors enjoy broad discretion in criminal cases, there is abundant room for extralegal factors to influence their charging decisions, plea offers, and sentencing recommendations—as indeed they do (Lynch, 2013; O'Neal, Tellis, & Spohn, 2015). Attorneys play a prominent role in an adversarial justice system like that of the United States; thus, there are ample opportunities for psychological processes to produce bias and suboptimal outcomes.

Finally, police and parole officers make consequential legal decisions and are therefore good candidates for psychological investigation. Interest in these legal actors is growing, as evidenced by the existence of organizations like the Society for Police and Criminal Psychology, which publishes the *Journal of Police and Criminal Psychology*. Little research has been conducted on parole board members, but what has been done suggests that their decisions can be studied empirically and involve basic psychological processes like attribution and person perception (Lindsey & Miller, 2011; Miller, Lindsey, & Kaufman, 2014).

Whereas parole boards, even in jurisdictions where their hearings are open to the public, perform their activities mostly out of the public eye, law enforcement officers are highly visible in their communities. Police behavior is a major factor in citizens' compliance with the law (Tyler, 2006); understanding police behavior is especially important in an era when police–citizen tensions are unusually high and new technologies (e.g., cellphones, bodycams) have increased the public scrutiny of police–citizen interactions. Despite their specialized training, research shows that compared to laypeople, police are not especially knowledgeable about the factors that affect eyewitness memory (Wise et al., 2011), better eyewitnesses themselves (Vredeveldt & van Koppen, 2016), or better able to detect deception and true versus false confessions (Kassin et al., 2005; Vrij, 2004). As police are often the initial point of contact for eyewitnesses and suspects, and subsequent decision points (e.g., whether to charge, go to trial, etc.) are contingent on these initial encounters, a better understanding of police psychology would be invaluable.

What Münsterberg (Probably) Could Not Have Foreseen

Three aspects of contemporary law-psychology, which seem like established facts from an early 21st-century perspective, likely would have caught Münsterberg by surprise: clinical-forensic and correctional psychology, technological innovations, and specialty courts. Although Münsterberg practiced what we would regard nowadays as clinical psychology, professional psychology essentially did not exist at the time. Münsterberg lived and worked at a time of great scientific ferment: Röntgen discovered X-rays in 1895, Freud published *The Interpretation of Dreams* in 1900, Pavlov delivered his first major paper on classical conditioning in 1903, Einstein's annus mirabilis was in 1905, Sherrington published his detailed theory of synaptic activity in 1906, and Rutherford described the atomic nucleus in 1911. Because at this time psychology and even social science as a whole were somewhat inchoate, he could not have anticipated how the various social scientific disciplines and subdisciplines would coalesce, diverge, and intersect with the legal system. It also would have been difficult for him to foresee technological discoveries that would be applied in forensic contexts or changes in court structures themselves, such as specialty courts. In this section, we briefly connect Münsterberg's work in experimental law-psychology to two closely related subdisciplines—clinical-forensic and correctional psychology—and discuss recent technological and administrative developments that raise fundamental psychological questions when applied to the legal system.

Clinical-Forensic Psychology

Clinical psychology, as we know it today, did not really exist in the early 20th century. Considering that psychological distress has existed since the beginning of human history, attempts to alleviate it presumably have as well (Benjamin, 2005). As recently as the 18th and 19th centuries, "there were many psychological practitioners who operated under a variety of labels such as phrenologist, physiognomist, graphologist, mesmerist, spiritualist, seer, psychic, mental healer, and psychologist" (Benjamin, 2005, p. 3); and, of course, physician. By the turn of the 20th century, treatment of mental illness was almost exclusively the purview of physicians, especially those who specialized in psychiatry and/or neurology (Hunt, 2007); as described in Chapter 1, this included Hugo Münsterberg. As psychologically inclined physicians like Freud, Jung, and others increasingly employed psychotherapy rather than biomedical treatments, and psychology began to coalesce as a distinct scientific discipline, nonmedical psychologists started gravitating toward clinical practice. By the late 1890s and first decade of the 20th century, Lightner Witmer had established the first psychological clinic in the United States (and possibly the world), given the new discipline the name of "clinical psychology," and called for a program of doctoral training (Benjamin, 2005; Witmer, 1907). One of the consequences of this growing interest in therapeutic psychology was tension between clinical and experimental psychology in the early years of the American Psychological Association (APA; see Chapter 1), as well as between clinical psychology and psychiatry, both of which continue today. Despite these tensions, by the middle of the 20th century, clinical psychology was well established as a profession, spurred in large part by the assessment and treatment needs posed by World Wars I and II and the wars' aftermath (Benjamin, 2005).

It nonetheless took a while for the courts to recognize clinical psychologists as experts. Given physicians' much lengthier involvement in legal cases, and perhaps also due to the higher prestige of an MD versus a PhD, the justice system preferred psychiatric expert testimony on matters of mental health and criminal behavior until the middle of the 20th century (Heilbrun et al., 2009). Yet as clinical psychology became more established as both a scientific discipline and a part of the mainstream health care establishment, clinical psychologists gradually began finding themselves called to provide evidence in court. They were first clearly recognized as expert witnesses in *Jenkins v. U.S.* (1962), and as their involvement in the justice system grew, the field of clinical-forensic psychology grew as well (Ogloff & Douglas, 2013). The American Board of Forensic Psychology was founded in 1977, followed by the American Academy of Forensic Psychology a year later (Kaslow, 2018). The APA recognized forensic psychology as a specialty area within psychology in 2001, and it has developed its own standards, training programs, and specialty guidelines (Ogloff & Douglas, 2013).

Definitions of clinical-forensic psychology vary; Ogloff and Douglas (2013, p. 374), following the Forensic Psychology Specialty Council, define it as "the professional practice by psychologists . . . when they are engaged regularly as experts and represent themselves as such, in an activity primarily intended to provide professional psychological expertise to the legal system." Like clinical psychologists as a whole, forensic psychologists perform many roles in the legal system—assessment, diagnosis, prediction, prevention, and treatment (Benjamin, 2005)—with an emphasis on specialized clinical psychological assessments (Heilbrun et al., 2009; Melton et al., 2007;

Ogloff & Douglas, 2013). These functions performed by forensic psychologists comprise a key element of contemporary psychology and law, figuring prominently in professional meetings, books and journal articles, and federally funded research. Yet except for some brief and tantalizing hints in his chapter on crime prevention (e.g., criminal responsibility; see Chapter 10), Münsterberg pays little attention to clinical-forensic topics like psychopathy, competency, and risk and threat assessment. These issues come up not only with respect to offenders, but also with respect to victims, litigants, and witnesses (e.g., competency of child witnesses or mentally ill victims). It likely would have been unfathomable to Münsterberg that nonphysicians would assess and treat such persons.

Related to forensic psychology, the professional field of correctional psychology developed to address the psychological needs of prison inmates at roughly the same time—that is, in the mid-20th century. Prior to that time, little attention was paid to prisoners' mental health needs. The field emerged in reaction to indeterminate sentencing, defective delinquency laws, scant efforts at offender treatment besides occasional psychoanalytic approaches, and poor working conditions for prison psychologists (Brodsky, 2007; Dvoskin, Spiers, & Brodsky, 2007). The American Association for Correctional Psychology was founded as the Society of Correctional Psychologists in 1953 (currently, after multiple name changes, it is the International Association for Correctional and Forensic Psychology; Bartol & Freeman, 2005). Because large numbers of prisoners have a history of mental illness and/or trauma, their psychological needs are particularly acute (Crighton & Towl, 2008). Moreover, treating them can have collateral benefits—making them better improves the safety of those around them while they are incarcerated (i.e., other prisoners and corrections officers), those with whom they interact after release (e.g., family members, neighbors, employers), and society at large. Indeed, the major goals of correctional psychology are to enhance prisoners' well-being, reduce prisoners' risk of reoffending, and improve protection of the public (Crighton & Towl, 2008).

Technology

New technologies have acquired all sorts of psychologal applications. Newer polygraphs do a better job of detecting deception than older versions (National Resource Council, 2003; see Chapter 6); and neuroimaging and other kinds of neuroscientific evidence have been used, with some degree of success, to predict dangerousness (Jones, Wagner, Faigman, & Raichle, 2013), lying (see Chapter 5), and true versus false memories (Schacter, Chamberlain, Gaesser, & Gerlach, 2012). In each of these instances, both courts and researchers have expressed concerns about whether such evidence is sufficiently reliable to present in court and can be weighed properly by jurors (e.g., Bornstein & Greene, 2017; Hunter, Schweitzer, & Ware, 2019). In addition, the precise implementation is unclear: If a witness is suspected of lying, having a false memory, or being at high risk of future dangerousness, at what point do the authorities administer the test? What are the test's parameters? How strong must the suspicion be, or should all witnesses be tested? Will courts be required to invest in their own fMRI machines? Who pays for the machines, the technicians who run them, and the experts who testify about the results? These questions, which are not trivial, indicate that the technology might have outpaced a careful consideration of its application—of course, that is not unusual. Münsterberg himself was such a technological innovator (Hale, 1980; see Chapter 1) that he undoubtedly would have been pleased by the many technological advances that have brought psychology and law closer together.

Another area in which technological developments present psycholegal implications is forensic science. Forensic science evidence is an increasingly prominent component of criminal cases, and to less of an extent of civil cases as well. Münsterberg certainly could not have foreseen the advent of DNA testing, which has become so central to the movement to exonerate the falsely convicted. Although some rudimentary forensic science techniques existed in his day—for instance, Francis Galton's scholarly treatise *Finger Prints*, published in 1892, laid the foundation for the use of fingerprint identification in criminal cases—he could hardly have anticipated the explosion in biometrics, fiber analysis, ballistics, and other techniques. Such evidence has become so widespread, and so popular in media portrayals, that there are concerns jurors will expect to encounter forensic evidence at trial, and that it will exert an outsized influence on their decisions (evidence of such a "CSI effect" is mixed; see, e.g., Schweitzer & Saks, 2007).

Unfortunately, many of the fields that comprise forensic science developed without a sound empirical foundation (Faigman et al., 2014; Mnookin, 2018; National Research Council, 2009), and a number of studies have demonstrated cognitive biases in forensic examiners and their interpretation of evidence, as well as instances of outright fraud (National Research Council, 2009; Saks, 2018; Saks & Koehler, 2005). These problems are especially rife in the case of pattern identification evidence, such as fingerprints, bullets, bite marks, and signatures (Mnookin, 2018). Mistaken or misleading forensic evidence doubtless contributes to the many wrongful conviction cases in which forensic science errors play a part (Saks & Koehler, 2005). According to the Innocence Project, unvalidated or improper forensic science was the second leading cause of wrongful convictions (behind only eyewitness misidentification), present in 47% of the first 325 DNA exonerations (https://www.innocenceproject.org/causes-wrongful-conviction./).

Recording media, both visual and auditory, were nascent technologies in Münsterberg's day. Louis Daguerre developed the first practical photographs in the late 1830s, and Thomas Edison invented the phonograph in the late 1870s; motion pictures came along in the late 1880s/early 1890s and were an interest of Münsterberg's (see Chapter 1). These recording technologies have become steadily more user-friendly, affordable, and portable, to the point that they are now virtually ubiquitous. Governmental surveillance captures citizens' visual images and telephone conversations—often without their consent—and those same citizens record one another (and themselves) incessantly on their cell phones and other devices. Apart from the privacy concerns posed by these technologies, they raise a host of new questions related to eyewitness memory.

For example, legal authorities often scan CCTV images for evidence of wrongdoing or when searching for a known perpetrator. If the CCTV image leads to an arrest and subsequent prosecution, jurors could have the task of determining whether the defendant is the same person shown in the CCTV tape (a process known as *simultaneous identity matching*; Davis & Valentine, 2009). Laypeople's ability to perform simultaneous identity matching is surprisingly poor, and errors increase due to factors known to have a negative effect on eyewitness identification, such as a change in the target's appearance because of disguise or the passage of time. For example, Davis and Valentine (2009, Experiment 2) found that the error rate ranged from 23% to 55%, depending on experimental condition (presence of disguise, warning that the video was a year old, target presence/absence). In many cases, the CCTV videos may be of poor quality, brief duration, and taken years before trial, all of which could depress performance further. At a more mundane level, TSA and customs agents engage in this activity hundreds or thousands of times a day when they match a passport or driver's license photo to the person standing before them. The potential consequences of errors in such situations are every bit as serious as they are in the courtroom.

As prevalent as surveillance is, social media are perhaps even more so. Users have devised new and innovative ways of using social media, and these applications are finding their way into the courts. For example, both authors have been consulted in cases in which crime victims conducted their own Facebook searches for their assailant, notifying the police after recognizing someone they believed to be the perpetrator. The police then questioned the person and showed the witness a lineup containing his picture. Not surprisingly—considering the witness had already made a Facebook identification—the witness picked him out of the lineup. This "Facebook ID" scenario likely involves psychological processes very similar to those that arise in cases of unconscious transference (e.g., mugshot searches, discussed in Chapter 3; see McGorrery, 2015).

The proliferation of ever-more-powerful computers, in conjunction with greater social connectivity, has spawned new types of crimes or greatly expanded opportunities for committing existing crimes—identify theft, fraud, hacking, piracy, phishing, and cyberbullying, to mention only a few. The distance created by the technology distinguishes cybercrime from more "traditional" forms of crime. For example, cyberbullying—using technology (e.g., social websites, email, texting) to inflict intentional and repeated harm, typically among youth (Notar, Padgett, & Roden, 2013)—differs from traditional bullying in several respects. Cyberbullies can be anonymous or pretend to be someone else, they do not witness their victims' reactions, and the act of bullying is neither spatially nor temporally limited (Jenkins, Demaray, Dorio, & Eldridge, 2019). These characteristics could make the experiences of cyberbullies and other cybercriminals, as well as the experiences of their victims, different from those of perpetrators and victims in more "traditional" crimes. They necessarily pose investigatory challenges also, as in most cases, identification of the perpetrator is accomplished through an analysis of electronic data and not via sensory means, as in eyewitness and earwitness identification.[3]

Specialty Courts

Specialty courts, also referred to as problem-solving courts, have existed in the United States for more than a century (Gatowski, Dobbins, & Summers, 2013). These courts typically address either specific categories of offenses, such as domestic violence, drugs, prostitution, gambling, or animal cruelty; or specific groups of offenders, such as veterans, juveniles, the homeless, persons with mental illness, or parolees (Kaplan, Miller, & Wood, 2018; Miller, 2018; Wiener & Brank, 2013). Specialty courts tend to focus on the underlying social issues that are related to crime for these classes of offenders, address criminogenic risks and potential recidivism, and emphasize rehabilitation more than punishment (Kaplan et al., 2018; Nolan, 2009). They are often situated within a therapeutic jurisprudence framework, which emphasizes the capacity of laws and courts to yield therapeutic outcomes for those with whom they come into contact (Wexler & Winick, 1996). Although specialty courts are on the rise in the United States, where they arguably first developed, they are now a global phenomenon. Yet whether countries have specialty courts at all, the sorts of problems they address, and how the courts operate vary greatly (Miller, 2018; Nolan, 2009).

Specialty courts raise a host of psychological issues. First and foremost, many of them concentrate on the mental health needs of offenders, as in mental health courts, drug courts, homelessness courts, gambling courts, and veterans' courts. Other psychological implications include the effect on judges' decision making of effectively making them case managers as well as fact finders; how best to measure specialty courts' success, in terms of recidivism and/or improvement in the underlying issues that led

[3] Whether identifying cybercriminals is harder or easier than identifying criminals in a lineup, or more or less susceptible to error, is beyond the scope of the present chapter. The preceding chapters have discussed many of the issues associated with witness identification; we suspect that using electronic means to identify cybercriminals has its own set of challenges.

to offenders' involvement in the criminal justice system (e.g., mental illness, poverty, joblessness); and perceptions of both offenders and victims of experiencing dispute resolution via a specialty court as opposed to traditional means of justice administration. In this sense, then, they are a prime example of how substantive and procedural changes in the legal system can create new opportunities for psychologists to improve the administration of justice. Even though Münsterberg probably could not have foreseen this particular opportunity—or many others—specialty courts are entirely consistent with his larger thesis and ethos: Namely, psychologists have much to offer the legal system.

What Are We Missing Now?

At the time of this writing, *On the Witness Stand* is 110 years old, and the American Psychology-Law Society is almost 50 years old. What will be the big issues in psychology and law 110 years from now, in 2128? Or even in 2028? This is admittedly blatant—and arguably irresponsible, if not impossible—speculation. We would argue, however, that it is worthwhile to engage periodically in such speculation. The research questions that preoccupy a discipline at a given point in time are driven by many factors, such as social and historical forces (e.g., war, disease, civil rights), the overarching zeitgeist, and of course the personalities and talents of individual scholars (Hunt, 2007). So undoubtedly most of our predictions will prove to be wrong, and topics we do not consider will prove to be important in the coming decades. Nevertheless, our close examination of Münsterberg's work, and how the field looks 110 years later, has shown us the value of pausing periodically to take stock—to look back, as well as forward. Our predictions here have an easy element and a hard element. The easy piece is to predict that the issues Münsterberg could not readily have foreseen, but that are currently garnering significant attention from both the psycholegal research community and the courts, will continue to increase in importance. The hard piece is predicting what we are missing entirely. Given the difficulty of identifying topics of future import that are presently overlooked completely, our discussion necessarily emphasizes the relatively easy predictions—that is, things that are present in the field now but that we expect will rapidly increase in importance. Relatedly, we can ask the converse question: whether topics that are currently garnering a lot of empirical attention will fade from the scene.

With respect to recent trends that we expect to grow in importance, we single out several candidates: First, we would subsume several research topics under the rubric of identifying truth—whether it be a true (versus an erroneous) memory, a true (versus a false) confession, or a knowingly true statement (as opposed to a lie)—via mechanical means, such as neurophysiological tests. Second, in light of the growing prison population and rapidly changing face of the US correctional system, we foresee much more research on corrections: alternatives to incarceration, the effects of privatization, and more research on how to structure incarceration so as to facilitate prisoner reentry and reduce recidivism. Relatedly, we expect to see more innovative treatments for offenders with mental illness. Third, we anticipate an increase in the use of actuarial methods, rather than, or in addition to, human decision makers. Because we are trying to predict the future here, we make no claim that this list is exhaustive or even representative, and we will not be at all surprised if other topics turn out to supplant the ones we have chosen. Nonetheless, we will be surprised if the topics we have chosen do not contribute to at least some significant scientific and policy advances. With respect to currently important topics that we expect to become less prominent over time, we offer one nomination: the death penalty.

Identifying Truth

Witnesses and suspects sometimes lie, and they are sometimes honestly mistaken. Münsterberg was certainly not the first one to notice this, but his extensive discussion of the psychological processes underlying these phenomena is one of the major contributions of *On the Witness Stand*. As the previous chapters show, people—whether police officers, attorneys, professional judges, or laypeople/jurors—are not very knowledgeable about the factors that distinguish accurate from mistaken or deceitful witnesses or suspects; accordingly, they are not very adept at telling one from the other. Yet it goes without saying that determining truthfulness is at the heart of the criminal justice system. How could it be improved?

Chapter 5 describes some of the new lie detection procedures that take advantage of brain scanning and brain imaging (e.g., functional magnetic resonance imaging or fMRI). Early experimental findings on the procedures' ability to identify liars from truth tellers are promising. Similarly, some research has found that true and false memories have different neurophysiological characteristics (Johnson et al., 2012; Schacter et al., 2012). True statements, compared to false statements (errors or lies), also have different linguistic characteristics (Laney & Loftus, 2010; Vrij, 2008). These same principles could plausibly be extended to distinguishing true from false confessions.

However, there are several reasons for caution in extrapolating from these findings to real-world forensic contexts. First, what counts as high (e.g., better than chance) accuracy in the laboratory might not be adequate for forensic situations requiring a higher standard of proof. And even in the laboratory, some studies have found reliable biomarkers, but others have not (e.g., Laney & Loftus, 2010; Schacter et al., 2012). Second, even if a neurophysiological marker can distinguish *on average* between two groups, such as liars and truth tellers, it cannot say definitively whether a given witness or suspect is lying or telling the truth—though it would be relevant as one piece of evidence, among others, making one or the other hypothesis more likely. Third, there are practical considerations: Who would administer the brain scan to suspects? At what point in the process? And at whose expense? Finally, overcoming these obstacles would still leave ethical considerations. Replacing human evaluators of evidence with mechanical ones, even for only a narrowly circumscribed set of judgments, might have the advantage of improving truth determinations; but it would come with the cost of eliminating the flexibility, nuance, and personal touch that are inherent in human judgment.[4]

Despite these limitations, it seems certain that as technology continues to advance, techniques for imaging the brain, and for correlating brain activity or physiological indicators with forensically relevant behavior and cognitive performance, will develop further. Artificial intelligence is also likely to play a role. For example, machine learning (e.g., natural language processing) is already being used to analyze contracts and other legal documents (Marr, 2018); this same technique could potentially be applied to analyzing witnesses' and suspects' statements for veracity. One thing we can be sure of is that as technology advances, the cheaters and criminals will find more sophisticated ways to cheat and beat the system.

Advances in Correctional Psychology and Treating Mentally Ill Offenders

The intertwined phenomena of mass incarceration and prison overcrowding in the late 20th/early 21st-century United States have led to a number of correctional reforms, such as the privatization of prisons, revised sentencing guidelines, and alternatives to incarceration like increased community-based supervision (e.g., home confinement, with or without electronic monitoring). Little is known about the implications of these changes for recidivism, prisoner or correctional workers' well-being, or public safety—yet they pose significant risks as well as benefits. For example, private prisons—while potentially more cost-effective than government-run prisons—pay their workers less and are often more dangerous environments for correctional workers and prisoners alike (Bauer, 2018). If the greater efficiency of private prisons entails the provision of fewer services and programs, then prisoners' mental and emotional well-being could suffer. Insofar as mental health issues

[4] Arguably, a sufficiently sophisticated mechanical test could incorporate human characteristics of flexibility and nuance, but we leave that argument for another day. It would nonetheless be difficult, if not impossible, for a machine to fully capture the personal element involved in human judgment in forensic contexts. One could still argue, of course, that the "human touch" is an unnecessary and maybe even undesirable attribute of justice administration; we leave that argument for another day as well.

are widespread in prison populations (Prins, 2014), reducing services and/or making the detention environment more stressful would only exacerbate the problem.

These ill effects of incarceration can be lessened by alternatives like home confinement (i.e., house arrest). Home confinement, with or without electronic monitoring, is becoming increasingly prevalent—roughly 20% of adults and juveniles under community-based supervision are monitored electronically (Development Services Group, 2014). Despite electronic monitoring's clear cost savings compared to incarceration, and offenders' ability to continue working or attending school, evidence on whether it reduces recidivism is mixed (Development Services Group, 2014). Moreover, it raises a host of empirical questions that are largely unanswered: For what types of offenders (and for what kinds of offenses) is electronic monitoring more/less effective? What are the psychological effects, both pro and con, of electronic monitoring compared to traditional community-based supervision? How does it affect offenders' families? Does the prospect of home confinement with electronic monitoring pose less of a deterrent to crime than the prospect of incarceration? The importance of these questions is likely to increase as new technologies make electronic monitoring more practical, efficient, and affordable.

Although clinical-forensic psychology is extremely broad, it has concentrated the bulk of its efforts on assessment and evaluation (e.g., violence risk, various sorts of competency); in these efforts it has been quite successful, developing ever more reliable instruments and techniques (Melton et al., 2007)—a trend that is likely to continue, to the field's benefit. Less attention has been paid to the treatment of offenders with mental illness (Heilbrun & Griffin, 1999). It is beyond the scope of the present work to explore reasons for this comparative neglect, which might include factors like the criminal justice system's deemphasis of rehabilitation as a punishment goal and the resistance to treatment of some offense categories, such as sexual violence and child sexual abuse (e.g., Seto, 2008). We also do not mean to imply that forensic psychologists have been ignoring treatment altogether, as numerous treatment-focused regimens exist, in both prisons and the community (e.g., educational, skills-based, behavioral, and rehabilitative programs; see Heilbrun & Griffin, 1999; Hollin, 2013); we merely suggest, rather, that much work remains to be done.

Actuarial Methods

Although they are not a new topic in psychology and law, we expect actuarial risk assessment instruments to become more common and to be used in novel contexts. Actuarial methods are already widely used to predict dangerousness and recidivism for purposes of sentencing or civil commitment, especially for certain classes of offenders, such as sex offenders (e.g.,

Rettenberger, Rice, Harris, & Eher, 2017). The use of such instruments is still somewhat controversial (e.g., Hart & Cooke, 2013; Litwack, 2001), but they have consistently been shown to predict recidivism, especially violent recidivism, reasonably well (e.g., Rettenberger et al., 2017; Singh, Grann, & Fazel, 2011); moreover, they do so better than intuitive clinical judgments (Hanson & Morton-Bourgon, 2009), although not necessarily better than structured judgments by professional clinicians that can incorporate data from the same kinds of instruments (Fazel, Singh, Doll, & Grann, 2012).

Structured risk assessment tools are currently quite common. For example, Neal and Grisso (2014) found that a large (n = 434), international sample of forensic mental health clinicians used some sort of structured tool in nearly all criminal risk evaluations: 89% of violence risk assessments and 97% of sex offender risk assessments. These data suggest that actuarial risk assessment instruments, either on their own or in conjunction with clinical judgment, will soon be—if they are not already—the standard method of predicting violence risk in forensic settings, although work remains to be done in determining precisely how to use them and how (or whether) to combine them with clinical judgment (Hart & Cooke, 2013). According to one recent paper, "[t]he development and distribution of standardized psychological instruments for the assessment of recidivism risk in sexual and violent offenders is one of the most pioneering and influential improvements in the last decades of risk prediction research" (Rettenberger et al., 2017, p. 624). Thus, predicting their increased use seems like something of a no-brainer.

Of perhaps greater relevance to predicting future trends, there are signs that actuarial methods will also be used for other kinds of tasks. For example, in August 2018 California became the first state to eliminate cash bail (scheduled to take effect in October 2019); several other states have curtailed the practice (Fuller, 2018). Under the new system, rather than being evaluated based on their ability to post bail, suspects will be assessed in terms of their risk to public safety and the risk that they will fail to appear in court (Fuller, 2018). California is still in the process of figuring out how to make these assessments, but it seems likely that some sort of actuarial risk assessment instrument will be part of the decision-making calculus. This provides a new opportunity for psycholegal scholars, as some of the relevant risk factors presumably overlap with those used for other purposes—that is, predicting violence and the risk to public safety seem to go hand in hand. However, other risk factors, such as those predicting failure to appear, are almost certainly different. Criminal defendants fail to appear in court for a variety of reasons (Bornstein, Tomkins, Neeley, Herian, & Hamm, 2013), many of which appear to have little to do with their potential for violence (e.g., work or other scheduling conflicts, transportation problems). In the future, actuarial tools might be used in making any number of other decisions, such as determining eligibility for pretrial diversion programs, specialty courts, or parole—further expanding the multifarious situations in which mental health professionals already conduct psychological evaluations for the courts (Melton et al., 2007).

Death Penalty Research: On Its Way Out?

Research on psychological elements of capital punishment, such as conviction proneness of death-qualified jurors, jurors' comprehension of and ability to follow capital jury instructions, and the role of extralegal factors (e.g., race/ethnicity) in sentencing, has been a prominent topic within psychology and law for several decades, inspired largely by the US Supreme Court's jurisprudence on the issue (e.g., *Furman v. Georgia*, 1972; for review, see Bornstein & Greene, 2017; Haney, 2005). However, there is evidence that capital punishment is on the decline in the United States: According to the Death Penalty Information Center, only 30 states and the federal government currently have the death penalty, the lowest number in years, and three of those states (Colorado, Pennsylvania, and Oregon) are under gubernatorial moratoria (https://deathpenaltyinfo.org/states-and-without-death-penalty).[5] Eight of those death penalty abolitions and all of the moratoria have occurred since 2007, suggesting that policymakers' support for the death penalty is waning. Public support has also declined substantially since the mid-1990s. In 1996, 78% of Americans favored the death penalty for people convicted of murder; this figure reached a four-decade low of 49% in 2016, increasing slightly to 54% in 2018 (Oliphant, 2018; see also Hritz, Royer, & Hans, 2019). Concurrently, the number of capital trials, death sentences, and executions have all declined in recent years (Bornstein & Greene, 2017; Hritz et al., 2019).

Assuming these trends continue, they raise the question: Why conduct research on capital juries? On the one hand, capital trials seem to be a crucible for studying psychological variables that exist to a smaller degree in many jury trials, such as media influence, emotional responding, gruesome and complex evidence, and highly consequential decisions. On the other hand, the death decision is qualitatively different from other jury tasks in many respects—that is, "death is different," owing to a variety of procedural (e.g., death qualification, weighing of aggravating and mitigating circumstances) and substantive factors (e.g., prosecutors' litigation strategies, nature of the offense and penalty; see, generally, Haney, 2005). Thus, it would be reasonable to expect psycholegal scholars to lose interest in conducting death penalty research, journal editors and book publishers to lose interest in publishing it, and readers to lose interest in reading it. Death penalty research has been of great value to the field—and it seems likely that the research conducted by psychologists and other social scientists has contributed to declining public and legislative support for capital punishment—but it is entirely possible that

---

[5] The legislature of an additional state, Nebraska, abolished the death penalty in 2015, but Nebraska voters reinstated it in 2016.

within a generation or two, it will have outlived both its scientific and its practical usefulness.

One factor in the decline of capital jury trials is, arguably, the decline in all kinds of jury trials—civil and criminal, state and federal (Bornstein & Greene, 2017; Galanter, 2004). One could therefore argue that jury research, as a whole, will diminish in volume and importance in the coming years. This is certainly possible, but we think it is unlikely. Jury trials are increasing outside the United States (Hans et al., 2017), continue to be a hallmark of the American justice system as enshrined in the Constitution, and offer a unique opportunity for direct civic participation (Gastil, Deess, Weiser, & Simmons, 2010) and the expression of community sentiment (Hans, 2014). In addition, the psychological processes that underlie jury decision making in noncapital trials, at both the individual and group levels, are common to decision making in other domains—involving, as they do, fundamental processes of weighing evidence and possible outcomes, hypothesis testing, persuasion, story construction, group behavior, and so on (Bornstein & Greene, 2017; Devine, 2012). Thus, a decline in empirical research on capital juries would not jeopardize the field of jury research as a whole.

Conclusions

The list of topics covered in the present chapter—both of things Münsterberg addressed and of those he did not—is necessarily incomplete; it illustrates only some of the many ways in which psychology and law has grown over the past century and will undoubtedly continue to expand. Münsterberg recognized early on that the more science and law work together, the more both stand to benefit. And this need is only becoming greater: "As the knowledge of science and the procedures of law evolve, the need for this 'cross-pollination' becomes ever more necessary" (Baltimore, Tatel, & Mazza, 2018, p. 191). For psychology and law as a discipline, this growth is, by and large, a good thing—it shows that psychology's relevance to the legal system transcends whatever questions happen to be the issues of the day. However, it also runs the risk of "balkanization," according to which subdisciplines become so large and focused in their own right that they cease to talk to one another, leading psychology and law to lose any sort of unifying theme (Hart, 2002, p. 3). This raises the question: "Is there something at the heart of psychology and law that connects all of the field's diversity, bonding it across time and its diversified subfields?" (Grisso, 2018, p. 21).

According to Grisso (2018), the heart of psychology and law lies in its dual commitments to science and advocacy. "Committed to science and advocacy": that would have been a fitting epitaph for Hugo Münsterberg. As one of the most prominent and successful members of the first generation of experimental psychologists, and director of the psychology laboratory at the

United States' preeminent institution of higher learning, Münsterberg was nothing if not committed to science. He trained students in research methods, invented tools for scientific investigation, and studied a staggering array of empirical questions. By today's subdisciplinary nomenclature, he could be classified as a physiological, cognitive, social, personality, industrial-organizational, legal, or even clinical psychologist—though he would fit most comfortably as a general applied psychologist. His commitment to science as a serious undertaking never wavered.

As *On the Witness Stand* makes clear, his commitment to advocacy—the *uses* of science for the benefit of society—did not waver either. Humble about psychology's potential applications he was not. Münsterberg was an early proponent of using psychology in the courts and other venues (e.g., the workplace), advocating so strongly for his science's relevance to practical matters that he endured a significant backlash, including ad hominem attacks, from both the popular and the academic press (see Chapters 1 and 2). In an era when most psychologists were opposed, in their efforts to establish psychology as a legitimate science, to venturing outside the laboratory, Münsterberg was the most vocal advocate for psychology of his generation. Although many others made significant and lasting contributions to psychology and law at the same time as Münsterberg, and even earlier, in his dual commitments to science and advocacy, he rightfully deserves to be considered, if not the sole founder of the field, then its most noteworthy early figure.

In his obituary of Münsterberg, William Stern (1917) eulogized him as follows: "In Münsterberg psychology loses one of its most important leaders and most stimulating thinkers, whose thoughts will fructify both theory and practice long after his premature death" (p. 188). More than 100 years later, it is evident that Münsterberg has fulfilled Stern's prediction. His ideas have fructified the field in ways too numerous to count, and they continue to do so. A contemporary reappraisal, taking into account where the field of psychology and law stands in the first quarter of the 21st century, makes it clear that his influence continues. It would not be at all surprising if that were still the case another century from now.

References

Agosta, S., Pezzoli, P., & Sartori, G. (2013). How to detect deception in everyday life and the reasons underlying it. *Applied Cognitive Psychology, 27*, 256–262.

Akehurst, L., Köhnken, G., Vrij, A., & Bull, R. (1996). Lay persons' and police officers' beliefs regarding deceptive behaviour. *Applied Cognitive Psychology, 10*, 461–471. doi:10.1002/(SICI)1099-0720(199612)10:6<461::AID-ACP413>3.0.CO;2-2

Allen, J. J., Iacono, W. G., & Danielson, K. D. (1992). The identification of concealed memories using the event-related potential and implicit behavioral measures: A methodology for prediction in the face of individual differences. *Psychophysiology, 29*, 504–522.

Allwood, C. M., & Granhag, P. A. (1999). Feelings of confidence and the realism of confidence judgements in everyday life. In P. Juslin & H. Montgomery (Eds.), *Judgement and decision making: Lens-modeling and process tracing approaches* (pp. 123–146). Hillsdale, NJ: Lawrence Erlbaum.

Almerigogna, J., Ost, J., Bull, R., & Akehurst, L. (2007). A state of high anxiety: How non-supportive interviewers can increase the suggestibility of child witnesses. *Applied Cognitive Psychology, 21*, 963–974. doi:10.1002/acp.1311

Altman, C. M., Schreiber Compo, N., McQuiston, D., Hagsand, A. V., & Cervera, J. (2018). Witnesses' memory for events and faces under elevated levels of intoxication. *Memory, 26*, 946–959. doi:10.1080/09658211.2018.1445758

Alvarez, M. J., Miller, M. K., & Bornstein, B. H. (2016). "It will be your duty . . . :" The psychology of criminal jury instructions. In M. K. Miller & B. H. Bornstein (Eds.), *Advances in psychology and law* (Vol. 1, pp. 119–158). New York, NY: Springer. doi:10.1007/978-3-319-29406-3_4

Amendola, K. L., & Wixted, J. T. (2015). Comparing the diagnostic accuracy of suspect identifications made by actual eyewitnesses from simultaneous and sequential lineups in a randomized field trial. *Journal of Experimental Criminology, 11*, 263–284. doi:10.1007/s11292-014-9219-2

American Institute of Criminal Law and Criminology (1910). *Proceedings of the first national conference on criminal law and criminology.* Chicago, IL: Northwestern University Press.

Anastasi, A. (1964). *Fields of applied psychology.* New York, NY: McGraw-Hill.

Anthony, T., Copper, C., & Mullen, B. (1992). Cross-racial facial identification: A social cognitive integration. *Personality and Social Psychology Bulletin, 18*, 296–301.

Areh, I. (2011). Gender-related differences in eyewitness testimony. *Personality and Individual Differences, 50*, 559–563. doi:10.1016/j.paid.2010.11.027

Arnold, G. F. (1906). *Psychology applied to legal evidence and other constructions of law.* Calcutta: Thacker, Spink & Co.

Ashcraft v. Tennessee, 322 U.S. 143 (1944).

Assefi, S. L., & Garry, M. (2003). Absolut memory distortions: Alcohol placebos influence the misinformation effect. *Psychological Science, 14*, 77–80.

Babiak, P., Folino, J., Hancock, J., Hare, R. D., Logan, M., Mayer, E. L., . . . Woodworth, M. (2012, July). Psychopathy: An important forensic concept for the 21st century. *FBI Law Enforcement Bulletin, 81*, 3–8.

Bain, S. A., Baxter, J. S., & Ballantyne, K. (2007). Self-monitoring style and levels of interrogative suggestibility. *Personality and Individual Differences, 42*, 623–630. doi:10.1016/j.paid.2006.08.021

Baker, L. A., Barton, M., & Raine, A. (2002). The southern California twin register at the University of Southern California. *Cambridge University Press, 5*, 456–459. doi:10.1375/136905202320906273

Baker, L. A., Jacobson, K. C., Raine, A., Lozano, D. I., & Bezdjian, S. (2007). Genetic and environmental bases of childhood antisocial behavior: A multi-informant twin study. *Journal of Abnormal Psychology, 116*, 219–235. doi:10.1037/0021-843X.116.2.219

Baldwin, J. M. (1903). *Mental development in the child and the race: Methods and processes* (2nd ed., corrected). New York, NY: Macmillan.

Baltimore, D., Tatel, D. S., & Mazza, A. (2018). Bridging the science-law divide. *Daedalus, 147*(4), 181–194. doi:10.1162/DAED_a_00528

Barclay, C. R., & Wellman, H. M. (1986). Accuracies and inaccuracies in autobiographical memories. *Journal of Memory and Language, 25*, 93–103.

Barland, G. H. (1988). The polygraph test in the USA and elsewhere. In A. Gale (Ed.), *The polygraph test: Lies, truth and science* (pp. 73–95). London, UK: Sage.

Barnes, H. E. (1948). *An introduction to the history of sociology.* Chicago, IL: University of Chicago Press.

Barnier, A. J., Dienes, Z., & Mitchell, C. J. (2008). How hypnosis happens: New cognitive theories of hypnotic responding. In M. R. Nash, A. J. Barnier, M. R. Nash, & A. J. Barnier (Eds.), *The Oxford handbook of hypnosis: Theory, research, and practice* (pp. 141–177). New York, NY: Oxford University Press.

Barnier, A. J., & McConkey, K. M. (1992). Reports of real and false memories: The relevance of hypnosis, hypnotizability, and context of memory test. *Journal of Abnormal Psychology, 101*, 521–527.

Barrash, J., Tranel, D., & Anderson, S. W. (2000). Acquired personality disturbances associated with bilateral damage to the ventromedial prefrontal region. *Developmental Neuropsychology, 18*, 355–381.

Bartol, C. R., & Bartol, A. M. (2006). *Current perspectives in forensic psychology and criminal justice*. Thousand Oaks, CA: Sage.

Bartol, C. R., & Freeman, N. J. (2005). History of the American Association for Correctional Psychology. *Criminal Justice and Behavior, 32*, 123–142. doi:10.1177/0093854804272893

Baudouin, C. (1921; transl. by E. & C. Paul). *Suggestion and autosuggestion: A psychological and pedagogical study based upon the investigations made by the new Nancy school*. New York, NY: Dodd, Mead & Co.

Bauer, S. (2018). *American prison: A reporter's undercover journey into the business of punishment*. New York, NY: Penguin.

Beard, G. M. (1878). The scientific study of human testimony. *Popular Science Monthly, 13*, 53–64.

Beaver, K. M., Boutwell, B. B., & Barnes, J. C. (2014). Social support or biosocial support? A genetically informative analysis of social support and its relation to self-control. *Criminal Justice and Behavior, 41*, 453–470. doi:10.1177/0093854813504918

Beaver, K. M., DeLisi, M., Wright, J. P., Boutwell, B. B., Barnes, J. C., & Vaughn, M. G. (2013). No evidence of racial discrimination in criminal justice processing: Results from the national longitudinal study of adolescent health. *Personality and Individual Differences, 55*, 29–34. doi:10.1016/j.paid.2013.01.020

Beer, J. S., John, O. P., Scabini, D., & Knight, R. T. (2006). Orbitofrontal cortex and social behavior: Integrating self-monitoring and emotion-cognition interactions. *Journal of Cognitive Neuroscience, 18*, 871–879. doi:10.1162/jocn.2006.18.6.871

Behrman, B. W., & Davey, S. L. (2001). Eyewitness identification in actual criminal cases: An archival analysis. *Law and Human Behavior, 25*, 475–491.

Behrman, B. W., & Richards, R. E. (2005). Suspect/foil identification in actual crimes and in the laboratory: A reality monitoring analysis. *Law and Human Behavior, 29*, 279–301.

Bell, B. E., & Loftus, E. F. (1989). Trivial persuasion in the courtroom: The power of (a few) minor details. *Journal of Personality and Social Psychology, 56*, 669–679. doi:10.1037/0022-3514.56.5.669

Bem, D. J. (1966). Inducing belief in false confessions. *Journal of Personality and Social Psychology, 3*, 707–710. doi:10.1037/h0023226

Ben-Shakhar, G. (2008). The case against the use of polygraph examinations to monitor post-conviction sex offenders. *Legal and Criminological Psychology, 13*, 191–207. doi:10.1348/135532508X298577

Ben-Shakhar, G. (2012). Current research and potential applications of the concealed information test: An overview. *Frontiers in Psychology, 3*, 1–11. doi:10.3389/fpsyg.2012.00342

Ben-Shakhar, G., & Elaad, E. (2002). Effects of questions' repetition and variation on the efficiency of the guilty knowledge test: A reexamination. *Journal of Applied Psychology, 87,* 972–977.

Ben-Shakhar, G., & Elaad, E. (2003). The validity of psychophysiological detection of information with the Guilty Knowledge Test: A meta-analytic review. *Journal of Applied Psychology, 88,* 131–151. doi:10.1037/0021-9010.88.1.131

Ben-Shakhar, G., & Furedy, J. J. (1990). *Theories and applications in the detection of deception: A psychophysiological and international perspective.* New York, NY: Springer-Verlag.

Benjamin, L. T. (2005). A history of clinical psychology as a profession in America (and a glimpse at its future). *Annual Review of Clinical Psychology, 1,* 1–30. doi:10.1146/annurev.clinpsy.1.102803.143758

Benjamin, L. T. (2006). Hugo Münsterberg's attack on the application of scientific psychology. *Journal of Applied Psychology, 91,* 414–425. doi:10.1037/0021-9010.91.2.414

Benjamin, L. T., & Baker, D. B. (2004). *From séance to science: A history of the profession of psychology in America.* Belmont, CA: Thomson/Wadsworth.

Benton, D. (2007). The impact of diet on antisocial, violent and criminal behaviour. *Neuroscience and Biobehavioral Reviews, 31,* 752–774. doi:10.1016/j.neubiorev.2007.02.002

Benton, D., Kumari, N., & Brain, P. F. (1982). Mild hypoglycaemia and questionnaire measures of aggression. *Biological Psychology, 14,* 129–135. doi:10.1016/0301-0511(82)90020-5

Benton, D., & Owens, D. (1993). Is raised blood glucose associated with the relief of tension? *Journal of Psychosomatic Research, 37,* 723–735. doi:10.1016/0022-3999(93)90101-K

Benton, T. R., McDonnell, S., Ross, D. F., Thomas, N., & Bradshaw, E. (2007). Has eyewitness research penetrated the American legal system? A synthesis of case history, juror knowledge, and expert testimony. In R. C. L. Lindsay, D. F. Ross., J. D. Read, & M. P. Toglia (Eds.), *The handbook of eyewitness psychology, Vol. 2. Memory for people* (pp. 453–500). Mahwah, NJ: Erlbaum.

Bergold, A. N., & Heaton, P. (2018). Does filler database size influence identification accuracy? *Law and Human Behavior, 42,* 227–243. doi:10.1037/lhb0000289

Bigelow, K. M., & Morris, E. K. (2001). John B. Watson's advice on child rearing. *Behavioral Development Bulletin, 1,* 26–30.

Binet, A. (1900). La suggestibilité [On suggestibility]. *Bibliothèque de pédagogie et de psychologie* (Vol. 3). Paris, France: Schleicher Frères.

Binet, A. (1905). La science du témoignage (travaux de l'année 1904). *L'Année Psychologique, 11,* 128–136.

Birbaumer, N., Veit, R., Lotze, M., Erb, M., Hermann, C., Grodd, W., & Flor, H. (2005). Deficient fear conditioning in psychopathy: A functional magnetic resonance imaging study. *Archives of General Psychiatry, 62,* 799–805. doi:10.1001/archpsyc.62.7.799

Bjork, J. M., Chen, G., & Hommer, D. W. (2012). Psychopathic tendencies and mesolimbic recruitment by cues for instrumental and passively obtained rewards. *Biological Psychology, 89,* 408–415. doi:10.1016/j.biopsycho.2011.12.003

Blackstone, W. (1979). *Commentaries on the Laws of England.* 4 vols. Facsimile reprint ed. of the 1st ed. of 1765–69. Chicago, IL: University of Chicago Press.

Blair, I. V., Lenton, A. P., & Hastie, R. (2002). The reliability of the DRM paradigm as a measure of individual differences in false memories. *Psychonomic Bulletin & Review, 9,* 590–596.

Blair, R. R. (2009). The amygdala and ventromedial prefrontal cortex: Functional contributions and dysfunction in psychopathy. In S. Hodgins, E. Viding, A. Plodowski, S. Hodgins, E. Viding, & A. Plodowski (Eds.), *The neurobiological basis of violence: Science and rehabilitation* (pp. 123–136). New York, NY: Oxford University Press.

Bloom, R. M. (2002). *Ratting: The use and abuse of informants in the American justice system.* Westport, CT: Praeger.

Blumenfeld, H. (2002). *Neuroanatomy through clinical cases.* Sunderland, MA: Sinauer.

Blumenthal, J. A. (2010). Property law: A cognitive turn. *Psychonomic Bulletin & Review, 17,* 186–191.

Bond, C. J., & DePaulo, B. M. (2006). Accuracy of deception judgments. *Personality and Social Psychology Review, 10,* 214–234. doi:10.1207/s15327957pspr1003_2

Bond, C. J., & DePaulo, B. M. (2008). Individual differences in judging deception: Accuracy and bias. *Psychological Bulletin, 134,* 477–492. doi:10.1037/0033-2909.134.4.477

Bonnie, R. J., & Grisso, T. (2000). Adjudicative competence and youthful offenders. In T. Grisso, R. G. Schwartz, T. Grisso, & R. G. Schwartz (Eds.), *Youth on trial: A developmental perspective on juvenile justice* (pp. 73–103). Chicago, IL: University of Chicago Press.

Borawick v. Shay (1994). 68 F.3d 597 (2nd Cir. 1995).

Bornstein, B. H. (2017a). Jury simulation research: Pros, cons, trends and alternatives. In M. B. Kovera (Ed.), *The psychology of juries* (pp. 207–226). Washington, DC: American Psychological Association.

Bornstein, B. H. (2017b). *Popular myths about memory: Media representations versus scientific evidence.* Lanham, MD: Lexington Books.

Bornstein, B. H., Deffenbacher, K. A., McGorty, E. K., & Penrod, S. D. (2012). Effects of exposure time and cognitive operations on facial identification accuracy: A meta-analysis of two variables associated with initial memory strength. *Psychology, Crime & Law, 18,* 473–490.

Bornstein, B. H., Golding, J. L., Neuschatz, J., Kimbrough, C., Reed, K., Magyarics, C., & Luecht, K. (2017). Mock juror sampling issues in jury simulation research: A meta-analysis. *Law and Human Behavior, 41,* 13–28.

Bornstein, B. H., & Greene, E. (2017). *The jury under fire: Myth, controversy, and reform.* New York, NY: Oxford University Press.

Bornstein, B. H., & Hamm, J. A. (2012). Jury instructions on witness identification. *Court Review, 48,* 48–53.

Bornstein, B. H., Hullman, G., & Miller, M. K. (2013). Stress, trauma, and wellbeing in the legal system: Where do we go from here? In M. K. Miller & B. H. Bornstein (Eds.), *Stress, trauma, and wellbeing in the legal system* (pp. 293–309). New York, NY: Oxford University Press.

Bornstein, B. H., & Kleynhans, A. J. (2019). The evolution of jury research methods: From Hugo Münsterberg to the modern age. *Denver Law Review, 96*, 813–829.

Bornstein, B. H., Laub, C. E., Meissner, C. A., & Susa, K. J. (2013). The cross-race effect: Resistant to instructions. *Journal of Criminology, 2013*, 1–6, doi:10.1155/2013/745836

Bornstein, B. H., & McCabe, S. G. (2005). Jurors of the absurd? The role of consequentiality in jury simulation research. *Florida State University Law Review, 32*, 443–467.

Bornstein, B. H., & Meissner, C. A. (2008). Introduction: Basic and applied issues in eyewitness research: A Münsterberg centennial retrospective. *Applied Cognitive Psychology, 22* (6), 733–736.

Bornstein, B. H., & Penrod, S. D. (2008). Hugo who? G.F. Arnold's early contributions to psychology and law. *Applied Cognitive Psychology, 22*, 759–768.

Bornstein, B. H., O'Bryant, S., & Zickafoose, D. J. (2008). Intuitions about arousal and eyewitness memory: Effects on mock jurors' judgments. *Law and Psychology Review, 32*, 109–129.

Bornstein, B. H., & Robicheaux, T. R. (2009). Methodological issues in the study of eyewitness memory and arousal. *Creighton Law Review, 42*, 525–547.

Bornstein, B. H., Tomkins, A. J., Neeley, E. M., Herian, M. N., & Hamm, J. A. (2013). Reducing courts' failure-to-appear rate by written reminders. *Psychology, Public Policy, & Law, 19*, 70–80.

Bornstein, B. H., Wiener, R. L., & Maeder, E. M. (2008). Pioneers in interdisciplinary legal education: A history of the UNL law-psychology program. In A. G. Gless (Ed.), *The history of Nebraska law* (pp. 174–194). Athens, OH: Ohio University Press.

Bornstein, B. H., & Zickafoose, D. J. (1999). "I know I know it, I know I saw it': The stability of the confidence-accuracy relationship across domains. *Journal of Experimental Psychology: Applied, 5*, 76–88.

Bothwell, R. K., Deffenbacher, K. A., & Brigham, J. C. (1987). Correlation of eyewitness accuracy and confidence: Optimality hypothesis revisited. *Journal of Applied Psychology, 72*, 691–695.

Boyce, M., Beaudry, J., & Lindsay, R. C. L. (2007). Belief of eyewitness identification evidence. In R. C. L. Lindsay, D. F. Ross., J. D. Read, & M. P. Toglia (Eds.), *The handbook of eyewitness psychology Vol. 2. Memory for people* (pp. 501–525). Mahwah, NJ: Erlbaum.

Braffman, W., & Kirsch, I. (1999). Imaginative suggestibility and hypnotizability: An empirical analysis. *Journal of Personality and Social Psychology, 77*, 578–587.

Brainerd, C. J., & Reyna, V. F. (2005). *The science of false memory*. New York, NY: Oxford University Press.

Braun, K. A., Ellis, R., & Loftus, E. F. (2002). Make my memory: How advertising can change our memories of the past. *Psychology & Marketing, 19*, 1–23.

Bray, C. (2006, June 3). "Hell, someone's cut this girl in half!" *The Telegraph*. Available at https://www.telegraph.co.uk/culture/books/3652732/Hell-someones-cut-this-girl-in-half.html

Brennan, P. A., & Mednick, S. A. (1993). Genetic perspectives on crime. *Acta Psychiatrica Scandinavica, 87*(Suppl 370), 19–26. doi:10.1111/j.1600-0447.1993.tb05357.x

Brennan, P. A., Mednick, S. A., & Raine, A. (1997). Biosocial interactions and violence: A focus on perinatal factors. In A. Raine, P. A. Brennan, D. P. Farrington, & S. A. Mednick (Eds.), *NATO ASI series: Series A: Life sciences, Vol. 292. Biosocial bases of violence* (pp. 163–174). New York, NY: Plenum Press. http://dx.doi.org/10.1007/978-1-4757-4648-8_10

Brewer, N., Caon, A., Todd, C., & Weber, N. (2006). Eyewitness identification accuracy and response latency. *Law and Human Behavior, 30*, 31–50.

Brewer, N., Weber, N., & Semmler, C. (2007). Eyewitness identification. In N. Brewer & K. D. Williams (Eds.), *Psychology and law: An empirical perspective* (pp. 177–221). New York, NY: Guilford Press.

Brewer, N., & Wells, G. L. (2006). The confidence-accuracy relationship in eyewitness identification: Effects of lineup instructions, foil similarity, and target-absent base rates. *Journal of Experimental Psychology: Applied, 12*, 11–30.

Briggs, J., Harrison, C., Mcinnes, A., & Vincent D. (1996). *Crime and punishment in England: An introductory history.* Abingdon, Ozon: Routledge.

Brigham, J. C., Bennett, L. B., Meissner, C. A., & Mitchell, T. L. (2007). The influence of race on eyewitness memory. In R. C. L. Lindsay, D. F. Ross, J. D. Read, & M. P. Toglia (Eds.), *Handbook of eyewitness psychology, Vol. 2. Memory for people.* (pp. 257–281). Mahwah, NJ: Lawrence Erlbaum.

Brigham, J. C., Maas, A., Snyder, L. D., & Spaulding, K. (1982). Accuracy of eyewitness identifications in a field setting. *Journal of Personality and Social Psychology, 42*, 673–681.

Brigham, J. C., Van Verst, M., & Bothwell, R. K. (1986). Accuracy of children's eyewitness identifications in a field setting. *Basic and Applied Social Psychology, 7*, 295–306.

Brodes v. State, 614 S.E. 2d 766 (Ga. 2005).

Brodsky, S. L. (2007). Correctional psychology and the American Association of Correctional Psychology. *Criminal Justice and Behavior, 34*, 862–869. doi:10/1177/0093854807301993

Broomhall, L. (2005). Acquired sociopathy: A neuropsychological study of executive dysfunction in violent offenders. *Psychiatry, Psychology and Law, 12*, 367–387. doi:10.1375/pplt.12.2.367

Brower, M. C., & Price, B. H. (2001). Neuropsychiatry of frontal lobe dysfunction in violent and criminal behaviour: A critical review. *Journal of Neurology, Neurosurgery & Psychiatry, 71*, 720–726. doi:10.1136/jnnp.71.6.720

Brown v. Board of Education of Topeka, 347 U.S. 483 (1954).

Brown v. Mississippi, 297 U.S. 278, (1936).

Brown, E., Deffenbacher, K., & Sturgill, W. (1977). Memory for faces and the circumstances of encounter. *Journal of Applied Psychology, 2*, 311–318.

Brown, M. R. (1926). *Legal psychology: Psychology applied to the trial of cases, to crime and its treatment, and to mental states and processes.* Indianapolis, IN: Bobbs-Merrill.

Brown, N .N., Gudjonsson, G., & Connor, P. (2011). Suggestibility and fetal alcohol spectrum disorders: I'll tell you anything you want to hear. *Journal of Psychiatry & Law, 39*, 39–71.

Brown, R. E. (1994). *The Death of the Messiah, From Gethsemane to the Grave, Volume 1*. New York, NY: Doubleday.

Bruck, M., & Melnyk, L. (2004). Individual differences in children's suggestibility: A review and synthesis. *Applied Cognitive Psychology, 18*, 947–996. doi:10.1002/acp.1070

Brunner, H. G., Nelen, M., Breakefield, X. O., Ropers, H. H., & van Oost, B. A. (1993). Abnormal behavior associated with a point mutation on the structural gene for monoamine oxidase A. *Science, 262*, 578–580.

Buckhout, R. (1974). Eyewitness testimony. *Scientific American, 231*, 23–31.

Burckhardt, J. (1998). *The Greeks and Greek civilization*. New York, NY: St. Martin's Press.

Burtt, H. E. (1931). *Legal psychology*. New York, NY: Prentice-Hall.

Buydens-Branchey, L., Branchey, M., Hudson, J., & Fergeson, P. (2000). Low HDL cholesterol, aggression and altered central serotonergic activity. *Psychiatry Research, 93*, 93–102. doi:10.1016/S0165-1781(99)00126-2

Cairns, H. (1935). *Law and the social sciences*. London, England: Kegan Paul, Trench Trubner and Co.

Callahan, L. A., Steadman, H. J., McGreevy, M. A., & Robbins, P. C. (1991). The volume and characteristics of insanity defense pleas: An eight-state study. *Bulletin of The American Academy of Psychiatry & The Law, 19*, 331–338.

Calvillo, D. P. (2014). Individual differences in susceptibility to misinformation effects and hindsight bias. *Journal of General Psychology, 14*, 393–407. doi:10.1080/00221309.2014.954917

Calvillo, D. P., Parong, J. A., Peralta, B., Ocampo, D., & Van Gundy, R. (2016). Sleep increases susceptibility to the misinformation effect. *Applied Cognitive Psychology, 30*, 1061–1067. doi:10.1002/acp.3259

Candel, I., Merckelbach, H. L., Loyen, S., & Reyskens, H. (2005). "I hit the Shift-key and then the computer crashed": Children and false admissions. *Personality and Individual Differences, 38*(6), 1381–1387. doi:10.1016/j.paid.2004.09.005

Cardeña, E., & Carlson, E. (2011). Acute stress disorder revisited. *Annual Review of Clinical Psychology, 7*, 245–267. doi:10.1146/annurevclinpsy-032210-104502

Caspi, A., McClay, J., Moffitt, T., Mill, J., Martin, J., Craig, I. W., . . . Poulton, R. (2002). Role of genotype in the cycle of violence in maltreated children. *Science, 297*, 851–854. doi:10.1126/science.1072290

Cattell, J. M. (1895). Measurements of the accuracy of recollection. *Science, 2*, 761–766.

Cautin, R. L. (2009). The founding of the Association for Psychological Science: Part 1. Dialectical tensions within organized psychology. *Perspectives of Psychological Science, 4*, 211–223.

Ceci, S. J., & Bruck, M. (1995). *Jeopardy in the courtroom: A scientific analysis of children's testimony*. Washington, DC: American Psychological Association.

Ceci, S. J., & Friedman, R. D. (2000). The suggestibility of children: Scientific research and legal implications. *Cornell Law Review, 86*, 33–108.

Ceci, S. J., Huffman, M. L. C., Smith, E., & Loftus, E. F. (1994). Repeatedly thinking about a non-event: Source misattributions among preschoolers. *Consciousness & Cognition, 3*, 388–407.

Chabris, C. F., Weinberger, A., Fontaine, M., & Simons, D. J. (2011). You do not talk about Fight Club if you do not notice Fight Club: Inattentional blindness for a simulated real-world assault. *I-Perception, 2*(2): 150–153. doi:10.1068/i0436

Cheit, R. E. (2014). *The witch-hunt narrative: Politics, psychology, and the sexual abuse of children*. New York: Oxford University Press.

Chojnacki, D. E., Cicchini, M. D., & White, L. T. (2008). An empirical basis for the admission of expert testimony on false confessions. *Arizona State Law Journal, 40*, 1–45.

Christiaansen, R. E., Ochalek, K., & Sweeney, J. D. (1984). Individual differences in eyewitness memory and confidence judgments. *Journal of General Psychology, 110*, 47–52.

Christianson, S. A., & Hübinette, B. (1993). Hands up! A study of witnesses' emotional reactions and memories associated with bank robberies. *Applied Cognitive Psychology, 7*, 365–379.

Christov-Moore, L., Simpson, E. A., Coudé, G., Grigaityte, K., Iacoboni, M., & Ferrari, P. F. (2014). Empathy: Gender effects in brain and behavior. *Neuroscience and Biobehavioral Review, 46*, 604–627.

Cirincione, C., Steadman, H. J., & McGreevy, M. A. (1995). Rates of insanity acquittals and the factors associated with successful insanity pleas. *Bulletin of The American Academy of Psychiatry & The Law, 23*, 399–409.

Clancy, S. A. (2005). *Abducted: How people come to believe they were kidnapped by aliens*. Cambridge, MA: Harvard University Press.

Clancy, S. A., McNally, R. J., Schacter, D. L., Lenzenweger, M. F., & Pitman, R. K. (2002). Memory distortion in people reporting abduction by aliens. *Journal of Abnormal Psychology, 111*, 455–461.

Claparède, E. (1906). La psychologie judiciaire. *L'année Psychologique, 12*, 274–302.

Clark, S. E. (2012). Costs and benefits of eyewitness identification reform: Psychological science and public policy. *Perspectives on Psychological Science, 7*, 238–259. doi:10.1177/1745691612439584

Clarke, J., Prescott, K., & Milne, R. (2013). How effective is the cognitive interview when used with adults with intellectual disabilities specifically with conversation recall? *Journal of Applied Research in Intellectual Disabilities, 26*, 546–556. doi:10.1111/jar.12049

Clifasefi, S. L., Takarangi, M. K., & Bergman, J. S. (2006). Blind drunk: The effects of alcohol on inattentional blindness. *Applied Cognitive Psychology, 20*, 697–704.

Clifford, B. R. (1983). Memory for voices: The feasibility and quality of earwitness evidence. In S. M. A. Lloyd-Bostock & B. R. Clifford (Eds.), *Evaluating witness evidence* (pp. 189–218). Chichester, England: Wiley.

Clifford, B. R., Rathborn, H., & Bull, R. (1981). The effects of delay on voice recognition accuracy. *Law and Human Behavior, 5*, 201–208.

Cloninger, C. R., & Gottesman, I. I. (1987). Genetic and environmental factors in antisocial behavior disorders. In S. A. Mednick, T. E. Moffitt, & S. A.

Stack (Eds.), *The causes of crime: New biological approaches* (pp. 92–109). Cambridge, UK: Cambridge University Press.

Cloninger, C. R., Sigvardsson, S., Bohman, M., & von Knorring, A. L. (1982). Predisposition to petty criminality in Swedish adoptees, II: Cross-fostering analysis of gene-environment interaction. *Archives of General Psychiatry, 39*, 1242–1247.

Cochrane, R. E., Grisso, T., & Frederick, R. I. (2001). The relationship between criminal charges, diagnoses, and psycholegal opinions among federal pretrial defendants. *Behavioral Sciences and the Law, 19*, 565–582. doi:10.1002/bsl.454

Colloff, M. F., & Flowe, H. D. (2016). The effects of acute alcohol intoxication on the cognitive mechanisms underlying false facial recognition. *Psychopharmacology, 233*, 2139–2149. doi:10.1007/s00213-016-4263-4

Cook, S., & Wilding, J. (1997). Earwitness testimony: Never mind the variety, hear the length. *Applied Cognitive Psychology, 11*, 527–541.

Cooper, R. M., & Zubek, J. P. (1958). Effects of enriched and restricted early environments on the learning ability of bright and dull rats. *Canadian Journal of Psychology/Revue canadienne de psychologie, 12*, 159–164. doi:10.1037/h0083747

Correll, J., Park, B., Judd, C. M., & Wittenbrink, B. (2007). The influence of stereotypes on decisions to shoot. *European Journal of Social Psychology, 37*, 1102–1117. doi:10.1002/ejsp.450

Correll, J., Park, B., Judd, C. M., Wittenbrink, B., Sadler, M. S., & Keesee, T. (2007). Across the thin blue line: Police officers and racial bias in the decision to shoot. *Journal of Personality and Social Psychology, 92*, 1006–1023. doi:10.1037/0022-3514.92.6.1006

Costa, P. T., Terracciano, A., & McCrae, R. R. (2001). Gender differences in personality traits across cultures: Robust and surprising findings. *Journal of Personality and Social Psychology, 81*, 322–331.

Costanzo, M., Shaked-Schroer, N., & Vinson, K. (2010). Juror beliefs about police interrogations, false confessions, and expert testimony. *Journal of Empirical Legal Studies, 7*, 231–247.

Crawford, W. R. (1948). Representative Italian contributions to sociology: Pareto, Loria, Vaccaro, Gini, and Sighele. In H. E. Barnes (Ed.), *An introduction to the history of sociology* (pp. 553–584). Chicago, IL: University of Chicago Press.

Crighton, D. A., & Towl, G. J. (2008). *Psychology in prisons* (2nd ed.). Malden, MA: BPS Blackwell.

Crocker, C. B., & Kovera, M. B. (2011). Systematic jury selection. In R. L. Wiener & B. H. Bornstein (Eds.), *Handbook of trial consulting* (pp. 13–31). New York, NY: Springer.

Cummings, J. L., & Miller, B. L. (2007). Conceptual and clinical aspects of the frontal lobes. In B. L. Miller, J. L. Cummings, B. L. Miller, J. L. Cummings (Eds.), *The human frontal lobes: Functions and disorders* (2nd ed., pp. 12–21). New York, NY: Guilford Press.

Cutler, B. L. (2009). *Expert testimony on the psychology of eyewitness identification*. New York, NY: Oxford University Press.

Cutler, B. L., Dexter, H. R., & Penrod, S. D. (1990). Nonadversarial methods for sensitizing jurors to eyewitness evidence. *Journal of Applied Social Psychology, 20*, 1197–1207.

Cutler, B. L., & Penrod, S. D. (1989). Forensically relevant moderators of the relation between eyewitness identification accuracy and confidence. *Journal of Applied Psychology, 74*, 650–652.

Cutler, B. L., Penrod, S. D., & Martens, T. K. (1987). Improving the reliability of eyewitness identification: Putting context into context. *Journal of Applied Psychology, 72*, 629–637.

Cutler, B. L., Penrod, S. D., & Stuve, T. E. (1988). Juror decision making in eyewitness identification cases. *Law and Human Behavior, 12*, 41–55.

Cutler, B. L., & Wells, G. L. (2009). Expert testimony regarding eyewitness identification. In K. S. Douglas & J. L. Skeem (Eds.), *Psychological science in the courtroom: Consensus and controversy* (pp. 100–123). New York, NY: Guilford Press.

Dalenberg, C. J., Brand, B. L., Gleaves, D. H., Dorahy, M. J., Loewenstein, R. J., Cardeña, E., . . . Spiegel, D. (2012). Evaluation of the evidence for the trauma and fantasy models of dissociation. *Psychological Bulletin, 138*, 550–588. doi:10.1037/a0027447

Dallenbach, K. M. (1913). The relation of memory error to time interval. *Psychological Review, 20*, 323–337.

Damaser, E., Whitehouse, W. G., Orne, M. T., Orne, E. C., & Dinges, D. F. (2010). Behavioral persistence in carrying out a posthypnotic suggestion beyond the hypnotic context: A consideration of the role of perceived demand characteristics. *International Journal of Clinical and Experimental Hypnosis, 58*, 1–20.

Damasio, A. R. (1994). *Descartes' error: Emotion, rationality and the human brain.* New York, NY: Putnam.

Danckert, J., Maruff, P., Ymer, C., Kinsella, G., Yucel, M., de Graaff, S., & Currie, J. (2000). Goal-directed selective attention and response competition monitoring: Evidence from unilateral parietal and anterior cingulate lesions. *Neuropsychology, 14*, 16–28. doi:10.1037/0894-4105.14.1.16

Dasse, M. N., Elkins, G. R., & Weaver, C. I. (2015). Hypnotizability, not suggestion, influences false memory development. *International Journal of Clinical and Experimental Hypnosis, 63*, 110–128.

Daubert v. Merrell Dow Pharmaceuticals, 509 U.S. 579, 113 S. Ct. 2786 (1993).

Davidson, R. J. (1994). On emotion, mood, and related affective constructs. In P. Ekman & R. J. Davidson (Eds.), *The nature of emotion: Fundamental questions* (pp. 51–55). New York, NY: Oxford University Press.

Davies, G., & Hine, S. (2007). Change blindness and eyewitness testimony. *Journal of Psychology: Interdisciplinary and Applied, 141*, 424–434.

Davis, D., & Loftus, E. F. (2007). Internal and external sources of misinformation in adult witness memory. In M. P. Toglia et al. (Eds.), *Handbook of eyewitness psychology, Vol. 1. Memory for events* (pp. 195–237). Mahwah, NJ: Erlbaum.

Davis, D., Loftus, E. F., Vanous, S., & Cucciare, M. (2008). "Unconscious transference" can be an instance of change blindness. *Applied Cognitive Psychology, 22*, 605–623.

Davis, J. P., & Valentine, T. (2009). CCTV on trial: Matching video images with the defendant in the dock. *Applied Cognitive Psychology, 23*, 482–505. doi:10.1002/acp.1490

Day, D. V., Schleicher, D. J., Unckless, A. L., & Hiller, N. J. (2002). Self-monitoring personality at work: A meta-analytic investigation of construct validity. *Journal of Applied Psychology, 87*, 390–401. doi:10.1037//0021-9010.87.2.390

Deffenbacher, K. A. (1980). Eyewitness accuracy and confidence: Can we infer anything about their relationship? *Law and Human Behavior, 4*, 243–260.

Deffenbacher, K. A., Bornstein, B. H., McGorty, E. K., & Penrod, S. D. (2008). Forgetting the once-seen face: Estimating the strength of an eyewitness's memory representation. *Journal of Experimental Psychology: Applied, 14*, 139–150.

Deffenbacher, K. A., Bornstein, B. H., & Penrod, S. D. (2006). Mugshot exposure effects: Retroactive Interference, mugshot commitment, source confusion, and unconscious transference. *Law and Human Behavior, 30*, 287–307.

Deffenbacher, K. A., Bornstein, B. H., Penrod, S. D., & McGorty, E. K. (2004). A meta-analytic review of the effects of high stress on eyewitness memory. *Law and Human Behavior, 28*, 687–706. doi:10.1007/s10979-004-0565-x

DePaulo, B. M., Lindsay, J. J., Malone, B. E., Muhlenbruck, L., Charlton, K., & Cooper, H. (2003). Cues to deception. *Psychological Bulletin, 129*, 74–118. doi:10.1037/0033-2909.129.1.74

DePaulo, B. M., & Pfeifer, R. L. (1986). On-the-job experience and skill at detecting deception. *Journal of Applied Social Psychology, 16*, 249–267.

Development Services Group, Inc. (2014). *Home confinement and electronic monitoring: Literature review.* Washington, DC: Office of Juvenile Justice and Delinquency Prevention. Retrieved from https://www.ojjdp.gov/mpg/litreviews/Home_Confinement_EM.pdf

Devenport, J. L., & Cutler, B. L. (2004). Impact of defense-only and opposing eyewitness experts on juror judgments. *Law and Human Behavior, 28*, 569–576.

Devenport, J. L., Kimbrough, C. D., & Cutler, B. L. (2009). Effectiveness of traditional safeguards against erroneous conviction arising from mistaken eyewitness identification. In B.L. Cutler (Ed.), *Expert testimony on the psychology of eyewitness identification* (pp. 51–68). New York, NY: Oxford University Press.

Devenport, J. L., Stinson, V., Cutler, B. L., & Kravitz, D. A. (2002). How effective are the cross-examination and expert testimony safeguards? Jurors' perceptions of the suggestiveness and fairness of biased lineup procedures. *Journal of Applied Psychology, 87*, 1042–1054.

Devine, D. J. (2012). *Jury decision making: The state of the science.* New York, NY: NYU Press.

Devine, D. J., Clayton, L. D., Dunford, B. B., Seying, R., & Pryce, J. (2001). Jury decision making: 45 years of empirical research on deliberating groups. *Psychology, Public Policy, and Law, 7*, 622–727.

Devinsky, O., Morrell, M. J., & Vogt, B. A. (1995). Contributions of anterior cingulate cortex to behaviour. *Brain: A Journal of Neurology, 118*, 279–306. doi:10.1093/brain/118.1.279

Dewsbury, D. A., & Bolles, R. C. (1995). The founding of the Psychonomic Society. *Psychonomic Bulletin & Review, 2*, 216–233.

Dhingra, K., & Boduszek, D. (2013) Psychopathy and criminal behaviour: A psychosocial research perspective. *Journal of Criminal Psychology, 3*, 83–107. doi:10.1108/JCP-06-2013-0014

Diamond, B. L. (1980). Inherent problems in the use of pretrial hypnosis on a prospective witness. *California Law Review, 68*, 313–349. doi:https://doi.org/10.15779/Z38VF2D

Doerner, J. K., & Demuth, S. (2010). The independent and joint effects of race/ethnicity, gender, and age on sentencing outcomes in U.S. federal courts. *Justice Quarterly, 27*, 1–27. doi:10.1080/07418820902926197

Doherty-Sneddon, G., & Phelps, F. G. (2005). Gaze aversion: A response to cognitive or social difficulty? *Memory and Cognition, 33*, 727–733.

Dolan, M., & Park, I. (2002). The neuropsychology of antisocial personality disorder. *Psychological Medicine, 32*, 417–427. doi:10.1017/S0033291702005378

Donders, F. C. (1868/1969). Over de snelheid van psychische processen. (On the speed of mental processing.) *Acta Psychologica, 30*, 412–431.

Doob, A. N., & Kirshenbaum, H. M. (1973). Bias in police lineups—Partial remembering. *Journal of Police Science and Administration, 18*, 287–293.

Douglass, A. B., Neuschatz, J. S., Imrich, J., & Wilkinson, M. (2010) Does post-identification feedback affect evaluations of eyewitness testimony and identification procedures? *Law and Human Behavior, 34*, 282–294.

Douglass, A. B., & Smalarz, L. (2019). Post-Identification feedback to eyewitnesses: Implications for system variable reform. In B. H. Bornstein & M. K. Miller (Eds.), *Advances in psychology and law* (Vol. 4, pp. 101–135). New York, NY: Springer.

Douglass, A. B., & Steblay, N. K. (2006). Memory distortion in eyewitnesses: A meta-analysis of the post-identification feedback effect. *Applied Cognitive Psychology, 20*, 859–869.

Doyle, J. M. (2005). *True witness: Cops, courts, science, and the battle against misidentification*. New York, NY: Palgrave Macmillan.

Driscoll, L. N. (1994). A validity assessment of written statements from suspects in criminal investigations using the SCAN technique. *Police Studies, 17*, 77–88.

Drivdahl, S. B., & Zaragoza, M. S. (2001). The role of perceptual elaboration and individual differences in the creation of false memories for suggested events. *Applied Cognitive Psychology, 15*, 265–281. doi:10.1002/acp.701

Drivdahl, S. B., Zaragoza, M. S., & Learned, D. M. (2009). The role of emotional elaboration in the creation of false memories. *Applied Cognitive Psychology, 23*, 13–35. doi:10.1002/acp.1446

Drizin, S. A., & Leo, R. A. (2004). The problem of false confessions in the post-DNA world. *North Carolina Law Review, 82*, 891–1007.

Dunning, D., & Perretta, S. (2002). Automaticity and eyewitness accuracy: A 10 to 12-second rule for distinguishing accurate from inaccurate positive identifications. *Journal of Applied Psychology, 87*, 951–962.

Dunning, D., & Stern, L. B. (1994). Distinguishing accurate from inaccurate identifications via inquiries about decision processes. *Journal of Personality and Social Psychology, 67*, 818–835.

Duren v. Missouri, 439 U.S. 357 (1979).

Durham v. United States, 214 F.2d 862 (D.C. Cir. 1954).

Dusky v. United States, 362 U.S. 402 (1960).

Dvoskin, J. A., Spiers, E. M., & Brodsky, S. L. (2007). Correctional psychology: Law, ethics, and practice. In A. M. Goldstein (Ed.), *Forensic psychology: Emerging topics and expanding roles* (pp. 605–632). Hoboken, NJ: Wiley.

Dysart, J. E., Lindsay, R .C. L., MacDonald, T. K., & Wicke, C. (2002). The intoxicated witness: Effects of alcohol on identification accuracy from showups. *Journal of Applied Psychology, 87*, 170–175.

Ebbesen, E. B., & Konecni, V. J. (1975). Decision making and information integration in the courts: The setting of bail. *Journal of Personality and Social Psychology, 32*, 805–821.

Eich, E. (2007). Context: Mood, memory and the concept of context. In H. L. Roediger, Y. Dudai, & S. M. Fitzpatrick, *Science of memory: Concepts* (pp. 107–110). New York, NY: Oxford University Press.

Eichenbaum, H. (2012). *The cognitive neuroscience of memory* (2nd ed.). New York, NY: Oxford.

Eisen, M. L., Goodman, G. S., Qin, J. J., Davis, S., & Crayton, D. (2007). Maltreated children's memory: Accuracy, suggestibility, and psychopathology. *Developmental Psychology, 43*, 1275–1294. doi:10.1037/0012-1649.43.6.1275

Eisen, M. L., & Lynn, S. J. (2001). Dissociation, memory and suggestibility in adults and children. *Applied Cognitive Psychology, 15*, 49–73. doi:10.1002/acp.834

Eisen, M. L., Qin, J., Goodman, G. S., & Davis, S. L. (2002). Memory and suggestibility in maltreated children: Age, stress arousal, dissociation, and psychopathology. *Journal of Experimental Child Psychology, 83*, 167–212.

Eisen, M. L., Smith, A. M., Olaguez, A. P., & Skerritt-Perta, A. S. (2017). An examination of showups conducted by law enforcement using a field-simulation paradigm. *Psychology, Public Policy, and Law, 23*, 1–22. doi:10.1037/law0000115

Ekman, P. (1997). Deception, lying, and demeanor. In D. F. Halpern, A. E. Voiskounsky, D. F. Halpern, A. E. Voiskounsky (Eds.), *States of mind: American and post-Soviet perspectives on contemporary issues in psychology* (pp. 93–105). New York, NY: Oxford University Press.

Ekman, P. (2001). *Telling lies: Clues to deceit in the marketplace, politics and marriage*. New York, NY: Norton. (Original work published 1985).

Elaad, E. (1990). Detection of guilty knowledge in real-life criminal investigations. *Journal of Applied Psychology, 75*, 521–529. doi:10.1037/0021-9010.75.5.521

Elaad, E. (1997). Polygraph examiner awareness of crime-relevant information and the guilty knowledge test. *Law and Human Behavior, 21*, 107–120.

Elaad, E. (1998). The challenge of the concealed knowledge polygraph test. *Expert Evidence, 6*, 161–187.

Elaad, E. (1999). The challenge of the Concealed Knowledge Polygraph Test. *Expert Evidence, 6*, 161–187. doi:10.1023/A:1008855511254

Elaad, E., Ginton, A., & Ben-Shakhar, G. (1994). The effects of prior expectations and outcome knowledge on polygraph examiners' decisions.

Journal of Behavioral Decision Making, 7, 279–292. doi:10.1002/bdm.3960070405

Elaad, E., Ginton, A., & Jungman, N. (1992). Detection measures in real-life criminal guilty knowledge tests. *Journal of Applied Psychology, 77*, 757–767. doi:10.1037/0021-9010.77.5.757

Epstein, J. (2009). Expert testimony: Legal standards for admissibility. In B. L. Cutler (Ed.), *Expert testimony on the psychology of eyewitness identification* (pp. 69–89). Oxford, England: Oxford University Press.

Erdelyi, M. H. (1994). The empty set of hypermnesia. *International Journal of Clinical and Experimental Hypnosis, 42*, 379–390. doi:10.1080/00207149408409366

Escobedo v. Illinois, 378 U.S. 478 (1964).

Evans, J. R., Schreiber Compo, N., & Russano, M. (2009). Intoxicated witnesses and suspects: Procedures and prevalence according to law enforcement. *Psychology, Public Policy and Law, 15*, 194–221.

Fabian, J. M. (2010). Neuropsychological and neurological correlates in violent and homicidal offenders: A legal and neuroscience perspective. *Aggression and Violent Behavior, 15*, 209–223. doi:10.1016/j.avb.2009.12.004

Faigman, D. L., Blumenthal, J., Cheng, E., Mnookin, J., Murphy, E., & Sanders, J. (2014). *Modern scientific evidence: The law and science of expert testimony*. Eagan, MN: Thomson Reuters/West.

Fairchild, G., Van Goozen, S. H., Stollery, S. J., & Goodyer, I. M. (2008). Fear conditioning and affective modulation of the startle reflex in male adolescents with early-onset or adolescence-onset conduct disorder and healthy control subjects. *Biological Psychiatry, 63*, 279–285. doi:10.1016/j.biopsych.2007.06.019

Fava, M., Abraham, M., Pava, J., Shuster, J., & Rosenbaum, J. (1996). Cardiovascular risk factors in depression: The role of anxiety and anger. *Psychosomatics: Journal of Consultation and Liaison Psychiatry, 37*, 31–37. doi:10.1016/S0033-3182(96)71595-5

Fawcett, J. M., Russell, E. J., Peace, K. A., & Christie, J. (2013). Of guns and geese: A meta-analytic review of the "weapon focus" literature. *Psychology, Crime & Law, 19*, 35–66. doi:10.1080/1068316X.2011.599325

Fazel, S., Singh, J.P ., Doll, H., & Grann, M. (2012). Use of risk assessment instruments to predict violence and antisocial behaviour in 73 samples involving 24,827 people: Systematic review and meta-analysis. BMJ: *British Medical Journal, 345*, e4692. doi:10.1136/bmj.e4692

Fazio, R., & Denney, R. L. (2015). Assessment of neurophysiological and neuropsychological bases for violence. In C. A. Pietz, C. A. Mattson, C. A. Pietz, & C. A. Mattson (Eds.), *Violent offenders: Understanding and assessment* (pp. 425–451). New York, NY: Oxford University Press.

Feingold, A. (1994). Gender differences in personality: A meta-analysis. *Psychological Bulletin, 116*, 429–456. doi:10.1037/0033-2909.116.3.429

Feingold, G. A. (1914). The influence of environment on identification of persons and things. *Journal of the American Institute of Criminal Law and Criminology, 5*, 39–51.

Ferguson, Z. (2015, March 26). Where is John Mark Karr, The man who falsely confessed to JonBenet Ramsey's murder, and what is he doing now? *Bustle*.

Available at https://www.bustle.com/articles/72098-where-is-john-mark-karr-the-man-who-falsely-confessed-to-jonbenet-ramseys-murder-what
Finkel, N. J. (1988). *Insanity on trial.* New York, NY: Plenum.
Finkel, N. J. (1995). *Commonsense justice: Jurors' notions of the law.* Cambridge, MA: Harvard University Press.
Fisher, R. P., & Geiselman, R. E. (1992). *Memory-enhancing techniques in investigative interviewing: The cognitive interview.* Springfield, IL: Charles C. Thomas.
Fisher, R. P., Geiselman, R. E., & Amador, M. (1989). Field test of the cognitive interview: Enhancing the recollection of actual victims and witnesses of crime. *Journal of Applied Psychology, 74*, 722–727.
Fisher, R. P., & Schreiber, N. (2007). Interviewing protocols to improve eyewitness memory. In M. P. Toglia, J. D. Read, D. F. Ross, & R. C. L. Lindsay (Eds.), *Handbook of eyewitness psychology, Vol. 1. Memory for events* (pp. 53–80). Mahwah, NJ: Lawrence Erlbaum.
Fitzgerald, R. J., Oriet, C., & Price, H. L. (2016). Change blindness and eyewitness identification: Effects on accuracy and confidence. *Legal and Criminological Psychology, 21*, 189–201.
Fitzgerald, R. J., & Price, H. L. (2015). Eyewitness identification across the life span: A meta-analysis of age differences. *Psychological Bulletin, 141*, 1228–1265. doi:10.1037/bul0000013
Flowe, H. D., Finklea, K. M., & Ebbesen, E. B. (2009). Limitations of expert psychology testimony on eyewitness identification. In B. L. Cutler (Ed.), *Expert testimony on the psychology of eyewitness identification* (pp. 201–221). New York, NY: Oxford University Press.
Flowe, H. D., Takarangi, M. K. T., Humphries, J. E., & Wright, D. S. (2016). Alcohol and remembering a hypothetical sexual assault: Can people who were under the influence of alcohol during the event provide accurate testimony? *Memory, 24*, doi:10.1080/09658211.2015.1064536
Forgas, J. P. (2010). Affect in legal and forensic settings: The cognitive benefits of not being too happy. In B. H. Bornstein & R. L. Wiener (Eds.), *Emotion and the law: Psychological perspectives* (pp. 13–44). New York, NY: Springer.
Forgas, J. P., Goldenberg, L., & Unkelbach, C. (2009). Can bad weather improve your memory? An unobtrusive field study of mood effects on eyewitness memory. *Journal of Experimental Social Psychology, 45*, 254–257.
Forgas, J. P., Vargas, P., & Laham, S. (2005). Mood effects on eyewitness memory: Affective influences on susceptibility to misinformation. *Journal of Experimental Social Psychology, 41*, 574–588.
Forrest, K. D., Woody, W. D., Brady, S. E., Batterman, K. C., Stastny, B. J., & Bruns, J. A. (2012). False-evidence ploys and interrogations: Mock jurors' perceptions of ploy type, deception, coercion, and justification. *Behavioral Sciences and the Law, 30*, 342–364.
Fox, S. G., & Walters, H. A. (1986). The impact of general versus specific expert testimony and eyewitness confidence upon mock juror judgment. *Law and Human Behavior, 10*, 215–228.
Frank, M. G., & Feeley, T. H. (2003). To catch a liar: Challenges for research in lie detection training. *Journal of Applied Communication Research, 31*, 58–75.

Frazier v. Cupp, 394 U.S. 731 (1969).
Frenda, S. J., Patihis, L., Loftus, E. F., Lewis, H. C., & Fenn, K. M. (2014). Sleep deprivation and false memories. *Psychological Science, 25*, 1674–1681. doi:10.1177/0956797614534694
Freud, S. (1901/1960). *The psychopathology of everyday life* (trans. by A. Tyson). New York, NY: W.W. Norton.
Frijda, N. H. (1994). Varieties of affect: Emotions and episodes, moods, and sentiments. In P. Ekman & R. J. Davidson (Eds.), *The nature of emotion: Fundamental questions* (pp. 59–67). New York, NY: Oxford University Press.
Frye v. United States, 293 F. 1013 (D.C. Cir. 1923).
Fulero, S. M. (1999). A history of Division 41 (American Psychology-Law Society): A rock and roll odyssey. In D. A. Dewsbury (Ed.), *Unification through division: Histories of the divisions of the American Psychological Association* (Vol. 4) (pp. 109–127). Washington, DC: American Psychological Association.
Fuller, T. (2018, August 28). California is the first state to scrap cash bail. *New York Times*. Retrieved from https://www.nytimes.com/2018/08/28/us/california-cash-bail.html.
Furedy, J. J., Davis, C., & Gurevich, M. (1988). Differentiation of deception as a psychological process: A psychophysiological approach. *Psychophysiology, 25*, 683–688.
Furman v. Georgia, 408 U.S. 238 (1972).
Furumoto, L. (1980). Mary Whiton Calkins (1863–1930). *Psychology of Women Quarterly, 5*, 55–68. doi:0361-6843/80/1500-0055$00.95
Gabbert, F., Hope, L., & Fisher, R. P. (2009). Protecting eyewitness evidence: Examining the efficacy of a self-administered interview tool. *Law and Human Behavior, 33*, 298–307. doi:10.1007/s10979-008-9146-8
Gajos, J. M., & Beaver, K. M. (2016). The effect of omega-3 fatty acids on aggression: A meta-analysis. *Neuroscience and Biobehavioral Reviews, 69*, 147–158. doi:10.1016/j.neubiorev.2016.07.017
Galanter, M. (2004). The vanishing trial: An examination of trials and related matters in federal and state courts. *Journal of Empirical Legal Studies, 1*, 459–570.
Gallo, D. A. (2010). False memories and fantastic beliefs: 15 years of the DRM illusion. *Memory & Cognition, 38*, 833–848.
Galton, F. (1892). *Finger prints*. London, England: Macmillan.
Ganis, G. (2015). Deception detection using neuroimaging. In P. A. Granhag, A. Vrij, & B. Verschuere (Eds.), *Wiley series in the psychology of crime, policing and law. Detecting deception: Current challenges and cognitive approaches* (pp. 105–121). Hoboken, NJ: Wiley-Blackwell.
Ganis, G., Rosenfeld, J. P., Meixner, J., Kievit, R. A., & Schendan, H. E. (2011). Lying in the scanner: Covert countermeasures disrupt deception detection by functional magnetic resonance imaging. *Neuroimage, 55*, 312–319.
Garrett, B. (2011). *Convicting the innocent: Where criminal prosecutors go wrong.* Cambridge, MA: Harvard University Press.
Garry, M., Manning, C. G., Loftus, E. F., & Sherman, S. J. (1996). Imagination inflation: Imagining a childhood event inflates confidence that it occurred. *Psychonomic Bulletin & Review, 3*, 208–214.

Gastil, J., Deess, E. P., Weiser, P., & Simmons, C. (2010). *The jury and democracy: How jury deliberation promotes civic engagement and political participation*. New York, NY: Oxford University Press.

Gatowski, S. I., Dobbin, S. A., & Summers, A. (2013). Exploring the value-added of specialized problem-solving courts for dependency cases. In R. L. Wiener & E. Brank (Eds.), *Problem solving courts: Social science and legal perspectives* (pp. 33–53). New York, NY: Springer.

Gawrylowicz, J., Memon, A., & Scoboria, A. (2014). Equipping witnesses with transferable skills: The Self-Administered Interview. *Psychology, Crime & Law, 20*, 315–325. doi:10.1080/1068316X.2013.777961

Gawrylowicz, J., Ridley, A. M., Albery, I. P., Barnoth, E., & Young, J. (2017). Alcohol-induced retrograde facilitation renders witnesses of crime less suggestible to misinformation. *Psychopharmacology, 234*, 1267–1275. doi:10.1007/s00213-017-4564-2

Gay, P. (1988). *Freud: A life for our time*. New York, NY: W.W. Norton.

Geiselman, R. E., & Callot, R. (1990). Reverse versus forward recall of script-based texts. *Applied Cognitive Psychology, 4*, 141–144. doi:10.1002/acp.2350040206

Geiselman, R. E., Fisher, R. P., Cohen, G., Holland, H., & Surtes, L. (1986). Eyewitness responses to leading and misleading questions under the cognitive interview. *Journal of Police Science & Administration, 14*, 31–39.

Geiselman, R. E., & Mendez, B. A. (2005). Assistance to the fact finder: Eyewitness expert testimony versus attorneys' closing arguments. *American Journal of Forensic Psychology, 23*, 5–15.

Geiselman, R. E., Putman, C., Korte, R., Shahriary, M., Jachimowicz, G., & Irzhevsky, V. (2002). Eyewitness expert testimony and juror decisions. *American Journal of Forensic Psychology, 20*, 1–16.

Geraerts, E. (2012). Cognitive underpinnings of recovered memories of childhood abuse. In R.F. Belli (Ed.), *True and false recovered memories: Toward a reconciliation of the debate* (pp. 175–191). New York, NY: Springer. doi:10.1007/978-1-4614-1195-6_6

Geraerts, E., Raymaekers, L., & Merckelbach, H. (2008). Recovered memories of childhood sexual abuse: Current findings and their legal implications. *Legal and Criminological Psychology, 13*, 165–176.

Geraerts, E., Schooler, J. W., Merckelbach, H., Jelicic, M., Hauer, B. J. A., & Ambadar, Z. (2007). The reality of recovered memories: Corroborating continuous and discontinuous memories of childhood sexual abuse. *Psychological Science, 18*, 564–568.

Gerrans, P. (2014). Pathologies of hyperfamiliarity in dreams, delusions and déjà vu. *Frontiers in Psychology, 5* (Art. 97), 1–10. doi:10.3389/fpsyg.2014.00097

Gerrie, M. P., Garry, M., & Loftus, E. F. (2005). False memories. In N. Brewer & K. D. Williams (Eds.), *Psychology and law: An empirical perspective* (pp. 222–253). New York, NY: Guilford Press.

Gill, C. D. (1989). The admissibility of hypnotically refreshed testimony: *Rock v. Arkansas. Boston College Law Review, 30*, 573–599.

Glenn, A. L., & Raine, A. (2014). Neurocriminology: Implications for the punishment, prediction and prevention of criminal behavior. *Nature Reviews Neuroscience, 15*, 54–63. doi:10.1038/nrn3640

Global Deception Research Team. (2006). A world of lies. *Journal of Cross-Cultural Psychology, 37*, 60–74.

Goldenweiser, A. (1948). The psychosociological thought of Wilhelm Wundt. In H. E. Barnes (Ed.), *An introduction to the history of sociology* (pp. 216–226). Chicago, IL: University of Chicago Press.

Golding, S. L., Skeem, J. L., Roesch, R., & Zapf, P. A. (1999). The assessment of criminal responsibility: Current controversies. In A. K. Hess, I. B. Weiner, A. K. Hess, & I. B. Weiner (Eds.), *The handbook of forensic psychology* (pp. 379–408). Hoboken, NJ: John Wiley & Sons.

Golomb, B. A., Stattin, H., & Mednick, S. (2000). Low cholesterol and violent crime. *Journal of Psychiatric Research, 34*, 301–309.

Goodsell, C. A., Neuschatz, J. S., & Gronlund, S. D. (2009). Effects of mugshot commitment on lineup performance in young and older adults. *Applied Cognitive Psychology, 23*, 788–803.

Gotz, M. J., Johnstone, E. C., & Ratcliffe, S. G. (1999). Criminality and antisocial behavior in unselected men with sex chromosome abnormalities. *Psychological Medicine, 29*, 953–962.

Granhag, P. A., Andersson, L. O., Strömwall, L. A., & Hartwig, M. (2004). Imprisoned knowledge: Criminals' beliefs about deception. *Legal and Criminological Psychology, 9*, 103–119. doi:10.1348/135532504322776889

Granhag, P. A., & Hartwig, M. (2008). A new theoretical perspective on deception detection: On the psychology of instrumental mind-reading. *Psychology, Crime & Law, 14*, 189–200. doi:10.1080/10683160701645181

Granhag, P. A., & Vrij, A. (2005). Detecting deception. In N. Brewer & K. Williams (Eds.), *Psychology and law: An empirical perspective* (pp. 43–92). New York, NY: Guilford Press.

Green, J. P., Lynn, S. J., & Malinoski, P. (1998). Hypnotic pseudomemories, prehypnotic warnings, and malleability of suggested memories. *Applied Cognitive Psychology, 12*, 431–444.

Green, J. P., Page, R. A., Rasekhy, R., Johnson, L. K., & Bernhardt, S. E. (2006). Cultural views and attitudes about hypnosis: A survey of college students across four countries. *International Journal of Clinical and Experimental Hypnosis, 54*, 263–280.

Greene, E., Wilson, L., & Loftus, E. F. (1989). Impact of hypnotic testimony on the jury. *Law and Human Behavior, 13*, 61–78. doi:10.1007/BF01056163

Greenwald, A. G., McGhee, D. E., & Schwartz, J. L. (1998). Measuring individual differences in implicit cognition: The implicit association test. *Journal of Personality and Social Psychology, 74*, 1464–1480.

Grisso, T. (1991). A developmental history of the American Psychology-Law Society. *Law and Human Behavior, 15*, 213–231.

Grisso, T. (2018). The evolution of psychology and law. In T. Grisso & S. L. Brodsky (Eds.), *The roots of modern psychology and law* (pp. 1–27). New York, NY: Oxford University Press.

Grisso, T., Steinberg, L., Woolard, J., Cauffman, E., Scott, E., Graham, S., . . . Schwartz, R. (2003). Juveniles' competence to stand trial: A comparison of adolescents' and adults' capacities as trial defendants. *Law and Human Behavior, 27*, 333–363. doi:10.1023/A:1024065015717

Gronau, N., Ben-Shakhar, G., & Cohen, A. (2005). Behavioral and physiological measures in the detection of concealed information. *Journal of Applied Psychology, 90*, 147–158.

Gross, H. (1897/1918). *Kriminal-psychologie* [Criminal psychology: A manual for judges, practitioners, and students]. Translated by H .M. Kallen. Boston, MA: Little, Brown & Co.

Gudjonsson, G. H. (1997). *The Gudjonsson suggestibility scales manual*. Hove, UK: Psychology Press.

Gudjonsson, G. H., Hannesdottir, K., Agustsson, T. P., Sigurdsson, J. F., Gudmundsdottir, A., Pordardottir, P., Tyrfingsson, P., & Petursson, H. (2004). The relationship of alcohol withdrawal symptoms to suggestibility and compliance. *Psychology, Crime & Law, 10*, 169–177. doi:10.1080/10683160310001609979

Gudjonsson, G. H., Hannesdottir, K., Petursson, H., & Tyrfingsson, T. (2000). The effects of alcohol withdrawal on memory, confabulation, and suggestibility. *Nordic Journal of Psychiatry, 54*, 213–220.

Gudjonsson, G. H., Vagni, M., Maiorano, T., & Pajardi, D. (2016). Age and memory related changes in children's immediate and delayed suggestibility using the Gudjonsson Suggestibility Scale. *Personality and Individual Differences, 102*, 25–29.

Guo, G., Ou, X. M., Roettger, M., & Shih, J. C. (2008). The VNTR 2 repeat in MAOA and delinquent behavior in adolescence and young adulthood: Associations and MAOA promoter activity. *European Journal of Human Genetics, 16*, 626–634. doi:10.1038/sj.ejhg.5201999

Guthrie, C., Rachlinski, J. J., & Wistrich, A. J. (2001). Inside the judicial mind. *Cornell Law Review, 86*, 777–830.

Guthrie, R. V. (2003). *Even the rat was white: A historical view of psychology* (2nd ed.). New York, NY: Pearson.

Hagsand, A., Roos af Hjelmsäter, E., Granhag, P. A., Fahlke, C., & Söderpalm Gordh, A. (2017). Witnesses stumbling down memory lane: The effects of alcohol intoxication, retention interval, and repeated interviewing. *Memory, 25*, 531–543. doi:10.1080/09658211.2016.1191652

Hakun, J. G., Ruparel, K., Seelig, D., Busch, E., Loughead, J. W., Gur, R. C., & Langleben, D. D. (2009). Towards clinical trials of lie detection with fMRI. *Social Neuroscience, 4*, 518–527. doi:10.1080/17470910802188370

Hale, M. (1980). *Human science and social order: Hugo Münsterberg and the origins of applied psychology*. Philadelphia, PA: Temple University Press.

Hall, D. F., Loftus, E. F., & Tousignant, J. P. (1984). Postevent information and changes in recollection for a natural event. In G. L. Wells & E. F. Loftus (Eds.), *Eyewitness testimony: Psychological perspectives* (pp. 124–141). Cambridge, England: Cambridge University.

Hancock, M., Tapscott, J. L., & Hoaken, P. N. (2010). Role of executive dysfunction in predicting frequency and severity of violence. *Aggressive Behavior, 36*, 338–349.

Haney, C. (2005). *Death by design*. Oxford, England: Oxford University Press.

Hans, V. P. (2014). What's it worth? Jury damage awards as community judgments. *William & Mary Law Review, 55*, 935–969.

Hans, V. P., Fukurai, H., Ivkovic, S. K., & Park, J. (2017). Global juries: A plan for research. In M. B. Kovera (Ed.), *The psychology of juries* (pp. 131–157). Washington, DC: American Psychological Association.

Hanson, R. K., & Morton-Bourgon, K. E. (2009). The accuracy of recidivism risk assessments for sexual offenders: A meta-analysis of 118 prediction studies. *Psychological Assessment, 21*, 1–21. doi:10.1037/a0014421

Hare, R. D., Frazelle, J., & Cox, D. N. (1978). Psychopathy and physiological responses to threat of an aversive stimulus. *Psychophysiology, 15*, 165–172. doi:10.1111/j.1469-8986.1978.tb01356.x

Hare, R. D., Hart, S. D., & Harpur, T. J. (1991). Psychopathy and the DSM-IV criteria for antisocial personality disorder. *Journal of Abnormal Psychology, 100*, 391–398. doi:10.1037/0021-843X.100.3.391

Harker v. Maryland, 800 F.2d 437 (4th Cir. 1986).

Harmon v. State, 700 P.2d 212 (Okla. Crim. App. 1985).

Hart, S. D. (2002, Fall). President's column: The state of the division. *American Psychology-Law Society News, 22*, 2–3, 8.

Hart, S. D., & Cooke, D. J. (2013). Another look at the (im-)precision of individual risk estimates made using actuarial risk assessment instruments. *Behavioral Sciences and the Law, 31*, 81–102. doi:10.1002/bsl.2049

Hartwig, M., Granhag, P. A., & Luke, T. (2014). Strategic use of evidence during investigative interviews: The state of the science. In D. C. Raskin, C. R. Honts, & J. C. Kircher (Eds.), *Credibility assessment: Scientific research and applications* (pp. 1–36). Oxford, UK: Academic Press.

Hartwig, M., Granhag, P. A., & Strömwall, L. A. (2007). Guilty and innocent suspects' strategies during police interrogations. *Psychology, Crime & Law, 13*, 213–227. doi:10.1080/10683160600750264

Hartwig, M., Granhag, P. A., Strömwall, L. A., & Andersson, L. O. (2004). Suspicious minds: Criminals' ability to detect deception. *Psychology, Crime & Law, 10*, 83–95. doi:10.1080/1068316031000095485

Hasel, L. E., & Kassin, S. M. (2009) On the presumptions of evidentiary independence: Can confessions corrupt eyewitness identifications? *Psychological Science, 20*, 122–126. doi:10.1111/j.1467-9280.2008.02262.x.

Hashtroudi, S., Parker, E. S., DeLisi, L. E., Wyatt, R. J., & Mutter, S. A. (1984). Intact retention in acute alcohol amnesia. *Journal of Experimental Psychology: Learning, Memory, and Cognition, 10*, 156–163.

Heaps, C., & Nash, M. (2001). Comparing recollective experience in true and false autobiographical memories. *Journal of Experimental Psychology: Learning, Memory, & Cognition, 27*, 920–930.

Heath, B. (2012). Federal prisoners use snitching for personal gain. *USA Today*. Retrieved from https://www.usatoday.com/story/news/nation/2012/12/14/jailhouse-informants-for-sale/1762013/

Heilbrun, K., & Griffin, P. (1999). Forensic treatment: A review of programs and research. In R. Roesch, S. D. Hart, & J. R. P. Ogloff (Eds.), *Psychology and law: The state of the discipline* (pp. 241–274). New York, NY: Kluwer/Plenum.

Heilbrun, K., Grisso, T., & Goldstein, A. M. (2009). *Foundations of forensic mental health assessment*. New York, NY: Oxford University Press.

Heinz, T., & Pezdek, K. (2001). The effect of exposure to multiple lineups on face identification accuracy. *Law and Human Behavior, 25*, 185–198.

Henderson, K. S., & Levett, L. M. (2018). Investigating predictors of true and false guilty pleas. *Law and Human Behavior, 42*, 427–441. doi:10.1037/lhb0000297

Henkel, L. A., Coffman, K. J., & Daily, E. M. (2008). A survey of people's attitudes and beliefs about false confessions. *Behavioral Sciences and the Law, 26*, 555–584. doi:10.1002/bsl.826

Henmon, V. A. C. (1911). The relation of the time of a judgment to its accuracy. *Psychological Review, 18*, 186–201. doi:10.1037/h0074579

Hildebrand Karlén, M. H., Roos af Hjelmsäter, E., Fahlke, C., Granhag, P. A., & Gordh, A. S. (2015). Alcohol intoxicated eyewitnesses' memory of intimate partner violence. *Psychology, Crime & Law, 21*, 156–171. doi:10.1080/1068316X.2014.951644

Hilgard, E. R. (1965). *Hypnotic susceptibility.* Oxford, England: Harcourt, Brace & World.

Hilgard, E. R. (1977). The problem of divided consciousness: A neodissociation interpretation. *Annals of the New York Academy of Sciences, 296*, 48–59.

Hillbrand, M., & Spitz, R. T. (1999). Cholesterol and aggression. *Aggression and Violent Behavior, 4*, 359–370. doi:10.1016/S1359-1789(98)00009-3

Hilliar, K. F., Kemp, R. I., & Denson, T. F. (2010). Now *everyone* looks the same: Alcohol intoxication reduces the own-race bias in face recognition. *Law & Human Behavior, 34*, 367–378. doi:10.1007/s10979-009-9204-x

Hippchen, L. J. (1976). Biochemical approaches to offender rehabilitation. *Offender Rehabilitation, 1*, 115–123. doi:10.1300/J418v01n01_11

Ho, D. E., & Kramer, L. (2013). The empirical revolution in law. *Stanford Law Review, 65*, 1195–1202.

Hodgson, R., & Davey, S. J. (1887). The possibilities of mal-observation and lapse of memory from a practical point of view. *Proceedings of the Society for Psychical Research, 4*, 381–495.

Hoge, S. K., Bonnie, R. J., Poythress, N., Monahan, J., Eisenberg, M., & Feucht-Haviar, T. (1997). The MacArthur adjudicative competence study: Development and validation of a research instrument. *Law and Human Behavior, 21*, 141–179.

Hollin, C. R. (2013). *Psychology and crime: An introduction to criminological psychology* (2nd ed.). London, England: Routledge.

Hollins, T. S., & Perfect, T. J. (1997). The confidence-accuracy relation in eyewitness event memory: The mixed question type effect. *Legal and Criminological Psychology, 2*, 205–218.

Honts, C. R., Amato, S., & Gordon, A. K. (2001). Effects of spontaneous counter-measures used against the comparison question test. *Polygraph, 30*, 1–9.

Hope, L., Gabbert, F., & Fisher, R. P. (2011). From laboratory to the street: Capturing witness memory using the Self-Administered Interview. *Legal and Criminological Psychology, 16*, 211–226. doi:10.1111/j.2044-8333.2011.02015.x

Hornak, J., Bramham, J., Rolls, E. T., Morris, R. G., O' Doherty, J., Bullock, P. R., & Polkey, C. E. (2003). Changes in emotion after circumscribed surgical lesions of the orbitofrontal and cingulate cortices. *Brain: A Journal of Neurology, 126*, 1691–1712. doi:10.1093/brain/awg168

Horry, R., Memon, A., Wright, D. B., & Milne, R. (2012). Predictors of eyewitness identification decisions from video lineups in England: A field study. *Law and Human Behavior, 36*, 257–265. doi:10.1037/h0093959

Horselenberg, R., Merckelbach, H., & Josephs, S. (2003). Individual differences and false confessions: A conceptual replication of Kassin and Kiechel (1996). *Psychology, Crime & Law, 9*, 1–8.

Horselenberg, R., Merckelbach, H., Smeets, T., Franssens D., Peters, G. Y., & Zeles, G. (2006). False confessions in the lab: Do plausibility and consequences matter? *Psychology, Crime & Law, 12*, 61–75. doi:10.1080/10683100420003O3076

Horvath, E. S., Jayne, B. P, & Buckley, J. P. (1994). Differentiation of truthful and deceptive criminal suspects in behavioural analysis interviews. *Journal of Forensic Sciences, 39*, 793–807.

Hosch, H. M., & Platz, S. J. (1984). Self-monitoring and eyewitness accuracy. *Personality and Social Psychology Bulletin, 10*, 289–292.

Hoskins, L. L., Roth, R. M., & Giancola, P. R. (2010). Neuroimaging of aggression: Empirical findings and implications. In A. J. Horton, L. C. Hartlage, A. J. Horton, L. C. Hartlage (Eds.), *Handbook of forensic neuropsychology* (pp. 137–174). New York, NY: Springer.

Houston, K. A., Meissner, C. A., & Evans, J. R. (2014). Psychological processes underlying true and false confessions. In R. Bull (Ed.), *Investigative interviewing* (pp. 19–34). New York, NY: Springer. doi:10.1007/978-1-4614-9642-7_2

Houts, M. (1956). *From evidence to guilt.* Springfield, IL: Charles C. Thomas.

Hritz, A. C., Royer, C. E., & Hans, V. P. (2019). Diminishing support for the death penalty: Implications for fair capital case outcomes. In C. J. Najdowski & M. C. Stevenson (Eds.), *Criminal juries in the 21st century: Contemporary issues, psychological science, and the law* (pp. 41–59). New York, NY: Oxford University Press.

Hubbs-Tait, L., Nation, J. R., Krebs, N. F., & Bellinger, D. C. (2005). Neurotoxicants, micronutrients, and social environments: Individual and combined effects on children's development. *Psychological Science in the Public Interest, 6*, 57–121. doi:10.1111/j.1529-1006.2005.00024.x

Humphreys, G., Hodsoll, J., & Campbell, C. (2005). Attending but not seeing: The "other-race" effect in face and person perception studied through change blindness. *Visual Cognition, 12*, 249–262.

Hunt, M. (2007). *The story of psychology.* New York, NY: Anchor Books.

Hunter, S., Schweitzer, N. J., & Ware, J. M. (2019). Neuroscience and jury decision-making. In C. J. Najdowski & M. C. Stevenson (Eds.), *Criminal juries in the 21st century: Contemporary issues, psychological science, and the law* (pp. 221–243). New York, NY: Oxford University Press.

Hurlock, E. B. (1930). The suggestibility of children. *Journal of Genetic Psychology, 37*, 59–74.

Hyman, I. E., & Billings, F. J. (1998). Individual differences and the creation of false childhood memories. *Memory, 6*, 1–20. doi:10.1080/741941598

Hyman, I. E., Husband, T. H., & Billings, F. J. (1995). False memories of childhood experiences. *Applied Cognitive Psychology, 9*, 181–197.

Hyman, I. E., & Loftus, E. F. (2002). False childhood memories and eyewitness memory errors. In M. L. Eisen, J. A. Quas, & G. S. Goodman (Eds.), *Memory and suggestibility in the forensic interview* (pp. 63–84). Mahwah, NJ: Erlbaum.

Iacono, W. G. (2001). Forensic "lie detection": Procedures without scientific basis. *Journal of Forensic Psychology Practice, 1*, 75–86.

Iacono, W. G. (2015). Forensic application of event-related brain potentials to detect guilty knowledge. In P. A. Granhag, A. Vrij, & B. Verschuere (Eds.), *Detecting deception: Current challenges and cognitive approaches* (pp. 81–103). Hoboken, NJ: Wiley-Blackwell.

Inbau, F. E., & Reid, J. E. (1962). *Criminal interrogation and confessions.* Baltimore, MD: Williams & Wilkins.

Inbau, F. E., Reid, J. E., Buckley, J. P., & Jayne, B. C. (2001). *Criminal interrogation and confessions* (5th ed.). Burlington, MA: Jones & Bartlett Learning.

Jacobs, P. A., Brunton, M., Melville, M. M., Brittain, R. P., & McClemont, W. F. (1965). Aggressive behavior, mental subnormality and the XYY male. *Nature, 208*, 1351–1352.

Jakob, R. (1992). On the development of psychologically oriented legal thinking in German speaking countries. In F. Lösel, D. Bender, & T. Bliesener (Eds.), *Psychology and law: International perspectives* (pp. 519–525). Berlin, Germany: Walter de Gruyter.

James, W. (1890). *Principles of psychology.* New York, NY: Henry Holt.

Janet, P. (1889/1973). L'automatise psychologique [Psychological automatism.] Paris: Centre National de las Recherche Scientifique (Original work published in 1889).

Jelinek, L., Hottenrott, B., Randjbar, S., Peters, M. J., & Moritz, S. (2009). Visual false memories in post-traumatic stress disorder (PTSD). *Journal of Behavior Therapy and Experimental Psychiatry, 40*, 374–383.

Jenkins v. U.S., 307 F.2d 637 (D.C. Cir. 1962).

Jenkins, L. N., Demaray, M. K., Dorio, N. B., & Eldridge, N. (2019). The law and psychology of bullying. In B. H. Bornstein & M. K. Miller (Eds.), *Advances in psychology and law* (Vol. 4, pp. 197–234). New York, NY: Springer.

Johnson, M. E., & Hauck, C. (1999). Beliefs and opinions about hypnosis held by the general public: A systematic evaluation. *American Journal of Clinical Hypnosis, 42*, 10–20. doi:10.1080/00029157.1999.10404241

Johnson, M. K., Hashtroudi, S., & Lindsay, D. S. (1993). Source monitoring. *Psychological Bulletin, 114*, 3–28.

Johnson, M. K., & Raye, C. L. (1981). Reality monitoring. *Psychological Review, 88*, 67–85.

Johnson, M. K., Raye, C. L., Mitchell, K. J., & Ankudowich, E. (2012). The cognitive neuroscience of true and false memories. In R.F. Belli (Ed.), *True and false recovered memories: Toward a reconciliation of the debate* (pp. 15–52). New York, NY: Springer.

Johnson, R., Pfefferbaum, A., Kopell, B. S. (1985). P300 and long-term memory: Latency predicts recognition performance. *Psychophysiology, 22*, 497–507. doi:10.1111/j.1469-8986.1985.tb01639.x

Jones v. State, 537 S.E.2d 80 (Ga. 2000).

Jones, A. M., Bergold, A. N., Dillon, M. K., & Penrod, S. D. (2017). Comparing the effectiveness of *Henderson* instructions and expert testimony: Which safeguard improves jurors' evaluations of eyewitness evidence? *Journal of Experimental Criminology, 13*, 29–52. doi:10.1007/s11292-016-9279-6

Jones, O. D., Wagner, A. D., Faigman, D. L., & Raichle, M. E. (2013). Neuroscientists in court. *Nature Reviews Neuroscience, 14*, 730–736.

Juslin, P. (1994). The overconfidence phenomenon as a consequence of informal experimenter-guided selection of almanac items. *Organizational Behavior and Human Decision Processes, 57*, 226–246.

Juslin, P., Olsson, N., & Winman, A. (1996). Calibration and diagnosticity of confidence in eyewitness identification: Comments on what can be inferred from the low confidence-accuracy correlation. *Journal of Experimental Psychology: Learning, Memory, and Cognition, 22*, 1304–1316. doi:10.1037/0278-7393.22.5.1304

Kalven, H., & Zeisel, H. (1966). *The American jury*. Boston, MA: Little, Brown.

Kandel, E., & Mednick, S. A. (1991). Perinatal complications predict violent offending. *Criminology, 29*, 519–529. doi:10.1111/j.1745-9125.1991.tb01077.x

Kaplan, J., Cutler, B. L., Leach, A.-M., Eastwood, J., & Marion, S. (2019). Evaluating coercion in suspect interviews and interrogations. In B. H. Bornstein & M. K. Miller (Eds.), *Advances in psychology and law* (Vol. 4, pp. 1–40). New York, NY: Springer.

Kaplan, J. R., Fontenot, M. B., Manuck, S. B., & Muldon, M. F. (1996). Influence of dietary lipids on agonistic and affiliative behavior in Macaca fascicularis. *American Journal of Primatology, 38*, 333–347. doi:10.1002/(SICI)1098-2345(1996)38:4<333::AID-AJP4>3.0.CO;2-#

Kaplan, J. R., Manuck, S. B., & Shively, C. A. (1991). The effects of fat and cholesterol on social behavior in monkeys. *Psychosomatic Medicine, 53*, 634–642. doi:10.1097/00006842-199111000-00005

Kaplan, T., Miller, M. K., & Wood, E. F. (2018). Looking backwards, looking forward: How the evolution of specialty courts can inform the courts of tomorrow. *Court Review, 54*, 14–24.

Kaslow, F. W. (2018). The founding and early years of the American Board of Forensic Psychology. In T. Grisso & S. L. Brodsky (Eds.), *The roots of modern psychology and law* (pp. 195–206). New York, NY: Oxford University Press.

Kassin, S. M. (2007). Coerced-internalized false confessions. In M. P. Toglia, J. D. Read, D. F. Ross, & R. C. L. Lindsay (Eds.), *Handbook of eyewitness psychology, Vol. 1. Memory for events* (pp. 175–192). Mahwah, NJ: Erlbaum.

Kassin, S. M. (2014). False confessions: Causes, consequences, and implications for reform. *Policy Insights from the Behavioral and Brain Sciences, 1*, 112–121.

Kassin, S. M. (2015). The social psychology of false confessions. *Social Issues and Policy Review, 9*, 25–51. doi:10.1111/sipr12009

Kassin, S. M., Bogart, D., & Kerner, J. (2012). Confessions that corrupt: Evidence from the DNA exoneration case files. *Psychological Science, 23*, 41–45. doi:10.1177/0956797611422918

Kassin, S. M., Drizin, S. A., Grisso, T., Gudjonsson, G. H., Leo, R. A., & Redlich, A. D. (2010). Police-induced confessions: Risk factors and recommendations. *Law and Human Behavior, 34*, 3–38. doi:10.1007/s10979-009-9188-6

Kassin, S. M., Ellsworth, P. C., & Smith, V. L. (1989). The "general acceptance" of psychological research on eyewitness testimony: A survey of experts. *American Psychologist, 44*, 1089–1098.

Kassin, S. M., & Fong, C.T . (1999). "I'm Innocent!": Effects of training on judgments of truth and deception in the interrogation room. *Law and Human Behavior, 23*, 499–516.

Kassin, S. M., & Gudjonsson, G. H. (2004). The psychology of confessions: A review of the literature and issues. *Psychological Science in the Public Interest: A Journal of the American Psychological Society, 5*, 33–67. doi:10.1111/j.1529-1006.2004.00016.x

Kassin, S. M., & Kiechel, K. L. (1996). The social psychology of false confessions: Compliance, internalization, and confabulation. *Psychological Science, 7*, 125–128. doi:10.1111/j.1467-9280.1996.tb00344.x

Kassin, S. M., Meissner, C. A., & Norwick, R. J. (2005). "I'd know a false confession if I saw one": A comparative study of college students and police investigators. *Law and Human Behavior, 29*, 211–227. doi:10.1007/s10979-005-2416-9

Kassin, S. M., & Neumann, K. (1997). On the power of confession evidence: An experimental test of the fundamental difference hypothesis. *Law and Human Behavior, 21*, 469–484.

Kassin, S. M., & Sukel, H. (1997). Coerced confession and the jury: An experimental test of the "Harmless Error" rule. *Law and Human Behavior, 21*, 27–46. doi:10.1023/A:1024814009769.

Kassin, S. M., Tubb, V. A., Hosch, H. M., & Memon, A. (2001). On the "general acceptance" of eyewitness testimony research: A new survey of the experts. *American Psychologist, 56*, 405–416. doi:10.1037//0003-066X.56.5.405

Kassin, S. M., & Wallace, D. B. (2012). Harmless error analysis: How do judges respond to confession errors? *Law and Human Behavior, 36*, 151–157. doi:10.1037/h0093975

Kassin, S. M., & Wrightsman, L. (1985). *The psychology of evidence and trial procedure*. Beverly Hills, CA: Sage.

Kebbell, M. R., & Wagstaff, G. F. (1997). Why do the police interview eyewitnesses? Interview objectives and the evaluation of eyewitness performance. *Journal of Psychology: Interdisciplinary and Applied, 131*, 595–601. doi:10.1080/00223989709603841

Keren, G. (1987). Facing uncertainty in the game of bridge: A calibration study. *Organizational Behavior & Human Decision Processes, 39*, 98–114.

Key, K. N., Neuschatz, J. S., Bornstein, B. H., Wetmore, S. A., Luecht, K. M., Dellapaolera, K. S., & Quinlivan, D. S. (2018). Beliefs about secondary confession evidence: A survey of laypeople and defense attorneys. *Psychology, Crime and Law, 24*, 1–13. doi:10.1080/1068316X.2017.1351968

Key, K. N., Wetmore, S. A., Neuschatz, J. S., Gronlund, S. D., Cash, D. K., & Lane, S. (2017). Lineup-fairness affects postdictor validity and "don't know" responses. *Applied Cognitive Psychology, 31*, 59–68.

Kirsch, I., & Braffman, W. (2001). Imaginative suggestibility and hypnotizability. *Current Directions in Psychological Science, 10*, 57–61.

Kirsch, I., Cardeña, E., Derbyshire, S., Dienes, Z., Heap, M., Kallio, S., . . . Whalley, M. (2011). Definitions of hypnosis and hynotizability and their relation to suggestion and suggestibility: A consensus statement. *Contemporary Hypnosis & Integrative Therapy, 28*, 107–115.

Kirsch, I., Montgomery, G., & Sapirstein, G. (1995). Hypnosis as an adjunct to cognitive-behavioral psychotherapy: A meta-analysis. *Journal of Consulting and Clinical Psychology, 63*, 214–220. doi:10.1037/0022-006X.63.2.214

Klaver, J. R., Lee, Z., & Rose, V. G. (2008). Effects of personality, interrogation techniques and plausibility in an experimental false confession paradigm. *Legal and Criminological Psychology, 13*, 71–88.

Kleinmuntz, B., & Szucko, J. J. (1984). Lie detection in ancient and modern times: A call for contemporary scientific study. *American Psychologist, 39*, 766–776.

Klemfuss, J. Z., & Ceci, S. J. (2012). Legal and psychological perspectives on children's competence to testify in court. *Developmental Review, 32*, 268–286. doi:10.1016/j.dr.2012.06.005

Klobuchar, A., Steblay, N. K. M., & Caligiuri, H. L. (2006). Improving eyewitness identifications: Hennepin County's blind sequential lineup pilot project. *Cardozo Public Law, Policy & Ethics Journal, 4*, 381–413.

Kobler, F. (1914). Ein rechtspsychologisches Experiment. *Zeitschrift für angewandte Psychologie, 8*, 317–325.

Kocab, K., & Sporer, S. L. (2016). The weapon focus effect for person identifications and descriptions: A meta-analysis. In M. K. Miller & B. H. Bornstein (Eds.), *Advances in psychology and law (Vol. 1)* (pp. 71–117). New York, NY: Springer. doi:10.1007/978-3-319-29406-3_3

Koenigs, M. (2012). The role of prefrontal cortex in psychopathy. *Reviews in the Neurosciences, 23*, 253–262. doi:10.1515/revneuro-2012-0036

Köhnken, G., Milne, R., Memon, A., & Bull, R. (1999). The cognitive interview: A meta-analysis. *Psychology, Crime, & Law, 5*, 3–27. doi:10.1080/10683169908414991

Kovera, M. B. (2017). *The psychology of juries*. Washington, DC: American Psychological Association.

Kovera, M. B., & McAuliff, B. D. (2000). The effects of peer review and evidence quality on judge evaluations of psychological evidence: Are judges effective gatekeepers? *Journal of Applied Psychology, 85*, 574–586.

Krafka, C., & Penrod, S. D. (1985). Reinstatement of context in a field experiment on eyewitness identification. *Journal of Personality and Social Psychology, 49*, 58–69.

Krix, A.C ., Sauerland, M., Raymaekers, L. H. C., Memon, A., Quaedflieg, C. W. E. M., & Smeets, T. (2016). Eyewitness evidence obtained with the Self-Administered Interview is unaffected by stress. *Applied Cognitive Psychology, 30*, 103–112. doi:10.1002/acp.3173

Krug, K. (2007). The relationship between confidence and accuracy: Current thoughts of the literature and a new are of research. *Applied Psychology in Criminal Justice, 3*, 7–41.

Kukucka, J., & Kassin, S. M. (2014). Do confessions taint perceptions of handwriting evidence? An empirical test of the forensic confirmation bias. *Law and Human Behavior, 38*, 256–270. doi:10.1037/lhb0000066

Kuna, D. P. (1978). One-sided portrayal of Münsterberg. *American Psychologist, 33*, 700.

LaBar, K. S., Gatenby, J. C., Gore, J. C., LeDoux, J. E., & Phelps, E. A. (1998). Human amygdala activation during conditioned fear acquisition and extinction: A mixed-trial fMRI study. *Neuron, 20*, 937–945.

Labkovsky, E., & Rosenfeld, J. P. (2012). The P300-based, complex trial protocol for concealed information detection resists any number of sequential countermeasures against up to five irrelevant stimuli. *Applied Psychophysiology and Biofeedback, 37*, 1–10.

Lamb, M. (2001, Fall). Who was Wonder Woman? Long-ago LAW alumna Elizabeth Marston was the muse who gave us a superheroine. *Boston University Alumni Magazine*. Retrieved from https://web.archive.org/web/20070104060542/http://www.bu.edu/alumni/bostonia/2001/fall/wonderwoman/.

Lampinen, J. M., Neuschatz, J. S., & Cling, A. D. (2012). *The psychology of eyewitness identification*. New York, NY: Psychology Press.

Landy, F. J. (1992). Hugo Münsterberg: Victim of visionary? *Journal of Applied Psychology, 77*, 787–802.

Lane, S. M. (2006). Dividing attention during a witnessed event increases eyewitness suggestibility. *Applied Cognitive Psychology, 20*, 199–212. doi:10.1002/acp.1177

Lane, S. M., & Meissner, C. A. (2008). A "middle road" approach to bridging the basic-applied divide in eyewitness research. *Applied Cognitive Psychology, 22*, 779–787. doi:10.1002/acp.1482

Laney, C., & Loftus, E. F. (2010). Truth in emotional memories. In B. H. Bornstein & R. L. Wiener (Eds.), *Emotion and the law: Psychological perspectives* (pp. 157–183). New York, NY: Springer. doi:10.1007/978-1-4419-0696-0_6

Langdale, A. (2002). *Hugo Münsterberg on film: The photoplay: A psychological study and other writings*. New York, NY: Routledge.

Langleben, D. D., Loughead, J. W., Bilker, W. B., Ruparel, K., Childress, A. R., Busch, S. I., & Gur, R. C. (2005). Telling truth from lie in individual subjects with fast event-related fMRI. *Human Brain Mapping, 26*, 262–272. doi:10.1002/ hbm.20191.

Langleben, D. D., & Moriarty, J. C. (2013). Using brain imaging for lie detection: Where science, law, and policy collide. *Psychology, Public Policy, and Law, 19*, 222–234.

Lassiter, G. D., Clark, J. K., Daniels, L. E., & Soinski, M. (2004). Can we recognize false confessions and does the presentation format make a difference? Paper presented at the annual meeting of the American Psychology-Law Society, Scottsdale, AZ.

Laub, C. E., Kimbrough, C., & Bornstein, B. H. (2016). Is an ear as good as an eye? Safeguards to help jurors use different kinds of identification testimony. *American Journal of Forensic Psychology, 34*(2), 33–56.

Laub, C. E., Wylie, L. E., & Bornstein, B. H. (2013). Can the courts tell an ear from an eye? Legal approaches to voice identification evidence. *Law & Psychology Review, 37*, 119–158.

Laurence, J., & Perry, C. (1983). Hypnotically created memory among highly hypnotizable subjects. *Science, 222*, 523–524. doi:10.1126/science.6623094

Lawson, R. B., Graham, J. E., & Baker, K. M. (2007). *A history of psychology: Globalization, ideas, and applications*. Upper Saddle River, NJ: Pearson/Prentice-Hall.

Leal, S., Vrij, A., Warmelink, L., Vernham, Z., & Fisher, R. P. (2015). You cannot hide your telephone lies: Providing a model statement as an aid to detect deception in insurance telephone calls. *Legal and Criminological Psychology, 20*, 129–146. http://dx.doi.org/10.1111/lcrp.12017

Le Bon, G. (1896). *The crowd* [orig. published as *La psychologie des foules]*. London, England: Ernest Benn.

Legault, E., & Laurence, J. (2007). Recovered memories of childhood sexual abuse: Social worker, psychologist, and psychiatrist reports of beliefs, practices, and cases. *Australian Journal of Clinical & Experimental Hypnosis, 35*, 111–133.

Lehman, E. B., McKinley, M. J., Thompson, D. W., Leonard, A. M., Liebman, J. I., & Rothrock, D. D. (2010). Long-term stability of young children's eyewitness accuracy, suggestibility, and resistance to misinformation. *Journal of Applied Developmental Psychology, 31*, 145–154.

Leichtman, M. D., & Ceci, S. J. (1995). The effects of stereotypes and suggestions on preschoolers' experiences. *Developmental Psychology, 31*, 568–578.

Leippe, M. R., & Eisenstadt, D. (2007). Eyewitness confidence and the confidence-accuracy relationship in memory for people. In R. C. L. Lindsay, D. F. Ross, J. D. Read, & M. P. Toglia (Eds.), *The handbook of eyewitness psychology, Vol. 2: Memory for people* (pp. 377–425). Mahwah, NJ: Lawrence Erlbaum Associates.

Leippe, M. R., & Eisenstadt, D. (2009). The influence of eyewitness expert testimony on jurors' beliefs and judgments. In B. L. Cutler (Ed.), *Expert testimony on the psychology of eyewitness identification* (pp. 169–199). Oxford, England: Oxford University Press.

Leo, R. A., & Liu, B. (2009). What do potential jurors know about police interrogation technique and false confession? *Behavioral Sciences & the Law, 27*, 381–399. doi:10.1002/bsl.872

Leonard, D. P., Imwinkelried, E. J., Kaye, D. H., Bernstein, D. E., & Mnookin, J. L. (2015). *The new Wigmore: A treatise on evidence* (5 vols.). South Holland, Netherlands: Wolters Kluwer.

Levin, D. T., & Simons, D. J. (1997). Failure to detect changes to attended objects in motion pictures. *Psychonomic Bulletin & Review, 4*, 501–506.

Levin, D. T., Simons, D. J., Angelone, B. L., & Chabris, C. F. (2002). Memory for centrally attended changing objects in an incidental real-world change detection paradigm. *British Journal of Psychology, 93*, 289–302.

Levine, L. J., Burgess, S. L., & Laney, C. (2008). Effects of discrete emotions on young children's suggestibility. *Developmental Psychology, 44*, 681–694. doi:10.1037/0012-1649.44.3.681

Levine, T. R., Kim, R. K., & Blair, J. P. (2010). (In)accuracy at detecting true and false confessions and denials: An initial test of a projected motive model of veracity judgments. *Human Communication Research, 36*, 81–101.

Levy, S. (1955). Hypnosis and legal immutability. *Journal of Criminal Law, Criminology, and Police Science, 46*, 333–346. doi:10.2307/1139416

Liebman, J. I., McKinley-Pace, M. J., Leonard, A. M., Sheesley, L. A., Gallant, C. L., Renkey, M. E., & Lehman, E. B. (2002). Cognitive and psychosocial correlates of adults' eyewitness accuracy and suggestibility. *Personality and Individual Differences, 33*, 49–66.

Lindsay, D. S., & Johnson, M. K. (1987). Reality monitoring and suggestibility: Children's ability to discriminate among memories from different sources. In S. J. Ceci, J. Toglia, & D. F. Ross (Eds.), *Children's eyewitness memory* (pp. 91–121). New York, NY: Springer-Verlag.

Lindsay, D. S., & Read, J. D. (1994). Psychotherapy and memories of childhood sexual abuse: A cognitive perspective. *Applied Cognitive Psychology, 8*, 281–338.

Lindsay, D. S., & Read, J. D. (1995). "Memory work" and recovered memories of childhood sexual abuse: Scientific evidence and public, professional, and personal issues. *Psychology, Public Policy & Law, 1*, 846–908.

Lindsay, R. C. L., Ross., D. F., Read, J. D., & Toglia, M. P. (2007). *The handbook of eyewitness psychology (Vol. 2): Memory for people*. Mahwah, NJ: Erlbaum.

Lindsay, R. C. L., & Wells, G. L. (1985). Improving eyewitness identifications from lineups: Simultaneous versus sequential lineup presentation. *Journal of Applied Psychology, 70*, 556–564.

Lindsay, R. C. L., Wells, G. L., & O'Connor, F. J. (1989). Mock-juror belief of accurate and inaccurate eyewitnesses: A replication and extension. *Law and Human Behavior, 13*, 333–339.

Lindsay, R. C. L., Wells, G. L., & Rumpel, C. M. (1981). Can people detect eyewitness-identification accuracy within and across situations? *Journal of Applied Psychology, 66*, 79–89.

Lindsey, S. C., & Miller, M. K. (2011). Discretionary release decisions of actual and mock parole board members: Implications for community sentiment and parole decision-making research. *Psychiatry, Psychology and Law, 18*, 498–516. doi:10.1080/13218719.2011.625619

Linnoila, V. M., & Virkkunen, M. (1992). Aggression, suicidality, and serotonin. *The Journal of Clinical Psychiatry, 53*(10, Suppl), 46–51.

Litwack, T. R. (2001). Actuarial versus clinical assessments of dangerousness. *Psychology, Public Policy, and Law, 7*, 409–443. doi:10.1037//1076-8971.7.2.409

Liu, J., Raine, A., Venables, P. H., & Mednick, S. A. (2004). Malnutrition at age 3 years and externalizing behavior problems at ages 8, 11, and 17 years. *The American Journal of Psychiatry, 157*(6), 593–600. doi:10.1176/appi.ajp.161.11.2005

Locker, L., & Pratarelli, M. E. (1997). Lexical decision and the detection of concealed information. *Journal of Credibility Assessment and Witness Psychology, 1*, 33–43.

Loftus, E. F. (1976). Unconscious transference in eyewitness identification. *Law and Psychology Review, 2*, 93–98.

Loftus, E. F. (2005). Planting misinformation in the human mind: A 30-year investigation of the malleability of memory. *Learning & Memory, 12*, 361–366.

Loftus, E. F., & Bernstein, D. M. (2005). Rich false memories. In A. F. Healy (Ed.), *Experimental cognitive psychology and its applications* (pp. 101–113). Washington, DC: American Psychological Association.

Loftus, E. F., Miller, D. G., & Burns, H. J. (1978). Semantic integration of verbal information into a visual memory. *Journal of Experimental Psychology: Human Learning and Memory, 4*, 19–31.

Loftus, E. F., & Pickrell, J. E. (1995). The formation of false memories. *Psychiatric Annals, 25*, 720–725.

Lombroso, C. (1876/2006). *L'uomo delinquent [Criminal man]*. Translated by M. Gibson & N.H. Rafter. Durham, NC: Duke University Press.

Lombroso, C. (1899/1911). *Le crime: Causes et remèdes [Crime: Its causes and remedies]* Translated by H. P. Horton. Boston, MA: Little, Brown.

Los Angeles County Grand Jury (1990). Investigation of the involvement of jailhouse informants in the criminal justice system in Los Angeles County. *Los Angeles County Grand Jury.*

Lykken, D. T. (1959). The GSR in the detection of guilt. *Journal of Applied Psychology, 43*, 385–388. doi:10.1037/h0046060

Lynch, M. (2013). Institutionalizing bias: The death penalty, federal drug prosecutions, and mechanisms of disparate punishment. *American Journal of Criminal Law, 41*, 91–131.

Lynn, S. J., & Rhue, J. W. (1991). An integrative model of hypnosis. In S. J. Lynn & J. W. Rhue (Eds.), *Theories of hypnosis: Current models and perspectives* (pp. 397–438). New York, NY: Guilford Press.

Lynn, S. J., Laurence, J., & Kirsch, I. (2015). Hypnosis, suggestion, and suggestibility: An integrative model. *American Journal of Clinical Hypnosis, 57*, 314–329.

Lynn, S. J., Matthews, A., & Barnes, S. (2009). Hypnosis and memory: From Bernheim to the present. In K. D. Markman, W. P. Klein, J. A. Suhr, K. D. Markman, W. P. Klein, & J. A. Suhr (Eds.), *Handbook of imagination and mental simulation* (pp. 103–118). New York, NY: Psychology Press.

Lynn, S. J., Vanderhoff, H., Shindler, K., & Stafford, J. (2002). Defining hypnosis as a trance vs. cooperation: Hypnotic inductions, suggestibility, and performance standards. *American Journal of Clinical Hypnosis, 44*, 231–240.

Maeder, E. M., & Pica, E. (2014). Secondary confessions: The influence (or lack thereof) of incentive size and scientific expert testimony on jurors' perceptions of informant testimony. *Law and Human Behavior, 38*, 560–568. doi:10.1037/lhb0000106

Malpass, R. S. (2006). A policy evaluation of simultaneous and sequential lineups. *Psychology, Public Policy, and Law, 12*, 394–418. doi:10.1037/1076-8971.12.4.394

Malpass, R. S., & Devine, P. G. (1981). Eyewitness identification: Lineup instructions and the absence of the offender. *Journal of Applied Psychology, 66*, 482–489.

Malpass, R. S., Tredoux, C. G., & McQuiston-Surrett, D. (2007). Lineup construction and lineup fairness. In R. C. L. Lindsay, D. F. Ross., J. D. Read, & M. P. Toglia (Eds.), *The handbook of eyewitness psychology, Vol. 2. Memory for people* (pp. 155–178). Mahwah, NJ: Lawrence Erlbaum.

Malpass, R. S., Tredoux, C. G., Schreiber Compo, N., McQuiston-Surrett, D., MacLin, O. H., Zimmerman, L. A., & Topp, L. D. (2008). Study space analysis for policy development. *Applied Cognitive Psychology, 22*, 789–801.

Mann, S., Vrij, A., & Bull, R. (2004). Detecting true lies: Police officers' ability to detect suspects' lies. *Journal of Applied Psychology, 89*, 137–149. doi:10.1037/0021-9010.89.1.137

Manson v. Brathwaite, 432 U.S. 98 (1977).

Marion, S. B., Kukucka, J., Collins, C., Kassin, S. M., & Burke, T. M. (2016). Lost proof of innocence: The impact of confessions on alibi witnesses. *Law and Human Behavior, 40*, 65–71. doi:10.1037/lhb0000156

Marks, D. F. (1973). Visual imagery differences in the recall of pictures. *British Journal of Psychology, 64*, 17–24. doi:10.1111/j.2044-8295.1973.tb01322.x

Marr, B. (2018, May 23). How AI and machine learning are transforming law firms and the legal sector. *Forbes*. Retrieved from https://www.forbes.com/sites/bernardmarr/2018/05/23/how-ai-and-machine-learning-are-transforming-law-firms-and-the-legal-sector/#d01035132c38

Marsh, A. A., Finger, E. C., Fowler, K. A., Adalio, C. J., Jurkowitz, I. N., Schechter, J. C., . . . Blair, R. R. (2013). Empathic responsiveness in amygdala and anterior cingulate cortex in youths with psychopathic traits. *Journal of Child Psychology and Psychiatry, 54*, 900–910. doi:10.1111/jcpp.12063

Marsh, A. A., Finger, E. C., Mitchell, D. V., Reid, M. E., Sims, C., Kosson, D. S., . . . Blair, R. R. (2008). Reduced amygdala response to fearful expressions in children and adolescents with callous-unemotional traits and disruptive behavior disorders. *The American Journal of Psychiatry, 165*, 712–720. doi:10.1176/appi.ajp.2007.07071145

Marston, W. M. (1917). Systolic blood pressure symptoms of deception. *Journal of Experimental Psychology, 2*, 117–163. doi:10.1037/h0073583

Marston, W. M. (1920). Reaction–time symptoms of deception. *Journal of Experimental Psychology, 3*, 72–87.

Martire, K. A., & Kemp, R. I. (2011). Can experts help jurors to evaluate eyewitness evidence? A review of eyewitness expert effects. *Legal and Criminological Psychology, 16*, 24–36.

Matsuda, I., Nittono, H., & Allen, J. J. (2012). The current and future status of the concealed information test for field use. *Frontiers in Psychology, 3*, 532.

Maus, H. (1962). *A short history of sociology*. New York, NY: Philosophical Library.

Mazzoni, G., Loftus, E. F., & Kirsch, I. (2001). Changing beliefs about implausible autobiographical events: A little plausibility goes a long way. *Journal of Experimental Psychology: Applied, 7*, 51–59.

Mazzoni, G., & Lynn, S. J. (2007). Using hypnosis in eyewitness memory: Past and current issues. In M. P. Toglia, J. D. Read, D. F. Ross, & R. C. L. Lindsay (Eds.), *The handbook of eyewitness psychology, Vol I: Memory for events* (pp. 321–338). Mahwah, NJ: Lawrence Erlbaum.

Mazzoni, G., & Memon, A. (2003). Imagination can create false autobiographical memories. *Psychological Science, 14*, 186–188.

McAllister, H. A., Bregman, N. J., & Lipscomb, T. J. (1988). Speed estimates by eyewitnesses and earwitnesses: How vulnerable to postevent information? *Journal of General Psychology, 115*, 25–35.

McAllister, H. A., Dale, R. H. I., & Keay, C. E. (1993). Effects of lineup modality on witness credibility. *Journal of Social Psychology, 133*, 365–376.

McAuliff, B. D., Nemeth, R. J., Bornstein, B. H., & Penrod, S. D. (2003). Jury decision making in the 21st century: Confronting science and technology in court. In D. Carson & R. Bull (Eds.), *Handbook of psychology in legal contexts* (2d ed.) (pp. 303–327). Chichester, England: Wiley.

McCarty, D. G. (1929). *Psychology for the lawyer.* New York, NY: Prentice-Hall.

McCloskey, M., & Zaragoza, M. (1985). Misleading postevent information and memory for events: Arguments and evidence against memory impairment hypotheses. *Journal of Experimental Psychology: General, 114*, 1–16.

McConkey, K. M. (1986). Opinions about hypnosis and self-hypnosis before and after hypnotic testing. *International Journal of Clinical and Experimental Hypnosis, 34*, 311–319.

McDonald, K. P., & Ma, L. (2016). Preschoolers' credulity toward misinformation from ingroup versus outgroup speakers. *Journal of Experimental Child Psychology, 148*, 87–100. doi:10.1016/j.jecp.2016.03.011

McFarland, G. W. (1993). *The "Counterfeit Man": The true story of the Boorn-Colvin murder case.* Amherst, MA: University of Massachusetts.

McGorrery, P. (2015). The limited impact of Facebook and the displacement effect on the admissibility of identification evidence. *Criminal Law Journal, 39*, 207–218.

McQuiston-Surrett, D. E., Malpass, R. S., & Tredoux, C. G. (2006). Sequential vs. simultaneous lineups: A review of methods, data, and theory. *Psychology, Public Policy & Law, 12*, 137–169.

Meares, J. (2016). *Dangerous women and reasonable men: Gender and eyewitness testimony at the turn of the twentieth century.* Master's thesis, University of Canterbury.

Mecklenburg, S. H. (2006). *Report to the legislature of the state of Illinois: The Illinois pilot program on double-blind, sequential lineup procedures.* Springfield, IL: Illinois State Police.

Mednick, S. A., Gabrielli, W. F. Jr., & Hutchings, B. (1984). Genetic influences in criminal convictions: Evidence from an adoption cohort. *Science, 224*, 891–894. doi:10.1126/science.6719119

Meijer, E. H., & Verschuere, B. (2010). The polygraph and the detection of deception. *Journal of Forensic Psychology Practice, 10*, 325–338.

Meijer, E. H., & Verschuere, B. (2015). The polygraph: Current practice and new approaches. In P. A. Granhag, A. Vrij, & B. Verschuere (Eds.), *Wiley series in the psychology of crime, policing and law. Detecting deception: Current challenges and cognitive approaches* (pp. 59–80). Hoboken, NJ: Wiley-Blackwell.

Meijer, E., Verschuere, B., & Ben-Shakhar, G. (2011). Practical guidelines for developing a CIT. In B. Verschuere, G. Ben-Shakhar, E. Meijer, B. Verschuere, G. Ben-Shakhar, & E. Meijer (Eds.), *Memory detection: Theory and application of the Concealed Information Test* (pp. 293–302). New York, NY: Cambridge University Press. doi:10.1017/CBO9780511975196.017

Meissner, C. A., & Brigham, J. C. (2001). Thirty years of investigating the own-race bias in memory for faces: A meta-analytic review. *Psychology, Public Policy & Law, 7*, 3–35.

Meissner, C. A., & Sporer, S. L., & Schooler, J. W. (2007). Person descriptions as eyewitness evidence. In R. C. L. Lindsay, D. F. Ross, J. D. Read, & M. P.

Toglia (Eds.), *Handbook of eyewitness psychology, Vol. 2. Memory for people* (pp. 3–34). Mahwah, NJ: Lawrence Erlbaum.

Meissner, C. A., Sporer, S. L., & Susa, K. J. (2008). A theoretical and meta-analytic review of the relationship between verbal descriptions and identification accuracy in memory for faces. *European Journal of Cognitive Psychology, 20,* 414–455.

Meixner, J. B., Labkovsky, E., Rosenfeld, J. P., Winograd, M., Sokolovsky, A., Weishaar, J., & Ullmann, T. (2013). P900: A putative novel ERP component that indexes countermeasure use in the P300-based concealed information test. *Applied Psychophysiology and Biofeedback, 38,* 121–32. doi:10.1007/s10484-013-9216-7

Meloy, J. R. (2006). Empirical basis and forensic application of affective and predatory violence. *Australian and New Zealand Journal of Psychiatry, 40,* 539–547.

Melton, G. B., Petrila, J., Poythress, N. G., & Slobogin, C. (2007). *Psychological evaluations for the courts: A handbook for mental health professionals and lawyers* (3rd ed.). New York, NY: Guilford Press.

Memon, A., Havard, C., Clifford, B., Gabbert, F., & Watt, M. (2011). A field evaluation of the VIPER system: A new technique for eliciting eyewitness identification evidence. *Psychology, Crime & Law, 17,* 711–729. doi:10.1080/10683160903524333

Memon, A., Mastroberardino, S., & Fraser, J. (2008). Münsterberg's legacy: What does eyewitness research tell us about the reliability of eyewitness testimony? *Applied Cognitive Psychology, 22,* 841–851. doi:10.1002/acp.1487

Memon, A., Meissner, C. A., & Fraser, J. (2010). The Cognitive Interview: A meta-analytic review and study space analysis of the past 25 years. *Psychology, Public Policy, and Law, 16,* 340–372. doi:10.1037/a0020518

Mercer, K. D., Selby, M. J., & McClung, J. (2005). The effects of psychopathy, violence and drug use on neuropsychological functioning. *American Journal of Forensic Psychology, 23,* 65–86.

Mertens, R., & Allen, J. J. (2008). The role of psychophysiology in forensic assessments: Deception detection, event-related potentials, and virtual reality mock crime scenarios. *Psychophysiology, 45,* 286–298.

Meyer-Lindenberg, A., Buckholtz, J. W., Kolachana, B., Hariri, A. R., Pezawas, L., Blasi, G., . . . Raichle, M. E. (2006). Neural mechanisms of genetic risk for impulsivity and violence in humans. *PNAS Proceedings of The National Academy of Sciences of The United States of America, 103*(16), 6269–6274. doi:10.1073/pnas.0511311103

Meyer, E. C., & Lynn, S. J. (2011). Responding to hypnotic and nonhypnotic suggestions: Performance standards, imaginative suggestibility, and response expectancies. *International Journal of Clinical and Experimental Hypnosis, 59,* 327–349.

Milgram, S. (1974). *Obedience to authority.* New York, NY: Harper & Row.

Miller, M. K. (2018). An eleven-factor typology of factors encouraging or discouraging the development of problem-solving courts in various countries. Unpublished manuscript.

Miller, M. K., Lindsey, S. C., & Kaufman, J. A. (2014). The religious conversion and race of a prisoner: Mock parole board members' decisions, perceptions,

and emotions. *Legal and Criminological Psychology, 19*, 104–130. doi:10.1111/j.2044-8333.2012.02063.x
Milling, L. S., Coursen, E. L., Shores, J. S., & Waszkiewicz, J. A. (2010). The predictive utility of hypnotizability: The change in suggestibility produced by hypnosis. *Journal of Consulting and Clinical Psychology, 78*, 126–130. doi:10.1037/a0017388
Milne, R., Sharman, S. J., Powell, M. B., & Mead, S. (2013). Assessing the effectiveness of the cognitive interview for children with severe intellectual disabilities. *International Journal of Disability, Development and Education, 60*, 18–29. doi:1 0.1080/1034912X.2013.757137
Miranda v. Arizona, 384 U.S. 436 (1966).
Mitchell, J. P., Banaji, M. R., & Macrae, C. N. (2005). The link between social cognition and self-referential thought in the medial prefrontal cortex. *Journal of Cognitive Neuroscience, 17*(8), 1306–1315. doi:10.1162/0898929055002418
Mnookin, J. L. (2018). The uncertain future of forensic science. *Daedalus, 147*(4), 99–118. doi:10.1162/DAED_a_00523
Moffitt, T. E. (2005). The new look of behavioral genetics in developmental psychopathology: Gene-environment interplay in antisocial behaviors. *Psychological Bulletin, 131*, 533–554. doi:10.1037/0033-2909.131.4.533
Monahan, J. (2018). Predictions of violence. In T. Grisso & S. L. Brodsky (Eds.), *The roots of modern psychology and law* (pp. 143–157). New York, NY: Oxford University Press.
Monahan, J., & Walker, L. (2011). Twenty-five years of *Social Science in Law. Law and Human Behavior, 35*, 72–82. doi:10.1007/s10979-009-9214-8
Monahan, J., & Walker, L. (2018). *Social science in law: Cases and materials* (9th ed.). Westbury, NY: Foundation Press.
Moon, M. R., & Khin-Maung-Gyi, F. (2009). The history and role of Institutional Review Boards. *AMA Journal of Ethics, 11*, 311–321.
Moore, C. C. (1907). Yellow psychology. *Law Notes, 11*, 125–127.
Moore, L. (2004). *Con men and cutpurses: Scenes from the Hogarthian underworld.* London, England: Penguin Books.
Moore, U., & Callahan, C. (1943). *Law and learning theory: A study in legal control.* New Haven, CT: Yale Law.
Morgan, C. A., Hazlett, G., Doran, A., Garrett, S., Hoyt, G., Thomas, P., Baranoski, M., & Southwick, S. M. (2004). Accuracy of eyewitness memory for persons encountered during exposure to highly intense stress. *International Journal of Law and Psychiatry, 27*, 265–279.
Moskowitz, M. J. (1977). Hugo Münsterberg: A study in the history of applied psychology. *American Psychologist, 32*, 824–842.
Mossman, D., Noffsinger, S. G., Ash, P., Frierson, R. L., Gerbasi, J., Hackett, M., . . . Wall, B. W. (2007). AAPL practice guideline for the forensic psychiatric evaluation of competence to stand trial. *Journal of the American Academy of Psychiatry and the Law Online, 35*(Suppl. 4), S3–S72.
Mote, P. M., Neuschatz, J. S., Bornstein, B. H., Wetmore, S. A., & Key, K. N. (2018). Secondary confessions as post-identification feedback: How jailhouse informant testimony can alter eyewitnesses' identification decisions. *Journal of Police and Criminal Psychology, 33*, 375–384. doi:10.1007/s1189

Münsterberg, H. (1898). The danger of experimental psychology. *Atlantic Monthly, 81*, 159–167.
Münsterberg, H. (1899). Psychology and mysticism. *Atlantic Monthly, 83*, 67–85.
Münsterberg, H. (1901). *American traits from the point of view of a German*. Boston, MA: Houghton Mifflin Co.
Münsterberg, H. (1907). "Yellow psychology": Dr. Münsterberg replies to Mr. Moore. *Law Notes, 11*, 145–146.
Münsterberg, H. (1908). *On the witness stand: Essays on psychology and crime*. New York, NY: Doubleday.
Münsterberg, H. (1909a). *Psychology and the teacher*. New York, NY: D. Appleton & Co.
Münsterberg, H. (1909b). *Psychotherapy*. New York, NY: Moffat, Yard & Co.
Münsterberg, H. (1910a). *American problems from the point of view of a psychologist*. New York, NY: Moffat, Yard & Co.
Münsterberg, H. (1910b). My friends the spiritualists: Some theories and conclusions concerning Eusapia Palladino. *Metropolitan Magazine, 31*, 559–572.
Münsterberg, H. (1913a). *American patriotism and other studies*. New York, NY: Moffat, Yard & Co.
Münsterberg, H. (1913b). *Psychology and industrial efficiency*. Boston, MA: Houghton Mifflin.
Münsterberg, H. (1913c). The case of Beulah Miller: An investigation of the new psychical mystery. *The Metropolitan, 16-18*, 61–62.
Münsterberg, H. (1913d). The mind of the juryman with a side-light on women as jurors. *The Century Illustrated Monthly Magazine, 86*, 711–716.
Münsterberg, H. (1914a). *Grundzüge der psychotechnik*. Leipzig, Germany: J.A. Barth.
Münsterberg, H. (1914b). *Psychology and social sanity*. New York, NY: Doubleday, Page.
Münsterberg, H. (1914c). *Psychology general and applied*. New York, NY: D. Appleton & Co.
Münsterberg, H. (1914d). *The war and America*. New York, NY: D. Appleton & Co.
Münsterberg, H. (1915a). *Business psychology*. Chicago, IL: LaSalle Extension University.
Münsterberg, H. (1915b). *The peace and America*. Leipzig, Germany: Bernhard Tauchnitz.
Münsterberg, H. (1916/1970). *The photoplay: A psychological study*. New York, NY: D. Appleton & Co. (reprinted by Arno Press & the *New York Times*).
Münsterberg, H. (1917). Twenty-five years in America: The first chapter of an unfinished autobiography. *The Century Illustrated Monthly Magazine, 94*, 34–48.
Münsterberg, H., Ribot, T., Janet, P., Jastrow, J., Hart, B., & Prince, M. (1910). *Subconscious phenomena*. Boston, MA: Richard G. Badger/Gorham Press.
Murray, D. M., & Wells, G. L. (1982). Does knowledge that a crime was staged affect eyewitness performance? *Journal of Applied Social Psychology, 12*, 42–53.
Murrey, G. J., Cross, H. J., & Whipple, J. (1992). Hypnotically created pseudomemories: Further investigation into the "memory distortion or response bias" question. *Journal of Abnormal Psychology, 101*, 75–77.

Nahari, G., & Ben-Shakhar, G. (2011). Psychophysiological and behavioral measures for detecting concealed information: The role of memory for crime details. *Psychophysiology, 48*, 733–744. doi:10.1111/j.1469-8986.2010.01148.x

Nahari, G., Vrij, A., & Fisher, R. P. (2012). Does the truth come out in the writing? Scan as a lie detection tool. *Law and Human Behavior, 36*, 68–76. doi:10.1037/h0093965

Nahari, G., Vrij, A., & Fisher, R. P. (2014). Exploiting liars' verbal strategies by examining the verifiability of details. *Legal and Criminological Psychology, 19*, 227–239. doi:10.1111/j.2044-8333.2012.02069.x

Narby, D. J., & Cutler, B. L. (1994). Effectiveness of voir dire as a safeguard in eyewitness cases. *Journal of Applied Psychology, 79*, 724–729.

Nash, M. (1987). What, if anything, is regressed about hypnotic age regression? A review of the empirical literature. *Psychological Bulletin, 10*, 42–52.

Nash, R. A., & Wade, K. A. (2009). Innocent but proven guilty: Eliciting internalized false confessions using doctored-video evidence. *Applied Cognitive Psychology, 23*, 624–637. doi:10.1002/acp.1500

Natapoff, A. (2009). *Snitching: Criminal informants and the erosion of American justice.* New York, NY: NYU Press.

National Institute for Health and Clinical Excellence. (2009). *Antisocial Personality Disorder: Treatment, Management, and Prevention.* London, UK: NICE.

National Research Council. (2003). *The polygraph and lie detection. Committee to review the scientific evidence on the polygraph. Division of behavioral and social sciences and education.* Washington, DC: The National Academic Press.

National Research Council. (2009). *Strengthening forensic science in the United States: A path forward.* Washington, DC: National Academies Press.

National Research Council. (2014). *Identifying the culprit: Assessing eyewitness identification.* Washington, DC: National Academies Press.

Neal, T. M. S., & Grisso, T. (2014). Assessment practices and expert judgment methods in forensic psychology and psychiatry. *Criminal Justice and Behavior, 41*, 1406–1421. doi:10.1177/0093854814548449

Neath, I., & Surprenant, A. M. (2015). *Human memory* (3rd ed.). Belmont, CA: Wadsworth.

Neil v. Biggers, 409 U.S. 188 (1972).

Neisser, U. (1967). *Cognitive psychology.* New York, NY: Appleton-Century-Crofts.

Neuschatz, J. S., & Cutler, B. L. (2008). Eyewitness identification. In J. Byrne (Ed.), *Cognitive psychology of memory, Vol. 2 of Learning and memory: A comprehensive reference, 4 vols.* (pp. 845–865). Oxford, UK: Elsevier.

Neuschatz, J. S., Lawson, D. S., Swanner, J. K., Meissner, C. A., & Neuschatz, J. S. (2008). The effects of accomplice witnesses and jailhouse informants on jury decision making. *Law and Human Behavior, 32*, 137–149. doi:10.1007/s10979-007-9100-1

Neuschatz, J. S., Wetmore, S. A., Key, K. N., Cash, D. K., Gronlund, S. D., & Goodsell, C. A. (2016). A comprehensive evaluation of showups. In M. K. Miller & B. H. Bornstein (Eds.), *Advances in psychology and law, Vol. 1* (pp. 43–69). New York, NY: Springer. doi:10.1007/978-3-319-29406-3_2

Neuschatz, J. S., Wilkinson, M. L., Goodsell, C. A., Wetmore, S. A., Quinlivan, D. S., & Jones, N. J. (2012). Secondary confessions, expert testimony, and unreliable testimony. *Journal of Police and Criminal Psychology, 27*, 179–192.

Niedzwienska, A., Neckar, J., & Baran, B. (2007). Development and validation of the Implicit Memory Theory Scale. *European Journal of Psychological Assessment, 23*, 185–192. doi:10.1027/1015-5759.23.3.185

Nogrady, H., McConkey, K. M., & Perry, C. (1985). Enhancing visual memory: Trying hypnosis, trying imagination, and trying again. *Journal of Abnormal Psychology, 94*, 195–204. doi:10.1037/0021-843X.94.2.195

Nolan, J. L. (2009). *Legal accents, legal borrowing: The international problem-solving court movement.* Princeton, NJ: Princeton University Press.

Notar, C. E., Padgett, S., & Roden, J. (2013). Cyberbullying: A review of the literature. *Universal Journal of Educational Research, 1*, 1–9. doi:10.13189/ujer.2013.010101

Nudd, T. (2012, July 17). Colgate Sells Dental Floss with Help From Photoshop Disasters. Retrieved June 09, 2016, from http://www.adweek.com/adfreak/colgate-sells-dental-floss-help-photoshop-disasters-141945--

Odinot, G., Wolters, G., & van Koppen, P. J. (2009). Eyewitness memory of a supermarket robbery: A case study of accuracy and confidence after 3 months. *Law and Human Behavior, 33*, 506–514. doi:10.1007/s10979-008-9152-x

Ogloff, J. R. P. (2000). Two steps forward and one step backward: The law and psychology movement(s) in the 20th century. *Law and Human Behavior, 24*, 457–483.

Ogloff, J. R. P., & Douglas, K. S. (2013). Forensic psychological assessments. In J. R. Graham & J. A. Naglieri (Eds.), *Handbook of psychology (Vol, 10): Assessment psychology* (2nd ed., pp. 373–393). Hoboken, NJ: John Wiley & Sons.

Ogloff, J. R. P., Tomkins, A. J., & Bersoff, D. N. (1996). Education and training in psychology and law/criminal justice: Historical foundations, present structures, and future developments. *Criminal Justice and Behavior, 23*, 200–235.

Oliphant, B. (2018, June 11). Public support for the death penalty ticks. *Pew Research Center Fact Tank*. Retrieved from http://www.pewresearch.org/fact-tank/2018/06/11/us-support-for-death-penalty-ticks-up-2018/

O'Neal, E. N., Tellis, K., & Spohn, C. (2015). Prosecuting intimate partner sexual assault: Legal and extra-legal factors that influence charging decisions. *Violence Against Women, 21*, 1237–1258. doi:10.1177/1077801215591630

OR. REV. STAT. § 136.675 (1990).

Orchard, T. L., & Yarmey, A. D. (1995). The effects of whispers, voice-sample duration, and voice distinctiveness of criminal speaker identification. *Applied Cognitive Psychology, 9*, 249–260.

Orne, M. T. (1962). On the social psychology of the psychological experiment: With particular reference to demand characteristics and their implications. *American Psychologist, 17*, 776–783.

Orne, M. T. (1972). Can a hypnotized subject be compelled to carry out otherwise unacceptable behavior? *International Journal of Clinical and Experimental Hypnosis, 20*, 101–117. doi:10.1080/00207147208409281

Orne, M. T. (1979). The use and misuse of hypnosis in court. *International Journal of Clinical and Experimental Hypnosis*, *27*, 311–341. doi:10.1080/00207147908407571

Orne, M. T., Dinges, D. F., & Orne, E. C. (1984). On the differential diagnosis of multiple personality in the forensic context? *International Journal of Clinical and Experimental Hypnosis*, *32*, 118–169.

Orne, M. T., & Evans, F. J. (1965). Social control in the psychological experiment: Antisocial behavior and hypnosis. *Journal of Personality and Social Psychology*, *1*, 189–200. doi:10.1037/h0021933

Ortiz, J., & Raine, A. (2004). Heart rate level and antisocial behavior in children and adolescents: A meta-analysis. *Journal of the American Academy of Child and Adolescent Psychiatry*, *43*, 154–162. doi:10.1097/00004583-200402000-00010

Ost, J., Blank, H., Davies, J., Jones, G., Lambert, K., & Salmon, K. (2013). False memory ≠ false memory: DRM errors are unrelated to the misinformation effect. *PloS ONE*, *8*, e57939. doi:10.1371/journal.pone.0057939

Ost, J., Foster, S., Costall, A., & Bull, R. (2005). False reports of childhood events in appropriate interviews. *Memory*, *13*, 700–710. doi:10.1080/09658210444000340

Ost, J., Vrij, A., Costall, A., & Bull, R. (2002). Crashing memories and reality monitoring: Distinguishing between perceptions, imaginings, and false memories. *Applied Cognitive Psychology*, *16*, 125–134. doi:10.1002/acp.779

Page, R. A., & Green, J. P. (2007). An update on age, hypnotic suggestibility, and gender: A brief report. *American Journal of Clinical Hypnosis*, *49*, 283–287.

Palmer, F. T., Flowe, H. D., Takarangi, M. K. T., & Humphries, J. E. (2013). Intoxicated witnesses and suspects: An archival analysis of their involvement in criminal case processing. *Law & Human Behavior*, *37*, 54–59. doi:10.1037/lhb0000010

Palmer, M. A., Brewer, N., Weber, N., & Nagesh, A. (2013). The confidence-accuracy relationship for eyewitness identification decisions: Effects of exposure duration, retention interval, and divided attention. *Journal of Experimental Psychology: Applied*, *19*, 55–71. doi:10.1037/a0031602

Palmer, M. A., Sauer, J. D., & Holt, G. A. (2017). Undermining position effects in choices from arrays, with implications for police lineups. *Journal of Experimental Psychology: Applied*, *23*, 71–84. doi:10.1037/xap0000109

Paterline, B. A. (2016). Forensic hypnosis and the courts. *Journal of Law and Criminal Justice*, *4*, 1–7.

Paterson, H. M., Luppino, D., Calderwood, C., MacDougall, H. G., Taubert, J., & Kemp, R. I. (2017). Can training improve eyewitness identification? The effect of internal feature focus on memory for faces. *Psychology, Crime & Law*, *23*, 927–945. doi:10.1080/1068316X.2017.1346099

Patihis, L., Frenda, S. J., LePort, A. K. R., Petersen, N., Nichols, R. M., Stark, C. E. L., McGaugh, J. L., & Loftus, E. F. (2013). False memories in highly superior autobiographical memory individuals. *Proceedings of the National Academy of Sciences*, *110*, 20947–20952.

Patrick, C. J., Cuthbert, B. N., & Lang, P. J. (1994). Emotion in the criminal psychopath: Fear image processing. *Journal of Abnormal Psychology*, *103*(3), 523–534. doi:10.1037/0021-843X.103.3.523

Pawlenko, N. B., Safer, M. A., Wise, R. A., & Holfeld, B. (2013). A teaching aid for improving jurors' assessments of eyewitness accuracy. *Applied Cognitive Psychology, 27*, 190–197. doi:10.1002/acp.2895

Payne, B. K. (2001). Prejudice and perception: The role of automatic and controlled processes in misperceiving a weapon. *Journal of Personality and Social Psychology, 81*, 181–192.

Payne, D. G. (1987). Hypermnesia and reminiscence in recall: A historical and empirical review.

Peirce, C. S., & Jastrow, J. (1884). On small differences in sensation. *Memoirs of the National Academy of Sciences, 3*, 73–83.

Pennington, N., & Hastie, R. (1993). The story model for juror decision-making. In R. Hastie (Ed.), *Inside the juror* (pp. 192–221). Cambridge, England: Cambridge University Press.

Penrod, S. D., & Bornstein, B. H. (2007). Methodological issues in eyewitness memory research. In R. C. L. Lindsay, D. F. Ross, J. D. Read, & M. Toglia (Eds.), *Handbook of eyewitness psychology (Vol. 2): Memory for people* (pp. 529–556). Mahwah, NJ: Erlbaum.

People v. Romero, 745 P.2d 1003 (Colo. 1987).

People v. Worthington, 38 P. 689 (Cal. 1894).

Perfect, T. J. (2004). The role of self-rated ability in the accuracy of confidence judgements in eyewitness memory and general knowledge. *Applied Cognitive Psychology, 18*, 157–168.

Perfect, T. J., Hollins, T. S., & Hunt, A. L. R. (2000). Practice and feedback effects on the confidence-accuracy relation in eyewitness memory. *Memory, 8*, 235–244.

Perillo, J. T., & Kassin, S. M. (2011). Inside interrogation: The lie, the bluff, and false confessions. *Law and Human Behavior, 35*, 327–337.

Perry, C. (1997). Admissibility and per se exclusion of hypnotically elicited recall in American courts of law. *International Journal of Clinical and Experimental Hypnosis, 45*, 266–279. doi:10.1080/00207149708416128

Peth, J., Vossel, G., & Gamer, M. (2012). Emotional arousal modulates the encoding of crime-related details and corresponding physiological responses in the Concealed Information Test. *Psychophysiology, 49*, 381–390. doi:10.1111/j.1469-8986.2011.01313.x

Pezdek, K., Blandón-Gitlin, I., & Gabbay, P. (2006). Imagination and memory: Does imagining implausible events lead to false autobiographical memories? *Psychonomic Bulletin & Review, 13*, 764–769.

Pezdek, K., Finger, K., & Hodge, D. (1997). Planting false childhood memories: The role of event plausibility. *Psychological Science, 8*, 437–441.

Philippon, A. C., Cherryman, J., Bull, R., & Vrij. A. (2007). Lay people's and police officers' attitudes towards the usefulness of perpetrator voice identification. *Applied Cognitive Psychology, 21*, 103–115.

Piaget, J. (1932). *The moral judgment of the child*. Oxford, England: Harcourt, Brace.

Pigott, M. A., Brigham, J. C., & Bothwell, R. K. (1990). A field study of the relationship between quality of eyewitnesses' descriptions and identification accuracy. *Journal of Police Science and Administration, 17*, 84–88.

Piquero, N. L., & Davis, J. L. (2004). Extralegal factors and the sentencing of organizational defendants: An examination of the Federal Sentencing Guidelines. *Journal of Criminal Justice, 32*, 643–654. doi:10.1016/j.jcrimjus.2004.08.001

Plant, E. A., & Peruche, B. M. (2005). The consequences of race for police officers' responses to criminal suspects. *Psychological Science, 16*, 180–183.

Plant, E. A., Peruche, B. M., & Butz, D. A. (2005). Eliminating automatic racial bias: Making race non-diagnostic for responses to criminal suspects. *Journal of Experimental Social Psychology, 41*, 141–156.

Platz, S. J., & Hosch, H. M. (1988). Cross-racial/ethnic eyewitness identification: A field study. *Journal of Applied Social Psychology, 18*, 972–984.

Podlesney, J. A. (2003). A paucity of operable case facts restricts applicability of the guilty knowledge technique in FBI criminal polygraph examinations. *Forensic Science Communications, 5*(3), Retrieved from http://www.fbi.gov/hq/lab/fsc/backissu/july2003/podlesny.htm. Accessed 6 June 2014.

Poole, D. A., Lindsay, D. S., Memon, A., & Bull, R. (1995). Psychotherapy and the recovery of memories of childhood sexual abuse: U.S. and British practitioners' opinions, practices, and experiences. *Journal of Consulting and Clinical Psychology, 63*, 426–437. doi:1 0.1037/0022-006X.63.3.426

Popplestone, J. A., & McPherson, M. W. (1994). *An illustrated history of American psychology*. Akron, OH: University of Akron Press.

Porter, S., Birt, A. R., Yuille, J. C., & Lehman, D. R. (2000). Negotiating false memories: Interviewer and rememberer characteristics relate to memory distortion. *Psychological Science, 11*, 507–510.

Porter, S., Juodis, M., ten Brinke, L., Klein, R., & Wilson, K. (2010). Evaluation of a brief deception detection training program. *Journal of Forensic Psychiatry & Psychology, 21*, 66–76.

Porter, S., & ten Brinke, L. (2009). Dangerous decisions: A theoretical framework for understanding how judges assess credibility in the courtroom. *Legal and Criminological Psychology, 14*, 119–134.

Porter, S., Woodworth, M., & Birt, A. R. (2000). Truth, lies, and video- tape: An investigation of the ability of federal parole officers to detect deception. *Law and Human Behavior, 24*, 643–658.

Porter, S., & Yuille, J. C. (1996). The language of deceit: An investigation of the verbal clues to deception in the interrogation context. *Law and Human Behavior, 20*, 443–458. doi:10.1007/BF01498980

Porter, S., Yuille, J. C., & Lehman, D. R. (1999). The nature of real, implanted, and fabricated memories for emotional childhood events: Implications for the recovered memory debate. *Law and Human Behavior, 23*, 517–537.

Powys, J. C. (1914). *The war and culture: A reply to Professor Münsterberg*. New York, NY: G. Arnold Shaw.

Price, W. H., & Whatmore, P. B. (1967). Behaviour disorders and pattern of crime among XYY males identified at a maximum security hospital. *British Medical Journal, 1*(5539), 533–536.

Prins, S. J. (2014). Prevalence of mental illnesses in U.S. state prisons: A systematic review. *Psychiatric Services, 65*, 862–872. doi:10.1176/appi.ps.201300166

Quas, J. A., Goodman, G. S., Bidrose, S., Pipe, M. E., Craw, S., & Ablin, D. S. (1999). Emotion and memory: Children's long-term remembering, forgetting, and suggestibility. *Journal of Experimental Child Psychology, 72*, 235–270. doi:jecp.10.1006/1999.2491

Quas, J. A., Rush, E. B., Yim, I. S., Edelstein, R. S., Otgaar, H., & Smeets, T. (2016). Stress and emotional valence effects on children's versus adolescents' true and false memory. *Memory, 24*, 696–707. doi:10.1080/09658211.2015.1045909

Quas, J. A., Rush, E. B., Yim, I. S., & Nikolayev, M. (2014). Effects of stress on memory in children and adolescents: Testing causal connections. *Memory, 22*, 616–632. doi:10.1080/09658211.2013.809766

Quinlivan, D. S., Neuschatz, J. S., Jimenez, A., Cling, A., Douglass, A. B., & Goodsell, C. A. (2009). Do prophylactics prevent inflation? Post-identification feedback and the effectiveness of procedures to protect against confidence-inflation in earwitnesses. *Law and Human Behavior, 33*, 111–121. doi:10.1007/s10979-008-9132-1

Ragozzino, M. E. (2007). The contribution of the medial prefrontal cortex, orbitofrontal cortex, and dorsomedial striatum to behavioral flexibility. In G. Schoenbaum, J. A. Gottfried, E. A. Murray, S. J. Ramus, G. Schoenbaum, J. A. Gottfried, . . . S. J. Ramus (Eds.), *Linking affect to action: Critical contributions of the orbitofrontal cortex* (pp. 355–375). Malden, MA: Blackwell.

Raine, A. (1993). *The psychopathology of crime: Criminal behavior as a clinical disorder.* San Diego, CA: Academic Press.

Raine, A. (2002). Biosocial studies of antisocial and violent behavior in children and adults: A review. *Journal of Abnormal Child Psychology, 30*, 311–326. doi:10.1023/A:1015754122318

Raine, A. (2013). *The anatomy of violence: The biological roots of crime.* New York, NY: Vintage Books.

Raine, A., Brennan, P., & Mednick, S. A. (1994). Birth complications combined with early maternal rejection at age 1 year predispose to violent crime at age 18 years. *Archive of General Psychiatry, 51*, 984–988.

Raine, A., Brennan, P., & Mednick, S. A. (1997). Interaction between birth complications and early maternal rejection in predisposing individuals to adult violence: Specificity to serious, early-onset violence. *American Journal of Psychiatry, 154*, 1265–1271.

Raine, A., Meloy, J. R., Bihrle, S., Stoddard, J., LaCasse, L., & Buchsbaum, M. S. (1998). Reduced prefrontal and increased subcortical brain functioning assessed using positron emission tomography in predatory and affective murderers. *Behavioral Sciences & the Law, 16*, 319–332

Raine, A., Stoddard, J., Bihrle, S., & Buchsbaum, M. (1998). Prefrontal glucose deficits in murderers lacking psychosocial deprivation. *Cognitive and Behavioral Neurology, 11*, 1–7.

Raine, A., Venables, P. H., Dalais, C., Mellingen, K., Reynolds, C., & Mednick, S. A. (2001). Early educational and health enrichment at age 3–5 years is associated with increased autonomic and central nervous system arousal and orienting at age 11 years: Evidence from the Mauritius Child Health Project. *Psychophysiology, 38*, 254–266. doi:10.1017/S0048577201990067

Rao, U., Carlson, G. A., & Rapport, M. D. (1991). Serum cholesterol and aggressive behavior in psychiatrically hospitalized children. *Acta Psychiatrica Scandinavica, 83*, 77–78. doi:10.1111/j.1600-0447.1991.tb05515.x

Raskin, D. C., & Esplin, P. W. (1991). Statement validity assessment: Interview procedures and content analysis of children's statements of sexual abuse. *Behavioral Assessment, 13*, 265–291.

Raskin, D. C., & Honts, C. R. (2002). The comparison question test. In M. Kleiner (Ed.), *Handbook of polygraph testing* (pp. 1–47). San Diego, CA: Academic Press.

Ratchford, M., & Beaver, K. M. (2009). Neuropsychological deficits, low self-control, and delinquent involvement: Toward a biosocial explanation of delinquency. *Criminal Justice and Behavior, 36*, 147–162. doi:10.1177/0093854808325967

Ratcliff, R. (1978). A theory of memory retrieval. *Psychological Review, 85*, 59–108.

Read, J. D., & Desmarais, S. L. (2009). Lay knowledge of eyewitness issues: A Canadian evaluation. *Applied Cognitive Psychology, 23*, 301–326.

Read, J. D., Tollestrup, P., Hammersley, R., McFadzen, E., & Christensen, A. (1990). The unconscious transference effect: Are innocent bystanders ever misidentified? *Applied Cognitive Psychology, 4*, 3–31.

Read, J. D., Yuille, J. C., & Tollestrup, P. (1992). Recollections of a robbery: Effects of arousal and alcohol upon recall and person identification. *Law and Human Behavior, 16*, 425–446.

Redlich, A. D. (2004). Law & psychiatry: Mental illness, police interrogations, and the potential for false confession. *Psychiatric Services, 55*, 19–21. doi:10.1176/appi.ps.55.1.19

Redlich, A. D., & Goodman, G. S. (2003). Taking responsibility for an act not committed: The influence of age and suggestibility. *Law and Human Behavior, 27*, 141–156. doi:10.1023/A:1022543012851

Redlich, A. D., Summers, A., & Hoover, S. (2009). Self-reported false confessions and false guilty pleas among offenders with mental illness. *Law and Human Behavior, 34*, 79–90. doi:10.1007/s10979-009-9194-8

Reed, K., Dellapaolera, K. S., Thimsen, S., & Bornstein, B. H. (2018). An empirical analysis of law-psychology journals: Who's publishing and on what? In M. K. Miller & B. H. Bornstein (Eds.), *Advances in psychology and law, Vol. 3* (pp. 285–299). New York, NY: Springer. doi:10.1007/978-3-319-75859-6_9

Rehnman, J., & Herlitz, A. (2007). Women remember more faces than men do. *Acta Psychologica, 124*, 344–355. doi:10.1016/j.actpsy.2006.04.004

Reisberg, D., & Heuer, F. (2007). The influence of emotion on memory in forensic settings. In M. P. Toglia, J. D. Read, D. F. Ross, & R. C. L. Lindsay (Eds.), *Handbook of eyewitness psychology, Vol. 1: Memory for events* (pp. 81–116). Mahwah, NJ: Lawrence Erlbaum.

Reisberg, D., Pearson, D. G., & Kosslyn, S. M. (2003). Intuitions and introspections about imagery: The role of imagery experience in shaping an investigator's theoretical views. *Applied Cognitive Psychology, 17*, 147–160. doi:10.1002/acp.858

Relinger, H. (1984). Hypnotic hypermnesia: A critical review. *American Journal of Clinical Hypnosis, 26*, 212–225. doi:10.1080/00029157.1984.10404165

Rensink, R. A., O'Regan, K., & Clark, J. J. (1997). To see or not to see: The need for attention to perceive changes in scenes. *Psychological Science, 8*, 368–373.

Rettenberger, M., Rice, M. E., Harris, G. T., & Eher, R. (2017). Actuarial risk assessment of sexual offenders: The psychometric properties of the Sex Offender Risk Appraisal Guide (SORAG). *Psychological Assessment, 29*, 624–638. doi:10.1037/pas0000390

Richardson, A. (1977). Verbalizer-Visualizer: A cognitive style dimension. *Journal of Mental Imagery, 1*, 109–126.

Ridley, A. M., & Clifford, B. R. (2004). The effects of anxious mood induction on suggestibility to misleading post-event information. *Applied Cognitive Psychology, 18*, 233–244. doi:10.1002/acp.963

Ridley, A. M., & Clifford, B. R. (2006). Suggestibility and state anxiety: How the two concepts relate to a source identification paradigm. *Memory, 14*, 37–45. doi:10.1080/09658210444000494

Ridley, A. M., & Clifford, B. R., & Keogh, E. (2002). The effects of state anxiety on the suggestibility and accuracy of child eyewitnesses. *Applied Cognitive Psychology, 16*, 547–558. doi:10.1002/acp.813

Ridley, A. M., Gabbert, F., & La Rooy, D. J. (2013). *Suggestibility in legal contexts: Psychological research and forensic implications*. Chichester, UK: Wiley-Blackwell.

Rigoni, M. E., & Meissner, C. A. (2008). Is it time for a revolution in the interrogation room? Empirically validating inquisitorial methods. Paper presented at Meeting of the American Psychology-Law Society, Jacksonville, FL.

Rilling, J. K., Glenn, A. L., Jairam, M. R., Pagnoni, G., Goldsmith, D. R., Elfenbein, H. A., & Lilienfeld, S. O. (2007). Neural correlates of social cooperation and non-cooperation as a function of psychopathy. *Biological Psychiatry, 61*, 1260–1271. doi:10.1016/j.biopsych.2006.07.021

Roberts, P. (2002). Vulnerability to false memory: The effects of stress, imagery, trait anxiety, and depression. *Current Psychology, 21*, 240–252. doi:10.1007/s12144-002-1016-9

Robinson, E. S. (1935). *Law and the lawyers*. New York, NY: Macmillan.

Rock v. Arkansas, 483 U.S. 44 (1987).

Roediger, H. L., III, & McDermott, K. B. (1995). Creating false memories: Remembering words not presented in lists. *Journal of Experimental Psychology: Learning, Memory, and Cognition, 21*, 803–814.

Roediger, H. L., Watson, J. M., McDermott, K. B., & Gallo, D. A. (2001). Factors that determine false recall: A multiple regression analysis. *Psychonomic Bulletin and Review, 8*, 385–407.

Roediger, H. L., Wixted, J. H., & Desoto, K. A. (2012). The curious complexity between confidence and accuracy in reports from memory. In L. Nadel & W. P. Sinnott-Armstrong (Eds.), *Memory and law* (pp. 84–118). New York, NY: Oxford University Press.

Rogers, R., Harrison, K. S., Hazelwood, L. L., & Sewell, K. W. (2007). Knowing and intelligent: A study of Miranda warnings in mentally disordered defendants. *Law and Human Behavior, 31*, 401–418. doi:10.1007/s10979-006-9070-8

Rolls, E. T. (2000). The orbitofrontal cortex and reward. *Cerebral Cortex, 10*, 284–294. doi:10.1093/cercor/10.3.284

Rosenfeld, J. P. (2011). P300 in detecting concealed information. In B. Verschuere, G. Ben Shakhar, & E. Meijer (Eds.), *Memory detection: Theory and application of the concealed information test* (pp. 63–89). Cambridge, UK: Cambridge University Press.

Rosenfeld, J. P. (2018). *Detecting concealed information and deception: Recent developments*. Cambridge, MA: Elsevier.

Rosenfeld, J. P., Ben-Shakhar, G., & Ganis, G. (2012). Detection of concealed stored memories with psychophysiological and neuroimaging methods. In L. Nadel & W. P. Sinnott-Armstrong (Eds.), *Memory and law* (pp. 263–303). New York, NY: Oxford University Press.

Rosenfeld, J. P., Cantwell, B., Nasman, V. T., Wojdac, V., Ivanov, S., & Mazzeri, L. (1988). A modified, event-related potential-based guilty knowledge test. *International Journal of Neuroscience, 42*, 157–161.

Rosenfeld, J. P., & Labkovsky, E. (2010). New P300-based protocol to detect concealed information: Resistance to mental countermeasures against only half the irrelevant stimuli and a possible ERP indicator of countermeasures. *Psychophysiology, 47*, 1002–1010.

Rosenfeld, J. P., Soskins, M., Bosh, G., & Ryan, A. (2004). Simple, effective counter-measures to P300-based tests of detection of concealed information. *Psychophysiology, 41*, 205–219.

Ross, D. R., Ceci, S. J., Dunning, D., & Toglia, M. P. (1994). Unconscious transference and mistaken identity: When a witness misidentifies a familiar but innocent person. *Journal of Applied Psychology, 79*, 918–930.

Rowland, L. W. (1939). Will hypnotized persons try to harm themselves or others? *The Journal of Abnormal and Social Psychology, 34*, 114–117. doi:10.1037/h0055818

Rusconi, E., & Mitchener-Nissen, T. (2013). Prospects of functional magnetic resonance imaging as lie detector. *Frontiers in Human Neuroscience, 7*, 594. doi:10.3389/fnhum.2013.00594

Russano, M. B., Meissner, C. A., Narchet, F. M., & Kassin, S. M. (2005). Investigating true and false confession within a novel experimental paradigm. *Psychological Science, 16*, 481–486.

Saks, M. J. (2018). Applying social psychology to law and the legal process. In T. Grisso & S. L. Brodsky (Eds.), *The roots of modern psychology and law* (pp. 44–60). New York, NY: Oxford University Press.

Saks, M. J., & Koehler, J. J. (2005). The coming paradigm shift in forensic identification science. *Science, 309*, 892–895.

Salzberg, H. C., & DePiano, F. A. (1980). Hypnotizability and task motivating suggestions: A further look at how they affect performance. *International Journal of Clinical and Experimental Hypnosis, 28*, 261–271. doi:10.1080/00207148008409851

Santana, E. J. (2016). The brain of the psychopath: A systematic review of structural neuroimaging studies. *Psychology & Neuroscience, 9*, 420–443. doi:10.1037/pne0000069

Sartori, G., Agosta, S., Zogmaister, C., Ferrara, S. D., & Castiello, U. (2008). How to accurately detect autobiographical events. *Psychological Science, 19*, 772–780.

Sauer, J., Brewer, N., Zweck, T., & Weber, N. (2010). The effect of retention interval on the confidence-accuracy relationship for eyewitness identification. *Law and Human Behavior, 34*, 337–347. doi:10.1007/s10979-009-9192-x

Sauerland, M., & Sporer, S. L. (2009). Fast and confident: Postdicting eyewitness identification accuracy in a field study. *Journal of Experimental Psychology: Applied, 15*, 46–62. doi:10.1037/a0014560

Schacter, D. L., Chamberlain, J., Gaesser, B., & Gerlach, K. D. (2012). Neuroimaging of true, false, and imaginary memories: Findings and implications. In L. Nadel & W. P. Sinnott-Armstrong (Eds.), *Memory and law* (pp. 233–262). Oxford, UK: Oxford University Press.

Schacter, D. L., Dawes, R., Jacoby, L. L., Kahneman, D., Lempert, R., Roediger, H. L., & Rosenthal, R. (2008). Policy forum: Studying eyewitness investigations in the field. *Law and Human Behavior, 32*, 3–5. doi:10.1007/s10979-007-9093-9

Scheflin, A. W., & Frischholz, E. J. (1999). Significant dates in the history of forensic hypnosis. *American Journal of Clinical Hypnosis, 42*, 84–107. doi:10.1080/00029157.1999.10701726

Schneider, S. L., & Laurion, S. K. (1993). Do we know what we've learned from listening to the news? *Memory & Cognition, 21*, 198–209.

Schneider, W. H. (2005). The establishment of institutional review boards in the U.S.: Background history. Unpublished manuscript. Retrieved from http://www.iupui.edu/~histwhs/G504.dir/irbhist.html.

Schreiber Compo, N., Carol, R. N., Evans, J. R., Pimentel, P., Holness, H., Nichols-Lopez, K., . . . Furton, K. G. (2017). Witness memory and alcohol: The effects of state-dependent recall. *Law and Human Behavior, 41*, 202–215. doi:10.1037/lhb0000224

Schreiber Compo, N., Evans, J. R., Carol, R. N., Kemp, D., Villalba, D., Ham, L. S., & Rose, S. (2011). Alcohol intoxication and memory for events: A snapshot of alcohol myopia in a real-world drinking scenario. *Memory, 19*, 202–210. doi:10.1080/09658211.2010.546802

Schreiber Compo, N., Evans, J. R., Carol, R. N., Villalba, D., Ham, L. S., Garcia, T., & Rose, S. (2012). Intoxicated eyewitnesses: Better than their reputation? *Law & Human Behavior, 36*, 77–86. doi:10.1037/h0093951

Schwartz, B. L. (2014). *Memory: Foundations and applications* (2nd ed.). Thousand Oaks, CA: Sage.

Schweitzer, N. J., & Saks, M. J. (2007). The CSI Effect: Popular fiction about forensic science affects the public's expectations about real forensic science. *Jurimetrics, 47*, 357–364.

Scott, S., Briskman, J., & O'Connor, T. G. (2014). Early prevention of antisocial personality: Long-term follow-up of two randomized controlled trials comparing indicated and selective approaches. *American Journal of Psychiatry, 171*, 649–657. doi:10.1176/appi.ajp.2014.13050697

Seamon, J. G., Philbin, M. M., & Harrison, L. G. (2006). Do you remember proposing marriage to the Pepsi machine? False recollections from a campus walk. *Psychonomic Bulletin & Review, 13*, 752–756.

Segal, J. A., & Spaeth, H. J. (1993). *The Supreme Court and the attitudinal model.* Cambridge, England: Cambridge University Press.

Seto, M.C . (2008). *Pedophilia and sexual offending against children: Theory, assessment, and intervention*. Washington, DC: American Psychological Association. doi:10.1037/11639-000

Seymour, T. L., & Kerlin, J. R. (2008). Successful detection of verbal and visual concealed knowledge using an RT-based paradigm. *Applied Cognitive Psychology, 22*, 475–490.

Seymour, T. L., Seifert, C. M., Shafto, M. G., & Mosmann, A. L. (2000). Using response time measures to assess "guilty knowledge." *Journal of Applied Psychology, 85*, 30–37.

Shaboltas, A. (2017). Forensic and criminal psychology in Russia: History of development and current state. In P. A. Granhag, R. Bull, A. Shaboltas, & E. Dozortseva (Eds.), *Psychology and law in Europe: When West meets East* (pp. 3–15). Boca Raton, FL: CRC Press.

Shapiro, P. N., & Penrod, S. (1986). Meta-analysis of facial identification studies. *Psychological Bulletin, 100*, 139–156

Shaw, J. I., & Skolnick, P. (1999). Weapon focus and gender differences in eyewitness accuracy: Arousal versus salience. *Journal of Applied Social Psychology, 29*, 2328–2341. doi:10.1111/j.1559-1816.1999.tb00113.x

Sheehan, P. W., Green, V., & Truesdale, P. (1992). Influence of rapport on hypnotically induced pseudomemory. *Journal of Abnormal Psychology, 101*, 690–700.

Sheehan, P. W., & Tilden, J. (1983). Effects of suggestibility and hypnosis on accurate and distorted retrieval from memory. *Journal of Experimental Psychology: Learning, Memory, and Cognition, 9*, 283–293. doi:10.1037/0278-7393.9.2.283

Sherrin, C. (1998). Jailhouse informants in the Canadian criminal justice system, Part II: Options for reform. *Criminal Law Quarterly, 40*, 157–187.

Shih, J. C., Ridd, M. J., Chen, K., Meehan, W. P., Kung, M., Seif, I., & De Maeyer, E. (1999). Ketanserin and tetrabenazine abolish aggression in mice lacking monoamine oxidase A. *Brain Research, 835*, 104–112. doi:10.1016/S0006-8993(99)01478-X

Sigurdsson, J. F., & Gudjonsson, G. H. (1997). The criminal history of "false confessors" and other prison inmates. *The Journal of Forensic Psychiatry, 8*, 447–445.

Sigursdsson, J. F., & Gudjonsson, G. H. (2001). False confessions: The relative importance of psychological, criminological and substance abuse variables. *Psychology, Crime, and Law, 7*, 275–289.

Silver, E., Cirincione, C., & Steadman, H. J. (1994). Demythologizing inaccurate perceptions of the insanity defense. *Law and Human Behavior, 18*, 63–70. doi:10.1007/BF01499144

Simon, L. (1996). *William James remembered*. Lincoln, NE: University of Nebraska Press.

Simons, D. J., & Chabris, C. F. (1999). Gorillas in our midst: Sustained inattentional blindness for dynamic events. *Perception, 28*, 1059–1074.

Simons, D. J., & Levin, D. T. (1997). Change blindness. *Trends in Cognitive Sciences, 1*, 261–267.

Simons, D. J., & Schlosser, M. D. (2017). Inattentional blindness for a gun during a simulated police vehicle stop. *Cognitive Research: Principles and Implications, 2*, 37. doi:10.1186/s41235-017-0074-3

Singh, J. P., Grann, M., & Fazel, S. (2011). A comparative study of violence risk assessment tools: A systematic review and metaregression analysis of 68 studies involving 25,980 participants. *Clinical Psychology Review, 31*, 499–513. doi:10.1016/j.cpr.2010.11.009

Skeem, J. L., Douglas, K. S., & Lilienfeld, S. O. (2009). *Psychological science in the courtroom: Controversies and consensus*. New York, NY: Guilford Press.

Skeem, J. L., & Golding, S. L. (2001). Describing jurors' personal conceptions of insanity and their relationship to case judgments. *Psychology, Public Policy, and Law, 7*, 561–621. doi:10.1037//1076-8971.7.3.561

Slater, A. (1994). *Identification parades: A scientific evaluation*. Police Research Award Scheme, Police Research Group, Home Office.

Slesinger, D., & Pilpel, E. M. (1929). Legal psychology: A bibliography and a suggestion. *Psychological Bulletin, 26*, 677–692.

Smalarz, L., & Wells, G. L. (2014). Post-identification feedback to eyewitnesses impairs evaluators' abilities to discriminate between accurate and mistaken testimony. *Law and Human Behavior, 38*, 194–202.

Smith, M. C. (1969). Effect of varying channel capacity of stimulus detection and discrimination. *Journal of Experimental Psychology, 82*, 520–526. doi:10.1037/h0028354

Smith, N. (2001). *Police Research Series Paper: Vol. 135. Reading between the lines: An evaluation of the Scientific Content Analysis technique (SCAN)*. London, England: Home Office, Research, Development and Statistics Directorate.

Smith, S. M., Lindsay, R. C. L., & Pryke, S. (2000). Postdictors of eyewitness errors: Can false identification be diagnosed? *Journal of Applied Psychology, 85*, 542–550.

Smith, S. M., Lindsay, R. C. L., Pryke, S., & Dysart, J. E. (2001). Postdictors of eyewitness errors: Can false identifications be diagnosed in the cross-race situation? *Psychology, Public Policy, and Law, 7*, 153–169.

Soderstrom, H., Tullberg, M., Wikkelsö, C., Ekholm, S., & Forsman, A. (2000). Reduced regional cerebral blood flow in non-psychotic violent offenders. *Psychiatry Research: Neuroimaging, 98*, 29–41. doi:10.1016/S0925-4927(99)00049-9

Sommer, A. (2012). Psychical research and the origins of American psychology: Hugo Münsterberg, William James and Eusapia Palladino. *History of the Human Sciences, 25*, 23–44. doi:10.1177/0952695112439376

Sorgi, P. J., Hallowell, E. M., Hutchins, H. L., & Sears, B. (2007). Effects of an open-label pilot study with high-dose EPA/DHA concentrates on plasma phospholipids and behavior in children with attention deficit hyperactivity disorder. *Nutrition journal, 6*, 16. doi:10.1186/1475-2891-6-16

Spanos, N. P., Burgess, C. A., Burgess, M. F., Samuels, C., & Blois, W. O. (1999). Creating false memories of infancy with hypnotic and non-hypnotic procedures. *Applied Cognitive Psychology, 13*, 201–218. doi:10.1002/(SICI)1099-0720(199906)13:3<201::AID-ACP565>3.0.CO;2-X

Spanos, N. P., Gwynn, M. I., Comer, S. L., Baltruweit, W. J., & de Groh, M. (1989). Are hypnotically induced pseudomemories resistant to cross-examination? *Law and Human Behavior, 13*, 271–289.

Spanos, N. P., Menary, E., Gabora, N. J., DuBreuil, S. C., & Dewhirst, B. (1991). Secondary identity enactments during hypnotic past-life regression: A sociocognitive perspective. *Journal of Personality and Social Psychology, 61*, 308–320.

Spanos, N. P., Quigley, C. A., Gwynn, M. I., Glatt, R. L., & Perlini, A. H. (1991). Hypnotic interrogation, pretrial preparation, and witness testimony during direct and cross-examination. *Law and Human Behavior, 15*, 639–653.

Spence, S. A., Farrow, T. F., Herford, A. E., Wilkinson, I. D., Zheng, Y., & Woodruff, P. W. (2001). Behavioural and functional anatomical correlates of deception in humans. *Neuroreport, 12*, 2849–2853.

Spiegel, D., & Spiegel, H. (1987). Forensic uses of hypnosis. In I. B. Weiner & A. K. Hess (Eds.), *Handbook of forensic psychology* (pp. 490–507). Oxford, UK: Wiley.

Spiegel, H., & Spiegel, D. (1978). *Trance & treatment: Clinical uses of hypnosis.* New York, NY: Basic Books.

Spielberger, C. D., Gorsuch, R. L., Luschene, R., Vagg, P. R., & Jacobs, G. A. (1983). *State-Trait Anxiety Inventory for Adults*. Palo Alto, CA: Consulting Psychologists Press.

Spillmann, J., & Spillmann, L. (1993). The rise and fall of Hugo Münsterberg. *Journal of the History of the Behavioral Sciences, 29*, 322–338.

Sporer, S. L. (1982). A brief history of the psychology of testimony. *Current Psychological Reviews, 2*, 323–340.

Sporer, S. L. (1992). Post-dicting eyewitness accuracy: Confidence, decision times and person descriptions of choosers and non-choosers. *European Journal of Social Psychology, 22*, 157–180.

Sporer, S. L. (1993). Eyewitness identification accuracy, confidence, and decision times in simultaneous and sequential lineups. *Journal of Applied Psychology, 78*, 22–33.

Sporer, S. L. (1994). Decision times and eyewitness identification accuracy in simultaneous and sequential lineups. In D. F. Ross, J. D. Read, & M. P. Toglia (Eds.), *Adult eyewitness testimony: Current trends and developments* (pp. 300–327). New York, NY: Cambridge University Press.

Sporer, S. L. (1996). Psychological aspects of person descriptions. In S. L. Sporer, R. S. Malpass, & G. Koehnken (Eds.), *Psychological issues in eyewitness identification* (pp. 53–86). Mahwah, NJ: Erlbaum.

Sporer, S. L. (2001). Recognizing faces of other ethnic groups: An integration of theories. *Psychology, Public Policy, and Law, 7*, 36–97. doi:10.1037//10076-8971.7.1.36

Sporer, S. L. (2006). The science of eyewitness testimony has come of age. *Psychological Science in the Public Interest, 7*, i–ii.

Sporer, S. L. (2008). Lessons from the origins of eyewitness testimony research in Europe. *Applied Cognitive Psychology, 22*, 737–757. doi:10.1002/acp.1479

Sporer, S. L., Penrod, S., Read, D., & Cutler, B. (1995). Choosing, confidence, and accuracy: A meta-analysis of the confidence-accuracy relation in eyewitness identification studies. *Psychological Bulletin, 118*, 315–327.

Sporer, S. L., & Schwandt, B. (2006). Paraverbal correlates of deception: A meta-analysis. *Applied Cognitive Psychology, 20*, 421–446. doi:10.1002/acp.1190

Sporer, S. L., & Schwandt, B. (2007). Moderators of nonverbal indicators of deception: A meta-analytic synthesis. *Psychology, Public Policy, and Law, 13*, 1–34. doi:10.1037/1076- 8971.1.13.1.1
Stager, G. L., & Lundy, R. M. (1985). Hypnosis and the learning and recall of visually presented material. *International Journal of Clinical and Experimental Hypnosis, 33*, 27–39. doi:10.1080/00207148508406633
State v. Gray, 39 P. 1050 (Kan. 1895).
State v. Henderson, 27 A. 3d 872 (N.J. 2011).
State v. Hurd, 432 A.2d 86 (N.J. 1981).
Steadman, H. J. (1979). *Beating a rap? Defendants found incompetent to stand trial.* Chicago, IL: University of Chicago Press.
Steblay, N. K. (1997). Social influence in eyewitness recall: A meta-analytic review of lineup instruction effects. *Law and Human Behavior, 21*, 283–297. doi:10.1023/A:
Steblay, N. K. (2011). What we know now: The Evanston Illinois field lineups. *Law and Human Behavior, 35*, 1–12. doi:10.1007/s10979-009-9207-7
Steblay, N. K. (2012). How I got started: Field experiments, meta-analysis, and eyewitness memory. *Applied Cognitive Psychology, 26*, 823–824. doi:10.1002/acp.1838
Steblay, N. K. (2018). All is not as it seems: Avoidable pitfalls in the interpretation of lineup field data. *Psychology, Public Policy, and Law, 24*, 292–306. doi:10.1037/law0000171
Steblay, N. K., & Bothwell, R. K. (1994). Evidence for hypnotically refreshed testimony: The view from the laboratory. *Law and Human Behavior, 18*, 635–651. doi:10.1007/BF01499329
Steblay, N. K., Dysart, J. E., Fulero, S., & Lindsay, R. C. L. (2001). Eyewitness accuracy rates in sequential and simultaneous lineup presentations: A meta-analytic comparison. *Law and Human Behavior, 25*, 459–473. doi:10.1023/A:1012888715007
Steblay, N. K., Dysart, J. E., & Wells, G. L..(2011). Seventy-two tests of the sequential lineup superiority effect: A meta-analysis and policy discussion. *Psychology, Public Policy, and Law, 17*, 99–139. doi:10.1037/a0021650
Steblay, N. K., Wells, G. L, & Douglass, A. B. (2014). The eyewitness post identification feedback effect 15 years later: Theoretical and policy implications. *Psychology, Public Policy, & Law, 20*, 1–18. doi:10.1037/law0000001
Steblay, N. M. (1992). A meta-analytic review of the weapon focus effect. *Law and Human Behavior, 16*, 413–424.
Stephenson, G. M. (1984). Accuracy and confidence in testimony: A critical review and some fresh evidence. In D. J. Muller, D. E. Blackman, & A. J. Chapman (Eds.), *Psychology and law: Topics from an international conference* (pp. 229–248). Chichester, UK: Wiley.
Stephenson, G. M., Clark, N. K., & Wade, G. S. (1986). Meetings make evidence? An experimental study of collaborative and individual recall of a simulated police interrogation. *Journal of Personality and Social Psychology, 50*, 1113–1122.
Stern, P. C. (2002). *The polygraph and lie detection: Report of the national research council committee to review the scientific evidence on the polygraph.* Washington, D.C.: The National Academies Press.

Stern, W. (1904/2000). Wirklichkeitsversuche. *Beiträge zur Psychologie der Aussage, 2*, 1–31. Reprinted and translated in U. Neisser & I. E. Hyman (Eds.), *Memory observed: Remembering in natural contexts* (2nd ed.) (pp. 199–213). New York, NY: Worth.

Stern, W. (1917). Münsterberg: In memoriam. *Journal of Applied Psychology, 1*, 186–188.

Stinson, V., Devenport, J. L., Cutler, B. L., & Kravitz, D. A. (1996). How effective is the presence-of-counsel safeguard? Attorney perceptions of suggestiveness, fairness, and correctability of biased lineup procedures. *Journal of Applied Psychology, 81*, 64–75.

Stinson, V., Devenport, J. L., Cutler, B. L., & Kravitz, D. A. (1997). How effective is the motion-to-suppress safeguard? Judges' perceptions of the suggestiveness and fairness of biased lineup procedures. *Journal of Applied Psychology, 82*, 211–220.

Stovall v. Denno, 388 U.S. 293 (1967).

Strömwall, L. A., & Granhag, P. A. (2003). How to detect deception? Arresting the beliefs of police officers, prosecutors and judges. *Psychology, Crime & Law, 9*, 19–36. doi:10.1080/10683160308138

Strömwall, L. A., Granhag, P. A., & Hartwig, M. (2004). Practitioners' beliefs about deception. In P. Granhag, L. Strömwall, P. Granhag, & L. Strömwall (Eds.), *The detection of deception in forensic contexts* (pp. 229–250). New York, NY: Cambridge University Press. doi:10.1017/CBO9780511490071.010

Suchotzki, K., Verschuere, B., Van Bockstaele, B., Ben-Shakhar, G., & Crombez, G. (2017). Lying takes time: A meta-analysis on reaction time measures of deception. *Psychological Bulletin, 143*, 428–453.

Sucic, I., Tokic, D., & Ivesic, M. (2015). Field study of response accuracy and decision confidence with regard to lineup composition and lineup presentation. *Psychology, Crime & Law, 21*, 798–819. doi:10.1080/1068316X.2015.1054383

Supreme Judicial Court Study Group on Eyewitness Evidence: Report and Recommendations to the Justices. (2013). Downloaded from http://www.mass.gov/courts/docs/sjc/docs/eyewitness-1390evidence-report-2013.pdf (9/8/17).

Swanner, J. K., Beike, D. R., & Cole, A. T. (2010). Snitching, lies and computer crashes: An experimental investigation of secondary confessions. *Law and Human Behavior, 34*, 53–65. doi:10.1007/s10979-008-9173-5

Tapp, J. L. (1976). Psychology and the law: An overture. *Annual Review of Psychology, 27*, 359–404.

Taylor v. Louisiana, 419 U.S. 522 (1975).

Technical Working Group for Eyewitness Evidence. (1999). *Eyewitness evidence: A guide for law enforcement*. Washington, DC: United States Department of Justice, Office of Justice Programs.

Tenney, E. R., MacCoun, R. J., Spellman, B. A., & Hastie, R. (2007). Calibration trumps confidence as a basis for witness credibility. *Psychological Science, 18*, 46–50. doi:10.1111/j.1467-9280.2007.01847.x

Terman, L. M. (1921). The status of applied psychology in the United States. *Journal of Applied Psychology, 5*, 1–4.

Thomas, A. K., & Loftus, E. F. (2002). Creating bizarre false memories through imagination. *Memory & Cognition, 30*, 423–431.

Thorne, B. M., & Henley, T. B. (2005). *Connections in the history and systems of psychology* (3rd ed.). Boston, MA: Houghton Mifflin.

Tiedens, L. Z., & Linton, S. (2001). Judgment under emotional certainty and uncertainty: The effects of specific emotions on information processing. *Journal of Personality and Social Psychology, 81*, 973–988.

Toglia, M. P., Read, J. D., Ross., D. F., & Lindsay, R. C. L. (2007). *The handbook of eyewitness psychology, Vol. 1: Memory for events.* Mahwah, NJ: Lawrence Erlbaum.

Tollestrup, P. A., Turtle, J. W., & Yuille, J. C. (1994). Actual victims and witnesses to robbery and fraud: An archival analysis. In D. F. Ross, J. D. Read, & M. P. Toglia (Eds.), *Adult eyewitness testimony* (pp. 144–160). Cambridge, England: Cambridge University Press.

Tomes, J. L., & Katz, A. N. (1997). Habitual susceptibility to misinformation and individual differences in eyewitness memory. *Applied Cognitive Psychology, 11*, 233–251.

Toro, R., Leonard, G., Lerner, J. V., Lerner, R. M., Perron, M., Pike, G. B., . . . Paus, T. (2008). Prenatal exposure to maternal cigarette smoking and the adolescent cerebral cortex. *Neuropsychopharmacology, 33*, 1019–1027. doi:10.1038/sj.npp.1301484

Tow, P. M., & Whitty, C. M. (1953). Personality changes after operations on the cingulate gyrus in man. *Journal of Neurology, Neurosurgery & Psychiatry, 16*, 186–193.

Tracy, P. E. (2003). *Who killed Stephanie Crowe? The anatomy of a murder investigation.* True Crime Publications.

Tranel, D., Bechara, A., & Denburg, N. L. (2002). Asymmetric functional roles of right and left ventromedial prefrontal cortices in social conduct, decision-making, and emotional processing. *Cortex, 38*, 589–612. doi:10.1016/S0010-9452(08)700248

Tranel, D., Gullickson, G., Koch, M., & Adolphs, R. (2006). Altered experience of emotion following bilateral amygdala damage. *Cognitive Neuropsychiatry, 11*, 219–232. doi:10.1080/13546800444000281

Trovillo, P. V. (1939). History of lie detection. *Journal of Criminal Law and Criminology, 30*, 104–119.

True, R. M. (1949). Experimental control in hypnotic age regression states. *Science, 110*, 583–584. doi:10.1126/science.110.2866.583

Tryon, R. C. (1940). Studies in individual differences in maze ability, VII: The specific components of maze ability, and a general theory of psychological components. *Journal of Comparative Psychology, 30*, 283–335. doi:10.1037/h0054238

Tyler, T. R. (2006). *Why people obey the law.* Princeton, NJ: Princeton University Press.

United States v. Prince-Oyibo, 320 F. 3d 494 (4th. Cir. 2003).

United States v. Semrau, 693 F.3d 510 (6th Cir. 2012).

United States v. Skeens, 494 F. 2d 1050 (D.C. Cir. 1974).

United States v. Wade, 388 U.S. 218 (1967).

Valentine, T., & Mesout, J. (2009). Eyewitness identification under stress in the London Dungeon. *Applied Cognitive Psychology, 23*, 151–161. doi:10.1002/acp.1463

Valentine, T., Pickering, A., & Darling, S. (2003). Characteristics of eyewitness identification that predict the outcome of real lineups. *Applied Cognitive Psychology, 17,* 969–993.

van Koppen, P. J., & Lochun, S. K. (1997). Portraying perpetrators: The validity of offender descriptions by perpetrators. *Law and Human Behavior, 21,* 661–685.

van Oorsouw, K., Merckelbach, H., & Smeets, T. (2015). Alcohol intoxication impairs memory and increases suggestibility for a mock crime. *Applied Cognitive Psychology, 29,* 493–501. doi:10.1002/acp.3129

van Wallendael, L. R., Cutler, B. L., Devenport, J., & Penrod, S. (2007). Mistaken identification = erroneous conviction? Assessing and improving legal safeguards. In R. C. L. Lindsay, D. F. Ross, J. D. Read, & M. P. Toglia (Eds.), *The handbook of eyewitness psychology, Vol. 2: Memory for people* Mahwah, NJ: Erlbaum.

van Wallendael, L. R., Surace, A., Hall Parsons, D., & Brown, M. (1994). "Earwitness" voice recognition: Factors affecting accuracy and impact on jurors. *Applied Cognitive Psychology, 8,* 661–677.

Van Zandt, T. (2000). ROC curves and confidence judgments in recognition memory. *Journal of Experimental Psychology: Learning, Memory, and Cognition, 26,* 582–600.

Veit, R., Lotze, M., Sewing, S., Missenhardt, H., Gaber, T., & Birbaumer, N. (2010). Aberrant social and cerebral responding in a competitive reaction time paradigm in criminal psychopaths. *Neuroimage, 49,* 3365–3372. doi:10.1016/j.neuroimage.2009.11.040White,

Verschuere, B., Prati, V., & de Houwer, J. (2009). Cheating the lie detector: Faking in the autobiographical Implicit Association Test. *Psychological Science, 20,* 410–413.

Verschuere, B., Suchotzki, K., & Debey, E. (2015). Detecting deception through reaction times. In P. Granhag, A. Vrij, & B. Verschuere (Eds.), *Detecting deception: Current challenges and cognitive approaches* (pp. 269–291). West-Sussex, England: Wiley-Blackwell.

Vidmar, N., & Hans, V. P. (2007). *American juries: The verdict.* Amherst, NY: Prometheus Books.

Virkkunen, M., de Jong, J., Bartko, J. J., Goodwin, F. K., & Linnoila, M. (1989). Relationship of psychobiological variables to recidivism in violent offenders and impulsive fire setters: A follow-up study. *Archives of General Psychiatry, 46,* 600–603. doi:10.1001/archpsyc.1989.01810070026003

Visu-Petra, G., Buş, I., & Miclea, M. (2011). Detecting concealed information from a mock crime scenario by using psychophysiological and Rt-based measures. *Cognitie, Creier, Comportament/Cognition, Brain, Behavior, 15,* 19–37.

Visu-Petra, G., Miclea, M., & Visu-Petra, L. (2012). Reaction time-based detection of concealed information in relation to individual differences in executive functioning. *Applied Cognitive Psychology, 26,* 342–351. doi:10.1002/Acp.1827

Vredeveldt, A., Charman, S. D., Blanken, A., & Hooydonk, M. (in press). Effects of cannabis on eyewitness memory: A field study. *Applied Cognitive Psychology.* doi:10.1002/acp.3414

Vredeveldt, A., & van Koppen, P. J. (2016). The thin blue line-up: Comparing eyewitness performance by police and civilians. *Journal of Applied Research in Memory and Cognition, 5*, 252–256. doi:10.1016/j.jarmac.2016.06.013

Vrij, A. (1994). The impact of information and setting on detection of deception by police detectives. *Journal of Nonverbal Behavior, 18*, 117–137.

Vrij, A. (2000). *Detecting lies and deceit: The psychology of lying and implications for professional Practice*. Chichester: John Wiley & Sons.

Vrij, A. (2004). Why professionals fail to catch liars and how they can improve. *Legal and Criminological Psychology, 9*, 151–181.

Vrij, A. (2005). Criteria-based content analysis: A qualitative review of the first 37 studies. *Psychology, Public Policy, and Law, 11*, 3–41.

Vrij, A. (2008). *Detecting lies and deceit: Pitfalls and opportunities* (2nd ed.). Chichester, England: Wiley.

Vrij, A. (2015). A cognitive approach to lie detection. In P. A. Granhag, A. Vrij, & B. Verschuere (Eds.), *Deception detection: Current challenges and new approaches* (pp. 205–229). Chichester, UK: Wiley.

Vrij, A., & Fisher, R. P. (2016). Which lie detection tools are ready for use in the criminal justice system? *Journal of Applied Research in Memory and Cognition, 5*, 302 307. doi:10.1016/j.jarmac.2016.06.014

Vrij, A., Fisher, R. P., & Blank, H. (2017). A cognitive approach to lie detection: A meta-analysis. *Legal and Criminological Psychology, 22*, 1–21. doi:10.111/lcrp.12088

Vrij, A., Fisher, R., Mann, S., & Leal, S. (2006). Detecting deception by manipulating cognitive load. *Trends in Cognitive Sciences, 10*, 141–142. doi:10.1016/j.tics.2006.02.003

Vrij, A., & Graham, S. (1997). Individual differences between liars and the ability to detect lies. *Expert Evidence, 5*, 144–148.

Vrij, A., Granhag, P. A., & Porter, S. (2010). Pitfalls and opportunities in nonverbal and verbal lie detection. *Psychological Science in the Public Interest, 11*, 89–121. doi:10.1177/1529100610390861

Vrij, A., Hope, L., & Fisher, R. P. (2014). Eliciting reliable information in investigative interviews. *Policy Insights from Behavioral and Brain Sciences, 1*, 129–136. doi:10.1177/2372732214548592

Vrij, A., Leal, S., Granhag, P. A., Mann, S., Fisher, R. P., Hillman, J., & Sperry, K. (2009). Outsmarting the liars: The benefit of asking unanticipated questions. *Law and Human Behavior, 33*, 159–166. doi:10.1007/s10979-008-9143-y

Vrij, A., Mann, S., & Fisher, R. P. (2006a). An empirical test of the Behaviour Analysis Interview. *Law and Human* Behavior, *30*, 329–345. doi:10.1007/s10979-006-9014-3

Vrij, A., Mann, S., & Fisher, R. P. (2006b). Information-gathering vs accusatory interview style: Individual differences in respondents' experiences. *Personality and Individual Differences, 41*, 589–599. doi:10.1016/j.paid.2006.02.014

Vrij, A., Mann, S. A., Fisher, R. P., Leal, S., Milne, R., & Bull, R. (2008). Increasing cognitive load to facilitate lie detection: The benefit of recalling an event in reverse order. *Law and Human Behavior, 32*, 253–265. doi:10.1007/s10979-007-9103-y

Vrij, A., Mann, S., Leal, S., & Fisher, R. (2010). "Look into my eyes": Can an instruction to maintain eye contact facilitate lie detection? *Psychology, Crime & Law, 16*, 327–348. doi:10.1080/10683160902740633

Vrij, A., Mann, S., Leal, S., Vernham, A., & Vaughan, M. (2016). Train the trainers: A first step towards a science-based cognitive lie detection training workshop delivered by a practitioner. *Journal of Investigative Psychology and Profiling, 13*, 110–130. doi:10.1002/jip.1443

Vrij, A., & Semin, G. R. (1996). Lie experts' beliefs about nonverbal indicators of deception. *Journal of Nonverbal Behavior, 20*, 65–80. doi:10.1007/BF02248715

Wade, K. A., Garry, M., Read, J. D., & Lindsay, D. S. (2002). A picture is worth a thousand lies: Using false photographs to create false childhood memories. *Psychonomic Bulletin & Review, 9*, 597–603.

Wagstaff, G. F. (2009). Is there a future for investigative hypnosis? *Journal of Investigative Psychology and Offender Profiling, 6*, 43–57.

Wagstaff, G. F., Brunas-Wagstaff, J., Cole, J., Knapton, L., Winterbottom, J., Crean, V., & Wheatcroft, J. (2004). Facilitating memory with hypnosis, focused meditation, and eye closure. *International Journal of Clinical and Experimental Hypnosis, 52*, 434–455.

Wagstaff, G. F., Cole, J., Wheatcroft, J., Anderton, A., & Madden, H. (2008). Reducing and reversing pseudomemories with hypnosis. *Contemporary Hypnosis, 25*, 178–191.

Wagstaff, G. F., Green, K., & Somers, E. (1997). The effects of the experience of hypnosis, and hypnotic depth, on jurors' decisions regarding the defense of hypnotic automatism. *Legal and Criminological Psychology, 2*, 65–74. doi:10.1111/j.2044-8333.1997.tb00333.x

Wagstaff, G. F., Vella, M., & Perfect, T. (1992). The effect of hypnotically elicited testimony on jurors' judgments of guilt and innocence. *The Journal of Social Psychology, 132*, 591–595. doi:10.1080/00224545.1992.9713898

Wagstaff, G. F., Wheatcroft, J. M., & Jones, A. C. (2011). Are high hypnotizables especially vulnerable to false memory effects? A sociocognitive perspective. *International Journal of Clinical and Experimental Hypnosis, 59*, 310–326.

Wald, M., Ayres, R., Hess, D. W., Schantz, M., & Whitebread, C. H. (1967). Interrogations in New Haven: The impact of Miranda. *Yale Law Journal, 76*, 1519–1648.

Waldstein, S. R., Polefrone, J. M., Bachen, E. A., Muldoon, M. F., Kaplan, J. R., & Manuck, S. B. (1993). Relationship of cardiovascular reactivity and anger expression to serum lipid concentrations in healthy young men. *Journal of Psychosomatic Research, 37*, 249–256. doi:10.1016/0022-3999(93)90033-C

Walsh, W. J., Isaacson, H. R., Rehman, F., & Hall, A. (1997). Elevated blood copper/zinc ratios in assaultive young males. *Physiology & Behavior, 62*, 327–329. doi:10.1016/S0031-9384(97)88988-3.

Warden, R. (2004). The snitch system: How incentivized witnesses put 38 innocent Americans on death row. *Northwestern University School of Law, Center on Wrongful Convictions*. Retrieved from http://www.law.northwestern.edu/legalclinic/wrongfulconvictions/documents/SnitchSystemBooklet.pdf ("Snitch System").

Weber, N., Brewer, N., Wells, G. L., Semmler, C., & Keast, A. (2004). Eyewitness identification accuracy and response latency: The unruly 10–12 second rule. *Journal of Experimental Psychology: Applied, 10*, 139–147.

Webert, D. (2003). Are the courts in a trance? Approaches to the admissibility of hypnotically enhanced witness testimony in light of empirical evidence. *American Criminal Law Review, 40*, 1301–1655.

Weiss, K. J., Watson, C., & Xuan, Y. (2014). *Frye*'s backstory: A tale of murder, a retracted confession, and scientific hubris. *Journal of the American Academy of Psychiatry & Law, 42*, 226–233.

Weiss, K. J., & Xuan, Y. (2015). You can't do that! Hugo Münsterberg and misapplied psychology. *International Journal of Law and Psychiatry, 42–43*, 1–10. doi:10.1016/j.ijlp.2015.08.001

Weld, H. P., & Danzig, E. R. (1940). A study of the way in which a verdict is reached by a jury. *American Journal of Psychology, 53*, 518–536.

Weld, H. P., & Roff, M. F. (1938). A study in the formation of opinion based upon legal evidence. *American Journal of Psychology, 51*, 609–628.

Wells, G. L. (1978). Applied eyewitness-testimony research: System variables and estimator variables. *Journal of Personality and Social Psychology, 36*, 1546–1557.

Wells, G. L. (2008). Field experiments on eyewitness identification: Towards a better understanding of pitfalls and prospects. *Law and Human Behavior, 32*, 6–10. doi:10.1007/s10979-007-9098-4

Wells, G. L., & Bradfield, A. L. (1998). "Good, you identified the suspect": Feedback to eyewitnesses distorts their reports of the witnessing experience. *Journal of Applied Psychology, 83*, 360–376.

Wells, G. L., & Lindsay, R. C. L. (1983). How do people infer the accuracy of eyewitness memory? Studies of performance and a metamemory analysis. In S. M. A. Lloyd-Bostock & B. R. Clifford (Eds.), *Evaluating witness evidence* (pp. 41–55). Chichester, UK: John Wiley & Sons.

Wells, G. L., & Murray, D. (1984). Eyewitness confidence. In G. L. Wells & E. F. Loftus (Eds.), *Eyewitness testimony: Psychological perspectives* (pp. 155–170). New York, NY: Cambridge University Press.

Wells, G. L., & Quinlivan, D. S. (2009). Suggestive eyewitness identification procedures and the Supreme Court's reliability test in light of eyewitness science: 30 years later. *Law and Human Behavior, 33*, 1–24. doi:10.1007/s10979-008-9130-3

Wells, G. L., Memon, A., & Penrod, S. D. (2006). Eyewitness evidence: Improving its probative value. *Psychological Science in the Public Interest, 7*, 45–75. doi:10.1111/j.1529-1006.2006.00027.x

Wells, G. L., & Smalarz, L., & Smith, A. M. (2015). ROC analysis of lineups does not measure underlying discriminability and has limited value. *Journal of Applied Research in Memory and Cognition, 4*, 313–317.

Wells, G. L., Small, M., Penrod, S. D., Malpass, R. S., Fulero, S. M., & Brimacombe, C. A. E. (1998). Eyewitness identification procedures: Recommendations for lineups and photospreads. *Law and Human Behavior, 22*, 603–647.

Wells, G. L., Steblay, N. K., & Dysart, J. E. (2015). Double-blind photo lineups using actual eyewitnesses: An experimental test of a sequential versus

simultaneous lineup procedure. *Law and Human Behavior, 39*, 1–14. doi:10.1037/lhb0000096
Wells, W. (2014). The Houston police department eyewitness identification experiment: Analysis and results. Retrieved from http://www.lemitonline.org/research/projects.html
Wetmore, S. A., Neuschatz, J. S., & Gronlund, S. D. (2014). On the power of secondary confession evidence. *Psychology, Crime & Law, 20*, 339–357. doi:10.1080/1068316X.2013.777963
Wexler, D. B., & Winick, B. J. (1996). *Law in a therapeutic key: Developments in therapeutic jurisprudence.* Durham, NC: Carolina Academic Press.
Whipple, G. M. (1909). The observer as reporter: A survey of the "psychology of testimony." *Psychological Bulletin, 6*, 153–170.
Whipple, G. M. (1910a). *Manual of mental and physical tests.* Baltimore, MD: Warwick & York.
Whipple, G. M. (1910b). Recent literature on the psychology of testimony. *Psychological Bulletin, 7*, 365–368.
Whipple, G. M. (1912). Psychology of testimony and report. *Psychological Bulletin, 9*, 264–269.
Whipple, G. M. (1913). Psychology of testimony and report. *Psychological Bulletin, 10*, 264–268.
Whipple, G. M. (1914a). Psychology of testimony and report. *Psychological Bulletin, 11*, 245–250.
Whipple, G. M. (1914b). Review of the principles of judicial proof, as given by logic, psychology and general experience, and illustrated in judicial trials. *Journal of Criminal Law and Criminology, 5*, 316–317.
Whipple, G. M. (1915). Psychology of testimony. *Psychological Bulletin, 12*, 221–224.
Whipple, G. M. (1917). Psychology of testimony. *Psychological Bulletin, 14*, 234–236.
White, S. F., Marsh, A. A., Fowler, K. A., Schechter, J. C., Adalio, C., Pope, K., . . . Blair, R. R. (2012). Reduced amygdala response in youths with disruptive behavior disorders and psychopathic traits: Decreased emotional response versus increased top-down attention to nonemotional features. *The American Journal of Psychiatry, 169*, 750–758. doi:10.1176/appi.ajp.2012.11081270Yang
Whitehouse, W. G., Dinges, D. F., Orne, E. C., & Orne, M. T. (1988). Hypnotic hypermnesia: Enhanced memory accessibility or report bias? *Journal of Abnormal Psychology, 97*, 289–295. doi:10.1037/0021-843X.97.3.289
Wiener, R. L., & Bornstein, B. H. (2011). *Handbook of trial consulting.* New York, NY: Springer.
Wiener, R. L., & Brank, E. (2013). *Problem solving courts: Social science and legal perspectives.* New York, NY: Springer.
Wigmore, J. H. (1904). *A treatise on the Anglo-American system of evidence in trials at common law.* Boston, MA: Little, Brown.
Wigmore, J. H. (1909). Professor Muensterberg and the psychology of testimony. *Illinois Law Review, 3*, 399–445.
Wigmore, J. H. (1970). *Evidence* (Vol. 3) (revised by J. H. Chadbourn). Boston, MA: Little, Brown.

Williams, G. (1955). *The proof of guilt: A study of the English criminal trial.* London, England: Stevens and Sons.

Wilson, J. P., Bernstein, M. J., & Hugenberg, K. (2016). A synthetic perspective on the own-race bias in eyewitness identification. In B. H. Bornstein & M. K. Miller (Eds.), *Advances in psychology and law (Vol. 2)* (pp. 241–270). New York, NY: Springer.

Wilson, S. C., & Barber, T. X. (1978). The Creative Imagination Scale as a measure of hypnotic responsiveness: Applications to experimental and clinical hypnosis. *American Journal of Clinical Hypnosis, 20*, 235–249.

Winograd, E., Peluso, J. P., & Glover, T. A. (1998). Individual differences in susceptibility to memory illusions. *Applied Cognitive Psychology, 12*, S5–S27. doi:10.1002/(SICI)1099-0720(199812)12:73.0.CO;2-D

Wise, R. A., Pawlenko, N. B., Safer, M. A., & Meyer, D. (2009). What U.S. prosecutors and defense attorneys know and believe about eyewitness testimony. *Applied Cognitive Psychology, 23*, 1266–1281.

Wise, R. A., & Safer, M. A. (2004). What U.S. judges know and believe about eyewitness testimony. *Applied Cognitive Psychology, 18*, 427–443.

Wise, R. A., Safer, M. A., & Maro, C. M. (2011). What U.S. law enforcement officers know and believe about eyewitness factors, eyewitness interviews and identification procedures. *Applied Cognitive Psychology, 25*, 488–500. doi:10.1002/acp.1717

Wistrich, A. J., Guthrie, C., & Rachlinski, J. J. (2005). Can judges ignore inadmissible information? The difficulty of deliberately disregarding. *University of Pennsylvania Law Review, 153*, 1251–1345.

Witkin, H. A, Mednick, S. A, Schulsinger, F., Bakkestrom, E., Christiansen, K. O., Goodenough, D. R., . . . Stocking, M. (1976). Criminality in XYY and XXY men. *Science, 193*, 547–555. doi:10.1126/science.959813

Witmer, L. (1907). Clinical psychology. *The Psychological Clinic, 1*, 1–9.

Wixted, J. T., Mickes, L., Clark, S. E., Gronlund, S. D., & Roediger, H. L. (2015). Initial eyewitness confidence reliably predicts eyewitness identification accuracy. *American Psychologist, 70*, 515–526. doi:10.1037/a0039510

Wixted, J. T., Mickes, L., Dunn, J. C., Clark, S. E., & Wells, W. (2016). Estimating the reliability of eyewitness identifications from police lineups. *Proceedings of the National Academy of Sciences, 113*, 304–309. doi:10.1073/pnas.1516814112

Wixted, J. T., Mickes, L., & Fisher, R. P. (2018). Rethinking the reliability of eyewitness memory. *Perspectives on Psychological Science, 13*, 324–335. doi:10.1177/1745691617734878

Wixted, J. T., & Wells, G. L. (2017). The relationship between eyewitness confidence and identification accuracy: A new synthesis. *Psychological Science in the Public Interest, 18*, 10–65. doi:10.1177/1529100616686966

Woody, W. D., & Forrest, K. D. (2009). Effects of false-evidence ploys and expert testimony on jurors' verdicts, recommended sentences, and perceptions of confession evidence. *Behavioral Sciences & the Law, 27*, 333–360.

Woody, W. D., Forrest, K. D., & Yendra, S. (2013). Comparing the effects of explicit and implicit false-evidence ploys on Mock Jurors' verdicts, sentencing recommendations, and perceptions of police interrogation. *Psychology, Crime and Law, 20*, 603–617. doi:10.1080/1068316X.2013.804922

Wright, D. B., Boyd, C. E., & Tredoux, C. G. (2001). A field study of own-race bias in South Africa and England. *Psychology, Public Policy, and Law, 7*, 119–133.
Wright, D. B., & McDaid, A. T. (1996). Comparing system and estimator variables using data from real line-ups. *Applied Cognitive, 10*, 75–84.
Wright, D. B., & Sladden, B. (2003). An own gender bias and the importance of hair in face recognition. *Acta Psychologica, 114*, 101–114. doi:10.1016/S0001-6918(03)00052-0
Wright, L. (1994). *Remembering Satan: A case of recovered memory and the shattering of an American family*. New York, NY: Knopf.
Wrightsman, L. S. (2006). *The psychology of the Supreme Court*. Oxford, England: Oxford University Press.
Wundt, W. (1918). *Völkerpsychologie (Vol. 9): Das recht*. Leipzig, Germany: Alfred Kröner.
Wylie, L. E., Hazen, K. P., Hoetger, L. A., Haby, J. A., & Brank, E. M. (2018). Four decades of the journal *Law and Human Behavior*: A content analysis. *Scientometrics, 115*, 655–693. doi:10.1007/s11192-018-2685-y
Wylie, L., Patihis, L., McCuller, L., Davis, D., Brank, E. M., Loftus, E. F., & Bornstein, B. H. (2014). The misinformation effect in elderly witnesses. In M. P. Toglia, D. F. Ross, J. Pozzulo, & E. Pica (Eds.), *The elderly eyewitness in court* (pp. 38–66). New York, NY: Psychology Press.
Yaling, Y., & Raine, A. (2009). Prefrontal structural and functional brain imaging findings in antisocial, violent, and psychopathic individuals: A meta-analysis. *Psychiatry Research: Neuroimaging, 174*, 81–88.
Yang, Y., & Raine, A. (2009). Prefrontal structural and functional brain imaging findings in antisocial, violent, and psychopathic individuals: A meta-analysis. *Psychiatry Research: Neuroimaging, 174*, 81–88. doi:10.10016/j.psycychresns.2009.03.012
Yapko, M. D. (1994). Suggestibility and repressed memories of abuse: A survey of psychotherapists' beliefs. *American Journal of Clinical Hypnosis, 36*, 163–171.
Yarmey, A. D. (1993). Adult age and gender differences in eyewitness recall in field settings. *Journal of Applied Social Psychology, 23*, 1921–1932.
Yarmey, A. D. (1995). Earwitness speaker identification. *Psychology, Public Policy, & Law, 1*, 792–816.
Yarmey, A. D. (2004). Eyewitness recall and photo identification: A field experiment. *Psychology, Crime & Law, 10*, 53–68. doi:10.1080/1068316021000058379
Yarmey, A. D. (2007). The psychology of speaker identification and earwitness memory. In R. C. L. Lindsay, D. F. Ross, J. D. Read, & M. P. Toglia (Eds.), *Handbook of eyewitness psychology* (pp. 101–136). Mahwah, NJ: Erlbaum.
Yarmey, A. D., Yarmey, A. L., Yarmey, M. J., & Parliament, L. (2001). Commonsense beliefs and the identification of familiar voices. *Applied Cognitive Psychology, 15*, 283–299.
Yates, S. Q. (2017, Jan. 6). *Memorandum for heads of department law enforcement components: All department prosecutors*. Washington, D.C.: U.S. Department of Justice. Retrieved from https://www.justice.gov/opa/pr/justice-department-announces-department-wide-procedures-eyewitness-identification

Young, P. C. (1952). Antisocial uses of hypnosis. In L. Cron (Ed). *Experimental hypnosis* (pp. 376–409). New York, NY: Macmillan.

Yuille, J. C., & Cutshall, J. L. (1986). A case study of eyewitness memory of a crime. *Journal of Applied Psychology, 71*, 291–301.

Yuille, J. C., & Tollestrup, P. A. (1990). Some effects of alcohol on eyewitness memory. *Journal of Applied Psychology, 75*, 268–273.

Zani v. State, 758 S.W.2d 233 (Tex. Crim. App. 1988).

Zanni, G. R., & Offermann, J. T. (1978). Eyewitness testimony: An exploration of question wording upon recall as a function of neuroticism. *Perceptual and Motor Skills, 46*, 163–166.

Zapf, P., Green, D., & Rosenfeld, B. (2011). Competency to stand trial and criminal responsibility research. In B. Rosenfeld & S. D. Penrod (Eds.), *Research methods in forensic psychology* (pp. 156–173). Hoboken, NJ: Wiley.

Zaragoza, M. S., & Lane, S. M. (1998). Processing resources and eyewitness suggestibility. *Legal and Criminological Psychology, 3*, 305–320.

Zhu, B., Chen, C., Loftus, E. F., Lin, C., He, Q., Chen, C., Li, H., Xue, G., Lu, Z., & Dong, Q. (2010). Individual differences in false memory from misinformation: Cognitive factors. *Memory, 18*, 543–555. doi:10.1080/09658211.2010.487051

Zimbardo, P. G. (1967). The psychology of police confessions. *Psychology Today*, 1, 17–27.

Zimbardo, P. G. (2007). *The Lucifer effect: Understanding how good people turn evil*. New York, NY: Random House.

Zuckerman, M., DePaulo, B. M., & Rosenthal, R. (1981). Verbal and nonverbal communication of deception. In L. Berkowitz (Ed.), *Advances in experimental social psychology* (Vol. 14, pp. 1–57). New York, NY: Academic Press.

Index

Tables and figures are indicated by *t* and *f* following the page number

For the benefit of digital users, indexed terms that span two pages (e.g., 52–53) may, on occasion, appear on only one of those pages.

The UK Regulatory Framework Post-Brexit: 'Law Unbound'

Edited by

Paul Craig
Vilija Vėlyvytė

OXFORD
UNIVERSITY PRESS

OXFORD
UNIVERSITY PRESS

Great Clarendon Street, Oxford, OX2 6DP,
United Kingdom

Oxford University Press is a department of the University of Oxford.
It furthers the University's objective of excellence in research, scholarship,
and education by publishing worldwide. Oxford is a registered trade mark of
Oxford University Press in the UK and in certain other countries.

Revised Edition published in 2026

Published in the United States of America by Oxford University Press
546 Fifth Avenue, New York, NY 10036, United States of America.

British Library Cataloguing in Publication Data
Data available

Library of Congress Control Number: 2026937104

ISBN 9780198969808

DOI: 10.1093/9780198969815.001.0001

Printed and bound by
CPI Group (UK) Ltd., Croydon, CR0 4YY

MIX
Paper | Supporting
responsible forestry
FSC® C013604
FSC
www.fsc.org

The manufacturer's authorized representative in the EU for product safety is
Oxford University Press España S.A. of Parque Empresarial San Fernando de Henares,
Avenida de Castilla, 2 – 28830 Madrid (www.oup.es/en or product.safety@oup.com).
OUP España S.A. also acts as importer into Spain of products made by the manufacturer.

Contents

Abbreviations

ACRS	Afghan Citizens Resettlement Scheme
AI	artificial intelligence
AIMFD	Alternative Investment Fund Managers Directive
ARAP	Afghan Relocation and Assistance Policy
ASCM	Agreement on Subsidies and Countervailing Measures
BN(O)	British National Overseas
BTOM	Border Target Operating Model
CAA	Civil Aviation Authority
CAT	Competition Appeal Tribunal
CCPs	central clearing counterparties
CCRAR	Consolidated Credit Rating Agency Regulation
CDPA	Copyright, Designs and Patents Act
CEAS	Common European Asylum System
CETA	EU–Canada Comprehensive Economic and Trade Agreement
CFR	Charter of Fundamental Rights of the EU
CJEU	Court of Justice of the EU
CMO	commercial market operator
CMU	Capital Markets Union
CPTPP	Comprehensive and Progressive Agreement for Trans-Pacific Partnership
CRA	credit rating agencies
CSD	Central Securities Depositaries Regulation
CTA	Common Travel Area
DBT	Department for Business and Trade
DCTS	Developing Countries Trading Scheme
DHSC	Department for Health and Social Care
DSA	Digital Services Act
DUAA	Data (Use and Access) Act
DUP	Democratic Unionist Party
EAW	European arrest warrant
ECA	European Communities Act
ECHR	European Convention on Human Rights
ECJ	European Court of Justice
ECtHR	European Court of Human Rights
EEC	European Economic Community
EFSA	European Food Safety Authority
EHIC	European Health Insurance Card

ELTIF Regulation	European Long-term Investment Fund Regulation
EMIR	European Market Infrastructure Regulation
EPPS	Environmental Principles Policy Statement
ERG	European Research Group
ESAs	European Supervisory Authorities
ETA	electronic travel authorization
ETIAS	entry–exit system and travel authorization system legislation
EUIPO	EU Intellectual Property Office
EUTMs	EU trade marks
EuVECA and EuSEF Regulations	European Venture Capital and European Social Entrepreneurship Fund Regulations
EUWA	European Union (Withdrawal) Act
EUWAA	European Union (Withdrawal Agreement) Act
EV	electric vehicles
EVEL	'English votes for English laws'
FRFR	Financial Services Future Regulatory Framework Review
FSA	Food Standards Agency
FSMA	Financial Services and Markets Act
FTA	free trade agreement
GATS	General Agreement on Trade in Services
GB	Great Britain
GBER	General Block Exemption Regulations
GDP	gross domestic product
GHIC	Global Health Insurance Card
GPA	Agreement on Government Procurement
GSP	General System of Preferences
HRA	Human Rights Act
HSE	Health and Safety Executive
IAS Regulation	International Accounting Standards Regulation
ILO	International Labour Organization
IMA	Illegal Migration Act
IMF	International Monetary Fund
LPF	level playing field
MEDP	Migration and Economic Development Partnership
MEO	market economy operator
MFA	Minimal financial assistance
MFN	most favoured nation
MHRA	Medicines and Healthcare Products Regulatory Agency
MMF Regulation	Money Market Fund Regulation
MRLs	maximum residue levels
NCA	National Crime Agency
NDPBs	non-departmental public bodies
NI	Northern Ireland
NPPS	National Procurement Policy Statement
ODR	online dispute resolution

OEP	Office for Environmental Protection
OIM	Office for the Internal Market
OLAF	European Anti-Fraud Office
OPSS	Office for Product Safety and Standards
OSA	Online Safety Act
PEM	Pan-European-Mediterranean zone
PPNs	Procurement Policy Notes
PRIIPs	Packaged Retail and Insurance-based Investment Products Regulation
REULA	Retained EU Law (Revocation and Reform) Act
ROOs	rules of origin
RRA	Race Relations Act
SAU	Subsidy Advice Unit
SCA	Subsidy Control Act
SCO	safe country of origin
SDA	Sex Discrimination Act
SGEI	services of general economic interest
SIS	Schengen Information System
SPCs	supplementary protection certificates
SPEI	services of public economic interest
SPUC	Society for the Protection of the Unborn Child
SSC	social security coordination
SSoPI	Subsidies or Schemes of Particular Interest
STC	safe third country
TCA	Trade and Cooperation Agreement
TFEU	Treaty on the Functioning of the European Union
TPD	Temporary Protection Directive
UCITS	Undertakings for Collective Investment in Transferable Securities Directive
UKIMA	Internal Market Act
UKSC	Supreme Court of the United Kingdom
UNCHR	United Nations High Commissioner for Refugees
UNCRPD	United Nations Convention on the Rights of Persons with Disabilities
WA	Withdrawal Agreement
WTO	World Trade Organization
WTR	Working Time Regulations 1998

Contributors

Chloë Anthony is Assistant Professor in Law, School of Law, Politics and Sociology, University of Sussex, United Kingdom. https://orcid.org/0000-0002-6341-8944

Kenneth A. Armstrong is Emeritus Fellow, Sidney Sussex College, University of Cambridge, Cambridge, United Kingdom. https://orcid.org/0000-0001-6997-8566

Sue Arrowsmith KC (hon), BA, DJur is Professor Emerita, School of Law, University of Nottingham, United Kingdom

Catherine Barnard is Professor of European Law, School of Law, University of Cambridge; Fellow, Trinity College Cambridge

Gavin Barrett, LLB, PhD, DALF, Barrister at Law is Professor of EU Constitutional and Economic Law, Sutherland School of Law, University College Dublin, Ireland. https://orcid.org/0000-0002-6961-1454

Andrea Biondi, PhD is Advocate General, European Court of Justice, Luxembourg, Luxembourg

Catherine Briddick is Andrew W. Mellon Associate Professor of International Human Rights and Refugee Law, Refugee Studies Centre, University of Oxford, Oxford, United Kingdom. https://orcid.org/0000-0001-7754-4784

Luke R.A. Butler is Professor of Public Procurement Law and Regulation, University of Nottingham, United Kingdom

Fiona Costello is Assistant Professor, University of Birmingham, Birmingham, United Kingdom. https://orcid.org/0000-0002-5648-7837

Cathryn Costello is Full Professor of Global Refugee and Migration Law, University College Dublin, Dublin, Ireland, Faculty of Law, University of Oxford, United Kingdom. https://orcid.org/0000-0002-6915-9939

Paul Craig, FBA, KC (hon) is Emeritus Professor of English Law, St John's College, Oxford, United Kingdom

A.C.L. Davies, FBA is Professor of Law and Public Policy, Faculty of Law, University of Oxford, United Kingdom

James Devenney is Professor of Transnational Commercial Law, University of Reading, United Kingdom; University College Dublin, Ireland; Dalian Maritime University, China

Sionaidh Douglas-Scott, BA (Hons) MA LLM LLD (hon) is Anniversary Chair in Law, Law Department, Queen Mary University, London, United Kingdom

Elizabeth Fisher is Professor of Environmental Law, Faculty of Law and Corpus Christi College, University of Oxford, United Kingdom

Filippo Fontanelli is Professor of International Law and Practice, University of Edinburgh, United Kingdom

Sandra Fredman, FBA, KC (hon) is Professor of the Laws of the British Commonwealth and the USA, Faculty of Law, University of Oxford, Oxford, United Kingdom, Oxford University, United Kingdom. https://orcid.org/0000-0002-4132-1164

Geraint Howells, LLB, LLD is Established Professor, Law, University of Galway, Galway, Ireland, University of Manchester, Manchester, United Kingdom. https://orcid.org/0000-0002-4946-7301

Jeff King, BA Hons, LLB/BCL, MSt, DPhil is Professor of Law, Faculty of Laws, University College London, London, United Kingdom. https://orcid.org/0009-0001-2963-5590

Totis Kotsonis, PhD is Head of Subsidies, Procurement and Trade, Pinsent Masons LLP, London, United Kingdom

Emily Lydgate is Professor of Environmental Law, University of Sussex, United Kingdom, Centre for Inclusive Trade Policy, United Kingdom. https://orcid.org/0000-0002-3799-0015

Orla Lynskey is Professor of Law and Technology, University College London, United Kingdom

Christopher McCrudden, FBA MRIA is Emeritus Professor of Human Rights and Equality Law, Queen's University Belfast, United Kingdom, and L Bates Lea Global Professor of Law, University of Michigan, Law School, USA

Valsamis Mitsilegas is Professor of European and Global Law and Dean, School of Law and Social Justice, University of Liverpool, Liverpool, United Kingdom. https://orcid.org/0000-0001-6424-7289

Niamh Moloney is Professor of Financial Markets Law, Law School, London School of Economics and Political Science, United Kingdom

Katherine Nolan is Assistant Lecturer, School of Social Science, Law, and Education, Technological University Dublin, Ireland. https://orcid.org/0000-0002-5412-7408

Steve Peers, PhD is Professor of Law, Royal Holloway Law School, Royal Holloway, University of London, United Kingdom

Gavin Phillipson, BA, LLM (Cantab) SFHEA is Professor of Public Law and Human Rights, Law School, University of Bristol, Bristol, United Kingdom. https://orcid.org/0000-0002-9326-8983

Justine Pila is Professor of Law, University of Oxford, United Kingdom

Barry Rodger, LLB (Hons), Dip LP, BCL (Oxon), LLM is Professor, The Law School, University of Strathclyde, Glasgow, United Kingdom. https://orcid.org/0000-0002-8588-433X

Andreas Stephan, PhD, MA, LLM, LLB is Professor of Competition Law, School of Law, University of East Anglia, Norwich, United Kingdom. https://orcid.org/0000-0002-9839-7338

Vilija Vėlyvytė is Lecturer, EU Law, Dickson Poon School of Law, King's College London, United Kingdom. https:// orcid.org/0009-0008-8085-1695

Chris Willett, LLB, PhD, Certificate in Curriculum Development (Higher Education) is Professor of Commercial Law, University of Essex, Colchester, United Kingdom

Alison L. Young is Professor, University of Cambridge, United Kingdom, Law Commission of England and Wales, United Kingdom

1
Post-Brexit Regulation: 'Law Unbound'

Paul Craig and Vilija Vėlyvytė

1 Introduction

The objective of this book is readily apparent from its title. It is to provide a comprehensive analysis of the UK's post-Brexit regulatory framework, and to do so against the conceptual frame of the 'Law Unbound', thereby reflecting the animating impulse of the Brexit campaign to take back sovereign control over the regulatory domain. In contemporary legal scholarship, 'unbound' generally signals liberation from constraint—conceptual, institutional, or territorial.[1] In this book we use 'law unbound' in three distinct senses.

First, the literal juridical sense: UK law is no longer bound by EU membership and, to an extent circumscribed by the Withdrawal Agreement and the Trade and Cooperation Agreement (TCA), by EU law. Second, the sovereignty claim: being unbound in terms of regulatory autonomy, epitomized by the Leave campaign's call to 'take back control'. Third, the aspirational register found in contemporary legal scholarship: being unbound as a promise of wider possibilities. The chapters analyse the first sense, and subject the latter two to critical scrutiny: how far regulatory autonomy truly extends once legal, economic, and geopolitical interdependencies are considered; and whether the freedoms created by legal unbinding have in fact delivered the advantages implied in that promise.

The inquiry is timely. A decade on from the referendum and five years after the end of the transition period, sufficient practice has accumulated—in institutions and across many areas of economic and social policy—to permit assessment on the basis of what has been done rather than what was forecast or claimed. The intervening period has generated legislation, case law, administrative practice, and international negotiations that together render the contours of the new settlement more legible. It is now possible to test what 'unbound' has meant in practice: where regulatory discretion has been used, where it has been deliberately curtailed by domestic choices, and

[1] See, eg, R Delgado, AK Wing, and J Stefancic, *The Law Unbound! A Richard Delgado Reader* (Paradigm Publishers 2007); L Raible, *Human Rights Unbound: A Theory of Extraterritoriality* (OUP 2020); *AJIL Unbound* (American Journal of International Law) <www.cambridge.org/core/journals/american-journal-of-international-law/ajil-unbound>; *Chicago Unbound* (University of Chicago Law School) <https://chicagounbound.uchicago.edu>; *European Law Unbound Society* <https://europeanlawunbound.eu>

Paul Craig and Vilija Vėlyvytė, *Post-Brexit Regulation: 'Law Unbound'* In: *The UK Regulatory Framework Post-Brexit: 'Law Unbound'*. Edited by: Paul Craig and Vilija Vėlyvytė, Oxford University Press. © Oxford University Press 2026.
DOI: 10.1093/9780198969815.003.0001

where new bilateral commitments with the EU have written constraints back in. The same period has also begun to reveal, empirically, emerging consequences—some benefits as well as costs—of the post-Brexit settlement.

The book is divided into three Parts—Institutional, Economic, and Social—with due consideration for the linkages between the respective Parts. Part I considers the institutional dimension of Brexit. The chapters examine the impact of Brexit on the constitution, Parliament, government, regulators, courts, devolved governments, and Northern Ireland. The objective, broadly conceived, is to provide a picture of the UK institutional framework as it has developed after Brexit. While there are distinct chapters on the topics set out above, the respective authors consider the interplay between the UK's governing branches—the Parliament, government, courts, regulators, and devolved governments—in the development of post-Brexit law and policy, and how this process has affected the institutional position and power of those branches. This inquiry facilitates the drawing of broader conclusions concerning the implications of Brexit for the UK's constitution, including the distribution of powers among the UK's governing branches and between central and devolved governments. It also facilitates understanding of the ways in which the UK institutional structure has shaped post-Brexit legislation.

Part II turns to the impact of Brexit in discrete economic areas, with separate chapters on goods, services, financial services, competition, subsidy control, public procurement, digital and data regulation, and intellectual property. This is followed by Part III, which examines the impact of Brexit in the social domain, with chapters on citizens' rights, immigration law and policy, asylum and refugee law, equality law, employment law, healthcare, consumer law, environmental law, food law, and criminal law.

The chapters have been structured to facilitate comparison between topics and contain a set of cross-cutting themes. Thus, the institutional chapters in Part I begin by considering the pre-Brexit position, with a brief outline of the impact of EU membership on the constitutional position and power of the institution concerned. This is followed by post-Brexit legal change, where the focus is on the implications of the principal domestic legislation that shaped the UK's exit from the EU—including the European Union (Withdrawal) Act 2018, the UK Internal Market Act 2020, the European Union (Future Relationship) Act 2020, and the Retained EU Law (Revocation and Reform) Act 2023—on the constitutional position and power of the institution concerned. There is then consideration of post-Brexit constitutional and political change. The changes depend on the particular institution, but they include matters such as the extent to which the UK Parliament has taken back control in a post-Brexit world; the effect of Brexit on the relationship between the legislature and the executive; how far the form and substance of devolved power have changed in a post-Brexit world; and the legal interpretive challenges for the courts post-Brexit.

The chapters in Parts II and III are also structured to facilitate comparison and cohesion. The chapters begin with pre-Brexit regulation, with a brief outline of the principal contours of the EU legal regime pre-Brexit. This is followed by post-Brexit regulation, which includes the principal regulatory changes, including those under way or proposed, in the relevant area. Special attention is given to legislation that has, inter alia, replaced retained EU law, such as the UK Internal Market Act 2020, Agriculture Act 2020, Environment Act 2021, Professional Qualifications Act 2022, Subsidy Control Act 2022, Procurement Act 2023, Financial Services and Markets Act 2023, and Product Regulation and Metrology Act 2025. The chapters in Parts II and III then address post-Brexit legality, connoting the consistency of regulatory changes with the UK's obligations under the Withdrawal Agreement and the Trade and Cooperation Agreement, including the provisions on the level playing field and non-regression. The chapters conclude with broader reflections, in the form of a post-Brexit empirical and normative analysis. The precise content of such analysis necessarily varies as between chapters. However, there are central themes, such as the extent to which there has been regulatory divergence in the post-Brexit world; the rationale for such divergence insofar as it exists; whether it is active or passive; the economic impact of regulatory change; the territorial impact on the devolved areas of Scotland, Wales, and Northern Ireland, including the extent to which post-Brexit change has affected the pre-existing division of competence between Westminster and the devolved areas; and post-Brexit legislative developments at the EU level which can affect the extent of regulatory divergence between the UK and EU.

This introductory chapter reflects the structural dimensions of the chapters in the subsequent Parts of the book. It draws together and highlights themes that emerge from the individual chapters, thereby helping to provide an overview of the UK Regulatory Framework post-Brexit, and the extent to which the law has been unbound.

2 The Institutional Dimension

(a) Pre-Brexit Position

The impact of EU membership on the constitutional and institutional structure of the UK pre-Brexit was at one and the same time significant and expected. The UK's unwritten constitution vested sovereign power in Parliament, with no substantive constraints, and, albeit more contentiously, no procedural constraints. This constitutional regime was then overlaid by a political regime of first past the post, which vested controlling power in the government, which would normally assume office on the basis of a minority of the vote, but without the need for a coalition. There were tensions, as Alison Young and Jeff King note,[2] between the Westminster and Whitehall models of government, with the former emphasizing the importance of Parliament as the

[2] Chs 2 and 4.

controlling elected body within the UK system, while the latter stressed ministerial power as the driving force behind fulfilment of electoral commitments.

The formal contours of this regime were not per se affected by EU membership. However, the substantive reality was that EU accession markedly altered the domestic institutional structure. This was readily apparent from the implications of membership that were known when we joined the club, 14 years after its inception. The EU had competence over significant policy areas that expanded with subsequent Treaty amendments; EU law came with the architecture developed by the EU courts, notably direct effect and primacy, which were accommodated in the UK legal order;[3] EU rules shaped the regulatory frame in the important areas to which it applied;[4] and UK national courts rapidly became accustomed to applying EU law in cases that came before them.[5]

This substantive reality also had consequences for the territorial division of power within the UK. EU rules were equally applicable throughout the UK, thereby overlaying any territorial division of competence within the UK. The EU rules could also have more specific implications, as in the case of Northern Ireland, where EU fundamental rights and equality law underpinned the Northern Ireland human rights and equality provisions introduced in the run-up to the Belfast–Good Friday Agreement and thereafter. Chris McCrudden relates how the legislative and executive power over devolved matters vested in the Northern Ireland Assembly and the Northern Ireland Executive was limited by requirements not to act contrary to the ECHR and EU law.[6]

(b) Post-Brexit Change: Constitutional, Political, and Legal

The formal dimensions of the UK constitution were not per se changed by Brexit. To the contrary, they were affirmed. The oft-repeated motif of the Leave campaign to 'take back control' spoke to the desire to reunite the formal dimension with substantive reality, such that the UK, through its sovereign Parliament, controlled its own destiny. It is nonetheless clear that Brexit cast into sharp relief tensions in the UK constitution and institutional structure, which in turn gave a very distinctive meaning to the idea of taking back control.

Thus, as Alison Young notes, Brexit provided the circumstances in which inherent weaknesses of the UK constitution led to a diminution of checks and balances as between the executive, legislature, and judiciary, fuelled by the idea of acting in line with the wishes of the people.[7] In related vein, Jeff King notes how 'Brexit supplied the

[3] Ch 6.
[4] Ch 5.
[5] Ch 6.
[6] Ch 8.
[7] Ch 2.

occasion, and conjured the passions, that led to a decisive augmentation of executive power that parliamentary observers considered unprecedented', with the consequence that 'taking back control' meant placing very considerable law-making powers that had previously been shared with the EU in the hands of the executive.[8]

This was manifest in the tensions between the Westminster and Whitehall views of the UK constitutional and institutional system. The executive espousal of the Whitehall view was unsurprising, but not always successful in the complex political machinations that occurred after the Brexit referendum and before the exit deal was struck. The Westminster view, as represented primarily by the House of Commons, was evident in the rebellion led by Dominic Grieve leading to legislative amendments giving increased power to the legislature over the approval of the Withdrawal Agreement, which was the foundation for the three legislative rejections of Theresa May's proposed agreements, leading to her demise. The tensions between the Whitehall and Westminster views continued throughout the period leading to conclusion of the Withdrawal Agreement and the TCA. In relation to the former, Boris Johnson used his newly secured majority to remove the meaningful votes provisions from section 13 of the European Union (Withdrawal) Act 2018. In relation to the latter, Parliament was presented with the mammoth TCA with scant time to understand the document on which future relations between the UK and EU would turn.[9]

The distinctive meaning to the idea of taking back control was also manifest, as Jeff King relates, in the very extensive use of delegated powers by the executive in the principal legislation giving effect to Brexit, and in statutes enacted thereafter. There was no meaningful parliamentary accountability. The problem was exacerbated by increased recourse to skeleton clauses in legislation that conferred very wide powers on the executive to create regulatory schemes in the future. This led to repeated protest by the House of Lords Secondary Legislation Scrutiny Committee, the Delegated Powers and Regulatory Reform Committee, and the Constitution Committee, albeit with limited impact.[10] The desire for augmentation of executive power post-Brexit was further manifest in relation to the two inquiries launched by the government seeking to curb powers of judicial review, although the outcome was not as far-reaching as some had feared.[11]

Brexit also enabled the executive to modify the regulatory architecture after the UK left the EU. Pre-Brexit, EU law set the substantive criteria for regulators in areas that fell within EU competence, and the attendant regime for regulatory independence. Post-Brexit, there could be substantive amendment of the legislation applied by regulators, but the imperatives that regulators should consider were also modified. There was, as Kenneth Armstrong shows, an increased politicisation of regulators as governments sought to align regulatory policy with strategies to drive economic growth.[12]

[8] Ch 4.
[9] Ch 4.
[10] Ch 4.
[11] Ch 4.
[12] Ch 5.

He acknowledges that this politicisation and realignment has roots deeper than Brexit, while emphasizing the cumulative effect of the financial crisis, the COVID-19 pandemic, and Brexit, which created the economic context for government efforts to harness regulators as agents of growth.

There is, moreover, no doubt that the role of UK courts post-Brexit has changed. While there are instances where direct effect and primacy are still applicable, most notably concerning the Withdrawal Agreement and Northern Ireland, in the great majority of instances this is no longer the focus. Nor is this surprising in a post-Brexit world. The principal judicial focus is rather to navigate the complex legal terrain provided by the Brexit legislation, which includes specification as to the courts' powers within that overall architecture. This in turn generates, as Paul Craig shows,[13] challenging questions as to general principles of interpretation, and how they have changed in a post-Brexit world; how the courts have exercised the powers allowing them to depart from CJEU judgments delivered prior to IP completion day; how UK courts use the power to consider post-IP completion day EU case law where it is 'relevant' to the matter before the UK court; and rival judicial visions as to how causes of action under the European Union (Withdrawal) Act 2018 should be conceptualized.

There are nonetheless aspects of academic debate post-Brexit which raise issues concerning the status of UK constitutional law pre-Brexit, and the extent to which it has been modified in the post-Brexit legal world. Gavin Phillipson considers what lessons can be drawn from the UK's membership of the EU and recent case law on the Withdrawal Agreement for the long-debated issue as to whether Parliament can, to any degree, bind its successors.[14] This is particularly apposite with respect to debates concerning constitutional statutes and implied repeal, and the possibility of manner and form constraints on parliamentary sovereignty. Gavin Phillipson argues, based on the case law pre- and post-Brexit, that Parliament may endow statutes with resistance to implied repeal, but contends that it is more doubtful as to whether statutes that Parliament does not appear to have so endowed can nevertheless be judicially characterized as 'constitutional' due to the importance of their subject matter. Statutes may therefore be found to be constitutional because Parliament endowed them with such status through wording of the kind used in the European Communities Act 1972 and the European Union (Withdrawal) Act 2018, but Phillipson questions whether the case law has established that courts can decide that the constitutionally significant subject matter of legislation justified such status as a matter of common law. He argues further that there is a real distinction between requirements relating to the form of words used to repeal legislation and the manner of such repeal, so far as the latter connotes the need for special majorities and the like. The former are regarded as compatible with democratic rule and parliamentary sovereignty, the latter not.

[13] Ch 6.
[14] Ch 3.

(c) Post-Brexit Change: Scotland and Wales

The studies in this book reveal the significant impact of Brexit on devolved government.[15] They can be broadly conceptualized as procedural, substantive, and institutional, although there is inevitably some overlap between these categories.

In procedural terms, there was perforce an underlying tension from the outset resulting from the fact that although England and Wales voted to leave the EU, Scotland and Northern Ireland voted to remain. It also became clear that Scotland and Wales preferred a future relationship with more engagement between the UK and the EU than was evident in UK government policy and the eventual outcome of Brexit. However, the devolved governments had, as Sionaidh Douglas-Scott shows,[16] scant voice in the Brexit negotiations, in part due to the relations with the EU being treated as a foreign policy matter and thus a reserved power for the UK government, and in part because the machinery for discourse between Westminster and the devolved governments was used sparingly to say the least.[17] A further procedural dimension concerns the status of the Sewel convention post-Brexit. There is little doubt that it has diminished in importance, as exemplified by the fact that lack of devolved parliamentary consent was ignored when major Brexit legislation, such as the UK Internal Market Act 2020 (UKIMA), was passed in Westminster.[18]

In substantive terms, Brexit had a profound effect on the distribution of competences between Westminster and the devolved governments. The reality pre-Brexit was that many devolved matters relating to issues such as agriculture and goods were regulated primarily by the EU, with the consequence that EU law provided UK-wide harmonization. Brexit could then have signalled a revitalization of devolved competence, consequent on the repatriation of competences on leaving the EU. This has, however, been qualified by enactment of legislation, such as the UKIMA, which significantly curtailed the autonomy of devolved governments in the salient area.[19] The objective is to ensure free movement of goods across the four nations, thereby largely removing regulatory divergence as powers return from Brussels to each of them. There is a touch of irony in the fact that the underlying ideas that shape UKIMA draw liberally on concepts fashioned in EU law, such as mutual recognition and non-discrimination. There have, in addition, been Supreme Court decisions embodying what Alison Young has termed a 'move towards muscular unionism, with a strong protection of parliamentary sovereignty having an impact on the perception of the horizontal division of power in the UK'.[20]

15 Chs 7–8.
16 Ch 7.
17 Ch 7.
18 Chs 1, 7.
19 Chs 1, 7, 9.
20 Ch 1.

In institutional terms, the reality of the division of power between the UK government in Westminster and the devolved governments has altered as a result of the procedural and substantive factors adumbrated above. There have been other factors inclining to the same conclusion. The very complexity of Brexit legislation, including decisions as to which pieces of EU law to amend, repeal, or retain, has compromised transparency, clarity, and accountability, thereby increasing the complexity of the devolution process.[21] This has been further exacerbated by institutional devices, such as Common Frameworks within the context of the UKIMA 2020.[22]

(d) Post-Brexit Change: Northern Ireland

The singularity of Northern Ireland serves to explain its treatment in a separate chapter of this book. Borders was a key issue dealt with in the Withdrawal Agreement. In a post-Brexit world, the border between Northern Ireland and the Republic of Ireland constituted a land border between the UK and the EU, and was therefore addressed in the negotiations. The delineation of a border is not normally problematic. It is achieved through customs posts, border crossings, and the like. However, all parties wished to prevent a hard border between Northern Ireland and Ireland, for reasons that were part security and part economics. The return of a hard border could jeopardize the peace process between Northern Ireland and the Republic of Ireland. The free flow of goods and people between the two was the norm, and thus a hard border would be economically disruptive in a post-Brexit world. While the desire to avoid a hard border was shared by all parties, the consequential difficulty was that Northern Ireland constituted a border for the EU when the UK ceased to be a member state. If there was no hard border, there was a danger that EU rules on customs and trade could be flouted by goods entering the EU via Ireland, having come across the soft border from Northern Ireland, having entered via any third country. The Northern Ireland backstop was to be the solution to this problem. A hard border was to be avoided, but rules would be put in place to secure the EU's interests in relation to customs and trade regulation after the end of the transition period, pending completion of a trade agreement between UK and EU that would obviate the problem. The issue was addressed in a Protocol attached to the Withdrawal Agreement.

Chris McCrudden reveals the infamous trilemma that Brexit thus presented for Northern Ireland:[23] how to maintain the absence of North–South barriers; while preventing new barriers between Northern Ireland and the rest of the UK; while at the same time permitting significant regulatory divergence between the UK and the EU. It was not possible to secure all three preferences.

[21] Ch 7.
[22] Ch 9.
[23] Ch 8.

The 'solution' encapsulated in the Ireland–Northern Ireland Protocol to the EU–UK Withdrawal Agreement was to limit the East–West dimension via a regulatory 'border' between Northern Ireland and Great Britain. Northern Ireland effectively remained within the Single Market for goods and EU customs arrangements, the corollary being increased regulatory controls for goods travelling between Great Britain and Northern Ireland. EU law continued to apply in Northern Ireland in such instances, including the Charter of Rights, CJEU case law, and references to the CJEU from national courts.

The singularity of Northern Ireland had, as Chris McCrudden relates, complex legal and political consequences. In legal terms, there were distinctive provisions in the Brexit legislation relating to Northern Ireland, which generated a raft of important legal challenges in which the courts were forced to grapple with difficult issues that interrelated with other complex legal instruments, such as the Belfast–Good Friday Agreement. In political terms, there was dissatisfaction by unionist parties with the rift between Northern Ireland and the rest of the UK, which led to further legal challenges and the modification of the Northern Ireland Protocol through the Windsor Framework.

3 The Economic and Social Dimension

(a) Pre-Brexit EU Regulation

It is important to be mindful at the outset of a point that is both trite and important in equal measure, which is that the impact of EU regulation on the subject-matter areas covered by this book varied in scope and intensity. In some areas it was all-embracing and detailed, leaving relatively little room for national manoeuvre; in other areas the coverage was more limited, and less prescriptive; yet elsewhere, it was betwixt and between these positions. The significance of EU regulation was also affected by the nature of UK regulation of the relevant area when the UK joined the EU.

For example, in relation to goods, EU membership entailed adherence to comprehensive EU rules concerning movement of goods between member states, and between the EU and third countries.[24] In public procurement, it involved the adoption of detailed hard law obligations of a kind that had not hitherto existed in the UK.[25] Food law was characterized by harmonized EU regulatory requirements.[26] EU competition law prescribed a comprehensive set of EU rules relating to cartels, dominant undertakings, and mergers, which differed markedly from UK pre-accession competition law.[27] There was a comprehensive and mandatory EU regime concerning

[24] Ch 9.
[25] Ch 14.
[26] Ch 25.
[27] Ch 12.

state aid and subsidies.[28] The EU developed a wide-ranging body of environmental law, albeit with some room for national adaptation.[29] EU financial regulation underwent substantial expansion from 1966 onwards, culminating in a comprehensive rulebook that governed capital markets, investment, banking, and insurance across member states, normally through directly applicable regulations and detailed directives. The system underpinned a financial services 'passport' that permitted firms to operate cross-border with authorization from their home state.[30] Citizens' rights were protected through EU Treaty provisions, regulations, directives, and case law.[31] Intellectual property developed into a central element of the EU's agenda and was extensively Europeanized through unitary EU-wide rights, harmonization of national IP rights, harmonized enforcement regimes, and EU case law.[32] There was considerable EU coverage of employment law, notwithstanding the more limited Treaty competence in this area.[33] In consumer law there was a very considerable volume of EU regulation pre-Brexit, which covered many important areas of consumer policy, but allowed discretion through national case law.[34] By way of contrast, UK data protection law predated EU law by more than a decade, but the EU General Data Protection Regulation became the 'gold standard' data protection legislation.[35]

The relationship between EU and UK law could also be symbiotic, as in the case of the law relating to equality, where EU equality law was shaped by developments initiated in the UK as much as UK equality law was shaped by the EU. The binding nature of EU law served moreover to entrench equality law in the UK, notwithstanding the absence of a UK written constitution, thereby protecting the right to equality in the UK against erosion.[36]

In other areas, the coverage of EU law was less complete and/or less efficacious. The regulation of services is a prominent example. Services constitute more than 70 per cent of the EU's economic output, and 80 per cent of the UK's economic output. They are governed by an admixture of Treaty provisions and EU legislation. However, a single market for services has not been fully attained. Guaranteeing market access and establishing non-discrimination are insufficient to liberalize services trade, since access may also be impeded by barriers to authorization, licensing, or certification formalities, while mutual recognition of professional qualifications and free movement of persons is also important.[37]

In yet other areas, such as asylum, the pre-Brexit picture was more complex. This was in part for temporal reasons, since asylum law was brought into EU law post-1997

[28] Ch 13.
[29] Ch 24.
[30] Ch 11.
[31] Ch 17.
[32] Ch 16.
[33] Ch 21.
[34] Ch 23.
[35] Ch 15.
[36] Ch 20.
[37] Ch 10.

through the Treaty of Amsterdam. It was in part for substantive reasons, because the UK negotiated the right to engage selectively in EU asylum and immigration policies. This is important given the centrality of immigration and asylum in the Brexit campaign, and in post-Brexit government policy. The claim that the UK needed to leave the EU to 'take back control' in this area is, as Catherine Briddick and Cathryn Costello emphasize, misleading.[38] The picture was also more complex in relation to cooperation in criminal matters, where UK policy was a blend of influencing and shaping the development of EU criminal law, while at the same expressive of concern that European integration in criminal matters would unduly threaten state sovereignty.[39] In healthcare, because the EU lacked an explicit competence to regulate national health systems, the NHS and UK healthcare provision were shaped primarily through the exercise by the EU of other competences not specific to health, above all the internal market competence.[40] In immigration law, the UK had an opt-out, such that many EU measures were inapplicable to the UK.[41]

(b) Post-Brexit Legality

(i) The Withdrawal Agreement and the Trade and Cooperation Agreement: Subject Matter

Brexit signified the UK leaving the EU, the corollary being that it could make its own laws in its sovereign capacity. There are nonetheless legal boundaries in this respect, flowing from the Withdrawal Agreement[42] and the Trade and Cooperation Agreement (TCA).[43]

The Withdrawal Agreement dealt with people, money, borders, and transitional issues. Part One dealt with 'Common Provisions'. It established core legal precepts that shaped much that came thereafter, such as the continued application of direct effect and primacy of EU law to the provisions of the Withdrawal Agreement, insofar as they met the criteria for direct effect. Parts Two to Five were concerned with substantive issues: citizens' rights, separation, transitional issues, and financial provisions. Part Six covered institutional provisions. The issues were addressed in considerable detail, as attested to by the fact that the Withdrawal Agreement ran to 185 densely

38 Ch 19.
39 Ch 26.
40 Ch 22.
41 Ch 18.
42 European Union (Withdrawal Agreement) Act 2020; Agreement on the withdrawal of the United Kingdom of Great Britain and Northern Ireland from the European Union and the European Atomic Energy Community, [2019] OJ C384 I/01.
43 The Trade and Cooperation Agreement between the European Union and the European Atomic Energy Community, of the One Part, and the United Kingdom of Great Britain and Northern Ireland, of the Other Part, [2020] OJ L444/14, [2021] OJ L149/10.

worded Articles, plus the Northern Ireland Protocol, nine Annexes, and a Political Declaration, which covered 198 pages of the EU's Official Journal.

This was, however, dwarfed by the TCA, which weighed in at 2530 pages. It brought new meaning to the phrase the 'devil is in the detail'. The TCA sets the terms for trade between the UK and EU post-Brexit. The nature of the UK–EU trade agreement was shaped, as Filippo Fontanelli shows, by the respective negotiating imperatives of the EU and the UK, with the consequence that the TCA fell short of the level of integration in other EU FTAs.[44] The provisions concerning the Level Playing Field in Title XI TCA are divided by subject matter, with different chapters dealing with competition, state aids, state-owned enterprises, taxation, labour and social standards, environment and climate, other instruments for trade and sustainable development, and horizontal provisions. The provisions are complex, and differ to some extent for each subject matter area. The salient issue for the purposes of this book is the extent to which such provisions circumscribe the UK's legislative and regulatory autonomy in a post-Brexit world.

(ii) The Withdrawal Agreement: Practical Impact

The Withdrawal Agreement is not relevant to all chapters in this book; to the contrary, its relevance is confined to certain topics. There is, for example, no substantive coverage of asylum in the Withdrawal Agreement or the TCA. However, where relevant it has been central to the framework of legal rules that apply in the post-Brexit world. This is particularly so in relation to citizens' rights and to Northern Ireland, and the latter can have an indirect impact on other areas, such as employment law and healthcare.[45] The Withdrawal Agreement preserved important elements of cross-border access to healthcare.[46]

In relation to citizens' rights the Withdrawal Agreement provides the architectural frame for the rights of EU citizens living in the UK post-Brexit. However, as Catherine Barnard and Fiona Costello show,[47] applicants face considerable difficulties in realizing their rights under the Withdrawal Agreement. Whereas prior to Brexit they could prove their residency rights by showing an EU passport or ID card, post-Brexit all EU nationals who were resident in the UK before December 2020 had to apply under the EU Settlement Scheme to continue that lawful residence. This entailed very considerable administrative burdens, more especially because to benefit fully from their free movement rights and enjoy equal access to social assistance, individuals had to be 'exercising their Treaty rights', by demonstrating that they were a worker or a self-employed person.

[44] Ch 9.
[45] Chs 21, 22.
[46] Ch 22.
[47] Ch 17.

(iii) The Trade and Cooperation Agreement: Practical Impact

The TCA's relevance differs as between different areas covered by this volume. There is no doubt that, for example, it is central to post-Brexit relations concerning trade in goods, setting the architecture for customs duties and rules of origin between the UK and EU. The likely economic impact of the TCA on UK producers flowing from customs checks on goods imported into the UK from the EU led to repeated delays in implementation of the relevant TCA provisions by the UK.[48] While conclusion of the TCA involved protracted negotiations, post-Brexit there has in general terms been legal *détente*, such that while permanent negotiations continue, invocation of the TCA to contest UK or EU measures affecting trade in goods have been rare.[49] The TCA level playing field rules nonetheless provide some insurance against regulatory arbitrage, while shaping bilateral talks. As Filippo Fontanelli explains, this reflects the underlying political calculus: actively lowering domestic standards threatens retaliation; actively raising them burdens exporters and consumers. This leads to the path of least resistance, in terms of managed proximity.

There is equally no doubt that the TCA is significant in the context of criminal justice. Security and criminal justice cooperation are covered by a separate part of the TCA Agreement. The TCA reflects, as Valsamis Mitsilegas reveals, the parties' willingness to achieve a high degree of cooperation in several areas, including surrender and the European Arrest Warrant, mutual legal assistance, and UK participation in EU criminal justice bodies and agencies.[50] The detailed TCA provisions provide the regulatory framework for these areas of criminal justice.

The impact of the TCA is, unsurprisingly, not always the same, given, inter alia, that the provisions concerning the level playing field differ in different areas. However, the general conclusion is that such provisions have been less constraining on the UK post-Brexit than might have been thought when the TCA was initially agreed. Where UK legislation has been enacted that coheres with TCA obligations it should not be assumed that this was motivated or caused by the need to comply with the TCA rules on the level playing field. There are, nonetheless, some areas where the TCA provisions have shaped subsequent UK legislation.

The general pattern is exemplified by employment law, where the TCA includes a 'non-regression' clause and a commitment to comply with certain international labour standards, the object being to ensure that the UK could not use its departure to gain a competitive advantage over other member states by lowering its existing standards of social protection. However, Anne Davies shows that these provisions are not easy to invoke in practice, because of a lack of clarity in their drafting, the difficulty of proving the impact of a change in employment law on trade, and the general unwillingness of parties to trade agreements to disrupt a successful economic relationship

[48] Ch 9.
[49] Ch 9.
[50] Ch 26.

by invoking a social clause.[51] Moreover, while provisions in the Labour government's Employment Rights Act 2025 cohere with those in the TCA, there is no evidence that they were motivated by TCA commitments. The causality issue is also evident in the context of consumer law, where the forces that drove the Product Regulation and Metrology Act 2025 are less TCA compliance, and more the desire to reduce impediments to trade between the UK and the EU.[52]

The general pattern whereby the TCA provisions have been less effective than might initially have been imagined is further evidenced by state aid and subsidies.[53] This issue was a major concern during the TCA negotiations, which is unsurprising given the centrality of state aid to a level playing field. The UK duly enacted the Subsidy Control Act 2022 (SCA), which mirrors in certain respects the substantive criteria concerning state aid in EU law. However, the devil is once again in the detail, and in the way in which the SCA has been applied. There are, as Andrea Biondi and Totis Kotsonis demonstrate, some significant substantive differences as between the EU and UK regimes, and also in relation to enforcement, with the consequence that the Commission has questioned whether the UK's subsidy control regime represents the 'effective' control of subsidies that Article 366 TCA demands.

The issue concerning the efficacy of the TCA provisions is exemplified, albeit in a somewhat different way, by services. In this context, the TCA has had limited impact on post-Brexit freedom of action because the TCA provisions are, as Gavin Barrett shows,[54] pretty thin. This was in part because certain services, such as financial services, were not mentioned; in part because the obligations were limited to market access and non-discrimination; and in part because there are numerous EU and national reservations in the TCA. The relative thinness of the TCA provisions is also evident in other areas, such as competition law, where, as Barry Rodger and Andreas Stephan demonstrate, the TCA merely requires a competition law regime in relation to anti-competitive agreements, abuse of dominance, and anti-competitive mergers, policed by an independent competition authority.[55] It is further apparent in relation to food law, where Emily Lydgate and Chloë Anthony link the thinness of the provisions and the limits of the level playing field enforcement mechanisms to the Conservative government's desire to retain regulatory autonomy for post-Brexit food law.[56] The limited impact of the TCA provisions is also a feature of intellectual property law, since core IP rules are already embedded in international law and retained EU law, leaving little for the TCA to add.[57]

[51] Ch 21.
[52] Chs 9, 23.
[53] Ch 13.
[54] Ch 10.
[55] Ch 12.
[56] Ch 25.
[57] Ch 16.

(c) Post-Brexit Regulation: A Conceptual Framework

The chapters in Parts II and III provide detailed specification of the post-Brexit legislation enacted in the different areas covered by this study. Reference will be made to some of this legislation and regulation in the ensuing analysis. However, the primary objective of the current chapter is to provide an analytical overview of the picture post-Brexit. This is facilitated by the conceptual framework set out below.

(i) Divergence: The Substantive Dimension

The chapters in the book provide a rich and illuminating analysis concerning the extent to which there has been divergence between UK and EU law in the areas studied. It is readily apparent that there are differences not only as between different areas, but also within a particular area. It would be a simple world if we could make neat demarcations, with definitive conclusions that a particular area unequivocally demonstrated divergence or not, as the case may be. However, the real world is neither neat nor simple. While definitive conclusions can sometimes be drawn in relation to a particular topic, this is not always the case. It may then be helpful to have a conceptual framework concerning divergence through which to navigate the detailed terrain in later chapters.

Active divergence is expressive of the adoption of new UK rules that are different from EU law in a post-Brexit world. This must be qualified by consideration of causality. In some instances, the enactment of the new rules was a conscious choice to depart from EU law, pursuant to the legislative freedom attendant on Brexit. In other instances, the legislative motivation for the new rules was not primarily a desire to depart from EU law, but rather expressive of a modified policy agenda in that particular area, where the resultant legislation addressed issues that might not be covered by EU law, or did so in a somewhat different manner.

Passive divergence connotes the fact that EU rules in the relevant area have changed and that UK law has not mirrored such change. It is axiomatic that EU regulatory provisions change with the effluxion of time. This is in part for exogenous reasons, such as the need to respond to the challenges of AI. It is in part for endogenous reasons, such as internal policy changes within the EU, or the realization that the regulatory status quo is working imperfectly. It is also important to note that passive divergence by the UK may be intentional or unintentional. The former is expressive of a conscious choice by the UK not to follow or mirror the new EU rules. The latter captures the scenario where the UK government has not considered the issue one way or another. Governments are busy; so too individual ministers. They work within bounded rationality, and subject to constraints of time, knowledge, and resource. It is then perfectly possible that the change in EU law may not feature on the government's agenda, or that of the minister.

Inactive divergence captures the situation where UK law differs from EU law in a post-Brexit world, primarily because the UK has no coherent policy in the relevant area. It bears affinity to passive divergence, but is nonetheless distinctive. In areas characterized by inactive divergence it is not simply that the UK government fails to keep up with particular EU law developments, whether intentionally or unintentionally. The underlying rationale for differentiation is, at one and the same time, both more general and simpler, which is that the UK government does not have a coherent policy for the relevant domain. It does not know what it wishes to do in that area. This may be the result of absence of expertise on a topic that has long been regulated by the EU. It may be the result of rival factions in government, which are unable to resolve their differences. It may be that the issue is not regarded as sufficiently important to feature on the government's agenda. It may be for an admixture of such reasons.

Continued convergence is expressive of the fact that the UK chooses to follow central precepts of EU law in a post-Brexit world. This is not inconsistent with the idea of 'Law Unbound', since it is axiomatically expressive of UK sovereignty to continue with a certain substantive body of legal rules that are felt to work well. Having said that, alignment with EU law can also be the result of post-Brexit recognition of economic and social reality. It should nonetheless be noted that *continued convergence* as used here can connote a formal legislative mechanism whereby the UK can track and adopt the new EU rules in the relevant area. *Continued convergence* can also capture a less formal modality of connection.

(ii) Divergence: The Institutional Dimension

There are, as we noted at the outset of this chapter, linkages between the institutional dimensions of Brexit, discussed in Part I, and the economic and social dimensions considered in Parts II and III. The linkage is evident in relation to divergence, and speaks directly to the underlying idea of taking back control that animated the Brexit debate.

It is important and simple in equal measure: there is no necessary connection between the degree of substantive convergence/divergence considered above, and the modality through which post-Brexit regulation is made. There are instances where the relevant post-Brexit legal rules are fully debated in Parliament, leading to legislation, in which the sovereign Parliament expresses the wish to diverge from, or retain, the pre-existing EU law. There are instances where the post-Brexit position is enshrined in legislation, but where the statute accords broad discretion to the minister as to whether to depart from or continue to follow EU legal rules. There are areas where the legislature is silent, in the sense that there is no formal statute or secondary legislation, such that the choices are effectively made by the administration or regulatory agency with authority over the relevant area. The extent to which the UK legislature can be said to have taken back control differs markedly in these three instances.

(iii) Divergence: The Territorial Dimension

There are also linkages between the territorial dimensions of Brexit addressed in Part I and the economic and social dimensions discussed in Parts II and III. There are three more particular such aspects that impact on economic and social divergence/

convergence within the UK in a post-Brexit world: there are those that flow most directly from the differential treatment of Northern Ireland; there are those relating to legislation enacted by a devolved legislature concerning continued alignment with EU law in a post-Brexit world; and there are those that result from the structure and application of post-Brexit UK legislation.

(d) Post-Brexit Regulation: The Emerging Picture

The conceptual framework provides a helpful lens through which to view post-Brexit developments. However, further inquiry reveals nuances not only as between the preceding categories, but also within them. It also demonstrates that a particular area may exhibit elements of, for example, active divergence, passive divergence, and some continued convergence,[58] leading to some drift away from EU law.[59] It is, in addition, important to be mindful of causality, as exemplified by asylum law. Thus, as Catherine Briddick and Cathryn Costello show, the claim that it was necessary to exit the EU to manage migration rested on two connected false premises: that it was EU membership that constrained government action in this domain; and that post-Brexit, the UK would be free of such constraints.[60]

(i) The Substantive Dimension: Active Divergence

Active divergence captures, as noted earlier, the adoption of UK provisions that differ from those in the EU. This may be reflective of a conscious desire to depart from EU law; it may alternatively be because of changes in the domestic political agenda that are not directly related to EU law. This duality is evident from the studies covered in the book, which also reveal the nuance within particular areas, such that active divergence in a particular area may be accompanied by developments that reduce the degree of difference between UK and EU law.

This is readily apparent from consideration of financial services.[61] Niamh Moloney charts the post-Brexit story, noting that UK financial regulation was a natural candidate for the 'take back control' agenda, given the strength of the City of London, its significance to UK gross domestic product, and the potential for financial regulatory reform to drive competitiveness and economic growth. She recounts the ways in which UK financial regulation is experiencing the largest reform exercise since the global financial crisis, which extends across all domains of financial regulation—institutional, legislative, and technocratic—concluding that the potential for active divergence is significant. It is exemplified by the Financial Services and Markets Act 2023, which shifts financial regulation away from legislation to a more flexible system

[58] See, eg, Ch 25; Ch 22.
[59] See, eg, Ch 20.
[60] Ch 19.
[61] Ch 12.

with considerable rulemaking power exercised by regulators. However, Moloney also notes three factors that moderate the divergence. These factors do not deny differences between the UK and the EU in a post-Brexit world, but qualify the differences.

First, financial regulation is highly dynamic, such that it is in an almost permanent state of revision, reform, and expansion in all major financial systems. Second, the normative extent of the divergence thus far is contestable, and the baseline normative framework for financial regulation has not changed since withdrawal, this being to secure financial stability, market efficiency/integrity, and investor/consumer protection. Third, the EU approach has itself changed towards a more deregulatory approach that is attentive to growth and competitiveness, with the consequence that the gap between the political interests and policy prescriptions in the new UK regime and that in the EU is not that significant.

The nuanced nature of post-Brexit development is also evident in relation to procurement. Sue Arrowsmith and Luke Butler relate how the UK government decided to press forward with an overarching hard law framework for domestic procurement objectives in the Procurement Act 2023. The Act retained and extended certain aspects of the EU regime. However, active divergence was evident in the decision intentionally to roll back certain EU constraints on contracting authority discretion and through the adoption of a single regulatory framework to replace four separate sets of regulations; it is also likely to emerge from judicial interpretation. There is, nonetheless, evidence of continued convergence, such that many of the Act's provisions draw on, and often paraphrase, concepts from the EU procurement directives.

The need for care when evaluating post-Brexit change is manifest in a different way in the context of state aid and subsidies. The Subsidy Control Act 2022 borrows liberally from EU concepts of state aid. There are nonetheless marked differences between the respective regimes. Thus, as Andrea Biondi and Totis Kotsonis show,[62] the UK's post-Brexit subsidy control regime represents a significant departure from the EU's state aid system by adopting a decentralised, principles-based approach. This model provides greater flexibility and speed, but it also introduces notable challenges in terms of consistency and enforcement. The UK regime is predicated on self-assessment by public authorities, which allows decisions to be made more quickly. However, the new regime also has significant costs. There is limited oversight; decentralisation places heavy reliance on individual authorities' interpretation of the subsidy control principles, creating a risk of inconsistent application; and enforcement is circumscribed both by very short time limits for bringing claims and by the deferential approach of the Competition Appeal Tribunal.

The duality in the sense of active divergence, reflective in part by conscious desire to depart from EU law and in part by change in the domestic political agenda that is not directly related to EU law, is further exemplified by employment law. The Labour government's Employment Rights Act 2025 is a major piece of legislation, which

[62] Ch 13.

addresses multiple important issues. However, as Anne Davies shows,[63] this is primarily because the Labour government's priorities for employment law are different to the EU's regulatory priorities. Insofar as UK law exceeds the protection afforded by the EU, the principal motivation is the desire to tackle employment practices that are exploitative and unfair to workers.

The complex nature of post-Brexit change is also apparent in the context of environmental law. Environmental law is, as Liz Fisher explains, inherently 'messy' given the range of topics it covers.[64] This is attested to by post-Brexit environmental law, where there has been legal change—some structural, some policy-based, some noticeable, and some less so. Thus, the Environment Act 2021 contains a new governance structure, coupled with substantive provisions addressing different issues in environmental law, often amending or consolidating pre-existing EU regimes. There is nonetheless also much that remains. However, UK public law institutions, including devolved legislatures and courts, now bear the full responsibility for UK environmental law.

This complexity is further exemplified by healthcare. Vilija Vėlyvytė shows how Brexit has taken UK healthcare out of EU legal frameworks for cross-border care, workforce mobility, and medicines regulation, but that the regulatory freedom promised by 'Law Unbound' has been realized only in part and unevenly. The causes vary as between different areas of healthcare. Thus, in relation to workforce policy, the claims of control mask persisting reliance on overseas labour, while plans for expanding domestic workforce remain uncertain amid unresolved questions of funding, training capacity, and pay. In relation to medicines, reforms to the Medicines and Healthcare Products Regulatory Agency assert formal autonomy, but the reality is that whether, and when, medicines become available in Great Britain remains deeply influenced by added trade frictions, domestic drug-pricing policy, and, ultimately, market size—pressures that have already prompted pragmatic re-binding.[65]

Active divergence is further evidenced in the sphere of digital and data regulation. The EU and UK acknowledged the need for regulation of digital platforms. However, while there are high-level commonalities between the EU Digital Services Act 2022 and the UK Online Safety Act 2023, there are very significant differences in terms of the detailed specification of the obligations and responsibilities under the respective pieces of legislation.[66] Active divergence is also manifest in relation to other aspects of digital and data regulation. Legislation that was viewed until recently as an indispensable safeguard for fundamental rights in a digitised world is now perceived by the UK government as an undesirable brake on innovation. There has, moreover, been a marked diminution of enforcement in the sphere of data protection which has dropped off the cliff-edge in recent years, as regulators prioritise economic growth.[67]

[63] Ch 21.
[64] Ch 24.
[65] Ch 22.
[66] Ch 15.
[67] Ch 15.

There are elements of active divergence in other areas, where the UK government has chosen not to follow a particular EU regulatory measure, or to modify the UK approach to the particular problem. This is exemplified by intellectual property law, where the UK decided not to implement the Digital Single Market Directive, driven by a desire to pursue its own copyright path and concerns over the EU's increasingly interventionist regulation of the digital economy.[68] A comparable pattern can be observed in competition law, where the EU's Digital Markets Act and the UK's Digital Markets, Competition and Consumers Act 2024 share common policy objectives, but diverge in ways that reflect the UK's post-Brexit regulatory autonomy.[69] More radical divergence occurred in the context of asylum, where UK legislation post-Brexit, such as the Nationality and Borders Act 2022 and the Illegal Migration Act 2023, departed from relevant EU law, and in certain respects constituted repudiation of the UK's international obligations to refugees.[70] Divergence is evident yet again in the context of immigration law, where, as Steve Peers shows,[71] UK law post-Brexit has changed considerably in relation to matters such as visas, student admissions, and labour migration, although it should be remembered that EU law had limited purchase in relation to immigration because of the UK opt-out.

(ii) The Substantive Dimension: Passive Divergence

Passive divergence is, unsurprisingly, evident in several areas, where there have been developments in EU law that have not been matched or mirrored in post-Brexit UK.

It is exemplified by the law relating to intellectual property where, as Justine Pila recounts,[72] there have been significant EU developments following the EU's 2020 IP Action Plan, with commitments to enhanced IP protection; greater use and deployment of IP among small and medium-sized enterprises; greater access to and 'sharing' of IP-protected assets; improved enforcement; and a 'fairer' playing field globally. There have been a plethora of more particular EU legislative initiatives designed to effectuate these objectives. Pila notes that the initiatives are indicative of the scope of EU involvement in IP, and that UK initiatives have been minimal by comparison.

A further striking instance of passive divergence is apparent in the realm of digital and data regulation concerning AI. The EU adopted a comprehensive legislative instrument in the form of the EU AI Act, while the UK eschewed any such legislative framework, preferring instead to rely on existing regulatory provisions. The UK approach was driven, as Orla Lynskey and Katherine Nolan recount, by the desire to be more high-tech-friendly, hoping thereby to benefit from economic growth as a result.[73] The degree of such divergence may nonetheless be narrowing somewhat as a

[68] Ch 16.
[69] Ch 12.
[70] Ch 19.
[71] Ch 18.
[72] Ch 16.
[73] Ch 15.

result of the EU Omnibus legislative proposals, including those relating to the digital sector, designed to simplify the law and reduce regulatory burdens.

There are, unsurprisingly, elements of passive divergence in other areas, given that EU regulation has continued apace post-Brexit. Passive divergence is apparent in consumer law, where the EU consumer agenda has developed in relation to matters such as representative actions, product safety, and product liability rules, with which the UK has not kept pace.[74] In competition law the EU revised and renewed its key Block Exemption Regulations (BERs) post-Brexit, some of which are more ambitious and incorporate broader policy objectives, but the UK initially retained the former EU BERs and later replaced them with UK-specific instruments that largely mirrored the old EU approach.[75] In consumer law, there have been some divergences as the EU advances its consumer acquis in response to technological developments.[76] In the law relating to goods, there has been passive divergence as new EU product standards have opened regulatory gaps with the UK, although these gaps may be closed through the Product Regulation and Metrology Act 2025.[77] In criminal justice there has been passive divergence as a result of CJEU case law narrowing the concept of mutual trust between the UK and the EU in a post-Brexit world.[78] Passive divergence is also evident in environmental law, with ongoing EU legislative developments and CJEU case law,[79] and in healthcare, where reforms of the EU regulatory architecture for the pharmaceutical sector diminish the plausibility of the UK's post-Brexit claim to regulatory agility in this area.[80]

(iii) The Substantive Dimension: Inactive Divergence

Inactive divergence captures, as adumbrated above, the situation where UK law differs from EU law in a post-Brexit world, primarily because the UK has no coherent policy in the relevant area.

It is exemplified by intellectual property, where, as Justine Pila explains,[81] UK law post-Brexit is characterized by the absence of a clear vision for IP after fifty years of EU membership, with the consequence that there is no coherent post-Brexit vision for IP or what it should seek to achieve, which stands in marked contrast to the hive of EU activity. This in turn generates the inquiry as to whether, having 'taken back control', the UK will develop a coherent direction for IP policy. These problems have been further compounded by the public controversy which IP reforms have attracted, and the problems thereby posed for the UK government.

[74] Ch 23.
[75] Ch 12.
[76] Ch 23.
[77] Ch 9.
[78] Ch 26.
[79] Ch 24.
[80] Ch 22.
[81] Ch 16.

(iv) The Substantive Dimension: Continued Convergence

There are areas where the UK regulatory framework post-Brexit continues to draw on foundational precepts drawn from EU law, notwithstanding divergences in certain respects.[82] There are other areas, such as competition law, where the dominant theme thus far is continued convergence. The Competition Act 1998 continues to govern this area, with its key provisions on agreements and abuse of a dominant position[83] reflecting the relevant provisions under EU law.[84] The 1998 Act was amended post-Brexit, in part to accommodate the fact that the investigative and adjudicatory regime had changed and in part to accord the UK regulatory authorities broad discretion to depart from pre-Brexit EU competition law principles and CJEU case law on a variety of grounds if they wished to do so.[85]

However, as Barry Rodger and Andreas Stephan show,[86] the UK regulatory authorities have shown little inclination thus far to utilize this discretionary power to tread a distinctive path. The Competition and Markets Authority (CMA) and the courts have relied on established EU law principles, the clear implication being that they will continue to do so for the foreseeable future, subject to any compelling arguments about the rationale for a divergent approach to be taken under UK law. In substantive terms, there is some divergence in relation to soft law guidelines and the regulation of digital markets, while in institutional terms the CMA's role has perforce changed post-Brexit. This does not alter the dominant theme, which is continued adherence to the competition law precepts developed by the Commission and EU Courts pre-Brexit.

There is also evidence of continued convergence in relation to consumer law, as apparent in the analysis of Geraint Howells, Chris Willett, and James Devenney.[87] This is exemplified by the Digital Markets, Competition and Consumers Act 2024, which broadly followed the EU Digital Markets Act. The Product Regulation and Metrology Act 2025 (PRMA) contains important provisions for voluntary alignment in the consumer protection arena. Product regulations may provide that a product requirement is to be treated as met if a requirement of relevant EU law specified in product regulations is met.[88] The Secretary of State may also by regulations make provision, in relation to the marketing or use of products in the UK, which corresponds, or is similar, to a provision of relevant EU law, for the purpose of reducing or mitigating the environmental impact of products.[89]

The PRMA is also relevant more generally for the law relating to goods, which reveals shifting government objectives over time. The initial Conservative post-Brexit

[82] See, eg, Ch 14, procurement law.
[83] Competition Act 1998, ss 2, 18.
[84] Arts 101–102 TFEU.
[85] Competition Act 1998, s 60A(7).
[86] Ch 12.
[87] Ch 23.
[88] Product Regulation and Metrology Act 2025, s 2(7).
[89] ibid s 1(2).

promise of a bonfire of red tape post-Brexit was, as Filippo Fontanelli shows,[90] quietly ditched by the Sunak administration, given the fears voiced by business concerning the costs of increased regulatory diversity for UK firms trading in the EU that would have to comply with two sets of regulations. The Labour government elected in 2024 took this a step further, seeking to engineer and embrace convergence, the PRMA being the most prominent but by no means the only example of such policy.

Shifting government objectives over time is also evident in the context of food law.[91] The initial approach was reflective of general Conservative government policy concerning Brexit, which was maintenance of regulatory autonomy in a post-Brexit world. There are areas where this has persisted under the Labour government post-2024. Its approach has nonetheless been more nuanced. Thus, the Labour government agreed to negotiate a Common Sanitary and Phytosanitary Area with the EU, which will re-introduce dynamic alignment with EU food law in a wide range of areas, with the consequence that the majority of plant and animal products traded between the UK and the EU will not be subject to regulatory compliance checks and controls. It has been taken forward through the Common Understanding concluded in May 2025. In the area of migration, Steve Peers recounts the efforts to agree a youth mobility scheme between the UK and the EU.[92]

There are other areas where the UK government would like to continue to follow EU law but is unable to do so, because the EU is unwilling to agree to continuance of the status quo ante. This is exemplified by services, where the UK would like to continue with mutual recognition of professional qualifications, or something closely akin thereto. However, the EU has been resistant, reluctant to allow cherry-picking of the benefits of the Single Market, the consequence being that the Common Understanding of May 2025 was silent on the issue, while the relevant provisions in the TCA do not suffice in this respect. The Common Understanding was also vague with respect to other service issues, such as the difficulties post-Brexit for those engaged in cultural and artistic exchanges.[93]

There can also be elements of continued convergence as to policy objectives, even though the detailed legislative instruments in UK and EU law post-Brexit differ. We see this in the context of the law relating to asylum. The post-Brexit law is complex and reveals elements of active and passive divergence. There are nonetheless, as Catherine Briddick and Cathryn Costello demonstrate,[94] areas of important policy convergence amidst the divergence, as both the UK and the EU seek to grapple with large numbers of migrants. They identify three such areas. Externalization connotes returns to faraway states, to which the applicant has no connection, such as Rwanda. Criminalization captures the expanded use of criminal law in the UK and EU to tackle

[90] Ch 9.
[91] Ch 25.
[92] Ch 18.
[93] Ch 12.
[94] Ch 19.

irregular migration. Selectivity speaks to bespoke schemes for different groups of protection-seekers, such as those from Ukraine or Hong Kong.

(v) The Institutional Dimension

The analysis in the preceding section included the institutional dimension, there being no necessary connection between the degree of substantive convergence/divergence and the modality through which post-Brexit regulation is made. In some areas, Parliament might truly take back control; in other areas, there can be an accretion of executive power.

This is exemplified by food law, where, as Emily Lydgate and Chloë Anthony show, there has been an admixture of active divergence, passive divergence, and continued convergence. However, they also noted that the substantive regulatory changes were not as significant as the changes to the processes of regulatory formation, implementation, and enforcement, with evidence of consolidation of executive power, expansion of non-legislative approaches to policy-making and regulation, and fragmentation of food standards across the UK. Lydgate and Anthony rightly emphasize the significance of the processes and principles that underpin the approval of new regulation, and conclude that while formal regulatory sovereignty exists in a post-Brexit world, accountability and transparency have suffered due to the expansion of executive power over legislative approval processes. Formal regulatory sovereignty cannot be equated with improved democratic accountability.[95]

This tension is more generally apparent in the Product Regulation and Metrology Act 2025, which accords the minister very broad discretionary power to make regulations 'which correspond, or are similar, to a provision of relevant EU law for the purpose of reducing or mitigating the environmental impact of products'. It provides power for dynamic EU alignment with little democratic accountability. The criteria for the invocation of such powers are, moreover, open-textured, and the EU law to which UK law may be aligned is framed in broad terms as 'relevant EU law'.[96] There is, moreover, much in post-Brexit environmental law that is executive in nature, as attested to by the importance of policy documents such as environmental improvement plans and policy statements.[97]

(vi) The Territorial Dimension

There are, as noted above, linkages between the territorial dimensions of Brexit addressed in Part I and economic and social divergence/convergence within the UK in a post-Brexit world.

First, and most obvious, there is divergence that flows from the differential treatment of Northern Ireland. A consequence of the desire to ensure the continuance of open borders between Ireland and Northern Ireland was that the latter effectively

[95] Ch 25.
[96] Product Regulation and Metrology Act 2025, s 1(2).
[97] Ch 24.

remained within the Single Market for goods and EU customs arrangements, to which EU law applied. This in turn meant increased regulatory controls for goods travelling between Great Britain and Northern Ireland,[98] with implications for diverse areas, including healthcare.[99] In political terms, the differentiation was unwelcome to the Northern Ireland Unionist Party. In economic terms, it had trade-distortive effects: it undermined Northern Ireland producers, who had to comply with two sets of rules while competing with products subject only to EU rules; and it hindered trade between Great Britain and Northern Ireland, because GB producers that sold into Northern Ireland had to comply with EU rules. The political and economic tensions created by the original version of the NI Protocol were the rationale for the amendments introduced by the Windsor Framework, which was designed, inter alia, to allow some GB goods to enter NI without having to comply with all EU rules, where the risk of their movement to the EU via Ireland was judged to be low. The complexities of the Windsor Framework amendment to the Northern Ireland Protocol, including the provisions on the 'Stormont Brake' and the ways in which the UK government has rendered new EU provisions applicable to NI without always consulting the Northern Ireland Assembly, are charted in subsequent chapters.[100] There is, moreover, a related, albeit distinct, cause of divergence between GB and Northern Ireland, flowing from the repeal or amendment of retained/assimilated EU law. Thus, to the extent that there is an overlap between retained/assimilated EU law and provisions of the Northern Ireland Protocol concerning trade and customs arrangements, any departure in GB from that EU law, with no change in the position in Northern Ireland because of the Protocol, leads to greater divergence between the law in GB and Northern Ireland.

The second territorial dimension that impacts on economic and social divergence relates to legislation enacted by a devolved legislature concerning continued alignment with EU law in a post-Brexit world. It is axiomatic that Scotland, Wales, and Northern Ireland can exercise their devolved powers so as to enact legislation that differs from that in the rest of the UK, provided that they remain within the sphere of their devolved competence. That is indeed the very *raison d'etre* of devolution. The fact that this occurs in a post-Brexit world is not therefore in itself indicative of divergence. What is salient for this study is the enactment of legislation by a devolved legislature designed to ensure continuity with EU law, as exemplified by the UK Withdrawal from the European Union (Continuity) (Scotland) Act 2021, which makes provision for Scottish law to keep pace with EU standards and regulations in devolved areas, even though the UK has left the EU. It empowers Scottish Ministers to make regulations securing such alignment, and obliges them when doing so to maintain or advance standards relating to environmental protection, animal health, plant health, equality and human rights, and social protection. The regulations are subject to the affirmative procedure before the Scottish Parliament and the executive must

[98] Ch 8.
[99] Ch 22.
[100] Chs 8, 9.

report annually on use of the alignment power.[101] The bulk of the UK Withdrawal from the European Union (Continuity) (Scotland) Act 2021 concerns environmental governance, including a framework for environmental principles and the creation of a new body, Environmental Standards Scotland.[102]

The third territorial aspect to economic and social convergence/divergence results from the structure and application of post-Brexit UK legislation. This is manifest most markedly in the United Kingdom Internal Market Act 2020, discussed in preceding sections of this chapter[103] and in other chapters of the book,[104] which reduces regulatory divergence as between the four nations at the expense of the autonomy of the devolved regions. The territorial implications of UK legislation are also evident in other areas, as exemplified by the complexities surrounding the application of the Procurement Act 2023 to the devolved regions. Thus, while the Act is predicated on application to England and Wales, Scotland, and Northern Ireland, and would therefore seem indicative of convergence, the reality is that the exact extent of the Act's application is different in each nation and very complex.[105]

4 Conclusion

There will be no attempt to summarize all findings of this chapter, more especially given that it draws together themes from the rich scholarship in subsequent chapters. Suffice it to say the following. The analytical architecture developed in the preceding pages will, it is hoped, be helpful when reading particular chapters to situate the discussion therein within the broader contours of other subject-matter areas.

It is clear that while exit from the EU signifies 'law unbound' in the literal juridical sense adumbrated at the outset of this chapter, the Withdrawal Agreement and the TCA continue to impose constraints that vary as between different subject-matter areas.

It is also clear that the second sense of 'law unbound' as embodied in the sovereignty claim of regulatory autonomy, epitomized by the Leave campaign's call to 'take back control', is nuanced, both institutionally and substantively. In institutional terms, taking back control has often vested further power in the executive rather than the sovereign legislature, and has accorded increased power to the Westminster legislature/executive, at the expense of those in Scotland, Wales, and Northern Ireland. In substantive terms, the post-Brexit economic and social regulatory landscape is mixed, both within and as between different areas, featuring elements of active divergence,

[101] https://www.parliament.scot/chamber-and-committees/committees/current-and-previous-committees/session-6-constitution-europe-external-affairs-and-culture-committee/business-items/continuity-act.
[102] Ch 24.
[103] Section 2(c).
[104] Chs 7, 9.
[105] Ch 15.

passive divergence, inactive divergence, and continued convergence. This is unsurprising, given the diversity of the subject matter covered within this book, and the plethora of different considerations that shape the emerging law within any one particular area.

The third sense of 'law unbound' that features in the aspirational register found in legal scholarship connoting a sense of wider possibilities is perforce open to rival interpretations, both as to its particular meaning and realization. Viewed from a more abstract perspective, it connotes the loosening of constraint as to the factors that shape and frame the law in a particular area. However, the reality is that there are always constraints, and there are also trade-offs as to the costs and benefits of any particular type of constraint. EU membership perforce imposed limits on national freedom of action, but so too does membership of any club. You cannot belong to a club and expect full decisional autonomy; you cannot expect to win every decisional contest; and you cannot have your cake and eat it too.

There is on reflection an admixture of irony, paradox, and tragedy in the Brexit saga. The irony of Brexit is that during its EU membership there were relatively few instances of serious disagreement by the UK as to the direction of EU policy, and in those instances where it wished to hold back, such as economic and monetary union, or aspects of the area of freedom, security, and justice, the UK secured an opt-out. The paradox of Brexit is that in certain instances, such as illegal migration, it has rendered UK control more difficult and less efficacious than hitherto. The tragedy of the Brexit debate was that the Remain campaign never felt able to present a positive case for EU membership, relying almost exclusively on the deleterious economic consequences that would flow from exit. There have been, and will continue to be, such consequences, as well as some opportunities, but that was only ever part of the story.

It is noteworthy that as this book goes to press, the Labour government is seeking closer ties to the EU, including through legislation that will allow the UK some measure of dynamic alignment with EU regulatory provisions, which can be effectuated through ministerial sponsored secondary legislation. The fate of such initiatives remains to be seen, so too does their longevity given that the Conservative and Reform parties predictably voiced strong opposition to them. Their opposition to the use of secondary legislation to attain such ends has more than a touch of constitutional irony, given the widespread use of statutory instruments, backed up with Henry VIII clauses, in the legislation attendant on Brexit.[106]

[106] For comment, see Mark Elliott, https://publiclawforeveryone.com/2026/04/13/the-constitutional-implications-of-dynamic-alignment-with-eu-rules/.

PART I

THE INSTITUTIONAL

2

The UK Constitution

Alison L. Young[*]

1 Introduction: Plus ça Change?

23 June 2016—the day of the UK's 'Brexit' referendum—is clearly a historical moment. It also had clear political consequences. The then Prime Minister, David Cameron, had campaigned for the UK to remain in the European Union.[1] The majority referendum vote in favour of Leave led to his resignation. The Brexit process also caused the resignation of his successor, Theresa May, following her inability to obtain the support of the House of Commons for the first Withdrawal Agreement negotiated between her government and the European Union.[2]

What is harder to determine is whether the referendum triggered a constitutional moment or crisis, or merely illustrated gaps in the UK's constitution.[3] Brexit did require the UK constitution to find answers to novel questions, filling areas of constitutional silence. Most notably, legal disputes arose as to whether the prerogative power of foreign relations, which includes the power to withdraw from as well as to enter into international treaties, would include a power to withdraw from the EU Treaties, with 11 members of the UK Supreme Court concluding that the prerogative power could not be used.[4]

Brexit was also the catalyst for a series of constitutional firsts or novelties, used to resolve tensions between the institutions of the constitution. For example, it led to the first use of the Fixed-Term Parliaments Act 2011 to hold an early general election on 8 June 2017. In 2019, having failed to obtain the requisite two-thirds majority of the whole House of Commons in favour of an early general election, Parliament passed the Early Parliamentary General Election Act 2019 to hold an early general election on 12 December 2019. Finally, the Dissolution and Calling of Parliament Act 2022

[*] I currently hold the role of Law Commissioner for Public Law and the Law in Wales. This article was written in a personal capacity and does not reflect the views of the Law Commission.

[1] https://www.gov.uk/government/speeches/david-camerons-departing-words-as-prime-minister.

[2] https://www.gov.uk/government/speeches/prime-ministers-statement-in-downing-street-24-may-2019.

[3] See, eg, C Kirkland and S Deva, 'Weakness Not Crisis: Brexit and the UK Constitution' [2023] British Politics 603; D Wincott, G Davies, and A Wager, 'Crisis, What Crisis? Conceptualising Crisis, UK Pluri-culturalism and Brexit Politics' (2021) 55 Regional Studies 9; V Barbé, 'Parliamentary Law and the Institutional Crisis in the UK During Brexit' (2023) 3 International Journal of Parliamentary Studies 94.

[4] *R (Miller) v Secretary of State for Exiting the European Union* (*Miller 1*) [2017] UKSC 5, [2018] AC 61.

Alison L. Young, *The UK Constitution* In: *The UK Regulatory Framework Post-Brexit: 'Law Unbound'*. Edited by: Paul Craig and Vilija Vėlyvytė, Oxford University Press. © Oxford University Press 2026. DOI: 10.1093/9780198969815.003.0003

repealed the 2011 Act, moving the UK back from fixed-term to five-year maximum-term Parliaments where the government requests that the Monarch dissolves Parliament, thereby triggering a general election. The first two were used to resolve a perceived constitutional problem—the concern that a government with a small majority may be unable to shepherd required legislation for Brexit through Parliament, or the impasse created by Parliament blocking the government's proposed plans for Brexit and the defeat of a programme motion for necessary legislation. The 2022 Act demonstrated a policy choice to return the government's ability to request a dissolution of Parliament, tipping the balance of power in favour of the executive over the legislature.

Other changes occurred not through the law, but through changes to parliamentary practices or novel interpretations of parliamentary procedures. Most notable was the use of Standing Order No 24, which provides a Member of Parliament with the opportunity to table an emergency debate.[5] On 3 September 2019, an emergency debate was used to vote on a motion to suspend Standing Order No 14, which prioritises government business, on 4 September 2019. Instead, the day would be used to vote on all three stages of the European Union (Withdrawal) Bill 2019 (No 2)—colloquially referred to as the Benn–Burt Bill—in the House of Commons. The Bill was then agreed to in the House of Lords. The ensuing Act required the then Prime Minister, Boris Johnson, to seek an extension to the negotiation period for a Withdrawal Agreement with the EU, should Parliament fail to vote in favour of the current agreement by a set deadline. This prevented the Prime Minister from implementing his policy choice to leave the EU with no deal should a deal fail to be approved by the House of Commons.

Brexit also posed a daunting legal challenge. With the UK having been a member of the European Union for more than forty years, EU law had become enmeshed in the UK's legal system, with a majority of the UK Supreme Court regarding EU law as a source of domestic law.[6] To leave with no provisions designed to preserve EU law within the UK legal system post-Brexit could give rise to a legal vacuum. However, the whole purpose of Brexit was to enable the UK to enact its own laws, changing EU laws when desirable.

In the immediate aftermath of Brexit, academic commentary drew on the potential of Brexit to provide an opportunity to move the UK away from a political to a legal constitution,[7] or as a moment through which to strengthen the UK's political constitution.[8] Neither fully materialized. The changes to the UK constitution have been more subtle. While the main defining features of the UK constitution remain, there have been changes as to relative powers between the institutions of the UK

[5] https://publications.parliament.uk/pa/cm201719/cmstords/1020/body.html.

[6] *Miller 1* (n 4) [60]–[68].

[7] V Bogdanor, 'Brexit, the Constitution and the Alternatives' (2016) 27 King's Law Journal 314; B Ackerman, 'Why the UK Needs a Written Constitution and Cannot Wait for Parliament to Write One' (2018) 89 Political Quarterly 584; V Bogdanor, *Beyond Brexit: Towards a British Constitution* (Tauris 2019).

[8] M Gordon, 'Parliamentary Sovereignty and the Political Constitution(s): From Griffith to Brexit' (2019) 30 King's College Law Journal 125 and 'Referendums and in the UK Constitution: Authority, Sovereignty and Democracy after Brexit' (2020) 16 European Constitutional Law 213.

constitution and the way in which those occupying roles in these institutions have used these powers. Arguably, this demonstrates a strength of the UK constitution to flex to accommodate what might have otherwise been a constitutional collapse. However, I will also argue that it demonstrates a key weakness in the constitution, particularly as regards its susceptibility to populism. This weakness was not caused by Brexit; rather, Brexit and the Brexit referendum provided the circumstances through which this weakness was illustrated.

This chapter will first set out how the legal change required to enable the UK to exit the European Union without undermining legal certainty provided a subtle means of constitutional change, offering a potential quasi-constitutional protection of liberal market principles. It will then set out how Brexit provided an opportunity for what appears to be a relatively minor modification of the key constitutional principles of parliamentary sovereignty: the separation of powers and the rule of law. The final section will explain how Brexit and the referendum provided for a wider political change in the behaviour of institutions of the constitution, particularly as concerns the dangers of populism.

2 From EU to Assimilated Law

(a) Legal Domestication

The UK is described as a dualist state. Unincorporated international treaties cannot be relied on in a UK court in and of themselves. For a treaty, once ratified, to be relied upon in national courts, it needs to be incorporated into domestic law. This is normally through legislation from the UK Parliament, with the Scottish Parliament, the Senedd Cymru, and the Northern Ireland Assembly also having the power to implement international treaties which fall within their competences. European Union law was incorporated into UK law through the provisions of the European Union Act 1972. This provided for a novel means of incorporation. The Act did not just incorporate the provisions of EU law in existence at the time the UK ratified the EU Treaties and became a member state of the EU.[9] It also provided the means through which future provisions of EU law generated by the EU could be incorporated into UK law.[10]

The European Communities Act 1972 was repealed post-Brexit, this repeal coming into effect on 31 January 2020.[11] Following this date, the UK entered into a transition period, where the UK negotiated its future arrangement with the European Union. During this period, the UK's relationship with the EU was governed by the Withdrawal Agreement. Article 4 of this Agreement required most provisions of EU law to continue to have direct effect and supremacy in the UK, although the UK was

[9] European Communities Act 1972, s 1(2).
[10] ibid s 2(1).
[11] European Union (Withdrawal) Act 2018 (EUWA 2018), s 1 (as originally enacted).

no longer represented in the EU institutions and UK citizens no longer had the right to vote for Members of the European Parliament. This was achieved through the preservation of the effect of the European Communities Act 1972 during this transition period.[12]

The European Union (Withdrawal) Act 2018 (EUWA) provided the means through which provisions of EU law were preserved, as well as ensuring that necessary modifications could be made to UK law to accommodate Brexit, providing the means through which EU laws could be modified post-Brexit. Legal certainty was maintained through the incorporation of a 'snapshot' of EU law as of exit day.[13] This included ensuring that domestic laws enacted under the ECA 1972 would remain in force after this legislation was repealed.[14] However, not all elements of EU law were preserved. Most notably, the EU's Charter of Fundamental Rights and Freedoms did not become part of domestic law.[15] Also, it provided a means through which necessary modifications could be made to UK legislation in order to remedy deficiencies, for example if UK legislation referred to an EU institution or to EU legislation.[16]

EU law became a part of UK law, referred to as retained EU law.[17] Although a form of domestic law, retained EU differed from domestic law. First, the source of retained EU law was different. Retained EU law was either made by the EU institutions[18] or derived from case law of the European Court of Justice.[19]

Second, it had a different status from UK law, being repealed in a different manner. Retained EU law made by the EU institutions was known as retained direct EU law. This was further divided into retained direct principal EU law and retained direct minor EU law. The former referred to provisions of EU law made through the ordinary law-making procedure, which required the consent of the European Parliament and the Council. Its provisions had a similar status to primary legislation, being modified either by an Act of Parliament or by delegated legislation enacted under a Henry VIII clause.[20] The latter referred to all other provisions of direct EU law. They were treated in a similar manner to delegated legislation, capable of being overturned by either primary or secondary legislation.[21] It was also easier for domestic courts to depart from retained EU case law. The UK Supreme Court, and other final courts of appeal, were no longer bound by retained EU case law.[22] This was later expanded to the Court of Appeal and its equivalents.[23]

[12] ibid ss 1A and 1B (as amended by the European Union (Withdrawal Agreement) Act 2020).
[13] ibid ss, 2, 3, and 4 (as originally enacted).
[14] ibid s 2(2)(a) (as originally enacted).
[15] ibid s 5(4).
[16] ibid s 8 (as originally enacted).
[17] ibid s 21 (as originally enacted).
[18] ibid s 3 (as originally enacted).
[19] ibid s 4 and s 6(7) (as originally enacted).
[20] ibid s 7(2) (as originally enacted).
[21] ibid s 7(3) (as originally enacted).
[22] ibid s 6(4) (as originally enacted).
[23] The European Union (Withdrawal) Act 2018 (Relevant Court) (Retained EU Case Law) Regulations 2020.

Third, retained EU law was interpreted differently from domestic law, the 'validity, meaning and effect' being determined in accordance with retained EU case law and retained general principles of EU law.[24] Fourth, retained EU law had a different force from other provisions of domestic law. The 2018 Act preserved the supremacy of EU law as regards conflicts arising between retained EU law and legislation enacted prior to exit day.[25] Consequently, were a conflict to arise with a provision of domestic law enacted prior to 31 December 2022, retained EU law would still be able to disapply or quash that provision.

Since 1 January 2024, retained EU has been renamed as assimilated law.[26] However, not all retained EU law became assimilated law. The Retained EU Law (Revocation and Reform) Act 2023 (REULA) revoked specific retained EU provisions listed in the First Schedule to the Act.[27] The remaining provisions of UK legislation implementing EU law and legislation made by the EU institutions were preserved as assimilated law. However, other provisions of retained EU law—for example, former directly effective provisions of EU law—are no longer part of UK law.[28] Nor are the general principles of EU law.[29]

In addition, the differences between retained EU law and domestic law were removed, with assimilated law more closely resembling domestic law. The meaning of assimilated law is not determined through an analysis of EU case law or the general principles of EU law. Instead, assimilated law that was originally enacted by European Union institutions and did not require implementation by domestic law 'must, so far as possible, be read and given effect in a way which is compatible with all domestic enactments'.[30]

It is also now easier for UK courts to depart from assimilated EU case law than to depart from retained EU law. It is still the case that the Court of Appeal and Supreme Court, and their equivalents, are not bound by assimilated case law. When deciding whether to depart from retained EU case law, these courts applied the test used by the Supreme Court when departing from its own case law—which, although expressed broadly, is exercised cautiously in practice.[31] Since 1 January 2024, the higher court determining whether to depart from assimilated case law must have regard to 'the

[24] European Union (Withdrawal) Act 2018, s 6(3) (as originally enacted). See also *Lipton v BA City Flyer Ltd* [2021] EWCA Civ 454 (per Green LJ). This case was appealed to the Supreme Court, which did not engage with the obiter dictum of the Court of Appeal. See also S Drake and J Shaw, 'Clarifying the Duties of the UK Judiciary Post-Brexit: *Lipton v BA City Flyer Ltd*' (2022) 85 MLR 1261.

[25] EUWA 2018 (n 11) s 5.

[26] Retained EU Law (Revocation and Reform) Act 2023 (REULA 2023), s 5.

[27] ibid s 1.

[28] ibid s 2.

[29] ibid s 4.

[30] EUWA 2018 (n 11) s 5 (A2)(a).

[31] Practice Statement (HL: Judicial Precedent) [1966] 1 WLR 1234, which enables the House of Lords, now the Supreme Court, to depart from its own precedents when 'it is right to do so'.

fact that decisions of a foreign court are not (unless otherwise provided) binding', 'any changes of circumstances which are relevant', and the extent to which the case law 'restricts the proper development of domestic law'.[32] The Act also provides a means by which lower courts can make a reference to a higher court to determine whether assimilated case law should be followed,[33] as well as a means whereby the law officers may refer a case to a higher court and intervene in cases determining whether UK courts should depart from assimilated case law.[34]

It is also easier to repeal assimilated law than it was to repeal retained EU law. All assimilated law can be repealed by both primary and secondary legislation.[35] More fundamentally, REULA abolished the principle of supremacy.[36] Where there is a conflict between domestic law and assimilated direct EU legislation, domestic law prevails, regardless of whether the domestic legislation in question was enacted prior to or after exit day. Where an incompatibility arises, a court must make an incompatibility order as regards assimilated law.[37]

The main purpose of REULA was to facilitate the ability of the UK governments and administrations to modify provisions of assimilated law found in secondary legislation and EU law that had been incorporated into domestic law through secondary legislation. REULA empowers ministers to restate,[38] revoke, and replace these provisions.[39] However, any replacement of assimilated EU law must not increase a regulatory burden.[40] One oddity is that it is possible for the executive, when it considers it appropriate to do so, to provide that the restatements of assimilated law may provide that its provisions have 'an effect that is equivalent to' the supremacy of EU law.[41] Similarly, until 23 June 2026, national authorities have the power to reproduce the effect of directly effective provisions of EU law that would otherwise cease to be assimilated law.[42] It is also possible for national authorities to reproduce an effect equivalent to the supremacy of EU law for these restatements or reproductions.[43] If this effect is preserved, then the restatement of secondary retained EU law has supremacy over domestic law. If the restatement were to conflict with other provisions of domestic law, the court must issue a declaration of incompatibility as regards the other domestic provision.[44]

32 EUWA 2018 (n 11), s 6(5) as amended by the Retained EU Law (Revocation and Reform) Act 2023.
33 ibid s 6A (as amended by the Retained EU Law (Revocation and Reform) Act 2023).
34 ibid s 6B and 6C (as amended by the Retained EU Law (Revocation and Reform) Act 2023).
35 ibid Sched 8, para 3.
36 REULA 2023 (n 26) s 3.
37 EUWA 2018 (n 11) s 6D(2).
38 REULA 2023 (n 26) ss 11 and 12.
39 ibid s 14.
40 ibid s 14(5).
41 ibid s 11(6).
42 ibid s 12(8).
43 ibid s 12(6).
44 EUWA 2018 (n 11) s 6D(2).

(b) A New Internal Market

In addition to ensuring legal continuity post-Brexit, the UK also needed to re-regulate in areas that had previously been regulated through EU laws.[45] The modification that has had the largest constitutional impact is the re-regulation of the UK's internal market. During the UK's membership of the European Union, the UK's market was regulated through EU law provisions. This provided for both negative and positive regulation of the market. To the extent that English, Welsh, Scottish, Northern Irish, or UK law impacted on market access, EU law provisions facilitating the free movement of goods, services, labour, and capital helped to create a common market through negative harmonization. Provisions that impacted on these free movement provisions would be contrary to EU law, unless they were applied equally to domestic goods and were justified as a proportionate restriction on free movement for a legitimate aim. Positive market integration arose from the competence of the EU institutions to enact measures to create and regulate the EU's internal market. These provisions no longer apply in the UK post-Brexit, requiring the provision of an alternative means to regulate an internal market, or to allow for market divergence across England, Scotland, and Wales.[46]

The UK Internal Markets Act 2020 (UKIMA) provides the means through which the UK currently regulates its own internal market. In a manner similar to the EU, UKIMA provides a form of negative harmonization, recognizing the principles of mutual recognition and non-discrimination for goods and services. As such, a good that is able to be sold in either England, Wales, or Scotland can also be sold in the other two nations. However, UKIMA does not fully replicate the EU's internal market. The key differences stem from the UK being a union of nations with a system of asymmetrical devolution, whereas the EU is a grouping of states that transferred competence to supranational institutions of the EU.

First, there are substantive differences. UKIMA does not apply to labour and capital. In addition, there are fewer possible justifications for derogating from free movement provisions.[47] Second, although UKIMA does not place a limit on the capacity of the devolved legislatures to enact provisions that may limit the free movement of goods or services, the practical effect of this legislation is limited. For example, the

[45] The most important provisions can be found in the Fisheries Act 2020, the Agricultural Act 2020, and the Environment Act 2021. In addition, the Trade Act 2021 and the Immigration and Social Security (Withdrawal) Act 2021 provided for the implementation of new Trade Agreements and Immigration provisions post-Brexit.

[46] 'The Windsor Framework' CP806, February 2023 (https://assets.publishing.service.gov.uk/media/63fccf07e90e0740d3cd6ed6/The_Windsor_Framework_a_new_way_forward.pdf) currently regulates the situation in Northern Ireland, requiring Northern Ireland to comply with internal market regulations found in the EU in order to preserve the open land border between Northern Ireland and Ireland.

[47] K Armstrong, 'The Governance of Economic Unionism after the UK Internal Markets Act' (2022) 85 MLR 635; T Horsley, 'Constitutional Reform by Legal Transplantation: The UK Internal Markets Act 2020' (2022) 42 OJLS 1143.

Senedd Cymru might enact legislation prohibiting the manufacture of a specific good in Wales due to safety concerns. If that good were available for sale in Scotland or England, it would have to be made available for sale in Wales too, unless justified as a proportionate restriction on the free movement of goods, even if it could not be manufactured in Wales. This could potentially undermine the effect of the legislation.[48] The same is not true of England. The UK Westminster Parliament enacts legislation for England as well as the UK. If it wished, the Westminster Parliament could modify or repeal the provisions of UKIMA. This is not possible for the devolved legislatures.[49]

Third, there is not the same ability for collaboration and coordination across England, Scotland, and Wales. There is the ability to create common frameworks, formed collaboratively by the governments of England, Scotland, and Wales, through intergovernmental communications. These provide a means through which to ensure market harmonizations through positive means. However, common frameworks are only exempt from the provisions of mutual recognition and non-discrimination when UK government ministers add the common framework to the list of exemptions set out in a Schedule to the Act.[50] This might undermine the aim of collaboration.

UKIMA is a means through which to maintain an internal market in the UK. However, it also marks a change to the UK's constitution, through a statutory commitment to a specific understanding of market economics. The UK's predominantly political constitution, however, had largely left such matters to politics, providing a constitutional framework through which different governments could introduce different market policies. While it is possible for UKIMA to be repealed, if this is recognized as a constitutional statute it may be more difficult to achieve, providing a form of quasi-constitutionalism of a particular understanding of markets and free trade.[51]

3 Constitutional Endurance

The UK constitution is a predominantly political constitution, with a constitutional monarchy formed from a union of states with devolution of power from Westminster to Scotland, Wales, and Northern Ireland. This is as accurate post- as it was pre-Brexit. The UK is still a constitutional monarchy. Brexit did not see a move towards an entrenched constitution. Nor was there a major change to the devolution settlements post-Brexit. Although the Wales Act 2017 did move Wales from a conferred powers to a reserved powers model, this was set in train prior to the Brexit referendum and completed before Brexit. The Northern Ireland Protocol, now the Windsor Framework,

[48] *R (Counsel General for Wales) v Secretary of State for Business, Energy and Industrial Strategy* [2022] EWCA Civ 118; N Kilford, 'The Market Access Principles and the Subordination of Devolved Competence' (2024) 75 NILQ 1.

[49] UK Internal Markets Act 2020, s 54, which adds the Act to the list of those that cannot be modified by the devolved legislatures.

[50] ibid s 10.

[51] Horsley (n 47).

has modified the situation in Northern Ireland. But this has not led to a border poll, giving the people of Northern Ireland the opportunity to vote for Northern Ireland to join Ireland or to remain part of the United Kingdom.

A similar argument can be made when we turn to an analysis of the key constitutional principles of the United Kingdom. The Westminster Parliament still enjoys parliamentary sovereignty. While this may have been challenged prior to Brexit through the recognition of the primacy of directly effective provisions of EU law, it is not the case that Brexit has removed this challenge. There are still some provisions of the Withdrawal Agreement that have direct effect and primacy post-Brexit, posing a similar challenge to parliamentary sovereignty. This challenge was also resolved in a similar manner. Although the EU's Charter of Fundamental Rights and Freedoms was not preserved as either retained or assimilated law, this has had little effect on the protection of the rule of law or human rights in the UK constitution. The relative institutional roles of the legislature, courts, and executive have also remained largely unchanged.

(a) Parliamentary Sovereignty

It may seem odd to argue that parliamentary sovereignty has largely remained unchanged. During the UK's membership of the European Union, the United Kingdom at least partially accepted the primacy of directly effective EU law.[52] To the extent that domestic legislation contradicted directly effective EU law, the former could be disapplied, providing the means through which EU law prevailed.[53] However, the principle of supremacy was not preserved post-Brexit. First, retained EU law only prevailed over domestic law enacted prior to Brexit. From 1 January 2024, domestic law prevails, with the requirement of the courts to make declarations of incompatibility of EU law that contradicts domestic law. Assimilated law is also to be interpreted in a manner so as to be compatible with all domestic law. Legislation also reinforced the status of parliamentary sovereignty. Section 38 of EU (WA) states: 'it is recognised that the Parliament of the United Kingdom is sovereign.'[54] This would appear to indicate a move away from the situation pre-Brexit, where Parliament's sovereignty had been reduced, to a restoration of Parliamentary sovereignty post-Brexit.

However, this is an overly simplistic account. There are situations in which some laws post-Brexit have a similar effect to the supremacy of directly effective provisions of EU law. First, as discussed above, the executive has been given broad powers to revoke, restate, or replace secondary assimilated or retained law. REULA empowered

[52] *R v Secretary of State for Transport, ex p Factortame Ltd* [1990] 2 AC 85; *Thoburn v Sunderland City Council* [2002] EWHC 195 (Admin), [2003] QB 151; *R (HS2 Action Alliance Ltd) v Secretary of State for Transport* [2014] UKSC 3, [2014] 1 WLR 324.

[53] *Benkharbouche v Embassy of the Republic of Sudan* [2017] UKSC 62, [2017] 3 WLR 957.

[54] European Union (Withdrawal Agreement) Act 2020, s 38(1).

the executive, until the end of 2023, to restate secondary retained EU law—that is, secondary legislation that was enacted in order to implement European Union law.[55] If a national authority were to restate secondary retained EU law then, following the restatement of this provision, the provision would not be one that enjoyed supremacy. However, it is possible for the executive, when it considers it appropriate to do so, to provide that the restated secondary retained EU law has 'an effect that is equivalent to' the supremacy of EU law.[56] Similarly, until 23 June 2026, national authorities have the power to reproduce the effect of directly effective provisions of EU law that would otherwise cease to be assimilated law,[57] as well as to restate secondary assimilated law.[58] It is also possible for national authorities to reproduce an effect equivalent to the supremacy of EU law for these restatements or reproductions.[59] If this effect is preserved, then the restatement of secondary retained EU law has supremacy over domestic law. If the restatement were to conflict with other provisions of domestic law, the court must issue a declaration of incompatibility as regards the other domestic provisions.[60]

The bigger challenge to the assertion that Brexit returned sovereignty to the UK Parliament stems from the incorporation of certain provisions of the Withdrawal Agreement, specifically those relating to the rights of EU citizens remaining in the UK post-Brexit and provisions of the Windsor Framework. These provisions have direct effect and primacy in domestic law, through legislative provisions worded in a similar manner to the European Communities Act 1972.

The European Communities Act 1972 provided that 'any enactment passed or to be passed . . . shall be construed and have effect subject to' the provisions of the Act which incorporated EU law into domestic law.[61] Section 7A(1) of EUWA provides for the incorporation of the provisions of the Withdrawal Agreement into domestic law, referring to 'rights, powers, liabilities, obligations and restrictions from time to time created or arising by or under the withdrawal agreement'. Section 7A(2) clarifies that these provisions are to be 'recognised and available in domestic law' and 'enforced, allowed and followed accordingly'. Finally, section 7A(3) sets out that 'every enactment . . . is to be read and has effect subject to subsection (2)'—in other words, that all legislation is to be read and have effect subject to the rights and so on of the Withdrawal Agreement and citizenship provisions which have effect in domestic law.

The impact of this provision was discussed in the recent Supreme Court case of *Allister*, concerning a presumed contradiction between provisions of the then Northern Ireland Protocol, now the Windsor Framework, and Article VI of the Act of Union 1801.[62] *Allister* did not concern a conflict between the provisions of the

[55] EUWA 2018 (n 11) s 11(1) and 11(7).
[56] REULA 2023 (n 26) s 11(6).
[57] ibid s 12(8).
[58] ibid s 12(1).
[59] ibid s 12(6).
[60] EUWA 2018 (n 11) s 6D(2).
[61] European Communities Act 1972, s 2(4).
[62] *Re Allister's Application for Judicial Review (Northern Ireland)* [2023] UKSC 5, [2023] 2 WLR 457.

Windsor Framework and legislation enacted post-Brexit. Nevertheless, the conclusion of the court is instructive as to the impact of Brexit on parliamentary sovereignty. The Supreme Court concluded that, to the extent that there was a conflict between the Act of Union and the Windsor Framework, this conflict was resolved by the wording of section 7A(3) of EUWA. As such, the Act of Union was to be read subject to the provisions of the then Northern Ireland Protocol. Given the similarities between the wording of the 2018 Act and the 1972 Act, were a conflict to arise between the Windsor Framework and later legislation, this too would be resolved in favour of the provisions of the Windsor Framework applying section 7A(3).[63]

The legal position regarding parliamentary sovereignty, therefore, would appear to be unchanged. It is still possible for some aspects of law, specifically the Windsor Framework and citizenship provisions, to disapply UK legislation. In the same way as prior to Brexit, it may be the case that, were an Act of Parliament enacted post-Brexit to specifically state that its provisions take effect notwithstanding the provisions found in the Withdrawal Agreement, this later legislation would prevail. The only difference is as to the breadth of provisions that may disapply an Act of Parliament. During the time of the UK's membership of the EU, directly effective provisions of EU law covered a wider range of potential legal policies. This is limited to a narrow field post-Brexit. Also, as concerns restated provisions of retained or assimilated law, this is a choice of UK institutions, as opposed to being required by EU law.

(b) Other Constitutional Principles

Legally, the balance of powers between the legislature, the executive, and the judiciary remains the same. The legislation used to implement the necessary legal changes post-Brexit did provide sweeping powers to the executive. However, the role of the executive remained the same. Parliament decided to delegate these powers to the executive, including determining any limits on the scope of these executive powers and the extent to which Parliament can scrutinise delegated legislation enacted under these provisions. There may be a difference in the scale of powers delegated to the executive, but there is nothing new in how these powers were obtained or are subject to both political and legal oversight.

Courts were used to determine key issues concerning Brexit. Again, this is best understood as a change in the number of constitutional cases decided by the courts in a relatively short period of time, and a turn to using court cases when political means of challenge appeared to be fruitless. However, the courts determined these cases

[63] K Majewski, '*Re Allister*: The End of "Constitutional Statutes"', UK Const L Blog (21 February 2023) (https://ukconstitutionallaw.org/); M Elliott and N Kilford, 'Nothing to See Here? *Allister* in the Supreme Court' (2024) 28 Edinb L Rev 95; A L Young, '*Re Allister's Application for Judicial Review*: The Importance of Constitutional Wisdom', in L Graham and J Russell (eds), *Public Law in the Supreme Court* (Routledge 2026) 114.

through an analysis of legal principles, with applicants applying to the courts through the usual process of judicial review. Despite being provided with the opportunity to do so, the Supreme Court did not modify the separation of powers by giving legal effect to a constitutional convention, specifically concluding that the Sewel Convention was not legally enforceable in the courts.[64] Nor is there any evidence of the courts extending the scope of their powers to review legislation beyond that currently provided through the Human Rights Act 1998, or through the potential modification of parliamentary sovereignty discussed in the previous section.

Nevertheless, the decision of the Supreme Court in the two *Miller* cases has had an impact on the separation of powers in two ways. First, these cases furthered the extent to which legislation and the common law limit the scope of prerogative powers—that is, those powers that reside in the Crown that stem from the common law as opposed to legislation. In the first *Miller* case, the Supreme Court established that prerogative powers could not be used to modify domestic law or change domestic rights. Nor could they be used to frustrate statutory provisions.[65] In the second *Miller* case, two constitutional principles of the common law—parliamentary sovereignty and parliamentary accountability—were used to limit the scope of a prerogative power.[66]

The recognition of the common law principle of parliamentary accountability illustrates the second change to the separation of powers. The Supreme Court recognized that, as far as the common law was concerned, one of the roles of the legislature is to hold the executive to account. The accountability of the executive to Parliament is supplementary to the accountability of the executive to the courts. The Supreme Court, therefore, provided further support for a checks-and-balances model of the separation of powers in the UK. Coupled with parliamentary sovereignty, this requires Parliament to hold the government to account. The legislature, not the executive, is the most important institution in the UK constitution.

As with the changes to parliamentary sovereignty, the modification of the separation of powers is minimal. It is also difficult to see this arising from Brexit per se. Rather, the circumstances of Brexit provided the opportunity for the Supreme Court to draw on and clarify long-standing principles of the UK constitution to resolve a legal issue concerning the scope of specific prerogative powers. Brexit merely provided an opportunity for the court to clarify its interpretation of the separation of powers.

The *Miller* decisions also provided an opportunity for the courts to uphold the rule of law, demonstrating that the executive has to act within the confines of the law, be this legislation or the common law. However, Brexit has also weakened the rule of law, again in a less dramatic way than some feared. The main change has been through the removal of the EU's Fundamental Charter of Fundamental Rights. This did not provide the main means through which the UK protects human rights. The Charter only

[64] *Miller 1* (n 4) [136]–[151].
[65] *Miller 1* (n 4).
[66] *R (Miller) v Prime Minister, Cherry v Advocate General for Scotland* [2019] UKSC 41, [2020] AC 373.

applied when the UK was acting within the sphere of EU law. Nevertheless, it provided a stronger means of upholding rights, given that UK legislation contravening the provisions of the Charter could be disapplied, whereas that contradicting Convention rights could only be interpreted in a manner compatible with Convention rights and, where this was not possible, be declared incompatible with Convention rights.[67]

The UK's key constitutional principles, therefore, have also stayed largely the same, although the scope of their application may have changed. Also, to the extent that change has occurred, this has often been through the application of long-standing principles of the constitution. Brexit provided an opportunity for case law which provided these clarifications, rather than requiring or providing for these modifications.

4 Constitutional Change

When examined predominantly through a lens of legal rules, institutional roles, and key defining concepts, Brexit appears to have caused little change to the UK constitution. However, a different pattern emerges when we examine the political realities of the relationships between institutions of the constitution. This change in political realities provided the stimulus for a series of potential and actual constitutional changes which had the potential to undermine the rule of law and threaten the stability of the territorial constitution.

(a) The Relationship between the Legislature and the Executive

The Supreme Court in the second *Miller* decision relied on the common law principle of parliamentary accountability. Parliament holds the government to account for its actions. The first phase of the Brexit process appeared to support this description of the separation of powers in the UK constitution. The European Union (Notification of Withdrawal) Act 2017 provided the opportunity for Parliament to empower the executive to notify the EU of the UK's intention to withdraw from the EU Treaties. This provided Parliament with the opportunity to place conditions on the power of the government. However, no conditions were made. The House of Lords had amended the Bill to require a parliamentary vote on the final agreement with the EU. During the debates in the Commons, which rejected this motion, the Secretary of State for Exiting the European Union made a commitment that the 'Government will bring forward a motion on the final agreement to be approved by both Houses of Parliament before it is concluded'.[68]

[67] Human Rights Act 1998, ss 3 and 4. See HRA ss 3 and 4. See *Benkharbouche* (n 53), which illustrates the difference between remedies available under the Human Rights Act 1998 and those available under EU law.

[68] HC Deb vol 623, Col 41 (13 March 2017).

This political promise became section 13 of EUWA, which required that the Withdrawal Agreement and the framework for a future relationship with the EU could not be ratified by the UK unless approved by a resolution of the House of Commons.[69] The House of Lords was also required to debate a motion taking account of the resolution of the House of Commons. Should no agreement be reached, the Act required the government to make statements to the house, these statements in turn being debated by a motion in neutral terms.

This provided for a specific modification to the separation of powers. International treaties are normally negotiated by the UK government. Although the House of Commons has a potential veto power over international agreements, this is almost impossible to apply in practice. The House of Commons can delay the ratification of a Treaty, through continually resolving not to ratify a Treaty. If the House of Lords resolves not to ratify a Treaty, the Treaty can nevertheless be ratified following a ministerial statement and the lack of a vote in the House of Commons against the ratification of the Treaty.[70] These provisions can be difficult to apply in practice, particularly in the House of Commons, where it can be difficult for backbench and opposition MPs to table a motion to vote against the ratification of a Treaty. Section 13, therefore, effectively changed the balance of power over the ratification of a Treaty, placing more power in the hands of the House of Commons.

In addition to modifying the relationship between the executive and the legislature, the so-called meaningful votes triggered by these provisions were part of a pattern of the shifting nature of relations between these two institutions of the constitution over the Brexit process. The House of Commons voted against the first Withdrawal Agreement.[71] This led to a series of events which appeared to move the balance of power between the legislature and the government in favour of the government. There were two further defeats of the Withdrawal Agreement;[72] a series of votes against prevailing government policy on Brexit, alongside a vote in favour of asking for an extension to the Article 50 TEU negotiation period;[73] and indicative votes on the nature of a possible Withdrawal Agreement.[74] There were also two successful Private Members' Bills.[75] The first required the Prime Minister to seek an extension to the Article 50 negotiation period, a policy that was accepted by the Prime Minister before the Bill became an Act. The second set a deadline by which the Commons had to vote in favour of a Withdrawal Agreement, failing which the Prime Minister was required to seek a further extension of the negotiation period. Not only is it incredibly rare for Private Members' Bills to become Acts of Parliament in the UK, but this is only normally

[69] EUWA 2018 (n 11), s 13(1)(b).

[70] Constitutional Reform and Governance Act 2020, ss 20 to 25; A Lang and M Mendez, 'Parliament's Engagement with Treaties' in A Horne, L Thompson and B Yong (eds), *Parliament: Legislation and Accountability* (3rd edn, Hart 2022) Ch 7.

[71] HC Deb vol 652, cols 1020–1129 (15 January 2019).

[72] HC Deb vol 656, cols 208–300 (12 March 2019) and HC Deb vol 657, cols 60–145 (25 March 2019).

[73] HC Deb vol 656, cols 553–654 (14 March 2019).

[74] HC Deb vol 657, cols 825–878, cols 879–885, and cols 893–910 (1 April 2019).

[75] The European Union (Withdrawal) Act 2019 and the European Union (Withdrawal) (No 2) Act 2019.

achieved when the Bill has the backing of the government, rather than changing governmental policy.

The then Prime Minister, Boris Johnson, became frustrated by what he regarded as a 'zombie Parliament'—a Parliament that was unable to achieve the government's policies.[76] Having failed to prorogue Parliament for a period that would have made it impossible for the House of Commons to prevent the UK leaving the EU with no deal, he tried, and failed, to obtain the votes of two-thirds of the members of the House of Commons to trigger an early parliamentary general election, leading to the enactment of the Early Parliamentary General Elections Act 2019, which set a date for the general election on 12 December 2019.

The general election delivered a strong majority for Johnson's conservative government. This changed the relative relationship between the legislature and the executive in favour of the government—in favour of the executive over the legislature. For example, the European Union (Withdrawal Agreement) Act 2020 was passed by the House of Commons in three days—despite the earlier version of this Bill, placed before the House of Commons prior to the early general election, effectively being left in limbo after the House of Commons voted against a programme motion which would have only provided three days of debate on the Bill, perceived as insufficient time to debate such an important Bill.[77] The 2020 Act repealed section 13 of EUWA, removing the requirement for the House of Commons to vote to approve the Withdrawal Agreement as a condition of its ratification,[78] as well as stating that the usual provisions for ratification of an international treaty did not apply.[79] It also provided that a minister may not agree to an extension of the negotiation period.[80]

These events saw a modification and later restoration of the relative balance of powers between the legislature and the executive. Although triggered by Brexit, they did not solely arise due to Brexit. Other factors also played a role. The 2017–19 government did not have a majority. It was a minority government with a confidence-and-supply agreement from a small political party. This made it easier for opposition and backbench MPs to defeat the government. This was combined with Brexit cutting across party lines, meaning that more MPs were willing to vote against party lines. Some felt so strongly about Brexit that they were willing to risk their future careers to prevent a no-deal Brexit. The Private Members' Bills were also only achievable due to the way in which the Speaker was willing to interpret and apply parliamentary standing orders, the Speaker being prepared to defend Parliament even if this meant providing novel interpretations. Article 50 TEU also imposed a timetable on the Withdrawal Process that could not be unilaterally changed by the government.

[76] HC Deb vol 664, cols 774–780 (25 Sep 2019).
[77] HC Deb vol 666 col 825–930 (22 Oct 2019).
[78] European Union (Withdrawal Agreement) Act 2020, s 31.
[79] ibid s 32.
[80] ibid s 33.

This changed the usual position, where the government is in charge of the parliamentary timetable.[81]

Brexit, therefore, did not create a long-term change in the relationship between the executive and the legislature. This may explain why the events of 2019 did not create a long-term modification towards a strong legislature checking the powers of the executive. If anything, they provided a catalyst to modify the balance of powers back to favouring a strong executive, particularly through the repeal of the Fixed-term Parliaments Act 2011. The only possible long-lasting change is to the interpretation of Standing Order No. 24. Having set a precedent for its use, it may open the door to being used in the future as a means through which to facilitate a motion to vote against the ratification of a Treaty or against delegated legislation. However, to date it has not been used for these purposes, it being unlikely to be successful where the government has a large majority in the House of Commons.

(b) The Relationship between Westminster and the Devolved Governments

Legally, the devolution structure that existed prior to Brexit has remained in place. However, as with the nature of the relationship between the legislature and the executive, the relationship between Westminster and the devolved legislatures and governments has changed. Most notably, the Sewel Convention has been put under strain, causing a rebalance of power in practice away from the devolved nations towards Westminster, as illustrated above through the workings of the UK Internal Markets Act 2020.

Tension between the devolved executives and legislatures arose given the outcome of the Brexit vote. Although the UK as a whole voted to leave the European Union, England and Wales voted to leave whereas Scotland and Northern Ireland voted to remain. Following the Brexit vote, Scotland and Wales set out their respective policies on the future relationship with Europe, both of which preferred a future relationship with more engagement between the UK and the EU than the UK government's policy and the eventual outcome of Brexit.[82] The devolution settlement reserved international law to the UK government. There are inter-governmental mechanisms that enable the Westminster government to collaborate with the devolved executives. In particular, the Joint Ministerial Committee (European Negotiations) was formed to facilitate this process. However, this was criticized by the devolved governments for meeting infrequently, and for the fact that the UK government determined

[81] Standing Order No 14.

[82] 'The Scottish Government, Scotland's Place in Europe' (2016), https://www.gov.scot/binaries/content/documents/govscot/publications/corporate-report/2016/12/scotlands-place-europe/documents/00512073-pdf/00512073-pdf/govscot%3Adocument/00512073.pdf and the Welsh Government and Plaid Cymru, 'Securing Wales's Future: Transition from the European Union to a New Relationship' (2017), https://www.gov.wales/sites/default/files/publications/2018-10/white-paper-securing-wales-future.pdf.

when meetings would take place. The Committee was also only a consultative body, meaning that the Westminster government could ignore the views of the devolved governments. The lack of transparency of these meetings also meant that it was hard for others to hold the UK government to account for its actions.

Both the Scottish Parliament and the Senedd Cymru enacted legislation in their own Parliaments to provide an alternative means of preserving EU law in Scotland and Wales.[83] Both originally voted against a legislative consent motion for the UK Parliament's European Union (Withdrawal) Bill, with the Senedd Cymru voting in favour of the Bill following government amendments to the Bill. A number of key pieces of Brexit legislation were enacted without the consent of the devolved legislatures. Evidence presented to the House of Lords Select Committee on the Constitution suggested that Brexit marked a deterioration in the relationship between the UK government and the devolved executives.[84] There is also evidence of a growing pattern of legislation being enacted without the consent of the devolved governments, as well as disagreement between the Westminster and the devolved governments as to the scope of application of the Sewel Convention.[85]

Further tension was evidenced in the desire of the Scottish government to hold a second independence referendum. The first Scottish independence referendum took place after the Westminster government made an order under section 30 of the Scotland Act 1998. The UK government refused to make a further order to enable a second independence referendum, leading to the Scottish government wishing to introduce legislation in the Scottish Parliament to hold a second referendum. However, the Lord Advocate refused to certify the Bill as being within the competence of the Scottish Parliament, leading to a reference to the UK Supreme Court which confirmed that the Bill was beyond competence.[86] Tensions led to the establishment of a new inter-governmental framework, designed to facilitate greater cooperation between Westminster and the devolved governments.[87]

The outcome of the Brexit referendum and tensions during the Brexit negotiations and the implementations of Brexit has created a change in inter-governmental relations. However, while Brexit was the catalyst for these changes, the Covid-19 pandemic facilitated the improvement of inter-governmental relations. The pandemic required cross-UK cooperation on issues of health policy, which is devolved to Scotland, Wales, and Northern Ireland. However, issues remain as to the scope of

[83] The European Union (Legal Continuity) (Scotland) Bill 2018 and the Law Derived from the European Union (Wales) Act 2018.

[84] House of Lords, Select Committee on the Constitution, 'Respect and Co-operation: Building a Stronger Union for the 21st Century', 10th Report of Session 2021–22, HL Paper 142.

[85] House of Lords Select Committee on the Constitution, 'The Governance of the Union: Consultation, Co-operation and Legislative Consent', 1st Report of the Session of 2024–25, HL Paper 13, Ch 4. See also S Tierney, 'The Territorial Constitution and the Brexit Process' (2019) 72 CLP 59.

[86] *Reference by the Lord Advocate of Devolution Issues under paragraph 34 of Schedule 6 of the Scotland Act 1998* [2022] UKSC 31, [2022] 1 WLR 5435.

[87] https://assets.publishing.service.gov.uk/media/61df0068e90e07037ba76b4c/The_Review_of_Intergovernmental_Relations.pdf.

the Sewel Convention and the extent to which Westminster legislation continues to be implemented without the consent of the devolved governments and legislatures. Recent decisions of the Supreme Court have also raised concerns of a move towards muscular unionism, with a strong protection of parliamentary sovereignty having an impact on the perception of the horizontal division of power in the UK.[88]

(c) The Relationship between Courts and the Executive

It is perhaps unsurprising that litigants turned to the courts as a potential means of challenging decisions of the executive concerning Brexit. This use of the court to resolve issues of constitutional uncertainty provided an indirect challenge to parliamentary sovereignty, while reinforcing the rule of law. The *Miller* cases were regarded by some academics as a potential challenge to parliamentary sovereignty as they provided an opportunity for the court to determine key constitution principles without the input of the legislature.[89] In turn, they provided an opportunity to reinforce the rule of law. The law provided clear limits on the powers of the executive, including through the common law placing limits on the scope of prerogative powers.

Following the 2019 general election, the incoming government was elected on a manifesto which included a commitment to 'update the Human Rights Act and administrative law', focusing on redressing a perceived move towards stronger rights protections, promising to ensure that judicial review 'is not abused to conduct politics by another means'.[90] There were two main reviews designed to achieve these objectives: independent reviews of the Human Rights Act 1998[91] and of judicial review.[92]

The latter had minimal impact, giving rise to the Judicial Review and Courts Act 2022, which modified one area of judicial review. The former gave rise to a further government consultation exercise,[93] leading to the British Bill of Rights Bill 2020. The Bill was designed to weaken the connection between UK courts and the European Court of Human Rights.[94] It also proposed to weaken the extent to which courts could protect rights, removing the requirement, found in section 3 of the Human Rights Act 1998 (HRA), that courts should interpret legislation, so far as it is possible to do so, in a

[88] M Elliott and N Kilford, 'The Supreme Court's Defence of Unqualified Law-making Power: Parliamentary Sovereignty, Devolution and the Scotland Act 1998' (2021) 81 CLJ 4.

[89] M Gordon, 'The Prorogation Case and the Political Constitution', UK Const L Blog (30 Sept 2019) (https://ukconstitutionallaw.org/); S Tierney, 'Prorogation and the Courts: A Question of Sovereignty', UK Const L Blog (17 Sep 2019) (https://ukconstitutionallaw.org/).

[90] Conservative Party, 'Our Plan: Manifesto 2019', 48 (https://cchq2019.webflow.io/our-plan).

[91] The Independent Human Rights Act Review, https://www.gov.uk/guidance/independent-human-rights-act-review.

[92] The Independent Review of Administrative Law, https://www.gov.uk/government/consultations/judicial-review-reform.

[93] Ministry of Justice, 'Human Rights Act Reform: a Modern Bill of Rights. A Consultation to reform the Human Rights Act 1998' CP 588, December 2021, https://consult.justice.gov.uk/human-rights/human-rights-act-reform/supporting_documents/humanrightsreformconsultation.pdf.

[94] Bill of Rights Bill 2022, clauses 1 and 3.

manner compatible with Convention rights,[95] while retaining the power of the courts to make a declaration of incompatibility.[96] Other provisions of the Bill made it harder for courts to protect positive rights;[97] required courts to regard that Parliament, when passing any legislation, had decided that this legislation 'strikes an appropriate balance' between rights and legitimate interests;[98] and gave 'the greatest possible weight to the principle that, in a Parliamentary democracy' any decision as to the balance between rights and other interests 'should be properly made by Parliament'.[99]

However, the Bill of Rights Bill did not proceed beyond its first reading. In June 2023, the then Lord Chancellor, Alex Chalk, announced to the House of Commons that the government no longer wished to proceed with the Bill.[100] Nevertheless, future legislation was enacted which provided a weakening of the protection of human rights in specific areas, most notably in immigration law[101] and prisoners' rights.[102]

Academic commentary has also pointed to a modification in the behaviour of the judiciary, with a greater recognition of the constitutional role of the courts requiring a process of checking the executive, which does not require the courts to stray into a determination of policy.[103] This is a further indication of a pattern of a perceived change in behaviour, with courts providing a strong protection of the rule of law during the Brexit process, followed by a reaction of the executive that the courts were straying too far into the domain of politics, and a perception, by some, of a move away from a strong protection of rights by the courts.

However, as with other accounts of modifications in the behaviour of institutions of the constitution, these changes are not a result of the Brexit process alone. Rather, they arise from a combination of the referendum, a minority government, and an ensuing strong majority government. This could be explained as a normal pattern of behaviour in the UK constitution. Any perceived changes are more a result of a government wishing to use its control of Parliament to initiate legislative changes to implement its particular vision of the UK constitution. These changes are then open to further modification if a government of a different political persuasion gains a majority in Parliament and can, therefore, enact legislation implementing a different constitutional vision, including through the way in which that government exercises its powers. However, there are also concerns that Brexit has instigated deeper changes to the UK constitution.

[95] ibid clause 1(2)(b) and Sched 5, para 2.
[96] ibid clause 10.
[97] ibid clause 5.
[98] ibid clause 7(2)(a).
[99] ibid clause 7(2)(b).
[100] HC Deb, vol 735, col 145 (27 June 2023).
[101] For example, both the Illegal Migration Act 2023 and the Safety of Rwanda (Asylum and Immigration) Act 2024 contain provisions which specifically exclude s 3 of the Human Rights Act 1998.
[102] The Victims and Prisoners Act 2024 specifically excludes s 3 of the Human Rights Act 1998 as regards determinations of certain rights of prisoners.
[103] L Graham, 'Has the Supreme Court Become More Restrained in Public Law Cases?' (2024) 87 MLR 1073.

5 Populism or Business as Usual?

The main threat to the constitutional principles of the UK came not from Brexit per se but from the use of the referendum, which supported a policy choice that was not the same as that of a majority of members of Parliament. This challenged the traditional understanding of parliamentary sovereignty in the UK constitution. While the sovereignty of Parliament may be justified as a means of upholding the political sovereignty of the people, the role of the people is normally relegated to participation in elections.[104] The referendum modified the role of the people. Although the Brexit referendum was only advisory, it was regarded as politically binding. The 2019 early parliamentary general election provided a further opportunity to reinforce the outcome of the referendum. The election was motivated, at least in part, by a desire to achieve Brexit and a belief held by the Prime Minister and his government that the wishes of the people to achieve Brexit were being thwarted by Parliament.[105] This provided an opportunity for the UK constitution to move towards populism.

Populism is an elusive concept. Nevertheless, it has three key features. First, populism focuses on the importance of the will of the people. Political decisions are made and supported because they are cast as decisions that implement the will of the people. Second, populism favours popular as opposed to parliamentary sovereignty. Third, populism is agonistic. It relies on antagonism between the people and elite institutions. Populist leaders argue that they alone represent the will of the people. Other institutions of the constitution—such as the legislature or the courts—represent elite institutions designed to control populist leaders, preventing them from implementing the will of the people. Populism does not regard politics as a means of finding consensus. Rather, it sees politics as an agonistic process, thriving on conflict and disagreement where the will of the people triumphs over the will of the elites.

In addition to these key features, populist leaders homogenize the will of the people, selecting one group of the people as representing the true will of the people, rather than recognizing that 'the people' are often composed of a wide range of groups and interests. Populist leaders also often use rhetoric as opposed to deliberation.[106] Political decisions reflect emotions and dismiss the claims of experts regarding the correct solution. These two further elements are regarded as explaining why populism harms democracy and why it can give rise to authoritarian governments.[107]

There were clear signs of populism throughout the Brexit process.[108] However, Brexit provided the circumstances in which inherent weaknesses of the UK

[104] M Gordon, 'Parliamentary Sovereignty and the Political Constitution(s): From Griffith to Brexit' (2019) 30 Kings College Law Journal 125.

[105] AL Young, *Unchecked Power? How Recent Constitutional Reforms Are Threatening UK Democracy* (Bristol University Press 2024) Ch 1.

[106] J-W Müller, *What is Populism?* (University of Pennsylvania Press 2016).

[107] Young (n 105) Ch 2.

[108] Young (n 105).

constitution led to a weakening of checks and balances. Many of these checks and balances rely on those who constitute the executive, legislature, and judiciary acting in a particular manner. A reliance on acting in line with the wishes of the people provided an opportunity for those in power to advocate an undermining of these checks and balances in order. The will of the people was more important than the controls of experts or elites, such as the legislature and the courts.

In the aftermath of Brexit, some of the checks and balances have been restored. The general election of 2024 also returned a large majority government of a different political persuasion from the previous one. This has seen a continence in a change of behaviour that was initiated by the previous government under the Prime Ministership of Rishi Sunak. For example, the new Ministerial Code provides for a stronger role of the Independent Adviser on Ministerial Interests, enabling them to conduct investigations of their own initiation into alleged breaches of the Code.[109] This helps to provide a better means through which to oversee the behaviour of ministers, rather than merely relying on the Prime Minister to decide whether an alleged breach of the code is serious enough to warrant investigation. Although provisions which limited human rights protections have not been overturned, their effect has been minimised through policy changes regarding immigration laws. There is also less evidence of the use of rhetoric following the resignation of Boris Johnson as Prime Minister.

These events perhaps mark a different, more positive impact of Brexit on the UK constitution. The Brexit referendum and the Brexit process illustrated the thin line between features of the UK's predominantly political constitution and populism. In doing so, it illustrated the need for an effective constitutional balance between the legislature, the executive, and the courts, as well as between Westminster and the devolved Parliaments and governments. This experience may provide a means of shoring up the UK constitution, through illustrating the potential dangers of populism.

6 Conclusion

Despite the legal, political, and constitutional impacts of Brexit, key features of the UK constitution have largely remained unchanged. The UK is still a predominantly political constitution, with legal checks and balances over the executive, which largely uphold the sovereignty of Parliament. It remains a constitutional monarchy, with powers devolved to Scotland, Wales, and Northern Ireland. Although there have been changes in the way in which institutions of the constitution act, including a move towards granting more power to the executive and threats to reduce the powers of the court to check the powers of the executive and uphold human rights, Brexit did not cause a major constitutional change. Where change did occur, it was either marginal, or has been partially changed back, or was caused by factors other than Brexit

[109] Ministerial Code, para 2.6.

alone. This is true, for example, in the changed nature of the relationship between Westminster and the devolved legislatures and governments.

Nevertheless, the Brexit process illustrated the thin line between the UK's predominantly political, centralized constitution and populism. The outcome of the referendum, which diverged from that wanted by a majority of MPs at the time, provided an opportunity for populism to take hold. Populism is agonistic. So is the Westminster Parliament. However, whereas populism relies on popular sovereignty and the will of the people overriding the will of elitist institutions, the UK constitution is grounded on parliamentary sovereignty, supplemented by experts deliberating on political choices to provide political as well as legal checks over government, which normally has a strong majority in Parliament. The referendum provided a means for populism to cause a split between the people and the elites, giving rise to an opportunity for political actors to rely on rhetoric and to homogenize the will of the people, pushing the UK towards a populist government.

This experience may provide the opportunity for deeper reflection on the nature of the UK's constitution, particularly as regards the need to uphold political and legal checks and balances, as well as to engage in more deliberative policy making that is also more able to reach out to and reflect the wishes of the many diverse groups found in the UK. Only time will tell whether this will lead to further change in the UK constitution or provide a roadmap for future populist turns.

3
Parliament

Gavin Phillipson

> *Factortame* is still in play since the rights and obligations under the Withdrawal Agreement must prevail over any inconsistent domestic law.[1]

1 Introduction: Parliament Unbound?

The purpose of this chapter is to provide an answer to the following, specific question. What lessons can we draw from the UK's membership of the EU and recent case law on the Withdrawal Agreement[2] for a long-debated issue: can Parliament, to any degree, 'bind its successors?' It gives an answer to that question in the form of seven propositions, which I summarize at the outset, and defend in the chapter as a whole. The seven propositions are as follows.

Proposition 1: We now know that Parliament may, through the use of sufficiently clear words, indicate that a given statute cannot be implicitly displaced or repealed simply by the subsequent enactment of legislation inconsistent with it. Acts that contain such 'priority rules'[3] may usefully be referred to as 'constitutional statutes',[4] precisely because they have this elevated status. Laws LJ in *Thoburn*[5] was right that this is the legal *effect* of a statute being recognized as 'constitutional'. However (*Proposition 2*), his assertion that *only* the common law can bestow this elevated status onto statutes—an argument endorsed by several leading scholars[6] to critique the Divisional Court decision in *Miller I*[7]—has always been wrong.

[1] *Re NIHRC's Application* [2024] NIKB 44, [57] (hereafter '*NIHRC*').
[2] Agreement on the withdrawal of the United Kingdom of Great Britain and Northern Ireland from the European Union and the European Atomic Energy Community, [2019] OJ C384 I/01.
[3] This is Mark Elliott's useful phrase: see his 'Sovereignty, Primacy and the Common Law Constitution: What Has EU Membership Taught Us?' in M Elliott, J Williams, and A Young, *The UK Constitution after Miller: Brexit and Beyond* (Hart 2018) 225 (hereafter 'Elliott').
[4] As seen below, this was first postulated in *Thoburn* (n 5); accepted in dicta of the Supreme Court in *H v Lord Advocate* [2012] UKSC 24, [32], per Lord Hope, and considered further in *R (HS2 Alliance Ltd) v Secretary of State for Transport* [2014] UKSC 3, esp. [207] (hereafter '*HS2*').
[5] *Thoburn v Sunderland City Council* [2002] EWHC 195 (Admin); [2003] QB 151 (hereafter '*Thoburn*').
[6] D Feldman, 'Brexit, the Royal Prerogative, and Parliamentary Sovereignty' UK Const L Blog (8 Nov 2016); Mark Elliott and Hayley Hooper, 'Critical Reflections on the High Court's Judgment in *R (Miller) v Secretary of State for Exiting the European Union*' UK Const L Blog (7 Nov 2016).
[7] *R (Miller) v Secretary of State for Exiting the European Union* [2016] EWHC 2768, [2017] 1 All ER 158.

Gavin Phillipson, *Parliament* In: *The UK Regulatory Framework Post-Brexit: 'Law Unbound'*. Edited by: Paul Craig and Vilija Vėlyvytė, Oxford University Press. © Oxford University Press 2026. DOI: 10.1093/9780198969815.003.0004

Proposition 3: We now know that provisions in two statutes had or have this elevated status—the European Communities Act 1972 (ECA) and the European Union (Withdrawal) Act 2018 (EUWA), as amended. Such status is confirmed by the fact that the courts have given effect to the priority rules in both these statutes via the actual disapplication of subsequent legislation inconsistent with them: in relation to the ECA, in *Factortame*;[8] in relation to EUWA the disapplication, in *Dillon*,[9] of key parts of the Northern Ireland Legacy Act 2023.

Proposition 4: Such priority rules thus have effect, but only for as long as they are in force. They are subject either to ordinary express repeal—which removes them permanently—or to express *suspension (disapplication)* by a subsequent statute via what are known as 'notwithstanding clauses' (provisions that direct the courts to apply this statute 'notwithstanding' the priority rule in the earlier statute). The latter point is not established definitively by case law, but will be argued to be by far the most plausible interpretation of that case law. Hence the effect of these priority rules in legislation is to impose a requirement of linguistic *form—express* repeal or disapplication—on future Parliaments.

Proposition 5: It follows that the *only* change these constitutional statutes and decisions on them have made is to the judge-made rule of implied repeal, whose application to those statutes they suspend. Hence the dramatic claims by Wade that such suspension in *Factortame* amounted to a legal revolution[10] or—pace Nick Barber—'the death of parliamentary sovereignty'[11] are wide of the mark. Since such statutes leave Parliament free to repeal or amend any law through its ordinary procedures, they leave the core of parliamentary sovereignty wholly untouched.

Proposition 6: It remains an open question whether the common law may *additionally* badge certain statutes as constitutional because of the importance of their subject matter, *à la Thoburn*. While the post-Brexit decision of *Allister* lends no active *support* to this claim, it does *not*—contrary to some views[12]—refute or undermine it. Finally, we have *Proposition 7*: Parliament's proven ability to impose such requirements of form must be sharply distinguished from the *theory* that it can also impose requirements of 'manner'—better referred to, following Goldsworthy, as imposing binding restrictive *procedures* on its future self, via for example referendum locks or requirements for two-thirds majorities.[13] For this and other reasons, this chapter will

[8] *R v Secretary of State for Transport, ex p Factortame Ltd* (No 2) [1991] 1 AC 603 (hereafter 'Factortame'). Other examples of disapplication include *R v Secretary of State for Employment ex p EOC* [1995] 1 AC 1; *Benkharbouche v Secretary of State for Foreign and Commonwealth Affairs* [2017] UKSC 62.

[9] *In re Dillon and others—NI Troubles (Legacy and Reconciliation) Act 2023* [2024] NICA 59 ('*Dillon*'), on appeal from judgment of the High Court: [2024] NIKB 11.

[10] HWR Wade, 'Sovereignty—Revolution or Evolution?' (1996) 112 LQR 568.

[11] N Barber, 'The Afterlife of Parliamentary Sovereignty' (2011) 9(1) *I*CON* 144; *The United Kingdom Constitution* (Oxford University Press 2021) 56 and Ch 5 generally.

[12] K Majewski, '*Re Allister*: The End of Constitutional Statutes', UK Const L Blog (21 Feb 2023), https://ukconstitutionallaw.org/.

[13] J Goldsworthy, *Parliamentary Sovereignty: Contemporary Debates* (Cambridge University Press 2010) Ch 7 ('Goldsworthy, *Debates*').

argue, *contra* Mike Gordon, that the phrase 'manner and form' should be consigned to the constitutional dustbin:[14] the two pathways are categorically distinct and should be kept firmly apart in future analysis.

In order to defend these propositions, this chapter will first briefly rehearse the challenge to Diceyan orthodoxy posed by the *Factortame* saga, and the radically different interpretation of that saga suggested in *Thoburn*. It will then turn to *Miller I*[15] and the important but, I will argue, largely overlooked light that the judgments in that case shed on these issues. The chapter will then consider three important post-Brexit cases that examine the continuing effect on parliamentary sovereignty of key provisions of the main Brexit legislation—EUWA 2018, as amended by the European Union (Withdrawal Agreement) Act 2020, which gives effect to the Withdrawal Agreement between the UK and the EU (WA). It will argue that the decisions in *NIHRC* and *Dillon* shed clear light both on what happened in *Factortame* and on the position we have now reached, post-Brexit, with 'constitutional statutes' and their suspension of implied repeal. This section will also explain why, as contended above, the Supreme Court decision in *Allister*[16] does *not* spell the death-knell of the constitutional statute,[17] and actually leaves that notion undisturbed. Finally, it will turn to Proposition 7, to make the argument that the above developments should *not* be read as opening the door to the 'manner and form' school, at least in what I will contend is its controversial form.

2 Diceyan Orthodoxy and the EU Supremacy Challenge

Under the traditional doctrine of the 'positive' and 'negative' aspects of parliamentary sovereignty, the following propositions were advanced by Dicey, and are still taught to law students to this day.[18] Dicey defined the negative aspect as follows:

(a) no person or body outside Parliament is recognized by the law as having a right to override or set aside any legislation of Parliament at all.

[14] *Parliamentary Sovereignty in the UK Constitution: Process, Politics and Democracy* (Hart 2015) (hereafter 'Gordon'). While I disagree with much of Gordon's analysis, this book in my view remains by far the most subtle, nuanced, and erudite modern defence of the 'manner and form' theory of parliamentary sovereignty.

[15] *R (Miller) v Secretary of State for Exiting the European Union* [2017] UKSC 5; [2017] 2 WLR 583 (hereafter '*Miller I*').

[16] *Re Allister and Others v Secretary of State for Northern Ireland* [2023] UKSC 5 ('*Allister*').

[17] As contended by K. Majewski, '*Re Allister*: The End of Constitutional Statutes', UK Const L Blog (21 Feb 2023), https://ukconstitutionallaw.org/.

[18] AV Dicey, *An Introduction to the Study of the Law of the Constitution* (10th edn, Macmillan 1959) 40.

The positive aspect was said to entail three further propositions, of which the first two are material:

(b) there is no law which Parliament cannot change;
(c) there is therefore no distinction between constitutional and other laws.

(a) Factortame

Paul Craig's chapter in this volume explains the details of the *Factortame* judgments and readers unfamiliar with them are referred to that account.[19] In brief, section 2 of the European Communities Act 1972 (ECA) gave domestic effect to the corpus of EU law as it existed 'from time to time', without the need for further enactment, and, famously, section 2(4) provided that all UK statutes, including those 'to be passed', would take effect 'subject to' the requirements of directly effective EU law. This is what was referred to above as the 'priority rule' established in the ECA. Section 2(4) thus purported to change in some way the normal rule under which such subsequent statutes would have 'impliedly repealed' the application of inconsistent provisions of EU law in the UK, and/or the provisions of the ECA that gave them domestic effect. How significant this was only became apparent when the famous *Factortame* litigation arose, and the UK courts 'disapplied' a statute passed sixteen years after the ECA—the Merchant Shipping Act 1988—because of its incompatibility with EU law. The starkly different contemporary reactions to this remarkable ruling are well known, ranging from William Wade's characterization of what had happened as a peaceful 'revolution'[20] to Trevor Allan's measured response arguing that it was merely a sensible 'evolution', with many other views in between.[21] What is striking, reading the literature now, is how polarized views remain, nearly forty years later. Nick Barber for example has a quasi-Wadean view of *Factortame* as representing 'the death of parliamentary sovereignty';[22] in contrast, his Oxford colleague Richard Ekins has most recently reiterated his stout denial that Britain's membership of the EU saw even a modest adjustment to Diceyan orthodoxy.[23] As already indicated, I will argue that recent decisions make reasonably clear that the change brought about in *Factortame* was a relatively modest and pragmatic adjustment to the rule of implied repeal only. While Barber and others appear to assume that the rule of implied rule is an inherent and important aspect of parliamentary sovereignty, I will follow Goldsworthy[24] in arguing the contrary.

[19] Ch 6.
[20] Wade (n 10).
[21] TRS Allan, 'Parliamentary Sovereignty: Law, Politics and Revolution' (1997) 113 LQR 443.
[22] Barber (n 11). Barber refines this dramatic claim as referring only to the 'old view' of sovereignty, but in my view even this attaches undue importance to the doctrine of implied repeal.
[23] 'Legislative Freedom and its Consequences' in R Johnson and Y Yi Zhu (eds), *Sceptical Perspectives on the Changing Constitution of the United Kingdom* (Hart 2023). He expounds this position more comprehensively (though in this author's view still implausibly) in 'Legislative Freedom in the United Kingdom' (2017) 133 LQR, 582–605.
[24] J Goldsworthy, *The Sovereignty of Parliament: History and Philosophy* (Oxford University Press, 1999) 14–15 ('hereafter 'Goldsworthy, *History*').

(b) The Alternative Analysis in *Thoburn*: The ECA as But One in a Category of Statutes Recognized as 'Constitutional' by the Common Law

Before going any further, we must briefly remind ourselves of the highly influential analysis of Laws LJ in *Thoburn* of what had happened in *Factortame*, and how sharply it differs from the explanation judicially proffered in *Factortame* itself. As Paul Craig has explained, Lord Bridge's reasoning in that decision was 'explicitly grounded on the idea that the decision concerning [the adjustment to] sovereignty was made by Parliament and not the courts'[25]—characterized as Parliament's 'voluntary acceptance' of some degree of limitation on its sovereignty as the necessary price for joining the European club. Laws LJ in *Thoburn* rejected this approach, and argued for an entirely different explanation. He claimed first that 'the House of Lords [in *Factortame*] effectively accepted that section 2(4) [ECA] could not be impliedly repealed'—so that it continued to give domestic effect even to provisions of EU law incompatible with the later 1988 Act. This meant, he said, that the 'ECA is a constitutional statute: that is, it cannot be impliedly repealed'.[26] However, crucially, he argued that this result 'derived, *not* from EU law, but purely from the law of England: the *common law* recognises a category of constitutional statutes'. These he defined as those that importantly 'condition the relationship between the individual and the state' or affect 'fundamental constitutional rights'.[27] Laws LJ went on to suggest that the ECA was but one among a class of constitutional statutes, which, he said, included among other examples 'the Magna Carta, the Bill of Rights 1689, the Act of Union, the Reform Acts [on the franchise], the Human Rights Act 1998, the Scotland Act 1998 and the Government of Wales Act 1998'.[28] Such constitutional statutes, Laws LJ wrote, can only be repealed by express words or 'words so specific that the inference of an actual determination to effect the result contended for [is] irresistible'.[29]

Crucially, he was insistent that it was *only* the common law that could recognize and denote a statute as 'constitutional'. This, he claimed, was because:[30]

> The Legislature cannot, according to our constitution, bind itself as to the form of subsequent legislation, and it is impossible for Parliament to enact that in a

[25] P Craig, 'Sovereignty of the United Kingdom Parliament after Factortame' [1991] YBEL 221, 252. Of course, as Craig shrewdly acknowledges, this was doubtless partly because the judges did not wish to be seen as having taken a political choice 'at 'the boundary of the legal system' (quoting HWR Wade, 'The Basis of Legal Sovereignty' [1955] CLJ 186, 192, 196).

[26] *Thoburn* (n 5) [69].

[27] ibid [62]. The full quote defines a constitutional statute as 'one which (a) conditions the legal relationship between citizen and State in some general, overarching manner, or (b) enlarges or diminishes the scope of what we would now regard as fundamental constitutional rights' (ibid).

[28] ibid.

[29] ibid [63].

[30] ibid [42], citing well-known *obiter* of the Court of Appeal in *Ellen Street Estates v Minister of Health* [1934] 1 KB 590, 597.

> subsequent statute dealing with the same subject-matter there can be no implied repeal.

The claim, then was that Parliament[31]

> *cannot* stipulate against implied repeal any more than it can stipulate against express repeal . . . The British Parliament has not the authority to authorise any such thing. Being sovereign, it cannot abandon its sovereignty.

I have previously critiqued this reasoning,[32] arguing that the remarkable equation Laws LJ makes here, of restrictions on express and implied repeal, cannot withstand analysis: the former would amount to a substantive restriction on the freedom of action of future Parliaments, while the latter is a mere requirement of linguistic form, which leaves Parliament free to repeal any law. I also pointed out that Laws LJ himself appears to accept in *Thoburn* that the suspension of implied repeal by the common law in relation to those Acts the courts deem to have the status of 'constitutional statutes' 'preserves the sovereignty of the legislature'. This makes a nonsense of his suggestion that, were *Parliament* to stipulate against implied repeal, it would somehow be 'abandon[ing] its sovereignty'.[33] And this in turn completely undermines his claim that implied repeal *can* be suspended, but *only* by the courts, not Parliament itself.[34]

Having rehearsed these points, we can now turn to the fresh light shed by *Miller I* on this controversy.

3 Overlooked Lessons from *Miller I*

(a) *Miller I*: Suspension of Implied Repeal via Parliamentary Intention

Barber notes that Lord Bridge's statement in *Factortame* that provisions of EU law 'should be treated as supreme in those areas to which they apply'[35] 'coyly left open the possibility' that courts might later 'conclude that this scope was limited by aspects of

[31] *Thoburn* (n 5) [59].

[32] G Phillipson, 'EU Law as an Agent of National Constitutional Change: *Miller v Secretary of State for Exiting the European Union*' (2017) 36(1) YBEL 46, 87–90; available https://doi.org/10.1093/yel/yex012.

[33] ibid 90. The 'preserves the sovereignty' claim is in *Thoburn* (n 5) [64].

[34] My argument here is distinct from Wade's famous contention that the norm of parliamentary sovereignty is a rule that, uniquely, 'can stand against a statute' because, while, on one level, being a rule of common law, it is at a deeper level 'the ultimate political fact upon which the whole system of legislation hangs' and hence a norm beyond the reach of Parliament: Wade (n 25) 186–89. My argument, in contrast, is confined *only* to the rule of implied repeal, which I contend is a useful rule giving practical effect to sovereignty, but not essential to it.

[35] *Factortame No 2* (n 8) 659.

the UK constitution'.[36] This indeed is precisely what the courts concluded in *Miller I*. As the Supreme Court, in an important passage in that judgment, wrote:[37]

> [L]egislation which alters the domestic constitutional status of EU institutions or of EU law is not constrained by the need to be consistent with EU law. In the case of such legislation, there is no question of EU law having primacy, so that such legislation will have domestic effect even if it infringes EU law (and that would be true whether or not the 1972 Act remained in force).

This first of all firmly puts to bed the most more radical interpretations of *Factortame* suggested at the time, whereby, as Elliott puts it,[38]

> the EU legal system and the primacy it enjoys [were] understood to have overwhelmed, or inundated, the domestic legal system: the latter has become subservient to the former; the rules of the constitutional game are laid down no longer by domestic but by EU law; and EU law thus *always* trumps domestic law.

Under this view, the only way to have reversed this position, restoring the primacy of UK statute law, would have been withdrawal from the EU.[39] The passage just quoted plainly rebuts this suggestion, by clarifying that Parliament had always been capable of modifying 'the domestic constitutional status of EU law' during the UK's membership of the EU, regardless of the ECA. In doing so, the Supreme Court thereby followed, while fleshing out, the *obiter* suggestions by the Court in *HS2* that 'the application of [the EU law] doctrine [of the supremacy of EU law] in *our* law depends upon the [ECA] 1972';[40] hence, clashes between EU law and fundamental domestic constitutional principles would necessarily be 'resolved by our courts as an issue arising under the constitutional law of the United Kingdom'.[41] We may also recall that this position had been expressly affirmed by Parliament in 2011 in a provision which stated in terms that 'directly applicable or effective EU law . . . falls to be recognised and available in law in the United Kingdom *only* by virtue of [the 1972] Act or [under] any other Act'.[42]

Thus, this provision, *Miller I*, and the above dicta from *HS2* all agree that the status of EU law in domestic law throughout remained a matter of UK constitutional law that Parliament could change at any time. As the majority in *Miller I* bluntly put it: EU

[36] Barber, *The UK Constitution* (n 11) 78.
[37] *Miller I* (n 15) [67].
[38] Elliott (n 3), at 226. Support for this view is found in obiter comments of Lord Denning in *Bulmer v Bollinger* [1974] Ch 401, 418, Hoffmann J in *Stoke on Trent City Council v B&Q* [1991] 4 All ER, 221, 223–24, and V Bogdanor 'Imprisoned by a Doctrine: The Modern Defence of Parliamentary Sovereignty' (2012) 32(1) OJLS 179, 184–86.
[39] Craig (n 25) floats this possibility.
[40] *HS2* (n 4) [79].
[41] ibid.
[42] European Union Act 2011, s 18 (since repealed).

law could 'only enjoy a status in domestic law which [the principle of parliamentary sovereignty] allows'.[43]

It would appear to follow from this that the courts would also have given effect to a statute that was not seeking to alter the status of EU law in general, but which Parliament had expressly provided was to have effect 'notwithstanding the provisions of the ECA 1972 or any directly effective rule of EU law'.[44] If the priority rule in the ECA could be removed or altered by Parliament by express repeal, presumably it could also be disapplied in relation to a particular statute. As the majority said in *Miller I*, 'EU law cannot be implicitly displaced by the mere enactment of legislation which is inconsistent with it'.[45] But legislation expressly displacing EU law in terms would be a different matter. Recall that Lord Bridge was explicit that s 2(4)

> has precisely the same effect as if a section were incorporated in [the Merchant Shipping Act] which in terms enacted that the provisions with respect to registration of British fishing vessels were to be without prejudice to the directly enforceable [EU law] rights of nationals of any Member State of the [EU].[46]

But such an implied provision could not sensibly be 'read into' a statute that expressly proclaimed the opposite—that it was to have effect notwithstanding the ECA and EU law. Hence it follows from the above that a statute that was incompatible with EU law but included such a notwithstanding clause would have been given effect.

The overall conclusion then is that the effect of section 2(4) was *only* to suspend the doctrine of implied repeal. While it is true, as several scholars have pointed out, that section 2(4) does not *in terms* seek to 'exempt [the ECA] from the doctrine of implied repeal',[47] that result follows from the fact that the section 2(4) priority rule, like any other statutory provision, only applies for as long as it remains in force. It was therefore always subject to Parliament's ability to direct that it be set aside, whether by express repeal *or* override. Hence, when read in light of the overall doctrine of parliamentary sovereignty, section 2(4) only imposed a requirement of form—express words—on subsequent legislation in order for it to be given effect despite its inconstancy with the ECA.[48] In other words, it suspended the normal operation of the

[43] *Miller I* (n 15) [67].

[44] It is even possible that express words might not always be necessary. As Laws LJ puts it in *Thoburn* (n 5), the same result could follow from 'words so specific that the inference of an actual determination to effect the result contended for was irresistible' [36].

[45] *Miller I* (n 15) [66].

[46] [1990] 2 AC 85.

[47] Elliott (n 3) 234 and Gordon (n 14) 60 make the same point, as did G Marshall back in 2002: 'Metric Measures and Martyrdom by Henry VIII Clause' (2002) 118 LQR 493, 500. Elliott (ibid) points out that 'the words "shall . . . have effect subject to" suggest that, for as long as the section 2(4) priority rule remains in force, domestic law that is incompatible with directly effective EU law is inapplicable, period, rather than inapplicable unless a contrary intention is manifested in express terms.' Barber appears actually to endorse this as the correct reading of the ECA: (n 11) (*I*CON*), though strangely, he seems simply to proceed on the basis that this is the meaning of intention of the provision, without actually arguing for it.

[48] Hence, I clearly overstated matters when I previously claimed that 'the plain words' of section 2(4) disclosed a clear parliamentary intention to suspend implied repeal (n 32) 46.

doctrine of implied repeal, something indeed suggested more than forty-five years ago by Lord Denning and a fairly impressive array of senior scholars.[49] In turn, this means that the famous claim in *Ellen Street Estates* that Parliament can do no such thing[50] can no longer be treated as good law. This then is the case for propositions 1, 3 (as it relates to the ECA), 4, and 5.

(b) Does the *Thoburn* Analysis of the ECA Survive *Miller*?

Both Nick Barber and Mark Elliott have sought to suggest that it might. Barber indeed claims that the majority in *Miller I* 'explicitly support[ed]' the characterization by Laws LJ in *Thoburn* 'of the nature and implications of the [ECA]'.[51] We have seen that the majority recognized the ECA as a constitutional statute in the sense that it was not subject to ordinary implied repeal. But on the key element of the *Thoburn* analysis—that it is *the courts alone* who decide whether a given statute is 'constitutional'- the majority in *Miller I* appeared to take a different view. On this, they followed *Factortame*'s clear attribution of the special status of the ECA to Parliament itself, rather than, as Laws LJ and his defenders would argue, to the common law. This is actually evident in both judgments given in that case. The Divisional Court put it thus.[52]

> Since in enacting the ECA as a statute of major constitutional importance, *Parliament has indicated* it should be exempt from casual, implied repeal by Parliament itself, still less can it be thought to be likely that Parliament nonetheless intended that its legal effects could be removed by the Crown through the use of its prerogative powers.

Likewise, the majority judgment in the Supreme Court said of EU law as a new source of law in the UK's legal systems:[53]

[49] Denning said that if the UK Parliament legislated in express terms to override the ECA/EU law, it would be 'the duty of the courts to follow the statute of our Parliament': *McCarthys Ltd v Smith* [1979] 3 All ER 325, 329. The same thing was suggested by Hartley who argued that courts could treat s 2(4) 'as a rule of interpretation to the effect that Parliament is presumed not to intend statutes to override [EU] law, unless and until 'Parliament clearly and expressly states in a future Act that it is to override [EU] law' (Hartley (*Foundations of European Community Law*) 243, quoted by Craig (n 25) 251). Gordon also considers that a UK court would have been bound to accede to a direct instruction by Parliament to disapply the s 2(4) priority rule in such circumstances: Gordon (n 14) 158–59 and 182–83; A Tomkins, *Public Law* (Clarendon 2003) 119–20; J Eekelaar, 'The Death of Parliamentary Sovereignty—A Comment' (1997) 113 LQR 185, 185; Goldsworthy, *History* (n 24) 244 and *Debates* (n 13) 198.

[50] *Ellen Street Estates* (n 30). I am indebted to Tom Adams for this point.

[51] *Thoburn* (n 5) 76.

[52] *R (Miller) v Secretary of State for Exiting the European Union* [2016] EWHC 2768, [2017] 1 All ER 158, [88] (emphasis added).

[53] *Miller I* (n 15) [81] (emphasis added).

> [T]he source in question was brought into existence by Parliament through primary legislation [the ECA], *which gave that source an overriding supremacy* in the hierarchy of domestic law sources.

The Supreme Court judgment made the same point in saying that, while the 'constitutional effect of the 1972 Act was unprecedented', the 'unprecedented state of affairs' that it wrought 'will last only so long as Parliament wishes'.[54] This directly follows the approach of Lord Bridge in *Factortame*, who emphasized that 'it was "*by virtue of*" *section 2(4)* of the 1972 Act that the impugned provisions of the Merchant Shipping Act 1998 only had effect "subject to" relevant EU law rights'.[55]

Elliott, however, contends that it is by no means clear that *Miller I* rejects the *Thoburn* common law analysis. He notes that while the Supreme Court said that the ECA's invulnerability to ordinary implied repeal was 'clear' from section 2(4) itself, 'in the very next sentence' the majority writes that the ECA 'accordingly has a constitutional character, as discussed by Laws LJ in *Thoburn*'.[56] However, this rather equivocal sentence is a long way from endorsing the specific contention of Laws LJ that *only* courts can endow statutes with such a character. More plausibly the majority meant simply that the ECA has a constitutional character in the way defined by Laws LJ—that it is not subject to implied repeal. Elliott points out that the passage in *Thoburn* referred to by the majority here includes Laws LJ's assertion that 'Parliament cannot bind its successors by stipulating against repeal, wholly or partly, of the 1972 Act', and that it 'cannot stipulate as to the manner and form of any subsequent legislation'.[57] But it hardly appears credible to suggest that a Supreme Court which has just said 'it is clear' *from section 2(4)* ECA 'that EU law cannot be implicitly displaced by the mere enactment of legislation which is inconsistent with it' could be taken to have then immediately endorsed a suggestion that Parliament can stipulate no such thing.[58] While the reference to the reasoning in *Thoburn* is undoubtedly ambiguous, it must be read in light of the remainder of the reasoning of the Supreme Court—that it was section 2(4) itself which achieved the result seen in *Factortame*, as Lord Bridge himself said in deciding that case.[59] If further evidence is needed, this position has also been expressly endorsed by Lord Neuberger (speaking extrajudicially) when he said:[60]

[54] ibid [60].

[55] As Gordon (n 14) 178 also points out, calling it the 'central theme' of Lord Bridge's speech: 'Parliament, through the enactment of the ECA, was solely responsible for the domestic primacy of EU norms.'

[56] Elliott (n 3) 234.

[57] ibid 235.

[58] The same goes for the other reference in the preceding para 66, which observes that 'the issue' (the effect of the ECA) 'was informatively discussed by Laws LJ in *Thoburn*, paras 37–47', another carefully noncommittal formulation.

[59] Craig (n 25) 252.

[60] Lord Neuberger, speech, 'Who Are the Masters Now?' (April 2011) at para 40, available at http://webarchive.nationalarchives.gov.uk/20131202164909/http:/judiciary.gov.uk/Resources/JCO/Documents/Speeches/mr-speech-weedon-lecture-110406.pdf.

> When the courts scrutinise the validity of Acts of Parliament, and refuse to apply them where they are in conflict with European Union law, as happened in *Factortame (No 2)*, they do not so in the teeth of Parliament. They do so precisely because that is what Parliament has chosen to give the courts the power to do.

The courts, he said, do this 'pursuant to Parliament's direction'; hence '[t]he fact that the courts can review legislation, and set it aside . . . is thus not in any way a refutation of Parliamentary sovereignty: on the contrary, it is an instance of its operation'.[61] From all this it follows that the *Miller I* referencing of the Laws LJ analysis is best read as endorsing the broad notion that there are constitutional statutes, defined as those not subject to implied repeal, but *without* endorsing either Laws LJ's much criticized definition of such statutes[62] or his trenchant assertion that *only* the common law can denote them.[63] Thus, the argument previously made that the Divisional Court in *Miller I* 'mis-states the process by which a statute comes to be regarded as "constitutional"' by wrongly suggesting that this could be so 'because the legislature intended it to have that status'[64] no longer appears sustainable. This, then, is the case for Proposition 2.

There remains the more subtle and interesting point made by Elliott, doubting whether parliamentary instruction *alone* was sufficient to modify the ordinary doctrine of implied repeal. This will be considered below, in section 4(c), once we have considered how the courts have dealt with the Withdrawal Agreement.

4 The Special Status of the Withdrawal Agreement: Mirroring the Effect of the ECA

We may now turn to consider the continuing impact of the *Factortame* experience, post-Brexit, by considering the important decisions in *Allister*, *NIHR*, and *Dillon*. From these, I will argue as follows: first, nothing in any of these decisions casts doubt on the notion of there being 'constitutional statutes', whose effect is that their provisions are not subject to ordinary implied repeal.[65] Second, they strongly confirm that *Parliament* can give a statute, or statutory provision, such a heightened constitutional status via its clear intention, subject to judicial affirmation.[66] Third, such affirmation has been readily forthcoming; indeed, courts have found such parliamentary

[61] ibid.

[62] There would be good reasons for such caution: the Laws LJ test for a constitutional statute has been subject to withering criticism, both for vagueness and for its over- and under-inclusiveness; see, eg, Barber (n 11) 80; Feldman, 'The Nature and Significance of "Constitutional" Legislation' [2013] LQR 343.

[63] Something that Elliott, departing somewhat from his previous stance (n 6), seems now to reject: 'the analysis in *Thoburn* goes too far [in] treating the ECA's status as a matter that is purely for the common law constitution, such that legislative intention has no part to play' (Elliott (n 3) 247). This is discussed further below in section 4(c).

[64] Feldman; Hooper and Elliott (n 6).

[65] This will encompass proposition 5 from the Introduction.

[66] Proposition 1, ibid.

intention even though the statutory words manifesting it are *not* actually as explicitly future-acting as those used in section 2(4) ECA. Fourth, the consequences are that, in the limited field to which it applies, the Withdrawal Agreement, and the EU law to which it gives effect, has the same superior status in relation to other statutes—including subsequent enactments—as did the ECA. All this means that the significant but limited and specific effect the UK's membership of the EU had on the doctrine of sovereignty lives on, post-Brexit.[67] I will deal first with *Allister*, which concerns the first of these arguments.

(a) *Allister:* 'The End of "Constitutional Statutes"?'

Allister concerned a clash between Article VI of the 1800 Act of Union between Great Britain and Ireland and EUWA. As noted above, EUWA (as amended by the 2020 Act) gives domestic effect to the Withdrawal Agreement (WA). Article 4(2) of the WA obliges the UK to ensure compliance with the Article 4(1) obligation to make sure the WA and 'the provisions of [EU] law made applicable by [it] have the same legal effects in UK domestic law' as in the rest of the EU, in particular by ensuring its judicial authorities have power to 'disapply inconsistent or incompatible domestic provisions'. The Court of Appeal in *Dillon* summarized the effect of Article 4—whose 'import . . . can hardly be overstated'—very clearly:[68]

> [C]ertain [EU] law continues to apply in the circumstances mandated by the WA. In addition, provisions of the WA itself are to have the same legal effects as they produce within the EU. Those laws and provisions of the WA shall be capable of being relied upon directly so far as they have direct effect and may give rise to the remedy of disapplication of primary legislation.

The Court of Appeal had previously found, in *Secretary of State for Work and Pensions v AT*,[69] that 'the Withdrawal Agreement takes precedence over inconsistent UK law in Article 4(2)'. This is because of section 7A EUWA, whose wording, the High Court said in *Dillon*, 'mirrors that of section 2 of the [ECA]' in providing (per subsection (1)) that 'all such rights, powers, liabilities, obligations, and restrictions from time to time created or arising by or under the Withdrawal Agreement' and all related remedies and procedures 'are without further enactment to be given legal effect or used in the [UK]'; under subsection (2) are to be '(a) recognised and available in domestic law, and (b) enforced, allowed and followed accordingly'; and, finally and crucially

[67] Furthermore, this impact may apply well beyond the scope of the Withdrawal Agreement given significant *obiter dicta* at the highest level that there are other 'constitutional statutes', like the Scotland Act and the Human Rights Act, that have nothing to do with the EU: *H v Lord Advocate* (n 4) and *HS2* (n 4) [207].

[68] *Dillon* (n 9) [57].

[69] [2023] EWCA Civ 1307, [106].

(subsection (3)), that '[e]very enactment (including an enactment contained in this Act) is to be read and has effect subject to subsection (2)'.

Allister was concerned with a clash between the above provisions and a statute enacted centuries *earlier*—the 1800 Act of Union. Why then was the case not a straightforward exercise in applying the later statute? The answer is that there was a strong argument that the 1800 Act of Union was a constitutional statute. If that was right, it would mean that it could not be merely impliedly repealed in the normal way, simply by identifying an inconsistency with a provision in any later statute. But what we had in *Allister* was *not* such a situation: the later provision in the EUWA expressly provided that it should prevail over 'every enactment'.[70] Consequently, the Supreme Court said,[71] section 7A did not *repeal*, but only *modified* (suspended, subjugated), Article VI of the 1800 Act. On the constitutional status of the statutes involved, the Supreme Court said this:[72]

> The debate as to whether . . . the Acts of Union are statutes of a constitutional character, whether the 2018 and 2020 Acts are also statutes of a constitutional character, and as to the correct interpretative approach when considering such statutes or any fundamental rights, is academic. Even if it is engaged in this case . . . the suspension, subjugation, or modification of rights contained in an earlier statute may be effected by express words in a later statute. The most fundamental rule of UK constitutional law is that . . . the Crown in Parliament, is sovereign and that legislation enacted by Parliament is supreme . . . The answer to any conflict between the [WA] and any other enactment whenever passed or made is that those other enactments are to be read and have effect subject to the rights and obligations which are to be recognised and available in domestic law by virtue of section 7A(2).

Majewski notes that this judgment 'affirms Parliament's ability to enact "subject to" clauses to the effect that other enactments, including later Acts of Parliament, are to be read and given effect *subject to* some other rules'. This, he says, means 'that there is little—if anything—left for the *Thoburn* doctrine to do . . . it is legally redundant'.[73] But it is hard to see why this follows.

The simplest and most attractive way of reading *Allister* is as follows: the notion of 'constitutional statutes' is there to prevent particularly significant enactments (for the constitution or for fundamental rights) being subject to casual, implied repeal. Assuming *Thoburn* is partly right, a constitutional statute may be 'recognized' by the courts, who will then disapply the normal rule of implied repeal. We now also know that Parliament can itself make clear through statutory language that this is to be the

[70] EUWA, s 7A(3).
[71] *Allister* (n 16) [67]–[68].
[72] ibid [66]. Note that insofar as Allister's interpretation of s 7A(3) as applying to 'any other enactment whenever passed or made' suggested that it applied to subsequent legislation, it was technically obiter (since the case before the Court concerned a statute long in the past, the Act of Union 1800).
[73] Majewski (n 17).

case. It did so in section 2(4) ECA (on its true construction) and has done so again in section 7(A)(3) EUWA.

The Supreme Court in *Allister* did not need to decide whether the Act of Union 1800 was a constitutional statute, because, *even if it was*, Parliament in 2020 had expressed the clear intention that the incorporated WA was to prevail over 'every' enactment.[74] Therefore, even if the Supreme Court had decided that the Act of Union *was* a constitutional statute, it would have made no difference—it would have been overridden anyway, due to the clear intention of Parliament in 2020. The issue of the possible constitutional status of the 1800 Act therefore did not have to be decided and remained moot, or, as the Supreme Court said, 'academic'. Hence, *Allister*, far from spelling the 'end of constitutional statutes', does nothing to cast doubt on them.

Having established the first of my four arguments set out at the beginning of this section, I now turn to the remaining three.

(b) *Dillon* and *NIHRC:* The WA Legislation as 'Constitutional'

> The remedy of [statutory] disapplication . . . is entirely orthodox.[75]

As Chris McCrudden further explains in this volume, the Northern Ireland Troubles (Legacy and Reconciliation) Act 2023 ('the Legacy Act') provided for conditional immunities or 'amnesties' from prosecution for serious crimes committed during the 'Troubles' and also made sweeping inroads into the ordinary regime of civil liability, by 'ending Troubles-related civil proceedings, and making protected material inadmissible in civil proceedings and coroners' proceedings'.[76] The issue for our purposes is the incompatibility that the High Court and Court of Appeal found between these provisions and Article 2 of the Northern Ireland Protocol to the WA, now known as the Windsor Framework (WF). Article 2(1) of the WF imposes an obligation on the UK to ensure that no diminution of the rights, safeguards, and equality of opportunity arises for individuals who are resident in Northern Ireland as a result of the UK's withdrawal from the EU.

In *Dillon* the Court of Appeal, in agreement with the High Court, found that Article 2(1) was directly effective in domestic law by virtue of section 7A of EUWA[77] and that it was 'self-evident' that the Legacy Act resulted in a diminution of the relevant

[74] Majewski (ibid) argues that s 7(A)(2) does not expressly indicate that the words 'every enactment' includes the 1800 Acts of Union, and neither does this conclusion seem 'irresistible' in the light of the words used. I disagree: 'every' statute is fairly clear language.

[75] *NIHRC* (n 1) [17].

[76] McCrudden, Ch 8.

[77] Art 4(1) WA provides that 'legal or natural persons shall . . . be able to rely directly on the provisions contained or referred to in this Agreement which meet the conditions for direct effect under Union law'.

rights.[78] Hence the Legacy Act was found to be incompatible with the WF, which is part of the WA. In deciding what the appropriate remedy was, attention focused on the wording of section 7(A) EUWA, which was said by the High Court to 'mirror' the effect of section 2 ECA. In fact, the former, as noted above, is very close in wording to section 2 ECA, but does *not* include the distinctive phrase in section 2(4) that the duty to read all legislation as subject to the ECA includes 'every enactment passed, *or to be passed*'. The Court of Appeal in *Dillon* may have recognized this by saying that the terms of section 7A 'closely resemble' (rather than 'mirror') the terms of section 2(4) ECA; indeed, the Court of Appeal in *Allister* said only that the effect of EUWA is to subjugate primary legislation to the Withdrawal Agreement 'in the event of any conflict with a *previous* enactment'.[79] Nevertheless, as we saw above, the Supreme Court in *Allister* has pronounced (albeit strictly *obiter*) that its effect is the same. As Lord Stephens said:[80]

> A clear answer has been expressly provided by Parliament . . . to any conflict between the Protocol and any other enactment *whenever passed or made* is that those other enactments are to be read and have effect subject to the rights and obligations which are to be recognised and available in domestic law by virtue of section 7A(2).

So, the words 'every enactment', despite *not* stating in terms that this includes Acts not yet passed, have been read by both the Supreme Court and the Court of Appeal as meaning just that. Ronan Cormacain observes of section 7A that 'if Parliament uses the same words [as in s 2 ECA] it means the same thing'.[81] To which we can observe that, apparently, it means the same thing even it *doesn't* use exactly the same words.

On the issue of disapplication of incompatible legislation, the Court of Appeal quoted Humphreys J in *NIHRC*:[82]

> Read together, the provisions of article 4 of the WA and section 7A of the Withdrawal Act are juridically aligned to the approach to the supremacy of EU law under the 1972 Act and *Factortame*. In the circumstances where domestic law is inconsistent with the provisions of the WA and laws made applicable by article 4, the latter take precedence and domestic law is disapplied. *This outcome does not occur*

[78] The rights lost were said to include access to courts in relation to civil remedies and to inquests, access to police and Ombudsman inquiries and victims' rights protected under Article 11 of the Victims' Directive to request a review of a decision not to prosecute: *Dillon*, para 129.

[79] *Allister*, (Northern Ireland Court of Appeal), [194].

[80] *Allister* (n 16) [66] (emphasis added); obiter because *Allister* did not concern a clash between EUWA and a *subsequent* statute. Lord Stephens in the words emphasized—'*whenever passed or made*'—was referring to s 20(1) EUWA which, as he notes at [65], states that '"enactment" means an enactment whenever passed or made.'

[81] https://ukconstitutionallaw.org/2024/05/23/ronan-cormacain-seeking-asylum-on-the-outgoing-tide-of-eu-law-supremacy-of-eu-law-in-northern-ireland-under-the-windsor-framework/.

[82] *NIHRC* (n 1) 152 (emphasis added).

> *at the whim of the courts but represents the will of Parliament as articulated in the Withdrawal Act.*

Thus, both the High Court and the Court of Appeal in *Dillon* readily agreed that legislation, like the Legacy Act 2023, passed *subsequent* to the Withdrawal Agreement Act 2020 that is incompatible with it nevertheless does *not* impliedly repeal it. It followed that, as the Court of Appeal said (agreeing with the High Court),[83] '[p]ursuant to section 7A(3), every enactment—which, naturally, includes the Legacy Act'—that is incompatible with the WA 'must be disapplied (i.e. 'stripped of "effect")'.[84] The Court indeed said that 'section 7A *mandates* disapplication to the extent of any inconsistency with the WA'.[85]

Subject to receiving a different outcome in the Supreme Court, we may now seek to summarize the constitutional lessons of *Dillon* and *NIHRC*. The answers were suggested above and support propositions 1 and 3 from the Introduction: these rulings strongly confirm that *Parliament* can endow a statute with constitutional status via its clear intention; as discussed further below, that intention has to be affirmed by the courts but, in the post-Brexit case law, they have shown themselves very ready to find such intention *even though* the statutory words manifesting such intent are *not* as express as those used in section 2(4) ECA. The result is that the Withdrawal Agreement, and the EU law to which it gives effect, have the same superior status in relation to other statutes—including subsequent enactments—as did the ECA.

(c) Jurisprudential Lessons

What deeper lessons might these cases teach? As we saw above in relation to *Factortame* and *Miller I*, Elliott rejected the idea that 'Parliament straightforwardly immunised section 2(4) against implied repeal', so that we can 'understand the elevated status of section 2(4) in terms of *nothing more* than mechanical curial implementation of parliamentary intention'; he also denied that the Supreme Court in *Miller I* endorsed such a view.[86] This appears to signal a shift from his previous full-blooded endorsement of the *Thoburn* view that *only* the courts can, as it were, badge a statute as constitutional,[87] to a more defensible position that Parliament can indeed convey an intention that a given statute shall have this status, but that the courts still have an important role to play.[88] In fleshing out what he thinks this role should be,

[83] In *Dillon* (n 9) the High Court similarly found that 'any provisions of the 2023 Act which are in breach of the WF should be disapplied', [527].

[84] *Dillon* (n 9) [154(c)] Court of Appeal.

[85] ibid [158].

[86] Elliott (n 3) 235.

[87] Elliott (n 6).

[88] I also set out here a more jurisprudentially rooted account of the respective role of courts and Parliament in this area than I previously offered, Phillipson (n 32) 42–47.

instead of 'a brittle distinction between legislation whose repeal is and is not subject to special conditions' such as express words, Elliott argues that 'the better view is that resistance to repeal is a matter of degree rather than [a] binary'.[89] Under this approach, there should be a judicial assessment of 'the degree of fundamentality' a given provision should be afforded, which should be 'inform[ed] by' Parliament's intention but not simply determined by it. Instead, he says, its degree of constitutional status should be assessed by asking whether 'it reflects a norm that sounds deeply within the common law constitution'.[90] This suggestion is given partial support by the fact that *HS2* did indeed appear to suggest—without resolving the matter—that there might be 'a hierarchy of constitutional statutes', with the Bill of Rights, Article IX occupying a higher rank in that hierarchy even than the ECA.[91]

In what follows, I offer a jurisprudential account of the role that the courts have to play in these cases through the framework of Hart's analysis of the Rule of Recognition. It is important to understand that the nomenclature of the capital-R 'Rule of Recognition' is actually shorthand for that *set* of rules that identifies valid sources of law, which includes the doctrine of implied repeal. These rules can be changed if the senior officials who work the system agree;[92] Goldsworthy glosses this as meaning that all three branches must agree to such a change.[93] Taking the instance of the ECA, that means the government drafted the legislation, Parliament approved and passed it, and the courts gave it effect. Thus, Elliott is correct to say that the change to the rule of implied repeal was not brought about by Parliament alone. There might be cases where Parliament appeared to draft a clause constraining its successors in some way, but courts did not read it as having that effect.[94] Under this analysis, contrary to the *Thoburn* model, government and Parliament together take the initiative by presumptively badging legislation as having a constitutional character through its drafting. But that then has to be *confirmed* by the courts via their interpretation and application of the provision in question. All three branches are then involved in making the change, as Goldsworthy suggests. This analysis then confirms that the courts do at the least have a formal role to play—they must accept the change to the

[89] Elliott (n 3) 239.

[90] ibid 240.

[91] Elliott elsewhere described *HS2* as proposing 'a far richer constitutional order in which the differential normative claims of constitutional and other measures fall to be recognised and calibrated in legal terms'. <http://ukconstitutionallaw.org/2014/01/23/mark-elliot-reflections-onthe-hs2-case-a-hierarchy-of-domestic-constitutional-norms-and-the-qualified-primacy-of-eu-law/>.

[92] This ability to change the rules of recognition does not apply to the Supreme Rule within it (which for the UK is Parliament's ability to make or unmake any law): it was probably the Supreme Rule that the Supreme Court in *Miller I* had in mind when it pronounced at [60] that membership of the ECA had not changed 'the rule of recognition'. For explanation of this point, see R Craig, 'A Simple Application of the Frustration Principle: Prerogative, Statute and Miller' [2017] PL Issue Nov Supp (Brexit Special Issue 2017) 25, 45–46; Phillipson (n 32) 70–72.

[93] Goldsworthy, *History* (n 24) 240. This flows from his assertation that the fundamental rules bestowing law-making authority on Parliament (and for that matter, the courts) exist via 'a consensus among the most senior officials of the legal system, in all three branches of government, legislative, executive, and judicial'.

[94] A possible example might be the apparent referendum lock in s 1 of the Scotland Act 2016 and s 1 of the Wales Act 2017.

rule of implied repeal proposed by Parliament and government for it to come about—and did so in *Factortame*.

Having established this basic point, we may now compare the post-Brexit case law to Elliott's sketch of the substantial and demanding role he thinks courts should play under his view of constitutional adjudication. From this analysis, two insights emerge.

First, there is no indication of the kind of deep and nuanced reasoning Elliott espouses in the cases we have looked at. Far from the courts engaging in the kind of 'rounded approach' in which parliamentary intention is but one factor, to be assessed along with other, deep 'unlegislated' norms, judges seem to engage in pretty much the 'mechanical curial implementation of parliamentary intention' that Elliott deplores. The courts in *Dillon*, for example, might have looked more deeply at the underlying values of the Legacy Act, perhaps seeing it as an important attempt to move on from, rather than endlessly relitigating, traumatic episodes from the Troubles in Northern Ireland.[95] But there is no hint of such an analysis. Instead, judicial attention focused overwhelmingly on the text of the WA and section 7A EUWA. This was said (somewhat misleadingly) to 'mirror' that of section 2(4) ECA, thus allowing courts straightforwardly to read across from *Factortame* the duty to disapply even subsequent incompatible legislation.

The second point is that all this was done *while expressly disclaiming* any creative aspect to this judicial reasoning, by arguing that the outcome straightforwardly 'represents the will of Parliament as articulated in the Withdrawal Act'.[96] For the courts, post-Brexit, the eagerness to ascribe the peculiar constitutional force of the statutes under consideration to Parliament's intention *alone* is, if anything, even stronger than it was during the UK's membership of the EU.

This brings me to my final argument in this section: my contention that, rather than simply deploring this 'mechanical' judicial approach, we can make sense of it by developing further the Hartian analysis just considered. Let us assume that *Factortame* *is* explicable on the basis that all three branches had agreed on a change to one of the rules of recognition—implied repeal. This would give rise to a new position, in which Parliament can suspend the operation of implied repeal to a given statute (or particular provisions in it) by sufficiently clear drafting. If we assume that that change had already come about, it explains why the role of the court in post-Brexit cases like *Dillon* was a minimal one. The courts had already 'agreed' with the other branches of government that the rule governing implied repeal had changed: the new rule is that sufficiently clear wording in a given Act can suspend its application to that statute. As a result, all the courts needed to do in these cases was the relatively straightforward interpretive task of deciding whether the wording in section 7A was sufficiently clear to have this effect. To put it another way, once the change in the underlying rule had been accepted in *Factortame*, courts could simply get on with applying it in subsequent

[95] I do not mean to suggest that such arguments are plausible, or imply anything about what weight, if any, should be invested in them; I am merely noting them as possible.
[96] *NIHRC* (n 1) [17].

cases. If this is analysis is accepted, it would explain why the courts in these cases justified the outcome as simple obedience to legislative language. Nor does this rationale require courts specifically to reason in terms of the rules of recognition: they might more straightforwardly think of *Factortame* as the crucial precedent establishing that implied repeal *can* be suspended, making the judicial task of deciding whether section 7A had also done this much simpler and less momentous.

5 What Do We *Know* about How Far Parliament May Bind Its Successors?

The last section of this chapter turns to the broader question indicated by its heading above. Since it is concluded that Parliament can—and has—imposed requirements of form on its successors, does that mean it can also impose requirements of 'manner', such as the need for super-majorities to repeal certain legislation? After all, the literature in this area has long discussed whether Parliament can bind itself as to 'manner and form'. This section answers this question with a firm 'No', by drawing a sharp distinction between these two types of restriction. As I have previously argued, a restriction based merely on linguistic 'form'—that is, a requirement that a future statute must use clear words in order to override or displace a previous statute—amounts to no real restriction upon the freedom of action of a future Parliament. It is a moment's work for a draftsman to insert such words into a statute. As Goldsworthy puts it, 'a Parliament that can only effectively legislate if it uses a particular form of words, to ensure that its intentions are unmistakeable, is still free to legislate whenever it wishes to do so'.[97] By contrast, a requirement, say, that a two-thirds majority must be used to overturn a previous statute amounts to a very real fettering of future Parliaments, and thus a very real entrenchment of the provision in question, because such majorities, unlike the strokes of a draftsman's pen, are not at the disposal of a government.[98]

Gordon has, however, contested this argument, contending that 'to view the satisfaction of an express language requirement' as requiring nothing more than the draftsmen's pen[99]

> fails to acknowledge the impact such provisions are designed to have on the legislature itself. For the purpose of such requirements is to force Parliament to confront explicitly and directly the consequences of the change in the law it intends to make, rather than bury controversial change in obscure or ambiguous language, and thus prompt clear attempts to justify such action as part of the legislative process.

[97] Goldsworthy (n 24) 245.

[98] H Fenwick and G Phillipson, *Text, Cases and Materials on Public Law and Human Rights* (3rd edn, Routledge 2011) 194.

[99] Gordon (n 14) 94.

Gordon cites in support a famous passage in *Simms* as making the point that such a requirement[100]

> means that Parliament must squarely confront what it is doing and accept the political cost. Fundamental rights cannot be overridden by general or ambiguous words. This is because there is too great a risk that the full implications of their unqualified meaning may have passed unnoticed in the democratic process.

Gordon thus claims 'the requirement that express language be used as part of the process of legislating is therefore designed to change that very process',[101] something that, he argues, also shows the conceptual unity of 'manner and form' restrictions.

This objection is, however, unpersuasive. The 'form' restriction on this account may well result in parliamentarians looking more closely at the clause in question—subjecting it to more 'anxious scrutiny'; this in turn may force ministers into an explicit defence of what is being done. But the change here is not to *procedure*, it is to *the quality or nature of legislative debate*. Under such a restriction a majority in Parliament can still pass a Bill in the normal way—provided only that they can win the political argument that the clause in question is necessary or beneficial. In contrast, a change in procedure to (say) require a two-thirds majority would mean that majority decision-making was disabled: the provision that a majority wished to change would remain part of the law regardless. This appears wide open to the majoritarian complaints about judicial review of legislation advanced by Waldron—disabling majorities from bringing about democratically mandated legislative change.[102] As such it is clearly categorically different from a stipulation against implied repeal, which merely requires clarity from the government and a clear political decision by the governing majority that the change should indeed be made; as has been observed, a requirement of candour is hardly incompatible with democracy.[103]

The other difference is that a requirement to use express legislative words may or may not make some difference to legislative debate—it depends whether the governing party cares greatly about the provision it is expressly overriding or repealing. If it does not then the inclusion of such words will make little or no difference. In contrast, requirements of (say) a two-thirds majority *inevitably* impose themselves—their whole purpose is to stop simple majorities in Parliament being able to repeal the specified legislation. Hence Gordon's argument that 'manner' and 'form' restrictions alike 'alter the process by which law is made'[104] is unpersuasive. As a result, the conceptual distinction between the two types of restriction holds.

[100] *R v Secretary of State for the Home Department, ex p Simms* [2000] 2 AC 115, 131, cited by Gordon, ibid.
[101] Gordon (n 14) 94.
[102] See, eg, J Waldron, 'The Core of the Case Against Judicial Review' (2006) 1115 Yale LJ 1346.
[103] Indeed, Gordon (n 14) 337 himself concedes that 'it may well be democratically desirable to insist that some especially controversial forms of legislative action must be expressed with particular clarity to be legally effective, so long as they are still susceptible to being determined on a simple majority basis'.
[104] ibid 96.

There is moreover a further difference between restrictions on the required form of legislative drafting and those changing legislative procedures: as we have seen, there is now clear evidence that Parliament can bind itself as to the linguistic *form* of future legislation; there is no such evidence upholding binding restrictions as to manner, such as requirements for two-thirds majorities or referendums before certain legislation could be amended or repealed.

To substantiate this statement, we need briefly to consider the well-known case of *Jackson*—a case concerning the nature of legislation passed under the Parliament Act procedure.[105] There, two of their Lordships appeared to give active support to the 'manner and form' school. Thus Lady Hale, noting that Parliament had, by the 1911 Act, redefined the procedure necessary to produce a valid Act of Parliament, suggested that, since Parliament could *remove* requirements necessary to create a valid Act (in this case, the consent of the House of Lords), 'it may very well be that it can redefine itself upwards, to require a particular parliamentary majority (e.g. a two-thirds one)'.[106] Lord Steyn was more definite, saying simply that 'Parliament could for specific purposes provide for a two-thirds majority', citing with approval writers who had advanced this view.[107]

In addition to these dicta, it is also sometimes assumed that the *outcome* of *Jackson*—which rejected the Wadean argument that legislation passed under the Parliament Act procedure must be a form of delegated legislation—lends some kind of support to a key argument of the 'manner and form' school. This is the contention that legislation could redefine what 'Parliament' *is*, for the purposes of repealing or amending that legislation, thereby allowing for entrenchment by way of two-thirds majorities, referendum locks, and the like. Goldsworthy, however, disagrees that *Jackson* provides support for this view, and, I think, persuasively. He argues that while such procedural requirements are designed to *restrict* Parliament's ordinary law-making power—and thus entrench particular pieces of legislation—all the Parliament Acts did were to provide for an *alternative* means of legislating. No restriction on Parliament was achieved (or attempted), and nothing was entrenched. This distinction between 'alternative and restrictive procedures' is, as he says, crucial: the former 'does not limit Parliament's law-making powers or its practical ability to exercise them';[108] it simply provides an alternative means of exercising those powers. This I think is clearly correct.[109] It is also the case that a subsequent Parliament could simply abolish the Parliament Act

[105] *Jackson v A-G* [2006] 1 AC 262.
[106] ibid [163].
[107] ibid [81].
[108] Goldsworthy, *Debates* (n 13) 177.
[109] I therefore respectfully disagree with Alison Young's suggestion that the implication of the majority judgment in *Jackson* is that s 2(1) of the 1911 act is 'entrenched' in that it binds future Parliaments (A Young, *Parliamentary Sovereignty and the Human Rights Act* (Bloomsbury, 2008) 194). I do so for the reason Goldsworthy gives, which is that s 2(1) can be repealed or amended at any time by Parliament using the ordinary legislative procedure. This cannot sensibly be described as 'entrenchment', Goldsworthy, *Debates* (n 13) 178.

procedure. Thus, it has no equivalence to the notion of procedural requirements placed on a subsequent Parliament that *it cannot simply repeal.*[110]

There is a final difficulty with the school which argues that Parliament *is* (or should be) able to impose restrictive procedures on its successors. The problem is that this claim does not provide an answer as to *what kinds* of laws Parliament should be able to protect in this manner. Such protective restrictions are usually imposed (by written Constitutions) to ensure the protection of a Bill of Rights or other fundamental aspects of the constitutional order. The difficulty is that the assertion that Parliament can bind itself like this is not by its nature inherently limited in this way, but is put *in general terms*, as if any law passed by Parliament could be thus protected. The problem with such a view, of course, is that to grant such a power to Parliament would amount to a direct and comprehensive threat to democracy. For if Parliament could, whenever it wished, provide that a given law could only be repealed by a two-thirds majority, then any Parliament could in theory protect *any* legislation it passed by providing that it could not be repealed or modified except by such a super-majority. In such a case, a new government, elected on a different policy platform set out in its manifesto, might take through Parliament a statute repealing the previous one, but passed in the ordinary manner, only to find it declared *ultra vires* in the courts. Unlike codified Constitutions—which set out *a specific set* of foundational rights principles that are entrenched against legislative change—if Parliament's sovereignty included the ability to impose restrictive procedures on its future self whenever it wanted to, then in principle *any* piece of ordinary political legislation could be thus entrenched.[111] And as Gordon himself argues,[112]

> democratic decision-making should [proceed] on the basis of a simple majority, and higher thresholds cannot legitimately be imposed to make an elevated level of agreement necessary before outcomes can be determined.

Thus, the rule that Parliament cannot bind itself in this way is not merely a technical matter of constitutional law: it protects the democratic rights of future majorities to reverse the decisions of previous ones.[113] Any proponent of Parliament's ability to

[110] I therefore also disagree with Gordon's argument (n 14, 198–200) that *Jackson* represents a clear shift to 'manner and form' theory, at least as I understand the term. Gordon uses it very expansively simply to mean Parliament's ability to alter legislative procedure. In my view, such legislation is uncontroversial (see, eg, s 19 of the Human Rights Act) because it does not 'bind' future Parliaments, which remain free to repeal them at any time. I am therefore unconvinced that examples such as the referendum locks in the 2011 Act show the 'manner and form' school in action. The key contention of the 'continuing' theory of sovereignty was not that Parliament cannot reform legislative procedure, or even require referendums; it was simply that it cannot *entrench* those new procedures against ordinary (express) repeal.

[111] Heuston appears to have envisaged the manner and form approach operating to restrain a future Parliament from trampling on basic moral principles: R Heuston, *Essays in Constitutional Law* (Stevens 1964) 6.

[112] Gordon (n 14) 289.

[113] TRS Allan has made a similar argument: 'Parliamentary Sovereignty: Law, Politics and Revolution' (1997) 113 LQR 443, 447, 446. See also I Jennings, *Law and the Constitution* (5th edn, University of London Press 1959) 24.

thus procedurally restrict its successors must therefore incorporate within his or her argument some suggested definition as to the areas of law which Parliament should be able to protect and those which it must *not* be able to, as well as an indication of permissible and impermissible changes to the legislative process. Even were that to be done, no such stipulations could bind Parliament, absent their inclusion in a new codified constitutional settlement. Gordon, for one, is clear that no limitations of this could have legal effect, so that we would have to trust to political constraints to inhibit Parliament from egregiously entrenching particular policies by means of, for example, super-majority requirements.[114]

For this democratic reason and due to the absence of evidence that Parliament has ever successfully entrenched a procedural restriction on its ability to legislate on a given matter, I remain deeply sceptical about the argument that we should accede to version of 'manner and form' theory that allows Parliament to bind its successor in this way.[115] While requirements such as referendum locks or super-majorities remain in force, a court might require compliance with them, but I see no reason to believe that a court would somehow seek to invalidate the express repeal of even purportedly 'entrenched' referendum locks or super-majority requirements. On the other hand, as we have seen, Parliament *has* successfully disapplied the ordinary rule of implied repeal—via both section 2(4) ECA and section 7A WA—and this raises no conceptual difficulties because the requirement of express repeal or override places no substantive restriction on Parliament's ability to amend or repeal any law it wishes.

This leads to the final point of this section—that the language of 'manner and form' is obfuscatory, serving to actively obscure the very real doctrinal and conceptual distinctions we have explored between imposing mere requirements of linguistic form (clearly now within Parliament's capacity) and restrictive requirements of procedure (unproven and subject to potent objections). I would therefore issue a plea that this phrase be consigned to the constitutional dustbin. Instead, as Goldsworthy suggests, we should speak of imposing restrictions of 'procedure *or* form'.[116]

6 Conclusion

The argument of this chapter has been narrowly confined to defending the propositions set out in the Introduction. In particular, its key finding that Parliament may, with the agreement of the courts, endow statutes with resistance to implied repeal in

[114] 'While there would be no legal limits on Parliament's capacity to use the power imagined by the manner and form theory, there would necessarily be a range of democratic political conditions structuring the exercise of that authority', Gordon (n 14) 306. Gordon also argues that political prudence (refraining from doing something lest one's political opponents do the same when they are in power) would restrain Parliament in this area and that extreme bad-faith entrenchment could be met with (hopefully peaceful) revolutionary change, 314–17.

[115] In contrast, as noted above (n 110), I have no problem with what I consider the uncontroversial aspect of 'manner and form' theory which merely allows Parliament to reform the legislative process.

[116] Goldsworthy (n 13) Ch 7.

no way rules out the notion that courts may still decide—à la *Thoburn*—that statutes that Parliament does *not* appear to have so endowed should nevertheless be *judicially* deemed to be 'constitutional' due to the importance of their subject matter. If this is right there would be two means by which statutes may be found to be constitutional: by Parliament endowing them with such status by the kind of wording seen in the ECA and EUWA, *or* by courts deciding that their constitutionally significant subject matter justified such status as a matter of common law.

It does, however, remain the case that the relevant passages supporting the common law view[117] are all *obiter*; further, as we have seen, the references by the Supreme Court in *Miller I* to the analysis of Laws LJ in *Thoburn* fall a long way short of expressly endorsing this common law power when read in the context of the judgment as a whole and the landmark decision in *Factortame*. Finally, it remains the case that we have never actually seen a court disapply a subsequent, inconsistent statute on this basis—and nor is there evidence that the other branches of government have accepted that they can.[118] Hence the legal status of the common law hypothesis remains ambiguous, whereas the existence of what we might term *legislatively denoted* constitutional statutes has now been established beyond doubt.[119]

[117] In *Thoburn* (n 5), *HS2* (n 4), and *H v Lord Advocate* (n 4).

[118] As Goldsworthy's analysis (n 13) applying Hart (discussed above in section 4(c)) would require.

[119] It might be argued that the analysis in this chapter shows that Dicey's 'negative aspect' of parliamentary sovereignty (above, section 2) has also gone, since courts have 'set aside' enactments of Parliament. On this however, Tom Adams argues ('The Dead Man and the Constitution' (2026) forthcoming CLJ) that this is simply a dimension of the positive aspect: courts may set aside Acts of Parliament but only 'if empowered by Parliament' to do so—a characterization I contend fits the propositions argued for in this chapter.

4
The Executive

Jeff King

1 Introduction

The Brexit period in UK constitutional politics was framed by the Leave campaign as a political movement to 'take back control' from the European Union. Precisely where control would be lodged was ambiguous. Any attempt in the UK constitution to neatly divide the executive (or government) from Parliament, and put them against one another, is fraught, for reasons shortly to be explored. It is nevertheless fair to say that the saga that followed the Leave result in the 2016 Brexit referendum resulted in an unambiguous and constitutionally significant accretion of power to the UK government based in Westminster. It did so in three ways.

Brexit created a new narrative of Parliament versus the people, with the government on the people's side, and a populist style that decried political pluralism, elites, and institutions. That led to tensions between Parliament and the executive which ultimately resulted in the latter strengthening its legal position and the political support for it (see section 4 of this chapter). The experience also severely aggravated the pre-existing problem of excessive delegated law-making powers (section 5). And lastly, it energized a campaign against public law and courts, which impacted political culture and led to several Acts of Parliament that increased executive immunity from judicial review (section 6). However, the origin, rationale, and possible longevity of none of these developments can be understood without considering the two political preludes to such events, namely the impact of EU membership on the UK government before the Brexit referendum (section 2) and the events that followed the referendum but preceded the 2017 general election (section 3).

As for the future, it is too early to know whether these consequences will be enduring. Whether the UK executive under any party would want to relinquish any of this power is unclear, perhaps pious. A former political secretary to the Labour Prime Minister Tony Blair, John McTernan, was candid in his views, argued for at length in the Financial Times: '[t]here have been many moves to strengthen the executive over the past 14 years. Labour should exploit them.'[1]

[1] John McTernan, 'Starmer Should Use Powers the Tories Will Leave Behind' *Financial Times* (London, 12 April 2024) 15.

Jeff King, *The Executive* In: *The UK Regulatory Framework Post-Brexit: 'Law Unbound'*. Edited by: Paul Craig and Vilija Vėlyvytė, Oxford University Press. © Oxford University Press 2026. DOI: 10.1093/9780198969815.003.0005

2 First Prelude: Pre-Brexit Impact of EU Membership on the UK Government

The UK's system of parliamentary government is based on a simple formula. Parties secure seats based on a plurality of votes in any constituency, and form a government if able to command the confidence of the House of Commons. The electoral system typically delivers stable majorities in the Commons. There was coalition government only once in the post-Second World War period (2010–15), with periods of National Government (akin to a grand coalition in other European nations) during economic crisis and war in the early twentieth century. This meant parties were used to winning, and governments used their majority to dominate the legislative process both in terms of the bills introduced and how they progressed through both Houses. Perceived as a comparatively weak Parliament in terms of policy power, the situation is buttressed by a variety of constitutional conventions recognizing the primacy of the Commons over the House of Lords, and legal supremacy of the Commons secured by the Parliament Acts 1911 and 1949. Under this 'winner takes all' system of politics, legitimacy is seen to stem from a clear electoral mandate converted into a capacity to deliver. It is the polar opposite of systems mired in gridlock, protracted coalition talks, and unstable coalitions that obscure or dampen manifesto pledges. Seen more cynically, the UK order is a 'spoils' system of 'elective dictatorship' which works to the unmitigated benefit of the two main political parties, which trade in near-absolute power.[2]

Membership of the EU necessarily placed significant constraints on that model of government. In form, the constraints were identical to those placed on executives in other member states. In practice, there was a pre-existing tradition of uncompromising government, a commitment to what Bruce Ackerman had described as a 'monist' constitutional conception of democracy,[3] and a discomfort credibly described as 'constitutional' with the idea of the UK Parliament being subject to any higher normative order. It is reflected nationally in the perennial absence of any political support among the leading parties, and the majority of the academy, for a written and entrenched constitution for the UK.[4] Yet the discomfort was also plainly

[2] At certain moments, members of each main party proposed constitutional reform. The long-standing Conservative Lord Chancellor in two Cabinets, Lord Hailsham (Quentin Hogg), proposed a set of constitutional reforms to disable the 'elective dictatorship' that both parties had previously used to great profit. Lord Hailsham, *The Dilemma of Democracy: Diagnosis and Prescription* (Harper Collins 1978). And the Labour Party inaugurated a new system of devolved government and 'brought rights home' under the Human Rights Act 1998. For the most part, however, a significant reduction in executive power such as an entrenched constitution, fully federal arrangements, or serious consideration of a proportional representation voting system, were off the table.

[3] To be contrasted with the 'dualist' notion familiar to systems with written and entrenched constitutions and organs with constituted rather than inherent constitutional power. See B Ackerman, *We the People: Foundations Vol. 1* (Harvard University Press 1991) Ch 1.

[4] This is not my view, J King, 'The Democratic Case for a Written Constitution' (2019) 72 CLP 1. However, the opposing piece, J Murkens, 'A Written Constitution: A Case Not Made' (2021) 41 OJLS 956 is representative of the more common view.

exacerbated by the fact that "foreign bodies" produced law that had direct effect in the UK and supremacy over the UK Parliament. Political sovereignty, constitutional tradition, and free movement of persons were the three key points of tension that an electorally responsive executive always had to navigate.

Britain joining the EEC in 1972 was driven by the Conservative Party and met with a lukewarm reception by the Labour Party. The Labour Manifesto in the February 1974 election referred to 'a draconian curtailment of the British Parliament to settle questions affecting vital British interests' but it only called for renegotiation.[5] Following that renegotiation by Harold Wilson's freshly elected Labour government in the spring 1975, a government White Paper setting out the case for remaining was put to a Commons vote. Of Labour MPs, 145 voted in favour and 137 against, and even among ministers the vote was 45 to 38 in favour.[6] However divisive at the time, the membership question was settled by national referendum in 1975; hence between 1970 and 2015 the election manifestos of both parties (and all Liberal and Liberal Democratic parties) in all elections but one advocated negotiating to join or remaining a member.[7] It was only the Labour Manifesto of 1983—the one famously derided by the Labour MP Gerald Kauffman as 'the longest suicide note in history'—which called clearly for withdrawal from the EU.[8] The support of the Conservatives and Labour was pragmatic, and that of the Liberal Democrats internationalist. The curtailment of formal sovereignty was well understood on all sides.

There was nevertheless a journey to contemporary Euroscepticism that is the essential political backdrop to the Brexit event. The 1997 Conservative election manifesto mentions that '[s]ome . . . would like to build a federal Europe' and that they 'will not allow Britain to be part of a federal European state'.[9] This theme is recalled again in the 2001 election, before which Labour's manifesto responds by claiming that '[u]nlike the Conservatives, we see Europe as an opportunity not a threat'.[10] Such scepticism was nourished by the creation in 1993, by the Conservative MP Sir Michael Spicer, of the European Research Group (ERG). It would later be called 'the most influential [research group] in recent political history' by one leading journalist,[11] and its members were proclaimed the 'shock troops of the Eurosceptic right' by another.[12] Several of the key ministers in the Brexit process were chairs of the group, including Steve Baker, Jacob Rees-Mogg, and Suella Braverman. While this group affected Conservative Party policy internally, an external threat was the growing popular attraction to the

[5] Edward Scott, 'Party Policies on Europe at General Elections Since 1970' (House of Lords Library Briefing, 15 April 2019) 2.

[6] N Thomas-Symonds, *Harold Wilson: The Winner* (Weidenfeld & Nicolson, 2022) 379.

[7] ibid.

[8] See (n 5).

[9] ibid 10.

[10] ibid 11.

[11] Sebastian Payne, 'Disaffected Tory MPs Take Comfort in Research Groups' *Financial Times* (London, 1 December 2020) <https://www.ft.com/content/66bdf66d-165b-4b3e-ab53-2a09f56c02af> accessed 5 May 2020.

[12] T Shipman, *Fall Out* (rev edn, William Collins, 2018) 62.

United Kingdom Independence Party (UKIP). Founded in 1993, by 1999 UKIP had secured 9 per cent of the vote in elections to the European Parliament.[13] David Cameron's quip in 2006 that the party consisted of 'fruitcakes', 'loonies', and 'closet racists'[14] was altogether overconfident about the electoral threat they would come to represent. By 2014, UKIP's share of European parliamentary elections had climbed to 24 per cent. Its successor party, Reform, was by 2025 polling ahead of both the Conservative and Labour parties for elections to the UK Parliament.

Following thirteen years out of power, the Conservatives entered government as the dominant coalition partner with the pro-European Liberal Democrats in 2010. Prime Minister Cameron had to walk a fine line between maintaining that coalition and his own pro-EU membership sympathies on one side, and appeasement of a significant and belligerent Eurosceptic Tory backbench element on the other. A few actions in this Parliament took on constitutional significance. The first was the passage of the European Union Act 2011, an instrument instituting so-called national referendum locks on any substantial devolutions of further competence to EU jurisdiction and which included the 'sovereignty clause' in section 18, a provision that affirmed the UK Parliament as the source of any EU law's authority in the UK.[15] The second was courting ever greater hostility towards the European Convention on Human Rights. The Conservatives had in 2010 campaigned on a promise to 'replace the Human Rights Act with a UK Bill of Rights', reaffirming the commitment to 'scrap' it in 2015.[16] While coalition with the Liberal Democrats ruled out any such project, it did not stop the UK from pushing for the Brighton Declaration which affirmed, politically rather than juridically, the member state margin of appreciation in interpreting the Convention's requirements.[17] This took place amid cross-party fury over the ECtHR's prisoner voting judgment[18] and an increasingly hostile set of statements from the UK judiciary, such as 'Strasbourg has spoken; the case is closed'.[19] In barely twenty years, the most publicly visible senior UK judges had moved from a narrative of 'time to incorporate'[20]

[13] Richard Cracknell, 'European Parliament Elections: How Has the UK Voted in the Past?' (House of Commons Library, 21 May 2019) <https://commonslibrary.parliament.uk/european-parliament-elections-how-has-the-uk-voted-in-the-past/> accessed 9 May 2025.

[14] Ros Taylor, 'Cameron Refuses to Apologise to UKIP' *The Guardian* (4 April 2006) <https://www.theguardian.com/politics/2006/apr/04/conservatives.uk> accessed 5 May 2025.

[15] Select Committee on the Constitution, *European Union Bill* (HL 2010-11, 121) paras 60–67.

[16] Conservative Party, 'Invitation to Join the Government of Britain' (The Conservative Manifesto, 2010) 79 <http://media.conservatives.s3.amazonaws.com/manifesto/cpmanifesto2010_lowres.pdf> accessed 9 May 2025; Conservative Party, 'Strong Leadership. A Clear Economic Plan. A Brighter, More Secure Future' (The Conservative Manifesto, 2015) 60 <https://www.theresavilliers.co.uk/sites/www.theresavilliers.co.uk/files/conservativemanifesto2015.pdf> accessed 9 May 2025.

[17] European Court of Human Rights, 'High Level Conference on the Future of the European Court of Human Rights' (Brighton Declaration, Brighton, 19–20 April 2012) <https://www.echr.coe.int/documents/d/echr/2012_brighton_finaldeclaration_eng> accessed 9 May 2025.

[18] CRG Murray, 'Playing for Time: Prisoner Disenfranchisement under the ECHR after *Hirst v United Kingdom*' (2011) 22 King's LJ 309.

[19] *Secretary of State for the Home Department v AF (FC) and another and one other action* [2010] 2 AC 269 [118].

[20] Sir Thomas Bingham, 'The European Convention on Human Rights: Time to Incorporate' (Denning Lecture 1993, Bar Association for Commerce, Finance and Industry); Lord Hoffmann, 'Human Rights and the House of Lords' (1999) 62 MLR 159.

to transparent attacks on the Convention's core legal concepts and the Strasbourg Court's supervisory role.[21] A third constitutional innovation was Cameron's successful gambit to hold a national referendum on an alternative vote system in 2011,[22] and then to legally authorise the Scottish Government to hold a Scottish independence referendum in 2014.[23] 'No' votes in both gave Cameron political victories and in turn a taste for referendums. The promise of an 'in–out referendum' duly entered the Conservatives' 2015 election manifesto.[24] All three led to a fresh role for 'the people' as actors in the UK constitution. Lastly, the Liberal Democrats succeeded in obtaining support for what became the Fixed-term Parliaments Act 2011, an instrument that removed the Prime Minister's power to call an election at will and replaced it with a five-year statutory timetable, a super-majority requirement to trigger an early election outside that new schedule, and a new statutory procedure for managing non-confidence votes.[25] This new regime proved consequential across 2019.

3 Second Prelude: Between the Referendum and the 2017 Early General Election

Within weeks of election victory in May 2015, Prime Minister Cameron's government introduced the European Union Referendum Bill, which was passed by December.[26] Unlike the Act providing for the Alternative Vote referendum,[27] the 2015 Act did not direct the government to put through specific plans in the event of a 'yes' vote. The Prime Minister leveraged the coming referendum in his efforts to negotiate a much-discussed 'deal' with the EU allowing the UK to opt out of the 'ever closer union' principle of EU relations, and to constrict access to benefits and various other items.[28] Agreed on 19 February 2016, the deal had a hard time in the press.[29] With the

[21] Lord Sumption, 'The Limits of Law' (27th Sultan Azlan Shah Lecture, Kuala Lumpur, 20 November 2013) <https://www.sultanazlanshah.com/pdf/2021/SAS_Lecture_27.pdf> accessed 9 May 2025. See also Lord Hoffmann, 'The Universality of Human Rights' (Judicial Studies Board Annual Lecture, 19 March 2009) <https://conservativehome.blogs.com/files/hoffmann_2009_jsb_annual_lecture_universality_of_human_rights.pdf> accessed 5 May 2025.

[22] Feargal McGuinness and Jeremy Hardacre, 'Alternative Vote Referendum 2011' (Research Briefing, House of Commons Library 19 May 2011) <https://commonslibrary.parliament.uk/research-briefings/rp11-44/> accessed 5 May 2025.

[23] The Electoral Commission, *Scottish Independence Referendum: Report on the Referendum Held on 18 September 2014* (December 2014) <https://www.electoralcommission.org.uk/sites/default/files/pdf_file/Scottish-independence-referendum-report.pdf> accessed 9 May 2025.

[24] Conservative Party, 'Strong Leadership. A Clear Economic Plan. A Brighter, More Secure Future' (The Conservative Manifesto, 2015) 72–73 <https://www.theresavilliers.co.uk/sites/www.theresavilliers.co.uk/files/conservativemanifesto2015.pdf> accessed 9 May 2025.

[25] Fixed-Term Parliaments Act 2011, ss 1, 2.

[26] European Union Referendum Act 2015.

[27] Parliamentary Voting System and Constituencies Act 2011, ss 8(1), 9 and Sched 10.

[28] T Shipman, *All Out War* (rev edn, William Collins 2017) Ch 8.

[29] Roy Greenslade, 'Most of the National Press Lashes David Cameron's EU "Settlement"' (*The Guardian*, 3 February 2016) <https://www.theguardian.com/media/greenslade/2016/feb/03/most-of-the-national-press-lashes-david-camerons-eu-settlement> accessed 10 October 2025.

referendum looming, it remained entirely unclear whether Michael Gove and Boris Johnson, the two leading lights of what became the Leave campaign, were actually in favour of leaving. In a 'bolt from the blue', Gove published an essay supporting Leave on 20 February 2016. On that same weekend, Boris Johnson's position was so ambiguous that after he had prepared a newspaper column to outline it, 'even his closest friends, allies and family were unsure . . . whether he'd press send to the editor on the Remain or the Leave columns.'[30] The UK voted on 23 June 2016, by a thin majority, to leave the EU. England and Wales voted to leave by narrow margins; Northern Ireland to remain by a small margin; and Scotland to remain by a large margin.

His voice cracking with emotion, Cameron resigned the morning the result was announced. Theresa May was elected unopposed, on an 'anyone but Boris' internal party campaign, to the leadership of the Conservative Party, which led to her appointment by the Queen as Prime Minister.[31] Yet May had inherited two intersecting headaches, above and beyond the territorial constitution's set of policy problems explored elsewhere in this volume.[32] The Conservatives had a majority of only eleven seats, excluding the Speaker, and the House of Commons was notoriously pro-Remain. Before the referendum, only 24 per cent of MPs had declared for Leave.[33] The confluence of the two meant she had a tenuous mandate to deliver on her own interpretation of what the Leave result required.

The story of the first of two litigations brought by Gina Miller, which resulted in a Supreme Court holding on 25 January 2017 that an Act of Parliament would be required to trigger Article 50 of the Treaty of the European Union, has been told and analysed elsewhere.[34] The Cabinet politics of the decision are what concerns the analysis here. Two weeks prior to the stunning loss at the Divisional Court, the Brexit Minister, David Davis, told the PM 'I think we're going to lose, whatever our lawyers say'; he had already taken early charge of drafting what became the European Union (Notification of Withdrawal) Act 2017.[35] The bill was introduced two days after the Supreme Court's 24 January 2017 judgment. A group of formerly Remain-backing Conservative Party members engaged in early discussion of whether the Bill should be used as an occasion to propose that Parliament play a stronger role in the oversight of negotiations. On 7 February Labour MP Chris Leslie moved an amendment that called for a parliamentary vote on any 'new deal or treaty', and up to twenty Tory MPs threatened to support it.[36] In clever inner-party politics, the former Conservative Attorney General Dominic Grieve MP drafted a compromise deal and put it to Prime Minister May. It was that the government would commit in Parliament to giving a

[30] A Seldon and R Newell, *Johnson at 10* (Atlantic Books 2023) 62–63.
[31] Shipman, *All Out War* (n 28) Ch 29.
[32] Chs 7 and 8.
[33] Elise Uberoi, 'Brexit: The People vs. Parliament?' (House of Commons Library 8 July 2016) <https://commonslibrary.parliament.uk/brexit-the-people-vs-parliament/> accessed 9 May 2025.
[34] In addition to other chapters in this volume, see NW Barber, Tom Hickman, and Jeff King, 'Reflections on Miller' (2018) 8 UK Supreme Court Yearbook 212 (which puts the case in legal and academic context).
[35] T Shipman, *Fall Out: A Year of Political Mayhem* (William Collins 2018) 116.
[36] ibid 118.

parliamentary vote on not only the withdrawal arrangements but also the future relationship.[37] Taking him up on it, the rebellion was bought off and the Notification of Withdrawal Bill was passed unamended in the Commons, with various Lords' amendments rejected in ping-pong between the Houses. The most notable of the amendments was Tory-led (by Michael Heseltine), and demanded a 'meaningful' parliamentary vote.[38] Ultimately rejected at that point, the legal framework for such a meaningful vote would at a later time become section 13 of the European Union (Withdrawal) Act 2018. The Notification of Withdrawal Bill passed with a very large majority and gained Royal Assent on 16 March 2017. The White Paper outlining legislative plans for withdrawal followed shortly after.[39]

Prime Minister May gave notice of the UK's intention to leave the European Union on 29 March 2017, triggering the two-year negotiating window. Seeking to strengthen her parliamentary majority for the battles lying ahead, the Prime Minister called for an early general election, the necessary parliamentary motion being passed on 19 April 2017. Contrary to pollster predictions, the result was a disaster for her. Winning 317 seats, she formed a minority government which had to resort to a supply-and-confidence arrangement with the notably conservative Democratic Unionist Party (DUP) of Northern Ireland, whose ten seats still only delivered an extremely slim majority.[40]

4 Brexit: Exacerbated Tensions Between Westminster and Whitehall

These events set the scene for a change in constitutional culture, which arose from the period of instability across the 2017–19 session of Parliament. It led to a more domineering form of government–Parliament relations, and a more uncompromising mode of governance represented by populist oratory, references to the 'will of the people',[41] and combative ministerial styles. Two high-profile public interventions exhibited this tension in plain terms. The first was a statement on 19 March 2020 by the Prime Minister, Theresa May, to the public of the UK. It appealed to them over the heads of the elected Parliament.[42]

> You the public have had enough. You are tired of the infighting. You are tired of the political games and the arcane procedural rows. Tired of MPs talking about nothing

[37] ibid 119.

[38] ibid.

[39] Department for Exiting the European Union, *Legislating for the United Kingdom's Withdrawal from the European Union* (White Paper, Cm 9446, 2017).

[40] Gail Bartlett and David Torrance, 'The 2017–19 Government at Westminster: Governing as a Minority' (Briefing Paper Number 08103, House of Commons Library 31 March 2020) <https://researchbriefings.files.parliament.uk/documents/CBP-8103/CBP-8103.pdf> accessed 9 May 2025.

[41] For a critique of this tendency, see A Weale, *Will of the People: A Modern Myth* (Polity Press 2018).

[42] Prime Minister Theresa May, Government Statement (20 March 2019) https://www.gov.uk/government/speeches/pm-statement-on-brexit-20-march-2019 accessed 10 October 2025.

> else but Brexit when you have real concerns about our children's schools, our National Health Service, and knife crime. You want this stage of the Brexit process to be over and done with. I agree. I am on your side. It is now time for MPs to decide.

This statement was compared by some at the time with a political style familiar to the early days of fascism.[43] The second exemplary statement was made by the then Leader of the House of Commons, the Conservative Party frontbencher Jacob Rees Mogg MP. In a reply to a question in debate, he said:[44]

> AV Dicey said that all conventions have 'one ultimate object, to secure that Parliament or the Cabinet . . . shall in the long run give effect to the will . . . of the nation'. These conventions are being disregarded today, and so, by extension, is the will of the nation. Parliament sets itself against the people. Sovereignty comes from the people to Parliament. It does not come to Parliament out of a void. If Parliament tries to challenge the people, this stretches the elastic of our constitution near to breaking point.

Crucial to the political tendencies leaning in this direction was a perception that the 20–2019 Parliament played a key role in blocking a satisfactory exit process, and that there was something constitutionally problematic about it doing so. Some contended, persuasively in my view, that there was a tension evident between the 'representative' and 'responsible' understandings, or Westminster versus Whitehall views, of the government–Parliament relationship.[45] The Westminster view is that Parliament and the Commons sit at the centre of the system and exercise oversight and control. The Whitehall view is that ministers are the centre of the system because effective government requires them to act authoritatively. At the extreme end of this view, in Howarth's words, 'parliament is peripheral' and frequently a 'side-show'.[46] Howarth's definition may accurately describe how it is seen by a number of insiders—he would know[47]—but it is also important to see the basis for the (Whitehall) view that there was something constitutionally problematic with the conflict that followed across 2018–19.

Under the UK constitution the Crown enjoys prerogative powers to conduct treaty relations and ratify international treaties. Part II of the Constitutional Reform and

[43] Lea Ypi, 'Theresa May's Trumpian Statement Was Reminiscent of a Sovereign Dictator' (*The New Statesman*, 21 March 2019) <https://www.newstatesman.com/politics/uk/2019/03/theresa-may-s-trumpian-statement-was-reminiscent-sovereign-dictator> accessed 10 October 2025.

[44] HC Deb 3 September 2019, vol 664, col 101.

[45] David Howarth, 'Westminster versus Whitehall: Two Incompatible Views of the Constitution' (UK Const L Blog, 10 April 2019) <https://ukconstitutionallaw.org/> accessed 8 May 2025; AH Birch, *Representative and Responsible Government: An Essay on the British Constitution* (George Allen and Unwin 1964).

[46] Howarth, iibid.

[47] A law professor at Cambridge, he was also an MP for Cambridge between 2006 and 2010, and a frontbench member of the Liberal Democrats.

Governance Act 2010 introduced a new procedure for parliamentary oversight of treaties, but it does not confer a straightforward veto, let alone the power to oversee treaty negotiations. Yet it was common ground that this type of procedure alone was not fit for the significance and complexity of Brexit. After all, the European Union Act 2011 had itself imposed, on Eurosceptic initiative, significant parliamentary and popular constraints over executive treaty-making with the EU. What was far from common ground, however, was the appropriate extent and character of parliamentary oversight of any negotiations of the withdrawal agreement and the future relationship. The Whitehall view was that government could brief Parliament and discuss certain relevant matters. The Westminster view was that there must be a 'meaningful vote' on the terms of either, meaning veto powers and a vote on the plans.

The view supporting a meaningful vote view more or less prevailed up until 2019. Politically, the crucial moment was on 13 December 2017, when Dominic Grieve MP led a faction of eleven Tory rebels that secured a government defeat in the Commons and the amendment of what became section 9(1) of the European Union (Withdrawal) Act 2018. As introduced, the provision conferred delegated powers to implement the Withdrawal Agreement. Grieve's amendment provided that such powers could exist 'subject to the prior enactment of a statute by Parliament approving the final terms of withdrawal of the United Kingdom from the EU'.[48] A year and a half onwards, one special adviser said that 'the moment her premiership fell was the meaningful vote defeat'.[49] The second and equally consequential meaningful vote revision was that which inserted what became section 13 into the 2018 Act, which provided for 'parliamentary approval of the outcome of negotiations with the EU'. This section would not permit the ratification of the Withdrawal Agreement unless a copy of the Withdrawal Agreement and Future Relationship Agreement were laid before each House and approved by the House of Commons, the Lords had had the chance to debate it, and an Act of Parliament had been passed which contained provisions for the implementation of the withdrawal agreement.[50] The legislative tussle over the creation of section 13 was another occasion on which the government and others alleged that Parliament was creating a constitutional 'inconsistency' or even 'absurdity' by creating powers to issue instructions to government on negotiating positions.[51]

Section 13 would become the foundation for the series of meaningful votes that Prime Minister May's government would come to lose in spectacular fashion. After the Prime Minister's initial 'Chequers Plan' triggered the resignations of her Brexit Secretary (David Davis) and Foreign Secretary (Boris Johnson), it was also rejected by

[48] T Shipman, *No Way Out: Brexit from the Backstop to Boris* (William Collins 2024) Ch 2, which explores the politics of the rebellion.

[49] ibid 28.

[50] European Union (Withdrawal) Act 2018, sub-ss 13(1)(a)–(d).

[51] The argument is explored in Alison Young, 'European Union (Withdrawal) Bill and the Meaningful Vote: Constitutional Inconsistency or Constitutional Inconvenience?' (UK Const L Blog, 20 June 2018) <https://ukconstitutionallaw.org/> accessed 8 May 2025.

the EU.[52] May's government nevertheless reached a Withdrawal Agreement deal with the EU on 14 November 2018.[53] The next critical move was on 9 January 2019, when Grieve put forward a proposal that a business of the house motion in the House of Commons could be amended and a substantively new motion be substituted for it.[54] Such motions, by convention, were treated as unamendable if they were put 'forthwith'. The Clerk of the Commons advised the House of Commons Speaker, John Bercow, that there was such an applicable convention. Bercow reportedly replied: 'Well, it may be a convention, David, but it isn't an unbreakable rule.'[55] The intent behind Grieve's amendment was to trial the possibility of Parliament seizing control of the order paper from the government's established control, in particular to provide parliamentary time to pass legislation that was then under behind-the-scenes discussion.

With the 29 March 2019 negotiating deadline looming, the first meaningful vote on the Agreement was held on 15 January 2019. It was defeated by a majority of 230 votes—the largest defeat in parliamentary history, with 118 Conservative MPs voting with the opposition against the deal.[56] The second meaningful vote was 12 March, lost by a majority of 149 votes (75 of which were Conservatives).[57] May then requested and received from the European Council an extension of the deadline to 12 April. A third meaningful vote on 29 March was lost by fifty-eight votes (34 Conservatives). The diverse grounds for these losses were visible in the preference distribution that became evident in the two rounds of so-called indicative votes held on 27 March and 1 April respectively. In the first of these, fully eight options were laid out by MPs, including no-deal, customs union, revoking Article 50 notice, and a second referendum.[58] None secured a majority of votes, though the proposal for a customs union fell short by just six votes in the first round and three in the second. In the result, Parliament could deliver clear majorities for opposition, but none in favour of anything. A multitude of factions lobbied for different options.

[52] Sam Coates, 'Davis Triggers Cabinet Crisis with Resignation; Brexit Secretary "Fed Up" over May's Approach; Ally Also Quits, Raising Fears of More to Come' *The Times* (London, 9 July 2018) 1; Rob Merrick, 'Boris Johnson Resigns as Foreign Secretary Following Theresa May's Chequers Brexit Deal; Second Cabinet Resignation Comes Just 30 Minutes Before the Prime Minister Has to Face the Mounting Anger of Leave-Backing Tory MPs in the Commons' *The Independent* (9 July 2018) <https://www.independent.co.uk/news/uk/politics/boris-johnson-resigns-foreign-secretary-brexit-theresa-may-david-davis-chequers-cabinet-summit-a8438836.html> accessed 11 October 2025; Oliver Wright, Sam Coates, and Bruno Waterfield, 'Humiliation for May as EU Rejects Brexit Plan; Leaders Warn Chequers Blueprint "Will Not Work"'; *The Times* (London, 21 September 2018) 1, 4.

[53] See Antony Seely and others, 'The UK's EU Withdrawal Agreement' (Briefing Paper No 08453, HC Library 11 April 2019) < https://researchbriefings.files.parliament.uk/documents/CBP-8453/CBP-8453.pdf> accessed 8 May 2025.

[54] Shipman (n 48) 338–47.

[55] ibid 342.

[56] ibid Appendix I (detailing the results of the three meaningful votes and two rounds of indicative votes). Ch 20 details the politics of MV1.

[57] ibid.

[58] ibid 674–75. See further Maddy Thimont Jack, 'Indicative Votes on Brexit' (*Institute for Government*, 17 December 2018) <https://www.instituteforgovernment.org.uk/article/explainer/indicative-votes-brexit> accessed 9 May 2025.

Almost immediately after this episode, the technique of taking control of the order paper was used to facilitate the passage of what became the European Union (Withdrawal) Act 2019. The 'Cooper–Letwin Act' was introduced on 3 April and received Royal Assent on 8 April. It provided that immediately after the Act came into force, a Minister of the Crown must move a motion in the House of Commons which if passed would force the Prime Minister to seek an extension of the negotiating period to the specified date in the motion. Following the enactment of this provision, the negotiating period was extended to 31 October 2019. This episode also prompted significant consternation, with some arguing (implausibly in my view)[59] that the Bill was constitutionally suspect and it would have been appropriate for the government to advise the monarch to withhold Royal Assent to it when presented.[60]

Events moved quickly from this point onwards. With her leadership extremely bruised, and following significant Conservative losses at local council elections across the country, May announced her intention to resign on 24 May.[61] Following a leadership campaign, Boris Johnson was elected leader on 23 July, and Parliament went into summer recess two days later, resuming on 3 September. By that point an Order in Council had been made on 28 August 2024 which provided that Parliament should be prorogued at some time between 9 and 12 September until 14 October—just two weeks shy of the extended negotiating deadline. While that Order was quashed in the dramatic unanimous Supreme Court judgment considered elsewhere in this volume, it was machinations within Parliament that would once again prove more consequential for the executive and relations between Whitehall and Westminster. Hilary Benn, Alistair Burt, and other MPs introduced the European Union (Withdrawal) (No 2) Act 2019 on 4 September, and it completed all stages by 6 September, receiving Royal Assent on 9 September, the day before prorogation took effect. To obtain parliamentary time for the bill, the MPs had moved an emergency motion to that effect. The 21 Conservative Party rebels who had supported it had the whip removed.[62] Section 1 of the Act created a binding legal obligation on the Prime Minister to secure approval of MPs for either a Withdrawal Agreement or leaving the EU without an Agreement, and if neither had occurred by 19 October the law obliged the Prime Minister to seek an extension from the European Council for a further four months. Section 2 obliged the Prime Minister to report to both Houses of Parliament on progress in negotiations by 30 November and move a motion seeking approval of the report. The Act's schedule provided the identical wording of the letter the Prime Minister must send to the European Council. In the result, Johnson—who had said he would rather 'die in

[59] Jeff King, 'Can Royal Assent to a Bill Be Withheld If So Advised by Ministers?' (UK Const L Blog, 5 April 2019) <https://ukconstitutionallaw.org/> accessed 8 May 2025.

[60] Richard Ekins and Stephen Laws, 'Stop This Power Grab by MPs or Chaos Governs' *The Sunday Times* (31 March 2019).

[61] Theresa May, 'Prime Minister's Statement in Downing Street: 24 May 2019' (24 May 2019) <https://www.gov.uk/government/speeches/prime-ministers-statement-in-downing-street-24-may-2019> accessed 9 May 2025.

[62] This included two former Chancellors of the Exchequer, seven former Cabinet members, and various others.

a ditch' than send the letter[63]—sent an unsigned letter asking for an extension and a second letter explaining that he didn't believe they should grant the extension.[64] The episode was no doubt humiliating for him. Having taken no-deal off the table, the Opposition relented and granted the Prime Minister the early election he had by that point asked for three times and been denied. In one such denial, the Attorney General Geoffrey Cox actually shouted in the House of Commons that 'This Parliament is a disgrace!'[65] Johnson had also by that point reached a Withdrawal Agreement deal with the EU on 19 October, but still required a Withdrawal Agreement Bill to be put through Parliament. He hence needed the extension he sought from the EU, which was ultimately granted to 31 January 2020.

In the resulting general election held on 12 December, Johnson won a comfortable majority, with 365 of the 650 seats in the House of Commons. His principal campaign slogan and manifesto pledge was to 'get Brexit done'.[66] The foregoing year of parliamentary insurgency sowed the seeds for his administration's style of government.

First, his advisers took the view that the Fixed-term Parliaments Act 2011 had contributed to the gridlock and instability of the previous year. The Joint Committee reviewing the operation of the Act and the HL Constitution Committee found only modest support for that claim.[67] The manifesto commitment to repeal it was realized in the Dissolution and Calling of Parliament Act 2022, which not only 'revived' the prerogative of dissolution (returning it to the Prime Minister's hands), but in section 3 made any advice on dissolution non-justiciable.

The second set of actions was to dispense with parliamentary controls over the government's negotiations with the EU. The European Union (Withdrawal Agreement) Act 2020 was based on a previous bill that had fallen with the dissolution. It was introduced in early January and passed on 23 January. Section 31 repealed the all-important 'meaningful votes' provision (section 13) of the European Union (Withdrawal) Act 2018. The reintroduced bill also removed provisions providing for parliamentary oversight of negotiations for the future relationship, something

[63] Kate Devlin, Fariha Karim, and Richard Ford, 'I'd Rather Die in a Ditch than Ask for Brexit Delay, Says Johnson' *The Times* (London, 6 September 2019) 6.

[64] 'Brexit: PM Sends Letter to Brussels Seeking Further Delay' *BBC* (20 October 2019) <https://www.bbc.co.uk/news/uk-politics-50112924> accessed 9 May 2025.

[65] HC Deb, vol 664, col 660 (25 September 2019).

[66] Conservative Party, 'Get Brexit Done: Unleash Britain's Potential' (The Conservative and Unionist Party Manifesto, 2019) 48 <https://cdn.prod.website-files.com/5da42e2cae7ebd3f8bde353c/5dda924905da587992a064ba_Conservative%202019%20Manifesto.pdf> accessed 9 May 2025.

[67] Joint Committee on the Fixed-Term Parliaments Act, *Report* (2019–21, HL 253, HC 1046) paras 54, 60: 'We acknowledge the political events of 2019 were extreme, and the Fixed-term Parliaments Act was not the sole source of difficulty. There is a risk of gridlock in any system which does not guarantee that a Government can either get its business through or can be sure of securing an election. The extent to which the risk of gridlock is a price worth paying for the benefits of fixed-term Parliaments is a political judgment Parliament itself must make'; HL Select Committee on the Constitution, *A Question of Confidence? The Fixed-term Parliaments Act 2011* (2019–21, HL 121) para 149: 'The Fixed-term Parliaments Act 2011 was not the cause of the political deadlock in the 2017–19 parliament, but without the Act the deadlock would not have lasted as long.'

the Constitution Committee observed to be a 'matter of regret'.[68] It recommended that the government set out what its process would be for consultation and engagement with Parliament and the devolved authorities in respect of future relationship negotiations.[69]

Apart from the continued abuse of delegated powers, considered below, the other major action in this final period of government–Parliament relations was the introduction and extremely rapid passage of the European Union (Future Relationship) Act 2020. The Trade and Cooperation Agreement with the EU was signed on 24 December, and the deadline for concluding the Agreement, the end of the 'transition period', was 31 December 2020. Passed in a single day, the Act disapplied parliamentary oversight (section 36), but more importantly it incorporated huge amounts of law, in a fashion scarcely possible for MPs to digest. For example, section 26 provided that the Social Security Protocol (more than 100 pages of dense text) would 'form part of domestic law' and prevail over any inconsistent existing law. Section 29 is the most unfortunate provision, but also exemplifies the way in which hasty law-making leads to the marginalization of MPs. It provides essentially that any change that is required to be made in UK domestic law in order to give effect to the Agreements is deemed by section 29 to have taken such effect.[70] The provision was of uncertain import and led to litigation in which the Court of Appeal offered a broad view of its effect, but in which ultimately the Supreme Court reversed and sought to contain or read down the breadth of the provision.[71] Of perhaps most significance, it is not at all clear that it was legally necessary to pass such a bill so quickly. It could have been possible to provide for provisional application of the regime, together with a sunset provision, allowing fuller parliamentary consideration and confirmation at a later time.[72]

5 Brexit: A Vast Increase in Delegated Powers

Delegated powers were a site of significant constitutional controversy before Brexit. The Hansard Society completed its landmark report *The Devil is in the Detail* in 2014,[73] in which it found that the system needed complete overhaul due to severe problems with the perfunctory nature of parliamentary scrutiny and the steady expansion of

[68] Select Committee on the Constitution, *European Union (Withdrawal Agreement) Bill* (HL 2019–21, 5) paras 114–15.

[69] ibid.

[70] Jeff King, 'Looking Back at the EU Future Relationship Act' (*UCL European Institute*, 11 January 2021) <https://ucleuropeblog.com/2021/01/11/looking-back-at-the-eu-future-relationship-act/#:~:text = On%20that%20day%2C%20the%20European,Kingdom%20on%2024%20December%202020.> accessed 10 October 2025.

[71] *Lipton v BA Cityflyer Ltd* [2024] UKSC 24, [2025] AC 154.

[72] See (n 68).

[73] Ruth Fox and Joel Blackwell, *The Devil Is In the Detail: Parliament and Delegated Legislation* (Hansard Society 2014). The report is not published online. For more background, see J King, 'The Province of Delegated Legislation', in E Fisher, J King, and AL Young (eds), *The Foundations and Future of Public Law: Essays in Honour of Paul Craig* (Oxford University Press, 2020).

delegated power. In its inquiry into legislation, the Lords Constitution Committee observed that '[t]here has been an upward trend in the seeking of delegated powers in recent years and this should cease'.[74] Erskine May was also candid in admitting that '[c]riticism of the volume of delegated legislation and its lack of scrutiny by Parliament has frequently been made by committees of both Houses and by outsiders'.[75]

The European Union (Withdrawal) Bill was introduced on 13 July 2017, and brought the simmering dissatisfaction to the boil. Important aspects of the 2018 Act are detailed elsewhere in this volume, including about its delegated powers provisions in relation to devolved governments.[76] The core purpose of the Act was to take a snapshot of EU law and convert it to 'retained EU law', retaining its supremacy, and to use a suite of delegated powers to tailor the retained EU law so that it fit the UK statute book and was independent of any interoperation with EU law and institutions. The government argued in the White Paper preceding the Bill that '[t]he Great Repeal Bill will not aim to make major changes to policy or establish new legal frameworks in the UK beyond those which are necessary to ensure the law continues to function properly from day one'.[77] The initial reaction was nevertheless harsh. The Constitution Committee found that the bill 'weaves a tapestry of delegated powers that are breath-taking in terms of both their scope and potency', constituting 'an unprecedented and extraordinary portmanteau of effectively unlimited powers upon which the Government could draw'.[78] The Delegated Powers and Regulatory Reform Committee (DPRRC) announced it as 'one of the most important Bills in the constitutional history of the United Kingdom', with 'wider Henry VIII powers than we have ever seen', and with a delegated powers framework 'notable for its width, novelty and uncertainty'.[79] And Lord Wilson of Dinton (Crossbench), who was Cabinet Secretary and Head of the Home Civil Service before taking up a peerage in 2002, called it 'the dream of tyrants through the ages. It is something which is repugnant to the history of this country and the development of our legal system.'[80]

The legal scope of the Act has been examined exhaustively elsewhere, including the progress of its provisions on delegated powers.[81] The 'main powers in connection with withdrawal' are found in sections 8 (correcting deficiencies in EU law), 9

[74] Select Committee on the Constitution, *The Legislative Process: Delegated Legislation (sixteenth report)* (HL 2017–19, 225) para 25.

[75] M Hutton and others (eds), *Erskine May's Treaties on the Law, Privileges, Proceedings and Usages of Parliament* (25th edn, LexisNexis Butterworths 2019) 667.

[76] See, eg, Chs 2 (constitution) by Alison Young, and Chs 7 (devolution) and 8 (Northern Ireland) by Sionaidh Douglas Scott and Christopher McCrudden respectively.

[77] See (n 39) para 1.21.

[78] Select Committee on the Constitution, *European Union (Withdrawal) Bill: Interim Report (third report)* (HL 2017–19, 19) para 2.

[79] Delegated Powers and Regulatory Reform Committee, *European Union (Withdrawal) Bill (twelfth report)* (HL 2017–19, 73) paras 1, 9 and 15.

[80] HL Deb 7 March 2018, vol 789, col 1178.

[81] P Craig, 'Constitutional Principle, the Rule of Law and Political Reality: The European Union (Withdrawal) Act 2018' (2019) 82 MLR 319; see also King (n 73) for a focus on the delegated powers provisions as the bill progressed through Parliament.

(implementation of the withdrawal agreement) (both read together with Schedule 7), 11, and Schedule 2 (analogous powers of devolved authorities). The basic model (found in section 8) is that a Minister of the Crown may make by regulations 'such provision as the Minister considers appropriate to prevent, remedy or mitigate . . . any failure of EU law to operate effectively' or 'any other deficiency in retained EU law'.[82] Section 8(5) clarifies that any regulation under section 8(1) can be a Henry VIII power.[83] The government confirmed during passage that not only would it be able to enact further, so-called tertiary legislation under the instruments created under this power, but that such tertiary secondary legislation would not itself be subject to parliamentary scrutiny.[84] That meant delegated powers could create procedures for creating new law (for example, a new regulatory body), where the new powers were subject to no accountability.

On its face it seems breathtakingly wide. Section 8(2) however contains a list of deficiencies—this limits the scope of application. And section 8(3) allows ministers to make regulations proclaiming something to be a deficiency in retained EU law. Furthermore, evidence of the outright abuse of these powers is somewhat patchy, contrary to predictions that many (including myself) had given.[85] The 2018 Act is comparatively circumscribed by comparison with the extraordinarily wide powers in the Retained European Union (Revocation and Reform) Act 2023, considered further below. The ethos motivating the practice was broadly if not uniformly consistent with the reassurance by the Secretary of State for Exiting the European Union, David Davis, at second reading of the Bill in the House of Commons, that 'bringing in significant new policy changes is not the task at hand'.[86] The government had also made a range of concessions during passage, including adding a sunset clause, creating a sifting committee that could recommend upgraded scrutiny on 'proposed negative' instruments, and for a specific procedure for identifying new 'deficiencies' in section 8(3).[87]

However, the problem was not so much one of bad faith abuse of powers as a democratic deficit arising from a volume of law-making being funnelled through entirely inadequate accountability procedures. As Alexandra Sinclair and Joe Tomlinson clarify, there were 622 Brexit statutory instruments made in the 2017–19 session of Parliament, 142 of which were Henry VIII instruments amending primary legislation.[88] Their key finding—also matched in my own experience examining instruments

[82] European Union (Withdrawal) Act 2018, ss 8(1)(a) and (b).

[83] See also ss 9(2), 11 (read in conjunction with Sched 2, para. 1(3)), and 23(2).

[84] Such was a concern for the Delegated Powers and Regulatory Reform Committee and subject of an amendment to the bill moved by Lord Lisvane, HL Deb 12 March 2018, vol 789, col 1472, but the government held to its initial position: Delegated Powers and Regulatory Reform Committee, *European Union (Withdrawal) Bill: Government Response* (HL 2017–19, 119) at Appendix 1.

[85] King (n 73).

[86] HC Deb 7 September 2017, vol 628, col 351.

[87] See King (n 73) 165–67 for discussion and citations, also of concessions not given.

[88] Alexandra Sinclair and Joe Tomlinson, *Plus ça Change: Brexit and the Flaws of the Delegated Legislation System* (*Public Law Project*, 13 October 2020) <https://publiclawproject.org.uk/resources/plus-ca-change-brexit-and-the-flaws-of-the-delegated-legislation-system/> accessed 8 May 2025.

and reports on them by the Secondary Legislation Scrutiny Committee—was that the volume and character of the instruments coming in for scrutiny made them incredibly opaque. Many such instruments were extensive schedules of repeals that needed to be read in tandem with another legal instrument, an exceedingly difficult task even for a trained lawyer. And since it was a foregone conclusion that the instrument would be made unamended, there was little motivation for MPs to wrestle with the detail. Debates in the Commons delegated legislation committees lasted on average 18 minutes, and no measures were rejected.[89] Sinclair and Tomlinson conclude that the vast bulk of the powers were simply 'rubber stamped'.[90]

The 2018 Act was only one site for the growth of problematic delegated powers. In areas that were opened up following exit, busy ministers were not ready with detailed regulatory structures and so often inserted skeleton clauses into legislation to confer very wide powers to create regulatory schemes in the future. A practice of doing this led the House of Lords Secondary Legislation Scrutiny Committee, the Delegated Powers and Regulatory Reform Committee, and the Constitution Committee to write to senior members of government on 25 September 2020 to complain about the abuse of skeleton provisions in other, sectoral-related withdrawal legislation.[91] Examples given included the Immigration and Social Security Co-ordination (EU Withdrawal) Bill and the Medicines and Medical Devices Bill.[92] The report of the DPRRC on the latter bill described it as conferring 'very wide powers to almost completely rewrite the existing regulatory regimes for human and veterinary medicines and medical devices'.[93] With the Agriculture Bill, the DPRRC concluded that even after revisions based on its previous report, the bill still contained a 'significant transfer of power from the EU to Ministers of the Crown' and that it was a 'framework for future regulatory changes rather than . . . detailed changes that can be debated here and now'.[94] Relatedly, the use of delegated powers to complete the scheme of unfinished business arising from the implementation of the Trade and Cooperation Agreement—the future relationship, in other words—is also a large area of complex post-Brexit policy making left to delegated powers.[95] The whole of the Trade and Cooperation Agreement was negotiated without significant parliamentary oversight (see section 4 of this chapter) and section 31 confers an 'implementation power' that enables relevant national authorities to make regulations as considered appropriate to implement the various agreements comprising the future relationship. Left to the last minute, the

[89] ibid.
[90] ibid.
[91] The correspondence can be found on the Secondary Legislation Scrutiny Committee's webpage: <https://committees.parliament.uk/committee/255/secondary-legislation-scrutiny-committee/publications/3/correspondence/> accessed 8 May 2025.
[92] Also discussed in *Government by Diktat* (n 100).
[93] Delegated Powers and Regulatory Reform Committee, *Medicines and Medical Devices Bill (nineteenth report)* (HL 2019–21, 109) para 28.
[94] Delegated Powers and Regulatory Reform Committee, *Agriculture Bill* (HL 2019-21, 69) para 5.
[95] European Union (Future Relationship) Act 2020, s 31.

bill was introduced on 30 December 2020 and became law that same day. Thus even the creation of the skeleton provisions had no serious accountability.[96]

The Covid-19 pandemic struck in March 2020, which led to a notable increase in the use of delegated powers to govern. This practice was the same worldwide.[97] The Coronavirus Bill, numbering more than 300 pages, was passed hastily in Parliament across a few days in late March 2020, but it was anyway not the source of the delegated powers broadly used to manage the pandemic.[98] Whether such powers were abused is a topic examined elsewhere.[99] The question here is whether the precedent for expanded delegated powers during the withdrawal process, combined with necessary but sweeping use of such powers to handle the pandemic, led to an unsatisfactory general exacerbation of the problem of delegated powers. The DPRRC and the Secondary Legislation Scrutiny Committee were unambiguously of the view that they had done so, and made this the theme of their coordinated but separately issued reports on the problem of delegated powers in this period.[100] The SLSC report was candid in its conclusions:[101]

> [W]e believe, like the DPRRC and others, that a critical moment has been reached when it is imperative that efforts are made to re-set the relationship between Parliament and government—and not to how it was immediately before Brexit and the pandemic but afresh, to reflect the modern conditions of government.

Published in November 2021, the government had had plenty of time to digest and respond to those reports before it decided to introduce two other bills containing what amounted to the most extraordinarily wide creation of delegated powers of the entire process. The Northern Ireland Protocol Bill, abandoned in 2023, would have conferred powers on ministers to disapply and make changes to the application of the critically important Northern Ireland Protocol. The DPRRC found that the Bill

[96] See further Jeff King, 'Looking Back at the Future Relationship Act' (*UCL European Institute Blog*, 11 January 221) <https://ucleuropeblog.com/2021/01/11/looking-back-at-the-eu-future-relationship-act/> accessed 10 May 2025.

[97] See J King and OLM Ferraz (eds), *Comparing Covid Laws: A Critical Global Overview* (Oxford University Press 2026).

[98] Coronavirus Act 2020. The primary source was the Public Health (Control of Diseases) Act 1984. The 2020 Act did however confer, in Scheds 18 and 19, public health regulation-making powers based on the 1984 Act's template on the Scottish government and the Department of Health in Northern Ireland (as there was at the relevant time no Northern Ireland Executive formed).

[99] See the report of the Beatson Commission, Bingham Centre for the Rule of Law, *Independent Commission on UK Public Health Emergency Powers* (May 2024) <https://binghamcentre.biicl.org/documents/164_icukphep_final_report.pdf> accessed 10 January 2025. I sat as a Commissioner and adviser to the Secretariat of this Commission. See also, and mid-way through the pandemic, Public Administration and Constitutional Affairs Committee, *Coronavirus Act 2020 Two Years On (seventh report)* (HC 2021–22, 978); Select Committee on the Constitution, *COVID-19 and the Use and Scrutiny of Emergency Powers (third report)* (HL 2021–22, 15).

[100] Delegated Powers and Regulatory Reform Committee, *Democracy Denied? The Urgent Need to Rebalance Power between Parliament and the Executive* (HL 2021–22, 106); Secondary Legislation Scrutiny Committee, *Government by Diktat: A Call to Return Power to Parliament* (HL 2021–22, 105).

[101] ibid para 2.

'is a skeleton bill that confers Ministers a license to legislate in the widest possible terms' that 'represents as stark a transfer of power from Parliament to the Executive as we have seen throughout the Brexit process. The Bill is unprecedented in its cavalier treatment of Parliament, the EU, and the Government's international obligations.'[102] It would however not take long for this precedent to be superceded. The Retained European Union (Revocation and Reform) Act 2023 transformed 'retained EU law' into 'assimilated law'. Yet unlike the scheme of the 2018 Act, this Act was candid about conferring delegated powers to rewrite policies previously regulated under EU law. Sections 11–16 confer various powers, but section 14 is the most sweeping. It creates 'powers to revoke or replace'. Under this provision, the UK or devolved governments can revoke 'any secondary retained EU law' without replacing it; revoke and replace it with provision to 'achieve the same or similar objectives'; or revoke it 'and make such alternative provision as [it] considers appropriate'.[103] Under schedule 5 of the Act, the powers to revoke and replace with alternative provisions are subject to the affirmative scrutiny procedure, as are regulations conferring powers to make tertiary legislation. But the default scrutiny procedure is otherwise the negative procedure.[104] The DPRRC noted its objections to the European Union (Withdrawal) Bill but found that 'the powers conferred by the current Bill are even more significant' because the 'very large body' of retained EU law 'will be placed in the hands of Ministers. What becomes of it will depend on how Ministers choose to exercise the regulation-making powers in the Bill.'[105] The Bill is 'sufficiently lacking in substance not even to be described as "skeletal"'.[106] They called it 'hyper-skeletal'.[107] Relating it to their ordinary function, they observed as follows:[108]

> We criticise wide regulation-making powers in Bills covering just one policy area. Here we have very wide powers to make provision across multiple areas. If we were considering an open-ended delegated power in, say, an Employment Bill allowing Ministers to re-write the law on working time, we would express concern. This Bill is tantamount to creating scores of such powers.

Very unusually, the Committee recommended that five of the six most important provisions of the bill should be removed altogether.[109] Typically, that did not slow

[102] Delegated Powers and Regulatory Reform Committee, *Northern Ireland Protocol Bill (seventh report)* (2022–23, HL 40) para 4.

[103] Section 11(2) defines 'secondary retained EU law' as 'any retained EU Law that is not primary legislation' and 'any retained EU law that is primary legislation the text of which was inserted by subordinate legislation'. The field thus covers a vast area of policy.

[104] Sch 5, s 5. Under sch 5, s 6, however, proposed negative instruments are subject to a sifting procedure in which committees of the Commons and Lords can recommend upgrade to affirmative scrutiny.

[105] Delegated Powers and Regulatory Reform Committee, *Retained EU Law (Revocation and Reform) Bill (twenty-fifth report)* (HL 2022-23, 147) paras 7, 8.

[106] ibid para 8-9.

[107] ibid para 63.

[108] ibid para 10.

[109] ibid para 63.

the government down, though powers in section 14 are due to retire (sunset) on 23 June 2026.

The Labour government, elected in June 2024, took no steps to repeal this provision. And as noted in section 6 below, that government has appealed a successful judicial review against the use of Henry VIII powers to give a definition of 'serious disruption to the life of the community' in the Public Order Act 1986. Nevertheless, in his Bingham Lecture on the Rule of Law the Attorney General appointed in 2024 announced a particular concern with the abuse of delegated powers.[110] Not long afterwards, the government issued a revised *Cabinet Office Guide to Making Legislation* with updated and improved provisions on resort to delegated legislation, including a new 'delegated powers toolkit' offering extended guidance on whether to take such powers and if so what mode of parliamentary scrutiny is appropriate.[111] Such updates make reference to the reports of the Secondary Legislation Scrutiny Committee and DPRRC, and underscore the importance of responding in good faith to the latter's reports. Time will tell whether such changes have any impact.

6 Post-Brexit: The Curtailment of Public Law Controls

Another consequence of the shifts in constitutional temperament occasioned by the Brexit crisis was a high-level political campaign against judicial control of government. What set the tone was the exploitation of anti-lawyer rhetoric by the most senior members of government, including a succession of Prime Ministers. Though hostility to human rights law was palpable since 2010, there was a notable uptick in 2020, where at the Conservative Party annual conference both Prime Minister Johnson and his Home Secretary Priti Patel engaged in hostile comments about lawyers, particularly those representing asylum-seekers.[112] In 2022, the Prime Minister accused the Leader of the Opposition of being a 'lefty lawyer' during Prime Minister's Questions,[113] a remark which was technically accurate, but designed to evoke and nourish hostile attitudes towards law and pin them on his opponent. By 2023, following another set of acid remarks about lefty lawyers by Prime Minister Sunak and his Home Secretary Suella Braverman, the chair of the Bar Council of England and

[110] Lord Richard Hermer, 'The Rule of Law in an Age of Populism: The Attorney General's 2024 Bingham Lecture on the Rule of Law' (Honourable Society of Grays' Inn, 14 October 2024) <https://www.gov.uk/government/speeches/attorney-generals-2024-bingham-lecture-on-the-rule-of-law> accessed 8 May 2025.

[111] Cabinet Office, *Cabinet Office Guide to Making Legislation* (2025) ch 15 and Appendix E. The revision was issued in early 2025.

[112] 'Boris Johnson and Priti Patel "Should Apologise for Lawyer Attacks"' (*BBC News*, 26 October 2020) <https://www.bbc.co.uk/news/uk-54687081> accessed 10 October 2025; see also CJ McKinney, '5 Times the Johnson Government Complained about "Lefty Lawyers"' (*Legal Cheek*, 15 June 2022) <https://www.legalcheek.com/2022/06/5-times-the-johnson-government-complained-about-lefty-lawyers/> accessed 10 October 2025.

[113] HC Deb 8 March 2023, vol 728, col 297.

Wales, Nick Vineall KC, declared that such remarks 'betray a startling and regrettable ignorance of about the role of lawyers in society'.[114] Much of this verbal hostility can be traced to dissatisfaction about human rights law and the role of a right-wing think tank, the Policy Exchange, whose Judicial Power Project had been busy since 2015 with its focus on reducing what it perceived to be the excessive influence of judicial control of the executive in the preceding fifteen years.[115] It hosted a series of public events with government ministers, including many frontbenchers in the party.

The hostility quickly morphed from rhetorical and argumentative into real legislative change. I noted above the Conservative manifestos of 2010 and 2015 calling for repeal of the Human Rights Act 1998. The manifesto of 2017 had Brexit on its hands, but by 2019 the Party picked up the subject again with greater vigour. In the manifesto of that year, it made the following promise:[116]

> We will update the Human Rights Act and administrative law to ensure that there is a proper balance between the rights of individuals, our vital national security and effective government. We will ensure that judicial review is available to protect the rights of the individuals against an overbearing state, while ensuring that it is not abused to conduct politics by another means or to create needless delays.

True to this commitment, the government established the Independent Review of Administrative Law, which reported in March 2021,[117] and the Independent Human Rights Act Review, reporting in October 2021.[118] Both reports found that there was in fact no clear case for major reform at the present time. Beaten but unbowed, the government anyway introduced the UK Bill of Rights Bill in 2022. The Bill sought various reforms to the human rights scheme, including an elimination of the existing strong interpretive presumption that primary legislation be read consistently with Convention rights,[119] ending recourse to the jurisprudence of the Strasbourg Court, and the creation of new legal tests in the application of rights provisions that foreseeably put the UK on a collision course with the European Court of Human Rights. Reporting on the Bill of Rights Bill, the cross-party parliamentary Joint Committee on Human Rights concluded the reform project was a 'case not made' and recommended the government abandon its plans.[120] The Bill ultimately fell with the fortunes of its

[114] The Bar Council, 'PM and Home Secretary Attacks on Lawyers Betray a Startling Ignorance' (*The Bar Council*, 8 March 2023) <https://www.barcouncil.org.uk/resource/pm-and-home-secretary-attacks-on-lawyers-betray-a-startling-ignorance.html> accessed 10 October 2025.

[115] For a critical discussion that also represents my view, see P Craig, 'Judicial Power, the Judicial Power Project and the UK' (2017) 36 University of Queensland LJ 355.

[116] Conservative Party, 'Get Brexit Done: Unleash Britain's Potential' (The Conservative and Unionist Party Manifesto, 2019) 48 <https://cdn.prod.website-files.com/5da42e2cae7ebd3f8bde353c/5dda924905da587992a064ba_Conservative%202019%20Manifesto.pdf> accessed 9 May 2025.

[117] Ministry of Justice, *The Independent Review of Administrative Law* (Cm 407, 2021).

[118] Ministry of Justice, *The Independent Human Rights Act Review* (Cm 586, 2021).

[119] That is, it would have not replaced the repealed s 3 of the Human Rights Act 1998.

[120] Joint Committee on Human Rights, *Legislative Scrutiny: Bill of Rights Bill* (2022–23, HL 132, HC 611); 'Committee Urges Government Not to Proceed with the Bill of Rights Bill' (*UK Parliament*, 25 January

chief sponsor, Dominic Raab MP—who resigned after an independent ethics review determined he had bullied his civil servants.[121]

Having abandoned the primary human rights reform campaign, the government continued the fight in a lower-key fashion by opting for ad hoc legislative disapplication of provisions of the Human Rights Act 1998. For instance, in the Overseas Operations (Service Personnel and Veterans) Act 2021, section 11 controls judicial discretion by mandating certain considerations in cases concerning overseas operations, and imposing short time constraints on overseas armed forces proceedings.[122] The Illegal Migration Act 2023 went much further, legislatively disapplying section 3 of the Human Rights Act 1998 and enabling removal of persons even when such removal would be otherwise unlawful for violating Convention rights under section 6 of the Human Rights Act 1998.[123] The Safety of Rwanda (Asylum and Immigration) Act 2024 went furthest of all, disapplying nearly the whole of the Human Rights Act 1998, apart from the section 4 power to issue a declaration of incompatibility, which itself poses no legal obstacle to removing asylum-seekers.[124] Indeed, the saga leading to the Rwanda Act is itself of a piece with developments of that time. The government's policy of removing asylum-seekers who enter the UK without lawful permission to the state of Rwanda was initially trialled using executive powers under existing immigration law. The policy was comprehensively quashed in a unanimous Supreme Court judgment that found that such removals would be unlawful under UK law because there was a real risk of ill-treatment by reason of refoulement by Rwanda to their country of origin.[125] The government reacted swiftly to the 23 November judgment by introducing the Safety of Rwanda (Asylum and Immigration) Bill to the House of Commons on 7 December 2023. The unusual section 1(2)(b) proclaims that 'this Act gives effect to the judgement of Parliament that the Republic of Rwanda is a safe country'. The remaining provisions enact a legal fiction that officials must consider Rwanda to be safe for removal purposes (section 2), disapply the provisions of human rights law (section 3), and block any court from requiring ministers to abide by an interim measures judgment of the European Court of Human Rights (section 5). Such

2023) <https://committees.parliament.uk/committee/93/human-rights-joint-committee/news/175586/committee-urges-government-not-to-proceed-with-the-bill-of-rights-bill/> accessed 9 May 2025.

121 Adam Tolley KC, *Formal Complaints about the Conduct of the Right Honourable Dominic Raab MP, Deputy Prime Minister, Lord Chancellor and Secretary of State for Justice: Investigation Report to the Prime Minister* (Investigation Report, 20 April 2023). Tolly was appointed as an independent but the office of the Independent Adviser was vacant at the time, with Tolley acting on ad hoc appointment.

122 Criticized in Joint Committee on Human Rights, *Legislative Scrutiny: The Overseas Operations (Service Personnel and Veterans) Bill (ninth report)* (2019–21, HL 155, HC 665) paras 95–96.

123 see Joint Committee on Human Rights, *Legislative Scrutiny: Illegal Migration Bill (twelfth report)* (2022–23, HL 208, HC 1241) paras 75–90.

124 Joint Committee on Human Rights, *Safety of Rwanda (Asylum and Immigration) Bill (second report)* (2023–24, HL 62, HC 435) paras 83–95.

125 *R (AAA and others) v Secretary of State for the Home Department* [2023] UKSC 42.

techniques of legislative disapplication of the Human Rights Act 1998 were also used in sections 69–72 of the Victims and Prisoners Act 2024.[126]

The tendency to cabin judicial review was not limited to human rights law. Section 2 of the Dissolution and Calling of Parliaments Act 2022 claims to 'restore' the prerogative powers of the Crown to dissolve Parliament and call a new Parliament, and provides in section 3 that a court or tribunal may not question, among other things, 'the limits or extent of such powers'. The provisions of the Illegal Migration Act 2023 contained many limits on judicial oversight of immigration practices, leading the Constitution Committee to report that the '[t]he cumulative impact of the ouster and partial ouster provisions in the Bill gives rise to very considerable constitutional implications' and that 'the Bill provides an unusual degree of power to the executive'.[127] Both such instruments followed the dramatic attempt in the Internal Market Bill, introduced in 2020, to disapply any judicial recourse to all of international law and UK public law when considering the legal validity of statutory instruments made by the executive in relation to the implementation of the essential EU–UK Brexit instrument the Northern Ireland Protocol. The provisions led to a blistering report by the Constitution Committee[128] and a revolt in the House of Lords on 9 November 2020 in which it voted to support the amendment of Lord Judge (a noted judicial critic of excessive delegated powers) removing Part IV in its entirely from the bill.[129] It was not reinstated by the House of Commons during further legislative proceedings.

The reforms to public order law contained in the Police, Crime, Sentencing and Courts Act 2022 and Public Order Act 2023 follow this tendency.[130] Among its other features, the Public Order Act 1986 provides the scheme under which the police may control public assemblies and public processions. Section 14 allowed a senior police officer to impose conditions on an assembly where the officer reasonably believes that it may, among other things, create a 'serious disruption to the life of the community'. The 2022 Act mentioned above introduced Henry VIII powers to allow government to amend this definition, and in the first batch of 'serious disruption' regulations it defined such disruption as constituting something 'more than minor'.[131] These regulations were held ultra vires by the High Court and Court of Appeal, both finding that 'serious disruption' entailed a higher threshold for disruption than the 'more than

[126] While these provisions remain valid law, the Labour government elected in 2024 has laid concrete plans for the repeal of the Illegal Migration Act and Safety of Rwanda Act and has not brought the provisions of the Victims and Prisoners Act into force at the time of writing.

[127] Select Committee on the Constitution, *Illegal Migration Bill* (HL 2022–23, 200) paras 27, 10.

[128] Select Committee on the Constitution, *United Kingdom Internal Market Bill* (2019–21, HL 151).

[129] HL Deb, vol 807, col 1279ff (9 Nov 2020). See also Igor Judge, 'Ceding Power ot the Executive: The Resurrection of Henry VIII' (Lecture, King's College London, 12 April 2016) <https://www.kcl.ac.uk/law/newsevents/newsrecords/2015-16/Ceding-Power-to-the-Executive—Lord-Judge—130416.pdf> accessed 11 October 2025.

[130] Joint Committee on Human Rights, *Legislative Scrutiny: Police, Crime, Sentencing and Courts Bill, Part 3 (Public Order) (second report)* (2021–22, HL 23, HC 331) 3–27; R Martin, 'Convicting Peaceful Protesters: Proportionality's Proper Place at Criminal Trial' (2024) 44 OJLS 342.

[131] The Public Order Act 1986 (Serious Disruption to the Life of the Community) Regulations 2023 (SI 2023/655), regs 1(2), 3(2); Public Order Act 1986, s 14(2A).

minor' standard envisaged—and so the regulations amounted to an unlawful attempt to expand executive powers beyond the remit afforded by the parent act.[132] Although the saga entailed another abuse of delegated powers, it also demonstrated how the government sought to reduce and replace judicial discretion to manage the appropriate balance between the freedom of assembly and the state interest in public order.

7 Conclusion

Whether or not the UK's exceptionally powerful position for the executive in Parliament and hence in the constitution is best described as an 'elective dictatorship' (Hailsham) or more positively as an 'efficient secret' (Bagehot) is a matter of debate. But what is beyond debate is that Brexit supplied the occasion, and conjured the passions, that led to a decisive augmentation of executive power that parliamentary observers considered unprecedented. A review of the experience can only lead to one conclusion—that 'taking back control' meant placing much of the law-making powers that had previously been shared with the institutions of the European Union in the hands of the executive, at least in the near term. It also, however, left an imprint on the constitution that reached beyond those areas previously within EU competency. By casting the role of Parliament as an antagonist to rather than protagonist for democracy in the United Kingdom, by increasing the range and strength of delegated powers to an unprecedented degree, and by legislating to control public law and reduce judicial review of executive power, the Brexit experience will in the final analysis have significantly exacerbated the UK constitutional problem of outsized executive power.

[132] *R (National Council on Civil Liberties) v Secretary of State for the Home Department* [2024] EWHC 1181 (Admin), [2024] 1 WLR 5398, affirmed [2025] EWCA Civ 571.

5
Regulators

Kenneth A. Armstrong

1 Introduction

In this chapter, and as a means of offering an overarching perspective on the detailed substantive contributions to this volume, the analysis presented brings to the fore the effects on United Kingdom (UK) regulators of the UK's withdrawal from the European Union (EU)—'Brexit'. The point of departure is less Brexit itself and more where Brexit sits in the longer-run phenomenon of regulatory state-building in the UK.[1] The chapter situates detailed analysis of the effects of Brexit against the backdrop of the rise of the UK regulatory state and its 'Europeanization' during the decades of the UK's membership of the EU (sections 2 and 3). Two fundamental orientations emerge: the organizational form of the regulatory state, and normative positions on the desirability or otherwise of exercises of depoliticized public power at arm's length from (national) government. If the UK's membership of the EU can be understood as driving changes in where and how power is exercised, then de-membership requires us to consider the effects of withdrawal from the EU on the capacities and capabilities of UK regulators (section 4), as well as issues around the re-politicization of regulators outside of EU membership (section 5). Recognizing also that regulatory cooperation inside and outside of the EU is changed by Brexit, the analysis identifies frameworks for cooperation with European regulators under the EU–UK Trade and Cooperation Agreement (TCA),[2] as well as through efforts by UK regulators to reach out to regulators beyond Europe (section 6).

The central purpose of this chapter is to uncover and explain the effects of Brexit on UK regulators both in terms of the organization of regulatory functions and the purposes which regulators are required to pursue. The approach taken—an understanding of domestic institutions as mediating the forces of change generated by Brexit and a recognition of the variegated patterns of adaptation across policy sectors—also

[1] One of the best accounts of this process from a political science perspective can be found in M Moran, *The British Regulatory State: High Modernism and Hyper-innovation* (Oxford University Press 2003).

[2] Trade and Cooperation Agreement between the European Union and the European Atomic Energy Community, of the one part, and the United Kingdom of Great Britain and Northern Ireland, of the other part [2021] OJ L149/10.

Kenneth A. Armstrong, *Regulators* In: *The UK Regulatory Framework Post-Brexit: 'Law Unbound'*. Edited by: Paul Craig and Vilija Vėlyvytė, Oxford University Press. © Oxford University Press 2026. DOI: 10.1093/9780198969815.003.0006

has potential to resonate with two broader literatures on European integration. Scholarship on 'Europeanization' often highlights the manner in which domestic institutions mediate the demands of EU membership.[3] What emerges from the analysis presented here is that 'de-Europeanization' is also heavily mediated by domestic institutional factors. When we turn to the literature on the effects of EU integration on non-member states, we find the suggestion that it is the functionally differentiated design of regulatory regimes within EU policy making that dictates—more than high-level agreements—the effects of EU policies beyond EU borders.[4] If that is true for non-member states, then the experience of Brexit creates a useful vantage point from which to reflect on the dynamics of EU–UK interaction following membership in the regulatory domains featured in this chapter.

2 Regulatory State-Building

The 'regulatory state' refers both to a range of institutional structures and to normative ideas about the displacement of 'government' with 'governance', the relationship between the state and the market, and the challenge of securing accountability when assessing and managing social and economic risks.[5] As Moran carefully explained, the 'image' of the regulatory state has its origins in the US, beginning with efforts to liberalize trade and increase competition at the end of the nineteenth century and into the early decades of the twentieth century.[6] What changed in the post-war period was the creation of rule-making and rule-enforcing agencies to tackle an expanding range of social risks. It is the emergence of institutions for economic and social regulation that give the regulatory state its particular organizational form.

A phenomenon that emerged in the US gained traction around the world. In the case of the UK, a not dissimilar pattern of evolution can be seen. Sectoral economic regulations for public utilities were created as government sought to relinquish state ownership of industries through their privatization.[7] What really expanded the size and reach of the regulatory state—and in doing so, extended government's influence over the market—was risk regulation. As the state took on tasks to protect consumers and workers, and to manage new environmental, health, and even financial risks, a preferred means of bringing expertise and science into public policymaking was through the creation of regulatory agencies. The regulators analysed in this chapter—regulators of medicines, food, consumer products, chemicals, competition, financial

[3] Cf SJ Bulmer, 'Domestic Politics and European Community Policymaking' (1982) 21 JCMS 349.

[4] Cf S Lavenex and F Schimmelfennig, 'EU Rules beyond EU Borders: Theorizing External Governance in European Politics' (2009) 16 JEPP 791.

[5] For a constitutional perspective on these issues see D Oliver, T Prosser, and R Rawlings (eds), *The Regulatory State: Constitutional Implications* (Oxford University Press 2010).

[6] See (n 1).

[7] C Graham and T Prosser, *Privatising Public Enterprises: Constitutions, the State and Regulation in Comparative Perspective* (Oxford University Press 1991).

services, and aviation safety—are examples of the regulatory state as it evolved over time in the UK, including during the more than forty years of EU membership.

These regulatory bodies populated the UK's administrative landscape and, as is demonstrated in section 4(a), a key characteristic of the UK's version of the regulatory state is its differentiated institutional forms and constitutional status. Importantly then, 'the' regulatory state is really a phenomenon with characteristics that are particular not just to geographical locations, but even within countries to their own forms of government and their constitutional and legal frameworks. As is explored in section 3, what becomes of significance is how the distribution of public authority and political control within the regulatory state changed through EU membership. It is against the background of the Europeanization of the regulatory state that we can then judge the effects of de-Europeanization through Brexit.

In recalling briefly the rise of the regulatory state, our purpose is not just to recognize the distinctive organizational shape of regulatory policymaking and its particularistic manifestation in different political and constitution settings. Another reason is to highlight the ambiguities around normative justifications for regulation based on depoliticized, expert-driven, and technocratic decision-making. The challenge for the design of the regulatory state is how to reap the benefits of functionally differentiated regulation informed by specialized knowledge and professionalized decision-making while not diminishing political oversight and accountability.[8] Yet, conceiving of this governance architecture merely as 'de-politicization' risks masking an important underlying tension or even a pathology of regulation. It is a point of tension which the Europeanization of the regulatory state reproduced rather than resolved. To the extent that Brexit was a critique of this Europeanized regulatory state, withdrawal from the EU requires us to reconsider the degree to which domestic regulator can or should be insulated from political influence. This is something explored in more detail in section 5.

3 The Europeanized Regulatory State

Any exploration of how Brexit has affected regulation in the UK necessarily has to come to terms with what impact EU membership had in the first place. In doing so, we also confront an enduring characterization of the EU as the manifestation of the regulatory state in Europe.[9] As was identified in the previous section, this characterization refers both to the institutional forms of EU decision-making and to normative expectations about the balance between expert, and politically accountable, forms of regulation.

[8] See, eg, C Scott, 'Accountability in the Regulatory State' (2000) 27(1) JLS 38.

[9] See, eg, JA Caporaso, 'The European Union and Forms of State: Westphalian, Regulatory or Post-Modern?' (1996) 34 JCMS 29; M Lodge, 'Regulation, the Regulatory State and European Politics' (2008) 31 West European Politics 280; G Majone, 'The Rise of the Regulatory State in Europe' (1994) 17 West European Politics 77.

The organizational forms of EU activities are of obvious significance for present purposes. Withdrawal from the EU entailed detaching the UK's political, administrative, and court structures from the EU's political and judicial institutions. It also brought UK regulators outside the multiple European agencies that sprang up to manage a range of economic and social risks as markets became integrated into a single European market.[10] Importantly—and bringing to the fore a significant feature of the EU's regulatory style—Brexit would also remove the UK from networks that distributed regulatory powers across a range of European and domestic regulatory bodies.[11] It is this networked style of governance—the linkages across and between regulatory structures at a domestic and European level—that means it is preferable to refer to a 'Europeanized' rather than a 'European' regulatory state, as it better captures the co-evolution of structures and processes for regulation that occurred through EU membership.

It should be said that from a normative perspective, claims and counter-claims about the nature and extent of an EU legitimacy crisis, especially in the post-Maastricht period, have their origins in the EU's distinctive regulatory style of governance.[12] All of which is to acknowledge, as Moran identified, that the image of the EU as a form of regulatory state is not without a certain degree of baggage given the ambiguities and tensions around depoliticized and highly legalised forms of (networked) European governance. Of course, there is more to EU membership than this image of a legalistic, hierarchical, functionally differentiated and multi-level technocracy. The style of governance associated with the EU regulation of the EU single market also produced attempts to fashion new modes of governance that were less hierarchical and left space for greater experimentalism in the authorship and elaboration of rules, norms, and standards.[13] But rightly or wrongly, Brexit drew inspiration from discontents associated with beliefs that the regulatory state had moved decision-making outside of recognizable structures of political accountability as functions transferred to EU institutions and agencies, and as the networking of decision-making obscured the ownership and accountability of decision-making.

The fundamental normative question that Brexit poses is whether a process of de-Europeanization ought also to result in a re-politicization of regulation in some sort

[10] These agencies include the European Food Safety Authority, the Agency for the Cooperation of Energy Regulators, the European Securities and Markets Authority, the European Medicines Agency, the European Banking Authority, the European Chemicals Agency, and the European Union Aviation Safety Authority. See, eg, E Chiti, 'European Agencies' Rulemaking: Powers, Procedures and Assessment' (2013) 19 ELJ 93; E Chiti, 'An Important Part of the EU's Institutional Machinery: Features, Problems and Perspectives of European Agencies' (2009) 46 CMLRev 1395.

[11] D Coen and M Thatcher, 'Network Governance and Multi-level Delegation: European Networks of Regulatory Agencies' (2008) 28 Journal of Public Policy 49.

[12] G Majone, *Dilemmas of European Integration: The Ambiguities and Pitfalls of Integration by Stealth* (Oxford University Press 2009).

[13] CF Sabel and J Zeitlin, *Experimentalist Governance in the European Union: Towards a New Architecture* (Oxford University Press 2010); J Scott and DM Trubek, 'Mind the Gap: Law and New Approaches to Governance in the European Union' (2002) 8 ELJ 1; KA Armstrong, 'The Character of EU Law and Governance: From "Community Method" to New Modes of Governance' (2011) 63 CLP 179.

of way. Section 5 attempts to provide an answer to that question by examining how Brexit has or has not changed the statutory mandates or purposes of UK regulators in order to better align regulators with domestic political priorities. Our task in what follows in section 4 is to begin to capture how de-membership and de-Europeanization has changed the organization and delivery of regulatory policy.

4 The Impact of Brexit on the Organization of UK Regulation

By the time the UK left the EU and entered into a period of transition, there were nearly 300 public bodies carrying out a wide range of functions, from the purely advisory to those deeply engaged in regulatory work. Although Brexit will have affected the operations of a large number of these organizations, the focus of this chapter remains on the principal agencies engaged in managing social and economic risks.

In the subsections that follow, the analysis drills down into the effects of Brexit upon the organization of regulation in the UK. To put this in context, it is necessary to locate different regulatory agencies within the diverse and differentiated constitutional and institutional landscape of public bodies in the UK. Although the focus is upon UK-level regulators, it should be kept in mind that devolved responsibilities for the environment and for health mean that some regulators have a more confined jurisdictional reach and collaboration between regulators may be a feature of a particular policy area; for example, the Food Standards Agency works with Food Standards Scotland in elaborating the post-membership regulatory regimes for food and feed safety across the UK. Throughout the discussion, reference is made to a range of different regulatory bodies, and the aim is to illustrate key points and themes rather than to undertake a systematic comparative exercise, which would be beyond the remit of this chapter. Rather, the aim is to provide evidence for the central claim of this chapter that the effects of Brexit are managed and mediated through underlying and differentiated regulatory regimes and structures, resulting in variegated patterns of adaptation and change.

(a) The Institutional Landscape for Regulation

The heterogeneity of the UK's public administration beyond government departments has been the focus of attempts to categorize and rationalize the use of different types of 'arm's-length bodies'.[14] In 2016 the outcome of a classification review was

[14] Cabinet Office, *Review of the Administrative Classification of Public Bodies Within the United Kingdom: a Discussion Paper* (6 December 2014): https://assets.publishing.service.gov.uk/government/uploads/system/uploads/attachment_data/file/371650/Classification_Review_Discussion_Paper.pdf.

published. Bodies which are expected to perform functions at arm's length from government now fall into three categories: executive agencies; non-ministerial departments; non-departmental public bodies. As the UK left the EU and entered into a transition period, thirty-eight arm's-length bodies were 'executive agencies', while another twenty were non-ministerial departments. The remaining 237 bodies took the form of non-departmental public bodies.

Executive agencies do not have a separate legal personality and form part of the relevant government department. The budgets of executive agencies are part of the budget of the relevant department and so susceptible to the effects of spending reviews and budgetary constraints. But agencies function autonomously and at arm's length from government in their regulatory activities, with annual reports detailing their operations and financial position. For instance, the Medicines and Healthcare Products Regulatory Agency (MHRA) is an executive agency founded in 2003 with the Department for Health and Social Care (DHSC) as the parent department. Another executive agency is the Animal and Plant Health Agency, established in 2014, with the Department for the Environment and Rural Affairs as the parent ministry.

Non-ministerial departments are distinct legal entities operating similarly to government departments, but whose specialized functions means that direct political oversight is judged to be unnecessary. They are fewer in number—twenty as of 31 March 2020—and include some of the major regulatory authorities, including the Food Standards Agency (FSA), established in 2000. The Competition and Markets Authority (CMA)—formed in 2013 from the merger of the Office of Fair Trading with the Competition Commission—is also constituted as a non-ministerial department. The sectoral economic regulators—the Office of Rail and Road, the Office of Gas and Electricity Markets, and the Water Services Regulation Authority—are also constituted as non-ministerial departments.

The vast bulk of arm's-length public bodies are non-departmental public bodies (NDPBs). The Health and Safety Executive (HSE)—whose wide-ranging responsibilities include chemicals regulation as well as the health and safety protection of workers—was established in 1975 and operates as a non-departmental body sponsored by the Department for Work and Pensions.

It would be enough to highlight the way in which the UK regulatory landscape has evolved and differentiated into these three broad types of public body. But that does not completely capture the range of forms of UK regulators. Other regulators have a statutory corporate form. The Civil Aviation Authority (CAA), founded in 1972, is a statutory corporation. The more recently constituted Financial Conduct Authority and Prudential Regulation Authority—like their earlier incarnation as the Financial Services Authority—take the corporate form of companies limited by guarantee.

One of the UK's newest regulators—the Office for Product Safety and Standards (OPSS)—was established as the UK's product safety regulator in 2018 and unlike the other regulators studied here, its creation assumed that the UK would leave the EU with product safety becoming a regulatory responsibility of the OPSS outside of EU membership. And unlike other regulators, it is simply part of a government department—the Department for Business and Trade (DBT)—rather than separate from its departmental sponsor. This direct political oversight is consistent with calls by those advocating withdrawal from the EU to bring decision-making within accountable political structures.

Regulator	**Type of 'arm's-length' public body**			**Other**	
	Executive agency	**Non-ministerial department**	**Non-departmental public body**	**Corporate body**	**Office within a department**
Medicines and Healthcare Products Regulatory Agency	X				
Animal and Plant Health Agency	X				
Food Standards Agency		X			
Competition and Markets Authority		X			
Sectoral Economic Regulators		X			
Health and Safety Executive			X		
Civil Aviation Authority				X	
Financial Conduct Authority and Prudential Regulation Authority				X	
Office for Product Safety and Standards					X

The Europeanization of the regulatory state did not, therefore, have the effect of harmonizing or homogenizing regulatory structures, and instead the diverse manifestation of the regulatory state reflected the UK's uncodified constitution of public authority. The forces and vectors of institutional change—to the extent that they exist—reflect domestic political imperatives. After all, the rise of the sectoral economic regulators at the end of the twentieth century derived from the politics of privatization and the creation of new regulators as an alternative to state control of industries.

One clearly identifiable source of influence upon the organization landscape is the pressure exerted by constrained public finances and the wider economic environment. Following the financial crisis of the early twenty-first century, the 2010–15 Coalition government promised a 'bonfire of the quangos' in a bid to cut costs. As a consequence of the review of public bodies, more than 100 were axed. Importantly, for those bodies that remained, in April 2011 the Cabinet Office announced the triennial review of NDPB. By the time of the 2016 referendum, triennial reviews had been replaced by 'tailored reviews' of all public bodies at least once during the lifetime of a Parliament.[15] Revised Cabinet Office guidance issued in 2019 exhorted tailored reviews to understand how a public body would respond to the UK's departure from the EU.[16] A new programme of reviews of public bodies was launched in 2022, with the Cabinet Office publishing lists of bodies to be prioritized for review, including the CAA and the Health and Safety Executive—their inclusion resulting from the significant effects of Brexit on the regulation of aviation safety and chemicals respectively. Subsequent reviews brought in other regulators, including the CMA. On the one hand, these post-Brexit reviews follow the pattern of earlier reviews of public bodies, with the Covid-19 pandemic once again putting public spending under the spotlight. On the other hand, statements made by the then Brexit Opportunities and Government Efficiency Minister Jacob Rees-Mogg suggested that the review and reform of public bodies was part of a wider ambition to bring decision-making back under the control of ministers (aligned with the Brexit mantra of 'taking back control').[17]

In section 5 the analysis picks up this discussion in reflecting on how regulators' role, mandate, and purpose as public bodies has been 'politicized' both before and after the 2016 referendum. In doing so, the analysis also considers the implications of the 2024 general election. For the moment what has emerged is a clear understanding of the heterogeneity of the UK's regulatory landscape even despite waves of initiatives intended to review and reform public bodies. But if the diverse constitutional and legal forms of regulators have endured, to what extent is that differentiation and diversity—of itself or in combination with other sources of influence—a means of explaining how regulators have managed and mediated the effects of Brexit? In the subsection that follows, some answers to that question can be found.

(b) Charting the Effects of Brexit

As the other chapters in this volume reveal in detail, Brexit has had profound implications for the legal frameworks governing a wide range of regulated sectors. Gaining analytical purchase on the effects of Brexit at an organizational level is not without its difficulties as we wrestle with unpicking the shorter- and longer-term effects some five years on from the UK's formal exit. This analysis looks to the periods before the

[15] House of Commons Library, Public Bodies, Briefing Paper CBP8376, 19 Jan 2021.

[16] Cabinet Office, Tailored Reviews: Guidance on the Reviews of Public Bodies (May 2019): https://assets.publishing.service.gov.uk/media/5ce2bd47e5274a4bf48201ad/Tailored_Review_Guidance_on_public_bodies_-May-2019.pdf.

[17] J Rees-Mogg, 'Public Bodies Reform', Written Statement 26 Apr 2022, HCWS784.

referendum and after EU exit to identify changes, particularly in terms of the staffing and funding of UK regulators. Drawing on evidence presented in the annual reports and financial statements of major UK regulators, some significant findings are made about the diversity of the experience of Brexit for these bodies.

Something to highlight at the outset is the significant amount of funding allocated by the UK government for preparations for EU exit. According to the National Audit Office, more than £6bn was allocated for EU exit preparations, of which around £2bn was additional staff costs and around £1.5bn services, including building new IT and other infrastructure as the UK lost access to EU-wide systems.[18] Part of those budgets were allocated to regulators to support their adaptation to Brexit. As another National Audit Office report spotlighted, an anticipated effect of Brexit was the need for regulators to increase their capacities and capabilities for carrying out regulatory work that had previously been undertaken by, or in collaboration with, EU agencies and the regulatory authorities of EU member states.[19] The report highlighted the need, for example, for the FSA to take on additional staff to undertake risk assessments for regulated products and to undertake veterinary checks. With the UK leaving the EU's chemicals regulation regime (REACH), the National Audit Office reported a 46 per cent increase in staffing at the HSE. The CMA also took on new staff as merger control and augmented antitrust responsibilities returned to the UK.

As we will explore, regulators have experienced changes in their staffing and funding in different ways. But it needs to be recognized that maintaining and increasing staffing posed challenges for UK regulators. For the FSA, the lack of sufficient numbers of qualified people to carry out veterinary checks was also exacerbated by the absence of arrangements for the mutual recognition of qualifications for those professionals who qualified as vets outside the UK. For the CMA, its pool of competition lawyers was shared with a private sector that could attract talent without the restrictions on salary levels faced by a public regulator. Some agencies also experience high turnover rates and conscious restructuring programmes as UK regulators transitioned out of EU membership. While all regulators faced a similar challenge as their regulatory responsibilities changed, we need to look more closely at individual agencies to understand the effects of Brexit on the human and financial resources available to regulators. It is apparent that some agencies experienced significant challenges as sources of funding changed and as new skills were sought to maintain or expand the capacity of regulators to operate in a post-membership regulatory environment.

As was noted in the previous subsection, UK regulators have diverse constitutional and institutional forms. Regulators also come in different shapes and sizes, meaning that Brexit had a range of effects depending not only on the extent of functional change that withdrawal from the EU entailed, but also somewhat on the size and shape of the organizations as the UK left the EU. For a regulator like the OPSS, as it only came into existence in January 2018, its whole organizational existence as the UK's product

[18] National Audit Office, The Cost of EU Exit Preparations, HC 102 (2019–21).
[19] National Audit Office, Regulating after EU Exit, HC 61 (2022–23).

safety regulator has been lived in the context of the UK's withdrawal from the EU. Its staffing levels grew—with more than 350 staff in 2024/25—as did its budget—from an initial annual budget of £12m to over £60m in 2023/24 (all government funding).

If we look at a regulator like the Financial Conduct Authority (FCA), its size and financing are clearly of a very different scale to that of the OPSS. By financial year 2024/25 the FCA had more than 5,000 permanent staff (up from around 3,500 prior to the 2016 referendum). The FCA is funded through the fee income it receives from the firms it regulates, and the Financial Services and Markets Act gives the FCA powers to raise fees to meet its costs, including its increased staff costs. So unlike other UK regulatory agencies, it does not receive, nor is it dependent upon, UK government funding. As a corporate body separate from government, staff of the FCA are not civil servants and so not restricted by civil service remuneration structures. For the financial year ending 31 March 2025, regulatory fee income had risen to £760m from £507m in the year to 31 March 2016. As Figure 5.1 shows, this rise in income allowed the FCA to manage its increased staff costs. Significantly, the figures suggest an ability of the FCA to manage and adapt to the pressures which Brexit created.

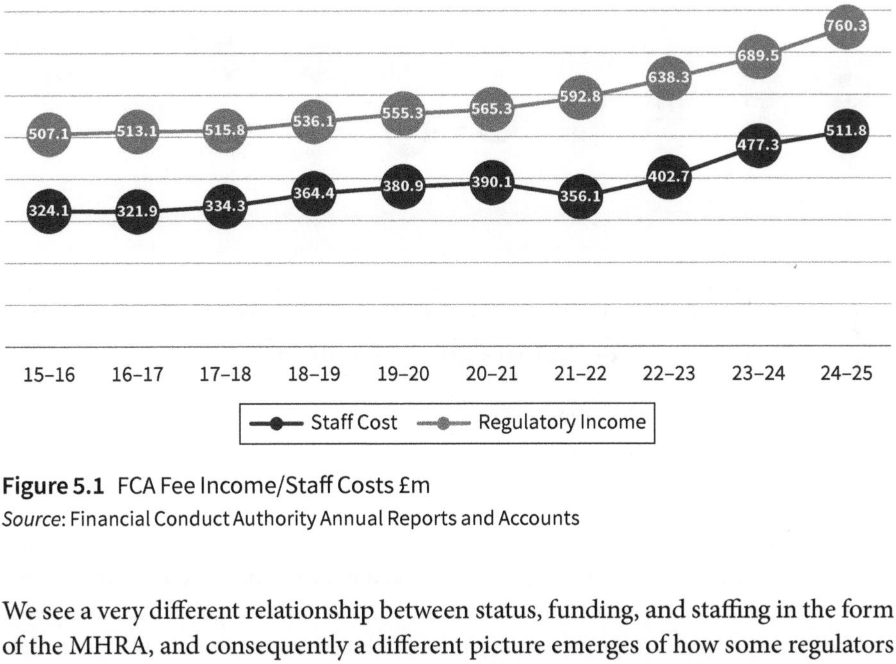

Figure 5.1 FCA Fee Income/Staff Costs £m
Source: Financial Conduct Authority Annual Reports and Accounts

We see a very different relationship between status, funding, and staffing in the form of the MHRA, and consequently a different picture emerges of how some regulators have adapted to Brexit. Established as an executive agency, the MHRA's funding model was until 2022 as a 'trading fund'. As such it was primarily funded from the fee income obtained from its regulatory functions, including market authorizations (licensing of new drugs) and market vigilance (for companies with existing licences). As a trading fund, the MHRA had significant control over its finances, while Treasury rules required the agency to generate a 3.5 per cent return. Although sponsored by the DHSC, the MHRA acted outside departmental financial boundaries.

Government finance was limited to payment for specific regulatory services. From April 2022, the trading fund was revoked and the MHRA brought within departmental budget and financial control.[20] All of this reflects the significant impact of Brexit on the sources of finance available to the agency. Trading income fell below its pre-referendum levels to less than £100m in three consecutive financial years from 2018 to 2021 before recovering and increasing to more than £150m. Staff costs fell in three consecutive financial years from 2020 to 2023 as the MHRA undertook a major transformation programme with a view to cutting 20 per cent of its headcount. In response to freedom of information requests, it was reported that this transformation programme was a response to Brexit and financial pressures as well as key policy reviews on life sciences and a more patient-focused approach to medicines and medical devices. Exit packages totalling £7m for around 160 people were agreed between 2020 and 2023. But like other agencies, staff costs rose again, albeit in line with increased trading income (Figure 5.2).

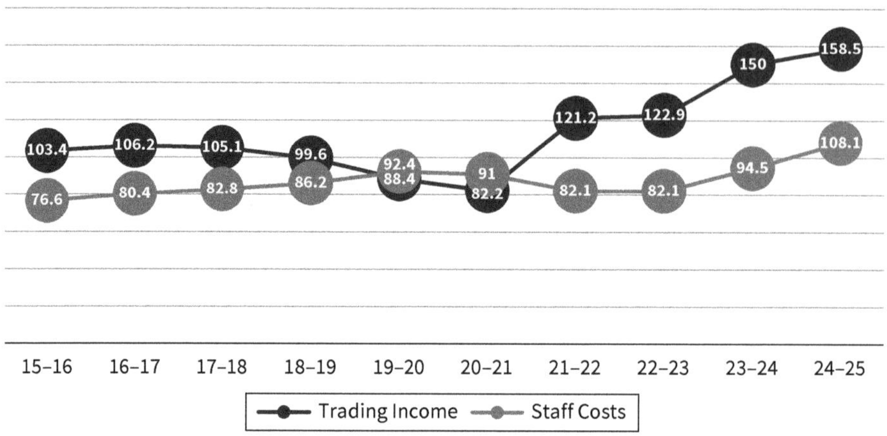

Figure 5.2 MHRA Trading Income/Staff Costs
Source: MHRA Annual Reports and Accounts

What is also striking about the MHRA is that the income it derives from its licensing operations (market authorizations), which peaked at more than £50m for the financial year 2017–18, showed a significant decline in the following five financial years and has not recovered to pre-referendum levels. Licensing income is also a smaller share of total trading income compared to pre-referendum levels. What had previously been a profit-making activity for the MHRA as a result of EU membership and its leading role in both centralized and decentralized medicines approval, from 2019/20 became a loss-making aspect of the agency's regulatory work (Figure 5.3).

[20] The Medicines and Healthcare Products Regulatory Agency Trading Fund (Revocation) Order 2022.

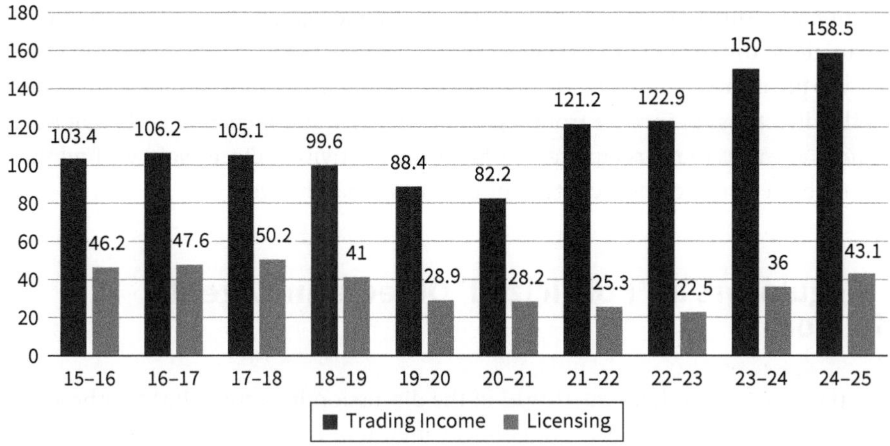

Figure 5.3 Licensing Income £m
Source: MHRA Annual Reports and Accounts

It should be noted that in 2018/19 the MHRA received £6m in funding from the DHSC to help the agency manage the process of EU exit (including significant changes to a large number of IT systems with which the MHRA was connected to the European regulatory regime). The significant revenue drop in 2019/20 was partly mitigated by increased funding from the DHSC of £12.6m. In 2020/21 £12.8m of EU exit funding was provided, but still against a backdrop of decreasing trading income and an agency that was also dealing with the Covid-19 pandemic. Posting deficits of around £40m per annum between 2023 and 2025, the MHRA relied on funding of more than £60m per annum to generate a surplus.

We can contrast both the FCA and the MHRA with the position of the CMA, whose primary funding comes from HM Treasury. Staff costs are clearly a principal expenditure for any regulator. At the CMA, staff costs of around £50m up until 2018/19 steadily rose until they had more than doubled in the financial year 2024/25. Following a targeted voluntary redundancy scheme that aimed at removing around twenty-five posts, an organization with a FTE headcount below 700 in 2016/17 (of whom less than 600 were permanent staff) grew to more than 1100 staff (of whom around 1000 were permanent roles). At the end of 2024 the CMA launched a workforce reduction plan with a stated aim of reducing staff costs by more than £5m, representing a reduced headcount of around 100 roles. The agency also experienced periods with a high turnover of staff, with recruitment also challenged by competition from the private sector. The CMA also experienced significant leadership problems, with high-profile departures of two of its chairs (meaning the agency had three chairs and an acting chair) within a decade.

Although we can point to similar trends for UK regulators—rising headcounts and staff costs, with short-term EU exit funding to help organizations manage the UK's exit from the EU—it is really the underlying financial models that have come under pressure, with different agencies able to adapt and manage change better than others. In part these differences are explained by the formal status of regulators and their ability to pivot fee structures to a changing environment. But in a case like the MHRA, it is the direct loss of income from regulatory activity and increased costs that have required agencies to restructure and refocus their activities. Once again we find that Brexit is both a pretext and a context for organizational change.

5 Regulators as 'Politicized' Objects and Agents of Reform

It is appropriate to pick up the thread of the discussion in section 4(a) that brought to light public bodies as objects of political attention. Consistent with the approach taken throughout this chapter, Brexit as a political moment and as a source of influence is reconstructed within a longer time frame that reaches back to pre-referendum political agendas and projects forward beyond the immediacy of exit.

Taking a longer view, we can see some of the contradictions and tensions around the relationship between, on the one hand, the growth in arm's-length bodies and the rise of the regulatory state and, on the other hand, anxieties around political accountability. Sectoral economic regulators and 'Next Steps' agencies were created in the 1980s and 1990s as government sought to withdraw from public ownership and take the delivery of public services out of government departments. The rise of the regulatory state—despite its differentiated institutional manifestations—also chimed with the aspiration to take regulation out of the hands of politicians. As we saw, successive governments sought effective and efficient regulation through programmes of review and reform of public bodies. Governments of different political parties promised to regulate better and smarter. In this context, Brexit presents itself as a disruption; an opportunity to change direction or reset patterns of relations between politicians and regulators. But to what extent has Brexit re-politicized or repurposed the activities of regulators? If understood as a critique of the Europeanized regulatory state, did Brexit then offer an alternative vision and trajectory for de-Europeanized regulation?

Cutting through the rhetoric and febrile politics of Brexit, and looking instead for ways of providing a distinctive legal analysis, one way of approaching the issue is to evaluate whether the statutory mandates of regulators have changed, or the purposes of regulation realigned with new political priorities and, if so, whether such changes and realignments are due to Brexit or other causal influences. Distinct from the other contributions to this volume, the focus here is not upon the impact of Brexit upon the regulatory frameworks derived from EU law, but instead more specifically upon regulators as objects—and as agents—of reform.

The report of the Taskforce on Innovation, Growth and Regulatory Reform (TIGRR) exemplifies a political vector linking issues of growth, competitiveness, and innovation to regulatory reforms capable of being delivered outside of EU membership. Much of that report operates at an instrumental level and connects to other programmes to review and replace retained EU law. However, the TIGRR report is noteworthy in spotlighting the role of regulators. The Taskforce was established by the Johnson government with terms of reference to 'scope out and propose options for how the UK can take advantage of our newfound regulatory freedoms'. What is striking is the Taskforce's recommendation to make changes to the statutory mandates of key candidate regulators. If implemented, regulators would be expected to promote competitiveness and innovation in order to drive economic growth. For illustrative purposes, three of these regulators—the CMA, the FCA, and the CAA—will be discussed. What emerges from this analysis is a sense of an increased politicization of regulators—with political influence exerted through a range of means—as governments have sought to align regulatory policy with strategies to drive economic growth. This politicization and realignment has roots deeper than Brexit; but cumulatively, the economic effects of the financial crisis, the Covid-19 pandemic, and Brexit created the economic context for government efforts to harness regulators as agents of growth.

To better understand the context in which UK regulators might also be expected to support economic growth, it needs to be recalled that back in the summer of 2013, the then Conservative–Liberal Democrat coalition government published its draft Deregulation Bill. Announced as a part of Cabinet Office initiatives to cut red tape, the Bill included a new 'growth duty' to apply to the functions of a large number of regulators. Section 108(1) of the Deregulation Act 2015 (which became operational in 2017) requires specified regulators 'to have regard to the desirability of promoting economic growth'. The test to be applied by regulators is one familiar to EU lawyers—is the exercise of the regulatory function both necessary and proportionate? More substantive guidance is given to regulators by ministers under section 110 and regulators must have regard to that guidance when exercising their functions. Different 'drivers' of growth—including innovation, competition, and productivity—are identified in the guidance. Although regulators are not statutorily obliged to report on how their strategies and policies meet the growth duty, voluntary reporting is encouraged.

The CMA and sectoral 'economic' regulators were outside the scope of the growth duty. Instead, under the Enterprise and Regulatory Reform Act 2013 which brought the CMA into existence, section 25 gave the CMA the purpose of seeking to promote competition both within and outside the UK, for the benefit of consumers. Sitting alongside its statutory duty, the UK government also published a non-statutory and non-binding 'Strategic Steer' setting out the high-level priorities to which the CMA would be expected to 'have regard', including strong economic growth. While respecting its operational independence particularly in competition cases, the intention behind the steer was to enhance the CMA's accountability for its performance.

As a consequence of the UK's exit from the EU, the CMA's role as a regulator inevitably changed, not least as merger control and subsidy control functions were repatriated. What is of interest here, however, is whether Brexit had any impact on the statutory or strategic context in which the CMA might be expected to exercise its functions, particularly with respect to government priorities on growth, competitiveness, and innovation as envisaged in the TIGRR report. In a consultation launched in July 2021, the UK government sought views not only on reforms to the application and enforcement of UK competition and consumer law, but also on the CMA's contribution to the government's wider ambitions for economic growth, competitiveness, and productivity. In particular, and repeating its respect for the CMA's operational independence, the consultation asked whether its non-binding strategic steers to the CMA should be updated more regularly than once per Parliament to reinforce ministerial expectations of how the CMA would align with political priorities. In its response to the consultation, the government concluded that such steers would remain non-binding and continue to respect operational independence, but their frequency would vary as and when ministers felt it appropriate to produce updated strategic steers. In turn the CMA would be expected to demonstrate how its work aligned with and delivered upon these priorities. In this way, political imperatives around growth, competitiveness, and productivity would be felt by the regulator less through express changes to its statutory mandate and more through extra-statutory ministerial influence.

The election of a UK Labour government in July 2024 was consequential for UK regulators. Against a weak economic backdrop and the constraints of fiscal rules, accelerating economic growth was a central pillar of the economic strategy of the new Labour Chancellor. Crucially for present purposes, the expectation that regulators would help deliver that growth was underscored by a Christmas Eve letter to UK regulators signed by the Prime Minister. In that letter—and in an accompanying Action Plan from the Chancellor—regulators were asked 'to go further to prioritise growth and facilitate investment'. Regulators were asked to identify five concrete and measurable proposals that could be taken within a year and 'with a tolerable level of risk'. Regulators were also asked to identify obstacles to reform. These letters—sent to the CMA, the FCA, the CAA, and other UK regulators—elicited responses from each regulator setting out their plans. It was widely reported that the unexpected departure of the CMA's chair in January 2025—only appointed to the role in 2022 after a lengthy appointment process—signalled the UK government's discontent with the CMA's level of ambition in aligning regulatory policy with government growth priorities. The broader point to take away is a governance relationship that evolved not through statutory changes to the mandate of the CMA, nor even through statutory guidance, but rather through multiple channels of political influence and pressure emanating not only from the CMA's sponsoring department but also from the offices of the Prime Minister and Chancellor.

One statutory change is worth noting, however. The Digital Markets, Competition and Consumer Act 2024 amended the CMA's statutory mandate under section 25 of the Enterprise and Regulatory Reform Act 2013 to place a general duty on the CMA to 'expedite' proceedings. The significance of this is a recognition that when it comes to the interface between 'regulation' and 'competitiveness', slow decision-making by regulators is seen as a problem that undermines the effectiveness and competitiveness of regulation. A highly prescriptive 2025 ministerial steer to the CMA reflected the ambition behind the government's 'new approach', underlining the need for swift decision-making.[21]

How does the experience of other regulators compare to that of the CMA? The trajectory of change for the FCA was different and reflected a more specific political focus on how financial services would be regulated outside of the EU's regulatory regimes. The Financial Services and Markets Act 2023 added a secondary statutory objective to the mandate of the FCA (alongside its primary duty to protect consumers and the integrity of financial markets), to require it, 'subject to alignment with relevant international standards', to meet international competitiveness and medium to long-term growth objectives. While this secondary duty does not apply to individual authorization decisions, it does apply to the FCA's rule-making and policy functions. But what is striking about the FCA's five-year 2025–30 strategic plan is its knitting together of both the Conservative UK government's 'Smarter Regulation' initiative[22] and the Labour UK government's new approach to regulation and economic growth.[23] In this strategy, the FCA's top two priorities are to be a 'smarter regulator' and to support 'sustained economic growth'. It is a strategy that says nothing explicitly about Brexit but instead reflects core post-Brexit themes of reforms to UK financial services regulation, including a 'rebalancing' of regulation that seeks not to eliminate risks but allow for a greater level of 'informed' risk-taking. In this regard, the FCA appears not as a passive object of reform but rather as a willing and collaborative agent of change.

A different example of 'active' engagement by regulators with growth-oriented reforms can be seen when we turn attention to the CAA. Certain of the CAA's regulatory functions were already within the scope of the Deregulation Act's growth duty and so also subject to the statutory guidance on its application. It will be recalled that reporting requirements for compliance with the duty are voluntary, but since 2020 the CAA has reported on how it complies with the duty, first as part of its annual report and then subsequently as a stand-alone report. One aspect of its 2025 report is the CAA's claim to be supporting economic growth by reducing the barriers to trade for exporters which arose as a consequence of the UK's departure from the EU, with the CAA pointing to a series of bilateral agreements with other regulators to reduce

[21] Department for Business and Trade, Strategic Steer to the Competition and Markets Authority (May 2025): https://www.gov.uk/government/publications/strategic-steer-to-the-competition-and-markets-authority/strategic-steer-to-the-competition-and-markets-authority. For its part, the CMA has adopted a '4Ps' approach as its response to the pressures from government. These refer to: Pace; Predictability; Proportionality; Process.

[22] Department for Business and Trade, Smarter Regulation: Delivering an Environment for Innovation, Investment and Growth, CP 1089 (May 2024). It is worth noting that DBT took over the Cabinet Office's work on Brexit-related regulatory reform (including revision and reform of retained EU law) and rolled it into DBT's 'Smarter Regulation' work. In this way, Brexit's regulatory dimension has been mainstreamed within government.

[23] Financial Conduct Authority, Strategy 2025–30: https://www.fca.org.uk/publication/corporate/our-strategy-2025-30.pdf.

duplication of regulatory efforts. But what is also apparent is that the CAA's growth duty reporting activities—including quarterly updates—align with the CAA's response to the Prime Minister's and Chancellor's demands for UJ regulators to pursue growth and innovation in the sectors they regulate.

It will be recalled that the TIGRR report recommended giving a wider set of regulators express competition and innovation duties. Candidate regulators included not only the CMA, the FCA, and the CAA but also the economic regulators—OFCOM, OFGEM, OFWAT. Instead, in July 2023 the UK government launched a consultation on whether to extend the 'growth duty' under the Deregulation Act to the economic regulators. In 2024 a statutory instrument did just that.[24] It should be noted, however, that criticism of the effectiveness of post-privatization economic regulators emerged more strongly within domestic politics with a particular focus on the structure and regulation of the water industry. In the summer of 2025 the UK government announced that the water regulator OFWAT would be abolished.

The conclusion we might draw is that UK regulators do not inhabit a depoliticized sphere of decision-making. Brexit is not the immediate cause of this politicization. For more than a decade, UK governments have sought through various means to align regulators with political priorities of which the pursuit of economic growth has assumed a paramount position. Expectations of regulators—and their leadership—have intensified. These political shifts cut across the realms of economic and risk regulation, reflecting not only the context of Brexit but a range of discontents and demands that run more deeply through domestic politics.

6 International Regulatory Cooperation after EU Membership

During its membership of the EU, the relationship between domestic UK regulators and their counterparts in EU institutions and agencies, as well as the regulatory authorities of EU (and also EEA) member states, became a dominant context for 'international' regulatory cooperation. Through its external trade policy, the EU also created legal frameworks that brought EU and domestic regulatory authorities into relationships with regulatory authorities in third countries. Brexit would take the UK out of these networks for regulatory cooperation. In the subsections below, post-membership regulatory cooperation is explored in two ways. The analysis begins with consideration of UK–EU cooperation under the auspices of the EU–UK TCA. What emerges from that analysis is once again a highly differentiated range of effects with sectors organized under different legal frameworks. Attention then turns to the wider international context in which UK regulators may seek collaborative partnerships beyond relations with the EU and its member states.

[24] Economic Growth (Regulatory Functions) (Amendment) Order 2024 No 587.

(a) Regulatory Cooperation through the TCA

When thinking about post-membership regulatory cooperation, a helpful place to start is the EU–UK TCA. An important point to stress at the outset is that whatever it says about regulatory cooperation has to be reconciled with the driving ethos of the Agreement, namely, the maintenance of the parties' regulatory autonomy. This is particularly reflected in Article 340 TCA, which provides:

> Each Party shall be free to determine its approach to good regulatory practices under this Agreement in a manner consistent with its own legal framework, practice, procedures and fundamental principles underlying its regulatory system.

This tension between the driving force of regulatory state-building through Europeanized (and international) regulatory networks and the political demands of autonomy (of which Brexit was the ultimate product) sets the context for the analysis in the final section of how UK regulators find themselves in the post-membership landscape of regulatory cooperation.

The TCA is not silent on examples of future regulatory cooperation between UK and EU regulatory authorities. Article 98 TCA envisages cooperation between EU and UK authorities in the field of technical regulations, standards, and conformity assessment procedures, with assistance from the Technical Barriers to Trade Specialist Committee. It is noteworthy that this cooperation is also with respect to these activities at international, regional, and national levels, in line with the structure of technical harmonization at these levels. Although somewhat different from the examples of risk regulation by public agencies, cooperation and coordination of the work of standards bodies is a significant part of the broader regulatory landscape in which the UK's OPSS operates.

The TCA also has very specific provisions for regulatory cooperation in certain sectors. For example, a particular example of cooperation between a UK regulator and its European counterpart can be found in Article 318 TCA, which anticipates cooperation between the EU's Agency for Cooperation of Energy Regulators and the UK's respective energy regulator.

More detailed provisions for cooperation can be found for chemicals regulation and aviation safety. Annex 13 on chemicals commits UK and EU authorities to cooperation in international forums and to each implement common standards and guidelines developed by such bodies. Article 7 of the Annex also commits the EU and UK, on a voluntary basis, to engage in regulatory cooperation to facilitate trade. Nonetheless, the kinds of exchanges of information envisaged are rendered more difficult outside of EU systems and databases to which the UK lost access when it left the EU. The TCA also lays down more specific provisions for the aviation sector. Importantly, Part Two, Heading Two, Title II (Aviation Safety) and Annex 30 provide inter alia for the 'reciprocal recognition' of certificates relating to airworthiness, environmental standards, and design and production. As 'competent authorities' and 'technical agents', the UK's CAA and the EU Aviation Safety Agency are tasked with cooperating with one another (and the competent authorities of member states) in implementing the TCA's provisions.

If the approach to regulatory cooperation in the areas of chemicals regulation and aviation safety was to enshrine in the TCA a legal framework for engagement between UK and EU authorities, then a different approach was taken for competition regulation. While restating the autonomy of the parties to maintain their own competition regimes, the content of those regimes is effectively to be modelled on the substance of the EU competition regime (Article 359 TCA). Article 361 TCA then recognizes the importance of cooperation between UK, EU, and member state competition authorities, both at a general policy level and more specifically when it comes to enforcing rules in respect of the same economic activity. Under the TCA, exchanges of information are permitted. But the crucial point is that the TCA envisages in Article 361(4) the inclusion in a separate agreement—recognized as forming part of the TCA—of measures

> on cooperation and coordination between the European Commission, the competition authorities of the member states and the United Kingdom's competition authority or authorities, which may include conditions for the exchange and use of confidential information.

In June 2023, the Council of the EU authorized the European Commission to open negotiations with the UK on the separate agreement envisaged in Article 361(4) TCA. Those negotiations were finalized in October 2024 and in May 2025 the Commission published a proposal for a Council Decision to sign an agreement with the UK on cooperation on the application of competition law.[25] The EU–UK Competition Cooperation Agreement between the CMA, the European Commission, and member state authorities was signed on 25 February 2026.

So looking across chemicals, aviation, and competition, we find different approaches being taken within the TCA in creating the frameworks of 'Cooperation' between UK and EU regulatory authorities. Outside of these sectors, we are left with more general provisions within the TCA on regulatory cooperation. Part Two, Heading One, Title X on 'Good Regulatory Practices and Regulatory Cooperation' is relevant. Article 351 TCA states that:

> The Parties may engage in regulatory cooperation activities on a voluntary basis, without prejudice to the autonomy of their own decision-making and their respective legal orders. A Party may refuse to engage in or it may withdraw from

[25] COM 2025 (232) final.

> regulatory cooperation activities. A Party that refuses to engage in or that withdraws from regulatory cooperation activities should explain the reasons for its decision to the other Party.

Here, and throughout this Title, we see at play the tension between promoting cooperation and the protection of autonomy. It is also noteworthy that the cooperation envisaged is over regulatory 'measures' (regulations, directions, primary and secondary legislation) between regulatory 'authorities' (the European Commission, UK Government and devolved administrations). This is cooperation over regulatory rule-making—and thus to be read in the context of the TCA's 'Level Playing Field' obligations—rather than cooperation between regulators in the implementation, application, and enforcement of regulatory frameworks.

We can better understand the implications of Brexit for those regulators that do not benefit from specific cooperation frameworks within the TCA if we consider medicines regulation. Here, the balance tipped towards regulatory autonomy and away from regulatory cooperation, despite the MHRA's stated preference for 'continued participation within the European Medicines Agency', including following its rules and contributing towards its costs.[26] Indeed, such was the concern that the MHRA would be taken out of the European regime for medicines approval that efforts were made to amend domestic legislation to require the UK government to reach an agreement with the EU as a legal framework for regulatory cooperation. In mid-2018, MPs voted for an amendment to the Trade Bill that would seek to leverage future trade negotiations to bring the UK back into the European medicines regulatory regime.[27] However, that version of the Bill never passed into law and what became the Trade Act 2021 did not reproduce the clause in the earlier Bill. As a result of its withdrawal from the EU, the MHRA was also no longer represented in the Heads of Medicines Agencies, which established a network of thirty European medicines regulators.

Brexit also meant that the UK ceased to have access to the Mutual Recognition Agreements (MRAs) which the EU has concluded with external trade partners. Although the MRAs do not impose the same legal discipline as applies to recognition of a European Medicines Agency (EMA) or EU/EEA national marketing authorization, they facilitate the import of pharmaceuticals from third country trade partners, allowing, for example, imports without a need to repeat batch testing undertaken outside the EU. So what is also striking is that not only does the TCA not provide a sectoral legal framework for EU–UK medicines cooperation, the EU has also not concluded an MRA with the UK in the way it has done with other trade partners.

[26] See MHRA Annual Report and Accounts 2018–19, p 15.

[27] Clause 17 of the Bill stated: 'It shall be the objective of an appropriate authority to take all necessary steps to implement an international trade agreement, which enables the UK to fully participate after exit day in the European medicines regulatory network partnership between the European Union, European Economic Area and the European Medicines Agency.'

Food safety regulation is another field where Brexit has significantly reduced the capacity of UK regulators to engage with European and international partners. At a technological level, the UK's FSA lost access to the European alert system for notification and exchange of information between regulators about risks in the food and feed chains. At a leadership level, the UK had participated in the Heads of Food Safety Agencies (HoA) network, bringing together leaders from the agencies of the EU/EEA member states as well as Turkey and the Balkan states. Meeting biannually in line with the rotating presidency of the EU Council and with specialized working groups, this network focuses on the enforcement of EU-derived food safety law. But as a consequence of Brexit, the UK was formally requested to leave the network, which it did in February 2022.

(b) International Cooperation

It would be misleading to focus solely on the UK's post-membership regulatory cooperation with the EU and its member states. Indeed, for some, the opportunity of Brexit and regulatory autonomy is also the capacity to seek to influence the design and content of regulation at a global level. Autonomy also creates a space for unilateral action that has the effect of changing the UK's relationship with its international partners. In this subsection, examples are given of how UK regulators are engaging in cooperative activities at an international level.

The MHRA adopted a new International Recognition Procedure (IRP) which became operational from 1 January 2024. While retaining the right to refuse, the MHRA can offer a domestic licence to a drug approved by regulators in Australia, Canada, Switzerland, Singapore, Japan, and the United States and, importantly, the European regulators (EMA and competent authorities of EU/EEA states).[28] It is worth noting, in particular, the cooperation that the MHRA has with its counterparts in Australia, Canada, Singapore, and Switzerland. These four countries established a consortium in 2007, of which the MHRA became the fifth member in 2020—the Access Consortium. The FSA also now focuses on other international networks—the International Network of Food Safety Authorities (INFOSAN)—and international organizations—the World Health Organization—to develop its collaborations with other regulators and to seek influence in international standard setting (including the Codex Alimentarius). For the CMA, while it may have entered into a new cooperation agreement with the European Commission, it too cooperates with competition regulators in wider international forums such as the International Competition Network.

The issue for regulators is not always about creating or entering new networks, but about what role they can now play as a national regulator in international forums

[28] Following a consultation, the UK government also decided to continue to accept batch testing undertaken in EU/EEA states and states covered by MRAs.

outside of EU membership. In the field of banking supervision, the UK sits alongside the European Central Bank and banking regulators from a total of twenty-eight jurisdictions in setting common standards under the auspices of the Basel Committee on Banking Supervision. But it is worth reflecting that this organization was founded in 1974 with members from the then G10 countries, including the UK, the US, France, and Japan. This ought to remind us that not only is international cooperation a continually evolving landscape, but also the position of UK regulators within that landscape changed during and after EU membership. Outside the EU, the task for many UK regulators is about re-establishing their voice and position within forums and networks of which they have been members for many years. Circling back to a central theme of this chapter, if we are to make sense of how Brexit has impacted on UK regulators, we need to start not with Brexit itself, but with the longer-run patterns of regulatory state-building understood as a domestic process that was internationalized and Europeanized. As subsection (a) identifies, de-Europeanization is variegated and incomplete across different regulatory sectors. And as this subsection also suggests, differentiated strategies of internationalization are being pursued outside of EU membership.

7 Conclusions

It is often remarked that Brexit is a process rather than an event. But even that insight requires some qualification. If we are to understand what effects Brexit is producing, we also need to be clear about what EU membership changed in the first place. In more conceptual terms, de-membership and de-Europeanization have a lot in common with EU membership and Europeanization. Particularly important for this study is the role of national regulators in mediating and adapting to EU membership and to the UK's departure from Europeanized regulatory regimes.

If Brexit is not merely an event, nor is it a singular phenomenon that creates easily predictable and uniform effects. As is clearly demonstrated here, while all regulators faced common challenges in preparing for EU exit and experienced similar requirements for financial and human resources, the impact on UK regulators is also highly differentiated. Part of the explanation for that differentiation lies in domestic factors, including the formal status of different regulators in the UK's uncodified constitutional and administrative landscape. Another explanatory factor is variegated patterns of governance within EU regulatory policy itself.

As many of the chapters in this volume narrate, the UK's withdrawal from the EU unleashed a large number of policy consultations and reviews about how best to adapt domestic regulatory frameworks to life outside the EU, and that, necessarily, has had implications for the functions exercised by UK regulators. What this contribution adds to those discussions is its identification of an intensifying trend by government to view regulators as objects and as agents of economic reform. Brexit may be the context in which this politicization of regulators is increasing, but the trajectory of change stretches back through decades of initiatives to reform regulon and to align public bodies with political priorities.

What also emerges from the findings of this chapter is that UK regulators have very different legal and organizational frameworks within which to engage in international cooperation. The EU–UK TCA creates different frameworks for cooperation in the areas of chemicals and aviation than it does for competition. Important areas of risk regulation such as medicines and food safety leave UK regulators outside of important IT and data-sharing systems as well as network meetings of regulators. All of this underlines how different Brexit feels for individual UK regulators. The next step is to evaluate and conceptualize how these regulators adapt to change over time and what longer-term legacies both EU membership and Brexit have for these organizations.

6

Courts

Paul Craig

1 Introduction

This chapter analyses the role of the courts in a post-Brexit world. In section 2 there is a brief overview of the foundational adjudicative principles applicable pre-Brexit, and how they were applied in the UK. The focus then shifts in section 3 to post-Brexit legal change, and the role assigned to the courts. This can only be understood through examination of the more general and complex post-Brexit statutory architecture. This is further complicated by the fact that the initial 2018 legislative framework has been significantly modified by later legislation. These important issues are explained in section 3. This then sets the scene for section 4, which considers in detail the post-Brexit role of the courts, how they have interpreted the legislative regime, and how they have construed their powers within that regime. The post-Brexit implications for courts and parliamentary sovereignty, and for courts and devolution, are considered in other chapters.[1]

2 Pre-Brexit: Foundational Adjudicative Principles

Pre-Brexit, UK courts were bound by the foundational principles of EU law in the same manner as all other national courts. This included the principle of direct effect, as well as the attendant jurisprudence on indirect effect and related doctrine developed by the CJEU as qualifications to the absence of horizontal effect of directives.[2] The principle of direct effect was recognized by section 2(1) of the European Communities Act 1972, while section 3 recognized the authority of ECJ case law.

[1] See Chs 3, 7, 8.

[2] M Rasmussen, 'Revolutionizing European Law: A History of the *Van Gend en Loos* Judgment' (2014) 12 ICON 136; JHH Weiler, '*Van Gend en Loos*: The Individual as Subject and Object and the Dilemma of European Legitimacy' (2014) 12 ICON 94; P Craig and G de Búrca, *EU Law, Text, Cases and Materials* (8th edn, Oxford University Press 2024) Ch 8; K Lenaerts and J Gutierrez-Fons, 'Van-Gend en Loos: A Star is Born' in P Craig and R Schütze (eds), *Landmark Cases in European Law, Volume 1: The Constitutional Cases* (Hart 2024) Ch 1.

Paul Craig, *Courts* In: *The UK Regulatory Framework Post-Brexit: 'Law Unbound'*. Edited by: Paul Craig and Vilija Vėlyvytė, Oxford University Press. © Oxford University Press 2026. DOI: 10.1093/9780198969815.003.0007

The principle of the primacy of EU law is foundational to the EU legal order,[3] and was applicable to the UK in the pre-Brexit world. When the UK joined the EEC it was felt that the traditional doctrine of parliamentary sovereignty would pose problems in this regard, given that this was commonly taken to mean that Parliament had the power to do anything other than to bind itself for the future.[4] In theory this made it very difficult for the primacy of EU law over later UK legislation to be guaranteed, since the ECA 1972, which incorporated EU law and rendered it domestically binding, seemed vulnerable to any later Act of Parliament that contravened or contradicted it, expressly or impliedly.

The UK courts nonetheless showed the capacity of the common law to adapt to changed circumstance. Prior to *Factortame*, the predominant approach was to use principles of construction to assume that when Parliament enacted the 1972 European Communities Act it intended any inconsistency with EU law to be resolved by giving primacy to EU law,[5] provided that there was no indication that Parliament expressly intended to depart from a provision of EU law, the assumption being that if the latter were to occur then the courts would follow the will of Parliament.[6] Thus, where an apparently conflicting provision of English law was capable of being read in conformity with EU law, this was the proper approach to take.

This approach was affirmed and developed in *Factortame*. The dictum of Lord Bridge is crucial in this respect,[7] although it remains unclear why an issue of this importance was not central to the other judgments. There were three related lines of argument in Lord Bridge's dictum. There was the contractarian argument based on voluntary agreement: the UK knew when it joined the EEC in 1972 that the EEC claimed sovereignty and that the UK therefore joined on those terms. There was a functional argument: the primacy of Community law was inherent in the very idea of the EEC, since it could only operate on such terms. If EEC law were not supreme then each member state could pick and choose the Community laws that it wished to comply with. The very idea of a level playing field that was central to the Community would then collapse. The third dimension to the argument was statutory interpretation: the UK joined the EEC through the European Communities Act 1972, section 2(4) of which stated that in the event of a clash between EEC law and national law, EEC law should prevail.[8]

[3] K Alter, *Establishing the Supremacy of European Law: The Making of an International Rule of Law in Europe* (Oxford University Press 2001); A Bobić, *The Jurisprudence of Constitutional Conflict in the European Union* (Oxford University Press 2022); Craig and de Búrca (n 2) Ch 10; B de Witte, 'Costa and the Primacy of EU Law' in Craig and Schütze (n 2) Ch 2.

[4] P Craig, 'United Kingdom Sovereignty after *Factortame*' (1991) 11 YBEL 221; P Craig, 'Britain in the European Union', in J Jowell, D Oliver, and C O'Cinneide (eds), *The Changing Constitution* (8th edn, Oxford University Press 2015) Ch 4.

[5] *Shields v E Coomes (Holdings) Ltd* [1979] 1 All ER 456, 461.

[6] *Macarthys v Smith* [1979] 3 All ER 325, 329; *Garland v British Rail* [1983] 2 AC 751, 771; *Pickstone v Freemans* [1989] AC 66; *Litster v Forth Dry Dock Co Ltd* [1990] 1 AC 546; *Webb v EMO* [1993] 1 WLR 49.

[7] *Factortame Ltd v Secretary of State for Transport (No 2)* [1991] 1 603, 658.

[8] See, for discussion, Craig (n 4); W Wade, 'Sovereignty—Revolution or Evolution?' (1996) 112 LQR 568; T Allan, 'Parliamentary Sovereignty: Law, Politics and Revolution' (1997) 113 LQR 443; D Nicol, *EC Membership and the Judicialization of British Politics* (Oxford University Press 2001) Ch 7.

Subsequent case law reinforced this position.[9] However, later courts also emphasized that acceptance of the primacy of EEC law was rooted firmly in UK law. It was the domestic acceptance of primacy that was emphasized in *Thoburn*.[10] This approach was affirmed by the Supreme Court in *HS2*, where Lord Reed made clear that application of the primacy doctrine in UK law 'itself depends upon the 1972 Act', with the consequence that a conflict between national and EU law 'has to be resolved by our courts as an issue arising under the constitutional law of the United Kingdom'.[11]

The preceding approach served the UK well during its membership of the EU. However, it was never fully tested. The UK courts were never faced with a situation in which Parliament expressly stated that it was derogating from a particular provision of EU law, while still remaining within the EU. We do not know what would have happened in such circumstances. The courts might have retreated to Diceyan orthodoxy, such that the latest express will of Parliament prevailed. They might have held that an express derogation from EU law was not possible while the UK remained within the EU. Nor did the UK courts face a *Kompetenz-Kompetenz* challenge, which would have tested the metes and bounds of Lord Bridge's conclusion that 'there is nothing in any way novel in according supremacy to rules of Community law in those areas to which they apply'.[12] Nor yet again did the UK courts have to grapple with the intricacies of the European Union Act 2011, which introduced a far-reaching regime of statutory and referendum 'locks'.[13]

In the absence of such difficulties, the UK courts could continue to give priority to EU law in the event of a clash with UK law. This was more especially so given that the Supreme Court in *HS2* endorsed the idea of constitutional statutes, with the consequence that the ECA 1972, which was recognized as such a statute, was protected from implied repeal.[14]

The UK courts did not, therefore, cause problems for the primacy of EU law of a kind posed by the courts of other member states. They moulded constitutional precepts of sovereignty to comport with the reality of UK membership of the EEC. The broader implications of this reasoning in a post-Brexit world will be considered below.

The pre-Brexit judicial story would, however, be incomplete without mention of the two Supreme Court decisions concerning the scope and application of prerogative power that arose out of the Brexit process. In *Miller 1*[15] the Supreme Court decided that the government could not trigger Article 50 TEU to begin withdrawing from the EU without statutory authorization from Parliament. In *Miller 2*,[16] the Supreme Court held that the Prime Minister's decision to prorogue Parliament at a crucial time

[9] *Equal Opportunities Commission v Secretary of State for Employment* [1994] 1 WLR 409.

[10] *Thoburn v Sunderland City Council* [2003] QB 151.

[11] *R (HS2 Action Alliance Ltd) v Secretary of State for Transport* [2014] UKSC 3, [79], [203]–[205]; P Craig, 'Constitutionalizing Constitutional Law: HS2' [2014] PL 373.

[12] *Factortame* (n 7) 658.

[13] P Craig, 'The European Union Act 2011: Locks, Limits and Legality' (2011) 48 CMLRev 1881.

[14] *HS2* (n 11) [207].

[15] *R (Miller) v Secretary of State for Exiting the European Union* [2017] UKSC 5.

[16] *R (Miller) v Prime Minister, Cherry and others v Advocate General for Scotland* [2019] UKSC 41.

during the Brexit process was null, void, and of no legal effect. The cases concerned structural constitutional review, in which the Supreme Court demarcated the ambit of legislative and executive power, the latter being exercised through the prerogative. They provoked a large volume of academic commentary both for and against the decisions. In my view, both decisions were correct.

The rulings forced courts and commentators alike to confront ambiguities in the well-known constitutional precepts through which limits to prerogative power are commonly expressed: the prerogative cannot be used to alter the law of the land or affect rights, and it cannot be deployed so as to circumvent statute that covers the same ground. The cases were also of lasting importance for the more general methodological lessons as to how we resolve the ambiguities adverted to above. The twin lessons in this respect are in some ways remarkably simple. The boundaries of particular doctrinal precepts can only be resolved if we articulate the background values that inform them, and use these as the touchstone to help us determine contested issues as to the reach of doctrine. The other lesson is that when determining the doctrinal issue, we ensure that the answer, whatsoever it might be, coheres with related constitutional principles.

The *Miller* cases also contain lessons about the relationship between the 'legal' and the 'political'. Underlying many significant constitutional cases there is often a political story. It takes two to tango. It takes two sides to engage in litigation. Ms Miller brought the first case because the government was determined to trigger Article 50 TEU without securing statutory approval. Why it chose to be intransigent in this respect is one dimension of the 'political' that informs this story; the consequence of its losing is yet another.

3 Post-Brexit Legal Change: The Role Assigned to the Courts

The role of the courts in a post-Brexit world can only be understood in the light of the complex legislative architecture through which the UK exited the EU. The architecture will be explicated in this section, and the interpretive issues faced by the courts pursuant to this legal framework will be examined in the section that follows.

(a) The EUWA: The Initial Statutory Architecture

The post-Brexit legislative architecture is to be found principally in the European Union (Withdrawal) Act 2018, as amended (EUWA) and the Retained EU Law (Revocation and Reform) Act 2023 (REULA).

Prior to Brexit, EU law took effect in the UK through the European Communities Act 1972. It was natural for the ECA to be repealed when the UK left the EU. This repeal took effect through the EUWA, section 1. However, the EUWA 2018, section 1A, provided that the ECA continued to have effect in the UK after exit day, which was 31 January 2020, until the end of the implementation period, which was 31 December 2020, IP completion day.[17]

The initial strategy was embodied in the EUWA 2018, which converted the EU legal *acquis* into UK law. This might seem strange, given that the UK had left the EU, but it was readily explicable. The UK had been a member of the EU since 1972, and many areas of life were regulated by EU law. EU directives had already been transformed into UK law. There was, however, much EU law, such as regulations, that was directly applicable, taking effect in domestic law when enacted by the EU, without the need for further national legislation. The ECA 1972, section 2(1), furnished the legal foundation for direct applicability and direct effect within the UK constitutional order. The regulatory architecture in any area was typically an admixture of Treaty provisions, plus directives, regulations, and decisions, which could take the form of legislative acts, delegated acts, and implementing acts.[18] It would in theory have been possible to scrap this regulatory material in the event of Brexit. However, this would have led to chaos. The EU rules regulated matters from product safety to creditworthiness of banks, from securities markets to intellectual property, and from the environment to consumer protection. There could not simply be a legal void in these areas, and pre-existing UK law would often not exist.

This was the rationale for the initial EUWA strategy.[19] The foundational premise was that the entirety of the EU legal *acquis* was converted into UK law. Parliament could then decide, in two stages, which measures to retain, amend, or repeal. Stage one was to ensure that the EU rules retained as domestic law were fit for legal purpose when we left the EU, since there could be provisions that did not make sense in a post-Brexit world, such as reporting obligations to the Commission. Stage two was the period post-Brexit, when Parliament could decide at greater leisure whether it wished to retain these rules. The EUWA, sections 2–4, as originally enacted, dealt respectively with the conversion of different types of EU law into UK law.

Section 2 EUWA[20] dealt with the saving of EU-derived domestic legislation, stipulating that it continued to have effect in domestic law on and after the end of the implementation period as it had prior thereto. EU-derived domestic legislation was defined principally by reference to enactments made pursuant to the ECA 1972, section 2(2), which was the legislative mechanism through which enactments to give effect to EU law were made.[21] This was typically done through a statute, or secondary legislation, that brought EU directives, which are not directly applicable, into domestic law.

[17] European Union (Withdrawal Agreement) Act 2020; Agreement on the withdrawal of the United Kingdom of Great Britain and Northern Ireland from the European Union and the European Atomic Energy Community, [2019] OJ C384 I/01, Art 127.
[18] Arts 289–291 TFEU.
[19] P Craig, 'Constitutional Principle, the Rule of Law and Political Reality: The European Union (Withdrawal) Act 2018' (2019) 82 MLR 319.
[20] As amended by the European Union (Withdrawal Agreement) Act 2020, s 25(1).
[21] EUWA, s 1B(7).

EU-derived domestic legislation could also include enactments that changed UK law to render it compatible with EU regulations,[22] or which otherwise related to the EU or to the European Economic Area.[23] Section 2 EUWA was necessary because although such directives had been incorporated into UK law, through for example a statutory instrument made pursuant to section 2(2) ECA, the general principle of UK law is that if the parent statute is repealed, the secondary measures enacted pursuant to it are also repealed. This would have placed in jeopardy important UK legislation that owed its origin to EU directives.

Section 3 EUWA[24] was concerned with the incorporation of direct EU legislation, and provided that, so far as operative immediately before the implementation period completion day, it formed part of domestic law thereafter. Direct EU legislation was defined in section 3(2). It covered, subject to certain exceptions,[25] directly applicable EU regulations, decisions, and tertiary legislation.[26] However, in order to be preserved, these measures must have been applicable in the UK during the implementation period by virtue of Part IV of the Withdrawal Agreement, which dealt with transition.[27] This meant that any such regulations, decisions, or tertiary legislation that were not applicable during the transition/implementation period would not be retained.

Section 3 EUWA was necessary because of repeal of the ECA 1972. Section 2(1) ECA gave legislative authorization for directly applicable EU law within the UK, thereby obviating the need for legislation to implement any particular EU regulation. This was fine while we remained in the EU. However, Brexit, and repeal of the ECA, meant that thousands of EU regulations that constituted UK law in many important areas would be lost, unless they could be retained post-Brexit, hence section 3 EUWA.

Section 4(1) EUWA was concerned with the saving of rights that had been part of UK law through section 2(1) ECA. These directly effective rights took effect in UK law via section 2(1) ECA, and they were preserved post-Brexit by section 4(1) EUWA. The entire body of directly effective rights was brought into UK law, subject to qualifications in section 4(2) EUWA.

Section 5(1) EUWA as initially enacted provided that the principle of the supremacy of EU law did not apply to any enactment or rule of law passed or made on or after the end of the implementation period, which was 31 December 2020. However, this was qualified by section 5(2) EUWA, which stated that 'accordingly, the principle of the supremacy of EU law continues to apply on or after IP completion day so far as relevant to the interpretation, disapplication or quashing of any enactment or rule of law passed or made before IP completion day'. This meant that if there was a conflict

22 EUWA, s 1B(7)(c)(ii).
23 EUWA, s 1B(7)(d).
24 As amended by the European Union (Withdrawal Agreement) Act 2020, s 25(2).
25 EUWA, s 3(2)(a)(i), (iii), Sched 6.
26 Tertiary legislation, as defined by EUWA, s 20, in effect means a delegated regulation or decision made pursuant to Art 290 TFEU, or an implementing regulation or decision made pursuant to Art 291 TFEU.
27 EUWA, s 3(2)(a)(ai).

between pre-IP completion day domestic legislation and retained EU law, the latter took precedence. It also meant that pre-IP completion day domestic law should be interpreted, as far as possible, in accordance with retained EU law. The policy rationale underlying section 5(2) was legal certainty: prior to IP completion day, EU law had supremacy over domestic law, and it was felt that this should therefore continue. The House of Lords Constitution Committee was, however, critical of this provision.[28] Section 5(1) EUWA was further qualified by section 5(3).

(b) The REULA: The Revised Statutory Architecture—Nomenclature, Direct Effect, and Supremacy

The revised strategy is contained in the Retained EU Law (Revocation and Reform) Act 2023 (REULA 2023). The general objective is to facilitate the amendment, restatement, or revocation and replacement of retained EU law (REUL) and assimilate the REUL remaining in force after the end of 2023 by removing the special EU law features attached to it. The changes made by the REULA take effect as amendments to the EUWA 2018.

The REULA changed the nomenclature after the end of 2023 from retained EU law, retained case law, and the like to assimilated law and assimilated case law.[29] The REULA removed general principles of EU law from the category of assimilated law,[30] and also revoked 587 measures that had hitherto been regarded as retained law.[31]

Section 2 of the REULA 2023 repealed section 4 of the EUWA 2018 from the end of 2023. The category of retained EU law concerning directly effective rights was therefore removed. This was an expected change, since the idea that directly effective rights derived from, for example, EU Treaty articles concerning free movement could still be applicable in a post-Brexit world made no sense.

Direct effect does, however, continue to operate in UK law pursuant to the EUWA, sections 7A and 7B. These sections were added to the EUWA by the European Union (Withdrawal Agreement) Act 2020, to implement Article 4 of the Withdrawal Agreement.[32] Article 4(1) provides that the provisions of the Withdrawal Agreement, and the provisions of Union law made applicable by the Withdrawal Agreement, shall produce in the UK the same legal effects as they produce within the Union and its member states. Accordingly, 'legal or natural persons shall in particular be able to rely directly on the provisions contained or referred to in this Agreement which meet the conditions for direct effect under Union law'. Article 4(2) then stipulates that the UK

[28] House of Lords, Select Committee on the Constitution, European Union (Withdrawal) Bill (HL 69, 2018) [81]–[88].
[29] REULA, s 5.
[30] ibid s 4.
[31] ibid s 1.
[32] Withdrawal Agreement (n 17); *Revenue and Customs Commissioners v Perfect* [2022] EWCA Civ 330.

must ensure through primary legislation that its judicial and administrative authorities can disapply inconsistent or incompatible domestic provisions.

The obligation in Article 4 of the Withdrawal Agreement was given effect in UK law by section 7A EUWA. It applies to all rights, powers, liabilities, obligations, and restrictions from time to time created or arising by or under the Withdrawal Agreement, and all such remedies and procedures from time to time provided for by or under the Withdrawal Agreement, as in accordance with the Withdrawal Agreement, are without further enactment to be given legal effect or used in the United Kingdom. These rights, powers, liabilities, and so on are to be recognized and available in domestic law, and enforced, allowed, and followed accordingly.

Section 7A(3) EUWA provides that every enactment (including an enactment contained in this Act) is to be read and has effect subject to the above. Section 20 EUWA defines enactment to mean an enactment whenever passed or made. This means that even a subsequent UK statute will be read subject to section 7A. It is open to Parliament to make clear that it is derogating from section 7A, pursuant to the principle of parliamentary sovereignty. However, the presumption is that unless Parliament makes clear that it is doing so, the directly effective rights in section 7A will survive.

Section 3 REULA 2023 abolished the principle of the supremacy of EU law from the end of 2023, subject to limited exceptions, so far as it had been preserved by the EUWA section 5. Section 5(A1) EUWA as amended states that the principle of supremacy is not part of domestic law after the end of 2023 in relation to any enactment or rule of law (whenever passed or made). Section 5(A2) EUWA reinforces this by stating that any provision of assimilated direct legislation must, so far as possible, be read and given effect subject in a way that is compatible with all domestic enactments, and is subject to all domestic enactments, so far as it is incompatible with them.[33]

There are, however, qualifications/exceptions to this schema. The principal qualification is in section 5(7) EUWA, which provides that sections 5(A1)–(6) are subject to relevant separation agreement law. This means that the supremacy of EU law, and the obligation to interpret national law consistently with EU law, continue to operate in relation to relevant provisions of the Withdrawal Agreement.[34] The other significant qualification is that section 5(A3) EUWA provides that the interpretive obligation in section 5(A2) EUWA can be displaced by regulations made under section 7(1) REULA. A minister can make a regulation pursuant to section 7(1) REULA, which reverses the interpretive assumption in section 5(A2) EUWA, such that the obligation is to interpret the domestic enactment to be compatible with the specified assimilated law. No such regulation can be made after 23 June 2026.

[33] This is subject to the exception in EUWA, s 5(A3).
[34] Withdrawal Agreement (n 17).

(c) The REULA: The Revised Statutory Architecture—The Role of the Courts

Section 6 EUWA, as amended by section 6 REULA,[35] deals with the role of UK courts when interpreting assimilated law, which is defined in section 6(7) EUWA to mean 'anything which, on or after IP completion day, continues to be, or forms part of, domestic law by virtue of section 2 or 3 or subsection (3) or (6) above, (as that body of law is added to or otherwise modified by or under this Act or by other domestic law from time to time)'.

Section 6(1) EUWA embodies the logical consequence of leaving the EU: a court or tribunal is not bound by any principles laid down, or any decisions made, by the CJEU on or after the implementation period completion day, and cannot refer any matter to it on or after IP completion day. This is subject to several exceptions specified in the Withdrawal Agreement,[36] where a reference may or must be made to the CJEU.[37]

Section 6(2) EUWA deals with the extent to which the UK courts may have regard to any post-exit EU case law. Many thousands of EU laws were retained pursuant to sections 2–3 EUWA. These rules continue to exist in the EU and will be interpreted by the EU courts. The logic of exit from the EU demands that we should not be bound by such post-IP completion day CJEU rulings, hence section 6(1). However, such rulings may be uncontroversial and helpful for UK courts when interpreting the same rules that have been retained in UK law. This is the rationale for section 6(2) EUWA, which provides that 'a court or tribunal may have regard to anything done on or after IP completion day by the European Court, another EU entity or the EU so far as it is relevant to any matter before the court or tribunal'.

Section 6(3) EUWA, as amended, deals with the relevance of pre-IP completion day case law when assessing the validity of assimilated EU law. It provides that 'any question as to the validity, meaning or effect of any assimilated law is to be decided, so far as that law is unmodified on or after IP completion day and so far as they are relevant to it, in accordance with assimilated case law[38] and having regard (amongst other things) to the limits immediately before IP completion day of EU competences'. Section 6(3) therefore legitimates reference to EU and domestic case law decided prior to IP completion day, on or after IP completion day, when determining the validity, meaning, or effect of law that has been assimilated pursuant to sections 2–3 EUWA, insofar as it is unmodified and insofar as the assimilated case law is relevant. Section 6(6) further provides that section 6(3) does not prevent the validity, meaning, or effect of any assimilated law that is modified on or after IP completion day from

[35] REULA, s 6 comes into effect on a date specified by a minister in a regulation, REULA, s 22(3).
[36] Withdrawal Agreement (n 17) Arts 136, 138, 158, 160, 174–75, Northern Ireland Protocol Arts 12(4), 12(7).
[37] EUWA, ss 6(6A), 7C.
[38] Defined in EUWA, s 6(7): assimilated domestic case law and assimilated EU case law.

being decided as provided in section 6(3) if doing so is 'consistent with the intention of the modifications'.

Section 6(3) and section 6(6) EUWA are, however, subject to qualifications contained in sections 6(4), 6(5), and 6(5A) EUWA, as amended by section 6 REULA. They deal with the extent to which specified courts can depart from assimilated EU case law[39] and assimilated domestic case law.[40] Thus, section 6(4) EUWA provides that the Supreme Court; the High Court of Justiciary, subject to certain qualifications; and a relevant appeal court are not bound by assimilated EU case law.[41] In deciding whether to depart from assimilated EU case law, the Supreme Court and the High Court of Justiciary must apply the same test as in deciding whether to depart from its own case law (section 6(5) EUWA), and so too must other courts that are given the power to depart from assimilated EU case law.[42]

There is, however, a revised version of section 6(5) EUWA, as amended by section 6 REULA, which has not yet been brought into force.[43] It provides that in deciding whether to depart from any assimilated EU case law by virtue of section 6(4)(a), (b), or (ba), the higher court concerned must, inter alia, have regard to: the fact that decisions of a foreign court are not (unless otherwise provided) binding; any changes of circumstances that are relevant to the assimilated EU case law; and the extent to which the assimilated EU case law restricts the proper development of domestic law.

There is in addition section 6(5ZA), which is not yet in force. It deals with the circumstances in which a higher court can depart from its own assimilated domestic case law if it considers it right to do so having regard, inter alia, to: the extent to which the assimilated domestic case law is determined or influenced by assimilated EU case law from which the court has departed or would depart; any changes of circumstances that are relevant to the assimilated domestic case law; and the extent to which the assimilated domestic case law restricts the proper development of domestic law.

The REULA introduced important new provisions into the EUWA 2018, concerning references as to the meaning of retained case law within the UK domestic legal system. The provisions take effect from a date to be appointed. Section 6A EUWA provides that a court or tribunal (other than a higher court) may refer one or

[39] Defined in EUWA, s 6(7): any principles laid down by, and any decisions of, the European Court, as they have effect in EU law immediately before IP completion day and so far as they relate to anything to which ss 2 or 3 EUWA applies, provided that they are not excluded by s 5 or Schedule 1 (as those principles and decisions are modified by or under this Act or by other domestic law from time to time).

[40] Defined in EUWA, s 6(7): any principles laid down by, and any decisions of, a court or tribunal in the United Kingdom, as they have effect immediately before IP completion day and so far as they (a) relate to anything to which section 2 or 3 applies, and are not excluded by section 5 or Schedule 1 (as those principles and decisions are modified by or under this Act or by other domestic law from time to time).

[41] EUWA, s 6(4)(ba) provides that a relevant court or relevant tribunal is not bound by any retained EU case law so far as is provided for by regulations under subsection (5A), which in effect enables a minister to denominate further courts and tribunals that are not bound by assimilated EU case law, but this power ceased to operate after IP completion day, s 6(5D).

[42] EUWA, s 6(5); European Union (Withdrawal) Act 2018 (Relevant Court) (Retained EU Case Law) Regulations 2020 (SI 2020/1525).

[43] The date is to be appointed.

more points of law which arise on retained case law and are relevant to proceedings before it if it is bound by the retained case law, and it considers that the point or points of law are of general public importance. The court or tribunal can make a reference on its own motion, or pursuant to an application by a party to the proceedings. If the reference relates to retained case law of the Supreme Court, it is to be made to that court, otherwise to the appropriate appeal court. Section 6B EUWA makes provision for law officers to make such references, while section 6C EUWA allows law officers to intervene where a higher court is considering an argument by a party that it should depart from retained case law.

Section 6D(1)(a) EUWA makes provision for incompatibility orders. Such an order must be issued where a court or tribunal finds that a provision of assimilated direct legislation is incompatible with any domestic enactment.[44] The court or tribunal has discretion as to the terms of the incompatibility order.[45]

4 Post-Brexit Legal Change: The Courts and Interpretation

There is no doubt that the role of UK courts post-Brexit has changed. While there are, as noted above, instances where direct effect and primacy are still applicable, most notably concerning the Withdrawal Agreement and Northern Ireland, in the great majority of instances this is no longer the focus. Nor is this surprising in a post-Brexit world. The principal judicial focus is rather to navigate the complex legal terrain provided by the Brexit legislation, which includes specification as to the courts' powers within that overall architecture. This section analyses the relevant legislation and underlying principles, and considers how they have been interpreted by the courts thus far.

(a) Post-Brexit: General Principles of Interpretation

The discussion begins with consideration of general principles of interpretation, and how they have changed in a post-Brexit world. Lord Sales has provided valuable insights in this respect.[46] He rightly notes that there are challenges post-Brexit in identifying the purposes of retained law without the EU's institutional assistance. The very fact that the preliminary reference procedure has, subject to limited exceptions, now

[44] EUWA, s 6D(1)(b) also makes provision for the converse situation where, exceptionally, and pursuant to regulations, the domestic regulation is to be read subject to the assimilated legislation, pursuant to REULA, s 7(1).

[45] EUWA, s 6D(4)–(5).

[46] Lord Sales, 'Retained EU Law: Purposive Interpretation when the Constitutional Architecture Changes' (2024) 49 ELRev 3. See also M Brenncke, 'Statutory Interpretation and the Role of the Courts after Brexit' (2019) 25 EPL 637.

gone means that UK courts can no longer seek the CJEU's assistance when there are doubts as to the interpretation of assimilated EU law, which have not been resolved in existing EU jurisprudence.[47]

It is, moreover, necessary to decide which general EU purposes remain relevant to the UK in the post-Brexit landscape.[48] As Lord Sales states, these purposes were partly inherited through the pre-exit caselaw of the CJEU, but 'it might be going too far to suggest that the UK law should inherit all the purposes of EU law, especially where those purposes are associated with European integration'.[49]

> The effectiveness of EU law partly relies on uniform application and interpretation in all member states. Requiring UK courts to interpret retained EU law, which is now solely UK domestic law, in a way that achieves the EU's common market objectives or ensures uniform application by the UK and its EU counterparts is not in itself obviously a purpose which is relevant in a post-Brexit legal system. With the change in the constitutional architecture wrought by Brexit, it is not unreasonable to expect that this will be another reason for divergence between the Court of Justice and UK courts in their interpretations, at least in areas of law that from an EU perspective are crucial to European integration.
>
> However, there are a number of other purposes underlying EU law that may remain relevant to the UK after Brexit, especially those that were not unique to the EU framework and telos but which relate to broader common economic or social aims. This may be significant in areas such as consumer rights, workers' rights, environmental protection standards, and data protection. In the latter area, the UK courts may identify a common interest in maintaining a high level of data protection in line with EU standards to allow data to flow efficiently across borders.[50]

Lord Sales argues persuasively that UK courts should adopt a purposive approach to assimilated EU law, at least as the most appropriate starting point.[51] However, he also notes that there will be instances where it is necessary for the UK courts to 'aim off' purposive interpretations given by the CJEU,[52] while recognizing that this can create problems of legal certainty.[53]

> To address these challenges, it will be important for UK courts to provide clear and well-reasoned explanations when they consider it is appropriate to 'aim off' from purposive interpretations of retained EU law. It is to be hoped that this should include detailed reasoning to explain why a particular interpretation is chosen; clear

47 ibid 7–8.
48 ibid 7.
49 ibid 8–9.
50 ibid 9.
51 ibid 10.
52 ibid 12.
53 ibid 12–13.

articulation of how the interpretation aligns with the domestic legal system and the specific context of the case; consideration of the potential impact of competing interpretations on legal certainty and an effort to mitigate any negative consequences; and consistency in interpretation between domestic cases whenever possible to minimise conflicting judgments. As always, clear and transparent judicial decision-making is essential in achieving as much certainty as is feasible.

(b) Post-Brexit: Departing from CJEU Case Law

The previous section considered general issues of statutory interpretation in a post-Brexit world. We now consider how the courts have exercised the powers given by section 6 EUWA, which allow them to depart from CJEU judgments delivered prior to IP completion day.

The Court of Appeal decision in *TuneIn*[54] considered whether a UK court should depart from pre-IP completion day EU law, in a case concerning breach of copyright. The law on this issue included EU directives. The meaning of the term 'communication to the public' in the EU directives had been interpreted by the CJEU on numerous occasions.[55] The defendant argued that the Court of Appeal should exercise the power to depart from the CJEU case law in certain respects.

Arnold LJ declined to do so. He noted that the criterion for the power to depart in section 6(5A) was whether the Supreme Court would depart from one of its decisions, a power that had been narrowly construed. The same test is applicable to other courts given the power to depart from assimilated EU law.[56]

Arnold LJ proffered several reasons why the power should not be exercised in the instant case:[57] there had been no change in the domestic legislation; there had been no change in the international legislative framework; the interpretation of 'communication to the public' was inherently difficult, and the CJEU case law had considered the issue frequently and in-depth; the academic commentary on the CJEU case law was evenly balanced; case law from other jurisdictions was not relevant because the legislative framework differed; to jettison the CJEU case law and consider the issue afresh would create considerable uncertainty; and the departure from CJEU case law contended for by the defendant would not determine the case in their favour. Sir Geoffrey Vos MR added that '[i]t would be undesirable for one nation to depart from the [Court of Justice's] approach without an exceptionally good reason'.[58] The value of preservation of legal certainty was recognized as having high status under the Withdrawal Act.

[54] *TuneIn Inc v Warner Music UK Ltd* [2021] EWCA Civ 441.
[55] ibid [67], [70]–[72].
[56] SI 2020/1525 (n 42).
[57] *TuneIn* (n 54) [78]–[89].
[58] ibid [198]. See also, *Merck Serono SA v Comptroller-General of Patents, Design and Copyright* [2025] EWCA Civ 45.

By way of contrast, Arnold LJ, giving judgment for the Court of Appeal, decided to depart from CJEU case law in *Industrial Cleaning Equipment*,[59] which was a trade mark dispute between rival users of the acronym ICE. Arnold LJ reached this conclusion for the following reasons: the CJEU decision was an isolated ruling;[60] neither the AG's Opinion nor the Court's judgment contained any analysis of the issue, 'but simply stated a bald conclusion';[61] the ruling was at variance with cases decided by the General Court;[62] and legal certainty would not be jeopardized by departing from the particular CJEU ruling.[63]

The preceding decisions are well reasoned and show a balanced approach by the UK courts in deciding whether to depart from pre-IP day CJEU case law.

It remains to be seen how far the approach changes when the amendments to section 6(5) EUWA introduced by section 6 REULA come into effect. The amendment was set out above,[64] and the revised criteria for departure are considerably broader than in the original version of section 6(5) EUWA. UK courts under the revised version should consider that decisions of foreign courts are not binding; any changes of circumstances that are relevant to the assimilated EU case law; and the extent to which the retained EU case law restricts the proper development of domestic law. The change in wording was noted in *E-Accounting Solutions Ltd v Global Infosys Ltd*,[65] and it will likely have an impact on the willingness to depart, more especially as the time when the UK was within the EU becomes more distant.

(c) Post-Brexit: Using Post-Brexit CJEU Case Law

UK courts can consider post-IP completion day EU case law so far as it is 'relevant' to the matter before the UK court. The determination of relevance can clearly vary from case to case.

In *TuneIn*, Arnold LJ regarded a post-IP completion day CJEU decision as 'highly persuasive':[66] it was relevant to the case; it was a Grand Chamber decision; and it refined an extensive body of twenty-four retained EU judgments on the topic, which had been followed in the UK.

In *Tower Bridge GP*,[67] by way of contrast, the Court of Appeal decided not to follow a post-IP completion day CJEU decision when interpreting UK VAT legislation that had implemented the requirements of the EU Principal VAT Directive. It reached this

[59] *Industrial Cleaning Equipment (Southampton) Ltd v Intelligent Cleaning Equipment* [2023] EWCA Civ 1451.
[60] ibid [84].
[61] ibid [83].
[62] ibid [85].
[63] ibid [86].
[64] See text accompanying (n 43).
[65] *E-Accounting Solutions Ltd v Global Infosys Ltd* [2023] EWHC 2038 (Ch), [13].
[66] *TuneIn* (n 54) [91].
[67] *Tower Bridge GP Ltd v HMRC* [2022] EWCA Civ 998.

conclusion because the CJEU decision broke new ground and was 'at odds with the previous jurisprudence of the court'.[68]

It is, however, likely, as noted by Lord Sales,[69] that CJEU case law, whether delivered before or after IP completion day, will become less persuasive over time, because legislative and policy changes in the UK and EU level will lead to divergence in interpretation, unless the UK consciously seeks to mirror new developments or pursue policies of equivalence.

(d) Complete Code versus Interpretation Act: *Lipton*

A leading decision on the interpretation of the post-Brexit legal regime is *Lipton v BA Cityflyer Ltd*.[70] The case concerned a claim for compensation for a delayed flight pursuant to Regulation 261/2004 that had since become part of retained EU law under the EUWA, albeit with some amendment by a statutory instrument. The immediate legal issue was whether the fact that a pilot fell ill, and could not therefore attend work, constituted 'extraordinary circumstances' under the Regulation, so as to obviate the need to pay compensation. The claim was begun before Brexit. The Supreme Court held that the pilot's absence for this reason did not constitute 'extraordinary circumstances' for the purpose of the EU Regulation.

However, the case is of interest because the parties proffered rival analyses as to how the cause of action should be conceptualized post-Brexit. The majority, Lord Sales and Lady Rose, with whom Lady Simmler agreed, favoured the Complete Code Analysis, while Lord Lloyd-Jones in dissent adopted the Interpretation Act Analysis. The following extract encapsulates the meaning of the rival analyses.[71]

> The Complete Code analysis: This approach regards the Withdrawal Act 2018 as a complete code by which Parliament dealt comprehensively with the application in the United Kingdom of EU law following IP completion day. According to the Complete Code analysis, where a set of facts occur pre-Brexit which, having regard to EU law which applied at that time, gives rise to a cause of action, the claimants right to pursue that cause of action is brought forward as part and parcel of the bringing forward of the law itself under whichever of sections 2, 3 or 4 is relevant. The scope of that cause of action is subject then to whatever limitations are placed upon it by other provisions of the Withdrawal Act 2018 as is clear, for example, from the provisions restricting Francovich damages claims.

[68] ibid [119].

[69] Sales (n 46) 12.

[70] [2024] UKSC 24. See also, *Umbrella Interchange Fee Claimants v Umbrella Interchange Fee Defendants* [2024] EWCA Civ 1559.

[71] ibid [59].

> The Interpretation Act analysis. This approach regards the Withdrawal Act 2018 as bringing forward only the instrument containing the EU law but not causes of action that have accrued by virtue of the application of the instrument prior to Brexit. According to the Interpretation Act analysis, where a set of facts occurs pre-Brexit which, having regard to an EU law which applied at the time, gives rise to a cause of action, the claimants right to pursue that cause of action is saved by the application of section 16 of the Interpretation Act. This is subject, of course, to those provisions of the Withdrawal Act 2018 which limit or erode that cause of action in some way after Brexit.

A preliminary issue was as to whether the original or amended version of Regulation 261/2004 should govern the case. The Court of Appeal had held that it was the latter, but the majority rejected this in part because Parliament was taken to legislate in accord with the rule of law, with the consequence that it was the law in place when the event occurred that governed the action, not a version amended thereafter, and in part because EUWA section 3 stated that it was the text of the EU regulation in force at IP completion day that was determinative.[72]

It was acknowledged that on the facts of the case the outcome would be the same on the Complete Code Analysis (CCA) or the Interpretation Act Analysis (IAA), but the majority held that the CCA was preferable. The arguments are long and complex. What follows is a distillation of the principal strands of the reasoning.

First, Regulation 261/2004 had an effect in EU law pre-IP completion day in two ways: it specified the law to be applied for the future and conferred rights of action when the rules were broken. The EUWA, section 3(3)(c), brought both dimensions into UK law. It rendered Regulation 261/2004 binding in its legal form pre-IP completion day, which continued to bind post-IP completion day, subject to amendment or repeal. The majority held that this reading cohered with the aim of the EUWA, which was to provide a clear and comprehensive treatment of retained EU law in a post-Brexit world.[73]

Second, the majority held that the CCA view was consistent with sections 3 and 4 EUWA.[74] Proponents of the IAA argued that section 3 EUWA brought Regulation 261/2004 into domestic law, but not the accrued rights that flowed therefrom when the Regulation was breached. The majority responded by pointing to section 4(2) EUWA, which carved out from section 4(1) rights, powers, liabilities, and the like flowing from section 3, thereby showing that section 3 brought not only the Regulation itself into domestic law, but also the rights flowing therefrom. The majority reinforced this by arguing that it did not make conceptual sense to distinguish between the Regulation itself and the rights that flow therefrom, since 'the purpose of legislation is to impose obligations and confer rights'.[75]

72 ibid [66]–[67].
73 ibid [84]–[87].
74 ibid [92]–[96].
75 ibid [96].

Third, the majority held that the CCA was also consistent with section 6 EUWA, such that the UK courts, when resolving the dispute, were not bound by CJEU case law post-Brexit, and could depart from pre-IP CJEU case law in certain circumstances.[76] It was, said the majority, not clear how section 6 was engaged on the IAA, since the application of section 6 was premised on the cause of action being 'retained EU law', which it would not be on the IAA, since it was not something that continued to be, or formed, part of EU law by virtue of sections 2–4 EUWA. The majority held that it would then follow on the IAA view that UK courts could be bound by post-Brexit CJEU rulings at least until the end of IP completion day, and possibly thereafter, for as long as such accrued causes of action might last; and that national courts would not be free to depart from pre-IP CJEU rulings.[77]

Lord Lloyd-Jones agreed with the majority on the substantive issue concerning the meaning of 'extraordinary circumstances' in Regulation 261/2004. However, he espoused the IAA in preference to the CCA. The argument is complex and detailed, and therefore, as with the argument of the majority, only the essence of the dissenting opinion can be presented here.

First, Lord Lloyd-Jones held that the applicable law was EU law, since this was the law in force when the claim accrued in 2018, and this was the basis on which Regulation 261/2004 itself applied. By way of contrast, the majority considered that the applicable law was retained EU law. He identified the essential point of difference with the majority as being whether 'the legislative provisions on retained EU law have only prospective effect'.[78] For Lord Lloyd-Jones, the plaintiffs gained accrued rights from Regulation 261/2004 pre-Brexit, enforceable in the UK through the ECA 1972, section 2(1), which were unaffected by the EUWA 2018.[79] This conclusion was predicated on the general common law principle that conduct and events were governed by the law in force when they took place. It followed that subsequent legislative changes did not generally have retrospective effect, subject to clear evidence to the contrary.[80] The EUWA 2018 was intended to secure continuity and legal certainty and to avoid a vacuum in the UK statute book, by bringing EU law into domestic law as from IP completion day. It was not intended to make provision retrospectively in respect of rights that had already accrued under EU law before withdrawal.[81]

Second, the accrued rights derived from Regulation 261/2004 were preserved in UK law through the Interpretation Act 1978, section 16(1)(c) of which provides that where an Act repeals an enactment, the repeal does not, unless the contrary intention appears, 'affect any right, privilege, obligation or liability acquired, accrued or incurred under that enactment'. Thus, on this view, repeal of the ECA 1972, which was

[76] ibid [107].
[77] ibid [108].
[78] ibid [193].
[79] ibid [194].
[80] ibid [196].
[81] ibid [197].

the legal foundation for the application of EU law in UK law, did not affect rights accrued thereunder prior to its repeal.[82]

Third, Lord Lloyd-Jones argued that neither the text of the EUWA 2018 nor the Explanatory Notes to the Bill provided any support for the view that it was intended to preserve rights and obligations derived from EU law that had already accrued as EU rights in domestic law. In the words of Lord Lloyd-Jones, 'if that was the legislative intention it is astonishing that it does not say so expressly'.[83] This conclusion was, said His Lordship, reinforced by the fact that where the EUWA 2018 did intend that certain provisions of EU law should not apply to matters arising before IP completion day, and thus where the 2018 Act was intended to operate with retroactive effect in relation to causes of action that accrued before IP completion day, it made express provision to that effect.[84] Lord Lloyd-Jones held that the language of sections 2–4 EUWA was not apt to transpose accrued rights and obligations into retained EU law, and that this would have to be inferred from those sections.[85] He felt that 'the more natural reading of these sections is that they were intended to put on the UK statute book a snapshot of EU law as it stood on IP completion day with prospective effect and with no effect on pre-existing causes of action'.[86] Lord Lloyd-Jones rejected in this respect the argument advanced by the majority that section 4(2) EUWA showed that section 3 EUWA was intended to cover not merely the retained EU law, but also the rights that flow therefrom. This was, said Lord Lloyd-Jones, to confuse the existence of a right with a cause of action flowing from that right.[87]

Fourth, Lord Lloyd-Jones rejected the majority's argument based on section 6 EUWA, which has been set out above. He held that section 6(1) EUWA, which stipulated that UK courts were not bound by EU case law after IP completion day, was not, as the majority contended, dependent on characterization of the law as retained EU law. That wording only appeared in the heading to section 6, and was not part of sections 6(1) or (2). The powers and duties contained therein could therefore apply to causes of action that accrued prior to the EUWA.[88] Lord Lloyd-Jones acknowledged that the power to depart from CJEU case law in section 6(4) EUWA was indeed expressly framed in terms of departure from 'retained EU case law', but held that the best reading of such provisions was that the power to depart from retained EU case law conferred by section 6(4) EUWA only applied in cases where the cause of action accrued after IP completion day.[89]

It is readily apparent that the contending arguments are complex, and the preceding analysis is, as noted above, merely a precis of lengthier argumentation. Space

[82] ibid [199]–[201].
[83] ibid [202].
[84] ibid [204].
[85] ibid [206]–[217].
[86] ibid [205].
[87] ibid [213]–[216].
[88] ibid [229]–[233].
[89] ibid [234]–[243].

precludes detailed analysis of the pros and cons of the respective arguments. Suffice it to say the following. The weight of academic opinion thus far favours the IAA favoured by Lord Lloyd-Jones.[90] The most important dimensions of the respective arguments are, in my view, that concerning retrospectivity and the argument from section 6 EUWA. The argument that the EUWA 2018 should not be construed as having retrospective impact on accrued rights is put forcefully by Lord Lloyd-Jones and favours the IAA, more especially given the fact that when the EUWA does have such an impact the legislation states this clearly and with specificity. The argument concerning section 6 EUWA, more especially that concerning section 6(4), tends to favour the majority view and lends weight to the CCA.

(e) EUFRA section 29: *Lipton*

There is an aspect of the decision in *Lipton* which warrants separate treatment. It concerns the interpretation of section 29 of the European Union (Future Relationship) Act 2020 (EUFRA). The lesson concerning what follows may be summarized as 'legislate in haste, reap the consequences thereafter'. Section 29(1) provides as follows:

> Existing domestic law has effect on and after the relevant day with such modifications as are required for the purposes of implementing in that law the Trade and Cooperation Agreement or the Security of Classified Information Agreement so far as the agreement concerned is not otherwise so implemented and so far as such implementation is necessary for the purposes of complying with the international obligations of the United Kingdom under the agreement.

The rationale for section 29 was temporal exigency. The normal procedure for addressing inconsistencies between a treaty and existing UK law is through statutory instruments, facilitated by Henry VIII clauses. Section 31 EUFRA contains the now routine HVIII clause. However, the Trade and Cooperation Agreement[91] was agreed at the eleventh hour, and there was therefore no time to make the requisite statutory instruments. Section 29 was the legislative response to this problem.

It is important to note that it is not merely an interpretive obligation. It is expressive of substantive change: existing law 'has effect' on and after exit day with such 'modifications' as necessary to implement the TCA, assuming that the inconsistency has not otherwise been addressed. The phrase 'existing law' can clearly cover the common law

[90] S Whittaker, 'Retaining European Law in the United Kingdom' (2021) 137 LQR 477; J Williams, 'Accrued EU Law Rights: A Guide for the Perplexed', EU Relations Law (blog) 5 Jan 2022, https://eurelationslaw.com/blog/accrued-eu-law-rights-a-guide-for-the-perplexed; C Vajda, 'Accrued EU Law Rights Encounter Some Brexit Turbulence: *Lipton v BA Cityflyer Ltd*' (2024) 49 ELRev 632.

[91] Trade and Cooperation Agreement between the European Union and the European Atomic Energy Community, of the one part, and the United Kingdom of Great Britain and Northern Ireland, of the other part [2021] OJ L149/10.

as well as statute. Common law provisions that are inconsistent with the TCA will, therefore, fall within section 29.

The interpretation of section 29 was considered by the Supreme Court in *Lipton* because it had featured in Green LJ's judgment in the Court of Appeal.[92] Green LJ held that section 29 transposed the TCA into domestic law. It followed, said Green LJ, that if the relevant provision of domestic law was inconsistent with the corresponding provision of the TCA then the 'inconsistent or incomplete provision is amended or replaced, and the gap is plugged',[93] through recourse to section 29. Green LJ concluded that there was, on the facts of *Lipton*, no inconsistency between the amended version of Regulation 261/2004 and the corresponding provision of the TCA. However, if there had been, the former would have been modified to be consistent with the latter through section 29.

The Supreme Court rejected this reading of section 29. It pointed to the fact that Article 5 TCA states that the TCA does not confer rights on individuals, nor can it be invoked directly in national courts. The Supreme Court concluded that since the aim of Brexit was to remove the influence of EU law from domestic law, 'it would be entirely inconsistent with that aim' and with the wording of Article 5 to 'interpret section 29 as having such an intrusive and automatic effect in our law'.[94]

The Supreme Court did not, however, specify exactly what could in its view be achieved through section 29 EUFRA. It merely stated that if in a future case a party sought to argue that the effect of section 29 was to modify the wording of some existing domestic law, then the court should consider the meaning and effect of section 29 afresh, while adding pointedly that the court 'should not have regard to what has been said by the Court of Appeal in this case'.[95]

The Supreme Court's reasoning based on Article 5 TCA is undoubtedly forceful. It will, nonetheless, be difficult for subsequent courts to decide precisely what can be achieved through section 29.

Consider the following scenario, which is an instance of collateral attack. A customs authority sues a trader for non-compliance with existing UK customs law. The trader responds by claiming rightly that the customs law is inconsistent with TCA provisions, and that therefore the national law must now, in the light of section 29, bear a meaning that is consistent with the TCA. If the trader can successfully make this argument, then it is able to rely on TCA provisions in national law. The conceptual foundation for this is UK law, in the form of section 29, which carries the force of parliamentary sovereignty. However, the consequence is that TCA provisions thereby become enforceable in national courts.

Consider a second scenario, which takes the form of direct attack. A trader instigates an action concerning public procurement. It argues that existing UK law

[92] [2021] EWCA Civ 454, [78].
[93] ibid [82].
[94] *Lipton* (n 70) [79].
[95] ibid [80].

embodies procedures that are inconsistent with the TCA provisions on procurement, and that therefore, in accordance with section 29, the existing law must have effect with the requisite modifications. It can be assumed for the sake of argument that procedures such as those in the TCA would be regarded as giving rise to individual rights if they formed part of UK law. If the trader can do this, then it is able to rely on TCA provisions in national law.

The following considerations are relevant in this regard. It might appear counter-intuitive for the TCA to be legally enforceable in UK courts, given the wording of Article 5 TCA. However, it would be problematic for the defendant/claimant in the previous scenarios not to be able to rely on the TCA provision. There would, for example, be serious legal problems with enabling a customs authority to sue a trader on the basis of a law that no longer contains the legal provisions that constitute the offence, since they have been 'modified' and 'have effect' subject to the TCA through section 29 EUFRA.

It should also be borne in mind that Article 5 TCA is not denuded of all effect, even if some form of direct effect operates through section 29 EUFRA. This is because section 29 only operates in relation to existing law, and therefore the denial of direct effect in the TCA would continue to operate in relation to post-EUFRA legislation. Thus, a trader could not rely on section 29 EUFRA to complain that legislation enacted in 2022 was inconsistent with the TCA. The other limit is that section 29 only operates where there is existing law that is inconsistent with the TCA. It does not cover the situation where there is no national law on the matter.

The final consideration is that insofar as Article 5 TCA is compromised, it is through the will of Parliament as expressed in section 29 EUFRA. This is important, given that Article 5 is framed as follows: 'nothing in this Agreement or supplementary agreement shall be construed' as giving rise to enforceable rights. This does not preclude Parliament from choosing to do so, or enacting legislation that has this effect, more especially given that section 29, thus construed, would avail UK and EU traders alike, assuming that the existing UK law was inconsistent with TCA provisions.

5 Conclusion

There is, as noted earlier, no doubt that the role of the courts has changed in a post-Brexit world. While the UK remained in the EU, the UK courts, like the courts of all other member states, were also EU courts, in the sense that they had the power and duty to apply EU law whenever it was relevant in the cases that came before them. Direct effect, indirect effect, and the primacy of EU law were the principal modalities through which this occurred. UK courts duly applied such precepts while we remained in the EU, and there was little, if any, pushback of the kind practised by constitutional courts in some other member states.

The judicial role is now very different. While there are instances where the precepts of EU law are still applicable, most notably in relation to the Withdrawal Agreement and Northern Ireland, the principal judicial focus in a post-Brexit world has been the application of the post-Brexit legislative regime, including interpretation of the powers of the courts within that regime. This has posed new challenges for the courts, flowing in part from the very complexity of the post-Brexit legislative architecture and in part from the inherently difficult issues concerning the interpretation and application of the judicial powers themselves, as set out in section 6 EUWA.

7

Devolved Governments

Sionaidh Douglas-Scott

1 Pre-Brexit Position

The UK introduced devolution in 1998 as a means of transferring greater power to its constituent nations.[1] Before 1998, the UK was a fairly centralized state, but with some diversity due to its different historical relationships with Scotland, Wales, and Northern Ireland. For example, although Wales had been absorbed into the English legal and administrative system by the sixteenth century, Scotland was an independent state until 1707, when it chose to enter a union with England. Under that union, Scotland retained its separate legal and education systems and Church, and parliamentary sovereignty was simply not mentioned in the Acts of Union of 1706/07. Ireland was different again, having first been subject to constraints and supervision from London and then from 1801 having been in an Act of Union with the UK, until the greater part of Ireland became independent in 1922. However, Northern Ireland remained in the UK, operating an early form of devolution, until its Parliament, Stormont, was abolished in 1972 and direct rule by Westminster established. By 1973, the *Kilbrandon Report on the Constitution* suggested that representative institutions be set up in Scotland and Wales.[2] However, due to the addition of a last-minute threshold requirement, the 1979 devolution referendums in Scotland and Wales were lost. It took almost another twenty years for devolution to come to Scotland, Wales, and Northern Ireland. This resulted in the 1998 Devolution Acts, which consisted of the Scotland Act 1998, the Government of Wales Act 1998, and the Northern Ireland Act 1998, which domestically implemented much of the Belfast/Good Friday Agreement.

Although initially these devolution settlements were different in nature, subsequent amendments changed this (although devolution has always operated somewhat differently in Northern Ireland). (Perhaps) over-simplifying matters, we might summarize the present situation in the following way.

[1] Namely, Scotland, Wales, and Northern Ireland. But not everyone would accept that Northern Ireland is a 'nation'.

[2] *Royal Commission on the Constitution 1969–1973*, Vol 1 Report (HMSO 1973).

Sionaidh Douglas-Scott, *Devolved Governments* In: *The UK Regulatory Framework Post-Brexit: 'Law Unbound'*.
Edited by: Paul Craig and Vilija Vėlyvytė, Oxford University Press.
DOI: 10.1093/9780198969815.003.0008

First, each devolved nation has a devolved parliament or assembly with legislative powers, elected on a wholly or partial proportional representation basis, and a devolved government. Second, these legislative powers are limited in number, with certain matters reserved to the Westminster Parliament.[3] Third, there exists no completely autonomous sphere of self-rule within the devolved nations, as UK sovereignty has been preserved in all matters to the UK Parliament.[4]

In this way, devolution was crafted to protect parliamentary sovereignty. Nonetheless, the Sewel Convention was generally applied, according to which Westminster 'will not normally legislate with regard to devolved matters' without the consent of the devolved parliaments, and indeed this convention was written into legislation in the Scotland Act 2016 and Wales Act 2017. However, since Brexit the status of the Sewel Convention has become questionable, since the lack of devolved parliamentary consent was ignored when major Brexit legislation was passed in Westminster.[5] Nonetheless, the UK Parliament itself, in primary legislation, committed to the permanence of the Scottish and Welsh Parliaments[6] (even if there is scepticism as to the strength of this commitment, due to the doctrine of parliamentary sovereignty). Thus, one might posit a confirmation of the importance of the devolution settlement, and the significance of devolved autonomy.

Devolved funding is provided largely through the Block Grant, which apportions funds from the UK's Consolidated Fund (the aggregate tax revenue from all four nations). Devolved governments can choose how to spend this according to policy priorities. Changes to the allocation of this funding are calculated by the Barnett Formula, which reflects per capita changes in UK government spending on 'comparable' public services in England. Although most taxes are set by the central government in London, devolved governments also have tax-raising powers of their own—so, for example, 31 per cent of total tax revenue in Scotland is now devolved.[7] This means that revenue from some taxes goes directly to the devolved governments and their Block Grant is proportionately reduced. However, the UK government can also circumvent the Barnett Formula altogether—as it did with £1bn funding for Northern Ireland delivered as part of the Conservative–DUP confidence-and-supply agreement from 2017 to 2019.[8] Although the Scottish and Welsh governments objected to this, their attempts at a legal challenge failed. The UK Internal Market Act 2020 also gives the UK government the power to spend money directly in devolved areas, through the

[3] Notably, Wales, unlike Scotland, has no separate legal jurisdiction.

[4] See, eg, s 28(7) Scotland Act 1998 which states: 'This section does not affect the power of the Parliament of the United Kingdom to make laws for Scotland.'

[5] The EU Withdrawal Act 2018 was adopted without legislative consent from Scotland and the EU Withdrawal Agreement Act 2020 adopted without legislative consent from Scotland, Wales, and Northern Ireland. Both the Scottish and Welsh Parliaments refused legislative consent to the Internal Market Act 2020 and EU (Future Relationship) Act 2021.

[6] Scotland Act 2016, s 1; Wales Act 2017, s 1.

[7] https://www.instituteforgovernment.org.uk/explainer/tax-and-devolution 2018.

[8] See, eg, '£1 Billion for Northern Ireland Won't Buy Off the DUP on Brexit', *New Statesman* (29 Oct 2018).

UK Shared Prosperity Fund, even where it does not have policy competence over those areas, and without the consent of the relevant devolved ministers—a matter that has become contentious.

However, England, the largest of the four nations, lacks its own parliament. This was seen as giving rise to the 'West Lothian Question' (named after the West Lothian constituency, whose MP, Tam Dalyell, raised the issue), whereby MPs elected to Westminster from devolved nations could vote on matters in England (such as education) which were devolved competences in Scotland, Wales, Northern Ireland, and so on and for which English MPs had no vote for those territories. The day after Scotland's first independence vote, in 2014, then Prime Minister Cameron announced outside 10 Downing Street that the question of English votes for English laws required a decisive answer and that any new powers for Scotland must be balanced by a reassessment of the voting power of devolution MPs at Westminster. This, at one and the same time, seemed to downplay the issue of greater autonomy for Scotland, and also concretized into the issue of 'English votes for English laws' (EVEL). A new procedure for EVEL was introduced as a 2015 reform which brought changes to the standing orders of the House of Commons.[9] Notably, this highly complex change gave English MPs a veto power over legislation concerning England only and was not a form of devolution to England. It was in any case abandoned in July 2021, and to date there has been little demand for English devolution.[10] The problem of how, if at all, England fits within devolution is sometimes referred to as 'the English question'. To date, the main development that could be described as taking any form of devolution in England has been that of devolution of executive powers to England's 'metro' mayors.[11]

The past two decades have, according to Tierney, seen a 'gradual dispersal of powers'[12] to devolved territories, although the UK is still not a federal state, despite Bogdanor's description of it as 'quasi-federal' in 2001.[13] Devolution is, however, a bit of a mixed picture.

On the one hand, two factors about the way devolution evolved illustrate how it might seem to challenge parliamentary sovereignty. First, very generally speaking, a 'reserved powers' model of devolution now operates in Scotland, Wales, and Northern Ireland. This means that all legislative power is devolved except those matters expressly reserved to the UK. And a considerable amount of power has been devolved. For example, in Scotland, most areas are devolved except defence and foreign relations, currency, constitutional matters, social security, immigration and citizenship, trade and industry, and most of income tax. Second, it is also worth noting that, in

[9] D Gover and M Kenny, 'Answering the West Lothian Question? A Critical Assessment of "English Votes for English Laws" in the UK Parliament' (2018) 71 Parliamentary Affairs 760.

[10] In 2004 North East England voters rejected elected regional assemblies in a referendum.

[11] 'Metro Mayors', at https://www.instituteforgovernment.org.uk/explainer/metro-mayors-devolution.

[12] S Tierney, 'Drifting towards Federalism? Appraising the Constitution in the Light of the Scotland Act 2016 and Wales Act 2017' in R Schütze and S Tierney (eds), *The United Kingdom and the Federal Idea* (Hart 2018) 101.

[13] V Bogdanor, *Devolution in the UK* (Oxford University Press 2001).

the earlier years of devolution, the UK government operated a fair amount of what has been described as 'permissive autonomy',[14] which meant considerable self-rule by devolved institutions. In this respect, UK devolution looked to have given rise to something akin to the 'self-rule' of federalism, with 'quasi-sovereign' institutions in its devolved territories.

Yet on the other hand, UK devolution always lacked the 'shared rule' that characterizes federalism. Reserved areas tend to overlap with powers that are often shared under federalism. But with devolution all the reserved powers are exercised by London, and relations between the UK government and devolved governments remained almost entirely informal, based on Concordats, memoranda of understanding, and a somewhat dysfunctional Joint Ministerial Committee of executives that rarely met before Brexit. Devolved institutions lack enforceable legal powers in these areas. Even legislative relations between Westminster and the devolved parliaments were regulated by the informal 'Sewel Convention', by which the UK Parliament would not normally legislate on devolved matters without the consent of the devolved legislatures—a political convention which, even after its translation into legislation, was held by the UK Supreme Court, almost inexplicably, to be nonetheless a mere convention and not legally enforceable.[15]

This lack of shared rule means that, for example, devolved governments seem to be in a weak situation when it comes to international affairs, including Brexit but also treaties more generally. This absence of shared rule also means that the UK government has over the past few years refused to accept that Scotland might have any power to hold another independence referendum, insisting this falls within reserved powers and is for the UK government alone to determine.

All in all, there is something to be said for the description, by Sandford and Gormley-Heenan, of 'Schrodinger's devolution', namely 'the idea that, since 1999, Scotland, Wales and Northern Ireland both have and have not experienced fundamental constitutional change, on which claims to territorial autonomy can be founded'.[16]

As well as being a devolved state, the UK is often described as a 'union' state. This term is usually used to distinguish the UK from both a federal and a 'unitary' state.[17] But why is the UK not a unitary state? That latter term implies a unified state, with a unitary political centre, shared governing institutions, and legal and administrative standardization—an overall, undifferentiated polity. In contrast, the term 'union state' denotes a state where the centre does not directly control in every part of the territory. The UK is composite in nature, and a plurality and diversity of arrangements exist over its composite parts.

[14] C Jeffrey, 'The Unfinished Business of Devolution' (2007) 22 Public Policy and Administration 92.

[15] *R (Miller) v Secretary of State for Exiting the European Union* [2017] UKSC 5.

[16] M Sandford and C Gormley-Heenan, '"Taking Back Control", the UK's Constitutional Narrative and Schrodinger's Devolution' (2020) 73 Parliamentary Affairs 108.

[17] S Rokkan and D Urwin, *Economy, Territory, Identity: Politics of West European Territories* (Sage 1983).

2 Post-Brexit Legal Change

UK devolution took place after the UK joined the EEC (now EU) in 1973. Notably, EU membership insulated devolved nations from a unitary UK-wide approach, by, for example, distributing EU funds on a basis more beneficial to some parts of the UK than others.

In the referendum on the UK's EU membership, the UK as a whole voted to leave. However, 62 per cent of Scotland's voting electorate, and 56 per cent of those voting in Northern Ireland, voted to remain. Although the SNP had argued in Westminster that there should be majorities in all four UK nations for a decision to leave the EU, this approach was rejected by the UK government. The UK's departure from the EU caused a major change to the UK constitution. But unlike the case for amendments to federal constitutions, there was no requirement for devolved participation in or consent to this major constitutional change. The devolved governments were similarly unable to play any important part in the Brexit negotiations due to the relations with the EU being treated as a foreign policy matter and thus a reserved power for the UK government. This was despite specific devolved government proposals, such as the 2016 Scottish Government's *Scotland's Place in Europe*, which argued for continued Single Market membership, possibly through the European Economic Area (EEA).

(a) EU Withdrawal Act 2018

An early indication of problems to come was furnished by the European Union (Withdrawal) Act 2018 (EUWA). This complex legislation had the task of preparing UK domestic law for the post-Brexit world, and transferred most EU laws into domestic law, in what has been described as a massive 'cut and paste' exercise. It also provided for repeal of the European Communities Act 1972.

Notably, during the UK's EU membership, many devolved matters, such as agriculture, fell under EU rather than UK competence, and EU rather than UK law had provided UK-wide harmonization. This meant that, post-Brexit, not only would there be no UK-wide harmonization in many areas (such as the UK Internal Market), but also devolved governments would inevitably be impacted by repatriation of EU competences to the UK, because in fact, many of those competences were devolved ones.

Importantly for this chapter, EUWA set out significant and controversial provisions—sections 10, 11, and 12, along with schedules 2 and 3—regarding devolution. As noted, UK devolution operates on a reserved powers model, which appeared to be undermined when, in the act of 'taking back control' from the EU, UK government legislation (in an earlier draft of EUWA 2018) proposed to return all former EU competences to Westminster by default, even if the powers in question were devolved, such as agriculture and environment. This was justified as necessary to ensure a functioning UK Internal Market post-Brexit, but even a redraft of the relevant provision could not prevent accusations by the Scottish government of a 'power grab' by London.

Part of the problem was that, in transferring a huge swathe of EU regulation into domestic law (in what EUWA termed 'retained EU law'), it was recognized that much of this regulation would have to be altered if it was to be functional post-Brexit. So EUWA provided UK government ministers with the power to repeal or amend this law to address 'deficiencies'—a provision that vastly increased executive power. Most controversial was section 12 EUWA, which, to summarize a convoluted provision, even after it had been redrafted, enabled the UK government unilaterally to limit devolved powers in areas of retained EU law, and so override consent.

As a result, even after a redraft of section 12, EUWA continued to be opposed by the Scottish government (but not the Welsh), which saw it as overriding a fundamental constitutional principle of the devolution settlement. And so the Scottish Parliament refused to grant consent to the relevant sections of EUWA.

This did not stop EUWA from being adopted in Westminster, given that the UK Supreme Court held in the first *Miller* case (discussed below) that the Sewel Convention, even set out in legislation, nonetheless remained a convention only, and not legally binding. However, this section 12 EUWA power (which allowed UK ministers to temporarily freeze the ability of devolved legislatures to amend retained EU law) was in fact never used and has now been repealed.

(b) Scottish Continuity Bill Legislation and Litigation

As noted, the Scottish Parliament refused to consent to EUWA 2018, and in March 2018 the Scottish Parliament adopted the UK Withdrawal from the European Union (Legal Continuity) (Scotland) Act 2018 by ninety-five votes to thirty-two. This Bill shared its structure and approach with the UK EUWA 2018, seeking to complement it. However, it diverged from EUWA in some areas: for example, it did not exclude the EU Charter of Fundamental Rights and allowed Scotland to keep pace with EU developments in future. It also, in section 17 (in contrast to the UK EUWA), required consent of Scottish Ministers should UK ministers wish to alter or repeal retained EU law within devolved areas. This Bill was challenged by the UK government and the lawsuit made constitutional history, being the first ASP referred to the UK Supreme Court by the Attorney General under section 33 of the Scotland Act 1998.

Later in 2018, the Supreme Court, applying the familiar test of whether a provision had 'more than a loose or consequential connection to a reserved matter',[18] found only section 17 outside the Scottish Parliament's competence,[19] due to enactments unilaterally adopted by the UK government in EUWA (subsequent to adoption of the

[18] *Martin v Most* [2010] UKSC 10, [49].
[19] *A Reference by the Attorney General and the Advocate General for Scotland* [2018] UKSC 64.

Scottish Continuity legislation) which prohibited the EUWA's own modification—that is, which made it, in now familiar terms, a 'protected statute'. However, it is hard not to conclude that the Continuity Bill was competent when adopted by the Scottish Parliament. If so, surely it follows that the UK government may challenge any devolved legislation it dislikes, thus suspending its application while the matter is *sub judice*, and in the meantime adopt its own 'protected legislation', which by coming into force automatically trumps the devolved legislation.

(c) European Union (Withdrawal Agreement) Act 2020 (EUWAA)

A Withdrawal Agreement[20] was agreed between the EU and the UK government on 17 October 2019 and entered into force on 1 February 2020, after the UK Parliament had adopted EUWAA 2020 and the EU had approved the Withdrawal Agreement. From that date the UK was no longer an EU member, although there was a transition period until 31 December 2020, during which most EU law continued to apply in the UK. This Agreement (sometimes known as the 'divorce' agreement) principally dealt with three matters: the UK's financial obligations; the situation of EU citizens in the UK and UK citizens in the EU post-Brexit; and the Northern Ireland Protocol.

However, it contained some provisions more specifically relevant to devolution. It amended EUWA powers to correct deficiencies in this body of 'retained EU law', extending the power by eleven months so it could be used until two years after the transition period ended (rather than exit day). Further, EUWAA was notably adopted without the consent of any of the devolved legislatures. According to Ian Blackford MP, then SNP leader at Westminster: 'We are faced with a situation which is completely unprecedented when the government in Edinburgh, Belfast and in Cardiff has not given consent to this Act of Parliament. That appears to completely contravene the devolution settlement.'[21]

(d) EU–UK Trade and Cooperation Agreement/European Union (Future Relationship) Act 2020

These measures are another piece of the Brexit jigsaw in that they set out Britain's future trading relationship with the EU. This UK statute was the main vehicle for implementation of the Trade and Cooperation Agreement which the UK had agreed with the EU. The Trade and Cooperation Agreement does not require the UK government

[20] Agreement on the withdrawal of the United Kingdom of Great Britain and Northern Ireland from the European Union and the European Atomic Energy Community, 2019/C 384 OJ C 384, 12.11.2019.

[21] 'Boris Johnson's Brexit Bill Becomes Law', *The Guardian* (23 January 2020).

to adopt European standards of regulation, but there is a 'non-regression' clause which enables the EU to retaliate should the UK resile on standards.

(e) Retained EU Law (Revocation and Reform) Act 2023

Under the Retained EU Law (Revocation and Reform) Act 2023 (REULA), 'retained EU law', the category that had been created by EUWA 2018, ceased to exist as a specific category of domestic law on 1 January 2024. Any remaining retained EU law instead became 'assimilated law'. Such laws no longer need be interpreted in accordance with EU law principles, but, under REULA, assimilated EU law may still be revoked, amended, or replaced—although more easily. Both UK government ministers and devolved government ministers may adopt these regulations. Until June 2026 (when the new power expires), the UK government has a duty to report on its reform of assimilated law. On 23 January 2025 the UK government published its third statutory assimilated law report, noting that 6,901 items of assimilated law had been identified, across around 400 policy areas, out of which 2,395 had been either revoked or reformed.

How will this interact with any Common Frameworks (discussed below) agreed in that area? Are they in danger of being overridden when formerly retained, now assimilated, EU law is amended or repealed? This is a potential danger, given no secure legal protection exists for Common Frameworks. It is also clear that devolved governments have taken a different approach to former EU law than the UK government. In its Third Bi-Annual Scottish Government REULA Update (February 2025) the Scottish government stated that its policy 'continues to be that there is no intention to revoke or reform assimilated law simply because it is . . . retained' from EU membership, continuing that it would consider UK government proposals 'on a case-by-case basis'.

However, it may be that 'the Labour Government's approach to reform of legacy EU laws is different from that of its Conservative predecessor'.[22] As a result, Angus Robertson MSP, Cabinet Secretary for Constitution, External Affairs and Culture, welcomed the UK government's position, writing that 'in my view the tenor of the latest UK report gives a greater confidence than has been in place since the Brexit referendum that the Scottish Parliament's custodianship over devolved Scots law is understood'.[23]

The UK House of Commons also suggested in a recent *Insight* paper that the current UK government may be 'more willing' than its predecessor to reform assimilated

[22] 'A Shift in Approach? Assimilated Law Reform and the Change of Government' (HC, Research Briefing, 15 November 2024).

[23] Angus Robertson MSP, at https://www.parliament.scot/-/media/files/committees/constitution-europe-external-affairs-and-culture-committee/correspondence/2025/third-biannual-reul-act-report--letter-to-ceeac-convener--february-2025.pdf.

law to 'align with EU rules where this would reduce divergence and regulatory friction within the UK's internal market'.[24]

(f) Internal Market Act 2020

(i) General

This is very significant legislation. It aims to provide the framework for a UK Internal Market after Brexit. Federal States have specific provisions to ensure internal market policy harmonization. For example, the German Federation has certain exclusive powers under Article 73(5) German Constitution, although Länder also have considerable competences of their own, some including treaty making.

Although the 2020 UK White Paper preceding the UK Internal Market Act asserted that '[t]he UK Internal Market has for centuries been at the heart of our economic and social prosperity as a country',[25] this claim is not particularly persuasive. The 1707 Acts of Union contained no reference to a single UK market, and the union of Scotland and England was mostly a customs union.[26]

Notwithstanding, the UK's departure from the EU necessitated a UK Internal Market and the Internal Market Act (UKIMA) was drafted and adopted extremely quickly in 2020—albeit that the draft Bill's initial conflict with the Northern Ireland Protocol necessitated redrafting to remove offending clauses that violated international law. Notably, UKIMA was adopted without consent from Scotland and Wales, who feared the Act would inflict new limits on the exercise of their devolved powers. It is also notable that UKIMA is a 'protected' enactment, meaning that devolved institutions may not modify[27] it—that is, they may not set aside or override its market access principles even if perceived to have a harmful effect on devolved regulation.

(ii) Market Access Principles of 'Mutual Recognition' and 'Non-discrimination'

UKIMA 2020 relies on two major principles: that of mutual recognition and that of non-discrimination.

Although devolved nations may set their own regulations in devolved areas, the mutual recognition provision prevents them from applying these to goods and services already lawfully marketed elsewhere in the UK (this also extends to goods imported into the UK from third countries such as the USA), unless very limited

[24] 'Assimilated Law Reform: Moving towards Alignment?', *Insight* (4 February 2025).

[25] UK Internal Market (CP 278, 2020) 1.

[26] See, eg, M Keating, https://www.centreonconstitutionalchange.ac.uk/news-and-opinion/response-internal-market-white-paper.

[27] UKIMA, s 54.

exceptions apply. Similarly, the non-discrimination principle prohibits devolved governments from enacting laws that discriminate against goods and services from other parts of the UK, unless very limited exceptions apply. These principles apply separately in relation to goods and services and, although these terms are familiar from EU trade law, their operation is somewhat different, and much narrower, in UKIMA.

The mutual recognition principle under section 2 UKIMA applies to all rules governing product requirements (a familiar term from EU law). These are rules that concern goods themselves, including their ingredients, composition, packaging, and labelling. Under UKIMA, mutual recognition may be refused only in limited circumstances, for example combatting the spread of pests, diseases, or unsafe foodstuffs.[28] Unlike under EU law, there is no possibility of justification for more general threats to public health, or for environmental, consumer, or employment protection.

The non-discrimination principle under section 5 UKIMA, which includes both direct and indirect discrimination, applies to goods with a 'relevant connection' to another part of the UK.[29] This principle concerns 'manner of sale requirements' (what in EU law came to be known as 'selling arrangements'), such as licensing provisions, price requirements, place or time of sale, or advertising regulation. Direct discrimination may be defended only on very limited grounds, for example to reduce the spread of disease, or if justified on the basis of a 'public health emergency' (section 10(1)). Indirect discrimination may be justified if necessary to achieve a legitimate aim, such as the protection either of the life or health of humans, animals, or plants, or public safety and security (section 8(1) and (6)).

Part 2 of the Act sets out rules governing internal trade in services.[30] Under sections 10 and 18 UKIMA, the UK government may adopt regulations creating exclusions for both goods and services from market access principles.[31] (Such regulations may, but do not have to, implement an agreement forming part of a Common Framework—see below).

(iii) Monitoring/Enforcement

The Act establishes a new Office for the Internal Market (Part 4 & Sched 3 UKIMA) which must publish annual reports on the operation of UKIMA and five-yearly reports on its effectiveness. The Office's role is advisory, and enforcement itself is the province of trading standards authorities, regulators, and possibly courts where necessary.

The default position of the market access principles is that if a product is lawfully produced in one UK territory it should be automatically sold in other territories. If not, there could be a legal challenge—although the mechanisms are not particularly

[28] ibid s 10(1) and Schedule 1.

[29] ibid ss 5, 7, and 8.

[30] Rules on services apply only by default, where mutual recognition for goods under Part 1, or professional qualifications/regulations under Part 3, do not apply, ibid s 17(5).

[31] See, eg, UKIMA 2020 (Exclusions from Market Access Principles: Single-use Plastics) Regulations 2022.

clear (at this stage). Notably, violation of the market access principles results in disapplication of the relevant legislation.

(iv) Implications for Devolution

The Scottish government described UKIMA as 'perhaps the single most significant threat to the devolution settlements established over a quarter of a century ago'.[32] Mark Drakeford described it as 'the single most damaging act to the Union in the whole 20-plus years of devolution'.[33] UKIMA does not expressly restrict devolved autonomy, in the sense that any devolved provision/action inconsistent with its market access principles is still lawful. However, any such measure may be disapplied and not enforced against non-devolved products if they conflict with the Act. This means that, although devolved institutions may legislate within their areas of devolved competence to fulfil policy objectives, they may be unable to enforce those measures against goods from elsewhere in the UK. This may result in a competitive disadvantage against the devolved product, especially in the case of goods from England, which, given its size, dominates the rest of the UK. Therefore, devolved governments are losing their territorial autonomy, in that their regulation may no longer apply to all trade activity within their territory. This exerts 'a powerful "chilling effect"' on devolved policy-making.[34] Particular policy choices of the Scottish and Welsh governments, such as on single-use plastics or bottle deposit schemes, well illustrate the problem—namely that devolved policy innovation may be frustrated due to incompatibility with products conforming to policy developed elsewhere in the UK (usually England).

A perhaps predictable consequence was that, soon after UKIMA received Royal Assent, the Counsel General for Wales commenced judicial review seeking an advisory declaration on the constitutional implications of the UKIMA—the action, however, was rejected by the courts as 'premature'.[35]

The collapse of the Scottish government's Bottle Deposit recycling scheme (whereby a deposit of 20p added to the price of single-use drinks containers would be refunded if the item was returned for recycling) provides a good example. Given that this scheme would introduce different trading requirements in Scotland from England, it appeared to violate UKIMA by discriminating between goods originating from different parts of the UK. So the Scottish government applied to the UK government for a specific exemption from UKIMA. However, the UK government granted a partial exemption only, which did not cover glass.[36] This was seen as placing

[32] https://www.gov.scot/publications/scottish-government-position-paper-internal-market-act-2020/pages/3/ (3 April 2025).

[33] M Drakeford, oral evidence, Future governance of the UK (HL Constitution Committee, 14 July 2021).

[34] T Horsley, C Brown Swan, N McEwen, and L Whitten, 'Westminster Rules: The UK Internal Market Act' https://www.gla.ac.uk/media/Media_1114828_smxx.pdf; M Dougan, J Hunt, N McEwen, and A McHarg, 'Sleeping with an Elephant: Devolution and the UK Internal Market Act 2020' (2022) 138 LQR 650.

[35] *Counsel General for Wales v Secretary of State for Business, Energy and Industrial Strategy* [2022] EWCA Civ 118. Ultimately, the UK Supreme Court rejected the application for leave to appeal.

[36] On grounds that schemes elsewhere in the UK did not intend to include glass: https://commonslibrary.parliament.uk/will-glass-shatter-plans-for-uk-deposit-return-schemes/ (28 November 2023).

Scottish business at a competitive disadvantage, and in 2023 the Scottish government announced it would defer introduction of the scheme 'as a consequence of the UK Government's refusal to agree a full exclusion from the Internal Market Act'.[37] Since then, the Scottish government has faced litigation from firms that made preparations for the deposit scheme.[38]

On the other hand, under the Genetic Technology (Precision Breeding) Act 2023 gene-modified crops from England can now be sold in Scotland and Wales, although both devolved governments take issue with the policy and took no part in the UK Genetic Technology Bill. Furthermore, unlike the devolved governments, the UK Parliament may adopt primary legislation to disapply regulatory standards for any sector it wishes to protect. In this way, the devolved governments are put at a disadvantage twice over—first in terms of a regulatory race to the bottom due to the size and dominance of England's economy, and second due to Westminster's powers of parliamentary sovereignty.

In addition, UKIMA provides the UK government with spending powers in many devolved areas, thus compromising devolved governments' ability to take credit for funding policy innovations within their territories. If we add to this the UK Subsidy Control Act 2022, which replaces former rules on EU State Aid (such subsidies now becoming a reserved matter for the UK government), this strengthens a general impression of undermining devolved governments' ability to legislate in devolved areas.[39]

3 Post-Brexit Constitutional and Political Change

(a) Common Frameworks

(i) What Are They?

Another major piece of the post-Brexit jigsaw has been the establishment of 'Common Frameworks' of shared governance over policy areas where there is an element of devolution, so as to ensure common UK approaches.[40] Such frameworks only apply where a policy competence has been returned from the EU, and the enticement of the Common Framework proposal, a new concept in UK law, was that they would supposedly provide devolved governments with as much discretion over policy as they had possessed in the EU. Such frameworks tend to be technical in nature and the

[37] Scottish Government: https://www.gov.scot/news/deposit-return/

[38] *Biffa Waste Services Limited v Scottish Ministers* at https://www.bbc.com/news/articles/c5yrgzvgld5o.

[39] See, eg, Michael Russell MSP describing it as 'radically undermining the powers and democratic ability of the Scottish Parliament'. *After Brexit: The UK Internal Market Act and devolution* (Scottish Government, 8 March 2021).

[40] *Common Frameworks: Building a Cooperative Union* (HL Common Frameworks Scrutiny Committee, March 2021).

majority of them fall within the remit of the UK Department for the Environment, Food and Rural Affairs.

The Common Framework Principles were agreed between the UK, Scottish and Welsh governments in October 2017.[41] Examples of areas in which frameworks have been established include Resources and Waste, Fisheries Management and Support, Food Compositional Standards and Labelling, Agricultural Support, and Animal Health and Welfare. In 2021, the House of Lords Common Frameworks Scrutiny Committee noted thirty-two active framework policy areas.[42] It was also agreed in 2017 that Common Frameworks were necessary to ensure compliance with international obligations and enable the UK to negotiate new international trade agreements.

(ii) Legal Forms

Frameworks take a number of forms, which need not be primary legislation. They may instead be formulated as soft law, such as a Memorandum of Understanding. Indeed, to date, they are non-statutory in form and capable of producing only political rather than legal constraints. Their content may be devised as harmonization or common standards, or minimum standard requirements or mutual recognition. So they may in fact leave considerable freedom to devolved governments to develop their own policy.

Each Common Framework identifies which former EU competence is at issue. It also contains procedures that set out notification requirements (should there be changes made by government to retained/assimilated EU law) as well as processes to manage divergence, and procedures for disputes.

(iii) Scrutiny

Scrutiny has been a major concern. A House of Lords Common Frameworks Scrutiny Committee was established and committees in the Scottish Parliament and Senedd have scrutinised provisional frameworks and made recommendations on their improvement prior to finalisation. The HL Scrutiny Committee noted:[43]

> [D]uring much of their evolution, frameworks have been developed behind closed doors and with minimal stakeholder engagement or parliamentary scrutiny, and the vast majority are unfinished and have still not been published despite being operational.

[41] JMC (EU Negotiations) Communique, 2017, https://assets.publishing.service.gov.uk/government/uploads/system/uploads/attachment_data/file/652285/Joint_Ministerial_Committee_communique.pdf.

[42] *Common Frameworks: Building a Cooperative Union*, Annexe 4.

[43] *Common Frameworks: Building a Cooperative Union.*

Aside from problems with scrutiny, reflections on Common Frameworks have been relatively positive, partly because they are perceived by devolved ministers as 'mutually negotiated and agreed between governments, rather than imposed by the UK Government'.[44]

(iv) Interaction with UKIMA

On the other hand, there has been much criticism of perceived damage inflicted on Common Frameworks by UKIMA. Indeed, it was initially argued that UKIMA was unnecessary because common issues were much better dealt with by Common Frameworks. Although UKIMA permits the UK government to exempt completed Common Frameworks from its application, the Scottish government noted that[45]

> the Common Frameworks programme has been put under strain by the unilateral—and wholly unnecessary—imposition of the Internal Market Act in 2020, and then by UK Ministers' failure to honour assurances offered in both Houses of Parliament to follow agreed processes, and allow policy divergence agreed through a Common Framework to be excluded from the Act's effects.

(b) New Forums for Negotiation and Regular Engagement between Ministers

Since the post-1998 devolution settlement, there have existed soft law devices such as Concordats, Guidance notes and Memorandums of Understanding (MoU), to ensure cooperation between central and devolved governments.[46] In 1999 a MoU was agreed between the four administrations, providing a framework for intergovernmental relations in the UK.[47] This MoU established a forum of ministers from UK and devolved governments, the Joint Ministerial Committee (JMC), which operated on three levels: plenary, functional, and official. However, this JMC provided devolved governments with no legal rights. Under the Concordats and MoU, the UK government had to consult devolved administrations over formulation of the UK position and involve devolved administrations in negotiations relating to devolved matters. However, these measures are not legally binding, so devolved nation positions are not ensured. Thus, UK devolution left the UK's intergovernmental relations

[44] HL Select Committee on the Constitution, *The Governance of the Union: Consultation, Co-Operation and Legislative Consent*, September 2024.

[45] https://committees.parliament.uk/writtenevidence/124908/pdf/ at 4.

[46] See, eg, P Bowers, 'Concordats and Devolution Guidance Notes', HC RP, 2005, SN/PC/3767 for an early example.

[47] Updated October 2013: Cabinet Office, 'Devolution: Memorandum of Understanding and Supplementary Agreements' https://www.gov.uk/government/publications/devolution-memorandum-of-understanding-and-supplementary-agreement.

informal and the inter-UK government machinery and EU formation of the JMC(E) were perceived as functioning inadequately by the devolved governments.

It became evident that there had been a decline in relations between devolved administrations and the UK government. This deterioration had been driven by a number of factors, Brexit, the Covid pandemic, pursuit of independence in Scotland, and continued interruption of devolved government in Northern Ireland among them.

Two initiatives revealed an awareness of the need to mend intergovernmental structures—the review of Lord Dunlop into UK government Union capability,[48] and the UK government's own policy paper on the review of intergovernmental relations.[49] As a result, new intergovernmental structures, currently in place, were introduced in January 2022.[50] These take the form of a new three-tier intergovernmental relations structure (but still divided into plenary, functional, and official) which has official terms of reference and a more regular meetings agenda. The new system also set up a more formal dispute resolution process. The Labour government in power from July 2024 also set up a Minister for Intergovernmental Relations, based in the Cabinet Office, with responsibility for devolution.

The Council of the Nations and Regions was established in autumn 2024 by the incoming Labour government. It derives from a proposal originating with former Prime Minister Gordon Brown's *Commission on the UK's Future*.[51] The Council includes the Prime Minister, the First Ministers of the three devolved administrations, and the mayors of England's combined authorities, and is designed to facilitate partnership between them on cross-cutting issues and strategic questions. The intention is that it meet bi-annually, and its first meeting was on 11 October 2024 in Edinburgh, where it discussed investment and UK Industrial strategy. Although the Council arises from Labour government policy to improve relations between the UK government and the devolved governments, its interaction with other intergovernmental forums, such as the British–Irish Council, is not particularly clear.

However, any machinery for intergovernmental relations will only be as effective as its members allow, and their goodwill is key. Relations between the different governments of the UK are especially important regarding trade. Disputes can strain intergovernmental relationships, as the bottle deposit scheme and Gender Recognition Bill issues (discussed below) have demonstrated. Moreover, disputes have also come about over post-Brexit funding. There has been concern over UK government control of funds under the UK Shared Prosperity Fund (which replaces former EU structural

[48] Cabinet Office, The Dunlop Review into UK Government Union Capability (24 March 2021): https://www.gov.uk/government/publications/the-dunlop-review-into-uk-government-union-capability.

[49] Cabinet Office and Department for Levelling Up, Housing and Communities, Policy Paper: Review of Intergovernmental Relations (13 January 2022) https://www.gov.uk/government/publications/the-review-of-intergovernmental-relations.

[50] D Torrance, *Intergovernmental Relations in the UK*, at https://researchbriefings.files.parliament.uk/documents/CBP-8371/CBP-8371.pdf.

[51] *A New Britain: Renewing Our Democracy and Rebuilding Our Economy: Report of the Commission on the UK's Future* (Labour Party 2022).

funding), as well as the UK government's powers under UKIMA to dispense financial support throughout the UK, including in devolved areas.[52]

Certain strains on intergovernmental relationships merit further consideration, and three issues present particular cause for concern: the functioning of the Sewel consent mechanism; litigation over legal competence; and the possibility of independence disputes.

(c) The Sewel Convention

From the earliest days of devolution, it was agreed that it might at times be expedient if the UK Parliament itself could legislate on a devolved matter (for example, if comprehensive legislation were needed for the whole UK). Lord Sewel made the now famous statement at the time of the 1998 Scotland Act debate in the House of Lords that 'we would expect a convention to be established that Westminster would not normally legislate with regard to devolved matters in Scotland without the consent of the Scottish Parliament'.[53]

Thus the 'Sewel Motion' or Legislative Consent Motion (LCM) was born. In the earlier days of devolution, such motions were quite frequently used, and consent given. Notably, the UK government's Devolution Guidance (DG) Note 10 (which is not legally binding) appeared to give a wider understanding to the Sewel Convention for Scotland.[54] DG Note 10 states that a UK Bill requiring Scottish parliamentary consent under the Sewel Convention is one which 'contains provisions applying to Scotland and which are for devolved purposes, **or** *which alter the legislative competence of the Parliament or the executive competence of the Scottish Ministers*'.[55]

In 2016, the Sewel Convention was given a statutory basis by the Scotland Act 2016, section 2,[56] which inserted a new subsection (8) into the Scotland Act 1998, section 28, which now reads: 'But it is recognized that the Parliament of the United Kingdom will not normally legislate with regard to devolved matters without the consent of the Scottish Parliament',[57] although section 28(7) still states that 'This section does not affect the power of the Parliament of the United Kingdom to make laws for Scotland'.

However, it seems that the Scotland Act 2016, section 2, failed to transform the convention into a statutory obligation. In *Miller*, the UK Supreme Court determined that the UK government may not trigger Article 50 by use of the prerogative alone,[58] but also determined the status of the Sewel Convention, finding that, notwithstanding

[52] N Newson, *Union of the United Kingdom: Under Stress?* (HL Library, 16 June 2022).
[53] HL Deb vol 592, col 791, 21 July 1998.
[54] A different DG Note 9 applies to Wales.
[55] DG Note 10: 'Post-Devolution Primary Legislation Affecting Scotland' (Cabinet Office, 23 August 2011) para 4 (emphasis added).
[56] See also, Wales Act 2017, s 2.
[57] Notably this did not follow the fuller wording in DG Note 10.
[58] *R (Miller) v Secretary of State for Exiting the European Union* [2017] UKSC 5.

its incorporation in the Scotland Act 2016, the measure remains a convention, not a legally enforceable obligation. This was a controversial decision given the delicate state of UK–Scottish constitutional politics, which provided the context for enactment of the Scotland Act 2016. The Supreme Court explained that its finding was compelled by the wording of the Scotland Act itself, because '[w]e would have expected Westminster to have used other words if it were seeking to convert a convention into a legal rule justiciable by the courts'.[59] Yet it does seem strange to include a provision in legislation that is not intended to create any legal effect.

But there are other problems with the wording of Scotland Act, section 2, and Wales Act 2017, section 2. First, what is meant by the term 'normally'? Was any Brexit legislation abnormal? But surely, if 'normally' just means what the UK government interprets it as, then it is unhelpful or redundant? And so it proved. Substantial pieces of Brexit legislation, the EUWA 2018, the EU WAA 2020, and UKIMA were passed without the legislative consent of some or all devolved parliaments. A second complaint was that the new statutory provisions referred only to 'devolved matters'. This was felt to misrepresent the scope of the Sewel Convention, which had evolved to cover both devolved policy areas and situations where the UK Parliament varied the legislative competence of the Scottish Parliament or government, as in DG Note 10.

(d) Post-Brexit Problems with Sewel

Miller did not signal the end of worries about the Sewel Convention. For some time, it had been clear that the Sewel Convention was suffering difficulties. For example, in 2022, the Scottish Parliament's Constitution, Europe, External Affairs and Culture Committee (CEEAC) pinpointed a 'fundamental difference of viewpoint' between the UK and devolved governments regarding the convention, which had provoked a worsening of relations.[60] Although prior to 2018 the UK Parliament had not legislated without devolved consent,[61] since then the UK Parliament has on numerous occasions adopted legislation in the absence of consent from at least one of the devolved legislatures, even in the case of legislation unrelated to Brexit.[62] A more general complaint was made by all devolved governments regarding the absence of advance notice and consultation on UK Bills that concern devolved matters.

Indeed, there has been much consideration[63] of possible options to strengthen the Sewel Convention. There exists a range of possible reforms, such as placing the Sewel

[59] ibid [148].

[60] *The Impact of Brexit on Devolution* (Scottish Parliament: CEAAC Report, 2022).

[61] At least not in those cases where it had acknowledged that Sewel was engaged.

[62] For a list of such UK legislation: The Governance of the Union: Consultation, Co-Operation and Legislative Consent (HL Select Committee on the Constitution, September 2024).

[63] For example: The Governance of the Union: Consultation, Co-Operation and Legislative Consent; Scottish Parliament, CEAAC: How is Devolution Changing Post EU, Mccorkindale Adviser's Briefing 2023; also A Paun and K Shuttleworth, at https://www.instituteforgovernment.org.uk/sites/default/files/publications/legislating-by-consent-sewel-convention.pdf; Welsh Government, *Reforming Our Union: Shared Governance in the UK* (2019).

Convention on a statutory footing, introducing new political commitments to respect devolved autonomy, updating the Devolution Guidance Notes, or even establishing a new constitutional settlement. While some recommend legislation, there is scepticism over this, given that the attempt to place Sewel on a legislative footing in the 2016 Scotland Act seemed unable to alter its political status. However, amendment to remove the terms 'it is recognised that' and 'not normally' could be beneficial. Ambiguity over Sewel's scope could also be cleared up to make it unequivocal that it applies both to the policy arm and to institutional powers, as DG Note 10 suggests. Indeed, there is some strong support for updating the DG Notes, given that they are outdated in not taking account of Brexit, Common Frameworks, or new institutional structures. The DG Notes also make outdated references to the 'Scottish Executive' rather than the Scottish government and the 'National Assembly for Wales' instead of the Senedd. The most far-reaching of possible changes would be to institute a new constitutional settlement, entrenching the requirements of Sewel in some way. However, this would involve a fundamental re-organization of the state and would depend on there being an appetite for wider constitutional overhaul.

(e) Legal Disputes over Legislative Competence

Although legal challenges to devolved legislative competence took place in the past, these have become more numerous since Brexit. This has been partly due to the breakdown in intergovernmental relations and problems with Sewel detailed in the preceding paragraphs—so courts have been seen as productive avenues for settling disputes that could not be dealt with by other means.

(i) The Gender Recognition Reform (Scotland) Bill

But in addition, the UK government's powers to block laws passed in the devolved legislatures has been a further cause of controversy following the use of Scotland Act 1998, section 35,[64] to 'veto' the Gender Recognition Reform (Scotland) Bill in January 2023. This was the first use of a provision seen as there to be used only in the last resort. The then Welsh First Minister, Mark Drakeford MS, criticized the use of section 35 as setting a 'very dangerous precedent' for devolution.[65]

In December 2022, the Scottish Parliament (by a considerable majority) had adopted the Gender Recognition Reform (Scotland) Bill, which if it came into force would establish a specific Scottish process for obtaining a Gender Recognition

[64] Under s 35 Scotland Act 1998 the Secretary of State for Scotland may prohibit the Scottish Parliament's Presiding Officer from presenting a Bill for Royal Assent if the Secretary of State reasonably believes the Bill incompatible with international obligations, national security or defence interests or where legislation would have 'an adverse effect' on reserved matters.

[65] 'Gender Reform: Drakeford Says Scottish Law Block is Dangerous Precedent', *BBC News* (17 January 2023).

Certificate under the UK-wide Gender Recognition Act 2004. Gender recognition is a devolved matter in Scotland, and the Bill's proposals were designed to facilitate a legal change of gender in Scotland, including by removing the need for a medical diagnosis and reducing the minimum age from 18 to 16. However, the Secretary of State for Scotland issued a 's35 order', vetoing the Bill from obtaining Royal Assent. The Scottish government brought an application for judicial review, arguing that the UK government had made impermissible use of section 35 to block the Bill because it disagreed with its policy. The UK government's argument was that the Scottish Bill would have adverse consequences on reserved matters, most particularly the Equality Act 2010, under which 'sex' is a protected characteristic. The Scottish Court of Session decided in favour of the UK government, holding that a rational basis existed for the section 35 order and rejecting the argument that any policy disagreement over gender reform underlay the Secretary of State's decision. The Scottish government decided that it would not appeal against the Court's judgment,[66] with the result that the Bill could not be submitted for Royal Assent. A further twist was the *For Women Challenge* to the (different) Gender Representation (Scotland) Act,[67] which seems to have gathered further support after the success of the earlier challenge to the Gender Recognition Act.[68]

(ii) The Treaty Incorporation Bill References

In 2021, in the *Treaty Incorporation Bill References*,[69] the UK Supreme Court upheld the UK government's challenge to two Bills adopted by the Scottish Parliament on grounds they exceeded the Scottish Parliament's powers. Both Bills implemented treaties into Scots law, one incorporating the UN Convention on the Rights of the Child, the other the European Charter of Local Self-Government. Although both Bills were unanimously approved by MSPs and certified by the Presiding Officer as within the Scottish Parliament's powers, the Court held that both Bills placed obligations on UK ministers that exceeded devolved powers,[70] by modifying section 28(7) Scotland Act (in what Elliott described as 'a highly unconvincing judgement that reads the Scottish Devolution settlement unnecessarily narrowly'[71]). This significant judgment on legislative competence was perhaps a harbinger of how the Supreme Court would determine the competence of a future Scottish independence referendum Bill, which is examined in the next section.

[66] https://www.gov.scot/news/section-35-judicial-review/

[67] *For Women Scotland v Scottish Ministers* [2025] UKSC 16. This was a successful challenge to the Gender Representation on Public Boards (Scotland) Act 2018 on the ground that it unlawfully combined the separate characteristics of sex and gender reassignment under the Equality Act by extending the definition of 'women' to include people who self-identified as women.

[68] A McHarg, *The Contested Boundaries of Devolved Legislative Competence* (Bennett Institute for Public Policy 2023) 14.

[69] [2021] UKSC 42.

[70] *Reference by the Attorney General and the Advocate General for Scotland* [2021] UKSC 42.

[71] M Elliott and N Kilford, 'Devolution in the Supreme Court: Legislative Supremacy, Parliament's "Unqualified" Power, and "Modifying" the Scotland Act', UK Const L Blog (15 October 2021).

(iii) Other Litigation

There have been fewer challenges to devolved legislation in Wales. The challenge brought to UKIMA was, as noted, dismissed as premature. However, the Senedd enacted the Environmental Protection (Single-use Plastic Products) (Wales) Act in 2023, which makes it an offence to supply or offer to supply unnecessary, commonly littered single-use plastic products to a consumer in Wales. It has been suggested that this legislation might operate as a test case, as many of the products prohibited by the Welsh Act, such as plastic bags, are legally available to consumers in England, and there was no exclusion obtained from UKIMA provisions from the UK government.[72]

Aside from that, devolved governments have participated in other key litigation cases. The Scottish government intervened in the first *Miller* case to argue that the EU (Notification of Withdrawal) Bill would require devolved consent under the Sewel Convention—an argument that failed, as already discussed. The Welsh government intervened in *Miller I* and also the *Scottish Continuity Bill* case.[73]

(f) Independence

Another major challenge has been the resurfacing of a desire in Scotland for an independence referendum. On 23 November 2022, the UK Supreme Court held that the Scottish Parliament lacked the legal power to legislate for a second independence referendum.[74] This was not the first time that the issue of Scottish independence had been raised. In September 2014, a Scottish independence referendum was held and the proposal 'Should Scotland be an independent country?' rejected by a margin of 10.6 per cent.[75] During that independence campaign, the pro-UK 'Better Together' alliance conspicuously argued that Scotland could only retain its EU membership by remaining in the UK. This of course was not so, and since then, Brexit has taken place.

In June 2022 the Scottish government reanimated its campaign for independence, the main feature of which was a draft independence referendum Bill,[76] with the question, 'Should Scotland be an independent country?' The Lord Advocate, Dorothy Bain KC (the Scottish Government's principal Law Officer), immediately referred the Bill to the UK Supreme Court under Schedule 6 Scotland Act 1998, querying whether it related to reserved matters and so was outside the competence of the Scottish Parliament. The Lord Advocate argued that this Bill (unlike its 2014 precedent) was framed as a 'consultative referendum', and as such it could not per se end the Union.

[72] McHarg (n 68) 13.

[73] *Miller; Continuity Bill Reference* [2018] UKSC 64. There were also challenges from Northern Ireland: *re McCord & Agnew* [2017] UKSC 5; *JR80* [2019] NICA 58; *Re Allister* [2023] UKSC 5.

[74] *Independence Referendum Reference* [2022] UKSC 31.

[75] A McHarg, T Mullen, A Page, and N Walker (eds) *The Scottish Independence Referendum: Constitutional and Political Implications* (Oxford University Press 2016).

[76] Available at https://www.gov.scot/publications/scottish-independence-referendum-bill/.

Further steps would have to be taken. The UK government countered that it related to reserved matters that might only be legislated by the UK Parliament.

(i) The Supreme Court Judgment and Supreme Court and Devolution More Generally

In a unanimous judgment, the Supreme Court found that the draft Bill related to reserved matters and so the Scottish Parliament lacked the power to legislate for an independence referendum. The Court applied standard case law, finding that a statutory provision relates to a reserved matter if it has more than a 'loose or consequential' connection with it. Applying this test, it found that, even if the referendum had no immediate legal consequences, it would have important political consequences, and thus more than a loose or consequential connection with the reserved matters of the Union of Scotland and England and the sovereignty of the UK Parliament.

The result of this lawsuit was perhaps not so very surprising. First, although the case was acknowledged by the Court to be of constitutional importance, it was nonetheless heard by only a five-judge panel including the present Supreme Court President, Lord Reed (not by the full Court that decided the *Miller* cases). Lord Reed was not Supreme Court President during the *Miller* cases, and it has been argued that the 'Reed Court' differs in judicial approach from its predecessor. For example, Conor Gearty argued[77] that the Reed Court inclines toward legal formalism—in that it takes a narrow reading of the rule of law, adopts a close reading of legal texts, and eschews broader arguments, such as those relevant to Scottish independence which rest on the principle of democracy, or on unincorporated human rights such as self-determination.

Furthermore, in previous case law the Supreme Court has taken a narrow approach to devolution. In *Miller I*, it found the Sewel Convention to be a mere political convention and legally unenforceable. Notably, in pre-Brexit case law, it took the view that devolution statutes should be interpreted in the same way as any other legislation[78]—a very Diceyan approach that rejected the earlier suggestion of Lord Hoffmann in *Robinson* that the Northern Ireland Act was 'in effect a constitution' and should thus be interpreted 'generously and purposively'.[79] In the 2018 *Scottish Continuity Bill* and 2021 *Treaty Incorporation Bill References* cases, the Supreme Court also interpreted Scottish devolution narrowly, finding it could not be applied to undermine the sovereignty of the Westminster Parliament. In contrast, however, in *Miller I*, the Supreme Court interpreted the 'effect' of actions widely, finding that the UK government could not use the prerogative to trigger Article 50 TEU and start the process of leaving the EU because its direct effect would lead to repeal of the ECA 1972, and only Parliament could repeal legislation. Therefore, it was perhaps unsurprising that the Court

[77] C Gearty, 'In the Shallow End', *London Review of Books* (22 January 2022).

[78] *Reference re Local Government Byelaws (Wales) Bill* [2012] UKSC 53; *Imperial Tobacco* [2012] UKSC 61.

[79] *Robinson v Secretary of State for Northern Ireland* [2002] UKHL 32, [11].

considered that even a 'consultative' referendum could have wide effects, even if not legal ones, because it might ultimately lead to the breakup of the UK.

Put together, these elements (the impact of UKIMA on devolved competence, the tendency to ignore the Sewel Convention, and the challenge to the power of devolved parliaments to legislate within the field of devolved competence) may be seen as an onslaught on devolution and an attack on devolved autonomy. Ultimately, the courts, and most particularly the Supreme Court, have not offered much succour to devolution in this context.

4 Post-Brexit Conclusion

In conclusion, the impact of post-Brexit changes has undermined key assumptions of devolution, primarily by weakening local decision-making over devolved competences. The huge complexity of Brexit legislation has also compromised transparency, clarity, and accountability and vastly increased the complexity of the devolution process. Even the introduction of devices such as Common Frameworks has increased the multifarious nature of the post-Brexit intergovernmental landscape.

In July 2024, the UK elected a Labour government in the UK general election. The Labour Party election manifesto had committed to a 'reset' of the relationship between the devolved governments and the UK government.[80] The manifesto also detailed more specific commitments,[81] including the production of a new MoU on the Sewel Convention and the establishment of a Council of the Nations. It also committed to new arrangements for the allocation of post-Brexit structural funds to devolved governments.

Since being in power, the UK government has published a White Paper on English devolution, *Power and Partnership: Foundations for Growth.*[82] As noted at the outset of this chapter, little has occurred to date on the English devolution front—with the exception of an executive devolution in England, which has seen some prerogative powers of UK government ministers transferred to elected 'metro' mayors in England. The short-lived EVEL changes to UK Parliamentary procedures introduced by David Cameron were abolished in 2021. However, the UK government's English Devolution White Paper contains some detail on its plans for a 'devolution revolution' in England. These include the intention to extend devolution to all of England, the substitution of unitary authorities for two-tier local government, and further powers including flexibility in funding for mayors.

In July 2025, the Government introduced the English Devolution and Community Empowerment Bill into the House of Commons. This Bill is intended to set up a new

[80] *Change: Labour Party Manifesto 2024* (13 June 2024).
[81] Paragraph 30 *Manifesto.*
[82] https://www.gov.uk/government/publications/english-devolution-white-paper-power-and-partnership-foundations-for-growth.

framework for devolution of powers to local government and combined authorities in England. The Bill was still going through Parliament at time of writing.

Since being in office, the government also launched a review of and consultation on the Internal Market Act[83] (although this was not included as a manifesto commitment). It has also, as noted, established a new ministerial post—that of Minister for IG Relations, based in Cabinet Office, with responsibility for devolution.

It is too early to predict how the government's new initiatives and future plans for devolution may work out in practice, especially given the national and global issues which are commanding a lot of financial and other bandwidth at present. However, the following issues merit further consideration and can be sorted roughly into four groups.

First, there are issues concerning intergovernmental relations, and how they might be reformed to work better in future. There are many questions. Might any initiatives be able to counter the somewhat 'muscular unionism' that seemed to have developed under previous administrations?[84] Should intergovernmental relations perhaps be placed on a statutory footing? How might the new Council of the Nations and Regions contribute to intergovernmental relations, and also, how is it expected to interact with existing intergovernmental structures? Further, how might scrutiny of intergovernmental relations be delivered in the UK Parliament? Should there be an increased role for the House of Lords in such scrutiny? What would be the role of interparliamentary relations in the scrutiny of devolution and intergovernmental relations? By what means might interparliamentary relations be strengthened? And what form will the government's proposed new MoU on the Sewel Convention take, and will it have any more formal legal status than at present?

Second, what might be the implications for increasing the scope and status of devolution within England for devolution in Scotland, Wales, and Northern Ireland?

Third, will the UK government devolve any further powers to Scotland, Wales, and Northern Ireland in addition to planning to improve intergovernmental relations between them? Will there be any further moves toward Scottish independence, and if so, how will the government handle them?

Fourth, what will be the UK government's approach to the UK Internal Market and potential regulatory divergence between the UK nations? It has become clear that UKIMA has made it harder for devolved administrations to adopt regulatory policies perceived to interfere with economic efficiency and market integration. This has a knock-on effect on devolution more generally and how the UK constitution functions overall, and undermines notions of a voluntary Union long held in devolved nations (especially but not only Scotland).

[83] https://www.gov.uk/government/consultations/uk-internal-market-act-2020-review-and-consultation.

[84] M Kenny, P Rycroft, and J Sheldon, *Union at the Crossroads: Can the British State Handle the Challenges of Devolution?* (Bennett Institute/Constitution Society 2021).

8
Northern Ireland

Christopher McCrudden

Introduction: 'Here Be Dragons'

The Northern Ireland regulatory framework post-Brexit presents an intriguing, if complex, legal, constitutional, and political landscape, with an international treaty, the Ireland–Northern Ireland Protocol (now the Windsor Framework), interacting awkwardly with parliamentary sovereignty, the UK devolution settlement, European Union law, and general international law. The aim of this chapter, perhaps somewhat optimistically, is to provide a roadmap for those who must navigate the terrain.[1]

The phrase 'law unbound' refers, I understand, to a claim that the United Kingdom has enhanced freedom, following its departure from the European Union, and is now able, independently, to develop its own laws and regulatory frameworks, allowing it to shape its legal landscape unconstrained by the EU. Thus defined, the phrase has, thus far, little real purchase in Northern Ireland. Instead, the more pertinent concept is 'juridification', referring, as Colin Scott has described, to 'an overall sense of a shift towards law as the basis for governance'.[2] Part of the reason for this shift is the continuing status of EU law, directly and indirectly, in that part of the United Kingdom. Rather than less (EU) law, Brexit has produced more law in Northern Ireland, probably including more EU law, and certainly more international law, and with that significant constitutional uncertainty and instability. More intriguingly, perhaps, the obligations that the Withdrawal Agreement impose on the United Kingdom regarding Northern Ireland may yet have real effects in terms of the regulatory freedom that the United Kingdom as a whole thought it possessed.

After this introduction, the chapter is structured in five sections. First, I consider the impact of EU membership on Northern Ireland pre-Brexit. Second, I consider post-Brexit legal change in Northern Ireland, focusing on the implications for Northern Ireland regulatory law of the Ireland–Northern Ireland Protocol (now renamed the Windsor Framework[3]), which is the principal element of the EU–UK

[1] The heading of this section refers to the medieval practice of illustrating uncharted areas of maps where potential dangers were thought to exist with dragons and other mythological creatures.

[2] C Scott, 'Juridification' in P Cane and J Conaghan (eds), *New Oxford Companion to Law* (Oxford University Press 2008).

[3] See Windsor Political Declaration by the European Commission and the Government of the United Kingdom, 27 February 2023, https://commission.europa.eu/publications/windsor-political-declaration-european-commission-and-government-united-kingdom_en.

Christopher McCrudden, *Northern Ireland* In: *The UK Regulatory Framework Post-Brexit: 'Law Unbound'*.
Edited by: Paul Craig and Vilija Vėlyvytė, Oxford University Press. © Oxford University Press 2026.
DOI: 10.1093/9780198969815.003.0009

addition to the other provisions in the Withdrawal Agreement protecting EU citizens' rights applying to the UK as a whole, and in addition to the various protections for human rights in the Trade and Cooperation Agreement regarding continued membership of the ECHR and the incorporation of the ECHR into domestic law (both of which are considered in other chapters).

3 Post-Brexit Legal Change

In this section of the chapter, I consider the implications for Northern Ireland of two of the principal pieces of domestic legislation that shaped the UK's exit from the EU: the European Union (Withdrawal Agreement) Act 2020, which amended the European Union (Withdrawal) Act 2018, and the Retained EU Law (Revocation and Reform) Act 2023.

(a) European Union (Withdrawal Agreement) Act 2020

The Withdrawal Agreement and the Protocol were incorporated into domestic UK law in the European Union (Withdrawal Agreement) Act 2020, which amended the European Union (Withdrawal) Act 2018 in significant respects. The legal status of the Protocol in Northern Ireland law is protected in domestic law, in particular, under Section 7A of the European Union Withdrawal Act 2018, as amended.

The first case to establish this involved the unlikely issue of abortion. Some background will be useful at this point. In 2018, the UK Supreme Court considered whether the restrictions on abortion in Northern Ireland which prevailed at the time offended Article 8 ECHR.[6] The court's decision refusing standing to the NIHRC meant that there was no possibility of making a declaration of incompatibility under section 4 of the Human Rights Act 1998. However, a majority of the court (Lady Hale, Lord Mance, Lord Kerr, and Lord Wilson) considered that the law in Northern Ireland on abortion was disproportionate and incompatible with Article 8 insofar as it prohibited abortion in cases of (a) fatal (as distinct from serious) foetal abnormality, (b) pregnancy as a result of rape, and (c) pregnancy as a result of incest. If an individual victim did return to court in relation to the present law, the majority indicated that a formal declaration of incompatibility would in all likelihood be made.

A cross-party consensus in Westminster was determined that abortion reform should be legislated for at Westminster over the heads of Stormont. This group took advantage of the suspension of the Assembly between 2017 and 2020 to achieve this, but in a somewhat peculiar way. The Northern Ireland (Executive Formation etc) Act 2019 placed a duty on the Secretary of State for Northern Ireland to ensure that the

[6] *In re NIHRC* [2018] NI 228, [2018] UKSC 27.

Withdrawal Agreement applying a unique set of regulatory requirements to Northern Ireland.[4] Third, the implications for Northern Ireland of the principal domestic legislation that shaped the UK's exit from the EU are examined. Fourth, the effect of Brexit on the constitutional status of Northern Ireland will be examined, including how far the form and substance of devolved power have changed in a post-Brexit world, how far Brexit placed strains on powers exercised by the devolved governments, and the relationship with the Republic of Ireland. Fifth, and lastly, the likely future for Northern Ireland of developments in the EU, and changes flowing from the elections of President Trump and a new UK government in 2024, are briefly assessed.

1 Impact of EU Membership on Northern Ireland Pre-Brexit

The impact of EU membership on Northern Ireland pre-Brexit must be seen in the context of the overall governance arrangements existing in Northern Ireland, and in turn these need to be situated in the context of the Belfast–Good Friday Agreement (B–GFA), the peace agreement concluded between the UK and Ireland, and all but one of the major political parties in Northern Ireland, in April 1998. The Agreement, substantially incorporated into Northern Ireland law by the Northern Ireland Act 1998, remains key to understanding Northern Ireland governance arrangements, both pre- and post-Brexit.

Central to the B–GFA was the recognition that there were three strands of relationships, each of which was jointly and severally critical to creating and maintaining peace in Northern Ireland. Strand One required the establishment of a devolved Executive and Assembly in Northern Ireland on a power-sharing basis—simply put, without power-sharing, there would be no devolved government. Strand Two required the recognition of North–South relationships on the island of Ireland through the creation of bodies that would encourage the promotion of an all-island perspective on a modest list of issues of common concern. In practical terms, however, Strand Two meant a significant reduction in the importance of the border between Northern Ireland and the Republic of Ireland, both economically and politically. Strand Three required the recognition of an East–West dimension, meaning the relationship between Ireland and Britain. Coupled with this new architecture were significant commitments on human rights and equality, including the incorporation of the ECHR into domestic law. Constitutionally and legally, the architecture that the B–GFA approved is still in force.

There are, therefore, significant elements in Northern Ireland governance that are *sui generis* so far as the rest of the United Kingdom is concerned. However, it would be

[4] On this see C McCrudden (ed), *The Law and Practice of the Ireland–Northern Ireland Protocol* (Cambridge University Press 2022).

misleading if a description of Northern Ireland governance did not also point to the extent to which Northern Ireland shares several elements of orthodox UK constitutional law and practice. Northern Ireland is an integral part of the United Kingdom. The UK Parliament is the sovereign authority, and parliamentary sovereignty remains the cornerstone of Northern Ireland constitutional law, as it is in the rest of the United Kingdom. From the perspective of UK constitutional developments, Northern Ireland is one of three jurisdictions in which devolution has taken place. Northern Ireland governance arrangements share some of the most important aspects of the devolution of powers that operate in Scotland and Wales.

Even in these respects, Northern Ireland does have its particularities. Northern Ireland political parties are distinct from GB-based parties, which do not stand for election in Northern Ireland (with the exception of the tiny Conservative Party). While parliamentary sovereignty remains, there is explicit provision made in section 1 of the Northern Ireland Act 1998 for a constitutional referendum on Irish unification, if the Secretary of State for Northern Ireland considers that a majority might vote in favour of unification. Devolution in Northern Ireland looks very different from that in Scotland and Wales in several respects.

Scotland, Wales, and Northern Ireland have different distributions of governmental functions (what is sometimes termed 'asymmetric devolution'). The three jurisdictions now have very different internal constitutional structures, with Northern Ireland's unique system of power-sharing (or, more correctly, consociational) government, and its unique relationship with the Republic of Ireland, now playing a significant role in shaping the exercise of government. Perhaps of most significance, Northern Ireland remains a fragile society, in which political issues soon become constitutional, and constitutional issues soon lead to resort to the courts. The courts are then faced with the distinctly important task of remaining relevant, while at the same time remaining legitimate.

The impact of EU membership on Northern Ireland pre-Brexit, therefore, must be seen in the context of these commonalities and differences with the rest of the UK, as well as the common EU membership of the United Kingdom and the Republic of Ireland. The UK's membership of the EU increasingly led to EU law providing important underpinnings to both the law and the spirit of the B–GFA. The effective disappearance of the land border between the Republic of Ireland and Northern Ireland, together with the cessation of violence, contributed to the growth of an all-island economy. The EU provided significant funding to peace-related and community relations-related projects, and some significant infrastructure projects received EU funding. Diplomatically, prior to the B–GFA in particular, common membership provided significant opportunities for informal trust-building between Ireland and the UK in the margins of EU meetings. EU fundamental rights and equality law underpinned the Northern Ireland human rights and equality provisions introduced in the run-up to the B–GFA and following that Agreement. The legislative and executive power over devolved matters, vested in the Northern Ireland Assembly and the

Northern Ireland Executive, was limited by requirements not to act cont ECHR and EU law.

2 The Ireland–Northern Ireland Protocol

So far as Northern Ireland was concerned, Brexit presented the now in Trilemma: (i) how to maintain the absence of North–South barriers (Strand 2), same time as (ii) preventing new barriers between Northern Ireland and the rest UK (Strand 3), at the same time as (iii) permitting significant regulatory diverg between the UK and the EU. It soon became clear that the UK could satisfy two o three of these preferences. One had to give, and eventually the UK opted to limit East–West dimension, with the creation of a regulatory 'border' (in heavy quotat marks) between Northern Ireland and Great Britain. This was encapsulated in t Ireland–Northern Ireland Protocol to the EU–UK Withdrawal Agreement.

The Withdrawal Agreement (including the Ireland–Northern Ireland Protoco addressed the Trilemma in two main ways. First, in order to continue the open border policy between Ireland and Northern Ireland, Northern Ireland effectively remained within the single market for goods and the EU customs arrangements. (This is a brief and necessarily simplistic summary of the original Articles 5 and 7–11 of the Protocol.) This meant increased regulatory controls for goods travelling between Great Britain and Northern Ireland. A limited degree of Northern Ireland democratic control was introduced under which the Assembly was able to reject these arrangements at periodic intervals. Where Articles 5 and 7–11 of the Protocol apply—basically, where the customs and single market provisions apply—EU law as such applies. The Charter of Fundamental Rights continues to apply; dynamic alignment continues to apply (subject to the Windsor Framework which is considered below); the courts must apply relevant CJEU jurisprudence, current and future; references to the CJEU remain possible from Northern Ireland courts, and breaches are subject to European Commission infringement proceedings before the CJEU.

Second, various other provisions were introduced into the Protocol going beyond the trade and customs provisions. The existing 'Common Travel Area' arrangements between the UK and Ireland, which predated EU membership and provided for freedom of movement and residence of UK and Irish citizens, among other important mechanisms that recognized the close relationship between the two countries, were preserved. The B–GFA was to be protected 'in all its dimensions', and there was an agreement that human rights protections should not be 'diminished', implemented in Article 2. This sought to protect those equality and human rights provisions of the B–GFA which were underpinned by EU law (the 'no diminution' obligation).[5] This is in

[5] For an account of the human rights and equality provisions of the B-GFA, see C McCrudden, 'The origins of "civil rights and religious liberties" in the Belfast-Good Friday Agreement' (2024) 75 NILQ 443.

wide-ranging recommendations for Northern Ireland abortion reform in paragraphs 85 and 86 of the inquiry into the UK of the UN Committee on the Elimination of All Forms of Discrimination against Women should henceforth be implemented in Northern Ireland law.[7]

In compliance with this duty under the 2019 Act, the Secretary of State made several sets of regulations. These included the Abortion (Northern Ireland) Regulations 2021 which were made to address the gaps in commissioning abortion services in Northern Ireland and conferred on the Secretary of State a power to direct ministers, departments, and other public agencies to take action for the purpose of implementing the CEDAW report. The judicial review challenge, by SPUC, the Society for the Protection of the Unborn Child, was to these 2021 Regulations and the directions made under them. SPUC's challenge was unsuccessful both in the High Court and in the Court of Appeal.[8] It comprised several grounds, but I shall focus on the two most interesting of these for the purposes of this chapter.

SPUC argued, first, that the powers of the Secretary of State were limited to those that would be exercisable by the Assembly, and that the Assembly could not legislate in the area of international relations. The Court of Appeal agreed that the Regulations must fall within the legislative competence of the Assembly to be *intra vires*. However, the Court disagreed with SPUC's argument that the Secretary of State was in fact legislating in the area of international relations. The Court said that the provision of abortion services comes within the remit of health; health is a transferred matter; therefore, prima facie, the Assembly has competence.

Second, SPUC argued that the Secretary of State was acting contrary to Article 2 of the Northern Ireland Protocol by virtue of his non-compliance with another UN Convention, namely the United Nations Convention on the Rights of Persons with Disabilities ('the UNCRPD'), which prohibits discrimination on the basis of disability. SPUC argued that the UNCRPD had become *EU* law by virtue of the EU ratifying the Convention in its own name. Further, as EU law, the Convention had entered Northern Ireland law prior to the UK's exit from the EU. Article 2 of the Protocol protected rights under the UNCRPD from being diminished due to Brexit. As a result, SPUC argued, the provisions of the Regulations that permit abortion without time restrictions where the foetus is suffering from severe foetal abnormality, such as Down's Syndrome, were contrary to the Convention because they discriminate on grounds of disability.

The Court of Appeal rejected the Protocol-based challenge. Abortion is not within the competence of the EU and therefore the Convention-as-EU-law, even if it applied to abortion as a matter of international law, could not have direct effect as EU law in

[7] Committee on the Elimination of Discrimination against Women, Inquiry concerning the United Kingdom of Great Britain and Northern Ireland under article 8 of the Optional Protocol to the Convention on the Elimination of All Forms of Discrimination against Women, CEDAW/C/OP.8/GBR/1, 6 March 2018.

[8] *SPUC Pro-Life Limited's Application for Judicial Review* [2022] NIQB 9; [2024] 2 CMLR 20, [2023] NICA 35 (permission to appeal to the Supreme Court subsequently refused).

Northern Ireland. Instead, it agreed with the arguments put forward by the Equality Commission which had intervened in the case (I was representing the Commission) that the UNCRPD-as-EU-law cannot be relied on by SPUC as limiting the Secretary of State's powers regarding abortion. There was also a further problem with SPUC's use of Article 2 of the Protocol. In order to establish a breach of Article 2, SPUC needed to establish that a right included in the relevant part of the B–GFA was engaged, and this it had failed to do. Although the Protocol point lost, the case was highly significant, not least because the Court of Appeal held that, as a result of Article 2 of the Protocol and Section 7A of the 2018 Withdrawal Act, the human rights and equality provisions of the 1998 Agreement have now taken on a direct legal significance that has not previously been recognized in Northern Ireland courts.

As significant, the provisions of the Protocol continue to have supremacy and incompatible domestic legislation must be disapplied with respect to Northern Ireland. Effectively, this means that section 7A replicates section 2 of the European Communities Act 1972, protecting the priority of the Protocol in domestic law in much the same way as section 2 gave priority to EU law in domestic law. Although the Supreme Court does not appear to like the term and, as we shall see, did not refer to this concept in *Allister*,[9] section 7A is a 'constitutional' provision, in Sir John Laws' sense of the term.[10] This provision is not subject to implied repeal and therefore subjects future legislation to this set of obligations, unless section 7A were to be expressly repealed or amended.

Or, at least, that is the way the Northern Ireland courts have consistently interpreted the relationship between Article 2, the Withdrawal Agreement, and section 7A since the *SPUC* case, particularly in the highly significant *Dillon* judgment in the Northern Ireland Court of Appeal.[11] The Northern Ireland Troubles (Legacy and Reconciliation) Act 2023 provided extensively for immunity from prosecution of 'Troubles-related' crimes, ending Troubles-related civil proceedings, and making protected material inadmissible in civil proceedings and coroners' proceedings. The High Court considered that these provisions were incompatible with several provisions of the ECHR, but also with Article 2 WF as incorporated into UK law by section 7A, and they were disapplied.[12] The Secretary of State for Northern Ireland appealed, and the Northern Ireland Court of Appeal largely upheld the High Court's judgment, while differing in some respects from its approach.

The NICA considered that section 7A incorporated EU law with continuing effect into UK domestic law post-Brexit, including rights, obligations, remedies, and so on arising 'by or under' Article 4 of the Withdrawal Agreement. The WA was plainly

[9] *In the matter of an application by Allister and others for Judicial Review* [2024] AC 1113, [2023] UKSC 5.
[10] J McGarry and S Spence, 'Constitutional Statutes—Roots and Recognition' (2020) 41 Statute Law Review 378.
[11] *Dillon* [2024] NICA 59.
[12] *Dillon* [2024] 3 CMLR 34, [2024] NIKB 11.

an international treaty to which the Vienna Convention on the Law of Treaties 1969 (Vienna) could apply. The UK and Ireland were parties to it. It also applied to the interpretation exercise to be conducted by the court in relation to the human rights and equality part of the B–GFA. Article 2 WF was directly effective: the non-diminution guarantee was expressed in clear, unambiguous terms, and was a straightforward negative obligation assumed by the UK. Therefore, it was incorporated through section 7A of the 2018 Act. Further, that had been Parliament's intention when section 7A was introduced.

Significantly, the effect of any breach of Article 2 resulted in the disapplication of the offending provision, based on section 7A of the 2018 Act, which mirrored section 2 of the European Communities Act 1972. By Article 4(2) of the Withdrawal Agreement, the UK was obliged to ensure compliance with the Protocol, including by empowering its judicial authorities to 'disapply inconsistent or incompatible domestic provisions'. Section 7A was the domestic primary legislation by which the UK had fulfilled that obligation, and it clearly mandated disapplication of an offending provision. It followed that disapplication was the correct remedy, which was distinguishable from the discretionary remedy of a declaration of incompatibility under the HRA. As we shall see, that judgment has been appealed by the Secretary of State for Northern Ireland to the Supreme Court.

Some of the rights and obligations established by Article 2 of the Protocol are given effect to in Northern Ireland law by relying on what would have been the direct effect, pre-Brexit, of the relevant EU Directives in domestic law. This is most obviously so in the case of the anti-discrimination directives which were legislated into Northern Ireland law in a series of provisions, such as the Sex Discrimination Order 1976. Where these provisions underpinned rights listed in the B–GFA, Article 2 applies to prevent any diminution of those rights. As a result, the UK's implementation of the EU Directives prior to Brexit must either remain in place post-Brexit, or be replaced with something equivalent. Otherwise, there would be a 'diminution' of the rights under Article 2. There is no obligation on the UK to retain these underpinning directives as such, or the transposing domestic legislation, but there is a continuing obligation to achieve the same effects, an obligation of result.

(b) Retained EU Law (Revocation and Reform) Act 2023

So, for the purposes of this chapter, there is a critical distinction to be made between EU law that underpins the Protocol (directly or indirectly) and EU law that does not underpin the Protocol. This distinction is significant because of the continuing debate over 'retained' EU law in the United Kingdom generally. The concept of 'retained EU law' was established, of course, by the European Union (Withdrawal) Act 2018 to ensure legal certainty and continuity immediately after Brexit, by preserving all EU and EU-derived law as it stood immediately before the UK's departure, including the retained EU law that applied in Northern Ireland.

Under the 2018 Act, where the Protocol did not apply, the arrangement for retained EU law in Northern Ireland applied in very similar terms to that in Great Britain, except that the devolved administrations in Scotland and Wales could amend, replace, or repeal in areas of devolved responsibility. Thus, the provisions of UK law that applied in England, Scotland, and Wales regarding 'retained EU law' under the Withdrawal Acts (including the non-application of the Charter and EU general principles, no post-exit dynamic alignment, and no further references to the CJEU) applied in those areas of Northern Ireland law that were not covered by the Protocol. But only in those areas.

Where EU law does not directly apply but the obligation to achieve the equivalent effect that EU law would have produced when the UK was a member of the EU constitutes the basis for compliance with the Protocol (as is the case with Article 2), the restrictions that applied under the 2018 Act did not apply in Northern Ireland. Thus, dynamic alignment applied, which required Northern Ireland law to follow and implement any changes in EU law that continued to apply (including changes in the jurisprudence of the Court of Justice). So too, EU general principles and the EU Charter of Fundamental Rights continued to apply in the context of the interpretation of retained EU law that implemented Protocol obligations in Northern Ireland.

That has been confirmed by the High Court and the Northern Ireland Court of Appeal in a series of cases, which (apart from *Alistair*) all involve issues arising from Article 2 and range broadly, including on issues that arise from policies affecting the whole of the UK. The Northern Ireland Human Rights Commission argued successfully, for example, that parts of the Illegal Migration Act 2023 constituted a diminution in rights, contrary to Article 2.[13] Most importantly, as we have seen, Article 2 has been used to claim that parts of the controversial Northern Ireland Legacy Act must be suspended, and this claim was upheld by the Northern Ireland Court of Appeal. This judgment is currently before the Supreme Court, having been appealed against by the UK government. We shall see what the Court makes of these in due course, but the important point is that such cases, using EU law in this way, are inconceivable in London, or in Cardiff, or in Edinburgh.

Against this background we can consider the Retained EU Law (Revocation and Reform) Act 2023, which came into effect on 1 January 2024. Several hundred pieces of retained EU law were set out in the Schedule to the Act that were revoked or assimilated by 31 December 2023. Any laws not listed in the revocation schedule were retained automatically. The Act also accomplished several further aims: it repealed the principle of supremacy of EU law from UK law by the end of 2023; it repealed directly effective EU law rights and obligations in UK law by the end of 2023; it abolished general principles of EU law in UK law by the end of 2023; it established a new rule requiring retained direct EU legislation to be interpreted and applied consistently

[13] *In re NIHRC and JR 295 (Illegal Migration Act 2023)* [2024] 3 CMLR 18, [2024] NIKB 35.

with domestic legislation, rather than the other way round; and it created a suite of powers that allowed retained EU law to be revoked or replaced, restated or updated, and removed or amended. The Act also changed the way *courts* can depart from retained EU case law. Section 7 introduced a new test, which encouraged the courts to depart from retained case law more often and may result in large amounts of law being changed. The Act also changed the way that some types of retained EU law can be modified, such as 'downgrading' retained directly effective EU legislation so this can be amended by secondary legislation, and removing additional parliamentary scrutiny requirements that previously applied when modifying some types of EU-derived domestic secondary legislation. In some respects, then, the 2023 Act did change the goalposts, but so far as Northern Ireland is concerned, again only where the Protocol does not apply.

In most respects the impact of the new Act in Northern Ireland will, therefore, be direct only where the Protocol does not apply. Effectively, what applies in England, Scotland, and Wales applies in Northern Ireland, but (to repeat) only in those areas of activity where the Protocol does not apply. And, as before, devolved administrations may choose to keep or repeal different aspects of retained EU law. Northern Ireland is unlikely to diverge significantly from England in those areas where the Protocol does not apply.

Where the Protocol *does* apply, the *direct* effect of the new REUL Act should be minimal. I will mention three important respects in which the legal order before the new Act came into effect remains the case in Northern Ireland.

First—I emphasize again that we are talking about areas where the Protocol applies—the Protocol continues to have priority over domestic law. That is by virtue of several provisions in the 2018 Act, but particularly the crucial section 7A of the 2018 Act. That is not to say that Parliament could not repeal or amend section 7A, but it is an important limitation of the Retained EU Law Act that the Act did not repeal or amend section 7A, unlike what was threatened under the UK Internal Market Bill and the Northern Ireland Protocol Bill, neither of which were proceeded with.

Second, the provisions abolishing the principle of the supremacy of retained EU law do not have any direct implications with regard to areas covered by the direct EU law that applies in Northern Ireland—not retained EU law, but direct EU law. The fact that retained EU law is not made supreme in the UK does not matter in these circumstances because under section 7A, the EU law that applies directly in Northern Ireland has been given supremacy. Altering the status of retained EU law does not affect the continuing supremacy of EU law. Where the Article 2 requirement applies and retained EU law is part of the way in which the Article 2 obligations are met, the abolition of the supremacy of EU law in general also makes no difference because Article 2 requires that retained EU law to have priority in Northern Ireland. That is again guaranteed under section 7A.

Third, as regards the role of the courts and retained case law, we have also seen that there are specific provisions in the Protocol that require, in certain circumstances, judicial interpretation to conform to CJEU jurisprudence, particularly with regard to the single market and customs arrangements in Articles 5 and 7–10. In those areas, it will not be optional; the courts must apply CJEU jurisprudence, dynamically as well, so current and future jurisprudence. With regard to Article 2, and particularly with regard to the Annex 1 directives—that is, basically the EU anti-discrimination directives—those will also be interpreted in the light of CJEU jurisprudence, current and future. If a directive is not listed in Annex 1, but is still retained EU law that underpins a B-GFA right, the courts are required to interpret it in conformity with CJEU jurisprudence as at the end of the transition period.

So, where the Protocol does apply, the *direct* effect of the new REUL Act should be minimal, but only if the selection of those provisions that will be repealed or assimilated is carried out with the utmost care. The practical danger is that a wholesale removal of EU retained law by Whitehall departments that does not take into account its relationship with Article 2 or the other articles I have mentioned could unintentionally lead to the diminution of the protected rights. We have seen that retained EU law is currently part of the structure of law that underpins the B-GFA provisions on human rights and equality. If the UK government were to attempt to remove the retained EU law that underpins these rights in Northern Ireland, without replacing it with something equivalent, that would lead to a diminution in the rights and therefore a breach of Article 2.

These direct effects aside, the main effects of the new REUL Act will be *indirect*. By calling them indirect, however, I do not intend to downplay the significance of these effects. Britain now has the potential to diverge significantly from Northern Ireland because the 2023 Act provides Great Britain (i.e. England, Scotland, and Wales) with the opportunity to depart significantly from European legal requirements that continue to apply in Northern Ireland.

So, as far as the courts are concerned, for example, the more freedom to depart from Court of Justice jurisprudence that the courts in England, Wales, and Scotland have, the more potential divergence there will be with the courts in Northern Ireland which do not have that freedom. In this context the role of the Supreme Court is particularly intriguing, because the same provision if it arises in England, Wales, and Scotland may be given one interpretation under this increased freedom to depart, but the court will not have the freedom to depart if the case arises with regard to the same provision in Northern Ireland. In this context, the dilemma encapsulated in the function of the Supreme Court as being a Supreme Court for England, Scotland, and Wales as well as for Northern Ireland is well to the fore.

The indirect effects go beyond affecting the role of the courts. To the extent that retained EU law overlaps with the provisions of Articles 5 and 7–10, and in particular with the provisions in Annex 2, any departure in GB from that retained EU law, with the position in Northern Ireland remaining the same because of the Protocol, will lead to greater divergence between GB and Northern Ireland. In other words, amending, replacing, or repealing retained EU law in GB has potential implications for opening up divergence with Northern Ireland in the areas where Articles 5 and 7–10 continue to apply EU law directly in Northern Ireland. To the extent that we are concerned with divergence between Northern Ireland and the rest of the UK—effectively with the UK internal market—the ball is in the court of the UK government.

4 Post-Brexit Constitutional and Political Change in Northern Ireland

These points hint at a larger set of significant constitutional issues, to which we now turn. We have seen that, in attempting to address the Trilemma, the UK and the EU agreed in the Protocol to downplay the East–West dimension, in order to preserve Strands One and Two of the B–GFA from the effects of Brexit. As the effects of this compromise sank in, the adverse reactions of unionist politicians and commentators to these provisions dominated Northern Ireland politics. Their concern was that the regulatory barriers to trade in goods flowing from West to East (GB to NI) would ultimately weaken the Union between Northern Ireland and the rest of the United Kingdom. The trade issue became, quite quickly, a constitutional issue. In attempting to resist these aspects of the Protocol, unionists used two main tactics: litigation and political bargaining.

As regards the first of these, a loose coalition of unionist politicians challenged the trade-in-goods provisions of the Protocol in the domestic courts on constitutional grounds, which ultimately came before the Supreme Court in *Re Allister's Application for Judicial Review*.[14] In a short, unanimous judgment, this challenge was dismissed. The judgment of Lord Stephens for a unanimous Supreme Court consisted largely of one response to the elaborate, but ultimately fatally flawed, challenges by the leaders of political unionism: what is it about parliamentary sovereignty that you don't understand? Parliament had spoken. What the Queen-in-Parliament enacts is the law, and the most recent enactment trumps all others. Dicey, pure and simple. No need to consider high-falutin' concepts like constitutional statutes.

As a result, all the arguments of the unionist leaders were rejected. Is the Protocol contrary to the trade provisions of the Acts of Union of Ireland and Great Britain of 1800 and, if it is, is the implementing legislation thus ultra vires? Answer: no. Even if the Protocol does go against elements of the Acts of Union (which the Court does not decide), the incorporation of the Protocol into UK law suspended the Acts of Union to the extent required to accomplish compliance with the Protocol. Section 7A of the European Union (Withdrawal) Act of 2018, as amended in 2020, indicated a clear parliamentary intention to do so.

Did the incorporation of the Protocol constitute a breach of the commitment to 'consent' in Section 1 of the Northern Ireland Act (and, ultimately, of the B-GFA)? This promises that Northern Ireland remains part of the United Kingdom unless the majority of the people of Northern Ireland consent to that change in a referendum.

[14] [2024] AC 1113, [2023] UKSC 5.

Again, no, replies the Court; didn't you read what we said on this precise issue in *Miller 1*?[15] The consent principle in section 1 relates only to the right to determine whether Northern Ireland remains part of the United Kingdom or joins a united Ireland, and applies to no other constitutional change.

Alternatively, argued the unionists, the cross-community consent requirement in the Northern Ireland Assembly, provided for in the Northern Ireland Act, applies. This, they said, renders *ultra vires* a key part of the legislation implementing the Protocol, namely the Democratic Consent Regulations which permit the Northern Ireland Assembly to vote on whether or not to keep the provisions of the Protocol relating to trade, but without the need for cross-community consent. Wrong again, said the Supreme Court; see above on parliamentary sovereignty.

Taking the *Allister* case to the Supreme Court was always more about the theatrics of resistance than anticipation of a legal victory. It was one of several weapons used to try to destabilize the Ireland–Northern Ireland Protocol. Another of these weapons was boycott, a term of resistance coined in Ireland, of course, and one that both Sinn Féin and the Democratic Unionist Party have taken to their hearts. It is primarily a political device but with real legal implications, as several of the cases before the local courts demonstrated. To understand these cases, it will be useful to recall that there have been two periods recently when the devolved institutions were effectively mothballed: between January 2017 and January 2020, and from 2022 until February 2024.

Even during the period when there was a functioning Assembly and Executive (2020–22), DUP ministers refused to carry out some of their functions as a protest against the Protocol. There have been several cases challenging that stance, with the first arising in the High Court in 2021 in *Re Napier's Application*, in which Scoffield J held that the relevant minister was clearly acting *ultra vires* when he refused to attend meetings of the North–South Ministerial Council contrary to the Northern Ireland Act.[16] After the minister refused to change his stance, the issue then became what the appropriate remedy should be. In a controversial decision, Scoffield J declined an application to issue an order of mandamus, arguing that the appropriate remedy was political rather than legal.[17] Perhaps the sight of a DUP minister being hauled off to gaol to purge his contempt played a role in this decision.

In 2023, the courts returned to the issue in *Rooney*,[18] in which there was a challenge to the written instructions of the DUP Minister of Agriculture, Environment and Rural Affairs to the civil servants in his Department to cease all those checks relating to animals and various agri-food goods moving from Great Britain into Northern Ireland. These checks were required to comply with the UK's legal obligations arising from the Protocol. Colton J held that the minister and the department had a statutory obligation to implement the checks on these goods under section 7A of the European

[15] *R (Miller) v Secretary of State for Exiting the European Union* [2017] 2 WLR 583, [2017] UKSC 5.
[16] [2021] NIQB 86.
[17] [2023] NI 1, [2021] NIQB 120.
[18] [2023] NIKB 3.

Union (Withdrawal) Act. By issuing his instructions, the minister was in breach of his clear legal obligations. The Court granted certiorari to quash the decision.

These cases arose from events when the Assembly and Executive were operational in the period 2020–22. However, the ultimate resistance by the DUP to the Protocol was their boycott of the institutions of devolved government itself, from February 2022, leading to the collapse of power-sharing. Politically, this contributed to a two-year political standoff in which the United Kingdom government attempted first to persuade the European Union to modify the Protocol to become more acceptable to unionist opinion, and then to persuade unionists to accept whatever modifications were extracted from the EU.

The first element in the government's two-pronged strategy ultimately resulted in an agreement between the UK and the EU, whereby the Protocol (now renamed 'the Windsor Framework') introduced some changes into the Protocol arrangements.[19] (None of these changes affected the operation of Article 2, by the way). I will mention only two main changes. First, the Windsor Framework provided for a potentially looser set of regulatory obligations regarding East–West trade in goods, introducing the concept of red and green lanes (which have come into operation at the time of writing). The Windsor Framework also redrew the scope of Articles 5 and 7–11, but only insofar as the number of provisions of EU law that apply—as set out in Annex 2—is now reduced somewhat.

Second, the Windsor Framework provided that in the context of EU law applying in Northern Ireland in the areas of trade and customs, regulatory alignment would be subject to the so-called Stormont Brake. This led to the amendment of Article 13 (one of only two provisions of the Protocol that required redrafting). The Stormont Brake has established a complicated set of procedures under which members of the Northern Ireland Assembly could trigger a requirement that the UK government consider whether to veto dynamic alignment in certain limited circumstances. Although agreed in March 2023, the Stormont Brake only became operational with the restoration of the Northern Ireland Executive and Assembly in February 2024. This provision was triggered by the requisite number of MLAs in one case in January 2025, but with the result that the UK nevertheless continued with implementing the contested provision.[20]

Having secured these modifications in March 2023, the government then turned to the second element in the strategy, which was to persuade the DUP to return to government armed with a new set of commitments built around the newly minted Windsor Framework. These changes were initially not sufficient to satisfy the Democratic Unionist Party, which continued to object to the regulatory controls on East–West trade that the Protocol had introduced, still considering that the controls weakened

[19] See Windsor Political Declaration by the European Commission and the Government of the United Kingdom, 27 February 2023, https://commission.europa.eu/publications/windsor-political-declaration-european-commission-and-government-united-kingdom_en.

[20] House of Commons Library, The Stormont Brake in Action, 28 January 2025.

the Union. These objections led to the DUP leaving the power-sharing Executive, precipitating the collapse of the Executive and Assembly. As a result, Northern Ireland had no functioning devolved government. Instead, Northern Ireland civil servants functioned as a shadow government. The UK government resisted the imposition of full-blown Direct Rule from London (not least because of the opposition of the Irish government), and minimal political accountability was provided for by the Secretary of State for Northern Ireland reporting to Westminster, which (understandably) was mostly occupied by other matters.

There then followed sustained negotiations between the UK government and the DUP, and the publication of a Command Paper, entitled 'Safeguarding the Union', which its then leader, Sir Jeffrey Donaldson, considered offered important reassurances.[21] Others within the DUP were more sceptical, considering the commitments by the government to have been significantly oversold. After a closely fought battle within the party the DUP agreed to the government's terms, including a return to the Assembly and the reinstitution of the Executive.

The constitutional issues have not, however, gone away; they have simply changed shape somewhat. In his negotiations with the government, Sir Jeffrey received public assurances that Article 2 WF would not lead to asylum and migration policy being different in Northern Ireland from that in the rest of the UK. 'The important starting point is that the Windsor Framework applies *only* in respect of the trade in goods—the vast majority of public policy is entirely untouched by it.'[22] In attempting to justify that position legally, the UK government published a letter to Sir Jeffrey which contained an Annex in which the government set out its approach to Article 2 WF, which was, essentially, that significant parts of Article 2 were non-justiciable.[23] This then formed part of the offer by the UK government to the DUP to encourage it to go back into government, thus restoring the Assembly and the Executive.

The courts were not party to this new interpretation of Article 2, however. As we have seen, the Northern Ireland Human Rights Commission sought judicial review of the Home Secretary and the Secretary of State for Northern Ireland regarding the provisions of the Illegal Migration Act 2023 ('the IMA'). The Commission considered that the IMA would have significant adverse effects on asylum seekers in Northern Ireland, in particular by creating barriers for individual legal challenges removing the ability to appeal and judicially review decisions in most circumstances. One of the grounds for seeking judicial review was an alleged breach of Article 2 of the Protocol.

The Commission identified a series of provisions in the IMA that it considered fell short of the minimum standards required by several EU Directives that were in force in Northern Ireland prior to the UK's exit from the EU, in particular the 2005 Procedures Directive, which provides for minimum standards for granting and withdrawing refugee status. The Commission argued that sections 2(1), 5(1), and 6 of the

[21] HM Government, *Safeguarding the Union*, CP1021, January 2024.
[22] CP1021, para 46, emphasis added.
[23] Home Office Letter to Sir Jeffrey Donaldson, 28 January 2024.

IMA required removal in specified cases even if a protection or human rights claim had been made. This appeared to be incompatible, the Commission argued, with Article 7(1) of the Procedures Directive, which requires that a person may remain in the UK until an asylum claim has been properly determined. Had the UK remained in the EU, such reductions in rights would, in the view of the NIHRC, have been unlawful. The High Court agreed. Humphreys J suspended significant parts of the IMA so far as it applied in Northern Ireland, in practice rejecting each element of the legal approach set out in the Donaldson Annex. The government then attempted to argue for its interpretation of Article 2 in the *Dillon* case before the Northern Ireland Court of Appeal, which also rejected the government's approach.

The Supreme Court has now agreed to hear an appeal from the Court of Appeal on this issue. This case is of singular constitutional significance in Northern Ireland, involving as it does the issue of the extent to which, post-Brexit, EU human rights norms continue to apply in Northern Ireland where they constituted underpinnings of the domestic implementation of rights protected in the B–GFA. The position of the previous Secretary of State for Northern Ireland changed between the High Court and the Court of Appeal, with the government launching a sustained argument that would render Article 2 of little legal significance in the future. Three particular issues frame the case. First, is Article 2 fully justiciable? The Secretary of State argues that it is not, reneging on commitments as to the meaning of section 7A and the legal status of Article 2 given just after the 2020 Act was passed, suggesting now that Article 2 is not 'directly effective' and thus section 7A does not apply. The second issue concerns the relationship between the ECHR as incorporated by the Human Rights Act 1998, the Charter of Fundamental Rights, and Article 2, with the Secretary of State submitting that EU human rights law effectively ceases to apply when the ECHR applies. The third issue considers the remedies available: if a breach of Article 2 is found to have been occasioned by primary legislation, is the default remedy the disapplication of the offending legislation, a considerably more effective remedy than is available under the Human Rights Act? The Secretary of State opposes disapplication of primary legislation.

5 Future Developments: Trump, Starmer, VDL, and the 'Reset'

The bulk of developments discussed in this chapter occurred during and resulted from choices made by the previous Conservative administration. An obvious question is what difference the new Labour administration has made or may make in the future, so far as Northern Ireland is concerned. Writing in September 2025, more than a year after the general election, there is relatively little practical change to be noted. If anything, the policies of the previous government have been retained. One indication of this has been the attitude of the new government to the attempts by the previous government following the negotiations with the DUP to argue that, in effect, Article

2 of the Protocol is largely non-justiciable and considerably more limited in scope than the Northern Ireland courts have hitherto interpreted it to have. The incoming administration has retained this approach in its appeal to the Supreme Court from the judgment of the NICA in *Dillon*.

That is not to say that the new government may not in the future have significant impact on the post-Brexit regulatory architecture and practice in Northern Ireland. As this is being written, the government is continuing to engage with the European Union with a view to negotiating a broad 'reset' in relations between the UK and the EU. This takes place in a context in which changes in the United States administration are having profound effects on geopolitics and the world economy, developments that leave the United Kingdom exposed and needing to ensure close relations with the EU *and* the United States at the same time as the two blocs appear to be drifting apart. The choices made in that context may well have significant effects in Northern Ireland. The closer the UK gets to the EU (in particular, by retaining or expanding the use of EU standards in food, agriculture, and safety), the less significant will be the Irish Sea 'border'. And the more the UK departs from these standards in order to secure an economic agreement (sometimes expansively termed a 'trade deal') with the United States, the greater will be the effect of that border.

There is, however, another significant Northern Ireland dimension which, if neglected, may yet create significant difficulties. At this point, I will turn from the somewhat intoxicating detail to consider two broader issues which seem to arise from what I have said so far. The first relates to the issue of trust; the second to the Rule of Law.

The issue of trust and distrust arises between multiple sets of political actors, including between the Northern Ireland parties and between Northern Ireland political actors and GB political actors. But the trust relationship I want to focus on primarily is that between the UK and the EU, and between Ireland and the UK. I do not think it is controversial that trust has been a scarce commodity in the long years since the referendum in 2016.[24] Unless trust is re-established between the UK and the EU, and between Ireland and the UK, operating the Windsor Framework in the way envisaged is likely to prove next to impossible, with Northern Ireland being collateral damage. There are signs perhaps that there is greater trust recently at a personal level between Commission President Ursula von der Leyen and Prime Minister Sir Keir Starmer, but there must be a question whether that inter-personal trust is sustainable if it is not underpinned by greater institutional trust between the EU and the UK. And that is rather slower in being re-established. In the context of the forthcoming 'reset' review, this has potentially critical implications.

One of the ways in which trust can be restored is by a firm commitment to uphold previous bargains, which brings me to the second point, concerning the Rule of Law. The willingness of previous UK governments to threaten continually to breach

[24] C McCrudden, 'Law and a Crisis of Trust: Human Rights and the Negotiation of Article 2 of the Ireland-Northern Ireland Protocol' (2023) 70 Irish Jurist 156.

the Rule of (International) Law caused real damage to trust relations, both personal and institutional. In recent years, we have seen: a threat to breach international law in the Internal Market Bill; a unilateral, and probably unlawful, extension of grace periods; a threat to the Protocol in the Northern Ireland Protocol Bill, accompanied by the embarrassing justification based on the doctrine of 'necessity'; anonymous briefings prior to the conclusion of the Windsor Framework that judgments adverse to the UK by the CJEU and the international arbitration body would simply be long-fingered and not implemented; and the sweeping re-interpretation of Article 2 in the Donaldson Annex. To misquote Oscar Wilde: to breach international law once looks like carelessness; to breach it (or to threaten to breach it) on multiple occasions looks like strategy.

If we think that trust between the UK and the EU needs to be restored, it seems obvious that the continual threats to breach or simply turn its back on international law are likely to do nothing to help restore that trust—rather the opposite. In light of all this, a key question is whether the UK government will implement the Windsor Agreement in good faith, and without breaching the B–GFA, both agreements being binding in international law. Riding on that decision is the likelihood of successful negotiations for a reset with the EU. Successful negotiations with the EU are unlikely unless the UK reaffirms its commitment to the liberal rules-based international order and adherence to the Rule of Law, even when it means short-term political embarrassment. Surely the penny has dropped by now that the EU as a law-based institution cannot possibly have stable, friendly, co-operative relationships with the UK otherwise.

So far as the position of Northern Ireland is concerned, the more immediate major issue that has emerged is the impact of the radical new tariff policy of the Trump Administration and the potential reaction of the EU and the UK to the twists and turns of a continually evolving story. This is because the United States currently distinguishes between the United Kingdom and the EU in the level of tariffs imposed on particular goods. Since Ireland is a member of the EU and the UK is not, exports of certain goods from Northern Ireland to the United States will attract a lower tariff than exports of the same goods from Ireland to the United States, thus securing an advantage for Northern Ireland exporters. If the EU retaliates, however, and imposes reciprocal tariffs on incoming goods from the United States, but the UK does not, the problem that arises complicates the picture. As (effectively) a continuing member of the EU Customs Union, Northern Ireland importers would be required under the Protocol to impose those tariffs on US goods but importers in Great Britain would not, placing importers in Northern Ireland at a disadvantage in comparison with those importing the same goods in Great Britain. As a result, it may be necessary to invoke Article 16 of the Protocol, allowing suspension of the Protocol in certain, tightly defined, circumstances. Needless to say, the different treatment of goods North and South would also make the Irish land border of economic significance, and the incentives for smuggling to take advantage of these differences may be considerable.

6 Conclusion

We are back, by way of a rather circuitous route, to our friend the Trilemma. The more EU law is replaced, amended, or withdrawn for Great Britain, the more divergence there is going to be with Northern Ireland in the areas of the single market and customs. The more divergence there is, the more the Union between Northern Ireland and Great Britain looks weakened, so far as unionists are concerned, and the greater the difficulty unionists will have in maintaining a commitment to power-sharing. That will be a choice for the UK government to make. If it chooses to drift away from the EU in areas that are covered by the Protocol in Northern Ireland, it will be choosing to strengthen the regulatory border in the Irish Sea, contrary to the logic of the Windsor Framework. Perhaps ironically, the Trump Administration's policies may, however, drive the UK back into the arms of Europe, with the consequently greater stabilization of Northern Ireland, politically as well as economically.

PART II

THE ECONOMIC

9
Goods

Filippo Fontanelli

1 Introduction

Brexit disrupted the rules governing trade in goods from, to, and within the United Kingdom (UK). In preparation for Brexit and in its wake, the UK has run a permanent regulatory laboratory to weather the storm. This chapter offers a chronology, overview, and assessment of these regulatory experiments, which are still ongoing.

UK goods move along four *vectors*: with the members of the European Union (EU); with non-EU countries—either through Free Trade Agreements (FTAs) or under World Trade Organisation (WTO) terms. Additionally, goods are traded, internally, across the UK's four nations, including between Great Britain (GB) and Northern Ireland (NI). The regulatory framework draws on distinct sources. Besides trade-specific rules (FTAs, customs regulations), measures not primarily about import/export can still hinder foreign goods' access to the UK market or UK goods' ability to sell abroad. Regulatory diversity within the UK can also obstruct internal trade.

Distinguishing between EU and non-EU trade remains crucial. First, the Brexit pledge involved a supposed trade-off: the UK would offset the loss of privileged EU trade with new global agreements. Second, the Trade and Cooperation Agreement (TCA) and the gravity of trade (neighbouring trade being quicker, easier, and cheaper) impose factual or legal constraints on deals with third countries.

Brexit's upheaval of EU–UK relations may seem unrelated to trade with non-EU countries. In fact, the link is strong. First, third country trade, previously handled by the Commission for the EU bloc, is the main macro-indicator of how 'taking back control' has fared. Second, UK trade with non-EU economies belongs here because it shows how Brexit triggered deregulation (ending dozens of FTAs), re-regulation (replicating them), and regulatory pioneering (using new competence to negotiate fresh deals).

The regulatory fever over intra-UK trade (including NI), perhaps counterintuitively, is another Brexit side effect. EU regulations were lifted like a lid, exposing what boiled beneath. Legitimate differences between devolved nations and the impossibility of a customs border in Ireland have created new, often intractable, fronts of regulation.

This chapter, after a concise account of trade regulation before Brexit (section 2), analyses the post-Brexit framework (section 3). Section 4 reviews cases where the

Filippo Fontanelli, *Goods* In: *The UK Regulatory Framework Post-Brexit: 'Law Unbound'*. Edited by: Paul Craig and Vilija Vėlyvytė, Oxford University Press. © Oxford University Press 2026. DOI: 10.1093/9780198969815.003.0011

TCA was invoked to challenge UK practice. Section 5 offers a general assessment of how the UK is embracing and managing regulatory autonomy vis-à-vis the EU.

2 Pre-Brexit Regulation of Trade in Goods

Before Brexit, the UK traded goods (a) within the EU under EU law, and (b) with third countries under the terms of applicable EU FTAs (if any), under WTO law, under preferential unilateral schemes, or, with non-WTO members, under ad hoc regulations. The regulation of intra-UK trade (c), including between NI and GB, was largely uncontroversial.

(a) Trade with the EU

Within the EU 'Internal Market', a free trade area, goods circulate freely between EU member states (MS) under the rules of the EU Treaties (Treaty on the European Union and Treaty on the Functioning of the European Union) and secondary legislation.

The principles underpinning freedom of circulation are: negative integration (banning discrimination and barriers such as tariffs and quotas); regulatory harmonization and convergence (requiring or encouraging MS to adopt similar standards); and mutual recognition of non-harmonized standards (goods meeting one MS's rules are exempt from compliance in the destination MS). By removing border checks, reducing regulatory diversity, and curbing its hindering effects, EU law enables a depth of trade integration unmatched by other inter-State systems and close to that of a single jurisdiction. MS may restrict trade only to pursue social aims through proportionate measures.

(b) Trade with Non-EU Countries

The EU's free trade area is also a customs union. Besides removing barriers to *internal* (intra-EU) trade, the MS' *external* economic policies and measures are unified, as illustrated by the EU bloc's participation in the WTO as a single member. A single EU tariff applies to foreign goods, irrespective of where they enter the EU, and the EU as a whole negotiates trade agreements with third countries.

While in the EU, the UK delegated to Brussels trade regulation. Non-EU imports in the UK faced the EU tariff, and UK goods enjoyed the preferential benefits granted by the FTAs between the EU and third countries (for example, Canada, Japan, Korea, Ukraine).

As regards all countries with which the EU had no FTA, trade with the UK followed one of these three models (still current for the EU): (1) the EU grants unilateral preferences to most countries, on account of their development status, through reduced tariffs, under the various iterations of the so-called General System of Preferences (GSP); (2) with all other WTO countries—for example, US, China, and India—trade occurs under basic WTO terms: non-discrimination (against imports, or across trade partners under the most-favoured-nation (MFN) principle), elimination of quantitative restrictions, tariffs at capped rates; (3) with non-WTO countries, the EU can adopt any tariffs and regulations it wants.[1]

(c) The UK Internal Market and Northern Ireland

Regulatory barriers to intra-UK trade were barely visible before Brexit. Prior to the UK's accession to the EU's precursor in 1973, regulatory divergence among the four nations was negligible. Afterwards, even where diversity could have emerged, EU rules largely pre-empted it, ensuring unhindered flows of goods within the UK. Brexit re-shored EU regulatory competences to the UK, some devolved to the four nations, and brought intra-UK trade governance under the shadow of regulatory diversity. This prompted the UK to adopt the UK Internal Market Act (UKIMA) in 2020.

Similarly, EU free circulation allowed a soft border between NI and Ireland, the UK's only land border with the EU. This was convenient: the 1998 Good Friday Agreement between the UK and Ireland, which ended the Troubles,[2] was facilitated by the EU Internal Market. Brexit threatened to reintroduce border checks, undermining the peace settlement. To preserve its fragile structure, the UK and EU regulated NI's post-Brexit status through *sui generis* rules, many affecting trade in goods.

3 Post-Brexit Regulation of Trade in Goods

Post-Brexit, we must distinguish again: (a) UK–EU trade, governed by the TCA; (b) trade with non-EU countries; (c) intra-UK trade at large; and (d) trade with NI.

(a) Trade with EU Countries: TCA

The TCA, in force since 1 January 2021, is a standard FTA. It replicates the EU single market's negative integration (removing tariffs and quantitative restrictions), but not its positive drivers: regulatory harmonization, convergence, or mutual recognition. Its regulatory thinness reflects the UK's aim to escape EU rules, to which the EU

[1] The EU agreed to replicate WTO terms with Azerbaijan and Serbia.

[2] S Weatherill, 'Comparative Internal Market Law: The UK and the EU' (2021) 40 YBEL 431, 434: 'the "Good Friday" . . . Agreement . . . acknowledges that the majority of the population of Northern Ireland wishes to remain part of the UK but also that a substantial minority of that population wish instead for a single state on the island of Ireland, and it puts in place a process, underpinned by institutional support, within which to manage these tensions peacefully.'

responded uncharitably, withholding concessions granted to other FTA partners and demanding commitments it sought from none.

The TCA must be judged for what it is—a typical FTA—not for what it cannot be. It eliminated customs duties just as they would otherwise have risen after Brexit. Yet it inherits little from the former UK–EU relationship and should not be seen as a reduction of the UK's past single market privileges. Rather, it is better understood as an enhancement of the no-deal baseline, creating a preferential but non-exclusive relationship. Without it, UK–EU goods trade would face tariffs like those applicable between the UK and China or Brazil. Against that baseline, the TCA is a major improvement; comparisons with EU membership are analytically unhelpful.

The TCA also falls short of the integration levels in other EU FTAs.[3]

> The Norwegian model (with full access to the EU single market) was discarded due to the UK's intransigence on the freedom of movement of EU citizens, the jurisdiction of the Court of Justice of the EU and the observance of EU regulations—all things that Norway accepts. The Turkish model (FTA with customs union) would have prevented the UK's much-anticipated objective of managing independently its external trade policy, and was ruled out too. The Swiss model (FTA with extensive regulatory integration through mutual recognition agreements) could not square with the UK's longing for regulatory autonomy, just like the Ukrainian model (FTA with extensive concessions on services), since Ukraine has committed to progressive regulatory alignment with EU rules.

Ultimately, the drafters followed the EU–Canada Comprehensive Economic and Trade Agreement (CETA), with variations dictated by the geographical proximity and the size of the reciprocal trade.

(i) Customs Formalities and Rules of Origin: General

Even without tariffs, goods are subject to customs checks. Authorities must ensure incoming merchandise meets regulatory standards and verify eligibility for TCA duty-free treatment based on origin.

The UK's handling of customs processes for EU *imports* is part of its regulatory response to Brexit. By contrast, UK *exports* to the EU now face the checks applied to third country goods, a clear downgrade from pre-Brexit circulation.[4] For instance, UK exports must obtain an export health certificate (EHC) and pass customs checks on compliance with the EU requirements.[5] The UK cannot unilaterally lift these constraints; deeper integration depends on bilateral arrangements such as mutual

[3] F Fontanelli, 'The Law of UK Trade with the EU and the World after Brexit' (2023) 34(1) King's LJ 3, 11–12.

[4] Instances of industries affected: shellfish, fisheries, small shipments.

[5] Impact: https://www.thegrocer.co.uk/news/uk-food-exporters-have-spent-over-200m-on-vet-paperwork-since-brexit/693897.article/.

recognition of standards, conformity assessments, or regulatory alignment. In this vein, the UK has raised issues in the Trade Partnership Committee about trade in seed potatoes and bivalve molluscs, asking the EU to ease its sanitary and phytosanitary (SPS) protocols. So far, no breakthrough has followed, the EU insisting the same SPS measures apply to all imports.

(ii) Customs Formalities: EU Goods Compliance with UK Regulatory Standards

UK border checks on EU imports have been repeatedly postponed, to avert the inflationary effects resulting from the additional delay and costs.[6] While the UK has established a complex Border Target Operating Model (BTOM) for checks on EU imports, the roll-out of its various components has been sketchy at best.

Take veterinary certificates: after much delay, checks on EU animal products started only in April 2024. However, still in September 2024 commentators said:

> [O]f course, . . . there have been very few checks, anyway, since January 2021 and, even as EHCs and inspection requirements have been introduced this year, they are currently being performed at such a low level as to be almost negligible.[7]

To minimize delays and costs, the UK has also set the frequency of checks at its minimum, raising concerns about the safety of the products imported (from EU and non-EU countries alike).[8]

Another revealing story concerns the requirement that EU imports have Safety and Security declarations. After countless announcements and delays, it came into effect in January 2025, while border checks on 'medium-risk' fruit and vegetables were further postponed first until July 2025,[9] and then—when the prospect emerged of a SPS agreement—until January 2027.[10]

Compliance costs for traders operating across jurisdictions, in the absence of mutual recognition, are ultimately a function of regulatory diversity.[11] Additionally,

[6] European Parliament, *Implementation of the EU–UK TCA* (Apr 2025) Research Briefing: 'The EU introduced the requirements from 1 January 2021, while the UK has been phasing them in to avoid massive trade disruption', https://www.europarl.europa.eu/RegData/etudes/BRIE/2025/765779/EPRS_BRI(2025)765779_EN.pdf-

[7] PIGWORLD, 'What a New Veterinary Agreement with the EU Could Mean for the UK Pig Sector' (6 September 2024) https://www.pig-world.co.uk/news/news-analysis/what-a-new-vet-agreement-with-the-eu-could-mean-for-the-pig-sector.html.

[8] Financial Times, 'Food from Outside EU Enters Britain Unchecked, Customs Agents Warn' (4 July 2024) https://www.ft.com/content/37899d72-40f6-4e77-8bfa-6e89d499cddf.

[9] Concurrently, some goods were re-classified as low risk, allowing them to skip checks altogether (pears, apples).

[10] DEFRA, 'Fruit and Veg Import Checks Will Not Be Introduced This Summer' (2 June 2025) https://planthealthportal.defra.gov.uk/latest-news/fruit-and-veg-import-checks-will-not-be-introduced-this-summer/.

[11] See Section 5(a)(iii).

and irrespective of the substantive content of these standards, the process of demonstrating and ascertaining compliance entails unavoidable costs.[12]

> Dynamic alignment with EU regulations is not sufficient to ease trade facilitation challenges. It requires binding institutional actions and recognition of conformity assessment bodies and procedures across the border.

For this reason, alongside coordination of their standards (which accept that *mutual recognition of standards* is not a realistic prospect), the UK and EU have also discussed the *mutual recognition of conformity assessment bodies*, to contain at least the costs of these processes.[13] In other words, the EU and UK could agree to entrust bodies based in each other's territory with certifying products' conformity with their own standards (for example, the EU would trust certifications of UK goods' compliance with EU standards, issued by UK bodies). At the time of writing, the EU has not agreed to include this item in the 'reset' agenda.[14]

(iii) TCA: Rules of Origin

For goods to obtain TCA duty-free treatment, customs authorities must ascertain that they were 'wholly obtained' in the EU or the UK, or substantially transformed there. Detailed rules of origin (ROOs) determine whether different goods meet these requirements and the formalities bearing on traders certifying the goods' provenance. The cost of these formalities can exceed the tariff payable for third country exports, so some businesses forego the duty-free benefit,[15] driving down the preference utilization rate.

ROOs impose an inevitable burden on tariff-free trade, because the tracking formalities and verification checks are costly. However, the precise impact of such burden depends on the specific ROO rules—that is, how to qualify for duty-free treatment. Two instances of post-Brexit ROO manoeuvring merit discussion.

First, Brexit threatened the viability of value chains across UK and EU (for example, UK-manufactured cars fitted with German engines and Italian leather seats). Some goods previously 'wholly obtained' in the EU became partly UK and partly EU after Brexit, possibly failing the conditions for duty-free treatment in the destination market. To avert that risk, the UK and EU agreed that any content originating from *either* territory counted towards origin in the *other* one. However, after Brexit the UK

[12] UKTPO, 'UK'S Conformity Assessment and Accreditation: Key Issues for the UK–EU Reset' (5 August 2025) Briefing Paper 86, https://www.uktpo.org/2025/08/05/briefing-paper-86-uks-conformity-assessment-and-accreditation-key-issues-for-the-uk-eu-reset/.

[13] Financial Times, 'Brussels Rebuffs UK Bid to Prise Open Access to EU Single Market' (25 April 2025) https://www.ft.com/content/f893a566-fd17-4915-ad0b-bdd2bd622987.

[14] Financial Times, 'EU Certificates Deal Could Boost Key UK Exports by a Quarter, Study Finds' (18 May 2025) https://www.ft.com/content/ff1c4d5d-67e3-446f-b80a-542898e5ba1d.

[15] UKTPO, 'How Much Free Trade in UK Free Trade Agreements?' (July 2024) Briefing Paper 83, https://blogs.sussex.ac.uk/uktpo/publications/how-much-free-trade-in-uk-free-trade-agreements/#preferenceBP83.

has left the Pan-European-Mediterranean zone (PEM), a so-called cumulation zone gathering the EU and twenty-seven neighbouring countries. PEM members consider raw and semi-processed materials from anywhere inside the PEM, and incorporated into final goods, as counting towards its declared origin; for example, a good qualifies as 'made in the EU' even if it incorporates Algerian and Moroccan raw materials. Since the UK is not in the PEM and the TCA does not offer cross-cumulation,[16] goods traded that contain (non-EU, non-UK) PEM inputs might lose TCA benefits. Current calls for the UK to rejoin the PEM seek to remedy this situation,[17] but the EU seems now unwilling to support this move.[18]

Second, the TCA ROOs relating to electric vehicles (EV)[19] require cars to have at least 40 per cent of UK/EU content for UK/EU provenance and duty-free treatment. On 1 January 2024 this threshold was supposed to rise to 45 per cent, before rising further to 55 per cent in 2027. Cars failing to meet these thresholds are considered as made outside the UK/EU and face a 10 per cent MFN duty in either territory. In 2023, the EU and UK agreed to maintain the initial regime (the 40 per cent threshold), due to the European industry struggling to scale up the production of batteries, which account for a large share of the cars' value. The step scheduled for 2024 would have caused many EV cars traded between UK and EU—still relying heavily on Chinese and other non-TCA components—to incur tariffs. The more lenient ROO was therefore extended until the end of 2026.

(iv) TCA: Level Playing Field

The TCA guarantees a 'level playing field' (LPF) for UK–EU trade. The formula signals the risk of either economy gaining an unfair export advantage and commits to monitoring it. Such unfairness can arise from two types of policies: government support for local producers (subsidies, state aid) and deregulation that lowers or removes the costs of local production.

The TCA polices race-to-the-bottom competitiveness more closely than any other FTA.[20] The UK's insistence on deviating from EU rules alarmed the EU, as it foreshadowed deregulation in matters previously governed by EU law.[21]

> Advanced social policies are not just noble, they are also expensive: higher standards equal higher production costs, and in turn lower the competitiveness of

[16] Cross-cumulation allows cumulating inputs from multiple countries that are not joined by a trade agreement. For instance, countries A and B can agree in their FTA that inputs from C count towards the threshold in the ROO between them.

[17] Anna Jerzewska, 'Should the UK Rejoin PEM?' (March 2025) UKTPO Working Paper, https://www.uktpo.org/wp-content/uploads/2025/03/SHOULD-THE-UK-REJOIN-PEM_UKTPO_WP.pdf.

[18] Financial Times, 'EU Blocks Britain's Attempts to Join Pan-European Trading Bloc' (2 July 2025) https://www.ft.com/content/0cb56d25-b08a-42cc-83bf-2979208a6745.

[19] Annex 5 to the TCA.

[20] On labour matters specifically, US FTAs contain innovative obligations and enforcement schemes: see K Claussen and CP Bown, 'Corporate Accountability by Treaty: The New North American Rapid Response Labor Mechanism' (2024) 118 AJIL 98.

[21] Fontanelli (n 3) 17–18.

locally produced goods on foreign markets, where identical products are cheaper to make. Conversely, the loosening of domestic standards can boost the competitiveness of one country's products abroad.

The TCA prohibits the parties from lowering the protection of various public interests, and exhorts them to increase it. An ad hoc bilateral body monitors compliance with the LPF rules and a panel of experts can be asked to investigate allegations of breaches. If one is ascertained, the panel can authorize retaliation, including through increased tariffs, to remove the unfair distortions and rebalance UK/EU trade relations.

(b) Trade with Non-EU Countries

UK trade with non-EU countries occurs under several rules. The UK enjoys (and grants) preferential market access to several countries through FTAs, mostly spawned out of pre-existing EU FTAs through the 'roll-over' project. With all other countries, it either trades under WTO terms or grants unilaterally development-based preferences.[22]

(i) The Global MFN Tariff and the Developing Countries Trading Scheme

Initially, the prospect of a no-deal Brexit led the UK to propose various MFN tariff schemes, as an alternative to simply adopting the EU tariff. These aimed to lower tariffs on critical EU imports and prevent sudden price spikes on consumer and intermediate goods. Under the MFN rule, the same tariff reductions would have automatically applied to equivalent non-EU imports.[23]

The TCA dispelled the risk of tariffs on EU goods, but the issue remained of choosing an MFN tariffs scheme applicable to non-EU WTO members (minus FTA partners and GSP beneficiaries). Formulating a Schedule of Concession[24] from scratch would have alerted dozens of WTO members, which could object to any increase of the EU baseline rates. Wisely, the UK chose instead to inherit the EU Schedule and tweak it downwards, removing or reducing tariffs across the board (to all third countries' benefit). The new 'Global Tariff' scheme simplified the applicable rates, removed duties on around 2000 goods,[25] and reduced tariffs by around 1 per cent on average.

Something similar occurred with the unilateral EU preferences for developing countries. Initially, the UK simply replicated the EU GSP and GSP + schemes. In late

[22] Brexit changed nothing about UK trade with non-WTO countries.

[23] See UK Government, 'Non-preferential Tariff Rates and Quotas on Imports if the UK Leaves the EU with No Deal (8 October 2019) https://www.gov.uk/government/publications/temporary-rates-of-customs-duty-on-imports-after-eu-exit/mfn-and-tariff-quota-rates-of-customs-duty-on-imports-if-the-uk-leaves-the-eu-with-no-deal.

[24] The document attached to the GATT recording the bound rates that each WTO member grants to each product.

[25] This was possible with tariffs on goods supported by EU protectionist concerns (eg dishwashers, garden shears, and Christmas trees).

2022, it launched the Developing Countries Trading Scheme (DCTS), which grants deeper concessions. The DCTS covers a wider set of products and more countries, uses more generous ROOs, and removes conditionality requirements.

(ii) The Roll-over Continuity Project

To retain the preferences previously enjoyed under EU FTAs, the UK carried out a 'roll-over' of these treaties.[26] Essentially, the UK agreed with almost all EU FTA partners that, after Brexit, new treaties replicating the EU FTA terms would enter into force with the UK. More than thirty roll-over treaties were concluded (some with multiple partners), ensuring continuity of trade. Practically, each pre-Brexit EU FTA split into two complementary agreements: one with the EU and one with the UK.

The continuity project required specific adjustments. First, several EU FTAs containing regulatory commitments (mutual recognition, services arrangements, regulatory alignment) were simplified into basic tariff-free agreements. Second, many UK FTAs include 'cross-cumulation' rules mirroring the TCA's simple-cumulation ROOs, allowing UK and EU inputs to count toward proving, respectively, UK or EU origin. This preserves the fiction of interchangeability: without it, goods with substantial EU components that previously qualified under the EU FTA might no longer meet origin requirements for duty-free treatment under the UK-only FTA.

(iii) FTAs with New Countries

With the roll-over deals, the UK gained experience as an autonomous FTA negotiator before Brexit took effect. Beyond convincing dozens of partners to maintain existing arrangements, the UK faced ad hoc complications that sometimes required solutions beyond minor adjustments.

For example, the roll-over treaty with Iceland, Liechtenstein, and Norway was replaced by a new FTA in 2021, while fresh deals with Canada and Israel were negotiated to accommodate potential UK divergence from EU regulations. The UK also added digital trade provisions to treaties with Ukraine and Singapore. The Comprehensive Economic Partnership with Japan (October 2020), modelled on the EU–Japan FTA, was hailed as the first major, genuinely new agreement concluded autonomously by the UK.

Beyond the continuity project, the UK pursued talks with non-EU countries, betraying some performative urgency. Early deals with Australia and New Zealand (2021–22) were widely described, including by a former Environment Secretary, as generous to UK counterparts, granting duty-free access for exports of lamb, dairy, and most agricultural products. In December 2024 the UK joined the Comprehensive and Progressive Agreement for Trans-Pacific Partnership (CPTPP), overlapping with several pre-existing bilateral agreements among its members; the UK's only new trade

[26] J Larik, 'Imitation as Flattery: The UK's Trade Continuity Agreements and the EU's Normative Foreign Policy' (2023) 34 EJIL 801.

partners are Malaysia and Brunei,[27]and the economic effects of joining this FTA deal are modest.[28]

In 2022–24, the UK advertised several negotiations. The results ranged from insignificant (for example, the so-called trade agreements with individual US states[29]) to interlocutory (for example, the updates on the talks with India and the US).

Somewhat paradoxically, the weakening of global compliance with WTO rules, confirmed by the incoming US administration in 2025, created new opportunities. The UK could design preferential agreements, both to appease the US and to forge new alliances, without major legal constraints. The 2025 deals with the US and India are best understood in this context.[30]

(iv) The Economic Prosperity Deal with the US

On 2 April 2025, the US announced new tariffs on imports: a 10 per cent MFN tariff across the board, plus country-specific additional components, proportional to the US trade deficit with each.[31] These tariffs would cover all goods not already hit by product-specific ones (for example, 25% on cars and car components of any origin except Canada and Mexico; 50% on steel). Gradually, all new tariffs (country-specific, product-specific, 10% baseline) entered into force, with sparse exemptions and suspensions.[32] As these tariffs were ultimately abrogated by the US Supreme Court in February 2026, new ones replaced them and further ones still were announced.

This move foreshadowed an era in which countries, fearing losing access to its market, negotiate directly with the US. Beforehand, most countries observed the WTO rule: only bilateral preferential agreements covering 'substantially all trade' between them are valid.[33] A comprehensive UK–US agreement meeting the WTO requirements, despite periodic optimism, is beyond reach.[34] Outside WTO constraints, however, a US–UK deal was indeed possible, and it was quickly negotiated.

A narrow 'US–UK Economic Prosperity Deal' (EPD) was agreed in May 2025. The UK grants preferential market access to US goods, and in return is spared from some of the new US product-specific tariffs, gaining a competitive edge over other

[27] The UK already had roll-over or fresh agreements with Australia, Canada, Chile, Japan, Mexico, New Zealand, Peru, Singapore, and Vietnam.

[28] Removing tariffs from Malaysia's palm oil might clash with the EU's measures against indirect land use change, but those measures in turn were found to be WTO-illegal, see WTO, Case DS593/R, *EU–Certain Measures Concerning Palm Oil and Oil Palm Crop-Based Biofuels*, panel report of 10 January 2025.

[29] See, eg, UK Government, 'UK Signs Trade Pact with Second Biggest US State—Texas' (13 March 2024) at https://www.gov.uk/government/news/uk-signs-trade-pact-with-second-biggest-us-state-texas.

[30] BBC, 'Four Things You Need to Know about UK–India Trade Deal' (6 May 2025) https://www.bbc.co.uk/news/articles/c99p2mlyep5o: 'US President Donald Trump's introduction of tariffs on goods entering America has prompted other world leaders to consider striking free-trade deals with one another.'

[31] This is an evident breach of the MFN rule requiring tariffs to apply to all countries equally, outside free trade agreements or development-based preferences.

[32] Tariffs on Chinese goods are suspended until November 2025 at the time of writing.

[33] Article XXIV(5) and (8) GATT.

[34] A comprehensive deal with the US is considered unviable due to the US demands on market access for its agri-food products, see NFU, 'NFU Warns Agriculture Has "Nothing More to Give" ' on US Trade' (9 July 2025) https://www.nfuonline.com/updates-and-information/us-trade-deal-board-meeting/.

countries. Specifically, the UK lowered its tariffs and/or tariff-rate quotas on US cars and agricultural products (including beef and bioethanol), while the US grants a lower tariff quota on UK cars, car components, steel, and aluminium, and/or reduces the 25 per cent tariff on these goods altogether, irrespective of quotas.

The EPD currently exists only as 'General terms'. A binding document covering more areas is still outstanding, which would cover also trade in pharmaceutical products and regulatory arrangements, such as specific mutual recognition agreements.[35] The anchoring value of these 'General terms' is unclear, in a context of continuous developments. Already in September 2025, the UK plan to obtain duty-free treatment for (at least a quota of) its steel exports faltered; the US instead offered to freeze the 25 per cent rate, rather than impose the freshly increased 50 per cent rate imposed to all other countries.[36]

Incidentally, and *pace* the cautious wording, the EPD marks the UK's first move into clearly WTO-illegal territory, and litigation cannot be ruled out.

(v) The FTA with India

In July 2025 the UK and India signed an FTA, which will enter into force after the ratification process. It covers most trade (unlike the EPD) and reflects positively on the UK's record as an autonomous negotiator: India has no FTA with EU, China, or the US.

In keeping with WTO law, it covers substantially all trade (more than 90% of tariff-lines will qualify for duty-free both ways). India's duties on UK goods will fall from 15 per cent to 3 per cent on average. The historically resistant Indian tariff on UK whisky will drop from 150 per cent to 75 per cent immediately, then gradually lower to 40 per cent in ten years. Indian tariffs on cars will gradually lower from 100 per cent to a tariff-rate quota of 10 per cent. The FTA reciprocal concessions are services-heavy, but among the preferences for goods trade, UK operators will have 'guaranteed and unprecedented access' to India's lucrative government procurement market.[37]

(c) The UK Internal Market

The UK enacted the Internal Market Act (UKIMA) in 2020.[38] It aims to ensure the free movement of goods (and services) across the four nations, despite potential

[35] Simon Lester, 'The "General Terms" of the US–UK Trade Deal: A Few Answers, Still Lots of Questions' (11 May 2025) IELP Blog, https://ielp.worldtradelaw.net/2025/05/the-general-terms-of-the-us-uk-trade-deal/?utm_medium = twitter&utm_source = dlvr.it.

[36] The Guardian, 'Plan to Slash US Steel Tariffs Shelved Hours before Donald Trump's UK Visit' (16 September 2025) at https://www.theguardian.com/politics/2025/sep/16/plan-slash-us-steel-tariffs-shelved-ahead-donald-trump-visit.

[37] India is not a party to the WTO General Procurement Agreement, so this was not already the case.

[38] UKIMA 2020.

regulatory divergence as powers return from Brussels to each of them.[39] To achieve this, it draws on the EU principle of free movement, which effectively guaranteed intra-UK trade in the past, and its corollaries.

The UKIMA introduced into UK legislation the 'market access principles' of mutual recognition[40] and non-discrimination.[41] Under these principles, intra-UK trade[42] is immune from local regulations that hinder trade flows access—inadvertently or for protectionism. Stringent 'relevant requirements' for local production, which prohibit the sale of non-compliant products, cannot block goods lawfully produced or first imported elsewhere in the UK. For example, Wales can require Welsh producers to add health warnings on drink labels. However, drinks produced or imported elsewhere in the UK that do not meet these rules can still be sold in Wales, undermining the policy's purpose and Welsh producers. Relevant requirements also cannot discriminate against goods from other parts of the UK. Ultimately, UKIMA overrides nation-specific laws that threaten goods' free movement within the UK.

The UKIMA market access principles exempt some measures with incidental trade-limiting effects. These include SPS (focused on diseases and pests), food safety rules, and public health emergencies. This list is narrower than the EU or WTO equivalents, and the limited range of devolved powers reduces the need to monitor intra-UKIMA barriers in non-devolved areas, such as product safety outside food and drink or data protection.[43] However, the UKIMA does not list environmental protection—a devolved competence—as a legitimate aim. Therefore, and pending future reforms, environment preservation cannot justify departures from mutual recognition and non-discrimination, save for risks connected to the use of fertilizers and pesticides.

Whereas the EU complements negative integration with positive one (regulatory convergence and harmonization), the UKIMA proposes to accompany the market access principles with a system of 'Common Frameworks'.[44] Through this system, established in 2017, the four nations can disclose their plans to diverge from the UK baseline and hold consultations; this process can lead to codifying local rules as scheduled UKIMA exceptions.[45] Alternatively, UK-wide schemes accommodating or coordinating different standards can be negotiated. This system aims to reduce diversity, through a participated process run in the shadow of mutual recognition.

[39] KA Armstrong, 'The Governance of Economic Unionism after the United Kingdom Internal Market Act' (2022) 85 MLR 635, 638–39. For a comparison, Weatherill (n 2).

[40] UKIMA 2020, s 2.

[41] UKIMA 2020, s 5.

[42] Market access within the UKIMA covers goods moving from NI to Great Britain, but not the other way around. On NI's status within the UKIM, see the following section.

[43] Weatherill (n 2) 456.

[44] UKIMA 2020, s 10(2), (4).

[45] T Horsley and J Hunt, 'Internal Market Governance by Consensus rather than Conflict? Common Frameworks and the Potential for Positive Harmonisation' (2024) 74 NILQ 68.

(d) Trade with Northern Ireland—the NI Protocol

The borderless arrangement between NI and Ireland is essential for the Good Friday Agreement, so its roll-over after Brexit was presumed. Without checks on the Irish border, however, GB goods imported into the NI—and non-compliant with EU rules—could enter the EU unnoticed, undercutting the EU's interest to police its border adequately. To address this risk without erecting a hard border in Ireland, the NI Protocol to the EU–UK Withdrawal Agreement[46] requires EU rules on goods to apply in NI (unlike in GB), and NI to stay in the EU customs union. This obviates the need for checks on the Irish border: goods on both sides are presumed EU-compliant.

For NI producers, this arrangement increases regulatory costs, imposing two different rulebooks at once. This duplication affects also GB goods entering the NI, which undergo the same customs procedures (including checks and paperwork) as UK goods directed to EU countries. This is true also for GB goods which end up sold/consumed in NI. The trade impact is intuitive.[47]

> [T]his made it more costly to export from GB to NI, and certain goods (like seed potatoes) were banned outright. Moreover, as the EU updated its rulebook, this regulatory gap grew. For example, an EU ban on the food colouring E171 meant supermarkets in Great Britain could no longer export breads and cakes containing that additive to Northern Ireland.

Effectively, a new EU–UK customs border operates in the Irish Sea. The NI Protocol imposes time and cost hindrances on GB–NI trade, besides the regulatory adaptation costs described.

4 Post-Brexit Legality

To reach a deal, the UK and EU engaged in wearisome confrontations; post-Brexit, legal *détente* set in. Permanent negotiations continue, but invocations of the TCA to contest UK or EU measures affecting trade in goods are rare.

[46] On the NI Protocol, see C McCrudden (ed), *The Law and Practice of the Ireland–Northern Ireland Protocol* (Cambridge University Press 2021).

[47] Joël Reland, 'Regulatory Divergence and the Windsor Framework' (14 February 2024) UK in a Changing Europe, https://ukandeu.ac.uk/explainers/regulatory-divergence-and-the-windsor-framework/.

(a) The Sand Eels Arbitration

The UK and Scotland prohibited sand-eel fishing in their waters in March 2024, on environmental grounds (sand eels are important for the sustenance of seabirds). This measure amounts to a ban on production, and thus affects trade in goods. The ban damages EU fishing vessels (mostly Danish) holding almost the entire fishing quota for sand eels under the TCA. The EU sued the UK in arbitration,[48] invoking the TCA rules on the joint management of fish stocks.

In mid-2025, the tribunal found partially in the EU's favour. It held that the UK ban was disproportionate and failed to balance adequately economic and environmental considerations. However, the ban's Scottish portion (issued by Scottish authorities and covering Scottish waters) was considered reasonable and sufficiently well-grounded. The UK announced that the ban will remain in place. It provided additional reasons, to bring it into compliance with the tribunal's award, amid fishermen's protests that this was a cosmetic move.

This case displays an atypical interaction between regulation and trade. Businesses normally want protection against regulatory relaxation abroad (in markets where they seek to compete, and whence competing goods originate); the LPF mechanism protects against this imbalance. Instead, the extraterritorial nature of fishing concessions under the TCA (EU operators can fish in UK waters) establishes a different dynamic: stringent UK regulation affects disproportionately foreign operators. With the costs of environmental measures falling mostly on foreigners, the UK found little internal resistance to adopt and maintain the ban, and it behoved the EU to question the measure's reasonableness on its operators' behalf.

The current UK proposal to ban bottom trawling (a fishing method) on environmental grounds could anticipate a similar clash. Its costs would hit mostly EU operators, and the EU could challenge it under the TCA.

(b) Level Playing Field

The TCA LPF Trade Specialised Committee consults regularly on matters that can trigger the LPF mechanism.

Thus far, the Committee's discussion has not led to either party alleging a breach of the TCA. Its agenda largely covers matters different from, or incidental to, trade in goods (subsidy control, digital markets, competition policy, etc). Discussion around standards affecting the production of goods is ongoing, especially regarding EU unilateral measures accelerating regulatory divergence (see section 5(a)(ii) below). At the latest meeting (October 2024), for instance, the Committee discussed the

[48] This was the first TCA arbitration.

implementation of the UK and EU Emission Trading Schemes, the Due Diligence Directive, and the Forced Labour Regulation.[49]

DEFRA published in April 2025 a report on the state of UK environmental regulation, largely EU-inherited.[50] It found that much of it needs updating and streamlining, and called 'for a radical repositioning and repurposing' of this field. Any deregulation effort flowing from this plan could engage the LPF provisions, and trigger the EU's scrutiny on the effects of relaxing environmental standards.

5 Post-Brexit Analysis: Managing Divergence

Brexit promised deregulation: divergence from EU standards was a goal, not a side effect.

Regulatory divergence between two jurisdictions increases trading costs. UK goods produced lawfully in the GB might be non-compliant with EU rules (and *vice versa*), hence market access might depend on bearing adaptation costs and new paperwork.[51]

> UK exports to the EU can no longer be automatically deemed compliant with EU regulatory requirements and hence have to be subjected to various conformity checks, customs formalities, and inspections at the borders.

For the same reasons, EU rules' application in NI means that UK–EU divergence creates attrition also on GB–NI trade.

Some *procedural* costs are inherent. Even assuming identical standards, border checks and conformity assessment procedures hinder goods' circulation. The cost of *substantive* compliance, instead, depends on the standards' similarity: the wider the gap between them, the harder to observe both. Ultimately, ease of trading is a function of the UK–EU regulatory proximity (through dynamic alignment, automatic mirroring, or other forms of convergence). Besides trying to coordinate with the EU, the GB must design and manage regulatory divergence *unilaterally*, that is, decide how to respond to the EU's reforms, and whether/how to deviate from the EU baseline.[52] For NI, obviously, the choice is constrained.

[49] Fourth Trade Specialised Committee on Level Playing Field for Open and Fair Competition and Sustainable Development under the EU–UK Trade and Cooperation Agreement—minutes of meeting of 3 October 2024, published on 10 September 2025.

[50] UK Government, 'An Independent Review of Defra's Regulatory Landscape (2 April 2025) https://www.gov.uk/government/publications/delivering-economic-growth-and-nature-recovery-an-independent-review-of-defras-regulatory-landscape/an-independent-review-of-defras-regulatory-landscape-foreword-and-executive-summary#executive-summary.

[51] Ruby Acquah and others, 'Regulatory Intensity and the EU Single Market: implications for the UK' (May 2024) UKTPO Briefing Paper 80, 2 at https://www.uktpo.org/wp-content/uploads/Publications/Briefing-Papers/UKTPO-2024-BP-80.pdf.

[52] Section 5(a)(i).

The relationship between UK and EU standards can take three different shapes: convergence; passive divergence (GB slips back); and active divergence (GB rules innovate upwards, but the EU does not follow).

(a) Regulatory Impact: Convergence and Divergence

After Brexit, the GB was cautious to promote divergence when it could affect trade in goods. Standards less stringent than EU ones (active backtracking) expose the UK to the LPF mechanism and social discontent; conversely, more stringent standards (active divergence) undercut GB exports' competitiveness and raise EU imports' consumer prices. Neither move seems ideal.

There has been little active divergence to report. The systematically postponed border checks and customs processes tell a clear story: even when it is planned, divergence is often avoided. Instead, passive divergence has been common. Embraced at first, the repercussions of passive divergence are now more tightly monitored and managed, with the goal of keeping EU standards in view.

(i) Maximum Deregulation: The Great Repeal Plan (Aborted)

Between 2020 and 2022, the UK government professed the intention to eliminate as much EU-inherited regulation as possible, promising a 'bonfire of red tape'.[53] While leaner regulation normally lubricates business, most UK operators voiced strong opposition, fearing the costs of increased regulatory diversity between the GB and two of their biggest markets (EU and NI). The Sunak administration silently let this plan fizzle out.[54]

(ii) The 'Reset': Embracing or Engineering Convergence

In 2024, the Labour government changed course, calling for a 'reset' of the bilateral rapport. In trade, rapprochement to the EU requires adding some substance to the TCA's regulatory shallowness. GB approximation to EU standards is no longer anathema. The sovereignty-based red lines have repositioned: freedom of movement or reversing Brexit remain non-starters, but the possibility of the UK's subordination to EU rules is quietly accepted. Active divergence appears less likely than between 2021 and 2024, despite sparse performative declarations.[55]

[53] Independent, 'Liz Truss Promises "Red Tape Bonfire" with Review of all EU Law by End of 2023' (22 July 2022) at https://www.independent.co.uk/news/business/liz-truss-promises-red-tape-bonfire-with-review-of-all-eu-law-by-end-of-2023-b2129521.html.

[54] Guardian, 'The Right's Brexit "Bonfire of Red Tape" Was Just Wind and Smoke. And Even Tories Want More Regulation Now (2 May 2024) https://www.theguardian.com/commentisfree/article/2024/may/02/brexit-bonfire-red-tape-tories-voters-business.

[55] See, for example, 'UK Government, Regulatory Innovation Office to Help Streamline Regulation, Helping UK's World-leading Fintech Sector' (1 July 2025).

Between 2024 and 2025, this policy of regulatory convergence 'kicked-off in earnest'[56] and alignment tools were entrenched in legislation. A regulation of September 2024[57] extends the UK courts' duty to interpret retained EU law following the EU case law.[58] In trade matters, the clearest example is the 2025 Product Regulation and Metrology Act (PRMA) authorizing the UK government to mirror EU product regulations in UK law, aligning the two regulatory regimes on a rolling basis via secondary legislation.[59] The PRMA's precise focus is ambiguous (the text oscillates between product safety and environmental protection), but it confers wide-ranging powers to approximate UK law to EU standards. Moreover, the PRMA stipulates the unilateral and indefinite equivalence of EU conformity marking (CE) to UKCA marking.[60] Unilateral recognition covers also EU-certified construction materials and medical devices, making them marketable in the UK.

Besides these systemic mechanisms, ad hoc alignment is also pursued on specific fronts. For instance, responding to the EU CBAM, the UK proposed a carbon border adjustment mechanism to prevent carbon-embedded products' leakage from the EU to the UK. In parallel, the UK wants to link its Emission Trading Scheme (ETS) to the EU's, to qualify for exemption under the EU CBAM.[61] A smaller but revealing example is the UK plan to replicate the 2024 EU measure imposing the USB-C charger as standard for all small electronic devices.

Alongside unilateral efforts to reduce divergence, cooperative plans are under way, moving quite slowly. Work on an SPS agreement, to increase UK agri-food exports,[62] started in May 2025. The UK has declared it will seek a 'bespoke' SPS deal, presumably different from the EU ones with Switzerland and New Zealand. The former removes border checks on the goods covered;[63] the latter—much thinner on regulation, and product-specific—removes most physical checks but does not dispense from veterinary certificates.[64] However, the Swiss agreement presupposes significant regulatory

[56] Joël Reland, 'UK–EU Divergence Tracker Q4 2024–Q2 2025 (2025)', UK in a Changing Europe 4 https://ukandeu.ac.uk/reports/uk-eu-divergence-tracker-q4-2024-q2-2025/.

[57] The Retained EU Law (Revocation and Reform) Act 2023 (Commencement No. 2 and Saving Provisions) (Revocation) Regulations 2024, made on 17 September 2024.

[58] Preventing Section 6 of the Retained EU Law Act from taking effect, which would have removed that obligation as of October 2024.

[59] Product Regulation and Metrology Act 2025, made on 21 July 2025, see s 1(2): 'The Secretary of State may also by regulations make provision, in relation to the marketing or use of products in the United Kingdom, which corresponds, or is similar, to a provision of relevant EU law for the purpose of reducing or mitigating the environmental impact of products.'

[60] Between 2021 and 2024 the UK had repeatedly postponed the imposition of the UKCA marking requirement.

[61] UK Government, 'Draft Legislation: Carbon Border Adjustment Mechanism' (24 April 2025) at https://www.gov.uk/government/consultations/draft-legislation-carbon-border-adjustment-mechanism.

[62] Emily Lydgate and Alex Carson-Taylor, 'An EU-UK SPS Agreement: The Perils and Possibilities of (Re)alignment' (3 December 2024) CITP Briefing Paper 17; Ignacio García Bercero, 'EU–Switzerland: A New Approach to Partial Integration into the Single Market? (29 January 2025) Bruegel at https://www.bruegel.org/first-glance/eu-switzerland-new-approach-partial-integration-single-market.

[63] Anton Spisak, The New EU–Swiss Deal: What It Means and the Lessons It Holds for the UK-EU 'Reset' (17 March 2025) CER Insight, https://www.cer.eu/sites/default/files/AS_swiss_eu_reset_17.3.25.pdf.

[64] US Department of Agriculture, 'Overview of UK–EU Engagement on a Potential SPS Agreement' (15 April 2025) Report UK2025-0014.

alignment (in fact, Switzerland's rules on GMOs and animal welfare are *stricter* than the EU's).[65] Conversely, the New Zealand deal covers a negligible amount of NZ imports. Neither fits perfectly the UK–EU scenario. Unsurprisingly, to achieve this SPS deal, the UK appears ready to accept 'dynamic alignment' with EU standards on agri-food products.[66] This would mark the first episode of open rule-taking after Brexit, epitomizing the 'reset' approach promoted by the Labour government.

(iii) Passive Divergence

In several trade-affecting matters, EU and UK standards have diverged. A pre-Brexit suspicion proved largely correct: on average, the UK would lag behind EU's reforms (passive divergence).

Most significantly, passive divergence was triggered by the suite of EU measures incentivizing non-EU businesses' obedience to EU values.[67] These measures condition foreign products' access to the EU market to various social and environmental requirements. The Carbon Border Adjustment Mechanism regulation, the Corporate Sustainability Due Diligence and Reporting directives (CSDD and CSDR), the Forced Labour regulation, and the Deforestation regulation use this approach.

Interestingly, these measures were not conceived to block non-compliant UK imports: they focus on products from non-European countries where these values are not adequately protected. For instance, the UK ETS mirrors the EU one: the risk of carbon leakage inherent in UK–EU trade is low. However, even when the standards' similarity ensures continued market access, these measures impose careful regulatory management, and burden UK trade with administration and certification processes. The Commission's Omnibus Package of April 2025 aims to simplify and reduce the coverage of the CSDD, CSDR,[68] and CBAM,[69] diminishing their ambition and the regulatory gap with the UK. In turn, the effects on UK trade will be softer.

Besides these wide-reaching EU instruments, selected episodes of divergence help with mapping the regulatory landscape as of October 2025. Evidently, passive divergence is the most common occurrence.

Various new EU product standards opened regulatory gaps with the UK. Namely, the EU restricted 'forever chemicals' and the permissible uses of several pesticides

[65] Swiss Federal Council, 'Factsheet: Agreement on Agriculture and Food Safety' (June 2025), https://www.europa.eda.admin.ch/dam/en/sd-web/jmq4IaLOjyeF/008%20Faktenblatt%20Landwirtschaft%20und%20Lebensmittelsicherheit%20(EN).pdf.

[66] UK Government, 'UK–EU Summit—Common Understanding' (19 May 2025) Policy Paper, point 27, https://www.gov.uk/government/publications/ukeu-summit-key-documentation/uk-eu-summit-common-understanding-html.

[67] These include environmental protection, human rights, labour standards, carbon pricing, and supply-chain sustainability.

[68] European Commission, Omnibus Package (1 April 2025) at https://finance.ec.europa.eu/news/omnibus-package-2025-04-01_en.

[69] European Parliament, 'CBAM: Parliament Adopts Simplifications to the EU Carbon Leakage Instrument (10 September 2025) press release, https://www.europarl.europa.eu/news/en/press-room/20250905IPR30181/cbam-parliament-adopts-simplifications-to-the-eu-carbon-leakage-instrument.

(including glysophate) and 'substances of human origin'; regulated the labelling of honey and other products through 'breakfast directives'; set new targets on the recycled content of packaging and proposed 'ecodesign' requirements; advanced plans to implement 'right2repair' obligations; updated its regulations on the labelling of chemical substances, on geographical indications, and on general product safety; banned mercury in dentistry products and goods containing microplastics; introduced a geographical indication protection for craft and industrial products; is considering introducing minimum standards of cats' and dogs' welfare; and required all vehicles to fit speed limiters and comply with 'Euro 7' emission standards.[70]

In the current *rapprochement* climate and with the PRMA up the government's sleeve, some of the items on this list might be soon targeted for realignment. The UK government has already taken steps to promote the recyclability of electrical waste,[71] held a consultation about aligning with EU rules on machinery safety through the PRMA, and extended producer responsibility for packaging.[72]

(iv) Active Divergence

Active divergence has been scarcer. The long-discussed import ban on *foie gras*, furs, and animal trophies—which cannot be produced in the UK, but can be imported—has not materialized.[73] On mandatory labelling on the packages' recyclability, the UK dropped its plans after the EU noted the trade effects of this product requirement in NI.

The UK plans to launch a deposit return scheme (DRS) for plastic bottles and cans in England and NI in 2027, ahead of comparable EU rules coming into effect in 2029. Scotland can now revive its DRS, which it had shelved due to the chilling effect of UKIMA. Wales is currently holding consultations on a DRS covering also single-use glass.

Recent reforms on the governance of genomic techniques straddle passive and active divergence. An EU proposal to simplify GMO classification (distinguishing between gene editing and genetic modification)[74] follows a comparable UK 2023 measure.[75] However, these measures liberalize some gene-editing techniques, so any

[70] For a detailed account of each measure, the regulatory divergence it entails, and the consequences for the UK, see the quarterly 'UK–EU Divergence Trackers' published by UK in a Changing Europe, https://ukandeu.ac.uk/.

[71] UK Government, 'Online Giants to Pay Their Fair Share for Electrical Waste' (10 December 2024) https://www.gov.uk/government/news/online-giants-to-pay-their-fair-share-for-electrical-waste.

[72] NI Assembly, DAERA response to DSC questions on EU Packaging and Packaging Waste Regulations (PPWR) (January 2025) https://www.niassembly.gov.uk/globalassets/committee-blocks/windsor-framework-democratic-scrutiny-committee/reg-eu-20241143/reg-eu-202540/2/daera---ppwr-questions-jan-2025.pdf.

[73] The Animal Welfare (Live Exports) Bill seeks to ban the export of live animals for fattening and slaughter. If this measure enters into effect the EU will not contest it, as it does not restrict access to the UK market.

[74] Commission, Proposal for a new Regulation on plants produced by certain new genomic techniques (5 July 2023) COM(2023) 411 final.

[75] Genetic Technology (Precision Breeding) Act 2023.

discrepancy (for instance, the EU measure not covering animals) could warrant re-alignment from the UK side, especially if the SPS deal is concluded. The repercussions of this scenario, also regarding the UKIMA and NI angles, are well synthesized as follows.[76]

> The EU is likely to ask the UK to come into line with its somewhat less liberal regime. Alternatively, the UK could push for gene editing policy to be part of the 'short list of limited exemptions' to be included in the SPS deal. This would lead to regulatory divergence between England and the EU as well as rest of the UK (given gene editing is a devolved policy), with implications for ease of export. The more exemptions the UK government negotiates the more friction would remain in GB-EU and GB-NI trade arrangements.

The UK introduced a national 'REACH' registry for chemicals, alternative to the EU one. The UK REACH registration process is leaner than the EU one (and therefore attracted criticism for lowering safety standards); however, businesses have lamented the duplication and costs involved. The registration deadline has been pushed back to late 2026, and later deadlines apply to smaller businesses (2028 and 2030).

(b) Economic Impact

Comparing the TCA to EU membership (instead of other FTAs) is analytically unhelpful, but a before/after-Brexit assessment of trade trends is legitimate. Brexit made UK–EU trade more costly, contracting trade flows and increasing prices. These trade effects (reducing the amount and variety of UK goods exported to the EU) showed up in the data shortly after Brexit.[77]

After falling sharply in 2021, UK–EU exports recovered, but 2024 numbers were still 18 per cent below the 2019 level in real terms,[78] with certain sectors hit harder (agri-food exports declined 34%).[79] According to one estimate, 16,400 businesses stopped exporting to the EU after Brexit.[80] EU imports are also below the pre-Brexit peak in absolute terms.[81]

The hallmarks of this deterioration are the increased costs of living (inflation of consumer prices) and doing business (due to more expensive exporting and

[76] Divergence tracker (n 56) 25.
[77] J Du and others, 'How Did Brexit Affect UK Trade?' (2023) 18 Contemporary Social Science 266, 280.
[78] House of Commons Library, Statistics of UK Trade with the EU (22 April 2025) Research Briefing no. 7851, 10, at https://researchbriefings.files.parliament.uk/documents/CBP-7851/CBP-7851.pdf.
[79] Divergence tracker (n 56) 7.
[80] UK Government, The UK's Trade Strategy (25 July 2025) Policy Paper, 20.
[81] House of Commons (n 78) 11.

importing processes). While the economic volatility of the 2020–25 period makes precise attribution difficult, one recent study found that '[t]he Brexit effect accounted for over 25% of the total inflation variation [of 7% between 2016 and 2024] or . . . a 0.8 percent higher average annual inflation.'[82] Partially, this Brexit-specific effect resulted from currency depreciation (which was insufficient to boost exports), but the majority relates to trade barriers raised after 2021. The NI situation is exceptional also in this regard: by retaining smooth access to the EU, exports appear to have in fact increased after Brexit.[83]

Largely, liberal ROO cumulation provisions in the TCA and UK FTAs prevented capital flight due to tariff-shopping: as far as tariff preferences go, producing in the UK or the EU remains largely comparable.

(c) Territorial Impact within the UK

Insofar as regulatory fragmentation between Westminster and the devolved areas could affect trade in goods, the original post-Brexit plan was that the UKIMA would neutralize it. Concurrently, the UK initially accepted that GB–NI trade would be encumbered by the NI double-rulebook constraint. Both scenarios evolved over time, softening the initial stance, towards more bespoken and responsive models of managing pluralism.

(i) Softening UKIMA Market Access Principles

In summer 2025 the UK government reassessed the UKIMA, following Scotland and Wales's criticism of its chilling effect on devolved legislation.[84] Central to this exercise was the promotion of the Common Frameworks as 'a tool for all governments within the UK to manage instances of divergence which might cause unnecessary cost and trade barriers'.[85] Through this programme, devolved governments can seek, for their regulatory specificities in areas of devolved competences, acknowledgment and immunity from the market access principles (ie the application of local rules to goods produced elsewhere in the UK).

[82] Federico Di Pace and Riccardo Masolo, 'Brexit and the Cost of Living: A Tale of Two Phases' (2025) BCAM Working Paper 2503 14.

[83] BBC, 'NI Protocol: Economic Output May Grow but Prices Could Be Higher' (14 November 2022) at https://www.bbc.co.uk/news/uk-northern-ireland-63620632.

[84] UK Government, Response to the Review of the United Kingdom Internal Market Act 2020 and Public Consultation (15 July 2025) at https://assets.publishing.service.gov.uk/media/686fa10e2cfe301b5fb679d0/uk-government-response-to-the-review-of-the-united-kingdom-internal-market-act-2020-and-public-consultation.pdf.

[85] ibid 12, para 25.

The UK government's favoured use of the Common Frameworks appears now to be a 'four nations' approach. Local governments' proposals are pooled within a multilateral discussion, with a view to introduce an agreed framework of interoperability across national standards. Regulatory harmonization or convergence is the preferred endgame.[86] Alternatively, all other governments can grant an exception to the applicant government or, if there is no consensus, the latter can ask the UK government to authorize a 'reserve' exclusion.

The UK government acknowledged that the range of interests warranting exceptions from the UKIMA market access principles needs extending. It mentioned environmental protection and public health at large in this context, but no other interests.[87] Together with the UK's hesitation to change retained EU law, the inconvenience for a nation to diverge from UK standards probably explains why Scotland and Wales have so far seldom passed laws aligning with runaway EU standards, despite their stated intention to do so systematically.[88] This chilling effect is best exemplified by Scotland initially giving up a bottle-recycling scheme that it could not extend to the rest of the UK.

Some examples of regulatory pluralism in the UKIMA's shadow constraints are the Scotland-led prohibition of single-use plastic (SUP), the four-government approach to banning single-use vapes and wet wipes, and various measures affected by UKIMA's regulatory chill—such as the bans on peat and glue traps.

Scotland prohibited *single-use plastic*, SUP, for certain products in 2022 and obtained from the Secretary of State an UKIMA exclusion[89]—the first ever granted. Similar measures were subsequently taken in England and Wales, covering partially different lists of products, but restrictions on products not covered by the Scottish ban are not exempted from UKIMA. For its part, NI transposed in 2025 the EU SUP Directive, which covers more products. Table 9.1 provides an informative snapshot of the intricacies of autonomous regulations under the Common Frameworks, the UKIMA constraints, and the NI special regime:

[86] Thomas Horsley, 'The UK Internal Market: A Four Nations Strategy on Vaping?' (11 December 2023) UK in a Changing Europe, https://ukandeu.ac.uk/the-uk-internal-market-a-four-nations-strategy-on-vaping/.

[87] Review of UKIMA 2020 (n 84) 5, 14.

[88] Joël Reland, 'Regulating after Brexit' (2025) UK in a Changing Europe 24, https://ukandeu.ac.uk/reports/regulating-after-brexit/. Scottish Parliament, Constitution, Europe, External Affairs and Culture Committee, Annual Report on the Scottish Government's Policy of EU Alignment (21 November 2024); UK Withdrawal from the European Union (Continuity) (Scotland) Act 2021.

[89] The United Kingdom Internal Market Act 2020 (Exclusions from Market Access Principles: Single-use Plastics) Regulations 2022.

Table 9.1

SUP item	England	Scotland	Wales	Northern Ireland	Scope of UKIMA
Plastic stemmed cotton buds	Banned October 2020	Banned October 2019	Banned October 2023	Article 5 SUP Directive to be transposed in 2025	Not in scope—covered by exclusion
Plastic drinking straws		Banned June 2022			
Plastic drinks stirrers					
Plastic cutlery or chopsticks	Banned/restricted October 2023				
Polystyrene food containers, drinks containers, or cups				Article 5 SUP Directive to be transposed in 2025	
Plastic balloon sticks				Article 5 SUP Directive to be transposed in 2025	
Plastic plates					
Plastic bowls or trays		Considering proposals	Considering proposals	Considering proposals	In scope of UKIMA
Plastic carrier bags	No ban proposals	Charge exists for single-use plastic cups. The government ran a call for evidence for some products, eg food containers, bowls & trays, period products, sachets, tobacco filters, and packaging on fruit and vegetables. The call for evidence sought information on the impact the products had on the environment, the market in Scotland, and actions taken elsewhere on them.	To commence bans by May 2026	Considering proposals	
Polystyrene lids for cups (and food containers)				SUP Directive Article 4 consumption reduction to be transposed in 2025	
Plastic tobacco filters			No proposals *(There is arequirement to report on whether consideration has been given to add plastic sauce sachets)*	SUP Directive Article 7 labelling to be transposed in 2025	
Plastic sachets				Proposal in EU Packaging and Packaging Waste Regulation	

(continued)

Table 9.1 Continued

SUP item	England	Scotland	Wales	Northern Ireland	Scope of UKIMA
Plastic single-use cups				SUP Directive Article 4 consumption reduction to be transposed in 2025	
Single-use vapes	Banned from 1 June 2025	Banned from 1 June 2025	Banned from 1 June 2025	Banned from 1 June 2025	
Wet wipes containing plastic	Considering ban in 2026	Considering ban in 2026	Considering ban in 2026	Considering ban in 2026	
Oxo-degradable plastic products	No proposals	Committed to a ban. Currently gathering evidence	To commence bans by Spring 2026	Article 5 SUP Directive to be transposed in 2025	
Single-use disposable beverage cups charge	No proposals	Consultation has been held	No proposals	Considering options to implement Article 6 of SUP Directive for a reduction in SUP beverage cups	

Source: Office for the Internal Market, Report on the Impact of Restrictions on the Sale of Single-use Plastics on the Operation of the UK Internal Market (12 February 2025) OIM 14, 16–17.

In April and October 2024, respectively, the UK government announced the bans of *plastic-containing wet wipes and single-use vapes*. Both measures resulted from a 'four-government approach'[90] which, for the ban on wet wipes, built on inputs by DEFRA and the Welsh government. In these cases, the UK government strived to achieve regulatory uniformity rather than accommodate diversity, 'coordinating intra-UK regulatory policy prospectively as an exercise in shared, not self-rule'.[91]

England's proposal *to prohibit the sale of peat* (lawfully extracted and sold in Scotland and NI) is still at an early stage. Wales has announced a similar measure, while Scotland and NI have no plan to follow suit. Considering a likely prospect of regulatory fragmentation, the UK government noted UKIMA's chilling effect and 'the likelihood that retailers in England might rely on the Market Access Principles to obtain peat-based growing media from elsewhere in the UK once the ban was in place'.[92] A Scottish Environment LINK representative lamented the difficulty of finding four-nation coordination through the Common Frameworks:[93]

> All four Governments across the UK have a policy of seeking to move towards eliminating the use of peat in horticultural practice, . . . but none of them has been able to legislate for it, because they are all caught up in the common frameworks and/or the internal market act. No one wants to go first and be caught out by those processes. We have four Governments of different political persuasions that all have good policy and good intent, but none of them has been able to deliver on that because of the procedures. To me, that seems to be absurd.

For the same reason, Scotland suspended its plan to ban glue traps, after the UK government first refused to grant an UKIMA exclusion in April 2024.[94] In December 2024 the new government granted the exclusion, and plans are under way for a UK-wide ban.

(ii) Northern Ireland Trade under the Windsor Framework and the Stormont Brake

Regulatory and customs integration between Ireland and Northern Ireland preserved the Good Friday Agreement but created a divide between GB and NI, alarming the

[90] Office for the Internal Market, Report on the Impact of Restrictions on the Sale of Single-use Plastics on the Operation of the UK Internal Market (12 February 2025) at https://assets.publishing.service.gov.uk/media/67a9e9ea5dea3871ea1ceac4/Report_on_the_impact_of_restrictions_on_the_sale_of_single-use_plastics_on_the_operation_of_the_UK_Internal_Market_.pdf.

[91] Horslay and Hunt (n 45) 71.

[92] Report on UKIMA (n 90) Annex D, para 14.

[93] Scottish Parliament, Constitution, Europe, External Affairs and Culture Committee, Consultation and Review on the UKIMA 2020 (6 March 2025), statement of Lloyd Austin.

[94] Another pertinent example is Scotland's urging UK-wide derogations for using non-organic substances and non-organically reared livestock where these are not available on the market, see J Zglinski, 'The UK Internal Market: A Global Outlier?' (2023) 82 CLJ 530, 554–55; likewise, Scotland's failed adoption of a deposit return scheme relates to UKIMA's chilling effect, see T Horsley, 'Reforming the UK Internal Market: The UK Government's Response to the Review of the United Kingdom Internal Market Act 2020' (21 July 2025) UK Constitutional Law Association.

Unionist party. The trade-distortive potential of EU–UK regulatory divergence is twofold. First, it undermines NI producers, who must comply with two sets of rules while competing with products subject only to EU rules (and, after the Windsor Framework, some subject only to UK ones). Second, this dual-rulebook system significantly hinders GB–NI trade, as GB producers selling in NI must adapt to EU rules.

In January 2023, the EU and UK approved the Windsor Framework amending the NI Protocol to allow some GB goods to enter the NI without having to comply with EU rules.[95] The double regulatory constraint on GB goods is designed to prevent their uncontrolled reimportation into Ireland from NI; the Windsor Framework exceptions rest on assessing and managing that risk. GB goods judged at a low risk of crossing the Irish border and labelled 'not for EU' face reduced checks and benefit from the UKIMA-like recognition: compliance with UK standards makes them marketable in NI. Similar exceptions apply to medicines and plants, which can move across the Irish Sea on the basis of UK certifications and paperwork rather than the EU's. This arrangement has been crucial for GB food imports—extended since July 2025 to most retail goods—which make up the bulk of NI supermarket stock. However, the covered products must still comply with EU animal and plant health rules and product standards. NI producers, who are not exempted in the same way, can be disadvantaged.

A safeguard protocol applies in cases of passive divergence exposing NI to excessive regulatory costs: for new EU measures to apply in the NI, the UK government must have assessed and approved their impact on GB–NI trade first. Moreover, NI Parliament members can veto new EU rules with a 'significant impact specific to everyday life of communities in Northern Ireland', pulling the so-called Stormont Brake. In this scenario, if the EU and UK cannot find a solution the EU must accept the disapplication of its rules in NI, but is entitled to take countervailing measures, such as trade sanctions or dedicated labelling requirements.

Repeatedly, the UK government has added new EU rules to the Windsor Framework, authorizing their NI application,[96] sometimes without consulting the NI Parliament or overriding its views.[97] Twice, the NI activated the Stormont Brake (on geographical indications for craft products and chemicals' labelling), but unsuccessfully. The UK refused to grant an exception, but pledged to work towards aligning UK standards to the EU ones, filling the regulatory gap. Apparently, in the current course, the UK prefers to use the alignment stone to kill two problematic birds: regulatory divergence from EU and regulatory schizophrenia in NI.[98]

[95] Decision No 1/2023 of the Withdrawal Agreement Joint Committee on laying down arrangements relating to the Windsor Framework, 24 March 2023.

[96] Regulation 2023/2411 on Non-Agricultural Geographical Indications (GIs) [2023] OJ L 27/20/2023; Regulations 2024/1392 and 2024/1501 on Ukraine/Moldova tariff liberalisation [2024] OJ L 29/5/2024; Regulation 2024/1252 on Critical Raw Materials [2024] OJ L 3/5/2024.

[97] This has called into question the effectiveness of the Stormont Brake, see Lord Murphy of Torfaen, Independent Review of the Windsor Framework (September 2025) 16 at https://assets.publishing.service.gov.uk/media/68b59ad53f3e5483efdba87d/Independent_Review_of_the_Windsor_Framework_by_the_Rt_Hon_Lord_Murphy.pdf.

[98] Reland (n 88) 24.

6 Conclusions

Brexit was presented as a deregulatory project. In goods trade, its first-year effects fit that script: EU rules ceased to bind GB, internal divergence was chilled by the UKIMA, and the NI cordoned off the most sensitive risks. Four years on, that picture has changed.

First, on EU–UK relations, the TCA did what FTAs do best: eliminate tariffs and quotas and provide governance channels. However, it lacked the single market's positive integration tools (harmonization and mutual recognition). Border checks, rules of origin, conformity assessment, and product-specific regimes now structure market access. Where alignment matters most (agri-food, chemicals, automotive), frictions persist. The UK's Border Target Operating Model has been rolled out hesitantly; even where the UK has chosen minimal checks, exporters cannot circumvent the EU's formalities.

Second, the TCA's LPF rules provide an insurance policy against regulatory arbitrage. They have not (yet) produced headline disputes in goods, but shape the bilateral talks. The political economy is straightforward: actively lowering domestic standards threatens retaliation; actively raising them burdens exporters and consumers. The path of least resistance has been 'managed proximity': dynamic or selective alignment where the trade payoff is largest (for example, SPS, product safety), plus unilateral recognition (for example, CE/UKCA equivalence) where sovereignty costs are low.

Third, on external policy, the UK has moved quickly to salvage continuity (roll-overs), selectively update agreements (such as Japan, EEA, EFTA states), and add new ones (Australia, New Zealand, CPTPP). The 2025 context of eroding multilateral discipline complicates the path ahead, and the UK's record is erratic: the US EPD promises partial relief from the US's wrath but sits precariously with WTO legality, complicates the relationship with the EU, and offers limited benefits compared to comprehensive FTAs. The India FTA, by contrast, is WTO-compliant and commercially meaningful, but will test business capacity to navigate new origin, customs, and standards disciplines.

Fourth, internal governance has shifted from default suppression of divergence (through UKIMA market-access principles) to a more deliberative 'Common Frameworks' approach. This remains work in progress. Where four-nations coordination succeeded (single-use vapes, wet wipes), policy was delivered with minimal market distortion. Where it stalled (peat), UKIMA's backstop chilled experimentation. The 2025 softening, clearer gateways and wider grounds for justified exclusions, and a presumption in favour of negotiated interoperability demonstrate a more mature (and less absolute) conception of the internal market integrity. However, the UK's grasp on the Common Frameworks process bends its use towards harmonization rather than pluralism.

Fifth, NI illustrates both the costs of dual rulebooks and the value of legal engineering. The Windsor Framework's architecture has eased some GB–NI flows without abandoning EU SPS guarantees. The Stormont Brake adds a political circuit-breaker but its activation threshold is suspiciously high; the default remains technocratic risk-management. Over time, the most durable solution is likely the same as for GB–EU trade more generally: identify where certification and inspection costs most distort everyday commerce, and address them with targeted alignment or risk-managed exceptions.

Looking ahead, three strategic choices dominate: (1) pursue a few deep, standard-heavy accommodations with the EU (SPS, mutual recognition of conformity assessment in defined sectors, ETS linkage), rather than aiming for open-ended rapprochement; (2) entrench the PRMA for rolling alignment and transparency, so that divergence is intentional and costed rather than accidental; (3) use Common Frameworks to anticipate EU changes early, facilitating UKIMA workarounds and NI-specific fixes instead of retrofitting contrived 'four nations' solutions.

The optimal policy is often to choose interdependence on negotiated terms. The UK's emerging doctrine is to accept 'rule-triage' with a substantial element of rule-taking: align where market access depends on it, recognize foreign assurance where it lowers costs without surrendering one's standards, and diverge where there is a clear, evidenced domestic welfare gain.

10
Services

*Gavin Barrett**

1 Introduction: The Importance of Services

The importance of services to modern economies, including the UK's, can scarcely be overstated. The services sector is hugely significant, globally, at EU level, and for the UK. Paradoxically, political attention during the Brexit settlement negotiations was focused on trade in goods. Yet the economic importance of services is greater.

Globally, services represent more than two thirds of world GDP.[1] They account for a lower proportion (25%) of international trade but a growing one,[2] this growth being aided by advances in technology and by the interconnectedness and interdependence of modern economies. In developed economies, a remarkable 74 per cent of employees work in services.[3]

It has been estimated that services contribute more than 70 per cent of the EU's economic output.[4] They account for a lower proportion of cross-border trade, but a highly significant one. The EU collectively is the world's largest services trader,[5]

* My thanks to the organizers of and participants in the 'UK Regulatory Framework Post-Brexit: Law Unbound' Workshop, 13–15 May 2025, for their valuable comments and to Dr Edoardo Rossi and the University of Urbino for hosting me as a visiting researcher while completing this chapter. Any errors remain the author's responsibility.

[1] P Sauvé, 'Services Offer a Springboard to Jobs and Growth for Developing Countries', World Trade Bank blog, https://blogs.worldbank.org/en/trade/services-offer-springboard-jobs-and-growth-developing-countries (accessed 5 June 2025). See also, G Barrett, *Brexit and the Free Movement of Services: Challenges and Regulatory Solutions* in F Kainer and R Repasi (eds), *Trade Relations after Brexit* (Nomos/Hart 2019) 213, 213.

[2] In 2023, global trade in services expanded by 5% in real terms. See generally UNCTAD, 'Services Are Powering Growth. Here's How Developing Nations Can Catch Up', https://unctad.org/news/services-are-powering-growth-heres-how-developing-nations-can-catch (accessed 5 June 2025). Note also House of Lords EU Committee, 'Brexit: Trade in Non-financial Services', 18th Report of Session 2016–17 (HL Paper 135), 10.

[3] United Nations Conference on Trade and Development (UNCTAD), *Trade in Services* (September 2024) 13.

[4] World Economic Forum, 'These Are the EU Countries with the Largest Economies' (1 February 2023) https://www.weforum.org/stories/2023/02/eu-countries-largest-economies-energy-gdp/ (accessed 5 June 2025); European Commission, 'Single Market for Services', European Commission, https://single-market-economy.ec.europa.eu/single-market/services_en#:~:text = Services%20are%20crucial%20to%20the,for%20them%20to%20do%20business (accessed 5 June 2025).

[5] 2023 figures indicate EU services exports to third countries were worth €1.340bn with imports valued at €1.177bn: Eurostat, 'World Trade in Services' (June 2024) https://ec.europa.eu/eurostat/statistics-explained/index.php?title = World_trade_in_services#:~:text = Highlights,to%20trade%20within%20the%20EU (accessed 6 June 2025).

Gavin Barrett, *Services* In: *The UK Regulatory Framework Post-Brexit: 'Law Unbound'*. Edited by: Paul Craig and Vilija Vėlyvytė, Oxford University Press. © Oxford University Press 2026. DOI: 10.1093/9780198969815.003.0012

accounting for more than a quarter of global exports and close to a quarter of global imports.[6]

Service industries now account for 80 per cent of the UK's economic output.[7] The UK is the second largest individual state exporter of services in the world, exporting $584 billion worth of services in 2023, representing a comparatively impressive 15.3 per cent year-on-year growth. By way of context, the US was some way ahead as the world's leading exporter, supplying $1027 billion worth of global services. After the UK come Germany, Ireland, China, and France, in that order.[8] Services account for a large proportion of UK trade, by international standards—54 per cent of exports and 34 per cent of imports.[9] Unlike in the case of goods,[10] the UK has a surplus with the EU in services, exporting £184bn of services to it and importing £141bn worth.[11]

It is not commonly realized that the vast bulk of services exported by the UK is non-financial in nature, covering areas such as (i) so-called other business services (a catch-all category comprising professional and management consulting services,[12] technical and trade-related business services,[13] and research and development services); (ii) travel services; (iii) information computer and telecommunications services; and (iv) transport services. In the four quarters to the end of March 2025, such service exports had a total value of £334.2 billion (close to 65% of all services exports and 38% of UK exports as a whole). Financial service exports were worth £104.1 billion, corresponding to 20 per cent of total service exports and just under 12 per cent of exports generally.[14] Non-financial services also give rise to vastly more jobs.[15]

[6] In 2022, the EU was responsible for 25.2% of global service exports and 23.4% of imports: ibid.

[7] G Hutton and K Zaidi, 'Industries in the UK', House of Commons Library Research Briefing No 8353 (3 Oct 2024) 1–2.

[8] UNCTAD, *Trade in Services* (Sept 2024). Such statistics can mislead, however: it is particularly difficult to measure the impact of (a) foreign-controlled enterprises and subsidiaries providing services and (b) services provisions involving a person moving from one country to another.

[9] M Ward, 'Geographical Pattern of UK Trade', Research Briefing, House of Commons Library (13 Dec 2024) 5. In 2024, the value of UK exports was £873.5bn: £507.8bn worth of services, £365.7bn by goods (Department for Business and Trade, 'UK Trade in Numbers (Web Version)—Official Statistics (23 May 2025) https://www.gov.uk/government/statistics/uk-trade-in-numbers/uk-trade-in-numbers-web-version (accessed 6 June 2025).

[10] In 2024, UK goods exports to the EU were worth £177bn, mirroring its exports to the rest of the world, worth £181bn. The UK imported £302bn worth of goods from the EU (mirroring its imports from the rest of the world, worth £301bn).

[11] D Webb and M Ward, 'Statistics on UK Trade with the EU', Research Briefing, House of Commons Library (22 Apr 2025) 12–13; Department for Business & Trade, 'UK Trade in Numbers' (19 June 2025); (for earlier figures), House of Lords EU Committee Beyond Brexit: Trade in Services (HL Paper 248, March 2021) 3. All top three UK global exports are services, not goods: so-called other business services (worth £186.9bn in the four quarters to the end of March 2025); financial services (worth £104.1bn); and travel services (worth £67.7bn) (Department for Business & Trade (n 9) 7).

[12] Including legal, accounting, management consulting, public relations, advertising, and market research.

[13] Including architectural, engineering, and scientific services.

[14] Source: author's calculations, based on Department for Business and Trade, *UK Trade in Numbers* (19 Jun 2025).

[15] In March 2025 there were 33.98 million people aged 16 and over employed in the UK, B Francis-Devine and A Powell, 'UK Labour Market Statistics', House of Commons Library Research Briefing, 13

Liberalized EU services trade is difficult to achieve, notwithstanding its economic importance, and harder to bring about than in goods. Services exist in many forms. Some can be traded online. Others, such as medical or dental treatment, are provided in person and hence require the free movement of persons. Other services may be embedded in goods, for example computer software. The GATS provides for four kinds of service delivery: (i) cross-border provision from one state to another; (ii) the consumer crossing the border to the provider; (iii) provision via a subsidiary/branch of the service provider; and (iv) the service provider crossing the border temporarily.[16]

Guaranteeing market access and establishing non-discrimination are insufficient to liberalize trade in services, but merely the start of what is needed. Frequently, the greatest market access barriers are authorization, licensing, or certification formalities.[17] Mutual recognition of professional qualifications and free movement of persons may also be key, depending on the services.

The slowness of integration in the EU services field can also be explained by there being no equivalent to the Common Commercial Policy here, no harmonized trade policy for services trade with third countries.[18] A services single market is also a more recent development than in goods, with a Services Directive only since 2006. A single digital services market is still under construction.[19]

The EU single market in services (although the most integrated international market worldwide, and gradually deepening[20]) is less integrated than that in goods. Exclusion thus always seemed potentially less dramatic in its consequences for post-Brexit Britain.

Considerable integration has nonetheless occurred, requiring mutual member state confidence, mutual scrutiny, and pioneering harmonization techniques:[21]

May 2025. A staggering 84.8% of UK jobs are in services. Just 3.1% are directly in finance and insurance. However, many other jobs in services areas such as professional services are clearly related to activity in the financial services sector, Hutton and Zaidi (n 7) 3–4. TheCityUK, which represents UK-based financial and related services, claims more ambitiously that financial services employ almost 1.1m people in the UK (corresponding to 3.4% of all employees) and that more than 2.4 m people (7.5% of UK employees) work in financial and related professional services, TheCityUK, 'Key Facts about UK-based Financial and Related Professional Services 2024', https://www.thecityuk.com/media/kdwbete3/key-facts-about-uk-based-financial-and-related-professional-services-2024.pdf.

[16] Article I:2 GATS; and World Trade Organisation (Trade in Services and Investment Division), 'The General Agreement on Trade in Services—An Introduction' (Sept 2022) 3.

[17] J Jacobsson, 'Brexit and the Professional Services Sector—What Future for UK Professionals in Europe?', DCU Brexit Institute Working Paper 01-2020.

[18] House of Lords EU Committee, 'Brexit: Trade in Non-financial Services', 18th Report of Session 2016–17 (HL Paper 135) 86.

[19] See (n 18) 90. Note further conclusions of Draghi Report, *The Future of European Competitiveness*, https://commission.europa.eu/document/download/97e481fd-2dc3-412d-be4c-f152a8232961_en?filename = The%20future%20of%20European%20competitiveness%20_%20A%20competitiveness%20strategy%20for%20Europe.pdf, commented on in what follows.

[20] See (n 18) 29.

[21] ibid 10.

> [T]he deep integration of the EU has been possible because of mutual trust, (close enough) common values and effective policies to secure a level playing field across the member states. The presence of all these three elements, coupled with the powers of the Commission and the Court, is evident in the area of professional qualifications where the EU is a global pioneer in the systematic mutual recognition of qualifications among its member states.

2 Free Movement of Services in EU Law

In EU law, provision for free movement of services is made in Title IV, Chapter 3 TFEU, Articles 56–62. However, other primary and secondary EU law provisions also have a role.[22] Much of Title IV, Chapter 2 TFEU, concerning freedom of establishment, applies to services provision.[23] Cross-border service provision is also supported by horizontal secondary law measures, such as the 2006 Services Directive;[24] Decision 2018/646, (providing tools for the documentation of skills and qualifications, widely used through the Europass internet-based information system);[25] the European Qualifications Framework[26] (allowing comparison of qualifications obtained across different education and training systems); and the umbrella Directive 2005/36, consolidating professional qualifications recognition law, replacing much earlier legislation on the topic, and moving decisively away from the ambitious but time-consuming sectoral earlier harmonization approach.[27] (Some sectoral legislation remains in force, such as the 1977 Lawyers' Services Directive.[28]) There is also more general *legislation*, such as the 2004 Citizens' Directive,[29] providing for the free movement of

[22] See generally, P Craig and G de Búrca, *EU Law—Text, Cases and Materials* (8th edn, Oxford University Press 2024) Ch 23. B van Leeuwen, 'Repositioning Free Movement of Services: A Substantive Perspective on the Structure and Dynamics of the Internal Market' (2025) 62 CMLRev 1 provides a recent perspective on ECJ services case law.

[23] Art 62 TFEU applies Arts 51–54 TFEU to services.

[24] Directive 2006/123/EC of the European Parliament and the Council of 12.12.2006 on services in the internal market [2006] OJ L376/36; J Flower, 'Negotiating European Legislation: The Services Directive' (2007) 9 CYELS 217.

[25] Decision (EU) 2018/646 of the European Parliament and the Council of 18.4.2018 on a common framework for the provision of better services for skills and qualifications (Europass) and repealing Decision No 2241/2004/EC [2018] OJ L112/42.

[26] Recommendation of the European Parliament and the Council of 23.4.2008 on the establishment of the European Qualifications Framework for lifelong learning [2008] OJ C111/1.

[27] Directive 2005/36/EC of the European Parliament and the Council of 7.9.2005 on the recognition of professional qualifications [2005] OJ L255/22.

[28] Council Directive 77/249/EEC of 22.3.1977 to facilitate the effective exercise by lawyers of freedom to provide services [1977] OJ L78/17. General practitioners, nurses, veterinary surgeons, pharmacists, and architects have also been the subject of sectoral measures on mutual recognition of qualifications. There have also been directives concerning particular industries and sectors of the economy such as food and beverages, the coal trade, and the wholesale, intermediary, and retail sectors, see further Craig and de Búrca (n 22) 860 *et seq*.

[29] Directive 2004/38/EC of the European Parliament and the Council of 29.4.2004 on the right of citizens of the Union and their family members to move and reside freely within the territory of the member states [2004] OJ L158/77.

persons required by many service providers. Other services-relevant laws include health-relevant measures (for example, the Cross-Border Healthcare Directive[30]), worker-relevant measures (for example, the Posted Workers Directive[31]), and digitally related measures (for example, the Electronic Commerce Directive).[32]

3 Post-Brexit Regulation in the UK

(a) The Trade and Cooperation Agreement

Given what was then UK government willingness to tolerate supranational governance, it never seemed likely that a high level of EU–UK integration concerning services trade would emerge from the Brexit negotiations. Deterioration in conditions for EU–UK cross-border services provision duly occurred.

The Withdrawal Agreement of January 2020 contained—as might be expected, given its focus on UK departure rather than the economics of the subsequent mutual relationship—relatively little on services. It did provide for continued application of the *acquis*, including services-related rules, until the end of the year-long post-Brexit transition period on 31 December 2020.[33]

The Trade and Cooperation Agreement (TCA) was subsequently signed on 30 December 2020, formally entering into force on 1 May 2021.[34] Its more detailed provisions concerning services were welcomed by UK business, although perhaps mostly because the alternative was no deal.[35]

The TCA is a free trade agreement. These vary greatly in the market access they provide. What they have in common is that they provide only access. They do not exempt from the duty to comply with local regulations. In contrast, single market rules involve mutual recognition, harmonized rules, and a more level playing field regarding competition, social standards, environmental standards, and data protection. A single market involves a single regulatory space.[36] A free trade agreement involves two distinct ones.

[30] Dir 2005/36 (n 27) codifies ECJ case law on Art 56 TFEU, Case C-777/18 *WO* EU:C:2020:745, [65].

[31] Directive 96/71/EC of the European Parliament and of the Council of 16 December 1996 concerning the posting of workers in the framework of the provision of services [1997] OJ L18/1.

[32] Directive 2000/31/EC of the European Parliament and Council of 8.6.2000 on certain legal aspects of information society services, in particular electronic commerce, in the Internal Market [2000] OJ L178/1.

[33] Art 127(1).

[34] On approval by the European Parliament having been provisionally applied from 1 Jan 2021; I Borchert and M Morita-Jaeger, 'Taking Stock of the UK-EU Trade and Cooperation Agreement: Trade in Services and Digital Trade', UK Trade Policy Observatory Briefing Paper 53 (Jan 2021); K Lannoo, 'On the Fringes: EU–UK Financial Services under the TCA', CEPS (5 Mar 2021).

[35] G Riddell of Ernst and Young, quoted in House of Lords EU Committee, 'Beyond Brexit: Trade in Services' (n 11) 3.

[36] And, to some extent, a common administrative space with agencies concerned with the vindication of consumer rights.

Part Two, Heading One, Title II TCA covers services and investment. Financial services and audio-visual services, both highly important to the UK, went unmentioned, although a brief Joint Declaration[37] envisaged a Memorandum of Understanding establishing a framework for structured regulatory cooperation on financial services, which was done in late March 2021.[38]

Even for the services it covered, the TCA provided thin fare, offering trans-frontier service trade providers and investors merely the usual market access plus non-discrimination commitments commonly found in FTAs—something far removed from a single services market. In consequence,[39]

> as a general principle, UK service suppliers will have to comply with host-country rules in each EU Member State, in particular with regard to the recognition of professional qualifications but also in terms of licensing. The country-of-origin principle for regulating the cross-border trade of financial services, known as 'passporting', will also no longer apply. Overall . . . the TCA represents a major setback for services sectors, for some more so than for others.

Major service sectors such as professional and business services, financial services, aviation, and road haulage now faced substantial new barriers (notwithstanding efforts to show ambition regarding telecommunications, digital trade, and international maritime trade).[40]

Moreover, TCA provisions were made subject to an (expandable[41]) list of EU and national reservations. UK service exporters thus suddenly found themselves selling into a patchwork of national markets. Fundamentally differently to the case in goods (where goods supplied to the EU market might have to meet customs, health, or veterinary requirements but then enjoy free circulation), the member state in which UK services are being sold now takes on crucial significance. For small businesses,[42] such fragmentation constitutes a trade barrier. The uncertainty is even greater than might first appear since the reservation by each member state merely creates a *right*: in practice this right may not be relied on.[43]

Other hidden risks also lurk in the TCA. Although Part Two, Title III purports to facilitate digital trade,[44] Article 202 stipulates that nothing in the TCA shall prevent a party from adopting or maintaining measures on personal data protection

[37] Joint Declaration on Financial Services Regulatory Cooperation between EU and UK.

[38] J Brunsden and P Foster, 'UK and EU Reach Financial Regulation Deal in Breakthrough on Cooperation', *Financial Times* (26 Mar 2021). The Memorandum established a Joint UK–EU Financial Regulatory Forum to facilitate dialogue regarding financial services.

[39] Borchert and Morita-Jaeger (n 33) 2.

[40] ibid.

[41] Annex Servin-1 sets out current reservations. Annex Servin-2 allows the EU and UK to adopt new reservations in stipulated fields.

[42] Note evidence given by Federation of Small Businesses to House of Lords, House of Lords EU Committee *Beyond Brexit: Trade in Services* (n 11) 25.

[43] ibid 24.

[44] Art 196 TCA.

and privacy, including regarding cross-border data transfers. Since December 2025, the UK has benefited from extensions of two 2021 adequacy decisions with the UK, which will now maintain free data flow with the UK until 27 December 2031. After this, and once the legislative process on the UK's 2024 Data Bill ends, the Commission must assess whether the UK continues to provide adequate personal data protection.

The TCA was described by then-Prime Minister Boris Johnson, *inter alia,* as 'a comprehensive Canada-style free trade deal'.[45] In many respects it does resemble earlier EU FTAs, containing the usual provisions requiring market access,[46] national treatment,[47] most-favoured-nation treatment,[48] and the absence both of quotas and of requirements of local presence.[49] Yet this pales in comparison to what EU member states offer each other, reflecting a barren landscape at international level.

TCA provisions on legal services did go beyond earlier FTAs.[50] But the gains made were very limited: 'designated legal services' are merely 'legal services in relation to home jurisdiction law and public international law, excluding Union law',[51] and 'legal services' do not include legal representation before courts or administrative agencies.[52] Moreover, other Brexit-associated travails, such as loss of UK access to the Lugano Convention,[53] reduce UK-based legal dispute resolution services' attractiveness.

Three major TCA-applied limits are (i) those that apply regarding mobility of persons; (ii) those that apply to the recognition of professional qualifications, and (iii) the loss of mutual recognition of home state standards.

Regarding free movement of persons, the TCA established a mutual regime: various categories of business visitor obtained varying rights to enter and reside.[54] Apart from length-of-stay limits, there may also be work permit or visa requirements and even economic needs tests, depending on what national reservations have been made.[55] The overall impact of these new restrictions was expected to be severe and the new regime appears to have had a major impact, for example, on young persons providing seasonal tourism-related experiences (such as ski lessons) on the continent.

Second, with the TCA, full mutual recognition of professional status has ended;[56] UK nationals in the EU are third-country nationals and have to seek recognition

[45] Prime Minister's statement on EU negotiations of 24 December 2020 quoted in S Fella and others, *The UK–EU Trade and Cooperation Agreement: Summary and Implementation* (Briefing Paper 09106, 30.12.2020) 16.
[46] Arts 128 and 135 TCA.
[47] Arts 129 and 137 TCA.
[48] Arts. 130 and 138 TCA.
[49] Arts 132 and 136 TCA.
[50] See generally Part II, Heading One, Title II, Section 7 TCA.
[51] Art 193 TCA.
[52] ibid.
[53] J Brunsden and K Beioley, 'Brussels Opposes UK Bid to Join Legal Pact, Splitting EU States', *Financial Times* (12 May 2021).
[54] Annex Servin-3. Discussed in House of Lords EU Committee, 'Beyond Brexit: Trade in Services' (n 11) 28 *et seq.*
[55] Borchert and Morita-Jaeger (n 34).
[56] The TCA grants lawyers only very limited rights to advise on international and home jurisdiction law under home jurisdiction titles (Part Two, Chapter 5, Section 7 TCA).

for their professional qualifications through reliance on national EU member state rules.[57] This is an important limit. Most services are provided by people, and 'access to a country is of little value if one cannot practice one's profession there'.[58] Securing recognition of professional qualifications has accurately been characterized as being as crucial as market access.[59] Outside the 'complex system of mutual trust and mutual spying' which has allowed mutual recognition agreements to flourish within the EU,[60] agreed mutual recognition of professional qualifications occurs infrequently, and tends to be negotiated slowly. The weak mutual recognition provisions found in the TCA reflect this reality.

Third, limits stem from the loss of mutual recognition of home state standards, as in the ending of passporting in financial services, discussed below.

Ways exist around such limitations, such as establishing a business or branch within the EU which might profit from free movement rights. However, such remedies tend to be less open to small businesses.

(b) A Regional Perspective

Although service provision tends to be most closely associated with London, there are also regional perspectives and concerns.[61] Hence for example, as regards Northern Ireland, the all-Ireland services market which this region formerly constituted (thanks to common EU membership) has now been left with 'shaky legal foundations' post-Brexit.[62] Unlike the situation in goods, there is now a border, albeit one that does not require border controls and that is a 'soft' border for a number of other reasons as well. First, the single market in services is less solid than that in goods. Second, the services border can be avoided by establishing undertakings or branches on the other side, or obtaining professional qualifications there or citizenship.[63] Third, several factors are

[57] European Commission Notice to Stakeholders; Withdrawal of the United Kingdom and EU Rules in the Field of Regulated Professions and the Recognition of Professional Qualifications (Brussels, 21 June 2018). See also I. Jozepa, 'UK–EU Trade and Cooperation Agreement; Professional Qualifications', House of Commons Briefing Paper 9172, 25 March 2021,1; Anon., 'UK–EU Trade and Cooperation Agreement: Implications for Universities', Universities UK analysis (22 April 2021).

[58] Jacobsson (n 17) 2 and 4.

[59] ibid.

[60] K Nicolaides, 'Mutual Recognition: Promise and Denial, from Sapiens to Brexit' (2017) 70 CLP 1, quoted by Jacobsson (n 17) 12.

[61] G Barrett, 'Free Movement of Services' in C McCrudden (ed), *The Law and Practice of the Ireland-Northern Ireland Protocol* (Cambridge University Press 2022) Ch 21.

[62] Tweet by D Henig @DavidHenigUK, 26 February 2020.

[63] In 2024 the number of British applications to the Foreign Births Register, a citizenship route for people with Irish grandparents/parents, was 23,456 (A Borrett, 'Irish Citizenship Applications from Britain Hit Post-Brexit Peak', *Financial Times* (24 February 2025). Approximately 120,000 British nationals have acquired Irish citizenship this way since 2016. Approximately 90,000 other Britons have acquired EU passports by other routes, such as naturalization (M Vink, 'The Brexit Naturalisation Effect: An Update Eight Years After the Referendum', Blog post, EUI Global Citizenship Observatory (6 March 2025) https://globalcit.eu/the-brexit-naturalisation-effect-an-update-eight-years-after-the-referendum/. The entry into force of the British Nationality (Irish Citizens) Act 2024 in July 2025 eased conditions under which Irish citizens

moderating the damage done to the all-island services market by Brexit (for example, limited recourse by Ireland to reservations, the Common Travel Area's existence, cross-border similarity in professional regulations and legal structures, and the desire of Ireland to limit Brexit's impact on Northern Ireland). To some extent, Ireland can function as a stepping stone permitting Northern Irish (and UK) service providers to access the single market by permitting establishment and mutual recognition of professional qualifications in an EU member state with the same legal and organizational culture and language. Not every element of the EU-created all-island market in services can be reconstituted by such means, however. Small enterprises appear particularly vulnerable.

(c) The May 2025 Common Understanding: Resetting Relations?

The Labour government elected in July 2024 promised to 'reset' relations with the EU. Two objectives in the Labour Party election manifesto concerning this 'reset' related specifically to services, namely, the commitments (i) to help touring artists; and (ii) to reach agreement on recognizing professional qualifications, thus opening EU markets for affected service exporters. The Commission sought a mandate to open negotiations on creating the possibility for EU students to study in UK universities.[64] After the London UK–EU Summit of May 2025 (preceded by confidential negotiations), a European Commission–UK Government Common Understanding was published. Commitments regarding services were limited. They were also vague, required further negotiation, and were not legal texts. There was a commitment to work towards a balanced youth experience scheme, but on terms to be agreed. Moreover, although the Understanding recognized 'the value of travel and cultural and artistic exchanges, including the activities of touring artists', it committed the parties merely 'to continue their efforts to support travel and cultural exchange'. The Understanding was silent regarding mutual professional qualifications recognition and contained no more than a commitment to continue exchanges on smooth border management for the benefit

may obtain a UK passport (Anon, 'Easier Routes to British Citizenship Open Up for Irish', Law Society of Ireland Gazette, 9 July 2025).

[64] Recommendation for a Council Decision authorising the opening of negotiations for an agreement between the EU and the UK on youth mobility (COM/2024/169 final); C Coleman, 'Youth Mobility Schemes', House of Lords Library Briefing (27 Jan 2025) https://lordslibrary.parliament.uk/youth-mobility-schemes/ ; Scottish Parliament Information Centre, 'The European Commission's Proposal for an EU–UK Youth Mobility Agreement' (19 April 2024) https://spice-spotlight.scot/2024/04/19/the-european-commissions-proposal-for-an-eu-uk-youth-mobility-agreement/ (accessed 5 June 2025). Shortly before this book went to press, on 15 April 2026, it was announced that the EU and the UK had enabled the UK's association to Erasmus+ in 2027, by adopting an amendment to Protocol I of the EU–UK Trade and Cooperation Agreement, thereby facilitating *inter alia* renewed student exchanges between the UK and the EU.

of citizens.[65] The Understanding did not focus on services and EU resistance to UK cherry-picking the single market seemingly persists.

4 UK Legislative Developments since Brexit

Brexit led to the enactment of several statutes. The EU (Notification of Withdrawal) Act 2017 processed departure itself. The European Union (Withdrawal) Act 2018 then established the primacy of retained EU law over earlier legislation (but not legislation enacted from 2021). The European Union (Withdrawal Agreement) Act 2020 implemented the Withdrawal Agreement domestically, providing for direct application of its provisions.

The EU (Future Relationship) Act 2020 applied the TCA domestically, incorporating some provisions into UK law,[66] deploying a general implementation clause for others,[67] and empowering ministers/devolved administrations to implement others using secondary legislation.[68]

The Retained EU Law (Revocation and Reform) Act 2023 Act revoked much 'retained EU law', renaming the remainder 'assimilated law' and changing its status so that courts could depart from retained case law, disapplying EU law principles as interpretative guidance, and repealing unassimilated directly effective EU rights, thus creating the prospect of divergence from EU law in the services field and others.

The UK Internal Market Act 2020 sought to preserve the UK's internal market post-Brexit, enabling free work and trade freely across the entire UK.[69] Part 2 governs access to the UK services market. A service provider is a person who provides a service in the course of their business or intends to and who has a permanent UK establishment through which the business is wholly/partly conducted.

The 2020 Act establishes two UK market access principles: mutual recognition and non-discrimination. Under the former, someone authorized to provide services in one part of the UK requires no additional authorization requirements to provide them elsewhere in the UK. Under the latter (subject to limited justifications[70]), a regulatory requirement discriminating against a would-be service provider directly/indirectly is ineffective.

These principles apply only to new or substantively changed requirements, however. Existing requirements are excluded from their ambit.[71] However (and crucially,

[65] Paras 13–16 of the Understanding. A commitment to explore the participation of the UK in the EU internal electricity market (paras 18–21), involving a rather specialist topic, is not further examined here.

[66] EU (Future Relationship) Act 2020, ss 23–25 on road haulage services.

[67] ibid s 29.

[68] ibid s 31.

[69] Explanatory Notes to the Act.

[70] Direct discrimination is permitted to the extent it is a reasonably justified response to a public health emergency. Indirect discrimination is only justified if it can be reasonably considered a necessary means of achieving a 'legitimate aim'.

[71] Provisions that have entered into force after the Act but simply re-enact or replicate pre-existing requirements without substantively changing them do not come within the scope of the Act.

in practice), Schedule 2 lists an enormous list of services falling outside either or both principles.[72]

The Office for the Internal Market (OIM) (which is within the Competition and Markets Authority (CMA)) administers this internal market, but because of the above-mentioned exclusions has little services-related work.

The 2020 Act also introduced a professional qualifications recognition system, allowing professionals qualified in one part of the UK to access professions (access to which is legally regulated) in another without the need to requalify. These provisions apply only where new requirements are introduced, or existing ones are changed. Other provisions ensure equal treatment regarding the practice of a profession (unless differentiation is justified).

5 UK–Non-EU Country Agreements Concerning Services

(a) Rollover Treaties

The UK stopped benefiting from EU trade agreements with the end of the transition period on 31 December 2021. The UK government then sought to reach similar agreements with the countries concerned: so-called 'rollover' agreements.

The plan met with considerable success. Within six months, almost forty trade agreements had been reached. At the time of writing, the UK has agreements with more than seventy-eight countries (excluding the 27 EU member states covered by the TCA).[73]

There were some complications. Some such agreements were stripped of earlier deeper regulatory commitments (for example, arrangements on services) and rolled over as basic agreements ensuring tariff-free trade in goods.[74] Others were instead supplemented by further agreements (for example, the 2022 UK–Singapore Digital Economy Agreement providing for financial services and the 2022 UK–Ukraine Digital Trade Agreement providing for services). Some rollover agreements have now been replaced by newer deals, invariably covering services:[75] the UK–Japan Comprehensive Economic Partnership Agreement went beyond rollover terms in areas such as financial services.[76]

The UK also agreed several trade treaties with countries that had no free trade agreement with the EU when Brexit occurred.

[72] In consequence, the Office for the Internal Market Panel, which advises on the effective operation of the UK's internal market, receives hardly any queries concerning services.

[73] Figures up to date as of 7 Feb 2025.

[74] The agreements with Turkey, Switzerland, and South Korea lack substantial provisions on services.

[75] New Treaties were agreed with Norway, Liechtenstein, and Iceland (with a chapter on services and investment), Canada (covering services), and Israel (covering the right of establishment and supply of services).

[76] See Ch 8. This did not however go significantly beyond what was conceded to the EU by Japan.

(b) Australia

The 2021 UK–Australia Free Trade Agreement was the first such agreement. Chapter 8 addresses cross-border services trade and contains clauses on market access, non-discrimination, and most-favoured-nation status. It abjures both quotas and local presence requirements for services provision.[77] It establishes a Committee on Services and Investment to monitor Chapter 8's implementation. Financial services, audio-visual services, and (most) air services are, however, excluded. The agreement was criticized for being too favourable to Australia, particularly in its provisions concerning agriculture.[78] Independent modelling undertaken of the deal predicted UK output increase of merely 0.07 per cent in tradable industries, and an exports increase of 0.35 per cent.[79] The Government 2021 Impact Assessment estimated that the agreement would increase UK GDP by 0.06 per cent to 0.10 per cent by 2035, with a central estimated increase of 0.08 per cent.[80] Such limited overall effects are unsurprising. Australia accounted for less than 2 per cent of UK goods/services exports and less than 1 per cent of imports. Barriers to trade were already low, particularly regarding trade in services, as measured by the OECD's Services Trade Restrictiveness Index.[81]

(c) New Zealand

The 2022 UK–New Zealand Free Trade Agreement contained far more extensive provision on services: a chapter on free movement of services providing for market access, non-discrimination, and most-favoured-nation status and rejecting quotas and local presence requirements;[82] annexes on (respectively) professional services, professional qualifications recognition, and international maritime services; a separate chapter on financial services;[83] and an annex on cross-border financial services

[77] The Agreement also has an Annex making provision for express delivery services.

[78] G Parker, J Evans, J Pickard, P Foster, and J Smyth, 'UK Offers Australia a Tariff-free Trade Deal despite Farmers' Fears', *Financial Times* (21 May 2021). Just before this book went to print, in March 2026, the EU and Australia reached agreement on an arguably much less unbalanced trade deal (See A Bounds and N Fildes, 'EU and Australia clinch trade and security pacts', *Financial Times* (24 March 2026). Insofar as concerns services, the deal promised improved access for EU firms to the professional and business services, maritime transport and financial services markets, as well as setting rules on data flows and prohibiting data localization requirements, an important step for digital and tech companies.

[79] M Gasiorek and G Larbalestier, 'UK–Australia FTA—Elbow Bumps and All', UK Trade Policy Observatory, University of Sussex (16 June 2021); D Webb, 'UK–Australia Free Trade Agreement', House of Commons Library Research Briefing (12 May 2023) 19.

[80] Department for Business and Trade and Department for International Trade, 'UK–Australia FTA: Impact Assessment: Economic Assessment of the Impact of the Free Trade Agreement between the United Kingdom of Great Britain and Northern Ireland and Australia' (16 Dec 2021).

[81] D Webb, 'UK–Australia Free Trade Agreement', House of Commons Library Research Briefing (12 May 2023) 19 *et seq.*

[82] Ch 9.

[83] Ch 11.

trade. Separate chapters also cover telecommunications, temporary entry of business persons, investment, and digital trade.[84] A Services and Investment Sub-Committee monitors cooperation and considers possible expansions.

The agreement's economic effect is small, however. The UK government's Impact Assessment estimated GDP as only 0.03 per cent higher in 2035 because of the agreement, and even that was uncertain. This was because of the small volume of trade conducted with New Zealand and the fact that trade barriers were already fairly low in any case.[85]

The Trade (Australia and New Zealand) Act 2023 facilitated implementation of both the Australia and New Zealand trade agreements.

(d) Comprehensive and Progressive Agreement for Trans-Pacific Partnership

In December 2024 the UK joined the Comprehensive and Progressive Agreement for Trans-Pacific Partnership (CPTPP), an Asia-Pacific trade bloc made up of eleven countries: Australia, Brunei Darussalam, Canada, Chile, Japan, Malaysia, Mexico, New Zealand, Peru, Singapore, and Vietnam. The economic benefits are small. The government's impact assessment estimated a long-term increase in GDP of only £2 billion (0.06%), as the UK already had bilateral trade agreements with nine of eleven CPTPP countries, and conducted only limited trade with CPTPP countries anyway.

Service sectors were supposed to benefit significantly from the agreement. In 2022, services accounted for 45 per cent of UK trade with CPTPP countries. CPTPP provisions largely concern preventing market access barriers, ensuring UK services providers in key sectors will be treated equivalently to local businesses, and prohibiting residence and local office requirements. The services chapter applies to all services, absent national opt-outs. The CPTPP omits mutual professional qualifications recognition but merely encourages cooperation. It provides for electronic payment card services, and facilitates portfolio management across CPTPP countries. It also has a chapter on Temporary Entry for Business Persons.

Stakeholders generally welcomed the CPTPP provisions on services, even if noting their supersession by trade agreements with Japan, New Zealand, and Australia. The House of Lords International Agreements Committee did too, although cautioning that benefits might be more limited than the government suggested, highlighting the lack of CPTPP provisions on mutual recognition of professional qualifications.[86]

[84] Chs 12 to 15.

[85] House of Commons Library, 'New Zealand–United Kingdom Free Trade Agreement', House of Commons Library Research Briefing (12 May 2023).

[86] D Webb, 'The Comprehensive and Progressive Agreement for Trans-Pacific Partnership', House of Commons Library Research Briefing (16 Dec 2024).

(e) India

In May 2025 the UK concluded a free trade agreement with India, expected to be the world's third largest economy by 2028 and a particularly important service provider to the UK—the fourth largest in 2024, supplying 4.7 per cent of UK imports.[87]

Full details have not yet been published, only chapter summaries,[88] and agreement is outstanding in some areas.[89] However, there is a financial services chapter, seemingly (and typically for a free trade agreement) largely about market access and non-discrimination. The deal purportedly secures UK companies' ability to deliver financial services to Indian clients. Up to 74 per cent UK ownership/investment in Indian insurance/banking firms will be permitted. The importance of developing conditions for cross-border electronic payments is recognized and commitments are made to cooperate on FinTech, diversity in finance, promoting financial stability, and improving market integration. The deal includes non-discrimination rules and comprehensive transparency commitments regarding authorization of financial services firms and regulatory measures.[90]

The agreement seeks to reduce barriers to digital trade and promote the compatibility of digital trading systems, including through supporting legal recognition of electronic contracts and electronic authentication.[91]

An annex to the agreement covers professional services, committing the UK and India to identify and encourage mutually interested UK and Indian relevant bodies to enter into negotiations on arrangements for recognition of professional qualifications. It establishes a Professional Services Working Group as a forum for UK and Indian officials in this regard.[92]

Overall, this agreement is strikingly weak on services, hence complaints of a 'lack of progress'.[93] Thus the 'General Provisions and Exceptions' chapter will permit both parties to adopt measures otherwise contravening the agreement, incorporates the General Exceptions found in the GATS, and contains a provision recalling the exclusions and exceptions found elsewhere in the agreement applicable to the NHS.[94] The Law Society has further criticized the failure to include legal services in the agreement.[95]

[87] Department for Business and Trade, 'Factsheets—India' (2 May 2025).

[88] UK Government, 'UK–India Trade Deal: Conclusion Summary' (6 May 2025) https://www.gov.uk/government/publications/uk-india-trade-deal-conclusion-summary/uk-india-trade-deal-conclusion-summary#introduction.

[89] Negotiations on a bilateral investment treaty (BIT) are reportedly ongoing at the time of writing: 'UK–India Free Trade Agreement', Research Briefing, House of Commons Library (9 May 2025).

[90] See (n 88) 4.10.

[91] ibid 4.7.

[92] ibid 4.17.

[93] 'The Britain–India Trade Deal Is a Sign of Things to Come', *The Economist* (7 May 2025).

[94] See (n 88) 4.3.

[95] Law Society, 'UK–India Trade Deal Misses the Target on Legal Services Market Access', press release (6 May 2025).

(f) USA

The US approach to trade since Donald Trump took office is dominated by a focus on goods rather than services, in line with his political priorities. In March 2025, Trump imposed a 25 per cent tariff on aluminium, steel, and derivative goods imports from the UK. From 3 April, a 25 per cent tariff was imposed on passenger vehicles and light trucks. Tariffs of 25 per cent on automobile parts were implemented on 3 May. From 5 April 2025, a 10 per cent baseline tariff was imposed on imports from the UK, affecting most goods.[96]

Although the tariffs concern goods, not services, the danger existed that retaliatory action against US unilateralism might lead to conflict over services. Ultimately, there was no retaliation. Instead, negotiations quickly led to the 'US–UK Economic Prosperity Deal' (EPD) unveiled on 8 May 2025. As expected, this mainly relates to goods,[97] not services. However, service-related provisions exist: both countries confirm that 'they will negotiate an ambitious set of digital trade provisions *that will include within its scope services, including financial services*'.[98] They also confirm an intention to discuss high-standard commitments regarding, for example, intellectual property rights protection. The EPD also indicates vaguely that 'both countries intend to cooperate on the effective use of *investment security measures*,[99] export controls, and *[information and communication technology] vendor security*, building on the current levels of close alignment on trade and investment security measures'.[100] How seriously the agreement will be taken is unclear. Legally, it comprises seven non-legally binding proposals intended to be later formalized, implemented, and possibly expanded.[101] Beyond its non-legally binding nature, either party can terminate it simply by giving written notice.[102] Nonetheless, in June 2025, just before leaving the G7 summit in Alberta, Canada, President Trump signed an executive order purporting to implement the EPD in US law.[103]

[96] 'US Trade Tariffs', Research Briefing, House of Commons Library (17 Apr 2025).

[97] Goods such as beef, vehicles and automobile parts, steel, and aluminium merited specific mention. Tariffs on vehicle imports were to be reduced to 10%, but on a capped number of vehicles. The 25% automobile parts tariff remained.

[98] Clause 4(a) EPD. Emphasis added.

[99] Strategies and regulations designed to protect investors and the financial system from various risks.

[100] Clause 5(b) EPD. Emphasis added. Both parties committed vaguely to continuing to identify mutually beneficial services serving to increase economic integration in critical industries and defence preparedness, leveraging government policies, licences, programmes, and private-sector participation to facilitate such transactions (Clause 6 EPD).

[101] Clause 1 EPD.

[102] Clause 7(d) EPD. Scepticism has been expressed as regards how much financial value the agreement will bring (J Freedland, 'The Art of Dealing with Donald Trump? Don't Fight Him Alone', *The Guardian* (7 May 2025).

[103] A Williams, D Sheppard, and P Foster, 'Donald Trump Signs Executive Order to Implement US–UK Trade Deal', *Financial Times* (16 June 2025).

6 Post-Brexit UK Economic Performance

Establishing a precise link between Brexit and export trends presents challenges: other significant events with negative implications for trade, such as COVID-19, occurred almost simultaneously with Brexit making itself felt economically. Of course, no counterfactual exists with which prevailing circumstances can be compared. The Office for Budget Responsibility (the UK's fiscal watchdog) assumed from October 2018 onwards that the volume of both imports and exports in the wake of Brexit would be 15 per cent lower than if the UK had remained in the EU and that the resulting reduction in trade intensity would lead to a 4 per cent reduction in the potential productivity of the UK economy. It recently described these estimates as remaining broadly on track and as being broadly consistent with recently published studies.[104] However, the picture varies as between goods and services. By the end of 2023, growth in UK *goods* trade (exports and imports) had fallen to about 10 per cent below 2019 levels, while it was around 5 per cent *higher* for the rest of the G7: a 15 per cent differential in favour of the other G7 nations.

In contrast, UK *services* trade (recovering from an initial post-Brexit fall) was the highest in the G7 by 2023's end, at 12 per cent above 2019 levels, but rising by only about 9 per cent elsewhere in the G7: a 3 per cent differential in the UK's favour. By 2024, the UK exported £184bn of services to the EU and £324bn elsewhere: not far off a one third/two thirds split. The better relative UK performance in exporting services than goods has been ascribed to several factors: (i) global services trade (in which the UK has a relative advantage) growing faster than goods trade since 2008; (ii) increasing digitalization, rendering services trade easier and less dependent on physical proximity; (iii) post-Brexit trade barriers affecting goods trade more than services; and (iv) the lesser dependence of UK service exports on EU markets—only a third of service exports go to the EU compared to about half of goods exports.[105] The overall post-Brexit trade picture is more complex than simply comprising 'goods-where-the-news-is-bad-and-services-where-the-news-is good', however. Exports in some services (namely, those affected by Brexit restrictions, such as financial services and transport) have declined since 2019.[106] Others, many falling under the rubric of so-called other business *sectors* (for example, management consulting, research and development, and advertising) have driven the rise in post-Brexit services exports.[107] Recent research suggests Brexit has imposed substantial new frictions on UK services exports to the EU and concludes:[108]

[104] Office for Budget Responsibility, *Economic and Fiscal Outlook* (Mar 2024) 39.
[105] ibid.
[106] Financial services declined by 5.9% between 2019 and the end of 2023 and transport services by 2%, ibid 40.
[107] ibid 39–40. Travel was formerly in decline but since 2022 has returned to growth levels last seen in 2019.
[108] S Bhalotia, S Dhingra, and D Arnold, *Deglobalisation in Disguise? Brexit Barriers and Trade in Services* (Centre for Economic Performance Discussion Paper No 2110, LSE, June 2025) 31.

> UK services exports to the EU declined significantly in response to the new barriers, but there were no offsetting gains in non-EU markets. On average, Brexit-induced trade barriers reduced UK services exports by 15.8% in affected EU destinations of services . . . and total UK exports are estimated to have fallen by 4.1 to 5.1%.

The implication of this is that although the UK specialized in the right industries at the correct time, thus facilitating global sales by world-class companies, service exports would nevertheless have been better had Brexit not occurred.[109]

7 Particular UK Service Sectors

(a) Financial Services and Brexit

Financial services are examined in detail in this book by Moloney,[110] and therefore observations here will be kept limited. Financial services are a key industry, in which the UK exports far more than it imports. By 2023, exports were worth £91.8bn and imports worth £18.6bn.[111] Financial and insurance services contributed £208.2bn to the UK economy by 2023: 8.8 per cent of the entire UK economic output. The story of financial services since Brexit has not proven particularly happy, however. Exports declined 5.9 per cent in 2019–23, and this when service exports grew overall. The reasons are unclear, but trade barriers with the EU may have played some role: services such as banking are relatively highly regulated.[112]

The significance to the European economy of financial services provided from the UK nonetheless remains large. The EU is the UK's largest export market here, accounting for 34 per cent of exports worth £32bn (ahead of the US at 31%). This represents a relative decline, however, since as late as 2017, the EU accounted for 40 per cent of UK financial services exports. This relative decline was most pronounced in 2020 and 2021 (coinciding with the end of the Brexit transition period in January 2020).[113] Nevertheless, exports to the EU remain hugely significant.[114] Dependence, of course, is mutual. The UK economy relies on EU demand for financial services.

[109] C Giles, 'Don't Believe the Myth: Britain's Services Have Been Hit Hard by Brexit', *Financial Times* (9 July 2025).

[110] Ch 11.

[111] G Hutton, A Panjwani, and M Ward, *Financial Services in the UK*, House of Commons Library Research Briefing (18 November 2024), 21; K Alexander, C Barnard, E Ferran, A Lang, and N Moloney, *Brexit and Financial Services Law and Policy* (Hart 2018).

[112] Office for Budget Responsibility, 'Economic and Fiscal Outlook' (Mar 2024) 40.

[113] In cash terms, exports of financial services to the USA, Switzerland, Canada, Hong Kong, and Singapore increased by 78% between 2017 and 2023.Those to the EU also increased, but only by 29%, Hutton and others (n 111) 5.

[114] ibid 22. Since Brexit, there have also been changes in the EU countries the UK exports financial services to. Exports to Luxembourg and Ireland increased by 119% and 70% respectively from 2017 to 2023. Exports to the Netherlands declined by 38%, ibid 23.

EU member states, however, depend on the UK to supply them.[115] Nor is the trade all in one direction. In 2023, the EU accounted for 26 per cent of UK financial services imports (worth just under £5bn). Although this represents a relative decline since 2017 (when the EU accounted for 33% of UK financial service imports), and the US surpassed the EU as the largest source of financial service imports in 2019 and has remained ahead since, it is nonetheless a significant level of trade.[116] Unsurprisingly, there is rivalry between London and other financial centres such as Paris, Frankfurt, Luxembourg, Dublin, and Amsterdam in providing such services. Nevertheless, the provision of financial services is not a zero-sum game. In other words, it is not necessarily the case that a decline in the fortunes of London in providing financial services will be matched by any corresponding increase in the fortunes of EU financial services centres. The City of London constitutes a financial ecosystem within the continent of Europe of unique mass. If badly damaged, there is a danger that instead of financial centres in the EU profiting and correspondingly increasing their business, all concerned will lose and business pass to non-European locations such as New York or Tokyo. EU member states and the UK are thus to an undefined extent mutually dependent on each other when it comes to financial services.

Notwithstanding (or perhaps because of) the importance of financial services, the TCA offered no special treatment.[117] A Joint Declaration did envisage a Memorandum of Understanding on regulatory cooperation, without however any guarantee such dialogue would be significant. Subsequently the EU has appeared recalcitrant concerning key decisions, for example on equivalence.[118]

At the time of Brexit, two issues were prominent. One was the loss of passporting, where meeting regulatory requirements in one EU member state absolves a financial services provider from meeting equivalent requirements in the service recipient's state. The importance of this subject was probably exaggerated: passporting is a valuable EU law right, but within the financial services field a far from universal practice on the part of businesses established outside the EU. Non-EU businesses that establish a branch or subsidiary in an EU member state no longer need to invoke any special passporting regime benefiting third country states in any case: notably, 87 per cent of companies providing insurance to the EU-27 have already established a branch or subsidiary in the EU. Furthermore, equivalence regimes[119] exist regarding many financial services.[120]

[115] European Research Centre for Economic and Financial Governance, 'Implications of Brexit on EU Financial Services', Study for the ECON Committee, European Parliament (IP/A/ECON/2016-22) 9.

[116] Financial service imports from the EU are concentrated in a few countries, with France, Germany, and Ireland accounting for 61% of them, Hutton and others (n 111) 24–25.

[117] N Moloney, Financial Services under the Trade and Cooperation Agreement: Reflections on Unfinished Business for the EU and UK, DCU Brexit Institute Working Paper 3-2021, 2; A Shalchi, 'The UK–EU Trade Deal: Financial Services' (House of Commons Library Research Briefing (22 June 2021).

[118] House of Lords EU Committee, *Beyond Brexit: Trade in Services* (n 12) 12.

[119] The EU uses the unilateral, Commission-accorded discretionary system of equivalence (requiring approximate alignment with EU rules) to manage third-country access to its financial market, Moloney (n 117) 3. Equivalence is accorded slowly, however, and only if doing so suits EU interests.

[120] Not all—they are not, for example, available for retail and wholesale banking or for UCITs.

A second prominent issue was the EU's desire to see central counterparties involved in euro-denominated clearing moving to EU territory.[121] Much euro-denominated clearing takes place in the UK, but the continuation of this seemed less tenable once the UK resolved to leave the EU. The European Commission ultimately adopted a gradual approach to this issue. In January 2025, the Commission issued a decision extending equivalence for UK central counterparties for three years until 30 June 2028.[122] This was to provide time for the implementation of the European Market Infrastructure Regulation (EMIR 3),[123] which the EU hopes will improve the attractiveness and competitiveness of EU clearing markets. The EU ultimately clearer wishes to end perceived over-reliance on UK central counterparties, thereby reducing risks to its financial system. The three-year equivalence extension is designed to give EMIR 3 measures time to start taking effect, increasing clearing in the EU and reducing EU exposure to UK central counterparties.[124]

One key post-Brexit question was whether the UK would continue to align itself to European standards. The ultimate picture would emerge only gradually: there was no initial UK bonfire of financial services rules.[125] Sooner or later, a move away from full alignment seemed likely, however. This has now transpired, something seen in detail in the chapter in this volume by Moloney. Pre-Brexit, the financial services regime was based almost entirely on EU law, albeit the UK had a major influence on the shape of the legal framework's shape. Post-Brexit, as Moloney details, UK legislation is now changing both substantive rules and institutional arrangements, in the latter case with the Financial Services and Markets Act 2023, shifting financial regulation away from legislation to a more flexible and reactive system of delegated rules adopted by regulators. As regards substantive rules, a 'large-scale and multi-layered' reform agenda is being pursued—the largest such exercise since the EU-driven response to the Great Financial Crisis of 2008 onwards. This will gradually replace significant aspects of the assimilated law governing UK financial regulation under the Retained EU Law (Revocation and Reform) Act 2023.[126] As Moloney observes, this approach raises no difficulties with the TCA, which requires only mutual access and non-discrimination between the UK and the EU. The UK has been more liberal

[121] Central counterparties provide clearing services for trades in various financial products, assuming the credit risk as between the parties.

[122] Commission Implementing Decision (EU) 2025/215 of 30.1.2025 determining, for a limited period of time, that the regulatory framework applicable to central counterparties in the UK is equivalent, in accordance with Regulation (EU) No 648/2012 of the European Parliament and Council, OJ L, 2025/215, 31.1.2025.

[123] Regulation (EU) No 648/2012 of the European Parliament and Council of 4.7.2012 on OTC derivatives, central counterparties and trade repositories [2012] OJ L201/1.

[124] Statement by Commissioner Albuquerque (responsible for financial services) on Commission website at https://finance.ec.europa.eu/news/commission-extends-time-limited-equivalence-uk-central-counterparties-2025-01-31_en.

[125] Note UK Government assurance referred to in House of Lords EU Committee, *Beyond Brexit: Trade in Services* (n 11) 63.

[126] Niamh Moloney, Ch 11 in this volume.

regarding access to its market to date than the EU.[127] But this new approach involves a competitiveness-driven reduction of UK financial regulation in the UK, at the very time when deregulatory winds are already blowing in an EU given to highly detailed financial regulation. This may create pressure for further EU reform.

(b) Professional Services and Brexit

Professional and business services are a major services export: the biggest category of UK service exports consists of so-called other business services, covering services including accountancy, advertising, architectural, and legal services. The UK exported £185bn worth of these in 2023,[128] making it the second-largest exporter globally of professional and business services.[129] Brexit nonetheless dealt the export of such services a double blow. The first comprised restrictions introduced on the free movement of persons at this time. The second comprised the withdrawal of mutual recognition of professional qualifications between EU states and the UK, a particularly important issue for regulated industries such as medicine, law, accountancy, and architecture.

There is a general mechanism in the TCA envisaging the possibility of pan-European mutual recognition of qualifications, but such clauses in FTAs have a poor record in securing change. Moreover, where there are violations of the TCA, the new state-to-state enforcement method will be more cumbersome than the pre-Brexit possibility of reliance on national courts for relief. Small firms in particular (with comparatively fewer resources) can expect to be hit harder by the TCA regime than larger ones.

Remarkably, two thirds of the services trade growth seen since 2019 has involved 'other services'. The reasons for this may relate to (i) trade barriers for such services being lower than more highly regulated ones such as banking; (ii) particularly strong growth in service exports to the US; and (iii) possible circumvention of trade barriers by sales through foreign affiliates.[130] Although the Labour government elected in July 2024 gave a manifesto commitment to seek a mutual recognition agreement with the EU for professional qualifications, no accord was reached. The May 2025 Common Understanding was silent on this issue.

[127] N Moloney, 'Access to the UK Financial Market after the UK Withdrawal from the EU: Disruption, Design, Diffusion' (2024) EBOLR 25.

[128] D Webb, 'Services Exports Outpace Goods', House of Commons Library Insight (30 Aug 2024).

[129] UK Government, 'Professional and Business Services' (Business.gov.uk, 2025) https://www.business.gov.uk/invest-in-uk/investment/sectors/professional-and-business-services/#:~:text = The%20UK%20is%20the%20second,Levelling%20Up%20and%20Net%20Zero.

[130] Office for Budget Responsibility, 'Economic and Fiscal Outlook' (Mar 2024) 39–40.

(c) Creative Industries and Brexit

Creative service industries, including music and television, were left in considerable difficulties by Brexit, for several reasons. Most prominently, the TCA led to restrictions on the free movement of persons, which have proven harsh on groups, particularly those seeking to establish a public profile by touring. The effect, except for the most well-resourced UK acts, has been to render tours in the EU well-nigh impossible.[131] Difficulties include difficulty and expense in securing visas, the '90 days out of 180 days' limit on time spent in Schengen (particularly vexatious for musicians and technical experts working for more than one artist), the carnet system for transporting kit in the EU, and the application of customs rules to merchandise sales.[132] 2020 alone allegedly saw a 44.5 per cent drop in economic value added by creative industries.[133] The difficulties here gained political traction within the UK, but the EU has sought a more liberal approach on free movement generally as its price for change.[134] Although the Starmer government's election manifesto committed it to seek to help touring artists, the May 2025 Common Understanding committed the parties only 'to continue their efforts to support travel and cultural exchange', which does not augur well for change.

8 Post-Brexit Developments in the EU

Post-Brexit legislative developments at EU level also merit consideration: regulatory divergence is, after all, not merely occasioned by UK legislative changes. The EU legislative framework is not a stationary object and can be expected to change over time.

A renewed period of intense development may well be in the offing. In recent times, concerns have grown that market integration has lost momentum. The share of EU GDP represented by trade between member states decreased both for goods (to 23.8%) and for services (to 7.8%) in 2023.[135] The Commission recently noted that within the single market, cross-border services trade is less than a third of that in goods and (unlike goods) lower than services trade with non-EU countries.[136]

[131] The UK rejected an EU-proposed visa waiver agreement facilitating touring.

[132] M Buckley, 'The Creative Sector—Brexit Impacts and Solutions' (Independent Commission).

[133] ibid.

[134] P Foster, G Parker, and A Bounds, 'UK and EU Split over Youth Mobility Deal, Negotiating Document Shows', *Financial Times* (7 May 2024); S Fella, 'Resetting the UK's Relationship with the European Union', House of Commons Library Research Briefing (5 Mar 2025).

[135] European Commission, *The 2025 Annual Single Market and Competitiveness Report*, Communication from the Commission to the European Parliament, the Council, the European Economic And Social Committee and the Committee of the Regions COM(2025) 26 final, 3.

[136] ibid.

Some indication of what the future might hold for services trade within the EU came with the April 2024 publication of the Letta Report.[137] Under the heading 'Accelerating integration in the single market for services', several ongoing challenges hampering the frictionless operation of the single services market were identified. The continued prevalence of 60 per cent of the many barriers to free movement of services which had been identified as long ago as 2002 is noted, as is the linked nature of the provision of services and goods (with 40 per cent of value created in the manufacturing sector being directly fuelled by services)—and thus the vital nature of tackling of barriers to free movement of services and to free movement of goods. The now dissipated initial momentum generated by the entry into force of the 2006 Services Directive and the deceleration of progress in dismantling obstacles to the free movement of service is also pointed out, with barriers remaining deeply embedded. A renewed sense of determination is described as imperative so as to avoid denial of the full economic benefits envisioned by the single market.[138]

A multi-pronged approach and a number of specific reforms are proposed in the Letta Report in order to deal with these challenges. First, the Report calls for specific but highly varied types of restrictions that persist under the Services Directive to be addressed. These barriers encompass 'discriminatory practices based on nationality or place of residence, restrictions limiting service providers to operating in a single member state, the utilization of protectionist economic needs tests, authorization processes influence by entrenched competitor involvement, and hindrances to the smooth temporary provision of services across borders'.[139] Second, the Report argues that particular attention should be focused on the retail sector, where obstacles include a lack of political will in favour of further integration and localized protectionism obstructing market entry. Third, the view is expressed that harmonization in regulations concerning the posting of workers and an end to fragmented administrative burdens are needed and require coordinated EU-level intervention. Fourth, sector-specific strategies rather than broad attempts at market integration are called for, the tailoring of policies to the unique dynamics of individual service sectors (allowing for a more precise identification of integration barriers) being viewed as a more effective path to overcome challenges, accompanied by the Commission intervening where lack of political will is the problem. Fifth, the addressing of the persistence of barriers creating frictions even within sectors covered by specific directives is called for (with the example of divergences between member states in liability caps in the field of statutory audits being instanced as an example). Sixth, streamlining the cross-border provision of services through simplified procedures is proposed. Seventh, a process of mutual learning between member states for liberalization is counselled.

[137] E Letta, *Much More than a Market: Speed, Security, Solidarity* (April 2024), https://www.consilium.europa.eu/media/ny3j24sm/much-more-than-a-market-report-by-enrico-letta.pdf (visited 11 May 2025).
[138] ibid 109.
[139] ibid 109–10.

Overall, the impression is given that the process of creating a single market in services has a long way to travel, is not susceptible to easy solutions, and will require a combination of measures going well beyond the simple adoption of legislation. Some determination to follow this course seems now to be building up a head of steam, however.[140]

A further key report has been that by Draghi, which emphasizes the importance of digital services (although, in this case, the issues raised go further than merely facilitating the free movement of services). While Europe has been far from inactive in the digital field—with measures such as the Data and Data Governance Acts, the Cyber Resilience Act, and the AI Act, and sectoral initiatives such as the Net Zero Industry Act and the new European Health Dataspace[141]—the Draghi Report points to a record of relative failure, both in terms of generating new tech companies and diffusing digital tech into the economy, and observes that the main reason EU productivity diverged from the US in the mid-1990s was Europe's failure to capitalize on the first digital revolution led by the internet. The report points out that while some digital sectors are likely already 'lost', Europe still has an opportunity to capitalize on future waves of digital innovation even if the EU's competitive disadvantage will likely widen in cloud computing, with a market characterized by continuous massive investments, economies of scale, and multiple services offered by a single provider.[142]

The Draghi Report compares the EU unfavourably with the US, pointing out that in addition to the Information and Communications Technology sector, the US has high productivity growth in professional services and finance and insurance, reflecting strong ICT technology diffusion effects.[143] The Commission responded rapidly to the Draghi Report. In response, it published a so-called Competitiveness Compass in January 2025,[144] intended to frame the work of the Commission for the remainder of its mandate.[145] Acknowledging the need to remove the persistent barriers to the s as mapped out in the Letta Report, the Commission proposed that,[146]

> to improve the functioning of the s across all industries, a Horizontal Single market Strategy will modernise the governance framework, removing intra-EU barriers and preventing the creation of new ones, fostering collaboration with Member States, and proposing a new approach to implementation. A reinforced Single Market Enforcement Taskforce (SMET) will ensure transposition that avoids unnecessary burdens, as well as overall implementation and enforcement of EU legislation.

[140] Note also the Draghi Report conclusions, *The Future of European Competitiveness* https://commission.europa.eu/document/download/97e481fd-2dc3-412d-be4c-f152a8232961_en?filename = The%20future%20of%20European%20competitiveness%20_%20A%20competitiveness%20strategy%20for%20Europe.pdf.

[141] European Commission, 'A Competitiveness Compass for the EU' COM(2025)30 final, 5.

[142] ibid 24.

[143] ibid 27.

[144] ibid.

[145] ibid 26.

[146] ibid 20.

> Further harmonisation measures will be launched to reduce remaining legal fragmentation, in the twin interests of deepening the Single Market and simplification.

The combination of the Letta Report, the Draghi Report, and the Competitiveness Compass seems a strong indication of the prospect of a renewed drive within the EU to improve the operation of the Single Market, including in the services field, and that the EU that the UK left in 2020 may undergo considerable change in the near future.

9 Conclusion

Some relief has been provided from economic difficulties which might otherwise have been occasioned to the UK by a number of factors. One has been the Trade and Cooperation Agreement with the EU, which makes at least limited provision for services. Another is the large number of rollover agreements (however limited their individual effect might be) and new trade agreements with non-EU states. Many (although not all) of these make provision concerning services. Frequently, what is provided for will be market access and non-discrimination. But sometimes trade agreements go further than this, at times covering digital services, financial services, and mutual recognition of qualifications.

Also assisting the UK is the fact that exclusion from a Single Market in services is a less dramatic fate than would otherwise be the case in a situation in which the Single Market in services is only relatively imperfectly formed in any case. There are work-arounds for some exclusions from the Single Market (such as the ability of a company to establish a subsidiarity in an EU member state) to provide services to another EU member state. Furthermore, the self-interest of the EU in maintaining the nearby financial ecosystem that is the City of London (manifested, for example, in its repeated delays in legislating against offshore central counterparties) also works to the UK's advantage and helps to countermand the danger of the very natural wish of financial centres such as Frankfurt and Paris to compete with the City of London bearing disagreeable legislative fruit at EU level. However, this relatively benevolent scenario may not endure forever. Divergences may grow. It is notable that concern is growing in the EU at the relative failure of the Single Market when it comes to services, and more particularly digital services. This has already given rise to the Letta Report, the Draghi Report, and now the Commission Competitiveness Compass. These seem likely ultimately to lead to some evolution in the Single Market in services to which a now-exited UK is of course no longer a party. Added to this, the UK itself is adjusting its approach to financial services regulation to a more flexible, less cumbersome system, more responsive to market needs.[147] This may lead it to adopt very different rules and systems in the financial services sector. Continuing evolution of the law governing

[147] See further Niamh Moloney, Ch 11 in this volume.

services is to be expected in both the UK and the EU. This brings with it considerable risk of the two systems becoming increasingly out of line with one another. However, given that many of the same economic pressures apply to the EU and the UK alike, and their situation of mutual economic dependence in many respects, it might be that divergences between the two systems will not nonetheless become as numerous or great as quickly as might otherwise be the case.

11
Financial Services

Niamh Moloney

1 Introduction

The question of whether UK financial regulation has become 'unbound' has particular resonance with the current geopolitical setting. The prevailing instability in global financial regulation, which is tied to a shift in the underpinning political economy of the relationship between regulation and growth, is also reshaping UK regulation as it adjusts post-Brexit. Whether this reshaping represents significant divergence from the EU is considered in this chapter.

The financial services sector provides the economy with the financial intermediation essential for growth.[1] It 'intermediates' between suppliers of capital, including households, and seekers of capital, including industrial firms and governments, to support capital allocation and related risk taking. It does this by reducing the frictions and transaction costs associated with raising capital through bank loans and through market instruments such as shares and bonds, and by providing risk management services, including through insurance contracts, derivatives, and other market mechanisms for pricing, managing, and hedging risks. The sector also generates interconnected and highly dynamic risks which can crystallize in ways that are not yet fully understood, as evidenced by the severe market dislocation in March 2020 as the pandemic took root.[2] All major economies globally accordingly apply regulatory schemes, of immense intricacy and complexity, which serve the classic public interest trifecta of financial regulation: financial stability, market efficiency and integrity, and investor/consumer protection. Ensuring an optimal balance between a vibrant financial sector and an appropriately calibrated regulatory system remains, however, a defining challenge for financial regulation, particularly in times of heightened financial system risk.[3] The extent to which political regimes globally, and so their

[1] As is frequently referenced by the current UK government as regards the need to strengthen economic growth. See Chancellor of the Exchequer Rachel Reeves, Mansion House Speech, 15 July 2025.

[2] On the Covid disruption see Financial Stability Board, 'Holistic Review of the March Market Turmoil' (2020).

[3] On the current fragility in the risk environment as geopolitical and trade relationships evolve and market structure changes, see eg FSB Chair Letter to G20 Finance Ministers and Central Bank Governors, 21 April 2025.

Niamh Moloney, *Financial Services* In: *The UK Regulatory Framework Post-Brexit: 'Law Unbound'*. Edited by: Paul Craig and Vilija Vėlyvytė, Oxford University Press. © Oxford University Press 2026. DOI: 10.1093/9780198969815.003.0013

regulatory arrangements, bend towards and away from regulatory intervention varies over time and with economic/market conditions (the 'regulatory sine curve' phenomenon[4]). Regulatory and policy uncertainty at present is considerable as governments internationally—with the 2008 Global Financial Crisis receding in the rear-view mirror—look to deregulatory reform to drive growth.[5] In the UK, financial regulatory reform as a means for driving economic growth is a core government priority.[6]

The availability of this reform lever follows from the EU withdrawal. UK financial regulation was a natural candidate for the 'take back control' agenda,[7] given the might of the City of London and its significance to UK GDP,[8] but also the acute importance of its financial stability, regarded by the IMF as a global public good.[9] Further, the reach of post-financial crisis regulation, the massive scale and depth of the EU rulebook (given its distinct role in supporting integration and managing cross-border risk transmission), and the potential (if contested) for financial regulatory reform to drive competitiveness and economic growth[10] meant that financial regulation was always going to be a bellwether for the UK's appetite for material regulatory divergence.

As outlined in this chapter, control is, decisively, being taken back over UK financial regulation, in a political context framed by concern to use financial (de-)regulation to support economic growth and competitiveness. It is clear that how financial regulation is adopted is being re-ordered. But whether a deep rupture with the EU legacy regime is under way is less clear.

[4] JC Coffee, 'The Political Economy of Dodd–Frank: Why Financial Reform Tends to be Frustrated and Systemic Risk Perpetuated' (2012) 97 Cornell LR 1019.

[5] In its April 2025 World Economic Outlook, the IMF noted the risks of 'an excessive rollback of financial regulation' and the need to put a premium on robust prudential policies to safeguard financial stability: IMF, World Economic Outlook: A Critical Juncture Amid Policy Shifts (2025), 20 and 24.

[6] Financial services form part of the government's new industrial strategy, with the government committing to 'regulate not just for risk, but for growth' and to a 'competitive regulatory environment': UK Government, The UK's Modern Industrial Strategy. Financial Services Growth and Competitiveness Strategy, July 2025, 5 and 8.

[7] On the negotiations see N Moloney, 'Financial Services and Brexit: Unfinished Business for the UK and EU' in F Fabbrini (ed), *The Framework of EU–UK Relations* (Oxford University Press 2021) 115; E Howell, 'Post-"Brexit" Financial Governance: Which Dispute Settlement Framework Should Be Utilised' (2020) 83 MLR 128; E Ferran, 'The UK as a Third Country in EU Financial Services Regulation' (2017) 3 J of Fin Reg 40. For a political economy perspective see S James and L Quaglia, *The UK and Multi-level Financial Regulation: From Post-Crisis Reform to Brexit* (Oxford University Press 2020).

[8] The financial services sector represents 9% of total UK economic output, provides 1.2 million jobs, and accounts for more than half of the UK's surplus in services exports: 2025 Growth and Competitiveness Strategy (n 6) 7.

[9] Bank of England, Financial Stability in Focus. The FPC's Approach to Assessing Risks in Market-based Finance (2023).

[10] The extensive law and finance literature considers the contested empirical evidence on the relationship between law, regulation, and financial market development. For a review see G Schnyder, M Siems, and R Aguilera 'Twenty Years of "Law and Finance": Time to Take Law Seriously' (2021) 19 Socio-economic Rev 377. The related legal/institutionalist literature examines why rules matter to financial market efficiency. See K Langenbucher, *Economic Transplants: On Lawmaking for Corporations and Capital Markets* (Cambridge University Press 2017); S Deakin and others, 'Legal Institutionalism: Capitalism, and the Constitutive Role of Law' (2017) 45 JCE 188; K Pistor, 'A Legal Theory of Finance' (2013) 41 J of Comparative Economics 315.

2 Pre-Brexit Regulation

(a) The Single Rulebook

EU financial regulation has steadily extended its reach over member states since 1966, with the Segré Report's identification of financial market regulation as an integration tool, through the Single European Act/single market agenda era and the first use of mutual recognition for financial services (the since-repealed 1989 Banking Coordination Directive II), and on to the Financial Services Action Plan era (1999–2004), the first major reforming era for financial services.[11] By relating EU financial system growth to harmonized regulation and the single market 'passport',[12] the FSAP agenda laid the foundations of the current behemoth regulatory system. But the 2008–14 financial crisis-era reforms were decisive in shaping the EU's current system of financial market governance. When this reform period closed in 2014, a legislative 'single rulebook' of vast reach was in place, and an immense new administrative rulebook of a heavily proceduralized and granular quality was under construction. Over this period the move to 'more Europe', as a means for supporting market depth and stability, became embedded, supported by the UK.[13]

Between 2014 and 2020 legislative measures were adopted to refine the crisis-era reforms, reflecting the ratcheting effect of the crisis-era 'review clauses'. This period also saw a new generation of legislation, adopted in support of the Capital Markets Union (CMU) agenda which, since 2015, has framed EU financial services policy.[14] Designed to be transformative, and imbued with the longstanding EU political and institutional faith in the capacity of harmonized regulation to drive structural financial market outcomes, the CMU agenda was to support a deeper and more integrated capital market, and thereby to secure more diversified funding for businesses and households and widen the sources of risk capital needed to meet the EU's now significant investment needs. Since March 2025 the CMU agenda has been subsumed within the related Savings and Investments Union agenda, oriented in particular to household investment.[15]

The post-crisis period also saw a transformation in the EU's technocratic capacity. This followed the 2011 establishment of the three European Supervisory Authorities

[11] COM(1999)232.

[12] The financial services 'passport' allows financial firms authorized and supervised in their home member state to provide services/establish a branch in other (host) member states without further host regulation. Given the potential for cross-border risk transmission (which crystallized to catastrophic effect over the financial crisis), the passport is supported by a harmonized rulebook of immense scale and depth.

[13] The choice faced by the EU in repairing its financial system was often expressed as 'more Europe' (a closely integrated market governed by densely harmonized rules) or 'less Europe' (segmented national financial markets, more limited harmonization, and cross-border access based on locally regulated subsidiaries): Financial Services Authority, 'The Turner Review. A Regulatory Response to the Global Banking Crisis' (2009) 101–02.

[14] COM(2015) 468 and COM(2020) 590.

[15] COM(2025)124.

(ESAs), for banking (the European Banking Authority), markets (the European Securities and Markets Authority), and insurance (the European Insurance and Occupational Pensions Authority). The three ESAs are constituted as coordinating agencies, and charged with supporting supervisory convergence and coordination across the EU's national regulators and with supporting the single rulebook through the adoption of soft law and by advising the Commission on administrative rules. They can be associated with the burgeoning of the administrative and soft law 'rulebooks' since the financial crisis. Relatedly, national regulators' supervisory practices have become ever more 'Europeanized', steered by the ESAs' purposeful and often entrepreneurial exercise of their soft supervisory convergence and coordination powers.[16]

The financial markets segment of the single rulebook in 2020 usefully illustrates how the UK financial market was governed almost entirely by (most usually) directly applicable EU regulations and (increasingly less common) highly detailed directives (the latter implemented usually through Statutory Instruments or, where appropriate, the UK regulators' administrative rulebooks). EU law governed the foundational capital-raising process, including the disclosures required by 'issuers' of securities (firms raising funds on the public markets by selling shares or bonds) and the process governing the admission and 'listing' of those securities to and on trading venues (2017 Prospectus Regulation, 2004 Transparency Directive, and 2002 International Accounting Standards Regulation (IAS Regulation)).[17] A mighty harmonized legislative rulebook addressed the investment firms and trading venues that support capital-raising (2014 Markets in Financial Instruments Directive II (MiFID II) and 2014 Markets in Financial Instruments Regulation (MiFIR), and 2019 Investment Firm Directive (IFD) and Investment Firm Regulation (IFR)).[18] The regime also covered investment funds through a series of highly detailed legislative measures (2009 Undertakings for Collective Investment in Transferable Securities (UCITS) Directive, 2011 Alternative Investment Fund Managers Directive (AIMFD), 2013 European Venture Capital and European Social Entrepreneurship Fund Regulations (EuVECA and EuSEF Regulations), 2015 European Long-term Investment Fund Regulation (ELTIF Regulation), and 2017 Money Market Fund Regulation (MMF Regulation)).[19] A related legislative regime applied to retail market investment product disclosure (the 2014 Packaged Retail and Insurance-based Investment

[16] 'On the Europeanization of regulatory practice see T Bach, E Ruffing, and K Yesilkagit, 'The Differential Empowering Effects of Europeanization on the Autonomy of National Agencies' (2015) 28 Governance 285. In the financial market context see N Moloney, 'ESMA and the Evolution of the EU's Supervisory Model for Financial Markets' in J Bauerschmidt, D Fromage, and A Schirk (eds), *AMLA and the European Financial Agencies* (forthcoming 2026).

[17] Regulation (EU) 2017/1129 [2017] OJ L168/12; Directive 2004/109/EC [2004] OJ L390/38; and Regulation (EC) No 1606/2002 [2002] OJ L243/1.

[18] Directive 2014/65/EU [2014] OJ L173/349 and Regulation (EU) No 600/2014 [2014] OJ L173/84; and Directive (EU) 2019/2034 [2019] OJ L314/64 and Regulation (EU) 2019/2033 [2019] OJ L314/1.

[19] Directive 2009/65/EC [2009] OJ L302/32; Directive 2011/61/EU [2011] OJ L174/1; Regulation (EU) No 345/2013 [2013] OJ L115/1; Regulation (EU) No 346/2013 [2013] OJ L115/18; Regulation (EU) 2015/760 [2015] OJ L123/98; and Regulation (EU) 2017/1131 [2017] OJ L169/8.

Products (PRIIPs) Regulation).[20] Market 'gatekeepers' (such as firms that provide verification or signalling services) were addressed, including benchmark providers (2016 Benchmark Regulation)[21] and credit rating agencies (Consolidated Credit Rating Agency Regulation (CCRAR)).[22] The pathologies of market behaviour were covered, primarily through the market abuse regime (2014 Market Abuse Regulation) and the short selling regime (2012 Short Selling Regulation).[23] The post-trading process was also addressed, mainly through the sprawling EMIR (2012 European Market Infrastructure Regulation).[24] EMIR governs derivatives market stability by requiring 'central clearing counterparties' (CCPs) to be interposed between trading parties to the conclusion of derivatives contracts, and by imposing a host of related reporting and risk management requirements. Alongside, the 2014 Central Securities Depositaries (CSD) Regulation addresses the process through which securities trading contracts are 'settled' (or completed).[25] Specific transactions were addressed by the 2015 Securities Financing Transactions Regulation ('securities financing' relates to the use of securities as guarantees) and the 2017 Securitization Regulation ('securitization' relates to the economically significant process through which bank loans are transformed into marketable securities, and risk is thereby dispersed and the cost of funding reduced).[26]

Beyond financial markets, the legislative behemoth that is the Capital Requirements Directive/Regulation regime underpinned EU banking regulation, along with the related bank recovery and resolution regimes.[27] Insurance was governed by the leviathan Solvency II and related insurance distribution measures.[28]

All these legislative measures were amplified by an immense and dynamic administrative rulebook[29] and a dense thicket of soft law,[30] and supported by the mass of supervisory coordination-related measures deployed by the ESAs. Administrative rules were typically either directly applicable in the UK as administrative regulations or, as administrative directives, implemented through Statutory Instruments. Soft and supervisory coordination measures were implemented through supervisory practice by the UK regulators, including through incorporation in their 'rulebooks'.

[20] Regulation (EU) No 1286/2014 [2014] OJ L352/1.

[21] Regulation (EU) 2016/1011 [2016] OJ L171/1.

[22] The EU's rating agency regime encompasses Regulation (EU) No 1060/2009 [2009] OJ L302/1 (CRA I); Regulation (EU) No 513/2011 [2011] OJ L145/30 (CRA II); and Regulation (EU) No 462/2013 [2013] OJ L146/1 (CRA III). Directive 2013/14/EU [2013] OJ L145/1 regulates other financial institutions as regards over-reliance on ratings.

[23] Regulation (EU) No 596/2014 [2014] OJ L173/1 and Regulation (EU) No 236/2012 [2012] OJ L86/1.

[24] Regulation (EU) No 648/2012 [2012] OJ L201/1.

[25] Regulation (EU) No 909/2014 [2014] OJ L257/1.

[26] Regulation (EU) 2015/2365 [2015] OJ L337/1 and Regulation (EU) 2017/2402 [2017] OJ L347/35.

[27] Directive 2013/36/EU [2013] OJ L176/338 (Capital Requirements Directive IV (CRD IV)) and Regulation (EU) No 575/2013 [2013] OJ L176/1 (Capital Requirements Regulation (CRR)).

[28] Directive 2009/138/EC [2009] OJ L335/1.

[29] The investment firm administrative rulebook under MiFID II/MiFIR and IFD/IFR runs to some 90 separate sets of detailed administrative directives and regulations.

[30] Eg EBA has adopted more than 100 sets of typically lengthy and detailed Guidelines under the banking rulebook.

The intermeshing of the UK financial system with EU legislation, administrative rules, soft law, and supervisory practice, at the time of the 2020 withdrawal, was accordingly intricate and embedded. UK financial regulation took the form, for the most part, of directly applicable (or, given the level of specification in directives, de facto directly applicable) EU financial regulation.[31] Nonetheless, a distinct normative setting for UK financial regulation could be identified. The cornerstone Financial Services and Markets Act 2000 (FSMA) sets the framework for financial services regulation in the UK in that, inter alia, it constitutes the UK regulators (the Bank of England, as regards its financial regulation functions, the Prudential Regulation Authority, and the Financial Conduct Authority) and confers their delegated powers, including rule-making powers, and it also fixes the perimeter of UK financial regulation.[32] FSMA relatedly specifies the regulators' general objectives, and these provide a guide to the normative principles that shaped, and still shape, UK political priorities as regards financial regulation. These objectives, which relate to the foundational objectives of financial regulation, including financial stability, market efficiency and integrity, and investor/consumer protection,[33] are expressly or impliedly stated across the EU single rulebook. But the EU has not adopted an over-arching statement of objectives. In that respect, the UK remained and remains distinct.

(b) Law Unbound?

The extent to which the UK's new regulatory autonomy would lead to large-scale changes to financial regulation, and to active, material divergence from the EU, was not clear at the withdrawal, notwithstanding the 'take back control' political framing.

The UK's powerful incentive to secure for its financial system the public interest in a stable financial market that is embedded in the EU regime aside, there was cause for counselling against a dramatic rupture. The UK was a primary influence on the bulk of the single rulebook,[34] with negotiating reversals on key legislation rare.[35] In

[31] Albeit not entirely. The less dense harmonization of certain aspects of EU retail investor protection regulation eg allowed the UK to adopt a discrete regime in some respects, including for investment advice. Similarly, the UK adopted a distinct approach to senior manager accountability in firms, an area not closely addressed by EU regulation given its interconnection with enforcement.

[32] Through the Financial Services and Markets Act 2000 (Regulated Activities) Order 2001 (as frequently revised). FSMA also includes certain legislative regimes that pre-dated or supplemented the EU regime, including in relating to the process of 'listing' securities and in relation to market manipulation.

[33] The Financial Conduct Authority's 'general duty' is to ensure 'markets function well', and it has three related operational objectives concerning consumer protection, market integrity, and competition. The Prudential Regulation Authority's 'general objective' is to ensure the safety and soundness of regulated firms and protection of insurance policy holders. FSMA sect 1B-E (FCA) and sect 2B (PRA).

[34] See, eg, E Ferran, 'After the Crisis: The Regulation of Hedge Funds and Private Equity in the EU' (2011) 12 EBOLR 379.

[35] In one celebrated case, the UK, outvoted on the Short Selling Regulation (a prescriptive crisis-era measure, shaped by member state resistance, in some quarters, to short selling as an excess of advanced capitalism), brought a judicial review of its validity, but failed before the Court of Justice: Case C-270/12 *UK v Council and Parliament* EU:C:2014:18.

addition, much of the essentials of EU financial regulation reflected the international standards adopted by the International Standard Setting Bodies of the global financial system, most famously the 'Basel standards' on bank capital, liquidity, leverage, and risk management adopted by the Basel Committee. Here too the UK was influential in setting these standards.[36] There are strong incentives for cleaving to these standards, as the adoption of domestic rules based on international standards is traditionally associated with strong signalling effects as to the quality of domestic financial regulation, as well as with levelling the local playing field for international actors and so with international competitive advantage.[37] Further, the financial sector had clear interests in minimizing the transaction costs of adjusting their complex internal compliance structures and systems to new requirements. Finally, the prospect, if receding, of an 'equivalence' determination from the EU—and so easier access to the EU market as the EU would then, under relevant sectoral legislation, allow EU access by UK firms under the equivalent UK rules—further strengthened incentives to remain aligned with the EU.

On the other hand, securing regulatory autonomy was a driving UK concern, often expressed in its determination that the systemic City of London financial centre, and related fiscal risks, prohibited it from EU 'rule-taking'.[38] Regulatory autonomy was a political priority[39] but it had technocratic support.[40] Initial indications nonetheless suggested that any future reforms would reflect 'what is right for the UK' and not be in the form of large-scale de- (or-re)regulation.[41] Similarly, the UK regulators cautioned against any expectations of a 'bonfire of regulation'.[42]

3 Post-Brexit Regulation

(a) The Reform Process

The subsequent reform process, which is proving significant, can be explained in terms of orders of change to the two settings of financial regulation: broadly, the political/normative and the technocratic/administrative.

[36] Quaglia and James (n 7) and D Mugge (ed), *Europe and the Governance of Global Finance* (Oxford University Press 2014).

[37] PH Verdier, 'The Political Economy of International Financial Regulation' (2013) 88 Indiana LJ 1405.

[38] S James and L Quaglia, 'Rule Maker or Rule Taker? Brexit, Finance and UK Regulatory Autonomy' (2022) 43 Int'l Political Science Rev 390.

[39] UK Parliament, Financial Services Update Written Statement from the Chancellor of the Exchequer (HCWS309), 23 June 2020.

[40] See, eg, Bank of England Governor Bailey, Treasury Select Committee Hearing on the December Financial Stability Report, 6 January 2021.

[41] HM Treasury, Chancellor of the Exchequer Financial Services Statement, 9 November 2020.

[42] See, eg, Bank of England, Financial Stability Report, July 2019.

Third-order reform engages change to the normative setting for regulatory intervention.[43] In financial regulation, it is typically associated with financial crisis, close political attention, and consequent material legislative reform. This occurred over the financial crisis, for example, when financial stability emerged globally as a core priority for financial regulation. Second-order reform can be related to change to institutional settings, such as the construction or reform of agencies (also a feature of the global crisis-era reforms), or legislative reform without material normative change. It too is associated with political interests and choices, although it also engages technocratic reform. First-order reform, the business-as-usual refinement and revision that carries on in steady-state political and market conditions, has a more straightforwardly technocratic setting. A dominant feature of financial regulation, it engages less politically contested and more technical changes to legislation, the adoption/revision of administrative rules and soft law, and supervisory practice. All these orders of change can be traced in the reform process.

This process is unfolding in stages. Given the scale of EU financial regulation and the imperative that the UK financial system continued to operate safely, the first stage concerned the onshoring (or retention) of directly applicable legislation and rules. This was achieved under the EU (Withdrawal) Act 2018. The bulk of the single rulebook was retained (now 'assimilated', following the Retained EU Law (Revocation and Reform) Act 2023, and not interpreted in line with EU interpretation principles), without substantive policy changes. Technical revisions were made, such as currency substitutions, and essential institutionally oriented reforms were adopted, such as empowering the Financial Conduct Authority, which oversees UK financial markets, in place of ESMA.[44] So also were deletions of single market 'technology', such as the removal of EU supervisory coordination/convergence requirements and passporting arrangements. By way of example, the 2017 Prospectus Regulation, a cornerstone EU legislative measure governing the disclosures required of issuers of securities when they access public markets, was onshored as the 'UK Prospectus Regulation'.[45] Minor adjustments were made to address deficiencies and redundancies, but no substantive revisions were made.

Attention then turned to the construction of the new rulebook with the 2019 Financial Services Future Regulatory Framework Review (FRFR).[46] The FRFR took

[43] On the different orders of regulatory change see J Black, 'What Is Regulatory Innovation' in J Black, M Lodge, and M Thatcher (eds), *Regulatory Innovation: A Comparative Analysis* (Edward Elgar 2005) 1.

[44] Eg the authorization and supervision of UK credit rating agencies, located in ESMA, switched to the Financial Conduct Authority.

[45] By means of a statutory instrument: The Prospectus (Amendment etc) (EU Exit) Regulations 2019, 2019 No 1234. The onshoring was to 'ensure[s] the UK prospectus regime continues to function effectively once the UK leaves the EU. Without these provisions, the UK's primary capital markets . . . would not operate effectively . . . This would cause significant disruption to UK investors, issuers and the UK financial services sector as a whole, with further impacts on the integrity and attractiveness of the UK's capital markets.' Explanatory Memorandum, para 2.6.

[46] HM Treasury, Financial Services Future Regulatory Framework Review. Call for Evidence. Regulatory Coordination (2019). The initial reform agenda was set out in HM Treasury, Financial Services Future Regulatory Framework Review. Proposals for Reform (2021).

the form of a system-wide, policy- and institutionally oriented review. It necessarily addressed the institutional implications of the 'repatriation' of administrative financial rule-making from the EU to the UK. But it was also the vehicle for the delivery of the political imperative for substantive reform, and so has been a bellwether, since 2019, for the extent to which financial regulation would become 'unbound'.[47] Two major outcomes would follow: the institutional reform agenda, adopted by the Financial Services and Markets Act 2023; and the substantive reform agenda, which continues to evolve,[48] with its most recent iteration the July 2025 'Leeds Reforms'.[49] The following sections consider these outcomes.

(b) The Institutional Setting: the Financial Services and Markets Act 2023

(i) Revocation of Assimilated Law: The Design

The Financial Services and Markets Act 2023, which amends FSMA 2000, frames the reform process. In a combined second-order (legislative) and first-order (administrative) reform, it provides the mechanism for revoking and replacing assimilated EU financial law, and so sits alongside the Retained EU Law (Revocation and Reform) Act.[50] It revokes specified assimilated EU financial services law,[51] and it empowers government to save, restate, and, on an ongoing basis, revise such assimilated law.[52] Relatedly, it de facto re-orders the institutional setting of UK financial regulation: the UK regulators are being more fully embedded in the related administrative

[47] Politically, the reform process was designed to 'tak[e] advantage of the UK's new freedoms now we have left the EU', and was described as a 'once-in-a-generation opportunity to ensure that, having left the EU, the government maintains a coherent, agile, and internationally-respected approach to financial services regulation that is right for the UK': 2021 FRFR Proposals for Reform, n 46.

[48] The scale of the reform process led to the 'Regulatory Initiatives Grid', regularly updated by the Financial Services Regulatory Initiatives Forum (HM Treasury, the Bank of England, the Prudential Regulation Authority, the Financial Conduct Authority, and leading trade associations).

[49] UK Government, 'Leeds Reforms to Rewire Financial System, Boost Investment and Create Skilled Jobs across the UK' (15 July 2025).

[50] The Act also contains substantive new regimes, including the new legislative regime for 'critical third parties' that provide systemically significant IT services to financial firms. This regime is similar to the EU's 'DORA' (Digital Operational Resilience Act) Regulation (DORA was adopted in 2022 and so did not form part of the onshoring process: [2022] OJ L333/1).

[51] FSMA 2023 sect 1 repeals the assimilated EU law, subject to commencement by HM Treasury, and Schedule 1 revokes specific measures on days to be appointed. The schedule covers the main legislative measures under the single rulebook (including those noted in sect 1 above).

[52] FSMA 2023 sect 4 empowers the government to 'save' EU law into domestic legislation and modify the legislation by 'restating' it (through amendments or through new subordinate legislation), where this is necessary or desirable in connection with one or more of the specified purposes. These purposes are set out in sect 3(2) and reflect the normative setting of UK financial regulation, encompassing the general/primary and secondary objectives of the regulators as specified in FSMA and related to eg financial stability, the safety and soundness of firms, consumer protection, market efficiency and integrity, competition in the financial services sector, and competitiveness and economy growth.

rule-making process in that they are being empowered to amplify and revise the saved/restated law.

It was not operationally necessary to revoke the assimilated law. But it was a political priority, and it has remained so. It followed from this political priority that the institutional apparatus for the administrative rule-making which carries much of the weight of financial regulation had to be fit for purpose, politically and functionally. One option, if a cumbersome one, was to follow the pre-existing system under which Statutory Instruments were the main vehicle for adopting administrative rules (albeit EU rules). The political vision underpinning the Financial Services and Markets Act 2023, however, was to re-order the nature of UK financial regulation to make it more consistent with the original division of labour between high-level legislation (political action) and detailed rules (administrative/regulator action) set out in FSMA 2000 (before the explosion of EU regulation, initially under the 1999 FSAP and subsequently under the crisis-era reforms, meant that this division became blurred given the requirements for implementing EU law).[53]

The organizational design of UK financial regulation will therefore change. It is currently shaped by the earlier implementation, and more recent assimilation, of EU legislation, and so is heavily based on Statutory Instruments. Over time, it will become more a creature of regulators' rulebooks. New 'saving/restating' framework legislation will set the politically directed contours of the new regimes; and the non-majoritarian financial regulators—already equipped with rule-making power under FSMA—will be given specific new delegations thereunder to amplify and develop these regimes through administrative rules. The new legislative regimes will accordingly set those regimes' scope and core principles, provide the mandates for related administrative rules,[54] and specify the regulators' associated powers, including as regards enforcement.

In an indication of the importance of this shift, HM Treasury published in 2022 an illustrative statutory instrument, relating to the repeal of the UK Securitization Regulation (the assimilated EU Securitization Regulation 2017). The draft SI followed an earlier HM Treasury review of how the future regime should be designed. That review concluded that the new regime should bolster securitization standards to enhance investor protection and promote market transparency (the original normative framing of the EU regulation was therefore retained). It also found that the new regime should support and develop UK securitization markets to increase their contribution to the UK economy (the original EU normative framing was thereby expanded to incorporate UK political imperatives). The SI accordingly restated (with revisions

[53] The FSMA model as originally established in 2000 follows the familiar hierarchy of legislation and administrative action. FSMA sets out the regulators' objectives and mandates, establishes the perimeter for regulated activities, empowers HM Treasury to extend or contract this perimeter, and for some sectors sets legislative requirements. The UK financial regulators are charged under FSMA with setting regulatory requirements for firms in accordance with the FSMA framework.

[54] Usually in terms of the regulator being empowered to make designated activity rules relating to the specified activities.

where necessary) the assimilated law where appropriate, introduced new legislative provisions, and empowered the regulators to replace/restate/remove other provisions through administrative rule-making.[55] This model is now being applied across UK financial services regulation as the assimilated legislation is replaced.

This organizational model represents a classic expression of the political/administrative division of labour familiar from EU financial regulation and from financial regulation internationally.[56] But it has not, in practice, been a dominant feature of the UK financial rule-making process since 2000, notwithstanding the design of FSMA 2000, given the burgeoning EU regime. So while financial regulation is now embedded in the UK political system and a function of its political economy, it is at the same time becoming more a creature of technocratic design. Political interest in regulatory decision-making can therefore be expected to intensify.

(ii) Revocation of Assimilated Law: The Process

The revocation process, which will expand the rule-making space for the financial regulators, is well under way, operating in 'tranches'. Progress is tied to the related, policy-oriented reform agenda (noted ahead), which is being managed politically by HM Treasury and, as regards technocratic amplification, by the financial regulators. By way of example, the cornerstone Prospectus Regulation 2017, onshored as the UK Prospectus Regulation, has been replaced by the new and significantly deregulatory legislative framework set out in the Public Offer and Admission to Trading Regulations 2024, which is being amplified by extensive FCA rules. The scale of the reform exercise can be seen from HM Treasury's March 2024 update. It identified some 777 pieces of assimilated regulation relating to financial services, of which some 44 per cent (344 measures) had been removed.[57]

The revocation process will continue as parliamentary time allows. The financial markets-specific revocation agenda is notably extensive, reflecting the huge scale of EU financial markets regulation. But this mammoth exercise is taking place across the whole range of assimilated EU financial services regulation, including as regards cornerstone EU banking[58] and insurance[59] measures.

[55] HM Treasury, 'The Securitization Regulation—Illustrative Statutory Instrument. Policy Note' (2022).

[56] See, eg, J Mendes, 'Law and Discretion in Monetary Policy and in the Banking Union: Complexity between High Politics and Administration' (2023) 60 CMLRev 1579; C Ford, *Innovation and the State: Finance, Regulation and Justice* (Cambridge University Press 2017).

[57] HM Treasury, 'Building a Smarter Financial Services Regulatory Framework for the UK: The Next Phase' (2024).

[58] In the banking sector, the reform agenda has, while addressing the assimilated law, also been engaging with the UK implementation of the final set of financial-crisis-era Basel standards (the 'Basel 3.1' reforms) which are also currently being implemented by the EU.

[59] In the insurance sector, the reform agenda has been dominated by reform of the sprawling Solvency II regime, with significant reforms made to the 'matching adjustment' (a technical feature of Solvency II which determines the level of capital an insurance company is required to hold) through the Insurance and Reinsurance Undertakings (Prudential Requirements) Regulations 2023.

(iii) The Institutional Setting

At the heart of the supporting institutional reforms, which are of a second-order nature but which have a third-order, normative tilt, are the enhancements to the FSMA 2000 legitimation framework, given the enhanced rule-making capacity of the UK regulators. These enhancements have been achieved through classic accountability mechanisms, from revisions to the regulators' constitutive mandates and tasks, to new reporting requirements.

Chief among the reforms is the much-discussed revision of the regulators' FSMA mandates to include a new 'secondary objective' on growth and competitiveness.[60] The FCA, for example, is now charged with the secondary objective of 'facilitating, subject to aligning with relevant international standards, the international competitiveness of the economy of the UK (including in particular the financial services sector), and its growth in the medium to long term'.[61] Its 'strategic' (or primary) objective remains the same: the FCA is charged with 'ensuring that relevant markets function well', and has three related operational objectives concerning consumer protection, market integrity, and competition.[62] This deliberate tiering of objectives into strategic/primary and secondary cautions against reading this reform as a third-order normative change. It can, though, reasonably be read as a clear political direction to the regulators to be mindful of competitiveness and growth in delivering the primary objective, as has been repeatedly underlined by the Chancellor of the Exchequer in recent Mansion House speeches,[63] and as is evident from the political monitoring of the regulators' progress.[64]

Other accountability-related reforms include new duties (including to keep administrative rules under review) and new reporting obligations (including to the newly constituted House of Lords Financial Services Committee).[65] They do not, however, include the deeply contested regulatory 'call in' power, which would have enabled HM Treasury to make, amend, or revoke regulators' rules, and which was mooted during the Bill's passage but generated criticism that it could have undermined the regulators' operational independence.[66]

[60] See, eg, E Ferran, 'International Competitiveness and Financial Regulators' Mandates: Coming Around Again in the UK' (2023) 9 J of Fin Reg 30.

[61] FSMA, s 1B(4A) and 1EB. A similar formula and tiering governs the PRA.

[62] FSMA, s 1B(1)–(3).

[63] Chancellor of the Exchequer, Mansion House Speech, 14 November 2024, underlining financial services as one of the eight growth sectors in the government's industrial strategy, and that 'the UK has been regulating for risk, but not regulating for growth'. The 15 July 2025 Speech was similar in tone, noting new targets for the PRA and FCA to 'ensure that regulators are really regulating for growth'.

[64] In December 2024 the Chancellor requested that the financial regulators report on how they were securing the new secondary objective. For the FCA response see Letter from FCA CEO Nikhil Rathi, 16 January 2025.

[65] E Howell, 'The Post-Brexit Accountability of the Financial Conduct Authority: Developing Parliament's Institutional Capacity' (2023) 139 LQR 483.

[66] See, eg, Financial Services Consumer Panel, Response to Public Bill Committee's call for evidence on the Financial Services and Markets Bill (2022).

(c) Policy Reform

The substantive policy reform process, which is informing the revocation and replacement exercise, and which is also shaping the extent of EU divergence, is framed by the prevailing competitiveness and growth priority. It has been punctuated by a series of politically set reform agendas, starting with the previously noted 2019 FRFR. The subsequent December 2022 Edinburgh reform agenda—designed to 'help turbocharge growth and deliver a smarter and home-grown regulatory framework'—consolidated the reforms then in train with new proposals.[67] It was followed by the successor delivery agenda, launched in 2022.[68] This was designed to 'deliver a comprehensive FSMA model of regulation through the power established in the Financial Services and Markets Bill [now Act]'.[69] The policy review process continued following the 2024 change of government. Most recently, July 2025 saw the adoption of the Leeds reform agenda. Designed to, inter alia, 'make the UK the number one destination for financial services',[70] it proposed a series of reforms as part of the 2025 Financial Services Growth and Competitiveness plan, adopted under the 2025 Industrial Strategy.[71]

This policy agenda has varied in its level of ambition, as noted in section 5. Some of its reforms are significantly deregulatory of the assimilated law; others make substantial revisions but are more concerned with refining and correcting; still others constitute entirely new domestic regimes but reflect the wider regulatory zeitgeist and have been shaped by lessons learned from cognate EU measures (notably as regards green finance and digital/crypto assets). Overall, the reform agenda can reasonably be termed a substantial calibration of UK financial regulation, and a decisive expression of regulatory autonomy.

The reform of the cornerstone regime governing capital-raising by firms illustrates the scale of the exercise. This reform was initially shaped by the influential UK Listing Review (2021) (the Hill Review).[72] It warned of the depth of the competitiveness challenges and proposed reforms. Specialist reviews under the auspices of HM Treasury followed,[73] and were supported by related FCA reviews on the associated technical rules.[74] Extensive deregulatory reforms have since been made to the prospectus disclosure regime governing public offers, and more are expected.[75] Similarly

[67] HM Treasury, 'Edinburgh Reforms Hail Next Chapter for UK Financial Services', News Story (9 December 2022); and HM Treasury, 'Financial Services: The Edinburgh Reforms' (2022).

[68] HM Treasury, 'Building a Smarter Financial Services Framework for the UK: Policy Statement' (2022).

[69] HM Treasury, 'Building a Smarter Financial Services Framework for the UK: Delivery Plan' (2023).

[70] HM Treasury, 'Leeds Reforms to Rewire Financial System, Boost Investment and Create Skilled Jobs across the UK', New Story (15 July 2025).

[71] N 6. The financial market reforms, eg, relate to inter alia promoting household investment and revising how the FCA's 'consumer duty' rules apply in the wholesale (professional) markets.

[72] UK Listing Review (2021).

[73] Key staging posts included HM Treasury, 'UK Prospectus Regime Review: A Consultation' (2021) and the UK Secondary Capital Raising Review (2022) (the Austin Review).

[74] Key interventions included FCA, 'Primary Markets Effectiveness Review' (CP 21/21) (2021).

[75] Set out in framework legislation (the Public Offer and Admission to Trading Regulations 2024). The detail of the regime is set out in new FCA rules, primarily PS25/9 New Rules for the Public Offers and

wide-ranging and deregulatory reforms to the 'admission-to-listing' regime for firms' securities have followed.[76] In both cases FCA rules have been determinative, in an indication of how technocratic decision-making, within a politically set framework, is coming to define the shape of UK financial regulation.

4 Post-Brexit Legality

There is, with all this activity, little sign of potential TCA illegality. The TCA, as regards financial services, is primarily concerned with securing the core WTO rights of establishment (through branches and subsidiaries) and of non-discrimination.[77] Illegality is therefore most likely to take the form of breach of these access rights.

Since the withdrawal the UK has proved more accommodating than the EU, displaying an openness to third country, including EU, access.[78] At the political level, several HM Treasury equivalence decisions have supported EU firms' access to the UK,[79] in stark contrast with the EU's more parsimonious approach. The EU has made only one equivalence determination, in relation to the UK CCP regime, reflecting the importance of UK CCPs' clearing of certain interest-rate derivatives to EU financial stability.[80] New UK legislative frameworks for addressing third country access have also been adopted, notably for investment funds. The new 'Overseas Funds Regime' adopted in 2021[81] is designed to facilitate third country, including EU, investment fund access to the UK. Notably, it is based on an 'outcome-based' equivalence process and not on the more austere line-item equivalence associated with the EU approach, and so signals a strong political commitment to supporting access to the UK market. This commitment found practical expression in 2024 when EU 'UCITS' fund regulation (the UCITS fund segment represents the majority part of the EU investment fund market) was determined to be equivalent under the new regime, and so EU UCITS funds are not subject to additional UK requirements when marketed in the UK.

This openness has been mirrored at the technocratic level. For example, the FCA's 'temporary permissions' regime (the TPR) facilitated EU firms that had previously passported to the UK market. Prior to its 2023 closure, the TPR provided a temporary

Admission to Trading Regime (2025). Further deregulatory reforms were consulted on in FCA consultation CP25/2.

[76] Set out in FCA, PS24/6 Primary Markets Effectiveness Review: Feedback to CP23/31 and final UK Listing Rules (2024). Further reforms were consulted on in 2025 (CP25/2).

[77] On the treatment of financial services under the TCA see S Hall, 'What Does the Brexit Trade Deal Mean for Financial Services', UK in a Changing Europe Blog (27 December 2020).

[78] See further, N Moloney, 'Access to the UK Financial Market after the UK Withdrawal from the EU: Disruption, Design, Diffusion' (2024) EBOLR 25.

[79] Including in relation to credit rating agency, short selling, CCP, and financial reporting regulation. See eg HM Treasury, 'Equivalence Decisions for the EEA States' (9 November 2020).

[80] M Lehmann, 'CCP Supervision after Brexit: From Extraterritoriality to a Model of Shared Control' (2022) 18 CMLJ 5.

[81] Under the Financial Services Act 2021.

licence for EU firms in the process of obtaining full UK authorization. A similar regime governs temporary marketing permissions for investment funds (the TMPR) and is due to close at the end of 2026. The regulators also (re-)issued guidance on the use of third country branches and subsidiaries. The FCA, for example, underlined the key role played by international firms in the UK market, its commitment to maintaining 'open and vibrant' markets, and its intention to authorize branches and subsidiaries where the relevant regulatory requirements were met, and as long as good risk mitigations were in place.[82]

All the indications suggest this liberal direction of travel will continue. The milestone December 2023 Berne Financial Services Agreement between the UK and Switzerland marks a significant waypoint.[83] Taking the form of a Treaty governing UK–Switzerland financial services access, it allows market access on a significantly more liberal basis than does the EU. The Treaty is based on a deference model, as in theory is the EU's equivalence model in that the EU 'defers' to the third country once its equivalence requirements are met. But in design the Treaty is materially more facilitative than the EU's equivalence regime. The mutual recognition at the heart of the Treaty is based on alignment of the regulatory outcomes sought, and not on line-item equivalence. It is therefore based on substantive deference, in practice, to the respective party's regulatory regimes: the Treaty, in effect, reflects the respective right of each party to regulate as they see fit, while providing outcomes-based access. Notably, the access arrangements apply independently of any domestic rule changes or adoptions. By contrast, the EU equivalence regime is based on the notion of dynamic alignment: equivalence can be withdrawn where a third country does not adapt its rules to stay in step with any EU changes. Also unlike the EU regime, the Treaty contains procedural restrictions on the withdrawal of deference, and is supported by a discrete institutional structure for coordination and dispute resolution through a Joint Committee. Further, unlike the EU regime, which is piecemeal, the Treaty is cross-sectoral, spanning a range of financial services, and is designed to be dynamic, containing a mechanism for adding new sectors, including through five-yearly review periods. Overall, it represents a striking institutionalization of trust between the two regulatory systems. It thereby implies less of a concern for autonomy, and more of a concern to facilitate access. This engaged and liberal approach to international engagement has been sustained, with the 2025 Financial Services Strategy noting the government's commitment to an open and connected financial services sector.[84]

The recent institutionalization of technocratic relations can also be expected to limit the potential for illegality. The TCA provided for a Memorandum of Understanding on Cooperation and Dialogue (the MoU) to be adopted, but this stalled pending resolution of the fraught issues relating to the Northern Ireland Protocol. The subsequent

[82] FCA, 'Approach to International Firms' (2021).

[83] Agreement between the United Kingdom of Great Britain and Northern Ireland and the Swiss Confederation on Mutual Recognition in Financial Services 2023.

[84] See (n 6) 24.

remedial Windsor Framework unlocked the MoU, which was adopted in June 2023,[85] and the related EU–UK Financial Regulatory Framework met for the first time in May 2024, and has continued to meet regularly.[86] While the Forum does not directly address access arrangements, it provides a forum for engagement and for constructing a bespoke epistemic community which may come, as the political economy of the international standard setting process suggests,[87] to have political influence.

5 Post-Brexit Empirical and Normative Analysis

(a) Regulatory Impact

(i) Decisive Divergence?

Empirically, UK financial regulation is undergoing the largest reform exercise since the Global Financial Crisis. The reforms extend across all domains of financial regulation: institutional (the new FSMA legitimation arrangements and tasks for the UK financial regulators), legislative (the raft of retooled EU legislation and entirely new regimes), and technocratic (the new administrative rulebook). The potential for active divergence is significant.

Financial regulation is, however, highly dynamic. The pace at which markets and risks evolve, as well as the greatly enhanced technocratic capacity globally since the financial crisis, means that financial regulation is in an almost permanent state of revision, reform, and expansion in all major financial systems. The UK reform process, and the extent of active divergence, must be seen in this light. Even if the UK were politically inclined to converge to the EU rulebook, if only on grounds of administrative expediency, change and so divergence would have followed. The specificities of the risk profile of the globally systemic UK financial system, which is more heavily market-based than the other more bank-based (or loan-oriented) member state financial systems;[88] the slow pace at which EU financial regulation tends to evolve; and the need to adjust administrative rules nimbly would have led to continual UK reforms. Divergence of this form is active, but it is also compelled.

This form of necessary divergence aside, the normative extent of the divergence so far is contestable. The foundational architecture of UK financial regulation—the regulatory perimeter, the regulatory and supervisory tools used, and the institutional structure—remains more or less the same now as in 2020. Further, the baseline

[85] UK–EU Memorandum of Understanding on Financial Services Cooperation (27 June 2023).

[86] Joint Statement: EU–UK Financial Regulatory Forum, May 2024.

[87] See, eg, T Büthe and W Mattli, *The New Global Rulers: The Privatization of Regulation in the World Economy* (Princeton University Press 2011); A-M Slaughter, *A New World Order* (Princeton University Press 2004).

[88] See the Commission's annual European Financial Stability and Integration Reports, most recently 2025, and, on the implications for regulatory governance, L Quaglia, D Howarth, and M Liebe, 'The Political Economy of European Capital Markets Union' (2016) 54 JCMS 185.

normative framework for UK financial regulation has not changed since the withdrawal. Its driving concern remains—as over EU membership, and in common with the principles that expressly or impliedly shape EU financial regulation—to secure financial stability, market efficiency/integrity, and investor/consumer protection. Certainly, the UK regulators now have a wider rule-making space, but the political decision to delegate to regulators was originally taken with FSMA 2000. Substantively, the legacy EU system is still more or less in place, albeit with pockets of active deregulation and divergence, although there is also some evidence of a 'shadow' convergence dynamic emerging as the EU has moved to a more deregulatory posture. This is neither unexpected nor a failure to seize a paradigmatic opportunity. Given the dynamics of financial regulation, active divergence at scale, marking a decisive normative break with the EU, was always likely to be limited.

Financial regulation does not develop in a hermetically sealed domestic vacuum but is shaped by the international setting. Aside altogether from the well-charted association between robust and predictable regulation and strong markets and, thereby, competitive advantage,[89] the ISSBs exert a moderating effect. The complexity and systemic nature of risks, the tendency of financial markets to evolve structurally and to disintermediate away from traditional channels (such as the vast expansion since the financial crisis in 'non-bank financial intermediation', or the provision of credit and funding outside the banking perimeter[90]), and the sheer technical difficulty in drafting appropriate regulatory responses means that rule-making is often first trialled and tested through the epistemic communities constituted by the ISSBs. The new UK regime governing digital operational resilience, for example, adopted under FSMA 2023, is not dissimilar to the related EU regime (the 2020 Digital Operational Resilience Act), but reflects also the governing principles being developed by the Basel Committee.[91] Similarly, UK banking regulation is closely based on Basel standards.[92] The significance of the ISSBs as influences on UK financial regulation has been given a political imprimatur by the Financial Services and Markets Act 2023, with its direction to regulators to consider the secondary objective on growth and competitiveness with regard to alignment with international standards.[93] The influence of the ISSBs should not be overstated. Standards can be high-level and reflect politically driven compromises shaped by the state 'great powers' of international finance, and the current geopolitical setting is placing pressure on international cooperation channels. But it remains the case that international finance governance is a determinative factor shaping UK financial regulation and the extent to which active divergence is likely.

[89] See, eg, (n 10) and in the context of the US market, JC Coffee, 'Law and the Market: The Impact of Enforcement' (2007) 156 U Pa LR 229.

[90] See, eg, European Systemic Risk Board, NBFI Monitor (2024).

[91] Basel Committee on Banking Supervision, 'Principles for the Sound Management of Third Party Risk. Consultative Document' (2024).

[92] PRA, Implementation of the Basel 3.1 standards near-final part 2 (PS9/24) (2024).

[93] The PRA is subject to this requirement (FSMA s2H(1B)).

Further, the political preferences that shape financial regulation are not entirely dissimilar internationally, further reducing the likelihood of active divergence. The domestic political concerns that animate financial regulation differ, of course, reflecting, inter alia, the institutional structures of economies, structural market path dependencies, market risk settings, legacy crisis effects, household portfolio patterns, and the economic cycle. As outlined ahead, the current political preoccupation with competitiveness and growth is clearly a driving influence on the UK reform programme. But this preference, and the related regulatory design choices being pursued, are not uniquely UK phenomena. At one end of the spectrum, the US currently looks set to pursue a materially deregulatory agenda under the Trump administration. But closer to the UK's political setting, the EU is pivoting from its traditionally more dirigiste, 'market-shaping' approach to financial regulation[94] and tilting towards a more deregulatory approach that is highly attentive to growth and competitiveness. Political concern as to the EU's sluggish competitiveness and as to the scale of the current investment gap (in the region of some €700–800 billion annually) has become acute.[95] The need to strengthen competitiveness is now framing the EU's regulatory policies, reflecting the urgency of the 2024 Draghi Report.[96] This pivot was emerging in the wake of the Covid pandemic, given the constrained capacity of EU financial markets to fund the recovery. The material deregulation of the EU fundraising disclosure regime adopted in 2024 under the Listing Act can be associated with this period.[97] While not as radical as the UK's current deregulation of the fundraising regime (noted ahead), it is in many respects similar. Since then, and for the first time since the financial crisis, the reduction of regulatory costs, deregulation, and simplification have become EU, and not only UK, watchwords. The January 2025 Competitiveness Compass, for example, is designed to reduce regulatory burdens,[98] and significant deregulation has been proposed to the green finance regime.[99] The gap between the political interests driving the new UK regime and those shaping the current EU regime is not as large as might have been predicted in 2020, and the policy prescriptions being followed are not that different.

[94] 'Market-shaping' relates to the political preference for shaping markets through interventionist regulation. The UK is associated with more facilitative 'market-making' regulation that tends to rely more on disclosure than intervention. From the extensive political economy literature, see L Quaglia, 'The "Old" and "New" Politics of Financial Services Regulation in the EU' (2012) 17 New Political Economy 15.

[95] See, eg, Budapest Declaration on the New European Competitiveness Deal, November 2024.

[96] M Draghi, 'The Future of European Competitiveness. Part A. A Competitiveness Strategy for Europe' and 'Part B. The Future of European Competitiveness' (2024).

[97] The Listing Act reforms are contained in Directive (EU) 2024/2811 [2024] OJ L2024/2811, 14.11.2024; Directive (EU) 2024/2810 [2024] OJ, 14.11.2024; and Regulation (EU) 2024/2809 [2024] OJ L2024/2809, 14.11.2024.

[98] The Competitiveness Compass (COM(2025)30) has eg committed to a 25% reduction in the regulatory reporting burden.

[99] The February 2025 'Omnibus Simplification' package, refining the EU's sustainability reporting regime, represents a material deregulation: COM(2025)80 and COM(2025)84.

Relatedly, the much-examined political economy of financial regulation[100] does not shift easily, even as the source of regulation changes. The Global Financial Crisis, while receding, remains the origin story of financial regulation internationally, and there are few indications of political appetite for major deregulation and so divergence.[101] Certainly, there is an industry appetite for change.[102] Nonetheless, in certain areas—typically those concerned with risk management—the embedded costs of implementing EU rules, and of building the complex IT, reporting, and other systems that now support firms' intricate risk management and reporting systems, is a significant counterweight to the benefits of active divergence. Firms within groups that span the UK and the EU are unlikely to join a clamour for change if the result is a fragmented cross-group regulatory landscape and an inefficient use of capital and liquidity, the loss of scale and consolidation efficiencies, and a need for complex UK/EU systems to be knitted together.

(ii) Divergence, Calibration, and Competitiveness

The reform process is midstream, and the assimilated EU rulebook is of enormous scale, so the extent of the divergence emerging is not easily judged. Nonetheless, some observations can be hazarded.

The swathe of policy agendas, from the 2019 FRFR to the 2025 Leeds agenda, all commit to recasting UK financial regulation in order to, variously, deliver a more British style of regulation, deploy the new regulatory autonomy to reflect the UK risk, economic, and political settings, and deliver a simpler and more agile regulatory scheme. The framing concern, however, has been to strengthen the competitiveness of the UK financial market and to support growth. The competitiveness concern predates the withdrawal. The 2021 Hill Review identified significant weaknesses in the UK public equity market[103] and proposed reforms which have since been adopted. The competitiveness of the UK public equity market had, however, long been of concern,[104] and repeated attempts at reform had been made.[105] What is new (or at least heightened) is the political concern with wider economic growth and competitiveness, and the enrolling of financial services regulation in service of this aim.

[100] For a foundational EU assessment see J Story and I Walter, *The Political Economy of Financial Integration in Europe: The Battle of the Systems* (Manchester University Press 1997).

[101] The 2025 Financial Services Competitiveness Strategy notes financial stability as a pre-requisite to economic growth, and commits the government to upholding consumer protection, trust in markets, and tackling financial crime: n 6, 11.

[102] Exemplified in the financial markets area by the support for the significant deregulation proposed by the Austin Review of secondary capital-raising (ie deregulation of the rules applicable where issuers repeatedly raise capital in the public markets).

[103] Among its headline findings was that over 2015–20 London accounted for only 5% of initial public offers globally: 2021 Hill Review, n 72, 1.

[104] See, eg, the financial-crisis-era Kay Review of UK Equity Markets and Long-Term Decision Making (2012).

[105] For a historical perspective see D Cheffins and B Reddy, 'Law and Stock Market Development over Time: An Uneasy Match' (2023) 43 OJLS 725.

Nonetheless, the outcomes and the extent of the divergence are more in the nature of a calibrating divergence than a decisive break with the EU. Many of the reforms represent active divergence, but retain the core architecture of the relevant legacy EU regime, while seeking a more proportionate and flexible style of regulation, better aligned with the normative outcomes sought than the precursor EU regime. The replacement for the assimilated UK PRIIPs Regulation (a cornerstone investor protection measure which requires firms to produce summary template disclosures for certain 'packaged' investment products (PRIIPs)), for example, will be significantly different to the legacy EU measure.[106] The EU regime is highly standardized, encrusted with detailed specifications, and offers very little flexibility to firms; it has been the subject of significant criticism and is undergoing a troublesome review process. The new UK version (for 'Complex Composite Investments') will be materially different, although it follows the same basic design as the EU regime in that it mandates summary disclosures. But it does not contain standardized format or template requirements, it adopts a more flexible approach to the risk metrics which bedevilled the EU regime, and it brings in 'past performance' information (disclosures widely regarded as useful for investors but excluded from the EU regime given the need for compromise across the EU's banking, insurance, and asset management sectors). Similar concerns to deliver a more proportionate regime are animating the reforms of the assimilated investment fund regime. For example, a recasting of the EU legacy regime for alternative investment funds (broadly, non-retail funds) into a more proportionate system, tiered to reflect the scale and risk of different funds, is likely, but large-scale reform of its essential requirements is not expected.[107]

Other reforms are straightforwardly deregulatory and divergent. The reforms to the fundraising regime are notably so. The new regime governing the disclosures required of firms when they raise funds on the capital markets represents a significant deregulation of the EU regime as it stood in 2020. The scope of the prospectus disclosure obligation, for example, has been materially limited, mainly to initial public offers.[108] Alongside, the 'admission-to-listing' regime (which, in effect, governs the admission of securities to the largest segments of major UK trading venues) has been radically reformed.[109] The previous prohibition on 'dual class' shares has, for example, been removed (a reform which allows founder shareholders to entrench control by retaining enhanced voting rights, and which is associated with attracting fintech and social media firms), while the structure of the listing rules has been revised so that

[106] The Consumer Composite Investments (Designated Activities) Regulation 2024 (the legislative framework) and FCA, A New Product Information Framework for Consumer Composite Investments (CP24/30) (2024) (the developing rulebook).

[107] HM Treasury, Regulations for Alternative Investment Fund Managers (2025).

[108] Through the Public Offer and Admission to Trading Regulations 2024 and the associated new FCA rulebook (n 75).

[109] FCA, Primary Markets Effectiveness Review: Feedback to CP23/31 and final UK Listing Rules (PS24/6)(2024).

these rules are more heavily based on requiring disclosure to investors rather than, as previously, on more prescriptive, ex ante controls.

The fundraising reforms are currently among the most significant of the reform programme. Nonetheless, the extent to which they represent significant divergence is debatable. Certainly, the reformed prospectus regime represents an act of active divergence from the EU regime as that regime applied at the UK withdrawal. Since then, however, the EU has adopted material deregulatory reforms under the 2024 Listing Act. And in the case of listing, it was always open to the UK to undertake reforms. The EU listing regime at the withdrawal was minimal, not subject to maximum harmonization, and afforded member states very significant discretion—the UK was an outlier in its detailed regulation of listing. The withdrawal process did not therefore 'unbind' the UK, although it provided the political and institutional conditions for reform. Here too, the EU has moved to deregulate the previous minimal regime, with significant reform adopted under the 2024 Listing Act.

Yet other areas represent active divergence but divergence which could be argued as compelled, not discretionary. The innovative new regime governing mutual recognition for third country investment funds (outlined in section 4) represents material divergence from the EU's approach to third country equivalence. But, once outside the EU, the UK was required to develop its own regime, and the approach adopted reflects the UK's long tradition of a liberal approach to third country access.

Passive divergence (in that the EU regime diverges and the UK does not follow) can also be identified. At the technocratic level passive divergence is constant, as EU administrative rules and soft law are constantly adjusted. But it is also a consequence of the EU's ever-expanding legislative single rulebook, under its CMU/SIU agendas and in response to emerging risks. The UK is similarly and independently building new regimes in response to UK market developments and its changing risk environment, albeit with the benefit of learning from similar regimes adopted by the EU, and with similar motivations, post-withdrawal. These reforms include the evolving UK digital and crypto finance regime, which is similar but not identical to the EU's behemoth MiCAR.[110] The UK is not adopting a new, specific omnibus regime (the MiCAR approach), but is addressing different aspects of digital asset regulation separately, in a technology-agnostic manner, and delegating most of the technical detail to the regulators (by contrast with the highly specified and technically complex MiCAR).[111] Passive divergence is also a feature of those areas where the EU has regulated but the UK has chosen not to, most notably as regards green finance. The UK has, for example, chosen not to develop a UK 'taxonomy' for green finance investments,[112] by

[110] Markets in Crypto Assets Regulation ([2024] OJ L[2024] OJ L150/4).

[111] The UK was later in developing its regime than the EU, with the reform initially set out in HM Treasury, 'Future Financial Services Regulatory Regime for Crypto Assets' (2023). The reforms take the form, in part, of FCA rules addressing the financial promotion of crypto assets (the FinProm rulebook), following a revision of FSMA by the Financial Services and Markets Act 2023 to bring marketing of crypto-assets within the regulatory perimeter.

[112] HM Treasury, UK Green Taxonomy. Consultation Response (2025), noting inter alia the costs and complexity of other international taxonomies, and respondents' concerns relating to the EU version.

sharp contrast with the EU's globally leading but highly contested and complex taxonomy regime.[113]

The complex feedback loops developing between the UK and the EU as they look to the other's regulatory laboratories, and as they grapple with competitiveness and growth concerns and a fragile geopolitical risk setting, seem to go beyond divergence and convergence. Their evolving relationship might be regarded as a variant of the 'uploading'/'downloading'/'crossloading' dynamics associated with the national/EU adoption of international standards (the uploading of preferences to international bodies, the downloading of adopted standards into national/EU regimes, and the crossloading of these preferences to third countries through equivalence or similar regimes).[114] The unfolding UK and the EU dynamic might best be regarded as a form of peer monitoring, whereby they each monitor each other's regulatory innovations, sometimes leading, sometimes following, in an effort to download the most effective tool for their respective markets.

(b) Economic Impact

Calls for more liberal UK access to the EU market, and proposals for how this could be achieved, in the interests of the UK and the EU, are frequent.[115] From the UK side, the impact of Brexit on financial services over the long-term remains, however, unclear.[116] The short-term impact has not been significant,[117] with EU-oriented business finding alternative channels, including through subsidiaries and delegation arrangements. One commonly cited proxy concerns the City's waning ability to attract initial public offers (IPOs) and 'listings' of securities to its major trading venues. Its global position has been weakening in recent years,[118] with losses of major listings frequently dissected[119] and the admission-to-listing reforms an attempt at mitigation.[120] But this weakness predates Brexit; there are myriad factors at play, including

[113] Regulation (EU) 2020/852 [2020] OJ L198/13.

[114] L Quaglia, *The European Union and Global Financial Regulation* (Oxford University Press 2014).

[115] See, eg, CA Petit and T Beck, 'Financial Sector Cooperation between the EU and the UK—Looking beyond Brexit', DCU blog (16 May 2025).

[116] Including as regards financial services employment. For an analysis finding stagnant job growth rather than dramatic losses, but noting that the long-term effects were unclear, see S Hall and M Heneghan, 'Brexit and "Missing" Financial Services Jobs in the United Kingdom' (2023) 18 J of the Academy of Soc Sci 235.

[117] From an extensive literature and finding 'very limited impact' based on global financial flows, see P Iliopoulos, S Ioannou, and D Wójcik, 'The City of London after Brexit: Sticky Power in the Global Financial Network' [2024] Progress in Economic Geography.

[118] While a downward trend had been evident for some time, in 2025 IPO fund-raising in London fell to a 30-year low amidst growing concern as to the attractiveness of the UK equity market: E Herbert and P Mathurin, 'London IPO fundraising falls to 30-year low', *Financial Times*, 4 July 2025.

[119] Including the high-profile 2023 decision by its owner Softbank to list Arm (a leading chip manufacturer) in New York, not London: A Gross and others, 'FCA Regulator Blamed for Arm's Decision to Shun London Listing', *Financial Times*, 3 March 2023.

[120] In a sign of the concern, the Chancellor announced a new listings taskforce in the July 2025 Mansion House speech.

the global turn to private capital markets;[121] and the EU is also struggling to attract global listings. The scale, depth of liquidity, and global interconnectedness of the City of London, and related path dependencies, all counsel against predictions of short or even medium-term erosion of its strength; the Commission's 2023 extension of the UK's sole equivalence decision (for CCPs) to 2028[122] underlines the City's dominance in risk management.

One of the most eye-catching Brexit consequences was the flood of certain equity trading business from London in January 2021, given the requirement for certain transactions in EU shares to be carried out in 'equivalent' venues.[123] London would, however, recover much of the lost volume,[124] although it remains a totemic development. Certainly, structural change is occurring. Firms have, for example, established subsidiaries in the EU, including to benefit from passporting rights.[125] And EU regulators, in particular ECB Banking Supervision, have been alert to 'letter box operations', imposing requirements relating, inter alia, to management, capital, and volumes of frontline business and risk taking.[126] Logic suggests that once a bridgehead is in place—even for limited and functional reasons—business will follow over time.

Amid this uncertainty two claims can be made: UK financial regulation is changing and diverging from the EU; but it is unclear what the economic impact of this will be.

At a system level, the packaging and sequencing of the UK reform programme, and the focused political attention, is facilitating a reasonably consistent and macro-oriented reform programme, while also supporting compressed regulatory learning. The EU cannot replicate this form of concentrated reform exercise. And the emerging UK regulatory setting augurs well for a more agile and responsive regulatory regime, with potential for reduced transaction costs. All the evidence so far suggests that UK financial legislation is becoming significantly thinner and more focused on political choices than EU financial legislation, with technical detail being delegated to regulators who now have secondary objectives relating to competitiveness and growth. This model promises much in terms of more proportionate and risk-based rules, as well as more agile rule-making, not least given the capacity the UK regulators now have to make speedy revisions and to remove obsolescent rules. These are basic housekeeping tasks essential to effective financial regulation, but with which the EU

[121] B Cheffins and B Reddy, 'Will Listing Rule Reform Deliver Strong Public Markets for the UK' (2023) 86 MLR 176.

[122] Implementing Decision (EU) 2025/215 [2025] OJ L 2025/215, 31.1.2025.

[123] Some €6 billion of dealing in EU shares moved from the UK to EU trading venues, and Amsterdam replaced the City as the major EU centre for EU share trading: P Stafford, L Fletcher, and S Morris, 'London's Sway in Europe Put to Test as Rival Hubs Make Trading Inroads', *Financial Times*, 13–14 February 2021.

[124] By 2024 it had reclaimed its position as Europe's largest share trading hub: C Dorrell, 'London Continues to Roar Back as City Overtakes Amsterdam to Be Europe's Share Trading Hub', Cityam, 19 June 2024.

[125] Relocations have been the subject of an extensive political economy/financial literature. See eg S Donnelly, 'Post-Brexit Financial Services in the EU' (2023) 30 JEPP 787; R Panitz and J Glückler, 'Relocation Decisions in Uncertain Times: Brexit and Financial Services' (2022) 98 Economic Geography 119. Frankfurt, Luxembourg, and Dublin were the most common destinations.

[126] See, eg, ECB Banking Supervision, Supervisory Expectations on Booking Models (2018).

struggles, given the inter-institutional nature of administrative rule-making process and the constraints posed by the *Meroni* doctrine.[127] The emergent third country regime also augurs well, and is being supported by shouldering initiatives, including a 'concierge' service to facilitate third country actors seeking UK access.[128]

Whether or not the substantive reforms will support competitiveness and growth remains to be seen. The law and finance literature shows a correlation between the core elements of financial regulation and growth,[129] but the EU's long struggle to deepen its capital markets through regulation cautions against the transformative potential of specific legislative measures.[130] Directionally, though, the reforms can reasonably be associated with potential competitive advantage. The greater proportionality being embedded in UK financial regulation should reduce transaction costs and support competition; and specific deregulatory reforms, such as the prospectus and listing reforms, should facilitate, at least to some extent, capital-raising.

6 Conclusion

What then to conclude? UK financial regulation is clearly diverging from the EU regime, but not in its essentials. So far, the divergence is more in the nature of a calibration, if a material one. The nascent 'leading and following' dynamic which seems to be developing between the UK and EU suggests that a new form of competitive but also constructive convergence is emerging. The prospects for the TCA negotiation may therefore be improving, not least given the re-establishment of technocratic relations through the MoU.

The outcome of this period of regulatory re-setting is difficult to predict. Ultimately, financial system and associated economic growth depends on a host of factors, only one of which is regulation.[131] Nonetheless, it is incontestable that the core elements of UK financial regulation, and their normative concerns with supporting the public interest in financial stability, market efficiency/integrity, and consumer/investor protection, remain essential to financial system and economic growth. And these core elements and normative concerns remain, and will most likely continue to be, very similar to those at the heart of, and shaping, EU financial regulation.

[127] Case 9-56 *Meroni v High Authority* EU:C:1958:7.
[128] Trailed in the July 2025 Mansion House Speech.
[129] See (n 10).
[130] A slew of reviews have charted the persistent weaknesses in the EU capital market , despite years of regulatory reform. See, eg, ECMI, 'Time to Re-Energise The EU's Capital Markets' (2022) and Oxera, 'Primary and Secondary Equity Markets' (2020).
[131] C Mayer, 'Economic Development, Financial Systems and the Law' in N Moloney, E Ferran, and J Payne (eds), *The Oxford Handbook of Financial Regulation* (Oxford University Press 2015) 41.

12
Competition Law

Barry Rodger and Andreas Stephan[*]

Competition law was one of the less contentious areas of policy when the United Kingdom was in the process of negotiating the Trade and Cooperation Agreement (TCA). EU and UK competition law were closely aligned, and the UK played a key role in helping to build a system of market regulation that focused on consumer welfare and which was underpinned by economic evidence. In contrast to subsidy control, which was both politically contentious and resulted in a detailed set of prescriptive requirements, the TCA contains only simple provisions on competition law. These are that both sides 'shall maintain a competition law which effectively addresses' the three major areas of regulation: anti-competitive agreements (cartels), abuse of a dominant position (high concentrations of market power within one business), and mergers that might have significant anti-competitive effects.[1]

Nevertheless, Brexit brought about a fundamental change in the enforcement of competition law in the UK and has arguably created a greater regulatory burden for businesses, with the prospect of significant policy divergence arising between the two jurisdictions. This is because where previously the European Commission dealt exclusively with virtually all multi-jurisdictional competition cases, businesses trading in both the UK and the wider EU market may now be subject to enforcement action and regulation by both the European Commission and the UK's Competition and Markets Authority (CMA). Prior to Brexit, the CMA's role as a 'national competition authority' was largely limited to issues concerning only the UK's domestic market. The prospect of divergence has arisen because the TCA contains only a simple set of obligations, and because Brexit occurred while the core principles of competition law are increasingly being challenged by the growth of industrial policy, the implications of the digital economy, sustainability, and the transition to a net zero economy.

* Disclaimer: Andreas Stephan is a panel member for the Office for the Internal Market, which is part of the Competition and Markets Authority. The parts of this chapter that comment on the work of the CMA (in particular the section on the evolution of post-Brexit UK competition law) were written by Barry Rodger and do not reflect the views of Andreas Stephan or the CMA.

[1] Trade and Cooperation Agreement between the European Union and the European Atomic Energy Community, of the one part, and the United Kingdom of Great Britain and Northern Ireland, of the other part [2021] OJ L 149/10, Arts 359 and 360.

Barry Rodger and Andreas Stephan, *Competition Law* In: *The UK Regulatory Framework Post-Brexit: 'Law Unbound'*.
Edited by: Paul Craig and Vilija Vėlyvytė, Oxford University Press. © Oxford University Press 2026.
DOI: 10.1093/9780198969815.003.0014

In this chapter we begin by looking at the pre-Brexit competition law context, outlining the development of UK and EU competition law and the relationship between the two until the end of the transition period. We then provide a more detailed overview of the Brexit transformation, focusing on the immediate implications on competition law in the UK arising from the UK no longer being a member state. The third section provides an overview of the post-Brexit competition law reform, policy developments, and regulatory recalibration consequent upon EU withdrawal. Section 4 undertakes a normative and empirical analysis, focused on the regulatory, legal, and economic impact of the revised substantive and enforcement context in the UK. The chapter concludes by observing that, while there has so far been little explicit divergence in the legal rules and their interpretation by the CMA and courts (notably the Competition Appeal Tribunal), there are longer-term trends that potentially make greater divergence inevitable. This would likely raise costs, trade barriers, and uncertainty for businesses involved in trade across the two jurisdictions.

1 Pre-Brexit UK Competition Law Context

This section outlines three key aspects of the pre-Brexit framework for competition law enforcement in the UK. First it examines how the relationship between EU and UK competition law developed in the years leading to Brexit. Second, it explores a particular aspect of this relationship which was the requirement for the UK competition law prohibitions, introduced in the Competition Act 1998, to be interpreted consistently with EU law. Finally, this section considers merger control and the 'clear-line' boundary between substantive competence of the EU Merger Regulation rules and that of the domestic merger control rules. These issues are particularly significant in light of the post-Brexit transformation.

(a) Competition Law Rules in the UK Pre- and Post-Regulation 1/2003

Following the Second World War and even after it became a member of the EEC, the UK did not seek to promote competition through rules of prohibition. For example, cartel agreements within the UK were long subject to mandatory public registration and would only be prohibited if found to be against the public interest.[2] When the UK joined the European Community in 1973 it became subject to EU rules on agreements, abuse of dominance, and State Aid, where they had an effect on trade between

[2] Restrictive Trade Practices Acts of 1956 and 1968. See B Lyons, D Reader, and A Stephan, 'UK Competition Policy Post-Brexit: Taking Back Control while Resisting the Siren Calls' (2017) 5(3) Journal of Antitrust Enforcement 347–74.

member states. However, its domestic enforcement regime retained the registration system for anti-competitive agreements and an equally weak regime against exploitative and exclusionary behaviour.[3] There was no prohibition of abusive conduct, but simply a monopoly investigations system based around the public interest and allowing for prospective remedies but no sanctions. The public interest was also central to merger control, leading to some periods of unpredictable and inconsistent decision-making.[4]

A major shift in approach came with the Competition Act 1998 and Enterprise Act 2002. This legislation aligned UK competition law to EU law, by creating domestic equivalents to Articles 101 and 102 and adopting an economics-based system of merger control similar to that being developed by the EU at the time. The two Acts resulted in very significant institutional changes, in particular the creation of a competition authority independent of direct government control (the Office of Fair Trading and Competition Commission, now the Competition and Markets Authority, following the Enterprise and Regulatory Reform Act 2013).[5] They also gave competition powers to sector-specific regulators[6] and created the Competition Appeals Tribunal—a specialist body to hear appeals in competition cases.[7] The involvement of government in merger control was restricted to a limited set of interventions on public interest grounds, such as national security.[8] The Competition Act also introduced new investigative powers and penalties that brought the UK into line with the antitrust laws of the EU and many other jurisdictions,[9] and allowed for infringement decisions under either the Act or the Treaty (whether delivered by the Commission or the CMA), to be used in support of follow-on actions and damages claims.[10] Finally, it should be noted that the UK went further than simply emulating the EU system, as the Enterprise Act 2002 also provides for market investigations where it is perceived

[3] Restrictive Trade Practices Act 1976. See R Clarke, S Davies, and N Driffield, *Monopoly Policy in the UK: Assessing the Evidence* (Edward Elgar 1998) 16.

[4] See generally SRM Wilks, *In the Public Interest: Competition Policy and the Monopolies and Mergers Commission* (Manchester University Press 1999).

[5] I McNeil, 'Investigations under the UK Competition Act' in B Rodger and A MacCulloch (eds), *The UK Competition Act: A New Era for UK Competition Law* (Hart 2000) Ch 4.

[6] Rodger and MacCulloch (n 5); N Dunne, 'Concurrency', in B Rodger, P Whelan, and A MacCulloch (eds), *The UK Competition Regime: A Twenty-Year Retrospective* (Oxford University Press 2021). Concurrent competition law powers are also held by the following sector-specific regulators, who hold them 'concurrently' with the CMA: the Civil Aviation Authority (CAA), Financial Conduct Authority (FCA), Gas and Electricity Markets Authority (Ofgem), Northern Ireland Authority for Utility Regulation (NIAUR), Office of Communications (Ofcom), Office of Rail and Road (ORR), Payment Systems Regulator (PSR), and Water Services Regulation Authority (Ofwat).

[7] D Bailey, 'The Early Case-Law of the Competition Appeal Tribunal' in B Rodger (ed), *Ten Years of UK Competition Law Reform* (Edinburgh University Press 2010) Ch 2.

[8] D Reader, 'UK Merger Control: Finely Tailored but Time for a New Suit?' in Rodger, Whelan, and MacCulloch (n 6) Ch 7.

[9] McNeil (n 5).

[10] The ability to bring actions for damages was enhanced by the Consumer Rights Act 2015, which introduced opt-out collective actions. See for example B Rodger, 'The Consumer Rights Act 2015 and Collective Redress for Competition Law Infringements in the UK: A Class Act?' (2015) Journal of Antitrust Enforcement 258.

that competition is not working properly, and the ultimate remedy here is for the CMA to break up firms.[11]

Accordingly, excluding the merger control rules (and the EU State Aid rules[12]), the following sets of competition law rules were potentially applicable in the UK before Brexit:

At the EU level: Articles 101 and 102 TFEU could be enforced by the European Commission or National Competition Authorities (including the CMA) where conduct affects inter-state trade. Regulation 1/2003[13] aimed to ensure these Articles were applied effectively and uniformly, enabling national bodies to apply them fully. Generally, the Commission addresses only cross-border anti-competitive conduct;[14] but if the CMA investigated a case not taken up by the Commission, and inter-state trade was affected, it had to apply Articles 101 or 102 alongside UK law.[15]

At the UK level: The market investigation powers under the Enterprise Act 2002 (formerly monopoly investigations under the Fair Trading Act 1973) remained unchanged by EU withdrawal and are not discussed further here.[16] The Competition Act 1998's Chapter I and II prohibitions were modelled on Articles 101 and 102 TFEU, with section 60 requiring alignment with EU law. However, unlike the EU provisions, the UK rules required only an effect on UK trade. This allowed enforcement against anti-competitive conduct with no EU impact, meaning the prohibitions could apply not only to multinationals but also to smaller, local businesses whose practices directly affected UK consumers.

(b) Section 60 Competition Act 1998: Harmonized Substantive Law

Even before Regulation 1/2003 came into effect, section 60 of the 1998 Act contained a mechanism for keeping the UK competition law prohibitions under the Competition Act 1998 aligned with the EU law Treaty Prohibitions under Articles 101 and 102 TFEU (then Articles 81 and 82 EC), as follows: 'so far as is possible . . . questions arising [in relation to the investigation and enforcement of UK competition law] are dealt with in a manner which is consistent with the treatment of corresponding questions arising in Community Law.' It is notable that this consistency mechanism was not mandated by EU law. The UK legislator voluntarily took this approach on the

[11] C Ahlborn and W Leslie, '"Jack of All Trades, Master of None": The Ever-Increasing Ambit of the Market Investigation Regime' in Rodger, Whelan and MacCulloch (n 6) Ch 6.

[12] See, eg, L Hancher, PJ Slot, and T Ottervanger, *EU State Aids* (6th edn, Sweet & Maxwell 2021).

[13] Council Regulation (EC) No 1/2003 of 16 December 2002 on the implementation of the rules on competition laid down in Articles 81 and 82 of the Treaty [2003] OJ L1/1.

[14] Notice on cooperation between the Commission and the courts of the member states in applying Articles 81 and 82 of the EC Treaty [2004] OJ C101/54.

[15] Moreover, per Art 3(2), Ch 1 of the Act could not prohibit agreements that did not amount to infringements of Art 101(1) or which fulfilled the conditions of the efficiency exception contained in Art 101(3). Chapter II, on the other hand, could be stricter than Article 102.

[16] Ahlborn and Leslie (n 11).

basis that adopting a transplant of the EU rules would enhance deterrence and harmonized rules would be beneficial to avoid double regulatory burdens on business having to comply with two sets of different competition rules.[17]

The practical consequence of a combination of section 60 and Regulation 1/2003 was that UK authorities and courts were largely bound by the jurisprudence of the Court of Justice of the European Union (CJEU) and decisional practice of the Commission, so there was little substantive difference in cases whether Articles 101/102 or their UK domestic equivalents were being applied. Indeed, UK competition cases typically referred to both, even where the conduct was essentially confined to geographic markets within the UK.[18]

(c) Merger Control: Split Competence, the Community Dimension Threshold, and more Localized Mergers for CMA

The EU Merger Regulation 139/2004 applied where there was a Community dimension merger and accordingly the Commission had (more or less)[19] exclusive competence. The UK merger control rules under Part 3 of the Enterprise Act were only applicable (with limited exceptions) where a merger was not of a Community dimension and therefore did not fall within Regulation 139/2004 and the exclusive competence of the Commission. Accordingly, the relationship between the EU and the UK merger enforcement regimes was different from that in relation to the prohibitions, in that they were not overlapping. Where EU merger control applied, it precluded the exercise of national merger control rules. Moreover, the substantive tests were and remain different, in that the European Commission may block mergers that lead to a *significant impediment to effective competition*,[20] while the Enterprise Act test was (and remains) that of a *substantial lessening of competition*.[21] Nevertheless, the thrust of merger control at both EU and UK levels is economics-based, with similar theories of harm and analytical approaches. This is not to suggest that outcomes will always be identical (as discussed later), but there is certainly a high level of convergence between the two regimes and anticipated substantive outcomes.

[17] R Whish, 'The Competition Act 1998 and the Prior Debate on Reform' in Rodger and MacCulloch (n 5) Ch 1.

[18] B Rodger, 'Application of the Domestic and EU Antitrust Prohibitions: An Analysis of the UK Competition Authority's Enforcement Practice' [2019] JAE 86.

[19] Council Regulation (EC) No 139/2004 of 20 January 2004 on the control of concentrations between undertakings [2004] OJ L24/1, Arts 1, 9, 21.

[20] ibid Arts 2(2)–(3).

[21] Enterprise Act 2002, Pt 3, Ch 1.

2 Brexit Transformation

Following the UK's withdrawal from the EU, Regulation 1/2003 no longer applies in the UK and UK regulators and courts no longer apply the EU competition prohibitions. In addition, the CMA is no longer part of the European Competition Network (ECN), which is a framework established in 2004 to facilitate cooperation and coordination between the Commission and the national competition authorities of member states. This section provides an outline of the requirements imposed on the UK by the TCA, and reflects on the extent to which the role of the CMA would be transformed by Brexit. We also briefly consider ongoing implications for the development of private enforcement of competition law in the UK.

(a) TCA Requirements and Impact on Domestic Law

The Withdrawal Agreement and the EU–UK TCA[22] meant a decisive break with the EU, including the complete severance of the UK from EU law, except as it relates to some aspects of law in Northern Ireland.[23] Unlike some other areas of policy, competition law was not considered a controversial or challenging aspect of the TCA negotiations. Indeed, whereas areas such as subsidy control (State Aid) are highly prescriptive, the TCA merely contains an obligation to maintain a competition law regime in relation to anti-competitive agreements, abuse of dominance, and anti-competitive mergers, as well as an independent competition authority.[24] Apart from certain exceptions and caveats relating to specific industries, the agreement contains no detail on how these laws should be designed, or any minimum requirements for their application. In principle, therefore, one could suggest that there might be significant scope for divergence in policy and for the UK to forge its own approach to competition law over time.[25] Section 60A of the 1998 Act, replacing section 60, is particularly important in this context and will be discussed in the following section on Post-Brexit Competition Law Reform and Regulatory Changes.

Post-Brexit, anti-competitive agreements would continue to be exempted from the Chapter I prohibition, under section 9 of the 1998 Act (which mirrors the exemption defence criteria contained in Article 101(3) TFEU) or, under section 10 of the 1998 Act, where they fell within a retained EU Block Exemption Regulation. Key EU block exemption regulations were retained and adopted into UK law in the immediate post-Brexit period,[26] but with the ability for the Secretary of State (on recommendation

[22] TCA (n 1) Title XI: Level Playing field for open and fair competition and sustainable development.
[23] See HM Government Policy Paper, *The Northern Ireland Protocol* (10 December 2020).
[24] TCA (n 1) Ch 2 of Title XI.
[25] See discussion at sections 3 and 4.
[26] See further discussion at section 3.

of the CMA) to vary or revoke these.[27] They are considered in more detail later. In that context and in order to ensure legal certainty, the European Union (Withdrawal) Act 2018, section 6 provides that UK courts continue to be bound by EU case law that is delivered before exit day and relates to *retained* EU law.[28] Section 6(4) provides that the UK Supreme Court[29] can depart from any retained EU case law, applying the same test as it would in deciding whether to depart from its own precedent—namely 'whether it appears right to do so'.[30]

Following Brexit, the provisions contained in the Competition Act 1998 (anti-competitive agreements and abuse of dominance) and the Enterprise Act 2002 (mergers that lead to a substantial lessening of competition) were simply retained, but essentially became 'scaled up' in their application, to capture enforcement and regulation previously undertaken by the European Commission on the UK's behalf. A change to the wording of those statutory provisions was not necessary because all international infringements that were previously dealt with under Articles 101 and 102 TFEU 'may affect trade within the United Kingdom'.

As with the antitrust rules, the substance of the UK's merger control regime remained unchanged as a result of Brexit. The question of whether a merger had a *community dimension*—which would, pre-Brexit, have precluded the application of the UK merger control process—simply became irrelevant and the UK merger rules became applicable to all merger situations that met the UK's merger regulation thresholds.[31] An obvious consequence of this is that the EU's one-stop shop merger control by the Commission no longer applies in the UK and, consequently, firms operating in both jurisdictions must have any proposed merger cleared by both regulators, with the prospect of diverging merger review process outcomes where there are different assessments of the potential competition effects. Divergence will be significantly more likely if either the UK or the EU make greater use of interventions on grounds such as industrial policy, environment, or other wider public interest issues.[32]

(b) The CMA's Transformed Role

A key consequence of Brexit was the expected increase in the CMA's workload, as it became propelled from a national (NCA within the EU's own terms)[33] to an

[27] ibid.

[28] Note this is a different point from the s 60A requirement of consistency point as discussed at section 3.

[29] Extended to Scotland's High Court of Judiciary in specified cases.

[30] House of Lords Practice Statement of 26 July 1966. See Ministry of Justice, *Government response to the consultation on the departure from retained EU case law by UK courts and tribunals* (October 2020) CP 303. The test to be applied by the courts is no stricter than that of the Supreme Court.

[31] Reader (n 8).

[32] An example of this was the merger of Lloyds TSB and HBOS during the 2007 financial crisis. See A Stephan, 'Did Lloyds/HBOS Mark the Failure of an Enduring Economics-based System of Merger Regulation?' (2011) 62(4) NILQ 539–52.

[33] Reg 1/2003, Art 11.

international competition authority. In practice this was considered likely to result in a considerable degree of duplication of work by the European Commission and the CMA. The overlaps between the UK economy and EU member states mean the Commission is very likely to investigate many of the same cases, but may equally stop prioritizing some as its focus turns only to competition in the remaining twenty-seven member states.[34] The most significant anticipated increase in terms of case work and resources was in relation to merger control, where the CMA estimated its caseload was likely to increase by between 60 and 87 per cent based on the financial year ending 31 March 2017.[35] In the context of cartel enforcement, there were also concerns that the CMA could see a very significant rise in leniency applications and consequently its workload in that area, although, as discussed below, this has not fully materialized.[36]

(c) Impact on Private Enforcement

Enforcement of competition law involving private parties in litigation before the courts has developed significantly in the EU, and more specifically within the UK, over the past twenty-five years, facilitated by a range of legislative and institutional developments at EU and UK levels.[37] There were several factors at the time of Brexit which were considered likely to impact upon the continued role of the Competition Appeals Tribunal (CAT) (and High Court) as a key international forum for international competition litigation. In particular, it was thought that the incentives of litigating EU-wide (and beyond) cartels in the UK would become weak.[38]

The first category of issues concerns the scope and effect of EU competition law. First, EU law is to be treated as a foreign law; second, the territorial scope of EU law infringements will no longer extend to the UK.[39] Section 58A of the Competition Act was revised to the effect that EU Commission decisions will no longer be binding on the CAT and courts in the UK. Moreover, the reciprocal nature of the EU-wide recognition and enforcement provisions under the Brussels Ia Regulation regime were no longer in force.[40] Yet because of the introduction of a range of legal, procedural, and

[34] On priority setting in competition enforcement, see O Brook, 'Priority Setting as a Double-edged Sword: How Modernization Strengthened the Role of Public Policy' (2020) 16(4) Journal of Competition Law & Economics 435.

[35] Written evidence from the Competition and Markets Authority (CMP0002), reported in House of Lords European Union Committee, 'Brexit: Competition and State Aid', 12th Report of Session 2017-19 (2 February 2018) HL Paper 67, [73].

[36] See discussion at section 4.

[37] R Whish and D Bailey, 'The Role for Private Enforcement in Competition Law: Its Role and Development in the EU' in B Rodger, M Sousa Ferro, and F Marcos (eds), *Research Handbook on Private Enforcement in the EU* (Edward Elgar 2023) Ch 1; B Rodger, 'UK and Ireland', ibid Ch 15.

[38] The reform of s 60 interpretative requirements in relation to the Competition Act prohibitions post withdrawal (see s 60A) is significant, but less so in this specific context.

[39] *Iiyama Benelux Bv v Schott AG* [2016] 5 CMLR 15, (Ch); *Iiyama (UK) Ltd v Samsung Electronics Co Ltd* [2016] EWHC 1980 (Ch), [2016] 5 CMLR 16, [2018] EWCA Civ 220; *Media-Saturn Holding GmbH v Toshiba Information Systems* [2019] EWHC 1095 (Ch).

[40] Regulation (EU) No 1215/2012 of the European Parliament and of the Council of 12 December 2012 on jurisdiction and the recognition and enforcement of judgments in civil and commercial matters [2012]

institutional mechanisms in the legal systems of the UK, including the specialist CAT, the period post-Brexit has not demonstrated any downturn in levels of litigation, and indeed there has been a surge of damages actions, particularly collective claims, raised at the CAT in the past few years.[41]

The UK's attractiveness as a forum reflects the experience of the established competition law plaintiff and defence Bar in London, the availability of alternative forms of funding and incentives to litigate, and the experience and quality of the judiciary in competition law-related litigation. The remainder of this chapter will focus on public enforcement of competition law in the UK, and in particular the role of the CMA.

3 Post-Brexit Competition Law Reform and Regulatory Changes

This section will provide key coverage of legislative, policy, and regulatory changes to the UK competition law architecture consequent upon EU withdrawal. The key legislative change, modifying the consistency with EU law requirement, in section 60A will be outlined first, before three crucial areas of policy development are examined: in relation to Block Exemptions and Guidance generally, and then more specifically in relation to sustainability agreements and digital markets. This section will conclude with a brief exploration of the key regulatory development here in the form of the post-Brexit changes to institutional cooperation between the EU and UK competition authorities.

(a) Legislative Change: Section 60A and Potential Divergence in the Competition Act Prohibitions

As previously mentioned, no changes were necessary to the wording of the prohibitions themselves, which had been modelled on Articles 101 and 102 TFEU, but a statutory instrument was needed to remove key references to EU competition law.[42] The most important change was the revocation of section 60, in order to 'modify' the obligation for UK competition law to be absolutely consistent with the EU law prohibitions and their interpretation by the CJEU. Section 60 was replaced by section 60A,

OJ L351/1; B Rodger, 'EU Competition Law and Private International Law: A Developing Relationship', in I Lianos and D Geradin (eds), *Handbook on European Competition Law: Enforcement and Procedure* (Edward Elgar 2013) Ch 8; Rodger, 'Competition Litigation and EU Private International Law Rules', in Rodger, Sousa Ferro, and Marcos (n 38).

[41] B Rodger, 'An Analysis of the CAT Case-law on Private Damages Actions Following the Supreme Court in Merricks' [2023] 16 GCLR 147.

[42] Statutory Instrument, Exiting the European Union: Competition, The Competition (Amendment etc.) (EU Exit) Regulations 2019.

which requires the CMA and courts to avoid inconsistency with EU law, but only in relation to principles and decisions taken by the CJEU before 1 January 2021, and even then with flexibility to depart from those in certain appropriate circumstances.

Pre-Brexit,[43] the CMA and the CAT had, in interpreting and applying the domestic rules, expressly followed Commission decisions and CJEU case law,[44] and it is evident that during that twenty-year period pre-withdrawal, UK competition case law was virtually completely reliant on EU jurisprudence. Consequent to the new revised section 60A of the Act, there is now 'some' scope for the UK courts and authorities to diverge from EU law precedent.

The Competition (Amendment etc.) (EU Exit) Regulations replaced the Competition Act 1998, section 60 (the requirement of equivalence with EU law) with 'section 60A – Certain principles etc to be considered or applied from exit day'. This requires the CMA and UK courts and tribunals to ensure there be no inconsistency between the principles that it applies, and the decision that it reaches' and 'the principles laid down by the TFEU and the European Court before exit day, and any relevant decision made by that Court before exit day . . . in determining any corresponding question arising in EU law' (section 60A (2)).

They must also have regard to any relevant decision or statement of the European Commission made before exit day, unless withdrawn. This obligation does not exist where the principle is excluded by the Regulations (for example in relation to aspects of Article 101 that relate to trade between member states). However, further exclusions on this obligation are set out in section 60A(7), where the authority or court 'thinks that it is appropriate to act otherwise in light of one or more of the following':

(a) differences between the provisions of this Part under consideration and the corresponding provisions of EU law as those provisions of EU law had effect immediately before exit day;
(b) differences between markets in the United Kingdom and markets in the European Union;
(c) developments in forms of economic activity since the time when the principle or decision referred to in subsection (2)(b) was laid down or made;
(d) generally accepted principles of competition analysis or the generally accepted application of such principles;
(e) a principle laid down, or decision made, by the European Court on or after exit day;(f) the particular circumstances under consideration.

The modification to the consistent interpretation requirement introduced by section 60A can be seen as an attempt at that time to balance the need for legal certainty with ensuring that UK authorities and courts would have the freedom to develop their own

[43] Rodger (n 7); Rodger, Whelan, and MacCulloch (n 6).
[44] Whether in the CJEU's capacity as appeal court, or in giving preliminary rulings.

jurisprudence, according to the particular interests of UK markets and consumers. This was particularly important in the light of debate at that time regarding any ongoing role for the CJEU in the domestic legal framework generally. There was debate about which aspects of the enforcement of the domestic competition law rules might have a greater likelihood for a divergent approach to be adopted. There was general consensus in the period leading to UK withdrawal that the law on abuse of dominance was likely to provide greater scope for divergence, because it potentially covers more types of market behaviour and the case law was comparatively sparse, contradictory, and still very much developing.[45] Moreover, whereas there is general universal consensus on the opprobrium to be attached to most anti-competitive agreements, there has been considerably wider academic debate about the appropriate scope and range of conduct to be prohibited by an anti-competitive rule aimed at abusive unilateral conduct.[46]

There are two explicit contexts in which section 60A and the question of divergence may arise. The first is in relation to pre-Brexit established CJEU case law. One particular issue that might be considered is the extent to which the classic EU jurisprudence developed from *United Brands* might continue to provide the test for excessive pricing under UK law.[47] The second is where post-Brexit CJEU case law departs from earlier established jurisprudence, and here there is provision to *allow* UK competition law to diverge from that earlier case law and follow different, post-Brexit decisions and principles. The third aspect of potential divergence is not explicit in section 60A, and relates to post-Brexit CJEU jurisprudence on issues that have not been dealt with already by the competition case law. Here, it is suggested that although there are no formal mechanisms as such to follow that type of CJEU case law, it is likely to be highly persuasive (for the CMA, other regulators, and the courts/CAT) and cited before the courts in the UK in any subsequent (public enforcement or private enforcement) dispute on the same issue.

(b) Policy Development 1: Block Exemptions and Guidance

The competition law provisions contained in the TFEU and Competition Act 1998 are deliberately wide in their application and non-exhaustive in the types of prohibited behaviour they list. This is important because the prohibitions on cartels and abuse of dominance apply to all businesses across the economy, and market developments (such as the rise of Big Tech or the use of pricing algorithms) mean that new forms of anti-competitive behaviour can emerge over time. However, these wide-ranging

[45] See, eg, P Ibanez Colomo, 'The (Second) Modernisation of Article 102 TFEU: Reconciling Effective Enforcement, Legal Certainty and Meaningful Judicial Review' (2023) 14(8) Journal of European Competition Law & Practice 608.

[46] LL Gormsen, *A Principled Approach to Abuse of Dominance in European Competition Law* (Cambridge University Press 2010); P Akman, *The Concept of Abuse in EU Competition Law* (Hart 2012).

[47] See discussion further infra at Section 4.

prohibitions also risk having a chilling effect on legitimate economic activity that is of benefit to both consumers and the wider economy.[48] Examples of this include research and development agreements, standard setting, and also 'vertical agreements'—which are essential to most chains of production and systems of distribution and sales. EU competition law deals with these areas by giving the regulator the power to publish guidance that sets out its enforcement priorities and seeks to provide businesses with a level of certainty as to how they will be treated.[49] Soft law plays a significant role in EU competition law enforcement, as the Commission publishes guidelines across the whole spectrum of its work, from how to define a market to the calculation of fines.[50] While these soft law instruments are not legally binding, they provide considerable legal certainty and have the power to influence the development of future case law.

Beyond the publication of detailed guidelines, the Commission can also (under Article 103 TFEU) propose the adoption of appropriate regulations that define the scope of Articles 101 and 102. The most important of these are block exemption regulations (BERs) that essentially create safe harbours for certain forms of beneficial behaviour. These establish that agreements will not amount to an infringement of competition law so long as certain criteria are met (generally that the parties to the agreement do not have very high market shares) and that the agreement does not contain any harmful blacklisted clauses.

Since Brexit the EU has revised and renewed its key BERs, most notably the Vertical Block Exemption Regulation,[51] and the block exemptions for research and development and specialization agreements.[52] The UK initially retained the EU BERs to ensure certainty for businesses in the period immediately following the end of the transition period.[53] It has since begun replacing these with UK-specific instruments under the framework of the Competition Act 1998 (as amended by the Retained EU Law (Revocation and Reform) Act 2023). The Vertical Agreements Block Exemption Order 2022 (VABEO) came into force in the UK on 1 June 2022.[54] While it largely mirrors the EU VBER it replaced, there are some differences in relation to dual distribution agreements and restrictions on online sales.[55] By contrast, the updated and

[48] A Witt, 'The Enforcement of Article 101 TFEU: What Has Happened to the Effects Analysis?' (2018) 55 CMLRev 417.

[49] Art 17 TEU allows for laying down 'guidance within which the Commission is to work'.

[50] O Stefan, 'Soft Law Making at the European Commission: Not Much of a One-Institution Show' in M Elaintonio and others (eds), *Research Handbook on Soft Law* (Edward Elgar 2023) 253.

[51] Commission Regulation (EU) 2022/720 on the application of Article 101(3) of the Treaty on the Functioning of the European Union to categories of vertical agreements and concerted practices [2022] OJ L134/4.

[52] Commission Regulation (EU) 2023/1066 on the application of Article 101(3) to categories of research and development agreements [2023] OJ L143/9; Commission Regulation (EU) 2023/1067 on the application of Article 101(3) TFEU to categories of specialisation agreements [2023] OJ L143/20.

[53] Prior to Brexit the UK maintained a set of parallel exemptions under s 10 of the Competition Act 1998, which served as domestic equivalents to the EU BERs.

[54] The Competition Act 1998 (Vertical Agreements Block Exemption) Order 2022, SI 2022 No. 516.

[55] A Jones and K Slaney, 'The New EU and UK Vertical Regimes: Improvements, Divergences, and Missed Opportunities?' CPI Antitrust Chronicle, September 2022 https://papers.ssrn.com/sol3/papers.cfm?abstract_id = 4282648.

renewed EU BERs are arguably more ambitious and seek to incorporate broader policy objectives in a way that signal a break with the economics-focused orthodoxy of the past twenty-five years, as explained below.

The CMA plays a key role in shaping these types of potential divergence in policy. While one might expect there to be benefits for business in the UK remaining aligned to equivalent UK BERs, it is important to remember that the EU may decide to develop and shape these exemptions in ways that are not in the interests of UK businesses. In 2021, the CMA stated that it recognized the advantages of consistency, but signalled a willingness to diverge where those advantages do not outweigh the need to protect the UK economy and its consumers.[56]

We would expect this recommended approach to be true not just of BERs, but also of guidelines and soft law more generally.

A key test for this trade-off has come as a consequence of new draft guidance published by the European Commission in August 2024, in relation to the application of Article 102 (the prohibition of abuse of dominance).[57] It is considered by many as a partial retreat from the economics effects-based regime that had developed since 2008 with the UK's support and influence. The new guidance reaffirms form-based prohibitions for certain types of conduct (meaning effects-based economic analysis to determine whether the conduct is anti-competitive in a particular case is not appropriate). In addition, it appears to downgrade the use of a key economics analytical tool in such cases—the 'As Efficient Competitor Test', which was seen by some as a de facto safe harbour for certain forms of conduct.[58] By contrast, the UK has not yet published new guidance on Chapter II of the 1998 Act and has far less experience of enforcing this prohibition compared to that of anti-competitive agreements.[59] Given the criticisms of the revised EU approach, it appears likely that the UK will retain the previous (more economics-based) approach to abusive conduct while the EU evolves in a different direction.

(c) Policy Development 2: Sustainability Agreements

Environmental policy poses a major challenge for competition law and especially for the economics effects-based approach described above, but this time in the context of

[56] CMA, 'UK Competition Law: Vertical Agreements Block Exemption Regulation: CMA's Recommendation' (3 October 2021) CMA145, [3.8].

[57] Guidelines on the application of Article 102 of the Treaty on the Functioning of the European Union to abusive exclusionary conduct by dominant undertakings. Draft guidelines available, https://competition-policy.ec.europa.eu/public-consultations/2024-article-102-guidelines_en. Adoption of the new guidelines is still pending at the time of writing.

[58] See, eg, P Akman and others, 'The European Commission's Draft Guidelines on Exclusionary Abuses: A Law and Economics Critique and Recommendations' (2025) Journal of European Competition Law & Practice. E-publication ahead of print, https://academic.oup.com/jeclap/advance-article/doi/10.1093/jeclap/lpaf020/8074758.

[59] Although it is notable that the work of the Competition Appeal Tribunal is increasingly concerned with opt-out private action claims that allege an abuse of a dominant position.

anti-competitive agreements. As with R&D and vertical agreements, there are certain critics who believe that prohibitions on anti-competitive agreements are preventing businesses from working together to make supply chains, manufacturing, and service provision more sustainable.[60] However, unlike those other areas, the economic benefits of exempting sustainability agreements are less certain and harder to measure.[61] For example, a genuine R&D project might result in a new, better quality product, or help reduce prices paid by consumers within a period of 5–10 years. By contrast, a genuine sustainability agreement might actually increase prices (because the transition to net zero is costly) and its precise benefits for the planet or the long-term sustainability of the economy may not be easily identifiable. For example, the Dutch *Chicken of Tomorrow* case concerned a 2013 initiative by supermarkets, poultry farmers, and processors to replace conventionally farmed chickens with a more sustainable alternative.[62] The Dutch competition authority ruled that the agreement breached competition law and that the countervailing benefits could not justify exemption under the Dutch equivalent of the efficiency defence contained in Article 101(3). It was found to result in insufficient benefits to consumers and represent a restriction of consumer choice, with a lack of evidence as to consumers' willingness to pay more, and it was considered that less restrictive means to promote more sustainably reared chickens were available.[63] Competition authorities have been very reluctant to exempt such agreements, because of the danger that harmful cartel behaviour might escape regulation by being given the appearance of an arrangement that seeks to contribute to sustainability—known as 'greenwashing'.[64]

Political, societal, and business pressures for action on the environment have forced the European Commission, the CMA, and several other authorities to take action.[65] For example, following the controversy in the *Chicken of Tomorrow* case, the Dutch government proposed legislative change to explicitly permit some forms of sustainability agreements under Dutch competition law.[66] When in 2023 the European Commission published its revised guidelines on horizontal agreements, it included a new dedicated section on sustainability agreements.[67] For the first time,

[60] S Holmes, 'Climate Change, Sustainability, and Competition Law' (2020) 8(2) Journal of Antitrust Enforcement 354.

[61] J Nowag, 'Competition Law's Sustainability Gap? Tools for an Examination and a Brief Overview' (2022) 5(1) Nordic Journal of European Law 149.

[62] Netherlands Authority for Consumers and Markets, ACM's Analysis of the Sustainability Arrangements Concerning the 'Chicken of Tomorrow', Case No. 13.0195.66 (2015), discussed in M Campo Comba, 'EU Competition Law and Sustainability: The Need for an Approach Focused on the Objectives of Sustainability Agreements' (2022) 15(3) Erasmus Law Review 190.

[63] ibid.

[64] R Hahn and A May, 'The Danger of Greenwashing' in J Haucap and others (eds), *Competition and Sustainability* (Edward Elgar 2024) 215.

[65] OECD (2020), *Sustainability and Competition*, OECD Competition Committee Discussion Paper, https://www.oecd.org/content/dam/oecd/en/publications/reports/2021/10/sustainability-and-competition_27b106e0/18e2061c-en.pdf.

[66] M van de Sanden and H Butt, 'Competition Law and Sustainability Initiatives: Dutch Bill Provides More Leeway' Kluwer Competition Law Blog, 23 September 2019.

[67] European Commission (2023), 'Guidelines on the Applicability of Article 101 of the Treaty on the Functioning of the European Union to Horizontal Cooperation Agreements', C(2023) 3445 final.

the Commission recognized that agreements that pursue a genuine sustainability objective, such as reducing carbon emissions (or improving animal welfare), may fall outside the scope of Article 101, or benefit from the efficiency defence contained in Article 101(3). While this is a significant development, it amounts to a 'soft safe harbour' rather than an outright exemption.

Rather than integrating sustainability agreements into its horizontal guidance, the CMA published stand-alone guidance in October 2023,[68] which arguably takes a more progressive approach as compared to the European Commission. For example, it sets out clearer categories of agreements that are unlikely to breach competition law, allowing for wider societal environmental benefits to be considered, and it also provides greater assurance against financial penalties being imposed. The two sets of guidance are otherwise considered to be broadly consistent with each other.[69]

It remains to be seen whether either approach will open the door to new forms of sustainability coordination that do not give rise to possible liability, but this is an important area of potential divergence between the UK and the EU. As most large businesses operate in multiple jurisdictions and make use of global supply chains, it may be that most unilateral attempts to promote sustainability agreements will be ineffective unless reciprocated across key international jurisdictions.

(d) Policy Development 3: Digital Markets

A key economic transformation of the past twenty years is the rise of 'Big Tech' and in particular a small number of mainly US businesses that might be described as super dominant in markets including internet search and social media. In 2019 two influential reports were published in the UK and the EU—the Furman Review[70] and the Crémer Report.[71] Both of these concluded that traditional competition law enforcement was not enough to deal with the rapidly evolving challenges posed by digital markets. Competition law enforcement is limited by its *ex post* nature (when the harm cannot easily be undone), the level of resourcing and time needed to complete cases, and the difficulties associated with applying Article 102-type abuse of dominance prohibitions to new categories of behaviour that might be considered not to be 'competition on the merits'.[72] In the context of merger control (which in the EU requires prior

[68] Guidance on the application of the Chapter I provision of the Competition Act 1998 to environmental sustainability agreements between businesses operating at the same level of the supply chain, CMA 185 (12 October 2023).

[69] S Holmes, 'Sustainability and Competition Policy in Europe: Recent Developments' (2024) 15(8) Journal of European Competition Law & Practice 562.

[70] HM Treasury, 'Unlocking Digital Competition: Report of the Digital Competition Expert Panel' (13 March 2019).

[71] European Commission, 'Competition Policy for the Digital Era: A Report by J Crémer, Y-A de Montjoye and H Schweitzer' (2019).

[72] For a discussion, see C Fernandez, 'A New Kid on the Block: How Will Competition Law Get Along with the DMA?' (2021) 21(4) Journal of European Competition Law & Practice 271.

notification and is therefore *ex ante* regulation), acquisitions by Big Tech companies of small businesses that might otherwise become future challengers to their market dominance generally fell below merger review thresholds.[73] Both reports called for a more proactive regulatory approach to digital markets.

The issues raised in these reports, and the related literature, gave rise to new post-Brexit regulatory regimes in the EU and the UK. While the EU's Digital Markets Act (DMA)[74] and the UK's Digital Markets, Competition and Consumers Act 2024 (DMCC) share a common set of policy objectives, they diverge in ways that reflect the UK's post-Brexit regulatory autonomy. Fundamentally, the EU regulation is one is that is largely based on form, while the UK regime is based on standards. For example, both hinge on a designation of large tech companies that mean they are subject to the respective regulatory regime. Under the DMA, 'gatekeepers' are designated on the basis of objective, quantitative thresholds relating to factors such as turnover and number of users.[75] By contrast, the DMCC takes a more qualitative, discretionary approach. The CMA has the power to designate firms as having 'Strategic Market Status'[76] (essentially gatekeepers), but only following in-depth assessment of a range of factors. Another key difference is that gatekeepers under the DMA are subject to a uniform set of obligations that are self-executing and legally binding.[77] The DMCC by contrast allows the CMA to develop tailored codes of conduct for each SMS firm.[78] This is arguably a more agile approach to regulation and one that can better adapt to changes in digital markets over time. This potentially comes at the price of weaker outcomes (as the businesses have more opportunity to blunt the impact of regulation), although the CMA has more far-reaching remedies at its disposal under the DMCC, including the power to break up companies.[79] A final key difference is that DMA decisions are subject to a full merits review before the CJEU, while the CMA's DMCC decisions are subject only to judicial review on the usual public law grounds. Both regimes allow for greater oversight of mergers and acquisitions.

The new regimes are in their relative infancy, and it remains to be seen whether the clear differences in regulatory design result in diverging outcomes for Big Tech companies. The fact the DMA was adopted first and has a first mover advantage could potentially shape the enforcement of the DMCC, as the businesses subject to both

[73] Furman Review (n 70) [3.54]; C Turgot, 'Killer Acquisitions in Digital Markets: Evaluating the Effectiveness of the EU Merger Control Regime' (2021) 5 European Competition & Regulatory Law Review 112.

[74] Regulation (EU) 2022/1925 of the European Parliament and of the Council of 14 September 2022 on contestable and fair markets in the digital sector and amending Directives (EU) 2019/1937 and (EU) 2020/1828 (Digital Markets Act) [2022] OJ L265/1, 1.

[75] DMA, Art 3.

[76] Digital Markets, Competition and Consumers Act 2024, Ch 2.

[77] DMA Arts 5–7.

[78] Digital Markets, Competition and Consumers Act 2024, Ch 3.

[79] For a discussion of the two regimes see, O Andriychuk, 'The New EU and UK Regimes for Regulating Competition in Digital Markets: We Finally See What's on the Plate—But Do We Know How to Eat It?' (2024) 12(2) Journal of Antitrust Enforcement 195.

regulatory regimes will argue that diverging approaches might raise their costs of compliance and lead to worse outcomes for consumers.

(e) Regulatory Development: Cooperation with the European Commission Post-Brexit

A significant institutional consequence of Brexit was that it removed the CMA from the ECN. This organization, established in 2004, plays a key role in facilitating cooperation and allows a free flow of confidential information between the European Commission and each of the national competition authorities.[80] The CMA has always had an excellent working relationship with the European Commission and while the process of Brexit did not undermine this, the nature of the withdrawal process left both regulators without a formal mechanism for cooperation and paused the exchange of the sort of information previously facilitated by the ECN. The TCA chapter on competition law simply contains a statement to the effect that there should be cooperation and coordination, but this essentially provided for cooperation on a similar basis as that between any two competition regulators from different legal jurisdictions. Initially post-Brexit cooperation between the CMA and European Commission occurred on a discretionary, ad hoc basis. It was not until October 2024 that technical negotiations concluded on a proposed EU–UK Competition Cooperation Agreement.[81] The agreement will help to ensure that competition law investigations are brought to each other's attention at an early stage, allow for the coordination of investigations (involving either the Commission or a national competition authority as necessary), and set out clear principles of cooperation aimed at avoiding any conflicts between jurisdictions.

4 Post-Brexit Normative and Empirical Analysis

It is too soon to definitively analyse the normative implications of Brexit, as many developments described above are recent or still being implemented. For example, the UK's digital markets regime only came into effect in January 2025. However, we can identify some key enforcement developments. First, this section considers key aspects of the general direction of travel observed from CMA practice and policy statements. Then we analyse how the section 60A consistency requirement has been applied. Finally, we provide an empirical analysis of all Competition Act 1998 enforcement

[80] Notice on cooperation (n 14) 54–64.

[81] European Commission Press Release, European Commission adopts proposals to sign and conclude the EU-UK Competition Cooperation Agreement (20 May 2025) IP/25/1273; Department for Business and Trade, New UK–EU Competition Cooperation Agreement.

decisions in the post-Brexit period, to determine whether CMA practice has developed, evolved, or transformed since the period when the CMA was part of the ECN.

(a) The Evolution of Post-Brexit UK Competition Law

While the substance of the UK's competition law has largely stayed aligned with pre-Brexit EU law, there have been some important developments relating to the CMA's enforcement practices.

The first concerns its role in merger control, in relation to the proposed acquisition in January 2022 of games developer Activision by Microsoft. The case demonstrates the CMA's willingness to take independent decisions post-Brexit and not necessarily align with the conclusions of the European Commission. While the proposed merger was later cleared by the European Commission subject to certain remedies, on 26 April 2023 the CMA decided to block it because of concerns about the elimination of competition in the nascent cloud gaming market.[82] Unlike the European Commission, the CMA were not willing to accept proposed behavioural remedies.[83] The merger was eventually cleared in October 2023 following a restructure of the deal by Microsoft, which included the divestment of cloud streaming rights for Activision games for a period of fifteen years (among other measures).[84]

The CMA's initial decision to block the deal attracted criticism within the UK and around the world. Microsoft's president, Brad Smith, publicly stated it was 'bad for Britain' and sent a negative signal about the UK's openness to investment by tech companies.[85] The decision raised questions about whether it was appropriate for the UK to block such a substantial deal when it constituted only a small proportion of the global market, and about why there was not closer coordination between the CMA and the European Commission to avoid a divergent outcome. Ultimately, the more recent move to closer cooperation between the CMA and European Commission should make divergence in merger cases less likely.

The second key development, impacting the wider competition policy environment, concerns the way in which Keir Starmer's Labour government has shaped the strategic priorities of the CMA. Starmer's government came to power with a 'pro-growth' agenda, part of which was to reduce barriers that made it harder for businesses to invest and grow.[86] It is generally accepted that competition law is consistent with growth, as the promotion of rivalry tends to spur greater innovation. Yet in October

[82] CMA Press Release, 'Microsoft/Activision Deal Prevented to Protect Innovation and Choice in Cloud Gaming', 26 April 2023.

[83] European Commission Press Release, 'Mergers: Commission Clears Acquisition of Activision Blizzard by Microsoft, Subject to Conditions', 15 May 2023.

[84] CMA Press Release, 'New Microsoft/Activision Deal Addresses Previous CMA Concerns in Cloud Gaming'.

[85] Furious Microsoft Boss Says Confidence in UK "Severely Shaken"', BBC News, 27 April 2023.

[86] See 'Change: Labour Party Manifesto 2024', https://labour.org.uk/wp-content/uploads/2024/06/Change-Labour-Party-Manifesto-2024-large-print.pdf.

2024, the Prime Minister appeared to signal that the CMA's existing approach might not be consistent with the pro-growth agenda. Speaking to business leaders, he said:

> We will rip up the bureaucracy that blocks investment . . . and will make sure that every regulator in this country, especially our economic and competition regulators, take growth as seriously as this room does.[87]

In January 2025, it was reported that the Chair of the CMA, Marcus Bokkerink, resigned days after meeting with the Chancellor of the Exchequer and the Business Secretary. The Business Secretary appointed former Amazon UK boss Doug Gurr as CMA Chair 'in a bid to boost growth and support the economy'.[88] Gurr was confirmed as the permanent Chair in February 2026.

These developments took many competition lawyers by surprise. Apart from the obvious concerns relating to the CMA's independence as a regulator, it was not immediately obvious in what way the CMA's work might constitute an impediment to growth. If we take merger regulation, for example, the vast majority of acquisitions are cleared, either unconditionally or with some limited commitments, and it is extremely rare for a merger to be blocked outright.[89] Similarly, cartels and some forms of abuse of dominance are almost universally accepted as harmful, and the DMCC is intended to make it easier for rivals to enter tech markets and grow.[90]

In February 2025 the Department for Business issued a draft strategic steer, for the CMA to prioritize growth across investigations, tailor remedies in high-growth sectors, increase transparency, and improve engagement with business stakeholders.[91] The CMA responded by focusing on the 'Four Ps': proportionality, predictability, process, and pace, especially in relation to merger control. These had actually been announced in November 2024 but were developed further in response to the strategic steer.[92]

The events discussed in this section provide only a snapshot of the CMA's work and the wider policy setting during a very specific and challenging period of time, but their cumulative effect may be to reduce the regulator's appetite for taking risks.

[87] 'Keir Starmer Vows to Rip Up Bureaucracy to Unleash "Shock and Awe" of Investment', *Financial Times* (14 October 2024).

[88] 'Chair of Competition Watchdog Steps Down after Labour Intervention', *The Guardian* (21 January 2025).

[89] According to CMA data for 2024, 1,037 mergers were considered formally or informally. Only 38 were investigated at phase 1 and 6 at phase 2, and only 1 was blocked. Of all considered mergers only 0.2 were blocked or abandoned. See 'CMA Transparency Data: Annual Merger Investigation Outcomes' (3 July 2025), https://www.gov.uk/government/publications/phase-1-merger-enquiry-outcomes/annual-merger-investigation-outcomes.

[90] See CMA, 'Guidance on the Digital Markets Competition Regime Set Out in the Digital Markets, Competition and Consumers Act 2024' (19 December 2024).

[91] Department for Business & Trade, 'Draft Strategic Steer to the Competition and Markets Authority' (February 2025).

[92] CMA, 'Driving Growth: How the CMA Is Rising to the Challenge', Speech by Sarah Cardell, CMA Chief Executive, at Chatham House Competition Policy 2024 conference (21 November 2024).

In particular, the drive for more growth may make it less likely that the CMA will attempt to follow the European Commission's strategy of targeting international cases which affect its markets, or for it to take enforcement decisions which develop UK law in a potentially divergent way.

(b) Section 60A and Substantial Divergence in Practice

The new section 60A interpretation provision was discussed above. It is suggested that the CMA and the CAT are very unlikely to exercise the freedoms provided by section 60A in relation to clear and settled questions of competition law, developed over time by the CJEU. Potential divergence in the interpretation and application of aspects of the substantive rules of UK and EU competition law is probably inevitable to some extent by virtue of the fact that aspects of the scope and application of the law, particularly in relation to unilateral conduct, are still evolving or are unresolved, and whose effects (and therefore correct treatment in law) are still disputed by academics, policy-makers, and practitioners. There was some suggestion that it would be in the UK's interest to create a positive obligation on courts to *have regard to* EU law and precedent,[93] but this was not politically acceptable given the imperative to regain sovereignty. Neither would it necessarily have been in the UK's interests to retain such ties with EU law without any influence over its future direction. As alluded to above, the position is slightly different between pre-Brexit EU case law and post-Brexit EU case law. In relation to the latter, section 60A(8) makes it implicitly clear that the obligation created by section 60A(2) does not extend to principles laid down or decisions made by the European Court after exit day (ie from 1 January 2021). Nonetheless, it was anticipated and remains the case that any post-Brexit EU case law would continue to be *strongly persuasive* and that the CMA and CAT would likely adopt the same reasoning as future EU cases.[94] Although it remains very early in the cycle of case law post-Brexit both to ascertain any real developments generally in relation to the consistency 'requirement' and in particular regarding any post-Brexit CJEU jurisprudence, it is instructive nonetheless to analyse the way section 60A has been referred to in the case law in the UK courts since Brexit.

We identified twelve cases[95] through a Westlaw search, although in three cases there was in fact no mention of the provision.[96] *Roberts v Severn Trent Water Ltd*[97] involved a collective proceedings claim for abuse of dominance. The Proposed

[93] See, eg, Fingleton and others, 'The Implications of Brexit for UK Competition Law and Policy' (2017) 13(3) Journal of Competition Law and Economics 389, 395.

[94] Unless the UK is required to implement some EU rules (such as State Aid) as part of a free trade agreement, there is no basis in international law for CJEU case law to be given any kind of special status.

[95] Westlaw case law search using 'Competition Act 1998 section 60A'.

[96] *Stellantis Auto SAS v Autoliv AB* [2025] CAT 9; *Le Patourel v BT Group Plc* [2024] CAT 76; *HG Capital LLP v Competition and Markets Authority* [2023] CAT 52.

[97] [2025] CAT 17.

Class Representative's claim drew support from European Court case law,[98] and the Tribunal also observed that the domestic provisions mirrored the EU prohibitions in Articles 101 and 102, making reference to section 60A. It indicated that it was 'common ground' in the present proceedings that the pre-Brexit case law of the EU courts applies. In relation to a particular, novel argument that the prohibition on exploitative abuse would not apply, the Tribunal stressed the continued importance of the body of EU competition case law, adding that 'in over half a century of jurisprudence under EU competition law' that particular, novel argument was absent.[99] This demonstrated the potential difficulty in arguing against a well-developed line of established case law by the EU courts in the application of the mirror provisions under domestic law. Moreover, the CAT in *Bayerische* cited earlier case law to the effect that the notion of an undertaking (for determination under the Chapter I prohibition and Article 101) was 'an autonomous concept of EU law'.[100] The CAT further held that '[a]lthough, no doubt, in future, the understanding of what is an undertaking will be developed by the courts of the United Kingdom, for present purposes the law of the European Union constitutes the best source for defining this term'.[101]

Overall, there has been limited consideration of section 60A in the post-Brexit period. There has been no case law involving any successful argument for a divergent approach to the interpretation of any aspects of the EU prohibitions post-Brexit. The courts have relied on established EU law principles and the clear implication is that this will continue for the foreseeable future, subject to any compelling arguments for a divergent approach. This conservative approach is also reflected in the CMA's approach to section 60A and the continued reliance on EU law.[102] Thus far, CMA practice in its infringement decisions has continued to rely directly on EU jurisprudence and has a fairly standard footnote in explaining the law, throughout those infringement decisions, as follows: 'Following the UK's exit from the EU, the UK no longer has jurisdiction to apply Article 101 TFEU. However, EU case law applying Article 101 TFEU remains relevant pursuant to section 60A of the Act.'[103] Particularly in the Chapter II cases, the CMA has relied on EU case law, notably *United Brands*, in relation to determining whether pricing has been excessive.[104] There has been no evidence, at least in any of its formal infringement decisions, of any departure from existing EU principles on the basis provided for under section 60A.

[98] Case C-457/10 P *AstraZeneca v Commission* EU:C:2012:770.

[99] [2025] CAT 17, [78].

[100] *Bayerische Motoren Werke AG v Competition and Markets Authority* [2023] CAT 7, [40].

[101] ibid.

[102] See discussion in what follows on review of enforcement trends by the CMA at 'Economic Impact—Enforcement Trends'.

[103] Cf the longer formulation by certain regulators, for example Case CA98.2020.01, FCA, 30 November 2023, Anti-competitive conduct in the UK international money remittance sector.

[104] See, eg, CMA Decision in Case 50908, 21 July 2022, Unfair pricing in the supply of phenytoin sodium capsules in the UK,

(c) Economic Impact: Enforcement Trends

A key issue following EU withdrawal was how the CMA would develop its enforcement strategies. Research by Rodger had demonstrated that over the fifteen years leading up to withdrawal, the UK authorities had investigated very few infringements of EU competition law and had tended to focus on mainly localized infringements of the domestic rules.[105] This section considers the CMA's enforcement practice in relation to the prohibitions post-Brexit, and compares this with its enforcement activity in the period between the Competition Act's introduction and EU withdrawal.

We reviewed the CMA's public *register of decisions*[106] under the Competition Act 1998 prohibitions. We included all decisions between exit day and 1 April 2025 inclusive, and this led to us identifying twenty-seven decisions in total, including six decisions by concurrent regulators: one each by FCA, OFCOM, ORR, OFWAT, PSR, and OFCOM. In all, twenty-four decisions involved either an infringement or fine (16 cases) or a commitments decision (8 cases).[107]

They key outcomes from this empirical study of post-Brexit CMA enforcement of the UK prohibitions are as follows: there has been continued prioritization of the Chapter I prohibition[108] but there has clearly been a move away from very localized small cartels (with very minor fines), as evidenced by research in relation to the earlier period to 2019,[109] but a continued focus on the application of the prohibition to the presumptively illegal by-object restrictions. There have been many more Chapter II prohibition cases, but the reliance on commitments outcomes (where there is no finding of infringement or penalty imposed) is notable,[110] both compared to earlier periods and on a comparative basis with, for example, the output of DGComp of the European Commission.[111] There has been a continuation of the prioritization on anti-competitive conduct, particularly abusive excessive pricing under the Chapter II prohibition, in relation to certain drugs provided by the pharmaceutical industry for the NHS. In those cases the fines imposed have been considerable, although they have in some cases been reduced through the appeal process.[112] Another point of interest has been the increasing interest in potentially abusive behaviour by Big Tech businesses in the digital economy, although these have all been addressed by commitments, and

[105] Rodger (n 19).

[106] https://www.gov.uk/government/publications/ca98-public-register/ca98-register.

[107] A commitments decision is an informal resolution of a case without a formal, final infringement decision; undertakings propose solutions to deal with any potential competition concerns of the competition authority.

[108] Rodger (n 19) found that anti-competitive agreements cases alone counted for 67 per cent of all cases.

[109] ibid.

[110] ibid; Rodger found only 5 commitments outcomes between 2004 and 2019, although it should be noted that overall in that period there was only an infringement finding in 7 of all of the 37 cases (18.9 per cent) in which the abuse rules were considered.

[111] See https://competition-policy.ec.europa.eu/antitrust-and-cartels/european-competition-network/statistics_en.

[112] See for example, 1419/1/12/21 *Hg Capital LLP v Competition and Markets Authority* [2023] CAT 52.

this may perhaps be seen as a precursor to the new regime in the UK for dealing with digital markets, as discussed in section 3. The statistics in relation to abuse cases appear to demonstrate a continued historical reluctance by the UK competition authority to undertake abuse cases and/or and the difficulties in pursuing a case through to an infringement finding. Nonetheless, such abuse cases are incredibly resource-intensive, compared with the relatively straightforward task where there is evidence of a clear cartel-type infringement.

Compared to the earlier study, there has been a broadly similar level of infringement and fine decisions in the (just over) four-year sample here, with fifteen infringement and fine decisions, evidencing little change pre- and post-withdrawal. Between 2001 and 2019 a total of £707m in fines was imposed by the CMA (and its predecessor the Office for Fair Trading or OFT), an average of £37.2m per year. The limited level of fines imposed by the OFT under its competition law powers was criticized at an early stage by the National Audit Office.[113] In the period since Brexit to 1 April 2025, a total of circa £690 million fines has been imposed,[114] which is a considerable increase, although this is subject to subsequent reductions on appeal in some of the cases.[115] The increase in fines imposed may partly reflect the return to more frequent use of the leniency and settlement processes under the Chapter I prohibition compared to the period prior to Brexit, and also a shift from a focus on fairly localized horizontal cartel arrangements for which only relatively small fines could be imposed in light of the relevant market affected. Furthermore, the pre-Brexit study had identified only sixteen formal infringement decisions involving EU law by the OFT/CMA since Regulation 1/2003 came into force (until 2019) and all involved UK and EU law. Post-Brexit it was unlikely that we would see any radical change in terms of the CMA's approach to enforcement given the prior limited use of EU law and its application primarily to local cases and contexts only, contrary to the enforcement context envisaged by Regulation 1/2003 and the Commission's Network Notice. Ironically, post-Brexit we can observe enforcement in relation to wider infringements of the Chapter I prohibition compared to the predominant enforcement in the pre-Brexit period on very localized cartels. Combined with increased levels of fines generally and revitalized leniency and settlements policy, it may be suggested that the CMA post-Brexit has enhanced its record for deterrent competition law enforcement, at least in relation to anti-competitive agreements, whereas the reliance on commitments in relation to unilateral conduct is more concerning.

[113] See 'The UK competition regime—NAO report'.

[114] Circa £260 million in chapter 1 prohibition cases, and more than £430 million in chapter II prohibition cases (one case was also combined with chapter 1). However, note that some fines were subsequently reduced on appeal.

[115] See for instance, 1419/1/12/21 *Hg Capital LLP v Competition and Markets Authority* [2023] CAT 52, where the CAT reduced the fines in relation to unfair prices for liothyronine tablets by £17.2m.

5 Conclusion

Competition law did not feature prominently in the Brexit debate and was not politicized in the way that subsidy control and some other policy areas were during the transition period. This meant it was subject to only a general set of less prescriptive obligations under the TCA—essentially an obligation to maintain a system of competition law in relation to agreements, abuse, and mergers, and to have an independent regulator. This left the UK with considerable latitude (in principle at least) to assert regulatory autonomy and forge its own independent path in applying its competition law. The introduction of section 60A of the Competition Act 1998 and the political imperative to break any continued influence of the CJEU made this prospect all the more realistic. This chapter has outlined some examples of divergence, including in relation to soft law guidelines and most notably the regulation of digital markets. Yet despite these, there is little evidence of significant substantive departure from EU competition law norms. The UK and the EU remain (for the time being at least) aligned in their core competition policy objectives. This is likely to continue in the short to medium term, and the speed of divergence may depend as much on how rapidly EU competition law continues to evolve (possibly in directions that are not considered in the interests of UK consumers) as it does on the UK's appetite to depart from established pre-Brexit case law.

The more pronounced differences to date lie in the institutional framework and enforcement landscape. The CMA has had to adapt to the role of an international competition regulator, dealing with all anti-competitive conduct and mergers that may affect trade in the UK and not just smaller purely domestic cases. It has shown a willingness to exert regulatory autonomy during a period when there has been no formal cooperation agreement in place between UK and EU regulators, in stark contrast to when the UK was a member state and there was close coordination and information exchange through the ECN. UK regulators have also had to grapple with an evolving political landscape that is shaping their strategic priorities. The UK's enforcement authorities face increasing demands, and recent trends indicate a shift towards larger, cross-border cases, with a particular emphasis on the pharmaceutical and technology sectors. However, such developments likely reflect global enforcement patterns rather than a distinctively post-Brexit trajectory. Indeed, there appears to be limited political or institutional appetite in the UK for a markedly interventionist approach in areas such as merger control or digital markets regulation.

In the short and medium term, divergence in competition law may be limited by the realities of business compliance and the tendency to still treat the UK and the EU as one closely integrated market. Given the inherently high degree of international convergence in competition law, the UK is likely to maintain a broadly harmonized approach with the EU in core areas.

However, over the longer term, the evolution of industrial policy may create pressures for divergence. Further shifts away from economics-based frameworks towards more protectionist or politically driven priorities could result in increased regulatory friction, particularly in emergent and strategically significant domains such as climate change, sustainability, and the digital economy. Notwithstanding this potential, the foundational principles and application of competition law in the UK are expected to remain substantively aligned with those of the EU.

13 Subsidy Control

Andrea Biondi and Totis Kotsonis*

1 Introduction

During the UK–EU negotiations that ultimately led to the conclusion of the Trade and Cooperation Agreement (TCA)[1] that regulates the parties' post-Brexit trade relations, subsidy control emerged as one of the most contentious issues. The UK's starting position was that any subsidy control bilateral commitments should broadly mirror existing World Trade Organization (WTO) obligations, providing for example for the biannual notifications of subsidies, the ability to request consultations on subsidies of concern, and a commitment to use best endeavours to mitigate a subsidy's adverse effects. In contrast, the EU's starting position was that the UK should effectively implement domestically EU State Aid rules, including the obligation to refer questions of interpretation of EU law to the Court of Justice of the EU (CJEU).

In the end, the TCA subsidy control commitments represent a compromise between these two starkly different positions. Accordingly, while the TCA does not require the UK to implement EU state aid law, it requires it to establish and maintain an 'effective system of subsidy control' that ensures subsidies are granted in accordance with a set of core principles that largely mirror the principles that the European Commission applies when determining the compliance of State Aid measures with the internal market. Other core commitments include an obligation to establish or maintain an operationally independent authority with 'an appropriate role' in subsidy control as well as ensure that the UK courts have the power to impose effective remedies for the breach of subsidy control rules.[2]

As is often the case, the devil is in the detail, so that while the principles and specific commitments that were agreed under the TCA could have led to the

* The opinions are expressed in a strictly personal capacity. They do not represent the views of the Court of Justice of the European Union as a body or those of its members.

[1] Trade and Cooperation Agreement between the European Union and the European Atomic Energy Community, of the one part, and the United Kingdom of Great Britain and Northern Ireland (OJ L 149, 30.4.2021, pp. 10–2539).

[2] See further A Biondi, 'Preserving the Playing Field: Subsidies Regulation in the TCA' in F Fabbrini (ed), *The Law and Politics of Brexit* (Oxford University Press 2024) Vol 4, 218.

Andrea Biondi and Totis Kotsonis, *Subsidy Control* In: *The UK Regulatory Framework Post-Brexit: 'Law Unbound'*.
Edited by: Paul Craig and Vilija Vėlyvytė, Oxford University Press.
DOI: 10.1093/9780198969815.003.0015

implementation of a domestic subsidy control system which was broadly consistent with the EU's approach to State Aid regulation, they did not. In fact, nearly three years after the implementation of the Subsidy Control Act 2022 (SCA)[3]—the legislation which was primarily introduced to implement the TCA subsidy control commitments—the EU continues to express concerns as to the extent to which the UK has complied with its TCA obligation to put in place and maintain an effective subsidy control system.[4]

This chapter seeks to describe how the UK's post-Brexit subsidy control regime operates, highlighting how it differs from EU State Aid rules, and commenting on the extent to which the domestic regime has shortcomings that might limit its effectiveness.

2 Definition of a Subsidy

(a) Core Components of the Definition

Section 2 of the SCA defines a subsidy as financial assistance that:

(a) is given, directly or indirectly, from public resources by a public authority;
(b) confers an economic advantage to one or more enterprises;
(c) is specific, in that it benefits certain enterprises over others; and
(d) has, or is capable of having, an effect on competition or investment within the UK, or on trade or investment between the UK and another country.

This four-limb test mirrors the structure of the EU State Aid definition, but with subtle shifts in terminology and scope, a sort of pick-and-mix of elements derived both from EU State Aid law and from international regulation of subsides. For instance, 'public resources' replaces 'State resources', and 'specific' replaces 'selective'—a change that is arguably largely semantic but which reflects the UK's desire to put in place a legal vocabulary which is distinct from that used under EU State Aid rules.

(b) Financial Assistance

This includes not only direct grants and loans, but also guarantees, tax exemptions, favourable terms for the disposal of public assets, and even contingent liabilities such as indemnities. This mirrors the EU's broad interpretation of 'aid', which also encompasses any kind of support or market transaction that is considered to have a financial value for the recipient.

[3] Subsidy Control Act 2022.
[4] EU Statement at the 1st Trade Policy Review of the United Kingdom, 28 October 2025.

(c) Public Resources and Public Authority

The term 'public resources' is not defined in the SCA. However, the 'UK subsidy control regime: statutory guidance' ('the Guidance') states this should be interpreted broadly, and that resources are considered public where they have come under public control prior to being transferred to the relevant receiving enterprises, therefore including the resources of public authorities at any level of central, devolved, regional, or local government.[5]

Public resources include non-payment of government revenues that would otherwise be due, such as exemptions and reliefs from tax revenue.[6] The concept also includes the allocation of funds which are not in fact transferred but remain contingent liabilities, such as guarantees.

A transfer between private entities will not be treated as public resources, even where this is mandated by regulation. At the same time, a transfer of public resources may exist where resources paid for by private bodies transfer through a public authority or other body that is influenced or controlled by a public authority, where this results in a corresponding charge to government expenditure or forgoes government revenue that was otherwise due.[7] Again, this definition is consistent with EU State Aid rules which focus on the question of whether the resources remain under state control.

The definition of 'public authority' under the SCA is similarly broad, including any entity exercising functions of a public nature,[8] including public authorities at any level of central, devolved, regional, or local government and non-governmental bodies that are performing a public function.[9] However, legislative bodies such as Parliament and devolved legislatures are excluded. Separately, some bodies exercise a mix of public and private functions. In those cases, it is necessary to consider whether the financial assistance comes from public resources to determine whether the assistance might constitute a subsidy.[10]

The question of which is the public authority giving a subsidy is particularly important under UK subsidy control. This is on the basis that, unlike the position under EU State Aid rules, it is the grantor of the subsidy, rather than an independent regulator, which has an obligation to determine the question of subsidy control compliance. According to the SCA, the public authority must consider the so-called subsidy control principles before giving a subsidy and must not give the subsidy unless it is of the view that the subsidy is consistent with those principles.

[5] UK Subsidy Control Statutory Guidance, s 3.58 (30 June 2023), Para 15.4 2. It should be noted that the SCA, under s 79(6), compels all relevant stakeholders to have regard to the Guidance.

[6] Para 15.6 Guidance.

[7] ibid.

[8] SCA, s 6(1) SCA.

[9] Para 15.2 Guidance.

[10] Para 15.3 Guidance.

(d) Economic Advantage and the CMO Principle

A central test under both the UK and EU subsidy control regimes is whether the financial assistance in question confers an economic advantage on the recipient. In essence, this means determining whether the support places the enterprise in a better financial position than it would have been in under normal market conditions.[11]

Under the SCA, an enterprise is considered to receive an economic advantage if the financial assistance is provided on terms more favourable than those that could reasonably have been expected to be available on the open market. This mirrors the EU's 'market economy operator' (MEO) test, which asks whether a private investor, acting in accordance with normal market conditions, would have made the same decision. In the UK, this concept is referred to as the 'commercial market operator' (CMO) principle, and it serves as a functional equivalent to the MEO test.[12]

In line with EU State Aid law, the CMO principle focuses exclusively on commercial objectives. Public policy considerations are excluded from the analysis, as they would not influence the decisions of a rational private operator.[13]

The application of the CMO principle was considered by the Competition Appeal Tribunal (CAT), the judicial body responsible for most subsidy control challenges, in *Weis v Greater Manchester Combined Authority ('Weis')*.[14] In its decision, the CAT confirmed that public authorities have a broad margin of appreciation when assessing whether a measure constitutes a subsidy and that in this regard, statutory guidance does not constitute a rigid checklist. Instead, the public authority's own experience and market knowledge can be relevant in determining whether the terms of assistance are consistent with market norms.

In *Weis*, neither party submitted expert evidence to demonstrate whether the financial assistance was in line with market terms. Nonetheless, the CAT relied on its own expertise to assess what might reasonably have been available on the market. It also noted that the identity of the granting authority—particularly its prior experience with similar funding schemes—was a relevant factor in the analysis. At the time of writing, the CAT's ruling is subject to appeal, and it remains to be seen whether the Court of Appeal will endorse this flexible approach.

(e) Specificity

The specificity limb tests whether the measure favours certain enterprises over others.[15] Although 'specificity' is a term borrowed from the Agreement on Subsidies

[11] SCA, s 3(2).
[12] *Weis v Greater Manchester Combined Authority* [2025] CAT 41, [103].
[13] Para 15.60 Guidance.
[14] *Weis* (n 12).
[15] Para 2.22 Guidance.

and Countervailing Measures (ASCM) concept, the test in itself is conceptually similar to the EU's 'selectivity' criterion under Article 107(1) TFEU. Measures of general application, such as region-wide tax reliefs, are not considered specific, even if they disadvantage enterprises in other parts of the UK.[16]

(f) Enterprise

The term 'enterprise' aligns with the concept of 'undertaking' in EU law. It refers to any person or group of persons engaged in an economic activity, regardless of legal form, method of financing, or whether or not the activity is profit-making.[17] The SCA also recognizes that entities may perform both economic and non-economic functions, and only the former are relevant for subsidy control purposes.[18] Accordingly, the term may apply to charities and public bodies when they engage in an economic activity.

In the first ever subsidy control case before the CAT, *Durham Company Limited v Durham County Council ('Durham')*,[19] the CAT clarified that the concept of 'enterprise' under the SCA is narrower than the EU's 'undertaking' concept.

In the *Durham* case, Max Recycle alleged that Durham County Council had granted a subsidy to its own trade waste business by allowing it to use household waste resources, funded by public money, at below market cost. The CAT held that no subsidy was present under the SCA, on the basis that the Council was both the giver and the recipient of the alleged subsidy, and that no separate legal entity was involved in carrying out the economic activity. As such, the economic benefit merely circulated within a single entity. The CAT ruled that a public authority cannot simultaneously be an enterprise receiving a subsidy under the SCA. By contrast, under EU State Aid law, it is accepted that a public authority may qualify as an undertaking if it engages in economic activity, even where that activity is carried out within the same legal entity.

It is worth noting, however, that the conclusion under EU State Aid rules would likely have been the same, albeit reached via a different route. For example, it is an established principle under EU law that where a public entity exercises an activity which cannot be separated from the exercise of its own public powers, that activity is not economic in nature and therefore not subject to State Aid regulation.

(g) Effect on Competition and Trade

Perhaps the most significant divergence from EU law lies in the fourth limb of the definition. While the EU regime requires a potential effect on trade between member states, the UK test captures measures that affect international trade but also

16 ibid.
17 Paras 15.13–15.15 Guidance.
18 Para 15.17 Guidance.
19 *Durham Company Limited v Durham County Council* [2023] CAT 14.

competition and investment in the UK. This broader scope means that subsidies with purely domestic effects, previously outside the reach of EU State Aid rules, are now subject to scrutiny under the SCA.

3 Subsidy Control Principles and Energy and Environment Principles

(a) Subsidy Control Principles

As already noted, the SCA imposes an obligation on public authorities to self-assess proposed subsidies or subsidy schemes with the subsidy control principles. These are as follows:[20]

Principle A: Subsidies should pursue a specific policy objective in order to remedy an identified market failure or address an equity rationale (such as local or regional disadvantage, social difficulties, or distributional concerns).

Principle B: Subsidies should be proportionate to their specific policy objective and limited to what is necessary to achieve it.

Principle C: Subsidies should be designed to bring about a change of economic behaviour of the beneficiary. That change, in relation to a subsidy, should be conducive to achieving its specific policy objective, and something that would not happen without the subsidy.

Principle D: Subsidies should not normally compensate for the costs the beneficiary would have funded in the absence of any subsidy.

Principle E: Subsidies should be an appropriate policy instrument for achieving their specific policy objective and that objective cannot be achieved through other, less distortive, means.

Principle F: Subsidies should be designed to achieve their specific policy objective while minimizing any negative effects on competition and investment within the United Kingdom.

Principle G: Subsidies' beneficial effects (in terms of achieving their specific policy objective) should outweigh any negative effects, including, in particular, negative effects on competition and investment within the United Kingdom, and international trade and investment.

[20] Sch 1 SCA.

(b) Energy and Environment

In addition to the general subsidy control principles, subsidies and schemes relating to energy and environmental matters must also be evaluated against a distinct set of energy and environment principles. These principles serve to ensure that public financial support in these sectors aligns with broader policy objectives, such as sustainability, market integrity, and environmental responsibility.

Of these, Principles A and B apply universally to all subsidies concerning energy and the environment. Principle A stipulates that subsidies must be designed to incentivize the beneficiary either to contribute to the delivery of a secure, affordable, and sustainable energy system and a well-functioning, competitive energy market, or to enhance environmental protection in ways that would not occur in the absence of the subsidy. Principle B reinforces the polluter-pays principle, requiring that subsidies must not absolve the beneficiary of liabilities arising from its role as a polluter.

Beyond these foundational principles, additional energy and environment principles apply to specific categories of intervention. These include subsidies aimed at electricity generation adequacy, renewable energy production, and co-generation; partial exemptions from energy-related taxes and levies; and support for decarbonization and energy efficiency initiatives.[21] However, these principles are considerably less detailed than the equivalent EU Guidelines on State Aid for climate, environmental protection and energy.[22]

Ultimately, there are legitimate concerns as to the capacity of public authorities to carry out a subsidy control principles compliance assessment. This issue is discussed later in the chapter.

4 Categories of Subsidies

(a) Subsidy Schemes

A subsidy scheme must set out the criteria on the basis of which individual subsidies may be granted under that scheme. A subsidy scheme may be made either by:

(a) a public authority that is not a primary public authority for the giving of subsidies only by itself; or
(b) a primary public authority for the giving of subsidies by other public authorities, and itself if it wishes.[23]

[21] Principles C–I are explained in more detailed in Chapter 4 of the Guidance.
[22] Communication from the Commission—Guidelines on State aid for climate, environmental protection and energy 2022 (C/2022/481).
[23] SCA, s 10(2).

A primary public authority is defined as a minister of the UK, Scottish, or Welsh governments or a Northern Ireland department, or any other public authority which, in the exercise of its functions, makes a scheme for the giving of subsidies by other public authorities.[24]

A public authority may only make a subsidy scheme if it is of the view that any subsidies provided for by the scheme will be consistent with the subsidy control principles.[25] There is therefore no requirement to reconsider the subsidy control principles each time a subsidy is awarded under the scheme.[26] Instead, a subsidy that meets the criteria for reliance on the scheme will be deemed to satisfy the subsidy control principles. Accordingly, reliance on a pre-existing subsidy scheme can often provide for a much swifter process when granting subsidies, compared to the comparatively more burdensome requirements associated with granting a standalone subsidy.

Subsidies properly given under a scheme are not subject to review by the CAT.[27] However, if a subsidy which was purported to have been given under a scheme did not in fact comply with the terms of the scheme, then the subsidy should have been treated as a standalone subsidy and an assessment against the subsidy control principles should have been undertaken. An interested party may challenge such a subsidy on these grounds.[28]

(b) Streamlined Subsidy Schemes

A streamlined subsidy scheme (also referred to as a streamlined route) is, in essence, the UK equivalent of the General Block Exemption Regulations (GBER) under EU State Aid law. These schemes operate as targeted exemptions from the standard subsidy control requirements for specific, low-risk categories of subsidies. They enable public authorities to award subsidies in a compliant manner, provided the relevant conditions set out in the scheme are satisfied.[29]

Streamlined subsidy schemes may only be made by a Minister of the Crown and must be laid before Parliament after being made.[30]

In January 2022, the Department for Business, Energy and Industrial Strategy stated in a policy note that it intended to establish streamlined subsidy routes for categories of subsidies at especially low risk of causing market distortions, that promote UK strategic policy objectives, and which the government judges to be compliant

[24] ibid s 10(3).
[25] ibid s 12(3).
[26] ibid s 12(2).
[27] ibid s 70(2) and para 13.12 Guidance.
[28] Para 13.13 Guidance.
[29] SCA, s 10(4).
[30] ibid s 10(4) and (5).

with the subsidy control regime.[31] This led to the making of three streamlined subsidy schemes[32] in connection with the following:

(a) research, development and innovation, including subsidies for feasibility studies, industrial research, and experimental development projects;
(b) energy usage, including subsidies for energy demand reduction, green heat networks, and related skills training; and
(c) local growth, including subsidies for SMEs relating to business development projects, support for the employment of workers with disabilities, and support for the employment of disadvantaged workers.

In April 2025, the government announced in its response to a public consultation that it planned to create two further streamlined subsidy schemes in relation to arts and culture and community regeneration.[33]

In the UK subsidy control regime, streamlined subsidy schemes are deliberately limited in scope and value, reflecting a policy choice to encourage public authorities to undertake bespoke assessments using the subsidy control principles rather than defaulting to predefined exemptions. This contrasts with the EU approach, where the GBER provides a wide array of relatively clear-cut exemptions with comparatively high subsidy thresholds, enabling the majority of subsidies—estimated at around 95 per cent—to be granted with legal certainty and a minimal administrative burden. It has been argued that the UK's approach has resulted in unnecessary administrative effort for subsidies that would have easily qualified under the GBER framework.

(c) Services of Public Economic Interest

Subsidies relating to services of public economic interest (SPEI) are subject to additional provisions under the SCA. These provisions are conceptually similar to the EU State Aid rules governing services of general economic interest (SGEI), which also recognize that certain public services may require subsidy support to be delivered effectively. SPEI services refer to services provided to the public which, without subsidy, would not be supplied by the market in an appropriate way—or at all. Examples include transport in remote regions, social housing, and postal services.

Subsidies for SPEI services must be limited to what is necessary to deliver the services, having regard to the costs involved and reasonable profits to be made in

[31] Para 10, see: https://assets.publishing.service.gov.uk/media/63bedac8d3bf7f6c1e396904/subsidy-control-bill-policy-statement-streamlined-routes-objectives-operation.pdf (accessed 27 October 2025).

[32] See: https://www.gov.uk/government/publications/subsidy-control-act-2022-streamlined-routes (accessed 27 October 2025).

[33] https://www.gov.uk/government/consultations/refining-the-uk-subsidy-control-regime/public-feedback/consultation-response- refining-the-uk-subsidy-control-regime#creating-new-streamlined-routes-for-subsidies (accessed 27 October 2025).

performing the services.[34] SPEI subsidies must also be given in a 'transparent manner', defined in the SCA as being given in accordance with a written contract or other legally enforceable arrangement in writing, which sets out the applicable terms and other information specified in the SCA.[35]

The public authority giving the SPEI subsidy must check, at least once every three years and at the end of the delivery period, that the amount of subsidy continues to be limited to what is necessary to deliver the services, and must take steps to recover any overcompensation identified.[36]

When providing a SPEI subsidy, the public authority must ensure compliance with the subsidy control principles, but only insofar as compliance with the principles would not prevent the carrying out of the SPEI services.[37]

(d) Subsidies (Partially) Exempt from the SCA

Certain categories of subsidy are exempt or partially exempt from the subsidy control requirements, as described below.

(i) Minimal Financial Assistance

Minimal financial assistance (MFA) is concerned with low-value subsidies. The subsidy control requirements do not apply to MFA, apart from the transparency requirements in respect of MFA over £100,000.[38] A subsidy may qualify as MFA provided its value plus the value of all other relevant subsidies received by the enterprise over the 'applicable period' is no more than £315,000.[39] The applicable period is the elapsed part of the current financial year (that is, from 1 April) and the two financial years immediately preceding.[40] In this context, relevant subsidies include:[41]

(a) any other MFA given by a public authority;
(b) SPEI assistance (see below);
(c) State Aid given under the EU State Aid *de minimis* regulations[42] by virtue of the Northern Ireland Protocol as revised by the Windsor Framework. The Windsor

[34] SCA, s 29(2).
[35] ibid s 29(3)–(5).
[36] ibid s 29(6)–(7).
[37] ibid s 29(8).
[38] ibid s 36(1) and (4).
[39] ibid s 36(1).
[40] ibid s 36(2).
[41] ibid s 42(8).
[42] The EU State aid de minimis regulations include: a) Commission Regulation (EU) No 360/2012 of 25 April 2012 on the application of Articles 107 and 108 of the Treaty on the Functioning of the European Union to de minimis aid granted to undertakings providing services of general economic interest [2012] OJ L114/8; b) Commission Regulation (EU) No 1407/2013 of 18 December 2013 on the application of Articles 107 and 108 of the Treaty on the Functioning of the European Union to de minimis aid [2013] OJ L352/1; c) Commission Regulation (EU) No 1408/2013 of 18 December 2013 on the application of Articles 107 and 108 of the Treaty on the Functioning of the European Union to de minimis aid in the agriculture sector

> Framework requires the application of EU State Aid rules whenever a measure could impact the trade in goods or electricity between Northern Ireland and an EU member state.[43]

Accordingly, subsidies given lawfully under a scheme, or standalone subsidies that have been assessed as being compliant with the subsidy control principles, as well as State Aid measures granted by public authorities in EU member states, would not be relevant.

Certain procedural requirements must be complied with before MFA can be awarded.

First, the proposed recipient of MFA must be provided with a written 'MFA notification', which:

(a) explains that the proposed subsidy is intended to be given as MFA;
(b) specifies the gross value amount of the MFA; and
(c) requests written confirmation that the recipient will not exceed the MFA threshold of £315,000 as a result of the proposed MFA assistance.[44]

The MFA may only be given to the proposed recipient once such written confirmation has been received.[45]

Second, when providing the MFA, the public authority must also provide a written 'MFA confirmation' to confirm in respect of the subsidy:

(a) that it is given as MFA;
(b) the date on which it is given; and
(c) its gross value amount.[46]

[2013] OJ L352/9; and d) Commission Regulation (EU) No 717/2014 of 27 June 2014 on the application of Articles 107 and 108 of the Treaty on the Functioning of the European Union to de minimis aid in the fishery and aquaculture sector [2014] OJ L190/45.

43 The Northern Ireland Protocol provides for the establishment of a sort of tailored custom area that also includes the preservation of State Aid rules. Art 10 of the Protocol provides that State Aid provisions continue to apply to the UK 'in respect of measures which affect that trade between Northern Ireland and the Union which is subject to this Protocol'. The EU and UK reached a political agreement on resolving certain issues in Northern Ireland, the so-called Windsor Framework. Still the State Aid provisions have been left untouched. The Framework simply restates that 'for a measure to be considered to have a genuine and direct link to Northern Ireland and thus to have an effect on the trade between Northern Ireland and the Union that is subject to the Windsor Framework, that measure needs to have real foreseeable effects on that trade. The relevant real foreseeable effects should be material, and not merely hypothetical or presumed.' Joint Declaration of the Union and the United Kingdom in the Joint Committee established by the Agreement on the withdrawal of the United Kingdom of Great Britain and Northern Ireland from the European Union and the European Atomic Energy Community of 24 March 2023 on the application of Article 10(1) of the Windsor Framework (OJ L 102, 17.4.2023, pp. 88–89).

44 SCA, s 37(1)–(2).

45 ibid s 37(3).

46 ibid s 37(4)–(5).

A recipient of MFA is required to keep a written record of the MFA confirmation for at least three years beginning with the date on which the MFA is given.[47] Such records should enable the MFA recipient to respond to any future requests from public authorities regarding whether the MFA threshold has been exceeded during a given period.

(ii) SPEI Assistance

The subsidy control requirements do not apply to subsidies granted in the context of performing SPEI services where the value of the subsidies do not exceed £725,000 over the applicable period ('SPEI assistance').[48] As with MFA, the applicable period is the elapsed part of the current financial year and the two financial years immediately preceding, and the list of relevant subsidies is the same.[49]

Before providing SPEI assistance, the public authority must provide to the proposed recipient a 'SPEI assistance notification' which contains the same information as the MFA notification vis-à-vis the SPEI subsidy.[50] The public authority may proceed to give the SPEI assistance only once it has received confirmation from the proposed recipient that the SPEI assistance threshold has not been exceeded.[51] Upon providing the SPEI assistance, the public authority must provide to the recipient a SPEI assistance confirmation as described above. The SPEI assistance confirmation must be kept by the enterprise for at least three years beginning with the date on which the SPEI assistance is given.[52]

As with MFA, all SPEI assistance exceeding £100,000 must be advertised by the public authority on the subsidy control database within three months of confirming the decision to award the subsidy.[53]

(e) Other Exemptions

Additional exemptions are described in Chapters 3 and 4 of Part 3 of the SCA. The following types of subsidies and schemes benefit from the partial exemptions described:

First, subsidies given to compensate the damage caused by natural disasters or other exceptional occurrences.[54] These subsidies are exempt from the subsidy control requirements, with the exception of the transparency requirements. Reliance on this exemption is restricted to situations where a notice has been published by the

[47] ibid s 37(6)–(7).
[48] ibid s 38(1).
[49] ibid ss 38(2) and 42(8).
[50] ibid s 39(1)–(2).
[51] ibid s 39(3).
[52] ibid s 39(6)–(7).
[53] ibid s 38(1) and (4).
[54] ibid s 43. The reference to 'exceptional occurrences' does not include occurrences having only an economic effect.

Secretary of State declaring that the exemption applies in respect of the natural disaster or occurrence.

Second, subsidies given to respond to a national or global economic emergency.[55] These subsidies are exempt *only* from the SCA provisions relating to prohibited subsidies or subsidies subject to certain requirements, explained below. Accordingly, subsidies awarded via this route would still require assessment against the subsidy control principles. As with the exemption for natural disasters, reliance on this exemption is permitted only where the Secretary of State has published a notice declaring that this exemption may be relied on.

Third, subsidies granted under schemes made before the entry into force of the SCA (4 January 2023). These subsidies are exempt from the subsidy control requirements, although most of them are subject to the transparency requirements.[56]

Fourth, subsidies given (either standalone or under schemes) in the context of a large cross-border or international cooperation project.[57] Such subsidies are exempt from the requirement to consider the subsidy control principles provided the authority giving the subsidy or making the scheme is satisfied that the project's benefits are not limited to the enterprise, sector, or states participating and that it will have wider benefits through spillover effects that do not exclusively accrue to the UK, the relevant sector, and the beneficiary of the subsidy or subsidies concerned.

Fifth, subsidies or subsidy schemes relating to nuclear energy. The requirement to consider the energy and environment principles does not apply to such subsidies or schemes.[58]

The following types of subsidies benefit from full exemption, that is, the subsidy control requirements do not apply: subsidies for the purpose of safeguarding national security;[59] subsidies given by or on behalf of the Bank of England in pursuit of monetary policy;[60] subsidies and subsidy schemes covered by a financial stability direction, as given by the Treasury,[61] which must consult the Bank of England before giving a financial stability direction; subsidies given in accordance with the EU or UK passenger transport regulations;[62] subsidies given under EU State Aid rules in accordance with the Windsor Framework;[63] subsidies, or schemes to which Article 138 of the EU Withdrawal Agreement applies, relating to the UK's participation in the implementation of EU programmes and activities committed under the MFF

55 ibid s 44.
56 ibid s 48(1)(a) and (2).
57 ibid s 50.
58 ibid s 51.
59 ibid s 45.
60 ibid s 46.
61 ibid s 47.
62 ibid s 48(1)(b). Passenger transport regulations include: (i) Regulation (EC) No 1370/2007 of the European Parliament and of the Council on public passenger transport services by rail and by road; (ii) that Regulation as it has effect by virtue of regulation 28(2) of the Public Service Obligations in Transport Regulations 2023; or (iii) the Public Service Obligations in Transport Regulations 2023.
63 ibid s 48(3)(a).

2014–2020 or previous financial perspectives;[64] and subsidies which are permissible under Article 413 of the TCA, relating to taxation.[65]

(f) Prohibited Subsidies or Subsidies Subject to Certain Requirements

Chapter 2 of Part 2 of the SCA sets out the categories of subsidy which are prohibited and other subsidies which are subject to certain requirements.

(i) General Prohibitions

Subsidies in the form of a guarantee are prohibited where there is no limit as to the amount of the debts or liabilities that are guaranteed or there is no limit as to the duration of the guarantee.[66]

Subsidies that are contingent upon export performance relating to goods or services are prohibited, other than where the subsidy is in the form of short-term export credit insurance, or the export credit is permissible in accordance with the WTO's ASCM.[67]

Subsidies that are contingent upon the use of domestic over imported goods or services are prohibited, with the exception of subsidies given in relation to the audiovisual sector.[68]

Subsidies for the relocation of an enterprise's activities are generally prohibited where the public authority requires the recipient, as a condition of receiving the subsidy, to relocate all or part of its existing economic activities to a different area of the UK and the relocation of those activities would not occur but for the giving of the subsidy.[69] The general prohibition on relocation subsidies does not apply if: the effect of the subsidy is to reduce the social or economic disadvantages of the area that would benefit from the giving of the subsidy; there is an overall reduction in the social or economic disadvantages within the UK generally as a result of giving the subsidy; and the subsidy is designed to bring about a change in the size, scope, or nature of the recipient's existing economic activities.

Subsidies to insurers providing export credit insurance are prohibited, unless the subsidy is given subject to a condition that any export credit insurance provided by the insurer against marketable risks is provided on a commercial basis, and the subsidy is not used to directly or indirectly benefit the part of the insurer's business which provides export credit insurance against marketable risks.[70]

64 ibid s 48(3)(b).
65 ibid s 49.
66 ibid s 15.
67 ibid s 16.
68 ibid s 17. This section is without prejudice to Arts 132 and 133 TCA.
69 ibid s 18.
70 ibid s 27.

Subsidies for air carriers for the operation of routes are prohibited unless one or more of the following conditions are met: the air carrier is undertaking a public service obligation in accordance with Regulation (EC) No 1008/2008; the subsidy will provide benefits for society at large; or the subsidy is a start-up subsidy that will establish a new route to a regional airport, which will increase traveller numbers and stimulate regional development.[71]

(ii) Rescue and Restructuring

Subsidies for rescuing and restructuring 'ailing or insolvent' enterprises are prohibited unless certain requirements are met. An ailing or insolvent enterprise is one which would almost certainly go out of business in the short to medium term without subsidies, is unable to pay its debts as they fall due, or has assets with a value less than its liabilities.[72]

A public authority is prohibited from providing rescue support to an ailing or insolvent enterprise, unless the subsidy is granted during the preparation by the enterprise of a restructuring plan (discussed further below) and involves temporary liquidity support in the form of a loan or loan guarantee. In addition, the subsidy must contribute to an objective. Absent this, there must be some other exceptional circumstances which justify the subsidy being given.[73]

Restructuring subsidies for ailing or insolvent enterprises are prohibited, unless the enterprise has prepared a credible restructuring plan based on realistic assumptions, with a view to ensure the return of the enterprise to long-term viability within a reasonable time.[74] Except where the enterprise is a small or medium-sized enterprise, the enterprise or its owners, creditors, or new investors must have contributed significant funds to the cost of restructuring or have a contractual obligation to do so.[75]

As with rescue subsidies, restructuring subsidies must contribute to an objective of public interest by avoiding social hardship or preventing a severe market failure. Absent this, there must be some other exceptional circumstances which justify giving the subsidy.[76] With the exception of subsidies relating to circumstances which are unforeseeable and not caused by the beneficiary of the subsidy, a restructuring subsidy may only be given once five years have passed since the relevant enterprise received any previous restructuring subsidy.[77]

Different rules apply in respect of subsidies for restructuring an ailing or insolvent deposit taker or insurance company.[78]

[71] ibid s 28.
[72] ibid s 24(1).
[73] ibid s 19.
[74] ibid s 20(2)–(3).
[75] ibid s 20(4).
[76] ibid s 20(5).
[77] ibid s 20(6)–(7).
[78] ibid s 21.

(g) Subsidies and Schemes of Particular Interest

The following subsidies will be subsidies of particular interest provided they do not involve subsidies for rescuing an ailing or insolvent enterprise under section 19 SCA, subsidies for liquidating an ailing or insolvent deposit taker or insurance company under section 22 SCA, or subsidies to support liquidity provision for an ailing or insolvent deposit taker or insurance company under section 23 SCA:[79] subsidies over £25m (or if they are over £1m and they cumulate to more than £25m with other related subsidies given to the enterprise over the previous three financial years); subsidies granted in sensitive sectors[80] if they are over £5m (or if they are over £1m and they cumulate to more than £5m with other related subsidies given to the enterprise over the previous three financial years); subsidies over £1m for relocation of activities under section 18 SCA; and subsidies for restructuring under section 20 or 21 SCA will always be subsidies of particular interest.

A subsidy scheme of particular interest is a scheme which allows for one or more subsidies of particular interest to be given under it.[81] A public authority must request a report from the Subsidy Advice Unit (SAU) before giving/making Subsidies or Schemes of Particular Interest (SSoPI).[82]

(h) Subsidies and Schemes of Interest

Subsidies of interest are those which do not meet the subsidy of particular interest criteria but do meet one or more of the following criteria:[83] subsidies over £5m but no more than £25m (individually or cumulatively) which do not meet the subsidy of particular interest criteria; subsidies of £1m or less for relocation of activities under section 18 SCA; subsidies for rescuing an ailing or insolvent enterprise under section 19 SCA; subsidies for liquidating an ailing or insolvent deposit taker or insurance company under section 22 SCA; and subsidies to support liquidity provision for an ailing or insolvent deposit taker or insurance company under section 23 SCA.

A public authority may request a report from the SAU before giving/making a SSoPI.[84] The SAU will apply its 'Prioritisation Principles' to determine whether a referral merits its resources and attention.[85]

[79] Reg 3 SSoI/SSoPI Regulations.
[80] Manufacture of basic iron and steel and ferro-alloys, aluminium production, copper production, manufacture of motor vehicles, building of ships and floating structures, manufacture of motorcycles, manufacture of air and spacecraft and related machinery, production of electricity.
[81] Reg 3(6) SSoI/SSoPI Regulations.
[82] SCA, s 52(1)(a).
[83] Reg 4 SSoI/SSoPI Regulations.
[84] SCA, s 56(1)(a).
[85] Prioritisation principles, SAU Guidance.

5 The Subsidy Database

In terms of monitoring, the SCA places a lot of emphasis on transparency. The SCA requires that public authorities should 'enter' their decision in a publicly accessible subsidy database with information on the amount of the subsidy, the identity of the beneficiary, the subsidy's legal, and the policy objective which it pursues.

The subsidy database is maintained by the Department of Business and Trade. This publicly accessible platform records details of subsidies and subsidy schemes awarded by public authorities.

Public authorities are required to record in the subsidy database each subsidy they give, unless the subsidy is given under a subsidy scheme which has its own entry in the subsidy database and the subsidy does not exceed £100,000.[86] A subsidy which initially meets this exemption and is subsequently modified, such that it exceeds £100,000, will require its own entry in the database.[87]

Details of every non-exempt subsidy scheme must be recorded in the subsidy database. There is no minimum financial threshold.[88]

Where a subsidy or scheme is required to be entered into the subsidy database, it must be done within three months of the confirmation of the decision to give the subsidy or to make the subsidy scheme, except for standalone subsidies given in the form of a tax measure, where the entry must instead be made within one year beginning with the date of the tax declaration.[89] Public authorities must ensure that the entry made in the subsidy database is maintained for at least six years, or for the duration of the subsidy or scheme if longer.[90] The same deadlines apply for modifications, with the limitation period running from the date of the modification instead of the date of the confirmation of the decision.

Whether the subsidy database is sufficiently developed to ensure full transparency of subsidies granted is debatable, as discussed in section 9 below.

6 The Subsidy Advice Unit

The SAU was established to carry out the CMA's subsidy control functions under the SCA. The SAU's functions are twofold: providing independent, non-binding advice to public authorities on proposed SSoIs and SSoPIs; and monitoring and reporting on the effectiveness of the subsidy control regime within the UK.[91]

[86] SCA, s 33(1)(a) and 33(2).
[87] ibid s 33(6).
[88] ibid s 33(1)(b).
[89] ibid s 33(3).
[90] ibid s 33(4).
[91] ibid Pt 4.

The SAU's role is strictly advisory: it provides independent, non-binding advice when requested by public authorities or when directed to do so by the Secretary of State. This advice is intended to support decision-making, but does not carry legal force. The SAU cannot initiate investigations into subsidies, nor can it approve or prohibit the granting of subsidies. It also lacks the authority to examine complaints related to subsidy awards.

This strictly advisory role has attracted criticism. While the SAU is positioned as a safeguard within the UK's decentralized subsidy control framework, its lack of enforcement powers raises concerns about the effectiveness and consistency of the regime (see section 9).

The SAU's monitoring function—while potentially valuable—is still in its early stages. Its first statutory review of the regime's effectiveness is due in 2026. Until then, questions remain about whether the SAU has sufficient access to data and resources to carry out this role meaningfully, especially given its limited visibility into subsidies that are not referred for review.[92]

7 Enforcement and Remedies

(a) Role of the CAT

The CAT is the specialist judicial body responsible for, among other things, enforcing subsidy control rules. An interested party who is aggrieved by the making of a subsidy decision may apply to the CAT for a review of the decision.[93] 'Subsidy decision' refers to a decision by a public authority to give a subsidy or to make a subsidy scheme. 'Interested party' means a person whose interests may be affected by the giving of the subsidy or the making of the subsidy scheme (mostly competitors of the beneficiary), or the Secretary of State. This means the UK government itself can act to enforce the rules if necessary.

Importantly, initiating a challenge before the CAT does not, in itself, suspend the implementation of the subsidy decision. The subsidy may therefore be granted and paid out while proceedings are ongoing, unless the Tribunal issues an order to the contrary. The CAT does have the power to grant interim relief—for instance, an injunction to prevent a subsidy from being granted or a project from progressing—if a claimant applies for such relief and meets the applicable legal test.

[92] For a more positive view see D du Parc Braham and M Marsden, 'The UK's Subsidy Control Regime Subsidy Advice Unit Referrals—Tips and Best Practice' (2023) 4 European State Aid Law Quarterly.

[93] SCA, s 70(1).

(b) Time Limits for Applications to Review Subsidy Decisions

The SCA imposes strict time limits for bringing a challenge. An interested party must send a notice of appeal to the CAT within one month of the 'relevant date' of the subsidy decision.[94] The 'relevant date' from which the one-month period starts running depends on the specific circumstances. Other than in two specific circumstances (discussed below), the relevant date will be the 'transparency date', being the date on which details of the subsidy or scheme are published on the subsidy database. In circumstances where the duty to make an entry on the subsidy database does not apply, such as in the case of MFA subsidies below £100,000, the time limit for challenge runs from when the interested party first knew or ought to have known of the subsidy decision.

However, where a public authority fails to comply with a duty to record the giving of a subsidy on the transparency database, it is unclear whether the limitation period would run from the point of knowledge or remain suspended until the database entry is made. In the author's opinion, the better view is that failure to comply with the transparency obligation should prevent the limitation period from running, with time only starting upon compliance.

Further ambiguity arises when a public authority asserts that a measure is not a subsidy (for example, because the authority considers that public money was made available to an enterprise on commercial terms) and therefore no duty to make a database entry applies, but its assertion is disputed. In the author's view, normal judicial review principles should apply so that an interested party would have three months to challenge the public authority's decision to conclude that the measure did not constitute a subsidy.

The SCA accounts for scenarios where additional review processes occur. If a subsidy is referred to the SAU for a report, then the relevant date is delayed until the publication of the report on that referral. This gives challengers the benefit of the SAU's analysis before bringing a challenge.

An interested party may also make a 'pre-action information request' under section 76 SCA, explicitly for the purpose of deciding whether to challenge the subsidy decision. The request must be in writing and state that it is made in contemplation of an application for a review of a subsidy decision under section 70, on the ground that the decision did not comply with a requirement in Chapter 1 or 2 of Part 2 of the SCA.[95] Upon such a request, the public authority is obliged to respond in writing within twenty-eight days, providing any information that would enable or assist the potential claimant to assess whether the subsidy was given in accordance with those requirements.

[94] ibid s 71 SCA.
[95] ibid s 76(1)-(2).

If the interested party requests information from the public authority within one month of the transparency date, then the one-month period to challenge the subsidy decision will run from the date the authority notifies the interested party that it has provided information in response to the request (not from the original transparency date).[96] Essentially, a timely section 76 request extends the deadline, allowing the challenger to wait for additional details before deciding whether to proceed with a CAT appeal.

The CAT's ability to extend the time limits for review of subsidy decisions is limited; it may only do so where it is satisfied that exceptional circumstances justify an extension.[97]

(c) Standard of Review

Section 70(5) requires the CAT to apply the same principles as would be applied by the High Court on an application for judicial review in England and Wales or Northern Ireland, or, in Scotland, the same principles the Court of Session applies in its supervisory jurisdiction. In essence, this means that the CAT's role is to ensure the decision was lawful, rational, and procedurally proper under the SCA's requirements.

In practical terms, this means that a claimant must identify a failure to comply with the SCA's requirements. This might include the argument that the subsidy breached one of the SCA's prohibitions (such as giving an unlimited guarantee, or aiding a failing enterprise contrary to specific rules); or that the public authority did not properly consider the subsidy control principles, or could not reasonably conclude the subsidy was consistent with those principles. Broad 'merits' arguments—for instance, that the subsidy could harm competition or that the authority misjudged the economics—will only succeed if the claimant demonstrates that the decision was one that no reasonable authority properly applying the principles could have made.

In *R (British Gas Trading and E.ON) v Secretary of State for Energy Security and Net Zero*,[98] a judicial review claim was brought before the SCA came into force, at the time when the TCA subsidy control provisions were directly applicable.[99] The Court of Appeal confirmed that the standard for reviewing a public authority's assessment of compliance with the subsidy control principles is rationality, not proportionality. According to this judgment, it is for the authority to judge whether a subsidy is proportionate, while the Court's role is limited to determining whether that judgment was rational or otherwise unlawful under domestic grounds for judicial review.

[96] Section 98A(2)(a) of the Competition Appeal Tribunal Rules 2015.
[97] ibid s 98A(7).
[98] *R (British Gas Trading and E.ON) v Secretary of State for Energy Security and Net Zero* [2025] EWCA Civ 209.
[99] EU (Future Relationship) Act 2020, s 29(1) incorporated the subsidy provisions of the TCA into domestic law, with effect from 1 January 2021.

This position was also confirmed by the CAT in the first case brought under the SCA. In *The Durham Company (Max Recycle) v Durham County Council (2023)*, the CAT observed that subsidy cases would likely involve limited issues and little need for extensive evidence or disclosure, since the questions are primarily ones of lawfulness of a discrete decision.[100] A challenge under the SCA therefore does not constitute a reconsideration of the merits of the decision, but rather serves as a legal review to determine compliance with the statutory framework.

(d) Remedies

The CAT can grant the following relief where it finds that a subsidy decision violates the requirements of the SCA.[101] These have the same effect as the corresponding relief granted by the High Court in judicial review proceedings:[102]

It can grant a mandatory order. The CAT can mandate that the public authority take a specific action. This could be used to compel an authority to do something necessary to comply with the law, for instance to require an authority to reconsider a subsidy application properly in line with the subsidy control principles, or to terminate an ongoing subsidy scheme that is found to be in breach of the Act.

It can grant a prohibiting order. The CAT may issue an order prohibiting the public authority from taking an unlawful decision or action that it has not yet taken. This could forbid the authority from giving a subsidy or continuing granting subsidies under a scheme that has been found to be unlawful.

It can grant a quashing order. It can quash the subsidy decision, which nullifies the public authority's decision to grant the subsidy or establish the subsidy scheme. A quashing order invalidates the decision, so it is as if it had never been made.

It can grant declaratory relief. It can make a declaration, which is a formal statement of the legal position. A declaration might declare that a given measure was a subsidy and unlawful, or clarify the rights of parties. While a declaration does not directly compel action, it provides authoritative guidance and may accompany other orders or suffice if a formal statement of illegality is needed; for example, if a subsidy had already been spent and no further remedy is practical, a declaration still registers the legal breach.

It can award an injunction. The CAT may grant an injunction, which can either be interim or final, to restrain specific actions. As a final remedy, an injunction could permanently bar the granting of a subsidy.

The CAT also follows the same principles as the High Court in judicial review proceedings in deciding whether to grant relief. The CAT has the right to refuse relief where it considers that there has been 'undue delay' in making the application

[100] *Durham Company Limited v Durham County Council* [2023] CAT 14, [3].
[101] SCA, s 72.
[102] ibid s 72(2) and (5). Note that in Scotland, s 73 provides equivalent powers for the Court of Session.

for judicial review.[103] Further, the CAT is also empowered to refuse relief if the relief sought would be likely to cause substantial hardship or prejudice to others or be detrimental to good administration.[104] For instance, if unwinding a subsidy would severely harm a third party who relied on it, the CAT might weigh that in its decision. Additionally, the CAT must refuse relief in England and Wales (absent exceptional public interest) if it appears highly likely the outcome would not have been substantially different even if the conduct complained of had not occurred.[105]

A remedy specific to subsidy control is the recovery order. This allows the CAT to order that the subsidy must be recovered from the beneficiary, thereby removing the competitive advantage that the beneficiary received. Note that there is no obligation on the CAT to issue a recovery order. This is different from the EU State Aid regime, where it is settled law that the European Commission must order the recovery of aid following a finding that the aid was unlawful and incompatible with the internal market.[106]

(e) Appeals against CAT Decisions

An appeal lies to the Court of Appeal in England and Wales and Northern Ireland, and to the Court of Session in Scotland, on any point of law arising from a decision of the CAT. An appeal may be brought by a party to the proceedings before the CAT or any other person who has a sufficient interest in the matter. An appeal requires the permission of the CAT or the appellate court.[107]

(f) Misuse of Subsidies

A public authority which has given a subsidy has the right to recover from the beneficiary the whole or part of its amount to the extent that the subsidy is used for a purpose other than the purpose for which it was given.[108] This right may be enforced by the public authority granting the subsidy, rather than the CAT.

[103] ibid s 72(8)(a). While this a standard judicial review rule, in the author's view this is non-compliant with the UK's obligations under Art 373(3) TCA which require that a full one-month period is afforded to interested parties wishing to challenge the grant of a subsidy and to seek its recovery.

[104] ibid s 72(7).

[105] ibid s 72(9) SCA, applying s 31(2A) and (2B) Senior Courts Act 1981.

[106] Case C-183/91 *Commission v Greece* EU:C:1993:233, [16]; Case C-404/97 *Commission v Portugal* EU:C:2000:345, [38]; Case C-261/99 *Commission v France* EU:C:2001:179, [22]; Case C-390/98 *HJ Banks & Co Ltd. v Coal Authority* EU:C:2001:456, [74]; Case C-277/00 *Germany v Commission* EU:C:2004:238, [74]; Case C-529/09 *Commission v Spain* EU:C:2013:31, [90].

[107] SCA, s 75(1)-(4).

[108] ibid s 77.

8 Case Law and Emerging Trends

(a) First Judgments Issued by the CAT

The Durham Company (Max Recycle) v Durham County Council[109] case was the first judgment issued by the CAT under the SCA. It addressed a fundamental question: can a public authority grant a subsidy to one of its own in-house operations?

Max Recycle, a private waste collection firm, challenged Durham County Council's practice of using the same trucks and staff for both its statutory household waste service and its commercial waste service. Max Recycle argued that this arrangement allowed the Council to cross-subsidize its commercial operations using public resources, thereby undercutting private competitors and distorting competition.

The CAT dismissed the claim. While it acknowledged that the Council's commercial service likely benefited from lower operating costs due to shared resources, it concluded that no 'subsidy' had been granted within the meaning of the SCA. The Tribunal's reasoning turned on the statutory definition of a subsidy, which requires a public authority to confer an economic advantage on an 'enterprise'. Because the Council was both the provider and recipient of the alleged advantage, and its commercial operations were not legally distinct from the Council itself, the CAT held that no subsidy had been given. This interpretation diverges from EU State Aid law, which adopts a more functional approach and may treat different activities within the same legal entity as separate for the purposes of assessing aid.

The case also highlighted the CAT's commitment to procedural efficiency. The challenge was lodged in February 2023 and was heard in July, and the judgment was issued that same month. The Tribunal emphasized the need for subsidy reviews to be handled 'quickly and with a light touch'. Notably, the CAT's President imposed a cost-capping order to protect parties from excessive litigation costs, recognizing the public interest in enabling access to justice. However, the Court of Appeal later overturned this order, ruling that the CAT lacked jurisdiction to cap costs in statutory review cases under the SCA.

Weis v Greater Manchester Combined Authority[110] was the second CAT case. It concerned the application of the CMO principle to two development loans totalling around £120 million granted by Greater Manchester Combined Authority (GMCA) to a private developer for high-rise residential projects. Weis, a competing developer, argued that the loans were on terms no private lender would offer, amounting to an unlawful subsidy. GMCA maintained the loans were commercial and satisfied the CMO principle.

[109] *The Durham Company Limited (trading as Max Recycle) v Durham County Council* [2023] CAT 50.
[110] *Mr Aubrey Weis v Greater Manchester Combined Authority* [2025] CAT 41.

The CAT dismissed the challenge but adopted an approach that arguably goes beyond a conventional judicial review. Rather than limiting itself to assessing rationality, the CAT undertook its own analysis of market terms. It was not concerned by GMCA's failure to refer to statutory guidance and held that section 3(2) of the SCA was satisfied on the basis of very limited evidence—specifically, reference to a loan GMCA had made three to four years earlier—without any supporting expert reports.

The CAT also permits GMCA to defend the SCA challenge using material not considered at the time of the decision, including evidence created after the fact. This suggests a flexible and pragmatic approach to the CMO principle, but one that raises questions about the scope of the CAT's jurisdiction and the nature of obligations imposed by the SCA. This judgment is currently being appealed.

(b) Pending Cases before the CAT

The New Lottery Company Ltd & Ors v Gambling Commission[111] case concerns a £70 million grant from the National Lottery Distribution Fund (NLDF) to Camelot, the former operator of the National Lottery, for marketing activities. The NLDF is a statutory fund under government control, intended to support 'good causes' under the National Lottery Act 1993. Competitors of Camelot argue that the grant constitutes a subsidy and may distort competition in the lottery market. The case raises important questions about the use of public funds for promotional activities and whether such support meets the definition of a subsidy under the SCA.

Interestingly, the CAT declined permission to submit expert evidence in the form of a draft report challenging the econometric analysis, reasoning that such evidence was unnecessary given that the case was to be reviewed on the basis of irrationality.[112] The Tribunal also noted concerns that admitting expert evidence could increase costs and cause delay. This suggests a restrictive approach to admissibility of expert evidence in cases involving the CMO principle, and indicates that the CAT will adopt a traditional judicial review approach. This case will be heard in December 2025.

In *Bristol Airport v Welsh Ministers*,[113] Bristol Airport lodged a challenge in July 2025 against a subsidy package of up to £205 million awarded by the Welsh government to support Cardiff International Airport. The package includes capital investments aimed at expanding Cardiff's operations. This is the first case in which the CAT will directly assess the application of the subsidy control principles and the standard of analysis required under the SCA.

Notably, the SAU published a report on the proposed subsidy that was critical of the Welsh government's assessment. The SAU raised concerns about the adequacy of the analysis provided, including the justification for the subsidy amount and the

[111] *The New Lottery Company Ltd and Others v the Gambling Commission* [2025] CAT 54.
[112] ibid.
[113] *Bristol Airport Limited v Welsh Ministers* [2025] CAT 54, Case No: 1740/12/13/25.

evaluation of its potential impact on competition and investment. This case is expected to be an important test of how the CAT interprets and applies the subsidy control principles. It may also shed light on the weight the Tribunal gives to SAU reports and whether deficiencies identified by the SAU influence the CAT's judgment.

In *Zenobe Energy Limited v Ofgem* 1754/12/13/25, Zenobe Energy Limited, a private equity-backed company specializing in battery storage, brought a challenge against Ofgem concerning the introduction of a government-backed scheme to provide financial support for Long Duration Electricity Storage (LDES) projects. The claimant argues that the measure, funded through network charges, constitutes a subsidy under the SCA.

The case raises some significant questions. First is whether the scheme falls outside the scope of the SCA because Clause 25 of the Planning and Infrastructure Bill obliges Ofgem to implement it, and section 78 with Schedule 3 excludes financial assistance mandated by primary legislation. Second is the interpretation of section 2(1)(a) of the SCA, particularly what qualifies as 'from public resources' when funding is derived from network charges. Third is the definition of a 'subsidy scheme' and the degree of discretion required for a measure to be classified as such. These issues will test the boundaries of the SCA and clarify its application to statutory schemes in regulated sectors.

9 The Effectiveness of the UK Subsidy Control Regime

(a) Self-assessment by Public Authorities: Risks and Limitations

The SCA marks a significant departure from the former EU State Aid regime, shifting the responsibility for compliance from a central regulator to individual public authorities. Unlike the former EU State Aid regime, which required prior approval from the European Commission (other than where an exemption applies) before aid could be granted, the SCA places the onus on public authorities, ranging from central government departments to local councils, to self-assess proposed subsidies for compliance with the statutory principles before any award is made. In effect, this means that public authorities are required to act as regulators of their own decisions.

While the Guidance offers direction on demonstrating compliance, it is doubtful whether all public authorities have the required resources and expertise available to sufficiently analyse whether a subsidy decision is compliant with the subsidy control principles. After all, the assessment of compliance is not a mere box-ticking exercise; it demands substantive analysis and evidence. For instance, Principle B requires justification that the subsidy is the minimum necessary, which may involve considering alternative policy instruments or reduced subsidy amounts. Without prior experience, public officials may struggle to determine the sufficiency of their analysis for compliance purposes. Similarly, Principle F requires that the beneficial effects of a subsidy outweigh any negative effects on competition or investment. This necessitates a reasoned assessment of market impacts, a task for which smaller authorities may lack the necessary expertise. The SAU has, on several occasions, recommended that public authorities provide clearer and more detailed analysis to support their subsidy assessments. This includes requests for further explanation of eligibility criteria, a more complete analysis of affected sectors and sub-sectors, and fuller consideration of potential impacts on competition and investment.

The challenges of self-assessment are compounded by the fact that, although the SCA provides for voluntary and mandatory referrals of certain subsidies to the SAU prior to their award, public authorities are not obliged to implement the recommendations set out in SAU reports. This lack of enforceability may limit the reports' effectiveness in improving compliance. At the time of writing, no voluntary referrals have been made to the SAU.

While the self-assessment approach facilities the speedier grant of subsidies, it is the authors' view that, where public authorities lack the necessary expertise and resources to undertake a robust compliance analysis under the SCA, there is a real risk of unjustifiable distortions of competition within the UK internal market and inefficient use of public funds.

(b) Transparency: Gaps and Consequences

Given that public authorities are self-assessing whether subsidies are compliant with the SCA, and in the absence of a specialized regulator approving subsidies before these are granted, the proper function of the UK subsidy control system is contingent on the ability of interested parties to monitor actively and effectively the granting of such subsidies, and to take timely action (whether by seeking additional information regarding a particular subsidy or scheme or, ultimately, by pursuing legal proceedings).

In the authors' view, the subsidy database is insufficiently developed to facilitate this. The database does not currently offer email alerts or other configurable notifications, either generally or to track specific types of subsidies. As such, interested parties must manually check the database on a regular basis. Even then, users are unable to search or filter by public authority name on the website. This functionality is only available once the entire database has been exported as a spreadsheet for offline analysis.

Under the Subsidy Database Regulations, public authorities are not required to provide at least a summary as to the reasons why they consider that a particular subsidy or scheme complies with the subsidy control principles.[114] This would seem problematic, in that absent the disclosure of this information, it is difficult for businesses to take an informed view as to whether there is a real need to seek further

[114] Subsidy Control (Subsidy Database Information Requirements) Regulations 2022, SI 2022/1153.

information about a particular subsidy or scheme, potentially making unnecessary requests simply to gain access to relevant information that can demonstrate a subsidy or scheme's compliance.

(c) Enforcement: Limitation Periods and Remedies

The effective monitoring of subsidies—and the ability to challenge them where appropriate—is made more difficult by the notably short limitation period under the SCA. Interested parties must bring judicial review proceedings within one month of the relevant date, which is typically defined by reference to the publication of specific information about the subsidy by the granting authority.

This contrasts sharply with the EU State Aid regime, where the European Commission has the power to investigate and ultimately require the recovery of unlawful State Aid within a ten-year period from its grant. This limitation period has been criticized as excessive and detrimental to legal certainty, but it does have the benefit of creating an important incentive for public authorities and would-be beneficiaries to comply with EU State Aid law. It also means that, except in exceptional circumstances, where unlawful State Aid is found to have been granted, the beneficiary is required to repay the public funds received, together with interest, thereby removing the resulting distortion of competition from the EU internal market.

While the shorter limitation period under the SCA increases legal certainty for the beneficiary of a subsidy, it could be argued that such a short limitation period does not strike the right balance between the need for legal certainty and the public interest in a robust remedies system, and is much less effective at deterring and remedying unlawful distortions of competition in the UK internal market. The short limitation period may ultimately result in problematic subsidies and schemes remaining in place without anyone, including the state and the CMA, having the power to require public authorities to take effective action to remedy the non-compliance and remove unlawful distortions of competition from the market.

(d) Ministerial Powers: Constraints on Post-Award Referrals

The Secretary of State is given a number of powers under the SCA, including the power to require a public authority to request a report from the CMA in relation to a proposed subsidy or scheme[115] and, separately, the power to make a post-award referral to the CMA in relation to a particular subsidy or scheme.[116] In both cases, this right

[115] SCA, s 55.
[116] ibid s 66.

arises where the Secretary of State considers that there is a risk of non-compliance in relation to the grant of a subsidy or making of a scheme or there is a risk of negative effects on competition or investment within the UK.

However, these powers are constrained by strict time limits. Post-award referrals must be made within twenty working days of publication of information relating to the subsidy or scheme on the subsidy database, or, where there is no such transparency obligation, the date on which the subsidy was given or scheme made. That said, it is helpful that the SCA gives the Secretary of State the power to issue regulations that amend this period.[117] The authors would argue that there is a strong case for extending the window for referrals to ensure effective oversight and intervention.

10 Conclusion

The UK's post-Brexit subsidy control regime represents a significant departure from the EU's State Aid system by adopting a decentralized, principles-based approach. This model provides greater flexibility and speed, but it also introduces notable challenges in terms of consistency and enforcement.

One of the main strengths of the regime is that self-assessment by public authorities allows decisions to be made more quickly, reducing administrative delays and enabling faster responses to local needs. The absence of mandatory pre-approval for most subsidies further lowers the bureaucratic burden. In addition, the SAU offers guidance to public authorities, which can help improve compliance and interpretation of the subsidy control principles.

However, the regime also exhibits significant weaknesses. Oversight is limited because the SAU's role is purely advisory, and the recent increase in the threshold for mandatory referrals from £10 million to £25 million has further reduced scrutiny of large subsidies. Decentralization places heavy reliance on individual authorities' interpretation of the subsidy control principles, creating a risk of inconsistent application. It is also doubtful that smaller authorities possess the expertise required to conduct a full subsidy control assessment, which typically involves complex economic analysis. Compliance with the seven subsidies principles requires indeed a complex legal and economic analysis. For instance, under the seventh subsidy principle, any public authority is obliged to carry out a full analysis of how to calculate whether the likely benefits of a certain subsidy outweigh the risks to fairness of competition law. The Guidance specifically refers to the need for public authorities to use decisions in the fields of antitrust and merger control that have considered the product or services in question—not an easy task for public authorities to perform.[118]

[117] ibid s 60(8).

[118] A Stephan, 'Will the New UK Subsidy Control Regime Help Level up the Economy' (2024) 87 MLR 172.

Enforcement of the rules raises further concerns. The one-month time limit for bringing claims is notably short and arguably makes it difficult for private parties to challenge allegedly unlawful subsidies. These issues are compounded by the CAT's deferential approach, which emphasizes that it is for public authorities to undertake the full analysis, while the Tribunal will only intervene if that analysis is clearly irrational. The CAT has also shown a willingness to accept limited evidence to demonstrate that financial assistance aligns with market terms and therefore does not constitute a subsidy.

These concerns appear significant. Indeed, the European Commission has already openly questioned whether the UK's current subsidy control regime represents the 'effective' control of subsidies that Article 366 TCA demands. The Commission has parked these issues high on the agenda of the TCA's joint bodies (notably, the 'Trade Specialised Committee on Level Playing Field for Open and Fair Competition and Sustainable Development under the TCA') and has raised specific queries regarding the operation of the UK's subsidy database, the enforcement role and effectiveness of the SAU, the current state of enforcement by UK courts and tribunals, and the practical implementation of the remedy of recovery for unlawfully granted subsidies.[119]

In the EU Statement at the first Trade Policy meeting, it was emphasized that the EU considers it vital to enhance the effectiveness of the UK's subsidy control system to ensure a level playing field, especially given the close and important trading relationship between the UK and the EU.[120]

The EU's position serves as a reminder that the UK's greater flexibility comes with heightened scrutiny, and that maintaining the confidence of the EU in the UK's subsidy control regime is crucial for avoiding future TCA disputes.

Looking ahead, the SAU's statutory review (expected to conclude in 2026) will be a critical opportunity to assess whether the regime is sufficiently effective in supporting competition and investment in the UK while ensuring compliance with the UK's international commitments.

119 Minutes: Trade Specialised Committee on Level Playing Field for Open and Fair Competition and Sustainable Development under the EU–UK Trade and Cooperation Agreement, 9 October 2024.

120 EU Statement at the 1st Trade Policy Review of the United Kingdom, 28 October 2025.

14
Public Procurement

Sue Arrowsmith and Luke R.A. Butler

1 Public Procurement Regulation before Brexit

(a) The UK's Traditional Approach

To understand the regulatory landscape before Brexit and the impact of EU regulation afterwards, it is necessary to understand the UK's traditional approach to procurement.

At the risk of over-simplification, Civil Law systems typically have a tradition of regulating procurement through hard law to promote domestic objectives such as value for money.[1] They have traditionally[2] enacted a single and overarching regulatory framework for procurement; relied on rules that are legally binding *and* enforceable, including by suppliers; been detailed; imposed extensive constraints on discretion; and applied a relatively uniform approach across contracting authorities.

The UK, by contrast, had—until the post-Brexit reforms elaborated in section 3—never adopted a comprehensive hard law framework for promoting *domestic* objectives. While competitive tendering was important,[3] it was traditionally implemented through soft law,[4] most recently in Procurement Policy Notes (PPNs).[5] Some hard law always existed, but addressed discrete and limited areas only.[6] Regulatory rules (hard and soft) tended to include limited detail and to afford significant discretion,[7] adding

[1] S Arrowsmith, 'Public Procurement', in C Jansen, F van Ommeren, J Wolswinkel, and S Arrowsmith, *Optimizing Public Interests through Competitive Tendering* (Cambridge University Press, 2025) 37–120.

[2] S Arrowsmith, *The Evolution of Procurement Law in the United Kingdom: a Common Law Perspective on Regulating Contract Award Procedures*, https://papers.ssrn.com/sol3/papers.cfm?abstract_id = 4756144, 9–16.

[3] Public Accounts Committee in 1925, C Turpin, *Government Procurement and Contracts* (Longman 1989) 124–25.

[4] Turpin (n 3).

[5] Collected at https://www.gov.uk/government/collections/procurement-policy-notes.

[6] See, eg, Local Government Act 1972, s 135, Local Government Act 1988, s 17, prohibiting taking account of non-commercial considerations (both of which still apply) and the Compulsory Competitive Tendering (CCT) regime under the latter Act.

[7] On rules v discretion, a central debate in procurement, see S Kelman, *Procurement and Public Management: The Fear of Discretion and the Quality of Government Performance* (The AEI Press 1999); S Arrowsmith, 'The EC Procurement Directives, National Procurement Policies and Better Governance: The Case for a New Approach' (2002) 27 ELRev 3.

Sue Arrowsmith and Luke R.A. Butler, *Public Procurement* In: *The UK Regulatory Framework Post-Brexit: 'Law Unbound'*.
Edited by: Paul Craig and Vilija Vėlyvytė, Oxford University Press. © Oxford University Press 2026.
DOI: 10.1093/9780198969815.003.0016

further to the 'soft' nature of the system.[8] The government placed trust in discretion rather than rules, supported by promoting professionalism and professionalization.[9] All this left contracting authorities largely free to adopt their own approaches—for example, to the scope and content of tendering rules.

(b) EU Regulation

The EU regulates procurement primarily for single market objectives. The free movement obligations apply, and 'co-ordination' Directives contain detailed tendering rules,[10] originally introduced to prevent discrimination and remove obstacles to participation, such as inadequate information.[11] While generally adopting a limited harmonization approach,[12] the Directives now leave limited space for national regulation.

Directive 2014/24/EU[13] regulates most public contracts, while three sectoral Directives, covering utilities,[14] defence,[15] and concessions,[16] take a similar approach but provide more procedural flexibility. On enforcement, bespoke Directives[17] require 'effective' national remedies. The Directives apply only to contracts above certain financial thresholds. However, the free movement rules require not just non-discrimination but also transparency, including publicity, for *all* contracts of cross-border interest.[18]

[8] L Jiang, 'Developing Multilateral Rules on Government Procurement: the Value of Soft Law', in S Arrowsmith and R Anderson (eds), *The WTO Regime on Government Procurement: Challenge and Reform* (Cambridge University Press 2011) Ch 23.

[9] See, eg, *Setting New Standards: A Strategy for Government Procurement* (1995) Cm.2840; Cabinet Office, *Making a Difference: Reducing Bureaucracy in Central Civil Government Procurement* (2003); HM Treasury, *Transforming Government Procurement* (January 2007).

[10] See S Arrowsmith, *The Law of Public and Utilities Procurement* (3rd edn, Sweet and Maxwell vol 1 2014 and vol 2 2018).

[11] S Arrowsmith, 'The Purpose of the EU Public Procurement Directives: Ends, Means, and the Implications for National Regulatory Space for Commercial and Horizontal Procurement Policies' (2011/12) 14 CYELS 1; P Kunzlik, 'Neoliberalism and the European Public Procurement Regime' (2012–13) 15 CYELS 283.

[12] Case 31/87 *Gebroeders Beentjes v Netherlands* EU:C:1988:422.

[13] Directive 2014/24/EU of the European Parliament and of the Council of 26 February 2014 on public procurement and repealing Directive 2004/18/EC, [2014] OJ L94/65.

[14] Directive 2014/25/EU of the European Parliament and of the Council of 26 February 2014 on procurement by entities operating in the water, energy, transport and postal services sectors and repealing Directive 2004/17/EC, [2014] OJ L94/243.

[15] Directive 2009/81/EC of the European Parliament and of the Council of 13 July 2009 on the coordination of procedures for the award of certain works contracts, supply contracts and service contracts by contracting authorities or entities in the fields of defence and security, and amending Directives 2004/17/EC and 2004/18/EC, [2009] OJ L216/76.

[16] Directive 2014/23/EU of the European Parliament and of the Council of 26 February 2014 on the award of concession contracts, [2014] OJ L94/1.

[17] The initial directives were adopted in 1989 and 1992 and amended in 2007: Directive 2007/66/EC of the European Parliament and the Council of 11 December 2007 amending Council Directives 89/665/EEC and 92/13/EEC with regard to improving the effectiveness of review procedures concerning the award of public contracts [2007] OJ L335/31.

[18] Case C-324/98 *Telaustria Verlags v Telekom Austria and Herold Business Data AG* EU:C:2000:669, [61]–[62]; Case C-507/03 *Commission v Ireland* [2007] ECR I-9777.

EU law had a significant impact on UK procurement culture:[19] while many member states merely needed to adapt existing hard law systems to EU obligations, the UK had to introduce for the first time an extensive set of rules enforceable by suppliers. The UK initially purported to comply with the Directives with 'soft law' instructions,[20] but from 1991 transposed the Directives through regulations[21] under section 2(2) of the European Communities Act 1972. Those applying in England, Wales, and Northern Ireland at the time of Brexit were the Public Contracts Regulations 2015,[22] Utilities Contracts Regulations 2016,[23] Concession Contracts Regulations 2016,[24] and Defence and Security Public Contracts Regulations 2011,[25] with (slightly) different regulations in Scotland.[26] The first sections of this chapter focus on the Westminster jurisdiction, while section 4 examines issues around devolution.

The Regulations transposed the Directives largely by copying out the Directives' text, which was adequate given the clear, precise, and unconditional nature of most rules. The Supreme Court held that the Regulations did not go beyond EU requirements, rejecting an argument that 'contract' under the Regulations covered agreements that were contractual under English law but outside the Directives.[27]

The government continued to legislate occasionally on specific procurement issues, a recent example being the Public Services (Social Value) Act 2012 ('Social Value Act') requiring consideration of social value in certain procurements. There was no attempt, however, to integrate, consolidate, or streamline the various procurement rules into a single instrument or framework.

While the government maintained the traditional approach so far as possible, EU obligations had a significant impact on that approach. Thus EU-based tendering obligations gradually diminished the national regulatory space and hence scope for the traditional approach, including affording discretion to contracting authorities (for example, on supplier dialogue). In addition, the EU's 'hard' law approach precluded the government from taking full advantage of the benefits of soft law, such as adapting swiftly to new developments.[28] Further, exposure to hard law contributed to a new culture and gradual acceptance of the hard law approach, which substantially influenced the post-Brexit regime, as section 2 elaborates.

A final point important for any 'Brexit dividend' is that in the past decade or so the CJEU has interpreted the Directives as requiring certain procurement decisions to be made only on a case-by-case basis (precluding domestic rulemaking) *and* only by

[19] J Fernández Martín, *The EC Public Procurement Rules: A Critical Analysis* (Clarendon Press 1996).
[20] ibid Ch 10.
[21] Public Works Contracts Regulations 1991 SI 1991/2680; Public Supply Contracts Regulations 1991 SI 1991/2679.
[22] SI 2015 No. 102.
[23] SI 2016 No. 274.
[24] SI 2011 No. 1848.
[25] SI 2016 No. 273.
[26] See section 4 of this chapter.
[27] *Brent London Borough Council v Risk Management Partners* [2011] UKSC 7.
[28] See Arrowsmith and Treumer, 'Competitive Dialogue in EU Law' (on dialogue with suppliers) and Arrowsmith, *The Law of Public and Utilities Procurement*, vol 2, ch 19 (on electronic technologies).

individual contracting authorities.[29] It is beyond the scope of this chapter to critique this questionable development, the full implications of which, including for soft law regulation, are yet to be appreciated.

2 Post-Brexit Regulation

(a) The Transition Period and the Period to February 2025

To ensure compliance with the Withdrawal Agreement[30] the procurement Regulations were retained during the transition period with limited (mainly technical) adaptations.[31]

Those Regulations were also preserved at the end of that period to ensure stability pending reform and compliance with trade commitments. In particular, as early as June 2018 the government decided to retain open public markets (including with the EU) by negotiating accession to the World Trade Organization Agreement on Government Procurement (GPA),[32] which occurred on 1 January 2021. Despite the political popularity of discriminatory procurement, there seems never to have been serious thought of rolling back GPA commitments with loss of reciprocal access for UK suppliers. The GPA opens markets in a similar manner to the Directives by prohibiting discrimination and mandating tendering and supplier remedies, but with more skeletal obligations. The Directives seek to ensure that providing access to EU markets in accordance with their procedures and remedies suffices also for GPA compliance; hence continued application of the EU-derived UK Regulations ensured UK compliance. The GPA also provides the model for many other trade agreements of both the EU and (after Brexit) the UK, including the TCA; thus providing access rights under the Regulations to trading partners sufficed for compliance with other agreements, also. For major contracts the TCA[33] simply supplements the GPA, providing in particular mutual market access (based on GPA procedures and remedies) for certain utility sectors, private utilities, and services covered by the Directives but not the GPA itself. In the UK, the amended version of the EU-derived Regulations thus served to ensure compliance with the TCA.

The end of the transition period did, however, entail some substantial amendments,[34] including replacing the EU's Official Journal with the domestic FindATender

[29] See, eg, Case C-267/18 *Delta Antrepriză de Construcții și Montaj 93 SA* EU:C:2019:826.

[30] Agreement on the withdrawal of the United Kingdom of Great Britain and Northern Ireland from the European Union and the European Atomic Energy Community [2020] OJ L/29 ('Withdrawal Agreement'), Art 118.

[31] The Public Procurement (Amendment etc) (EU Exit) Regulations 2020 No 1319.

[32] Coverage is negotiated bilaterally between Parties, without any MFN obligation (that is, with no obligation to extend agreed coverage to other GPA Parties).

[33] The applicable obligations are set out in TCA Title VI.

[34] The Public Procurement (Amendment Etc) (EU Exit) Regulations 2020, SI 2020 No 1319; the Defence and Security Public Contracts (Amendment) (EU Exit) Regulations 2020, SI 2020 No 1450.

system. The government also removed EU access to defence and security contracts—no longer covered by trade agreements—in anticipation of losing access to equivalent EU markets.[35]

(b) The Scope for a New Approach after Brexit

Clearly, trade agreements entailed significant legal constraints even after Brexit; for major procurement they continued to necessitate a system of hard law enforceable by suppliers, making it impossible to revert fully to the pre-EU situation. However, the constraints were considerably less than under EU law.

First, post-Brexit agreements have less extensive coverage than EU rules; in particular, hard defence procurement and lower value contracts are not covered. They also do not include explicit rules determining when public bodies can procure from other public bodies without tendering, something the Directives regulate in detail.[36] Second, there are fewer explicit procedural constraints, including on discretion. Third, enforcement rules are much less stringent. For example, they do not require a standstill between award and contract or rules rendering contracts ineffective in certain cases.

Given that during EU membership the government maintained the traditional characteristics of the UK system so far as permitted, the most obvious response to Brexit would have been simply to copy out the trade rules into new legislation, and with remedies—where some choices were required—to introduce a new system (perhaps based on judicial review) that merely met minimum requirements.

Instead, however, as section 3 elaborates, the government rejected substantial aspects of the pre-Brexit model in favour of an even wider scope for hard law than applied during EU membership.

(c) The Reform Process and the Post-Brexit Legislation

In contrast with some areas, post-Brexit reform in procurement is essentially complete. The Westminster government announced its reform intentions on 4 November 2019[37] as being to build a 'bonfire of red tape' of EU procurement rules, including to improve SME access;[38] published a Green Paper, *Transforming Public*

[35] The Defence and Security Public Contracts (Amendment) (EU Exit) Regulations 2020, regs 3(2)(d), (f), (h) and (i), and added an exemption equivalent to that under Art 346 TFEU by reg 3A–3C.

[36] See, eg, Directive 2014/24, Art 12.

[37] After convening focus groups during the summer and creating a Procurement Transformation Advisory Panel (PTAP) in October. Arrowsmith convened the academic focus group, and was a member of PTAP. Views expressed in this chapter are solely those of the authors.

[38] C Hope, 'Boris Johnson Orders a "Bonfire" of Red Tape to give Small Firms a Bigger Slice of Government Contracts after Brexit', *The Telegraph* (4 November 2019) https://www.telegraph.co.uk/politics/2019/11/04/boris-johnson-orders-bonfire-red-tape-give-small-firms-bigger/, reporting an interview by Oliver Dowden, the Cabinet Office Minister at that time.

Procurement,[39] in December 2020; published its response to consultation in December 2021;[40] and introduced a Bill based largely on the Green Paper on 11 May 2022. This received Royal Assent as the Procurement Act 2023 on 26 October 2023 and came into force mainly on 24 February 2025. The Act is supplemented by Regulations, in particular the Procurement Regulations 2024,[41] and guidance.[42] The Act requires the government to publish a National Procurement Policy Statement (NPPS), to which contracting authorities must have regard.[43]

Despite its title, the Green Paper focused on regulatory reform rather than broader transformation. Some gaps in the Green Paper affected the quality of reform. For example, intentions over ongoing purchasing arrangements ('dynamic purchasing systems', 'framework agreements', and 'qualification systems' in EU terminology) were not clearly formulated,[44] probably because of technical complexity; public–public arrangements were not considered; and exclusion and debarment was addressed only to a limited extent. This resulted in some consultations after the Green Paper and proposals not being discussed.[45] Similarly, the Green Paper did not address topics such as devolution and defence.

In February 2025 the new Labour government published a new NPPS,[46] and mooted some further reforms,[47] including on social value[48] and expanding national security exemptions; but no radical change appears to be contemplated.

3 Analysis of the New Legislation

(a) The Reform Objectives: A Comprehensive Hard Law System, Expanding the EU's approach

The most striking feature of the Procurement Act 2023 conceptually is that, rather than continuing the approach of minimal hard law regulation, the government has introduced an overarching hard law framework for promoting *domestic* procurement

[39] Cabinet Office, *Transforming Public Procurement*, CP253 (December 2020) ('2020 Green Paper'), Ch.1, *passim*.
[40] Cabinet Office, *Transforming Government Procurement: Response to Consultation*, CP556 (December 2021).
[41] SI 2024 No 692.
[42] Cabinet Office, 'Procurement Act 2023—Guidance Documents', https://www.gov.uk/government/collections/procurement-act-2023-guidance-documents.
[43] Procurement Act 2023, s 13.
[44] The relevant material is in Ch 5 of the Green Paper.
[45] Cabinet Office, *Transforming Public Procurement Part 1: Consultation on Draft Regulations to Implement the Procurement Bill* (June 2023) and Cabinet Office, *Transforming Public Procurement Government: Response to Consultation on Draft Regulations Implementing the Procurement Act 2023* (22 March 2024).
[46] Cabinet Office, *National Procurement Policy Statement* (13 February 2025).
[47] Cabinet Office, *Public Procurement: Growing British Industry, Jobs and Skills, Consultation on Further Reforms to Public Procurement* (June 2025).
[48] See section 3b(v) of this chapter.

objectives[49] as well as implementing trade rules. These domestic objectives are effectively identified in section12(1), requiring contracting authorities to consider the importance of delivering value for money, maximizing public benefit, sharing information, and acting (and being seen to act) with integrity. Rules regulating tendering—such as advertising requirements and time limits for response—serve now not only to ensure compliance with trade obligations (which remains one function[50]), but also to support these domestic objectives.

This has important consequences, including that hard law continues to regulate procurements no longer governed by trade rules, notably hard defence procurements. Brexit offered an opportunity to roll back the hard law regime and replace it with soft law, but the government rejected that, accepting hard law as the new preferred tool of *domestic* regulation.

This conceptual change is also manifested in new hard law obligations aimed at domestic objectives. To a large extent these are not policies that reflect any 'Brexit dividend', however, as they were not precluded by the EU. They link to Brexit only in that the post-Brexit reform process presented the political opportunity for legislation.

First, in line with a global movement towards 'open contracting',[51] the government greatly extended information transparency, introducing hard law publication obligations going well beyond those of either the Directives or its own previous soft law by, for example, requiring publication of any intention to contract without advertising, and of contracts and contract amendments.[52] Importantly, publications must use the Open Contracting Data Standard (OCDS),[53] ensuring information can be read and analysed; this facilitates monitoring for both legal compliance and policy outcomes by both government and stakeholders. Related to this, a new single digital platform will hold all the information.[54]

Second, the government has legislated an extensive regime of exclusions for suppliers posing risks to the procurement system.[55] This involves some mandatory exclusions, including of suppliers formally found to have infringed certain rules (for example, convicted of offences of dishonesty, or found by courts or regulators to have engaged in anti-competitive agreements) and an obligation to consider exclusion on 'discretionary' exclusion grounds[56] (such as for certain other competition

[49] See the 2020 Green Paper, Ch 1; S Arrowsmith, 'The Conceptual Reorientation of Procurement Regulation in the UK: The New Objectives of the Post-Brexit Regulatory Regime and the Enhanced Role of Hard Law as a Domestic Policy Tool' (2024) 33 PPLRev 161.

[50] HL Deb 11 July 2022 vol 823, col 363GC; Explanatory Notes to the Procurement Act 2023, paras 12 and 23.

[51] As promoted in particular by the Open Contracting Partnership, a non-profit body. See https://www.open-contracting.org/.

[52] Procurement Act 2023, ss 44, 53 and 77. On the contents of notices see Procurement Regulations 2024, Part 2.

[53] See again https://www.open-contracting.org/. This intention was stated in the 2020 Green Paper and the details of publication in the Procurement Regulations 2024 are designed to comply with the standard.

[54] See Cabinet Office, *Guidance: Central Digital Platform and Publication of Information* (Oct 2024).

[55] For the policy intention and analysis see Cabinet Office, *Guidance: Exclusions* (updated Feb 2025).

[56] See, in particular, Procurement Act 2023, ss 26–30 and the related mandatory and discretionary exclusion ground set out in schs 6 and 7 respectively.

infringements). The policy is supported by a centralized regime, under which the Cabinet Office investigates whether grounds for general debarment exist,[57] promoting an approach that both is effective and avoids disproportionately burdening contracting authorities.

Also noteworthy is that the government decided substantially to retain the rigorous EU-based remedies regime.[58] This contains many features not found in judicial review or in purely 'domestic' remedies legislation (for example, on enforcing section 17 of the Local Government Act 1988).[59] This 'softer' domestic enforcement limited the practical impact of procurement rules, but the government has rejected this approach, even though largely compatible with trade obligations, in favour of the 'harder' EU approach.

Thus the UK has eschewed one of the major freedoms of Brexit for an approach that is in a sense even 'more European' than before.

What were the drivers of this? A number of (related) factors possibly played a part,[60] or at least provide a policy justification for this approach.

First, it possibly reflects a recognition of enforceable hard law as the accepted modern approach, as embodied in the UNCITRAL Model Law on Public Procurement 2011,[61] and as reflecting advantages of that approach in terms of, for example, supplier confidence and better compliance.[62] This approach is now widely applied not only in Civil Law countries but also in other market economies, including many developing countries that formerly followed UK tradition.[63]

This approach may also have been influenced by, among other things,[64] the new procurement culture, involving a familiarity with hard law and its acceptance (if not positive approval), and by the creation of a procurement law 'industry' of legal professionals and educators.

In this environment, rolling back hard law might also have led to greater judicial regulation through judicial review and/or an implied contract governing the tendering process; both doctrines had begun to evolve to control procurement prior to transposing the Directives but after that were relegated to a limited role, which left legal control to explicit legislation.[65] It was certainly desirable that regulatory rules in such a technical area should instead be crafted by the legislator.

[57] Procurement Act 2023, ss 59-66; S Arrowsmith, *Constructing Rules on Exclusions (Debarment) under a Post-Brexit Regime on Public Procurement: A Preliminary Analysis* (24 July 2020), SSRN: https://ssrn.com/abstract = 3659909.

[58] Procurement Act 2023, Pt 9.

[59] Arrowsmith, *The Law of Public and Utilities Procurement*, vol 2, Ch 22.

[60] Arrowsmith (n 49).

[61] UNCITRAL Model Law on Public Procurement 2011, Chapter VIII, 'Challenge Proceedings'.

[62] X Zhang, 'Supplier Review as a Mechanism for Securing Compliance with Public Procurement Rules: A Critical Perspective' (2007) 16 PPLRev 325.

[63] See, on Africa, G Quinot and S Arrowsmith (eds), *Public Procurement Regulation in Africa* (Cambridge University Press 2013).

[64] Arrowsmith (n 49).

[65] On implied contract see *Blackpool and Fylde Aero Club v Blackpool BC* [1990] 1 WLR 1195 as interpreted in *JBW Group v Ministry of Justice* [2012] EWCA Civ 8; and on judicial review S Bailey, 'Judicial

Finally, the 2020 Green Paper stated that the domestic objectives set out there 'underpin the regulatory framework and demonstrate [the Government's] commitment to tackling corruption in public procurement'.[66] This perhaps suggests that hard law was important from both a policy perspective and to highlight government objectives clearly to stakeholders.

(b) Active Divergence

While elements of the EU approach have thus been retained and even extended, others have been intentionally rolled back. As we have seen, the government highlighted procurement as an area benefiting from Brexit through a 'bonfire of red tape' and in its May 2023 paper on Smarter Regulation it claimed: 'We have already made leaps and bounds in leveraging post-Brexit regulatory freedoms—including in areas such as . . . procurement.'[67] In its Explanatory Notes to the Procurement Act the government stated that it 'aimed to speed up and simplify public procurement processes';[68] that previous rules were 'too restrictive and complex'; and that it aimed to create a regime that is 'is simpler and more flexible'.[69] The government's 2022 paper *The Benefits of Brexit* claimed that the planned reforms aimed at simplification and speeding up processes would generate social value and unleash innovation opportunities for SMEs, charities, and social enterprises.[70]

The specific measures implementing these intentions can be placed into three broad categories, which to some extent echo the Smarter Regulation agenda: removing constraints on discretion (flexibility), reducing cost and delay, and simplifying legislation. A fourth category of 'actively diverging' measures—one that the Green Paper did not refer to—consists of measures ruled out under EU law because of constraints over rulemaking and centralized decision-making (set out in section 1(b) of this chapter).

The reality is, however, that the significance of the legal reforms overall is limited and the most important of them are not in fact related to Brexit freedoms.

(i) Flexibility

The Procurement Act has, first, taken advantage of reduced regulation post-Brexit to roll back some constraints that the EU imposed on contracting authority discretion.

Review of Contracting Decisions' (2007) PL 444 and E Aspey, 'The Search for the True *Public Law* Element: Judicial Review of Procurement Decisions' (2016) PL 35.

[66] 2020 Green Paper, para 25.
[67] *Smarter Regulation*, section 4.
[68] ibid [10].
[69] ibid [11].
[70] HM Government, *The Benefits of Brexit: How the UK is Taking Advantage of Leaving the EU* (Jan 2022) 8, 17, 18, and 79.

One important change is that the Act allows contracting authorities to use for any procurement a 'competitive flexible procedure'[71] that permits both an iterative process and supplier dialogue. Those features have many potential advantages, such as allowing refinement of specifications, facilitating adjustment of offers to requirements, and addressing collusion.[72] EU rules treated such features with suspicion because of the potential for abuse and unfairness, allowing them under the public sector regime only under defined conditions,[73] although they are freely available for utilities, defence, and concessions. Another change is the introduction of more flexible rules on frameworks—agreements that, following a tendering exercise, set terms for future 'call-off' contracts—although the impact of this is limited by the fact that EU requirements are not clear and UK practice already adopted a very flexible approach.[74] Other examples are a new flexibility to modify concluded contracts in the event of known risks materializing[75] and a discretionary exclusion for poor performance which is broader than EU law allows.[76]

Most of these changes are helpful, but the main obstacles to commercial outcomes were already addressed in 2004 by introducing the competitive dialogue procedure and explicit rules on frameworks, such that none of the Act's reforms are really fundamental.

(ii) Speedier and Less Costly Procedures

Procedural burdens affect both contracting authorities and suppliers and can deter participation, especially by SMEs. The reforms in this area are not in general, however, directly related to Brexit. They involve introduction of the central digital platform (allowing suppliers to submit basic information once only) and high-level duties to consider whether barriers to SME participation can be reduced[77] and to ensure procedures are 'proportionate'.[78]

Active divergence from EU requirements is perhaps most likely to emerge in judicial interpretation: identification of speedier and less costly procedures as a reform objective is relevant for judicial interpretation.

71 Procurement Act 2023, s 20.

72 K Krueger, 'The Scope for Post-tender Negotiations in International Tendering Procedures' in S Arrowsmith and A Davies (eds), *Public Procurement: Global Revolution* (Kluwer Law International 1999) Ch 10; P Bajari and S Tadelis, 'Incentives and Award Procedures: Competitive Tendering vs. Negotiations in Procurement', in N Dimitri, G Piga, and G Spagnolo (eds), *Handbook of Procurement* (Cambridge University Press 2006) 121–42.

73 Directive 2014/24, Arts 26 and 32.

74 S Brunning, 'The Supply and Proliferation of Multi-supplier Framework Agreements in the UK' (2023) 32 PPLRev 15.

75 Procurement Act 2023, s 74(1) and sch 8, [5].

76 ibid sch 7, [12].

77 ibid s 12(4) and s 86(1).

78 ibid s 20(3).

(iii) Legislative Simplification

Simplification—making the procurement regime easier to understand and operate[79]—is manifested in several ways, including by eliminating rules and details that serve little or no purpose.

Notably, simplification has resulted from adopting a single regulatory framework that is relatively comprehensive, to replace four separate sets of Regulations. Importantly, this is accompanied by greater uniformity between sectors, including applying three main award procedures—an open procedure, competitive flexible procedure, and direct award—for all sectors, with free access to the first two procedures. These replace an unwarranted plethora of procedures available in different variations and under different conditions in different Directives.[80] This reform also simplified the legislation by removing duplication through overlapping procedures. The opportunity for uniformity here rested on the UK's policy decision to allow more flexibility for the public sector in line with the position that applied in other sectors.

Further simplification resulted from eliminating anomalous and disproportionate differences, such as by adopting a single set of rules for mixed contracts (those involving subject matter of different types or for different purposes)[81] to replace a myriad of EU rules for different types of mixed contract.

However, some sectoral differences remain, entailing retention of the concepts of concessions, utilities contracts, and defence and security contracts—unfortunately, largely using the lengthy and complex EU-based definitions. This continues many of the regime's complexities, including boundary rules to determine which regime applies. Most surprising is retention of the concessions concept. This has its roots in Civil Law and its use was criticized by many Common Law consultees, on the basis that concessions are simply one type of complex contract that can be regulated under general rules on complex contracts.[82] Under the Procurement Act the rules governing concessions are largely assimilated de jure as well as de facto to those for other contracts, but with different thresholds and a few special rules that seem unwarranted. The definition of concessions generated highly complex case law[83] when there is no clear reason for the separate concept.

The Act, like the Directive, includes a special 'light-touch' regime for certain social, health, education, and other services involving personal service to individuals. Full analysis is beyond the scope of this chapter but the need for special rules to give the

[79] S Arrowsmith, 'Modernising the EU's Public Procurement Regime: A Blueprint for Real Simplicity and Flexibility' (2012) 21 PPLRev 71.

[80] ibid.

[81] Procurement Act 2023, s 5.

[82] S Arrowsmith, 'Revisiting the Case against a Separate Concessions Regime in the Light of the Concessions Directive: A Specific Directive without Specificities?', in F Amtenbrink, G Davies, D Kochenov, and J Lindeboom (eds), *The Internal Market and the Future of European Integration* (Cambridge University Press 2019) 370–95.

[83] Procurement Act 2023, which defines concessions in s 8 in a similar manner to EU law.

desired flexibility (in some cases) and justification for those rules (in others, such as modification) is unclear to the authors.

The concept of a utilities contract is based on detailed definitions derived from the Directives. The utilities sector enjoys certain flexibilities, which include lower thresholds, additional exemptions,[84] and more flexible rules on using supplier lists,[85] reflecting flexibilities in the Directives which have also been included in the UK's trade agreements. A key rationale is that these trade agreements—like the Directives—apply in utilities sectors to procurement of public undertakings and, in certain sectors under the TCA, to some private bodies.[86]

With defence and security contracts, the government has, as with utilities and concessions, retained a detailed EU-based definition, and also widened it.[87] In this sector, the differences from the 'standard' regime are extensive and important—a domestic choice, since trade agreements do not apply. Adaptations include extensive exemptions and additional grounds for direct award. It might have been possible to develop a simpler (albeit less uniform) regime based largely on exemption and internal approvals processes. The reasons for regulating through exemptions *and* adaptation instead are not known, but the result of the chosen approach is that such contracts are legally regulated but difficult to challenge because of wide discretion under the exemptions and direct award procedure—a relatively 'soft' approach, albeit formally under hard law.

Finally, as with other post-Brexit rules, the government has to a significant extent used new terminology, including for many rules and concepts that are similar, and even identical, to previous ones. Presumably this is to facilitate understanding through familiar language,[88] to adapt to a different approach to interpretation, and to highlight that EU case law has no formal relevance. However, this causes considerable uncertainty.

(iv) Centralization and Rulemaking

As explained, there is a further important way in which Brexit has facilitated reform which the government itself has not highlighted, namely that the UK is no longer subject to the Directives' constraints on rulemaking and centralized decision-making as set out in section 1b. The latter constraint would make it impossible, for example, for the government to centralize decision-making on debarment in the way it is has done to make the policy effective, as set out in section 2a.

[84] Procurement Act 2023, sch 2, [5]–[6] on joint ventures and companies in the same group.

[85] ibid s 40.

[86] Procurement Act 2023, s 2. For private utilities the Procurement Act provides for even more departure from the general uniform regime of the Act than for other utilities.

[87] Adding a new category under Procurement Act 2023, s 7(1)(g).

[88] In accordance with *Office of the Parliamentary Counsel drafting guidance* (March 2024), available at: https://assets.publishing.service.gov.uk/media/660407d091a320001a82b06b/2024.03.19.Drafting-guidance.pdf, at 1.3, in particular paras 1.3.6–1.3.10.

(v) Enhancement of Social Value?

Much has been made of the reforms enhancing social value.[89] However, the actual impact of the Act in this area is actually quite limited, and largely unrelated to Brexit.

This complex subject cannot be considered in detail but, in summary, the EU rules—while imposing significant constraints—have recently evolved towards greater flexibility, reflecting a greater EU and national interest in using procurement to promote social value. This is manifested in the UK in, for example, the Social Value Act, emphasis on social value in the NPPS,[90] and a mandatory soft law social value model and 10 per cent social value weighting for civil central government procurement, introduced in 2020.[91]

Brexit's removal of TFEU constraints provides greater flexibility in low-value contracts, and in 2020 the government issued a PPN highlighting the new possibility for reserving contracts for local suppliers or groups thereof, such as local SMEs.[92] This potentially creates obstacles to commerce in the UK's internal market. However, for high-value contracts, previous legal constraints are largely retained, as the GPA requires such constraints.[93] The Procurement Act changed the wording of the basis for award from 'most economically advantageous tender' to 'most advantageous tender' to encourage use of non-economic criteria, but this is merely presentational.[94] The Act also includes duties to have regard to the importance of maximizing public benefit[95] and to reducing barriers to SME access,[96] but these are high-level duties that do not require concrete measures and do not reflect any 'Brexit dividend', being exercisable only within the same legal constraints as before Brexit.

It is also relevant to note here that the TCA appears to place some restrictions on governments' ability to prevent their own contracting authorities from applying social value measures,[97] echoing in this one specific area the Directives' recently developed doctrine of allocating procurement power away from member state central governments to individual contracting authorities, as set out in section 3b(iv).

[89] See, eg, *The Benefits of Brexit* (n 71) 8.

[90] NPPS, 24 Feb 2025.

[91] Cabinet Office, *Procurement Policy Note—Taking Account of Social Value in the Award of Central Government Contracts Action* Note 06/20 (Sep 2020); Cabinet Office, PPN 002, *Taking Account of Social Value in the Award of Contracts* (updated March 2025).

[92] Cabinet Office, PPN 005—*Reserving below threshold* (updated Feb 2025) and Local Government (Exclusion of Non-commercial Considerations) (England) Order 2026 No. 94. See also section 5 on Northern Ireland.

[93] Procurement Act 2023 s 23(2) requiring award criteria to be related to the subject matter of the contract.

[94] ibid s 19(1).

[95] ibid s 12(2)(b).

[96] ibid s 12(2)(4); and for lower value contracts in s 86.

[97] TCA, Art 285.

(vi) Reduced Judicial Activism

Finally, many EU constraints were imposed, or originally imposed, through creative CJEU rulings based on general principles.[98] However, judicial creativity, and the related uncertainty, is now inherently restricted by domestic interpretation techniques. The legislature has limited the potential for this further by omitting obligations of transparency and proportionality found in the Directives, replacing them with more precise obligations along with general duties to consider: for example, transparency is replaced by obligations to publish specified information plus the section 12 requirement to have regard to the importance of information sharing.

(c) The Continuing Influence of EU Law and Relevance of Pre-Brexit Case Law

While Brexit has led directly or indirectly to important reforms, the government has also retained much detail from EU-based law. Other than in the structure of tendering procedures—significantly changed with the new competitive flexible procedure—many of the Act's provisions draw on the Directives' concepts and frequently paraphrase previous provisions. A degree of similarity is to be expected as procurement laws globally tend to have a similar structure and features, often influenced by models such as the UNCITRAL Model Law and GPA. But even in that context the similarity between the Act and Directives is striking.

To an extent, this is driven by trade commitments. For example, the Directives' concepts are used directly in the GPA to define the scope of UK entity coverage, thus requiring the Act to cover these entities. However, in many cases the EU-based approach is not related to trade constraints.

Thus, as section 3a explained, the Procurement Act includes an EU-based remedies regime. This has only a few and limited modifications.[99] Remedies was in fact an area in which radical reform was mooted by stakeholders and the Procurement Transformation Advisory Committee—not based on Brexit freedoms but to leverage the political opportunity for legislation to implement a cheaper, swifter review forum than the courts. However, major reform was rejected, at least temporarily, in favour of measures to improve the court process[100] and some enhanced centralized enforcement.[101]

The Act also largely repeats, in a slightly reworded form, detailed rules on several matters not explicitly or significantly dealt with in trade agreements—for example,

[98] K Pedersen and E Olsson, 'The Role of European Court of Justice in Public Procurement' in C Bovis (ed), *Research Handbook on EU Public Procurement Law* (Edward Elgar 2016) Ch 13.
[99] Procurement Act 2023, ss 51(2), 101(1).
[100] 2020 Green Paper, Ch 7.
[101] Procurement Act 2023, Pt 10 on procurement oversight.

on permitted contract modifications,[102] and on awarding work to other public bodies without tendering[103]—and also imports the EU rules on e-invoicing.[104] This is not to say that the rules are identical, but they are substantially the same. Further, the Act includes a 'same treatment' obligation that echoes the EU equal treatment principle,[105] although it will not be interpreted in exactly the same manner.

In this context previous case law remains relevant,[106] albeit that the Act does not have any formal link with EU law. This is because of the need to interpret the legislation in compliance with trade agreements and because of the usual approach of domestic law in using past case law to interpret 'successor' legislation.[107]

(d) Smarter Regulation?

The *Smarter Regulation* paper of May 2023 was published after the Procurement Bill was introduced and, as section 3b observed, cited procurement as an example of leveraging Brexit for smarter regulation. Section 3b explained that this is indeed the case to an extent—reforms have rolled back on substantive constraints and on rules that created complexity without proportionate benefits. The paper *Smarter Regulation One Year On*[108] also highlights procurement, although the specific measures it references, as opposed to vague references to 'cutting red tape'—notably, greater information transparency—were never precluded by EU rules.

However, we have noted that much of the EU-based framework remains. In addition the reforms add new burdens, so that the new regime has arguably increased the overall weight of obligations, for example, through an extended transparency regime (including the burden of redactions)[109] and the new debarment regime, involving obligations to exclude, or consider excluding suppliers, on numerous grounds. It is beyond the scope of this chapter to conduct a cost–benefit analysis of these measures, but they clearly involve significant burdens for contracting authorities and, with exclusions, also for suppliers.

Other new provisions, such as the general duties under section 12, are, it is submitted, not consistent with smart regulation: such duties tend to become tick-box exercises,[110] adding burdens without value. The considerations listed in section 12 are

[102] Procurement Act 2023, s 74 and sch 8.
[103] Referred to in the EU context as the exemptions for 'public–public arrangements' and in the Act as vertical and horizontal exemptions, Procurement Act 2023, sch 2, [2]–[3].
[104] Procurement Act 2023, s 67.
[105] Procurement Act 2023, s 12(2).
[106] Arrowsmith (n 49).
[107] ibid.
[108] 16 May 2024, para 85. This para also refers to 'Faster competition processes for emergency buying' which could refer to s 42 of the Act, which we noted may or may not involve a 'Brexit dividend'.
[109] Permitted exemptions from publication duties are stated in s 94 of the Procurement Act 2023 and seem likely to be applied in practice.
[110] See, eg, Government Equalities Office, *Review of the Public Sector Equality Duty—Report of the Independent Steering Group* (6 Sep 2013).

more important as objectives relevant for interpretation than as enforceable duties and should have been cast as such.

As for unnecessary complexities, while some have been tackled as set out in section 2a, the reforms have not gone as far as they could have done. In particular, the new regime is insufficiently comprehensive. The government has not integrated within it the rules on procuring clinical health services,[111] or other legislation, such as the Social Value Act. According to the 2020 Green Paper, separate laws were kept because

> [I]n line with current practice, they are freestanding laws that may be updated from time to time in their own right. Including them in the single and uniform regulations would unhelpfully duplicate and complicate the legal framework.[112]

However, far from duplicating and complicating the framework, an integrated approach would simplify it and enhance accessibility.[113] In fact, the approach taken seems to reflect the practical difficulties of integration in the desired timeframe, especially given the involvement of government departments other than the Cabinet Office. The interactions between different rules create considerable complexities, as well as other burdens, including from parallel sets of remedies.

The novel rules in the Procurement Act also add complexity, not just from the inevitable need to learn them and from transitional arrangements for existing procurements, but also by virtue of their extensive and (in some cases unnecessarily) complex nature. The debarment rules, for example, are extremely detailed and complex; so too are the transparency rules, particularly the exceptions. While the new rules on frameworks agreements provide more flexibility, the drafting is unnecessarily complex.[114] As section 5 explains, rules governing territorial aspects are also enormously complex.

The burdens of this complexity are not mitigated through guidance, as they might have been. Guidance before Brexit fulfilled various functions: rulemaking through administrative instruction; providing recommendations and exhortations of good practice; informing stakeholders; explaining the rules; and providing interpretations.[115] The Cabinet Office's guidance on the Act,[116] with a few notable exceptions—such as the guidance on exclusions[117]—merely paraphrases or summarizes, rarely adding value. Where rules have been simplified by omitting detail, guidance does not fill in the gaps. For example, exceptions to the obligation to use electronic means are no longer stated[118] but depend on what is 'practicable', and electronic means are not

[111] Now found in the Health Care Services (Provider Selection Regime) Regulations 2023, SI No 1348.

[112] 2020 Green Paper, para 49.

[113] S Arrowsmith, *Transforming Public Procurement Law after Brexit: Some Reflections on the Government's Green Paper* (2021) 30 PPLRev 103, 107–09.

[114] Arrowsmith (n 113) 117–18.

[115] See, eg, OGC/Treasury, *Competitive Dialogue in 2008: OGC/HMT joint guidance on using the procedure* (2008).

[116] See https://www.gov.uk/government/collections/procurement-act-2023-guidance-documents.

[117] Cabinet Office, *Guidance: Exclusions* (updated Feb 24, 2025); Cabinet Office, *Guidance: Debarment* (updated 24 Feb 2025).

[118] As in, eg, Public Contracts Regulations 2015, reg 2022.

defined in detail. There was considerable interest and regulatory capacity in the early days of reform, but the 'procurement project' appears to have run out of steam, with anecdotal evidence suggesting that different bits of guidance were allocated to civil servants with varying expertise, simply to get it done.

(e) Recent Developments in EU Law: Passive Divergence?

Recent EU developments have mainly involved consolidation and extension of recent jurisprudence, notably allocating further regulatory space to contracting authorities and requiring case-by-case decisions.[119] This, as noted, raises questions about the possibility for member states at central level to use soft law to steer decisions, as well as their power to adopt hard law rules. The ability of the government to organize procurement free of such constraints may turn out to be a major benefit of Brexit.[120]

The EU announced in March 2026 an intention to introduce a proposal to reform the procurement rules following a recent evaluation[121] mooting possible procurement preferences for European products, and environmental and other measures, that the UK will remain free to adopt or reject, as with proposed reforms of defence and security rules;[122] but as yet actual reforms are uncertain.

(f) Trade Impact

Regulatory divergence in procurement rules themselves seems unlikely to affect trade in major civil procurement markets. The main potential impact will arise from any increase in general obstacles to trade with the EU, such as loss of mutual recognition for service providers. GPA standards on procurement award procedures and enforcement are widely accepted globally, and were accepted by the EU in GPA negotiations with the UK (concluded before Brexit), with only limited supplementary provisions added in the TCA. In this context mutual access to procurement depends on the coverage negotiated, which in the case of the EU–UK agreements is almost as broad for civil procurement as applied under the Directives.

[119] Case C-66/22 *Infraestruturas de Portugal* EU:C:2023:1016.

[120] See section 1b of this chapter.

[121] European Parliament, Legislative Train 03.2026, A New Plan for European's Sustainable Prosperity and Competitiveness, Public Procurement Act—Q2 2026. See the prior Commission Staff Working Document, Evaluation of Directive 2014/23/EU on Concessions, Directive 2014/24/EU on Public Procurement and Directive 2014/25/EU on Utilities (SWD(2025) 333 final) Brussels, 14 October 2025, SWD(2025) 332 final.

[122] Proposal for a Directive of the European Parliament and of the Council amending Directives 2009/43/EC and 2009/81/EC, as regards the simplification of intra-EU transfers of defence-related products and the simplification of security and defence procurement, COM/2025/823 final.

The Procurement Act 2023 aims to comply with the UK's trade agreements by affording suppliers rights under those agreements (who must be treated no less favourably than UK suppliers) to enforce the Act.[123] Inadvertent divergences are a risk as the Act does not directly copy the wording of trade commitments but, while the authors have not yet conducted a full analysis from this perspective, it is clear that if any such divergences do exist they are minor and technical only.

Similarly, the trade agreements' non-discrimination provisions require trading partners to treat UK suppliers no less favourably than national suppliers. Thus, where the EU is concerned UK suppliers have rights,[124] as before, to enforce the Directives in accordance with the remedies that apply to EU suppliers.

As the GPA is widely accepted as a global model, future agreements are likely be concluded under its umbrella or following the same model.

With procurement not covered by agreements, foreign suppliers do not enjoy mutual rights in either the UK or the EU. Whether to admit them is at the choice of contracting authorities. In the EU this follows from *Kolin*,[125] stating that EU exclusive competence entails that admission is only at the discretion of contracting authorities on a case-by-case basis and cannot be regulated, and in the UK is because the matter simply has not been the subject of regulation.

This is the position that now applies to an extent with contracts below GPA thresholds, which are no longer subject to any rules for cross-border tenders. However, these contracts are of limited interest for cross-border trade, as trade is generally carried out instead by established local branches and, importantly, the TCA requires national treatment in procurement for these.[126] However, the possibility set out in section 3b(v) for reserving contracts for suppliers based on a locality could impact the efficiency of the UK *internal* market.

We noted that UK suppliers have lost rights of access to certain defence and security contracts which trade agreements do not cover. However, it is questionable whether the Defence and Security Directive had any real impact on opportunities,[127] and this loss may thus have little impact. However, the UK has been treated as a third country for the purposes of EU collaborative defence procurement—currently a point of renegotiation.[128]

[123] Procurement Act 2023, Pt 7.

[124] Under these agreements albeit not under the Directives themselves (which confer no rights on third country suppliers): Case C-652/22 *Kolin İnşaat* EU:C:2024:910.

[125] ibid.

[126] TCA, Art 288.

[127] Report from the Commission to the European Parliament and the Council on the implementation of Directive 2009/81/EC on public procurement in the fields of defence and security, to comply with Article 73(2) of that Directive (SWD(2016) 407 final).

[128] L West, 'UK Seeks Closer Defence Procurement Ties with EU', UK Defence Journal (4 May 2025).

4 Territorial Impact

(a) Pre-Brexit Position on Devolved Procurement

Procurement is largely a devolved or transferred matter,[129] with the Welsh and Scottish governments and Northern Ireland Executive having power to determine rules for conducting and managing certain procurement.[130]

As section 1b indicated, rules implementing EU procurement law were largely uniform. A common set of Regulations applied for England, Wales, and Northern Ireland, minimizing the risk of the UK (the member state) infringing EU law. On devolution, only Scotland had power to implement Directives separately and adopted its own Regulations[131] (other than for defence).[132] However, these diverged from those adopted for England and Wales and Northern Ireland only in very limited ways.

Additionally, as with the Westminster jurisdiction, other jurisdictions also adopted a few additional hard law rules on, or affecting, procurement in their own regulatory space, as well as soft law measures. The most notable were (in Scotland) the Procurement Reform (Scotland) Act 2014, imposing, among other things, various duties relating to social value, and (in Wales) the Well-being of Future Generations (Wales) Act 2015 (WBFGA).[133]

Brexit raised many questions, although devolution remained largely unstudied given the historical focus on the UK's compliance with EU law.[134] For example, what would be the approach for Northern Ireland given its cross-border relationship with Ireland, an EU member state? Would common UK-wide rules still be preferable and would Scotland opt in, and, if not, what would be the approach?[135]

(b) Post-Brexit Position: An Overview

Three key themes emerge from a study of post-Brexit developments.

The first is that, as section 4 elaborates, what has eventuated is a common framework, but less so than under EU law and not as extensive as it could have been. The default position is that the Procurement Act 2023 section 126 simply states that 'This

[129] Scotland Act 1998; Northern Ireland Act 1998; Government of Wales Act 1998 and Government of Wales Act 2006.

[130] Cabinet Office, Guidance: Devolved Contracting Authorities, updated 26 June 2025, [1].

[131] The main Regulations in force before Brexit and currently are the Public Contracts (Scotland) Regulations 2015 SI 2015 No. 446.

[132] Public Contract Regulations 2015, Reg 1(7) and Sch 6, para 19.

[133] See, in particular, Part 2 of the Act.

[134] L Butler and J Thomas, 'Public Procurement and Devolution in the UK: Exploring the Laws of (Un) Intended Consequences' (2025) 33 PPLRev 366.

[135] On concerns over fragmentation of the internal market see S Arrowsmith, 'Reimagining Public Procurement Law: Proposals for Post-Brexit Reform' [2023] PL 69, 87.

Act extends to England and Wales, Scotland and Northern Ireland' and, as elaborated later, the Act is relevant in at least some respects in all the nations. However, the exact extent of the Act's application is different in each nation and very complex. Wales and Northern Ireland both chose to opt in to the Act, although with exceptions. Scotland, on the other hand, chose not to opt in to the Act's provisions in general, but instead substantially retained its existing law.

The second theme is that, although EU rules provided more constraints than current trade rules, it was not the case that nations could do very little on their own before Brexit and could do much more afterwards, such that Brexit offered a significant 'devolution dividend'; and actual internal divergence does not generally reflect any such dividend. Thus, many of the Procurement Act rules that do not apply or that differentially apply to devolved or transferred authorities were not set under EU law and would not be incompatible with it. Further, post-Brexit rules on social value in Wales unrelated to the Act (Scotland and Northern Ireland having not adopted post-Brexit reforms of that kind) are a product of the momentum for reform produced by moving from a largely market-based EU model to one focusing more explicitly on domestic objectives, and not directly connected with removal of EU constraints.[136] Differences also reflect the position of Northern Ireland, and the need to avoid a hard border with Ireland.[137]

A third theme is that post-Brexit developments have generated, or may generate, significant costs through the burdens of applying a complex legal framework. Even for UK suppliers the fact that even largely common rules now apply slightly differently, quite apart from (increased) nation-specific legislation, makes the rules governing each specific procurement more difficult to understand. Again, not enough has been done to reduce the burdens through guidance. The Cabinet Office has published basic guidance on devolved contracting authorities[138] but has not published its scheduled guidance on 'intra-UK procurement', perhaps anticipating Scottish legislation which has not been forthcoming. Wales has published guidance largely replicating the Cabinet Office approach[139] and Northern Ireland has issued no guidance.

It is difficult to discern from published documents each nation's rationale for aligning (or not) with the Procurement Act. The 2020 Green Paper gave little attention to the implications of devolution[140] and, with the exception of Wales,[141] there appeared to be little consultation.

[136] P Henty and R D'Souza, 'Embedding Social Partnership and Sustainability into Welsh Procurement: Social Partnership and Public Procurement (Wales) Act 2023' (2023) PPLRev, NA279-NA285.

[137] Thus the discriminatory policy in Cabinet Office PPN 11/20 December 2020 is inapplicable for provision of goods into Northern Ireland.

[138] Cabinet Office, Guidance: Devolved Contracting Authorities (HTML), updated 19 May 2025.

[139] The guidance documents are available at: https://www.gov.wales/procurement-act-2023-guidance-documents accessed 27 July 2025.

[140] L Butler and S Brunning, 'Scoping Coverage of Above-threshold contracts in the Procurement Act 2023: Towards Uniformity, Simplification, and Flexibility' (2024) 4 PPLRev 193, 202–03.

[141] Welsh Government, Wales consultation on Public Procurement Secondary Legislation: Part 1, 19 Jun 2023.

Wales has given high-level justifications for opting in to the Procurement Act.[142] These included ensuring certainty, consistency, and continuity, and that 'maximum alignment' will ensure 'a level playing field' on both sides of the border 'whilst still allowing for devolved differences',[143] without undermining Wales' socially oriented legislation.[144] As will be elaborated, the Procurement Act contains specific provisions relating to Wales, but Wales has not clearly explained what is behind these. Also, following the legislative consent memoranda process,[145] Wales secured concurrent powers to make regulations adding or amending requirements in respect of these specific provisions (including prior Senedd consent on certain matters), which it has already exercised as set out later. Wales also introduced its own Health Service Procurement (Wales) Act 2024, and the Social Partnership and Public Procurement Act 2023 ('Social Partnership Act') to further its social value agenda. Welsh guidance has referred to a new approach to 'smarter public procurement in Wales',[146] but it is not clear whether this is intended to align with the smarter regulation agenda (something arguably belied by the amount of regulation).

The Northern Ireland Assembly has been virtually silent. It has generally secured a similar position on transferred Northern Ireland authorities and regulation-making powers as Wales but, unlike Wales, has not exercised its powers. The only limited exception is publication in June 2025 of a new Procurement Policy Statement.[147]

The Scottish government has also issued few public statements, prompting, in October 2024, a question to the Scottish Parliament on how Scotland will address the Procurement Act. In response, the Scottish government cited its earlier reforms in the Procurement Reform (Scotland) Act 2014, which were 'achieved in a way which was consistent with EU law', and stated that Scotland is best served 'by aligning with EU law where it is practical and sensible to do so'.[148]

Regardless, however, of the extent of opt-in to the Act, or of differential provisions or disapplication of certain rules, contracting authorities across the UK will generally need to know the full rules—for example, because of widespread use of UK-wide framework agreements as set out in section 4c(ii).

Further, to ensure the balance between exercising devolved powers and maintaining the integrity of the UK-wide regulatory frameworks, the Act includes provisions regulating the exercise of both Crown and devolved powers.[149] These would not look out

[142] Explanatory Memorandum to The Procurement (Wales) Regulations 2024, 11 Jun 2024.
[143] ibid [4.6]–[4.7].
[144] ibid [7].
[145] Pursuant to Standing Order (SO) 29.2.
[146] Information is available at https://www.gov.wales/smarter-public-procurement-wales accessed 25 July 2025.
[147] It has issued a Policy Statement: Northern Ireland Executive, Procurement Policy Statement, Issued: 06 June 2025. There is no designated provision for this in the Procurement Act in ss.13 and 14 (cf Wales); it appears to be published as a matter of convention.
[148] Question reference: S6W-30405 asked by Brian Whittle, MSP for South Scotland, Scottish Conservative and Unionist Party lodged 3 October 2024 and answered by Ivan McKee on 18 October 2024.
[149] Procurement Act 2023, Pt 11.

of place in the devolution Acts, but appear incongruous in a document purportedly providing a simplified means of guiding public buyers.

To address international trade implications, the Procurement Act provides for a Crown Minister or Scottish Ministers to make regulations to ensure that devolved Scottish authorities do not discriminate contrary to trade commitments[150] and to address trade disputes.[151]

These and other features of the Act's territorial application all add greatly to the legislation's complexity.

(c) Devolution under the Scheme of the Procurement Act

(i) Contracting Authorities Covered

The starting point is that the Procurement Act applies in its entirety to bodies within the definition of a contracting authority. With Wales, Scotland, and Northern Ireland, the Guidance (although not the Act) uses the term 'reserved authority'[152] for contracting authorities that are not 'devolved' or 'transferred' and thus covered in this way. An example appears to be the Ministry of Justice and its agencies procuring prison-related services, as the guidance refers to prisons as a reserved matter.[153]

For authorities which are 'devolved' or 'transferred', the Act applies to them *unless* they are excluded or provision is made for certain different rules to apply to them. As will now be explained, exclusion is the general position for devolved Scottish authorities, while for devolved Welsh authorities or transferred Northern Ireland authorities there are merely some different rules in limited respects.

The definitions of a devolved Welsh and transferred Northern Ireland authority are found in the provisions on the exercise of devolved ministerial powers. Thus, Welsh Ministers may only exercise a power for the purpose of regulating contracting authorities that are 'devolved Welsh authorities' within the meaning of the Government of Wales Act 2006, or those which are to be treated as such.[154] This covers those whose functions are exercisable wholly or mainly in relation to Wales, and are wholly or mainly functions that do not relate to reserved matters (thus covering, for example, utilities operating across borders, such as in Herefordshire and Powys).[155] Transferred Northern Ireland authorities are defined in similar terms.[156] Certain Procurement Act provisions do not apply to any of these authorities—for example, requirements to

[150] ibid s 91.
[151] ibid s 92.
[152] Cabinet Office, Guidance: Devolved Contracting Authorities, [9].
[153] ibid [20]. Although reserved authorities will be required to follow the rules applicable to Welsh devolved authorities if they participate in a devolved Welsh procurement arrangement, [21].
[154] Procurement Act 2023, s 111(1)–(4).
[155] Hansard, 9 Feb 2023.
[156] Procurement Act 2023, s 112.

comply with the NPPS,[157] requirements to publish contracts[158] or contract modifications,[159] and the prohibition on pre-qualification processes for low-value contracts;[160] while certain further requirements do not apply to Northern Ireland transferred authorities, including Part 6 of the Act, which contains rules regulating below-threshold contracts.[161] Policy reasons for the differences have not generally been articulated.

The Procurement Act defines a 'devolved Scottish authority' as an authority whose functions are exercisable only in or as regards Scotland and (a) none of its functions relate to reserved matters (as defined),[162] or (b) some do and some do not.[163] Such an authority is an 'excluded authority',[164] thus application of the Act is in general excluded, and existing Scottish regulations will continue to apply to such bodies. This definition would appear to mean, however, that the Act does apply to a contracting authority that exercises functions almost exclusively in or as regards Scotland, but also some elsewhere in the UK (even if its functions mainly relate to devolved matters), or whose functions relate to reserved matters but are only exercisable in Scotland.

(ii) Collaborative Procurement

An important complexity of devolution is cross-border collaboration. For example, a devolved Welsh authority may wish to procure jointly with or on behalf of a non-devolved authority. A reason Wales gave for opting into the Procurement Act was the need to follow the Act anyway for calling off from UK central government Crown Commercial Service frameworks, which would have a 'significant impact' given that call-offs under them by Welsh contracting authorities were valued at more than £295m in 2022/23.[165]

The Procurement Act provides for such arrangements and for the rules that apply.[166] Where the procurement is not a reserved procurement arrangement (to which the full Act applies) but is undertaken under a devolved arrangement, any rules specific to the nations will apply.

The Procurement Act did not initially address the need for devolved Scottish authorities to award contracts with, or call off from the frameworks of, other types of authority, and Regulations in 2024 amended the Act to address this. The Act now provides, first, that where a contract is to be awarded following a procedure or selection process carried out (a) jointly by a devolved Scottish authority and another authority, or (b) by a centralized procurement authority or equivalent,[167] under a procurement arrangement subject to the Act, the Act applies fully to the devolved Scottish

157 ibid s 13(10)(d).
158 ibid s 53(4).
159 ibid s 77(3).
160 ibid s 85(5).
161 ibid s 84(2)(b) and (c).
162 ibid s 2(12) provides that 'reserved matters' has the same meaning as in the Scotland Act 1998.
163 ibid s 2(6) and (8). See s 2(7) for utilities contracts.
164 ibid s 2(5).
165 Explanatory Memorandum to the Procurement (Wales) Regulations 2024, 11 June 2024, 12.
166 Procurement Act 2023, s 114.
167 ibid s 2(5)(a) and s 115A inserted by reg 47 PR 24.

authority. Second, where a devolved Scottish authority awards a contract based on a framework or dynamic market (or similar), select or modified Procurement Act provisions apply.[168] These rules are both complex and uncertain and Scotland only introduced further Regulations to address the permutations of cross-border procurement as late as 2025.[169]

(iii) Powers Exercisable in Respect of Devolved Procurement

As indicated, various Procurement Act provisions permit a Minister of the Crown, Welsh Ministers, or a Northern Ireland department[170] to make regulations relating to their jurisdiction. Unsurprisingly, most powers do not enable fundamental changes to procedural rules but mainly concern technical matters of detail.[171] The Welsh government has already exercised certain powers—for example, to specify services covered by the light-touch regime[172]—but this does not involve significant policy divergences.

(iv) Procurement Act Requirements in Respect of Devolved Authorities

Certain Procurement Act provisions apply to ministers in devolved nations or to devolved authorities not acting as contracting authorities. For example, if a contracting authority disregards a tender or excludes a supplier, it must give notice to an 'appropriate authority',[173] being a devolved authority in a devolved nation,[174] which may investigate whether to refer the matter to the Crown for inclusion on a debarment list.[175]

(d) Procurement Legislation Pursuing Nation-Specific Objectives

Outside the Procurement Act, Wales has built on its pre-existing 'well-being' policies since Brexit by adopting the Social Partnership Act, which Wales considers does not conflict with the Procurement Act.[176] This imposes many additional requirements

[168] Reg 47(2) and (3) and Sch 9A.

[169] Cross-Border Public Procurement (Miscellaneous Amendment) (Scotland) Regulations 2025 No. 392.

[170] Procurement Act 2023, s 123(1)(a)–(c).

[171] This includes powers to: specify or remove activities in utilities contracts (s 6(5)); specify services for light touch contracts (s 9(1); Reg 43 P(W)R 24); specify services for reserved public mutuals (s 33(8); Reg 43(2) P(W)R 24); amend the threshold for setting and publishing KPIs (s 52(5)); change what it means for an invoice to be in required electronic form (s 67); change the term in implied payment terms (s 68); change which international agreements are specified (s 89); make provision about notices (s 95); require sharing of information in a particular way (s 97(1)); amendment in relation to private utilities (s 121); interpretation (s 123); make consequential provision (s 125); amend Sch 1, para 3 or 5 (Sch 1, para 2; Sch 1, para 3; Sch 1, para 5. Reg.44 P(W)R 24); Sch 2 exempted contracts (Sch 2); Sch 4 utility contracts (sch 4).

[172] Reg 43 The Procurement (Wales) Regulations 2024.

[173] Procurement Act 2023, s 59(2) and (4).

[174] ibid s 59(6).

[175] ibid s 60(1)–(2).

[176] Welsh Government, 'Procurement Reform in Wales' (19 August 2024) [10].

on contracting authorities (defined differently to devolved Welsh authorities under the Procurement Act). These include seeking to improve well-being through procurement, setting and publishing objectives,[177] duties relating to social public works clauses,[178] publishing procurement strategies,[179] preparing an annual report,[180] and maintaining a published contracts register.[181] Such social legislation was already, however, possible before Brexit. It introduces yet another regulatory burden as well as increasing divergence between the nations, and its concrete benefits (like those of social value regimes in the other nations) remain to be proven, especially given financial constraints.

(e) Common Frameworks

Finally, before Brexit political concordats ensured that all nations adopted rules and policies compliant with EU law.[182] These have been replaced by a Common Framework for addressing issues arising in respect of coordinating devolved policies.[183] The procurement Common Framework is not regulated by the Procurement Act and Parliamentary Committees in Westminster and the nations have questioned the robustness of its governance arrangements and hence its value.[184] It remains to be seen whether this will be an effective forum for political resolution of procurement policy variances.

5 Conclusion

The post-Brexit procurement regime is already substantially complete, with the adoption of the Procurement Act 2023 and repeal (other than for transitional purposes) of the four sets of EU-based Regulations. The new legislation not only implements trade obligations—the function of the EU-based Procurement Regulations—but has been extended to promote domestic policy through hard law. One aspect of this is the adoption (through hard law) of new policies, including on information transparency and debarment. This effectively involves an extension, rather than a rollback, of the EU's regulatory approach, in large part attributable to the influence of

[177] Social Partnership and Public Procurement (Wales) Act 2023, s 24.
[178] ibid ss 25, 26, 28, 29, 34.
[179] ibid s 38.
[180] ibid s 39.
[181] ibid s 40.
[182] P Henderson, 'The Impact of Devolution on Public Procurement in the United Kingdom' (2003) 4 PPLRev 175.
[183] Common Framework for Public Procurement, Updated Provisional Framework Agreement, January 2022 CP 609.
[184] See, eg, A Stennett, 'The Public Procurement Common Framework', Research and Information Service Briefing Paper, Paper No 15/21 (18 February 2021), Northern Ireland Assembly.

EU membership. Further, the detail of the new law—its scope, obligations, and remedies regime—is substantially based on EU provisions, such that previous case law is likely to have a significant practical influence, even without a formal link to EU-based law. EU membership has clearly shaped the approach and content of the new regime, which is unrecognizable from that of the 1970s and has the general appearance more of an adapted version of EU law than a bespoke domestic regime.

As regards any Brexit dividend, most key elements of the post-Brexit regime that do not reflect EU provisions, including on information transparency, exclusion, and social value, are *not* directly connected with Brexit. They were never precluded by EU law and are linked only indirectly to Brexit, notably through the political reform opportunity that Brexit provided. There has been some degree of 'Brexit dividend' through active divergence, including by removing some constraints on contracting authority discretion and through some simplification. However, these changes are limited, and do not go as far as they could have done. They are also substantially counteracted by the uncertainty created by new terminology without adequate guidance, and accompanied by new complex and burdensome provisions, such as on transparency, debarment, devolution, and transition. Any claims that reforms facilitated by Brexit freedoms will enhance social value, opportunities for and innovation by SMEs and charities, or economic growth cannot be sustained. We suggested that the main benefit from Brexit might be freedom from CJEU-created constraints over rulemaking and centralized decision-making.

In terms of territorial application, more limited rules post-Brexit to an extent expanded scope for devolved action and there was no compulsion for other UK jurisdictions to follow the new Westminster domestic rules, such as on enhanced transparency. Nevertheless, Wales and Northern Ireland chose to opt in to the Procurement Act, with just limited modifications. Scotland, on the other hand, has continued largely to apply the pre-Brexit regime, including the EU-based Regulations. Post-Brexit there is therefore more internal divergence, and very much more complexity, the latter an obstacle to internal commerce.

Finally, from a trade perspective, in the most important markets the mutual EU–UK access that existed under EU law for major civil procurement—the most important market—is largely replicated by current trade agreements. Regulatory divergence does not have trade implications, and the main impact of Brexit on procurement seems likely to result from any negative impact of Brexit on more general market access rules. However, divergent and complex rules on territorial aspects and scope for local protectionism arising directly or indirectly from Brexit could have a negative economic impact.

15
Digital and Data Regulation

Orla Lynskey and Katherine Nolan

1 Introduction: From Common Ground to Splintered Terrains

The UK's departure from the European Union coincided with a time of significant change in EU digital governance. The impetus for this reform of the first generation of EU digital regulation was, and is, both social and technical. The movement from a unidirectional internet to the platform economy, and now the mainstreaming of so-called artificial intelligence (AI), brought about considerable social and economic change. The optimism associated with earlier technical advances was tempered by a range of challenges, including child safety, misinformation, and the vast power wielded by certain technology providers. This has resulted in a second generation of digital rules that are more interventionist, as well as more numerous,[1] than the first.[2] These new measures address a broader range of harms, incorporate a wider selection of regulatory tools, and are designed to regulate at scale. In the EU context it is plausible to claim that they reflect a move from whole economy regulation to whole society regulation given how much of daily life falls within their ambit. At the same time, both in the EU and the UK, great hopes have been placed in the digital sector (and particularly AI) as a source of economic growth. This being so, the role that law plays in shaping or constraining economic development in the tech sector is attracting increased attention.[3] Moreover, this sphere of regulation has been increasingly geopoliticized since Brexit, and US tech dominance has taken on new significance.[4] It is against the backdrop of this socio-technical and geopolitical change that digital and data regulation must be viewed.

[1] V Papakonstantinou and P De Hert, 'The Regulation of Digital Technologies in the EU: The Law-Making Phenomena of "Act-Ification", "GDPR Mimesis" and "EU Law Brutality"' (2022) Technology and Regulation 48.

[2] See E Bietti, 'A Genealogy of Digital Platform Regulation' (2023) 7 Georgetown Law Technology Review 1.

[3] Mario Draghi, 'The Future of European Competitiveness, Part A—A Competitiveness Strategy for Europe' (European Commission) <https://commission.europa.eu/topics/strengthening-european-competitiveness/eu-competitiveness-looking-ahead_en>.

[4] K Nolan, 'Geopolitics and EU Digital Law' in M Dawson and A Steinberg (eds) *Strategic Autonomy and the Geopolitics of EU Law* (Cambridge University Press 2026).

Orla Lynskey and Katherine Nolan, *Digital and Data Regulation* In: *The UK Regulatory Framework Post-Brexit: 'Law Unbound'*. Edited by: Paul Craig and Vilija Vėlyvytė, Oxford University Press.
DOI: 10.1093/9780198969815.003.0017

The story of digital and data regulation in the EU and the UK post-Brexit is best envisaged in two layers. Above the surface, both jurisdictions have introduced reform to the relevant legislative landscape. This may suggest that the two jurisdictions are moving in parallel. Nevertheless, on closer inspection, it is clear that the common ground between them (mainly in data law) pre-dates Brexit, whereas regulatory responses to societal challenges post-Brexit increasingly diverge. While digital platform regulation through the UK's Online Safety Act (OSA) and the EU's Digital Services Act (DSA) seek to address many of the same challenges, the approaches adopted differ in important ways. Regarding AI, the difference in regulatory response is even more pronounced. The scene becomes further complicated when we look below the surface. Here, important factors—commitment to human rights; enforcement capacity and culture; ideological approaches to digital policy—suggest that tectonic plates might be shifting in ways that will ultimately lead to a more fundamental rupture between the two regulatory regimes.

2 The Changing Legislative Landscape

This chapter addresses three aspects of digital and data regulation pre- and post-Brexit: laws concerning (i) data use; (ii) platform content responsibilities; and (iii) AI regulation. This is not an exhaustive account. Broader developments concerning digital policy as it intersects with competition in digital markets, platform responsibilities to workers, consumer protection in the online space, and intellectual property are addressed elsewhere,[5] and fall outside the scope of this chapter. Each of these three areas has seen significant change since Brexit. Digital and data regulation law is an increasingly complex legal patchwork; despite common starting points, and common societal and economic concerns, major reforms post-Brexit are driving increasing divergence.

(a) From Data Protection Law to Data Law

The logical substantive starting point for an analysis of EU digital law is data protection law. Practically, relevant technical developments (for example, digital platforms, 'AI' systems) necessarily entail data processing. Because data is a fundamental building block of digital society, data protection legislation necessarily engages with other forms of digital regulation. From a normative perspective, data protection is in a privileged position in the EU legal order, recognized as a fundamental right in primary law[6] and strictly safeguarded in EU jurisprudence. The most notable development in

[5] See Chs 12 on Competition, 16 on Intellectual Property, 20 on Employment, and 23 on Consumer law.
[6] Art 18 TFEU and Art 8 Charter.

this field since Brexit has been the flanking of data protection legislation with a raft of data laws as part of the EU Data Strategy.[7] In this section we discuss the transition from the EU General Data Protection Regulation (GDPR) to EU data law (with reference to the Data Act and the Data Governance Act) and, in the UK, the reform of the UK GDPR through the Data (Use and Access) Act (DUAA) 2025.

The key piece of digital and data regulation legislation unifying the UK and the EU is the GDPR, which entered into force in May 2018, pre-Brexit. The GDPR entered directly into the UK legal system as the 'UK GDPR', which formed part of a wider Data Protection Act 2018. The Act 'implemented' the elements of the GDPR which required further specification, as well as the EU Law Enforcement Directive, into UK law. It also contained provisions regulating national security data processing, which fall largely outside the scope of EU law.

While data protection law is well established in the UK, pre-dating EU data protection law by more than a decade,[8] the GDPR was pitched as 'gold-standard' data protection legislation. The GDPR adapted existing data protection legislation by specifying many of its provisions. For instance, an obligation of data protection by design and by default was introduced to further specify broadly worded principles such as data minimization.[9] Moreover, the law introduced a new layer of meta-regulation which imposed demonstrable accountability obligations on data controllers (those responsible for data-processing operations).[10] These new compliance obligations sought to ease data protection compliance and oversight at scale, a by-product of which was an increase in compliance costs for those subject to the law. While the law only introduced one entirely new right for individuals (data subjects)—the right to data portability[11]—the GDPR was presented to the public as a boon for rights protection in the digital age. Much of the enhanced rights protection was envisaged to stem from the increased effectiveness of the framework, both through accountability mechanisms and more robust supervisory powers for regulators.[12] The GDPR continues to serve as a common denominator for both legal frameworks. Nevertheless, the landscape around the GDPR has shifted in the intervening years. Both the UK and the EU legislative reforms reflect, albeit to differing degrees, a shift in emphasis away from the protection of fundamental rights when personal data are processed to emphasize the societal benefits of personal data processing.

In the UK, the Data Use and Access Act (DUAA) 2025 received Royal Assent in June 2025. The overall impact of the legislative changes introduced by the DUAA 2025 is to promote personal data processing at the expense of individual rights and

[7] A European strategy for data, COM(2020) 66 final.

[8] Data Protection Act 1984.

[9] GDPR, art 25.

[10] R Binns, 'Data Protection Impact Assessments: A Meta-Regulatory Approach' (2017) 7 International Data Privacy Law 22.

[11] GDPR, art 20.

[12] 'Safeguarding Privacy in a Connected World: A European Data Protection Framework for the 21st Century', COM(2012) 9 final.

interests. For example, Article 22 GDPR contained a qualified prohibition on the use of solely automated decision-making in situations where such automated decision-making would have a legal, or similarly significant, effect on individuals. The DUAA 2025 effectively removes this prohibition from the UK GDPR, thereby allowing the use of automated decision-making to make significant decisions about individuals without meaningful human input.[13] A qualified prohibition continues to apply only where the processing is based on 'special category data' (such as data concerning protected characteristics pursuant to equality law). The removal of such protections for individual rights at a time when the government plans to deploy automated decision-making widely in the public sector raises legitimate concerns.[14] Other rights, such as subject access rights and transparency rights, have been similarly degraded.[15]

Other changes introduced by the DUAA 2025 also shift the default in favour of ease of processing, even if at the expense of individual rights. Under the GDPR, a data controller needs a legal basis to process personal data. The introduction of a list of 'recognized legitimate interests' (including direct marketing, 'public security', and 'national security') will effectively expand the list of circumstances in which controllers can process data without being required to have specific regard for the impact on the rights and interests of affected individuals.[16] Similarly, the principle of purpose limitation is diminished. The principle stands for the idea that data that is processed for one purpose should not be further processed for another incompatible purpose.[17] Under the DUAA 2025, certain data can be further processed for new purposes if they are listed in a new annex of 'processing to be treated as compatible'[18] and it is not reasonable to expect it to obtain a new consent from data subjects. The combined impact of these changes is a degradation of rights in order to ease the path for increased data processing. More generally, the DUAA represents a deliberate step on the UK's part into the field of 'data law'. For instance, Part 1 DUAA establishes a 'smart data' scheme, putting the existing 'Open Banking' regime on a legislative footing and expanding the scheme to other sectors. The detail of this initiative will only be specified in secondary legislation. However, it has the potential to apply across many customer-facing sectors.

At EU level, although the GDPR remains the cornerstone of EU data law, legislative change has also sought to pave the way to increased processing of both personal and non-personal data. The EU Data Act[19] aims to make data more accessible

[13] DUAA, s 80.

[14] 'Letter to Peter Kyle: Keep Our Right Not to Be Subjected to Decisions Based Solely on AI' (6 December 2024) <https://www.openrightsgroup.org/press-releases/letter-to-peter-kyle-keep-our-right-not-to-be-subjected-to-decisions-based-solely-on-ai/> accessed 7 August 2025.

[15] DUAA, s 77(1)(b).

[16] Inserted into the GDPR by Sch 4 DUAA 2025.

[17] GDPR, art 5(1)(b).

[18] Inserted into the text via Sch 5.

[19] Regulation (EU) 2023/2854 of the European Parliament and of the Council of 13 December 2023 on harmonized rules on fair access to and use of data and amending Regulation (EU) 2017/2394 and Directive (EU) 2020/1828 (Data Act) [2023] OJ L2854, 22/12/23.

and usable by ensuring fairness in the allocation of the value of data among relevant actors. The Data Act contains, among others, provisions clarifying the conditions for business-to-business data-sharing where mandated by law,[20] specifying exceptional circumstances where business to government data sharing is mandated[21] and the minimum requirements cloud and edge computing service providers must meet to facilitate interoperability and switching.[22] The core component of the Data Act is Chapter II, which enables users of connected products and related services (for instance, a smart watch for fitness and the related app) to access the data that they co-create from the data holder. The rationale for the Act is economic: to maximize data value by empowering consumers and eliminating obstacles to data access and use.

Where the Data Act focuses on mandatory data sharing, the Data Governance Act (DGA)[23] applies to voluntary sharing of data. The DGA sets out the conditions for the re-use of certain categories of public sector data (complementing existing legislation in this area).[24] However, it also places a new class of actors—data intermediation services (DIS)—on a legal footing.[25] These DIS establish commercial relationships between data subjects and 'data holders', on the one hand, and data users, on the other, to facilitate the sharing of personal and non-personal data. This data sharing can occur through technical, legal, or other means and may even be for the purpose of exercising data subject rights pursuant to data protection law.[26] Although the ink is barely dry on this legislation, it will be repealed by the EU's Digital Omnibus Proposal (published in late 2025) if adopted.[27] The Data Act will become the core of EU Data Law, by integrating aspects of the DGA such as the rules on re-use of public sector information, lighter touch DIS rules, and further recalibrating data access requirements.[28]

Irrespective of the outcome of the Digital Omnibus legislative process, the adoption of these new legislative instruments at EU level[29] has a dual impact on the development of EU data law. First, it increases the risk of interpretative friction with the GDPR. The concepts used in these instruments are closely connected to those found in the GDPR yet not identical. For instance, the Data Act refers to 'data' (as opposed to the distinction between 'personal data' and 'non-personal data' adhered to in other

[20] Ch III.
[21] Ch IV.
[22] Ch VI.
[23] Regulation (EU) 2022/868 of the European Parliament and of the Council of 30 May 2022 on European data governance and amending Regulation (EU) 2018/1724 (Data Governance Act) [2022] OJ L 152/1.
[24] DGA, art 1(a).
[25] DGA, art 1(b).
[26] DGA, art 2(11).
[27] European Commission, Proposal for a Regulation of the European Parliament and of the Council on the simplification of the digital legislative framework (Digital Omnibus), COM(2025) 837 final, 19 November 2025.
[28] European Parliament, 'A Digital Omnibus: Identifying Interlinks and Possible Overlaps Between Different Legal Acts in the Field of Digital Legislation to Streamline Tech Rules' (Publications Office of the European Union 2024), PE 772.641 - February 2026, 21-22.
[29] See also Regulation (EU) 2025/327 of the European Parliament and of the Council of 11 February 2025 on the European Health Data Space and amending Directive 2011/24/EU and Regulation (EU) 2024/2847 [2025] OJ L327, 5/3/2025.

legislative instruments).[30] Moreover, this legislation grants rights to and imposes obligations on 'data holders' (which are currently defined differently under the Data Act and DGA).[31] Commentators highlight that there is significant uncertainty about how such concepts will interact with the related yet distinct concepts found in the GDPR,[32] which may discourage the precise data transactions that the DGA seeks to promote.[33] More fundamentally, these new instruments represent a normative step change from the GDPR. Indeed, the DGA has been characterized as 'an attempt by the EU to become an active player in promoting the monetization of personal data'.[34] It certainly reflects a shift in emphasis away from individual rights and towards the promotion of collective interests in personal data processing, a 'clash of policy objectives' observed by Carovano and Finck.[35] Indeed, although several changes proposed in the Digital Omnibus cut to the core of current reconciliation of rights and interests in the GDPR, the stated rationale for the Digital Omnibus is 'simplification' to enhance European competitiveness.[36] Its adoption would therefore likely exacerbate rather than mitigate this tension within Data Law.

In sum, through these legislative changes, both the UK and EU have shifted the legislative balance between fundamental rights protection and the potential commercial and societal benefits of increased personal data processing. Legislation that was viewed as an indispensable safeguard for fundamental rights in a digitized world just a few years earlier is now viewed by the UK government as an undesirable brake on innovation.[37] The same direction of travel is visible in the EU, albeit that, as discussed below, the constitutional status of the right to data protection in the EU is likely to temper the extent of the drift in emphasis away from fundamental rights protection.

[30] Regulation (EU) 2018/1807 of the European Parliament and of the Council of 14 November 2018 on a framework for the free flow of non-personal data in the European Union [2018] OJ L303/59.

[31] Data Act, art 2(13); DGA, art 2(8).

[32] B Lazarotto and G Malgieri, 'The Data Act: A (Slippery) Third Way beyond Personal/Non-Personal Data Dualism?' *European Law Blog* (4 May 2023) <https://europeanlawblog.eu/2023/05/04/the-data-act-a-slippery-third-way-beyond-personal-non-personal-data-dualism/> accessed 26 October 2023. K Nolan, 'Data Protection's Intersections: Reconciling Data Protection Requirements with Regulated Data Use Beyond the GDPR', in R Á Costello and M Leiser, *Critical Reflections on the EU's Data Protection Regime: GDPR in the Machine* (Bloomsbury Publishing 2024), https://dx.doi.org/10.2139/ssrn.5462717.

[33] T Groza and B Botero Arcila, 'The New Law of the European Data Markets: Demystifying the European Data Strategy' (2024) 24 Global Jurist 321, 35–37.

[34] L Vardanyan and H Kocharyan, 'The GDPR and the DGA Proposal: Are They in Controversial Relationship?' (2022) 9 European Studies 91.

[35] G Carovano and M Finck, 'Regulating Data Intermediaries: The Impact of the Data Governance Act on the EU's Data Economy' (2023) 50 Computer Law & Security Review 105830, 14.

[36] PT Kramcsák and B Lazarotto, "'Personal Data": More Than a Definition, a Quasi-Constitutional Stake in EU Law in the Era of the Digital Omnibus', European Law Blog, March 2026, https://doi.org/10.21428/9885764c.ebb7f452 (accessed 17 April 2026).

[37] 'Data (Use and Access) Bill [Lords]: Debate 12 February 2025', UK Parliament (8 November 2025) <https://hansard.parliament.uk/Commons/2025-02-12/debates/60F9F078-BE28-48A9-96BF-4B32B992C0E1/Data(UseandAccess)Bill[Lords]> accessed 11 August 2025.

(b) Platform Content Laws

Platform responsibility for content carried on digital platforms has also faced a significant project of reform since Brexit. The explosion of user-generated content enabled by Web 2.0 put pressure on the limited intermediary liability responsibility at the heart of platform content laws. This has led to a fundamental overhaul of platform content laws in both jurisdictions, with increasing attention to the role digital platforms play in shaping the environment in which digital benefits and harms emerge. This is however an area where the UK has seized the 'Brexit benefit' of going its own way. Therefore, while the new regimes seek to address many of the same harms and are likely to bring many of the same actors within their regulatory orbit, they differ in ways that are so significant as to make meaningful comparison between them difficult.

Prior to Brexit, the position in both jurisdictions was largely determined under the eCommerce Directive,[38] implemented in the UK by the Electronic Commerce (EC Directive) Regulations 2002. The eCommerce Directive was based on a notice and takedown framework, creating a series of exemptions from liability for intermediaries for unlawful content on their services provided they removed such content upon request. More specifically, immunities were conditionally available to intermediaries who were acting as 'mere conduits', caching content or hosting content on behalf of users.[39] In addition, member states were restricted from imposing general obligations on providers of such services to engage in monitoring of the information they transmit or store.[40] The aim of this law was, according to De Gregorio, 'to ensure the free movement of information society services and, at the same time, respect freedom of expression',[41] and thus in 2000, platform responsibility to moderate content was not yet a legislative concern.

However, gradually dissatisfaction with such intermediary immunity grew, as platforms took on increasing significance and the scale of illegal and harmful content increased. The first changes were incremental, with the adoption of sector-specific content obligations and restrictions concerning child abuse imagery[42] and terrorism

[38] Directive 2000/31/EC of the European Parliament and of the Council of 8 June 2000 on certain legal aspects of information society services, in particular electronic commerce, in the Internal Market ('Directive on electronic commerce') [2000] OJ L178/1.

[39] ibid Arts 12–14.

[40] ibid Art 15.

[41] G De Gregorio, 'The E-Commerce Directive and GDPR: Towards Convergence of Legal Regimes in the Algorithmic Society?' [2019] SSRN Electronic Journal 3 <https://www.ssrn.com/abstract = 3393557> accessed 24 June 2023.

[42] Directive 2011/93/EU of the European Parliament and of the Council of 13 December 2011 on combating the sexual abuse and sexual exploitation of children and child pornography, and replacing Council Framework Decision 2004/68/JHA [2011] OJ L335/1.

content,[43] and obligations for video-sharing platforms.[44] Platform responsibility for copyright infringement has also attracted legislative reform and judicial attention, considered elsewhere.

Ultimately, dissatisfaction prompted wholesale reform, and the 'second generation' of platform content laws were developed.[45] Thus, post-Brexit, platform content laws have been reformed through the DSA in the EU and the OSA in the UK. The DSA,[46] adopted by the EU in 2022, came fully into force on 17 February 2024.[47] The DSA amends the eCommerce Directive and substantially reforms EU law applicable to intermediary services, providing for a new framework of intermediary liability rules and platform obligations.[48] The UK has implemented a parallel reform of platform responsibilities in the OSA, which has been entering into force on a staggered basis, the first enforceable duties applicable in 2025.

When we compare the OSA and the DSA there are a number of basic commonalities, particularly the underlying political motivations, the actors captured, and the style of regulatory model adopted. As Law has written,[49] at a basic level both laws seek to achieve the same underpinning aim, namely greater levels of safety online. The DSA aims for 'a safe, predictable and trusted online environment that facilitates innovation and in which fundamental rights enshrined in the Charter, including the principle of consumer protection, are effectively protected'.[50] The OSA is framed in terms of an open-ended notion of online safety, with a 'general purpose of making the use of internet services regulated by this Act safer for individuals in the United Kingdom'.[51]

Both respond to the growth of the platform economy, as communications are now increasingly confined to the proprietary environments of privately operated platforms (from small-scale intermediaries to the hyper-scalers which attract most of the public and political attention).[52] Thus, the actors captured by the DSA and OSA are similar, and both regimes tailor their obligations according to the type and scale of the platform. Although there are slight differences in the scopes of application, the

[43] Directive (EU) 2017/541 of the European Parliament and of the Council of 15 March 2017 on combating terrorism and replacing Council Framework Decision 2002/475/JHA and amending Council Decision 2005/671/JHA [2018] OJ L88/6.

[44] Directive (EU) 2018/1808 of the European Parliament and of the Council of 14 November 2018 amending Directive 2010/13/EU on the coordination of certain provisions laid down by law, regulation or administrative action in member states concerning the provision of audiovisual media services (Audiovisual Media Services Directive) in view of changing market realities [2018] OJ L303/69.

[45] M Husovec, 'Rising Above Liability: The Digital Services Act as a Blueprint for the Second Generation of Global Internet Rules' (2023) 38 Berkeley Technology Law Journal 883.

[46] Regulation (EU) 2022/2065 of 19 October 2022 on a Single Market For Digital Services and amending Directive 2000/31/EC (Digital Services Act) [2022] OJ L277/1.

[47] Selected provisions came into effect earlier from 16 November 2022.

[48] DSA, art 1.

[49] S Law, 'Effective Enforcement of the Online Safety Act and Digital Services Act: Unpacking the Compliance and Enforcement Regimes of the UK and EU's Online Safety Legislation' (2024) 16 Journal of Media Law 263, 265.

[50] DSA, art 1(1).

[51] OSA, s 1(1).

[52] J Van Dijck, 'Seeing the Forest for the Trees: Visualizing Platformization and Its Governance' (2021) 23 New Media & Society 2801.

services falling within the ambit of the two laws will likely overlap considerably. The DSA applies to 'intermediary services' that have their place of establishment in the EU,[53] encompassing services that provide 'mere conduit' services, 'caching' services, and 'hosting' services.[54] Meanwhile, the OSA applies to either a 'user-to-user service' (services which facilitate the sharing of user-generated content),[55] 'regulated search service' (search engines),[56] or certain pornographic content providers.[57] Therefore, the DSA has a broader scope of application encompassing essentially all types of intermediaries (including, for example, online marketplaces), whereas the OSA is focused solely on content-based intermediaries. Both have extraterritorial dimensions.[58] As a result, many actors will be simultaneously captured by both the OSA and DSA where they operate across the UK and the EU, regardless of the place of their establishment.

There are also some basic similarities in terms of regulatory model because, as Farrand has written, both the OSA and DSA are 'co-regulatory in nature'.[59] Co-regulation generally combines some elements of industry self-regulation with state intervention (including legislation or forms of public institutional oversight).[60] Thus both regimes share an emphasis on cooperation with industry actors, a regulatory approach which has been criticized as having 'disregard for the structural power of private platform companies'.[61] Much like the GDPR, the DSA approach might be characterized as meta-regulation, as it envisages direct supervision of regulated actors, while the OSA approach is closer to classic self-regulation. As Farrand has noted, Ofcom has limited areas of oversight and the scope of obligations envisaged are narrower.[62]

Perhaps in an attempt to be more responsive to the changing socio-technical environment, both regulatory models are intended to be somewhat adaptive, with reliance on regulatory guidance to allow the regimes to evolve, often in cooperation with the regulated actors. Under the OSA, Ofcom is tasked with adopting various pieces of guidance and codes of practice. To date, two codes of practice have been adopted after the required public consultations; one concerning user-to-user services,[63] and one concerning search services.[64] The DSA envisages reliance on both voluntary codes of

[53] DSA, art 2(1).
[54] DSA, art 3(g).
[55] OSA, s 3(1).
[56] ibid s 3(4).
[57] ibid s 4.
[58] DSA, arts 2(1), 3(e); OSA, s 4(5-6).
[59] B Farrand, 'How Do We Understand Online Harms? The Impact of Conceptual Divides on Regulatory Divergence between the Online Safety Act and Digital Services Act' (2024) 16 Journal of Media Law 240, 257.
[60] CT Marsden, 'Internet Co-Regulation and Constitutionalism: Towards a More Nuanced View' [2011] SSRN Electronic Journal <http://www.ssrn.com/abstract = 1973328> accessed 12 May 2025.
[61] Bietti (n 2) 41. See also R Griffin, 'Procedural Fetishism in the Digital Services Act' [2025] European Journal of Legal Studies <https://data.europa.eu/doi/10.2924/EJLS.2025.LT.002> accessed 1 August 2025.
[62] Farrand (n 59).
[63] 'Illegal Content: Codes of Practice for User-to-User Services' (Ofcom 2025) <https://www.ofcom.org.uk/siteassets/resources/documents/online-safety/information-for-industry/illegal-harms/illegal-content-codes-of-practice-for-user-to-user-services-24-feb.pdf?v = 391889>.
[64] 'Illegal Content: Codes of Practice for Search Services' (Ofcom 2025) <https://www.ofcom.org.uk/siteassets/resources/documents/online-safety/information-for-industry/illegal-harms/illegal-content-codes-of-practice-for-search-services-24-feb.pdf?v = 391888>.

conduct and guidance from the Commission, and the Commission has held a public consultation and issued guidance in relation to child protection.[65] Additionally, both the OSA and DSA may be characterized as emphasizing procedural approaches,[66] particularly relying on strategies of risk assessment and mitigation. However, there is significant difference in how the relevant risks are characterized, as will be discussed further below. Both the OSA and DSA attempt to take a more systemic look at issues of platform-carried content than was seen under the eCommerce Directive, as there is greater emphasis on platform design and procedural protections.

Thus, there is quite a degree of superficial similarity between the regimes. However, when we look to the detail of each regime, there is notable divergence between the frameworks both substantively and procedurally. The classification of the types of regulated actor and the nature of the rules imposed on those actors are quite different. The DSA has a relatively complex regulatory framework, imposing tiered responsibilities based on the classification of type of intermediary. While liability for user-generated content is similar to that under the eCommerce Directive,[67] as Husovec explains, the major change under the DSA is the additional proactive responsibilities that have been applied to platforms when they engage in content moderation, 'and for some providers, what they need to think about when designing digital services'.[68] The level of obligation escalates on a tiered approach, whether an actor is classified as an 'intermediary service', a 'hosting service', an 'online platform', or a 'very large online platform or very large search engine' (VLOP or VLOS), and with some exceptions for small and micro organizations.

Pursuant to this system of tiered responsibility, all intermediaries are subject to transparency reporting obligations.[69] Hosting services, including online platforms, must implement mechanisms to respond to notices of illegal content.[70] Online platforms must also put in place procedural protections, including internal complaint-handling systems, facilitating 'trusted flaggers', processes concerning user suspension, and 'appropriate and proportionate measures' to protect minors.[71] Online marketplaces are subject to specific obligations relating to traceability of traders, compliance by design in its online interface, and rights to information of consumers.[72]

[65] 'ANNEX to the Communication to the Commission Approval of the Content on a Draft Communication from the Commission–Guidelines on Measures to Ensure a High Level of Privacy, Safety and Security for Minors Online, Pursuant to Article 28(4) of Regulation (EU) 2022/2065' (European Commission 2025) C(2025) 4764 final <https://digital-strategy.ec.europa.eu/en/library/commission-publishes-guidelines-protection-minors>.

[66] For criticism of such procedural approaches under the DSA, see Griffin (n 61); Agustina Del Campo, Nicolas Zara and Ramiro Álvarez-Ugarte, 'Are Risks the New Rights? The Perils of Risk-Based Approaches to Speech Regulation' (SSRN, 2025) <https://www.ssrn.com/abstract = 5161173> accessed 10 April 2025.

[67] DSA, arts 3–6.

[68] Husovec (n 45) 898.

[69] DSA, art 15.

[70] ibid arts 16–17.

[71] ibid arts 20–28.

[72] ibid arts 30–32.

The most onerous obligations apply to those platforms and search engines which are classified as VLOPs/VLOSs.[73] These actors are supervised directly by the Commission, and as of the time of writing, twenty-five actors have been so designated.[74] VLOPs and VLOSs now must conduct a risk assessment and mitigation exercise, with a focus on 'systemic risk', including dissemination of illegal content, effects on fundamental rights, on civic discourse, electoral processes, public security, gender-based violence, the protection of public health, minors, and serious negative consequences to physical and mental well-being.[75] They also face additional obligations relating to recommender systems, online advertising transparency, data access, and security.[76] They must be subject to independent audits to assess compliance with their obligations once a year,[77] establish compliance functions,[78] and face additional transparency reporting obligations.[79]

On the other hand, the OSA frames its obligations as 'duties of care', and applies a series of these across different types of services. Like the DSA, it subjects different types of services to different tailored duties of care, but the divisions drawn and nature of obligations imposed are distinct. First, all captured services are generally required to adhere to a series of duties about 'illegal content'.[80] Second, for those regulated services which are 'likely to be accessed by children', additional duties apply.[81] Third, the OSA envisages the categorization of services (Categories 1, 2A, and 2B) under secondary legislation (now implemented)[82] for the application of additional duties.[83] Bearing some similarity to the VLOPs and VLOSs, these additional duties have been extended to content recommender systems, search engines, services with direct messaging functionality which meet certain thresholds of monthly active UK users (in each case, in the millions). Fourth, additional rules are in place for services which host pornographic content, those rules being contingent on whether the content is professionally made or user-generated pornography.[84]

In each of these categories, we see quite a contrast to the DSA's approach. The specific rules to safeguard children, including the requirements to age verification or estimation,[85] and specific restrictions regarding pornographic content[86] do not have any

[73] ibid art 33.
[74] 'Supervision of the Designated Very Large Online Platforms and Search Engines under DSA | Shaping Europe's Digital Future' <https://digital-strategy.ec.europa.eu/en/policies/list-designated-vlops-and-vloses> accessed 11 August 2025.
[75] DSA, arts 34–35.
[76] ibid arts 38–40.
[77] ibid art 37.
[78] ibid art 41.
[79] ibid art 42.
[80] OSA, s 7(2).
[81] ibid s 7(4).
[82] The Online Safety Act 2023 (Category 1, Category 2A and Category 2B Threshold Conditions) Regulations 2025.
[83] C McGlynn, L Woods and A Antoniou, 'Pornography, the Online Safety Act 2023 and the Need for Further Reform' (2024) 16 Journal of Media Law 211, 222.
[84] ibid 223.
[85] OSA, s 12.
[86] ibid Pt 4.

express equivalent under the DSA. The DSA requires online platforms to put in place 'appropriate and proportionate measures' to protect minors, but is much less prescriptive in terms of what such measures might entail, unlike the OSA's emphasis on ensuring children do not get access to inappropriate content.[87] While the requirement that VLOSs and VLOPs must assess and mitigate systemic risks might also be interpreted to encompass some overlapping issues (and a number of pornographic websites have been so designated by the Commission), again the DSA is much less specific beyond naming protection of minors as relevant systemic risks.

These divergences in strategies are accentuated by different understandings of the nature of the harm or undesirable content which underpins both instruments. Farrand characterizes the distinction as the OSA emphasizing 'individualised harms' but that 'broader systemic harms impacting society are not included',[88] in contrast to a broader understanding under the DSA which 'reflects a drawing together of distinct policy fields concerning technology, security, and democracy at the level of the European Union.'[89] 'Moreover, the OSA remains anchored in a content-based approach.'[90] For instance, captured services providers' obligations are generally prescribed in terms of 'illegal content', being 'content that amounts to a relevant offence', and by relying on categories of criminal offence under UK law (including some offences under the OSA).[91] By contrast, the DSA is expressly concerned with 'systemic risk' associated with very large online platforms and search engines.[92] The scope of the rules also differ markedly, reflecting the different conception of harm underpinning both. Consumer and intellectual property issues are excluded from the OSA,[93] whereas the DSA expressly addresses these issues. For instance, online marketplaces are subjected to a number of specific rules focused on consumer safety and unfair competition.[94]

To compare the DSA and OSA is challenging, as these are two complex regimes. Nevertheless, there are high-level overlaps: similar political motivations, a reliance on co-regulatory techniques, attempts at drafting adaptive regimes, and a recognition that different forms of platforms should have differing responsibilities. However, looking to the specifics of the OSA and DSA, the nature of those responsibilities is quite different. This suggests that UK platforms which also operate in the EU will face a considerable additional compliance burden (and vice versa). One possibility is that we may see more convergence in practice. Cooperation with industry is built into both regimes, and actors who are subjected to both regimes may push for common

[87] DSA, art 28.
[88] Farrand (n 59) 254.
[89] ibid 257.
[90] McGlynn and others (n 83) 224.
[91] OSA, s 59(2).
[92] DSA, recitals 80–83; art 34.
[93] OSA, s 59(6).
[94] DSA, arts 30–32.

interpretations and approaches, while the adaptiveness of the regimes may give space to regulators to allow such convergence in practice.

(c) AI Law

Advances in, and popularization of, certain AI technologies and services mark the most significant socio-technical development since Brexit. This is also where we see the greatest contrast in regulatory strategy when we compare the UK and EU approaches. In short, the EU has taken a comprehensive approach to AI regulation based on a product safety approach, whereas the UK has decided not to introduce new AI laws in the hope of minimizing the regulatory burden and stimulating growth. Pre-Brexit, there was no specific legislation which was designed to address AI comprehensively, though aspects of the GDPR were (and remain) relevant, as well as other sectoral laws.[95]

The EU adopted the AI Act[96] on 13 June 2024, and its obligations come into effect on a staggered basis beginning on 1 August 2024. The AI Act applies to the providers or deployers of AI systems or general purpose AI models when they place such systems or models on the EU market.[97] It balances aims of promoting 'the uptake of human-centric and trustworthy artificial intelligence (AI), while ensuring a high level of protection of health, safety, fundamental rights enshrined in the Charter, including democracy, the rule of law and environmental protection, against the harmful effects of AI systems in the Union and supporting innovation.'[98]

The AI Act creates two systems of rules applicable to AI. First, AI systems which have identified purposes are subjected to a tiered system of rules depending on the classification of those purposes. AI systems deemed to have unacceptable levels of risk are prohibited; AI systems which are high risk are subjected to an extensive conformity assessment process; whereas limited risk systems have only to comply with certain transparency requirements. General purpose AI models are subjected to a separate series of rules.[99]

On the other hand, the UK government has not yet proposed dedicated AI legislation. Attempts have been made to advance a Private Member's Bill from the House

[95] UK copyright law had already anticipated authorship of computer-generated works, Copyright Designs and Patents Act 1988, s 9(3). Dedicated legislation for automated vehicles has also been introduced, Automated Vehicles Act 2024. CT Marsden, 'Generative AI Regulation in the UK', in P Hacker (ed), *The Oxford Handbook of the Foundations and Regulation of Generative AI* (Oxford University Press 2025) <https://doi.org/10.1093/oxfordhb/9780198940272.013.0043> accessed 6 August 2025.

[96] Regulation (EU) 2024/1689 of the European Parliament and of the Council of 13 June 2024 laying down harmonized rules on artificial intelligence and amending Regulations (EC) No 300/2008, (EU) No 167/2013, (EU) No 168/2013, (EU) 2018/858, (EU) 2018/1139 and (EU) 2019/2144 and Directives 2014/90/EU, (EU) 2016/797 and (EU) 2020/1828 (Artificial Intelligence Act). [2024] OJ L, 12/7/2024.

[97] ibid art 2.

[98] ibid art 1(1).

[99] M Almada and N Petit, 'The EU AI Act: Between the Rock of Product Safety and the Hard Place of Fundamental Rights' (2025) 62 CMLRev 85.

of Lords, but these attempts have not progressed to date.[100] The previous UK government used a White Paper to signal a 'pro-innovation' approach to AI, and this approach has been largely carried over by the Labour government which took power in 2024. Broadly, this approach relies on a principles-based approach to guide existing regulators,[101] justified on the basis that it would be premature to regulate before the risks associated with AI were better understood.[102] Subsequently, a commissioned independent AI Opportunities Plan states that '[t]he UK's current pro-innovation approach to regulation is a source of strength relative to other more regulated jurisdictions and we should be careful to preserve this'.[103] The UK government has endorsed almost all of the recommendations in this plan, including those which relate to reshaping existing regulators' roles to responsibility for enabling AI innovation.[104] While eventual legislation may yet emerge, particularly concerning copyright concerns which threatened to torpedo the DUAA legislative process,[105] to date comprehensive legislation has been presented as premature and soft policy instruments have been preferred.

One notable area of interest in terms of regional divergence will be the position of Northern Ireland. Articles 103–107 and 109 of the EU AI Act have been applied in Northern Ireland already under the Windsor Framework, due to the intersection between EU product safety law and the AI Act.[106] However, these provisions are addressed to the Commission, and thus are likely to have limited impact.[107] More significantly, though, the European Commission has set out a negotiating position that the AI Act ought to apply in Northern Ireland in its entirety under the Withdrawal Agreement insofar as free movement of products is concerned.[108] This is understood

[100] Artificial Intelligence (Regulation) Bill [HL] Bill 11 of 2023-2024; and Artificial Intelligence (Regulation) Bill [HL] (2025).

[101] 'A Pro-Innovation Approach to AI Regulation' (*GOV.UK*) <https://www.gov.uk/government/publications/ai-regulation-a-pro-innovation-approach/white-paper> accessed 28 July 2025.

[102] 'A Pro-Innovation Approach to AI Regulation: Government Response' (*GOV.UK*) <https://www.gov.uk/government/consultations/ai-regulation-a-pro-innovation-approach-policy-proposals/outcome/a-pro-innovation-approach-to-ai-regulation-government-response> accessed 28 July 2025.

[103] Matt Clifford, 'AI Opportunities Action Plan' (2025) <https://www.gov.uk/government/publications/ai-opportunities-action-plan/ai-opportunities-action-plan> accessed 28 July 2025.

[104] 'AI Opportunities Action Plan: Government Response' (*GOV.UK*) <https://www.gov.uk/government/publications/ai-opportunities-action-plan-government-response/ai-opportunities-action-plan-government-response> accessed 28 July 2025.

[105] Eleni Courea and Dan Milmo, 'UK Government Signals It Will Not Force Tech Firms to Disclose How They Train AI', *The Guardian* (6 June 2025) <https://www.theguardian.com/law/2025/jun/06/uk-government-signals-it-will-not-force-tech-firms-to-disclose-how-they-train-ai> accessed 8 August 2025. Department for Science, Innovation & Technology, Report on Copyright and Artificial Intelligence (18 March 2026) https://www.gov.uk/government/publications/report-and-impact-assessment-on-copyright-and-artificial-intelligence/report-on-copyright-and-artificial-intelligence accessed 17 April 2026.

[106] See Explanatory Memorandum, Secretary of State for Science, Innovation and Technology (17 July 2024) https://www.niassembly.gov.uk/globalassets/committee-blocks/windsor-framework-democratic-scrutiny-committee/uk-government-explanatory-memorandum-17-july-2024.pdf.

[107] Buick, in J Carson and S Farry, 'AI for NI: A Strategic Overview for the Adoption of Artificial Intelligence in Northern Ireland' (Ulster University Strategic Policy Unit 2025) 104 <https://www.ulster.ac.uk/__data/assets/pdf_file/0009/1735992/AIforNI-AStrategicOverviewFullDocument.pdf>.

[108] Proposal for a Council Decision establishing the position to be taken on behalf of the European Union in the Joint Committee established by the Agreement on the withdrawal of the United Kingdom of Great Britain and Northern Ireland from the European Union and the European Atomic Energy Community

to be currently under negotiation by the Withdrawal Agreement Joint Committee, and thus the final position is yet to be seen. The most recent press release associated with the meeting of the Joint Committee notes only that the committee 'took stock of the ongoing exchange of views on the implications of the Artificial Intelligence and Cyber Resilience Acts for the proper functioning of the Windsor Framework and agreed to work towards a conclusion at pace.'[109]

Stepping back, with the potential exception of Northern Ireland, a chasm will emerge over the coming years between the UK and the EU approach to automated systems, including AI. The EU has chosen to regulate AI systems as products although, unlike a washing machine, they are adaptive systems with their functioning dependent on both how they are developed and how they are deployed. This regulatory lens has attracted adverse scrutiny,[110] as have the regulatory vehicles used to bring the AI Act to fruition, most notably the Act's heavy reliance on private technical standards and certification processes.[111] Nevertheless, the benefit of the EU approach is that it provides some degree of operational clarity to the developers and deployers of AI systems, and of reassurance to those whose lives are impacted by such systems. In contrast, in the UK, important documents such as the White Paper are silent on fundamental rights and do not define key terms such as what constitutes a relevant 'AI risk'.[112] As Edwards notes, much of the political attention so far has been on the most speculative AI harms, diverting focus from less dramatic but more immediately tangible harms such as algorithmic management and surveillance at work or the automated denial of credit or welfare benefits.[113] The rift is neatly summarized by the sign-off to the White Paper which states that 'regulation is not always the most effective way to support responsible innovation', a position which stands in stark contrast to the EU approach. As will be discussed in the next section, this may be a reflection of the UK returning to its more libertarian roots now that its path is no longer confined by the EU's institutional and constitutional configuration.

as regards the adoption of a decision adding a newly adopted Union act to Annex 2 to the Windsor Framework, 23/4/2025. COM(2025) 118 final https://ec.europa.eu/transparency/documents-register/detail?ref = COM(2025)118&lang = en.

109 Joint statement by the UK Minister for the Cabinet Office Nick Thomas-Symonds and the European Commissioner, Maroš Šefčovič, 'Joint statement on the Withdrawal Agreement Joint Committee and Trade and Cooperation Agreement Partnership Council meetings' (2 February 2026) https://www.gov.uk/government/news/joint-statement-on-the-withdrawal-agreement-joint-committee-and-trade-and-cooperation-agreement-partnership-council-meetings-2-february-2026accessed 12 April 2026.

110 M Veale and F Zuiderveen Borgesius, 'Demystifying the Draft EU Artificial Intelligence Act' (2021) 4 Computer Law Review International 97.

111 N Smuha and K Yeung, 'The European Union's AI Act: Beyond Motherhood and Apple Pie?' in N Smuha (ed), *The Cambridge Handbook of the Law, Ethics and Policy of Artificial Intelligence* (Cambridge University Press 2025) <https://www.cambridge.org/core/product/identifier/9781009367783%23bp15/type/book_part> accessed 20 June 2025.

112 K Yeung and E Ahmed-Rengers, '"The Smartest, Healthiest, Safest and Happiest Place": A Response to the UK's "Pro-Innovation" AI White Paper' [2023] SSRN Electronic Journal <https://www.ssrn.com/abstract = 4487346> accessed 7 August 2025.

113 L Edwards, *'World Leading': AI Anarchy in the UK* (On file with authors).

3 What Lies Beneath: The Shifting Foundations of Digital Regulation

A solely doctrinal comparison of the legislative frameworks in the UK and the EU provides us with an incomplete picture of the potential for convergence or divergence. Equally important are influences that underpin the design and the interpretation of these instruments. Three factors are of particular salience in this sphere. These are, first, the differing constitutional roles played by fundamental rights; second, the enforcement ethos of both jurisdictions; and third, distinct political attitudes to the relationship of the State with Big Tech actors.

(a) Fundamental rights

Fundamental rights have long been foundational to digital law, with the rights to respect for private life, to data protection, and to freedom of expression playing a particularly prominent role. Widespread data processing engages privacy and data protection while the role of platforms in enabling the dissemination of user-generated content necessarily engages freedom of expression. How digital and data laws bite in practice when implemented by regulators and courts will therefore be determined to a large extent by the application of these rights. There is significant potential for divergence between the jurisdictions in this regard. UK law has historically not recognized a right to respect for private life,[114] much less a right to data protection, while freedom of expression (in particular press freedom) is comparatively well established, legally and culturally. For its part, the CJEU has embraced its role to uphold EU Charter rights post-2009. This is particularly evident in the data protection case law,[115] where the right to data protection[116] has been compared to the First Amendment in the US due to its robust protection by the CJEU.[117] The Charter rights to data protection and privacy have been drawn upon by the CJEU to dramatic effect in the interpretation of data protection legislation. Thus, the Court's interpretation of the concept of personal data, the notion of a controller, the legal bases for processing, and more have been shaped and justified by reference to underlying fundamental rights of individual data subjects.[118] Thus, even where legislative regimes in the EU and UK bear

[114] *Kaye v Robertson & Anor* [1991] FSR 62. More recently, a limited 'misuse of private information' was recognized in tort law, *Campbell (Appellant) v MGN Limited (Respondents)* [2004] UKHL 22.

[115] See, eg, in Cases C-293 and 594/12 *Digital Rights Ireland and Seitlinger* EU:C:2014:238; Case C-498/16 *Schrems v Facebook Ireland Ltd* EU:C:2018:37; Case C-311/18 *Data Protection Commissioner v Facebook Ireland* EU:C:2020:559.

[116] Art 16 TFEU; Art 8 of the Charter.

[117] B Petkova, 'Privacy as Europe's First Amendment' (2019) 25 ELJ 140.

[118] Including: Case C-131/12 *Google Spain and Google* EU:2014:317; Case C-434/16 *Nowak* EU:C:2017:994; Case C-252/21 *Meta Platforms Inc v Bundeskartellamt* EU:C:2023:537.

similarities, there are likely possibilities of divergence due to differing interpretations of that legislation.

It is less certain whether the CJEU will take a similar approach in the interpretation of the DSA or AI Act, but there is at least a relatively strong legislative basis for fundamental rights analysis to form part of judicial interpretation. Historically under the eCommerce Directive, fundamental rights have had relatively little influence on the interpretation of the intermediary liability rules. However, the DSA explicitly contains specific obligations to safeguard fundamental rights[119] and its recitals state that the law 'should be interpreted and applied in accordance with fundamental rights'.[120] Multiple obligations under the DSA are also framed in terms of fundamental rights impacts, including user restrictions,[121] systemic risk assessments,[122] and all mitigation measures adopted by VLOPs or VLOSs.[123]

Rooting the DSA generally (and some obligations specifically) in fundamental rights provides a strong basis for CJEU interpretation to be guided by a rights-based purposive reasoning. While it is only speculative at this stage, we have seen in the data protection context that such interpretative approaches can have a significant impact on the development of the law. The OSA, in contrast, is not framed around fundamental rights or civil liberties, but rather is focused on safety and particularly child protection. Indeed, there have been concerns that the OSA, in serving these overarching goals, might adversely impact rights, freedom of expression particularly.[124] Civil society have expressed concerns around potential overreach resulting in censorship.[125] Certain measures regarding child protection under the OSA have also been criticized as disproportionately interfering with privacy. The OSA's child assurance rules inspired a surge in downloads of virtual privacy networks to work around the checks[126] fulfilling warnings regarding efficacy.[127] Further, the additional burden that adults face to verify their age and the requirement to disclose extensive personal data to service providers raises concerns from a freedom of expression and data protection perspective. Nevertheless, the government has stood by the policy.[128] Therefore, in

119 G Frosio and C Geiger, 'Taking Fundamental Rights Seriously in the Digital Services Act's Platform Liability Regime' (2023) 29 ELJ 31, 43.

120 DSA, recital 153.

121 ibid art 14(4).

122 ibid art 34(1)(b).

123 ibid art 35(1).

124 E Judson, B Kira, and J Howard, 'The Bypass Strategy: Platforms, the Online Safety Act and Future of Online Speech' (2024) 16 Journal of Media Law 336.

125 'The UK Online Safety Bill: A Massive Threat to Online Privacy, Security, and Speech', *Electronic Frontier Foundation* (14 July 2023) <https://www.eff.org/pages/uk-online-safety-bill-massive-threat-online-privacy-security-and-speech> accessed 11 August 2025.

126 'VPNs Top App Store Charts as UK Age Verification Kicks In', *BBC* (28 July 2025) <https://www.bbc.com/news/articles/cn72ydj70g5o> accessed 11 August 2025.

127 V Nash and L Felton, 'Treating the Symptoms or the Disease? Analysing the UK Online Safety Act's Approach to Digital Regulation' (2024) 16 Policy & Internet 818, 826.

128 'Keeping Children Safe Online: Changes to the Online Safety Act Explained', *GOV.UK* (1 August 2025) <https://www.gov.uk/government/news/keeping-children-safe-online-changes-to-the-online-safety-act-explained> accessed 11 August 2025.

principle the UK and EU may drift further in terms of the protection of fundamental rights associated with platform regulation, due to a more explicit fundamental rights basis under the DSA combined with the prospect of interpretative divergence. In practice, the extent of this drift may depend on how the DSA is applied. For instance, relying on Article 28 DSA, the Commission has published a blueprint for a technical age verification solution which raises similar concerns to the UK approach.[129]

The extent to which the AI Act's interpretation or operation will be shaped by fundamental rights concerns is yet to be seen. Nevertheless, there is again a clear legislative basis to support strong fundamental rights-driven approaches by the judiciary. The purpose of the AI Act is framed in terms of the internal market and the uptake of 'human-centric and trustworthy' AI; 'while ensuring a high level of protection . . . fundamental rights enshrined in the Charter'.[130] Risk classification of AI systems are to be informed by risks to fundamental rights of natural persons,[131] and accordingly risk management is to be informed by risks to fundamental rights.[132] For certain public sector uses of AI systems, a fundamental rights impact assessment is required.[133] However, we should also acknowledge that the AI Act's risk-based approach has been questioned in terms of the coherence of 'risk' classifications with fundamental rights harms.[134] Naturally, the UK is not without human rights law post-Brexit, and the Human Rights Act 1998 may play an important part in driving judicial interpretations of the DUAA, the OSA, and any future digital and data laws. Nevertheless, the Charter, which has been so central to the Court's data protection case law, is no longer a basis of legislative interpretation (or indeed challenge).

Thus, interpretative divergence on the basis of fundamental rights driven interpretations of EU data and digital laws seems likely. It is a reliable feature of the CJEU's approach to data protection, and while it is yet to be seen whether this will translate into future DSA and AI Act case law, there is a strong legislative basis for rights-based approaches to be adopted.

Finally, as introduced, this is primarily a question of how formally distinct approaches to fundamental rights standards might lead to divergences in interpretation, but that does not answer the question as to the effectiveness of rights' protection. The EU has faced criticism that it does not always live up to its espoused rhetoric of fundamental rights protection.[135] Further, in the data protection context, not all EU

[129] European Commission, 'The EU Approach to Age Verification', https://digital-strategy.ec.europa.eu/en/policies/eu-age-verification accessed 17 April 2026.

[130] AI Act, art 1(1).

[131] ibid arts 6(3), 7(1)(b).

[132] ibid art 9(2)(a).

[133] ibid art 27.

[134] See, eg, I Kusche, 'Possible Harms of Artificial Intelligence and the EU AI Act: Fundamental Rights and Risk' [2024] Journal of Risk Research 1; Almada and Petit (n 99).

[135] See, eg, R Vatanparast, 'Designed to Serve Mankind? The Politics of the GDPR as a Global Standard and the Limits of Privacy' (2020) 80 Heidelberg Journal of International Law 819; P Terzis and J Van Hoboken, 'A Brussels Affect' (*Tech Policy Press*, 18 June 2024) <https://techpolicy.press/a-brussels-affect> accessed 17 July 2024.

institutions demonstrate the same commitment to fundamental rights standards.[136] The DSA has been criticized as inadequate, including for its proceduralism[137] and for risks of audit capture.[138] Concerns about the capacity of the AI Act[139] to respond to fundamental harms through the prism of risk mitigation have also been raised. For now, however, we suggest that the continued primary law status of the Charter, together with a strong legislative grounding for fundamental rights-based approaches, is likely to at least shape the interpretation of EU data and digital law at a judicial level, and provides a legal ground for a variety of legal challenges on foot of fundamental rights.

One point where the fundamental rights divergences may come to be tested post-Brexit is in the Northern Irish context, due to the special measures which have been put into place to safeguard fundamental rights in Northern Ireland. Fundamental rights protections are required to be equivalent across the island of Ireland according to the terms of the 1998 Belfast/Good Friday Agreement.[140] The Agreement led to the introduction of the Human Rights Act 1998 in the UK and the European Convention on Human Rights Act 2003 in Ireland.

Under Article 2(1) of the Protocol on Ireland/Northern Ireland to the Windsor Framework, the non-diminution of fundamental rights buttresses the 1998 Agreement. Article 2 has been relied upon by judiciary in Northern Ireland to disapply legislation[141] (though this matter is under appeal before the UK Supreme Court). In theory this could form a basis of challenge to UK data and digital laws which negatively affect the level of protection afforded to rights to privacy, data protection, or freedom of expression. Indeed, the initial data protection reform process prompted the Northern Ireland Human Rights Commission and Equality Commission to advocate for amendments to UK law to ensure no diminution of personal data protection in Northern Ireland.[142] Nevertheless, no regional divergence was reflected under the DUAA.

136 O Lynskey, M Murphy and K Nolan, 'Digital Empire or Digital Fiefdoms? Institutional Tensions and the EU Right to Data Protection' (2025) CYELS 1.

137 Griffin (n 61); Del Campo, Zara, and Álvarez-Ugarte (n 66).

138 J Laux, S Wachter, and B Mittelstadt, 'Taming the Few: Platform Regulation, Independent Audits, and the Risks of Capture Created by the DMA and DSA' (2021) 43 Computer Law & Security Review 105613.

139 Kusche (n 134); Almada and Petit (n 99).

140 K McNeilly and A O'Donoghue, 'Mapping the Tapestry: National and International Human Rights Frameworks in Northern Ireland and Ireland' 34 Irish Studies in International Affairs 1, 9.

141 *In the matter of an application by Martina Dillon, John McEvoy, Brigid Hughes and Lynda McManus for Judicial Review* [2024] NICA 59.

142 'Submission of the NIHRC and ECNI to the European Affairs Committee Inquiry on UK–EU Data Adequacy Agreements' (Northern Ireland Human Rights Commission and Equality Commission for Northern Ireland 2024) <https://www.equalityni.org/ECNI/media/ECNI/Consultation%20Responses/2024/NIHRC-ECNI-Sub-on-Data-Adequacy-Agreements-May-24.pdf> accessed 8 August 2025.

(b) Enforcement

A further undercurrent of the legislative landscape that may deepen cleavages between the UK and the EU is enforcement. The enforcement of the digital rulebook has been the subject of much attention and controversy in both jurisdictions in recent years, albeit for distinct reasons.

In the EU, much of the focus has been on how to design effective enforcement frameworks for digital regulation that involves a complex interplay of both domestic and EU regulators and courts.[143] The transnational enforcement of GDPR and cross-border cooperation between national authorities has been widely perceived as lacking.[144] The introduction of a harmonizing procedural regulation reflects such regulatory design difficulties. Perhaps as a result of the GDPR experience, subsequent legislative instruments have 'centralized' some aspects of enforcement with the Commission. For instance, the DSA empowers the European Commission to primarily oversee the regulated activities of VLOPs and VLOSEs, while national regulatory agencies regulate the activities of all other platforms and intermediaries. Similarly, under the AI Act the European Commission primarily handles enforcement for general purpose AI systems while national market surveillance authorities enforce the rest of the Act. This shift of regulatory enforcement capacity away from national regulators to the European Commission will theoretically eliminate the friction of horizontal regulatory cooperation and may therefore yield more efficient results. It is not without its challenges, however. It is dependent on the Commission taking this enforcement role seriously, and holding firm in the face of geopolitical pressures which discourage enforcement. Member states have also been slow to identify relevant regulators to enforce the AI Act, which may reflect the changing geopolitical context or, at least, some regulatory fatigue at domestic level as the tsunami of digital regulation beds down. Nevertheless, without downplaying the significant challenges that such composite EU-national administrative procedures pose and the degree to which geopolitical change has rattled EU nerves, it remains the case that the EU is committed in principle at least to the effective enforcement of its regulatory frameworks to achieve their primary objectives. The same may not be said of the UK.

In the UK, particularly post-Brexit, there has been an ostensible reorientation of key regulators away from the enforcement of their regulatory regimes towards 'economic growth'. It was widely reported in January 2025 that the Chair of the UK Competition and Markets Authority was removed from office on the grounds that the CMA was insufficiently attentive to growth concerns. The Chancellor had previously spoken about

[143] H Hofmann, 'New Regulatory Approaches under the EU's Legislation on Digitalisation: Introduction to the Special Edition of the EJRR "Charting the Landscape of Automation of Regulatory Decision-Making"' (2025) 16 EJRR 1.

[144] G Gentile and O Lynskey, 'Deficient by Design? The Transnational Enforcement of the GDPR' (2022) 71 ICLQ 799.

the need for regulators across all sectors to tear down regulatory barriers and for a 'cultural shift from excessively focusing on risk to helping drive growth'.[145] The UK's data protection regulator is transformed by the DUAA, which introduces an explicit requirement for the (now) Information Commission (IC) to take certain factors into account when exercising its functions, including a new duty to promote public trust and confidence in the processing of personal data and, on the other hand, a requirement to promote innovation and competition when exercising its functions. The SoS will also be able to exert strong indirect influence over the IC by appointing all non-executive members of the IC, who carry the balance of power in decision-making.

A more pressing, yet related, concern regards the effectiveness of the regulator. Data protection enforcement in the UK has dropped off a cliff-edge in recent years and stands in stark contrast to data protection enforcement in the EU. The 2024/25 ICO Annual Report reveals almost no enforcement of the law: only two fines for UK GDPR infringement, nine reprimands, and no enforcement notices in that period.[146] Investigations were also down by 80 per cent on 2023/24, while a staggering 70 per cent of complaints received no response within the ninety-day statutory timeframe. What appeared to be an enforcement gap post-Brexit has morphed into an enforcement void. The current Information Commissioner (who will become Chair of the IC for the duration of his mandate) has spoken publicly of his belief that the imposition of significant monetary penalties on Big Tech companies is ineffective in ensuring regulatory compliance.[147] The regulator has not provided any indication of what measures are being taken to ensure effective compliance, much less provided evidence of their effectiveness. There has been a similarly lax approach to public sector enforcement, following the introduction of a 'public sector approach' pursuant to which public authorities will only be fined if an infringement is 'egregious'. This public sector approach has subsequently been applied selectively to some charities and not others.[148] This begs the question of how public authorities can be held to account and compelled to introduce change when they violate data protection law. One such example is the Afghan data breach, which occurred in 2022 but was made publicly known in 2025 following the lifting of a super-injunction. The estimated cost of this breach to the taxpayer is £850 million and it is still unclear whether the breach resulted in any deaths.[149] As Baines notes, even if a fine was not felt appropriate, there

[145] 'Government Ousts UK Competition Watchdog Chair' (21 January 2025) <https://www.bbc.com/news/articles/c2d3e6zklxgo> accessed 8 August 2025.

[146] 'David Erdos: The UK Information Commissioner's Annual Report 2024/25: Surveying a Systematic Trend Away from Adequate Enforcement', *UK Constitutional Law Association* (22 July 2025) <https://ukconstitutionallaw.org/2025/07/22/david-erdos-the-uk-information-commissioners-annual-report-2024-25-surveying-a-systematic-trend-away-from-adequate-enforcement/> accessed 8 August 2025.

[147] Mark Sellman, 'Big Fines on Tech Companies Are Counter-Productive, Says Regulator' *The Times* (18 November 2024) <https://www.thetimes.com/business-money/companies/article/big-fines-on-tech-companies-are-counter-productive-says-regulator-bfkpc6xrk> accessed 8 August 2025.

[148] Jon Baines, 'ICO Fines: Are You Certain?' *informationrightsandwrongs* (29 July 2025) <https://informationrightsandwrongs.com/2025/07/29/ico-fines-are-you-certain/> accessed 8 August 2025.

[149] Sean Seddon, 'Afghan Data Breach: What We Do and Do Not Know', *BBC* (16 July 2025) <https://www.bbc.com/news/articles/c79qyl907lxo> accessed 8 August 2025.

was considerable exposure of risk to the underlying affected subjects and 'is surely something that the ICO should consider worthy of drawing to Parliament's attention by way of a statutory report'.[150]

Much like data protection law, the effectiveness of the OSA hinges to a significant—if not even greater—extent on the role played by Ofcom. Ofcom has not only a role in defining required conduct through the adoption of codes of practice, but also investigatory and sanctioning powers.[151] As the OSA is relatively recently adopted, and not all of its provisions are yet in force, it is premature to scrutinize Ofcom's approach too intensely. Many of its powers mirror those available to the ICO, thus reminding us that formal availability of powers does not mean effective enforcement. However, unlike under data protection law, the government may not associate the OSA so strongly with growth and competitiveness and therefore there may be less pressure on the regulator to act in an industry-friendly way. Indeed, early indications show that Ofcom is taking a robust approach to enforcement in relation to child protection.[152]

(c) Ethos/Vision of the Relationship between the State and Technology

A final point of potential cleavage between the UK and the EU concerns the relationship between the state and technology. There are two prongs to this. The first concerns the extent to which each jurisdiction conceives of its sovereignty in the face of technological development. The second concerns the way in which each jurisdiction uses regulation, or a lack thereof, to influence digital developments.

While both the UK and the EU have expressed their desire to bring technological development into the heart of government, the EU has become more cautious about its embrace of the infrastructure and services offered by certain actors. Debates about digital sovereignty, or more broadly the EU's 'strategic autonomy', increasingly dominate policy discourse in the EU. Though these terms are conceptually ambiguous, they share a common concern with EU independence in digital policy or infrastructure.[153] Historically, the EU has not treated technology development and commercialization as an urgent priority within its digital strategy. However, in the current geopolitical climate, the EU's dependence on US technology infrastructure and Chinese inputs looks increasingly fraught. Accordingly, the Commission has announced a number of initiatives to try and support *EU-led* innovation. A specific Commissioner for tech

[150] Jon Baines, 'Data Protection Risks to Life: Should More Be Done?' *Mishcon de Reya LLP* (7 August 2025) <https://www.mishcon.com/news/data-protection-risks-to-life-should-more-be-done> accessed 8 August 2025.

[151] OSA, Chs 4–6, Sch 13.

[152] L Woods, Ofcom's approach to OSA enforcement (7 April 2026, Online Safety Act Network) https://www.onlinesafetyact.net/analysis/ofcoms-approach-to-osa-enforcement/ accessed 15 April 2026.

[153] M Tambiama, 'Digital Sovereignty for Europe' (European Parliament 2020) PE 651.992.

sovereignty, security, and democracy has been designated.[154] Simultaneously, civil society and more than 250 European digital/tech CEOs have pitched the idea of a 'Eurostack', an initiative centred on three proposals—to buy European technology, to sell European technology, and to fund European technology.[155] Such debates have been largely absent in the UK as the government forges full steam ahead towards the digitization of the public sector.[156] In order to facilitate this, it has entered into partnerships with private actors such as Google and OpenAI for the delivery of public services.[157] While other prior initiatives in education and healthcare have avoided the constraints of public procurement,[158] the government states that this latest collaboration with Big Tech will 'operate in full compliance with all applicable public procurement laws'. It also adds, without further specification, that it 'may be subject to future commercial agreements'.[159]

A second point to note concerns the broad approach to regulation in both jurisdictions. To date, the EU has taken on the role of rule-setter for digital and data developments.[160] It has taken pride in, and deliberately sought to promote, a 'Brussels effect' whereby rules underpinned by EU values have been adopted in other jurisdictions.[161] Nevertheless, this commitment to values-driven digital regulation has wavered in recent years, in favour of a 'simplification' agenda, inspired by the Draghi Report.[162] The Draghi Report points to the European rulebook as an impediment to European competitiveness, and advocates for 'the will to reform the EU's governance, increasing the depth of coordination and reducing the regulatory burden'.[163] These rules are said to be a particular problem in the tech sector, as the report asserts that 'regulatory barriers constrain growth in several ways'.[164]

[154] 'Henna Virkkunen—European Commission' (14 July 2025) <https://commission.europa.eu/about/organisation/college-commissioners/henna-virkkunen_en> accessed 11 August 2025.

[155] 'Deploying the Eurostack: What's Needed Now' (2025) <https://eurostack.eu/wp-content/uploads/2025/06/eurostack-white-paper-final-19-05-25-3.pdf> accessed 11 August 2025.

[156] 'A Blueprint for Modern Digital Government', *gov.uk* (January 2025) <https://www.gov.uk/government/publications/a-blueprint-for-modern-digital-government/a-blueprint-for-modern-digital-government-html> accessed 11 August 2025.

[157] 'New Google Partnership Will Help Rid Taxpayer of "Ball and Chain" Legacy Tech and Aim to Upskill 100,000 Civil Servants in Tech and AI' (*gov.uk*) <https://www.gov.uk/government/news/new-google-partnership-will-help-rid-taxpayer-of-ball-and-chain-legacy-tech-and-aim-to-upskill-100000-civil-servants-in-tech-and-ai> accessed 11 August 2025; 'OpenAI to Expand UK Office and Work with Government Departments to Turbocharge the UK's AI Infrastructure and Transform Public Services' (*gov.uk*) <https://www.gov.uk/government/news/openai-to-expand-uk-office-and-work-with-government-departments-to-turbocharge-the-uks-ai-infrastructure-and-transform-public-services> accessed 11 August 2025.

[158] J Powles and H Hodson, 'Google DeepMind and Healthcare in an Age of Algorithms' (2017) 7 Health and Technology 351; O Lynskey, 'Automation in Education—Is EdTech a Threat to Public Values?' *LSE European Politics and Policy (EUROPP) blog* (27 July 2023) <https://eprints.lse.ac.uk/119927/1/europpblog_2023_7_27_automation_in_education_is_edtech_a_threat_to_public_values.pdf> accessed 11 August 2025.

[159] See n (157).

[160] A Bradford, *The Brussels Effect: How the European Union Rules the World* (Oxford University Press 2020); A Bradford, *Digital Empires: The Global Battle to Regulate Technology* (Oxford University Press 2023).

[161] Bradford, *The Brussels Effect*, ibid.

[162] Draghi (n 3).

[163] ibid 14.

[164] ibid 26.

As noted above, the Commission has taken up the cause of simplification to 'radically lighten the regulatory load for people, businesses and administrations in the EU'.[165] Its initial Omnibus proposals on both AI and the GDPR reflect a significant change in tack within the Commission, with the lauded rights-based approach to EU digital regulation making way for one that aspirationally promotes economic growth.[166] One example of this, for instance, is that the AI Omnibus proposal exempts high-risk models that are already on the market from the application of the AI Act.[167] As observed elsewhere, such an amnesty acts as invitation to AI providers to flood the market with systems deemed high-risk by the legislature before the Act comes fully into force.[168] Nevertheless, what shape the reopening of the digital acquis will ultimately take remains to be seen. While some simplification may be welcome, the appetite for drastic change appears to be limited.[169] Moreover, reservations have been expressed about reopening carefully negotiated and scrutinized provisions through the Omnibus method.[170] In sum, the UK has drifted from the EU values-based approach to regulation towards a more laissez-faire 'market-based' approach.[171] However, the EU's simplification agenda may herald a similar drift.

The UK and the EU are therefore faced with the same set of challenging geopolitical circumstances. The UK has responded by further embracing the existing Big Tech players for digital partnerships and promoting a reorientation of existing regulation around growth and competitiveness and a largely deregulatory pathway for AI. The EU is torn. It recognizes the longer-term democratic and strategic implications of its dependence on non-European technology and so is reorienting its digital industrial policy. Yet, the allure of technological innovation is proving to be strong, and its commitment to rights-based innovation is wavering in the name of 'simplification'.

165 A simpler and faster Europe: Communication on implementation and simplification < https://commission.europa.eu/document/download/8556fc33-48a3-4a96-94e8-8ecacef1ea18_en?filename = 250201_Simplification_Communication_en.pdf> accessed 28 April 2025.

166 GDPR Omnibus (n 27); Proposal for a Regulation of the European Parliament and of the Council amending Regulations (EU) 2024/1689 and (EU) 2018/1139 as regards the simplification of the implementation of harmonized rules on artificial intelligence (Digital Omnibus on AI) COM/2025/836 final.

167 ibid, Article 1(30) Digital Omnibus on AI.

168 F Bieker and K Nolan, 'European AI FOMO: The European Commission Sacrifices the Digital Acquis at the Altar of AI Hype' (*VerfBlog*, 29 January 2026) https://verfassungsblog.de/eu-digital-law-ai-fomo-omnibus/, DOI: 10.59704/8ea454b6677b517f, accessed 17 April 2026. See also, Ella Jakubowska, 'New European Commission: Our Takeaways on What to Expect' (*European Digital Rights (EDRi)*, 4 December 2024) <https://edri.org/our-work/new-european-commission-confirmed-our-takeaways-on-what-to-expect/> accessed 4 December 2024; Hannah Ruschemeier, 'The De-Regulatory Turn of the EU Commission' [2025] Verfassungsblog <https://verfassungsblog.de/the-de-regulatory-turn-of-the-eu-commission/> accessed 22 April 2025.

169 'Summary Conclusions of the Implementation Dialogue on the Application of the GDPR' (European Commission 2025) <https://commission.europa.eu/document/download/835dfd02-a38c-4cc3-ba53-5b0499e2b8b9_en?filename = Summary%20Conclusions%20Implementation%20Dialogue%20on%20the%20GDPR.pdf> accessed 7 August 2025.

170 A Alemanno, 'The Legality of Omnibus Legislation Under EU Law: A Preliminary Analysis of Omnibus I Simplification Directive of CSRD and CSDD and its Legal Consequences on the EU Legal Order' (09 November 2025). HEC Paris Research Paper No. LAW-2025-1588, Available at SSRN: https://ssrn.com/abstract=5727822, accessed 17 April 2026.

171 Bradford, *Digital Empires* (n 160).

4 Conclusion

Since Brexit, the divergence between UK and EU approaches to digital and data law has grown. In the legislative landscape, a common starting point with the GDPR and a shared desire to reap economic benefits of data use in both the EU and the UK has limited the divergence to some extent. But in the areas of platform governance and AI regulation, the UK has taken a different path. While there may be a largely shared socio-technical environment and many of the same political concerns influencing debates, there was little by way of predecessor EU regulation to create path dependencies. The DSA and OSA bear some superficial similarities, but their approach to regulation is quite different, shaped significantly by different ideas of harm. Whereas the EU has adopted comprehensive regulation based on ideas of risk assessment and mitigation under the AI Act, the UK has for now refrained from introducing legislation to constrain AI development.

We might then query what is driving this deepening cleavage between the regimes. The UK is no longer subject to the EU policy framework and therefore has more capacity to respond to local political concerns. This may to some degree explain the emphasis upon child protection found in the OSA, for example. The UK may also now be able to move more rapidly, with neither legislators nor regulators being subject to the need to build consensus across twenty-seven member states. But there is also the loss of medium to long-term policy planning and thinking. The OSA's flagship child age assurance approach, recently introduced, is already facing challenges of implementation. The UK's governmental policy on AI has been criticized for a lack of rigour.[172]

Legislative changes, we suggest, are only the surface level of what is changing. Below the surface, foundational aspects of data and digital law are also increasingly moving in different directions. Both the UK and EU are increasingly facing pressure to leverage economic benefits associated with the tech sector, but the response to these pressures differs. Commitment to robust enforcement of digital regulation is rapidly disappearing in the UK. While the EU is certainly not immune to the political headwinds that blow in the UK, there are institutional and constitutional safeguards that provide some stability. The continuing role for the Charter and judicial safeguarding of fundamental rights in the EU is likely to be a key safeguard in the digital and data space.

Where once the UK and EU digital and data law shared common ground, increasingly the terrain has splintered. Quite where any of this will resolve is beyond the ambitions of this chapter to predict, yet in forecasting for the future we must be attentive to what lies beneath the surface.

[172] Yeung and Ahmed-Rengers (n 112) 3.

16

Intellectual Property

Justine Pila

1 Introduction: Control but No Direction

This chapter studies the UK landscape of intellectual property law post-Brexit. To date there have been comparatively few such studies. Of those published, most appeared shortly after the 2016 Referendum and focused on the range of possible post-Brexit arrangements and their implications for IP.[1] Central concerns were the uncertainty that existed and the fate of specific initiatives, particularly the unitary patent system.[2] Also emphasized was the international consensus in IP, the benefits of harmonization in global markets for creative and informational products, and the limited scope and desirability of substantive UK–EU divergence in the light of these particularly.[3]

[1] See, eg, L McDonagh and M Mimler, 'Intellectual Property Law and Brexit: A Retreat or a Reaffirmation of Jurisdiction?' in M Dougan (ed), *The UK after Brexit* (Intersentia, 2017) 159; A George, 'Just Keep Calm & Carry On: The Impact of Brexit on Intellectual Property Laws in Britain and the European Union' (2017) 1 J IP Studs 90 and 'Restructuring Intellectual Property Jurisdiction Post-Brexit: Strategic Considerations for the European Union and Britain' (2017) 43 BJIL 131; R Arnold and others, 'IP Law Post-Brexit' (2017) 101 Judicature 65; L McDonagh, 'UK Patent Law and Copyright Law after Brexit' in *Brexit: The International Legal Implications* (BIICL, 2017) Paper No. 3; M Mimler, 'The Effect of Brexit on Trademarks, Designs and Other 'Europeanized' Areas of Intellectual Property Law in the United Kingdom' in *Brexit: The International Legal Implications* (BIICL, 2017) Paper No. 7; B Farrand, 'Bold and Newly Independent, or Isolated and Cast Adrift: The Implications of Brexit and Intellectual Property Law and Policy' (2017) 55 JCMS 1306; G Dinwoodie and R Cooper Dreyfuss, 'Brexit and IP: The Great Unraveling' (2018) 39 Cardozo LR 967; R Arnold, 'Divergence of UK Law from EU Law after Brexit: The Example of Intellectual Property' (2022) 12 QMJIP 172.

[2] See, eg, H Dunlop, 'What Now for the Unified Patents Court Following the Brexit Referendum?' [2016] EIPR 595; T Jaeger, 'Reset and Go: The Unitary Patent System Post-Brexit' [2017] IIC 254; A Ohly and R Streinz, 'Can the UK Stay in the UPC System after Brexit?' [2017] JIPL&P 245; MAG Sellens, 'The Viability of the Unitary Patent Package After the UK's Ratification of the Agreement on a Unified Patent Court' [2018] IIC 136; S Bross and M Lamping, 'Eyes Wide Shut' [2018] IIC 887; A McMahon, 'Brexit and the Unitary Patent Package: A Further Compromised Future?' (2018) 15 SCRIPTed 175; K Walsh, 'The Unitary Patent Package, the Court of Justice of the European Union, and Brexit: (Ir)reconcilable?' [2019] IPQ 91; W Tilmann, 'The UPC without the UK: Consequences and Alternatives' [2020] GRUR International 847; A Plomer, 'The Unified Patent Court and the Transformation of the European Patent System' [2020] IIC 791; D de Lange, 'EU Patent Harmonization Policy: Reconsidering the Consequences of the UPCA' [2021] JIPL&P 1–13. On the system itself see (n 19).

[3] See, eg, McDonagh (n 1); Dinwoodie and Dreyfuss (n 1); Farrand (n 1). Cf A Tsoutsanis, 'Back to the Future: From Brexit to IP 4.0—Reshaping Paris, Berne and TRIPS for the 21st Century' (2021) 16 JIPL&P 761.

Justine Pila, *Intellectual Property* In: *The UK Regulatory Framework Post-Brexit: 'Law Unbound'*. Edited by: Paul Craig and Vilija Vėlyvytė, Oxford University Press. © Oxford University Press 2026. DOI: 10.1093/9780198969815.003.0018

The current chapter expands the focus to consider post-Brexit developments, and highlights two features of the UK's IP landscape given little if any consideration previously: the absence of a clear vision for IP after fifty years of EU membership, and the challenges posed for the UK's democratically elected government by the public controversy which IP reforms have come in that period to attract. In combination these features can be seen to have impeded the UK's ability to exploit the opportunities for regulatory reset which Brexit promised, most clearly in the field of artificial intelligence (AI) and copyright. They also help to explain its failure to have embarked on any substantive review of assimilated EU provisions, or introduced other substantive legislative initiatives, in contrast to the continued hive of EU activity. If not addressed, they create a risk of the UK becoming suspended in time, and achieving its 'smarter regulation' goal of decreased regulation[4] by default rather than considered IP policy. At a time of significant geopolitical tension over issues at the heart of IP—including the regulation of AI, the responsibilization[5] of tech intermediaries, and fundamental rights—a suspended legislative framework and regulatory pivot to industry seems neither smart nor conducive to realizing the values of agility and proportionality to which post-Brexit UK governments have committed.[6] It will also impose an excessive burden on the courts to ensure the continued relevance of existing IP provisions, including by ensuring that they reflect their new, post-Brexit legal and policy context. Given this, a question moving forward is whether the UK, having 'taken back control',[7] will manage to find direction in IP. Important will be its capacity to formulate a coherent post-Brexit strategy which acknowledges its new 'second-mover' regulatory position while also heeding the dangers of sustained inaction in fields of fast-moving and disruptive technology, thereby resolving a tension in post-Brexit policy currently. Also needed is a clear and coherent vision for IP specifically, outlining its relationship to fundamental rights, and its role in regulating the development and exploitation of new technologies.[8]

[4] The 'smarter regulation' programme was established in May 2023 by the former (Conservative) government, and based on its earlier policy paper, 'The Benefits of Brexit: How the UK Is Taking Advantage of Leaving the EU' (2022). Central was a commitment to 'making regulation a last resort, not a first choice', and using alternatives to regulation, including standards and guidance, to meet the demands of fast-developing technology: DBT, 'Smarter Regulation to Grow the Economy' (10 May 2023) para 2.1; see also the government's 'smarter regulation' progress report, 'Smarter Regulation—One Year On' (May 2024), and collection, https://www.gov.uk/government/collections/smarter-regulation. The programme has essentially continued under the Labour government, which has committed to the same regulatory strategy since taking office in July 2024; see, eg, HM Treasury, 'Radical Action Plan to Cut Red Tape and Kickstart Growth' (17 March 2025); 'Better regulation' collection, https://www.gov.uk/government/publications/better-regulation-framework#full-publication-update-history.

[5] The term 'responsibilization' was 'developed in the governmentality literature to refer to the process whereby subjects are rendered individually responsible for a task which previously would have been the duty of another—usually a state agency—or would not have been recognized as a responsibility at all': A Wakefield and J Fleming (eds), *The SAGE Dictionary of Policing* (Sage Publications Ltd 2009) 276.

[6] 'The Benefits of Brexit' (n 4).

[7] UK Prime Minister, 'EU Exit: Taking Back Control of our Borders, Money and Laws while Protecting our Economy, Security and Union' (November 2018) Cm 9741.

[8] Cf IPO, 'IP for a Creative and Innovative UK: Strategy 2024 to 2027' (2 May 2024), discussed below; also IPO, 'IP Counter-Infringement Strategy 2022 to 2027' (4 February 2022).

2 Pre-Brexit Regulation: The Principal Contours of the EU Legal Regime Pre-Brexit

Traditionally conceived, IP comprises national, territorially defined rights of exclusion covering a wide range of intangible subject matter, from authorial works (literary and artistic property) to inventions, signs of commercial origin, geographical indications, plant varieties, and trade secrets (industrial property).[9]

In the early years of the European Union, the use of IP rights to partition domestic markets for goods and services along disparate national lines threatened to undermine the Treaty's free movement and competition guarantees, engendering a certain hostility towards IP.[10] An attitudinal change was prefigured by three judicial devices developed in the 1960s and 1970s: the distinction between the existence and exercise of IP rights, the former unaffected by the Treaty's guarantees and the latter needing to be restricted to accommodate them;[11] the autonomous EU law concept of the 'specific subject matter' of IP, the safeguarding of which was all that the Treaty's IP-protective provisions were held to require, leaving the wider array of IP rights conferred by member states amenable to EU restriction;[12] and the principle of rights exhaustion, preventing the use of IP rights to restrict the parallel importation of goods once marketed legitimately (with right holder consent) within EEA territory.[13] In combination these devices established the EU's competence to define and regulate IP rights under the internal market provisions of the early Treaty, confirmed the capacity of IP systems to support EU single market objectives, and paved the way for the development of an ambitious programme of EU law- and policy-making in IP.

In the decades since, IP has become central to the EU's agenda, and extensively Europeanized, via a process that can be seen to represent the EU's unique and distinctive mix of idealism and pragmatism; the Commission proceeding solely but steadily, often prompted by Court of Justice decisions, achieving what it can when it can through legislation and complementary soft law initiatives, adjusting as required to assuage social and industry concerns and criticisms.[14] On the eve of Brexit, it had succeeded in constructing an expansive regime, including the following:

[9] The distinction dates to the nineteenth century and was entrenched by the two foundational international agreements in IP, the 1883 Paris and 1886 Berne Conventions.

[10] The tension originated in the Rome Treaty's reservation of Member States' systems of property (EEC Art 222) and recognition of the protection of industrial and commercial property as an exception to the Arts 30 to 34 free movement and Art 85 competition guarantees (EEC Arts 36, 86).

[11] See Case 24/67 *Parke, Davis & Co. v Probel, Reese, Beintema-Interpharm and Cetrafarm* [1968] ECR 81.

[12] See Case 119/75 *Terrapin (Overseas) Ltd. v Terranova Industrie CA Kapferer & Co* [1976] ECR 01039.

[13] See Case 78/70 *Deutsche Grammophon Gesellschaft v Metro-SB-Grossmarkte* [1971] ECR 00487.

[14] For different accounts and perspectives, see Justine Pila and Ansgar Ohly (eds), *The Europeanization of Intellectual Property Law: Towards a European Legal Methodology* (Oxford University Press 2013).

- Three unitary IP rights and systems (EU trade marks (EUTMs),[15] Community (now EU) designs,[16] and Community plant variety rights[17]), supported by EU administrative bodies and courts, including national courts exercising jurisdiction for EU territory,[18] and supplementing national IP rights and systems harmonized along identical lines—with a fourth unitary right and system for patents about to commence,[19] and a fifth for supplementary protection certificates (SPCs) being considered.[20]
- Extensive harmonization of all other national IP rights and systems, including copyright and related rights, supplemented by 'European' database rights and resale rights for visual artists.[21]
- A harmonized IP enforcement regime governing the procedures and remedies available to protect all rights of IP, supported by the EU Intellectual Property Office (EUIPO)'s IP Observatory and the European Anti-Fraud Office (OLAF), and accompanied by separate measures for protecting trade secrets.[22]
- A harmonized e-commerce regime governing the provision of online services.[23]
- An extensive body of EU case law covering unitary and (harmonized) national IP rights.[24]
- An active programme of local and global IP law- and policy-making.

It bears emphasis that the UK had never been a passive 'taker' of this regime and had benefited considerably from its provisions;[25] and that it had also not

[15] Regulation (EU) 2017/1001 on the European Union trade mark [2017] OJ L154/1 (EUTM Regulation).
[16] Regulation (EU) 2024/2822 amending Council Regulation (EC) No 6/2002 on Community designs and repealing Commission Regulation (EC) No 2246/2002 [2024] OJ L 2822 (Designs Regulation).
[17] Council Regulation (EC) No 2100/94 on Community plant variety rights [1994] OJ L227/1.
[18] See, eg, Designs Regulation, Art 27; EUTM Regulation, Arts 123-126.
[19] The unitary patent system was established in 2012 as an enhanced cooperation measure involving all EU member states excluding Croatia and Spain by Regulation (EU) No 1257/2012 implementing enhanced cooperation in the area of the creation of unitary patent protection [2012] OJ L 361/1 (UP Regulation) and Regulation (EU) No 1260/2012 implementing enhanced cooperation in the area of the creation of unitary patent protection with regard to the applicable translation arrangements [2012] OJ L 361/89. It is supported by the EPC and the Unified Patent Court, the latter of which was established for this purpose by the (international) Agreement on a Unified Patent Court [2013] OJ C 175/1 and currently involves 18 EU member states.
[20] Proposal for a regulation on the unitary supplementary protection certificate for plant protection products COM(2023)221; Proposal for a regulation on the unitary supplementary certificate for medicinal products COM(2023)222.
[21] Directive 96/9/EC on the legal protection of databases [1996] OJ L 77/20; Directive 2001/84 on the resale right for the benefit of the author of an original work of art [2001] OJ L 272/32.
[22] Directive 2004/48/EC of the European Parliament and of the Council of 29 April 2004 on the enforcement of intellectual property rights [2004] OJ L147/45 (IP Enforcement Directive); Directive 2016/943 on the protection of undisclosed know-how and business information (trade secrets) against their unlawful acquisition, use and disclosure [2016] OJ L 157/1.
[23] Directive 2000/31/EC on certain legal aspects of information society services [2000] OJ L 178/1 (e-Commerce Directive).
[24] On the status of international IP agreements in the UK post-Brexit see Farrand (n 1).
[25] See, eg, A Harcourt, *Brexit and the Digital Single Market* (Oxford University Press 2023) Ch 2 (describing the UK's 'entrepreneurial' shaping of EU audio-visual policy and the regulatory benefits, this secured for its domestic communications and advertising industries).

seemed especially constrained by EU legislation which it (or its courts) did not support.[26]

3 Post-Brexit Regulation: Wider Regulatory Changes

Four types of EU–UK divergence in IP law have occurred: (1) those arising automatically and hence passively from the UK's withdrawal from the Union; (2) those resulting actively from the UK's decision not to retain/assimilate specific EU laws; (3) those resulting passively and perhaps actively from post-Brexit EU legal developments not replicated in the UK; and (4) those resulting actively from post-Brexit UK legal developments. A fifth type of divergence can also be identified as having resulted from incompatibilities between pre-Brexit EU and UK laws first acknowledged post-Brexit.

(a) Divergences Arising Automatically from Withdrawal

Post-Brexit IP arrangements were governed initially by the 2018 Withdrawal Agreement and the EU–UK political declaration negotiated in parallel under Article 50 TEU. The main aim of the Agreement's IP provisions was to 'save' the UK portion of rights derived from EU Regulations or reciprocity-based Directives, including by enabling their continued protection in the UK,[27] addressing the treatment of pending IP rights applications,[28] and confirming that IP rights which had previously been exhausted in the EU and UK under EU law would remain exhausted.[29] The political declaration looked to the longer-term future of IP law- and policy-making by making commitments concerning IP rights, subsequently given more concrete expression in the 2020 Trade and Cooperation Agreement (TCA).[30] To this end, the TCA recorded the EU's and UK's agreement to comply with existing international agreements and the 2012 Beijing Treaty on Audiovisual Performances;[31] to respect the principle of national treatment under the TRIPS Agreement;[32] to ensure certain minimum standards of protection across the fields of IP;[33] to make legal provision for the enforcement of IP rights in accordance with the IP Enforcement Directive,[34] and cooperate to support

[26] See, eg, J Cornwell, 'Injunctions and Monetary Remedies Compared: The English Judicial Response to the IP Enforcement Directive' [2018] EIPR 490.

[27] Withdrawal Agreement, Arts 54–58.

[28] ibid Arts 59–60.

[29] ibid Art 61.

[30] TCA, Art 219.

[31] ibid Art 222. The UK signed the Beijing Treaty in 2013 but has still not ratified it, continuing instead to consult on the best means of meeting its commitments: see (n 121).

[32] TCA, Art 224.

[33] ibid Arts 225–235 (copyright), 236–244 (trade marks), 245–249 (designs), 250–251 (patents and public health), 252–254 (trade secrets), and 255 (plant variety rights).

[34] ibid Arts 256–269.

their implementation through the newly created Trade Specialized Committee on IP;[35] to facilitate voluntary stakeholder initiatives to reduce IP infringement in certain ways;[36] and to use reasonable endeavours to agree rules for the protection and effective enforcement of GIs domestically.[37] The effect was to guarantee post-Brexit that the arrangements in place for IP would remain much as previously, with each party continuing to ensure high levels of protection and the effective enforcement of rights in pursuit of a seamless transition to a post-Brexit reality.

These commitments were implemented domestically by the European Union (Withdrawal) Acts 2018 and 2020 and the European Union (Future Relationship) Act 2020, supported by UK Regulations dealing with IP specifically. The Withdrawal Acts established as 'retained EU law' most EU law as it applied to the UK on 31 December 2020, as well as domestic legislation implementing EU IP Directives. This preserved the EU principles of supremacy and interpretive effect for retained EU law related to IP, such that any conflict between retained EU law and pre-Brexit domestic legislation would continue to be resolved in favour of the former. The EU (Future Relationship) Act implemented the TCA, including by means of a provision declaring existing domestic law to have effect with such modifications as required to ensure this.[38] And the UK (EU Exit) Regulations sought to make good on the UK's commitments in the field of IP specifically.[39] The most involved were the Intellectual Property (Copyright and Related Rights) (Amendment) (EU Exit) Regulations 2019, which amended the UK law of copyright and database rights to remove or change the range of cross-border mechanisms and arrangements which the UK's withdrawal from the EU had affected in the fields of copyright and database rights.

As a result of these and other post-Brexit provisions, the UK law of IP was extensively amended on 1 January 2021 (Implementation Period/IP completion day), including in the following ways:

- The protection conferred by unitary EU Trade Marks, EU Designs, and Community Plant Variety Rights ceased to extend to UK territory, with 'corresponding' UK rights created for existing right holders instead.
- UK lawyers and agents ceased to be eligible for rights of representation before the EUIPO.
- UK businesses and residents ceased to be eligible to register and hold .eu domain names.

[35] ibid Art 273.
[36] ibid Art 274.
[37] ibid Art 275.
[38] EU (Future Relationship) Act, s 29(1).
[39] Intellectual Property (Copyright and Related Rights) (Amendment) (EU Exit) Regulations 2019; Intellectual Property (Exhaustion of Rights) (EU Exit) Regulations 2019; Trade Marks (Amendment etc.) (EU Exit) Regulations 2019; Designs and International Trade Marks (Amendment etc.) (EU Exit) Regulations 2019; Patents (Amendment) (EU Exit) Regulations 2019; Customs (Enforcement of Intellectual Property Rights) Amendment) (EU Exit) Regulations 2019; Intellectual Property (Amendment etc.) (EU Exit) Regulations 2020.

- UK cultural heritage organizations ceased to be entitled to digitize orphan works (whose copyright owner cannot be identified) in their collections in reliance on the EU orphan works exception, needing instead to seek a licence under the UK's orphan works scheme and to limit the availability of licensed works to UK territory.
- UK citizens, residents, and businesses ceased to be eligible for the (reciprocity-based) EU *sui generis* database right conferring protection across EEA territory, and became limited instead to the UK database right conferring protection across UK territory.
- Broadcasters of content uplinked from the UK to an EEA state ceased to be able to rely on their clearance of rights in the UK, needing instead to obtain separate clearance for each EEA state—in contrast to broadcasters of content to the UK from an EEA state, which continued not to require separate clearance of rights unless the content was created in a state with lower levels of copyright protection.
- Right holders whose content was broadcast in the UK and then retransmitted by cable in the EEA ceased to be included in the collective rights management arrangements of EU law, needing instead to negotiate directly with the cable operator in each receiving state—in contrast to right holders whose content was broadcast in the EEA and then retransmitted by cable in the UK, whose rights continued to be exercisable exclusively through a licensing body.
- UK users of online content services ceased to be entitled (as of right) to 'port' the services (to access their content) to EEA states during periods of temporary residence, becoming dependent instead on the service provider's offer of portability after obtaining appropriate copyright clearance for the relevant states—with EEA users losing their corresponding right of portability to the UK.
- UK right holders and UK Collective Rights Management Organizations (CMOs) ceased to be entitled (as of right) to representation by EEA CMOs for online licensing of musical rights—in contrast to EEA right holders and CMOs, which retained their pre-Brexit rights of representation by UK CMOs.
- UK courts ceased to be designated EU courts governed by the Brussels I Regulation,[40] thereby losing their jurisdiction as such to determine the validity and infringement of unitary IP rights for EU territory.[41]
- UK territory ceased to be covered by the EU exhaustion principle, meaning that goods first marketed in the UK could no longer be resold in other EEA states without obtaining additional IP rights clearance in each of those states—in contrast to goods first marketed in the EEA, which could be resold in the UK without additional UK rights clearance (the so-called 'UK +' exhaustion principle).

[40] Regulation (EU) No 1215/2012 on jurisdiction and the recognition and enforcement of judgments in civil and commercial matters (recast) [2015] OJ L351/1.

[41] On 27 June 2024 the UK ratified the 2019 Hague Convention on the Recognition and Enforcement of Foreign Judgments in Civil or Commercial Matters (2 July 2019). The Convention took effect on 1 July 2025 and requires the recognition and enforcement in the UK of civil and commercial judgments issued in other Convention countries, and vice versa.

In addition to these amendments, the UK's withdrawal from the Union changed the legal and policy context with reference to which domestic IP measures are required to be interpreted. The extent of EU harmonization meant that before Brexit, most domestic IP legislation was construed with reference to its EU law and policy context, owing to the *Marleasing* principle of interpretive effect,[42] the widespread reliance of domestic IP legislation on autonomous concepts of EU law (interpreted by the Court of Justice), and the reproduction of harmonized industrial property provisions in Regulations governing corresponding unitary systems.[43] Given this, it was inevitable that the UK's departure from the EU would result in substantively different interpretations of domestic IP legislation by UK decision-makers,[44] especially given the early exclusion of the Charter from assimilated EU law under the 2018 Withdrawal Act.[45]

Indeed, a defining characteristic of EU IP law since the Lisbon Treaty has been the prominence given to the Charter in legislation and case law, particularly in the field of copyright, where its frequent invocation has supported the recognition of a third (human rights) legal tradition, supplementing the longstanding copyright and *droit d'auteur* traditions of common law and civil law states.[46] Even outside copyright, the Charter has become the central point of reference for determining the 'fair balance' required when interpreting EU IP provisions.[47] Aside from its methodological significance, this has resulted in substantive changes to IP law via creative interpretations of individual Charter provisions. An example is *Deckmyn v Vandersteen*,[48] where the Grand Chamber invoked the Article 21 right to non-discriminatory treatment to support a restrictive reading of the parody exception to copyright infringement as needing to take account of the interests of copyright owners in preventing the association of their works with discriminatory messages. Another is *Brüstle*, where the Grand Chamber invoked the Article 1 requirement that human dignity be respected and protected to support a broad interpretation of the exclusion from patentability of industrial uses of human embryos as precluding the patenting of any invention the original devising of which involved, at however early a stage, the destruction of a fertilized human ovum.[49] The result was similar in each case: a novel interpretation of

[42] Case C-106/89 *Marleasing SA v La Comercial Internacional de Alimentacio SA* [1990] ECR I-4135.

[43] See, eg, the substantive provisions of the EUTM Regulation with those of Directive (EU) 2015/2436 to approximate the laws of the member states relating to trade marks [2015] OJ L336/1.

[44] See, eg, *Industrial Cleaning Equipment (Southampton) Ltd v Intelligent Cleaning Equipment Holdings Co Ltd & Anor* [2023] EWCA Civ 1451.

[45] Withdrawal Act 2018, s 5(4).

[46] See P Goldstein and P Bernt Hugenholtz, *International Copyright: Principles, Law, and Practice* (4th edn, Oxford University Press 2019) Ch 1.

[47] See A Nari Lee and A Tischner, *Fairness in Intellectual Property Law* (Edward Elgar 2024) 141–82 ('Fairness, intellectual property and fundamental rights').

[48] Case C-201/13 *Deckmyn v Vandersteen* EU:C:2014:2132.

[49] Case C-34/10 *Brüstle v Greenpeace eV* [2011] ECR I-09821, [34]–[38], interpreting Biotech Directive Art 6(2)(c); confirmed in Case C-364/13 *International Stem Cell Corporation v Comptroller General of Patents, Designs and Trade Marks* EU:C:2014:2451. Compare the less expansive interpretation of EPC Rule 28(c) in G2/06 *WARF* (25 November 2008), and the distinction drawn under the UK Human Fertilisation and Embryology Act 1990 between the use of pre-14 and post-14 day embryos in scientific research and development.

an established exception to IP law based on an expansive and distinctively European conception of both the requirements of fundamental rights protection and the role of IP in regulating scientific and creative activities.

An important question moving forward is whether such interpretations will withstand the UK's withdrawal from the EU. Despite the UK's insistence that excluding the Charter from assimilated EU law would have no substantive impact,[50] it is difficult to see them doing so. Aside from the legal questions of the nature, scope, and interpretive significance of human rights post-Brexit, the UK's policy commitment to a more 'agile' and 'proportionate' regulatory method[51] signals a return to a more traditional approach in IP that is difficult to reconcile with either the *Deckmyn* or the *Brüstle* case. There is already some evidence for this in the context of parody, where the language of early post-Brexit case law reflects an approach more in keeping with US than EU perspectives in its emphasis on protecting the freedom of parodists to engage in critical commentary from unfair restriction by commercial interests.[52] This is consistent also with the UK's emphasis on leveraging the Charter's removal to create an environment more conducive to speech, and with the political support for withdrawing from the European Convention on Human Rights (owing to concerns over its expansive interpretation in the migration context particularly).[53] The result may then be a more conventional common law view of parody as entailing a balance between copyright and freedom of speech, and of art itself as 'political': valued by states and protected by copyright for its support of democracy and other societal benefits.[54] Similarly in the patent field, it will be open to the courts post-Brexit to abandon the CJEU's interpretation of the human embryos exclusion in preference for a more conventional common law reading of patentability as depending solely on the nature of the invention, without regard to how it came to exist, much less the 'rights' of any blastocyst embryo destroyed early in the process of devising it, or whether its protection might incentivize the commission of war crimes (as the Advocate-General in *Brüstle* considered[55]).

Finally, it remains to consider the effect on the future trajectory of domestic IP case law of the Retained EU Law (Revocation and Reform) Act 2023 (REUL Act),

[50] Withdrawal Act Explanatory Notes, [106]–[107].

[51] 'The Benefits of Brexit' (n 4).

[52] See, eg, *Shazam Productions Ltd v Only Fools* [2022] EWHC 1379 (IPEC). This is despite the Court's purported application of *Deckmyn*.

[53] See, eg, 'The Benefits of Brexit' (n 4), recording the government's early commitment to remove the reference to the Charter in the Communications Act 2003 (UK) 'due to our concerns about the chilling effect it has on free speech'. For evidence of a wider shift in UK approaches to freedom of speech post-Brexit see also the Higher Education (Free Speech) Act 2023 and related Office for Students' Regulatory Guidance 24 (June 2025). Leaving the ECHR is currently supported by the leaders of the Reform UK and Conservative parties, with the Labour Party supporting its retention but review.

[54] Cf N Netanel, 'Copyright and a Democratic Civil Society' (1996) 106 Yale LJ 283; J Rubenfeld, 'The Freedom of Imagination: Copyright's Constitutionality' (2002) 112 Yale LJ 1.

[55] EU:C:2011:138 (AG) [106]–[107]. Of relevance for *Deckmyn* also, see further Commission, 'Preserving Europe's Collective Memory for a Brighter Future', https://www.eacea.ec.europa.eu/preserving-europes-collective-memory-brighter-future_en.

introduced as part of the government's 'smarter regulation' programme,[56] and intended to encourage the UK's departure from established EU positions, including through the re-interpretation of domestic legislative provisions. To this end, the REUL Act enables the amendment of retained EU legislation by secondary UK legislation; makes it easier for Parliament to modify some types of EU-derived secondary UK legislation; abolishes the right to rely on directly effective EU rights, the supremacy of EU law (including the *Marleasing* principle of interpretive effect), and general EU law principles in respect of all enactments and legal rules whenever created; and requires the higher courts to have regard to certain factors when deciding whether or not to depart from retained case law. At the same time, the Act reinforces the 'business as usual' message of earlier measures by declaring that all but seven of the eighty-six identified retained IP-related laws are still to be retained (now 'assimilated'), with an assurance that the seven exceptions are inoperable, superseded by other domestic legislation, or no longer relevant, such that their revocation will have no 'policy effect'.[57] The result is a certain ambivalence regarding the intended and future impact of the REUL Act in IP.[58] Nevertheless, by removing previous interpretive constraints, the Act is likely to support further decisions such as *ICE v ICE* and *Shazam*, in which UK judges give effect to domestic legal and policy influences (including common law intuitions) when interpreting EU-derived provisions.

(b) Divergences Resulting from the UK's Decision not to Implement or Retain Specific EU Laws

Further divergences have also arisen as a result of EU and UK legal and policy developments post-Brexit. A significant cause of these has been the UK's decision not to implement Directives which were enacted before, but the transposition deadline for which post-dated, IP completion day, such as the Online Transmissions Directive and the DSM Directive.

The UK's decision on the eve of Brexit not to implement the DSM Directive, despite having supported its enactment as an EU member state, has been among the most consequential for its post-Brexit IP landscape. The reason is the significance of the Directive's provisions for the digital economy and creative industries, including the liability of online service providers for reproducing press publications (Article 15), the liability of content-sharing platforms for hosting IP-infringing content (Article

[56] See 'Smarter Regulation to Grow the Economy' (n 4) [4].

[57] IPO Guidance, 'IP and Retained EU Law: The Facts', 15 November 2022. For the complete list of retained EU IP measures see IPO Guidance, 'Retained EU Law for Intellectual Property', https://www.gov.uk/government/publications/intellectual-property-and-retained-european-union-law-the-facts/retained-eu-law-for-intellectual-property.

[58] See, eg, *E-Accounting Solutions Ltd v Global Infosys Ltd* [2023] EWHC 2038 (Ch); *Merck Serono v Comptroller-General of Patents* [2025] EWCA Civ 45; also P Johnson, '"Inverted Supremacy", "Weaker Precedent", and Other Uncertainties brought about by the Retained EU Law (Revocation and Reform) Act 2023' [2025] EIPR 634.

17), and the liability of AI model developers for using IP-protected content to train their models (Article 4). While presented as a function of the UK's desire to forge its own path in copyright, free from the constraints of EU law and policy, the decision can also be related to concern over the EU's direction in IP, including its increasing use of copyright as a mechanism for regulating the digital economy and redistributing the profits of large technology companies.[59] An example is its gradual extension of primary liability to restrict the safe harbour immunity of intermediaries under the e-Commerce Directive in an effort to close the 'value gap'[60] created by their indirect exploitation of copyright content without remunerating IP owners. Also sensitive has been the Directive's explicit targeting of large platforms, such as Facebook and YouTube,[61] owing to its support of a narrative regarding the EU's protectionist and censorial approach to regulation, and its discriminatory use of legislation to level the playing field between European and US technology companies; an approach the UK was unlikely to support given its wish to conclude a free trade agreement with the US.[62]

The question remains as to the UK's approach in the areas covered by the DSM Directive post-Brexit. Under sections 9(2)(d) and 11 of the CDPA, press publishers enjoy related rights in the typographical arrangements of their published editions, lasting for twenty-five years, and protecting against facsimile copying of the presentation and layout of their editions.[63] The result is something close to the protection of Article 15. As for the liability of online platforms for hosting copyright-infringing content, this will continue to be governed by the 'communication to the public' right under section 20 of the CDPA, implementing Article 8 of the 1996 WIPO Copyright Treaty, and having the meaning given to it by the CJEU in a voluminous body of case law interpreting (the corresponding) Article 3 of the Information Society Directive. Post-Brexit this is case law which the Court of Appeal has expressly declined to reject.[64] While the principles established by the Court of Justice have similar implications for the primary liability of online service providers as Article 17 of the DSM Directive has,[65] they do not address the value gap created by the platform economy

[59] See U Furgał, 'The Emperor Has No Clothes: How the Press Publishers' Right Implementation Exposes Its Shortcomings' (2023) 72 GRUR International 650.

[60] The term 'value gap' was used in a letter sent to the Commission in June 2016 by more than 1,000 recording artists and songwriters from across Europe objecting to the 'misuse' by online content-sharing platforms of the e-Commerce Directive's safe harbour provisions to distribute and monetize protected works and other subject matter with little if any remuneration of right holders. Closing it was a central aim of Art 17: see Commission, 'Questions and Answers—European Parliament's Vote in Favour of Modernised Rules Fit for Digital Age', https://ec.europa.eu/commission/presscorner/api/files/document/print/en/memo_19_1849/MEMO_19_1849_EN.pdf.

[61] DSM Directive, Art 17 applies only to platforms 'the main or one of the main purposes [of which] is to store and give the public access to a large amount of copyright-protected subject matter uploaded by its users, which it organizes and promotes for profit-making purposes', Art 2(b).

[62] Discussions on an agreement were commenced in May 2020 and shelved in 2021. On 16 June 2025, a US–UK Economic Prosperity Deal was concluded instead, committing to the reduction of certain tariffs.

[63] CDPA, ss 15, 17(5); *Newspaper Licensing Agency Limited v Marks & Spencer Plc* [2001] UKHL 38, [23]–[24].

[64] *TuneIn Inc v Warner Music UK Ltd* [2021] EWCA Civ 441.

[65] See, eg, Cases C-682-683/18 *Peterson v Google LLC* EU:C:2021:503, [102].

by normalizing IP licensing in the manner of Article 17 and its 'best efforts' copyright clearance regime.

In relation to the use of copyright material to develop AI models, the existing UK position is even further from that established by the DSM Directive. It derives from section 29A of the CDPA, which mirrors Article 3 of the DSM Directive by permitting copies of works to be made (by persons having lawful access to them) 'for the sole purpose of research for a non-commercial purpose', subject to sufficient acknowledgement unless this would be impractical or otherwise impossible. Missing from UK law is an equivalent to the Article 4 exception, which permits commercial text and data mining (TDM) of (lawfully accessed) works unless the right holder has 'expressly reserved' their rights 'in an appropriate manner'. This is difficult to reconcile with the UK's other post-Brexit commitment to develop a 'distinctive, pro-innovation approach to artificial intelligence regulation',[66] given which it is hardly surprising that reviewing the TDM exception has been a key policy aim since the 2016 Referendum.[67] In 2022, after its second public consultation on AI and IP, the government proposed a general exception to UK copyright and database rights to permit TDM 'for any purpose', with a view to ensuring that 'the UK's copyright laws are among the most innovation-friendly in the world'.[68] From an EU perspective, this was a remarkable proposal. By allowing works to be used without authorization (or remuneration) for commercial ends, it would have undermined the fundamental right to IP protection enshrined in Article 17(2) of the Charter, and entrenched a value gap of precisely the type which the DSM Directive had sought to address.[69] Adding insult to injury, it would have done so in service of a technology that is widely expected (and has already started) to displace human authorship and transform the creative industries.[70]

Given the significance of this, it is unsurprising that the UK proposal triggered a public outcry, and that the government was forced to rethink. There followed the Vallance Review, which recommended that it 'work with the AI and creative industries to develop ways to enable TDM for any purpose', and that a voluntary 'code of practice' on AI and copyright be developed.[71] The government accepted the recommendations

[66] See DSIT, 'White Paper: A Pro-Innovation Approach to AI Regulation' (29 March 2023).

[67] The government first consulted on AI and IP in 2020 (see n 121).

[68] IPO, 'Artificial Intelligence and Intellectual Property: Copyright and Patents—Government Response to Consultation' (June 2022) [62].

[69] The government's proposal followed its rejection of the recommendation of the CMS Committee that it consider introducing DSM Directive-inspired licensing, transparency, and other reforms 'to address the market distortions and the music streaming "value gap"' created by online content-sharing platforms (CMS Committee, 'Economics of Music Streaming' (HC 50, 15 July 2021) recommendations 4, 6, 9, 16, 23) in preference for industry solutions and allowing time to review the approaches of EU and non-EU states: see 'Economics of Music Streaming—Government Response' (HC 719, 21 September 2022). The CMS Committee responded by recommending that the government abandon its TDM proposal and clarify instead 'that licences are required to use copyrighted content in AI': 'Connected Tech: AI and Creative Technology' (HC 1643, 30 August 2023) recommendation 3.

[70] See, eg, D Thomas, 'How AI Is Transforming the Business of Advertising', *Financial Times* (11 February 2025).

[71] HM Treasury, 'Pro-Innovation Regulation of Technologies Review: Digital Technologies' (15 March 2023) 8–9 (Vallance Review).

and established a working party of tech developers and right holders to negotiate a code.[72] Unsurprisingly they failed to reach agreement, and the group was disbanded in early 2024, returning the government to its starting position on AI and copyright shortly before the Labour Party took office.[73]

Within days of commencing, the new government's Technology Secretary had commissioned a further review on AI and copyright, this time from Matt Clifford, Chair of the Advanced Research and Invention Agency. Echoing the tenor of Sir Patrick Vallance's Review, Clifford warned the government of the need for urgent action, noting that the EU had 'moved forward . . . with an approach that is designed to support AI innovation while also enabling rights holders to have control over the use of content they produce' while the UK fell behind, and recommending reform of the TDM regime to ensure that the UK remained 'at least as competitive as the EU'.[74] In a response published the same day, the government noted its launch the previous month of a new consultation on a 'TDM with opt out' exception modelled explicitly on Article 4 of the DSM Directive.[75]

Despite its shift, UK authors remained unhappy with the new TDM proposal, concerned at the feasibility of an opt out in practice, and accusing the government of 'committing theft, thievery on a high scale'.[76] Supported by crossbencher Baroness Beeban Kidron in the House of Lords, they demanded amendment of the Data (Use and Access) Bill before Parliament to require the providers of AI models to furnish right holders with sufficient information to enable them to identify any use of their copyright-protected subject matter in the generation or training of models later marketed domestically, so as to be able to exercise their rights.[77] The amendment was passed in the Lords by an overwhelming majority of 287 in favour and 118 against, only to be rejected two days later in the House of Commons. It continued to ping-pong between the Lords and Commons until the Bill was finally passed on 11 June 2025—without the Kidron amendment, but with a commitment to require the government 'to produce an economic impact assessment of the options available [on AI and copyright] and to report on key issues, including transparency, technical solutions, access to data and copyright licensing . . . approaches to models trained overseas and . . . how transparency and other requirements should be enforced'.[78]

[72] CMS Committee, 'Connected Tech: AI and Creative Technology—Government Response (HC 441, 11 January 2024).

[73] DSIT, 'A Pro-Innovation Approach to AI Regulation—Government Response' (10 February 2024) [29]–[30].

[74] DSIT, 'Independent Report: AI Opportunities Action Plan' (13 January 2025) recommendation 24.

[75] DSIT, 'AI Opportunities Action Plan: Government Response' (13 January 2025); IPO, 'Copyright and Artificial Intelligence' (December 2024) [9], [75], [97], [108], [113]-[124].

[76] Laura Kuenssberg, 'Elton John Brands Government "Absolute Losers" over AI Copyright Plans', *BBC* (18 May 2025); see also D Thomas, 'Elton John and Dua Lipa Urge Starmer to Back UK Artists in AI Copyright Row', *Financial Times* (10 May 2025).

[77] Data (Use and Access) Bill, Art 53(1)(d).

[78] As reported by Sir Chris Bryant, Minister of DSIT and the DCMS, in Parliament on 10 June 2025: *Hansard* vol 768, col 836. These commitments were given legislative expression in the Data (Use and Access) Act 2025, ss 135, 136.

The impact assessment and report were published in March 2026. Noting the large number of responses to its December 2024 consultation (11,520 in total), and the rejection by most of the proposed Article 4-style exception, the government declared that this was no longer its preferred option. It also deferred a final decision on the issue. 'We must take the time needed to get this right' it said, citing the 'limited and uncertain evidence on the impact of copyright on the development and deployment of AI in the UK', and the need 'to build this evidence base', and consider the wider legal, technological, and industry developments in the EU and US particularly.[79] In the meantime, it committed to take steps 'to help right holders control and license their work', explore options 'for supporting human creativity and artistry', and continue 'to seek input from voices across the economy, and engage with Parliament and technical experts to ensure any reform drives growth and supports adoption and diffusion of [AI].'[80]

Hence the fate of the UK's reform on copyright and AI remains unclear, seven years after the DSM Directive was enacted, one year after the EU finalized its voluntary AI Code of Practice to facilitate the implementation of Article 4 in practice,[81] and just as the Court of Justice prepares to hear its first referral on the requirements of Article 4.[82] The Technology Secretary reportedly regrets having ever consulted on the 'TDM with opt out' proposal, and from the government's 2026 report, it seems possible that no further legislative proposals of any form will be brought.[83] Whatever the case, the experience would seem to offer a lesson in how *not* to regulate in a field as complex, contested, and fast-moving as AI and IP. The most significant misstep was the government's failure to afford any strategic direction of its own to guide the process—or undertake appropriate economic impact assessments until forced to do so by Baroness Kidron's intervention—and its deferral instead to AI tech experts and representatives, including in formulating its proposals.[84] It is a mark of the anger generated by its approach that in May 2025, as the Kidron amendment was being considered, Sir Elton John described the government as 'absolute losers', and the Technology Secretary as 'a bit of a moron' in an interview with the UK's national broadcaster, the BBC.[85] Strategically too, the government's approach has undermined its regulatory agenda, including its first-mover ambition in AI, and done little to progress the debate or narrow the range of options canvassed. In fields as important economically and culturally as these, the UK's regulatory missteps risks damaging UK industry, and

[79] DSIT, 'Report on Copyright and Artificial Intelligence' (18 March 2026).
[80] ibid.
[81] The AI Code of Practice (10 July 2025) requires signatories to commit to implementing technical measures to prevent their AI models from generating content that reproduces copyright protected content: Measure 1.4.
[82] Case C-250/25 *Like Company Kft v Google Ireland Ltd.*
[83] J Bambridge, 'UK Minister Admits "Regret" over AI and Copyright Row', *Politico* (22 May 2025).
[84] See J Bambridge, 'How AI and Copyright Turned into a Political Nightmare for Labour', *Politico* (4 June 2025).
[85] Kuenssberg (n 76).

the UK reputationally, with the courts required in the meantime to formulate an approach using legislation from an earlier technological age.[86]

(c) Divergences Resulting from Post-Brexit EU Legal Developments

The third category of divergence results from post-Brexit EU legal developments. These include new and revised Regulations and Directives in IP, such as the 2023 Geographical Indications (Crafts and Industrial Products) Regulation,[87] and the 2024 revised versions of the Designs Regulation[88] and GI Regulation,[89] each of which has introduced substantive changes to different aspects of EU law that create correspondingly substantive divergences between the EU and UK IP regimes, in addition to further uncertainty for designers and businesses dealing with both. This category of divergence also includes the continued expansion of the already substantial volume of EU IP case law, clarifying and developing the EU IP *acquis* in ways too numerous to list.

Beyond such explicit EU IP developments are many others of relevance for IP. Among these are the 2024 AI Act and the 2022 Digital Services Act (DSA),[90] which contain detailed provisions on the transparency duties of (high-risk, general purpose, and other) AI model developers and the content moderation duties of online platforms respectively. These Acts, and especially the DSA, are also among the allegedly censorial and discriminatory EU regulations aimed at limiting speech and weakening the (US) technology industry which have caused such political and corporate ire in the United States recently,[91] with the DSA described by EU commentators as

[86] They have begun already with *Getty Images (US) Inc v Stability AI Limited* [2025] EWHC 2863 (Ch), currently under appeal. See also the trenchant criticisms of the UK's March 2023 White Paper on 'A Pro-Innovation Approach to AI Regulation' (n 66) by A Charlesworth and others, 'Response to the UK's March 2023 White Paper 'A Pro-Innovation Approach to AI regulation', https://papers.ssrn.com/ 204477368 (19 June 2023) and E Ahmed-Rengers and K Yeung, '"The Smartest, Healthiest, Safest and Happiest Place": A Response to the UK's "Pro-Innovation" AI White Paper', https://papers.ssrn.com/4487346 (4 August 2023).

[87] Regulation 2023/2411 on the protection of geographical indications for craft and industrial products and amending Regulations (EU) 2017/1001 and (EU) 2019/1753 [2023] OJ L 2411; C Budileanu, 'European Union Geographical Indications for Craft and Industrial Products: A Comparative Look at Geographical Indications for Other Types of Products' (2024) 1 LESIJ 24.

[88] Regulation (EU) 2024/2822 amending Council Regulation (EC) No 6/2002 on Community designs and repealing Commission Regulation (EC) No 2246/2002 [2024] OJ L 2822; A Kur and others, 'Substantive Law Aspects of the "Design Package"' (2023) 72 GRUR International 557.

[89] Regulation (EU) 2024/1143 on geographical indications for wine, spirit drinks and agricultural products, as well as traditional specialities guaranteed and optional quality terms for agricultural products [2024] OJ L 1143; I Kireeva and B O'Connor, 'Harmonising and Unifying the Protection of Geographical Indications in the EU: A Step-by-Step Approach' in A Zappalaglio and E Bonadio (eds), *The Future of Geographical Indications* (Edward Elgar 2025) 73.

[90] Regulation (EU) 2024/1689 laying down harmonized rules on artificial intelligence [2024] OJ L1689 and Regulation (EU) 2022/2065 on a Single Market For Digital Services and amending Directive 2000/31/EC [2022] OJ L277/1.

[91] See, eg, JD Vance, 'Remarks at the Munich Security Conference' (5 February 2025), https://www.presidency.ucsb.edu/documents/remarks-the-vice-president-the-munich-security-conference-0; M Zuckerberg interview with J Rogan (10 January 2025), https://youtu.be/7k1ehaE0bdU?si = hXR2wxEQ8L47tTNi.

horizontalizing the Charter by requiring online service providers to pay due regard to fundamental rights when implementing their duties, mirroring the approach in the *Deckmyn* case.[92]

Absent equivalent UK legislative provisions post-Brexit,[93] the duties of the developers and providers of AI models trained on IP-protected content and of internet services used to host, transmit, or store such content will continue to be governed by the comparatively sparse provisions of existing EU-derived measures. For internet service providers these include the 2000 e-Commerce Directive, implemented domestically by the e-Commerce Regulations 2002 and filled out by the courts in related (including assimilated EU) case law. In brief, this means that ISPs will be protected from primary liability for any infringing use of their services provided they have no actual or constructive knowledge of the infringement—without prejudice to their duties upon obtaining such knowledge to act expeditiously to stop the infringement, including by blocking or removing the infringing content, but without the additional duties of content moderation imposed by the DSA.[94] While the UK has also been willing to co-opt intermediaries in the fight against online IP rights and other infringements, it has done so primarily on an ad hoc basis via the issue of injunctive relief, rather than detailed regulatory instruments of the type supported by the EU in recent years.[95]

(d) Divergences Resulting from Post-Brexit UK Legal Developments

While significant divergences have been created by post-Brexit EU legal developments, the same is not true in the other direction, there having been few deliberate changes to established EU-derived positions in IP by UK law- or decision-makers. One counter-example is the decision of the Court of Appeal in *ICE v ICE* regarding trade mark acquiescence. Another is the expansion of the protection conferred on certain designs by the introduction of a second ('supplementary') unregistered design

[92] T Mast and C Ollig, 'The Lazy Legislature: Incorporating and Horizontalizing the Charter of Fundamental Rights through Secondary Union Law' (2023) 19 ECLR 462. See especially DSA, s 14(4); DSM Directive, recital 70.

[93] The UK's Online Safety Act 2023 explicitly excludes IP-infringing content from its definition of 'illegal content' in s 59(6)(a)(i).

[94] Of greatest relevance for IP, these include the duties (a) to maintain 'easy to access and user-friendly' notice and action systems that enable the electronic submission by users of 'sufficiently precise and adequately substantiated notices' of allegedly unlawful content (Art 16); (b) to include information regarding their content moderation 'policies, procedures, measures and tools' in their Terms and Conditions, expressed in 'clear, plain, intelligible, user-friendly and unambiguous language, and [made] publicly available in an easily accessible and machine-readable format' (Art 14(1)); and (c) to act in a diligent, objective and proportionate manner in applying and enforcing those policies, procedures, measures and tools, 'with due regard to the rights and legitimate interests of all parties involved, including the fundamental rights of the recipients of the service' (Art 14(4)).

[95] See, eg, *Wolverhampton City Council v London Gypsies and Travellers* [2023] UKSC 47.

right that covers reproductions for the purpose of repairing a complex product—shortly before the EU amended its own designs regime to introduce a permanent repair clause (to support the establishment of a spare parts market), among other changes of note, including the introduction of a new design right exception for 'critique and parody'[96] and an optional exclusion for designs that incorporate elements of cultural heritage.[97] A third is the decision to abandon at second reading a DSM Directive-inspired Copyright Bill to protect composers, lyricists, and musicians from the impact of the streaming market by creating an equitable remuneration right and related transparency duties for service providers—in order, counterintuitively, to create the possibility of 'industry-led solutions' to the industry-created problems which the Bill had sought to address.[98] And a fourth is the decision to abandon the pursuit of an EU-style TDM exception, for the moment at least. Aside from these deliberate divergences is the apparently unconscious one created by the exclusion of the Charter from assimilated EU law and the emphasis on freedom of speech in the post-Brexit interpretation of the copyright parody exception.

(e) Divergences which Pre-dated Brexit But Were Not Declared

A fifth type of divergence involves incompatibilities between EU and UK laws only declared after Brexit. *WaterRower* is an example of this.[99] As the Court acknowledged in that case, the UK restriction of copyright to works of artistic craftsmanship that have a certain aesthetic or artistic quality is inconsistent (and cannot be reconciled) with the so-called 'open' EU principle that copyright subsists in any and all works of authorship. Assuming that these positions are indeed incompatible, it is curious that their incompatibility was not declared and remedied before Brexit. Whatever the reason for this, the decision in *WaterRower* creates difficulties for the UK owing to its retention as assimilated EU law of cases supporting the 'open' approach, and will therefore require further consideration by the government or higher courts.[100]

[96] See S Jacques and E Derclaye, 'The Parody Exception in EU Design Law: A Catalyst for Creative Evolution, Innovation and Cultural Discourse' (2024) 46 EIPR 285.

[97] See B Justin Jütte and A Trapova, 'The Protection of Cultural Heritage by Designs' in I Stamatoudi (eds), *Research Handbook on Intellectual Property and Cultural Exchange* (Edward Elgar 2022) Ch 5.

[98] The Copyright (Rights and Remuneration of Musicians, etc) Bill would have introduced new rights to equitable remuneration and information regarding the use of their protected subject matter in an adapted version of the provisions of DSM Directive, Arts 19-22.

[99] *WaterRower (UK) Ltd v Liking Ltd* [2024] EWHC 2806 (IPEC).

[100] The UK's proposed review of its post-Brexit designs regime may provide an opportunity for this, owing to its concern with the definition of 'design', which seems to remain within the review's scope despite its restriction since 2022: see IPO, 'Survey on Priorities to Shape UK System for Protecting Designs' (7 February 2025).

4 Post-Brexit Regulation: Proposed Divergences

Looking to the immediate future, the position seems likely to continue as currently, with substantive EU IP law- and policy-making continuing at pace while the UK follows slowly behind, at risk of becoming suspended in time, as at IP completion day. Additional support for this is offered by the EU's 2020 IP Action Plan, which commits to several further actions in pursuit of longstanding EU IP policy objectives, including enhanced IP protection, greater use and deployment of IP among SMEs, greater access to and 'sharing' of IP-protected assets, improved enforcement, and a 'fairer' playing field globally.[101] Several of its actions have already been completed, including the roll-out of the unitary patent system, the revision ('modernization') of the industrial designs and GI systems, and the introduction of the DSA. Several others are also far-progressed, including an evaluation of the SPC system and establishment of a unitary SPC right; an evaluation of the plant variety rights systems; increased funds and assistance for SMEs applying for IP; the launch of additional IP-related education and training programmes; a new system to coordinate the compulsory licensing of IP in times of crisis; improved arrangements for SEP licensing; clarification of certain provisions of the Trade Secrets Directive; a review of the Database Directive; an expansion of OLAF's role in combating piracy and counterfeiting; and a new and ambitious IP enforcement toolbox. The number and range of these initiatives is indicative of the scope and depth of the EU's involvement in IP, and stands in contrast to the scope and depth of corresponding UK initiatives, which have been minimal by comparison. For example, the UK's current IP strategy outlines three policy goals—(a) to 'ensure that UK law incentivises innovation and creativity for the benefit of society', (b) to 'ensure that Intellectual Property rights are respected, and that enforcement of IP occurs nationally and internationally', and (c) to 'shape an IP system internationally that supports UK and global innovation'—with little detail regarding the means proposed for achieving each.

One important area of post-Brexit EU activity has been IP enforcement, which is also an area identified explicitly in the TCA as requiring attention and EU–UK collaboration post-Brexit,[102] and one of the strategic goals just mentioned.[103] The prominence given to enforcement is not surprising given the scale and impact of IP infringement globally—a point underlined by the US administration's characterization of insufficient protection as another non-tariff barrier imposed by foreign states.[104] Within the EU itself, IP rights are said to account for almost 50 per cent of GDP and 40 per cent of employment, with trade mark infringement (counterfeiting) having

[101] Commission Communication, 'Making the most of the EU's innovative potential: An intellectual property action plan to support the EU's recovery and resilience', COM(2020) 760 final.

[102] See (nn 34, 35).

[103] See 'IP for a creative and innovative UK: Strategy 2024 to 2027' (n 8).

[104] See US Executive Order 14257 'Regulating Imports With a Reciprocal Tariff To Rectify Trade Practices That Contribute to Large and Persistent Annual United States Goods Trade Deficits' (2 April 2025).

cost it €119 billion and 650,000 jobs in 2019 alone.[105] Of particular concern is the disparate impact on SMEs, which are said to face a 34 per cent lower survival rate than larger companies when affected by IP infringement. According to the Commission, so profitable and low-risk is IP infringement that it has replaced drug trafficking as the crime of choice among organized gangs.[106] Hence the urgency with which the 2004 IP Enforcement Directive was pursued, and the continued efforts to supplement it with other initiatives, including most recently harmonized criminal penalties, memoranda of understanding with online platform providers, and tech-driven enforcement procedures. These are among the proposals which the EU presented at the fourth EU–UK Trade Specialized Committee meeting in November 2024.[107] In contrast have been the UK's post-Brexit enforcement initiatives, which have been largely limited to providing 'guidance and signposting to help UK businesses navigate the SEP ecosystem' and launching a series of 'Choose Safe Not Fake', 'Fake Always Breaks', and 'Fake Toys Real Harms' anti-counterfeiting marketing campaigns.[108]

5 Post-Brexit Empirical and Normative Analysis

As has been seen, EU–UK regulatory divergence in IP has been overwhelmingly passive: the product of changes resulting automatically from the UK's withdrawal from the Union and the related redrawing of EU territory, and from post-Brexit EU legal developments.

Despite the foreseeability, and in some cases the inevitability, of these divergences, it is difficult to see them as Brexit dividends. Indeed, and subject to sector-specific responses and market conditions,[109] it seems likely that the exclusion of UK territory from the reach of unitary EU rights will reduce the likelihood of IP-related businesses

[105] Commission Recommendation, 'Combatting counterfeiting and enhancing the enforcement of intellectual property rights', COM(2024) 1739 final. The most recent UK figures (calculated using the EU's methodology) cover the period 2017–2019, and attribute 33.2 per cent of non-financial value added output, 19.2 per cent of employment, and 58.2 per cent of total goods export value, to industries with an above average use of registered IP rights (patents, trade marks, and registered designs): IPO, 'Use of Intellectual Property Rights Across UK Industries 2017 to 2019' (updated 9 June 2022). On the strong positive correlation between IP ownership and EU firm performance, see also EPO and EUIPO, *Intellectual Property Rights and Firm Performance in the European Union* (2nd edn, 2021).

[106] As reported by David Byrne, Member of the Commission, in the European Parliament on 9 March 2004 during the debate of Report A5-0468/2003 on the proposal for an IP Enforcement Directive [COM(2003) 46—C5-0055/2003—2003/0024(COD)].

[107] Commission, 'The fourth Trade Specialised Committee on Intellectual Property under the EU-UK Trade and Cooperation Agreement, 13 November 2024' (10 January 2025). The EU gave a further presentation on recently published reports concerning the impact on EU interests of IPR deficiencies in third world countries at the fifth Trade Specialized Committee meeting on 9 October 2025, alongside its latest IP enforcement data.

[108] ibid. The minutes of the 2024 and 2025 Specialized Committee meetings also reference reports by the UK of 'ongoing internal work' on enforcement transparency measures mirroring those of the EU, and enforcement-related work at WIPO and the OECD, without making clear what this work entails.

[109] Sectoral division is a feature of the responses to the government's consultation on the post-Brexit exhaustion regime: see IPO, 'UK's Future Exhaustion of Intellectual Property Rights Regime: Summary of Responses to the Consultation' (updated 15 May 2025).

operating, and IP-protected subject matter becoming available, within the UK; that the relocation from London of the pharmaceutical seat of the Unified Patent Court will weaken the UK's standing as a leading jurisdiction for pharmaceutical patenting, to the detriment of its legal service and pharmaceutical industries; that the inability of broadcasters to clear EEA rights from within the UK will make it a less attractive place for them to operate; that the move to a UK + exhaustion regime will be worse for UK industry and the public than the EU regime; and that the UK's exclusion from the EU table and 'ticket' will reduce its opportunities for supranational policy entrepreneurship to the further detriment of local industry. In short, it seems likely that Brexit will generate significant costs for the UK's IP-intensive industries.

The question remains whether the changed context with reference to which IP legislative provisions must now be drafted and interpreted will nevertheless produce opportunities for regulatory dividends that will come to outweigh these costs.

In principle, it is in the UK's interests that domestic legislative provisions are framed and interpreted having regard to UK contextual factors and policy objectives. Nevertheless, whether the result will be a substantively better regulatory environment and regime depends on one's assessment of those factors and objectives, as well as the quality of UK law- and policy-making in IP. And here, the signs are not encouraging. They also draw attention to two particular challenges which UK governments have faced: their limited regulatory experience in IP, and their greater political sensitivity and vulnerability to public opposition and criticism. The first of these helps to explain the government's failure to have formulated any clear and coherent post-Brexit vision for IP, and for what its protection in the future should seek to achieve.[110] The effects of the second have been exacerbated by that failure, and the government's related inability to defend the proposals it has submitted for public scrutiny.

(a) The UK's Limited Regulatory Experience

The different pace, ambition, and success of EU and UK IP initiatives since 2020 underlines their different regulatory experience. It bears remembering that the EU institutions have been actively engaged in IP law- and policy-making since the earliest years of the EEC Treaty, playing a central role also in shaping IP globally. Inevitably, they have had to weather significant public opposition and criticism over that period, with several EU measures—including the Biotech Directive, the Unitary Patent

[110] The government's inaction and lack of strategic direction in IP has been a source of growing frustration and criticism from the CMS Committee also, reflected in its 2023 recommendation 'that the Government take a more strategic approach to policymaking regarding cultural production and the creative industries', repeated in different ways subsequently: see CMS Committee, 'Economics of Music Streaming—Follow-up' (HC 874, 13 January 2023) recommendations 2–3; 'Connected Tech: AI and Creative Technology' (n 69) recommendations 3–6; CMS Committee, 'NFTs and the Blockchain: The Risks to Sport and Culture' (HC 598, 11 October 2023) recommendations 1–2; CMS Committee, 'Creator Remuneration' (HC 156, 10 April 2024) [39]–[40]; CMS Committee, 'British Film and High-end Television' (HC 328, 10 April 2025) [51]–[60].

Regulations, and the DSM Directive—having also been challenged constitutionally by one or other member state.

By contrast, the UK's activities in IP have been limited, constrained by EU law and policy, and focused inevitably on realizing such opportunities for policy intervention as these afford, rather than formulating and implementing an agenda for an independent state. It follows also that the UK has by and large avoided public criticism for its positions, such criticism having been directed to the EU institutions (including the Court of Justice) instead. This has particularly been the case as the EU approach has become more ambitious and distinctively 'European' in the ways outlined previously, reflecting the increased importance of intangibles globally, the increased complexity of the issues which their protection by IP creates, and the evolution of the EU economically, politically, and constitutionally. Even outside the EU, the IP landscape has changed considerably since the early 1970s, with IP rights more widely and deeply implicated in commercial and social life, and IP regimes correspondingly more politicized, adding new challenges for domestic law- and policy-making. A question raised by the UK's TDM experience is whether the government will be able to weather the public opposition and criticism which IP proposals have come to attract, and whether it will seek to avoid them by pursuing the easier path of non-regulatory solutions instead. This would be an ironic outcome of Brexit given the emphasis placed on democracy by the 'Leave' campaign. It also underlines the importance of a clear and coherent vision for IP to drive and anchor the government's future reform initiatives.

(b) Different Regulatory Approaches and Policies

This raises the further questions of what the UK 'believes' in IP, and what exactly its IP policy objectives are. For all the talk about taking back control, it is surprising how little attention has been given to this, and how unclear the answers remain.[111]

The EU position, entrenched further since 2016, stands as a model of clarity and coherence by comparison. In the EU conception, IP requires strong protection, and sufficient malleability to serve a range of economic and social aims, including the establishment and smooth functioning of a competitive single market, the regulation of technology-related activities, the promotion of European culture and heritage, and the protection of fundamental rights and interests. In recent years, these themes have been reflected in the EU's growing co-optation of technology companies (and their technologies) to ensure the protection and enforcement of IP rights and the redistribution of market returns from the commercial exploitation of protected subject matter via expanded conceptions of primary and secondary liability, the normalization of licensing, and such Rule of Law responsibilities as transparency, accountability, and

[111] Following a freedom of information request, the IPO disclosed its employment (as at 10 June 2019) of only 10 contractors (non-permanent employees) to work primarily or specifically on Brexit preparations or policy, in addition to one full-time secondee (from another government department or agency).

fundamental rights protection. This trend towards responsibilizing intermediaries can be seen to reflect the EU's distinctive mix of pragmatism and policy. Pragmatically, tech providers and developers are uniquely positioned and equipped to address IP infringement via *ex ante* and *ex post* interventions, making their co-optation as private regulators and police[112] essential if the EU is to address the ever-growing tide of piracy and counterfeiting so damaging to industries and the EU economy. Since the companies affected are overwhelmingly US companies, pressing them into the service of EU rights protection also serves the EU goals of creating a fair playing field conducive to involvement by EU-based SMEs, supporting EU technological sovereignty,[113] and promoting EU regulatory standards extraterritorially. So too as a matter of principle, responsibilizing tech firms to ensure the protection of EU citizens' rights and the transparency and accountability of the firms' activities reflects the European commitment to fundamental rights protection, and its collective memory of the dangers posed historically by companies that become 'too big',[114] and by the prioritizing of economic interests over social interests more generally; in the language of Polanyi, the dis-embedding of the economy from society.[115]

At the same time, the EU approach to IP distinguishes it from the approach of other jurisdictions, including the US, notwithstanding the commitment of each to the same international treaties and minimum standards of IP protection. Reflections of their difference can be seen in their approach to the issues outlined above, including gene patenting, parody and other copyright exceptions, and the duties of online intermediaries. They are also reflected in the discussions around AI and IP, including the duties of AI model providers and developers locally and extraterritorially. While the impact in practice of these differences varies, they are nevertheless significant, normatively and politically. Hence a key issue for the UK post-Brexit is what conception and approach to adopt as it accelerates its decoupling from the EU: the European conception and approach which many in the UK have grown accustomed to (and come to expect), or the more recognizably common law conception and approach of the US.

Until recently at least,[116] the UK had seemed most likely to pursue the latter, seeking thereby to align itself with the US at a sensitive moment geopolitically. This is consistent with its decision not to retain the Charter, its emphasis on a 'pro-business' and 'pro-innovation' approach to IP law and policy, its pursuit of a free trade agreement with the US, and its commitment to regulate in a different way, with more 'agility' and 'proportionality' than the EU is said to regulate with. Already these commitments can

[112] See L Belli and C Sappa, 'The Intermediary Conundrum: Cyber-Regulators, Cyber-Police or Both?' (2017) 8(3) JIPITEC 4620.

[113] See European Parliament, 'Report on European Technological Sovereignty and Digital Infrastructure' (11 June 2025).

[114] See T Wu, *The Curse of Bigness: How Corporate Giants Came to Rule the World* (Atlantic Books 2022).

[115] K Polanyi, *The Great Transformation* (Beacon Press 1944).

[116] Shortly before this book went to press, the government announced its intention to limit its deregulatory agenda in order to pursue closer economic ties with the EU amidst a deteriorating relationship with the US: see G Parker et al, 'Reeves to Limit Deregulatory Drive as She Seeks Closer UK Ties with EU', *Financial Times* (11 February 2026).

be seen to have influenced post-Brexit law and policy in IP, consciously or otherwise, including the proposals on AI and copyright, and the decisions not to implement the DSM Directive, not to proceed with the Copyright (Rights and Remuneration of Musicians, etc) Bill or other DSM-inspired reforms, not to replicate the content moderation duties of the DSA, and not to pursue other aspects of IP reform with the same commitment and energy as the EU continues to pursue them. A further factor in this regard has been the public controversy which new IP measures invariably generate. This has been underlined by the TDM experience, which raises the prospect of the UK seeking in the future to avoid the political fallout caused by controversial legislative initiatives either by limiting public consultation on them, or by seeking to avoid them altogether, in preference for other regulatory modalities. Aside from its implications for UK democracy, this would result in missed opportunities for the ambitious regulatory reset which the UK was promised before and after the Brexit Referendum.

6 Conclusion

Over the past sixty-plus years, intellectual property has been extensively Europeanized. Most national IP laws have been harmonized, five unitary (EU-wide) rights of industrial property have been created, and EU administrative and enforcement agencies have been established to oversee the licensing and protection of IP throughout EU territory. Given this extensive EU activity, leaving the Union has inevitably produced widespread effects. Most obviously, unitary right holders no longer enjoy protection within UK territory, the voluminous body of EU IP case law no longer produces the same domestic legal effects, EU rights management and enforcement arrangements no longer benefit UK right holders, and the UK government no longer enjoys the opportunities afforded by EU law- and policy-making for supranational policy entrepreneurship.

As at today, it is difficult to see these effects as having benefited the UK, and notable that the UK has fallen in the WIPO's Global Innovation Index from second (in 2014 and 2015) to fifth (in 2024) and sixth (in 2025).[117] Nevertheless, Brexit has also created opportunities for a regulatory reset in IP at a time of technological disruption and geopolitical tension over the EU's approach—including its responsibilization of technology companies, and its creative and expansive interpretation of fundamental rights in different parts of the IP regime. Whether the UK is able to exploit these opportunities to serve its interests remains to be seen, but current indications are mixed, if not discouraging. On the one hand, there is indeed evidence of a commitment post-Brexit to a regulatory reset involving greater reliance on non-regulatory (including market) solutions[118] and increased support for innovation, including at the

[117] For the rankings to 2025 see https://www.wipo.int/publications/en/details.jsp?id=4756&plang=EN.
[118] See, eg, (n 69) and text accompanying (n 98).

expense of IP rights and interests.[119] On the other hand, neither the government nor the Intellectual Property Office (responsible for domestic IP policy) has articulated any coherent strategy as might support this commitment, or shown any inclination to depart from assimilated EU positions in IP (to the extent permitted by international law and post-Brexit agreements). The main focus of the UK's post-Brexit IP activity has been consulting on issues, often more than once and with no concrete results.[120] While AI and IP—a flagship area of post-Brexit UK policy—had seemed an exception to this following the government's forced retreat from its original 'pro-innovation' approach to (post-Brexit) EU positions, even these positions have now been abandoned in preference for further consideration and consultation. Aside from extending the already considerable delays in providing much needed clarity on the UK position, the experience adds to an impression of legislative and policy stasis, particularly alongside the high level of EU activity. It therefore seems that if the UK does indeed achieve its 'smarter regulation' objective of decreased reliance on regulation, it will do so more by default than considered IP policy; and that the post-Brexit UK landscape in IP is at risk of being marked less by enhanced regulatory agility and proportionality than by limited regulatory vision and capacity, and, in an irony for those who supported Brexit to enhance UK democracy,[121] an inability or unwillingness to weather the controversy which IP legislative proposals have come to generate. At a time of widespread disruption to IP and industry caused by AI and other emerging technologies, the implications for society are significant.[122]

[119] See, eg, (nn 60–70) and accompanying text.

[120] See, eg, its consultations and surveys on AI and IP (7 September 2020, 29 October 2021, 17 December 2024), industrial designs (7 January 2022, 25 February 2025, 4 September 2025), standard essential patents (7 December 2021, 15 July 2025), and the implementation of the Beijing Treaty on Audiovisual Performances (23 April 2021, 14 September 2023).

[121] These include both positive concerns to see the UK 'take back control' of its law-making and negative concerns regarding the impact on UK law of the EU's so-called democratic deficit. On the latter see A Arnull, 'The Principle of Effective Judicial Protection in EU Law: An Unruly Horse?' (2011) 36 ELRev 51. For a sceptical, post-Brexit perspective see S Malinov, 'The Democratic Deficit of the EU: Breaking the Spell of a False Analogy' (2022) 20 European View 226.

[122] For a list of IP-intensive industries see IPO, 'Use of Intellectual Property Rights across UK industries', https://www.gov.uk/government/publications/use-of-intellectual-property-rights-across-uk-industries/use-of-intellectual-property-rights-across-uk-industries#conclusion.

PART III
THE SOCIAL

17
Citizens' Rights

Catherine Barnard and Fiona Costello

1 Introduction

Maria, exercising her EU free movement rights, came to the East of England[1] from Portugal in 2004. She moved straight into rented accommodation provided by the (informal) work agents who helped her move. The following day she started work in a poultry factory, at first as an agency worker, but in time she secured more permanent employment when she was directly employed by the factory. She subsequently moved out of the accommodation provided by the agency into another privately rented flat. Maria met her husband (also Portuguese) working in a chicken factory. She started learning English (and Lithuanian from the factory floor) after moving to the UK. Learning English eventually enabled her to leave the factory and find shop work. When her husband lost his job, he claimed Universal Credit (UC) as a qualified EU worker. In time, Maria had a child and was able to access free NHS care: proof of her EU citizenship sufficed to access these services. She was also eligible to claim Statutory Maternity Pay given her work history in the UK. In 2020 Maria, her husband, and their child successfully applied for EU settled status (SS) under the EU Settlement Scheme (EUSS), established as part of the Brexit arrangements under the Withdrawal Agreement. This means she can continue to enjoy these rights. Maria's siblings also now live in the UK, as does her husband's family, including his siblings and mother. Using their EU free movement rights, three generations of the same family all now live permanently in the UK. They visit Portugal only for holidays and family occasions.

If Maria wanted to move to the UK post-Brexit, her options would be much more limited. She would need to move under the UK's broader immigration law framework, which has no special carveout for EU/EEA nationals. In fact, there would be no route for her to move to work on a permanent basis in a chicken factory. She could come on a short-term poultry worker visa covering 2 October to 31 December in the same year. For this she would need to find a sponsor and meet the eligibility

[1] This case study is drawn from workers we interviewed in C Barnard and others, *Low-Paid EU Migrant Workers, the House, the Street, the Town* (Bristol University Press 2024), with some details changed for anonymity.

Catherine Barnard and Fiona Costello, *Citizens' Rights* In: *The UK Regulatory Framework Post-Brexit: 'Law Unbound'*.
Edited by: Paul Craig and Vilija Vėlyvytė, Oxford University Press. © Oxford University Press 2026.
DOI: 10.1093/9780198969815.003.0020

requirements. She would also need to pay a £319 application fee and have at least £1,270 in her bank for a minimum of twenty-eight days. Day 28 must be within thirty-one days of applying for this visa. She would need to prove her right to rent to her landlord, sharing the relevant immigration visa proof as required. The prospect of only three months' work weighed against the costs of coming to the UK would make this option less appealing for Maria. It is, perhaps, more likely that she would look to move to an EU member state, where her free movement rights are still available.

Maria's case highlights the stark contrast between the free movement rights enjoyed by EU citizens and the situation now the UK is no longer an EU member state. Free movement, the most vexed issue in the Brexit debate, has been stopped.

For those (EU citizens) already in the UK at the time of Brexit, Brexit represented a fundamental rupture in their lives.[2] Prior to Brexit, they could prove their residency rights simply by showing an EU passport or ID card, as Maria's case shows. No other paperwork or visa-related information was needed. Post-Brexit, all EU nationals (and their family members, and some others) resident in the UK before December 2020 had to apply under the EUSS to continue that lawful residence. They must now also provide a 'share code' to various actors (DWP, landlords, employers, and others) each time they need to prove their right to work, to rent, and so on in the UK. The administrative burden of applying for and managing this new status, for some, has been immense.[3]

This chapter analyses rights for EU nationals living in the UK, both pre- and post-Brexit. We will argue that the EUSS has maintained the vulnerabilities EU citizens were experiencing before Brexit in UK domestic law, namely that to benefit fully from their free movement rights and enjoy equal access to social assistance individuals had to be 'exercising their Treaty rights'. This requirement has been encoded into the EUSS, which offers two statuses: Pre-Settled Status (PSS) and Settled Status (SS). SS gives its holders an automatic 'right to reside' for the purpose of welfare benefits and other public funds. By contrast, those with only PSS do not get an automatic 'right to reside'; this group must show an additional right (i.e. they are exercising a Treaty right as a worker or self-employed person) to access public funds (such as social welfare, social housing, and the like).

In this chapter we will set out the pre-Brexit situation for EU citizens in the UK (section 2). We will then consider the post-Brexit framework (section 3) and how this is working in practice, including discussing ongoing issues with the implementation of the Withdrawal Agreement (section 4). We will also include empirical insights

[2] This chapter focuses on EU citizens in the UK. UK citizens in the EU also faced similar challenges (not outlined here in any detail); for more on this please see:< https://www.britishineurope.org/page/1016442-home>.

[3] M Sumption and M Fernández-Reino, 'Unsettled Status—2020: Which EU Citizens Are at Risk of Failing to Secure their Rights after Brexit?' (2020), published by The Migration Observatory. Available at https://migrationobservatory.ox.ac.uk/resources/reports/unsettled-status-2020/>.

from EU citizens living in the UK.[4] This will help to bring to life the experiences of those navigating the post-Brexit arrangements—particularly those more vulnerable. Our work will show that for many in this group (particularly those with PSS) their situation has not changed because the UK has carried over the pre-Brexit rules and application of rights. For those with settled status Brexit has, perhaps, made life more straightforward in respect of access to social assistance with an automatic right to reside. But, paradoxically, the more secure status has not convinced all SS holders, many of whom have been motivated to become British citizens (and who, our research shows, otherwise may not have undertaken the process[5]). Section 5 concludes.

2 Pre-Brexit Regulation

(a) Citizens' Rights

The status of EU citizenship was formally introduced by the Maastricht Treaty in 1992.[6] Under Article 20(1) of the Treaty on the Functioning of the European Union (TFEU), all nationals of EU member states are citizens of the EU. This citizenship is additional to (and does not replace) their national citizenship.[7] Article 20(2) TFEU lists the rights enjoyed by EU citizens. These include free movement and residence rights as well as political rights, such as the right to vote and stand as candidates in the European Parliament and municipal elections, to enjoy diplomatic protection of any member state in the territory of a third county, and to petition the European Parliament and apply to the European Ombudsman.[8] The details of those citizens' rights to free movement are fleshed out in the Citizens' Rights Directive 2004/38.[9] Free movement of workers and the self-employed, that is, those considered economically active, had already been permitted by the Treaty of Rome.[10] The Treaty of Maastricht extended this right, in Article 21 TFEU, to all nationals of the member states, including those who were economically inactive, subject to certain conditions, providing a basis for these rights in primary law.

[4] These insights are drawn from our earlier empirical work, funded by the ESRC. For more see Barnard and others (n 1).

[5] C Barnard, S Fraser Butlin, and F Costello, 'The Changing Status of European Union Nationals in the United Kingdom following Brexit: The Lived Experience of the European Union Settlement Scheme' (2021) Social & Legal Studies 365.

[6] However Barnard and Leinarte argue that 'the notion of European citizenship was not, as commonly thought, an idea developed by the Spanish government at Maastricht, but was in fact born at the same time as the initiatives to create a European Union (as opposed to the European Community) in the early 1970s'; for more, C Barnard and E Leinarte, 'The Creation of European Citizenship: Constitutional Miracle or Myopia?' (2022) 24 CYELS 24, 25.

[7] Art 20(1) TFEU.

[8] See further Case C-181/23 *Commission v Malta* EU:C:2025:283.

[9] [2004] OJ L158/77.

[10] Treaty of Rome: http://data.europa.eu/eli/treaty/teec/sign.

Article 21 TFEU says that every citizen of the Union shall 'have the right to move and reside freely within the territory of the member states, subject to the limitations and conditions laid down in the Treaties and by the measures adopted to give them effect'. The CJEU has recognized the direct effect of Article 21,[11] as a 'primary right'[12] to be interpreted broadly[13] and subject to the principle of proportionality.[14] In *Grzelczyk* the Court said—and has since repeated numerous times[15]—that EU citizenship was destined to be a fundamental status of the nationals of member states.[16] The Treaty provisions on EU citizenship are to be read in combination with Article 18 TFEU which prohibits any discrimination on grounds of nationality. Nic Shibhne neatly describes the 'Russian doll format' of how the various objectives of the EU fit together, with the 'internal market a central objective of the Union; free movement a central objective of the internal market; and non-discrimination a central objective of free movement'.[17]

(b) Free Movement: When, How Long, and Who?

EU citizens can rely on their free movement rights stemming from a number of different sources; for example, under Article 45 TFEU on the free movement of workers, Article 49 TFEU on freedom of establishment, and Article 21 TFEU on free movement of citizens (as outlined above), as well as secondary law protections such the Workers Regulation 492/11 and the Citizen's Rights Directive (CRD) 2004/38/EC.

The CRD gives every EU citizen the right to reside in another member state for an initial period of three months, with no conditions on their stay other than not being a burden on the social assistance scheme of the host state. The right to reside for more than three months is subject to certain conditions listed in Article 7 CRD as a worker or self-employed,[18] or as a student or a person of independent means (PIMs), the latter two groups being subject to the additional requirement of having comprehensive sickness insurance and sufficient resources. The CRD also gives rights to third country nationals to join their EU citizen family member (Section 3(c) below).[19] Article 45 TFEU and Regulation 492/11 give EU workers[20]/

[11] Case C-413/99 *Baumbast* EU:C:2002:493, [84]

[12] AG La Pergola in Case C-85/96 *Martinez Sala v Freistaat Bayern* EU:C:1998:217, [18].

[13] Cases C-523/11 and C-585/11 *Prinz and Seeberger* EU:C:2013:524, [25]

[14] Case C-200/02 *Zhu and Chen* EU:C:2004:639, [32]; Case C-408/03 *Commission v Belgium* EU:C:2006:192, [39]; Case C-162/09 *Lassal* [EU:C:2010:592, [29-31]; Case C-140/12 *Brey* EU:C:2013:565, [70].

[15] See the citations in Case C-181/23 *Commission v Malta* EU:C:2025:283, [43], [49], [92].

[16] Case C-184/99 *Grzelczyk* EU:C:2001:458, [31].

[17] N Nic Shuibhne, *The Coherence of EU Free Movement Law: Constitutional Responsibility and the Court of Justice* (Oxford University Press, 2013) 108–09.

[18] Article 7 CRD.

[19] Articles 2 and 3 CRD.

[20] Case 66/85 *Lawrie-Blum* EU:C:1986:284; Case 53/81 *Levin v Staatssecretaris van Justitie* EU:C:1982:105; Case 139/85 *Kempf* EU:C:1986:223.

jobseekers[21] rights to access,[22] look for, and take up employment in another member state; and to equal treatment in access to that employment, in conditions of employment[23] and in all other social and tax advantages[24] and vocational training.[25] It also provides for the right to stay there even after that employment has ended.[26] Within the framework of free movement, the most protected group are those who are in work, as their status as a 'worker' means they are entitled to equal treatment, including, for example, access to social assistance if needed. Economically inactive citizens who exercise their free movement rights, on the other hand, need to ensure they do not become a burden on the member state to which they have moved. It is to this issue that we turn next.

(c) Limitations and Qualifications

One important hallmark of life after Brexit for those with EU PSS (see section 4 below) is the legacy of the conditionality of their rights, particularly in accessing welfare benefits and housing assistance. In the following, we set out the pre-Brexit situation and the origins of this conditionality in EU law. As we saw above, Article 21 TFEU allows EU citizens the right to move and reside freely 'subject to the limitations and conditions laid down in the Treaties and by the measures adopted to give them effect'.

The tension between the fundamental aims of the internal market and the national measures adopted to give them effect has come before the European Court of Justice (CJEU) in several important cases in which the Court has played a central role in shaping the boundaries of these rights, particularly for economically inactive EU citizens. Under Directive 2004/38/EC, economically inactive citizens—such as students or persons of independent means—must demonstrate sufficient resources and comprehensive sickness insurance in order to stay beyond the initial three months in a host member state.

O'Brien says that 'Citizenship has come to define to whom we owe the greatest duty of social justice, and welfare the most important mechanism by which it is met'.[27] So how has the Court responded to that challenge. Its approach has evolved over time from initially a more expansive view to one of conditionality. In the expansionist period the Court adopted a rights-based approach to citizenship, focusing on the rights

[21] Case C-292/89 *R v Immigration Appeal Tribunal, ex p Antonissen* EU:C:1991:80; see also Art 14(2)(b) CRD.

[22] Case C-415/93 *Bosman* EU:C:1995:463.

[23] Art 7(1) of Regulation 492/2011; Cases C-259, 331 and 332/91 *Allué and Coonan v Universa degli studi di Venezia* EU:C:1993:333.

[24] Art 7(2) of Regulation 492/2011; Case 207/78 *Criminal Proceedings against Even* EU:C:1979:144.

[25] Art 7(3) of Regulation 492/2011.

[26] Art 45 TFEU. Limitations of these rights can only be justified on the grounds of public policy, public security, or public health (Art 45(3)). These exceptions are narrowly defined: Case 152/73 *Sotgiu v Deutche Bundespost* EU:C:1974:13.

[27] C O'Brien, *Unity in Diversity: EU Citizenship, Social Justice and the Cautionary Tale of the UK* (Hart 2017) 9.

and narrowing the scope of the limitations. This can be seen in the seminal cases such as *Grzelczyk*[28] (a student entitled to receive a minimum subsistence allowance on the same terms as nationals of the member state), *Bidar*[29](rights of a student who demonstrated a certain degree of integration in the host state to access a subsided loan after five years' residence), and *Collins*[30] (rights of a jobseeker with a 'genuine link' to the labour market of host state). These cases rely on integration into the host member state as the relevant criteria to access social benefits.

However, since the 2010s the Court has taken a more restrictive and cautious stance,[31] particularly in cases involving short-term residence and/or the perception of 'welfare tourism'. Perhaps best known is *Dano*,[32] where the Court said that, in the absence of satisfying the conditions of residence under Article 7(1)(b) CRD, economically inactive citizens were not entitled to equal treatment in respect of non-contributory social assistance. O'Brien says that '*Dano* sees the Court using a sledgehammer to crack an already cracked nut'.[33] The 'cracked nut' she refers to is welfare tourism, about which she explains that it 'was already widely accepted that the EU does not provide a mechanism for benefit tourism, or a right to reside "solely" for the purposes of claiming another state's social assistance'.[34] Nevertheless, in *Dano* the Court said:

> A Member State must therefore have the possibility, pursuant to Article 7 of Directive 2004/38, of refusing to grant social benefits to economically inactive Union citizens who exercise their right to freedom of movement solely in order to obtain another Member State's social assistance although they do not have sufficient resources to claim a right of residence.[35]

In *Brey* the Court had suggested that an individualized assessment had to be undertaken before refusal is made, reasserting the principle of proportionality. However, in *Dano* it accepted that individualized assessments were not necessary, a position confirmed in *Alimanovic*[36] (and others[37]), where the Court confirmed that that the member state could refuse grants of social assistance to economically inactive

[28] Case C-184/99 *Rudy Grzelczyk v Centre public d'aide sociale d'Ottignies-Louvain-la-Neuve* EU:C:2001:458.

[29] Case C-209/03 *The Queen, on the application of Dany Bidar v London Borough of Ealing and Secretary of State for Education and Skills* EU:C:2005:169.

[30] Case C-138/02 *Collins v Secretary of State for Work and Pensions* EU:C:2004:172.

[31] Case C-140/12 *Pensionsversicherungsanstalt v Peter Brey* EU:C:2013:565; Case C-333/13 *Dano v Jobcenter Leipzig* EU:C:2014:2358; Case C-67/14 *Jobcenter Berlin Neukölln v Alimanovic* EU:C:2015:597; I Shutes and S Walker, 'Gender and Free Movement: EU Migrant Women's Access to Residence and Social Rights in the UK' (2018) 44 Journal of Ethnic and Migration Studies 137, 137.

[32] Case C-333/13 *Dano* (n 31).

[33] O'Brien (n 27) 49.

[34] ibid.

[35] Case C-333/13 *Dano* (n 31) [78].

[36] Case C-67/14 *Alimanovic* (n 31).

[37] Case C-299/14 *García-Nieto* EU:C:2016:114.

individuals during the first three months. However, this now needs to be read in the light of *CG*,[38] a case involving access to Universal Credit (a non-contributory welfare benefit in the UK), where the CJEU said that the relevant authority had to satisfy itself that the refusal would not expose the claimant to an actual and current risk of violation of their rights under the EU Charter of Fundamental Rights (Section 4(b)) and the ability to live in 'dignified conditions'. In *Dano* the Court of Justice asserted that it did not have jurisdiction to answer the national authority's question about the Charter, as EU law was not engaged in the exercise of member states laying down the conditions for the grant of special non-contributory cash benefits.[39]

The shift in the Court's jurisprudence towards protecting host state interests can also be seen in *Commission v UK* concerning a potential breach of Regulation 883/2004 (coordination of social security systems).[40] The Commission argued that the 'right to reside' test (ie that the individual had to be exercising a Treaty right, eg as a worker under Article 45 TFEU),[41] introduced as supplementary to the habitual residency test which all people, including British nationals, needed to pass to access social security benefits in the UK, was indirectly discriminatory, placing an additional burden of proof on non-UK nationals. The CJEU found the test to be justified[42] and more than a decade later the right to reside test, as an additional test which forms part of the habitual residency test, continues to have great significance in the post-Brexit regulation and EU citizens' access to welfare benefits in the UK—an issue to which we will return in section 4.

In sum, the developing case law in the context of economically inactive citizens is complex, but the Court has consistently affirmed the right of member states to limit/refuse social assistance to economically inactive citizens. Where, however, the benefit is a 'social advantage', it can be paid to a migrant worker, including work seekers, on the same terms as nationals, unless there are objectively justified reasons why not.[43] Yet the general thrust of the recent case law is about defending 'the legitimate interests of Member States and the protection of public finances'[44] given the fear that unrestricted access (to host state social assistance) might 'lead to welfare migration and thus . . . be a fundamental challenge to the welfare state'.[45]

[38] C-709/20 *CG v Department for Communities in Northern Ireland* EU:C:2021:602.

[39] H Verschueren, 'Preventing 'Benefit Tourism' in the EU: A Narrow or Broad Interpretation of the Possibilities Offered by the ECJ in Dano?' (2015) 52 CMLRev 363, 387.

[40] Case C-308/14 *Commission v UK* EU:C:2016:436.

[41] Introduced by the Social Security (Persons from Abroad) Regulations (2006).

[42] Case C-308/14 *European Commission v United Kingdom of Great Britain and Northern Ireland* EU:C:2016:436. The Supreme Court in the UK had found the test to be indirectly discriminatory on the grounds of nationality in 2011, but that the discrimination was justified as a proportionate response to the legitimate aim of protecting the public purse: *Patmalniece (FC) v Secretary of State for Work and Pensions* [2011] UKSC 11. For more see: Research Briefing (2011): <https://researchbriefings.files.parliament.uk/documents/SN05972/SN05972.pdf>.

[43] Case C-731/21 *GV v Caisse nationale d'assurance pension* EU:C:2022:969.

[44] ibid [48].

[45] D Sindbjerg Martinsen, G Pons Rotger, and J Sampson Thierry, 'Free Movement of People and Cross-border Welfare in the European Union: Dynamic Rules, Limited Outcomes' (2019) 29(1) Journal of European Social Policy 84, 84.

However, research shows that there is no strong evidence for the 'welfare magnet hypothesis'. For example, Giulietti says 'empirical evidence suggests that immigration decisions are not made on the basis of the relative generosity of the receiving nation's social benefits'.[46] Our own work also shows little evidence of 'welfare tourism'. In fact, the precarity faced by many workers in their day-to-day working arrangements (in the poultry factories in and around Great Yarmouth) often puts welfare benefits out of reach because they cannot show habitual residency.[47] EU free movement has been accompanied by a 'more restrictive approach to EU migrants' entitlement to social benefits [that] has been evident . . . through the application of the conditions for residence rights'.[48] While the UK was not the only proponent in the EU to use restrictive measures,[49] it was one of the most proactive in implementing rights restrictions and conditionalities, particularly for economically inactive citizens, as the addition of the 'right to reside' test above shows.[50] In November 2014, the then Prime Minister David Cameron gave his famous 'EU speech'. He outlined the changes his government had already made to EU citizens' access to welfare benefits in the UK. He lamented the 'indefensible system where the State—our taxpayers—paid EU jobseekers to look for work indefinitely and even paid their rent while they did so', costing the British taxpayer £600 a month per jobseeker. He noted the changes: 'we've scrapped housing benefit for EU jobseekers. And we have limited benefits claims to three months for those EU migrants who have no prospect of a job. But now we are going to go further. We are overhauling our welfare system with a new benefit called Universal Credit', which EU jobseekers would not be able to claim. He added that if an EU jobseeker has not found work within six months, they will be required to leave.[51]

These tensions around EU citizens' access to welfare benefits and other social advantages on equal terms with nationals are still not resolved. Barnard and Leinarte argue that the practical implications of citizenship, such as 'how to manage immigration flows or the infrastructure changes needed in the host state to accommodate a significant number of arrivals of EU citizens (in particular in respect of housing and social welfare benefits)',[52] were left unaddressed for too long. They say that by the time the CJEU recognized these issues, it was too late for the UK. By then, the UK had already voted to leave the EU in the EU Referendum that Prime Minister Cameron had

[46] C Giulietti, 'The Welfare Magnet Hypothesis and the Welfare Take-up of Migrants' (2014) IZA World of Labor, 37; see also A Gago, 'All of the Same Type? The Use of Fears of "Welfare Tourism" to Limit the Access of EU Migrants to Social Benefits in the UK and Germany', in M Pomati, A Jolly, and J Rees (eds), *Social Policy Review 33 Analysis and Debate in Social Policy, 2021* (Bristol Policy Press 2021) <https://doi.org/10.51952/9781447359739.ch010>; SA Mantu and PE Minderhoud, 'Exploring the Limits of Social Solidarity. Welfare Tourism and EU Citizenship' (2016) 2 EU Law Journal 4 < http://dx.doi.org/10.21814/unio.2.2>.

[47] Barnard and others (n 1) Ch 6, 136–65.

[48] Shutes and Walker (n 31) 137.

[49] Gago (n 46) 203–22.

[50] The UK had some of the highest levels of internal free movement of EU citizens to the UK when it was a MS, with EUSS data showing more than 6 million EU citizens moved to the UK.

[51] Full text available at https://www.bbc.co.uk/news/uk-politics-30250299.

[52] Barnard and Leinarte (n 6) 26.

promised to deliver should his party be elected in the 2015 general election. It is to the consequences of this Referendum and the UK's exit from the EU ('Brexit') that we now turn.

3 Post-Brexit Regulation

(a) The Withdrawal Agreement

The UK voted to leave the EU by a narrow margin (52:48) in a referendum held in June 2016. A period of negotiation took place between the UK and the EU which culminated in two main international agreements: the Withdrawal Agreement (WA) and the Trade and Cooperation Agreement (TCA). The rights of EU nationals and others resident in the UK as of 1 January 2021 are guaranteed by three agreements: Part Two of the UK–EU Withdrawal Agreement, the EEA EFTA Separation Agreement, and the Swiss Citizens' Rights Agreement. These were implemented into UK law via the EU (Withdrawal Agreement) Act 2020. Under the terms of these agreements, the rights not only protect EU, EEA, and Swiss nationals together with their family members, but also extend to UK citizens resident in the EU, Norway, Iceland, Liechtenstein, and Switzerland. We shall focus on the rules which apply in the UK.

The WA gives indefinite leave to remain (ILR) to anyone who has resided legally in the UK in accordance with EU law for a continuous period of five years (this is called 'settled status' (SS)). Those who have resided in the host state for less than five years have the right to acquire ILR once they have completed five years of residency; before that, they can acquire limited leave to remain—known as 'pre-settled status' (PSS). As noted above, the UK required proof of continuous residence to acquire PSS or SS; applicants did not need to show, as they would if they were applying for UC, that they were exercising a Treaty right, for example working, being self-employed, studying, having independent means, or being a jobseeker.[53] The rights apply to EU (and EEA and Swiss) citizens who moved to the UK before the end of the transition period—31 December 2020—as well as to their non-EU family members (NEFM) and any children born to, or legally adopted by, those covered by the WA. Those with settled or PSS can be joined in the future by certain family members who have not gained settled status or PSS in their own right (section 3(c) below).

Article 27 of the WA preserves recognition of professional qualifications which people were using before the end of the transition period. Social security rights are also preserved (Article 30 WA). This means, for example, that periods of insurance, employment, or residence completed under the legislation of one member state are considered, when necessary, for the entitlement to a benefit under the legislation of

[53] However, whether or not this was intended to bestow additional rights was the subject ongoing litigation—see section 4.2.

another member state. The WA also lays out procedures for issuing residence documents (Article 18), with the aim of ensuring the process is not unnecessarily burdensome for applicants. As noted above, in the UK this scheme is the EU Settlement Scheme (EUSS). In the next section we will examine the application process and status outcomes for those navigating EUSS.

(b) The EU Settlement Scheme

To implement the rights set out in the Withdrawal (and other) Agreements the UK introduced the EUSS. Launched in March 2019, the deadline for 'in time' applications was 30 June 2021. Applications after this date were and continue to be permissible, but applicants need to demonstrate 'reasonable grounds' as to why they missed the 'in time' application window. From August 2023, the Home Office introduced a two-stage process for late applications, first deciding whether they accept the reasonable grounds provided for a late application and, if so, only then treating the application as valid. This change has important implications for applicants: they do not receive a 'certificate of application (CoA)' until after the Home Office accepts the reasonable grounds provided. Previously, applicants could use their CoA as proof of their right to rent, work, and so on prior to a final decision. This was good for applicants entitled to claim but was misused by those who were not. The latter started renting and working without any prospect of having a longer-term legal right to do so. Now, this additional step before receiving a CoA can mean delays for genuine applicants in being able to prove their rights.[54] But will not mislead those who are not. Another implication of this change is that if the Home Office finds the grounds provided are not reasonable, it will *reject* rather than refuse the application. Rejection removes the possibility of appeal for applicants.

By 31 March 2025, 8.5 million applications had been made, of which 50 per cent (4.1 million) were granted settled status, 35 per cent (2.9 million) were granted PSS, and 15 per cent had other outcomes.[55] The application is made entirely online via an app;[56] their status is also digital-only, something the UK negotiators pushed for.[57] The UK Home Office saw EUSS as a flagship programme for rolling out a digital future for all immigration status matters, such as those who hold BRPs (biometric residence permits), passport endorsements (such as ILR stamps), and vignette stickers in passports—more than three million people to date have needed to switch to an 'E-visa'.[58] Some have argued that digital-only status is indirectly discriminatory because

[54] For more on the decision backlog: https://the3million.org.uk/clear-eu-settlement-scheme-backlog.

[55] For more: https://www.gov.uk/government/statistics/immigration-system-statistics-year-ending-march-2025/how-many-grants-of-settlement-are-made-via-the-eu-settlement-scheme#settled-status.

[56] Although in limited circumstances a paper application route was available.

[57] J Tomlinson, J Maxwell, and A Welsh, 'Discrimination in Digital Immigration Status' (2021) Legal Studies 315.

[58] C Barnard and F Costello, 'eVisas: What, Why and When?' (December 2024), UK in a Changing Europe, https://ukandeu.ac.uk/evisas-what-why-and-when/.

it 'disadvantages various groups with protected characteristics—namely disability, age and race',[59] risking a 'digital Windrush'. Our own work,[60] and that of others,[61] has also shown the difficulties experienced by those more marginalized or vulnerable in navigating a digital-only application process and status. The campaigning organization The 3 Million[62] (ultimately unsuccessfully) campaigned for physical proof of status.

There have also been difficulties not only for status holders but also for those interacting with the scheme such as landlords and employers (and others). Some have argued that right to rent checks may lead to discrimination from landlords who may be less likely to rent to those for whom they need to undertake an immigration-checking process.[63] This reluctance may be exacerbated by the digital-only format of the immigration status, particularly for those landlords without relevant digital skills themselves—of which our research identified a number.[64] Take for example one European landlord, living in Great Yarmouth:

> A Dutch citizen, he had lived in the UK for forty-seven years and owns and rents out several properties in the town. He presented at an advice service, GYROS (the advice service in Great Yarmouth with which we have been working) with his old Nokia 3210 phone and said he was unable to use a computer. While GYROS could support him to make an application, in practical terms the status is totally unusable for him, with digital literacy issues and lacking access to a digital phone/laptop. He also faces significant barriers in undertaking right to rent checks for his tenants, many of them also EU citizens.[65]

However, our research in the town of Great Yarmouth, Norfolk also identified multiple examples of bad/unlawful practice, where landlords were not undertaking any right to rent checks and not providing their tenants with tenancy agreements or receipts for their rent. Great Yarmouth is a significantly deprived coastal town with poor standards of accommodation available, with many HMOs (houses of multiple occupation) which had previously been hotel accommodation but had fallen into disuse after tourist numbers to the town began to diminish.[66] The House in the title of our monograph *Low-Paid EU Migrant Workers: The House, the Street, the Town* was a good example of this. None of the eight residents of the HMO had any paperwork to prove their residency in the house nor any proof of payment of rent. Their bills were included in their rent. This meant they had no way of proving their tenancy, which

[59] Tomlinson, Maxwell, and Welsh (n 57) 316.
[60] Barnard, Fraser Butlin, and Costello (n 5).
[61] Sumption and Fernández-Reino (n 3).
[62] https://the3million.org.uk/.
[63] JCWI, 'Passport Please: The Impact of the Right to Rent Checks on Migrants and Ethnic Minorities in England' (February 2017), https://jcwi.org.uk/reportsbriefings/passport-please-2017/.
[64] Barnard and others (n 1) Ch 5.
[65] For more see Barnard and Costello, 'EUSS: Beyond the Cliff's Edge' (August 2021), UK in a Changing Europe, < https://ukandeu.ac.uk/euss-beyond-the-cliffs-edge/>.
[66] Barnard and others (n 1) Ch 5.

was crucial for applications to the EUSS. This meant some had to accept the less secure PS rather than SS, despite their long residency.

Although residency rights and their associated EUSS protections can last a lifetime, they may be lost if a person is absent from the UK for an extended period—more than five consecutive years for holders of SS, or more than two years for those with PSS (more below). These rules are more generous than those under EU law, where rights are lost after just two years of absence.

(c) Family Members of EU Citizens Post-Brexit

EU citizens' rights to free movement also include a right for their family members (including NEFMs) to accompany them.[67] Family members have the right to reside, to work, to study, and to receive benefits in the host member state.[68] Should family members not have such rights, the prospect of moving between member states to take up work might be less appealing/practical for EU free movers and therefore present a barrier to free movement. Reflecting the CRD provisions outlined above, family members include:

- spouse, civil partner, or unmarried partner (unmarried partners must be able to provide evidence of a long-term relationship before 31 December 2020, usually by demonstrating that they have been living together for more than two years);
- child or grandchild aged under 21;
- dependent child or grandchild of any age;
- dependent parent or grandparent.

The definition also extends to other family members, such as a durable partner (ie those who are not married but in a 'durable' relationship) and other dependent relatives for whom the member state may have a duty to facilitate entry and residence.[69] NEFMs therefore 'derive' their rights from their EU citizen family members who are exercising their Treaty Rights. This dependency can mean that 'this category of individuals is precarious as their rights depend entirely on their EU family member(s)'.[70]

Post-Brexit these groups (plus EEA EFTA nationals and Swiss nationals) all needed to make applications to the EUSS, either in their own right as an EU citizen or (if a third country national) as a family member of an EU citizen.

Those with settled or PSS can be joined in the future by certain family members who have not gained settled status or PSS in their own right. In the UK, this application is

[67] CRD Arts 4, 5, 7, 16, 23, and 24.

[68] CRD Art 23.

[69] CRD 3(2); Case C-1/05 *Yunying Jia v Migrationsverket* EU:C:2007:1; Case C-423/12 *Flora May Reyes v Migrationsverket* EU:C:2013:719.

[70] A Yong, 'A Gendered EU Settlement Scheme: Intersectional Oppression of Immigrant Women in a Post-Brexit Britain' (2022) 32(5) Social & Legal Studies, 756, 766.

made via the EU Settlement Scheme Family Permit Route.[71] A joining family member can apply with a valid passport and must be able to provide evidence of their relationship and that the relationship existed prior to December 2020.

Joining family members need to apply to the EUSS within three months of arriving in the UK.

As mentioned above, NEFMs may derive their rights from their EU citizen or British national family member. The different categories of derived right holders are known by the case names of CJEU decisions which gave the rights in the first place (Table 17.1).[72]

Table 17.1 Derived Rights Holders

'Zambrano' Carer	Primary carer of a British national child
'Surinder Singh' applications/'Lounes' applications	Family members of British citizens
'Chen' carers	The primary carer of a 'self-sufficient' EEA national child
'Ibrahim/Teixeira' cases	Child of an EEA national worker/former worker where that child is in education in the UK and the primary carer of the child

Those with a derived right to reside (Table 17.1) needed to apply to the EUSS via a paper application route, a more narrow and time-consuming application route which was available only in limited circumstances. According to the Home Office, paper application forms may be submitted by applicants who:

- are applying on the basis of a 'derivative' right to reside:
- do not hold a valid identity document and are unable to obtain one;
- are unable to apply using the online application form and cannot be supported to do so.

Those who need to make a paper application need to contact the Resolution Centre and ask for the application form; it cannot be automatically requested. Once this is received in the post, applicants can then complete and return it with relevant accompanying documents to prove residency and so on. This lengthier process can be compared to the online application route, for which Home Office marketing used an analogy of making a cup of tea to show how quick and simple it was to complete the online application process.[73]

[71] For more: https://www.gov.uk/family-permit.

[72] Case C-34/09 *Zambrano* EU:C:2011:124; Case C-370/90 *Surinder Singh* EU:C:1992:296; Case C-200/02 *Chen* EU:C:2004:639; Case C-310/08 *Ibrahim* EU:C:2010:80; Case C-480/08 *Teixeira* EU:C:2009:642.

[73] Barnard and Costello, 'EUSS, a Tale of Two Citizens' (December 2020), UKICE blog series, https://ukandeu.ac.uk/eu-settled-status-a-tale-of-two-citizens/.

The Home Office collects and reports on the outcomes of these applications under the various routes and Table 17.2 shows the outcomes across an almost five-year period showing, in total, more than 34,000 applications under these routes, with a further 760,000 non-EEA applications to the wider EUSS to date, showing the scale of non-EU family member applications to the scheme as a whole.[74]

Table 17.2 EUSS Statistics data, 28 August 2018 to 31 March 2025 (based on analysis by authors)

Applications	Chen	Family member of a British citizen	Ibrahim/ Teixeira	Zambrano
Application received	**2588**	**15,968**	**544**	**15,514**
Applications concluded	96%	97%	93%	98%
of which are Settled	29%	40%	41%	10%
of which are Pre-settled	42%	46%	21%	6%
of which are Refused	21%	7%	26%	77%
of which are Withdrawn or Void	3%	2%	3%	3%
of which are Invalid	2%	2%	3%	2%

Not all applications are successful. Most striking from the data above is the high levels of refusal of 'Zambrano' carers under the EUSS—more than 77 per cent of these applications are refused. In fact, the Zambrano carer route was subject to litigation in the UK,[75] which ultimately resulted in the Home Office updating its guidance to deem it lawful to refuse status under the EUSS if an individual already held another form of leave to remain, such as under Appendix FM.[76] Solanke has outlined the ongoing process of various British governments undermining the rights of Zambrano carers in the UK: 'the erosion of protection given in EU law began long before Brexit and the EU Referendum';[77] outlining among others the 'Zambrano amendments' which excluded Zambrano carers from access to mainstream benefits. This, she says, condemned families and British/European children to destitution in the UK.[78] The restrictive application of the provisions of the EUSS meant that most Zambrano carers were excluded from leave under Appendix EU and instead fall under Appendix FM, which requires ongoing renewal (subject to fees) as well as payment of the Immigration Health

[74] For more: https://www.gov.uk/government/statistical-data-sets/immigration-system-statistics-data-tables#eu-settlement-scheme.
[75] *SSHD v Akinsanya* [2022] EWCA Civ 37.
[76] EU Settlement Scheme: Zambrano Primary Carers, https://www. gov.uk/government/publications/eu-settlement-scheme-zambrano-primary-carers/eu-settlementscheme-zambrano-primary-carers.
[77] I Solanke, 'The Impact of Brexit on Black Women, Children and Citizenship' (2020) 58 JCMS 147, 148.
[78] ibid 151.

Surcharge, rather than a free application under the EUSS leading to ILR (a five-year route to settlement).

Yong argues that those making applications under these derived-rights routes are more likely to be marginalized women.[79] Our own empirical data supports this.[80] Following a number of Freedom of Information (FOI) requests to the Home Office, we were able to show that the majority of non-EU applications under the paper application route were women from (in order) Nigeria, Pakistan, Ghana, and India.[81] In fact, the gender breakdown of applications under the paper application route, which we obtained via FOI, is the only gender-related information available in the context of the EUSS as a whole. Our data makes clear that it is mostly women who were affected by the process of the more laborious and difficult paper application route as derived rights holders. As Yong concludes, 'the transitory regime of protection for EU citizens and their eligible family members of the EU Settlement Scheme entrenches the oppression of vulnerable women at the intersection of gender and immigration status under the law'.[82]

Having set out the initial context and process of the EUSS and who is eligible, in the next section we examine some of the (other) ongoing issues surrounding its application.

4 Post-Brexit Legality: Ongoing Issues

The responsibility for implementing Part Two of the WA on citizens' rights lies with the UK and each individual EU member state. In the UK, the Independent Monitoring Authority (IMA)[83] was established to oversee this implementation. UK courts can continue to hear relevant cases and, until 2028, refer matters to the CJEU. Any concerns regarding the WA's implementation can also be raised with the Joint Committee set up under the WA or the specialized committee on citizens' rights.

The implementation of the EUSS in the UK has been subject to several court decisions, including issues with the expiration of EUPS, access to welfare benefits for EUPS holders, and, more recently, the 'true cohort' of EU settled status holders in respect of housing (homeless) support.[84] In the following sections we will consider each

[79] Yong (n 70) 767.

[80] Barnard and Costello, 'EUSS: paper applications to a digital scheme', June 2021, for UKICE blog series, available: https://ukandeu.ac.uk/euss-paper-applications-to-a-digital-scheme/; Barnard and Costello, Paper applications to a digital scheme v2, February 2022, for the UKICE blog series, available here: https://ukandeu.ac.uk/paper-applications-to-a-digital-scheme/.

[81] https://ukandeu.ac.uk/euss-paper-applications-to-a-digital-scheme/

[82] Yong (n 70) 771.

[83] https://ima-citizensrights.org.uk/

[84] *Fertré v Vale of White Horse District Council* [2024] EWHC 1754 (KB), which concerns a decision by the local authority that Ms Fertre was not eligible for homelessness assistance based on her pre-settled status alone. Here the High Court ruled that a grant of status under the EU Settlement Scheme is a 'gateway status' giving the holder conditional rights only. In July 2025, the Court of Appeal upheld the High Court's ruling.

of these issues, as well as outlining the ongoing problems with late applications, the context of which was set out in section 3(b).

(a) EU Pre-Settled Status

(i) Expiration and Upgrade

The issue which has attracted the most litigation to date concerns the 'upgrading' of PS status (ie those who were only able to prove fewer than five years' continuous residence) to SS. Initially, it was thought that those who did not upgrade in time would become overstayers (ie they would lose their legal status), a particularly acute problem for those vulnerable workers in our research cohort. However, this was challenged through a judicial review initiated by the IMA.[85] The Divisional Court said that Article 13(4) WA provided lifelong protection for those granted residence rights in the UK under the WA. Once these rights were granted, they could not be revoked due to a failure to apply for further rights after the five-year period. Additionally, because Article 18 WA provides that individuals granted PS are entitled to permanent residence once they have fulfilled the five-year requirement, the High Court ruled that the EUSS was unlawful insofar as it denied the right to permanent residence for those with limited leave to remain (ie those with PSS).

In response to this decision, the Home Office first introduced a two-year extension for EUPS holders and later extended it to five years.[86] They also committed to automatically upgrading individuals to settled status where possible through automated checks, such as tax records. However, for many, the digital footprint required to prove their life in the UK is simply not being generated, as they may be in more informal work (cash in hand) or do not have formal rental agreements, as was the case with those in the house of our research. For more vulnerable individuals, this means they must still rely on available support to submit the necessary evidence to demonstrate their eligibility for SS.

(ii) EUPS and the 'Right to Reside' Test

The distinction between PSS and SS is important as each status has different rights attached to it, because one is a limited form of leave (PSS) and the other indefinite leave (SS). They also entail different approaches to the 'right to reside' test, for the purpose of claiming benefits, with SS granting an automatic right to reside, which PSS does not. PSS holders must prove an additional qualifying right to reside. These issues came to the fore in three cases before both EU and domestic courts: *Fratila*,[87] *CG*,[88]

[85] *R (Independent Monitoring Authority) v Secretary of State for the Home Department* [2022] EWHC 3274.

[86] For more: https://www.gov.uk/government/publications/eu-settlement-scheme-euss-status-automation/eu-settlement-scheme-euss-status-automation.

[87] *Fratila and another (AP) v Secretary of State for Work and Pensions* [2021] UKSC 53.

[88] Case C-709/20 *CG v Department for Communities in Northern Ireland* EU:C:2021:602.

and *AT*.[89] In all cases applicants had been refused access to UC as they held PSS and had no other 'qualifying' right to reside (ie they were not workers or self-employed). Both *CG* and *AT* concerned victims of domestic abuse; neither were in work and both had recently moved into a women's refuge for protection. In *CG*, a case whose facts arose before the end of the transition period, the Court of Justice found that before refusing social assistance benefits (UC), the relevant authority had to satisfy itself that the refusal would not expose the claimant to an actual and current risk of violation of their fundamental rights under the Charter of Fundamental Rights,[90] in particular Article 1 (human dignity), Article 7 (respect for private and family life), and Article 24(2) (rights of the child) of the Charter.

Similarly, in *AT* the First Tier Tribunal had said that without UC the claimant could not live in 'dignified conditions', therefore breaching her (and her child's) Charter rights. The Secretary for Work and Pensions (SSWP) appealed this decision on the basis that *CG* concerned those with PSS *before* the end of the transition period (December 2020), that the Charter only applied to member states when they were implementing EU law, and that this was not the case for the UK after the transition period. The Upper Tribunal held that *AT* could, nevertheless, rely on the EU Charter of Fundamental Rights after the end of the transition period.[91] This has been described as 'protection of the last resort';[92] that those EU citizens who do not have a qualifying right to reside for benefit purposes are nevertheless entitled to the protection of the Charter of Fundamental Rights. Nevertheless, these judgments provide some protection for individuals in situations such as *CG* and *AT* who are experiencing destitution and seek to rely on a safety net available to many others (ie Universal Credit).

More recently the case law and application of the Withdrawal Agreement/Charter has been extended beyond welfare benefits into eligibility for housing assistance/homeless duties. In *Hynek v Islington*[93] the judge found that PSS holders within the personal scope of the WA were entitled to equal treatment. Therefore, Hynek (an EU citizen with PSS in receipt of UC) was eligible for homelessness assistance. Similarly in *C v Oldham*,[94] a dependent family member of an EU citizen (at the time of the transition period) was also found eligible by the County Court for housing assistance, with these protected rights continuing after the individual was no longer dependent on her EU sponsor. However, the most recent case of *Fertre v Vale of White Horse District Council*[95] took a different line. Here the High Court ruled (and the Court of

[89] *Secretary of State for Work and Pensions v AT* [2023] EWCA Civ 1307.

[90] Available here: <https://eur-lex.europa.eu/legal-content/EN/TXT/HTML/?uri = CELEX%3A12012P%2FTXT>.

[91] The decision reaffirmed the ongoing relevance of the Charter where EU law rights under the Withdrawal Agreement are engaged.

[92] C O'Brien and A Welsh, 'Court of Appeal Decides the Secretary of State Is Wrong, Wrong, Wrong: The Charter Applies to People with Pre-Settled Status' (2024) 46(1) Journal of Social Welfare and Family Law 133–36.

[93] https://the3million.org.uk/sites/default/files/documents/JvIslington-Judgment-Final24May2024.pdf.

[94] *C v Oldham* [2024] EWCC 1.

[95] *Fertre v Vale of White Horse District Council* [2024] EWHC 1234.

Appeal upheld) that a grant of status under the EUSS was a 'gateway status' giving the holder conditional rights only.

These cases illustrate the tension that existed under EU law (and continues to exist for those states still in the EU) around the rights of *all* citizens to freely move and reside within the Member States of the EU. In particular, the question is how to treat those who are the most vulnerable but also the most burdensome on the state, namely those who are economically inactive and who lack sufficient resources to support themselves. These issues are now resurfacing in the application of WA law. UK courts, like the CJEU before them, are having to define the boundaries of protection for this group of rights holders under the WA in UK law. For those more vulnerable the best outcome to secure their rights is to ensure they can supply enough evidence to apply for SS and move to the more secure status, which offers them an automatic right to reside for the purposes of welfare benefits.

(iii) The 'True Cohort'

There is a further issue highlighted by the *IMA* decision. The EUSS was generous in the sense that it required individuals only to show residence in order to acquire PSS or SS, not that they were exercising a Treaty/CRD right in the UK before 31 December 2020. However, the UK government's position was (until recently) that this decision resulted in two cohorts: (1) a 'true cohort' of individuals with status under the scheme (who were exercising their Treaty rights on 31 December 2020 eg as workers or self-employed) and (2) those who were merely resident here (an 'extra cohort'). Only the true cohort held an automatic 'right to reside'. However, an amendment to the Border Security, Asylum and Immigration Bill (April 2025) tabled by the government stated that everyone who holds status under the EUSS will have enforceable rights under the WA, without the need to demonstrate that they were exercising Treaty rights at the relevant time. The Bill became an Act in December 2025. [96] Those who have been able to prove eligibility for SS based only on their residency and not on their 'qualified' residency (ie they were exercising treaty rights at the relevant time) have now gained an automatic right to reside for welfare benefits, which they may not have been eligible for otherwise. However, Zambrano carers and citizens who applied via the Surinder Singh route (section 3(c)) will not benefit from this amendment.[97] This again reinforces Solanke's point about a two-tier system of rights.

However, not all EU citizens in the UK have even now successfully been granted a status under the scheme, despite the distance from the application deadline. Some are still (or for the first time) navigating an application which is (post-June 2021) considered 'late'. It is to this group of people that we turn next.

[96] Now Section 45 of the Border Security, Asylum and Immigration Act 2025. For more: https://www.gov.uk/government/publications/border-security-asylum-and-immigration-act-2025-section-45/implementation-of-section-45-of-the-border-security-asylum-and-immigration-act-2025.

[97] For more: https://ima-citizensrights.org.uk/border-security-asylum-and-immigration-bill-clause-42/#:~:text=The%20IMA%20considers%20that%20it,their%20rights%20under%20the%20Agreements.

(b) Late Applications

The EUSS allows for late applications. As noted above, the deadline to make an in-time application was 30 June 2021, but applications have continued at pace since then, with on average 56,000 applications per month since the deadline.[98] In all, 250,000 grants of pre-settled status have been made from late applications,[99] showing the magnitude of the number of applicants who have needed to undertake this late application route. Some, who have lived in the UK for many years, did not think that that the EUSS applied to them, and our research shows examples of this.[100] Many who had already achieved and applied for EEA (PR) (permanent residency) believed this status meant that they did not need to make an application to the EUSS. Others were simply unaware of the existence of the scheme. Take Marianne,[101] a 59-year-old Portuguese woman who had been living in the UK since 2003:

> Marianne does not speak English and was not aware of the EUSS. She has cancer, mental health issues and suffers from diabetes and arthritis. She became aware of EUSS only when her benefits (which she'd been on since 2008) stopped.
>
> Although she has now been helped to make a late application, it is not enough to secure the continued payment of her benefits, and she is waiting on her CoA [certificate of application] to prove she has made an application. Evicted by her landlord, she is now considered 'intentionally homeless' due to rent arrears and other debts.
>
> When she was evicted she was unable to retrieve her documents, meaning she was able to provide only three years of evidence to support her EUSS application. She is homeless and reliant on food parcels pending a decision.

Marianne's case shows how quickly things can snowball for those unable to prove their immigration status, including an abrupt end to income, resulting debts, and in some cases, as this one, homelessness. Pre-Brexit Marianne could have proved her rights solely by showing her European passport, particularly in the context of her right to rent. This example shows starkly the impact Brexit has had on vulnerable individuals and just how far into their daily life it reaches.

Changes to how late applications are assessed were introduced in August 2023, owing in part to concerns that unmeritorious claims were being submitted, granting people not protected under the WA (eg those who arrived after December 2020) a

[98] For more: https://www.gov.uk/government/statistics/immigration-system-statistics-year-ending-june-2024/how-many-people-have-been-granted-settlement-via-the-eu-settlement-scheme#data-tables.

[99] https://the3million.org.uk/eu-settlement-scheme-statistics#:~:text = This%20analysis%20is%20compiled%20and,million%20(8%2C193%2C753)%20were%20concluded.

[100] Barnard and others (n 1) Ch 3.

[101] Names changed. This case study was also used in a blog post: Barnard and Costello, 'EUSS Applications: "Meritorious" Ones Suffer from Processing Delays; "Unmeritorious" Ones Benefit' (March 2022), UK in a Changing Europe.

'certificate of application (COA)' and therefore the right to work until a decision was made on their claim, which could take weeks or months (or longer). If refused, they could then submit another claim and follow the same process of CoA and refusal. We saw evidence of this in our research. For example, a family in Great Yarmouth had been incorrectly advised (in their country of origin) that they could still come to the UK and begin work via the EUSS. The family arrived in June 2021 and made an application to the EUSS and received a CoA. The mother was working, and her children were enrolled in the local school. However, her application was ultimately refused (because she arrived after the end of EU free movement in the UK). The CoA had given the family a false sense of security of future life in the UK until a final decision was granted. The mother believed that as she was already in work, was living in private rented accommodation, and had her children in school, it was impossible that she would not have the right to stay.

There are other consequences too. Take the case of Paula,[102] who arrived in the UK when seven months pregnant and had been helped by an advice shark to submit a (late) application. She was advised that she would be successful. She gave birth in an NHS hospital and now potentially faces medical bills of up to £10,000, in line with NHS overseas visitor charges, because she was not entitled to free medical treatment.

The changes to the late application process were intended to avoid situations such as these from occurring. However, it does mean that those with legally meritorious claims, as with Marianne above, can be subject to delays in decision-making while 'reasonable grounds' are assessed. This can lead to debt and even destitution while they are in limbo, unable to prove their rights.

(c) Extensions and Absences

Although EUSS is in principle a lifelong status, it can be lost in specific circumstances, for example extended absences from the UK. Those with SS can leave the UK for up to five consecutive years without losing their SS; for those with PSS the period for which they can be absent from the UK is reduced to two years. However, this latter group (holders of PSS) must also be aware that while absences of up to two years mean that pre-settled status will not be lost, cumulative absences can also interrupt their continuous residency. In order to apply for settled status, PSS holders must be able to prove more than five years' continuous residency in the UK.

After the *IMA* judgment,[103] the UK Home Office introduced, as we saw above, first, a two-year and then a five-year extension for PSS status. However, for some, the extensions are causing confusion. As the rules around absences were laid out until July 2025, some people may have (unknowingly) fallen out of eligibility for SS (absent for

[102] Name changed, also supported by GYROS.
[103] *Independent Monitoring Authority* (n 85).

more than 6 in 12 months) and still be being automatically granted an extension to their leave, without realizing their absences have (already) had an impact on their right to SS. Our previous research highlighted that some at the time mistakenly believed that an extended status meant the Home Office had disregarded any previous absences and the clock on their PSS started again.[104] The Home Office too recognized this confusion and in July 2025 amended the rules around absences to address this issue.[105] The new absences rule that applies from 16 July 2025 states that if PSS holders can prove they have been resident in the UK for at least thirty months in the past sixty months (instead of 6 in every 12 months), they will have completed a five-year continuous qualifying period. This will benefit those who might have otherwise fallen out of eligibility for SS or have been already refused SS based on their absences, who can now make a fresh claim, based on this broader approach to absences. It shows commendable pragmatism and responsiveness on the part of the Home Office to address this when it became clear it was an issue.

5 Conclusion

While EU free movement is about trans-border movement without barriers, Brexit has created an immigration category of EUSS status holders who must prove their right to remain in the UK before being able to access/continue their life in the UK. This is the greatest change for EU citizens in the UK post-Brexit. For those who can afford it,[106] British citizenship is considered the 'gold standard' for ultimate security in the UK. The security they had in the UK pre-Brexit is perceived by many as now lost, despite the UK's implementation of the EUSS to preserve their rights.[107] For many of those in our cohort this is not an option due to cost, but also to the absence of sufficient English-language skills to pass the Life in the UK test. However, this group nevertheless often report that they plan to apply for citizenship for their children. This will mean, in future, an increase in multi-citizenship families living in the UK—European parents/grandparents with British children and grandchildren. However, for those whose EU member states do not allow dual citizenship, giving up their European citizenship is a significant event.

The UK now hosts the largest diaspora of EU citizens in the world. Citizens' rights under the WA can last a lifetime, meaning that these rights will continue to be an important topic for decades. This also means that those with SS will have to continuously

[104] Barnard and Costello, 'Brexit, EU Citizens in the UK and the EUSS', (May 2025), UK in a Changing Europe.

[105] Statement of changes to the Immigration Rules: HC 836, 24 June 2025, available here: https://www.gov.uk/government/publications/statement-of-changes-to-the-immigration-rules-hc-836-24-june-2025.

[106] C Barnard and F Costello, 'From EU Citizenship to British Citizenship via the EU Settlement Scheme: Some Socio-Legal Reflections from the East Coast', in P Minnerop, V Roeben, R Schütze, and J Snell (eds), *EU Citizenship as an Independent Status: Between Form and Substance* (Oxford University Press, forthcoming); Barnard, Fraser Butlin, and Costello (n 5).

[107] Barnard, Fraser Butlin, and Costello (n 5).

and actively manage their status. For those more vulnerable, life in the UK both pre-and post-Brexit has many of the same markers of precarity. EU law and WA law continue to apply qualified and conditional rights.

For the EU, the reality of a multimillion-strong diaspora in the UK should mean that a good future relationship with the UK (and vice versa) is essential.

18
Immigration Policy

Steve Peers

1 Introduction

Migration was not the only issue in the Brexit referendum debate, but it was the most toxic. While the arguments largely focused on the impact of free movement and the perceived asylum crisis (as discussed in other chapters), the implementation of the Brexit vote led initially to a considerable liberalization of legal migration from the rest of the world to address concerns that British businesses would still need foreign workers (and universities would still need foreign students). Yet the consequent increase in net migration in turn fuelled a backlash that led to more restrictive policies—and a tentative turn back towards closer relations with the EU and its member states on migration issues.

The following chapter first examines the extent to which pre-Brexit regulation of this issue applied to the UK, followed by a detailed overview of post-Brexit divergence.

2 Pre-Brexit Regulation

A key feature of the EU legal regime on immigration policy pre-Brexit was that little of it applied to the UK—because the UK used its opt-out in this field far more than it did for asylum and civil law (from 1999),[1] or for criminal law.[2] As such this is an unusual subject for analysis from the perspective of post-Brexit divergence, because the UK was divergent already.

Indeed, one key post-Brexit feature is the widening of the scope of 'ordinary' immigration law on each side, with nationals of EU countries who are not covered by the Withdrawal Agreement (other than Irish people, who are subject to special rules)

[1] The UK's opt-out from immigration, asylum, and civil law measures was initially created with the entry into force of the Treaty of Amsterdam in May 1999, in conjunction with shifting these measures to the 'first pillar' of EU law (Community law, as it was then known). See generally S Peers, *EU Justice and Home Affairs Law* (Oxford University Press, 5th edn, 2023) Vol 1.

[2] The UK's opt-out widened in scope when criminal law and policing issues were also transferred to ordinary EU law in 2009, when the Treaty of Lisbon entered into force, coupled with the possibility to opt out of *pre*-Lisbon criminal law and policing measures after a five-year transition period, which the UK did in part ([2014] OJ L319).

Steve Peers, *Immigration Policy* In: *The UK Regulatory Framework Post-Brexit: 'Law Unbound'*. Edited by: Paul Craig and Vilija Vėlyvytė, Oxford University Press. © Oxford University Press 2026. DOI: 10.1093/9780198969815.003.0021

becoming subject to the UK rules on immigration for non-EU citizens, and UK citizens becoming subject to the immigration law of the EU and its member states—again, subject to a special relationship with Ireland.[3]

During membership—and particularly during the 2016 referendum campaign—it was often falsely claimed or implied that EU membership directly regulated non-EU immigration to the UK. This was only legally correct as regards asylum,[4] and for non-EU family of EU citizens who moved (including the non-EU family members of UK citizens who moved within the EU then back to the UK).[5] But there was always an argument that EU membership *de facto* constrained what the UK could do, that is, that so many EU nationals came to the UK that the UK could not be as liberal as it would have wanted to be as regards non-EU citizens; and as we shall see, the regulation of migration post-Brexit was rationalized by arguments about the consequences of ending free movement.

Be that as it may, there are four main areas of EU regulation as regards (non-asylum-related) immigration: visas, border controls, legal migration, and irregular migration. Examining in turn the main EU legislation applicable pre-Brexit, and the extent of UK opt-in to each area, for visa policy: the EU adopted a list of countries subject (or not) to a short-term visa requirement;[6] a visa code setting out procedures for applying for a short-term visa;[7] and a Visa Information System (VIS) database.[8] The UK opted out of all of these, due to its opt-out from the core of the Schengen system.[9]

On border controls, the EU has adopted: the Schengen Borders Code, setting out criteria for crossing borders;[10] the Schengen Information System (SIS), including list of persons to be refused entry;[11] the entry–exit system and travel authorization system legislation (ETIAS);[12] and the legislation setting up Frontex, the EU border control agency.[13] Again, the UK opted out of the legislation concerned due to its opt-out from the Schengen acquis; this opt-out was even reinforced by CJEU case law.[14] (The UK had access to the *police and criminal law data* in the SIS, as

[3] Ireland has opted out of EU immigration law nearly as comprehensively as the UK did (although post-Brexit Ireland has opted in to almost all EU asylum law: [2024] OJ L02/08/24).

[4] The UK opted in to the first phase of the legislation creating the Common European Asylum System, but only a limited part of the second phase legislation. See Ch 19.

[5] Arts 2(2) and 3(2), Directive 2004/38, [2004] OJ L158/37. On the latter group, see Case C-370/90 *Surinder Singh* [1992] ECR I-4265.

[6] Reg 539/2001, [2001] OJ L81/1, later codified (after many amendments) by Reg 2018/1806, [2018] OJ L 303/39.

[7] Reg 810/2009, [2009] OJ L 243/1, amended in particular by Reg 2019/1155, [2019] OJ L188/25.

[8] Reg 767/2008, [2008] OJ L218/60.

[9] On this point, the CJEU ruled that the UK could not opt in to a policing measure linked to the VIS, due to its opt-out from the core of Schengen: Case C-482/08 *UK v Council* [2010] ECR I-10413.

[10] Latest codified version: Reg 2016/399, [2016] OJ L77/1, as subsequently amended.

[11] At the time of Brexit, Reg 1987/2006, [2006] OJ L381/4, was applicable in practice as regards immigration data; the subsequent Reg 2018/1861, [2018] OJ L312/14, has applied in practice from March 2023 ([2023] OJ L 27/29). See also Reg 2018/1860, [2018] OJ L312/1, on the use of data for returns.

[12] Respectively Regs 2017/2226, [2017] OJ L327/20 and 2018/1240, [2018] OJ L236/1. The latter is not yet applied in practice.

[13] Most recently Reg 2019/1896, [2019] OJ L295/1.

[14] Case C-77/05 *UK v Council* [2007] ECR I-11459. See also Case C-137/05 *UK v Council* [2007] ECR I-11593, rejecting attempts to opt in to EU legislation on passport security, for the same reasons.

distinct from the migration control data, but lost access even to the former because of Brexit.)[15]

In the area of legal migration, the EU adopted Directives on: family reunion;[16] long-term residents;[17] non-work migration;[18] the Blue Card on highly skilled workers;[19] a single permit for workers;[20] and seasonal workers and intra-corporate transferees.[21] The UK opted out of all of these.

Finally, as regards irregular migration, the EU adopted measures prior to Brexit on: trafficking in persons (criminal law);[22] trafficking victims (migration law);[23] facilitation of illegal entry or stay;[24] employment of irregular migrants;[25] carrier sanctions;[26] advance passenger information;[27] the Returns Directive;[28] and readmission treaties.[29] The UK opted in to the criminal law measure on trafficking in persons after its adoption,[30] and was also covered by the measures on facilitation of illegal entry and stay, carrier sanctions, advance passenger information, and readmission treaties.

3 Post-Brexit Regulation

(a) EU Developments

At the EU level (for comparison's sake),[31] visa law has been amended post-Brexit in the form of some changes to the visa list Regulation;[32] amendments to the VIS;[33] and

[15] [2000] OJ L131/43.
[16] Directive 2003/86, [2003] OJ L251/12.
[17] Directive 2003/109, [2004] OJ L16/44, amended by Directive 2011/51, [2011] OJ L132/1.
[18] Directive 2004/114 on students, [2004] OJ L375/12; Directive 2005/71 on researchers [2005] OJ L289/15; amended and merged in Directive 2016/801, [2016] OJ L132/21.
[19] Directive 2009/50, [2009] OJ L155/17.
[20] Directive 2011/98, [2011] OJ L343/1; A Weatherburn, 'Working in Europe with a Single Permit: A Golden Ticket or Pie in the Sky?' (2024) 26 EJML 446.
[21] Directives 2014/36, [2014] OJ L94/375 and 2014/66 [2014] OJ L157/1. On the former, see L Palumbo, A Corrado, and A Triandafyllidou (eds), 'Special Issue: Migrant Labour in the Agri-food System in Europe: Unpacking the Social and Legal Factors of Exploitation', (2022) 24(2) EJML.
[22] Most recently (pre-Brexit) Directive 2011/36, [2011] OJ L101/1.
[23] Directive 2004/81, [2004] OJ L261/19.
[24] Directive 2002/90, [2002] OJ L328/17, and the parallel Framework Decision ([2002] OJ L328/1).
[25] Directive 2009/52, [2009] OJ L168/24. For the comparable UK rules as regards criminal penalties for employing illegal workers, see Immigration Act 2016, s 35.
[26] Directive 2001/51, [2001] OJ L187/45.
[27] Directive 2004/82, [2004] OJ L 261/24.
[28] Directive 2008/115, [2008] OJ L 348/98.
[29] For a list, see https://home-affairs.ec.europa.eu/policies/migration-and-asylum/irregular-migration-and-return/effective-firm-and-fair-eu-return-and-readmission-policy_en.
[30] Commission decision approving UK opt-in, [2011] OJ L 271/49.
[31] The following list includes only legislative measures, not secondary law or treaties with non-EU countries. On the major changes to EU asylum law, see Ch 19.
[32] In addition to Reg 2019/592, [2019] OJ L103 I/1 (UK post-Brexit), see Regs: 2023/850, [2023] OJ L110/1 (Kosovo); 2024/2495, [2024] OJ L23 September (some Serbs); and 2025/11, [2025] OJ L 01/14/25 (Vanuatu). A further amendment to Reg 2018/1806 (n 6) has been adopted: Reg 2025/2441, [2025] OJ L 10/10/2025 (visa suspension mechanism).
[33] Reg 2021/1134, [2021] OJ L248/11 (not yet applied). On the state of play of applying this law, see most recently COM (2025) 346, 1 Jul 2025.

other changes to visa law to provide for the digitalization of the visa application process.[34] As regards borders, the EU has amended the Schengen Borders Code[35] as well as the rules on advance passenger information,[36] and legislated for a transitional application of the entry–exit system.[37]

As for legal immigration, the EU has updated its legislation on the Blue Card and the single permit,[38] although a proposed update of the Long-term Residents Directive has not been agreed.[39] Negotiations to replace the Returns Directive and the legislation on facilitation of irregular migration are ongoing,[40] and the Directive on trafficking in persons (criminal law) has been amended.[41] As regards facilitation of irregular migration, the CJEU has delivered an important judgment in *Kinsa*, limiting the ability of member states to criminalize assistance to irregular migration in at least some cases.[42]

(b) UK Developments

On the UK side, in addition to extending general immigration law to non-Irish EU citizens not covered by the Withdrawal Agreement, there have been developments in the parallel areas of law and policy.

(i) Visas and Borders

As regards visas and borders, 'blue' passports for UK citizens were reintroduced not long after the Brexit vote.[43] Visa requirements for non-EEA citizens who were professional artists, musicians, or athletes travelling through Ireland were simplified.[44] The UK has rolled out an electronic travel authorization (ETA) scheme, comparable to the EU's (not yet operational) ETIAS scheme.[45] The UK has also been rolling out e-passport gates, although these are *not* identical to the EU's entry–exit system, which began operations in 2025.[46] While the changes to the UK's travel visa regime are by

[34] Regs 2023/2667 and 2023/2685, [2023] OJ L 07/12/23. This legislation is not yet applied in practice.

[35] Reg 2024/1717, [2024] OJ L 20/06/24.

[36] Regs 2025/12 and 13, [2025] OJ L 08/01/25.

[37] Reg 2025/1534, [2025] OJ L 23/07/25.

[38] Directives 2021/1883, [2021] OJ L 382/1 and 2024/1233, [2024] OJ L 30/04/24.

[39] COM (2022) 650, 27 April 2022. However, the EU has recently adopted a Reg on a talent pool of non-EU workers: Council doc 62/26, 18 March 2026.

[40] Respectively COM (2025) 101, 11 March 2025 and COM (2023) 755, 28 Nov 2023. See also the proposal to enhance Europol powers as regards smuggling of migrants (COM (2023) 754, 28 Nov 2023), which has been agreed but not yet formally adopted (Council doc 13302/25, 9 Oct 2025).

[41] Directive 2024/1712, [2024] OJ L 24/06/24.

[42] Case C-460/23 EU:C:2025:392.

[43] Home Office press release, 22 Dec 2017, <https://www.gov.uk/government/news/blue-uk-passport-to-return-after-eu-exit>.

[44] Home Office press release, 28 Feb 2019: <https://www.gov.uk/government/news/new-process-for-artists-and-sportspeople-entering-from-ireland>.

[45] Statement of Changes to the Immigration Rules, HC 1160, 9 Mar 2023, implementing s 75 of the Nationality and Borders Act 2022.

[46] See, for instance, Home Office press release, 30 Oct 2018: <https://www.gov.uk/government/news/epassport-gates-to-ease-travel-for-passengers-from-more-countries>.

and large different from changes in EU law,[47] the UK did reimpose visa requirements on Vanuatu at roughly the same time, and for the same reasons (concerns about investment citizenship schemes), as the EU.[48]

(ii) Legal Migration: Quasi-Protection Regimes

As regards various aspects of legal migration, one prominent feature of recent UK law is the introduction of special regimes within migration law that in fact aim at forms of protection. In particular there have been special regimes for Ukraine, Hong Kong, and Afghanistan.[49]

The scheme for Hong Kong, confirmed shortly after Brexit day as a response to China's national security law and applicable from early 2021 (ie just after the Brexit transition period ended), offered five years' stay, with a route to settlement and citizenship, and lower visa fees.[50]

The Ukraine scheme, introduced a month after Russia's full invasion of that country, created a Ukraine Family Scheme (wider family reunion rules for those with family in the UK), a Homes for Ukraine Sponsorship Scheme (where a sponsor was approved), and a Ukraine Extension Scheme (for Ukrainians already in the UK).[51] The Ukraine Family Scheme was ended in 2024, with the Homes for Ukraine scheme cut to eighteen months in duration, explicitly by comparison with the EU's Temporary Protection Directive.[52] Subsequently the new UK government created a new permission extension scheme for Ukraine.[53]

As for schemes for local Afghan staff who had assisted the UK, there were initial schemes for interpreters and those suffering intimidation,[54] subsequently supplemented (and eventually replaced) by the Afghan Relocation and Assistance Policy (ARAP).[55] The policy was wound up on the grounds that it had fulfilled its original

[47] Although see Nationality and Borders Act 2022, ss 70, 72, and 74, which provide for a visa sanctions regime in response to the perceived failure of other countries to readmit migrants, comparable to that introduced by EU law in 2019 (n 7).

[48] Statement of Changes to the Immigration Rules, HC 1715, 19 Jul 2023.

[49] Although it takes the form of a special protection regime; see also previously s 67 of the Immigration Act 2016, known as the 'Dubs Amendment', implemented by (*inter alia*) the Statement of Changes to the Immigration Rules, HC 1154, 15 Jun 2018.

[50] FCO/Home Office press releases, 1 Jul 2020, 22 Jul 2020, and 22 Oct 2020: <https://www.gov.uk/government/news/uk-to-extend-residence-rights-for-british-nationals-overseas-citizens-in-hong-kong>, <https://www.gov.uk/government/news/home-secretary-announces-details-of-the-hong-kong-bno-visa>, and <https://www.gov.uk/government/news/government-delivers-on-commitment-to-british-nationals-overseas-in-hong-kong>.

[51] Statement of Changes to the Immigration Rules, HC 1220, 29 Mar 2022. The Homes for Ukraine Sponsorship Scheme was extended later to include unaccompanied children: Statement of Changes to the Immigration Rules, HC 511, 20 Jul 2022. The Ukraine Extension Scheme was also later extended in time: Statements of Changes to the Immigration rules, HC 719, 18 Oct 2022 and HC 1496, 17 Jul 2023.

[52] Statement of Changes to the Immigration Rules, HC 556, 19 Feb 2024.

[53] Statement of Changes to the Immigration Rules, HC 334, 26 Nov 2024.

[54] They were granted the possibility to obtain settlement: Statement of Changes to the Immigration Rules, HC 1154, 15 Jun 2018. One scheme was widened to include interpreters made redundant: Dept of Defence and Home Office press release, 22 Oct 2020 (<https://www.gov.uk/government/news/more-afghan-interpreters-to-move-to-the-uk-as-scheme-extends>).

[55] Statement of Changes to the Immigration Rules, HC 1248, 4 Mar 2021. It was widened later that year: Statement of Changes to the Immigration Rules, HC 913, 14 Dec 2021.

purpose (having relocated over 21,000 people to the UK), along with the Afghan Citizens Resettlement Scheme (ACRS), which had resettled more than 12,800 people since 2021 (more than half of them children and a quarter of them women).[56]

(iii) Family Reunion

As regards family reunion, changes to the immigration rules in 2017 took account of UK Supreme Court case law which, although upholding the validity of the pre-existing minimum income requirement in light of Article 8 ECHR, nevertheless required other sources of income to be considered, and required assessment of proportionality and the best interests of the child.[57]

The biggest general change in this area was a decision to raise the income threshold in 2024, to £29,000, in order to reduce net migration—although that threshold was already higher than under EU family reunion law.[58] Other major changes relate to specific groups, as discussed further below: the removal, in 2023–24, of the facility for many students and all care workers to bring their dependants at all.

(iv) Student Admissions

Even prior to Brexit day, international students were encouraged by simplifying documentation for nationals of more countries.[59] More fundamentally, as part of the broader reform of immigration policy, admission as a student was simplified from 2020 (replacing the previous 'Tier 4' of UK immigration law).[60] The simplifications included a waiver of some documentation requirements, the removal of the eight-year time limit to obtain a degree, and greater facility to switch between migration categories. Also, a new route for graduates to remain was created from July 2021, allowing two years' work after completion of a degree (three years for PhD students),[61] paralleling (less generous) changes made in EU law several years previously.[62]

From 2023, concern about the levels of net migration led to a more restrictive approach. In order to reduce net migration, students could no longer bring dependants, except for those on research postgraduate schemes.[63] Students also lost the facility at this point to switch to a work permit before ending their studies. Most recently, the

[56] Statement of Changes to the Immigration Rules, HC 997, 1 Jul 2025.

[57] Statement of Changes to the Immigration Rules, HC 290, 20 Jul 2017, referring to *MM (Lebanon) & Others v the Secretary for the Home Department* [2017] UKSC 10 and *Agyarko & Ikuga v the Secretary for the Home Department* [2017] UKSC 11.

[58] Statement of Changes to the Immigration Rules, HC 590, 14 Mar 2024. For the comparable EU law, see Art 7(1), Directive 2003/86 (n 16), as interpreted by the CJEU in Case C-578/08 *Chakroun* [2010] ECR I-1839.

[59] Statement of Changes to the Immigration Rules, HC 1154, 15 Jun 2018.

[60] Statement of Changes to the Immigration Rules, HC 707, 10 Jun 2020.

[61] Statement of Changes to the Immigration Rules, HC 1248, 4 Mar 2021.

[62] Directive 2016/801 (n 18) Art 25: Member states must let graduates stay for nine months after graduation to seek work or self-employment, although they can check the likelihood of success after three months.

[63] Statement of Changes to the Immigration Rules, HC 1496, 17 Jul 2023.

graduate scheme was amended to reduce the period of stay after graduation from two years to eighteen months (the 3-year period for PhDs is unchanged), on the grounds that many graduates do not in fact obtain graduate-level jobs.[64] Finally, the current government's recent White Paper on immigration considers levying a fee of 6 per cent on international student fees; while not an immigration measure as such, any increased costs could impact on the number of foreign students.[65]

(v) Labour Migration

Even before Brexit day, government policy had adjusted to provide for more liberal rules for non-EU citizen workers: the doubling of Tier 1 'exceptional talent' visas from 1000 to 2000 in 2017;[66] the inclusion of 'leading fashion designers' and further TV and film applicants, and then architects, in Tier 1 in 2018;[67] the removal of doctors and nurses from the caps on Tier 2 skilled worker visas in 2018,[68] followed by the removal of PhD-level jobs from the cap in 2019;[69] the admission of trainee researchers to the Tier 5 route in 2018;[70] a new pilot scheme for seasonal agricultural workers, announced in 2018;[71] and the creation of 'start-up visa' and 'innovator visa' Tier 1 categories for entrepreneurs in 2019.[72]

On the other hand, policy developments during this time included some less liberal elements, such as an increase in the salary threshold for skilled workers (from £20,800 to £25,000 and then £30,000) in 2016 and 2017 (although there was a temporary waiver from the increase in the salary threshold for nurses, radiographers, paramedics, and STEM and Mandarin teachers,[73] extended in 2019);[74] an increase

[64] Statement of Changes to the Immigration Rules, HC 1333, 14 Oct2025.

[65] White Paper, 'Restoring control over the immigration system', 12 Mar 2025.

[66] Statement of Changes to the Immigration Rules, HC 309, 7 Dec 2017. These were issued to 'existing global leaders or promising future leaders in the digital technology, science, arts and creative sectors' as recognized by five designated bodies (Home Office press release, 15 Nov 2017): <https://www.gov.uk/government/news/government-doubles-exceptional-talent-visa-offer>.

[67] Statement of Changes to the Immigration Rules, HC 1154, 15 Jun 2018 and HC 1779, 11 Dec 2018.

[68] Statement of Changes to the Immigration Rules, HC 1154, 15 Jun 2018.

[69] Statement of Changes to the Immigration Rules, HC 2631, 9 Sep2019.

[70] Statement of Changes to the Immigration Rules, HC 1154, 15 Jun 2018; see also Home Office press release, 6 July 2018: <https://www.gov.uk/government/news/new-scheme-for-overseas-researchers-to-come-to-the-uk>.

[71] Statement of Changes to Immigration Rules, HC 1779, 11 Dec 2018. See also Home Office press release, 6 Sept 2018: <https://www.gov.uk/government/news/new-start-up-visa-route-announced-by-the-home-secretary>. The pilot, set to last for two years, provided for the admission of 2,500 workers for 6 months. It began on 6 March 2019, and ran until the end of 2020 (which turned out to coincide with the end of the Brexit transition period): Home Office press release, 6 March 2019: <https://www.gov.uk/government/news/seasonal-workers-pilot-opens>.

[72] Statement of Changes to the Immigration Rules, HC 1919, 7 March 2019, replacing the 'Graduate Entrepreneur' and 'Entrepreneur' categories. See previously Home Office press release, 13 Jun 2018: <https://www.gov.uk/government/news/new-start-up-visa-route-announced-by-the-home-secretary>. The two new schemes abolished or reduced the funding requirements, and the 'start-up' visa was granted for two years instead of one.

[73] Statement of Changes to the Immigration Rules, HC 667, 3 Nov 2016 and HC 1078, 16 Mar 2017.

[74] Statement of Changes to the Immigration Rules, HC 1919, 7 Mar 2019.

in the immigration health surcharge;[75] and tightening of the rules relating to investor visas.[76]

A wider reform of legal migration began with policy announcements in 2018,[77] which were explicitly linked to the end of free movement as the UK left the EU.[78] The introduction of this system began with the 'Exceptional Talent' route to entry for researchers becoming the uncapped 'Global Talent' route.[79] More broadly, a 'points-based immigration system' was introduced starting just before the end of the Brexit transition period,[80] which assigned points to those with 'specific skills, qualifications, salaries or professions', visas being awarded only to those with a sufficient number of points. The salary threshold was reduced to £25,600 (lowered for 'shortage occupations'), with a claim that 70 per cent of the EU workforce fell below it; the new rules were to apply equally to EU citizens. But the skilled worker definition was widened to include A-levels, not only degrees; the labour market test was dropped; and the cap on numbers was suspended.

Subsequent changes also confirmed this liberal trend. The seasonal workers pilot, which had only begun operations the previous year, was quadrupled to 10,000 workers for 2020.[81] Seasonal worker visas were then widened from the initial focus on fruit and vegetable-picking, in the run-up to Christmas 2021, to cover the poultry industry and haulage,[82] and then pork butchers.[83] A specific Health and Social Care visa

[75] Home Office press release, 11 Oct 2018: <https://www.gov.uk/government/news/increase-to-immigration-health-surcharge-gives-nhs-extra-funding>. The surcharge was created pre-referendum (in 2015), but increased at this point from £200/year to £400/year, with a lower rate for students and those on youth mobility schemes (£300/year). Permanent residents, modern slavery victims, and asylum-seekers were exempt.

[76] Statement of Changes to the Immigration Rules, HC 1919, 7 March 2019, requiring that funds be held for a longer period, unless the source of the funds can be shown.

[77] Home Office press release, 19 Dec 2018: <https://www.gov.uk/government/news/home-secretary-announces-new-skills-based-immigration-system>, referring to a removal of the cap on work visas, the abolition of labour market tests, and the widening of the skills threshold to include skills equivalent to A-levels.

[78] Home Secretary's statement to the House of Commons, 19 Dec 2018: <https://www.gov.uk/government/speeches/home-secretary-future-border-and-immigration-system>. The link with the end of free movement was emphasized further with the parallel introduction of a Bill to end it as a matter of UK law; the Bill, reintroduced after the 2019 election, eventually became the Immigration and Social Security (EU Withdrawal) Act 2020.

[79] Statement of Changes to the Immigration Rules, HC 56, 30 Jan 2020; see also Home Office press release, 27 Jan 2020: <https://www.gov.uk/government/news/boost-for-uk-science-with-unlimited-visa-offer-to-worlds-brightest-and-best>. This offered an accelerated route to settlement, with an exception to absence rules for work-related reasons, while preserving labour market flexibility for the migrants admitted on this basis and their dependants' access to the labour market. Also, the number of fast-track fellowships for top scientists increased from 62 to 120 (Home Office press release, 23 Dec 2019: <https://www.gov.uk/government/news/global-britain-to-attract-more-top-scientists-with-fast-tracked-entry>).

[80] Statement of Changes to the Immigration Rules, HC 813, 22 Oct 2020. See also Home Office press release, 18 Feb 2020: <https://www.gov.uk/government/news/home-secretary-announces-new-uk-points-based-immigration-system>.

[81] DEFRA press release, 19 Feb 2020: <https://www.gov.uk/government/news/10000-workers-to-boost-british-farming-sector>.

[82] Statement of Changes to the Immigration Rules, CP 542, 11 Oct 2021. Poultry-related admissions during the pre-Christmas period were later made permanent: Statement of Changes to the Immigration Rules, HC 719, 18 Oct 2022.

[83] Statement of Changes to the Immigration Rules, HC 803, 1 Nov 2021.

was created in 2020, including lower visa fees and an exemption from the NHS surcharge.[84] Care workers were added to the 'shortage occupations' list by 2022, not only lowering the pay threshold necessary to obtain visas, but furthermore lowering the skills requirements that would usually apply.[85] At the other end of the labour market, other changes made in 2022 liberalized entry of various categories of business-related migrants and created a new 'high potential individual' visa, issued to graduates of the top fifty non-UK universities for two years (bachelor's or master's graduates) or three years (PhD graduates).[86] A scheme was created for temporary permission to stay for victims of human trafficking or slavery;[87] this is (belatedly) comparable to an EU law which the UK never opted in to during its EU membership.[88] The entry route for innovators was liberalized, becoming an 'Innovator Founder' route.[89] Construction and related jobs, along with fishing jobs, were added to the shortage occupation list.[90]

On the other hand, there were some countervailing less liberal developments during this period, in particular the closure of the investor migration route due to concerns about abuse.[91]

However, the liberalization of labour migration, in conjunction with other immigration and asylum developments (small-boat crossings across the North Sea, the increase in the number of international students, the Hong Kong and Ukraine schemes) led to a considerable increase in net migration by 2023, and subsequent government immigration policy performed a number of U-turns in an attempt to reduce these numbers.

These U-turns began in early 2024, with an initial focus on care workers, 'in response to high levels of non-compliance and worker exploitation and abuse, as well as unsustainable levels of demand'. In the year to September 2023, '83,072 visas were granted for care workers and a further 18,244 visas for senior care workers, comprising 30% of all work visas granted'. Furthermore, 69 per cent of the 250,297 visas granted for work-related dependants were for Health and Care Worker dependants.[92] The government ended the right for care workers to bring in dependants, and limited the ability to sponsor them to regulated employers in the sector only.

More general changes to labour migration (in parallel to changes to family reunion) were made soon afterward, with a large jump in the usual salary threshold from £26,800 to £38,700.[93] The salary for the Health and Care visa and some others rose

[84] Home Office and Department of Health and Social Care press release, 14 July 2020: <https://www.gov.uk/government/news/government-launches-health-and-care-visa-to-ensure-uk-health-and-care-services-have-access-to-the-best-global-talent>.

[85] Statement of Changes to the Immigration Rules, HC 1019, 24 Jan 2022.

[86] Statement of Changes to the Immigration Rules, HC 1118, 15 Mar 2022.

[87] Statement of Changes to the Immigration Rules, HC 719, 18 Oct 2022.

[88] Directive 2004/82, [2004] OJ L261/24.

[89] Statement of Changes to the Immigration Rules, HC 1160, 9 Mar 2023.

[90] Statement of Changes to the Immigration Rules, HC 1496, 17 Jul 2023.

[91] Statement of Changes to the Immigration Rules, CP 632, 18 Feb 2022.

[92] Statement of Changes to the Immigration Rules, HC 556, 19 Feb 2024, explanatory memorandum.

[93] Statement of Changes to the Immigration Rules, HC 590, 14 Mar 2024. The previous rise to £26,200 was a small increase set out in an earlier Statement of Changes to the Immigration Rules, HC 1160, 9 Mar 2023.

to £29,000, with the shortage occupation list replaced by a minimum salary list, still setting out a 20 per cent discount from the general salary threshold (now amounting to a threshold of £30,960 in general cases, or £23,200 for health and social care cases).

This trend was continued after the change in government in 2024, with further changes in 2025 overhauling the labour migration system. The new policy cut back the number of occupations covered by the skilled worker route, raising the occupational skill threshold back to the level pre-2020: Regulated Qualifications Framework (RQF) level 6 or above, instead of level 3. The government acknowledged that '[t]he threshold was lowered from RQF level 6 in Immigration Rules changes made in 2020 . . . in part to help businesses adapt to the ending of free movement between the UK and EU'. But, in the new government's view, 'growth in visa numbers, and concerns about exploitation of overseas recruits, have been particularly seen in occupations below RQF level 6', justifying a lift in the threshold back to its previous level.[94]

However, there were transitional rules for those already on the skilled worker route, enabling them to 'renew their visas, change employment, and take supplementary employment, in occupations below RQF level 6'. But the transitional rules would 'not be in place indefinitely and will be reviewed in due course'.

As for the exceptions to the general rules, the Immigration Salary List was replaced by a Temporary Shortage List, for occupations below RQF level 6, with both lists to be phased out by the end of 2026. There were separate arrangements for adult social care, allowing 'in-country applications, for those switching from other visa routes, to continue for a transition period until 22 July 2028, at which point these occupations will be removed from the Immigration Salary List or Temporary Shortage List'.

The most recent changes to the rules are more modest, doubling the number of top non-EU universities whose graduates were covered by the High Potential Scheme (subject to national security caveats), but capping the numbers covered by this scheme at 8,000 per year.[95]

(vi) Irregular Migration

Finally, as for irregular migration, most of the changes in UK law are linked to asylum law issues, discussed in another chapter in this book. However, it is worth noting that the post-Brexit UK has increased penalties for smuggling of persons in the Nationality and Borders Act 2022,[96] paralleling the 2023 proposal to amend EU law.[97] However, those changes in UK law, dropping the requirement that liability for assisting illegal entry only applied where this was 'for gain',[98] diverged further from

[94] Statement of Changes to the Immigration Rules, HC 997, 1 Jul 2025, explanatory memorandum, referring to the discussion in the government's White Paper 'Restoring control over the immigration system', 12 Mar 2025.

[95] Statement of Changes to the Immigration Rules, HC 1333, 14 Oct 2025.

[96] Nationality and Borders Act 2022, s 41.

[97] COM (2023) 755, (n 40) Art 6.

[98] Nationality and Borders Act 2022, s 41(3), amending s 25A(1)(a), Immigration Act 1971.

EU law as interpreted by the CJEU.[99] The 2022 Act also increased the penalties for illegal entry,[100] a point not directly addressed by EU law (the case law on the Returns Directive says as a rule that only administrative law detention should apply during the removal process).[101]

(c) EU/UK Relations

A particular feature of post-Brexit UK immigration policy is the non-preferential treatment of the EU; that is, EU citizens are to be treated the same as any other non-citizens (other than Irish citizens) as regards immigration law.[102] This obviously reverses the position during EU membership, and is of course reciprocated by the EU (other than Ireland) too.[103] However, there are signs at the time of writing that this legal position may change, in three respects.

First, the EU and the UK agreed in principle—after much reluctance from the UK—to negotiate a youth mobility arrangement, as a part of the broader 'reset' of UK/EU relations agreed in May 2025.[104] The two sides agreed:

> [T]he European Commission and the United Kingdom should work towards a balanced youth experience scheme on terms to be mutually agreed. The scheme should facilitate the participation of young people from the European Union and the United Kingdom in various activities, such as work, studies, au-pairing, volunteering, or simply travelling, for a limited period of time. It should provide a dedicated visa path and ensure that the overall number of participants is acceptable to both sides.

This would be the first youth mobility scheme agreed by the EU as such, although its member states have agreed some such schemes bilaterally with non-member states; the EU Commission has not yet followed through on its plans to propose a more

[99] See *Kinsa* (n 42), compared to the wording of Art 1, Directive 2002/90 (n 24); more broadly, the underlying criminalization of assistance to *asylum-seekers* (not just irregular entrants) in UK law in s 25A of the Immigration Act 1971, as inserted by s 143 of the Nationality, Immigration and Asylum Act 2002, is hard to square with the *Kinsa* judgment. But note the exceptions to this obligation in s 25A(3), Immigration Act 1971, and the further defences for rescuers and as regards stowaways added by s 41(4), Nationality and Borders Act 2022.

[100] Nationality and Borders Act 2022, s 40.

[101] Case law beginning with Case C-61/11 PPU *El Dridi* EU:C:2011:268.

[102] Although UK law does reflect the provisions of the UK/EU Trade and Cooperation Agreement on provision of services and business visitors: Statement of Changes to Immigration Rules, CP 361, 31 Dec 2020.

[103] As regards visas, the UK and EU member states respectively are being treated the same as other countries subject to a visa waiver under the relevant laws.

[104] 'A Renewed Agenda for European Union–United Kingdom Cooperation Common Understanding' ('reset deal'), 19 May 2025, para 13. The EU and UK also agreed in principle that the UK should rejoin Erasmus, the student mobility programme (para 14, reset deal).

general framework (going beyond relations with the UK) for an EU youth mobility scheme.[105] As for the UK, it has a number of youth mobility treaties already.[106]

Of course, it might be argued that, given that the UK has many youth mobility arrangements already, a scheme with the EU would not really be treating the EU as a special case. The truth of this hypothesis will depend on the content of the scheme agreed (if a scheme is agreed) between the UK and EU, that is, whether it differs substantially from the youth mobility schemes which the UK has agreed with non-EU countries already.

On that point, the current UK schemes with other countries have some broad similarities, but differ somewhat by country. They apply to people who are either 18–30 or (for Australia, Canada, New Zealand, and South Korea) 18–35; the beneficiary can turn 30 or 35 (as the case may be) during the scheme. For some (Hong Kong and Taiwan) there is a ballot, to allocate the available 1,000 places a year. Applicants must pay both an application fee and the NHS surcharge; there is no recourse to public funds. Family reunion is a separate issue, although there is provision for children born in the UK while resident on the basis of the scheme. Youth visitors are entitled to work, study, or be self-employed, subject to some conditions. The usual period of maximum stay is two years, although an extension to three years is possible as regards Australia, Canada, and New Zealand. The arrangements with India are quite distinct, establishing an 'India Young Professionals Scheme' applicable to graduates (ie with a bachelor's degree), and subject to a separate ballot (3000 places/year).

How does this compare to the EU plans? The Council decision adopting the EU's negotiating mandate is published,[107] but the addendum to this decision—which sets out the substantive details of the EU's negotiation position—is not. All we know for sure is that the decision establishing the mandate refers to the power of member states to 'determine volumes of admission of third-country nationals in accordance with Article 79(5) TFEU'. In fact this gives a misleading impression of the content of Article 79(5), which is narrower in scope: it provides that this Article (the legal base for EU competence on non-EU immigration) 'shall not affect the right of Member States to determine volumes of admission of third-country nationals coming from third countries to their territory *in order to seek work, whether employed or self-employed*'.

On the other hand, the Commission's original request for a negotiation mandate (in response to the UK seeking to negotiate with only *some* member states) is fully published—although we do not know what amendments, if any, the Council may have made to it when adopting the decision setting out the negotiating mandate. Still, the Commission's proposal gives us a rough idea of what the EU negotiation position may be. In the Commission's view, there should be an EU-wide treaty with the UK because otherwise there would be 'differential treatment of Union nationals'. Obviously the UK has agreed in principle to this. The Commission also objects that an approach

[105] Commission Communication, Attracting Skills and Talent to the EU, COM (2022) 657, section 4.2.
[106] For an overview, see https://www.gov.uk/youth-mobility.
[107] [2025] OJ L 01/07/25.

based on traditional UK youth mobility schemes 'would not address the main barriers to mobility experienced by young people since the end of the transition period'—so it challenges the limits usually set by UK schemes. In particular, the Commission argues that an EU-wide agreement with the UK could address:[108]

> [A]n absence of quotas for beneficiaries; the avoidance of discretionary visa application procedures; the length of the mobility period within the eligibility period; the breadth of the purposes of stay; the possibility for beneficiaries to be accompanied by close family members; Union citizens benefiting from equal treatment compared to United Kingdom nationals in a number of cases.

The specific parameters proposed by the Commission included: limiting the agreement to young people, 'e.g. 18–30 years of age'; a 'reasonable' time limit, 'e.g. 4 years'; mobility is not limited to certain purposes (except services would be excluded), or subject to quota (even though the Commission's 2022 communication had referred to member states retaining the right to set quotas); 'common admission conditions';[109] '[r]elevant grounds for rejection' of an application; prior verification of the application; no intra-EU mobility (although the 2022 communication had referred to possible intra-EU mobility for an EU scheme); equality in working conditions (as further defined) as well as tuition fees;[110] waiver of UK healthcare fees; and conditions for family reunion. Visa fees 'should not be disproportionate or excessive'.[111]

However, as we have seen, the Council's decision on the negotiation mandate refers to member states' power to cap the number of entrants, that is, the possibility for member states to set a quota as regards work-seekers at least. The reset agreement also refers obliquely to numerical limits: the agreement 'should . . . ensure that the overall number of participants is acceptable to both sides'. Furthermore, the Commission's summary of member states' existing youth mobility schemes with non-EU countries indicates that these schemes 'are generally limited to solving the question of obtaining a visa/work permit but do not necessarily address issues such as university tuition fees or equal treatment to nationals. They are often also limited in terms of permissible volumes of admission.' In this light it would be extraordinary for the EU to insist that there must be no form of numerical cap on the UK side—although the form such a cap might take, the maximum numbers of people admitted, and the distribution of those numbers between member states could all be difficult issues.

The common understanding also agrees that the scheme should apply to 'various activities, such as work, studies, au-pairing, volunteering, or simply travelling, for a limited period of time' and 'should provide a dedicated visa path' (which implies prior

[108] COM(2024) 169, 18/04/24.

[109] The Annex (para 17) refers to a 'valid travel document, a valid comprehensive sickness insurance, and proof of sufficient means of subsistence (taking account of whether the applicant is working or not)'.

[110] But equal treatment 'should not extend to study and maintenance grants and loans or other grants and loans' (ibid, para 24 of Annex).

[111] ibid, para 23 of Annex.

verification). But much of the detail (age limits, time limits, equal treatment, visa fees, admission conditions, healthcare fees) is omitted. This leaves open to debate a lot of big differences between traditional UK schemes and the Commission proposal (if the details of that proposal were agreed by the Council as the EU's negotiation mandate), in particular as regards time limits, equal treatment (especially on tuition fees), visa fees, and healthcare fees.

Second, the UK and France have ratified a pilot migration deal, linking the issues of irregular migration and asylum.[112] While not an agreement with the EU, it was not concluded until after it had been notified to the EU Commission by France for consultation, in accordance with the EU decision concluding the Trade and Cooperation Agreement.[113]

The agreement applies to those entering the UK via small boats, if they are illegal entrants, aiming at their return to France within three months.[114] In return, migrants will be admitted into the UK from France; the numbers 'are intended to be regularly balanced during the period of the Agreement'.[115] The situation of those transferred is regulated by domestic law, which for France includes EU law.[116]

The treaty sets out both a procedure for readmission into France[117] and one for reciprocal admission into the UK.[118] The latter route applies to those in the territory of France, as further regulated by the UK's immigration rules.[119] This treaty will expire on 11 June 2026—the day before the application of the EU's asylum pact (surely not a coincidence)—although it may be renewed with the agreement of both parties.[120] In practice, by October 2025, the UK had removed more than forty migrants to France under the treaty;[121] it was not clear how many it had accepted in return.

Third, the EU and UK have provisionally agreed a treaty on the status of Gibraltar. According to the final text, the treaty will include, along with economic elements, provisions on a form of association with the Schengen system, alongside provisions on frontier workers and social security.[122] In particular, the EU and UK 'agreed to establish dual Gibraltar and Schengen border checks at Gibraltar port and airport—to

[112] Agreement between the Government of the United Kingdom of Great Britain and Northern Ireland and the Government of the French Republic on the Prevention of Dangerous Journeys, presented to Parliament August 2025 ('UK/France treaty').

[113] Art 9 of the Council decision concluding the TCA ([2021] OJ L149/2).

[114] Art 1(1), UK/France treaty. For the definition of 'small boat', see Art 2(1)(f).

[115] Art 1(2) and (3), UK/France treaty.

[116] Art 1(4) and (5), UK/France treaty.

[117] Arts 3–11, UK/France treaty.

[118] Arts 12–15, UK/France treaty.

[119] Art 12(1) and (2), UK/France treaty. Security risks, unaccompanied minors, and those previously removed from the UK are inadmissible (Art 12(6)). See the Statement of Changes to the immigration rules CP 1373, Aug 2025, adding a new Appendix UKEATS (UK/European Applicant Transfer Scheme) to the rules.

[120] Art 22, UK/France treaty. See also the review clause (Art 20).

[121] UK Gov press release, 19 Oct 2025, 'Record single flight of illegal migrants returned under new deal', at: <https://www.gov.uk/government/news/record-single-flight-of-illegal-migrants-returned-under-new-deal>.

[122] Joint statement, 11 June 2025: https://ec.europa.eu/commission/presscorner/detail/en/statement_25_1481.

be carried out in full cooperation between the EU and UK/Gibraltar authorities', removing Spain/Gibraltar land border checks. Spain will carry out the EU border checks, while checks for Gibraltar will be carried out as at present. There are also unspecified 'arrangements' for visas and residence permits.

4 Post-Brexit Legality

In relation to the divergences from (or links with) the EU post-Brexit, there has been some litigation as regards the Withdrawal Agreement—as discussed in the separate chapter on EU citizens.[123] Otherwise there has been little reason to address Brexit-related legal issues in this field, because the Withdrawal Agreement and Trade and Cooperation Agreement say little about migration directly (other than the acquired rights of UK and EU citizens in the Withdrawal Agreement).

As for the three types of post-Brexit links with the EU discussed above, any legal issues are only nascent, particularly in the advance of final texts in two cases. But some initial questions can be identified.

For the youth mobility treaty, the Council decision on a negotiation mandate has already identified Article 79 TFEU as the legal base, referring also (as noted above) to the reservation of member states' power to determine quotas of non-EU citizens as set out in Article 79(5). If this reservation is respected in the final agreement (and, as we have seen, the reset agreement suggests that it will be), there may be less reason to provide for the final text to be a 'mixed agreement', that is, needing to be ratified by both the EU and its member states (the Commission's proposal had left that point, and the legal base, open).[124]

We also know that—for the EU side at least—the youth mobility treaty is envisaged as a 'supplementing agreement' within the meaning of the Trade and Cooperation Agreement (TCA).[125] This means that it would be 'an integral part of the overall bilateral relations as governed by [that] Agreement and shall form part of the overall framework', with the implication that it will be interpreted in light of public international law (rather than EU law) and will not confer direct effect.[126] Similarly, it would be subject to the TCA rules on dispute settlement, termination, and suspension—although that adds only limited clarity, as the relevant rules in the TCA vary widely by subject matter.[127] In fact, the Commission proposal for further treaties with the UK on energy and sanitary standards, apparently taking the form of supplementing agreements,

[123] Ch 17.

[124] It is not required that a treaty falling within the shared competence of both the EU and its member states must always be a mixed agreement; see the example of the Trade and Cooperation Agreement itself, which was only concluded by the EU, not its member states.

[125] Recital 4 in the preamble to the Council decision (n 107), referring to Art 2 TCA, [2021] OJ L149/10.

[126] Arts 4 and 5.

[127] See the discussion of dispute settlement in S Peers, 'So Close, Yet So Far: The EU/UK Trade and Cooperation Agreement' (2022) 59 CMLRev 49.

would add further variations to the post-Brexit UK/EU legal framework (alignment with EU law, further jurisdiction for the CJEU)—although there is no suggestion that the agreement on youth mobility should follow that approach.

The same issues will arise for the agreement regarding Gibraltar: legal base, legal effect, role for the CJEU, competence, connection to the TCA framework, and extent of alignment with EU law. So far there is no indication of how these issues will be addressed, in the absence of a proposed treaty text; the joint statement does not address these points.

Finally, the UK/France migration treaty raises different issues: whether this particular treaty between a member state and a non-EU country is compatible with EU law. In practice, the Commission raised no public objection to the treaty when it was consulted, so presumably does not believe that the treaty falls within the exclusive competence of the EU, because 'its conclusion may affect common rules or alter their scope' (Article 3(2) TFEU). It is possible that a migrant objecting to the application of the scheme may raise this point. If the CJEU, were it to be asked, agrees with this argument, it would still be possible for the Commission to propose EU legislation to authorize France to conclude the treaty regardless (see Article 2(1) TFEU).[128] In practice, several French and British NGOs have challenged the application of the treaty in the French courts, apparently focusing on the process of applying the treaty in French law, rather than EU law arguments.[129]

On the UK side, the High Court, upheld by the Court of Appeal, blocked the removal of one migrant on the grounds that the Home Secretary had not followed the government's guidance as regards trafficking cases.[130] However, that guidance has since been amended, in response to the relevant litigation;[131] and in a later case, more generally the High Court was not convinced that it should issue interim relief to block removals to France, given that country's compliance with the ECHR in general.[132]

5 Post-Brexit Empirical and Normative Analysis

(a) Regulatory Impact

The UK government sold its more liberal labour migration policy for non-EU citizens starting in 2021 as a 'Brexit benefit'. While this was, as we have seen, inaccurate *legally*—the UK could always have had a more liberal (or *less* liberal) policy on non-EU

[128] For example, see the decision authorising France to negotiate with the UK as regards the Channel Tunnel, [2020] OJ L352/4.

[129] https://utopia56.org/marchandage-migratoire-entre-le-royaume-uni-et-la-france-quinze-associations-saisissent-le-conseil-detat/.

[130] *CTK v SSHD* [2025] EWCA Civ 1264.

[131] ibid [30]–[32].

[132] *LYD v SSHD* (KB), 22 Oct 2025: https://www.judiciary.uk/judgments/lyd-v-secretary-of-state-for-the-home-department-anonymity-order/.

labour migration policy from the EU, due to its opt-outs from EU immigration law—it could be argued that such an interpretation accurately reflects the *economics* of labour markets, given that free movement with the EU inevitably facilitated the access of EU citizens to work in the UK, while conversely the end of free movement reduced the number of EU citizens moving to the UK to work.

Likewise, the more liberal student migration policy adopted by the UK post-Brexit was also not a 'Brexit benefit' in the legal sense—the UK having opted out of EU law on migration of non-EU students (which does not regulate tuition fees anyway, even as regards an equal treatment rule). But as with labour migration, there is a sense in which this more liberal policy supported the supply of students for universities (rather than labour for employers) in the context of the declining numbers of EU students following the end of free movement. UK universities also benefited from being able to charge higher fees for such students, in the absence of an equal treatment rule.

EU law was going roughly in the same direction, to the extent that it regulates the same issues: it should not be forgotten that regulation of legal migration by the EU is only partial, with member states allowed to set higher standards in some areas, or to apply labour market quotas on admission of non-EU citizens, with more detailed regulation of non-EU labour migration confined to specific fields (highly skilled migrants, intra-corporate transferees, seasonal workers; the Single Permit Directive regulates equal treatment and procedural rules, not the grounds of admission for non-EU workers generally) and issues such as family reunion for non-EU students or levels of, and equal treatment in, tuition fees not regulated for them.

More precisely, the comparable developments between the UK and EU can be seen as regards advance travel authorization for short-term visits, and to a limited extent the use of border gates (although the UK use of this technology falls well short of the EU's entry–exit system). The EU's changes to the law on admission of students, researchers, and highly skilled workers have very broad similarities to the (initially) more liberal UK rules on this issue, particularly as regards a form of stays post-graduation (as an incentive for students) and more liberal entry rules. But the (initial) very liberal UK rules on admission of workers generally cannot be compared to EU law, given the limited harmonization of national law imposed by the latter.

Conversely, recent UK U-turns significantly tightening the law on labour migration, student migration, and family reunion have limited parallels in EU law, in part because of limited EU harmonization (there being no EU rules on admission of non-EU student family members, or pay thresholds for non-EU workers generally). As for family reunion, while EU rules are comparatively generous as regards income thresholds for sponsors, they do not apply to all sponsors, being limited to cases where the sponsor holds a residence permit valid for one year or more and where there is a reasonable prospect of the sponsor obtaining permanent residence.[133] While the UK has

[133] Directive 2003/86 (n 16) Art 3(1). Having said that, the UK has more flexibility to change the rules regarding acquisition of (EU) long-term residence than member states do, in the absence of amendments to EU law (ie Directive 2003/109, n 17).

more flexibility to regulate non-EU migration than EU member states, (a) it always had most of this flexibility, even as a member state; and (b) some of the areas most affected by recent UK U-turns would be outside the scope of EU law anyway.

(b) Economic Impact

Economists broadly argue that more liberal UK immigration law benefited the UK economy (including the university sector); it follows that reversing such policies has the opposite effect—although the UK has fallen short of prohibiting labour, student, or family migration, as the most passionate opponents of immigration would prefer. In the context of the current UK government, characterized by avowedly pro-growth policy aspirations, the immigration policy might be summarized, borrowing from Meat Loaf, as 'we'll do anything for growth—but we won't do that'.

(c) Territorial Impact

The post-Brexit migration policy of the UK has limited territorial distinctions, with the obvious exception of specific rules relating to Gibraltar if the UK/EU agreement on Gibraltar (summarized above) is approved. Although there are obvious differences between Northern Ireland and the rest of the UK, they relate more to the pre-existing Common Travel Area arrangements with Ireland, which are referred to (but do not stem from, and are not directly regulated by) the Withdrawal Agreement.[134] Within the EU, Ireland retains (and still uses) its opt-outs related to the Common Travel Area; but this was already the case when the UK was a member state, and has not been affected in practice by the UK's departure from the EU. As for the human rights standstill in the Windsor Framework, that is not applicable where the UK was not previously bound by EU law, due to exercising its opt-outs.[135]

6 Conclusion

Unlike many regulatory areas, non-EU migration to the UK was largely not regulated by EU law for the UK, partly due to UK opt-outs and partly due to limits on EU harmonization in this field. The impact of Brexit was therefore more indirect legally speaking, as the reduction in EU workers and students led to an attempt to liberalize the movement of their non-EU equivalents to compensate. The political impact of increased numbers has led to a U-turn—but this is, again, only indirectly a consequence

[134] See Ch 8.
[135] See *Shima Esmail* [2024] NIKB 64.

of Brexit, and some of the relevant changes to UK law would have been compatible with EU law (given the limits on harmonization) even had the UK remained a member state and opted in to that law.

While aspects of the UK liberalization of migration policy can be compared to EU developments, this comparison can only be partial due to the limits on EU harmonization; and while the reversal of policy does not reflect comparable EU developments, again there are limits on comparability due to the limits on harmonization. Overall, while the UK's sharp changes in migration policy post-Brexit can be linked back to Brexit, this link is economic rather than legal, and is diffused by both the UK's prior opt-outs and the limits on what the EU has harmonized in any event.

In parallel with the UK's U-turn on liberalization of policy, it has renewed links with the EU and its member states on issues related to migration. While this falls well short of a return to free movement, it is an indication that policies based on fully equal treatment of the EU with non-EU countries, and solutions related to relationships with non-EU countries, have at least been partly eschewed as time passes from the initial Brexit date.

19

Asylum in the UK

Catherine Briddick and Cathryn Costello[*]

1 Introduction: Sovereignty Myths

Promises that sovereignty would be regained, immigration and asylum controlled, and national identity reasserted were central to the Brexit referendum campaign of 2016 and the ultimate decision to leave the European Union (EU). To many analysts, the referendum was 'largely, if not entirely, about reducing immigration'.[1] A range of arguments in favour of Brexit employed populist,[2] sovereigntist,[3] and racist rhetoric,[4] in which asylum, labour, and other forms of migration were frequently conflated and portrayed as 'out of control'. This misframing was evident in campaign images of refugees from the 2015 'refugee crisis' walking in search of protection, fearmongering about the (illusory) prospect of Turkey's EU accession, and references to the 2004, 2007, and 2013 accessions of eastern and central European states. It also contributed to racial discrimination and violence. As Adrian Favell reminds us, Nigel Farage unveiled his 'Breaking Point' image on 16 June 2016, the same day that Labour MP Jo Cox was murdered 'by a white race supremacist in a West Yorkshire high street'.[5] An amorphous and undifferentiated conception of 'EU immigration' and the threat it posed to the body politic were decisive to both the decision to leave the EU and the changes to asylum law that followed.[6]

* Many thanks to Katie O'Sullivan for research assistance.

1 G Evans and A Menon, *Brexit and British Politics* (Polity Press 2017) 109.

2 C Joppke, 'Immigration in the Populist Crucible: Comparing Brexit and Trump' (2020) 8 Comparative Migration Studies 49.

3 J Agnew, 'Taking Back Control? The Myth of Territorial Sovereignty and the Brexit Fiasco' (2020) 8 Territory, Politics, Governance 259; A Menon and A Wager, 'Taking Back Control: Sovereignty as Strategy in Brexit Politics' (2020) 8 Territory, Politics, Governance 279; M Goodwin and C Milazzo, 'Taking Back Control? Investigating the Role of Immigration in the 2016 Vote for Brexit' (2017) 19 British Journal of Politics and International Relations 450.

4 A Favell, 'Crossing the Race Line: "No Polish, No Blacks, No Dogs" in Brexit Britain? or, The Great British Brexit Swindle: The Long View' in F Duina and F Merand (eds), *Europe's Malaise: The Long View* (Emerald Publishing 2020).

5 ibid 151.

6 On the former, see A Favell and R Barbulescu, 'Brexit, "Immigration" and Anti-discrimination' in P Diamond, P Nedergaard and B Rosamond (eds), *The Routledge Handbook of the Politics of Brexit* (Taylor & Francis 2018).

Catherine Briddick and Cathryn Costello, *Asylum in the UK* In: *The UK Regulatory Framework Post-Brexit: 'Law Unbound'*.
Edited by: Paul Craig and Vilija Vėlyvytė, Oxford University Press. © Oxford University Press 2026.
DOI: 10.1093/9780198969815.003.0022

Legally, the migration and protection issues that proved so central to the referendum campaign were always subject to UK 'control'. The UK had a right to selective participation in EU asylum policy, had a veto over new accessions, and had itself chosen to grant EU workers from the new member states unhindered access to the labour market in 2004. It is also the case that the UK received comparatively few of the refugees who fled to the EU in 2014/15. Post-Brexit, however, arrivals across all the main categories (for labour, study, and asylum) increased significantly.[7] Notable also are the large numbers of protection-seekers who were admitted under discretionary 'bespoke' schemes, including for those from Ukraine and Hong Kong.[8] This is something of a 'Brexit paradox', as leaving the EU was followed by more migration and protection-seeking overall.[9] From 2018 onwards, however, political and legal attention shifted to arrivals on 'small boats'.

In this chapter, we trace pre- and post-Brexit changes in UK and EU asylum law. Our starting point is that the UK's obligations to those in need of international protection continue to derive from international law, which in turn shapes the common law.

The 1951 Refugee Convention[10] defines 'refugees', obliges states to protect them from penalization and *refoulement*, and provides a set of important rights—rights that increase with refugees' degree of attachment to the host state. Wider protections against *refoulement* are also included in a broad array of international and regional human rights treaties, including the European Convention on Human Rights (ECHR).[11] *Non-refoulement* is, in addition, a norm of customary international law, one 'ripe for recognition' as *jus cogens*.[12] While the Refugee Convention does not contain a right to asylum as such, it does include the principle of non-penalization for irregular entry or stay. This protective provision, Article 31, reflects the drafters' understanding that refugees may be compelled to travel without permission in order to access a place of safety.[13]

[7] In February 2022, overseas care workers were given permission to work in the UK as Skilled Migrants. This change contributed to 'unusually high net migration' in 2022-3, see further Madeleine Sumption and Ben Brindle, 'The Ban on Care Workers' Family Members: What Will be the Impact?' (*Migration Observatory*, 5 April 2024) <https://migrationobservatory.ox.ac.uk/resources/commentaries/the-ban-on-care-workers-family-members-what-will-be-the-impact/> accessed 26 April 2024.

[8] M Benson, N Sigona, and E Zambelli, 'The UK's "Safe and Legal" Humanitarian Routes: From Colonial Ties to Privatising Protection' (2024) 95 Political Quarterly 263.

[9] We use the terms asylum-seeker and protection-seeker interchangeably here to capture a broad group of people seeking a protective status in the UK or EU, be that recognition as a Convention refugee, complementary/subsidiary protection, or another permission to remain.

[10] Convention relating to the Status of Refugees (adopted 28 July 1951, entered into force 22 April 1954) 189 UNTS 137.

[11] Convention for the Protection of Human Rights and Fundamental Freedoms (adopted 4 November 1950, entered into force 3 September 1953) ETS 5 (European Convention on Human Rights, as amended).

[12] C Costello and M Foster, 'Non-refoulement as Custom and *Jus Cogens*? Putting the Prohibition to the Test' in Maarten den Heijer and Harmen van der Wilt (eds), *Netherlands Yearbook of International Law 2015: Jus Cogens: Quo Vadis?* (TMC Asser Press 2016).

[13] C Costello (with Y Ioffe and T Büchsel), *Article 31 of the 1951 Convention Relating to the Status of Refugees* (UNHCR Legal and Policy Protection Series PPLA/2017/01, July 2017); C Costello and Y Ioffe, 'Non-penalization and Non-criminalization' in C Costello, M Foster, and J McAdam (eds), *The Oxford Handbook of International Refugee Law* (Oxford University Press 2021).

Our analysis proceeds as follows. We provide a brief overview of the EU's Common European Asylum System and the UK's former position therein. We then examine post-Brexit legal developments in the UK, which we understand as having three distinct phases—distortion, repudiation, and *potential* reset. Having mapped 'reforms' to EU asylum law, we consider UK and EU convergence and divergence in relation to externalization, criminalization, and selectivity. We conclude with a discussion of sovereignty myths and the rule of law.

2 The Common European Asylum System (CEAS) and the UK

(a) The CEAS and Its Development from 1990 to 2020: Protection vs Containment

The Common European Asylum System (CEAS) is a regional asylum framework that purports to be in accordance with the Refugee Convention and 'other relevant treaties', including the ECHR.[14] Asylum legislation, in particular the Qualification Directive(s), incorporates the Refugee Convention's approach to inclusion, cessation, and exclusion into EU law. It also elaborates on the refugee definition's key elements—persecution, grounds, and internal protection.[15] The Charter of Fundamental Rights of the EU (CFR) protects the right to asylum.[16]

The EU's commitment to protection in line with international standards is foundational to the CEAS. So too, however, is its role in containment—establishing and enforcing migration controls which tend to prevent those seeking protection from being able to do so safely and legally. Relatedly, the EU's promise of internal mobility for 'insiders', citizens and certain others, is secured alongside the immobilization of 'outsiders', those seeking protection in particular. As Cathryn Costello and Lilian Tsourdi have argued, these tensions, between protection and deflection, free movement and immobility, remain central to the CEAS' development and its response to 'crisis'.[17]

Cooperation by EU member states (MS) on asylum originated outside the framework of its Treaties and was linked to the gradual removal of internal border controls under the Schengen system.[18] Mobility, as part of the internal market, was crucial to

[14] Consolidated Version of the Treaty on the Functioning of the European Union [2012] OJ C 326/47 Art 78(1). See further E (Lilian) Tsourdi, 'Regional Refugee Regimes: Europe', in Costello, Foster, and McAdam (n 13).

[15] For an assessment see JC Hathaway, 'EU Accountability to International Law: The Case of Asylum' (2011) 33 Michigan Journal of International Law 1.

[16] Charter of Fundamental Rights of the European Union [2007] OJ C303/01, Art 18.

[17] E (Lilian) Tsourdi and C Costello, 'The Evolution of EU Law on Refugees and Asylum' in P Craig and G de Búrca (eds), *The Evolution of EU Law* (3rd edn, Oxford University Press 2021) Ch 25.

[18] Convention implementing the Schengen Agreement of 14 June 1985 between the Governments of the States of the Benelux Economic Union, the Federal Republic of Germany and the French Republic on the

European integration. In contrast, the Dublin Convention[19] established a different logic for asylum-seekers. It effectively prevented onward movement through criteria which allocated responsibility for determining claims, so that absent the possibility of certain kinds of family reunion, the country that admitted the asylum-seeker, physically or legally, was required to make a decision on their case.[20] This mechanism has profound effects on an asylum-seeker's chances of being recognized as a refugee. Even those who are granted a protective status remain largely excluded from EU movement, as there is no positive mutual recognition of asylum decisions. The Dublin system was, from the outset, beset with non-compliance as both states and asylum-seekers sought to evade its operation.

The first phase of EU asylum law followed the integration of asylum and migration into the EU Treaties by the Treaty of Amsterdam.[21] The first piece of binding legislation was the Temporary Protection Directive (the TPD).[22] Inspired by the EU's response to the flight from Kosovo, it remained a 'dead letter' until its first activation in 2022, in response to the unlawful Russian invasion of Ukraine.[23] Until then, it had been perceived as 'too generous' and liable to encourage further arrivals.[24]

The TPD was quickly followed by the Reception Conditions,[25] Qualification,[26] and Asylum Procedures Directives.[27] The Reception Conditions Directive set minimum standards in matters relating to accommodation and detention, financial and other support, and access to healthcare and to education. The most significant feature of the Qualification Directive was the inclusion of a status for those protected against

gradual abolition of checks at their common borders (with Final Act, procès-verbal and joint declaration) 3041 UNTS 137.

[19] Convention determining the State responsible for examining applications for asylum lodged in one of the Member States of the European Communities [1997] OJ C254/1.

[20] A Hurwitz, 'The 1990 Dublin Convention: A Comprehensive Assessment' (1999) 11 International Journal of Refugee Law 646.

[21] Treaty of Amsterdam amending the Treaty on European Union, the Treaties establishing the European Communities and certain related acts—Final Act [1997] OJ C340/1.

[22] Council Directive 2001/55/EC of 20 July 2001 on Minimum Standards for Giving Temporary Protection in the Event of a Mass Influx of Displaced Persons and on Measures Promoting a Balance of Efforts Between Member States in Receiving such Persons and Bearing the Consequences Thereof [2001] OJ L212/12.

[23] Council Implementing Decision (EU) 2022/382 of 4 March 2022 establishing the existence of a mass influx of displaced persons from Ukraine within the meaning of Article 5 of Directive 2001/55/EC, and having the effect of introducing temporary protection [2022] OJ L71/2.

[24] M Ineli-Ciger, 'Has the Temporary Protection Directive Become Obsolete? An Examination of the Directive and Its Lack of Implementation in View of the Recent Asylum Crisis in the Mediterranean' in C Bauloz, M Ineli-Ciger, and S Singer (eds), *Seeking Asylum in the European Union: Selected Protection Issues Raised by the Second Phase of the Common European Asylum System* (Brill/Nijhoff Publishers 2015). See further, J-F Durieux, 'Temporary Protection and Temporary Refuge', in Costello, Foster, and McAdam (n 13).

[25] Council Directive 2003/9/EC of 27 January 2003 laying down minimum standards for the reception of asylum seekers [2003] OJ L31/18.

[26] Council Directive 2004/83/EC of 29 April 2004 on minimum standards for the qualification and status of third country nationals or stateless persons as refugees or as persons who otherwise need international protection and the content of the protection granted [2004] OJ L304/12 (the Qualification Directive).

[27] Council Directive 2005/85/EC of 1 December 2005 on minimum standards on procedures in member states for granting and withdrawing refugee status [2005] OJ L326/13.

removal on some human rights grounds—'subsidiary protection'—in the UK context called 'humanitarian protection'.[28] The Qualification Directive also set out a restrictive, cumulative approach to 'particular social groups', one that departed from the accepted position in international refugee law.[29]

The Asylum Procedures Directive introduced inadmissibility and special decision-making processes, these rendering procedures less accessible, more complex, and less efficient.[30] The Directive also made provision for safe country practices—both safe country of origin (SCO) and safe third country (STC). STC practices originated in the notion of 'first country of asylum' (FCA)—that a refugee should stay where they already enjoyed protection, by virtue of their residence with legal status. Over time, FCA morphed into STC, the latter's scope expanding, but still requiring a connection between the protection-seeker and the relevant 'return' country. This approach to STCs provided the ostensible framework for the EU's extra-legal responses to the 2015 refugee crisis. Finally, during this period the Dublin II Regulation[31] replaced the Dublin Convention.

The second phase of EU asylum law involved recasting these Directives. The recast Qualification Directive[32] broadened the notion of family members and directly addressed persecution on the grounds of gender and sexual orientation.[33] The recast Asylum Procedures Directive[34] introduced yet further grounds to differentiate between procedures, but retained the 'connection requirement' for STCs.[35] The recast Reception Conditions Directive[36] addressed divergent approaches to scope, explicitly covering transit zones, MS' territorial waters and detention centres, and those applying for subsidiary protection.[37] The Dublin III

[28] J McAdam, *Complementary Protection in International Refugee Law* (Oxford University Press 2007) Ch 2.

[29] Compare Qualification Directive Art 10(d) with UNHCR, Guidelines on International Protection No. 1: Gender-Related Persecution within the context of Article 1A(2) of the 1951 Convention and/or its 1967 Protocol relating to the Status of Refugees (7 May 2002) UN Doc HCR/GIP/02/01, para 29.

[30] C Costello, 'The Asylum Procedures Directive and the Proliferation of Safe Country Practices: Deterrence, Deflection and the Dismantling of International Protection?' (2005) 7 European Journal of Migration and Law 35.

[31] Council Regulation (EC) No 343/2003 of 18 February 2003 establishing the criteria and mechanisms for determining the member state responsible for examining an asylum application lodged in one of the member states by a third-country national [2003] OJ L50/1.

[32] Directive 2011/95/EU of the European Parliament and of the Council of 13 December 2011 on standards for the qualification of third-country nationals or stateless persons as beneficiaries of international protection, for a uniform status for refugees or for persons eligible for subsidiary protection, and for the content of the protection granted (recast) [2011] OJ L337/9.

[33] On gender, see further C Querton, 'One Step Forward, Two Steps Back? Interpreting "Particular Social Group" in the European Union' (2022) 71 ICLQ 425.

[34] Directive 2013/32/EU of the European Parliament and of the Council of 26 June 2013 on common procedures for granting and withdrawing international protection (recast) [2013] OJ L180/60.

[35] C Costello and E Hancox, 'The Recast Asylum Procedures Directive 2013/32/EU: Caught between the Stereotypes of the Abusive Asylum Seeker and the Vulnerable Refugee' in V Chetail, P De Bruycker, and F Maiani (eds), *Reforming the Common European Asylum System: The New European Refugee Law* (Martinus Nijhoff 2015).

[36] Directive 2013/33/EU of the European Parliament and of the Council of 26 June 2013 laying down standards for the reception of applicants for international protection (recast) [2013] OJ L180/96.

[37] E (Lilian) Tsourdi, 'Reception Conditions for Asylum Seekers in the EU: Towards the Prevalence of Human Dignity' (2015) 29 Journal of Immigration, Asylum and Nationality Law 9.

Regulation[38] was complemented by the Eurodac Regulation,[39] the latter obliging MS to fingerprint asylum-seekers and document their admission and registration.

In 2015, very large numbers of refugees entered the EU irregularly, mostly on small boats making the short crossing from Turkey to the Greek islands. A significant proportion were refugees from the Syrian civil war.[40] Following the long-standing pattern, most evaded the Dublin system and moved onwards to seek protection in Germany and northern Europe. Notwithstanding the 'harmonization' of procedures and conditions that the first and second phase of the CEAS sought to ensure, detention and living conditions in some EU MS were so poor that courts blocked Dublin returns on this basis.[41]

The large numbers of refugees moving to and in Europe prompted waves of both solidarity and hostility. At the EU level, however, MS failed to cooperate to share responsibility, and so a solution was sought to deter arrivals. The EU–Turkey Statement was a political agreement 'to end the irregular migration'.[42] At its heart was the return to Turkey of those 'irregular migrants' who had sought protection in Greece. This 'temporary and extraordinary measure'[43] led to the transformation of Aegean Island 'Hotspots'[44] into mass detention spaces with squalid conditions. The CJEU declined jurisdiction to examine the legality of the agreement, finding that it was not an EU act.[45] However, in late 2024 the CJEU dealt a blow to the practice of returning asylum-seekers to Turkey, deeming it unlawful as Turkey did not, in fact, admit or readmit applicants for international protection.[46] The efficacy of the EU–Turkey deal remains contested. While some frame it as having effectively deterred arrivals, its impact is,

[38] Regulation (EU) No 604/2013 of the European Parliament and of the Council of 26 June 2013 establishing the criteria and mechanisms for determining the member state responsible for examining an application for international protection lodged in one of the member states by a third-country national or a stateless person (recast) [2013] OJ L180/31.

[39] Regulation (EU) No 603/2013 of the European Parliament and of the Council of 26 June 2013 on the establishment of 'Eurodac' for the comparison of fingerprints for the effective application of Regulation (EU) No 604/2013 establishing the criteria and mechanisms for determining the member state responsible for examining an application for international protection lodged in one of the member states by a third-country national or a stateless person and on requests for the comparison with Eurodac data by member states' law enforcement authorities and Europol for law enforcement purposes, and amending Regulation (EU) No 1077/2011 establishing a European Agency for the operational management of large-scale IT systems in the area of freedom, security and justice (recast) (2013) OJ L180/1.

[40] UN High Commissioner for Refugees (UNHCR), *International Protection Considerations with regard to people fleeing the Syrian Arab Republic, Update VI* (HCR/PC/SYR/2021/06, March 2021).

[41] *MSS v Belgium and Greece* [2011] 53 EHRR 28; *Tarakhel v Switzerland* App no 29217/12 (ECtHR, 4 November 2014).

[42] European Council, 'EU–Turkey Statement' (18 March 2016) <https://www.consilium.europa.eu/en/press/press-releases/2016/03/18/eu-turkey-statement/> accessed 26 September 2024.

[43] ibid.

[44] European Commission, *Communication from the Commission to the European Parliament, the Council, the European Economic and Social Committee and the Committee of the Regions: A European Agenda on Migration* (COM(2015) 240 final, 13 May 2015) 6.

[45] Case T-192/16 *NF v European Council* EU:T:2017:128.

[46] Case C-134/23 *Somateio 'Elliniko Symvoulio gia tous Prosfyges' and Astiki Mi Kerdoskopiki Etaireia 'Ypostirixi Prosfygon sto Aigaio' v Ypourgos Exoterikon and Ypourgos Metanastefsis kai Asylou* EU:C:2024:838.

at best, unclear.[47] What is undeniable is that the agreement contributed to the detention of refugees and others in conditions repeatedly condemned by the ECtHR as inhuman and degrading.[48]

(b) The UK in the CEAS: Highly Selective Participation

In 1997, when the Treaty of Amsterdam brought European asylum cooperation into EU law, the UK (and Ireland, with whom it has a common travel area) negotiated the right to engage selectively in EU asylum and immigration policies.[49] Accordingly, claims that it was necessary to leave the EU in order to regulate asylum are misleading, as the UK was able to decide when and how to participate in the CEAS.

The UK chose to opt in to the first phase of EU asylum law—the Temporary Protection, Reception Conditions, Qualification, and Asylum Procedures Directives. When this legislation was recast a decade later, the UK opted out of the main legislation, participating only in the recast of Dublin and Eurodac (Table 19.1).

Table 19.1 UK participation in CEAS: phase two instruments UK opt-in

2001 Temporary Protection Directive	Yes This Directive was not recast so the UK was bound by its original opt-in.
2011 Qualification Directive (recast)	No
2013 Eurodac Regulation	Yes
2013 Dublin III Regulation	Yes
2013 Reception Conditions Directive (recast)	No
2013 Asylum Procedures Directive (recast)	No

The consequences of the UK's opting out were, perhaps, not as significant as might be imagined. Core elements defining the scope of international protection, Convention refugeehood, and 'subsidiary protection' remained essentially unchanged during the recast process.[50] It is notable that the 'opt-in' exceptions were in relation to the Dublin

[47] G Ovacık, M Ineli-Ciger, and O Ulusoy, 'Taking Stock of the EU–Turkey Statement in 2024' (2024) 26 European Journal of Migration and Law 154.

[48] *AD v Greece* App no 55363/19 (ECtHR, 4 April 2023); *MB v Greece* App no 8389/20 (ECtHR, 23 November 2023); *JA and others v Italy* App no 21329/18 (ECtHR, 30 March 2023); *MA and others v Greece* App no 15192/20 (ECtHR, 3 October 2024).

[49] Treaty of Amsterdam amending the Treaty on European Union, the Treaties establishing the European Communities and certain related acts—Protocol on the position of the United Kingdom and Ireland [1997] OJ C340/99.

[50] See, eg, Case C-349/20 *NB and AB v Secretary of State for the Home Department* EU:C:2022:151 and the discussion of the UK's position in the CEAS and the relevance of post-2011 jurisprudence to the UK's application of Art 12(1)(a) of the Qualification Directive.

system, successive UK governments viewing it as a means of sending asylum-seekers elsewhere. In 2015, the then Minister of State for Security and Immigration, James Brokenshire MP, explained the UK position as follows:[51]

> The Government is fully committed to the system created by the Dublin Regulation, which determines which participating State is responsible for examining an application for international protection. The UK has opted in to all earlier proposals concerning the Dublin Regulation and the related Eurodac Regulation. Opting in to this single issue proposal concerning unaccompanied asylum seeking children is consistent with our strong support for the Dublin system as a whole, which has been of great benefit to the UK, enabling the removal of over 12,000 asylum individuals since 2003 to other participating States.

While the UK was able to have significant numbers of people removed under the Dublin system, over time, and with strategic litigation, the authorities responded to family reunification requests more frequently.[52] As a consequence, when the UK left the EU, Dublin operated as a legal *entry* route for asylum-seekers with close family members in the jurisdiction. The House of Lords' EU Committee was, therefore, concerned that UK withdrawal would result in[53]

> the loss of a safe, legal route for the reunification of separated refugee families in Europe. Vulnerable unaccompanied children would find their family reunion rights curtailed, as Dublin offers them the chance to be reunited with a broader range of family members than under current UK Immigration Rules.

3 Post-Brexit Legal Change in the UK: Distortion, Repudiation, and *Potential* Reset?

(a) International Obligations and UK–EU Agreements

The UK's obligations to those in need of international protection are determined by a range of international and regional instruments, as explained above. While the UK is primarily a dualist jurisdiction, international law permeates the UK legal system in many ways.[54] The UK has not incorporated the Refugee Convention into domestic

[51] 'European Union opt-in decision: Dublin Regulation and the Determination of Responsibility for Unaccompanied Asylum Seeking Children (Statement UIN HCWS219)', *UK Parliament* (23 January 2015) <https://questions-statements.parliament.uk/written-statements/detail/2015-01-23/HCWS219> accessed 16 July 2025.

[52] G Starfield, *Forging Strategic Partnerships: How Civil Organisers and Lawyers Helped Unaccompanied children Cross the English Channel and Reunite with Family Members* (Refugee Studies Centre Working Paper Series No 133, 2020).

[53] The European Union Committee, *Brexit: Refugee Protection and Asylum Policy* (48th Report of Session 2017–19, HL Paper 428, 11 October 2019) 3.

[54] See further, Lord Lloyd-Jones, 'International Law before United Kingdom Courts: A Quiet Revolution' (2022) 71 ICLQ 503.

law, as it did the ECHR with the Human Rights Act 1998. However, the 'primacy'[55] of the Refugee Convention has been affirmed in both primary legislation and judicial decisions. Thus, in *Sivakumaran* (1988)[56] Lord Keith observed that:[57]

> The United Kingdom having acceded to the Convention and Protocol, their provisions have for all practical purposes been incorporated into United Kingdom law.

The EU Qualification Directive was transposed into UK law by the Qualification Regulations[58] and relevant Immigration Rules.[59]

On 17 October 2019, the EU and UK reached an agreement on the UK's withdrawal from the EU. The Withdrawal Agreement and the related Political Declaration did not address asylum or related cooperation in any substantive way. In the Agreement, refugees are mentioned only where they are covered by provisions concerning social security co-ordination.[60] The Political Declaration makes brief reference to 'global challenges' such as 'illegal migration', pledging cooperation to 'tackle' it while 'recognising the need to protect the most vulnerable'.[61] The Withdrawal Agreement entered into force on 31 January 2020, providing for a transition period during which EU law continued to apply.

In the immediate post-Brexit transition period, as the UK and EU sought to negotiate a trade deal, the UK proposed two agreements to address matters covered by Dublin III—one on the transfer of unaccompanied asylum-seeking children,[62] and the other on cooperation on the return of irregular migrants.[63] EU negotiators rejected both on the basis that they fell outside their mandate.[64] The resulting EU–UK

55 Asylum and Immigration Appeals Act 1993, s 2.

56 *R v Secretary of State for the Home Department, Ex parte Sivakumaran* [1988] AC 958; [1988] 1 All ER 193.

57 ibid 990H.

58 The Refugee or Person in Need of International Protection (Qualification) Regulations 2006 No 2525.

59 The Immigration Rules are a unique form of subordinate legislation made under the Immigration Act 1971, s 3(2).

60 Agreement on the Withdrawal of the United Kingdom of Great Britain and Northern Ireland from the European Union and the European Atomic Energy Community (2019/C 384 I/01) [2019] OJ C384 I/1, Arts 30–32. Or in relation to the UK's military base in Cyprus. The UK did agree to honour agreements made in relation to the Trust Fund for Africa and the Facility for Refugees in Turkey, ibid Art 155.

61 Political Declaration setting out the framework for the future relationship between the European Union and the United Kingdom (2019/C 384 I/02) [2019] OJ C384 I/178 [90], [114].

62 'Draft Working Text for an Agreement between the United Kingdom of Great Britain and Northern Ireland and the European Union on the Transfer of Unaccompanied Asylum-seeking Children' (*GOV.UK*) <https://assets.publishing.service.gov.uk/media/5ec3b8c186650c27932664bf/DRAFT_Agreement_on_the_transfer_of_unaccompanied_asylum-seeking_children.pdf> accessed 9 May 2025.

63 'Draft Working Text for an Agreement between the United Kingdom of Great Britain and Northern Ireland and the European Union on the Readmission of Persons Residing Without Authorisation' (*GOV.UK*) <https://assets.publishing.service.gov.uk/media/5ec3b8d3d3bf7f5d43765d51/DRAFT_Agreement_on_the_readmission_of_people_residing_without_authorisation.pdf> accessed 9 May 2025.

64 Jennifer Rankin, 'Brexit: EU Rejects UK Proposal for Reuniting Child Asylum Seekers', *The Guardian* (3 September 2020) <https://www.theguardian.com/uk-news/2020/sep/03/brexit-eu-rejects-british-proposal-reuniting-child-asylum-seekers> accessed 9 May 2025.

Trade and Cooperation Agreement (UK–EU TCA)[65] did not address asylum but did place respect for democracy, the rule of law, and international human rights law at the centre of post-Brexit cooperation.[66] The related Joint Political Declaration also affirmed both parties' recognition of the 'importance of good management of migratory flows' and, therefore, the need for future 'bilateral discussions' on asylum and family reunion.[67]

(b) 'Small Boats', Legislative Change

At the end of the Brexit transition period on 31 December 2020, the Dublin III Regulation and those aspects of the CEAS that the UK had opted in to ceased to apply to the UK. As asylum did not feature heavily in the Withdrawal Agreement or the subsequent UK–EU TCA, it was not directly addressed in the first pieces of Brexit legislation, the European Union (Withdrawal) Act 2018 and the Immigration and Social Security Co-ordination (EU Withdrawal) Act 2020 (the latter of which repealed retained EU law relating to free movement).[68]

This position quickly changed with the increasing numbers of protection-seekers travelling to the UK by 'small boat'.[69] It is well understood that there are few safe and legal routes for refugees to enter the UK (or indeed, and as seen above, the EU). The presence of this particularly visible and dangerous 'irregular route' became and remains the focus of post-Brexit asylum policy. In part, the shift in routes appears to be a result of the suppression of previous irregular and dangerous pathways, such as stowing away on lorries entering the UK by boat or via the Channel Tunnel. It is unclear whether or not this increase in boat arrivals has contributed to an overall increase in irregular migration. However, in a trope familiar from other contexts, notably Australia, the need to 'stop the boats' and 'end smuggling' has informed sweeping legislative changes, which range from being in tension with to outright breach of the Refugee Convention, the ECHR, and other international instruments. Here, we

[65] Trade and Cooperation Agreement between the European Union and the European Atomic Energy Community, of the one part, and the United Kingdom of Great Britain and Northern Ireland, of the other part [2021] OJ L149/10.

[66] Steve Peers, 'Analysis 3 of the Brexit Deal: Human Rights and EU/UK Trade and Cooperation Agreement', *EU Law Analysis* (4 January 2021) <https://eulawanalysis.blogspot.com/2021/01/analysis-3-of-brexit-deal-human-rights.html> accessed 10 May 2025. The importance of the UK remaining a party to ECHR has also been affirmed by the CJEU, Case C-327/18 *PPU* EU:C:2018:733 [52].

[67] Declarations referred to in the Council Decision on the signing on behalf of the Union, and on a provisional application of the Trade and Cooperation Agreement and of the Agreement concerning security procedures for exchanging and protecting classified information [2020] OJ L444/1475, 1477–78.

[68] Immigration and Social Security Co-ordination (EU Withdrawal) Act 2020, s 3 does require the Secretary of State to review the ways in which protection claimants in an EU MS are able to enter the UK lawfully. See further, C Yeo and S Reardon-Smith, 'The Impact of Brexit on UK Asylum Law' (2018) 32 Journal of Immigration Asylum and Nationality Law 232.

[69] Peter William Walsh and Mihnea Cuibus, 'People Crossing the English Channel in Small Boats', *Migration Observatory* (18 July 2025) <https://migrationobservatory.ox.ac.uk/resources/briefings/people-crossing-the-english-channel-in-small-boats/> accessed 16 September 2025.

identify three phases in post-Brexit UK asylum law, in turn: (1) distortion; (2) repudiation; and (3) *potential* reset. Central to all three is the adoption of containment and deterrence policies that have been tried, and that have failed, elsewhere, policy transfers from the US and Australia to the UK and Europe being a well-established feature of the global refugee regime.[70]

(i) Distortion: The Nationality and Borders Act 2022

In March 2021, the Conservative government announced a 'New Plan for Immigration'.[71] It highlighted the UK's refugee resettlement schemes, rules on family reunion, and the route created for British National (Overseas) (BN(O)) status holders and their families in Hong Kong.[72] Simultaneously, the Plan framed all spontaneous asylum-seeking as 'illegal immigration', connected to criminal networks and placing 'unsustainable' pressure on public services.[73] The Nationality and Borders Act 2022 (NABA 2022) that followed contains provisions that purport to comply with international refugee law, but in fact distort it. This is particularly the case for asylum-seekers who arrive irregularly and who are imagined as transferable to STCs, as well as to core issues concerning the Convention refugee definition.

On STCs, NABA 2022 sought to enable the removal of asylum-seekers to a country with which they have no prior connection.[74] The change was justified on the basis that those seeking asylum should claim it in the first safe country they arrive in.[75] At the same time, the end of UK participation in the Dublin system meant that there was no longer a mechanism obliging EU neighbouring states to 'take back' asylum-seekers from the UK. The premise that people cannot travel to secure protection is, however, a false one. The Refugee Convention's non-penalization provision, Article 31, protects asylum-seekers and refugees from penalization for irregular entry and stay where they have 'come directly' from the country where their life or freedom is imperilled.[76] This wording is used in NABA 2022, but in terms which undermine the Convention's protective approach,[77] treating all those who stop in a country outside the UK as not having 'come directly' unless they can show that they could not seek

[70] See, eg, D Ghezelbash, *Refuge Lost: Asylum Law in an Interdependent World* (Cambridge University Press 2018).

[71] HM Government, 'New Plan for Immigration', *GOV.UK* (March 2021) <https://assets.publishing.service.gov.uk/government/uploads/system/uploads/attachment_data/file/972517/CCS207_CCS0820091708-001_Sovereign_Borders_Web_Accessible.pdf> accessed 10 May 2025.

[72] ibid 6.

[73] ibid 17.

[74] Nationality and Borders Act 2022, s 29 and Sch 4.

[75] HM Government (n 71) 18.

[76] UN High Commissioner for Refugees (UNHCR), *Guidelines on International Protection No. 14: Non-penalization of refugees on account of their irregular entry or presence and restrictions on their movements in accordance with Article 31 of the 1951 Convention relating to the Status of Refugees* (HCR/GIP/24/14 (23 September 2024)).

[77] UNHCR, 'UNHCR Observations on the Nationality and Borders Bill, Bill 141, 2021–22' (*UNHCR*, September 2021) <https://www.unhcr.org/uk/sites/uk/files/legacy-pdf/6149d3484.pdf> accessed 10 May 2025.

protection there.[78] Relatedly, the Act also extends the criminalization of irregular migration,[79] an already long-standing feature of UK law.[80]

On the refugee definition, NABA 2022 revoked the Qualification Regulations,[81] but rather than incorporate the Convention definition, the Act contained provisions which explicitly departed from established interpretations of it.[82] For instance, where a non-state actor is the persecutor, the protection-seeker has to show that the state (or a party or organisation controlling it/a substantial part of it) is unable or unwilling to provide 'reasonable protection', a dilution of the existing consensus on the effectiveness of state protection.[83] NABA 2022 also altered the established 'well-founded fear' standard, a change that again makes it harder for applicants to meet.[84] The Refugee Convention only protects where persecution is feared for particular reasons or grounds—race, religion, nationality, political opinion, or 'membership of a particular social group' (MPSG). The MPSG ground is the most complex and, relatedly, the one interpreted to respond to claims based on gender, sexual orientation, and gender identity.[85] The Act limits the interpretation of MPSG in a way that is more restrictive than that advocated by UNHCR or, indeed, adopted in relevant UK adjudication.[86] In addition, other provisions make claims more difficult to prove by, for example, allowing decision-makers to draw adverse credibility inferences in a broader range of circumstances.[87]

(ii) Repudiation: The Illegal Migration Act 2023 and Safety of Rwanda (Asylum and Immigration) Act 2024

NABA 2022 was followed by an attempt to externalize refugee protection, through first an agreement with Rwanda and the Illegal Migration Act 2023 (the IMA 2023) and

[78] Nationality and Borders Act 2022, s 37(1).

[79] ibid ss 40–41 introduced new offences of illegal entry and assisting unlawful immigration or asylum-seekers.

[80] A Aliverti, 'Making People Criminal: The Role of the Criminal Law in Immigration Enforcement' (2012) 16 Theoretical Criminology 417; C Costello, 'Victim or Perpetrator? The Criminalization of Migration and the Idea of "Harm" in the Labour Market Context' in *Criminality at Work* (Oxford University Press 2020).

[81] Nationality and Borders Act 2022, s 30(4). See also the Nationality and Borders Act 2022 (Commencement No. 1, Transitional and Saving Provisions) Regulations 2022 No 590.

[82] Nationality and Borders Act 2022, ss 30–38.

[83] ibid s 31(1)(c).

[84] ibid s 32 (balance of probabilities then reasonable likelihood, a divergence from reasonable likelihood).

[85] On the grounds and women's claims, see C Briddick, 'Resisting Domestic Violence' (2024) 36 International Journal of Refugee Law 106.

[86] Nationality and Borders Act 2022, s 33(2)–(5) provides for a cumulative approach to the delineation of PSGs (as adopted by the Qualification Directive). For a trip through the UK jurisprudence see: *Fornah v Secretary of State for the Home Department* [2006] UKHL 46; [2007] 1 All ER 671; *SB (PSG—Protection Regulations—Reg 6) Moldova CG* [2008] UKAIT 00002 and *AZ (Trafficked women) Thailand* CG [2010] UKUT 118 (IAC) (on the move from disjunctive to cumulative with the Qualification Directive). Then, *DH (Particular Social Group: Mental Health) Afghanistan* [2020] UKUT 00223 (IAC) which confirmed a return to the disjunctive approach). Then, *EMAP (Gang Violence—Convention Reason) El Salvador CG* [2022] UKUT 00335 (IAC) (confirmed the disjunctive approach, until the relevant provisions in the Nationality and Borders Act 2022 came into force).

[87] Nationality and Borders Act 2022, s 19 on adverse credibility and s 26 on the late provision of evidence (not currently or yet in force).

then, when that failed, a Treaty and further primary legislation. Externalization is a broad term used to describe[88]

> measures taken by States—unilaterally or in cooperation with other States—which are implemented or have effects outside their own territories, and which directly or indirectly prevent asylum seekers and refugees from reaching a particular 'destination' country or region, and/or from being able to claim or enjoy protection there.

In April 2022, the UK and Rwanda entered into a Migration and Economic Development Partnership (MEDP), a Memorandum of Understanding creating a mechanism for the 'relocation' of asylum-seekers from the UK to Rwanda. Those relocated would have their claims determined, but protection-seekers, including refugees and victims of trafficking, would remain in Rwanda indefinitely, irrespective of any decision made on their case.[89]

In parallel, the IMA 2023 created a strict statutory duty to deport all those who arrived irregularly 'as soon as is reasonably practicable'.[90] This duty to deport was accompanied by a requirement to disregard claims and a power to detain. It applied regardless of whether the person concerned had an application for international protection, as a victim of slavery or trafficking, or for judicial review.[91] Such claims were to be declared inadmissible, without being assessed. The IMA 2023 also significantly expanded the Secretary of State's detention powers. Those subject to the duty to deport could be held as long as 'reasonably necessary'.[92]

The IMA 2023 was an explicit repudiation of the UK's international obligations to refugees and others in need of international protection. In the words of the UN High Commissioners for Refugees and Human Rights, it sought to extinguish access to asylum for those who, fleeing persecution and other serious violations of human rights, are compelled to travel irregularly.[93] Central to this legislation was the prospect of deportation to a STC—in this case, Rwanda.[94]

In June 2022, the ECtHR made a rule 39 order to halt the government's first attempt to deport asylum-seekers to Rwanda.[95] In *R (AAA (Syria) and others)*

[88] UN High Commissioner for Refugees (UNHCR), *UNHCR Note on the 'Externalization' of International Protection* (28 May 2021) [5].

[89] *Memorandum of Understanding between the government of the United Kingdom of Great Britain and Northern Ireland and the government of the Republic of Rwanda for the provision of an asylum partnership arrangement* (13 April 2022).

[90] Illegal Migration Act 2023, s 2 and s 6. This was to apply to any person who arrived in the UK without permission and not 'directly' from a country in which their life and liberty was threatened.

[91] ibid s 5; on children see s 4, for whom there was a power, rather than a duty, to deport.

[92] ibid ss 11–12.

[93] 'UK Illegal Migration Bill: UN Refugee Agency and UN Human Rights Office Warn of Profound Impact on Human Rights and International Refugee Protection System', *UNHCR* (18 July 2023) <https://www.unhcr.org/uk/news/press-releases/uk-illegal-migration-bill-un-refugee-agency-and-un-human-rights-office-warn> accessed 31 October 2023.

[94] The first attempts to remove protection-seekers to Rwanda occurred before the passing of the Illegal Migration Act 2023. The 'success' of this Act was, however, predicated on there being another country prepared to decide claims deemed inadmissible in the UK.

[95] *NSK v UK (formerly KN v UK)* App no 28774/22 (interim measures) (ECtHR, 14 June 2022).

(2023)[96] the Supreme Court affirmed that returning someone to a country where their life or freedom would be threatened is prohibited by a range of international conventions and several acts of Parliament.[97] In relation to Rwanda there were[98]

> substantial grounds for believing that there is a real risk that asylum claims will not be determined properly, and that asylum seekers will in consequence be at risk of being returned directly or indirectly to their country of origin.

This ruling confirmed that the international legal regime introduced above has domestic legal consequences, including the creation of judicially enforceable obligations and protections. However, on 5 December 2023 the UK–Rwanda Asylum Partnership Treaty[99] was signed, domestic legislation being proposed shortly after to implement it. This legislation required decision-makers to treat Rwanda as a safe country, notwithstanding the Supreme Court's finding to the contrary. The government thus sought to circumvent the *AAA* ruling by creating a new 'mechanism',[100] one that was to enable deportation *notwithstanding* the issues identified by the Supreme Court—a mechanism that, when the Treaty and Act are considered together, operated to prevent individuals from challenging their deportation *to* and *from* Rwanda.[101] Notable also was the Safety of Rwanda (Asylum and Immigration) Act 2024's disapplication of key sections of the Human Rights Act 1998 and related attempts to prevent judges from having regard to interim measures indicated by the ECtHR.[102] In this respect, the Act can be seen as part of a broader attempt to detach the UK from the ECHR system.[103] Only the general election of July 2024 and the election of a Labour government averted the constitutional crisis that would have ensued had the Act been implemented.

[96] *R (AAA (Syria) and others) v Secretary of State for the Home Department* [2023] UKSC 42; [2023] 1 WLR 4433. For a critical engagement with this reasoning, see N Palmer, 'Distributing Mobility: Regressive "Safe Third Country" Agreements and Racialised Difference' (forthcoming, 2026) London Review of International Law.

[97] ibid [5], [19]–[33].

[98] ibid [105].

[99] Agreement between the Government of the United Kingdom of Great Britain and Northern Ireland and the Government of the Republic of Rwanda for the Provision of an Asylum Partnership Agreement to Strengthen Shared International Commitments on the Protection of Refugees and Migrants (Kigali, 5 December 2023) (UK–Rwanda Asylum Partnership Treaty).

[100] ibid Art 2(3)(a).

[101] The Act connects its provisions and commencement with the Treaty, Safety of Rwanda (Asylum and Immigration) Act 2024, s 10. See further, Catherine Briddick, 'When Treaties are Forbidden' (*VerfBlog*, 29 February 2024) <https://verfassungsblog.de/when-treaties-are-forbidden/> accessed 29 March 2024.

[102] Safety of Rwanda (Asylum and Immigration) Act 2024, s 3, s 5.

[103] See further, V Mitsilegas and E Guild, 'The UK and the ECHR after Brexit: The Challenge of Immigration Control' (2024) 5 European Convention on Human Rights Law Review 116.

(iii) A New Government and a *Potential* Reset?

In his first press conference as Labour Prime Minister after the July 2024 general election, Sir Keir Starmer announced an end to the Rwanda 'plan'.[104] The Home Secretary confirmed to Parliament that she had informed the Rwandan government that the UK would be ending the MEDP.[105] A Statutory Instrument was used to gut the Illegal Migration Act 2023, enabling claims to be processed and permission to remain granted.[106]

At the time of writing, the Border Security, Asylum and Immigration Bill 2025 is progressing though Parliament. This legislation will, if passed, repeal the Safety of Rwanda (Asylum and Immigration) Act 2024 in full.[107] It will also repeal most of the IMA 2023, bar certain provisions on detention and trafficking.[108] This would remove the duty to detain and deport from the statute book. It would also, however, leave intact a provision on modern slavery that mandates the disqualification of certain victims from protection,[109] contrary to the UK's obligations under the Council of Europe's Trafficking Convention.[110] The Bill would also leave NABA 2022 untouched, while introducing yet more criminal offences and expanding law enforcement powers.[111]

Relatedly, the UK has reached an agreement with France on a scheme that will enable the transfer of some of those who arrive irregularly by boat back to France.[112] In parallel, the UK will accept an equivalent number of individuals from France, those concerned being able to travel legally to the UK to make a claim for protection. At the time of writing, very small numbers of asylum-seekers have been returned to France, while a family were the first people to arrive in the UK.[113] UNHCR has tentatively welcomed this development, noting that[114]

[104] Sam Francis, 'Starmer Confirms Rwanda Deportation Plan "Dead"', *BBC News* (6 July 2024) <https://www.bbc.co.uk/news/articles/cz9dn8erg3zo> accessed 24 April 2025.

[105] 'Border Security and Asylum, Volume 752: debated on Monday 22 July 2024' (*Hansard, UK Parliament*) <https://hansard.parliament.uk/Commons/2024-07-22/debates/FBB2B906-592F-4047-A6E1-59D6DB97573A/BorderSecurityAndAsylum> accessed 24 April 2025.

[106] The Illegal Migration Act 2023 (Amendment) Regulations 2024 No. 815.

[107] Border Security, Asylum and Immigration Bill 2025, s 37.

[108] ibid s 38, which will repeal the Illegal Migration Act 2023, ss 1 to 6 and Sch 1; ss 7 to 11; ss 13 to 15 and Sch 2; ss 16 to 28; ss 30 to 51; ss 53 to 58; s 61 and 66. This leaves s 12 on detention and s 29 on modern slavery in place. See further M Gower and CJ McKinney, *Research Briefing: Border Security, Asylum and Immigration Bill: Progress of the Bill* (House of Commons Library, 2 May 2025).

[109] Broadening the public order disqualification in the Nationality and Borders Act 2022, s 63.

[110] Council of Europe Convention on Action against Trafficking in Human Beings (adopted 16 May 2005, entered into force 1 February 2008) CETS 197 Arts 3, 10 and 16. See also, GRETA, 'Written Evidence by the GRETA (IMB0024)' (*Joint Committee on Human Rights*, 5 April 2023) <https://committees.parliament.uk/writtenevidence/119915/pdf/> accessed 17 July 2025; Catherine Briddick, *Violence against Women and Regimes of Exception: Undoing Discrimination in Migration Law* (OUP 2025) Ch 6.

[111] Border Security, Asylum and Immigration Bill 2025, Ch 2.

[112] 'UK–France Leaders Declaration' (*GOV.UK*, 10 July 2025) <https://www.gov.uk/government/news/uk-france-leaders-declaration> accessed 17 July 2025; Agreement between the Government of the United Kingdom of Great Britain and Northern Ireland and the Government of the French Republic on the Prevention of Dangerous Journeys (London 29 July and Paris 30 July 2025) (UK–France Agreement).

[113] Kathryn Armstrong, 'First Migrants Arrive from France under "One In One Out" Deal', *BBC News* (24 September 2025) <https://www.bbc.co.uk/news/articles/cwywv34w00ro> accessed 28 September 2025.

[114] UNHCR, 'News Comment: UK–France Pilot Arrangement', *UNHCR* (10 July 2025) <https://www.unhcr.org/europe/news/press-releases/news-comment-ukfrance-pilot-arrangement> accessed 17 July 2025.

> if implemented in line with international law, standards and safeguards, the pilot could offer access to protection to asylum-seekers and refugees on both sides of the Channel, with the UK and France demonstrating a shared responsibility and commitment to supporting people fleeing war, violence and persecution.

However, there is much to question in the agreement. At its core are provisions which involve the detention and deportation of asylum-seekers, selected on the basis of their mode of arrival, potentially contrary to Article 31 of the Refugee Convention. It is also of a provisional nature.[115] That the UK will admit some protection-seekers directly is to be welcomed. As Amnesty International UK points out, however, the safe entry of such people 'depend[s] on someone else making the dangerous crossing controlled by smugglers'.[116] It is also significant that the Treaty replicates the one-for-one model of the ill-fated EU–Turkey deal, with all of its connotations of commodification and dehumanization. The apparent reset that followed the ending of the Rwanda plan appears to be animated by 'fantasies' of control and punishment.[117] The suspension of refugee family reunion in September 2025, and with it the denial of admission to those with some of the strongest moral and legal claims to it, only adds force to such arguments.[118]

4 Post-Brexit Legal Developments in the EU

The 2015 'crisis' and the EU's response to it had significant consequences in the UK, influencing public opinion and asylum legislation before and after Brexit.[119] In the EU, it informed a new wave of asylum legislation, but no fundamental re-think of the containment practices that had contributed to the crisis.[120] After almost a decade of legislative wrangling, a highly complex set of legislative measures has emerged: the so-called Pact on Migration and Asylum.

Within the Pact, the Asylum and Migration Management Regulation (AMMR)[121] replaces the Dublin III Regulation, the change of name obscuring what is, in essence,

[115] UK–France Agreement, Art 22. This provision states that the agreement will expire in June 2026 unless both sides agree to renew it.

[116] Amnesty International United Kingdom Section, 'UK–France Returns Deal', *Amnesty International* (11 August 2025) <https://www.amnesty.org.uk/resources/uk-france-returns-deal> accessed 16 September 2025.

[117] L Mayblin and others, '"Bringing Order to the Border": Liberal and Illiberal Fantasies of Border Control in the English Channel' (2024) 50 Journal of Ethnic and Migration Studies 3894.

[118] Nuni Jorgensen, 'Q&A: The UK's New Approach to Refugee Family Reunion', *Migration Observatory* (9 September 2025) <https://migrationobservatory.ox.ac.uk/resources/commentaries/qa-the-uks-new-approach-to-refugee-family-reunion/> accessed 16 September 2025.

[119] See further, GK Bhambra, 'The Current Crisis of Europe: Refugees, Colonialism, and the Limits of Cosmopolitanism' (2017) 23 ELJ 395.

[120] C Costello, 'Overcoming Refugee Containment and Crisis' (2020) 21 GLJ 17.

[121] Regulation (EU) 2024/1351 of the European Parliament and of the Council of 14 May 2024 on asylum and migration management, amending Regulations (EU) 2021/1147 and (EU) 2021/1060 and repealing Regulation (EU) No 604/2013 [2024] OJ L2024/1351, 22.5.2024.

continuity of approach.[122] Relatedly, the Eurodac Regulation[123] creates a fully-fledged Eurodac 'system', with increased information being gathered on applicants and being held for increased periods of time. The Crisis and Force Majeure Regulation[124] makes provision for derogations from the AMMR and provides for solidarity measures, where certain conditions are met.

The Asylum Procedure Regulation[125] provides for regular, accelerated, and border status determination processes. Accelerated procedures apply where a person is deemed to come from a 'safe country' and in a range of other situations, including those where, for example, there are grounds to think a person a danger to national security, or where an application is not considered to have been made in a sufficiently timely manner.[126] Border procedures apply where applications are made at external EU borders, in transit zones, and following disembarkation from a search and rescue operation.[127] Mobility restrictions are imposed,[128] and, when a claim is refused, the related Return Border Procedure Regulation[129] provides for detention and return.[130] The Screening Regulation[131] operates alongside these instruments, funnelling protection-seekers into the 'right' procedures and providing that those crossing an external border without permission, including following 'rescue', are not authorized to enter the jurisdiction they are in.[132]

The Qualification Regulation[133] leaves previous Directives' approaches to refugee and subsidiary protection broadly unchanged, but weakens protection for *sur place*

[122] ibid Pt III, Ch II, which establishes a hierarchy of criteria to allocate responsibility and which once again focuses on entry after considerations of family membership and unity are considered. Later, provision is made for an annual 'solidarity pool' and forum.

[123] Regulation (EU) 2024/1358 of the European Parliament and of the Council of 14 May 2024 on the establishment of 'Eurodac' for the comparison of biometric data in order to effectively apply Regulations (EU) 2024/1351 and (EU) 2024/1350 of the European Parliament and of the Council and Council Directive 2001/55/EC and to identify illegally staying third-country nationals and stateless persons and on requests for the comparison with Eurodac data by member states' law enforcement authorities and Europol for law enforcement purposes, amending Regulations (EU) 2018/1240 and (EU) 2019/818 of the European Parliament and of the Council and repealing Regulation (EU) No 603/2013 of the European Parliament and of the Council [2024] OJ L2024/1358, 22.5.2024.

[124] Regulation (EU) 2024/1359 of the European Parliament and of the Council of 14 May 2024 addressing situations of crisis and force majeure in the field of migration and asylum and amending Regulation (EU) 2021/1147 [2024] OJ L2024/1359, 22.5.2024.

[125] Regulation (EU) 2024/1348 of the European Parliament and of the Council of 14 May 2024 establishing a common procedure for international protection in the Union and repealing Directive 2013/32/EU [2024] OJ L2024/1348, 22.5.202 (Asylum Procedure Regulation).

[126] ibid Art 42.

[127] ibid Arts 43–45, Art 53.

[128] ibid Art 54.

[129] Regulation (EU) 2024/1349 of the European Parliament and of the Council of 14 May 2024 establishing a return border procedure, and amending Regulation (EU) 2021/1148 [2024] OJ L2024/1349, 22.5.2024.

[130] ibid Arts 1, 4–5.

[131] Regulation (EU) 2024/1356 of the European Parliament and of the Council of 14 May 2024 introducing the screening of third-country nationals at the external borders and amending Regulations (EC) No 767/2008, (EU) 2017/2226, (EU) 2018/1240 and (EU) 2019/817 [2024] OJ L2024/1356, 22.5.2024 (Screening Regulation).

[132] ibid Arts 5–6.

[133] Regulation (EU) 2024/1347 of the European Parliament and of the Council of 14 May 2024 on standards for the qualification of third-country nationals or stateless persons as beneficiaries of international

refugees and enables social security and assistance to be connected with integration measures.[134] The Reception Conditions Directive[135] develops standards on assistance, while making it conditional on residence in certain places and providing for its removal in cases of 'secondary movement'.[136]

Overall, this legislative package brings further complexity to EU asylum law, including yet more exceptional provisions which seek to limit access to asylum. Across Europe, court challenges to containment, deterrence, and externalization practices proliferate. While the Pact asserts its Refugee Convention and international law foundations, its instruments establish procedures which seek to manipulate the EU's external borders, legally excising spaces to restrict rights and further suppress mobility, including through detention.[137] It is notable that relevant provisions refer to the use of appropriate locations for particular procedures, those which take into account 'geography and existing infrastructures'[138]—'Hotspots'. This is not the only way in which the EU is doubling down on failed policies. The EU Commission has proposed yet more legislation: a regulation on the STC concept that enables (but does not require) states to deem 'safe' countries that asylum-seekers have no connection to.[139] Such an expansion of the concept would enable EU MS to enter into Rwanda-style externalization arrangements. All of this points to greater demands being made of courts, at a time when many are already under pressure from domestic autocratic moves.[140]

protection, for a uniform status for refugees or for persons eligible for subsidiary protection and for the content of the protection granted, amending Council Directive 2003/109/EC and repealing Directive 2011/95/EU of the European Parliament and of the Council [2024] OJ L2024/1347, 22.5.2024.

[134] ibid Art 5, Art 31.

[135] Directive (EU) 2024/1346 of the European Parliament and of the Council of 14 May 2024 laying down standards for the reception of applicants for international protection [2024] OJ L2024/1346, 22.5.2024 (Reception Conditions Directive).

[136] ibid Arts 8–9.

[137] See, eg, Screening Regulation (n 131) Arts 5, 6 and 8 (screening in border locations of those apprehended/disembarked following an unauthorized external EU border crossing); Reception Conditions Directive, Arts 8–10 (on geographical restrictions and detention); Asylum Procedure Regulation (n 125) Arts 30, 42–56 (on the accelerated asylum border procedure with residence requirement at the external border/transit zone). See further K Soderstrom, *An Analysis of the Fiction of Non-entry as Appears in the Screening Regulation* (ECRE, 16 September 2022).

[138] Screening Regulation (n 131) recital 10.

[139] Proposal for a Regulation of the European Parliament and of the Council amending Regulation (EU) 2024/1348 as regards the application of the 'safe third country' concept (Brussels, 20 May 2025, COM(2025) 259 final, 2025).

[140] See further, KL Scheppele, 'The Opportunism of Populists and the Defense of Constitutional Liberalism' (2019) 20 GLJ 314.

5 Externalization, Criminalization, and Selectivity

This brief overview of post-Brexit developments in the UK and EU reveals areas of convergence amid the divergence in three areas: externalization, criminalization, and selectivity.

On externalization, it will be recalled that when the UK opted into the Asylum Procedures Directive (first phase) it was bound by an approach to STCs which required there to be a connection between an asylum-seeker and the country that they were to be returned to. At the same time, the UK's place within the Dublin system and the obligatory character of the 'take back' requirement provided a means of returning protection-seekers to EU MS, in certain circumstances. 'Free' from the CEAS, the 'connection' requirement was assumed to no longer apply, so STC returns to faraway countries could be attempted, provided their cooperation could be gained. The plan to deport to Rwanda was, therefore, a direct progeny of Brexit. Pertinent forerunners to this policy include US processing in Guantanamo Bay, Australia's detention and 'protection' in Nauru and Papua New Guinea, the EU–Turkey Statement, and, notably, Israel's 'transfer' of Eritrean and Sudanese asylum-seekers to Rwanda and Uganda.[141] Denmark, also unconstrained by EU asylum law, has similarly sought to enter into a Rwanda 'scheme'.[142] Against this backdrop, the Commission's proposal to enlarge the STC concept in EU law, removing the 'connection requirement', is profoundly troubling. Steve Peers observes that the flaws of the Rwanda policy 'were so huge, they must have been visible from outer space'.[143] Yet, even following the ECtHR's intervention and the Supreme Court's judgment, they do not appear to be visible to the EU.

Criminalization, and the judicial responses to it, mark another area of post-Brexit UK and EU convergence and divergence. The use of the criminal law for acts which may be neither harmful nor wrongful warrants examination from first principles.[144] As explained above, the Refugee Convention protects asylum-seekers from penalization under certain circumstances. The UK has criminalized many aspects of irregular migration. Relatedly, the British courts have decided some of the leading cases on Article 31, noting its vitality in a world where refugees are increasingly denied the ability to travel safely or legally.[145] The potential for such protective interpretations

[141] International Refugee Rights Initiative (IRRI), *"I was left with nothing": "Voluntary" Departures of Asylum Seekers from Israel to Rwanda and Uganda* (8 September 2015); Ghezelbash (n 70).

[142] Nikolas Feith Tan, 'Externalisation of Asylum in Europe: Unpacking the UK–Rwanda Asylum Partnership Agreement', *EU Immigration and Asylum Law and Policy, Odysseus Network* (17 May 2022) <https://eumigrationlawblog.eu/externalisation-of-asylum-in-europe-unpacking-the-uk-rwanda-asylum-partnership-agreement/> accessed 23 May 2022.

[143] Steve Peers, 'Towards a Euro-Rwanda Policy? The Proposed New EU Asylum Law Rules on "Safe Third Countries"', *EU Law Analysis* (21 May 2025) <https://eulawanalysis.blogspot.com/2025/05/towards-euro-rwanda-policy-proposed-new.html> accessed 22 May 2025.

[144] Aliverti (n 80).

[145] *R v Uxbridge Magistrates Court and Another, ex parte Adimi* [1999] EWHC Admin 765; [2001] QB 667. See also *R v Mateta* [2013] EWCA Crim 1372; [2014] 1 WLR 1516.

of UK law was removed with the introduction of new offences in NABA 2022, with devastating consequences for those caught by them.[146] Here, a change in government has not yielded a change in approach. The Border Security, Asylum and Immigration Bill 2025 introduces still more offences. These may criminalize the provision of mutual and humanitarian assistance in circumstances where those concerned are not involved in 'smuggling' as defined by international law.[147]

Increasing criminalization can be seen in the law of many states in the Global North, and, within EU law, in the Facilitation Directive.[148] As *was* the case in the UK, there has been judicial pushback against such moves in some jurisdictions, the right to offer assistance, as a feature of humanity and solidarity, being judicially recognized and protected.[149] In *Kinsa* (2024),[150] the CJEU drew on the CFR and the Refugee Convention's Article 31 to prevent the over-criminalization of protection-seekers and to protect the rights of children.

Finally, selectivity. The UK has, post-Brexit, developed a number of bespoke schemes for different groups of protection-seekers, including but not limited to those from Ukraine and Hong Kong.[151] This preference for the 'invited' over the 'uninvited' initially appears to be an area where the UK is diverging from the EU. Historically, few EU MS have invited refugees—for political and geographical reasons, asylum-seekers tend to enter the EU irregularly and seek protection on arrival. However, the UK's Ukraine schemes parallel, to an extent, the temporary protection of Ukrainians currently offered by the EU. The EU has also, since 2015, made some moves to cooperate on resettlement.[152] In the Pact, the Resettlement and Humanitarian Admission Framework Regulation[153] establishes 'safe' pathways for some in need of protection and strengthens 'partnerships' with non-EU countries. The UK and EU are, therefore, once again converging, not in relation to the practice of humanitarian admissions, but in the framing of spontaneous asylum-seeking as undesirable, to be replaced by invitation-only pathways and tailored schemes.

[146] *R v Ashari Mohamed & Ors* [2023] EWCA Crim 211; [2023] 3 WLR 31.

[147] Which requires 'directly or indirectly, a financial or other material benefit', Protocol against the Smuggling of Migrants by Land, Sea and Air, supplementing the United Nations Convention against Transnational Organized Crime (adopted 15 November 2000, entered into force 28 January 2004) 2241 UNTS 507, Art 3. See further Immigration Law Practitioners' Association, *Briefing of the Immigration Law Practitioners' Association: Border Security, Asylum and Immigration Bill—House of Lords, Second Reading (2 June 2025)* (ILPA 2025).

[148] Council Directive 2002/90/EC of 28 November 2002 defining the facilitation of unauthorised entry, transit and residence [2002] OJ L 328/17.

[149] *R v Appulonappa* 2015 SCC 59; [2015] 3 SCR 754.

[150] Case C-460/23 *Kinsa* EU:C:2025:392.

[151] See further, Zoe Bantleman, 'Goodbye Refuge, Hello Bespokism', *Völkerrechtsblog* (10 March 2023) <https://voelkerrechtsblog.org/goodbye-refuge-hello-bespokism/> accessed 17 September 2025.

[152] N Welfens, 'The EU's Normative Justifications of Refugee Resettlement' (2024) 37 Journal of Refugee Studies 552.

[153] Regulation (EU) 2024/1350 of the European Parliament and of the Council of 14 May 2024 establishing a Union Resettlement and Humanitarian Admission Framework, and amending Regulation (EU) 2021/1147 [2024] OJ L2024/1350, 22.5.2024.

6 Conclusion: The Rule of Law

This chapter has offered an account of protection in Europe during and after the UK's departure from the EU. Our analysis, necessarily situated at a high level of generality, has traced the development of the CEAS and the way that the tensions that animate it have been resolved in different ways (mobility/immobility), for different people (citizens/others), and at different points (first phase/recast/Pact). We have also highlighted the UK's position within this shifting and contested terrain, one in which it remained, in the legal sense, 'in control' of asylum through a partial and selective engagement with the CEAS and its instruments. Claims that it was necessary to exit the EU in order to manage migration rested, consequently, on two connected false premises. The first was that it was *EU* membership that constrained government action in this domain. The second was that post-Brexit, the UK would be free of such constraints.

The paucity of the 'take back control' position in relation to asylum in particular became apparent in the legislative chaos that followed Brexit. The visibility of increasing irregular boat arrivals lends itself to moral panics and politicization. In the UK as elsewhere, such arrivals are readily portrayed and understood as a problem in need of a radical solution. In the Australian context, the 'Pacific solution' resulted in the human rights catastrophe of offshore detention and processing.[154] In the UK, it led to the Rwanda plan. Having first used primary legislation, in the form of NABA 2022, to distort the UK's obligations under the Refugee Convention, the then Conservative government moved to repudiate them altogether.

The 2024 change in government in the UK has yielded yet further legislative change, at least some of which can be understood as a 'reset' as 'new' Bills promise to repeal the 'old'. However, the agreement reached with France on returns and changes to family reunion prompt a further question, namely: reset to what? Successive UK governments have supported and implemented ever harsher policies towards those seeking asylum or other forms of protection, all with the aim of deterring irregular arrivals. This deterrence logic is rarely questioned in political debate, even though it has little empirical support.[155] The harshness of asylum policies does not significantly determine the numbers of protection-seekers coming to any particular country.[156] Even if efficacy could be established, treating one group of vulnerable people harshly—often

[154] B Boochani, *No Friend But the Mountains* (Picador 2018); M Gleeson, 'Protection Deficit: The failure of Australia's Offshore Processing Arrangements to Guarantee "Protection Elsewhere" in the Pacific' (2019) 31 International Journal of Refugee law 415.

[155] ER Thielemann, 'The Effectiveness of Governments' Attempts to Control Unwanted Migration' in CA Parsons and TM Smeeding (eds), *Immigration and the Transformation of Europe* (Cambridge University Press 2006); J Hagen-Zanker and R Mallett, *Journeys to Europe: The Role of Policy in Migrant Decision-Making* (ODI Insights, February 2016); H Crawley and J Hagen-Zanker, 'Deciding Where to Go: Policies, People and Perceptions Shaping Destination Preferences' (2019) 57 International Migration 20.

[156] L Abdelaaty, 'Do Rights Violations Deter Refugees?' (2023) 49 Journal of Ethnic and Migration Studies 110.

inhumanely and cruelly—in order to deter others should attract strong legal and ethical objections. Indeed, where deterrence practices entail violations of human rights, including inhuman and degrading treatment, UK courts have found such violations unlawful.[157] The politics of performative cruelty have, however, remained a consistent feature of UK asylum policy.[158]

Stepping back and comparing developments in both the UK and the EU post-Brexit, it is noticeable that while there has been a degree of divergence, there are also areas where changing asylum law has entailed convergence. On the latter, it is significant that notwithstanding swift and often successful legal challenges and a wealth of ethical, practical, and fiscal hurdles, European states and the EU continue to explore different modes of externalization. On the former, while increasing resort to criminalization and criminal penalties is a feature of both UK and EU law, the UK's criminalization of protection-seeking is, following NABA 2022, particularly extreme in terms of the range of conduct covered, the severity of sentences, and the intensity of enforcement.[159] Finally, the UK's and EU's interest in selective admission over spontaneous arrivals shares a vision of (sovereign?) control over refugee arrivals that is incompatible with the right to leave any country and the right to seek asylum.

We end here with some reflections on sovereignty and the rule of law. In 2004, Catherine Dauvergne argued that as 'globalizing forces' challenge and transform the nation, the role and place of migration law shifts to become the 'new last bastion of sovereignty'.[160] In response to diminishing power over economic policies, the flow of money and of ideas, states turn to migration laws to assert their 'nation-ness' and 'exemplify their sovereign control and capacity'.[161] More than twenty years later, developments in the UK following Brexit offer support for this analysis. The idea that the unbinding of the UK from EU law would increase the UK's room for manoeuvre in the asylum domain rested on accounts of 'sovereignty' and 'freedom' that sought to wish away international law, both as a source of obligation and as a foundation for cooperation. This larger system of interconnected rules, actors, and institutions was and indeed continues to be portrayed as alien and threatening.[162] Consonant with

[157] For example, s 55(1) of the Nationality, Immigration and Asylum Act 2002 made destitute those asylum seekers whose claims were deemed not to have been made as soon as was reasonably practical after their arrival in the UK. Excluded from welfare benefits and asylum support, those affected experienced homelessness, hunger, and ill health. The (then) House of Lords held that these practices violated Art 3 ECHR. *R (Limbuela) v Secretary of State for the Home Department* [2005] UKHL 66; [2006] 1 AC 396.

[158] On the so-called hostile environment, see S York, 'The "Hostile Environment"—How Home Office Immigration Policies and Practices Create and Perpetuate Illegality' (2018) 32 Journal of Immigration Asylum and Nationality Law 363; M Griffiths and C Yeo, 'The UK's Hostile Environment: Deputising Immigration Control' (2021) 41 Critical Social Policy 521.

[159] V Taylor, *'No Such Thing as Justice Here': The Criminalisation of People Arriving to the UK on "Small Boats"'* (Border Criminologies and the Centre for Criminology, University of Oxford, February 2024).

[160] C Dauvergne, 'Sovereignty, Migration and the Rule of Law in Global Times' (2004) 67 MLR 588, 588.

[161] ibid 595.

[162] For an extreme but illustrative example, see Alex Storey, 'Starmer's Attorney General stripped the UK of Her Sovereign Rights', *GB News* (2 Jan 2025) <https://www.gbnews.com/opinion/keir-starmer-attorney-general-richard-hermer> accessed 8 May 2025.

this worldview are contemporary calls for the UK to leave the ECHR and Refugee Convention.

In response to such developments, Dauvergne explores the 'protean potential' of the rule of law to inform principled and rights-protective decision-making.[163] In *AAA*, the Supreme Court affirmed that the prohibition on *refoulement* was a

> core principle of international law, to which the United Kingdom government has repeatedly committed itself on the international stage, consistently with this country's reputation for developing and upholding the rule of law.[164]

Decisions such as *AAA* indicate that, in some cases at least, the potential identified by Dauvergne for securing law's protective promise may indeed be realized.

[163] Dauvergne (n 160) 613.
[164] *R (AAA (Syria) and others)* (n 96) [26].

20
Equality Law

Sandra Fredman

1 Introduction

It is difficult to overstate the symbiotic relationship between EU and UK equality law. From the moment the UK entered the EU until the Brexit rupture, EU equality law was shaped by developments initiated in the UK as much as UK equality law was shaped by the EU. This was on all levels, including through the social partners, social dialogue, governmental policy-making, and activism. Similarly, throughout these decades, UK courts directly incorporated ECJ jurisprudence on equality into UK judgments, but also continued to influence ECJ perspectives through referrals to the ECJ and the work of UK lawyers. Moreover, EU law filled the gap created by the absence in the UK of a codified constitution containing an entrenched right to equality. Because of its binding nature on the UK Parliament, EU equality law played a crucial role in protecting the right to equality in the UK against erosion, especially during periods in which the government in power was rolling back workers' rights in other areas.

Brexit clearly opened up the possibility that this could be reversed, with moves to repeal all or part of the Equality Act 2010 (EA 2010). However, the fact that EU equality law was not simply imposed on the UK but developed collaboratively with healthy support from the UK legislature meant that this was never a real risk. Instead, the real issue which emerged is the extent of divergence from EU law. In practice, under the Coalition and post-Brexit Conservative governments, the Equality Act 2010 remained largely static, deprived of the ongoing dynamism of interaction with the EU. Some of the energy moved to developing the equality guarantee in Article 14 of the European Convention on Human Rights (ECHR), as incorporated through the Human Rights Act 1998 (HRA), which has itself become more robust in recent decades.[1] However, the HRA only binds the state, not private parties, and the ECHR does not operate directly in the field of employment, the heartland of both the EA 2010 and EU equality law. In any event, the HRA's continued existence has at times itself been

[1] S Fredman, 'Emerging from the Shadows: Substantive Equality and Article 14 of the European Convention on Human Rights' (2016) 16 HRLRev 273.

Sandra Fredman, *Equality Law* In: *The UK Regulatory Framework Post-Brexit: 'Law Unbound'*. Edited by: Paul Craig and Vilija Vėlyvytė, Oxford University Press. © Oxford University Press 2026. DOI: 10.1093/9780198969815.003.0023

precarious, especially because of successive manifesto promises by Conservative governments to repeal the HRA.

All this could be changing since the new Labour government came to power in 2024, armed with several manifesto promises to improve discrimination law, including in relation to equal pay, intersectionality, and sexual harassment at work. Here it is of particular interest to ask whether any proposed positive reform draws on developments in EU law, or simply proceeds without paying any further attention to our erstwhile close partner. Conversely, new developments in UK equality law create valuable precedents for EU law. This raises the question of whether policymakers will look to developments in EU law for inspiration and convergence. In particular, the EU Pay Transparency Directive contains a wealth of valuable provisions. Thus far, however, those tasked with drafting new amendments have shown little knowledge and even less enthusiasm for such an approach.

2 Pre-Brexit: The Role of EU Law in UK Equality Law

The development of equality law in the UK and that in the EU were closely intertwined from the entry of the UK to the EU.[2] Moreover, the relationship with the EU has not been one in which the EU simply imposed equality guarantees. This has been a constructive and reciprocal relationship. The UK was an active and important partner in developing EU equality law, whether through the social partners, the women's movement, litigation before the ECJ, or the law-making process itself. At the same time, EU equality law functioned as a quasi-constitutional right in the UK. In most jurisdictions, the right to equality is found in a constitutional bill of rights, which underpins statutory protection and protects against legislative attempts to weaken or repeal equality rights. The absence of a codified constitution in the UK means that a constitutional equality guarantee is lacking. Instead, anti-discrimination and equality law in the UK developed on a statutory basis, culminating in the Equality Act 2010 (EA 2010). EU equality went some way towards filling this gap. Under EU law, the principle of equal treatment is treated as a fundamental legal norm and the provisions of the equality directives should be interpreted in a way that provides effective and substantive protection against discrimination.[3] EU law is also clear that exceptions to equality rights and justifications for derogating from equality must be narrowly construed and rigorously justified.[4] Because of its binding nature, courts were required to interpret statutes consistently with EU law. This meant that UK domestic legislation had to be interpreted in a way that provided effective and substantive

[2] This section draws on S Fredman, *Discrimination Law* (3rd edn, Oxford University Press 2022) Chs 2 and 3.

[3] Case C-54/07 *Centrum voor Gelijkheid van Kansen en voor Racismebestrijding v Firma Feryn NV* [2008] ECR I-5187; Case C-415/10 *Meister v Speech Design Carrier Systems GmbH* EU:C:2012:417.

[4] Case C-341/09 *Petersen v Berufungsausschuss für Zahnärzte für den Bezirk Westfalen-Lippe* [2010] ECR I-47, [60]; Case C-447/09 *Prigge v Deutsche Lufthansa AG* EU:C:2011:573, [56], [72].

protection against discrimination[5] and that exceptions to equality rights and justifications for derogating from equality must be narrowly construed and rigorously justified.[6] Furthermore, Parliament was required to enact appropriate legislation and, in some contexts, individuals were given direct rights against their employers.[7]

Both these trends can be seen by a closer examination of equality law prior to Brexit. When the UK entered the EU in 1972, the Equal Pay Act 1970 had already been passed but was not due to come into effect until 1975. Similarly, both the Sex Discrimination Act 1975 (SDA) and the Race Relations Act 1976 (RRA) were adopted by the UK independently of its newly acquired EU membership. The SDA prohibited discrimination on grounds of sex or marriage in employment more generally, including recruitment, promotion, and training, while the RRA enacted a similar prohibition on discrimination, this time on grounds of race, colour, nationality, and ethnic or national origin. Both the SDA and the RRA also made it unlawful to discriminate in education and the provision of services, both of which were, at least on the face of it, outside the competence of the EU. Also of great importance was the introduction of a statutory conception of indirect discrimination, imported from the US disparate impact theory developed by the US courts in *Griggs v Duke Power*.[8]

However, EU law very quickly came to play a major role in the future of discrimination law, especially in relation to women's right to equality. In one sense, this was a surprising source of women's rights. At its inception in 1957, the EU was conceived of primarily as creating a common market, where competition was undistorted by domestic tariffs and restrictions. Protection of social rights was regarded as a matter for member states rather than the Community. Nevertheless, France, which already had an equal pay law, successfully argued that it would be placed at an unfair competitive disadvantage if other member states were permitted to pay women less for the same work. It was for this, primarily economic, reason that a right to equal pay for equal work for men and women was included in Article 119 of the Treaty of Rome.

In practice, however, Article 119 lay dormant until the mid-1970s, when it was ignited by a remarkable campaign by women at European level. A test case brought on behalf of a Belgian air stewardess, Gabrielle Defrenne, led to the landmark decision of *Defrenne v Sabena*,[9] in which the ECJ held that Article 119 was a source of rights which could be enforced in courts in member states even if there was no domestic legislation to this effect. Equally important was the Court's assertion in *Defrenne* that the social aims of the EU were on a par with its economic aims. The Community, it stated, 'is not merely an economic union, but is at the same time intended . . . to ensure social progress and seek the constant improvement of the living and working conditions of their peoples'.[10]

[5] Case C-54/07 *Firma Feryn* (n 3); Case C 415/10 *Meister* (n 3).
[6] Case C-341/09 *Petersen* (n 4) [60]; Case C-447/09 *Prigge* (n 4) [56], [72].
[7] Case 43/75 *Defrenne v Sabena* [1976] ECR 455 (ECJ).
[8] *Griggs v Duke Power Co* 401 US 424 (1971) (US Supreme Court).
[9] Case 43/75 *Defrenne* (n 7).
[10] ibid [10].

It was also at this time that the EU introduced the Equal Pay Directive, which provided not just for equal pay for the same work for men and women, but also for work of equal value.[11] The radical conception of equal value, itself taken from the ILO, was not yet part of UK equal pay legislation. It was only after a compliance case brought by the Commission against the UK that the scope of the Equal Pay Act was widened to include work of equal value.[12] At about the same time, the EU passed the Equal Treatment Directive, requiring member states to introduce legislation requiring equal treatment in employment.[13] This in turn led to further compliance proceedings against the UK, requiring the UK to amend the SDA to make it possible to declare void a provision in a collective agreement which discriminated on grounds of sex.[14]

Notably, however, the Equal Treatment Directive relied on a relatively bland conception of 'equal treatment' and did not at that point incorporate effects-based or indirect discrimination. This concept was incrementally incorporated into EU law through a series of judicial decisions, largely in cases brought by part-time women workers, many of them references from UK courts which were becoming accustomed to the concept of indirect discrimination. Thus, in *Jenkins v Kingsgate*,[15] the applicants, part-time workers, were paid less than full-time workers. Although all part-time workers were paid less than full-time workers, so that there was no direct discrimination, the applicants argued that this constituted indirect discrimination, in that a disproportionate number of part-time workers were women. In this and a series of further cases from various jurisdictions, the ECJ developed and reinforced a principle of indirect discrimination, affording predominantly female part-time workers a range of rights, including access to pensions.[16] Particularly important were the cases of *ex p EOC*[17] and *ex p Seymour Smith*,[18] in which resort was had to EU law to prevent erosion of part-time and fixed-term workers' employment rights by increasing their threshold to access these rights to five years, rather than the two years applicable to other employees. In these cases, UK law on indirect discrimination merged with EU law on migration to develop a specific EU conception.[19] However, it was not until the Burden of Proof Directive that a statutory definition of indirect discrimination was included in EU law.

Protection against pregnancy discrimination developed in the opposite direction, beginning with the groundbreaking EU law of *Dekker*,[20] which held that

[11] Council Directive 75/117/EEC of 10 February 1975 on the approximation of the laws of the member states relating to the application of the principle of equal pay for men and women [1975] OL L45/19.

[12] Case 61/81 *Commission of the European Communities v United Kingdom* [1982] ECR 2601.

[13] Council Directive 76/207/EEC of 9 February 1976 on the implementation of the principle of equal treatment for men and women as regards access to employment, vocational training and promotion, and working conditions [1976] OJ L39/40.

[14] Case 165/82 *Commission v United Kingdom of Great Britain and Northern Ireland* [1983] ECR 3431.

[15] Case 96/80 *Jenkins v Kingsgate (Clothing Productions) Ltd* [1981] ECR 911.

[16] Case 170/84 *Bilka-Kaufhaus GmbH v Weber von Hartz* [1986] ECR 1607.

[17] *R v Secretary of State for Employment, ex p Equal Opportunities Commission* [1994] IRLR 176 (HL).

[18] *R v Secretary of State ex p Seymour Smith and Perez* [1997] IRLR 315 (HL).

[19] Case C-237/94 *O'Flynn v Adjudication Officer* [1996] ECR I-2617.

[20] Case C-177/88 *Dekker v Stichting Vormingscentrum voor Jonge Volwassenen Plus* [1990] ECR I-3941.

discrimination on grounds of pregnancy was sex discrimination regardless of the specious requirement in other jurisdictions for a male comparator. This was consolidated in *Webb*,[21] a UK case, and a series of further cases. Parallel to the ECJ's development of this crucial protection was the legislative process, culminating in the Pregnant Workers' Directive[22] and later the Parental Leave Framework Directive.[23] In both of these processes, the social partners were consulted as part of social dialogue, and UK trade unions and other civil service organizations were actively involved in the process, as was the UK itself at the state level. Cross-fertilization soon followed, with pregnancy included as a separate ground of discrimination in the EA 2010.

The UK was well ahead of the EU in relation to discrimination provisions prohibiting both race and disability discrimination. As we have seen, the Race Relations Act 1976 was enacted independently of the EU. The Disability Discrimination Act followed in 1995, after much hard work by UK activists. But neither race nor disability were included in EU equality law until the Treaty of Amsterdam afforded the EU competence to legislate in this area.[24] This was rapidly followed by the Race Directive in 2000,[25] which included a statutory definition of indirect discrimination based on the EU conception of 'particular disadvantage', rather than the UK and US principle of disproportionate impact. This Directive also broke new ground in extending beyond employment and training to social protection, including social security and healthcare, social advantages, education, and access to and supply of goods and services available to the public, including housing.[26]

The Race Directive was accompanied by the Employment Directive, which incorporated disability, thereby catching up with the UK. But it also went well beyond. Its inclusion of religion and belief, sexual orientation, and, most surprisingly, age as grounds for discrimination significantly broadened the reach of binding EU equality law for the UK.[27] While these were originally incorporated in secondary legislation, the EA 2010 constituted a welcome consolidation of discrimination law in the UK. This now includes the definition of indirect discrimination used in EU law, based on 'particular disadvantage', and directly reflects the contours of EU law on age discrimination as well as sexual orientation and religion and belief.

[21] Case C-32/93 *Webb v EMO Air Cargo Ltd* [1994] ECR I-3567.

[22] Council Directive 92/85/EEC of 19 October 1992 on the introduction of measures to encourage improvements in the safety and health at work of pregnant workers and workers who have recently given birth or are breastfeeding [1992] OJ L348/1.

[23] Council Directive 96/34/EC of 3 June 1996 on the framework agreement on parental leave concluded by UNICE, CEEP and the ETUC [1996] OJ L145/4; amended by Council Directive 2010/18/EU of 8 March 2010 implementing the revised Framework Agreement on parental leave concluded by BUSINESSEUROPE, UEAPME, CEEP, and ETUC and repealing Directive 96/34/EC [2010] OJ L68/13.

[24] Treaty of Amsterdam, Art 19.

[25] Council Directive 2000/43/EC of 29 June 2000 implementing the principle of equal treatment between persons irrespective of racial or ethnic origin [2000] OJ L180/22.

[26] Race Directive, Art 3(1)(b).

[27] Council Directive 2000/78/EC of 27 November 2000 establishing a general framework for equal treatment in employment and occupation [20000] OL L303/16.

The EU also set the pace on rights for trans people, in parallel with the ECtHR. Momentum for change came initially from the ECJ, which was willing to develop the meaning of 'sex' to encompass some forms of gender identity. This was the route taken by the ECJ in the seminal case of *P v S* in 1996.[28] If a person was dismissed on the grounds of gender reassignment, the Court held, they were treated unfavourably compared to persons of the sex they were deemed to belong to before undergoing gender reassignment. Discrimination on the grounds of gender reassignment therefore fell within the EU prohibition of discrimination on grounds of sex. Legislative developments followed the judicial lead. The EU Directive on the principle of equal treatment between men and women in employment, known as the Recast Directive, now specifies in its preamble that it also applies to discrimination arising from gender reassignment.[29] Following the terminology used by the EU Directive, the UK EA 2010 includes 'gender reassignment' as a protected characteristic. In relation to disability, although the EU intervention was later than that in the UK, the ECJ has now, after some halting starts, taken the definition of disability further than originally seen in the UK, embracing the 'social model' of disability found in the Convention on the Rights of People with Disabilities.[30]

3 Divergence Post-Brexit

(a) Equal Pay and Pay Transparency

One of the main areas of interest, in relation to post-Brexit divergence, concerns equal pay, where the contrasting approaches of the ECJ and the UKSC are apparent in two crucial cases on the scope of comparison: *Asda*[31] and *Tesco*.[32] The primary rule is that a woman can only claim equal pay if she is paid less than a man doing equal work and employed by the same employer at the same establishment.[33] There is, however, a small exception. Under the EA 2010, A is permitted to compare herself with B if B is employed by the same employer at a different establishment in situations in which 'common terms apply at the establishments (either generally or as between A and B)'.[34] This opaque formulation has, however, given employers multiple opportunities to contest claims at this threshold stage, in an attempt to protract potentially very costly

[28] Case C-13/94 *P v S and Cornwall County Council* [1996] ECR I-2143.

[29] Directive 2006/54/EC of the European Parliament and of the Council of 5 July 2006 on the implementation of the principle of equal opportunities and equal treatment of men and women in matters of employment and occupation (recast) [2006] OJ L204/23, Preamble, para (3).

[30] Cases 335 and 337/11 *HK Danmark v Dansk Arbejdsgiverforening* EU:C:2012:775; Case C-354/13 *Fag og Arbejde (FOA), acting on behalf of Karsten Kaltoft, v Kommunernes Landsforening (KL), acting on behalf of the Municipality of Billund* EU:C:2014:2463.

[31] *Asda Stores v Brierley* [2021] UKSC 10.

[32] Case C-624/19 *K v Tesco Stores Ltd* EU:C:2021:429.

[33] EA 2010, s 79.

[34] ibid.

equal pay claims. It was this provision that Asda and Tesco, both large supermarkets, relied on. One claim, *Asda*, went to the UKSC and was decided entirely on domestic law. The other, *Tesco*, went to the ECJ and was resolved on EU law. The comparison between the reasoning is therefore a helpful test case on divergence.[35]

Asda v Brierley,[36] which reached the UKSC in 2021, was brought by 7,000 workers, overwhelmingly women, employed in Asda's retail stores. They claimed that their work was of equal value to that of the male workforce at Asda's distribution depots, who were paid substantially more and worked at locations separate from the retail stores. Asda argued that the retail workers and distribution workers were not employed on 'common terms' as required by the legislation, because they were at different locations and had different terms and conditions of employment. This was a question which had already reached the Supreme Court on three former occasions,[37] reflecting both the tenacity of employers and the murkiness of the statutory wording. The Supreme Court rejected Asda's argument. Lady Arden held that there was a short and direct answer to the case, provided by the earlier decision in *North*.[38] The single aim, which emerged from the three preceding decisions, was to enable claimants to use comparators from a different establishment if the latter's terms and conditions can be transposed either in fact or in theory to the claimants' establishment. This was the case on the facts before the Court.

EU law contains some promise of a clearer pathway to cross-establishment comparisons. As we have seen, in the foundational case of *Defrenne*,[39] the ECJ held that Article 119 EEC (now Article 157 TFEU), which requires member states to ensure the application of equal pay for men and women of equal work or work of equal value, was directly effective, both vertically and horizontally. However, the Court of Justice stated that inter-industry comparisons were too complex to give rise to directly enforceable rights without domestic legislation. Nevertheless, it left open the possibility of a comparison between employees in the 'same service'. This formula was refined in later cases to refer to a single source which was responsible for the inequality and could restore equal treatment.[40] It was this avenue which the shopworkers in the *Tesco* case[41] pursued in order to compare their work with better-paid workers in Tesco's distribution centres. They were successful before the ECJ. Importantly, the Court held that Article 157 TFEU could be relied on in relation to a comparator with the same employer but in different establishments, provided the employer of both the claimant and the comparator can be regarded as a 'single source', in that it was responsible for the inequality and could restore equal treatment. In this case, the Court held, Tesco

[35] S Fredman, 'Inching Forward: Preliminary Victory for Equal Value at Tesco and Asda' (2022) 51 ILJ 166.

[36] *Asda Stores* (n 31).

[37] *Leverton v Clwyd County Council* [1984] IRLR 28 (HL); *British Coal Corpn v Smith* [1996] ICR 515 (HL); *Dumfries and Galloway Council v North* [2013] UKSC 45 (SC).

[38] *North* (n 37).

[39] Case 43/75 *Defrenne* (n 7). See further *Scullard v Knowles* [1996] IRLR 344 (EAT).

[40] Case C-256/01 *Allonby v Accrington & Rossendale College* EU:C:2004:18.

[41] Case C-624/19 *K v Tesco Stores Ltd* (n 32).

Stores could constitute such a single source to which the pay and conditions of shop-workers and distribution centres may be attributed, and which could be responsible for any discrimination.

The EU concept of a 'single source' is a much simpler formula than the one developed by the UK Supreme Court. By permitting cross-establishment comparisons in most cases where the employer has control over setting terms and conditions, it sidesteps the complex requirements of the 'common terms and conditions' formula and the technicalities of the '*North* hypothetical'. However, its applicability in the UK after Brexit is unclear. The case fell within the eleven-month window specified in the Withdrawal Agreement for the CJEU to retain jurisdiction (IP completion day), making it applicable to the facts of the *Tesco* case itself. Whether it can continue to apply, however, is subject to the complex web of statutory provisions beginning with section 6 of the Withdrawal Act 2018 and further modified by the Retained EU Law (Revocation and Reform Act) 2023. What does seem clear is that the Supreme Court's power to depart from retained EU case law conferred by section 6(4) of the 2018 Act applies to cases in which the cause of action accrues after IP completion date.[42] In *Asda*, the Supreme Court held that, since the case could be resolved on the basis of the *North* hypothetical, it was unnecessary to decide whether the claimants could succeed on the basis of a 'single source' where the common terms requirement is not met.[43] This suggests that this might well be a situation in which the UKSC does continue to diverge, and in which approaches derived from ECJ case law will not receive a favourable hearing.

In the meanwhile, the Labour government is moving quickly to amend the Equality Act 2010 to fulfil its robust manifesto promises to reform equal pay provisions. One of the key areas concerns pay transparency. A weak form of pay transparency was introduced in 2017, requiring require large private and public sector employers (employing 250 or more workers) to report annually on the gender pay gaps in their institutions.[44] 'Gender pay gap' is defined more widely than equal pay for work of equal value to encompass the spread of pay across the whole establishment. This casts light on occupational segregation and disproportionate pay, as well as unequal pay for work of equal value. Employers must publish information not only about pay differences but also about differences in bonuses, including the proportions of male and female relevant employees who were paid bonus pay. The regulations also require employers to include the proportions of male and female relevant employees in the lower, lower middle, upper middle, and upper quartile pay bands. The information should be published on the government portal and the organization's website. Failure to comply with the reporting requirement can lead to hefty fines.

The reporting obligation depends for its efficacy entirely on the expected reputational risk to organizations with high gender pay gaps. There is no duty on

[42] *Lipton v BA Cityflyer Ltd* [2024] UKSC 24, [239].
[43] *Asda Stores* (n 31) [6].
[44] The Equality Act 2010 (Gender Pay Gap Information) Regulations 2017.

employers to take action to reduce the gap or indeed to even produce a plan to do so. Instead, government encourages employers to publish a narrative explaining why the pay gap exists, and to voluntarily produce and publish an action plan for closing it. In fact, about half published a plan in 2018/19.[45] Only in Wales is there a requirement on public sector employers to publish an action plan in cases in which the report reveals gender pay differences.

There was initially a high level of compliance with the duty, with 100 per cent of eligible employers fulfilling the obligation in 2019.[46] However, despite increasing transparency, the same names have continued to appear every year in the list of those with the worst records. Even more worrying is the fact that, while there has been a tiny narrowing of the gap in hourly pay, the bonus gap has soared.[47] Indeed, in 2019/20, as many as eighty-two companies reported a gender bonus gap of 100 per cent, many of them in the public sector.[48]

The Labour government, following its manifesto promises, has committed itself to reforming these provisions by requiring employers with 250 or more employees to develop, publish, and implement Gender Pay Gap Action Plans. This is therefore a key junction at which future reforms can attempt to converge or at least draw on EU post-Brexit developments. In this context, this takes the form of the EU Pay Transparency Directive,[49] adopted in May 2023, to be brought into force by member states by 7 June 2026. There are several key features in the Transparency Directive that would assist in creating effective action plans, which the government would do well to consider. Unlike the UK reporting regulations, the Directive requires relevant employers to take steps to remedy gender pay gaps revealed through the reporting process. Where differences in average pay for same work or work of equal value are not justified by objective, gender-neutral criteria, the employer should take measures to remove inequalities within a reasonable period of time in close cooperation with workers' representatives, the labour inspectorate, and/or the equality body.[50] The Directive sets out detailed measures to achieve this effect. For example, a Joint Pay Assessment is triggered when pay reporting demonstrates a difference in the average pay level between female and male workers of at least 5 per cent in any category of workers; the employer has not justified such a difference in the average pay level on the basis of objective, gender-neutral criteria; and the employer has not remedied such an unjustified difference in the average pay level within six months of the date of submission of the pay reporting. Joint pay assessments should lead to remedial measures which should lead to elimination of gender-based pay discrimination within a reasonable period of

[45] Fawcett Society, Global Institute for Women's Leadership and Thomson Reuters Foundation, *Gender Pay Gap Reporting: A Comparative Analysis* (Thomson Reuters, 2020) 24.

[46] ibid 17.

[47] The Equality Trust, *UK Gender Pay Gap Reporting 2017–2020: Patterns and Progress* (September 2020).

[48] ibid.

[49] Directive (EU) 2023/970 of the European Parliament and of the Council of 10 May 2023 to strengthen the application of the principle of equal pay for equal work or work of equal value between men and women through pay transparency and enforcement mechanisms [2023] OJ L132/21.

[50] ibid Art 9(10).

time. Crucially, the Directive recognizes that one of the key levers of compliance is the contracting power of the state. In particular, member states should consider requiring contracting authorities to include conditions ensuring compliance with the principle of equal pay in the performance of public contracts.[51]

(b) Sexual Harassment

There is also scope for the EU to benefit from developments in the UK. A key new reform concerns sexual harassment at work. Although sexual harassment has been included in the anti-discrimination statutes in both the UK and the EU for decades now, it is still widely prevalent in the workplace. Yet very few cases proceed to employment tribunals, with only 167 tribunal cases related to sexual harassment in 2023.[52] So there is an urgent need for a new approach to dealing with sexual harassment and other forms of harassment at work, which does not only depend on individuals bringing their complaints to tribunals. The key change which came into effect on 26 October 2024 was to shift the responsibility for compliance away from individuals and towards employers. This was further strengthened by the Employment Bill 2024. Under the newly incorporated section 40A of the Equality Act 2010,[53] 'An employer (A) must take all reasonable steps to prevent sexual harassment of employees of A in the course of their employment'. This is clearly a reform which the EU would also benefit from.

(c) Intersectionality

This is one area in which there have been developments on both sides of the Channel, where each could reciprocally benefit from the other. The provision for protection against discrimination on two grounds simultaneously in section 14 of the Equality Act 2010 was never brought into force by the ensuing Coalition and Tory governments. The current Labour government is, however, committed to bringing it into force. In the meanwhile, the EU Pay Transparency Directive incorporates intersectionality for the first time. Article 3(2)(e) states: 'For the purposes of this Directive, discrimination includes "intersectional discrimination", which is discrimination based on a combination of sex and any other ground or grounds of discrimination protected under [the Race] Directive 2000/43/EC or [the Employment Directive] 2000/78/EC'.[54] The preamble stresses that transparency would address intersectional discrimination where non-transparent pay settings allow for discriminatory practices on several

[51] ibid Art 24(1).
[52] https://www.peoplemanagement.co.uk/article/1890253/new-ehrc-guidance-sexual-harassment-does-mean-employers.
[53] Worker Protection (Amendment of Equality Act 2010) Act 2023; Employment Bill 2024.
[54] Dir 2023/970 (n 49) Art 3(2)(e).

discrimination grounds. Although the Directive is about gender-based pay discrimination, it emphasizes that disabled women, ethnic minority women, Roma women, young women, or elderly women may face intersectional pay discrimination, which needs to be addressed. This is a step beyond Article 14, which only allows a combination of two grounds; but it is confined to pay transparency. A synthesis between these provisions would widen section 14 to include multiple grounds and would widen EU law beyond pay issues.

4 Conclusion

The relationship between the UK and the EU in relation to equality law was one of positive and constructive collaboration. This co-ownership of equality law has meant that there was never a risk of a wholesale repeal of equality law and all its manifold EU inputs. However, in recent years there has been a drift away from EU law, including in the jurisprudence of the UK courts. With the new Labour government's energetic commitments to reforming equality law, a window of opportunity opens for further collaboration. However, despite many attempts to persuade policymakers to take this route, there does not appear to be much appetite. This is a pity, since there is still much to be gained from mutual cross-fertilization.

21
Employment Law

ACL Davies[*]

EU membership had a substantial influence over employment law in the UK, with regulation in many important areas being traceable to EU sources: equality (especially equal pay), working time, and non-standard forms of work, to name but a few. For some advocates of the UK's exit from the EU, freeing the labour market from 'Brussels red tape' was a significant objective. The Working Time Regulations 1998 (WTR) might be cited as an example of a measure which had a relatively low impact in practice (due to the possibility of getting a worker to opt out of the 48-hour maximum limit on the working week[1]) but which fitted into a narrative of unwanted bureaucracy limiting UK productivity.[2]

But anyone who was hoping for the repeal of the WTR immediately after 'exit day' has been disappointed. The Trade and Cooperation Agreement (TCA) includes a non-regression clause, which requires the UK to maintain the levels of employment and social protection in force at the time of its exit from the EU.[3] While this is drafted so as not to preclude all changes to employment law, it is at least arguable that it might be infringed by the repeal of a major piece of EU-derived legislation, which in turn opens up the possibility that the EU could impose tariffs on the UK. The TCA also requires the UK to comply with various international norms, such as ILO Conventions, in the social field.[4] In practice, most of the immediate changes to domestic legislation in the aftermath of the UK's exit were technical ones: dealing with cross-border issues no longer relevant to a non-member state and preserving rights that would have been lost as the status of EU law changed.

The outcome of the 2024 general election proved crucial in determining whether the next government would be inclined to test the boundaries of the non-regression clause or whether it would want to enact a significant programme of worker-protective legislation. The Labour Party's landslide victory heralded a new era for employment

* This chapter considers developments up to 16 April 2026.

1 C Barnard and others, 'Opting Out of the 48-Hour Week: Employer Necessity or Individual Choice?' (2003) 32 ILJ 223.

2 SI 1998/1833.

3 Trade and Cooperation Agreement (December 2020), UK Treaty Series No 8, 2021, Arts 386–387.

4 ibid Art 399.

ACL Davies, *Employment Law* In: *The UK Regulatory Framework Post-Brexit: 'Law Unbound'*. Edited by: Paul Craig and Vilija Vėlyvytė, Oxford University Press. © Oxford University Press 2026. DOI: 10.1093/9780198969815.003.0024

law, with an Employment Rights Bill (ERB) laid before Parliament within 100 days of the government taking office, and promises of further consultations and reforms to come.[5] But the EU has not stood still since Brexit either, with significant new directives coming into force arising out of the European Pillar of Social Rights and broader initiatives to regulate platform work.[6] These do not appear to have had much influence over developments at Westminster, where the government is focused on addressing longstanding domestic issues. The TCA does not require the UK to keep pace with new developments in EU law, as some had hoped, so some divergence is to be expected, but the TCA provides an option to invoke 'rebalancing measures' if the divergence has an impact on trade.[7] It is very difficult to determine when the threshold for this might be met.

This chapter proceeds in five sections. First, I explain how employment law varies across the four nations of the UK, and offer a brief overview of the EU-derived provisions of employment law before the UK's exit from the EU, for the benefit of the non-specialist reader. Second, I consider the immediate changes around the time of the UK's exit as the UK disentangled itself from EU law. Third, I examine the Northern Ireland Protocol and the Windsor Framework as they apply to employment and equality law.[8] Fourth, I analyse the main provisions of the TCA relating to employment law and consider their implications for the future of employment law in England, Wales, Scotland, and Northern Ireland (on topics not covered by the Protocol and Framework). Finally, in the fifth section, I offer a comparison of the EU's post-Brexit employment policy, on the one hand, with the Employment Rights Act 2025 (ERA 2025) and other ideas emerging from the Labour government at Westminster and the proposed Employment Bill in Northern Ireland, on the other, to assess the extent of the 'divergence' which has already developed. This chapter does not deal in detail with equality law and associated matters such as parental leave, which are covered in another contribution.[9]

1 Background Pre-Brexit

Although it is appropriate to speak of the exit of the 'UK' from the EU, employment law has never been a UK matter. Different rules apply in England, Wales, Scotland, and Northern Ireland, with the biggest differences between Northern Ireland and the other three nations. The relationship between national law and EU law post-Brexit is also different as between Northern Ireland and Great Britain, with the effect that the law in Northern Ireland is likely to remain more closely aligned to EU law. It is

[5] UK Government, *Next Steps to Make Work Pay* (October 2024).
[6] European Parliament, Council and Commission, *European Pillar of Social Rights* (2017).
[7] TCA (n 3) Art 411.
[8] The Protocol is part of the UK–EU Withdrawal Agreement (2020) and was amended by the Windsor Framework (2023).
[9] Ch 20.

difficult fully to capture these distinctions in a single chapter, but I explain the background here and return to the post-Brexit Northern Ireland position later on.

Employment law is a mix of statute and judge-made law in fields such as contract and tort. Looking first at statute, employment law is reserved to Westminster in respect of Scotland and Wales but largely devolved in Northern Ireland. While it is important to check the territorial extent of each piece of legislation, it is generally the case that employment law statutes passed by the Westminster Parliament nowadays extend to England, Wales, and Scotland, with limited applicability in Northern Ireland.[10] The statutory framework for Northern Ireland's employment law prior to devolution was always somewhat different: there was usually separate legislation for Northern Ireland, and while this generally mirrored that in Great Britain, this was not uniformly the case.[11] A distinctive approach to employment law has gradually emerged in Northern Ireland since the creation of the Assembly. The ERA 2025 has only very partial application in Northern Ireland,[12] but the Northern Ireland Executive is proposing its own Bill with some similar provisions, which I analyse below.[13] Even in Scotland and Wales, where employment law is not devolved, it is possible for differences to emerge in some circumstances. For example, the Senedd retained a version of the agricultural wages regime for Wales, using its devolved powers to regulate the sector.[14]

One of the consequences of EU membership was, of course, to set a baseline for employment law across the EU, and thus to reduce the extent to which the four nations of the UK could pursue their own agendas in the field. I turn now to an overview of that baseline. At the time of the UK's departure from the EU, there was competence to enact directives as measures of minimum harmonization in the following fields under Article 153(1) TFEU:

(a) improvement in particular of the working environment to protect workers' health and safety;
(b) working conditions;
(c) social security and social protection of workers;
(d) protection of workers where their employment contract is terminated;
(e) the information and consultation of workers;
(f) representation and collective defence of the interests of workers and employers, including co-determination . . .
(g) conditions of employment for third-country nationals legally residing in Union territory;

[10] The National Minimum Wage Act 1998 is an example of UK-wide legislation: s 56.

[11] Compare, eg, Employment Rights Act 1996 and the Employment Rights (Northern Ireland) Order 1996 (SI 1919/1996 (NI 16)). For an example of distinctive Northern Ireland legislation, see the Fair Employment and Treatment (Northern Ireland) Order 1998 (SI 1998/3162).

[12] ERA 2025, s 158.

[13] NI Executive Department for the Economy, *The 'Good Jobs' Employment Rights Bill* (April 2025).

[14] Agriculture Sector (Wales) Act 2014. See *Agricultural Sector (Wales) Bill—Reference by the Attorney General for England and Wales* [2014] UKSC 43.

(h) the integration of persons excluded from the labour market, without prejudice to Article 166;
(i) equality between men and women with regard to labour market opportunities and treatment at work.

These competences had been used as the basis for directives on health and safety and working time (with numerous specific and sectoral directives), the right to a written statement of terms and conditions of employment, information and consultation rights at national level and through European Works Councils, and rights in the event of collective redundancies, a transfer of the undertaking, or the insolvency of the employer.[15]

EU law also provided for a special process of negotiation between the social partners, the social dialogue, which could result in autonomous agreements to be implemented by the social partners at the national level (such as the agreement on 'telework'[16]) or in agreements to be implemented by means of a directive,[17] such as the Directive on Fixed-Term Work.[18] After a promising start, the social dialogue did not prove to be particularly productive, though it remains important that there is a duty on the Commission to consult the social partners during the process of proposing a directive to be agreed through the usual legislative route.[19]

Article 153(5) excluded some matters from the EU's competence: 'pay, the right of association, the right to strike or the right to impose lock-outs.' It is widely thought that the member states wished to preserve their national autonomy in relation to the economically sensitive matter of pay and the politically sensitive matters of freedom of association and the right to strike. However, the exact scope of the exclusion is contested, though the CJEU recently rejected most elements of a challenge to the Minimum Wage Directive on this basis.[20] More broadly, the exclusion of EU competence to enact directives on these topics does not amount to an exclusion of EU law more generally, as the well-known *Viking* and *Laval* cases demonstrated.[21] In these cases, examples of 'negative integration', the CJEU ruled on the compatibility of trade unions' exercise of their right to strike with the employer's internal market freedoms (freedom of establishment and freedom to provide services respectively).[22] An attempt to use the competence to regulate the internal market to

[15] Directives relating to equal treatment, equal pay, and parental leave rights are dealt with elsewhere. For a detailed account, see C Barnard, *EU Employment Law* (4th edn, Oxford University Press 2012), and for a historical overview, see J Kenner, *EU Employment Law: From Rome to Amsterdam and Beyond* (Hart 2003).
[16] Framework Agreement on Telework, 16 July 2002.
[17] Art 155 TFEU.
[18] Directive 1999/70/EC.
[19] Art 154 TFEU.
[20] Directive (EU) 2022/2041, and see Case C-19/23, *Denmark v Parliament and Council* EU:C:2025:865.
[21] Case C-438/05 *International Transport Workers' Federation v Viking Line ABP* EU:C:2007:772; Case C-341/05 *Laval un Partneri Ltd v Svenska Byggnadsarbetareforbundet* EU:C:2007:809.
[22] For discussion see ACL Davies, 'One Step Forward, Two Steps Back? The *Viking* and *Laval* Cases in the ECJ' (2008) 37 ILJ 126; M Freedland and J Prassl (eds), *Viking, Laval and Beyond* (Hart 2014). On negative integration more generally, see V Velyvyte, *Judicial Authority in EU Internal Market Law: Implications for the Balance of Competences and Powers* (Hart 2024).

enact a regulation addressing the perceived difficulties with the Court's approach was not successful.[23]

From a UK perspective, very few areas of employment law were untouched by EU law prior to the UK's exit. The clearest examples of purely domestic employment law are the National Minimum Wage, unfair dismissal law, and most aspects of trade union legislation.[24] The 'building blocks' of the law, such as the common law of the contract of employment, are also largely domestic in origin. Large swathes of employment law—on the topics outlined above—were based on EU law. Importantly, this is not to say that employment law in the UK would not have developed in any of the same directions in the absence of EU membership. While this may be true in some cases (domestic working time legislation seems unlikely), it is clearly incorrect in others. For example, the UK had begun to develop equality legislation before its entry into the EU and widened its list of protected characteristics before the EU did.[25] Even if EU exit had opened up the possibility of a wholesale repeal of employment law—which it did not—this would have been and remains unlikely in practice.

2 The Brexit Process

As Barnard has argued, the only sensible strategy for managing the UK's exit without generating considerable legal uncertainty was to preserve most EU-derived law in force after 'exit day'.[26] This was achieved through the device of 'retained EU law' under the European Union (Withdrawal) Act 2018. Immediate changes were only needed where the law made reference to EU obligations which were no longer applicable, or where it had cross-border applications. There were very few examples of either of these situations in employment law.[27]

The task of tidying up references to EU obligations was carried out through the Employment Rights (Amendment) (EU Exit) Regulations 2019.[28] For example, section 19(4) Employment Relations Act 1999, which allowed the Secretary of State to make regulations to implement EU obligations relating to part-time work, was repealed. The same instrument made provision for one of the few examples of employment law with cross-border relevance, the rules relating to European Works Councils

[23] Commission, Proposal for a Council Regulation on the exercise of the right to take collective action within the context of the freedom of establishment and the freedom to provide services (COM (2012) 130 final), known as 'Monti II'.

[24] See, generally, Z Adams and others, *Deakin and Morris' Labour Law* (7th edn, Hart 2021).

[25] See, eg, Equal Pay Act 1970; Disability Discrimination Act 1995.

[26] C Barnard, 'Retained EU Law in the UK Legal Orders: Continuity Between the Old and the New' in A Łazowski and A Cygan (eds), *Research Handbook on Legal Aspects of Brexit* (Edward Elgar 2022). 'Retained' EU law is now known as 'assimilated' law by virtue of the Retained EU Law (Revocation and Reform) Act 2023.

[27] Space precludes a discussion of the repeal of the Posted Workers (Enforcement of Employment Rights) Regulations 2016 (SI 2016/539) and the Posted Workers (Agency Workers) Regulations 2020 (SI 2020/384) by the Retained EU Law (Revocation and Reform) Act 2023.

[28] SI 2019/535.

(EWCs).[29] These rules put in place a process for large firms (Community-scale undertakings) with an operation in more than one member state to set up an EWC or similar mechanism for information and consultation. After the UK's exit from the EU, workers in the UK can no longer participate in the process of initiating a request for negotiations about an EWC,[30] though it is possible for an EWC to continue to operate under UK law after the UK's exit where certain conditions are met.[31] Whether workers in the UK continue to be covered by an EWC agreement depends on the terms of the agreement, though existing UK-based representatives on EWCs retain the usual rights and protections for worker representatives under the Regulations.[32]

3 Arrangements In Northern Ireland

The EU–UK Withdrawal Agreement made separate provision for Northern Ireland in the Northern Ireland Protocol.[33] This was amended in 2023 by an agreement known as the Windsor Framework. Although these agreements are principally concerned with trade in goods, they have some implications for employment and equality law, which I will consider briefly here.[34]

The UK's exit from the EU presented a particular difficulty in respect of the border between Ireland and Northern Ireland. A key commitment in the Belfast/Good Friday Agreement was that there should be no visible border, but the UK's exit meant that this would now be an external border of the EU, where a variety of checks would normally be applied. The compromise reached was that EU rules on customs and free movement of goods would continue to apply in Northern Ireland. This meant that checks on goods moving from Great Britain to Northern Ireland would need to be carried out when they entered Northern Ireland, because this was the point at which they gained access to the EU internal market. The Windsor Framework is intended to streamline this process by distinguishing between goods intended for Northern Ireland only and goods which might enter the EU internal market.

While all of this may seem far removed from employment law, the Protocol and the Framework both contain provisions intended to safeguard the equality and human rights provisions in the Belfast/Good Friday Agreement. It is these provisions which bring about a closer relationship between employment and equality law in Northern

[29] Directive 94/45/EC; 2009/38/EC (Recast), transposed by the Transnational Information and Consultation of Employees Regulations 1999 (SI 1999/3323), as amended.

[30] Due to the repeal of SI 1999/3323, regs 7–16.

[31] For discussion, see R Zahn, 'The Status of European Works Councils in UK Law Post-Brexit: A Commentary on *easyJet PLC v easyJet European Works Council* and *Olsten (UK) Holdings Limited v Adecco Group European Works Council*' (2024) 53 ILJ 746.

[32] SI 1999/3323, regs 25–33.

[33] See (n 8).

[34] For detailed analysis, see A Deb and CRG Murray, 'Article 2 of the Windsor Framework, the Legacy Act and the Illegal Migration Act: Adjusting to post-Brexit Realities' [2025] PL 477; C McCrudden, 'Human Rights and Equality' in C McCrudden (ed), *The Law and Practice of the Ireland-Northern Ireland Protocol* (Cambridge University Press 2021).

Ireland and the EU. They are applicable generally, not just in relation to trade in goods.[35] Article 2(1) of the Windsor Framework states:

> The United Kingdom shall ensure that no diminution of rights, safeguards or equality of opportunity, as set out in that part of the 1998 Agreement entitled Rights, Safeguards and Equality of Opportunity results from its withdrawal from the Union, including in the area of protection against discrimination, as enshrined in the provisions of Union law listed in Annex 1 to this Protocol, and shall implement this paragraph through dedicated mechanisms.

This has two important effects. First, the law in Northern Ireland must remain aligned with EU law in respect of the six equality directives listed in Annex 1.[36] This means that it must be amended to keep pace with EU developments in these areas, not just that it must not fall below the standards in place at the time of exit. Second, there must be no 'diminution' in the protection of any of the other rights listed in the relevant chapter (Rights, Safeguards and Equality of Opportunity—RSEO) of the Belfast/Good Friday Agreement.[37] This includes a broadly framed equality right, and a paper published jointly by the Equality Commission for NI and the NI Human Rights Commission (which have formal responsibility for monitoring the Framework) has identified a number of employment directives that may be covered, including those dealing with health and safety; pregnant workers; fixed-term, part-time, and agency work; and parental leave.[38] Of course, it remains to be seen in each of these cases whether a court would accept the argument that the relevant directive related to a right protected under the RSEO, with some of those just listed having more obvious connections than others.

Although these provisions have not yet been tested in the employment sphere, they are the subject of ongoing litigation in other contexts. At the time of writing, the Northern Ireland courts have accepted that the provisions are justiciable and that legislation bringing about a 'diminution' in rights protected by the Framework may be 'disapplied' by the courts.[39]

The upshot of this is that there is a much stronger commitment to maintain a subset of EU equality and employment law in force in Northern Ireland than there is in Great Britain under the terms of the TCA, to which we will now turn. It is particularly significant that this is enforceable in court because it means that individuals and groups

[35] Deb and Murray (n 34) 481.

[36] These are: Directive 79/7/EEC, Directive 2000/43/EC, Directive 2000/78/EC, Directive 2004/113/EC, Directive 2006/54/EC, and Directive 2010/41/EU.

[37] See *SPUC Pro-life Ltd v Secretary of State for Northern Ireland* [2023] NICA 35, [2024] 2 CMLR 20.

[38] NIHRC and ECNI Working Paper, *The Scope of Article 2(1) of the Ireland/Northern Ireland Protocol* (December 2022) https://nihrc.org/publication/detail/nihrc-and-ecni-working-paper-the-scope-of-article-21-of-the-ireland-northern-ireland-protocol.

[39] The leading cases are *Re Dillon's Application for Judicial Review* [2024] NIKB 11, [2024] 3 CMLR 34; and [2024] NICA 59; and *Re Northern Ireland Human Rights Commission's Application for Judicial Review* [2024] NIKB 35; [2024] 3 CMLR 18. *Dillon* is before the UK Supreme Court at the time of writing.

affected by a change in the law can challenge it, whereas under the TCA, any objections must be raised by the EU itself.

4 The TCA

In order to understand the constraints on the future development of domestic employment law, it is essential to examine the relevant provisions of the TCA.[40] This applies in all four nations of the UK, including to those parts of employment law in Northern Ireland not subject to the Windsor Framework. The TCA includes a 'non-regression' clause and a commitment to comply with certain international labour standards. It seems clear that the EU included these elements with a view to ensuring that the UK could not use its departure to gain a competitive advantage over the other member states by lowering its existing standards of social protection. More controversially, the TCA also makes provision for 'rebalancing measures' in the event of 'significant divergences' on labour and social standards, which could be used where differences have arisen not because of regression by the UK, but because of new standards adopted by the EU. The aim here is to protect the EU's ability to enact new measures in the field of employment law without incurring a competitive disadvantage as against the UK, to which such measures would no longer apply. This does not amount to a dynamic requirement for the UK to keep pace with new developments in EU law (of the kind found in Article 2 of the Windsor Framework in relation to equality directives in Northern Ireland), but it does mean that the UK may find itself confronted with adverse trade consequences if it chooses not to do so.

I argue that although these provisions may influence the future development of employment law in the nations of the UK, they will not be easy to invoke in practice, for three main reasons: a lack of clarity in their drafting, the difficulty of proving the impact of a change in employment law on trade, and the general unwillingness of parties to trade agreements to disrupt a successful economic relationship by invoking a social clause.[41]

In line with most commentators, I consider the TCA largely on the assumption that it will be used to stop the UK from diverging from the EU rather than the other way around, though its provisions are symmetrical. This is a common-sense assumption given the objectives of those who campaigned for the UK to leave the EU. However, major changes in the political complexion of the EU and the UK in the future could conceivably falsify this assumption.

[40] For an overview, see S Peers, 'So Close, Yet So Far: The EU/UK Trade and Cooperation Agreement' (2022) 59 CML Rev 49.

[41] For helpful analysis, see J Kenner, 'Brexit and Workers' Rights: Managing Divergence and Managing Trust' in Łazowski and Cygan (n 26); P Syrpis, 'The Influence of the EU on UK Labour Law—Before and After Brexit' (2022) 51 ILJ 802.

(a) Non-regression

The non-regression clause applies to 'labour and social levels of protection'.[42] This slightly odd phrase is defined in Article 386(1) to refer to 'overall' levels of protection in 'law and standards' relating to:

(a) fundamental rights at work;
(b) occupational health and safety standards;
(c) fair working conditions and employment standards;
(d) information and consultation rights at company level; or
(e) restructuring of undertakings.

Article 386(2) defines the same concept for the EU as 'labour and social levels of protection that are applicable to and in, and are common to, all Member States'. One noteworthy feature of these formulations is that they appear not to be confined to the social *acquis*. In relation to the UK, this could easily have been achieved by specifying the directives (and case law) applicable at the time of exit, and for the EU by reference to provisions 'applicable' by virtue of EU law. As I explore further below, this is of particular significance for fundamental rights, where EU law itself plays a supplementary role. Kenner suggests that the wording is broad enough to require the UK to maintain in place provisions in force at the time of exit that were not related to EU law at all.[43] One such example is the National Minimum Wage Act 1998, which is clearly a measure upholding 'fair working conditions', but is purely a matter of domestic law. If this interpretation were to be correct, it would suggest that the UK has taken on a greater burden of compliance than the member states, which are only obliged to maintain standards 'common to all Member States'. While this would include 'common' measures not derived from EU law, such as obligations under ILO Conventions ratified by all member states, it is not apt to cover matters of national law within the member states.

Nevertheless, the topics listed in the clause (with the exception of fundamental rights) do seem to match quite closely to the social *acquis*, suggesting that this may have been what the drafters had in mind when devising the clause.[44] Some of the phrases used can be traced relatively easily to particular directives: health and safety, information and consultation, and the 1970s directives on collective redundancies, acquired rights, and insolvency.[45] Paragraph (c) presumably captures most other employment law measures, such as the 'atypical' work directives, the Working

[42] TCA, Art 387.
[43] See (n 41) 333.
[44] Kenner (ibid) rightly points out that it does not include internal market measures such as the Posted Workers Directive (96/71/EC), as amended.
[45] See Barnard (n 15) for detail.

Time Directive (though that could also fall under health and safety), and the Written Statement Directive.[46] Of course, the concept of the *acquis* also encompasses the CJEU's jurisprudence in these various areas.

The most tricky to interpret is paragraph (a), on 'fundamental rights at work'. One comprehensive point of reference for 'fundamental rights at work' in EU law is, of course, the EU Charter. This was not 'retained' during the exit process, on the basis that it was no longer relevant because it applied to the EU institutions and to the member states when acting within the scope of EU law.[47] Of course, many aspects of the social *acquis* represent the detailed working-out of workers' rights, such as the right to paid holidays.[48] But this is already easily captured by the other provisions of Article 386(1). Another possibility is that this is a reference to international sources, though these are dealt with separately under Article 399, discussed further below.

While it is unfortunate that the scope of the non-regression clause is not as clear as it might have been, of greater practical significance is what exactly the idea of 'non-regression' entails in this context. This is set out in Article 387. Paragraph 1 affirms the parties' freedom to set their own levels of 'labour and social protection' in accordance with their international commitments, including the TCA itself. The crucial provision is paragraph 2:

> A Party shall not weaken or reduce, in a manner affecting trade or investment between the Parties, its labour and social levels of protection below the levels in place at the end of the transition period, including by failing to effectively enforce its law and standards.

This sets the end of the transition period as the date at which a party's level of protection is to be assessed for non-regression purposes. It also identifies failure to enforce standards as a form of regression alongside the obvious method of repealing or amending legislation, a point to which I return below.

The most significant element is the phrase 'in a manner affecting trade or investment between the Parties'. This captures the idea that only significant changes, giving one party an advantage in trading with the other or in attracting inward investment, will be caught by the clause. But it will not be easy to apply. If we take repealing the WTR as an example, Kenner notes that this would be quite a significant change to labour legislation in the UK and a clear departure from the law in force at the end of the transition period.[49] But its impact on trade and investment is much harder to assess. On the one hand, it might make the UK a more attractive place for firms to do business, on the basis that there is less regulation of working time, which can be

[46] Equality law is beyond the scope of this chapter but presumably fits here, or under (a).

[47] For discussion, see C Barnard, 'So Long, Farewell, Auf Wiedersehen, Adieu: Brexit and the Charter of Fundamental Rights' (2019) 82 MLR 350.

[48] Case C-173/99 *R v Secretary of State for Trade and Industry, ex p BECTU* [2001] ECR I-4881, [43].

[49] See (n 41) 338.

bureaucratic, and more flexibility to require workers to work the hours needed to complete particular tasks. On the other hand, the WTR already incorporate elements of flexibility—such as the notorious opt-out from the 48-hour maximum working week—and are not well enforced, so it is not clear how much impact their removal would have.[50] The EU would face an uphill struggle to prove the impact of such a measure on trade and investment.

The other element of the non-regression arrangements worth noting is their specific reference to enforcement. It is clear that the inclusion of enforcement was intended to address the scenario in which a party does not repeal protective measures but instead stops enforcing them. Article 388 spells this out in greater detail:

> For the purposes of enforcement as referred to in Article 387 each Party shall have in place and maintain a system for effective domestic enforcement and, in particular, an effective system of labour inspections in accordance with its international commitments relating to working conditions and the protection of workers; ensure that administrative and judicial proceedings are available that allow public authorities and individuals with standing to bring timely actions against violations of the labour law and social standards; and provide for appropriate and effective remedies, including interim relief, as well as proportionate and dissuasive sanctions...

It is quite striking (though in the context of the complexity of the agreement perhaps not surprising) that the UK agreed to this clause. Although there is some public enforcement of labour law in the UK in specific areas (health and safety (including working time), the National Minimum Wage, agency work, and gangmaster licensing), there is no general labour inspectorate.[51] The ERA 2025 has made provision to bring some existing enforcement agencies together into the Fair Work Agency (FWA) with broader responsibilities (for example, including holiday pay) and the possibility of adding more powers in the future, so the direction of travel may be towards a labour inspectorate, but it clearly did not exist at the time of agreement.[52] Critics of the current mechanisms for individual enforcement of employment rights would also question whether they comply with the provisions of the clause. The two most obvious problems are the failure to provide 'timely' recourse, given the long delays in getting to a tribunal hearing, and the absence of interim relief outside very limited areas (for example, unfair dismissal on trade union grounds).[53] On its face, the clause obliges the UK to rectify these deficiencies, but since it clarifies the meaning of enforcement in Article 387(2), the non-regression clause, it might be argued that the UK is simply obliged not to allow an ineffective system to become even worse.

[50] See (n 1).

[51] See ACL Davies, *Valuing Employment Rights: A Study of Remedies in Employment Law* (Hart 2024) Ch 2.

[52] ERA 2025, Part 5.

[53] ERA 1996, ss 128–132.

(b) International Labour Standards

Article 399 deals with the parties' commitments in the sphere of international labour standards and is worth considering separately.[54] Some parts of the Article are aspirational, committing the parties to 'promoting' the ILO's decent work agenda in trade (Article 399(1)) and in domestic law (Article 399(6)). However, there are also some stronger provisions requiring the parties to maintain certain standards in place. These do not have the 'impact on trade' proviso in Article 387, which could prove to be significant in practice.

Article 399(2) commits the parties to 'respecting, promoting and effectively implementing the internationally recognised core labour standards, as defined in the fundamental ILO Conventions', which relate to freedom of association and collective bargaining, forced labour, child labour, and non-discrimination.[55] This goes beyond promotion to compliance (respecting) and implementation. The ILO has recently added health and safety to the Declaration, and has designated two further conventions as fundamental as a result.[56] It is unclear from the drafting whether Article 399(2), coupled with the requirement in Article 399(3) to make 'continued and sustained efforts' to ratify the fundamental conventions, should be construed in a static way (applying only to those recognized at the time of the TCA) or dynamically, to cover this new development in the ILO. This is important because the UK has only ratified one of the two health and safety conventions now designated as fundamental.[57]

One of the common criticisms of the ILO Declaration is that its content is relatively thin, so from that perspective, a much more important provision is Article 399(5). This commits the parties to implementing the ILO Conventions they have ratified (not just the fundamental conventions) and to implementing their obligations under the European Social Charter. In the case of the UK, this refers to the obligations assumed under the 1961 Charter, since the UK has not ratified the 1996 revised version. In the labour law context, rights accepted by the UK include the right to just conditions of work (which deals with hours of work and holidays), the right to fair remuneration, and rights relating to freedom of association and collective bargaining.[58] Successive governments have been content to ignore the findings of the ILO bodies and the Committee of Experts in relation to the UK's failure fully to implement these various commitments, so their presence in the TCA could help to elevate them to greater

[54] For detailed analysis, see KD Ewing, 'The EU–UK Trade and Cooperation Agreement: Implications for ILO Standards and the European Social Charter in the United Kingdom' (2021) 32 King's Law Journal 306.

[55] See https://www.ilo.org/international-labour-standards/conventions-protocols-and-recommendations for a list.

[56] Occupational Safety and Health Convention, 1981 (No. 155); Promotional Framework for Occupational Safety and Health Convention, 2006 (No. 187).

[57] The UK has ratified No 187 but not No 155.

[58] For an overview, see https://www.coe.int/en/web/european-social-charter/united-kingdom.

prominence. Interestingly, Article 399(5) does not refer to the ECHR (although there are references elsewhere in the TCA[59]). Although the ESC is the more obviously 'social' instrument, some rights in the ECHR are highly relevant to employment law, including the Article 11 right to freedom of association and the Article 8 right to respect for private life, which has been used to tackle a range of issues, including workplace surveillance and unfair dismissal.[60] This is an unfortunate omission.

(c) Dispute Resolution

Given the various uncertainties about the meaning of the non-regression clause and the provisions relating to international agreements, the dispute resolution mechanism provided for under the TCA takes on particular significance. The non-regression clause is subject to the procedures set out in Articles 408, 409, and 410.[61] The provisions relating to international standards are subject to Articles 408 and 409.[62]

Under Article 408, provision is made for formal consultations between the parties.[63] If these do not result in an agreement, there is a possibility of making a referral to a panel of experts under Article 409. If the panel finds that one party is in breach, there must be further discussions between the parties to agree on measures to address the breach, with a further possibility of referral to the panel in the event of a disagreement. Under Article 409(19), a dispute may ultimately be taken to arbitration. Where it concerns non-regression (rather than compliance with international standards), Article 410 allows for the use of Articles 749 and 750, providing for the respondent to pay temporary compensation or the complainant to suspend some of its own obligations under the agreement.

(d) Rebalancing Measures

Under Article 411, there is a power to take 'rebalancing measures' in the event of 'significant divergences' on various matters, including labour and social standards, where they have 'material impacts on trade and investment'. This does not require proof that the non-regression clause has been breached. Rather, it acknowledges the fact that over time, non-regression becomes less relevant as the parties' legal systems diverge more generally, but that there could come a point at which that divergence becomes problematic from the perspective of trade. The Commission's 'frequently asked questions' make clear that this provision is intended to 'future-proof' the level playing field:

[59] Respect for human rights under Art 763 is an 'essential element' under Art 771, breach of which can lead to termination of the TCA.
[60] See, generally, A Bogg and others, *Human Rights at Work* (Hart 2024).
[61] Art 396(2).
[62] Art 407(2).
[63] Note that Art 389(1) seeks to avoid disputes by emphasizing dialogue between the parties.

> This might be relevant, for example in a situation where one Party would significantly increase its levels of protection related to labour or social standards, the environment or climate above the levels of the other Party. This may entail an increase in the costs of production and hence a competitive disadvantage.[64]

The implication here is that even if the UK maintained its existing social laws and standards in place in full compliance with other parts of the TCA, unilateral 'rebalancing' could still occur if the EU enhanced its own level of protection to the extent that it put itself at a competitive disadvantage. While this is by no means the same as a 'dynamic' clause requiring the UK to keep pace with new developments in EU law after its exit, it demonstrates that the UK cannot simply ignore what happens in the EU because of its potential impact on trade and investment. However, the rebalancing measures may not be easy to invoke. Under Article 411(2):

> Such measures shall be restricted with respect to their scope and duration to what is strictly necessary and proportionate in order to remedy the situation. Priority shall be given to such measures as will least disturb the functioning of this Agreement. A Party's assessment of those impacts shall be based on reliable evidence and not merely on conjecture or remote possibility.

The measures may be adopted after a short period of consultation between the parties, but they are subject to review by the arbitration tribunal.[65] More generally, the operation of Article 411 itself may be the subject of a review initiated by either side after the agreement has been in force for four years, a clear sign of how controversial the inclusion of these provisions was.[66]

(e) Conclusion

As other commentators have noted, there are a number of obstacles to the use of these provisions in practice. One is that there are many interpretive uncertainties which would need to be resolved. Another is the question, noted above, of whether any alleged 'regression' or 'divergence' has an impact on trade or investment, though this is not required under Article 399. But perhaps a bigger question is whether it would ever be politically feasible for the EU to disrupt the TCA because of a labour violation.[67] The EU has a longstanding policy of including clauses requiring, for example, compliance with certain ILO norms in trade agreements with third countries, but these

64 See https://ec.europa.eu/commission/presscorner/detail/en/qanda_20_2532.
65 Art 411(3).
66 Art 411(4).
67 KD Ewing, 'Implications of the Post-Brexit Architecture for Labour Law' (2017) 28 King's Law Journal 403.

are rarely invoked, despite widespread violations.[68] The EU–Korea FTA case has been much discussed, but precisely because it is exceptional.[69] In general terms, the parties' interests in maintaining trade flows typically override any concerns relating to labour rights.

5 Post-Brexit Developments

Employment law has continued to develop since the UK left the EU, both at EU level and within the nations of the UK themselves. I explore these developments here. It is clear that no significant 'regression' has taken place, but that there is a degree of 'divergence'. This has occurred because the Labour government's priorities for employment law in England, Wales, and Scotland are different to the regulatory priorities being pursued at EU level. It is possible that the agenda in Northern Ireland will align more closely with that in the EU, but it remains heavily influenced by what is going on elsewhere in the UK. It is difficult to assess whether the EU would have grounds for invoking Article 411 given the uncertainties surrounding its interpretation explored above. Given that the Labour government at Westminster is more sympathetic towards the EU than its predecessor, there may be strong political reasons for the EU not to pursue this option at present.

I begin by examining the three new EU Directives (transparent and predictable working conditions, minimum wage, and platform work) enacted since the UK's exit. These implement commitments made in the European Pillar of Social Rights.[70] I assess the extent of divergence by examining what changes would have been required to bring domestic law into line with these directives.[71] I then examine measures passed by the Conservative government between the UK's exit and the change of government in 2024. While there was a clear appetite in some quarters to see 'benefits' from the UK's exit in terms of greater deregulation, this government chose only to make minor changes to employment law, many of which were in fact worker-protective. The Labour government elected in 2024 has a very significant agenda in relation to employment law reform. The ERA 2025 is an enormous undertaking, running to more than 150 sections and more than 300 pages. I argue that it is largely concerned with addressing domestic matters and does not appear to be motivated in any obvious way by a desire for closer alignment with the EU. The Act applies principally to England, Wales, and Scotland, though some elements will take effect in Northern Ireland too.[72]

[68] J Harrison, 'The Labour Rights Agenda in Free Trade Agreements' (2019) 20 Journal of World Investment and Trade 705; L Van den Putte and J Orbie, 'EU Bilateral Trade Agreements and the Surprising Rise of Labour Provisions' (2015) 31 International Journal of Comparative Labour Law and Industrial Relations 263.

[69] For analysis, including comparison with the TCA, see T Novitz, 'Sustainable Labour Conditionality in EU Free Trade Agreements? Implications of the EU–Korea Expert Panel Report' (2022) 47 ELRev 3.

[70] See (n 6).

[71] For reasons of space, I take English law as my focus here.

[72] ERA 2025, s 158.

In April 2025, the Northern Ireland Executive announced that it would bring forward an Employment Bill addressing some of the same topics, which I consider towards the end of the section, noting some of the areas of closer alignment with the EU.[73]

It is important to note at the outset that the volume of material addressed in this section is huge and far from settled. It is not possible to consider every detail in this chapter. Nor is it possible to provide the usual employment law critique of the fairness and workability of the various measures under consideration. Instead, my focus is on assessing the extent of any divergences and commenting on the possible reasons for their occurrence.

(a) EU Developments

The European Pillar of Social Rights, proclaimed in 2017, has provided a fresh impetus to the EU's efforts in the field of social law.[74] The document included six groups of commitments relating to employment law: 'secure and adaptable employment', fair wages, 'information about employment conditions and protection in case of dismissals', worker participation, 'work–life balance', and health and safety and data protection. The Directive on Transparent and Predictable Working Conditions reflects the third of these commitments.[75] The Directive on Adequate Minimum Wages obviously reflects the second, but is also concerned with improving the coverage of collective bargaining on wages, so fulfils the fourth too.[76] The Directive on Platform Work has a strong emphasis on data protection as well as a concern with the precarious nature of this type of work.[77] I examine each in turn, from the perspective of regulatory divergence with the UK.

(i) Transparent and Predictable Work

The Directive on Transparent and Predictable Working Conditions was agreed in 2019, but had a post-Brexit implementation deadline of 2022.[78] The 'transparency' part of the Directive updates and enhances the protections previously afforded by the Written Statement Directive.[79] The 'predictability' is novel. Interestingly, English law had already begun to align with some of the provisions in the Directive prior to 2024, and does so even more clearly under the ERA 2025.

[73] See (n 13).

[74] For an overview, see S Garben, 'The European Pillar of Social Rights: An Assessment of Its Meaning and Significance' (2019) 21 CYELS 101.

[75] Directive (EU) 2019/1152 of the European Parliament and of the Council of 20 June 2019 on transparent and predictable working conditions in the European Union [2019] OJ L186/105.

[76] Directive (EU) 2022/2041 of the European Parliament and of the Council of 19 October 2022 on adequate minimum wages in the European Union [2022] OJ L275/33.

[77] Directive (EU) 2024/2831 of the European Parliament and of the Council of 23 October 2024 on improving working conditions in platform work OJ L, 11/11/2024.

[78] See (n 75) Art 21.

[79] Council Directive 91/533/EEC of 14 October 1991 on an employer's obligation to inform employees of the conditions applicable to the contract or employment relationship [1999] OJ L288/32.

The UK's implementation of the old Written Statement Directive is in sections 1-7B Employment Rights Act 1996 (ERA). This was amended in 2019 to cover workers as well as employees. It was also amended in 2018 to extend the information to be provided, so there is a close—though not exact—correspondence between the ERA provisions and the new Directive. For example, ERA makes reference to variable hours of work ('whether or not such hours or days may be variable, and if they may be how they vary or how that variation is to be determined'), but is much less detailed than the new Directive, which distinguishes between jobs with predictable and unpredictable hours and sets out specific requirements for each.[80]

Another important provision in the Directive is the requirement in Article 8 to limit probation periods to no more than six months. The ERA was amended to include a requirement to provide information about the probation period in the written statement, but no attempt was made to control its duration.[81] In fact, English law knows no concept of a probation period, other than the two-year 'qualifying period' for unfair dismissal law.[82] This means that the employee has no right to complain of unfair dismissal (except on 'automatically unfair' grounds, such as discrimination) until they have worked continuously for the employer for two years. The ERA 2025 will mirror the Directive by reducing the qualifying period to six months.[83] This will take effect in January 2027.[84]

Finally, the Directive seeks to improve the situation of workers with unpredictable or 'on demand' working arrangements.[85] The relevant measures include:

- A right to turn down a shift without 'adverse consequences' unless it is within 'predetermined reference hours and days' and reasonable notice is given
- A right to compensation for the late cancellation of a shift
- Measures to prevent the abuse of on-demand contracts, one option being a presumption of a contract with minimum hours based on hours previously worked over a reference period
- A right to request a contract with predictable hours after six months' service.

The Conservative government enacted the Workers (Predictable Terms and Conditions) Act 2023, which made provision for a version of the right to request a contract with predictable hours, with the qualifying period to be set out in regulations. This reflected a manifesto commitment and stemmed, in part at least, from the Taylor Review's recommendations about one-sided flexibility.[86] The legislation

[80] ERA s 1(4)(c); (n 75) Art 4(2)(l) and (m).
[81] ERA s 1(4)(ga).
[82] ERA s 108.
[83] ERA 2025, s 25.
[84] See https://www.gov.uk/government/publications/implementing-the-plan-to-make-work-pay-and-employment-rights-act/plan-to-make-work-pay-and-employment-rights-act-timeline-update.
[85] ibid Arts 10–12.
[86] M Taylor, *Good Work: The Taylor Review of Modern Working Practices* (July 2017).

drew on the right to request flexible working, a relatively well-established feature of domestic law, which requires the employer to consider the request within a specific timeframe and provides a list of reasons for turning a request down.[87]

The 2023 Act is repealed by the ERA 2025, which makes much more elaborate provision for what it refers to as zero-hours contracts.[88] These are:

- A right to be offered a contract with guaranteed hours based on the average hours worked over a reference period, expected to be 12 weeks.
- A right to reasonable notice of shifts, including cancellations and changes (reasonable notice to be specified in regulations).
- A right to a payment when a shift is cancelled, moved or curtailed at short notice (notice to be specified in regulations).

This aligns much more closely with the Directive, but with the more worker-protective option of providing a right to a guaranteed-hours contract rather than a right to make a request. There are concerns about the complexity of the new provisions—and the effect this might have on enforcement and compliance—but they contain some innovative measures to ensure that their scope is broad and to guard against evasion. In this area at least, the UK is now clearly keeping pace with and even exceeding the level of protection afforded by EU law. However, in a pattern that will become quite familiar in this discussion, there is no particular sense that EU law is the inspiration or motivation for the changes. Rather, the government is concerned to tackle zero-hours contracts on the basis that they are exploitative and unfair to workers.[89]

(ii) Minimum Wages

The Directive on Adequate Minimum Wages in the EU was agreed in 2022, with an implementation deadline of November 2024.[90] The short title is somewhat misleading as to the content, because the Directive does not oblige member states to introduce a statutory minimum wage, and because a significant part of the Directive is concerned with collective bargaining. The Treaty basis for the Directive is controversial. The EU has no competence over pay by virtue of Article 153(5) TFEU, but the Directive is based on Article 153(1)(b) empowering the EU to enact measures on 'working conditions'. The Commission's argument was that the Directive did not fall foul of the exclusion in Article 153(5) because the Directive does not seek to set a minimum level of pay, such as an EU-wide minimum wage. The CJEU has largely accepted this argument.[91] There are a few echoes of the Directive in recent developments in UK employment law, but it does not appear to be a significant influence.

[87] ERA ss 80F-I.
[88] Sections 1–8, and see DBT, *Zero Hours Contracts Factsheet* (n 83).
[89] DBT, ibid.
[90] See (n 76) Art 17. For analysis, see L Ratti and others (eds), *The EU Directive on Adequate Minimum Wages: Context, Commentary and Trajectories* (Hart 2024).
[91] See (n 20).

Chapter II of the Directive obliges member states which already have a minimum wage to take various steps to ensure that it is set at an adequate level, that it is not subject to excessive deductions, that the social partners are involved in setting and updating the rate, and that effective enforcement mechanisms are in place. The UK has had a statutory National Minimum Wage since 1998. The rate is reviewed annually by the Secretary of State,[92] taking into account the advice of the Low Pay Commission, which conducts a consultation exercise in which the social partners may (and do) participate.[93] The government provides a 'remit' to the LPC which sets out the factors to be taken into account when considering how the rate should be set. The Labour government amended this to include the cost of living, one of the factors member states may specify under the Directive.[94] Although the NMW is by no means perfect, it has a reasonably strict regime around deductions and has been enforced by HMRC, which has powers not only to recover arrears for workers but also to impose penalties on employers.[95] Had the UK remained in the EU, this aspect of the Directive would not have required major substantive changes to domestic law.

The provisions of Article 4 on collective bargaining, by contrast, would have posed more of a challenge, despite the UK's historical emphasis on collective bargaining as a regulatory tool. Article 4(1) requires member states to take steps to promote collective bargaining, and draws on some ideas familiar from the relevant ILO Conventions, including access to information to support collective bargaining, protection against discrimination for workers and representatives wishing to engage in collective bargaining, and protection for the autonomy of trade unions and employers' associations.[96] Although English law already provides basic protection in these areas, there are some obvious weaknesses. For example, there is specific protection against being offered inducements to give up collective bargaining (addressing the ECtHR's decision in *Wilson v UK*[97]), but there is no protection against detriment in this situation.[98]

Article 4(2) requires any member state with collective bargaining coverage of less than 80 per cent—in the UK in 2023 it was 39.2 per cent—to 'provide for a framework of enabling conditions for collective bargaining, either by law after consulting the social partners or by agreement with them. Such a member state shall also establish an action plan to promote collective bargaining.' This provision could not have been implemented by means of the traditional UK strategy of 'copying out'.[99] Of

[92] National Minimum Wage Act 1998, s 2.

[93] https://www.gov.uk/government/organisations/low-pay-commission.

[94] DBT, *National Minimum Wage and National Living Wage: Low Pay Commission Remit* (July 2024).

[95] Davies (n 51). The enforcement role is transferring to the Fair Work Agency under the ERA 2025.

[96] ILO, Freedom of Association and Protection of the Right to Organise Convention, 1948 (No. 87); Right to Organise and Collective Bargaining Convention, 1949 (No. 98).

[97] *Wilson v UK* (2002) 35 EHRR 20.

[98] Trade Union and Labour Relations (Consolidation) Act 1992, s 145B, but see s. 145B(4). Surprisingly, this has not been rectified in the ERA 2025, though a HRA challenge might be an option: ACL Davies, 'Article 11 in the Mirror: The Importance of Section 2 Human Rights Act 1998 in Understanding the Courts' Approach to Article 11 of the European Convention on Human Rights' Industrial Law Journal, dwaf014, https://doi.org/10.1093/indlaw/dwaf014.

[99] For discussion in another context, see C Barnard, 'The Working Time Regulations 1998' (1999) 28 ILJ 61.

course, the UK government could relatively easily have initiated discussions with the TUC and employers' umbrella organizations, and perhaps even produced a document of some kind, but a genuine commitment to the promotion of collective bargaining coverage requires wide-ranging effort. To take just one example, while collective bargaining coverage is always more extensive than trade union membership, because non-members as well as members benefit from collective agreements, measures to increase trade union membership must be an important starting point for increasing collective bargaining coverage. With membership levels of around 12 per cent in the private sector, this would be a significant challenge.[100]

The ERA 2025 includes a number of measures relating to freedom of association, collective bargaining, and the right to strike. Some of these would have been relevant to an action plan to increase collective bargaining coverage. First, the Act introduces a new duty on employers to inform workers that they have a right to join a trade union as part of the written statement.[101] This is intended to raise awareness of trade union membership.[102] Second, the Act gives trade unions a right of access to workplaces.[103] This will take the form of a request to the employer with the possibility of resolution by the CAC if the parties cannot agree on the terms of access. This is intended to provide unions with a way of organizing workplaces in which they have no, or very few, members. Third, the Act makes some changes to the statutory trade union recognition procedure under Schedule A1, with a view to facilitating its use.[104] These include removing the 40 per cent support requirement in a recognition ballot and replacing it with a simple majority, ensuring that a non-independent union cannot be recognized to block an application from an independent union, and removing the requirement to demonstrate to the CAC that the union would be likely to win a recognition ballot.

Nevertheless, there is no reason to believe that these measures were inspired by the Minimum Wage Directive. The Labour government is supportive of the trade union movement and is seeking to address its concerns. For example, the various improvements to Schedule A1 come after years of unsuccessful attempts by trade unions to tackle its flaws through litigation under the Human Rights Act 1998.[105]

(iii) Platform Work

The Platform Work Directive was finally agreed by the EU in October 2024, with a transposition deadline of December 2026.[106] The Directive has three main components. First, Article 5 seeks to ensure that a greater proportion of platform workers

[100] DBT, *Trade Union Statistics* (2024).
[101] Section 58.
[102] DBT, *Trade Unions Factsheet*, 11 (n 83).
[103] Section 59 and ibid 9–10.
[104] Section 60 and ibid 12–14.
[105] Davies (n 98).
[106] See (n 77).

can access employment rights by requiring member states to put in place a presumption that they have employment status. This applies where there are 'facts indicating direction and control', a formulation watered down from earlier drafts in which there was a list of facts giving rise to the presumption. Much will therefore depend on how member states implement the provision. Second, the Directive applies some protections to 'persons performing platform work' in Article 2(1)(c). Individuals within this definition do not get access to traditional employment rights, but they are covered by many of the rights relating to data collection and algorithmic management set out elsewhere in the Directive. For example, a person performing platform work is entitled to a written statement of the reasons for the termination of their access to the platform and to a review of that decision under Article 11. This brings me neatly to the third significant element of the Directive: its attempt to regulate platforms' activities in the sphere of data collection and surveillance. For example, Article 7 prohibits the collection of data relating to trade union membership and the processing of data to predict the exercise of rights relating to freedom of association and collective bargaining. This measure is an important building-block in preventing platforms from excluding trade union activists or undermining organizing efforts.

Had the UK remained in the EU, it is clear that changes would have been required to implement the Platform Work Directive. The Supreme Court's decision in *Uber*—a case involving platform workers—applied a purposive approach to worker status, noting that although the workers had freedom to choose when to work, their working lives were substantially controlled by the platform so that they were in need of the protection of employment law.[107] However, a decision on the facts of a specific case cannot amount to a presumption that all platform workers have 'worker' status. The UK would also have needed to implement the provisions relating to 'persons performing platform work' and algorithmic management.[108]

Interestingly, the ERA 2025 does not contain any equivalent provisions, and the government's policy paper makes no mention of platform work, though it does promise a consultation on surveillance at some point in the future.[109] On one view, this approach is preferable: algorithmic management techniques are already widespread throughout the labour market and are not confined to platform work.[110] It is possible that we will gain further insights into the government's views on platform working when it consults on employment status later in the Parliament.[111]

[107] *Uber BV v Aslam* [2021] UKSC 5, [2021] ICR 657.
[108] The Directive goes beyond the requirements of the GDPR (in force in the UK) in various respects.
[109] See (n 5) 14.
[110] For discussion, see J Adams-Prassl, 'What If Your Boss Was an Algorithm? Economic Incentives, Legal Challenges, and the Rise of Artificial Intelligence at Work' [2019] 41 Comparative Labor Law and Policy Journal 123.
[111] See (n 5) 14.

(b) Domestic Developments

I turn now to developments in domestic law since the UK's exit, other than those already analysed in parallel with changes in EU law. These can usefully be divided into changes under the Conservative government between 2021 and 2024, and much more extensive developments under the Labour government elected in July 2024.

(i) Changes 2021–2024

The Conservative government did not attempt any major post-Brexit reform to employment law. Instead, it made some minor changes to the rules on the transfer of undertakings and the WTR in England, Wales, and Scotland, using powers in the Retained EU Law (Revocation and Reform) Act 2023.[112] The consultation document preceding the changes stated that the government sought to retain 'important workers' rights' while removing 'unnecessary bureaucracy'.[113] No reference was made to the TCA, so it is difficult to tell whether the government's enthusiasm for workers' rights reflected its own policy objectives in employment law or a concern to avoid testing the boundaries of the non-regression clause. I offer a brief overview of the WTR changes here to illustrate the government's approach.

The reforms are a mix of deregulation, clarification, and restatement. In terms of deregulation, the changes reverse the effect of two CJEU decisions, *Robinson-Steele* and *CCOO*. In *Robinson-Steele*, the CJEU held that the practice of rolled-up holiday pay (adding extra money to a worker's hourly rate in respect of holiday pay, rather than paying them when they took holiday) was not permitted under the WTD because it would have the effect of deterring workers from taking the holiday to which they were entitled.[114] This ruling was ignored by many employers in the UK, who found the practice to be a convenient way of providing holiday pay to workers with irregular hours. Under the new rules, rolled-up holiday pay is permitted for irregular hours and part-year workers (as defined in the Regulations) and must be at least 12.07 per cent of pay.[115] In *CCOO*, the CJEU had ruled that member states were obliged to require employers to keep a record of each individual worker's daily working hours in order to demonstrate compliance with their WTD obligations.[116] Regulation 9 WTR only requires records to be kept in relation to night work and the 48-hour week, not in relation to other provisions of the WTR. The amendment makes clear that it does

[112] Employment Rights (Amendment, Revocation and Transitional Provision) Regulations 2023 (SI 2023/1426).

[113] DBT, *Retained EU Employment Law: A Government Response to the Consultation on Reforms to Retained EU Employment Law and the Consultation on Calculating Holiday Entitlement for Part-Year and Irregular Hours Workers* (November 2023).

[114] Case C-131/04 *Robinson-Steele v RD Retail Services Ltd* EU:C:2006:177.

[115] 12.07% is the statutory holiday entitlement as a percentage of the working weeks in a year.

[116] Case C-55/18 *Federacion de Servicios de Comisiones Obreras (CCOO) v Deutsche Bank SAE* EU:C:2019:402.

not require a record to be kept of an individual's hours provided that the employer can 'demonstrate compliance'.

In terms of clarification, the principal change brought about by the amending Regulations is to the rules on calculating the paid annual leave entitlements of irregular hours and part-year workers.[117] This issue was addressed by the Supreme Court in the *Harpur* case, but there was widespread dissatisfaction with the Court's approach.[118] This has been replaced with a calculation of holiday entitlement at 12.07 per cent of the hours worked by the worker in the previous pay reference period.

Finally, in terms of codification, the Regulations restate the CJEU's extensive case law on 'normal remuneration' for the purposes of calculating holiday pay,[119] and on the possibility of carrying over leave from one year to another in the event that the worker is unable to take holiday for various reasons.[120] While this changes the status of the law by detaching it from its CJEU source under section 11 of the Act, it provides much-needed clarity in two complex areas of law where a detailed knowledge of CJEU rulings was previously required in order to apply the WTR correctly.

(ii) Changes Post-2024: The 'Making Work Pay' Agenda

Had the outcome of the 2024 general election been different, we might have seen an ongoing project of 'tinkering' with assimilated law along the lines set out above, perhaps with some bolder attempts to push the boundaries of the non-regression clause. However, the Labour government has its own agenda for employment law set out in the policy document *Next Steps to Make Work Pay* and the ERA 2025.[121] Most of the Act's provisions are applicable to England, Wales, and Scotland, though a few (mainly relating to enforcement) also apply to Northern Ireland.[122] The Northern Ireland Executive is proposing its own Employment Bill, which I will deal with in the next section.

It is difficult to do justice to every detail of the government's agenda for employment law in Great Britain in this short chapter, and the task is further complicated by the fact that some aspects remain to be worked out, both in terms of how the Act will be implemented and what further measures will be adopted once additional consultations have taken place. Nevertheless, the overwhelming focus is on domestic concerns, with EU law playing a limited role as a possible source of inspiration for future developments. Bogg and Ford note that the government's policy document and the Act itself do not set out a grand vision for employment law,[123] in contrast to the

[117] See (n 112) reg 3.
[118] *Harpur Trust v Brazel* [2022] UKSC 21, [2022] ICR 1380.
[119] See (n 112) reg 3.
[120] ibid.
[121] See (n 5).
[122] Section 158.
[123] A Bogg and M Ford, 'From "Fairness at Work" to "Making Work Pay": A Preliminary Assessment of the Employment Rights Bill', UK Labour Law Blog, 14 October 2024.

Fairness at Work White Paper under the Blair government.[124] Instead, they reflect the politics of more challenging times:

> The primary focus is on the government's duty to tackle exploitation, abuse, unscrupulous employers and poor treatment of workers. The priority is to tackle bad work and to provide effective redress for wrongs.[125]

This does not mean that the reforms are not ambitious—in many respects, they are—but many of the initiatives are concerned with improving the effectiveness of the existing law rather than introducing wholly new ideas. The changes can be grouped into three main areas: individual employment law, collective labour law, and enforcement.

The Act contains a number of significant reforms to the employment rights of individuals. The 'crackdown' on exploitative zero-hours contracts and the removal of the two-year qualifying period for unfair dismissal were discussed above. Another important proposal is the ban on 'fire and rehire' practices. This expression describes a situation in which the employer seeks to change the employees' terms and conditions of employment and threatens them with dismissal if they refuse. In the Act, dismissing an employee for refusing to agree to a change in terms and conditions of employment, or dismissing the employee in order to rehire or replace them on different terms, will become an automatically unfair reason for dismissal, unless the employer can demonstrate that the changes were unavoidable because there was a threat to its viability.[126]

The Act also contains a number of reforms relating to collective labour law. Some of these were discussed above where they related to collective bargaining. The Act has repealed the rules imposing a higher ballot threshold on 'important public services',[127] along with the regime of 'minimum service levels' in those services.[128] Outside the public service context, the requirement of a 40 per cent turnout in a ballot will be repealed, so that a union will once again be able to call a strike based on a simple majority of those voting.[129] The notice to be given ahead of industrial action will be reduced from fourteen days to ten[130] and there will continue to be an 'expiry date' on ballots, but extended from six to twelve months.[131] All these changes are clearly designed to address the grievances of the trade union movement arising from the Trade Union Act 2016 and the Strikes (Minimum Service Levels) Act 2023, both of which were hugely unpopular.

Another set of changes relates to provisions derived from EU law, but the motivation for the changes is clearly domestic. The Collective Redundancies Directive

124 Department of Trade and Industry, *Fairness at Work* (May 1998).
125 Bogg and Ford (n 123).
126 Section 28.
127 Section 69.
128 Section 78.
129 Section 68.
130 Section 74.
131 Section 72.

requires member states to make provision for employers contemplating making a number of workers redundant to consult with representatives on ways of avoiding the redundancies, reducing the number of redundancies, or mitigating their consequences.[132] The Commission had to bring enforcement proceedings against the UK government in respect of the CRD in the early years,[133] but after a series of reforms, the Commission's 1999 implementation report gave the UK a clean bill of health in respect of this Directive.[134] The Act extends the requirement to consult to situations in which the employer is making a number (yet to be determined) of redundancies across the business as a whole, not just in a single establishment, and will double the maximum award that a tribunal can make to each employee in the event of a failure to consult, or to consult properly, from 90 days' pay to 180 days' pay.[135] The political motivation for these worker-protective changes is, of course, the notorious episode in which P&O Ferries dismissed all its employees and replaced them with agency workers, with no consultation.[136]

A third group of reforms in the Act relates to the enforcement of employment rights. As I noted in my discussion of the TCA, a significant commitment under the non-regression clause is to have an effective regime of labour inspection and individual enforcement of employment rights. The Act takes a number of positive steps in this regard, but there is no evidence to suggest that it is motivated by TCA commitments. It seems much more likely that it reflects an acceptance, for purely domestic reasons, that the current regime is flawed. One important development here is the creation of the FWA to bring together the existing public bodies with the power to enforce employment law (the Gangmasters and Labour Abuse Authority, the Employment Agency Standards Inspectorate, and the staff within His Majesty's Revenue and Customs responsible for the enforcement of the National Minimum Wage).[137] The new body will have some additional powers to enforce holiday pay and sick pay entitlements, and the government plans to expand its remit over time.[138] This could result in the body becoming more like the kind of labour inspectorate found in many other jurisdictions. In the meantime, individual litigation will remain the main method of enforcement for the vast majority of employment rights, though there are two significant reforms here too. First, the FWA will have the power to bring proceedings on behalf of individuals and or to support them with legal advice and assistance.[139] The impact of this will depend on the FWA's resources, but it could facilitate more test cases on important topics. Second, the Act extends the limitation period for

132 Directive 98/59/EC.
133 Case C-383/92 *Commission v UK* [1994] ECR I-2479.
134 Commission, *Implementation of the Directive Concerning the Approximation of the Laws of the Member States Relating to Collective Redundancies* (1999).
135 Sections 29–30.
136 See (n 5) 10.
137 ERA 2025 Part 5.
138 DBT, *Fair Work Agency Factsheet* (n 83).
139 Sections 116–117.

bringing a tribunal claim from three to six months.[140] This will give individual litigants more time to seek help.

Finally, there are a number of items on the government's future agenda which were much discussed by the Labour Party in opposition, but which do not feature in the Act. In some respects, it is easier here to see parallels with developments in the EU, where similar ideas are also under contemplation. There has been a consultation on tackling unpaid internships,[141] and the government has also indicated that it might pursue a code of practice on the right to disconnect.[142] At EU level, the Commission has recently proposed a Directive which would address terms and conditions for interns and tackle what the Commission refers to as 'bogus' internships, but which are better thought of as jobs disguised as internships.[143] Many member states have already enacted a right to disconnect—which often requires employers to negotiate with trade unions on the matter rather than to implement a specific set of entitlements—and the Commission, in response to an initiative from the Parliament, has commenced second-stage consultation with the social partners on 'fair telework' and the right to disconnect.[144]

It is at least possible that, having addressed a shopping list of problems in the Act, the government has taken some inspiration from developments elsewhere in the EU when thinking about its future plans for employment law. However, there is no obvious evidence to support this, and it is equally possible that the topics identified here are simply well-known issues that are the subject of discussion in many similar economies around the world. The position may become clearer if and when the UK government develops detailed proposals.

(iii) Changes in Northern Ireland

Space precludes a detailed assessment of the proposed Employment Bill in Northern Ireland. At the time of writing, the Executive has published its policy proposals but no draft Bill, so some details are yet to be worked out.[145] The proposals are organized around four themes: terms of employment, pay and benefits, voice and representation, and work/life balance. Many of the specific reforms to be enacted reflect what is going on in Great Britain: sometimes to implement changes which have already been made in Great Britain but not in Northern Ireland, and sometimes to keep pace with the ERA 2025. But there are some respects in which the Employment Bill will go

[140] Section 152.
[141] DBT, *Making Work Pay: Call for Evidence on Unpaid Internships* (July 2025), *Government Response to Making Work Pay: Call for Evidence on Unpaid Internships* (February 2026).
[142] See (n 5) 14.
[143] Commission, *Proposal for a Directive on Improving and Enforcing Working Conditions of Trainees and Combating Regular Employment Relationships Disguised as Traineeships ('Traineeships Directive')* (COM(2024) 132 final/2, March 2024).
[144] Commission, *Second-Phase Consultation of Social Partners under Article 154 TFEU on Possible EU Action in the Area of Telework and Workers' Right to Disconnect* (C(2025) 7020 final, July 2025).
[145] See (n 13).

further than the proposals in Great Britain, and it is clear from the policy paper that the Executive also takes inspiration from developments in the EU and in Ireland.

In terms of 'catching up', the Bill will include proposals to extend the written statement legislation to workers as well as employees,[146] and to increase the reference period for holiday pay calculations from twelve to fifty-two weeks.[147] And in terms of mirroring the ERA 2025, the Bill will introduce provisions to address zero-hours contracts—the right to move to a contract with regular hours, the right to reasonable notice of shifts, and the right to payment for cancellations at short notice—and provisions to make it easier for trade unions to access workplaces and to seek recognition.[148] There is a specific commitment to work with relevant agencies to consider how to increase collective bargaining coverage to 80 per cent, in line with the EU Directive, and to put in place a statutory code of practice on the right to disconnect, in line with the position in Ireland.[149] Admittedly, these bolder commitments do not involve specific legislative proposals, but they are much more explicit indicators of openness to ideas from the EU and other member states than we have seen from the Westminster government.

6 Conclusion

No attempt will be made to summarize the preceding discussion, but two points may be made in conclusion. First, although it seems likely that some people assumed that an advantage of the UK's exit from the EU would be greater flexibility to deregulate in the sphere of employment law, the exit arrangements do limit this option to some extent. Northern Ireland is under an obligation to keep pace with EU equality law, broadly defined, and for England, Wales, and Scotland, and Northern Ireland outside the equality context, there are the constraints of the non-regression clause and the requirement to uphold certain international labour rights and standards in the TCA. Although there are many interpretive uncertainties surrounding these provisions, it is noticeable that the Conservative government did not seek to test their boundaries. Second, the election of a Labour government at Westminster in 2024 means that the current domestic political focus is on a worker-protective agenda as set out in the ERA 2025, with Northern Ireland likely to adopt many similar measures. The EU has also continued to pursue a worker-protective agenda in line with the European Pillar on Social Rights. Interestingly, however, these agendas overlap rather than align. For example, the UK is likely to go beyond the Directive on Transparent and Predictable Working Conditions in relation to zero-hours contracts, and to improve its enforcement strategies in ways which fulfil commitments in the TCA. But

[146] ibid 11.
[147] ibid 16.
[148] ibid 9; 19–20.
[149] ibid 20; 17.

there is no evidence to suggest that relations with the EU (or a concern to avoid rebalancing measures) were the motivation for the changes. Some EU measures, such as the Directive on Platform Work, have been ignored completely, and other purely domestic issues have been vigorously pursued, notably in relation to the right to strike. The Northern Ireland Executive is pursuing similar policies but with some more explicit references to the EU. It remains to be seen whether the policy overlap will grow bigger or smaller in the future.

22
Healthcare

Vilija Vėlyvytė[*]

1 Introduction

This chapter examines how Brexit has reshaped the UK's regulatory framework for the provision of healthcare. It focuses on healthcare—rather than health law in the wider sense[1]—because it is here that the regulatory consequences of EU membership, and of withdrawal, have been most directly experienced by patients. The analysis builds on a rich body of scholarship that has charted the post-Brexit landscape for UK health governance and the NHS.[2] It carries the story forward by bringing the rapidly evolving regulatory picture into sharper contemporary focus and reading it through

* Thank you to Tamara Hervey and Mark Dayan for very thoughtful feedback on earlier drafts. All errors remain my own.

[1] Health law is generally understood to encompass rules governing both healthcare and public health. On the concept of EU health law, see TK Hervey and JV McHale, *European Union Health Law: Themes and Implications* (CUP 2015) Ch 3; TK Hervey, 'EU Health Law' in S Peers and C Barnard (eds), *European Union Law* (4th edn, OUP 2023).

[2] For a book-length account, see TK Hervey and others, *Not What the Bus Promised: Health Governance after Brexit* (Hart 2023) (Hervey, *Not What the Bus Promised*). See also N Fahy and others, 'How will Brexit Affect Health and Health Services in the UK? Evaluating Three Possible Scenarios against the WHO Health System Building Blocks' (2017) 390 The Lancet 2110 (Fahy and others, 'Three Possible Scenarios'); N Fahy and others, 'How Will Brexit affect Health and Health Services in the UK? An Updated Analysis' (2019) 393 The Lancet 949; N Fahy and others, 'Assessing the Potential Impact on Health of the UK's Future Relationship Agreement with the EU: Analysis of the Negotiating Positions' (2020) 16 Health Economics, Policy and Law 290; N Fahy and others, 'Impact on the NHS and Health of the UK's Trade and Cooperation Relationship with the EU, and Beyond' (2022) 17 Health Economics, Policy and Law 471. For research reports, see M Dayan and others, 'Understanding the Impact of Brexit on Health in the UK' (Nuffield Trust, 22 December 2020) <www.nuffieldtrust.org.uk/research/understanding-the-impact-of-brexit-on-health-in-the-uk> accessed 30 September 2025 (Nuffield Trust, Report 2020); M Dayan and others, 'Going It Alone: Health and Brexit in the UK' (Nuffield Trust, 20 December 2021) <www.nuffieldtrust.org.uk/research/going-it-alone-health-and-brexit-in-the-uk> accessed 30 September 2025 (Nuffield Trust, Report 2021); M McCarey and others, 'Health and Brexit Six Years On' (Nuffield Trust, 19 December 2022) <www.nuffieldtrust.org.uk/research/health-and-brexit-six-years-on> accessed 30 August 2025 (Nuffield Trust, Report 2022); M Dayan and others, 'The Future for Health after Brexit' (Nuffield Trust, 18 April 2024) <www.nuffieldtrust.org.uk/research/the-future-for-health-after-brexit> accessed 2 September 2025 (Nuffield Trust, Report 2024); Mark Dayan and others, 'Health in the UK after Brexit: Moving Apart or Stuck Together?' (Nuffield Trust, 21 March 2025) <www.nuffieldtrust.org.uk/research/health-in-the-uk-after-brexit-moving-apart-or-stuck-together> accessed 5 July 2025.

Vilija Vėlyvytė, *Healthcare* In: *The UK Regulatory Framework Post-Brexit: 'Law Unbound'*. Edited by: Paul Craig and Vilija Vėlyvytė, Oxford University Press. © Oxford University Press 2026. DOI: 10.1093/9780198969815.003.0025

the conceptual lens of 'Law Unbound' employed in this volume, which captures the core promise of Brexit to reclaim regulatory sovereignty. The chapter tests that promise across three domains—access to healthcare, workforce, and medicines—assessing how far law has been unbound in each while considering the structural and market constraints within which UK healthcare now operates post-Brexit.

It bears recalling that the EU has no general competence to regulate healthcare. The Treaties make clear that Union action must respect member states' responsibility for 'the organisation and delivery of health services and medical care'.[3] The EU may act in the field of 'public health' but its role is complementary in nature: it may support, coordinate, or supplement national policies but, save for limited exceptions, has no power to harmonize member state laws.[4] Despite these limitations, the Union's influence on national health systems has been substantial, channelled indirectly through *inter alia* internal market law—the free movement provisions, legislation giving effect to them, and the principle of mutual recognition.[5] These rules, while not all health-specific in origin, enabled UK patients' access to healthcare within the EU, facilitated recruitment of health professionals into NHS roles, and embedded the UK in a common regulatory regime for medicines.

The chapter argues that UK post-Brexit frameworks for access, workforce, and medicines amount to limited unbinding from the EU. Regulatory independence is asserted but only partly achieved: the UK remains tied to the EU through bilateral commitments—including, in places, the continuing application of EU law—while post-Brexit economic and market realities further narrow the scope for autonomous rule-making. More fundamentally, the chapter shows that post-Brexit 'control' has largely meant steering healthcare through external conditions the UK cannot fully set—legal in Northern Ireland, market-driven in Great Britain—so the system grows more complex while the benefits of going different ways remain uncertain.

The analysis proceeds as follows. Section 2, which examines access to healthcare, shows that the post-Brexit settlement has largely preserved reciprocal arrangements governing cross-border access, albeit on terms that are, in some respects, narrower and less secure than before. Section 3 addresses NHS workforce, where policy remains unsettled, having oscillated between reliance on overseas recruitment and ambitions to expand the domestic workforce. Section 4 turns to medicines, where regulatory reform has been pursued against structural constraints that limit the UK's capacity to function as a competitive launch market. Each section includes a discrete discussion of Northern Ireland, reflecting its unique position in the post-Brexit regulatory and legal landscape.

[3] See TFEU, Art 168(7). For a historical overview of EU competence in health, see M Guy and W Sauter, 'The History and Scope of EU Health Law and Policy' in TK Hervey, CA Young, and LE Bishop (eds), *Research Handbook on EU Health Law and Policy* (Edward Elgar 2017).

[4] TFEU, Art 6(a); Art 168(5) and (6). Note exceptions in Art 168(4).

[5] For a comprehensive account problematizing this, see V Vėlyvytė, *Judicial Authority in EU Internal Market Law: Implications for the Balance of Competences and Powers* (Hart 2022) Ch 2, ss I–II; ch 3, ss I–II.

2 Access

Among the most tangible benefits of EU membership was the ability of UK nationals and residents to access healthcare across the Union. Brexit did not end that access. The negotiated settlement preserved core entitlements to medical treatment in the EU—an outcome of real significance—albeit on terms that are, in some respects, narrower and less secure than before. The implications are most visible in Northern Ireland.

(a) Cross-border Healthcare Pre-Brexit

While access to healthcare remains primarily a matter of national competence, the EU regulates its cross-border dimensions, that is, entitlements to healthcare when moving within the Union. During UK membership of the EU, these entitlements also extended to UK nationals (and residents).

One set of rights arose under the EU's rules on the coordination of social security, consolidated in Regulation 883/2004 (Social Security Regulation).[6] These rules ensured continuity of healthcare cover for individuals whose employment or residence status created a cross-border element. This category included posted workers temporarily employed in another member state, frontier workers who lived in one state but were employed in another (a common situation on the island of Ireland), and pensioners who retired to another member state.[7] In such cases, individuals, and for the most part their family members,[8] were entitled to healthcare in the host state on the same terms as those insured there.[9] The costs were settled between states: for pensioners, by the state paying the pension; for frontier workers, by the state of employment. This framework was intended to ensure that the exercise of free movement rights did not entail the loss of healthcare cover.

In addition, EU law also provided rights to necessary healthcare during a temporary stay abroad and to planned treatment in another member state. The former, 'needs-arising' cover, entitled patients to emergency care or treatment that became medically necessary while abroad, including management of pre-existing or chronic conditions such as dialysis or chemotherapy.[10] Entitlement was demonstrated through the European Health Insurance Card (EHIC), which guaranteed access to publicly funded healthcare in the host state on equal terms with locals.

[6] Council Regulation (EC) 883/2004 on the coordination of social security systems [2004] OJ L166/1 (Reg 883/2004). The Regulation also covers EEA and Swiss nationals; the chapter refers to EU for simplicity.

[7] See, accordingly, Arts 12(1), 17, 24.

[8] ibid Arts 17–18 and Annex III, which limit family members' healthcare cover in the frontier worker's state of work to needs-arising healthcare.

[9] ibid Art 19. 'Insured' in this context refers to persons falling within the scope of a member state's social security system, whether on the basis of insurance contributions or residence (Art 1(c)).

[10] ibid Art 19(1). Note also para (2), which provides that a prior arrangement with the specialized unit may be required to confirm capacity to deliver the treatment.

Planned, or elective, healthcare, by contrast, concerned situations where patients travelled abroad specifically to obtain treatment. Two legal routes operated in parallel. The first, under the Social Security Regulation, entitled patients to public, state-funded care in another member state, subject to prior authorization by national health authorities—in the UK, the NHS and its devolved counterparts.[11] Authorization had to be granted where the patient's condition met the 'medical necessity' test (discussed below). Treatment was then provided under the same conditions of cost and access as for locals, even if more expensive than in the UK. Costs were settled directly between the two health systems, with patients liable only for any co-payments under the host state's rules.

The second route derived from the Directive on Patients' Rights,[12] which allowed patients to obtain certain treatments abroad and subsequently reclaim the cost from their home health system. Prior authorization was not the default: it could be required for care involving an overnight hospital stay and for interventions that were highly specialized or otherwise cost-intensive.[13] Treatments outside those categories—essentially outpatient (non-hospital) services—could be sought without prior authorization, provided that they formed part of the home state's benefits package. Moreover, care could, in principle, be sourced from either public or private providers, but reimbursement was capped at the cost of an equivalent state-funded treatment at home,[14] making it unlikely that patients using private providers would recover the full amount.

(b) Post-Brexit Restrictions

(i) Legal Framework

Brexit ended the free movement of people between the UK and the EU. Even so, the Withdrawal Agreement (WA)[15] and the Trade and Cooperation Agreement (TCA)[16] preserved important elements of cross-border access to healthcare. The WA secures continued application of the EU Social Security Regulation for those who had exercised free-movement rights before 31 December 2020—for example, UK pensioners resident in an EU member state, or frontier workers on the island of Ireland, where such work is commonplace.[17] Crucially, the rights conferred are directly effective and

[11] ibid Art 20.

[12] Council Directive 2011/24/EU on the application of patients' rights in cross-border healthcare [2011] OJ L88/45 (Dir 2011/24).

[13] ibid Art 8.

[14] ibid Art 7(4).

[15] Agreement on the Withdrawal of the United Kingdom of Great Britain and Northern Ireland from the European Union (2019) Cm 1227 (WA).

[16] Trade and Cooperation Agreement between the United Kingdom of Great Britain and Northern Ireland and the European Union (2020) Cm 1227 (TCA).

[17] WA, Part Two, Title III.

prevail over conflicting national legislation.[18] Individuals falling outside the personal scope of the WA—those who moved on or after 1 January 2021—are instead covered by the Protocol on Social Security Coordination (SSC) annexed to the TCA.[19] The Protocol largely reproduces the Regulation's protections and is directly enforceable in UK courts, but unlike the WA, it lacks supremacy over domestic law.[20] The outcome is a dual framework in which WA-based protections are the more secure because they may not be displaced by contradictory subsequent legislation, whereas provisions in the TCA may be so.[21]

The Protocol also maintains access to needs-arising healthcare,[22] a provision of particular importance for students on study visits abroad and for tourists, especially older travellers and those with chronic conditions.[23] After Brexit, UK residents demonstrate entitlement through the Global Health Insurance Card (GHIC), which replaced the EHIC.

Entitlements to planned treatment, by contrast, do not mirror the pre-Brexit position. The route under the Patients' Rights Directive has been discontinued, removing the only basis on which patients could independently seek (some limited forms of) treatment abroad, including from private providers, and subsequently reclaim costs from the NHS. What remains post-Brexit is the Regulation route, under which the NHS pays directly[24] for treatment obtained in another state.[25] This route is confined to public healthcare and is subject to a requirement of prior authorization at all times.

(ii) 'Medical Necessity', and the Right to Timely Healthcare

A related, if less visible, change concerns the criteria for granting prior authorization. Under EU law, refusals to do so were tightly circumscribed by the 'medical necessity' test. Where the treatment formed part of the home system's benefits, authorization could not lawfully be withheld if it was medically necessary—that is, equivalent care could not be provided in the patient's home member state within a medically justifiable timeframe (or without undue delay).[26] In applying that test, national

[18] By virtue of WA, Art 4 (1) and (2). Given effect in UK law by European Union (Withdrawal) Act 2018, s 7A (as inserted by European Union (Withdrawal Agreement) Act 2020). On this point, see Paul Craig, Ch 4.

[19] Protocol on Social Security Coordination (Annex to the Trade and Cooperation Agreement between the United Kingdom of Great Britain and Northern Ireland and the European Union) (2020) Cm 1227 (SSC), Arts 11, 15–16, 21–22.

[20] European Union (Future Relationship) Act 2020 (EUFRA 2020) s 26.

[21] So far, UK courts have not found any TCA obligations to be displaced by legislation enacted after the TCA.

[22] SSC, Arts 17, 25. Implemented in UK law by Healthcare (International Arrangements) Act 2019; Healthcare (European Economic Area and Switzerland Arrangements) (EU Exit) Regulations 2019, SI 2019/1293.

[23] Note SSC, Art 17(2), Appendix SSCI-2 to Annex SSC-7, replicating the Regulation's Art 19(2) requirement of prior arrangement with the unit providing care (see n 10).

[24] In strict terms, the payer is the Department of Health and Social Care (DHSC).

[25] SSC, Art 18. Given effect in UK law by EUFRA 2020 (n 20), s 26; Healthcare (EU Exit) Regs (n 22), reg 6.

[26] Reg 883/2004 (n 6) Art 20(2).

authorities were required to conduct an objective, patient-specific assessment, taking into account the individual's medical history, their current state of health, and the likely course of the condition.[27]

The landmark *Watts* judgment of 2006 illustrates the significance of this rule. Mrs Watts was refused NHS authorization for hip replacement surgery in France on the basis that she was already on the waiting list in the UK. She faced a wait of approximately one year, later reduced to three to four months after her condition deteriorated. The CJEU ruled that such a refusal was incompatible with EU law: once medical necessity was established, the NHS could not rely on the existence of a waiting list to deny authorization.[28] The Court thus recognized that patients were entitled to receive care within a timeframe consistent with their medical needs—in effect, a right to timely healthcare.[29]

The right to timely healthcare appears not to have survived Brexit. Article 18(2) SSC, which governs planned treatment, retains the earlier EU standard whereby authorization must be granted where treatment cannot be provided 'within a time limit which is medically justifiable'.[30] The legal context, however, has changed. Authorization decisions are no longer reviewable under EU law or subject to CJEU oversight and, arguably, now lie within NHS discretion. Against that backdrop, what qualifies as a 'medically justifiable' wait is likely to take into account domestic waiting-time targets, rather than rest solely on the individualized clinical assessments required under EU law. Evidence from Northern Ireland, where waits are the longest in the UK, suggests that the shift in approach has already occurred, as discussed below.

(c) Northern Ireland

Cross-border cooperation between Northern Ireland and Ireland plays an important role in healthcare provision on the island of Ireland. The two health systems operate a set of shared services and have joint staffing arrangements, while patients—particularly those in border regions—regularly travel to the other side for certain types of treatment. Brexit threatened to unsettle these arrangements, but that risk has largely been averted through the WA, the TCA, and a series of bilateral measures.[31] There have, however, been changes—some UK-wide, some specific to Northern

[27] ibid.

[28] Case C-372/04 *Yvonne Watts v Bedford Primary Care Trust and Secretary of State for Health* [2006] ECR I-4325, [113], [119]–[120], [123].

[29] See Vilija Vėlyvytė, 'Brits Still Have the Right to Timely Healthcare', *UK in a Changing Europe* (18 January 2024) <www.ukandeu.ac.uk/brits-still-have-the-right-to-timely-healthcare> accessed 29 April 2025.

[30] SSC, Art 18(2); Annex SSC-7, Art 23(2). See also NHS England, 'UK Planned Treatment Scheme: Guidance for commissioners from 1 January 2021' (4 June 2022), 14–15 <www.england.nhs.uk/wp-content/uploads/2016/03/S2-and-directive-commissioner-guidance-June-2022.pdf> accessed 8 July 2025.

[31] For comprehensive analysis, see Hervey, *Not What the Bus Promised* (n 2) Ch 6.

Ireland—that have narrowed the overall scope of entitlements post-Brexit. Those are the discontinuation of the Directive route, the loss of a justiciable right to timely (cross-border) healthcare, and uncertainty over long-term funding for service-level arrangements on the island of Ireland.

(i) The Common Travel Area

For historical reasons, British and Irish nationals occupy a distinctive status on the island, reflecting a long-standing commitment by both states to treat each other's citizens, for most purposes, as their own. That commitment is anchored in the Common Travel Area (CTA)—a web of bilateral arrangements, domestic provisions, and administrative practice between the UK and Ireland that predate EU membership.[32] The CTA accords reciprocal rights of residence, work, social security, and access to public services, including healthcare.[33] Healthcare entitlements have been carried over post-Brexit by a combination of bilateral arrangements, reaffirming continuity of the CTA-derived rights, and the WA/TCA, which occupy the space previously filled by EU law.

The revised Convention on Social Security allows Irish nationals resident in the UK and UK nationals in Ireland to continue accessing healthcare in both countries within a coordinated social security framework.[34] It is complemented by a Memorandum of Understanding (MoU),[35] signed in late 2020, which in addition secures cross-border access to necessary and planned care on terms broadly comparable to those of the TCA. Unlike the TCA, however, the MoU is not legally binding. The two governments have therefore agreed that the TCA prevails in cases of overlap, except where the MoU offers greater protection. In several respects it does: it broadens the range of documents (beyond GHIC/EHIC) that can establish entitlement to necessary care, maintains cross-border ambulance cooperation, and preserves enhanced access to free healthcare for frontier workers.[36]

[32] CTA also covers the Crown Dependencies of the Isle of Man, Jersey, and Guernsey. For academic commentary, see B Ryan, 'The Common Travel Area between Britain and Ireland' (2001) 64 MLR 831.

[33] For an analysis of CTA post-Brexit, see S de Mars and CRG Murray, 'With or Without EU? The Common Travel Area After Brexit' (2020) 21 GLJ 815.

[34] See, eg, Convention on Social Security between the Government of the United Kingdom of Great Britain and Northern Ireland and the Government of Ireland (1 February 2019) CP 49, replacing Convention on Social Security between the Government of the United Kingdom of Great Britain and Northern Ireland and the Government of Ireland, with Exchange of Notes (14 December 2004) Gr Brit T.S. No 30 (2007) (Cm 7277), Art 16. For detailed analysis see Hervey, *Not What the Bus Promised* (n 2) Ch 6.

[35] Memorandum of Understanding between the Government of the United Kingdom of Great Britain and Northern Ireland and the Government of Ireland concerning Common Travel Area Healthcare Arrangements (18 December 2020).

[36] ibid respectively: 3.2.b.ii; Annex A; 5.2. See also Department of Health and Social Care (DHSC), *Exchange of letters on UK–Ireland reciprocal healthcare arrangements* (23 February 2022) <www.gov.uk/government/publications/exchange-of-letters-on-uk-ireland-reciprocal-healthcare-arrangements> accessed 5 July 2025.

(ii) The WA and TCA

Non-Irish EU nationals—more than 5 per cent of the island's population[37]—fall outside the CTA.[38] In practice, however, those lawfully resident on the island stand in a position broadly comparable to that of British and Irish nationals.[39] The WA and TCA afford rights to necessary and planned cross-border care, and certain groups are covered by rules on the coordination of social security. Given the prevalence of cross-border employment on the island, protections for frontier workers are of particular salience.[40] As discussed earlier, frontier workers—and, to a large extent, their family members—retain entitlement to healthcare on both sides of the border.[41]

The principal legal change affecting both EU-26 and British and Irish nationals has been the discontinuation of the Directive route and, at a deeper level, the loss of a judicially enforceable right to timely healthcare. The Directive's option to obtain care from private providers—long used to alleviate Northern Ireland's exceptionally long waiting lists[42]—was briefly retained after withdrawal, albeit subject to prior authorization requirement in all cases.[43] It has since been replaced by schemes that operate on even stricter terms: prior authorization is mandatory, budgets are capped, and eligibility is confined to patients who have already waited more than a year (itself reduced from two).[44] This marks a clear departure from the EU law position: access

[37] Derived from data provided by the Central Statistics Office, *Census 2022 Profile 5—Diversity, Migration, Ethnicity, Irish Travellers, Religion* (31 May 2023) <www.cso.ie/en/csolatestnews/pressreleases/2023pressreleases/pressstatementcensus2022resultsprofile5-diversitymigrationethnicityirishtravellersreligion>, and Northern Ireland Statistics and Research Agency, *Census 2021 Main Statistics for Northern Ireland (Phase 1): Country of Birth* (22 September 2022) <www.nisra.gov.uk/system/files/statistics/census-2021-main-statistics-for-northern-ireland-phase-1-statistical-bulletin-country-of-birth.pdf> accessed 30 April 2025.

[38] Unless as family members of British and Irish nationals under the 2019 Social Security Convention (n 34). See esp Arts 1(1), 2(b), 16, 20.

[39] Note that to secure residence status post-Brexit, non-Irish EU citizens in Northern Ireland were required to apply for the EU Settlement Scheme. To that effect, see WA, Art 18; implemented in UK law by the Citizens' Rights (Application Deadline and Temporary Protection) (EU Exit) Regulations 2020, SI 2020/1209.

[40] See, eg, S McGuinness, A Bergin, and A Devlin, *A Study of Cross-Border Working on the Island of Ireland* (ESRI Working Paper No. 781, June 2024) <www.esri.ie/system/files/publications/WP781.pdf> accessed 30 April 2025, which estimates that there were between 17,827 and 19,282 frontier workers on the island of Ireland in 2021.

[41] Note that protection for family members under the TCA SSC is more limited than under the WA: their access to necessary healthcare in the worker's state of work is conditioned upon residence in the same State as the worker: SSC, Arts 15–16, Annex SSC-2. For a comprehensive account of frontier workers' status on the island of Ireland post-Brexit, see S de Mars and C O'Brien, 'Inevitably Diminished: Rights of Frontier Workers in Northern Ireland after Brexit' (2022) 73 NILQ 119.

[42] Nuffield Trust, Report 2025, 40–41. See also Donna Deeney, 'Fast-tracked Patients for Healthcare Scheme in Northern Ireland Will Now Miss Out' *Belfast Telegraph* (Belfast, 12 February 2020) <www.belfasttelegraph.co.uk/news/health/fast-tracked-patients-for-healthcare-scheme-in-northern-ireland-will-now-miss-out/38948796.html> accessed 6 October 2025.

[43] Department of Health (Northern Ireland), *Cross-Border Healthcare Directive Reinstated* (16 June 2021) <www.health-ni.gov.uk/news/cross-border-healthcare-directive-reinstated> accessed 30 April 2025.

[44] See, eg, Department of Health (Northern Ireland), 'Health Minister Expands EU Treatment Scheme' (8 September 2025) <www.health-ni.gov.uk/news/health-minister-expands-eu-treatment-scheme> accessed 5 July 2025 ('Minister Expands EU Treatment Scheme'). For detailed guidance, Department of Health (Northern Ireland), 'Waiting List Reimbursement Scheme' <www.online.hscni.net/our-work/travelfortreatment/wl-reimbursement/> accessed 8 September 2025.

is now primarily determined by waiting-list thresholds, with medical necessity (the basis for the right to timely healthcare) engaging only once that threshold is met. It follows that the right to timely healthcare, as understood in EU law, no longer exists post-Brexit, at least not in Northern Ireland.

Recent UK case law on waiting times lends weight to this view. In *Wilson and Anor*,[45] the first case of its kind, the High Court in Belfast was asked to consider whether excessive waiting times could give rise to an enforceable right to treatment. The applicants, Eileen Wilson and May Kitchen, had waited almost four and three years respectively following GP referrals. Colton J held that resolving the waiting list crisis required 'high level political decisions in relation to resources and . . . structural reform of the health service' and was 'not a matter for the courts'.[46] He further observed that it would not be in the public interest to advance the applicants ahead of others on the lists.[47] The judgment was upheld by the Court of Appeal, which added that even if a duty to the applicants existed, the authorities had discharged it by acting within their discretion given resource constraints.[48]

Wilson and Anor did not concern the right to timely healthcare as understood in EU law; it delineated the position on timeliness within UK public law. The broader implication, however, is that—absent EU law and CJEU oversight post-Brexit—domestic courts are unlikely to uphold (*Watts*-type) challenges to schemes that condition eligibility for cross-border treatment on a one-year wait or similar threshold.

From a systemic perspective, that outcome is not unwelcome. As Newdick argued in the context of EU law, judicializing access through individual 'medical necessity' claims tends to privilege articulate and better-resourced patients, pushing the most vulnerable further back—an uneasy fit with the fairness and solidarity that underpin a publicly funded service.[49] Normatively, therefore, the post-Brexit change is defensible. Nonetheless, it is a loss for individual patients and—together with the disappearance of the Directive route—marks a narrowing of entitlements relative to the pre-Brexit position. This, in turn, raises questions about compatibility with Article 2 of the Northern Ireland Protocol, which safeguards against the diminution of rights post-Brexit.[50]

45 *Re Wilson and Kitchen's Application for Judicial Review* [2023] NIKB 2.
46 ibid [74].
47 ibid [87].
48 *Wilson and Kitchen v Department of Health for Northern Ireland* [2023] NICA 54, [48], [64].
49 C Newdick, 'Citizenship, Free Movement and Health Care: Cementing Individual Rights by Corroding Social Solidarity' (2006) 43 CMLRev 1645.
50 To that effect, see WA (n 15), Protocol on Ireland/Northern Ireland (as amended by the Windsor Framework), Art 2 (NI Protocol). For commentary on Art 2 in relation to access to healthcare, see TK Hervey, *Access to Healthcare and Article 2 of the Ireland/Northern Ireland Protocol* (Northern Ireland Human Rights Commission 2022) <www.nihrc.org/uploads/publications/Access_to_Healthcare_and_Article_2.pdf> accessed 25 July 2025.

(iii) Beyond the CTA, WA, and TCA

Northern Ireland and Ireland also maintain a range of cross-border and all-island healthcare arrangements under which anyone covered by the national health system in either jurisdiction can access care, regardless of nationality. These arrangements are implemented through service-level agreements (SLAs) and memoranda of understanding, and are underpinned by Strand Two of the Good Friday agreement,[51] which mandates North–South cooperation, including in health.[52] A prominent example is Co-operation and Working Together (CAWT), a North–South partnership established in 1992 to improve access to health and social care in border regions. Covering roughly a quarter of the island and serving a population of 1.6 million, CAWT facilitates joint delivery of services including ambulance, chronic disease management, mental health, and children's services.[53] Crucially, access is determined by clinical need and does not depend on rights under the CTA, WA, the TCA, or previously EU law. This reduces the practical impact of the formal distinctions between categories of residents on the island with respect to cross-border entitlements.

CAWT is not without weaknesses. Like other SLAs, it lacks a formal legal basis. Strand Two of the Good Friday Agreement provides an institutional framework, but it does not establish CAWT as a matter of international law. Entitlements under CAWT therefore carry less legal security (though perhaps have more practical effect) than those provided under the WA or TCA. A second limitation is financial. CAWT has no statutory budget or permanent funding stream. Pre-Brexit, its projects were largely financed through EU programmes such as INTERREG III;[54] post-Brexit, funding has been secured through the EU PEACE PLUS Programme until 2027.[55] What follows thereafter is unclear, as the EU and the UK have not agreed on any successor programme. The healthcare benefits delivered through CAWT therefore come with a degree of precarity.

[51] The Agreement between the Government of the United Kingdom of Great Britain and Northern Ireland and the Government of Ireland (Good Friday Agreement, 1998).

[52] See, eg, House of Lords European Union Committee, *Brexit: Reciprocal Healthcare* (HL Paper 107, 2017–19), para 100 <www.publications.parliament.uk/pa/ld201719/ldselect/ldeucom/107/10710.htm> accessed 30 April 2025. For an in-depth discussion, see Hervey, *Not What the Bus Promised* (n 2) Ch 6.

[53] D Heenan, 'Cross-Border Cooperation in Health in Ireland' (2021) 32 Irish Studies in International Affairs 117, 130.

[54] For details, see P Clarke and J Jamison, *From Concept to Realisation: An Evaluation of CAWT* (Centre for Cross Border Studies 2000) <www.cawt.com/download/doc_library/corporate/ConceptRealisation.pdf> accessed 2 May 2025, Part I, 2.2.1.

[55] CAWT, 'Border Communities to Benefit from €34.6 Million EU Funding Award from the PEACEPLUS Programme to the CAWT Partnership' <https://cawt.hscni.net/border-communities-to-benefit-from-e34-6-million-eu-funding-award-from-the-peaceplus-programme-to-the-cawt-pArtnership/> accessed 30 April 2025.

(d) Interim Conclusion: Limited Unbinding

The post-Brexit settlement for cross-border healthcare reflects limited unbinding from EU law. Core routes are retained, if in some respects on narrower and weaker terms. The GHIC scheme still guarantees needs-arising healthcare, and comprehensive cover continues for pensioners, frontier workers, and posted workers through ongoing social security coordination. Rights under the WA are, however, more firmly entrenched in domestic law than those of post-2020 movers, whose TCA-based entitlements lack supremacy and thus remain open to legislative revision.

Access to planned treatment is where the UK has unbound itself from elements of EU law. The Directive route has been discontinued, removing access to private healthcare and a range of outpatient treatments that previously did not require prior authorization. Furthermore, with the UK no longer bound by CJEU case law on 'timely' healthcare, authorization decisions may be expected to give greater weight to waiting-list priorities, rather than being based solely on an individualized assessment of clinical need. Domestic courts are unlikely to second-guess that policy choice, given their broader stance on the justiciability of any putative right to timely healthcare. In practice, these changes are felt most in Northern Ireland, where cross-border care is woven into routine service delivery.

3 Workforce

The UK's health and social care sectors have long relied on overseas labour. Recruiting from abroad has historically been—and remains—the primary means of addressing workforce shortages. Brexit did not change this, but it transformed the legal and policy framework through which overseas recruitment takes place. The end of free movement created new barriers for EU-trained professionals, while the Health and Care Worker Visa opened a streamlined route for all overseas recruits. Since then, UK policy has been pulled between the immediate need to fill vacancies and the longer-term ambition of building a sustainable domestic workforce. Although the government presents the latter as a priority, the absence of a concrete plan for implementation undermines the credibility of this strategy.

(a) Restriction of EU Recruitment

The UK's post-Brexit immigration policy made one point unmistakable: EU nationals, who once had a right to live and work in the UK,[56] would no longer enjoy

[56] Directive 2004/38/EC on the right of citizens of the Union and their family members to move and reside freely within the territory of the member states amending Regulation (EEC) No 1612/68 and

preferential treatment over other foreign nationals. Unless holding settled or pre-settled status, they are now subject to the same immigration regime as anyone else.[57] For EU health professionals and care workers, this means having to obtain a visa to work in the UK. A dedicated route exists: the Health and Care Worker (HCW) Visa, introduced in 2020, streamlines the immigration process for doctors, nurses, allied health professionals, and, until recently, social care workers.[58] Like any visa, it is conditional and time-limited. Applicants must satisfy occupation, salary, and English-language requirements and secure sponsorship from a licensed employer. Leave is typically granted for five years, after which the visa must be renewed or converted to settlement.[59] The scheme is also highly policy-sensitive, with rules subject to revision at short notice, as later illustrated in relation to social care. In short, it is no substitute for the freedom of movement previously guaranteed under EU law.

A parallel shift has occurred in the recognition of professional qualifications. While the UK was a member state, it participated in the EU system for mutual recognition under Directive 2005/36/EC,[60] which enabled doctors, general care nurses, dentists, midwives, and other health professionals trained in the EU[61] to practise in the UK, and vice versa, without requalification. The WA preserved the recognition for EU qualifications obtained, or applied for, by 31 December 2020, but the TCA neither continued that system nor created a replacement. Recognition has now been repatriated to domestic regulators under the Professional Qualifications Act 2022 and sector-specific legislation. Within this framework, EU-trained health professionals would, in principle, follow the same routes as other international applicants, with their professional competence assessed on an individual basis, making recognition more bureaucratic and less predictable than under the Directive. Yet in healthcare, the picture is complicated by the 'standstill' regime: the UK has unilaterally chosen to maintain near-automatic recognition for many EEA and Swiss healthcare qualifications, exempting their holders from additional competence assessments.[62] In

repealing Directives 64/221/EEC, 68/360/EEC, 72/194/EEC, 73/148/EEC, 75/34/EEC, 75/35/EEC, 90/364/EEC, 90/365/EEC and 93/96/EEC [2004] OJ L158/77.

[57] To that effect, see Immigration and Social Security Co-ordination (EU Withdrawal) Act 2020, s 20.

[58] Health and Care Visa Guidance (updated 8 Aug 2025) <www.gov.uk/government/publications/health-and-care-visa-guidance-for-applicants/health-and-care-visa-guidance-accessible> accessed 12 July 2025. For more detailed discussion, see this book's chapter by Steve Peers, Ch 18.

[59] Recent proposals would extend the qualifying period for settlement to ten years. To that effect, see CJ McKinney and M Gower, *Changes to UK Visa and Settlement Rules after the 2025 Immigration White Paper* (House of Commons Library, Research Briefing, 3 July 2025) <commonslibrary.parliament.uk/research-briefings/cbp-10267> accessed 14 August 2025 (Changes to UK Visa and Settlement).

[60] For a version currently in force, see Directive 2013/55/EU amending Directive 2005/36/EC on the recognition of professional qualifications and Regulation (EU) No 1024/2012 (IMI Regulation) [2013] OJ L354/132 (Dir 2013/55).

[61] To be precise, this framework covers EEA and Switzerland; the chapter uses 'EU' and 'EU nationals' for simplicity.

[62] See European Qualifications (Health and Social Care Professions) (Amendment etc) (EU Exit) Regulations 2019, SI 2019/593; DHSC, 'Professional Qualifications—EU Exit Standstill Provisions: Review by the Secretary of State' (Decision, updated 7 Sept 2023) <www.gov.uk/government/publications/professional-qualifications-eu-exit-standstill-provisions-review-by-the-secretary-of-state/professional-qualifications-eu-exit-standstill-provisions-review-by-the-secretary-of-state> accessed 21 October 2025.

practical terms this largely preserves the pre-Brexit recognition arrangements, but on a unilateral and time-limited basis, with no assurance that they will survive the next review, expected in 2028.

The changes in immigration policy and uncertainty surrounding the recognition of qualifications have inevitably dulled the UK's appeal to EU health professionals. Nuffield Trust analysis shows that, post-Brexit, the EU/EEA share of professionals registering to practise in the UK has fallen sharply, with nursing most affected.[63] This trajectory may be read as evidence that the UK has indeed 'taken back control' of its borders. Yet, as the discussion below demonstrates, the control exercised has been highly selective: it has curbed EU migration while leaving the system's broader reliance on overseas labour largely intact.

(b) Non-EU Recruitment and Its Reversal

For health professionals trained outside the EU—who had never benefited from free movement—the HCW Visa reduced barriers to entry through lower fees and expedited processing, and thus quickly became the gateway to employment in the UK. As a result, recruitment to the NHS from outside the EU has increased sharply since Brexit. In England, nearly one in five NHS staff now report a non-British nationality, up from roughly one in eight before Brexit.[64] The shift has been most pronounced in medicine and nursing: in recent years, more than half of doctors and nearly half of nurses joining their registers trained outside the UK and EEA.[65]

Even with a rapidly growing international workforce, shortfalls persist. NHS England reported a vacancy rate of 6.7 per cent as of March 2025,[66] with a sustained rise projected over the coming decade.[67] The situation is similar in social care. The extension of the HCW Visa to frontline care roles in 2022[68] brought vacancies down

[63] Lucina Rolewicz, Billy Palmer, and Cyril Lobont, *The NHS Workforce in Numbers* (Nuffield Trust, February 2024) <www.nuffieldtrust.org.uk/resource/the-nhs-workforce-in-numbers> accessed 29 July 2025.

[64] Adam McCulloch, 'Record Proportion of International NHS Workers', *Personnel Today* (15 February 2024) <www.personneltoday.com/hr/record-proportion-of-international-nhs-workers/> accessed 28 July 2025.

[65] Lucina Rolewicz, Mark Dayan, Nina Hemmings and William Palmer, 'Immigration Crackdown Threatens NHS Workforce, Data Show', *BMJ* (1 December 2024) <www.bmj.com/content/390/bmj.r1554> accessed 28 July 2025; The Health Foundation, 'How Reliant Is the NHS in England on International Nurse Recruitment?' *The Health Foundation* (2024) <www.health.org.uk/features-and-opinion/features/how-reliant-is-the-nhs-in-england-on-international-nurse-recruitment> accessed 28 July 2025.

[66] NHS Digital, *NHS Vacancy Statistics, England, April 2015–March 2025, Experimental Statistics* (29 May 2025) <digital.nhs.uk/data-and-information/publications/statistical/nhs-vacancies-survey/april-2015-march-2025-experimental-statistics> accessed 28 July 2025.

[67] Calculation based on figures provided in NHS England, *NHS Long Term Workforce Plan* (30 June 2023) <www.england.nhs.uk/long-read/nhs-long-term-workforce-plan-2/> accessed 28 July 2025.

[68] Skills for Care, *The State of the Adult Social Care Sector and Workforce in England* (October 2025) 61 <www.skillsforcare.org.uk/Adult-Social-Care-Workforce-Data/workforceintelligence/resources/Reports/National/The-state-of-the-adult-social-care-sector-and-workforce-in-England-2025.pdf> accessed 1 November 2025.

from a peak of 10.7 per cent in 2021/22 to 7 per cent in 2025[69]—a material improvement, but far from sufficient to stabilize a chronically overstretched service.[70] Moreover, the consequences cut across both sectors: shortages in social care delay hospital discharge and lengthen waiting times,[71] while NHS gaps draw staff away from already fragile care providers.[72] Strain in one system thus spills into the other, leaving both more exposed.

As noted earlier, the government's immediate post-Brexit response to shortages was international recruitment. The emphasis has since shifted. Recent policy papers—the 2023 NHS Long Term Workforce Plan,[73] the 2025 Immigration White Paper,[74] and the 10-Year Health Plan for England released in the same year[75]—focus on reducing reliance on overseas labour and expanding domestic training. For the NHS, the policy is framed in measured terms: the 10-Year Health Plan proposes ending the service's 'dependency on international recruitment' by capping new overseas hires at 10 per cent by 2035. In social care, the approach is far more radical. The Immigration White Paper announces the closure of the dedicated visa route for care workers, as part of a wider effort to 'clamp down' on low-skilled migration.[76] That step follows earlier restrictions, including higher salary thresholds for the HCW visa and the removal of the right of care workers to bring dependants.[77] The overall message is clear: international recruitment, the headline remedy in the immediate post-Brexit period, has been relegated to a residual role, potentially subject to phase-out.

In principle, the emphasis on building a domestic workforce is sound. International recruitment can relieve immediate pressure, but it cannot substitute for tackling the structural drivers of shortages—insufficient training capacity, chronic underfunding across health and social care, and persistent retention problems linked to pay and working conditions.[78] The NHS Long Term Workforce Plan was presented as the first

[69] ibid 55.

[70] See, eg, Migration Advisory Committee 'Adult Social Care and Immigration (Accessible)' (Independent report, 27 April 2022) <www.gov.uk/government/publications/review-of-adult-social-care-2022/adult-social-care-and-immigration-accessible> accessed 20 March 2024.

[71] See, eg, NHS Confederation, 'NHS Leaders Warn that Social Care Workforce Crisis Risks Patient Safety' (28 July 2022) <www.nhsconfed.org/news/nhs-leaders-warn-social-care-workforce-crisis-risks-patient-safety> accessed 28 July 2025.

[72] See, eg, Lucina Rolewicz and others, *Waste Not, Want Not: Strategies to Improve the Supply of Clinical Staff to the NHS* (Nuffield Trust, Dec 2023), 3–4 <www.nuffieldtrust.org.uk/sites/default/files/2023-12/Waste%20not%20want%20not-WEB-pdf.pdf> accessed 28 July 2025.

[73] (n 66).

[74] Home Office, *Restoring Control over the Immigration System* (12 May 2025) <www.gov.uk/government/publications/restoring-control-over-the-immigration-system-white-paper> accessed 28 July 2025.

[75] DHSC, *Fit for the Future: 10-Year Health Plan for England* (Dec 2023) <https://assets.publishing.service.gov.uk/media/6888a0b1a11f859994409147/fit-for-the-future-10-year-health-plan-for-england.pdf> accessed 13 August 2025 (10-Year Health Plan).

[76] Immigration White Paper, paras 26–27; Changes to UK Visa and Settlement (n 58).

[77] See, eg, Home Office, 'New Laws to Cut Migration and Tackle Care Worker Visa Abuse' (11 March 2024) <www.gov.uk/government/news/new-laws-to-cut-migration-and-tackle-care-worker-visa-abuse> accessed 28 July 2025; Home Office, 'New Rules to Prioritise Recruiting Care Workers in England' (12 March 2025) <www.gov.uk/government/news/new-rules-to-prioritise-recruiting-care-workers-in-england> accessed 28 July 2025. Discussed in Skills for Care, Report 2025 (n 68) 61.

[78] UK overseas recruitment also raises ethical issues: Nuffield Trust, 'Research Reveals NHS Overreliance on Doctors from "Red List" Countries and Renewed Signs of Widespread Medicines Shortages' (Press

systematic attempt to address these issues. It promises to double medical school places and nearly double nursing training places by 2031, projecting an overall workforce increase of about 60 per cent by 2036/37.[79] The commitments are ambitious, but the Plan offers limited detail on implementation—in particular as regards placement capacity, educator supply, and, critically, long-term financing, on which any expansion of training depends.[80] The Labour government, for its part, has dismissed the Plan's projections as unrealistic and undertook to bring forward a refreshed workforce plan in 2025.[81] At the time of writing, no such plan has been published.[82]

The 2023 Plan also recognizes the importance of retention, as staff turnover—including among international recruits—remains high.[83] It pledges improvements to staff health and wellbeing, support for flexible work, enhancements to the physical working environment, career-development measures, and pension reforms to enable partial or phased retirement. As with the training proposals, the implementation detail is sparse and the commitments lack dedicated funding, relying instead on the assumption that improved retention will generate savings.[84] Equally telling is what is omitted: pay. Despite widespread dissatisfaction among NHS staff, neither the Plan nor the Labour government's 10-Year Health Plan contains any commitment on pay.[85] Absent credible action on pay, the prospects for retention remain uncertain, even if domestic training expands.[86]

Unlike healthcare, social care has no statutory long-term workforce plan. That absence is striking given the sector's precarious position: chronic underfunding has depressed pay and working conditions; providers face high turnover; and staffing models lean heavily on migrant labour.[87] The result is a workforce that is both hard

release, 24 March 2025) <www.nuffieldtrust.org.uk/news-item/research-reveals-nhs-overreliance-on-doctors-from-red-list-countries-and-renewed-signs-of-widespread-medicines-shortages> accessed 28 July 2025.

[79] See also Nuffield Trust, Report 2024 (n 2) 60–61, noting that similar plans of expansion have been announced in Wales and Scotland.

[80] Public Accounts Committee, *Access to Urgent and Emergency Care* (Seventy-Third Report of Session 2022–23, 25 October 2023) 9, 15–16 <committees.parliament.uk/publications/41812/documents/207351/default/> accessed 12 July 2025 (Public Accounts Committee Report). For concrete proposals regarding financing of higher medical education, see, eg, William Palmer and others, *Student Loans Forgiveness* (Nuffield Trust, September 2023) <www.nuffieldtrust.org.uk/sites/default/files/2023-09/Nuffield%20Trust%20-%20Student%20loans%20forgiveness_WEB_final.pdf> accessed 6 October 2025.

[81] 10-Year Health Plan (n 75) 97.

[82] Last checked April 2026.

[83] See, eg, Rolewicz and others (n 72) 3–4; Public Accounts Committee Report (n 80) 14.

[84] Jessica Holden, 'The NHS Long Term Workforce Plan Explained' (The King's Fund, 27 July 2023) <www.kingsfund.org.uk/insight-and-analysis/long-reads/nhs-long-term-workforce-plan-explained> accessed 13 June 2015.

[85] Saoirse Mallorie, 'NHS Workforce in a Nutshell' (The King's Fund, 10 May 2024) <www.kingsfund.org.uk/insight-and-analysis/data-and-chArts/nhs-workforce-nutshell> accessed 13 August 2025.

[86] To that effect, see also T Ferreira and AM Collins, 'The NHS Long Term Workforce Plan: An Ambitious Leap or a Misstep?' (2023) 116 J R Soc Med 368, likening training expansion plans to 'filling a leaking bucket' if issues of retention are not adequately addressed.

[87] Discussed in, eg, Migration Advisory Committee, 'Adult Social Care and Immigration' (n 70); Skills for Care, Report 2025 (n 68) 55; Mithran Samuel, 'Number of Overseas Care Recruits Plummets as Report Shows They Have Driven Workforce Recovery' (*Community Care*, 10 October 2024) <www.communityc

to grow and hard to retain. Seeking to chart a way forward, the government has commissioned an independent review of the sector, but the conclusions are not due until 2028. Moreover, the review's terms of reference require that recommendations be 'affordable' within strict fiscal limits.[88] Such constraints cast doubt on the likelihood of meaningful change.

(c) Northern Ireland

Given the centrality of workforce mobility to all-island and cross-border care, one might have expected the loss of free movement to destabilize service delivery. That has not occurred. The Nuffield Trust's most recent analysis suggests that day-to-day provision across the island has largely continued on pre-Brexit terms.[89] Several factors help explain this. The CTA insulates most North–South professional mobility from the new visa regime; the UK's standstill on recognition largely preserves pre-Brexit treatment of EU healthcare qualifications; and long-standing administrative and service-level cooperation, exemplified by CAWT, had already embedded cross-border staffing arrangements by the early 2000s, so that the EU mutual recognition framework added relatively little in practice. These arrangements seem unlikely to be seriously disrupted even if (or when) the government were to end the standstill regime.

(d) Interim Conclusion: Unbound but Dependent

Unbound from EU free movement, the UK health and care workforce model appears caught between reliance on overseas recruitment—itself subject to politically contingent terms—and domestic reform that has yet to materialize.

The NHS Long-Term Workforce Plan was presented as the first comprehensive strategy to expand the domestic workforce, but the commitment itself is not new. For decades—well before Brexit—successive governments made similar promises.[90] While earlier reforms delivered short-term gains,[91] they failed to secure lasting

are.co.uk/2024/10/10/number-of-overseas-care-recruits-plummets-as-report-shows-they-have-driven-workforce-recovery/> accessed 15 August 2025.

[88] DHSC, 'Independent Commission into Adult Social Care: Terms of Reference' (11 July 2025) <www.gov.uk/government/publications/independent-commission-into-adult-social-care-terms-of-reference/independent-commission-into-adult-social-care-terms-of-reference> accessed 22 July 2025.

[89] Nuffield Trust, Report 2025 (n 2) 12.

[90] See, eg, Department of Health, *The NHS Plan: A Plan for Investment, A Plan for Reform* (Cm 4818–I, July 2000), 50–58 <https://pns.dgs.pt/files/2010/03/pnsuk1.pdf> accessed 26 September 2025.

[91] See, eg, Geoffrey Rivett, '1998–2007: Labour's Decade' in *The History of the NHS* (Nuffield Trust) <www.nuffieldtrust.org.uk/chapter/1998-2007-labour-s-decade#toc-header-6> accessed 26 September 2025; DHSC, 'Up to 1,500 Extra Medical Training Places Announced' (Press release, 4 October 2016) <www.gov.uk/government/news/up-to-1500-extra-medical-training-places-announced> accessed 27 September 2025.

change because commitments were not matched by sustained investment and the infrastructure required for delivery.[92] The present strategy risks repeating this pattern. It sets ambitious projections without a clear account of how education and training capacity will be expanded and financed over time; and, while it acknowledges the importance of retention, it offers few concrete measures, with pay—the central retention lever—largely untouched. Social care still lacks a statutory workforce plan, and the recent closure of migration routes risks further destabilizing an already fragile sector, with predictable spillovers into the NHS.

The core weaknesses in UK health and care workforce planning are long-standing and domestic, so much would likely have looked similar even without Brexit. Brexit has nevertheless intensified pressures by removing the EU recruitment channel and placing workforce supply within a volatile visa regime. In doing so, it has put into sharp focus both the UK's dependence on international workers and the NHS' dependence on the government's broader immigration policy choices.

4 Medicines

The regulation of medicines is a field that shows with particular clarity the costs of being 'unbound' from EU law. Although Brexit formally restored the UK's regulatory autonomy by, largely, releasing it from the EU medicines regime, the exercise of that autonomy has been constrained by new trade barriers and the economic realities of a relatively small market. Against this backdrop, recurrent shortages, rising costs, and delays in patient access have become defining features of the UK's post-Brexit medicines landscape.

(a) Pre-Brexit Legal Framework

Prior to Brexit, the regulation of medicines in the UK was embedded within the EU internal market framework, which provided three main routes to authorization. The centralized procedure, mandatory for innovative and highly specialized therapies, entailed assessment by the European Medicines Agency (EMA) followed by a formal authorization by the European Commission, yielding a single licence valid across the EU and EEA.[93] A decentralized procedure, used for medicines outside the scope of

[92] See, eg, House of Commons Health Committee, *Workforce Planning* (Fourth Report of Session 2006–07, HC 171–I, 2007) <www.publications.parliament.uk/pa/cm200607/cmselect/cmhealth/171/171i.pdf> accessed 6 October 2025; J Beech and others, *Closing the Gap: Key Areas for Action on the Health and Care Workforce* (The Health Foundation, The King's Fund and Nuffield Trust 2019) <www.nuffieldtrust.org.uk/sites/default/files/2019-03/heaj6708-workforce-full-report-web.pdf> accessed 6 October 2025.

[93] Regulation (EC) No 726/2004 laying down Community procedures for the authorisation and supervision of medicinal products for human and veterinary use and establishing a European Medicines Agency [2004] OJ L136/1, Arts 3, 5(1), 9(1).

the centralized procedure, allowed simultaneous entry into multiple national markets for products not yet authorized, with one member state acting as a reference state and the others aligning with its evaluation.[94] Where a medicine was already licensed in one member state, the mutual recognition procedure enabled its marketing in others, subject only to narrow exceptions. Medicines authorized through any of these routes could therefore circulate freely within the EU.

(b) Post-Brexit Medicines Landscape

(i) Legal Change and Regulatory Reform

Post-Brexit, the UK is no longer part of the EU's authorization procedures or its system of mutual recognition.[95] Marketing authorizations must now be obtained from the Medicines and Healthcare products Regulatory Agency (MHRA) and carry no effect within the EU, where a separate application to the EMA remains necessary. The split is reinforced by new trade barriers. Medicines moving between Great Britain and the EU are subject to divergent packaging and labelling rules and additional import and customs formalities, each adding cost and delay.[96] Products exported from Great Britain to the EU must also undergo, in the EU, batch testing and certification by a Qualified Person, even where identical tests have already been carried out for the GB market.[97] Where a single, integrated regulatory regime existed pre-Brexit, there now stands a fragmented framework that duplicates regulatory obligations and makes market access slower and more expensive.

Inevitably, this makes the UK a less attractive base for manufacturing, given its relatively small domestic market,[98] while dependence on the EU—by far the largest source of UK medicines imports[99]—leaves national supply vulnerable to disruption. These risks are no longer hypothetical; they have materialized. The Nuffield Trust

[94] Directive 2001/83/EC on the Community code relating to medicinal products for human use [2001] OJ L311/67, Art 28.

[95] TCA, Annex TBT-2: Medicinal Products.

[96] See, eg, MHRA, *Import a human medicine* (Guidance, updated 29 January 2025) <gov.uk/guidance/import-a-human-medicine> accessed 30 July 2025.

[97] European Commission, 'Notice to stakeholders—Withdrawal of the United Kingdom and EU rules for medicinal products for human use and veterinary medicinal products' (Rev 3, 13 March 2020) 10–12 <www.ema.europa.eu/en/documents/regulatory-procedural-guideline/notice-stakeholders-withdrawal-united-kingdom-and-eu-rules-medicinal-products-human-use-and-veterinary-medicinal-products_en.pdf> accessed 21 October 2025. Discussed in Nuffield Trust, Report 2024 (n 2) 75–76.

[98] See Statista, *Market Share of the Leading 10 Global Pharmaceutical Markets in 2024* (Statista, 11 June 2025) <www.statista.com/statistics/245473/market-share-of-the-leading-10-global-pharmaceutical-markets/> accessed 13 July 2025, reporting that UK represents 2.8% of the global pharmaceuticals market.

[99] See, eg, House of Commons Business, Energy and Industrial Strategy Committee, *The Impact of Brexit on the Pharmaceutical Sector* (HC 2017–19, 382, 17 May 2018) Ch 6 'Trade Opportunities Post-Brexit', paras 54–57 <https://publications.parliament.uk/pa/cm201719/cmselect/cmbeis/382/38209.htm> accessed 25 July 2025, noting that the EU accounts for 73% of UK pharmaceutical imports and 44% of UK exports.

estimates that NHS England paid £220 million more in 2022–23 than it would have at previous prices for the same medicines.[100] The increase was largely driven by drug shortages, which doubled between 2022 and 2024, and showed little sign of easing by 2025.[101] Certainly, global factors—the pandemic, wider supply shocks, and the war in Ukraine—have played a role, but Brexit is consistently identified as an aggravating factor, and the UK recorded the weakest growth in medicines imports among the G7 over 2010–23.[102]

Confronted with these pressures, the UK has sought to reposition itself as a market for pharmaceutical innovation. The strategy has centred on reform of the MHRA, designed to streamline and modernize authorization processes while projecting regulatory autonomy post-Brexit. Key changes include a 150-day accelerated assessment, offering a quicker route to approval than the EMA's standard 210-day procedure,[103] and the Innovative Licensing and Access Pathway (ILAP), introduced in 2021 and updated in 2025,[104] which aims to close the gap between regulatory approval and clinical adoption by promoting early, coordinated engagement with the MHRA, National Institute for Health and Care Excellence (NICE), and NHS.[105] These domestic routes are complemented by the International Recognition Procedure (IRP),[106] launched in 2024, which allows the MHRA to rely on approvals granted by 'trusted' overseas regulators, including the EMA and US Food and Drug Administration; it replaces the earlier, transitional 'EC reliance' route used immediately after Brexit.[107]

Taken together, these reforms—among others not examined here[108]—project an industry-oriented system that promises a faster, smoother, and more predictable route into the UK pharmaceutical market. The reform of clinical trials follows

[100] Nuffield Trust, Report 2024 (n 2) 6–11.

[101] ibid; Liz Wells, 'Medicines Supply Issues "Distressing New Normal"' (Healthcare Management, 30 June 2025) <www.healthcare-management.uk/medicines-supply-issues-distressing-normal> accessed 28 July 2025.

[102] See, eg, Nuffield Trust, Report 2022 (n 2) 25–32; Nuffield Trust, Report 2024 (n 2) 16–21; Nuffield Trust, Report 2025 (n 2) 20–21.

[103] MHRA, 'Submission and Assessment Timetables for Innovative Medicines Applications' (Guidance, 3 April 2025) <www.gov.uk/guidance/submission-and-assessment-timetables-for-innovative-medicines-applications> accessed 28 July 2025.

[104] MHRA, 'Innovative Licensing and Access Pathway (ILAP)' (Guidance, updated 16 October 2025) <www.gov.uk/government/publications/innovative-licensing-and-access-pathway-ilap> accessed 31 October 2025.

[105] For commentary, see JA Levine, 'The Potential of an Innovative Licensing and Access Pathway Metapolicy on the United Kingdom's Life Sciences Strategy' (2025) 91 Br J Clin Pharmacol 3019.

[106] MHRA, 'International Recognition Procedure' (Guidance, updated 17 September 2025) <www.gov.uk/government/publications/international-recognition-procedure/international-recognition-procedure> accessed 21 September 2025.

[107] MHRA, 'European Commission (EC) Decision Reliance Procedure' (Guidance, updated 18 November 2022; withdrawn 21 July 2025) <www.gov.uk/guidance/european-commission-ec-decision-reliance-procedure> accessed 21 September 2025.

[108] For national assessment routes, see, eg, MHRA, 'Early Access to Medicines Scheme—Information for Applicants' (Guidance, 1 April 2025) <www.gov.uk/guidance/apply-for-the-early-access-to-medicines-scheme-eams> accessed 20 October 2025. For international collaborations, see MHRA, *Guidance: Project Orbis* (12 Aug 2025) <www.gov.uk/guidance/guidance-on-project-orbis> accessed 15 August 2025; MHRA, *Guidance: Access Consortium* (26 Feb 2024) <www.gov.uk/guidance/access-consortium> accessed 15 August 2025.

the same logic. Heralded as the 'biggest overhaul of clinical trial rules in 20 years',[109] the amendments to the Clinical Trials Regulations[110] due to enter into force in 2026 promise quicker approvals within a more streamlined and flexible framework, including a combined ethics and regulatory review and a simplified route for certain lower-risk trials.[111] Behind these various reforms lies a larger ambition: to recast the MHRA as an 'agile', world-leading regulator at the heart of the UK's post-Brexit vision of itself as a sovereign life sciences 'superpower'.[112]

The significance of these reforms, however, must be set in context. The EU has not stood still: since Brexit, it has brought into application its Clinical Trials Regulation[113] and the long-awaited Clinical Trials Information System (CTIS),[114] which streamline the authorization of multi-state trials; adopted a new framework for joint health technology assessment to support national pricing and reimbursement decisions for new medicines;[115] and given the EMA a reinforced statutory role in monitoring and managing medicines shortages.[116] In 2023, the Commission also tabled the 'pharma package', proposing a comprehensive revision of the EU's general pharmaceutical legislation.[117] Space precludes a detailed examination of these measures,[118] but their direction matters: the EU is expanding and modernizing its pharmaceutical regulation with a view to improving access, strengthening the security of supply, and maintaining the competitiveness of the European pharmaceutical industry. Against

[109] MHRA, 'MHRA to Streamline Clinical Trial Approvals in Biggest Overhaul of Trial Regulation in 20 Years' (Press release, 21 Mar 2023) <www.gov.uk/government/news/mhra-to-streamline-clinical-trial-approvals-in-biggest-overhaul-of-trial-regulation-in-20-years\> accessed 18 November 2025.

[110] Medicines for Human Use (Clinical Trials) Regulations 2004, SI 2004/1031, as amended by the Medicines for Human Use (Clinical Trials) (Amendment) Regulations 2025, SI 2025/538.

[111] For details, see Explanatory Memorandum to the Medicines for Human Use (Clinical Trials) (Amendment) Regulations 2025, SI 2025/538 <www.legislation.gov.uk/uksi/2025/538/pdfs/uksiem_2025 0538_en_001.pdf?>.

[112] Department for Business, Energy and Industrial Strategy, and others, 'Bold New Life Sciences Vision Sets Path for UK to Build on Pandemic Response and Deliver Life-changing Innovations to Patients' (Press release, 6 July 2021) <www.gov.uk/government/news/bold-new-life-sciences-vision-sets-path-for-uk-to-build-on-pandemic-response-and-deliver-life-changing-innovations-to-patients> accessed 1 June 2025.

[113] Regulation (EU) No 536/2014 on clinical trials on medicinal products for human use and repealing Directive 2001/20/EC [2014] OJ L158/1.

[114] EMA, 'Clinical Trials Information System' <www.ema.europa.eu/en/human-regulatory-overview/research-development/clinical-trials-human-medicines/clinical-trials-information-system> accessed 21 November 2025.

[115] Regulation (EU) 2021/2282 on health technology assessment and amending Directive 2011/24/EU [2021] OJ L458/1.

[116] Regulation (EU) 2022/123 on a reinforced role for the European Medicines Agency in crisis preparedness and management for medicinal products and medical devices [2022] OJ L20/1. See also Commission, 'Proposal for a Regulation of the European Parliament and of the Council laying a framework for strengthening the availability and security of supply of critical medicinal products as well as the availability of, and accessibility of, medicinal products of common interest, and amending Regulation (EU) 2024/795' COM (2025) 102 final, 11 Mar 2025.

[117] For details, see European Commission, *Reform of the EU Pharmaceutical Legislation* (26 April 2023) <www.health.ec.europa.eu/medicinal-products/legal-framework-governing-medicinal-products-human-use-eu/reform-eu-pharmaceutical-legislation_en> accessed 30 August 2025.

[118] For commentary, see I Abed and others, 'Commentary on the European Medicines Agency's Extended Mandate: Protecting Public Health in Times of Crisis and Improving Availability of Medicines and Medical Devices' (2023) 89 BJCP 5; M Dayan and others, 'Parallel, Divergent or Drifting? Regulating Healthcare Products in a Post-Brexit UK' (2023) 30 JEPP 1972, 2545–50.

that backdrop, the UK's claim to regulatory agility as a distinctive competitive advantage becomes increasingly difficult to sustain.

(ii) Institutional Capacity Constraints

Early evidence suggests that the UK's medicines reforms have yet to deliver on their promise. Despite new authorization pathways, UK approval times remain longer than those in the EU. Between December 2022 and December 2023, only four medicines were approved faster in the UK; fifty-six were approved later, and by March 2024 eight had not been approved at all.[119] The MHRA also initially struggled to meet its own statutory timelines,[120] although that record has since improved,[121] helped by a £10m government funding boost.[122] It is, however, telling that in 2024–25, nearly 40 per cent of all applications for marketing authorization proceeded via the IRP rather than full assessment by the MHRA, signalling continued reliance on overseas regulators.[123] These patterns point to persistent resource and capacity constraints, following the loss of EU-linked staff and funding.[124] As things stand, the UK's post-Brexit launch environment remains less agile than official rhetoric suggests.

(iii) Medicines Funding and Pricing Policy

A further constraint lies in the UK's highly restrictive medicines funding and pricing policy. The government devotes about 9 per cent of health spending to medicines, compared with an OECD average of roughly 16 per cent.[125] Two long-standing cost-containment mechanisms help explain this gap. First, the National Institute for Health and Care Excellence (NICE) applies a cost-effectiveness threshold that has been left essentially unchanged for more than two decades and not adjusted for inflation,[126] making it more difficult for clinically valuable but high-cost therapies to

[119] Nuffield Trust, Report 2024 (n 2) 31.

[120] Claire Duddy, 'Medicines Shortages', House of Commons Library Research Briefing CBP-9997 (4 September 2025), 13–14 <researchbriefings.files.parliament.uk/documents/CBP-9997/CBP-9997.pdf> accessed 21 October 2025.

[121] MHRA, 'MHRA Performance Data' (updated 20 November 2025) <www.gov.uk/government/publications/mhra-performance-data/mhra-performance-data> accessed 22 November 2025.

[122] MHRA, 'MHRA to Receive £10m from HM Treasury to Fast-track Patient Access to Cutting-edge Medical Products' (Press release, 15 March 2023) < www.gov.uk/government/news/mhra-to-receive-10m-from-hm-treasury-to-fast-track-patient-access-to-cutting-edge-medical-products> accessed 22 November 2025.

[123] Hannah Kuchler and Sarah Neville, 'UK Drugs Agency Outsources 40% of Applications after Brexit Turbulence' *Financial Times* (London, 20 July 2025) <www.ft.com/content/947e6379-d4cc-4b9f-b497-94497a915f9e> accessed 21 October 2025.

[124] Hannah Kuchler and Peter Foster, 'UK Medicines Regulator Needs More Resources, Drugmakers Say' *Financial Times* (London, 4 Dec 2024) <www.ft.com/content/808b6d62-472a-40c7-8238-6a6dba4e7bbe> accessed17 July 2025. See also Dayan and others, 'Parallel, Divergent or Drifting' (n 118) 2564. See also this book's chapter by Kenneth Armstrong, Ch 5.

[125] OECD, *Health at a Glance 2023: OECD Indicators* (OECD Publishing 2023) Ch 10, 'Pharmaceutical Expenditure' <www.oecd.org/en/publications/2023/11/health-at-a-glance-2023_e04f8239/full-report/pharmaceutical-expenditure_a58c1da0.html> accessed 30 July 2025.

[126] Eleanor Hayward, 'British Cancer Patients Will Suffer "Unless NHS Pays More for Drugs"' The Times (22 August 2025) <www.thetimes.com/uk/healthcare/Article/british-cancer-patients-drugs-medication-86rfg76fw> accessed 1 September 2025.

secure approval for NHS use. Second, government pricing agreements with industry cap permissible growth in NHS spending on branded medicines, with companies required to repay the excess. Where demand outpaced the cap, markedly so in some post-Covid years, repayment rates became unusually high: rebates exceeded 21 per cent of sales in 2023 and were set at 22.9 per cent in 2025, a level reported to be three to four times that of comparable schemes in Germany, Italy, and France.[127]

Industry has long argued that the combination of static thresholds and high rebates makes Great Britain commercially unattractive as a launch market, in most recent negotiations warning that continued investment and launch activity would be reconsidered absent reform.[128] Against that background, and in response to US tariff pressure, the government has revised the policy: from April 2026, NICE's threshold will increase by 25 per cent, and the payment percentage for newer medicines under the current branded medicines pricing scheme (VPAG)[129] will be capped at 15 per cent for 2026–28.[130]

It is too early to assess the longer-term implications.[131] Potentially, these reforms could strengthen the UK's standing as a life sciences base and support earlier patient access to innovative treatments.[132] There is, however, a caveat. The government has indicated that any increase in medicines expenditure is to be accommodated within the NHS's existing spending limits.[133] Higher medicines spending is thus likely to be offset elsewhere, whether through slower progress in reducing waiting times or tighter budgets for general practice and community services.[134] Whether the net effect will ultimately be positive is, therefore, uncertain.

More broadly, this episode suggests that outside the EU single market the UK negotiates from a weaker position and may be compelled to accept sharper trade-offs in order to secure, or retain, trade and inward investment.

[127] Association of the British Pharmaceutical Industry (ABPI), 'Delivering a Voluntary Scheme for Health and Growth' (Mar 2025) 11, 14–17 <www.abpi.org.uk/media/t4ih3u0o/abpi-vpag-report-20-march-2025.pdf> accessed 31 October 2025.

[128] See, eg, Hannah Kuchler, 'Higher Medicine Sales Tax Makes UK "Uninvestable", Warn Drugmakers' *Financial Times* (20 Mar 2025) <www.ft.com/content/9e6a19c6-074a-4386-8050-3a9517f0c524> accessed 31 October 2025.

[129] DHSC, 'VPAG 2024: Scheme Documents and Guidance' (7 Aug 2025) <www.gov.uk/government/collections/vpag-2024-scheme-documents-and-guidance> accessed 7 September 2025.

[130] See, eg, Office of the United States Trade Representative, 'U.S. Government Announces Agreement in Principle with the United Kingdom on Pharmaceutical Pricing' (Press release, 1 December 2025) <ustr.gov/about/policy-offices/press-office/press-releases/2025/december/us-government-announces-agreement-principle-united-kingdom-pharmaceutical-pricing> accessed 23 December 2025.

[131] This section was updated on 23 December 2025 to reflect the change in policy.

[132] For recent data on patient access, see, eg, Orban Holdgate, 'Comparing New Medicine Availability across Europe' (ABPI Blog, 12 June 2024) <www.abpi.org.uk/media/blogs/2024/june/comparing-new-medicine-availability-across-europe/>, reporting that by 2024 only 56% of EMA-approved medicines were available in England.

[133] Alice Inch, 'Changes to Medicines Policy: What You Need to Know' (NHS Confederation, 15 December 2025) <www.nhsconfed.org/publications/changes-medicines-policy-what-you-need-know> accessed 23 December 2025.

[134] See, eg, Sally Gainsbury and Huseyin Naci, 'The Tough Choices at the Heart of the Government's Dispute with Big Pharma' (Nuffield Trust, 8 Oct 2025) <www.nuffieldtrust.org.uk/news-item/the-tough-choices-at-the-heart-of-the-government-s-dispute-with-big-pharma> accessed 10 October 2025.

(c) Northern Ireland

Under the Northern Ireland Protocol, Northern Ireland remained aligned with EU internal market rules for goods.[135] This arrangement avoided the re-emergence of a hard border on the island of Ireland, with all the political ramifications such a border would entail. It also meant that medicines placed on the Northern Ireland market after Brexit had to comply with the EU legal framework, including rules on authorization, packaging, and labelling.[136] The regime applies equally to medical devices, which must bear a CE mark to be marketed in Northern Ireland post-Brexit.[137] Inevitably, this creates trade frictions, but the stakes for medicines were higher: given that around 80 per cent of Northern Ireland's medicines are sourced from Great Britain—where rules diverged post-Brexit—the Protocol's framework posed a serious risk of supply disruption, with potentially severe consequences for patients.[138]

As it turned out, the Protocol's medicines regime never fully took effect, and interim measures maintained uninterrupted flows until a permanent settlement was reached.[139] That settlement, formalized in the Windsor Framework in 2023, stipulates that from January 2025 all medicines placed on the Northern Ireland market must be authorized by the MHRA on a UK-wide basis.[140] To ensure that such medicines are not placed on or re-exported to the EU market, they must carry the label 'UK only'. Routine medicines—including most generics and over-the-counter products—remain aligned with certain rules of EU law, most notably on pharmacovigilance.[141] The purpose of this hybrid arrangement is to limit regulatory divergence for widely used products, thereby safeguarding EU supply into Northern Ireland.

The solution provided by the Windsor Framework is not without trade-offs: reliance on the MHRA carries a risk of delayed access to medicines in Northern Ireland compared to Ireland, where EMA authorizations continue to apply, and dual obligations on routine medicines add regulatory complexity for manufacturers. These drawbacks are, however, secondary to the Framework's central achievement—preserving the stability of medicines supply in Northern Ireland, which might otherwise have been jeopardized by a de facto regulatory border in the Irish Sea.

[135] For a comprehensive discussion, see this book's chapter by Filippo Fontanelli, Ch 9.
[136] See NI Protocol (n 50) (pre-Windsor text), Art 5(4) and Annex 2, Pt 20.
[137] NI Protocol (n 50), Art 5(4) and Annex 2, Pt 21.
[138] On this point, see *Not What the Bus Promised* (n 2) 110–29.
[139] See, eg, Council of the European Union, 'EU–UK Relations: The Council Adopts Legislation to Ensure Continued Supply of Medicines' (Press release, 12 April 2022) <www.consilium.europa.eu/en/press/press-releases/2022/04/12/council-adopts-directive-ensure-continued-supply-of-medicines/> accessed 1 May 2025.
[140] Implemented in UK law through Human Medicines Regulations 2012, SI 2012/1916, reg. 49 (1ZA)–(1ZC), as amended by the Human Medicines (Amendments relating to the Windsor Framework) Regulations 2024, SI 2024/832.
[141] ibid Pt 11 and Sch 12A.

(d) Interim Conclusion: Bound by Economic Realities

The reforms to the MHRA—now unbound from the EMA and EU medicines framework—articulate an ambition to position the UK as an agile, world-leading regulator. In practice, that vision has been weighed down by post-Brexit capacity constraints at the MHRA and by a highly restrictive medicines reimbursement and pricing regime (only very recently modified) that has weakened incentives to launch in the UK. Above all, scale is the most substantial, and least tractable, constraint: the UK is a comparatively small pharmaceuticals market, competing with a far larger EU that is modernizing its own framework. This structural reality, already anticipated in pre-Brexit analysis and visible across much of the life sciences sector,[142] has been consistently downplayed in official rhetoric.[143]

Policy delivery, however, has taken a more pragmatic turn, with the UK already engaging in 're-binding' with the EU. On the trade side, it has reduced certain compliance obligations for EU-sourced medicines, for example, by continuing to recognize EU batch testing and certification (without reciprocal action from the EU).[144] On the regulatory side, the UK continues to rely on EMA authorizations—initially via the EC Reliance Route and later through the IRP. The recent clinical trials reform points in the same direction, keeping the domestic framework closely aligned with the structure of the EU Clinical Trials Regulation (albeit without access to CTIS).[145] A similar pattern is emerging in the regulation of medical devices, where the government has both signalled an intention to recognize approvals from 'trusted' overseas regulators and announced plans to extend recognition of CE marking in Great Britain indefinitely.[146]

142 See, eg, Fahy and others, 'Three Possible Scenarios' (n 2) 6–7; Nuffield Trust, Report 2020 (n 2) 12–15; Nuffield Trust, Report 2021 (n 2) 14–21.

143 See, eg, 'Bold New Life Sciences Vision' (n 112); Department for Science, Innovation and Technology, and others, *Life Sciences Sector Plan to Grow Economy and Transform NHS* (gov.uk, 16 July 2025) <www.gov.uk/government/news/life-sciences-sector-plan-to-grow-economy-and-transform-nhs> accessed 23 July 2025. See also DHSC, 'The Future Strategy for Batch Testing of Medicinal Products in Great Britain: Government Response' (Consultation outcome, 15 December 2022) <www.gov.uk/government/consultations/the-future-strategy-for-batch-testing-of-medicinal-products-in-great-britain/outcome/the-future-strategy-for-batch-testing-of-medicinal-products-in-great-britain-government-response> accessed 29 July 2025, which frames the UK's 'independence' from the EU as freedom to decide whether and on what terms to accept batch testing conducted abroad.

144 DHSC, 'Batch Testing' (n 143).

145 Dayan and others, 'Parallel, Divergent or Drifting' (n 124) 2551, 2558. See also Explanatory Memorandum (Clinical Trials) (n 111), para 6.3, making explicit reference to EU Clinical Trials Regulation.

146 See MHRA, 'MHRA Announces Proposals to Improve Access to the World's Best Medical Devices for Patients and to Boost Economic Growth in Britain's Med Tech Sector' (Press release, 22 July 2025) <www.gov.uk/government/news/mhra-announces-proposals-to-improve-access-to-worlds-best-medical-devices-for-patients-and-to-boost-economic-growth-in-britains-med-tech-sector> accessed 17 August 2025.

These steps amount to an acknowledgement—by practice if not proclamation—of the limits of the UK's post-Brexit regulatory autonomy.[147] MHRA reform may yield useful innovations, but timely access to medicines ultimately depends on facilitating entry into Great Britain for products already licensed in major jurisdictions such as the EU and the US, and, more broadly, on maintaining sufficient regulatory compatibility with the EU to remain an attractive location for life sciences investment.

5 Conclusion: Unbound in Theory, Constrained in Practice

Brexit has taken UK healthcare out of EU legal frameworks for cross-border care, workforce mobility, and medicines regulation,[148] yet the promised regulatory freedom—'Law Unbound'—has been realized only in part and unevenly, with tangible consequences for patients and the NHS.

In cross-border healthcare, reciprocal arrangements have largely continued under the WA, TCA, and related instruments—reflecting mutual interest in protecting each party's nationals abroad—but the settlement is leaner in individual rights and, in places, offers less legal security than before. In workforce policy, claims of control mask persisting reliance on overseas labour, while plans for domestic expansion remain uncertain amid unresolved questions of funding, training capacity, and pay. With free movement ended, the health and care workforce is also more exposed to the volatility of domestic immigration rules. In medicines, MHRA reforms assert formal autonomy, but whether and when medicines become available in Great Britain remains deeply influenced by added trade frictions, domestic medicines funding and pricing policy, and ultimately market size—pressures that have already prompted pragmatic re-binding.

The limits of unbinding are most evident in Northern Ireland. Cross-border healthcare on the island remains grounded in the rights set out in the WA and TCA (as, previously, in EU law), and reliance on EU funding for CAWT continues post-Brexit. The Windsor Framework carves out an exception for medicines to Northern Ireland's general alignment with the EU single market for goods, but elements of EU pharmaceutical law continue to apply to ensure supply from the EU. The settlement is complex and deliberately hybrid: it works because Northern Ireland remains, by design, inextricably linked to EU law.

[147] Tension between regulatory autonomy and convergence has been identified as a recurring theme in post-Brexit governance of life sciences. See, eg, Dayan and others, 'Parallel, Divergent or Drifting' (n 124); M Quigley and others, 'The Shape of Medical Devices Regulation in the United Kingdom? Brexit and Beyond' (2023) 5 Law, Technology and Humans 21.

[148] For fuller accounts of clinical trials and medical devices (treated only briefly here), see (nn 146, 147, and 2).

Ultimately, even as the UK charts a path outside the EU, UK healthcare remains shaped by its European context: in Northern Ireland through law; in Great Britain, at the very least, through the gravitational pull of the EU single market. In this unfolding narrative, Brexit has fallen short of fulfilling its promise to 'take back control', with anticipated benefits still elusive and the regulatory landscape continuing to evolve in complexity.

23
Consumer Law and Policy

James Devenney, Geraint Howells, and Chris Willett

1 Pre-Brexit Regulation: The EU Legal Regime Pre-Brexit

(a) The Broad Reach of the EU Consumer *Acquis*

In few areas of law is Lord Denning's description of EU as an incoming tide more apposite than in relation to consumer law.[1] Starting modestly with rules on doorstep selling,[2] there were later controls on distance selling.[3] The rules went on to cover significant areas of consumer private law including unfair terms,[4] sale of goods,[5] product liability,[6] and consumer credit.[7] Regulatory controls were placed on unfair commercial practices[8] and product safety.[9] There were also rules to assist with dispute resolution through measures such as those on small claims[10] and online dispute resolution (ODR)[11] and to promote better enforcement.[12]

(b) Innovative Features of the EU Consumer *Acquis*

Information obligations imposed on traders have always been a key element used by policy-makers to redress information asymmetry between consumers and sellers. These obligations became more extensive under EU law and have arisen both indirectly through, for example, misleading omissions provisions in the Unfair Commercial Practices Directive,[13] and through direct obligations to inform.[14] The

[1] *Bulmer v Bollinger* [1974] Ch 401, 418.
[2] Dir 85/577/EEC.
[3] Dir 97/7/EC.
[4] Dir 1993/13/EC.
[5] Dir 1999/44/EC.
[6] Dir 1985/374/EEC.
[7] Dir 87/102/EEC and Directive 2008/48/EC.
[8] Dir 2005/29/EC.
[9] Dir 92/59/EEC and Dir 2001/95/EC.
[10] Reg (EC) No 861/2007.
[11] Reg (EU) No 524/2013.
[12] Reg (EC) No 2006/2004 and Regulations 2107/2394.
[13] Dir 2005/29/EC.
[14] Dir 2011/83/EU.

James Devenney, Geraint Howells, and Chris Willett, *Consumer Law and Policy* In: *The UK Regulatory Framework Post-Brexit: 'Law Unbound'*. Edited by: Paul Craig and Vilija Vėlyvytė, Oxford University Press.
 DOI: 10.1093/9780198969815.003.0026

use of the right of withdrawal was already known to UK law,[15] but has also been used far more extensively by the EU.[16]

The EU also reshaped some areas of UK consumer law by imposing new models of regulation. Three good examples are products liability, unfair terms, and unfair commercial practices. The UK had been discussing moving from negligence to strict products liability in response to the thalidomide scandal.[17] The EU created the level playing field that allowed strict liability to be introduced.[18] As regards unfair terms, the UK had punctual controls concentrated on exclusion and limitation clauses. The EU favoured a broad unfairness test. A central element of this was the good faith principle. Originally considered alien to the common law,[19] its meaning has become so accepted that the Law Commission advised against altering the wording to remove good faith, so as not to create more uncertainty.[20] The impact on fair trading law is even more remarkable. The notion of a general duty to trade fairly had been proposed by the Office of Fair Trading and rejected.[21] However, the EU introduced a broad prohibition on unfair commercial practices. In the area of enforcement there was also a significant change brought about by the EU. UK legislation had relied heavily on giving individuals private law rights or using criminal sanctions. Under the influence of the EU, the use by public bodies of injunctions and undertakings is now a common feature of the UK regulatory landscape.

Our conclusion would be that the EU consumer *acquis* had been well received into UK law, at least on the surface. The position is more nuanced when we look at its application in case law.[22]

(c) EU Law Removing UK Law

The earlier EU consumer law directives were minimal in nature and established a floor of consumer rights. There was then a distinct move by the EU to favour maximum harmonization directives that provided for both a floor and a ceiling to consumer protection. This was often subject to express exclusions that allowed scope for continued national law, often in relation to specific products or services. For example,

[15] See, eg, Consumer Credit Act 1975, ss 67-74.

[16] M Loos, Rights of Withdrawal, Centre for the Study of European Contract Law Working Paper Series No. 2009/04; G Howells, '*Pacta Sunt Servanda* and the Consumer's Right of Withdrawal' in N Witzleb (ed), *Contract Law in Changing Times: Asian Perspectives on Pacta Sunt Servanda* (Routledge 2023).

[17] *Royal Commission on Civil Liability and Compensation for Personal Injury*, Cmnd. 7054 (1978) and Law Commission and Scottish Law Commission, *Liability for Defective Products*, (Law Com No. 82, Scot Law Com No. 45).

[18] Dir 1985/374/EEC.

[19] G Teubner, 'Legal Irritants: Good Faith in British Law or How Unifying Law Ends Up in New Divergencies' (1998) 61 MLR 11; H Collins, 'Good Faith in European Contract Law' (1994) 14 OJLS 229.

[20] Law Commission, *Unfair Terms in Consumer Contracts: Advice to the Department for Business, Innovation and Skills* (March 2013) 6.42.

[21] *A General Duty to Trade Fairly* (OFT 1986).

[22] See section 1(f).

certain sectors, such as financial services, might be excluded. In the area of products liability Article 13 of the Product Liability Directive allowed for the continued application, *inter alia*, of sales of goods law.

(d) Continued National Developments

However, not all changes introduced to UK consumer law in the past few decades have resulted from the need to comply with EU law. Domestic reform has been possible, especially in areas such as unfair terms and sales law that have been subject to minimum harmonization directives. The Law Commission had reviewed consumer sales law on several occasions and the law has subsequently been amended based on those recommendations.[23] Furthermore, the UK led the way in extending conformity rules to digital content in the Consumer Rights Act 2015. That same legislation saw important changes to unfair terms by extending controls to all terms, not merely non-negotiated terms, and only excluding core terms and the price from assessment if they were not only transparent but additionally prominent.[24] The UK pushed ahead with providing an individual remedy for unfair commercial practices.[25]

(e) The Complexity of UK Law

UK law became more complex due to the need to blend the EU law with existing national legislation, especially in areas governed by minimal harmonization EU Directives. The Unfair Terms on Consumer Contacts Regulations,[26] implementing the EU rules, for a long time sat alongside the pre-existing controls in the Unfair Contract Terms Act 1977. However, the need to simplify the regime was recognized,[27] and was achieved by integrating the two regimes in the Consumer Rights Act 2015.

Consumer credit law became more complicated, partly because of the need to implement EU law, which often used different financial thresholds. Thus, EU rules might apply to some contracts, with existing national rules covering contracts outside the scope of EU rules. UK law became complicated also because implementing EU law became, for example, entangled with a broader move away from using the Consumer Credit Act 1974 towards a principles and rules-based handbook regime found in the consumer credit sourcebook (CONC) adopted by the Financial Conduct Authority. However, not all rules suit that format, so there is a complicated mixture of

[23] See, eg, Law Com 160, Scot Law Com 104, Sale and Supply of Goods (1987); Law Com No 317, Scot Law Com 217 *Consumer Remedies for Faulty Goods* (2009).
[24] Consumer Rights Act 2015, s 64(2).
[25] Law Com No 332, Scot Law Com 226, *Consumer Redress for Misleading and Aggressive Practices* (2012) and The Consumer Protection (Amendment) Regulations 2014.
[26] SI 1999/2083.
[27] Law Com No 292, Scot Law Com, 199, *Unfair Terms in Contracts*, (2005).

rules—some in legislation or statutory instrument, and others governed by the FCA sourcebook.[28]

(f) National Judicial Interpretation of EU Law

Moving away from the raw statutory provisions, it is in their case law application that one often finds the true soul of the legal regime. There are various examples which illustrate that the UK was able to put its own flavour on the relevant EU rules. Thus, in *A v National Blood Authority*[29] Burton J gave a very pro-claimant and pro-European interpretation of the Product Liability Directive. His views on how to establish a defect have, however, been criticized in two subsequent judgments involving artificial hips that were not held to be defective.[30] In essence, they considered that you could not legitimately expect a product not to fail if you had been warned of even a minor risk of it doing so. However, this is a more conservative application of the law than in many continental cases and would be hard to justify under subsequent reform to the directive both regarding the burden of proof and the restrictions of warnings exculpating otherwise defective products.[31] The judgments in the artificial hip cases sit well with some conservative common law academic criticisms of the defectiveness standard.[32]

One sees similarly conservative approaches being adopted by the courts to unfair terms legislation. The Supreme Court in *Parking Eye*[33] adopted the CJEU's 'agreement' test under which the court, in order to determine whether the term violates the concept of good faith, asks whether the trader, dealing fairly and equitably, could have reasonably assumed that the consumer would have agreed to the term had it been subject to individual negotiation.[34] However, the court did not seek to establish what a hypothetical negotiation might have achieved, but accepted the general practice of consumers in agreeing to the term as evidence that they agreed with it and also introduced the element of the trader having a legitimate interest in using the term. Likewise, as regards the exclusion from assessment of core terms, the UK Supreme Court refused to use unfairness to assess the fairness of banks charges.[35] It refused

[28] E Lomnika, 'The Reform of Consumer Credit in the UK' [2004] JBL129.

[29] [2001] 3 All ER 289.

[30] *Wilkes v DePuy* [2016] EWHC 3096 (QB) and *Gee v. DePuy*, [2018] EWHC 1208. For a decision on the factual finding of non-defectiveness of an artificial hip see the Supreme Court decision in *Hastings v Finsbury Orthopaedics Ltd* [2022] UKSC 19.

[31] Directive (EU) 2024/2853.

[32] C Newdick, 'The Future of Negligence in Product Liability' (1987) 103 LQR 288; C Newdick, 'The Development Risk Defence of the Consumer Protection Act 1987' (1988) 47 CLJ 455; C Newdick, 'Risk, Uncertainty and "Knowledge" in the Development Risk Defence' (1991) 20 Anglo-American Law Review 309–26; J Stapleton, 'Products Liabilty Reform: Real or Illusory? (1986) 6 OJLS 392; J Stapleton, 'Products Liability in the United Kingdom: The Myths of Reform' (1999) 34 Texas International Law Journal 45.

[33] *Parking Eye v Beavis* [2015] UKSC 67, [105], [108].

[34] Case C-415/11 *Aziz v Caixa d'Estalvis de Catalunya, Tarragona i Manresa (Catalunyacaixa)* EU:C:2013:164, [69]; Case C-621/17 *Kiss v CIB Bank Zrt*, EU:C:2019:820, [50].

[35] *Office of Fair Trading v Abbey National*, [2009] UKSC 6.

to accept the distinction between core and ancillary charges. This seemed out of line with the spirit of CJEU case law, as has subsequently been confirmed.[36]

The conclusion is that even in harmonized areas the courts, through interpretation of EU law, could give a national flavour to the law. A study of unfair commercial practices found the same phenomenon of national traditions affecting interpretation of unfairness.[37] This is possible structurally as the CJEU only interprets and does not apply law. Indeed, in the area of unfair terms, it stepped back from giving clear guidance on unfairness[38] to stress the role of the national courts in applying the directive's rules[39]—probably through fear of being overwhelmed. Also, national courts have a discretion to refer cases and the UK courts tended to be reticent to do so, if only for concern at the delays that might entail. Even the Supreme Court, which has a duty to refer, can invoke the *acte claire* doctrine to refuse a referral, as it did in the bank charges case despite the Court of Appeal holding the opposite view. Some see this decision as the court not wanting to impose a heavy burden on an already embattled banking sector post-Global Financial Crisis.[40]

Although the CJEU was often painted as interventionist, it also showed restraint in relation to challenges to UK implementation of EU law, as exemplified by *Commission v UK*[41] in relation to the development risks defence. The UK's wording certainly seems more pro-defendant than that of the directive, by introducing more subjective elements of assessing the producer's knowledge. Yet the Court was unwilling to accept there was a breach until this had been established in practice from case law.

(g) Cooperation Between Agencies

A noticeable feature of the landscape pre-Brexit was the cooperation between UK regulatory agencies and their counterparts and the Commission. This was formalized through the Consumer Protection Cooperation Regulation.[42] In the area of product safety there was information exchange through the RAPEX and other notification systems, and Prosafe provided a forum for market surveillance officials to come together. Under the Lamfalussy architecture national supervisors were involved in advising the Commission on financial services law. European consumer centres advised consumers on cross-border disputes and Fin-Net promoted cooperation between national ombudsmen in financial services.

[36] See, eg, Case C-224/19 *CY v Caixabank SA* EU:C:2020:578.

[37] B Duuinvoorde, *The Consumer Benchmarks in the Unfair Commercial Practices Directive* (Springer 2016).

[38] Case C-244/98 *Oceano Grupo Edutorial and Salvat Editores* EU:C:2000:346.

[39] Case C-237/02 *Freiburger Kommunalbauten GmbH Baugesellschaft & Co. KG v Ludger Hofstetter and Ulrike Hofstetter* [2004] ECR-I 3403.

[40] J Devenney, 'Gordian Knots in Europeanised Private Law: Unfair Terms, Bank Charges and Political Compromises' [2011] NILQ 33.

[41] Case C-300/95 [1997] ECR I-2649.

[42] Regulation (EU) 2017/2394.

2 Post-Brexit Regulation: Consumer Law and Policy

(a) Key Initial Repeals in the Field of Consumer Law and Policy

In this field, as in other fields, at an early stage the UK government indicated that, at least in the short term, much of the consumer *acquis* would be converted into domestic law. This was predominantly framed as a pragmatic solution for business;[43] but it might equally, in this context and while recognizing the complex nature of consumer decision making,[44] have been framed around consumer confidence.[45] This was given effect to by, *inter alia*, the European Union (Withdrawal) Act 2018, which retained most pre-existing core consumer law of an EU origin in domestic law. There were, however, three notable areas where repeals were made in the consumer law context.

First, Regulation (EU) No 524/2013 on consumer ODR[46] was repealed.[47] That Regulation had established a free multilingual European Online Dispute Resolution Platform. While recognizing the importance of effective dispute resolution for consumer rights and confidence,[48] Regulation (EU) No 524/2013 was not well used, with only approximately 200 cases across the EU enabled by it per year;[49] and it was ultimately repealed by the EU.[50] Second, while the Competition and Markets Authority (CMA) continues to have powers to seek undertakings and enforcement orders to prevent continued breaches that harm consumers collectively, the reach of those powers has been curtailed. It can continue to take action in the UK courts against UK businesses and businesses from EU countries where their activities harm UK consumers. However, post-Brexit, the CMA no longer can take action against such

[43] See HM Government, *The United Kingdom's Exit from and New Partnership with the European Union* (2017), Cm 9417, 1.1ff.

[44] See, eg, C Waddams Price and M Zhu, 'Empirical Evidence of Consumer Response in Regulated Markets' (2016) 12 Journal of Competition Law & Economics 113.

[45] On the impact of legal uncertainty in this field see, eg, EU Commission, Green Paper on policy options for progress towards a European Contract Law for consumers and businesses, COM(2010)348 final; C Willett, 'Re-Theorising Consumer Law' (2018) 77 CLJ 179, 181.

[46] Regulation (EU) No 524/2013 of the European Parliament and of the Council of 21 May 2013 on online dispute resolution for consumer disputes and amending Regulation (EC) No 2006/2004 and Directive 2009/22/EC [2013] OJ L165/1.

[47] See Consumer Protection (Amendment etc.) (EU Exit) Regulations 2018, reg 10.

[48] See, eg, OECD, Recommendation of the Council on Consumer Dispute Resolution and Redress (OECD/LEGAL/0356 (2024)).

[49] See Proposal for a Regulation of the European Parliament and of the Council repealing Regulation (EU) No 524/2013 and amending Regulations (EU) 2017/2394 and (EU) 2018/1724 with regard to the discontinuation of the European ODR Platform, 2023/0375(COD), section 1 of Explanatory Memorandum.

[50] Regulation (EU) 2024/3228 of the European Parliament and of the Council of 19 December 2024 repealing Regulation (EU) No 524/2013, and amending Regulations (EU) 2017/2394 and (EU) 2018/1724 with regard to the discontinuation of the European Online Dispute Resolution Platform.

businesses in their local courts.[51] This may mean UK consumers will sometimes go unprotected against activities that a business has been banned from continuing in its own country by a local court. Note also that the UK European Consumer Centres have gone. However, to some extent this has morphed into the UK International Consumer Centre, funded by the UK government and run by the Chartered Trading Standards Institute, to help consumers with cross-border complaints in the twenty-nine EU/EEA states and twelve states internationally with which partnerships have been formed.

Third, the 2006[52] and 2017[53] Consumer Protection Cooperation Regulations were repealed.[54] These provided for cooperation between member states' national enforcement agencies. While the CMA has said that it 'will seek to continue to work with EU enforcers as far as possible',[55] there were at least in the immediate aftermath of Brexit strained relations between the UK and EU that restricted cooperation between regulators. It remains to be seen if relations improve going forward, but one suspects it will be hard to build up to the same level of cooperation. On the other hand, in the field of product safety the UK–EU Trade and Cooperation Agreement provides a framework for ongoing exchanges,[56] which are also integral to the structure of the EU's Safety Gate.

(b) The Retained EU Law (Revocation and Reform) Act 2023

The original Retained EU Law (Revocation and Reform) Bill 2022 caused concern in consumer law circles, particularly around timeframes, for bodies such as the Consumers' Association,[57] the Chartered Institute of Trading Standards,[58] and Consumer Scotland (the statutory body for consumers in Scotland).[59] Ultimately the Retained EU Law (Revocation and Reform) Act 2023 was much more modest than originally proposed and it did not really affect core EU-derived consumer law.

[51] See amendments to Enterprise Act 2022, Pt 8 and Consumer Rights Act 2015, Sched 5 by the Consumer Protection (Enforcement) (Amendment etc.) (EU Exit) Regulations 2018. See now Digital Markets, Competition and Consumers Act 2024, particularly s 173.

[52] Regulation (EC) No 2006/2004 of the European Parliament and of the Council on cooperation between national authorities responsible for the enforcement of consumer protection laws [2004] OJ L364/1.

[53] Regulation (EU) 2017/2394 of the European Parliament and of the Council of 12 December 2017 on cooperation between national authorities responsible for the enforcement of consumer protection laws and repealing Regulation (EC) No 2006/2004 [2017] OJ L345/1.

[54] Reg 2006/2004 and Reg 2017/2394 were repealed by the Consumer Protection (Enforcement) (Amendment etc.) (EU Exit) Regulations 2019/203, reg 8.

[55] CMA, Guidance on the Functions of the CMA after the Transition Period, 5.15.

[56] Art 96.

[57] See: https://www.which.co.uk/news/article/consumer-rights-food-and-safety-laws-at-risk-of-being-scrapped-under-new-legislation-azzZF1N8tg2E.

[58] Retained EU Law (Revocation and Reform) Bill, Written Evidence Submitted by the Chartered Trading Standards Institute (CTSI) (REULB31).

[59] Retained EU Law (Revocation and Reform) Bill, Written Evidence Submitted by Consumer Scotland (REULB13).

(c) Consumer Law Reform in the UK

More generally, several proposals for reform of core consumer law in the UK appear to have stalled. This is so in areas inside and outside of the consumer *acquis*. An example of the latter is the reforms to the law on the passing of property in goods proposed by the Law Commission,[60] which seem to have been indefinitely postponed.[61] An example of the former is product liability, where, in 2021, the Law Commission tentatively suggested 'product liability and emerging technology' for its programme of law reform.[62] Yet in February 2023 the Law Commission concluded that the time was not right to establish a new programme of reform, noting that it had 'taken this decision in view of the Government's focus on priorities for the remainder of this Parliament'.[63] Subsequently, in a report mainly concerned with product safety reform, the government has alluded briefly to the need for modernizing product liability law, but concretely has only mentioned the possibility of extending the definition of product to include software and taking AI into account when assessing defectiveness.[64] The Law Commission has recently taken up the topic of product liability again.[65] The context, we would suggest, is a country hamstrung by Brexit, without—at least under the former government—a real vision for the future of UK consumer law or for achieving the competitive advantages which Brexit promised to deliver.[66]

[60] Law Commission Consultation Paper, *Consumer Sales Contracts: Transfer of Ownership* (Law Com 398, (2021)). This was the culmination of much work at the Law Commission: see Law Commission, *Consumer Prepayments on Retailer Insolvency* (Consultation Paper 221, 2015), Law Commission, *Consumer Prepayments on Retailer Insolvency* (Law Com 368, 2016); Law Commission Consultation Paper, *Consumer Sales Contracts: Transfer of Ownership* (Consultation Paper 246, 2020).

[61] See Law Commission Annual Report 2022-23 (Law Com, No 414) 54: 'However, any decision as to whether to implement the final draft Bill would need to balance a number of relevant considerations to ensure that the benefits justify the potential costs. In particular, during the course of our work, we identified a common practice among retailers of delaying the point at which the sales contract is formed until the goods are dispatched to the consumer. This would reduce the impact of our reforms which, like most consumer protections, depend on a sales contract being in place. The evidence we have received about the practice does not suggest that it causes consumer detriment in more general terms, but we think this, and the case for our reforms, should be kept under review.'

[62] See https://lawcom.gov.uk/14th-programme/.

[63] See https://lawcom.gov.uk/update-14th-programme-of-law-reform/.

[64] Department for Business, Energy and Industrial Strategy, *Smarter Regulation: UK Product Safety Review* (August 2023) at 42.

[65] Product liability—Law Commission, https://lawcom.gov.uk/project/product-liability/#4-Updates.

[66] Compare general policy statements such as wanting 'a more active pro-competition strategy to deliver more targeted and effective pro-competitive interventions' (Department for Business, Energy and Industrial Strategy, *Reforming Competition and Consumer Policy: Driving Growth and Delivering Competitive Markets that Work for Consumers* (2021) at 0.15). See also the UK government policy paper *Establishing a Pro-innovation Approach to Regulating AI* (CP 728, (2022)).

(d) Digital Markets, Competition and Consumers Act 2024

(i) Digital Markets

The Digital Markets, Competition and Consumers Act 2024 (DMCCA 24) broadly followed the EU Digital Markets Act (DMA)[67] in providing general competition/market structure rules for 'strategic market players' such as Google, Apple, Microsoft, and the like in digital markets.[68] It claims to be more flexible and principles-based than the EU approach that imposes a blanket set of obligations on all gatekeepers.

(ii) Consumer Protection

The DMCCA 24 also contains a number of consumer protection provisions which were heralded by soundbites around the establishment of 'a more active pro-competition strategy to deliver more targeted and effective pro-competitive interventions'.[69] Yet, although the DMCCA 24 does, for example, provide a (welcome)[70] sharpening of enforcement powers,[71] other changes are more modest. For example, it repeals[72] the consumer protection from the Unfair Trading Regulations 2008 (CPUTR 2008), which transposed the EU Unfair Commercial Practices Directive (UCPD), only to resurrect them, with some tweaks, in the DMCCA 24 itself.[73] The DMCCA 24 also makes it clear that drip pricing is not allowed, by requiring that the total price has to be provided or else there will be a material omission.[74] This makes express what is implicit within the UCPD.[75] A similar pattern can also be seen in relation to ADR notification duties.[76]

The impact of these tweaks, in terms of levels of protection, is mixed. For example, under the CPUTR 2008, following the UCPD, it was provided that if traders could reasonably foresee that a group of consumers were vulnerable to a practice, then this vulnerability should be taken into account in assessing whether the practice had sufficient effect on consumers to count as misleading or aggressive.[77] This rule stays in place, but as well as the criteria counting as vulnerability until now (age, physical or mental health, and credulity), the DMCCA 24 seems to have improved protection

[67] Regulation (EU) 2022/1925.
[68] Pt 2, rules, eg, on discriminatory terms, bundling or tying services, abuse of market power to dominate designated activities or in mergers.
[69] Department for Business, Energy and Industrial Strategy, *Reforming Competition and Consumer Policy: Driving Growth and Delivering Competitive Markets that Work for Consumers* (2021) at 0.15.
[70] K Beioley, 'CMA Chair Tyrie Steps Down Early Pointing to "Inherent Limits" of Role', *Financial Times* (18 June 2020).
[71] Digital Markets, Competition and Consumers Act 2024, Pt 3.
[72] ibid s 251.
[73] ibid Pt 4, Ch 1.
[74] ibid s 230.
[75] Guidance 4.2.8.
[76] Digital Markets, Competition and Consumers Act 2024, Pt 4, Ch 4.
[77] Consumer Protection from Unfair Trading Regulations 2008, SI 2008/1277, reg 2(5).

by including vulnerability to 'the product' and vulnerability based on 'the circumstances the [consumers] are in'.[78] Vulnerability to 'the product' might allow account to be taken, for example, of whether addictive digital interfaces might be likely to pressurize consumers who would otherwise not be vulnerable. Vulnerability based on the consumer's 'circumstances' might, for example, allow consideration of financial difficulties, which might make some consumers more susceptible than others to being misled or pressured by online loan offers. So, in this respect, the law in the UK may now be more protective than the UCPD, which does not recognize these forms of vulnerability and, as it is a full harmonization directive, does not allow for greater protection in the member states than is provided for by the UCPD itself.[79]

In other respects, however, the DMCCA 24 may reduce protection compared to the UCPD. For example, under the UCPD, and the CPUTR 2008, an aggressive practice could (and, in the case of the UCPD, still can) be established by *coercion*, *harassment*, or *undue influence* significantly impairing 'freedom of choice' and being likely to cause a consumer transactional decision that would not otherwise be taken.[80] In the case of *undue influence*, this had to involve impairment of freedom of choice in the form of an *uninformed* decision.[81] However, the overarching freedom of choice concept (in the UCPD and under the CPUTR 2008) which is applicable to *coercion* and *harassment* is wider. It arguably includes situations where consumers have limited power/choice but do what the trader wants because, for example, of addictive interfaces or threats to take enforcement action for disputed debts.[82] Here the consumer will usually make a well-informed choice. Indeed, it is exactly *because* they understand their lack of practical substantive choice that they give in to the harassment or coercion. However, the DMCCA 24 omits this broader overarching freedom of choice element. It refers solely to coercion, harassment, or undue influence affecting transactional decision making, while keeping the requirement that undue influence must involve uninformed decision making.[83] This might lead regulators and courts to conclude that, as with undue influence, there can only be an aggressive practice in the case of coercion or harassment if the consumer's *informed* decision making is impaired: so, if there is sufficient *transparency*, there can be no aggressive practice, even if the consumer has little power/choice. A consumer may, for example, make a purchase due to an addictive interface; yet there might be no unfair practice, even though leaving the site is in practice very hard, as long as it was made clear that the consumer could leave the site if they wished—the consumer has now made an informed decision to stay.

[78] Digital Markets Competition and Consumers Act 2024, s 247(3)–(4).

[79] Art 4.

[80] Unfair Commercial Practices Directive (n 13) Art 8; Consumer Protection from Unfair Trading Regulations (n 77) reg 7(1).

[81] Unfair Commercial Practices Directive (n 13) Art 2(j); Consumer Protection from Unfair Trading Regulations (n 77) reg 7(3)(b).

[82] *OFT v Ashbourne Management Services* [2011] EWHC 1237 (Ch), where threatening to report a consumer to a credit reference agency for a disputed debt was an aggressive practice.

[83] Digital Markets Competition and Consumers Act 2024, ss 228(1), 228(3)(b).

The Digital Markets, Competition and Consumer Bill also made a number of headlines when introduced, most notably around the subscription contract traps[84] and the regulation of fake reviews.[85] Subscription traps are a typical online problem where consumers might believe they are making one-off payments, but later discover they are trapped in an expensive long-term contract. The DMCCA 24 provisions on subscription contracts are complex, but essentially provide for a fourteen-day cancellation period as well as detailed pre-contract and subsequent information/warnings. This broadly reflects EU enforcement action against subscription traps under the UCPD.[86]

In respect of fake reviews, despite the headlines there were actually no provisions on fake reviews in the original Bill and, in fact, fake reviews could have easily been dealt with under pre-existing legislation![87] While the Bill was moving through Parliament the government did consult on fake reviews,[88] with the result that it was decided that there would be new banned practices[89] relating to fake reviews but the liability would only be civil liability.[90] This broadly follows the Modernization Directive (MD) provision[91] that it is a misleading omission (an unfair practice under the UCPD regime) if traders do not provide information about whether and how they are sure consumer reviews originate from those who have genuinely used the product.

(e) Glimpses of Continued Alignment

(i) Conservative Government Pre-2024

Thus, although voluntary alignment was controversial to many Brexit supporters, the Conservative government's DMCCA 24 broadly aligns with corresponding EU provisions. Another example from the Conservative era is the EU's Circular Economy Plan.[92] Here EU initiatives have been followed in the Eco-design for Energy Related Products and Energy Information Regulations 2021,[93] which in addition to covering

[84] J Reilly, 'MONEY TRAPS: Ministers Set to Crackdown on "Subscription Traps" Costing Brits £1.6bn per Year', *The Sun* (22 April 2023).

[85] J Clark, 'CRACK DOWN: Five New "Laws" to Stop Brits Being Ripped Off Including Fake Review Fines and a Subscription Trap Ban', *The Sun* (19 July 2021).

[86] European Commission, Study on Misleading "Free" Trials and Subscription Traps for Consumers in the EU (2017), https://op.europa.eu/en/publication-detail/-/publication/bf621260-9441-11e7-b92d-01aa75ed71a1; Guidance 2.96.

[87] Compare CMA, 'Press Release: CMA Intervention Leads to Further Facebook Action on Fake Reviews' (9 April 2021).

[88] Department for Business and Trade, *Smarter Regulation: Consultation on Improving Price Transparency and Product Information for Consumers* (September 2023).

[89] See now See Digital Markets, Competition and Consumers Act 2024, Sch 20, para 13. Note also s 237(8) (breach of Sch 20, para 13 not a criminal offence).

[90] Department for Business and Trade, *Government Response to Consultation on 'Smarter Regulation: Improving Consumer Price Transparency and Product Information for Consumers* (January 2024).

[91] Directive (EU) 2019/2161, Art 3(4)(c).

[92] https://environment.ec.europa.eu/strategy/circular-economy-action-plan_en.

[93] SI 2021/745.

design and labelling requirements introduce a right to repair by requiring manufacturers of certain products to make spare parts and information on repairs to be available to professional repairers.[94]

(ii) Labour Government 2024

The incoming Labour government's election manifesto[95] contained general commitments (such as the Green Prosperity Plan[96]) which would benefit consumers as well as specific consumer law commitments in relation to energy market regulation[97] and ticket touting.[98] The subsequent King's Speech contained a number of Bills which might impact generally on consumers (such as a Passenger Railway Services (Public Ownership) Bill, a Better Buses Bill and a Water (Special Measures) Bill) as well as more specific consumer measures in a Product Regulation and Metrology Bill.

The subsequent Product Regulation and Metrology Act 2025 may mark an important step in voluntary alignment in the consumer protection arena.[99] Here the UK had already taken a step in that direction by not requiring the UKCA mark to be used for many products if the CE marking was used.[100] The Act proposes enabling powers that would allow the UK to align with developing EU rules. It even gives an express power to adopt EU regulations making provision, in relation to the marketing or use of products in the United Kingdom, which corresponds, or is similar, to a provision of relevant EU law for the purpose of reducing or mitigating the environmental impact of products.[101] It also moves UK law into line with the EU's DSA by allowing enforcement action in relation to unsafe goods to be taken against online marketplaces.[102]

(f) The Role of the Courts

The courts also have a role to play in the future directions of consumer law and policy. The Supreme Court is not bound by 'retained EU case law' and, in deciding whether or not to depart from such case law, the Supreme Court (currently) has to apply the same tests as it would apply in deciding whether or not to depart from its own case law.[103] The European Union (Withdrawal Agreement) Act 2020, section 26(1), made it possible for regulations to be introduced making provision for other courts or tribunals not to be bound by 'retained EU case law'. This was done, for example in relation

[94] See, eg, Sched 13.
[95] Labour Party Manifesto, *Change* (June 2024).
[96] ibid 50.
[97] ibid 54.
[98] ibid 87.
[99] Even in the King's Speech there was a suggestion of voluntary alignment in respect of the proposed Product Regulation and Metrology Bill: see Prime Minister's Office, *The King's Speech 2024: Background Briefing Notes* (17 July 2024) 37.
[100] The Product Safety and Metrology etc (Amendment) Regulations 2024, SI 2024/696.
[101] Section 1(2).
[102] See, eg, ss 2 and 3.
[103] European Union (Withdrawal) Act 2018, s 6(5).

to the Court of Appeal, under the European Union (Withdrawal) Act 2018 (Relevant Court) (Retained EU Case Law) Regulations 2020.[104]

The Retained EU Law (Revocation and Reform) Act 2023, section 6 would have made changes, from 1 October 2024, to the European Union (Withdrawal) Act 2018, section 6, but that reform has now been paused. If that reform is brought into effect, the European Union (Withdrawal) Act 2018, section 6(5) would read:

> (5) In deciding whether to depart from any assimilated EU case law by virtue of subsection (4)(a), (b) or (ba), the higher court concerned must (among other things) have regard to—
> (a) the fact that decisions of a foreign court are not (unless otherwise provided) binding;
> (b) any changes of circumstances which are relevant to the assimilated EU case law;
> (c) the extent to which the assimilated EU case law restricts the proper development of domestic law.

The last factor is potentially the most relevant for future consumer decisions and it will be interesting to see how future courts handle some of the issues we considered in the previous case law.[105] For example, we noted above[106] that the Supreme Court applied the agreements test in assessing the unfairness of terms, but did so in a restricted way that took account of the trader's interests. The Supreme Court may now feel emboldened to state that should be the test even if the EU law differs. Equally, its preference in the bank charges case not to differentiate between core and ancillary terms might be maintained notwithstanding subsequent Court of Justice case law. Approaches of this sort could be said to align with common law tradition which has traditionally been resistant to substantive fairness interventions.[107]

It will be interesting to see how it approaches transparency, which has been so aggressively used by the Court of Justice to assist litigants, but has not yet been litigated in the UK. Although the Consumer Rights Act 2015 seems to go further as regards physical transparency by also requiring prominence, the UK courts might be less keen to ensure the consequences of the terms are understandable to the average consumer as well as being grammatically clear. This might be said to reflect common law tradition. In one sense, notwithstanding the UK legislative trajectory of relatively high standards of transparency, the *common law* tradition pulls in the direction of low standards of transparency. For example, the common law incorporation rules on standard terms generally[108] require only reasonable notice that terms exist, not that

[104] SI 2020/1525.
[105] See section 1(f).
[106] ibid.
[107] See S Lee and C Willett, 'Brexit Ideologies and UK Digital Consumer Law' in E Bergaimin and C Willett, *Consumer Protection and the Digital Economy: A Research Companion* (Routledge 2025).
[108] Aside from special prominence rules in the case of the most extreme or unusual cases of substantive unfairness: *Interfoto Picture Library v Stiletto Visual Programmes* [1988] 1 All ER 348.

they are immediately available or are expressed in a transparent manner, far less anything approaching the sort of rigorous spelling out of risks in the CJEU approach.[109] This is of course just conjecture and the UK courts may well be as supportive of consumer protection as the CJEU.

The conservative approach to assessing defectiveness in the artificial hip cases might be maintained on the basis that it accords with a significant strand in UK scholarship that argues the concept of defect, especially when there is a development risks defence, is conceptually incoherent and there is no logically discernible mid-point between strict and absolute liability.[110] Indeed, it might go further and move the standard in practice even closer to a fault-based one. Certainly one might imagine warnings being able to act as a protective shield to a greater extent than they will in EU law, especially given the recent reforms (not part of assimilated law) that do not treat a warning as sufficient to excuse an otherwise defective product. This is all of course conjecture. The courts seem to indicate they will be cautious in amending EU-derived law.[111] The one instance where they have done so to date was because there was no justification given for the ruling in the Court of Justice decision.[112]

3 Post-Brexit Legality: Consistency with the TCA

(a) EU–UK Trade and Cooperation Agreement: Consumer Law and Policy

The EU–UK Trade and Cooperation Agreement covers a wide variety of issues, including trade in goods and services (although not, for example, equivalences for financial services[113]), aviation and road transport, digital trade, and energy. In respect of consumer protection, the Preamble to the Agreement recognized the parties' autonomy in respect of consumer protection generally,[114] but also noted a *desire* that the 'Agreement contributes to consumer welfare through policies ensuring a high level of

[109] *Parker v South Eastern Railway* (1877) 2 CPD 416.
[110] See (n 32).
[111] See, eg, *Merck Serono v Comptroller-General of Patents* [2025] EWCA Civ 45.
[112] *Industrial Cleaning v Intelligent Cleaning Equipment* [2023] EWCA Civ 1451.
[113] See, however, Joint Declaration on Financial Services Regulatory Cooperation between the European Union and the United Kingdom (December 2020). See also Memorandum of Understanding establishing a framework for financial services regulatory cooperation between the European Union and the United Kingdom of Great Britain and Northern Ireland (June 2023). See also: https://www.gov.uk/government/publications/joint-statement-eu-uk-financial-regulatory-forum-october-2023/joint-eu-uk-financial-regulatory-forum-joint-statement-october-2023 and https://www.gov.uk/government/publications/joint-statement-eu-uk-financial-regulatory-forum-may-2024/joint-eu-uk-financial-regulatory-forum.
[114] Trade and Cooperation Agreement between the European Union and the European Atomic Energy Community, of the one part, and the United Kingdom of Great Britain and Northern Ireland, of the other part [2021] OJ L 149/10, see also Art 123(2).

consumer protection and economic well-being, as well as encouraging cooperation between relevant authorities'.[115] The Preamble also noted the opportunities presented by digital trade and the issue of 'unjustified barriers' in that area.

Explicit consumer protection provisions in the Agreement include: marking or labelling of products;[116] cooperation on market surveillance and non-food product safety and compliance;[117] particular postal services;[118] promoting transparent and reasonable rates for international mobile roaming services;[119] safety of medicinal products;[120] and air travel.[121] There are also commitments around digital trade, particularly in respect of building consumer trust.[122] The Agreement also refers on numerous occasions to 'fair competition' or the equivalent, which is of interest given the link between competition law and consumer law.[123]

(b) Current Position

The regulatory changes to date are unlikely to affect the level playing field. If anything, the Product Regulation and Metrology Act 2025 is seeking to provide the means for future alignment. One measure which could have caused serious disruption would have been insistence on the use of the UKCA marking instead of the CE marking. However, as noted above,[124] the government is now allowing continued reliance on the CE marking for many categories of products. In the product safety field there has been discussion of and support for developing smarter regulation digital means of complying with labelling requirements.[125] However, these moves are unlikely to cause a breach as the government notes that the EU is thinking along similar lines and that it will follow the EU developments closely.[126]

[115] ibid; see also Art 770.

[116] ibid, which, under Art 95(2)(a), 'shall only require information which is relevant for consumers or users of the product or information that indicates that the product conforms to the mandatory technical requirements'.

[117] ibid Art 96.

[118] ibid Art 162.

[119] ibid Art 181.

[120] ibid Annex 12.

[121] ibid Art 438(2): 'the Parties shall ensure that effective and non-discriminatory measures are taken to protect the interests of consumers in air transport. Such measures shall include the appropriate access to information, assistance including for persons with disabilities and reduced mobility, reimbursement and, if applicable, compensation in case of denied boarding, cancellation or delays, and efficient complaint handling procedures.'

[122] ibid Art 208.

[123] ibid Arts 355, 359.

[124] See section 2(e)(ii).

[125] Department for Business, Energy and Industrial Strategy, *Smarter Regulation: UK Product Safety Review* (August 2023).

[126] Department for Business and Trade, *Government Response to Product Safety Review and Next Steps* (2024).

4 Post-Brexit Empirical and Normative Analysis: Three Dimensions

(a) Regulatory Impact

(i) Overview

Prior to Brexit, the Conservative government made it clear that there was no fundamental desire to dismantle consumer rights derived from the EU. It is true that under the last government there was also some rhetoric about using the freedoms to improve the law and it also reported some negative comments about some EU measures, such as the EU's Product Safety Pledge.[127] Permitting e-labelling was seen as one way the UK could gain a competitive advantage. However, the Labour government is clearly trying to find ways to enhance alignment. Perhaps our biggest criticism is that the UK has not set out its stall as to its future approach to consumer law and policy. In a separate paper[128] we call for targeted distinctive alignment. There is certainly more of a sense that alignment is becoming a government policy, but the nature of the rationale for such alignment is not yet clear. It seems to be based on facilitating trade rather than any distinctive vision of consumer protection.

We have noted that positive UK legislative actions have not, to date, brought about serious divergences in the field of consumer law. Rather, we consider the greater risk is from the EU consumer agenda moving on and the UK not keeping pace with it. We will give four examples. The first is the lack of a representative action in the UK for consumer claims compared to the rest of Europe, which is a very stark reminder of how the enforcement landscape would potentially be different if we were still in the EU. The other three examples reflect the development of EU consumer law to address technological challenges. Product safety and product liability rules have both been amended, moving them beyond the UK law. As regards contractual rights, the EU has adopted rules for conformity of digital content and services. Ironically, the UK had, through its Consumer Rights Act 2015, been a leader in this space, but the EU has developed a more sophisticated regime.

(ii) Representative Actions

In practical terms, one of the most significant illustrations to date of Brexit's impact on UK consumer law is that the UK has not been required to introduce a representative action for consumers. The EU Representative Actions Directive[129] is based around the designation of qualified entities to bring actions to protect the collective

[127] Call for Evidence Product Safety Review, 10.

[128] Geraint Howells, Chris Willett, and James Devenney, 'The Acts and Scenes of the Brexit Consumer Law and Policy Melodrama … ' in Christian Twigg-Flesner and James Devenney (eds), *Disruption, Innovation and Re-alignment in UK Consmer Law and Policy* (Hart 2026).

[129] Directive (EU) 2020/1828 of the European Parliament and of the Council of 25 November 2020 on representative actions for the protection of the collective interests of consumers [2020] OJ L409/1.

consumer interest. Qualified entities can be public bodies or consumer organizations, so long as the latter meet specific criteria.[130] They are entitled to seek both injunctive and redress measures.[131] The effectiveness of these measures for providing consumer redress typically depends on whether they are opt-out regimes allowing the representative to claim for the harm caused to all affected consumers, and on the relevant funding options available to finance the litigation. The directive leaves it to member states to determine whether the mechanism adopted for redress measures is an opt-in or opt-out regime.[132] Third party funding is permitted if allowed under national law but there need to be controls to limit the influence of the funders.[133] So the effectiveness of the regime will depend heavily on the choices made by member states. The UK, by contrast, has no such general representative action procedure. It does have a collective redress procedure in the competition field,[134] which is very successful precisely because it allows opt-out claims that are financed by venture capital funds under damage-based fee agreements. The government has decided that any extension of the collective procedure to other areas will be on an incremental basis, after evaluating how collective redress in the competition field works in practice. There seems no appetite yet to extend the competition regime, whose very dynamic use may be a reason for hesitation in providing more collective redress mechanisms. In practice, many of the competition cases seem to be consumer cases where unfair terms are alleged to result in abuse of a dominant position.

(iii) Product Safety

The EU Directive has now been replaced by the General Product Safety Regulation,[135] which modernizes the law with respect to technology by considering factors such as the interconnectedness of products (internet of things)[136] and the evolving, learning, and predictive functionalities of AI products.[137] It also extends the potentially responsible parties to fulfilment services providers and, in limited circumstances, online platforms. The information and communication mechanisms have been reformed. The new structure, now named *Safety Gate*, has three elements: (i) Safety Gate Rapid Alert System (rapid non-food information exchange between national authorities and Commission); (ii) Safety Gate Portal (complaints from the public); and (iii) Safety Business Gateway (for businesses to fulfil their obligations to inform national authorities).

[130] ibid Art 4.
[131] ibid Art 7(4).
[132] Dir 2020/1828 (n 129) recital 43.
[133] ibid Art 10.
[134] G Howells, 'Class Actions in the UK and Ireland. A Tale of Two Common Laws Diverging Post-Brexit' [2024] EJCL 277.
[135] Regulation (EU) 2023/988 of the European Parliament and of the Council of 10 May 2023 on general product safety [2023] OJ L135/1.
[136] ibid Art 6(1)(b).
[137] ibid Art 6(1)(h).

The Labour government has stressed the importance of product safety by introducing, as noted above, the Product Regulation and Metrology Act 2025 in its first legislative session. One senses that an important aspect of this was to give it the freedom to continue to align with the EU moving forward where it chooses to do so. However, one of the important themes in the earlier *Product Safety Review*[138] was the desire to move to a more hazard-based regulation. This was clearly intended to signal a streamlined approach to regulation and be potentially deregulatory. How the tension between achieving a change in regulatory approach and seeking continued alignment with EU law works out will be an important touchstone for testing where the priorities lie going forward. Of course, it is possible that the EU would also be thinking of similar changes to promote its competitiveness, but unfortunately the UK is no longer able to directly influence these internal debates.

(iv) Product liability

The EU has adopted a new product liability[139] directive.[140] This brings software within the definition of a product;[141] introduces liability for substantially modified products;[142] extends the range of potential defendants to include authorized representatives, fulfilment service providers, online platforms in some circumstances, and substantial modifiers;[143] ensures that the features of AI, the internet of things, and cybersecurity risks are included within the definition of defectiveness;[144] takes account of the ability to update and upgrade software when determining the time to assess defectiveness and the state of scientific and technical knowledge for the purpose of the development risks defence;[145] expands damages to include psychological harm and destruction or corruption of data;[146] extends the expiry (long-stop limitation) period to bring a case to twenty-five years in the case of latent personal injury;[147] and introduces access to justice reforms on disclosure of evidence and the burden of proof.[148] It is unclear how far the UK will follow these reforms. It seems, based on the *Product Safety Review*, that the government will be open to including software within the strict products liability regime. However, it was not included in the Product Regulation and Metrology Act 2025.

[138] *Smarter Regulation UK Product Safety Review* (2023).
[139] J Devenney and G Howells, 'Developing Product Liability Networks for AI Systems in the Medical Context' (2025) 76 NILQ 118.
[140] Dir 2024/2863/EU.
[141] ibid Art 4(1).
[142] ibid Arts 4(180) and 8(2).
[143] ibid Art 8(1)(c) and 8(4).
[144] ibid Art 7(2)(c), (d) and (f).
[145] ibid Art 7(2)(f) and 11(1)(e).
[146] ibid Art 6.
[147] ibid Art 17(2).
[148] ibid Arts 9 and 10.

(v) Digital Content

Another key post-Brexit EU provision is the Digital Content and Services Directive 2019.[149] Digital content is data produced and supplied in digital form under a contract from a supplier to a consumer,[150] for example download of films, apps, games, and so on. A digital service is one allowing 'the consumer to create, process, store or access [digital] data . . . or . . . allowing . . . sharing . . . or any other interaction with [digital] data uploaded or created by the consumer or other [service] user',[151] for example storage and sharing of consumer data in the cloud, on phones, on social media, and so on, and processing of consumer data in the provision of money transfer and payment service. Since 2015 the UK, through the Consumer Rights Act 2015, has had similar rules for digital content, but digital services were not covered. Also, whereas the EU Directive covered digital content and services supplied in return for data, in UK law there needs to be a price paid—though there is power to extend this to cover contracts made using data by ministerial order.

Under the EU Directive both digital content and digital services must conform to the contract.[152] Conformity depends on express contractual provisions ('subjective' standards).[153] Crucially, it also includes non-excludable 'objective' requirements on fitness for purpose, quantity, accessories, instructions, compliance with trials and reviews, and updates, as well as on quality.[154] Where these conformity standards are breached, consumers have the right to have the digital content or service brought into conformity, price reduction, and/or termination.[155]

The EU seems to have benefited from the UK's experience to produce a more sophisticated set of rules. For example, when assessing conformity it made it clear that relevant factors include functionality, compatibility, accessibility, continuity, and security.[156] The EU Directive, unlike the UK Act, does not mention repair and replacement as specific remedies, but the recitals show the drafters were attuned to the digital context and cite issuing updates and providing a new copy as potential forms of cure.[157] The directive also considers how data should be handled once the contract has been ended.[158] Obligations to update have been introduced by the EU[159] and these provide for an innovative, potentially long-term post-contractual obligation.[160]

[149] Directive (EU) 2019/770 of the European Parliament and of the Council of 20 May 2019 on certain aspects concerning contracts for the supply of digital content and digital services [2019] OJ L136/1; J Morais Carvalho, 5/2019, EuCML.

[150] ibid Art 2(1).

[151] ibid Art 2(2); where the consumer is enabled to process data supplied by the trader—this seems to be both the supply of digital content and a digital service.

[152] Dir 2019/770 (n 149) Art 6.

[153] ibid Art 7, eg, on description, quantity and quality, functionality, compatibility, interoperability, fitness for particular purpose, accessories, instructions and updates.

[154] ibid Art 8.

[155] ibid Arts 14–18.

[156] ibid Art 8(1)(b).

[157] ibid recital 63.

[158] ibid Art 16.

[159] ibid Arts 7 and 8.

[160] See L Nogler and U Reifner (eds), *Life Time Contracts: Social Longterm Contracts in Labour, Tenancy and Consumer Credit Law* (Eleven, 2014).

(b) Economic Impact

To date it is hard to assess whether the regulatory burden will be significantly different post-Brexit in the EU or the UK. The lack of a representative action may be the most significant difference, but unless member states choose to make it opt-out and allow third party funding the EU Representative Actions Directive may not have a major impact. The EU has moved forward with some enhancements of the law to address technological developments. However, there are no signs yet that the UK will strike out in a remarkably different deregulatory route. Indeed, as regards product safety standards, the mood music is in favour of continued alignment. It is true that the UK is looking to enhance its competitiveness through more efficient regulation, but the Draghi report on *The Future of European Competitiveness* indicates that the EU is also likely to be developing its regulation in a more pro-business manner.

The precise economic impact of Brexit is, of course, keenly contested.[161] However, in March 2022 the Office for Budget Responsibility found that *goods* exports to the EU fell by 9 per cent in the fourth quarter of 2021 compared with 2019,[162] and this was not offset by exports to non-EU countries, which were down even more, by 18 per cent, in the same period.[163] In the same period, goods imported from the EU decreased by 18 per cent, whereas imports from non-EU countries increased by 10 per cent in the same period. Exports of *services* to the EU were down 5–10 per cent in the same period, while imports of services were down by about 30 per cent.[164] Some care needs to be taken with these figures given, for example, their proximity to the end of the transition period,[165] the delays in implementing full customs checks at the UK border,[166] and the current degree of regulatory alignment between the UK and EU in certain sectors, as well as distorting global factors such as the Covid-19 pandemic and the war in Ukraine (which impacted prices for energy, which is largely imported from outside the EU[167]).[168] Nevertheless, the Office of Budget Responsibility's most recent

[161] See, eg, R Freeman, K Manova, T Prayer and T Sampson, 'UK Trade in the Wake of Brexit' (Centre for Economic Performance Discussions Paper No.1847 (2022)).

[162] Office for Budget Responsibility, *The Latest Evidence on the Impact of Brexit on UK Trade* (March 2022). See also J Springford, *The Cost of Brexit* (Centre for European Reform, December 2021).

[163] ibid. In respect of services the Office for Budget Responsibility noted: 'UK services trade with the EU has fallen by more relative to 2019 levels than non-EU trade . . . However, much of this decline is likely to reflect the impact of the pandemic, particularly in sectors such as travel and transport that accounted for a greater proportion of pre-pandemic EU services trade than non-EU. UK service exports to the EU and rest of the world have recovered to around 5 and 10 per cent below 2019 levels while imports of services from the EU are still down by over 30 per cent.'

[164] ibid.

[165] 31 December 2020.

[166] Discussed by K Forster-van Aerssen and T Spital, *The Impact of Brexit on UK Trade and Labour Markets* (2023) ECB Economic Bulletin.

[167] Office for Budget Responsibility (n 162).

[168] ibid.

assessment[169] concludes that its 'assumptions about the impact of Brexit appear to be broadly on track'. Moreover, there is also evidence of emerging regulatory differences (and uncertainty about future directions[170]) impacting on UK businesses' trading (and possibly appetite for trading) in the EU[171]), as well as EU businesses' appetite to trade in the UK.[172] There is evidence that Brexit significantly worsened the cost of living crisis in the UK[173] and that trade frictions often manifest in a negative impact for the price sensitivity of consumers.[174]

(c) Territorial Impact

Northern Ireland poses a number of challenges for Brexit in general and post-Brexit trade in particular.[175] It has also been the backdrop to some of the straining of the relationship between the UK and EU. It has created issues for consumers in Northern Ireland, with the Northern Ireland Consumer Council reporting,[176] for example, issues with the supply, availability, delivery times, and costs of online shopping,[177] as well as Great Britain retailers no longer delivering to Northern Ireland.[178] Post-Brexit, the border between Northern Ireland and Ireland became a land border between the EU and the UK. One issue was how to protect trade between Ireland and the United Kingdom.[179] A related conundrum was how to ensure that goods crossing the border complied with relevant EU (or indeed UK) regulations without having a hard border

[169] Office for Budget Responsibility, *How Are Our Brexit Trade Forecast Assumptions Performing?* (March 2024).

[170] ibid.

[171] See, eg, British Chamber of Commerce, *Brexit at Three: Fresh Trade Challenges Growing* (December 2023): 'Almost two thirds (60%) of firms trading with the EU say it is now more difficult to do so than it was a year ago . . . Almost half (49%) of exporters disagree the Brexit deal is helping them grow sales . . . Two fifths (41%) of firms exporting under the Brexit deal say they face difficulties adapting to its rules on buying and selling goods.'

[172] See, eg, KPMG and British Chamber of Commerce in Germany, *100 Days of Brexit—An Interim Conclusion* (2021). See also https://kpmg.com/de/en/home/media/press-releases/2024/04/brexit-continues-to-be-a-burden-for-companies.html.

[173] See, eg, JD Bakker, N Datta, R Davies, and J De Lyon, *Brexit and Consumer Food Prices: 2023 Update* (Centre for Economic Performance, Brexit Analysis No 18, 2023).

[174] See, eg, R Freeman, K Manova, T Prayer and T Sampson, 'UK Trade in the Wake of Brexit' (Centre for Economic Performance Discussions Paper No 1847, 2022).

[175] See, eg, the University of Strathclyde's Fraser of Allander Institute, *The New Northern Ireland Protocol: Is Northern Ireland Stuck in the Middle?* (29 November 2021).

[176] Consumer Council, *Northern Ireland Consumers and EU Exit: An Overview of EU Exit Experiences in 2023* (2023).

[177] ibid 12.7.

[178] ibid 12.6.

[179] Department for Exiting the European Union, *The United Kingdom's Exit from and New Partnership with the European Union* (Cm 9417 (2017)) at 4.3: 'Maintaining our strong and historic ties with Ireland will be an important priority for the UK in the talks ahead. This includes protecting the Common Travel Area (CTA) . . . The UK and Irish economies are deeply integrated, through trade and cross-border investments, as well as through the free flow of goods, utilities, services and people. Annual trade between the UK and Ireland stands at over £43 billion, while around 60 per cent of Northern Ireland's goods exports to the EU are to Ireland.'

on the island of Ireland, which was politically very sensitive.[180] This conundrum became embroiled in the issue of the so-called backstop. The 'backstop' was replaced, in the revised EU–UK Withdrawal Agreement,[181] through the Revised Protocol on Ireland/Northern Ireland. This prevented the need for a hard border on the island of Ireland by aligning Northern Ireland to a limited set of EU rules including VAT and excise in respect of goods and, particularly important for the current chapter, some consumer-focused product requirements.

Yet this, in effect, created a border in the Irish Sea by, for example, creating checks on certain goods entering Northern Ireland from Great Britain. This was so even if the goods were to remain in Northern Ireland. This angered some communities in Northern Ireland[182] and was modified by the Windsor Agreement,[183] which created two lanes for goods coming into Northern Ireland from Great Britain: a green lane (for goods which would remain in Northern Ireland) and a red lane (for goods which would go on to the EU across the Northern Ireland/Ireland border).

Nevertheless, the Democratic Unionist Party (DUP), concerned about the potential detachment of Northern Ireland from the rest of the United Kingdom, refused to support the Windsor Framework and continued to boycott Stormont power-sharing until 30 January 2024, when it was widely reported that the DUP had endorsed a new trade deal for Northern Ireland proposed by the UK government. More detail followed on 31 January 2024 with the publication of the *Safeguarding the Union* policy paper.[184] A key focus of the deal was strengthening the UK internal market[185] through, for example, replacing the green lane with an internal market system,[186] establishing a new body (IntertradeUK) to champion trade within the UK,[187] and modifying the EU (Withdrawal) Act 2018 in connection with the Stormont Brake procedure set out in the Northern Ireland Protocol/Windsor Framework.[188] Significantly, as Northern Ireland remains subject to some EU laws (including consumer laws), there was to be a legal duty for ministers to consider whether Bills in the Houses of Parliament (which, for example, seek to move away from EU laws in England, Scotland, and Wales) would affect trade between Northern Ireland and the rest of the UK.[189] This was given effect by a new section 13C in the European Union (Withdrawal) Act 2018.[190] This was

[180] See, generally, F Cochrane, *Breaking Peace: Brexit and Northern Ireland* (Manchester University Press, 2020), particularly Ch 6. See also M Murphy, 'Northern Ireland and Brexit: Where Sovereignty and Stability Collide?' (2021) 29 Journal of Contemporary European Studies 405.

[181] See https://commission.europa.eu/strategy-and-policy/relations-non-eu-countries/relations-united-kingdom/eu-uk-withdrawal-agreement_en.

[182] See, eg, DUP, '7 Reasons the Irish Sea Border Must Go' (14 January 2022).

[183] See HM Government, *The Windsor Framework: A New Way Forward* (CP 806, 2023).

[184] Northern Ireland Office, *Safeguarding the Union* (CP 1021, 2024).

[185] See also the Windsor Framework (UK Internal Market and Unfettered Access) Regulations 2024, SI 163.

[186] *Safeguarding the Union* (n 184) [82]–[86].

[187] ibid [122]–[126].

[188] ibid [167]–[169].

[189] ibid [145]–[146].

[190] Inserted by Windsor Framework (Constitutional Status of Northern Ireland) Regulations 2024, SI 164, reg 3.

to be flanked by legislation which would prevent the UK government making new agreements with the EU which would create new barriers to trade between Northern Ireland and the rest of the UK.[191] This was given effect by a new section 38A in the European Union (Withdrawal Agreement) Act 2020.[192] The overall result of the foregoing is that it is now harder for the rest of the UK to move away from those consumer-focused EU laws which bind Northern Ireland.

5 Post-Brexit: Conclusion

There are no signs that EU consumer law will be dismantled in the UK. The Labour government has indicated it wants good relations with Europe to promote trade and the Product Regulation and Metrology Act 2025 paves the way for continued alignment. Yet, divergences are emerging. For the most part this is because the EU is moving ahead with its *consumer acquis*, mainly in response to technological developments. The UK is not dismantling EU law, but it is not keeping pace with it. When it does introduce domestic reform it certainly has a local flavour, derived at a minimum from drafting style, even if the underlying policy direction is aligned with the EU. It was probably always a myth that harmonized EU law would remove the need for local legal and compliance expertise. However, there are likely to be an increasing number of differences between the UK and EU which may in time affect the ease of trade. This certainly seems to be a negative consequence of Brexit, and the question is whether it is worthwhile introducing these new frictions into the system. If there were a new masterplan—Singapore-style deregulation or a more protective consumer regime—then one might argue some grit in the system was worthwhile. Absent a compelling vision, it seems regrettable.

A large unknown is also how court practice will develop. The common law has traditionally been seen as conservative and favouring certainty over broad flexible standards of the type introduced by the EU. One could imagine attempts to rein in the EU provisions, though common law judges have also shown themselves open to adapting principles to protect consumers. One suspects there will be a complex evolving story about interpretation in the UK courts of EU-inspired law post-Brexit. Also, the practical impact of reduced cooperation between UK and member state agencies may be a serious harm to practical enforcement. The good news is that this could be easily remedied if there is the will to do so. Doing so might be an important building block for building trust going forward.

[191] *Safeguarding the Union* (n 184) [69]-[71].
[192] Inserted by SI 164 (n 190) reg 2.

24
Environmental Law

*Elizabeth Fisher**

1 Introduction

What does it mean to make environmental law 'unbound' in light of Brexit? It is tempting to imagine it as a series of acts in which law and people become unconstrained by untying the binds of EU environmental regulation, so action is uninhibited by the EU legal order. UK environmental law can now unfurl and unfold. 'Un-' is a negative prefix. The image is of freeing the law from what is, and venturing out into unexplored negative space of the many things it could be. From this perspective, taking back control is about unimagined possibilities—legal, ideological, or otherwise.[1]

In this chapter, I present a different image of post-Brexit environmental law—one that is less about the negative space of possibility and more about the reality of what environmental law is. 'Taking back control' has involved the UK and its regions needing to take on more of the work of discharging the 'law jobs' that are inherent in environmental law.[2] There is no neat narrative. It has been a legally messy and dynamic process involving different actors, institutions, and developments.[3] It is a process that is ongoing. It is a process saturated in existing law and legal thought, and a study of those processes underscores how environmental law requires significant legal expertise—particularly in a post-Brexit legal world.

In this chapter, I begin with a sketch of the necessity and nature of environmental law and a brief explanation of pre-Brexit environmental law (section 2). I then chart the key legislative developments post-Brexit (section 3) and how they have evolved

* This chapter was completed with support from Leverhulme Trust MRF-2021-71. The views expressed in this chapter are my own academic views and are not those of the Office for Environmental Protection, of which I am a non-executive board member.

[1] Compare Jacob Rees-Mogg, 'Retained EU Law, Statement made on 22 September 2022' (Statement UIN HCWS298, UK Parliament), https://questions-statements.parliament.uk/written-statements/detail/2022-09-22/hcws298 accessed 8 November 2025 and Duncan French, 'Alternate Realities: Brexit and Pokémon' (OUP Blog 10 Oct 2016).

[2] On law jobs see K Llewellyn, 'The Normative, the Legal, and the Law-jobs: The Problem of Juristic Method' (1940) 49 Yale LJ 1355.

[3] In this regard it is more akin to a 'carrier bag' narrative, E Fisher, 'Telling Meaningful Stories about Climate Change and Public Law' (2025) 37 JEL 1.

Elizabeth Fisher, *Environmental Law* In: *The UK Regulatory Framework Post-Brexit: 'Law Unbound'*. Edited by: Paul Craig and Vilija Vėlyvytė, Oxford University Press. © Oxford University Press 2026. DOI: 10.1093/9780198969815.003.0027

the different law jobs involved in environmental law (section 4). In section 5, I conclude by discussing the legal expertise these jobs require.

Three points before starting. The analysis in this chapter is by no means exhaustive—environmental law is too sprawling a subject, and the developments post the referendum too numerous, for it to be possible to capture all developments in the space of 10,000 words. In this chapter, I focus primarily on the law relating to environmental problems within the UK; I thus leave out of the picture extra-territorial and trade issues. I also put to one side the Aarhus Convention on Access to Information, Public Participation in Decision-making and Access to Justice in Environmental Matters—an international Convention, aspects of which have been implemented through EU law directives.[4] Second, the starting point for analysis is the referendum, not the date on which the UK left the EU. This is because it was from 2016 onwards that there was debate about what the future of UK environmental law could and should look like. Third, in this chapter I am not focused on the substantive norms of environmental law and whether pre- or post-Brexit environmental law is 'better'. Rather, my focus is on the legal work that environmental law requires.

2 UK Environmental Law: Pre-Brexit

Environmental problems are situations where there is collective (albeit often contested) concern for the quality of the physical world.[5] That concern arises from real-world problems. Water pollution. Air pollution. The destruction of natural habitats. Climate change. Our down-to-earth reality is that we live in a physical world where our actions have consequences for others. Our pollution creates health risks. Our use of non-renewable resources is a zero-sum game. One community's choices about environmental quality have implications for others. And let us face it—we all produce sewage.

Environmental law is the law of environmental problems. It is a sprawling subject that stretches from localized problems (contaminated land) to global problems (climate change). The cause of problems can vary, as can the required response. Laws can relate to products, activities, and/or places. Given that environmental problems are collective problems, a significant part of environmental law is public law, and in particular administrative law.

Environmental law does not consist of a single environmental law 'job'. As will be discussed in section 3, at least seven can be identified in the public law context. These are: dealing with trouble cases; delineating jurisdiction; the defining of environmental

[4] See European Commission, 'The Aarhus Convention and the EU', https://environment.ec.europa.eu/law-and-governance/aarhus_en accessed 9 November 2025.

[5] E Fisher, B Lange, and E Scotford, *Environmental Law; Text, Cases and Materials* (2nd edn, Oxford University Press 2019) 23.

problems; the creation and operation of legal obligations; creating frameworks for the assembling and use of knowledge; administrative governance; and ensuring public institutions are accountable.[6]

The foundations of UK environmental law can be found in at least the nineteenth century, when laws were developed to address the serious consequences of industrialization and urbanization.[7] From the early 1970s to 2016, what is now the EU dominated the legal substance and legal imagination of UK environmental law.[8] This was because the EU from the early 1970s onwards developed a comprehensive and ambitious body of harmonized environmental law.[9] The catalysts for harmonization were 'common market' building and an explicit desire to develop an environment protection programme. The result was a sprawling collection of different forms of EU laws, legal norms, and governance structures concerned with environmental protection.[10]

In the mid-1990s it was said that 80 per cent of UK environmental legislation derived from the EU.[11] Much of that law related to environmental quality (air, water), nature, environmental assessment, and waste. EU institutions and norms played an important role in relation to all the different law jobs involved in environmental law. This was not just because EU laws defined environmental problems[12] and created obligations[13] but also because of the ability of the Commission to enforce EU law before the Court of Justice of the European Union (CJEU)[14] and because of the interpretative authority of that Court.[15]

With that said, UK law was not irrelevant—quite the opposite. First, most EU environmental laws are directives. Not only was the implementation and primary enforcement of EU environmental laws a task for UK public institutions (and thus UK public law), but EU directives were subsumed into UK law, often in the form of

[6] Fisher, 'Telling Meaningful Stories' (n 3) and on a longer discussion of law jobs see E Fisher, 'Public Law, the Levels of the Law, and Environmental Problems' Anuario De Derecho Público 2023 (Universidad Diego Portales 2024).

[7] B Pontin, 'Integrated Pollution Control in Victorian Britain: Rethinking Progress Within the History of Environmental Law' (2007) 19 JEL 173; B Pontin, *The Environmental Case for Brexit: A Socio-legal Perspective* (Hart 2020); S Coyle and K Morrow, *The Philosophical Foundations of Environmental Law: Property, Rights and Nature* (Hart 2004).

[8] I have discussed this in E Fisher, 'Executive Environmental Law' (2020) 83 MLR 163.

[9] E Fisher, 'Legal Imagination and European Union Environmental Law', in P Craig and G de Burca (eds), *The Evolution of European Union Law* (3rd edn, Oxford University Press 2021) Ch 27.

[10] S Kingston, V Heyvaert, and A Čavoški, *European Environmental Law* (Cambridge University Press 2017).

[11] R Lee, 'Always Keep a Hold of Nurse: British Environmental Law and Exit from the European Union' (2017) 29 JEL 155, 155.

[12] See, eg, Directive 2008/98/EC of the European Parliament and of the Council of 19 November 2008 on waste and repealing certain Directive [2008] OJ L312/3.

[13] Directive 2011/92/EU of the European Parliament and of the Council of 13 December 2011 on the assessment of the effects of certain public and private projects on the environment [2012] L26/1.

[14] Case C-56/90 *Commission v UK* EU:C:1993:307 (enforcement of bathing water directive).

[15] For a discussion in one area see E Fisher, 'Blazing Upstream? Strategic Environmental Assessment as "Hot" Law' in G Jones and E Scotford (eds), *The Strategic Environmental Assessment Directive: A Plan for Success* (Hart 2017).

delegated legislation.[16] While these environmental laws did give rise to both enforcement actions[17] and preliminary references,[18] they also gave rise to a rich body of national case law. Implementing laws, as well as the 'direct' and other effects of EU law, gave rise to a body of UK public law doctrine concerned with the implementation of EU environmental law.[19]

Second, and related to this, there were areas that EU environmental law only partially harmonized or that were not harmonized. Nature conservation is an example of the former,[20] and planning law an example of the latter. As planning law is the most important framework for delivering environmental laws (including EU laws) in the UK, that lack of harmonization was not insignificant.[21] Third, environmental law is dynamic, and new laws arise in response to new problems. In areas such as climate change, the EU did act,[22] but so did the UK—and initially in a way that was far more ambitious.[23]

Overall, EU and national law both played a role in discharging the seven environmental law jobs identified above, sometimes in tandem and sometimes as solely a national enterprise. In playing these roles, EU and UK law were entangled. Those entanglements were often manifest in UK legal disputes in which national courts were trying to determine what the implementation of EU environmental law norms required.[24] Sometimes these disputes raised questions of high constitutional principle,[25] sometimes they were about specific regimes,[26] and sometimes they raised more generic questions about administrative law norms.[27] In cases where environmental law was derived from EU law, EU law was the source of authoritative standards, but the legal cultures of the UK were the site for practical realization of any legal norm.

[16] For some examples currently on the books see Conservation of Habitats and Species Regulations 2017 SI 2017/1012 implementing Council Directive 92/43/EEC of 21 May 1992 on the conservation of natural habitats and of wild fauna and flora [1092] OJ L206/7; Environmental Assessment of Plans and Programmes Regulations 2004 implementing Directive 2001/42/EC of the European Parliament and of the Council of 27 June 2001 on the assessment of the effects of certain plans and programmes on the environment [2001] OJ L197/30.

[17] See, eg, Case C-6/04 *Commission v UK* EU:C:2005:372 (Habitats Directive—Directive 92/43/EEC).

[18] See, eg, Case C-290/03 *R (Diane Barker) v London Borough of Bromley* EU:C:2006:286 (EIA Directive).

[19] M Perraudeau, 'Back to the Future: Brexit, EIA and the Challenge of Environmental Judicial Review' (2019) 21 Env L Rev 6.

[20] Fisher, Lange, and Scotford (n 5) Ch 21.

[21] ibid Ch 19.

[22] Examples before 2016 include Directive 2009/28/EC of the European Parliament and of the Council of 23 April 2009 on the promotion of the use of energy from renewable sources and amending and subsequently repealing Directives 2001/77/EC and 2003/30/EC [2009] OJ L140/16 and Directive 2003/87/EC of the European Parliament and of the Council of 13 October 2003 establishing a scheme for greenhouse gas emission allowance trading within the Community and amending Council Directive 96/61/EC [2003] OJ L275/32.

[23] Climate Change Act 2008. For this reason, I will not focus much on climate change in this chapter.

[24] *Berkeley v Secretary of State For The Environment* [2000] UKHL 36 (EIA Directive).

[25] *R (HS2 Action Alliance) v The Secretary of State for Transport* [2014] UKSC 3 (parliamentary privilege and to a lesser extent sovereignty).

[26] *Morge v Hampshire County Council* [2011] UKSC 2.

[27] *Dover District Council v CPRE Kent* [2017] UKSC 79.

3 Legislative Developments: Post-Referendum

Given this situation, it was obvious to anyone working in environmental law that the outcome of the referendum was significant for UK environmental law. Post-referendum discussion focused on the need to ensure a robust legal architecture for environmental law to make it effective. The removal of the enforcement power of the Commission[28] and the rupture from CJEU jurisprudence were understood as particularly significant in this regard.[29] Overall, there was a concern that EU-derived environmental laws would become a form of 'zombie legislation'—on the books but lacking any legal means to give them legal significance.[30] At worst, Brexit could be a justification for deregulation by stealth, although the 2015 Conservative Manifesto contained an explicit commitment to environmental protection.[31] At the very least there was a practical issue about how to make environmental law 'work'—both in the present and in the future—given that the EU legal order was part of the structures and substance of UK environmental law. The response to this was legislative action.[32]

The European Union (Withdrawal) Act 2018 (EUWA)[33] made EU-derived national legislation 'retained' law[34] and continued to give the CJEU some legal relevance.[35] These two provisions, while of a general nature, were particularly important for environmental law given the above.[36] The 2018 Act also included section 16 that required a draft Bill to be published in six months that would give legal force to a set of environmental principles in relation to 'the making and development of policies by Ministers of the Crown'.[37] That section was repealed in 2020 as it was 'unnecessary or spent',[38] but before then it catalysed what ultimately become the Environment Act 2021.[39] As a catalyst, the principles listed in section 16 were a rough reiteration (with additions) of principles listed in section 191(2) TFEU that 'Union policy on the environment . . . shall be based on'. How significant these principles were to the operation of EU environmental law is open to question,[40] but they were understood to give coherence and legal weight to environmental laws.[41]

[28] M Lee, 'Accountability for Environmental Standards After Brexit' (2017) 19 Env Law Rev 89, 90; M Lee, 'Brexit and Environmental Protection in the United Kingdom: Governance, Accountability and Law Making' (2018) 36 J of Energy and Natural Resources Law 351.

[29] House of Commons Environmental Audit Committee, *The Future of the Natural Environment after the EU Referendum* (HC 599, 2017) 19.

[30] ibid 3, 20.

[31] ibid 39.

[32] ibid 41.

[33] For a more detailed discussion see Craig, Ch 6.

[34] European Union (Withdrawal) Act 2018, ss 2, 3, and 7.

[35] ibid s 6.

[36] See, eg, *Harris v Environment Agency* [2022] EWHC 2264 (Admin), [51]–[60]; *R (Misbourne Environmental Protection Ltd) v Environment Agency* [2021] EWHC 3094 (Admin), [18]–[22].

[37] EUWA, s 16.

[38] European Union (Withdrawal Agreement) Act 2020, s 36.

[39] For a discussion of the first Bill in this process see Fisher, 'Executive Environmental Law' (n 8).

[40] E Scotford, *Environmental Principles and the Evolution of Environmental Law* (Hart 2017).

[41] Green Alliance, *Environmental Governance in the UK A Post-Brexit Assessment* (Jan 2025) 6.

I have recounted elsewhere the early stages of the debate concerning the Environment Bill and I will not recount it here.[42] The Bill was introduced in 2019 and was ultimately passed in 2021. The Act has two distinct components. First, it creates a new governance structure to address the structural issues discussed above. Part One of the Environment Act 2021 (EA 2021) constitutes a regime of target-setting,[43] environmental improvement plans,[44] policy statements on environmental principles,[45] and a new body to monitor and hold public bodies accountable, the Office for Environmental Protection (OEP).[46]

The OEP is a unique accountability body with a mixture of monitoring obligations,[47] investigation and enforcement powers,[48] advice powers,[49] and reporting powers.[50] It can also initiate and intervene in court procedures.[51] The OEP has as a principal objective 'in exercising its functions' the requirement to 'contribute to (a) environmental protection, and (b) the improvement of the natural environment'.[52] Part One of the EA 2021 does not place such an obligation on any other body.

The Act also includes an obligation that any Second Reading Speech in relation to a Bill that is 'environmental law' must include a statement that the 'Bill will not have the effect of reducing the level of environmental protection provided for by any existing environmental law', or that such a statement is unable to be made but that 'Her Majesty's Government nevertheless wishes the House to proceed with the Bill'.[53] This is a backstop provision designed to address the dangers of incremental rollback of environmental protection. Overall, this new governance framework is very much 'executive' in nature.[54] The logic of environmental law is in policy documents such as environmental improvement plans and policy statements.

This framework is only one component of the EA 2021, however. The vast bulk of the Act contains provisions, some quite ambitious, in relation to a range of different environmental subject areas including biodiversity net gain,[55] waste producer responsibility,[56] and conservation covenants,[57] to name a few examples. This part of the Act is ad hoc, often amending other legislation,[58] and includes powers to consolidate or amend EU-derived regimes.[59] Different sections have also come into legal

[42] Fisher, 'Executive Environmental Law' (n 8).
[43] Environment Act 2021, ss 1–7.
[44] ibid ss 8–15.
[45] ibid ss 17–19.
[46] ibid ss 22–43.
[47] ibid ss 28–29.
[48] ibid ss 31–37.
[49] ibid s 30.
[50] ibid ss 29–30.
[51] ibid ss 38–39.
[52] ibid s 23(1).
[53] ibid s 20(3)–(4).
[54] Fisher, 'Executive Environmental Law' (n 8).
[55] Environment Act 2021, ss 98–101.
[56] ibid ss 50–51.
[57] ibid Part 7.
[58] ibid eg Sch 11 amending the Environment Act 1995.
[59] ibid eg Sch 21 (REACH) and ss 89–93 (water quality).

force at different times.[60] While the EA 2021 empowers and obliges the creation of new environmental laws, it also does not do much in explicitly removing EU-derived environmental laws.

The EA 2021 applies primarily to England and Northern Ireland. Scotland has followed a different path. The bulk of the UK Withdrawal from the European Union (Continuity) (Scotland) Act 2021 concerns environmental governance, including a framework for environmental principles and the creation of a new body—Environmental Standards Scotland.[61] Wales, in contrast, is still in the process of creating a new governance structure. The Environment (Air Quality and Soundscapes) (Wales) Act 2024 was passed in 2024 and an Environment (Principles, Governance and Biodiversity Targets) (Wales) Bill is currently being debated. Part of that Bill is the proposal for a new environmental accountability body for Wales.

Legislative reform has not stopped there. Many of the regulations that could have been 'sunsetted'[62] under the Retained EU Law (Revocation and Reform) Act 2023 were environmental law provisions.[63] While that did not eventuate, that Act has limited the legal relevance of EU legal norms. The Levelling-up and Regeneration Act 2023 (LURA 2023) which applies to England is essentially a new Planning Act—a topic, as noted above, never really in the province of EU law. That Act provides for greater central control and, as with the EA 2021, a greater role for policy.[64] It also allows for the replacement of the EU-derived regimes of environmental impact assessment and strategic environmental assessment with a new regime of environmental outcome reports.[65] That regime has, of the time of writing, yet to be introduced. There is also at the time of writing a new Planning and Infrastructure Bill being debated before Parliament.[66] It currently includes a new framework for environmental delivery plans for developments.[67]

The above discussion is not exhaustive. But what is obvious is that environmental law has been a topic that has not been left untouched in the post-referendum world. Environmental law in any jurisdiction is always 'messy', given the range of topics it covers.[68] Post-Brexit environmental law is particularly messy. There has been some legal change—some structural, some policy-based, some noticeable, and some less so. There is also much that remains—primarily in the form of delegated legislation. Some of this is UK-derived and some EU-derived (what is now 'assimilated law').[69]

[60] ibid s 147 and related delegated legislation.

[61] UK Withdrawal from the European Union (Continuity) (Scotland) Act 2021, s 19 and Sch 1.

[62] Section 1.

[63] https://www.gov.uk/government/publications/retained-eu-law-dashboard accessed 8 November 2025.

[64] R Ogden-Jones, 'Policies, Places and Practices: Why Environmental Law Scholars Should Care About the Levelling-Up and Regeneration Act 2023' (2024) 36 JEL 445.

[65] LURA 2023, Part 6.

[66] https://bills.parliament.uk/bills/3946 accessed 9 November 2025.

[67] Part 3.

[68] JB Ruhl, 'Thinking of Environmental Law as a Complex Adaptive System: How to Clean Up the Environment by Making a Mess of Environmental Law' (1997) 34 Houston Law Rev 935.

[69] Retained EU Law (Revocation and Reform) Act 2023, s 5.

The result is that while environmental law has always been fragmented, it is even more so now.[70] This is both between regions and also across subject areas. Even for those with decades of experience in the field, getting an accurate picture of the current legal landscape is not easy, not least because of the different dates on which different obligations come into force.[71] This is particularly the case when new legislation is not replacing existing regimes but often amending them and/or inserting new obligations into other pieces of legislation.[72] It is also important to remember that EU environmental law has also not stood still either in terms of legislative development[73] or in the case law of the CJEU.[74]

My sketch of these developments is not necessarily a criticism. My point is that all of this is an inevitable consequence of Brexit. Unbound environmental law is not so much an act of unshackling so that unrealized opportunities can be pursued. It is an act of UK public law institutions now bearing the full responsibility for existing UK environmental law. That includes devolved regions. Legislatures, administrative bodies, and courts and all levels of government are now doing all the work of environmental law—work that is embedded in existing regimes. While in the past, the doctrinal difficulties of applying EU environmental law were often attributed to the CJEU,[75] that is a narrative no longer available. Nor are the standard-setting processes, enforcement powers, and interpretative powers of EU institutions. I am not saying any of these were perfect. What I am saying is that the removal of them means that UK institutions must 'own' environmental law—all of it. The task of building and maintaining UK environmental law rests with UK public law institutions.

4 UK Environmental Law Jobs Now

It is useful to ponder further what that task entails. As noted above, environmental law consists of at least seven overlapping 'law jobs'—a phrase taken from the 'law jobs'

[70] For a discussion of overall developments see Green Alliance, *Environmental Governance in the UK: A Post-Brexit Assessment* (Jan 2025) 1.

[71] Consider the Planning Inspector's legal error in relation to the biodiversity net gain obligation in *NRS Saredon Aggregates Ltd v Secretary of State for Levelling Up, Housing and Communities* [2023] EWHC 2795 (Admin), [56].

[72] See, eg, the biodiversity net gain obligations in planning law, see s 98 and Sch 14, EA 2021 and the discussion in *R (Morris Homes (North) Ltd) v Westchurch Homes Ltd* [2025] EWHC 657 (Admin).

[73] Regulation (EU) 2021/1119 of the European Parliament and of the Council of 30 June 2021 establishing the framework for achieving climate neutrality and amending Regulations (EC) No 401/2009 and (EU) 2018/1999 ('European Climate Law') and Regulation (EU) 2024/1991 of the European Parliament and of the Council of 24 June 2024 on nature restoration and amending Regulation (EU) 2022/869 (Text with EEA relevance) [2021] OJ L243, 9/7/2021.

[74] See, eg, Case C-293/17 *Coöperatie Mobilisation for the Environment UA and Vereniging Leefmilieu v College van gedeputeerde staten van Limburg and College van gedeputeerde staten van Gelderland* EU:C:2018:882.

[75] *HS2 Action Alliance Ltd* (n 25) [158] and *R (Oss Group Ltd) v Environment Agency* [2007] EWCA Civ 611, [55].

theory of the American legal realist Karl Llewellyn.[76] It is a phrase that underscores the types of legal work that law entails. Llewellyn identified five general law jobs.[77] I identify seven, three of which overlap with Llewellyn's list, and four of which reflect the distinctive nature of environmental law.

The *first law job* that Llewellyn identified was dealing with 'trouble cases'[78] by addressing 'offense, grievance, dispute'.[79] As I have written about elsewhere, disputes are inevitable in relation to environmental problems.[80] Environmental law does not make those disputes go away. Quite the opposite. Laws that define environmental problems, the creation of legal obligations in relation to environmental problems, and calling decision-makers to account all give rise to legal disputes. Many of those disputes will be about how to craft laws, interpret legislation, and exercise discretion. Some of these disputes will be between those who value the environment differently, but disputes will also arise because competitors will bring actions in cases where a legal actor has got a benefit of not having a legal obligation imposed on them.[81]

Due to the directive-heavy nature of EU environmental law and the doctrine of direct effect, dispute resolution has overwhelmingly been at the national level. The CJEU, through the preliminary reference procedure, can provide authoritative interpretations of EU environmental law,[82] but the resolution of any dispute has been in national courts and tribunals (including the Planning Inspectorate). There are many examples of cases involving questions of EU law being resolved with no preliminary preference at all.[83] There are also many legal disputes in UK courts which raise no point of EU-derived law.[84]

Brexit thus did not change the sites of dispute resolution, but dispute resolution is evolving. Without the preliminary ruling procedure, adjudicating on interpretation is for national courts alone. Brexit is also giving rise to *more* environmental law disputes. In part this is because the legislative changes discussed above give rise to legal uncertainty which in turn gives rise to disagreement about what the law means.[85] But

[76] Llewellyn (n 2); KN Llewellyn and EA Hoebel, *The Cheyenne Way: Conflict and Caselaw in Primitive Jurisprudence* (University of Oklahoma Press 1941); and Llewellyn's unpublished course materials in William Twining, *Karl Llewellyn and the Realist Movement* (2nd edn, Cambridge University Press 2012) 552–72. See also Twining's discussion in Chs 8 and 9.

[77] Llewellyn (n 2).

[78] ibid 1375–76.

[79] ibid 1375.

[80] E Fisher, *Environmental Law: A Very Short Introduction* (Oxford University Press 2017) Ch 1.

[81] *R (Morris Homes (North) Ltd) v Westchurch Homes Ltd & Ors* [2025] EWHC 657 (Admin), failed challenge concerning biodiversity gain planning condition under the Environment Act 2021.

[82] For a discussion of the limits of this see V Heyvaert, J Thornton, and R Drabble QC, 'With Reference to the Environment: the Preliminary Reference Procedure, Environmental Decisions and the Domestic Judiciary' (2014) 130 LQR 413. See also S Bogojević, 'Judicial Dialogue Unpacked: Twenty Years of Preliminary References on Environmental Matters Initiated by the Swedish Judiciary' (2017) 29 JEL 263.

[83] See the discussion about the possibility of a preliminary reference in *HS2 Action Alliance Ltd* (n 25) [117], [127]–[128].

[84] See, eg, *Frack Free Balcombe Residents' Association v Secretary of State for Housing, Communities and Local Government & Ors* [2025] EWCA Civ 495.

[85] See, eg, *R (Rights: Community: Action Ltd) v Secretary of State for Housing, Communities and Local Government* [2025] EWCA Civ 990. For a discussion of this phenomenon see J Bell and E Fisher, 'Exploring a Year of Administrative Law Adjudication in the Administrative Court' [2021] PL 505.

disputes have also arisen because of uncertainty created by the removal of the EU legal system from the legal picture.[86] Questions have emerged concerning what type of enforcement powers public bodies have,[87] and when a court can provide a remedy.[88]

Some of these disputes relate to the *second law job*, what Llewellyn called 'arranging for the say and the manner of its saying'.[89] This job is defining where the authority of law comes from and what form law can take. Before Brexit, it was not just that EU law was supreme, but that different types of EU legal forms and norms were authoritative in all the devolved regions of the UK.[90] UK environmental law was shaped by the Treaties, directives, general principles of EU law, and preliminary references through EU law having effect in national law and national courts being under an obligation to make such law 'effective'.[91] There were also cases in which, after a preliminary reference, a national court needed to provide some form of remedy.[92]

As can be seen in the previous section, these legal obligations did not disappear in one swoop, but it is increasingly the case that it is only domestic legal norms that are authoritative. At the same time, there is growing divergence between the devolved regions as they adopt different pieces of legislation. Furthermore, new policy documents such as EIPs and EPPSs have authoritative value under the EA 2021. In short, there is the appearance of new and different types of legal work in relation to determining what the law is.

At the same time, the existing forms of what Llewellyn called 'channelling'[93] have remained relatively stable. This *third law job* of environmental law involves 'effective channelling, preventively and in advance, of people's conduct—and attitudes—toward one another'.[94] 'Channelling' is what we think of law regulating behaviour through the creation of duties, responsibilities, and rights, usually through legislation. Laws create duties on administrative decision-makers to consider environmental matters,[95] or to set standards that need to be met.[96] Legislation creates rights of third parties

[86] *CG Fry & Son Ltd v Secretary of State for Housing, Communities and Local Government* [2025] UKSC 35.

[87] *Natural England v Cooper* [2025] EWCA Civ 15 (standing of Natural England to request injunction to enforce EIA obligations).

[88] *R (Bradbury) v Awdurdod Parc Cenedlaethol Bannau Brycheiniog (Brecon Beacons National Park Authority)* [2025] EWCA Civ 489, [70]-[85]—concerning remedy in related to alleged breach of habitats regulations.

[89] Llewellyn (n 2) 1383.

[90] Consider, eg, how the House of Lords' reasoning in *Berkeley* (n 24) was shaped by the need to ensure 'substantial compliance' with the obligations of the EIA Directive.

[91] Consider, eg, the discussion of effectiveness in *Walton v The Scottish Ministers (Scotland)* [2012] UKSC 44, [134]–[140].

[92] *R (ClientEarth) v Secretary of State for the Environment, Food and Rural Affairs* [2015] UKSC 28 and the more complicated *R (Barker) v London Borough of Bromley* [2006] UKHL 52, [2007] 1 AC 470 which followed from Case C-290/03 (n 18).

[93] Llewellyn (n 2) 1376–83.

[94] ibid 1376.

[95] See, eg, EIA Directive (n 13) Arts 2 and 8.

[96] Directive 2008/50/EC of the European Parliament and of the Council of 21 May 2008 on ambient air quality and cleaner air for Europe [2008] OJ L152/1.

that administrative decision-makers will be entrusted with realizing.[97] As seen above, post-Brexit legislation has also introduced new obligations—targets under the EA 2021, biodiversity net gain, and the yet to be introduced environmental outcome reports being key examples. But at the same time, most of the formal legal obligations of UK environmental law remain the same. Thus, while the structures of authority are changing (see the last law job), the regimes derived from EU environmental law are currently not.

Many of those regimes relate to two law jobs which are distinctive (albeit not unique) to environmental law. The *fourth law job* concerns the defining of environmental problems. Environmental problems do not exist out in the world with little labels on them. Directives, Commission practice, and CJEU case law played an important role in framing environmental problems, often in quite distinctive ways. 'Nature' under EU environmental law was an EU-wide concept.[98] Chemicals were defined as market objects.[99] 'Waste' was defined by a directive and embedded in EU policy.[100] Preliminary references were thus particularly important in relation to environmental law and often focused on definitions, although not always with straightforward results. As Carnwath J (as he then was) noted in relation to Court of Justice case law concerning the definition of waste, 'a search for logical coherence in the Luxembourg case-law is probably doomed to failure'.[101] That was not so much due to the Court, but due to the wording of different directives, and more significantly the dynamic concept of waste.[102]

Post-Brexit, the task of defining environmental problems is the task of UK public law institutions. In most cases, the EU framing of environmental problems remains in areas such as waste[103] and water quality.[104] But in areas such as nature conservation, there have been more ambitious attempts to craft new regimes with new framings of environmental problems, albeit in ways that are not dissimilar to how EU environmental law is developing.[105] The emergence of problems such as climate

[97] Environmental Information Regulations 2004 (England and Wales) implementing Directive 2003/4/EC of the European Parliament and of the Council of 28 January 2003 on public access to environmental information and repealing Council Directive 90/313/EEC [2003] OJ L41/26. See E Fisher, 'Exploring the Legal Architecture of Transparency' in P Ala'i and R Vaughn (eds), *Research Handbook on Transparency* (Edward Elgar 2014).

[98] Fisher, Lange, and Scotford (n 5) Ch 21.

[99] E Fisher 'Chemicals as Regulatory Objects' (2014) 23 Review of European, Comparative and International Environmental Law 163.

[100] Fisher, Lange, and Scotford (n 5) Ch 16.

[101] *Oss Group Ltd* (n 75), [53].

[102] E Scotford, 'Trash or Treasure: Policy Tensions in EC Waste Regulation' (2007) 19 JEL 367.

[103] *The National Farmers' Union v Herefordshire Council & Ors* [2025] EWHC 536 (Admin), [58]–[83]. Environment Agency, 'Check If Your Material Is Waste' (11 July 2024) https://www.gov.uk/guidance/check-if-your-material-is-waste accessed 9 November 2025.

[104] EA 2021, s 93.

[105] Compare, eg, the use of targets (albeit of different sorts) in Reg 4, Environmental Targets (Biodiversity) (England) Regulations 2023 and Regulation (EU) 2024/1991 of the European Parliament and of the Council of 24 June 2024 on nature restoration and amending Regulation (EU) 2022/869 [2024] OJ 2024/1991.

change also gives rise to questions about whether existing legal regimes encompass them.[106]

The *fifth law job* concerns the assembly and utilization of knowledge about environmental problems. Environmental problems do not just need to be defined; knowledge about them needs to be gathered and integrated into decision-making. Directives thus imposed a series of assessment obligations on member states and other actors.[107] These mostly remain.

Those public assessment obligations relate to the *sixth law job* of environmental law—creating and maintaining regimes for administrative governance. Environmental legislation, whether directives or otherwise, often requires a significant role for local and central public administration in individualized decision-making[108] and different forms of standard-setting and plan creation.[109] In the UK it has been public law that has primarily governed this—both through how public institutions are constituted and through the judicial review doctrine of the courts.[110] Post-Brexit administrative regimes are far more fragmented across the regions. Effective and legitimate administrative governance is also a product of both administrative authority and capacity.[111] That capacity, particularly in local government, has always been lacking,[112] and Brexit has not changed that situation.[113]

Courts also have a role to play in administrative governance. They are not just enforcing environmental law obligations, but also dealing with the legal questions that arise in administering environmental legislation. These are questions about process, procedure, and how discretion should be exercised.[114] They are questions that overlap with the task of delineating legal obligations and enforcing them. Some of these questions involve the continued operation of regimes originally derived from

[106] *R (Finch (Weald Action Group)) v Surrey County Council* [2024] UKSC 20 (EIA Directive and climate change).

[107] See, eg, Air Quality Standards Regulations 2010 implementing Directive 2008/50/EC (n 96); Water Environment (Water Framework Directive) (England and Wales) Regulations 2017 implementing Directive 2000/60/EC of the European Parliament and of the Council of 23 October 2000 establishing a framework for Community action in the field of water policy [2000] OJ L327/1.

[108] See, eg, Reg 3, Town and Country Planning (Environmental Impact Assessment) Regulations 2017; and Reg 12, Environmental Permitting (England and Wales) Regulations 2016.

[109] See, eg, local development schemes under Part 2 of the Planning and Compulsory Purchase Act 2004; national policy statements under Part 2 of the Planning Act 2008; and environmental objectives and programmes of measures under Water Environment (Water Framework Directive) (England and Wales) Regulations 2017.

[110] See, eg, the discussion of s 10 of the Planning Act 2008 in *R (Friends of the Earth Ltd) v Heathrow Airport Ltd* [2020] UKSC 52, [114]–[134].

[111] E Fisher and S Shapiro, *Administrative Competence: Reimagining Administrative Law* (Cambridge University Press 2020) Ch 1.

[112] J Weston, 'Screening for Environmental Impact Assessment Projects in England: What Screening?' (2012) 29 Impact Assessment and Protect Appraisal 90.

[113] House of Lords Built Environment Committee, *The Impact of Environmental Regulations on Development* (HL Paper 254 2023) [125]–[130].

[114] For an earlier discussion of this see E Fisher, 'Law and Energy Transitions: Wind Turbines and Planning Law in the UK' (2018) 38 OJLS 528.

EU law.[115] Other cases concern new obligations, for example what it means to have 'due regard' to an environmental principles policy statement (see below).[116]

The *final law job* to mention is that of accountability. Much of the work of environmental law is public law work and, as seen above, administrative law work. Having aspirations to protect environmental problems is easy; delivering on those aspirations is harder. Lees and Pedersen for example have argued that modern environmental law can tend towards being 'performative'—that is, 'just for show'.[117]

The EU, through enforcement actions and preliminary references, was understood to be a major source of accountability in UK environmental law.[118] The creation of the OEP was designed to address the potential accountability vacuum. As noted above, it is a unique body. It is not an Ombudsman. It is not a court or tribunal. It receives and investigates complaints about significant failures of environmental law,[119] but can also be proactive, including giving advice[120] and intervening in legal proceedings.[121] It also has a significant monitoring function—including assessing how on track the government is in meeting its own environmental improvement plan.[122] Given the novelty of the regime, it is not surprising that the relationship between judicial review and OEP enforcement has also been raised in legal argument.[123] Brexit has thus given rise to a distinctive accountability structure in environmental law, albeit one that in many ways reflects a distinctly English tradition of non-legal accountability.[124] Some of the OEP's reporting functions also bear a similarity to the Royal Commission on Environmental Pollution which operated from 1970 to 2011.[125] It, like everything else, is still in the early stages of its evolution.

5 The Need for Legal Expertise

Seven law jobs is a lot—an academically cumbersome number, made even more ungainly by the fact that these different law jobs overlap. Defining environmental

[115] *Secretary of State for Environment, Food and Rural Affairs v R (Pickering Fishery Association)* [2025] EWCA Civ 378 (water framework directive).

[116] See section 5.

[117] E Lees and O Pedersen, 'Performative Environmental Law' (2025) 88 MLR 124.

[118] Lee, 'Brexit and Environmental Protection in the United Kingdom' (n 28).

[119] Environment Act 2021, ss 31–37.

[120] ibid s 30. See, eg, Office for Environmental Protection, 'OEP Gives Advice to Government on the Planning and Infrastructure Bill' (1 May 2025), https://www.theoep.org.uk/report/oep-gives-advice-government-planning-and-infrastructure-bill accessed 9 November 2025.

[121] ibid s 39. It has done this in *Fry* (n 86) and *Finch* (n 106) before the Supreme Court, and *Rights: Community; Action* (n 85) and *Secretary of State for Environment, Food and Rural Affairs v Pickering Fishery Association* (n 115) in the Court of Appeal.

[122] Office for Environmental Protection, *Progress in Improving the Natural Environment in England 2023/2024* (Jan 2025).

[123] *Wild Justice v The Water Services Regulation Authority* [2022] EWHC 2608 (Admin), [65]–[69].

[124] E Fisher, *Risk Regulation and Administrative Constitutionalism* (Hart 2007) Ch 2.

[125] S Owens, *Knowledge, Policy, and Expertise: The UK Royal Commission on Environmental Pollution 1970–2011* (Oxford University Press 2015).

problems gives rise to legal disputes. Administrative governance is about accountability. Delineating jurisdiction will bear on duties of assessment. Any form of regulation will result in disputes and a need for accountability.

Seven law jobs may be a lot, but a survey of them makes clear that environmental law is about *law*. That is an obvious point, but one worth making, as environmental law is often thought of as a subject that is strong on science and politics and weaker when it comes to legal content.[126] The 'law' of environmental law is also not just environmental law obligations—it is about a lot of other legal work that is not as visible and as obvious. In all cases, these different law jobs involve what Llewellyn called 'juristic method'.[127] He described that as 'the ways of handling "legal" tools to law-job ends, and of the on-going upkeep and improvement of both ways and tools'.[128] Juristic method is not just legal method. For Llewellyn it applies to all law jobs.[129] Such method is not just about legal doctrine, but also about spokesmanship, troubleshooting, giving advice, knowing the law, and understanding what a valid legal interpretation could be in a legal culture.[130] Juristic method is embedded in legal culture.[131]

Pre-Brexit, environmental law jobs and juristic method were spread across UK and EU institutions. Environmental law thus reflected both legal cultures. Post-Brexit, all law jobs are the responsibility of UK institutions and UK juristic method is the legal method of environmental law. Brexit has thus not resulted in unleashing unimagined possibilities in UK environmental law, but has resulted in UK public law institutions taking on the full burden of the legal work of environmental law. That may lead to new types of law being created, and the EA 2021 is an example of this, but that fact should not negate a legal reality—there is a lot of existing environmental law work to be done through the maintenance and ongoing operation of the laws that exist and through the legal work that regimes such as the EA 2021 are giving rise to.

That work requires legal expertise. By legal expertise I mean 'skills, experience, and knowledge' about law. Llewellyn described legal expertise as a 'craft'.[132] Another way to describe this expertise is that it is 'thick'.[133] It is both explicit and tacit, collective and individual, and ever evolving. It is embodied in institutions and communities. Environmental law has always required legal expertise.[134] While distinct, due to the

[126] E Fisher, 'On Being in the Back of the Book: Climate Change, Separation of Powers, and the Limits of Public Law Imagination', in M Leloup and others (eds), *Cambridge Handbook of Separation of Powers* (Cambridge University Press forthcoming).

[127] Llewellyn (n 2) 1392–95.

[128] ibid 1392.

[129] ibid 1393.

[130] Twining (n 76) 566.

[131] Elizabeth Fisher, 'Through "Thick" and "Thin": Comparison in Administrative Law and Regulatory Studies Scholarship' in P Cane, H Hofmann, E Chi Yeung, and P Lindseth (eds), *The Oxford Handbook of Comparative Administrative Law* (Oxford University Press 2020).

[132] Llewellyn (n 2) 1393. For Llewelyn's longer discussion of this see his unpublished course materials extracted in Twining (n 76) 561–58.

[133] Fisher and Shapiro (n 111) Ch 2.

[134] Fisher, 'Legal Imagination and European Union Environmental Law' (n 9). See also E Fisher, 'Law's Importance Does Not Come from It Being Wrapped in Plastic: On Future Proofing Environmental Law' in K Huhta, H van Asselt, and S Vesa (eds), *Future-proofing Law in a Time of Environmental Emergency* (Edward Elgar 2025).

polycentric and physical nature of environmental problems, that expertise is not unique.[135] It builds on existing legal expertise and has been a catalyst for the development of doctrines in other areas.[136] Environmental law is not just applied law, but also contributing to law writ large.

Post-Brexit, that legal expertise must be sourced in UK law. The creation and operation of this evolving body of law requires active legal work. By active, I do not mean activist. I mean that these laws confront lawyers with legal questions which they had not previously come across and so they need to keenly and conscientiously reflect on, apply, and often evolve existing legal concepts. To put the matter differently, the post-Brexit legal world in relation to environmental problems is requiring lawyers to up their intellectual game. As Lord Sales notes, it was 'inevitable' that[137]

> leaving the EU would lead to greater complexity and difficulty for lawyers and judges as they adjust to the new constitutional architecture of the UK and changes in the institutional and regulatory matrix in which a good deal of UK law is set.

UK public law norms and ideas are now the primary source of materials for this legal work—UK administrative law doctrines, in particular.

Rather obviously, this legal work arises in relation to new legal obligations, such as those under the EA 2021. Take, for example, the section 19(1) obligation in the Act that a 'Minister of the Crown must, when making policy, have due regard to the policy statement on environmental principles currently in effect'. The nature of that obligation was considered by the Court of Appeal in *Rights: Community: Action*.[138]

That case concerned a challenge to the lawfulness of a written ministerial statement—'Planning—Local Energy Efficiency Standards Update'. The legal framework and background are complicated and concerned different legislative obligations in planning, building standards, and energy efficiency in buildings.[139] The practical implications of the written ministerial statement were to limit the power of local authorities to set higher energy efficiency standards for new builds.[140] At the time it was issued there was no consideration of the EPPS—that only happened a little more than two months later after pre-action protocol correspondence, albeit it was done in good faith.[141] One question before the Court of Appeal was whether this was enough to discharge the duty under section 19 of the EA 2021. The other concerned

[135] E Fisher, 'Environmental Law as "Hot" Law' (2013) 25 JEL 347.

[136] See the discussion in Fisher, 'Law's Importance Does Not Come from It Being Wrapped in Plastic' (n 134). UK examples include *HS2 Action Alliance Ltd* (n 25) (constitutional law); *Empress Car Company (Abertillery) Ltd* [1998] UKHL 5; [1999] 2 AC 22 (criminal law); and *Bushell v Secretary of State for the Environment* [1981] AC 75(administrative law).

[137] Lord Sales, 'Retained EU Law: Purposive Interpretation when the Constitutional Architecture Changes' (2024) 49 ELRev 3–14, 14.

[138] *Rights: Community: Action* (n 85).

[139] ibid [13]–[54].

[140] ibid [2].

[141] ibid [6]

the interpretation of section 1 of the Planning and Energy Act 2008 and an argument that an 'error of interpretation' of that Act 'tainted' consideration of the relationship between the written ministerial statement and that Act.[142] That second ground is a reminder that legal questions are rarely isolated.

Regarding section 19, as the Court noted, 'much of the appellant's focus is on the allegedly "rearguard" nature of the EPPS assessment carried out in February 2024 after the decision to publish the 2023 WMS'[143] and whether this was a breach of section 19. The High Court had concluded it was not.[144]

The Court first turned to the wording of the EA Act 2021—not just to the wording of section 19, but also to the definition of 'making policy' in section 47, which states that it 'includes developing, adopting or revising policy'. As the Court noted:[145]

> [T]he duty applies at a number of stages in the 'making' of a policy. For example, the duty to have "due regard" to the EPPS applies when a policy is being developed and not simply at the point when a policy is adopted. It applies when a policy is being formulated and different policy options are being considered. Accordingly, it is necessary to be careful in the language used to deal with a situation where there was no regard to the EPPS at one material point but an EPPS assessment has been carried out subsequently.

Given this, and in light of other case law concerning planning policy and written ministerial statements,[146]

> [i]t would be wrong to say that a s.19 compliant EPPS assessment carried out subsequently has remedied the earlier breach of s.19 when the policy was adopted, or has retrospectively validated that decision. Instead, the court decides whether in the event of subsequent compliance with the s.19 duty, it would be appropriate to declare that the policy is unlawful or to quash the policy.[147]

In this case it concluded no.[148] In doing so, the CA also provided greater guidance on the nature of the section 19 duty. It stated:[149]

> [T]he duty in s.19 must be carried out in substance, with rigour and with an open mind. The duty is to have due regard to the matters specified in the EPPS that are

[142] ibid [63].
[143] ibid [82].
[144] *R (Rights Community Action Ltd) v Secretary of State for Levelling Up, Housing and Communities* [2024] EWHC 1693 (Admin).
[145] *Rights: Community: Action* (n 85) [85].
[146] ibid [88], *R (West Berkshire District Council) v Secretary of State for Communities and Local Government* [2016] EWCA Civ 441.
[147] *Rights: Community: Action* (n 85) [88].
[148] ibid [112].
[149] ibid [93].

> relevant to the assessment. It is not a duty to achieve a particular result or outcome. It is for the Minister to decide how much weight to give to the relevant matters. Provided that there has been a proper focus on the relevant principles, the court cannot interfere simply because it would have given greater or less weight to particular matters. The weight and extent of the s.19 duty are highly fact-sensitive and dependent on individual judgment.

That last sentence drew on legal analysis in relation to the very different public sector equality duty.[150] *Rights: Community: Action* is a good illustration of a new legislative obligation that is not interpreted in a vacuum. It is interpreted in light of existing doctrine. Not by repeating that doctrine, but by using it as a touchstone for rigorous analysis.

Interpreting new legal obligations is not the only active legal work happening post-Brexit. Recent appellate case law primarily concerns decisions made prior to Brexit. As such, while the preliminary reference procedure is no longer available, national laws in these pre-2020 cases are interpreted in line with the laws they are implementing.[151] More recent case law in the High Court is solely adjudicated on with reference to UK case law.[152] There are, however, exceptions to this. For example, regulation 3 of the Water Environment (Water Framework Directive) England and Wales Regulations 2017 requires certain decision-makers to comply with the obligations of the Water Framework Directive. This means that, without amendment of those regulations, any legal disputes invoke consideration of the obligations under the Directive.[153] The fundamental point remains however that it is for national courts alone to adjudicate on these disputes.

The significance of this can be seen in the recent UK Supreme Court case of *C G Fry & Son Limited v Secretary of State for Housing, Communities and Local Government.*[154] In this case, outline planning permission had been granted to a multistage housing development in 2015.[155] The site is near the Somerset Levels and Moors—an area designated under the international Ramsar Convention on Wetlands of International Importance Especially as Waterfowl Habitat and given legal protection under England due to section 37A of the Wildlife and Countryside Act 1981.

In June 2020 the third phase of the development was granted approval subject to the discharge of ten conditions. In August 2020 Natural England issued new advice on when an 'appropriate assessment' was required under regulation 63 of the Conservation of Habitats and Species Regulations 2017. Those regulations provide

[150] ibid [12] discussing *Hotak v Southwark London Borough Council* [2015] UKSC 30; [2016] AC 811. Note the recognition that the duties are different, see [57].
[151] *Finch* (n 106) [10].
[152] *R (Associated Petroleum Terminals (Immingham) Ltd) v Harbour Master for the River Humber* [2025] EWHC 1992 (Admin), [45]-[46]; *R (Hynot Ltd) v Secretary of State for Energy Security and Net Zero* [2025] EWHC 2644 (Admin), [37]–[62].
[153] *Secretary of State for Environment, Food and Rural Affairs v Pickering Fishery Association* (n 115).
[154] *C G Fry & Son Ltd* (n 86).
[155] ibid [6].

protection for species and sites protected under EU law (what are known as European sites).[156] Regulation 63 states that:

> (1) A competent authority, before deciding to undertake, or give any consent, permission or other authorisation for, a plan or project which—
> (a) is likely to have a significant effect on a European site . . . (either alone or in combination with other plans or projects), and
> (b) is not directly connected with or necessary to the management of that site, must make an appropriate assessment of the implications of the plan or project for that site in view of that site's conservation objectives.

Regulation 63 implements Article 6(3) of the Habitats Directive—an article that has catalysed a rich CJEU and national case law.[157] Specifically, the CJEU has stated that the duty to do an appropriate assessment must be interpreted in line with the precautionary principle.[158] Ramsar sites are not European sites, but national policy states they should be treated as such.[159]

Natural England's new advice was catalysed by a CJEU case concerning duties of appropriate assessment in relation to plans and projects that can result in increased nutrient loads in protected areas.[160] In 2021, relying on such advice, the relevant local planning authority withheld approval of the discharge of conditions until an appropriate assessment had been carried out. An appeal to a Planning Inspector,[161] the High Court, and the Court of Appeal confirmed this was lawful. While the appellant was not arguing that EU law was not legally relevant,[162] it was arguing that on a proper interpretation of the regulations, the duty to do an appropriate assessment could only apply at the outline planning permission stage.

The Supreme Court, consistent with the other decision-makers and rulings, disagreed.[163] What is striking is that in doing so it made clear that resolving the question did not require reference to

> the principles of interpretation in EU law because the Habitats Regulations are to be construed . . . by applying the conventional approach to statutory interpretation in domestic law, which includes the purposive approach. Despite this the Court of Appeal discussed the effect of the Withdrawal Act in obiter dicta in some detail

[156] These are special protection areas under the Directive 2009/147/EC of the European Parliament and of the Council of 30 November 2009 on the conservation of wild birds [2010] OJ L20/7 as amended and special areas of conservation under the Council Directive 92/43/EEC (n 16).

[157] See Fisher, Lange, and Scotford (n 5) Ch 21.

[158] See Case C-127/02 *Landelijke Vereniging tot Behoud van de Waddenzee and Nederlandse Vereniging tot Bescherming van Vogels v Staatssecretaris van Landbouw, Natuurbeheer en Visserij* EU:C:2004:482.

[159] *C G Fry & Son Ltd* (n 86) [181], National Planning Policy Framework 2021 (now [194], National Planning Policy Framework 2024).

[160] Case C-293/17 (n 74).

[161] *C G Fry & Son Ltd* (n 86) [12].

[162] ibid [14].

[163] ibid [56].

> (paras 37–53). It is not necessary for this court to deal with this part of their judgment; nor did we receive submissions which would assist us to do so. The points made in the judgments of the CJEU and the domestic courts referred to above are relevant because they serve to emphasise the purposes promoted by the Habitats Directive and the Habitats Regulations, which are already clear from the terms and context of those instruments.[164]

The bottom line is that it is UK precedent and UK doctrine that matter. While it is doctrinal development in light of past EU law, domestic doctrine is now the starting point.[165]

A second issue in the case concerned the legal effect of the policy that designated a Ramsar site as a European site, thus making regulation 63 apply to it. The Court, on an analysis of the framework for outline planning permission in the Town and Country Planning Act 1990, concluded while policy can be a material consideration,[166]

> [r]ights given by the planning legislation cannot be overridden or diluted by general policies laid down by central government, whether in the form of the NPPF [National Planning Policy Framework] or otherwise.

Such rights are given by outline planning permission.[167] As such, '[n]ational policy and new scientific advice of the kind in issue in this case' did not confer a power to impose a duty of appropriate assessment in relation to a Ramsar site 'because the operation of the conditions set out in the outline planning permission (and hence of the sub-conditions set out in the reserved matters approval) is determined by the interpretation of the conditions set out in the outline permission'.[168] The legal implications of policy guidance have their limits.[169]

These cases, and many others, are illustrating how post-Brexit environmental law is giving rise to legal work. Little of it is neat. Much of it builds on existing doctrine. Just as EU environmental law directives contributed much to the doctrine of direct effect,[170] new and existing environmental legislation will be contributing much to UK doctrine in the coming decades. It will be the legal gift that keeps on giving. That gift will require legal expertise. That point does not sit easily with the way in which environmental law is often imagined as an area of 'functionalist' law that is strong on policy and outcomes and weaker on law.[171] Nor does it sit easily with the idea of environmental law as an area of law in which public law doctrines are 'applied' but do not

164 ibid [59].
165 ibid [57].
166 ibid [62].
167 ibid [66].
168 ibid [70].
169 Note that the current version of the Planning and Infrastructure Bill will legislate that Ramsar sites will be treated as European sites (cl 98).
170 Fisher, 'Legal Imagination and European Union Environmental Law' (n 9).
171 For my critique of this in relation to climate change law see Fisher, 'Telling Meaningful Stories' (n 3).

evolve those doctrines.[172] But look across all public law systems, and environmental laws have shaped much public law thought.[173] It is important not to be in thrall to simplistic visions of environmental law, including the idea that Brexit unbinds environmental law. Those images have always been problematic and now that UK public law institutions bear the responsibility of environmental law it is particularly important not to be captivated by them.[174]

6 Conclusion

I suspect the analysis in this chapter is a bit of a narrative disappointment. I have not told a tale of untapped possibilities. I have not even told a tale that is very dramatic. In essence, what I have done is charted how environmental law is a messy subject that requires a lot of legal work. Brexit has not changed that. What it has done is make that work solely the task of UK institutions. Post-Brexit environmental law is a work in progress. For those who want to be able to tell a simple story of Brexit as a disaster or a success, the lack of neat conclusions and an end to the story will be frustrating. But as a story, what it underscores is the need to get on with a vast number of environmental law jobs.

A final word. Environmental law unbound is not an exercise in imagining the unimagined, although it is an exercise in legal imagination. By legal imagination I mean the mental constructs that lawyers use to think about law.[175] Legal imagination is always in operation because so much of legal thought involves speculation. An act of legal inquiry is an act of envisaging the possibilities of what law is and how it can be applied. Post-Brexit, what really matters is thus not just legal expertise but also UK legal imagination—not just in relation to environmental law obligations but also to the other law jobs that relate to environmental law. Administrative governance, accountability, assessment, defining environmental problems, delineating jurisdiction, and dealing with legal disputes will all need to be front and centre in the decades to come. There will be a lot to think about and a lot to do. As the cases and legislative reform in this chapter highlight, that work is already under way. What the chapter makes clear is that law unbound is not about freeing the law from what is, and venturing out into unexplored negative space. It is quite the opposite.

[172] Fisher, 'On Being in the Back of the Book' (n 126).
[173] Fisher, 'Legal Imagination and European Union Environmental Law' (n 9).
[174] Fisher, 'Law's Importance' (n 134).
[175] Fisher, 'Legal Imagination and European Union Environmental Law' (n 9) and Fisher, 'Telling Meaningful Stories' (n 3).

25 Food Law

Emily Lydgate and Chloë Anthony

Food law aims to address food safety risks and achieve animal welfare and environmental standards. In so doing, it helps to shape the natural environment, including land use, pollution levels, soil health, and biodiversity, and human health outcomes, including nutrition and exposure to contaminants and additives.[1] The need to safeguard UK standards and concerns about deregulating to match other countries emerged as defining issues post-Brexit. Demonstrating the strength of sentiment, surveys conducted by the Department of Business and Trade between 2019 and 2025 consistently found that the top concern about free trade agreements among the public was the threat to UK food safety.[2]

Because agri-food products are heavily regulated, including at borders, UK food law has important implications for trade. With respect to the EU, the UK's largest export destination, the UK has gone from seamless regulatory integration to 'third country' status, subject to full documentary, identity, and physical regulatory compliance checks. Food law has also fragmented within the UK. In the UK, food law and policy is devolved.[3] Post-Brexit, Northern Ireland's food law remains harmonized with that of the EU; Scotland has provided for, but not fully maintained, alignment with EU food law; and England and Wales' food law is uncoupled from the EU.

Post-Brexit UK food law domestic reform has been defined by the central UK government's desire to maintain full regulatory autonomy. Several cross-cutting studies tracking post-Brexit divergence in food and other standards have identified different types of regulatory divergence: internal divergence between the four countries of the UK; passive divergence, whereby the UK does not follow changes in EU law; active divergence, where changes in UK law are not matched by the EU; procedural divergence in regulatory processes between the UK and the EU; delayed divergence, where changes to assimilated EU law are planned or provided for, but have not been yet undertaken; and active and passive convergence.[4]

[1] European Environment Agency, *How Pesticides Impact Human Health and Ecosystems in Europe* (Apr 2023).

[2] Department for Business and Trade, Public Attitudes to Trade Tracker (updated 25 Mar 2025) at <https://www.gov.uk/government/collections/public-attitudes-to-trade-tracker>.

[3] Food Standards Agency, 'Four-Country Working: Guidance on Devolved Responsibilities and Collaborative Working across the UK' at <https://www.food.gov.uk/about-us/four-countryworking>.

[4] A Kolamunna, J McMahon, G Furey, and F Lalor, 'Impact of Brexit and Subsequent Food Regulatory Divergence on the Irish Food and Drink Industry' (2024) 19(9) Global Trade and Customs Journal 567;

Emily Lydgate and Chloë Anthony, *Food Law* In: *The UK Regulatory Framework Post-Brexit: 'Law Unbound'.*
Edited by: Paul Craig and Vilija Vėlyvytė, Oxford University Press. © Oxford University Press 2026.
DOI: 10.1093/9780198969815.003.0028

Previous research conducted by the authors examined post-Brexit changes to the UK's general food regulatory framework as well as to rules on pesticides, food hygiene, and labelling[5] as examples of food regulation spanning product, process, and presentation rules.[6] We found that formal changes to regulation, that is, active divergence, were not as significant and far-reaching as changes to the processes of regulatory formation, implementation, and enforcement. Three cross-cutting trends were identified: a consolidation of executive power; the omission of certain elements of the EU regime and expansion of non-legislative approaches to policy-making and regulation; and fragmentation of food standards across the UK.

The UK's regulatory rupture with the EU, and resultant re-shaping of its internal market, at the time of writing remain subject to further reform. While the Conservative government prioritized regulatory autonomy, the Labour government has agreed with the EU to negotiate a Common Sanitary and Phytosanitary Area.[7] This agreement promises to re-introduce dynamic alignment with EU food law in a wide range of areas, leading to 'the vast majority' of plant and animal products traded between Great Britain and the EU no longer being subject to regulatory compliance checks and controls.[8] Re-alignment with EU food law has profound implications for multiple dimensions of UK food law governance.

This chapter proceeds as follows. Section 1 briefly outlines EU food law, its intersection with the EU single market, and implementation in the UK before Brexit. Section 2 examines food law post-Brexit by providing an overview of the assimilated EU framework and the UK's internal market, as well as a case study of assimilated pesticide regulation, namely that of maximum residue levels in food. Section 3 offers an analysis of the UK's obligations with regard to food law under the EU–UK Withdrawal Agreement and Trade and Cooperation Agreement. Section 4 sets out key implications of a forthcoming Common Sanitary and Phytosanitary Area across domestic food law governance, considering different models for dynamically aligning with the EU.

We conclude that the 'taking back control' agenda was implemented by means of a transfer of power to the UK government and regulatory bodies so that regulatory

G Asiamah, 'Divorced But Co-habiting: A Co-evolutionary Perspective on EU–UK Regulatory Nexus Post-Brexit' (2024) Journal of European Integration (https://doi.org/10.1080/07036337.2024.2407094); LC Whitten, *EU Law Tracker: Report Four* (Feb 2025); E Lydgate and A Carson-Taylor, *An EU-UK SPS Agreement: the Perils and Possibilities of (Re)alignment* (Centre for Inclusive Trade Policy, Dec 2024); J Reland, *UK–EU Divergence Tracker Q2–Q3* (UK in a Changing Europe, Nov 2024); D Phinnemore and LC Whitten, *Mapping Post-EU Exit Regulatory Divergence in Northern Ireland* (May 2024).

[5] E Lydgate and C Anthony, 'Brexit, Food Law and the UK's Search for a Post-EU Identity' (2022) 85 MLR 1168.

[6] Drawing on van der Meulen and Wernaart's analytical framing of EU food law, in V van der Meulen and B Wernaart (eds), *European Food Law Handbook* (European Institute for Food Law, 2020) and B van der Meulen, 'The Structure of European Food Law' (2013) 2 Laws 69.

[7] HM Government, UK-EU Summit—Common Understanding (19 May 2025) at <https://www.gov.uk/government/publications/ukeu-summit-key-documentation/uk-eu-summit-common-understanding-html>, Arts 23–33.

[8] ibid Art 25.

sovereignty has meant a consolidation of executive power rather than improved democratic accountability. In re-aligning food law with the EU, the UK government could maintain an executive-led approach of regulation by ministers with little transparency or consultation. Alternatively, it could ensure that the formation of food law is inclusive of stakeholder priorities and accountable to devolved nations and Parliament. The latter would help to redress the Brexit-era notion that the only legitimate way to respect democratic outcomes in the UK is through regulatory independence from the EU.

1 Pre-Brexit Regulation, EU Food Law, and the EU Internal Market

UK food law was highly integrated with EU law and governance institutions before Brexit such that the National Audit Office reported in 2019 that around 90 per cent of UK food law and policy was made at EU level.[9] In a study of food safety law post-Brexit, Asiamah finds that[10]

> [t]he institutionalisation of regulatory principles, norms, and culture, resulting from decades of collaboration and coordination between the UK and EU, has deeply embedded these values within domestic institutions . . . This arrangement reflects the entrenched nature of regulatory frameworks influenced by a shared history and the mutual benefits derived from harmonised standards.

In the EU regime, regulatory functions are divided between member states, the European Commission, scientific agencies, and standing committees. The EU's legal framework for food safety regulation is found in the General Food Law of 2002,[11] and responded to two major events: the adoption of the WTO Agreement on Sanitary and Phytosanitary Measures, which was designed to prevent barriers to trade arising from domestic regulations relating to human, animal, and plant life or health; and the food safety crises of the early 1990s.[12] The framework, with subsequent amendments, establishes the roles of: the Commission in overseeing the implementation of EU food law; the European Food Safety Authority (EFSA) as the scientific agency providing advice and assessing risks; the Standing Committee on Plants, Animals, Food and Feed in assisting the Commission in developing food law; member states in enforcing food safety laws domestically; food businesses in implementing control systems as

[9] National Audit Office, *Ensuring Food Safety and Standards* (June 2019) HC 2217 11.

[10] Asiamah (n 4) 9.

[11] Regulation (EC) No 178/2002 of the European Parliament and of the Council of 28 January 2002 laying down the general principles and requirements of food law, establishing the European Food Safety Authority and laying down procedures in matters of food safety [2002] OJ L31/1 (General Food Law).

[12] European Commission, *White Paper on Food Safety* COM (1999) 719.

well as in compliance; and the Rapid Alert System for Food and Feed in responding to food safety risks. EU rules on delegated and implementing legislation also apply.

Alongside the General Food Law, EU food law includes requirements for regulatory harmonization in a wide range of areas in order to enable free movement of goods. These encompass positive listing systems that specify substances approved for food use, such as food additives and flavourings, and the establishment of thresholds for potentially harmful substances in food, including contaminants, toxins, pesticide residues, and veterinary drug residues. There are also non-harmonized areas of food law. In these areas, member states are obliged to mutually recognize each other's goods as achieving an equivalent level of protection.[13]

Mutual recognition allows food products legally produced and marketed in one member state to be sold in any other member state, even if they do not fully comply with the regulation in the destination country. However, member states can reject mutual recognition of imported goods under exemptions outlined in Article 36 TFEU and developed through case law of the Court of Justice of the European Union. These include public morality, policy, or security; protection of human, animal, or plant health and life; preservation of national treasures with artistic, historic, or archaeological value; and protection of industrial and commercial property. Member States may also cite 'overriding reasons of public interest', and are not obliged to mutually recognize products that violate mandatory requirements related to consumer protection or environmental protection.[14]

2 Post-Brexit Food Law and the UK Internal Market

(a) Assimilating EU Food Law

Translating EU regulation and regulatory processes into a UK context post-Brexit took place through the incorporation of EU laws into UK law. This created different categories of 'retained EU law' under the European Union (Withdrawal) Act 2018, which have been revised under the Retained EU Law (Revocation and Reform) Act 2023, and renamed as 'assimilated EU law'. As an EU Regulation, the General Food Law was incorporated directly into UK law.[15] While EU Exit secondary legislation amending the General Food Law, and other related EU laws, retained overarching aims and principles, governance arrangements and the constitution of the UK internal market changed profoundly. Ostensibly due to the need to proceed quickly to avoid a regulatory cliff edge, regulatory functions previously held by the Commission

[13] European Commission, 'Mutual Recognition of Goods' at <https://ec.europa.eu/growth/singlemarket/goods/free-movement-sectors/mutual-recognition_en>.

[14] Case C-302/86 *Commission v Denmark* EU:C:1988:421.

[15] European Union (Withdrawal) Act 2018, s 3.

and EU scientific agencies are transferred to GB ministers, and the roles of domestic regulatory bodies are not set out in the assimilated EU regime.[16]

Comparing the effectiveness of EU and UK regulation is challenging due to differences in geographical scope, lawmaking and institutional arrangements, and differences within and across policy areas. A cross-cutting trend in the incorporation of EU food law is the omission of explicit reference to EU bodies and procedures, and expansion of ministerial capacities to undertake regulatory functions, leading to the question of whether EU checks and balances are adequately replicated.[17] This is further in question due to amendments made by the 2023 Act which provides that 'no general principle of EU law is part of domestic law after the end of 2023'.[18] Due to the complexity of incorporating EU law domestically, detailed research is needed on the impact of removing the applicability of EU principles in UK law in relation to separation agreements, international agreements, domestic legislation, and case law, and in regulatory practice in individual areas of law.

A relevant example for this chapter is the precautionary principle, which is central to EU law as an environmental rule of law principle.[19] It is applied to risk management in EU food law to allow provisional measures where scientific uncertainty exists regarding potential harm to human health, in order to safeguard health protection.[20] The Environment Act 2021 provides for the precautionary principle, as well as other environmental principles, in a new Environmental Principles Policy Statement (EPPS) to which ministers must have regard when making policy.[21] Commenting during the passage of the Environment Bill, Lee and Scotford found that the new status for environmental principles 'undermines their legal significance to the greatest extent possible, despite their statutory foothold'.[22] In its advice on the draft EPPS, the Office for Environmental Protection found the precautionary principle to be narrowed in scope and not reflecting the usual understanding and application of the principle.[23] The 2021 Act and the EPPS expressly limit the application of the precautionary principle to environmental matters, although recognize that it may continue to apply in other areas of law, such as 'human health, food and safety'.[24]

[16] More specifically, the assimilated GFL replaces reference to the Community with Great Britain, removes references to EU institutions or replaces such references with powers for GB ministers (Chapter III), removes processes relating to the Rapid Alert System for Food and Feed and crisis management (Chapter IV), and removes rules on exercise of delegated powers (Chapter V). General Food Law (Amendment etc) (EU Exit) Regulations 2019, SI 2019/641 (as amended); Food and Feed Safety (Miscellaneous Amendments and Transitional Provisions) Regulations 2022, SI 2022/377.

[17] Lydgate and Anthony (n 5).

[18] European Union (Withdrawal) Act 2018, s 5(A4).

[19] Art 191(2) TFEU.

[20] General Food Law, Art 7.

[21] Defra, Environmental principles policy statement (EPPS) (Jan 2023) at <https://www.gov.uk/government/publications/environmental-principles-policy-statement/environmental-principles-policy-statement>.

[22] M Lee and E Scotford, 'Environmental Principles after Brexit: The Draft Environmental (Principles and Governance) Bill' (2019) (working paper) 4.

[23] Office for Environmental Protection, *A Review of the Implementation of the Duty to Have Due Regard to the Environmental Principles Policy Statement in England* (Feb 2025) 17.

[24] Environment Act 2021, s 19(5)(c); EPPS (2023) (n 20) footnote.

The assimilated General Food Law retains the general objectives of a high level of protection of human life and health and consumer interests (Article 5) and the general principles of risk analysis, including the precautionary principle (Article 7). Although the principle is retained, reference to taking the opinion of EFSA into particular account is removed, and not replaced with reference to UK agencies (Article 6). EFSA provides independent scientific advice on risks associated with the food chain, operationalizing the application of the precautionary principle. In the UK, the precautionary principle is operationalized through the scientific review processes of relevant agencies (in Great Britain, the Food Standards Agency, Food Standards Scotland, and the Health and Safety Executive). The lack of a formalized role for independent scientific advice in the assimilated framework does not preclude a robust risk assessment process, nor *de jure* weaken the precautionary principle, but makes the application of the precautionary principle more discretionary and less transparent.

While the procedures that apply the precautionary principle in the EU are no longer directly applicable to the UK post-Brexit, the changes outlined above, including weakening the extent to which it binds regulators and introducing a more informal approach to risk assessment, reveal an overall weakening of the principle. In contrast, the EU has continued to apply a stricter interpretation. Responding to concerns about risk assessment processes in the EU, a new regulation on transparency of EU risk assessment in the food chain was adopted in June 2019,[25] and a comprehensive update of EU official controls came into force in December 2019.[26] We further examine precaution in the example of pesticides regulation below.

Questions have arisen regarding the capacity of UK regulators to fulfil their functions post-Brexit. Examining the Health and Safety Executive's regulation of chemicals, the Food Standards Agency's regulation of food safety and standards, and the Competition and Markets Authority's role in enforcing competition and consumer protection law, the National Audit Office found expanded responsibilities for all regulators and delayed implementation of new GB regulatory regimes.[27]

> Leaving the EU has changed the operating environment for many UK regulators. They have new responsibilities for developing regulatory policy at a national rather than EU level, and they have taken on new regulatory functions previously carried out by the EU and its institutions. They have also lost access to a range of data sharing and cooperation arrangements.

[25] Regulation (EU) 2019/1381 of the European Parliament and of the Council of 20 June 2019 on the transparency and sustainability of the EU risk assessment in the food chain [2019] OJ L231/1. For background, see European Commission, 'Transparency and Sustainability of the EU Risk Assessment in the Food Chain' at <https://food.ec.europa.eu/horizontal-topics/general-food-law/transparency-and-sustainability-eu-risk-assessment-food-chain_en> and European Commission, *Executive Summary of the REFIT Evaluation of the General Food Law (Regulation (EC) No 178/2002)* SWD(2018) 38 final.

[26] Regulation (EU) 2017/625 of the European Parliament and of the Council of 15 March 2017 on official controls and other official activities performed to ensure the application of food and feed law, rules on animal health and welfare, plant health and plant protection products [2017] OJ L95/1.

[27] National Audit Office, *Regulating after EU Exit* (May 2022) HC 61, 5.

(b) Pesticides, Precaution, and Divergence

To understand post-Brexit regulation and the application of principles outlined in the General Food Law, it is instructive to consider a case study. We take pesticide regulation, and specifically the setting of maximum residue levels (MRLs) in food, to illustrate how divergence in food law has played out. The precautionary principle is applied to pesticide regulation in the EU through what is commonly called a 'hazard-based' approach to risk assessment: some pesticides are intrinsically hazardous and therefore too dangerous to be in use. In contrast, many non-EU countries, such as the US, follow a more permissive approach to pesticide approval based on the notion that risk can be mitigated, commonly referred to as the 'risk-based' approach.[28] The example of MRL regulation demonstrates the interaction between changes to legislative process and changes to legislative outcomes, through the lens of regulatory formation and the application of the precautionary principle. Though the precautionary principle is maintained in assimilated EU pesticide law, and the hazard-based approach was initially replicated through adoption of EU MRLs, the process by which standards are now set, implemented, and enforced has changed post-Brexit.

Regulation of plant protection products, or pesticides, encompasses approvals of active substances (and safeners, synergists, co-formulants, or adjuvants) and the authorization and sustainable use of pesticides, as well as the setting of MRLs in food and feed. The EU regime for MRLs was consolidated in 2005.[29] MRLs are defined in the EU Regulation as 'the upper legal level of a concentration for a pesticide residue in or on food or feed set in accordance with this regulation, based on good agricultural practice and the lowest consumer exposure necessary to protect vulnerable consumers'.[30] The EU MRLs Regulation is incorporated into UK law directly, with amendments, using powers provided in the 2018 Withdrawal Act.[31]

MRL procedures are set out in detail in the EU Regulation and technical guidelines.[32] In brief, the Commission proposes MRLs on the basis of scientific assessments provided by EFSA. The Commission prepares a draft regulation that is voted on by the Standing Committee on Plants, Animals, Food and Feed, which is made up of representatives from member states. If there is a qualified majority in favour, the regulation is submitted to the Council of Europe and the European Parliament.

[28] E Lydgate, PAN UK, and Sustain, *Toxic Trade: How Trade Deals Threaten to Weaken UK Pesticide Standards* (June 2020).

[29] Regulation (EC) No 396/2005 of the European Parliament and of the Council of 23 February 2005 on maximum residue levels of pesticides in or on food and feed of plant and animal origin [2005] OJ L70/1 (EU MRLs Regulation).

[30] ibid Art 3(d).

[31] Pesticides (Maximum Residue Levels) (Amendment etc) (EU Exit) Regulations SI 2019/577 (as amended).

[32] European Commission, *MRL setting procedure in accordance with Articles 6 to 11 of Regulation (EC) No 396/2005 and Article 8 of Regulation (EC) No 1107/2009* (23 September 2021) SANTE/2015/10595 Rev 6.1.

If no objections are raised, the regulation will enter into force twenty days after publication and the new MRLs will be approved for use six months after that. When the UK was an EU member state, designated authorities for MRLs were the Health and Safety Executive (HSE)[33] for England and Wales and Scottish Ministers for Scotland; the Department of Agriculture and Rural Development, now the Department for Agriculture, Environment and Rural Affairs, was and remains the designated authority for Northern Ireland.[34]

Post-Brexit, the HSE has expanded its role in pesticides regulation by undertaking responsibilities previously carried out by EFSA, the Commission, and member states, which includes implementing a new GB regime for pesticides in addition to decision-making on active substances, MRLs, and product authorizations.[35] While GB ministers have powers to exercise these functions directly, the HSE is the delivery body acting on a GB-wide basis on behalf of the Secretary of State and Welsh and Scottish Ministers.[36] The National Audit Office reported in 2022 that the HSE 'did not consider it had capacity to keep pace with the EU pesticides regime', and that Defra had extended expiry dates of active substances due for renewal to give time for the development of a GB active substance review programme; nevertheless, six urgent reviews were requested by the HSE in response to assessments made by the EU.[37]

In the assimilated EU MRLs Regulation,[38] references to harmonization of standards across the EU, to rules relating to member states' territories, and to exports to third countries are removed throughout.[39] Provision for the assessment of existing MRLs by EFSA and member states is replaced with powers for either the Secretary of State for England or Welsh or Scottish Ministers to review existing MRLs (Articles 10–13). GB ministers have longer time limits for their decisions than EFSA does in the EU regime. All Annexes to the EU Regulation, which contain MRL registers of products and active substances to which MRLs apply, are repealed and replaced by transitional rules until the end of December 2020, and are now found in an online GB statutory register.[40]

[33] Established under the Health and Safety at Work Act 1974.

[34] Pesticides (Maximum Residue Levels) (England and Wales) Regulations 2008, SI 2008/2570; Pesticides (Maximum Residue Levels) (Scotland) Regulations 2008, SI 2008/342; The Pesticides (Maximum Residue Levels) Regulations (Northern Ireland) 2008, SI 2008/433.

[35] National Audit Office (n 27) 42.

[36] ibid 43, 50.

[37] ibid 50.

[38] As amended by the Pesticides (Maximum Residue Levels) (Amendment etc) (EU Exit) Regulations 2019, SI 2019/557.

[39] More specifically, it repeals provisions in the EU Regulation relating to the assessment of existing MRLs by EFSA, and administrative review by the Commission (Arts 10, 11, and 13); sanctions for member states in relation to non-compliance with the Regulation (Art 34); emergency measures to be taken in the event of a health risk requiring immediate action (Art 35); coordination of applications between EFSA and members states (Ch VIII); procedure for the adoption of the EFSA's opinions and Committee procedure (Arts 44 and 45); reporting on the implementation of the Regulation to the Committee (Art 47); and procedures for the repeal and amendment of the Regulation (Art 48).

[40] HSE, 'The GB MRL (Maximum Residue Level) Statutory Register' at <https://secure.pesticides.gov.uk/MRLs/Main>.

References to EU bodies (EFSA, the Commission, the Standing Committee, the Council, and Parliament) are replaced by reference to the 'competent authority', defined in Article 3A of the assimilated EU Regulation as the Secretary of State for England, Welsh Ministers for Wales, and Scottish Ministers for Scotland, unless consent has been given to the Secretary of State to exercise their functions. As such, the assimilated regulation retains many of the principles and procedural requirements, but powers and responsibilities are consolidated to GB ministers separately. Although there is provision for coordination, with consent, in the assimilated EU regime, and as noted the HSE coordinates regulation of pesticides as the delivery body, there is greater potential for fragmentation of the regime.

On the evaluation of applications (Article 8), the EU Regulation requires submissions to EFSA, the Commission, and the Standing Committee, while the assimilated regulation establishes that competent authorities draw up evaluations either in accordance with uniform principles or by setting evaluation principles by means of secondary legislation in the constituent territories. The competent authority is responsible for preparing evaluation reports on applications and sharing them with other competent authorities. Decisions on applications (Article 14) in the EU Regulation are subject to EU rules on delegation and implementing legislation; in the assimilated regulation, competent authorities are responsible for decisions on applications and opinions, and may decide to set a new MRL, modify or delete an existing MRL, reject the application, or take no action.

The competent authority must, as in the EU Regulation, take account of: the scientific and technical knowledge available; the cumulative and synergistic effect of pesticide residues where measurable; assessments of risks to consumers with a high intake or high vulnerability; evaluations or decisions to modify the use of pesticides; rules on legal use of an active substance; and any other legitimate factors. However, the changes outlined show trends towards consolidation of power to GB ministers, and informalization of regulatory approval processes, with details of procedures for involvement of regulators being eliminated. As a result, risk assessment is more discretionary, with fewer checks and balances.

Both the EU and the UK have faced long-running civil society and judicial pressures on pesticides authorizations and MRLs setting. Although revisions to risk assessment and delegation have been implemented, legal challenges on pesticide regulation continue within the EU. Most recently, a landmark 2023 CJEU ruling on the granting of emergency authorizations for neonicotinoids confirmed the principle that 'when granting authorisations of plant protection products, the objective of protecting human and animal health and the environment should "take priority" over the objective of improving plant production'.[41] The Commission's

[41] Case C-162/21 *Pesticide Action Network ASBL v État Belge* EU:C:2023:30, [48]. For background see European Commission, 'Neonicotinoids' at <https://food.ec.europa.eu/plants/pesticides/approval-active-substances-safeners-and-synergists/renewal-approval/neonicotinoids_en>.

decision to renew the approval of glyphosate until 2033 is also currently being challenged.[42]

In July 2024, England's Office for Environmental Protection launched a formal investigation into Defra's compliance with environmental law, that is, nature conservation law and the precautionary principle, in granting emergency authorization for the use of neonicotinoid Cruiser SB on sugar beet seeds in 2023 and 2024.[43] A more responsive approach to concerns around pesticide control has been indicated by the Labour government. Defra halted the emergency authorization for Cruiser SB early in 2025[44] and issued a policy paper outlining tighter controls on the use of certain neonicotinoids (clothianidin, imidacloprid, and thiamethoxam); legislation is foreseen stopping their emergency use, as well as a review of guidance on emergency authorization rules, which will set out the role of the precautionary principle.[45] A UK Pesticides Action Plan was published in March 2025, reiterating existing domestic and international statutory obligations, and setting out pesticides reduction targets and measures to support alternatives to use of conventional pesticides.[46]

Since the end of the Brexit transition period in December 2020, the UK has diverged from EU pesticide law. Pesticide Action Network's analysis highlights significant divergence in two main areas: the granting of automatic extensions to active substance authorizations due to limited capacity of the regulator to undertake its review functions; and changes to well over 700 GB MRLs to bring these into alignment with weaker international standards set by the Codex Alimentarius.[47] The decision to bring a large number of UK pesticide MRLs in line with international standards, rather than maintaining alignment with the EU's stricter approach, reveals a weakening of the application of the precautionary principle. The lack of formalized processes and

[42] ClientEarth, 'Next Step: Glyphosate Approval Now in the European Court of Justice' (11 December 2024) at <https://www.clientearth.org/latest/press-office/press-releases/next-step-glyphosate-approval-is-now-in-the-european-court-of-justice/>. For background see European Commission, 'Glysophate' at <https://food.ec.europa.eu/plants/pesticides/approval-active-substances-safeners-and-synergists/renewal-approval/glyphosate_en>.

[43] Office for Environmental Protection, 'Emergency Authorisations for Neonicotinoid Pesticide Use' (8 July 2024) at <https://www.theoep.org.uk/investigation/emergency-authorisations-neonicotinoid-pesticide-use>.

[44] Defra, 'Statement of Reasons for the Decision on the Application for Emergency Authorisation of the Use of Cruiser SB on Sugar Beet Crops in England in 2025' (23 January 2025) at <https://www.gov.uk/government/publications/neonicotinoid-product-as-seed-treatment-for-sugar-beet-emergency-authorisation-application/statement-of-reasons-for-the-decision-on-the-application-for-emergency-authorisation-of-the-use-of-cruiser-sb-on-sugar-beet-crops-in-england-in-2025>.

[45] Defra, 'A New Approach to the Use of Certain Neonicotinoids on Crops Grown in England' (21.12.24) at <https://www.gov.uk/government/publications/a-new-approach-to-the-use-of-certain-neonicotinoids-on-crops-grown-in-england>.

[46] Defra, Welsh Government, Scottish Government, Northern Ireland Executive, *UK Pesticides National Action Plan 2025* (March 2025) at <https://www.gov.uk/government/publications/uk-pesticides-national-action-plan-2025>.

[47] Pesticide Action Network UK, *Divergence of GB and EU Pesticide Standards* (Apr 2025) at <https://www.pan-uk.org/site/wp-content/uploads/PANUK_Divergence_GB_EU_pesticides_14Apr2025.pdf>; Decision on the adoption of Codex MRLs (CCPR 2021); Decision on the adoption of Codex MRLs (CCPR 2022); Decision on the adoption of Codex MRLs (CCPR 2023); Decision on the adoption of Codex MRLs (CCPR 2024).

transparency for conducting risk assessment contributes to the discretionary nature of such decisions, and also makes tracking their rationale more difficult. In this way, regulation of MRLs demonstrates active and passive divergence in standards compared with the EU as well as procedural divergence.

(c) Food Law and the Internal Market

The repatriation of EU food law also took place in the context of profound changes to the UK internal market. Prior to Brexit, the supremacy of EU law over national legislation constrained divergence between Scotland, Wales, England, and Northern Ireland. The European Union Committee of the UK House of Lords described the EU in a 2017 report as 'part of the glue holding the United Kingdom together'.[48] For food law, this 'glue' took the form of harmonized regulatory requirements and ensured that food products meeting standards in one UK nation automatically complied with requirements throughout the entire UK internal market. Post-Brexit, the UK was no longer bound by EU harmonized regulation, and had to determine anew how to balance devolution with maintaining frictionless internal UK trade.[49]

The UK Internal Market Act 2020 (UKIMA) provides the legislative underpinning of the post-Brexit UK internal market. It introduces 'market access principles' of mutual recognition and non-discrimination. The UKIMA mutual recognition principle provides that goods made in or imported into one part of the UK can also be lawfully sold in other parts of the UK. If regulatory requirements of either Wales, Scotland, or England are met, the product can be placed on the market of each. Non-discrimination applies to selling arrangements, such as advertising regulations, licensing requirements, or requirements for display of goods, and prevents devolved nations from treating goods from other UK nations less favourably.[50] However, these principles do not apply to goods exported from Great Britain into Northern Ireland, where the Northern Ireland Protocol and the Windsor Framework ensure that agri-food products conform with EU food law.[51]

While the mutual recognition principle preserves devolved powers, rather than requiring that devolved nations conform with harmonized standards as they did in the EU, in practice devolved legislation will no longer apply to all relevant activity in the devolved territory.[52] Exclusions to the mutual recognition principle are narrower than

[48] European Union Committee, *Brexit: Devolution* (July 2017) HL Paper 9, [2].

[49] K Armstrong, 'Governing With or Without Consent—The United Kingdom Internal Market Act 2020' (UK Constitutional Law Association, 18 December 2020) at <https://ukconstitutionallaw.org/2020/12/18/kenneth-armstrong-governing-with-or-without-consent-theunited-kingdom-internal-market-act-2020/>.

[50] UK Internal Market Act 2020, Part 1.

[51] Agreement on the Withdrawal of the United Kingdom of Great Britain and Northern Ireland from the European Union and the European Atomic Energy Community, Protocol on Ireland/Northern Ireland UKTS No 3/2020; HM Government, *The Windsor Framework: a New Way Forward* (CP 806, 2023).

[52] M Dougan et al, *UK Internal Market Bill, Devolution and the Union* (UK in a Changing Europe 2020) 3.

in the EU and include 'threats to human, animal or plant health', covering movements of pests, outbreaks of foodborne illness, or product recalls due to safety concerns. They also include chemical regulation, fertilizers, and approval of new active substances for pesticides.[53] The latter exemption does not, however, include maximum residue levels for pesticides, which means that GB nations could still be obligated to import products that contain levels of residue prohibited domestically.

In parallel, Common Frameworks were developed to establish agreed UK, or GB, approaches to certain policy areas, implemented via legislative or 'non-legislative' frameworks; those addressing environment, food, and rural affairs are still subject to final approval by ministers.[54] Rather than being complementary, Armstrong characterizes Common Frameworks and UKIMA as rivals: the market power asymmetry of England vis-à-vis other devolved nations means that England can *de facto*, if not *de jure*, shape legislation in devolved nations.[55] UKIMA allows the list of exclusions from the market access principles to be extended if agreed upon as part of a common framework. The Secretary of State acts as a gatekeeper. They may amend the schedule of exemptions via an affirmative statutory instrument and, if consent from devolved nations is not forthcoming within a month, the Secretary of State may proceed.[56] This undermines key principles of the Common Frameworks programme, namely 'respect for the devolution settlement', that devolved competences will 'not normally be adjusted without consent', and a 'significant increase in decision-making powers for the devolved administrations'.[57] In 2025, the UK government introduced some reforms to expand permitted exclusions under UKIMA, signalling a greater level of responsiveness to concerns raised by devolved nations.[58]

3 UK Obligations under UK–EU Food Trade Law

UK–EU food law trade is bound by obligations in the UK–EU Trade and Cooperation Agreement chapter on Sanitary and Phytosanitary Measures (the TCA SPS Chapter).[59] Generally, SPS chapters in free trade agreements concern plant, animal, or human life and health. They address border controls and regulatory risk assessment to ensure that agri-food products moving between parties are safe. SPS chapters do not

[53] UK Internal Market Act 2020, Schedule 1.

[54] Cabinet Office, 'UK Common Frameworks' at <https://www.gov.uk/government/collections/uk-common-frameworks>.

[55] K Armstrong, 'The Governance of Economic Unionism after the United Kingdom Internal Market Act' (2022) 85 MLR 635.

[56] UK Internal Market Act 2020, s 10(2).

[57] Joint Ministerial Committee (EU Negotiations), 'Communique' (16 October 2017) at <https://www.gov.uk/government/publications/joint-ministerial-committee-communique16-october-2017>.

[58] HM Government, 'UK Government response to the review of the United Kingdom Internal Market Act 2020 and Public Consultation' (15 July 2025) at <https://assets.publishing.service.gov.uk/media/686fa10e2cfe301b5fb679d0/uk-government-response-to-the-review-of-the-united-kingdom-internal-market-act-2020-and-public-consultation.pdf>.

[59] UK/EU and EAEC Trade and Cooperation Agreement UKTS No 8/2021 (TCA), Ch 3.

normally address animal welfare and agri-food regulation not enforced at borders. The TCA SPS Chapter has unusually broad scope and application to food law, and includes additional provisions on animal welfare, antimicrobial resistance, and sustainable food systems.[60]

The TCA SPS Chapter does not provide for procedural or substantive regulatory harmonization. SPS chapters often include provisions that encourage parties to recognize the equivalence of each other's regulation, and conformity assessment processes, in order to reduce the need for regulatory compliance checks on food products moving between borders. The SPS Chapter of the Comprehensive and Progressive Trans-Pacific Partnership (CPTPP), to which the UK acceded post-Brexit, includes such an equivalence provision: it does not require parties to recognize the equivalence of each other's regulation, but they must respond expeditiously to requests to determine equivalence of regulation, explain the basis of their assessment, and justify any determination that measures are not equivalent.[61] Similar equivalence provisions were also negotiated in post-Brexit UK FTAs with Australia and New Zealand.[62]

The TCA SPS Chapter notably lacks such obligations. Although it does not rule out increased cooperation on regulation, it does not mandate either side to review or consider such proposals. The TCA established a Trade Specialised Committee on Sanitary and Phytosanitary Measures as a joint forum for discussion of SPS issues between the UK and EU.[63] This includes issues on development and application of SPS requirements and standards; concerns relating to SPS import conditions applied by the other party; and reviewing measures including certification to facilitate trade.[64] Formal committee meetings occur once a year. In these meetings, the EU has raised concerns about lack of transparency, in particular regarding frequent delays and changes to the UK's Border Target Operating Model, which determines the frequency with which EU agri-food exports will be subjected to border checks.[65]

The TCA also contains a chapter on the Level Playing Field for Open and Fair Competition and Sustainable Development. It includes a so-called non-regression obligation not to 'weaken or reduce, in a manner affecting trade or investment between the Parties, environmental levels of protection or climate levels of protection below the levels in place at the end of the transition period'.[66] The scope of this obligation extends to 'the management of impacts on the environment from agricultural or food production, notably through the use of antibiotics and decontaminants'.[67] The

[60] ibid Ch 3, Art 70. For a more detailed discussion of provisions in SPS chapters, see M Wagner, 'The Future of SPS Governance: SPS-Plus or SPS-Minus?' (2017) 51 Journal of World Trade 445.
[61] CPTPP, Ch 7, Art 7.8.
[62] UK/Australia Free Trade Agreement UKTS No 37/2023, Ch 6, Art 6.7; UK/New Zealand Free Trade Agreement UKTS No 36/2023, Ch 5, Art 5.6.
[63] TCA, Art 8(1)(d).
[64] TCA, Art 87.
[65] Defra, 'Fourth meeting of the Trade Specialised Committee on Sanitary and Phytosanitary Measures under the EU–UK Trade and Cooperation Agreement: minutes' (21 October 2024) at <https://www.gov.uk/government/publications/trade-specialised-committee-on-sanitary-and-phytosanitary-measures>.
[66] TCA, Art 391(2).
[67] TCA, Art 390(1).

Chapter also affirms the precautionary principle, stating that 'the lack of full scientific certainty shall not be used as a reason for preventing a Party from adopting appropriate measures to prevent serious or irreversible damage to the environment or human health'.[68] These obligations can be enforced through dispute settlement, including the imposition of remedies (in other words, temporary application of tariffs) for non-compliance.[69]

These provisions provide limited scope for the EU to argue that the UK has not upheld its food law obligations under the TCA post-Brexit. The inclusion of food law areas in the non-regression obligation is narrow, focusing on production and environmental impacts. Pesticide MRLs, where risk is evaluated with respect to human health, do not appear to be in scope. Even where areas are in scope, it seems unlikely that a dispute would result in the EU being authorized to impose remedies, in the form of additional temporary tariffs, against the UK.[70] Even if the UK domestically diverges, it has to meet EU requirements on decontaminants to access the EU single market, which would make it more difficult to argue that domestic changes affect trade. The provisions upholding the precautionary principle are aimed at ensuring that both sides are able to maintain the precautionary principle domestically rather than providing a basis for either side to challenge the other for its non-application. In sum, the SPS chapter provides no specific obligations to cooperate toward harmonizing food law, and level playing field enforcement mechanisms do not effectively address deregulation of food law.

4 A Common Sanitary and Phytosanitary Area: Implications for UK Food Law

(a) Context

The omission of an equivalence provision, or regulatory harmonization, in the TCA SPS Chapter underscores that the Conservative government wished to prioritize full regulatory autonomy for post-Brexit food law. This omission is noteworthy given the economic and political importance of bilateral agri-food trade, where the UK and EU are each other's single most important trade partner. The UK imported 24 per cent of the food it consumed domestically in 2023 from the EU.[71] As a 'third country', in EU trade terminology, Great Britain's agri-food exports are subject to full documentary, identity, and physical border checks to ensure regulatory compliance. Brexit has also resulted in intra-UK trade frictions for Great Britain's agri-food exports to Northern

[68] TCA, Art 356(2).

[69] TCA, Art 357.

[70] G C Leonelli, 'From Extra-territorial Leverage and Transnational Environmental Protection to Distortions of Competition: the Level Playing Field in the EU–UK Trade and Cooperation Agreement' (2021) 33 Journal of Environmental Law 611.

[71] Lydgate and Carson-Taylor (n 4).

Ireland.[72] Pursuant to the Northern Ireland Protocol and the Windsor Framework, Northern Ireland has maintained membership in the EU single market in order to preserve free movement of goods on the island of Ireland.[73] This has resulted in regulatory fragmentation, and the introduction of border checks on agri-food products exported from Great Britain to Northern Ireland.

To address these problems, the Labour Party set out early in its term in office that it intended to pursue an SPS agreement with the EU, and in May 2025 announced a Common Understanding with the EU that included a commitments to pursue a Common Sanitary and Phytosanitary Area.[74] SPS agreements harmonize or mutually recognize regulation on human, animal or plant life or health in exchange for reducing border requirements. Existing SPS agreements vary greatly. In general, the extent of reduction in border controls correlates with the depth and breadth of regulatory alignment. As an example of a shallow agreement, the EU–New Zealand veterinary (animal and animal product) agreement reduces physical inspection requirements and certificate protocols for product categories including red meat, poultry, dairy products, and seafood, but maintains documentary and identity verification.[75] The UK–New Zealand FTA provides a similar model for phytosanitary (plant and plant product) regulation, but is embedded in the UK–New Zealand FTA SPS chapter rather than free-standing.[76] It establishes mutual recognition of plant health certifications within designated pest-free areas, and maintains documentary and identity border checks. In contrast, the EU–Switzerland Common Food Safety Area is a deep agreement, characterized by broad alignment across EU and Swiss food law and the elimination of all border controls.[77]

The Common Understanding mandates the UK and EU to work towards SPS alignment and resembles the Swiss Common Food Safety Area more closely than the EU–New Zealand veterinary agreement. It has a broad sectoral scope: sanitary, phytosanitary, food safety, and consumer protection rules affecting agri-food products, live animals, pesticides, organics, and marketing standards. It promises to eliminate the 'vast majority' of certificates and controls for animals, plants, and animal and plant products between Great Britain and the EU. It will also be annexed onto the Windsor Framework, thus easing trade in agri-food products from Great Britain to Northern Ireland.[78]

[72] House of Lords European Affairs Committee, *Report from the Sub-Committee on the Protocol on Ireland/Northern Ireland: The Windsor Framework July* (2023) HL Paper 237, Ch 3 The Movement of Goods.

[73] Agreement on the Withdrawal of the United Kingdom of Great Britain and Northern Ireland from the European Union and the European Atomic Energy Community UKTS No 3/2020.

[74] HM Government (n 7).

[75] Agreement between the European Community and New Zealand on sanitary measures applicable to trade in live animals and animal products (26.2.1997) OJ L 57, 5.

[76] UK–New Zealand Free Trade Agreement, Ch 5, Arts 5.7, 5.13.

[77] Protocol to the Agreement between the European Community and the Swiss Confederation on Trade in Agricultural Products Establishing a Common Food Safety Area, concluded 29 January 2025, COM(2025) 0309 final, pending publication in OJ (C-series).

[78] European Commission, Recommendation for a COUNCIL DECISION authorising the opening of negotiations between the European Union and the United Kingdom of Great Britain and Northern Ireland on a common sanitary and phytosanitary area between the European Union and the United Kingdom in

The agreement requires dynamic alignment with EU rules. The UK gains consultation rights in EU decision-making processes (excluding Council participation) and access to relevant EU agencies and databases, but must provide appropriate financial contributions. Limited exceptions to dynamic alignment will be negotiated. These exceptions must maintain EU-level standards, enable free flow of EU goods in the UK market, and ensure that only EU-compliant goods enter the EU. The UK will retain targeted biosecurity and public health protection rights similar to EU member states. The Common SPS Area will utilize the institutional committee structure of the Trade and Cooperation Agreement. Existing TCA committees will support implementation of the treaty, and its independent arbitration panel will undertake dispute resolution, with the Court of Justice of the European Union maintaining ultimate authority over all EU law questions that arise within the agreement's scope.

Vis-à-vis other sectors, the depth and breadth of re-alignment being pursued in food law is unique, and signals a new era in UK–EU relations. The Conservative government emphasized the importance of regulatory and judicial independence.[79] EU negotiators also stated during Brexit negotiations that the EU would uphold the balance of rights and obligations in the Single Market and prevent the UK from harmonizing regulation in only the sectors of its choice, colloquially known as 'cherry-picking'.[80] The US and EU differ in their approach to the application of the precautionary principle. Successful conclusion of a UK trade agreement with the US, as well as accession to the CPTPP, whose SPS Chapter was initially drafted by the US, was positioned by some in the Conservative government as a way to solidify the UK's autonomy from the EU. This in turn cleared the path that some in government favoured: a pivot toward the US's less precautionary regulatory approach.[81] The agreement to work toward a Common SPS Area demonstrates that the rigid era of 'red lines' is yielding to a more pragmatic approach. It was agreed in the context of greater trade frictions with the US Trump Administration, and is significant in consolidating the UK's choice to follow the EU's regulatory risk assessment model.

Despite the fact that weakening of the precautionary principle has already occurred in assimilating EU food law post-Brexit, both the Conservative Party[82] and the Labour Party[83] promised to uphold UK food standards in the face of pressure

respect of Great Britain and to link the United Kingdom and the Union's greenhouse emissions trading systems, 16 July 2025, COM(2025) 408 final.

[79] Prime Minister's Office and the Rt Hon Boris Johnson MP, *Prime Minister's Statement on EU Negotiations* (24 December 2020) at <https://www.gov.uk/government/speeches/prime-ministers-statement-on-eu-negotiations-24-december-2020>.

[80] European Parliament, 'EU–UK Talks: MEPs United behind EU Stance, Rejecting UK Cherry-picking' (AFET INTA 12 June 2020) at <https://www.europarl.europa.eu/news/en/press-room/20200611IPR81004/eu-uk-talks-meps-united-behind-eu-stance-rejecting-uk-cherry-picking>.

[81] E Lydgate and M Gasiorek, *CPTPP and Agri-food Regulation: Crossing the EU-exit Rubicon?* (UKTPO Briefing Paper 60, July 2021).

[82] Conservative Party, 'Get Brexit Done: Unleash Britain's Potential—The Conservative and Unionist Party Manifesto 2019' (2019), 57.

[83] 'Britain reconnected' in The Labour Party, 'Change: Labour Party Manifesto 2024' (2024).

from trade partners. The Labour government upheld this promise in its Economic Prosperity Deal with the US Trump Administration in May 2025, which affirms that 'imported food and agricultural goods must comply with the importing country's SPS standards'.[84] Just as uncoupling the UK from EU food law prompted reforms of domestic governance examined above, re-alignment with EU food law also prompts significant reforms to both existing and future food law.[85] While the following analysis remains speculative, given that negotiations have not yet concluded, the governance questions raised below retain salience regardless of the final form that the agreement takes if utilized as benchmarks.

(b) Addressing Existing Divergence: Formal and Process Dimensions

Absent full Single Market membership, lines must be drawn between agri-food products and/or regulations that fall within the remit of an SPS agreement, and those that fall outside and are still subject to border checks. While the Common Understanding provides a sectoral list, set out in the proceeding section, some ambiguity remains regarding the precise scope of coverage. For example, marketing standards are included. Labelling requirements might be considered marketing standards, but are traditionally considered to be Technical Barriers to Trade rather than SPS regulation. This includes labelling requirements such as the Packaging and Packaging Waste Regulation,[86] which results in barriers to trade for UK agri-food exports to the EU. The scope and coverage of exceptions must also be agreed.

As the Common Understanding provides, the Common SPS Area will encompass not only formal re-alignment but also some process re-alignment: UK participation in EU agencies, including observer status at EFSA. With respect to enforcement, it will entail the UK's acceptance of the authority of the rulings of the CJEU. Sectoral process alignment may give rise to new areas of ambiguity regarding how regulation is made, applied, and enforced. Returning to the example of pesticides MRLs, an area where significant regulatory divergence has occurred, illustrates these ambiguities. Pesticides are explicitly listed as within the scope of the Common Understanding, eliminating any ambiguity regarding the necessity of re-alignment. Most obviously, the UK must re-set MRLs that have diverged and ensure that the active substances approved for use on the UK market match those used in the EU, reversing active, formal

[84] Department for Business and Trade, General Terms for the United States of America and the United Kingdom of Great Britain and Northern Ireland Economic Prosperity Deal (8 May 2025), part 2(a) at <https://www.gov.uk/government/publications/us-uk-economic-prosperity-deal-epd>.

[85] Lydgate and Carson-Taylor (n 4); J Du, O Shepotylo, and G Messenger, 'Would a Veterinary Agreement Be a Boost for UK–EU Agri-food Exports?' (UK in a Changing Europe, 17 June 2024); I García-Bercero, *A Trade Policy Framework for the European Union–United Kingdom Reset* (Breugel, November 2024).

[86] Regulation (EU) 2025/40 of the European Parliament and of the Council of 19 December 2024 on packaging and packaging waste OJ L 2025/40.

divergence. The UK will also need to address passive divergence by changing its domestic regulation to match new stricter EU pesticides regulation outlined above.

With respect to regulatory approvals processes, the UK's complete alignment with the EU seemingly obviates the need for independent interpretation and application of the precautionary principle. In practice, it appears likely that the UK's risk assessment will take place pursuant to EFSA's processes, which it will have some ability to influence via observer status. It will also have some ability to influence EU regulation through interventions in the Committee structure that will oversee the implementation of the Common SPS Area. However, in the event of a legal challenge to EU-aligned UK pesticides regulation, a confusing set of conflicting obligations faces the courts. On the one hand, the CJEU will act as the ultimate authority. However, pursuant to the Withdrawal Act, the UK has disapplied EU principles to UK law.[87]

Border enforcement emerges as another area of process re-alignment that may prove contentious. Post-Brexit, the UK introduced a new system of monitoring its borders, the Border Target Operating Model, part of its 2025 Border Strategy. The introduction of SPS checks and certification, and pre-notification requirements for exports from the EU, has been postponed seven times, creating uncertainty for the sector and border and port operators.[88] Subsequent to the announcement of negotiations toward the SPS Common Area, the UK government announced that controls still not introduced, which include checks on medium-risk fruits and vegetables and certification requirements for organics and marketing standards, would be postponed until early 2027, providing time for negotiations to conclude. This obviates once again the need for checks and, as a result, the UK's border controls remain light touch. Agri-food stakeholders have raised concerns about the adequacy of existing border controls within Great Britain.[89] Given the extent to which border controls with the EU will be waived, the UK will be responsible for enforcing the external boundary of the EU single market for many agri-food products. Thus concerns about the adequacy of UK border enforcement may now be raised by the EU.

(c) Dynamic Alignment: Revisiting the Basis of Power over UK Food Law

As set out above, due to ambiguous boundaries, an SPS agreement will involve some degree of 'opting in' and 'opting out' of alignment with EU food law. These

[87] European Union (Withdrawal) Act 2018, s 5(A4).

[88] Institute for Export, 'Final Stage of Post-Brexit Border Checks Delayed Again until July 2025' (17 September 2024) at <https://www.export.org.uk/insights/trade-news/final-stage-of-post-brexit-border-checks-delayed-again-until-july-2025/>.

[89] *Letter from the Chair of the Environment, Food and Rural Affairs Committee (Rt Hon Sir Robert Goodwill MP) to the Secretary of State for Environment, Food and Rural Affairs regarding SPS import checks*, House of Commons (30 January 2024) at <https://committees.parliament.uk/publications/43133/documents/214560/default/>.

considerations are a microcosm of the larger Brexit dilemma: how and where to draw the line between maintaining domestic control over regulation and ensuring frictionless trade with our major trade partner. This dilemma is likely to remain salient when the EU develops new food laws. Even presuming conformity with external formal and process requirements imposed by the EU as outlined in the Common Understanding, the domestic procedures established to govern dynamic alignment could vary. There is an important distinction between regulatory sovereignty, which the UK has achieved for food law, and accountability and transparency, which has suffered due to the expansion of executive power over legislative approval processes. In re-aligning its domestic regulation with the EU, the UK lessens its regulatory sovereignty, but it can do so in a way that entails greater or lesser democratic oversight.

The EU–Swiss Common Food Safety Area demonstrates how domestic democratic processes can be built into dynamic alignment provisions. While the treaty contains broad sectoral coverage, alignment with new EU regulation is not automatic.[90] Switzerland has up to two years, extended by one year if a referendum occurs, to meet its constitutional obligations vis-à-vis the implementation of new regulation. Until then, the regulation is applied provisionally, though Switzerland can argue that provisional application is not possible if it provides an explanation. If Switzerland does not align, and the issue cannot be resolved through the Joint Committee implementing the treaty, either side may refer the issue to an arbitral tribunal. Should Switzerland not implement the tribunal's decision, the EU can impose proportionate compensatory measures.

In this way, Switzerland preserves its ability to decide whether to align with new EU regulation, but must also accept a trade-off between dynamic alignment and full EU market access. Crucially, the decision whether to make this trade-off is based in Switzerland's domestic democratic procedures, including the possibility of a direct vote. The EU–UK Common Understanding similarly provides that, when undertaking dynamic alignment, the EU will respect the UK's constitutional and parliamentary procedures.[91] This provides the UK the room to determine what procedures are necessary to determine whether dynamic alignment is desirable in a particular case.

Two existing domestic models of unilateral EU alignment, outside the area of food law, illustrate the variability of existing models within the UK, while the Windsor Framework illustrates a treaty-based model. First, the Product Regulation and Metrology Act allows the Secretary of State to make regulations 'which correspond, or are similar, to a provision of relevant EU law for the purpose of reducing or mitigating the environmental impact of products'.[92] This introduces powers for dynamic EU alignment with little democratic accountability. The extent to which such powers will be invoked remains undefined. There is also little precision regarding which laws may be in scope; simply 'relevant EU law' is included. The approach to making this

[90] EU–Swiss Common Food Safety Area, Arts 14, 15, 20, and 21 in the following.
[91] Common Understanding, Art 27.
[92] Product Regulation and Metrology Act (2025), cl 1(2).

regulation is concentrated in the central UK government. Although it may be presumed that existing intergovernmental cooperation mechanisms will be utilized, this remains unspecified.

Second, the UK Withdrawal from the EU (Continuity) (Scotland) Act 2021 provides that Scottish law can continue to keep pace with EU standards and regulations in devolved areas, even though the UK has left the EU. It applies primarily to environmental standards, consumer protection, and certain aspects of employment law that fall within Scotland's devolved powers. While the aim is to prevent regulatory divergence from EU standards, there are criteria to determine whether alignment will be beneficial. Before using these powers, ministers must consider factors including the effects on Scotland's resources and relationships with the rest of the UK, the impact on trade, and whether the regulations would contribute to maintaining and advancing standards. Further, there is parliamentary oversight: Scottish Ministers must publish annual reports on how they have used the powers to align with EU law, which are laid before the Scottish Parliament. This creates transparency and enables Parliament to question ministers on how powers are being used.

Third, Northern Ireland already has post-Brexit experience of regulatory harmonization and dynamic alignment with EU SPS regulation. The Northern Ireland Protocol and the Windsor Framework include mechanisms for managing dynamic alignment with new EU legislation, as well as modifications to existing EU legislation.[93] The integration of new EU regulation is addressed in the Northern Ireland Protocol. New EU laws are not adopted automatically. Pursuant to Article 13(4), when the EU adopts a new act which falls under the scope of the Protocol, it must inform the UK. The parties can then discuss its impact on the operation of the Protocol. The Joint Committee that governs the Protocol can decide to adopt a decision adding the new EU act into the Protocol, or examine all further possibilities to maintain the good functioning of the Protocol.[94]

For modification of existing legislation, pursuant to the Windsor Framework, adoption can only be blocked if a cross-party group in the Northern Ireland Assembly agrees to apply the so-called Stormont Brake; further criteria must be met to ensure that its application is a last resort.[95] While this provides some scope for Northern Ireland oversight over legislative alignment, in practice these conditions give a much higher degree of automaticity to the updating of EU legislation in Northern Ireland.[96]

[93] For an overview, see J Curtis, *The Northern Ireland Protocol and Windsor Framework* (House of Commons Library, 1 February 2024).

[94] For example, Decision No 3/2020 of Joint Committee established by Agreement on the withdrawal of the UK from the EU and the EAEC of 17 December 2020 amending Protocol on Ireland and N Ireland to the Agreement UKTS No 14/2020.

[95] HM Government, Decision on the Withdrawal Agreement Joint Committee on laying down arrangements relating to the Windsor Framework (24 March 2023) at <https://www.gov.uk/government/publications/the-windsor-framework>.

[96] B Melo Araujo, 'The Windsor Framework and Its Impact for Northern Ireland and EU–UK relations' in F Fabbrini (ed), *The Law & Politics of Brexit: Volume V: The Trade and Cooperation Agreement* (OUP 2024).

The UK maintains the option to align dynamically; however, this option, described by Peers as the 'Westminster Brake'[97], is governed centrally by UK ministers, while the Stormont Brake gives the affected region, Northern Ireland, some oversight.

A Common Sanitary and Phytosanitary Area provides the opportunity to overcome regulatory fragmentation between nations in the UK's internal market. Alongside Northern Ireland's continued participation in the EU single market, the Scottish government maintains that alignment with EU law remains 'a priority', which may be achieved in a number of ways, including the so-called keeping pace power, but also through primary or secondary legislation, or non-legislatively, 'as appropriate'.[98] While the annual reports confirm that the powers under the Continuity Act have been made use of only once,[99] the overall intent to align with EU law is reiterated.

However, as food law is devolved, it is important that consent from devolved nations to negotiate the Common SPS Area, its coverage and exceptions, and decisions about whether to align dynamically with future regulation, are not simply assumed. While none of the UK's current models for managing dynamic alignment match the Swiss inclusion of a possible referendum, they demonstrate that the UK decision to align with EU regulation can be made more or less democratically accountable. At the very minimum, dynamic alignment should be subject to explicit criteria and reporting monitored by Parliament, stakeholder consultation, and agreement with devolved nations.

5 Conclusion

Great Britain's full and formal autonomy from EU food law has given rise to ongoing tensions. Intra-UK trade barriers between GB and Northern Ireland, public concerns about lowered food standards pursuant to trade agreements, and market access barriers for UK agri-food exports bound for the EU have all made the UK's lack of regulatory cooperation with the EU a controversial area. Since January 2021, the UK has diverged from EU food law in a number of dimensions; we focus here on the General Food Law and the example of pesticide MRLs. These changes underscore that, when taking stock of divergence, not only formal legislative change, but also processes and principles that underpin the approval of new regulation, are significant. These changes include concentration of regulatory powers in the executive, and lessening of formal requirements for provision of independent scientific evidence.

UK–EU food law trade is currently governed by the SPS and Level Playing Field Chapters of the Trade and Cooperation Agreement, which do not prohibit, but

[97] S Peers, 'Just Say No? The New "Stormont Brake" in the Windsor Framework' (EU Law Analysis, 5 March 2023) <https://eulawanalysis.blogspot.com/2023/03/just-say-no-new-stormont-brake-in.html>.

[98] Scottish Government, *UK Withdrawal from the European Union (Continuity Act) (Scotland) Act 2021—Regulation-making Power under Section 1: Statement of Policy* (July 2022).

[99] Scottish Government, *The Scottish Government's Policy of EU Alignment—Annual Reports 2023* (31 October 2023) 6.

provide strikingly little support for, the recognition of the equivalence of UK and EU food law. This is despite substantive regulatory harmonization during the UK's membership of the EU and until the end of the transition period, and the fact that the UK and EU are each other's most important trade partner for agri-food products. The prospect of a Common EU–UK Sanitary and Phytosanitary Area, agreed in principle but not concluded at the time of writing, is an inflection point for UK post-Brexit food law. 'Taking back control' has seen food law powers consolidated to Great Britain's ministers and the executive of the UK government. If EU regulatory re-alignment provides substantive powers for Parliament and devolved nations to review, and decide upon, whether to align on a case-by-case basis, it could, paradoxically, increase the robustness and accountability of domestic UK food law governance even while reducing the UK's regulatory sovereignty.

26
Criminal Justice

Valsamis Mitsilegas[*]

1 Introduction

The aim of this volume is to evaluate the United Kingdom (UK)'s post-Brexit regulatory framework and to do so against the conceptual frame of 'Law Unbound', thereby reflecting an animating impulse of the Brexit campaign, which was to take back sovereign control over the regulatory domain. The present contribution undertakes this evaluation in the field of criminal law, and more specifically in the field of EU–UK cooperation in criminal matters after Brexit.

There are two key distinguishing features of the relationship between the UK and EU criminal law to be considered when undertaking this evaluation. The first feature involves the ongoing (pre- and post-Brexit) tension between sovereignty and law enforcement effectiveness as regards UK participation in EU criminal law. While UK participation in European integration in criminal matters has been viewed by many politicians as a direct threat to state sovereignty and to the state's monopoly in exercising power in the field, this political reluctance to be part of an increasingly supranational EU criminal law has been accompanied by the prioritization, by both politicians and law enforcement and criminal justice practitioners, of enhancing criminal justice cooperation and law enforcement capabilities within the EU in order to enhance the security of the UK. The second feature, which distinguishes criminal law from other fields of regulation, involves the fact that cooperation in the field of criminal justice involves primarily operational action, rather than legislative production. There are of course legislative measures in the EU *acquis* (such as the Framework Decision on the European Arrest Warrant), which are key in determining the parameters of the UK position in the field pre- and post-Brexit, but as will be demonstrated, the key challenges after Brexit in terms of EU–UK criminal justice cooperation from a UK perspective involve not so much regulatory alignment with EU law, but rather operational capacity and capability within the limited legal avenues available to a non-EU member state.

* The author would like to thank John Doyle for his valuable insights on an earlier draft. The usual disclaimer applies.

Valsamis Mitsilegas, *Criminal Justice* In: *The UK Regulatory Framework Post-Brexit: 'Law Unbound'*. Edited by: Paul Craig and Vilija Vėlyvytė, Oxford University Press. © Oxford University Press 2026. DOI: 10.1093/9780198969815.003.0029

These two key features are central to understanding the post-Brexit UK position in the field of criminal law. In order to understand the present challenges fully, it is essential to begin by examining how the tension between sovereignty and law enforcement efficiency was reflected before Brexit. The chapter will then evaluate key provisions of the EU–UK Trade and Cooperation Agreement (TCA) in the field, before examining how the UK legal and operational systems have adjusted themselves post-TCA. The chapter will also include a specific section examining how the UK may have to adjust further in response to action by EU institutions—and in particular the Commission and the Court of Justice (ECJ)—in interpreting the TCA requirements. The conclusion will aim to evaluate the current framework and look forward to potential opportunities and challenges in the field of EU–UK cooperation in criminal matters.

2 UK Criminal Justice Cooperation Pre-Brexit

(a) The Ambivalent Relationship between the UK and European Criminal Law

In the pre-Brexit era, the UK developed an ambivalent relationship with the evolution of European integration in criminal matters.[1] This ambivalence was premised on the clash between the focus by the UK government and practitioners on effectiveness of law enforcement and security cooperation—and the use of the EU legal framework to achieve such effectiveness—on the one hand, and concerns regarding the adverse impact of integration in the sensitive area of criminal law on state sovereignty on the other.[2] To analyse the post-Brexit legal landscape of EU–UK cooperation it should not be forgotten that, as has been pointed out by the House of Lords (European Union Committee), the UK has been a leading protagonist in driving and shaping the nature and direction of cooperation at EU level on police and security matters.[3] A key example in this context has been the UK's leadership in securing the application of the principle of mutual recognition in the field of criminal law, an idea which was put forward by the then UK Home Secretary Jack Straw at the Cardiff European Council in 1998. This initiative is emblematic of the UK approach towards European integration in criminal matters: the UK has pushed for a system based on automaticity in inter-state cooperation, granting extraterritorial reach to national decisions, without this being envisaged to require initially any EU harmonization in the field and with EU member states thus not having to change their domestic criminal laws in order

[1] I have elsewhere described this relationship as uneasy: see V Mitsilegas, 'The Uneasy Relationship between the United Kingdom and European Criminal Law. From Opt-outs to Brexit?' (2016) Criminal Law Review 517.

[2] V Mitsilegas, 'European Criminal Law after Brexit' (2017) 28 Criminal Law Forum 219.

[3] House of Lords European Union Committee, *Brexit: Future UK–EU Security and Police Cooperation* (7th Report, session 2016-1) para 27.

to comply with Brussels-led legislation.[4] On the other hand, the United Kingdom has been reluctant to adopt EU legislation which would have an impact on domestic criminal procedure, in particular in the field of defence rights.[5] The UK has also led in the development of an EU model of data-driven law enforcement and surveillance. Key examples include the export of a model of intelligence-led policing to Europol[6] and the adoption of the controversial Data Retention Directive, which reflects a UK focus on large-scale surveillance.[7]

Yet these efforts by the UK to influence European criminal law have been combined by fears, at the political level, that European integration in criminal matters would threaten unduly state sovereignty. These fears were exacerbated by the changes in the constitutional framework underpinning criminal law brought about by the Lisbon Treaty, signifying in particular the end of unanimity in the Council and full powers for the Commission and the ECJ in the field of criminal law. The entry into force of the Lisbon Treaty has thus led to efforts by the UK to extend the pre-Lisbon provisions enabling UK 'opt-outs' in the field of EU migration law to the field of EU criminal law. Protocol 21 to the Lisbon Treaty extended the right of the UK not to participate in EU law to the whole of Title V TFEU on the Area of Freedom, Security and Justice, including criminal law measures.[8] The right not to participate also extended to legislation amending existing measures which were binding upon the UK. The UK government would decide on its participation in post-Lisbon measures on a case-by-case basis.[9] The Lisbon Treaty has also introduced the legal possibility for the development of EU criminal justice à la carte, in the Treaty legal basis enabling the establishment of a European Public Prosecutor's Office. Reflecting member states' concerns over the impact of such an agency on national sovereignty and legal diversity, Article 86 TFEU introduced an exception to the ordinary decision-making procedure by requiring the establishment of the Office by enhanced cooperation. The UK announced from the outset its non-participation in the Regulation establishing the European Public Prosecutor's Office.[10]

[4] V Mitsilegas, *EU Criminal Law* (Hart 2009) Ch 3.

[5] V Mitsilegas, *EU Criminal Law after Lisbon* (Hart 2016) Ch 6.

[6] Mitsilegas, 'European Criminal Law after Brexit' (n 3). UK officials have also held two Eurojust Presidencies (including the inaugural Presidency) and a key directorship of Europol.

[7] V Mitsilegas 'The Privatisation of Surveillance in the Digital Age' in V Mitsilegas and N Vavoula (eds), *Surveillance and Privacy in the Digital Age: European, Transatlantic and Global Perspectives* (Hart 2021) 101–58.

[8] Protocol 19 covers the United Kingdom's participation regarding the Schengen *acquis*.

[9] See Arts 3 and 4 of Protocol 21 to the Lisbon Treaty.

[10] The European Union Act 2011 imposed a 'referendum lock' on the UK's participation on the EPPO—European Union Act 2011, cl 11, s 6 and in particular s 6(5)(c); JR Spencer, 'The UK and EU Criminal Law: Should We Be Leading, Following or Abstaining?' in V Mitsilegas, P Alldridge, and L Cheliotis (eds), *Globalisation, Criminal Law and Criminal Justice: Theoretical, Comparative and Transnational Perspectives* (Hart 2015) 135–52.

(b) UK Participation Pre-Brexit

The United Kingdom has had a mixed record regarding participation in post-Lisbon EU criminal law pursuant to Protocol 21. In the field of mutual recognition, the United Kingdom participated in the one major judicial cooperation instrument adopted after Lisbon, the Directive on the European Investigation Order.[11] The UK participation in the Directive on the European Investigation Order may be seen to have come against the odds in view of the increasingly Eurosceptic political climate at Westminster, but may be explained by the necessity to ensure that the United Kingdom remains in the first category of countries in an increasingly integrated system of judicial cooperation in the field of evidence.[12] The picture was different with regard to the UK participation in post-Lisbon EU criminal procedural law measures granting rights to individuals. While the UK opted into the first measures adopted post-Lisbon on the rights of suspects and defendants in criminal procedure, it did not participate in key other instruments in the field, including in particular the Directive on the right of access to a lawyer.[13] The non-participation of the UK in this measure could come as a surprise given the fact that the Directive introduces minimum standards which would arguably lead to minimum—if any—legislative changes to domestic criminal procedure.[14] However, non-participation may be explained by the government's reluctance to participate in a constitutionalized post-Lisbon framework where institutions such as the Commission and the Court of Justice would have a say in evaluating the domestic implementation and proceeding to the interpretation of the terms of the Directive.[15]

[11] Directive 2014/41/EU of the European Parliament and of the Council of 3 April 2014 regarding the European Investigation Order in criminal matters [2014] OJ L130/1.

[12] House of Commons European Scrutiny Committee, The European Investigation Order and Parliamentary Scrutiny of Opt-in Decisions, Oral Evidence of Theresa May, HC 1416, Published on 15 September 2011, Q1: 'what we found was that the police were saying to us that they felt the EIO would be of significant benefit to them. Indeed, there was a concern that, if we were not part of the EIO, what we would see was that the requests from the UK would, frankly, go to the bottom of the pile in future, in relation to assistance that they wanted from police forces in other Member States.'

[13] Directive 2013/48/EU on the right of access to a lawyer in criminal proceedings and in European arrest warrant proceedings, and on the right to have a third party informed upon deprivation of liberty and to communicate with third persons and with consular authorities while deprived of liberty [2013] OJ L294/1. For a critique see D Giannoulopoulos, 'Fair Trial Rights in the UK Post Brexit: Out with the Charter and EU Law, In with the ECHR?' (2016) 7 New Journal of European Criminal Law 387, 389.

[14] Baroness Ludford has pointed out that UK concerns have been taken into account in negotiations: see Oral evidence by Dominic Raab MP to the Justice Sub-Committee of the House of Lords Select Committee on the European Union, Directive 2013/48/EU on the right of access to a lawyer, Tuesday 19 January 2016, Q3.

[15] The impact of the Court of Justice was a recurring theme in the Oral evidence by Dominic Raab MP to the Justice Sub-Committee of the House of Lords Select Committee on the European Union, Directive 2013/48/EU on the right of access to a lawyer, Tuesday 19 January 2016, QQ 2, 3, and 6. The government's review of the Balance of Competences in the field of criminal justice included an extensive section on the potential impact of the ECJ in the field post-Lisbon HM Government, see 'Review of the Balance of Competences between the United Kingdom and the European Union. Police and Criminal Justice' presented to the Parliament by the Secretary of State for Foreign and Commonwealth Affairs by Command of Her Majesty, December 2014, paras 3.11–3.21.

UK concerns regarding the impact of the entry into force of the Lisbon Treaty on the transfer of sovereign powers to the European Union in the field of criminal justice have resulted in a further political compromise in the Treaty of Lisbon, which addressed measures which had been adopted *before* the entry into force of the Lisbon Treaty, under the largely intergovernmental third pillar. Protocol No 36 on Transitional Provisions retained the pre-Lisbon limited powers of EU institutions with regard to third pillar law for a period of five years after the entry into force of the Lisbon Treaty.[16] At least six months before the end of that period, the United Kingdom could notify to the Council its non-acceptance of the full powers of the EU institutions in third pillar law.[17] In the case of a decision not to accept these powers, third pillar law ceases to apply to the UK,[18] but the latter may notify subsequently its wish to participate in such legislation which has ceased to apply to it.[19] This transitional period came to an end on 1 December 2014, a date that marked a significant step towards the constitutionalization of EU criminal law by granting EU institutions their full powers of scrutiny with regard to third pillar law still in force after Lisbon. The UK notified the Presidency of the EU that, pursuant to Article 10(4) of Protocol 36, it did not accept the powers of the EU institutions; accordingly, third pillar law would cease to apply in the UK from 1 December 2014.[20] However, the UK eventually indicated that it would seek to opt back in to thirty-five of the third pillar measures, including the European Arrest Warrant Framework Decision.[21] The majority of measures concerned the principle of mutual recognition in criminal matters (including the Framework Decision on the European Arrest Warrant), as well as a number of other key measures including legislation establishing Europol and Eurojust and legislation on Joint Investigation Teams and criminal records.[22]

As was the case with the UK's decision to participate in the post-Lisbon Directive on the European Investigation Order, the 'opting back in to' the Framework Decision on the European Arrest Warrant was supported by a number of relevant stakeholders and practitioners in the field of criminal justice.[23] Similarly, views of law enforcement practitioners were taken into account by the UK government in its subsequent

[16] Art 10(1) and 10(3) of Protocol 36 of the Lisbon Treaty. For a background to the transitional provisions see A Hinarejos, JR, Spencer and S Peers, *Opting Out of EU Criminal Law: What Is Actually Involved?* (CELS Working Paper, New Series, vol. 1, University of Cambridge Faculty of Law, September 2012).

[17] Art 10(4) of Protocol 36 of the Lisbon Treaty.

[18] ibid Art 10(4).

[19] ibid Art 10(5).

[20] UK notification out-put Council document (EC) 12750/13.

[21] Council Framework Decision (EC) 2002/584/JHA of 13 June 2002 on the European Arrest Warrant [2002] OJ L190/1 (EAW Framework Decision).

[22] See Annex to Council Decision (EC) 2014/836/EU [2014] OJ L343/11.

[23] House of Commons Home Affairs Committee, Pre-Lisbon Treaty EU Police and Criminal Justice Measures: The UK's Opt-in Decision, paragraphs 8–12. See also T May, 'Fight Europe by All Means, But Not Over This Arrest Warrant' *Daily Telegraph* (London, 9 November 2014) http://www.telegraph.co.uk/news/politics/conservative/11216589/Theresa-May-Fight-Europe-by-all-means-but-not-over-this-Arrest-Warrant.html last accessed 1 October 2025.

decision for the United Kingdom to opt back in to a series of measures related to the Prüm system of storage and exchange of personal data, including DNA data.[24] In her speech before the House of Commons, the then Home Secretary Theresa May stressed the views of senior law enforcement officers and stated that attempts to exchange data in other ways would require not only an intergovernmental agreement, but the building of separate systems.[25]

3 EU–UK Criminal Justice Cooperation Post-Brexit: The TCA

Security and criminal justice cooperation are covered by a separate part in the TCA Agreement: Part III on law enforcement and judicial cooperation in criminal matters. Part III is supplemented by a series of Annexes developing further implementing, definitional, or technical provisions. It is also accompanied by a series of notifications by the UK and the EU on behalf of the member states[26] (and by the EU separately).[27] The TCA reflects the parties' willingness to achieve a high degree of cooperation in several areas, most notably on surrender (post the EU cooperation on the European Arrest Warrant), money laundering and confiscation, and certain areas of data sharing. Yet key post-Brexit gaps are also notable: there are no provisions on substantive criminal law; cooperation on mutual legal assistance is limited; the TCA does not include provisions on transfer of prisoners; and the post-Brexit position of the UK as a third state does not allow full participation in EU criminal justice bodies and agencies and does not allow access to EU security and law enforcement databases. The present contribution will focus on three key elements of the TCA framework on criminal law: extradition and surrender; mutual legal assistance; and the UK participation in EU criminal justice bodies and agencies.[28] The focus will also be on the TCA provisions on human rights benchmarks which form the basis of the EU–UK relationship in the field of criminal law after Brexit.

[24] Council Decision (EC) 2008/615/JHA of 23 June 2008 on the stepping up of cross-border cooperation, particularly in combating terrorism and cross-border crime [2008] L210/1; Council Decision (EC) 2008/616/JHA of 23 June 2008 on the implementation of Decision 2008/615/JHA on the stepping up of cross-border cooperation, particularly in combating terrorism and cross-border crime [2008] L210/12; Council Framework Decision 2009/905/JHA of 30 November 2009 on Accreditation of forensic service providers carrying out laboratory activities [2009] L322/14.

[25] House of Commons Hansard Debates for 8 December 2015: Theresa May—cl.914, 916 respectively.

[26] See Council (EC) Notification (OJ C 117I); Council (EC) notification UK Competent Authorities (OJ C 117I) available at https://eur-lex.europa.eu/legal-content/EN/TXT/HTML/?uri = OJ:C:2021:117I:FULL&from = EN last accessed 1 October 2025.

[27] See EU–UK Trade and Cooperation Agreement—Notification by the Union [2020] OJ L 444/1486–148 available at https://eur-lex.europa.eu/legal-content/EN/TXT/HTML/?uri = CELEX:22020X1231(02)&from = EN accessed 1 October 2025.

[28] V Mitsilegas, *EU Criminal Law* (2nd edn, Hart 2022) Ch 12.

(a) Surrender and the Arrest Warrant

The TCA aims to provide a high degree of continuity with the previously applicable European Arrest Warrant (EAW) system. The pre-Brexit terminology of 'surrender' and of an 'arrest warrant' is maintained in the text: the heading of Title VII is 'surrender'; the basis of the system is a 'surrender decision';[29] and the objective of UK–EU cooperation is to base extradition on a mechanism of surrender pursuant to an arrest warrant.[30] Title VII on surrender replaces the corresponding provisions of the following conventions applicable in the field of extradition in relations between the UK, on the one side, and member states, on the other: (a) the European Convention on Extradition, done at Paris on 13 December 1957, and its additional protocols; and (b) the European Convention on the Suppression of Terrorism, as far as extradition is concerned.[31] Title VII is applicable in respect of European arrest warrants issued in accordance with Council Framework Decision 2002/584/JHA by a state before the end of the transition period where the requested person has not been arrested for the purpose of its execution before the end of the transition period.[32]

A number of key innovative elements of the EAW system remain in the TCA. Cooperation remains judicial. The 'Arrest Warrant' for the purposes of the TCA means a judicial decision issued by a state with a view to the arrest and surrender by another state of a requested person, for the purposes of conducting a criminal prosecution or executing a custodial sentence or detention order.[33] 'Judicial authority' means an authority that is, under domestic law, a judge, a court, or a public prosecutor; a public prosecutor is considered a judicial authority only to the extent that domestic law so provides.[34] In terms of scope of cooperation, an arrest warrant may be issued for acts punishable by the law of the issuing state by a custodial sentence or a detention order for a maximum period of at least twelve months or, where a sentence has been passed or a detention order has been made, for sentences or detention orders of at least four months.[35] Cooperation takes place on the basis of specific elements introduced in a form.[36] Cooperation is intended to be swift; the TCA has introduced cooperation with similar deadlines as the EAW. Mirroring Article 17 of the EAW FD, the TCA sets out strict time limits for the decision to execute the arrest warrant.[37] The latter must be dealt with and executed as a matter of urgency:[38] in cases where the requested person consents to surrender, the final decision on the execution of the arrest

[29] Art 613 TCA.
[30] Art 596 TCA.
[31] Art 629(1) TCA.
[32] Art 632 TCA.
[33] Art 598(a) TCA.
[34] Art 598(b) TCA.
[35] Art 599 TCA.
[36] Art 606, form contained in Annex 43 TCA.
[37] Art 615 TCA.
[38] Art 615(1) TCA.

warrant must be taken within ten days after the consent was given;[39] in other cases, the final decision on the execution of the arrest warrant shall be taken within sixty days after the arrest of the requested person, a deadline which can be extended by a further thirty days where this is not possible.[40] The TCA further mirrors the EAW FD (Article 23) in the provision on time limits for surrender.[41]

The TCA includes several grounds to refuse to execute an arrest warrant. As with the EAW system, mandatory grounds for non-execution are initially limited to age, amnesty, and *ne bis in idem*.[42] There are several grounds for optional non-execution, in a provision which includes details on the treatment of in absentia hearings.[43] The TCA includes a detailed provision on guarantees to be given by the issuing state in particular cases.[44] This incorporates the case law of the Court of Justice[45] in requiring guarantees if there are substantial grounds for believing that there is a real risk to the protection of the fundamental rights of the requested person; the executing judicial authority may require, as appropriate, additional guarantees as to the treatment of the requested person after the person's surrender before it decides whether to execute the arrest warrant.[46] The TCA contains a general provision on the rights of a requested person, outlining rights of information, translation, and interpretation and access to a lawyer.[47] However this provision is much less detailed than the series of EU Directives on procedural rights in criminal proceedings. In addition to these safeguards, surrender will not occur on the basis of a series of grounds related to non-compliance with the proportionality principle, the non-existence of dual criminality, the occurrence of political offences, and the existence of a nationality exception. All these elements constitute a departure from cooperation under the EAW model. If the executing judicial authority finds the information communicated by the issuing state to be insufficient to allow it to decide on surrender, it must request that the necessary supplementary information, in particular with respect to Article 597 (principle of proportionality), Articles 600 (grounds for mandatory non-execution of the arrest warrant) to 602 (political offence exception), Article 604 (guarantees to be given by the issuing state in particular cases), and Article 606 (content and form of the arrest warrant), be furnished as a matter of urgency and may fix a time limit for the receipt thereof, taking into account the need to observe the time limits provided for in Article 615.[48]

A further departure from the EAW system can be seen in the treatment of the principle of proportionality. Respect for the principle of proportionality underpins the

[39] Art 615(2) TCA.
[40] Art 615(3) and (4) TCA.
[41] Art 621 TCA.
[42] Art 600 TCA.
[43] Art 601 TCA.
[44] Art 604 TCA.
[45] See, in particular, Cases C-404 and 695/15 PPU *Aranyosi* and *Căldăraru* EU:C:2016:198.
[46] Art 601(c) TCA.
[47] Art 609 TCA.
[48] Art 613(2) TCA.

TCA surrender system: cooperation through the arrest warrant shall be necessary and proportionate, taking into account the rights of the requested person and the interests of the victims, and having regard to the seriousness of the act, the likely penalty that would be imposed, and the possibility of a state taking measures less coercive than the surrender of the requested person, particularly with a view to avoiding unnecessarily long periods of pre-trial detention.[49] Non-compliance with the proportionality principle may constitute a ground of refusal to recognize and execute an arrest warrant.[50] The inclusion of a specific provision on proportionality reflects a pre-Brexit debate led by the United Kingdom which called for the use of proportionality in order to curb what was deemed the overuse of the European Arrest Warrant system by states—in particular Poland—issuing EAWS for offences which fell within the scope of the EAW Framework Decision (FD) but were in essence minor or trivial.[51] This debate resulted in the inclusion of proportionality as a principle to be taken into account by the issuing authorities in the Directive on the European Investigation Order.[52] However, already pre-Brexit the United Kingdom went a step further by amending domestic law to treat non-compliance with proportionality as a ground of refusal to execute a warrant (and not merely as a requirement to be checked in the issuing state).[53] The UK approach treating non-compliance with proportionality as a ground for refusal at the executing state has been reflected in the TCA, where the principle plays a prominent role in the operations of the EU–UK surrender system.

Automaticity in the execution of arrest warrants under the TCA is further tempered by the watering down of a number of innovations introduced by the European Arrest Warrant Framework Decision. The TCA introduces a political offence exception to surrender.[54] It waters down the requirement of the abolition of the verification of dual criminality.[55] And it allows EU member states to refuse the surrender of own nationals to the UK.[56] In case of refusal to surrender on nationality grounds, an executing state must consider instituting proceedings against its own national which are commensurate with the subject matter of the arrest warrant, having taken into account the views of the issuing state. In circumstances where a judicial authority decides not to institute such proceedings, the victim of the offence on which the arrest warrant is based must be able to receive information on the decision in accordance with the applicable domestic law.[57] Where a state's competent authorities institute

[49] Art 597 TCA.

[50] Art 597(1) TCA.

[51] For an overview of the debate, see T Ostropolski, 'The Principle of Proportionality under the European Arrest Warrant—with an Excursus on Poland' (2014) 5 New Journal of European Criminal Law 167.

[52] Art 6(1)(a) and (b) respectively TCA.

[53] Section 157 of the Anti-Social Behaviour, Crime and Policing Act 2014 has amended s 21A of the Extradition Act 2003 to treat lack of proportionality as a ground for refusal (s 21A(1)(b)).

[54] Art 602 TCA.

[55] Art 599 TCA.

[56] Art 603 TCA. Notifications made by the European Union to the UK under Part Three of the UK–EU Trade and Cooperation Agreement are available here:
https://assets.publishing.service.gov.uk/media/66e94eeac069f68b7681bc1a/2024-09-12 + EU + Notifications + to + the + UK+-+Final + Version + Septmeber + 2024.pdf accessed 1 October 2025.

[57] Art 603(3) TCA.

proceedings against its own national in accordance with paragraph 3, that state must ensure that its competent authorities are able to take appropriate measures to assist the victims and witnesses in circumstances where they are residents of another state, particularly with regard to the way in which the proceedings are conducted.[58]

Another difference with the pre-Brexit operation of the European Arrest Warrant relates to the fact that the UK as a third country no longer has direct access to real-time EAW-related alerts inserted in the second-generation Schengen Information System (SIS II) post-Brexit. The operational gap resulting from the lack of UK access to SIS II after Brexit has been highlighted by UK law enforcement authorities, with the UK government attempting to mitigate this loss by using the Interpol I-24/7 system for alerts.[59] The challenges of replacing SIS with Interpol are twofold. From an operational/political perspective, it may prove an uphill struggle to persuade the authorities of EU member states to duplicate work by inserting alerts in both SIS II and Interpol systems.[60] From a fundamental rights point of view, reliance on Interpol may prove to be controversial in view of the challenging human rights record of a number of its members and reports of abuse of the Interpol Red Notice alerts system.[61]

(b) Mutual Legal Assistance

The general provisions on mutual legal assistance are contained in Title VIII. The latter does not replace, but merely supplements and facilitates, the application between the UK and EU member states of the 1959 European Convention on Mutual Assistance in Criminal Matters and its Additional Protocol of 1978.[62] A competent authority for the purposes of this Title is any authority which is competent to send or receive requests for mutual assistance in accordance with the provisions of the European Mutual Assistance Convention and its Protocols and as defined by states in their respective declarations addressed to the Secretary General of the Council of Europe. 'Competent authority' also includes Union bodies notified in accordance with point (c) of Article 690(7).[63] In addition to the channels of communication provided for under the European Mutual Assistance Convention and its Protocols, if direct transmission is provided for under their respective provisions, requests for mutual assistance may also be transmitted directly by public prosecutors in the UK to competent authorities of the member states.[64] In urgent cases, any request for mutual assistance,

[58] Art 603(4) TCA.

[59] Northern Ireland Affairs Committee, *Cross-Border Co-operation on Policing, Security and Criminal Justice After Brexit* (4th Report, session 2019-21, HC Paper 766) para 59.

[60] House of Lords, European Union Committee, *Beyond Brexit; Policing, Law Enforcement and Security* (25th Report, session 2019-21, HL Paper 250) para 86.

[61] For a critical view of Interpol governance and the misuse of Interpol Red Notices see House of Commons Foreign Affairs Committee, *In the Room: The UK's Role in Multilateral Diplomacy*, First Report of Session 2021–22, para 119.

[62] Art 633(1) TCA.

[63] Art 634 TCA.

[64] Art 641(1) TCA.

as well as spontaneous information, may be transmitted via Europol or Eurojust, in line with the provisions in the respective Titles of the TCA.[65]

Mutual assistance is based on a standard form developed by the Specialised Committee on Law Enforcement and Judicial Cooperation.[66] Time limits for the execution of requests are not as ambitious as the ones in the European Investigation Order (EIO) Directive. The requested state must decide whether to execute the request for mutual assistance as soon as possible and in any event no later than forty-five days after the receipt of the request,[67] as compared to the thirty-day limit set out in Article 12(3) of the EIO Directive. The TCA does not include the EIO commitment for the decision on execution to be taken and for investigative measures to be carried out with the same celerity and priority as for a similar domestic case (Article 12(1) EIO). The TCA mirrors the EIO by stating that a request for mutual assistance must be executed as soon as possible and in any event no later than ninety days after the decision authorizing the request,[68] and that if it is indicated in the request for mutual assistance that, due to procedural deadlines, the seriousness of the offence, or other particularly urgent circumstances, a shorter time limit is necessary, or if it is indicated in the request that a measure for mutual assistance is to be carried out on a specific date, the requested state shall take as full account as possible of that requirement.[69]

The text of the TCA mirrors the EIO Directive in introducing a proportionality test at the stage of issuing a request. The competent authority of the requesting state may only make a request for mutual assistance if it is satisfied that the following conditions are met: (a) the request is necessary and proportionate for the purpose of the proceedings, taking into account the rights of the suspected or accused person; and (b) the investigative measure or investigative measures indicated in the request could have been ordered under the same conditions in a similar domestic case.[70]

The text of the TCA reverts back to the European Mutual Assistance Convention and its Protocols on the grounds for refusal to execute a request for mutual legal assistance (which include political and fiscal offence exceptions and *ordre public* grounds) and adds to this list *ne bis in idem*, in cases where the person in respect of whom the assistance is requested and who is subject to criminal investigations, prosecutions, or other proceedings, including judicial proceedings, in the requesting state has been finally judged by another state in respect of the same acts, provided that, if a penalty has been imposed, it has been enforced, is in the process of being enforced, or can no longer be enforced under the law of the sentencing state.[71] The TCA allows for the establishment of Joint Investigation Teams but states that the relationship between

[65] Art 641(1) TCA.
[66] Art 635 TCA.
[67] Art 640(1) TCA.
[68] Art 640(2) TCA.
[69] Art 640(3) TCA.
[70] Art 636 TCA.
[71] Art 639 TCA. Oehmichen and Keith note that the TCA grounds for refusal are more extensive than those included in the EIO Directive: A Oehmichen and B Keith, 'Mutual Legal Assistance under the EU–UK Trade and Cooperation Agreement' (2021) 12 New Journal of European Criminal Law 222, 228.

member states within the Joint Investigation Team must be governed by Union law, notwithstanding the legal basis referred to in the agreement on the setting up of the Joint Investigation Team.[72] Overall, mutual legal assistance is a field where the TCA has demonstrated a markedly lower level of ambition in comparison to surrender, which means that cooperation may be significantly slower.

(c) Bodies, Offices, and Agencies

The TCA contains several provisions on UK relations with key EU criminal justice agencies, notably Europol and Eurojust. Title V of Part III is devoted to UK relations with Europol. A key change is that, as in the case of other EU databases after Brexit, the UK will no longer have direct access to the Europol Information System. Cooperation will continue on the basis of national contact points and the posting of UK liaison officers in the Hague[73] and via the exchange of information between a UK central contact point and Europol; however, this will not preclude direct exchanges of information between Europol and the competent authorities of the UK.[74] The UK has notified a wide range of authorities for the purposes of cooperation with Europol, enumerating specifically twenty-one authorities as well as any other authority that has statutory functions for any of the law enforcement purposes specified in Part 3 of the Data Protection Act 2018. The National Crime Agency has been designated as the UK national contact point for Europol (the UK Europol National Unit).

Part III of the TCA also contains provisions on UK cooperation with Eurojust,[75] which aims to provide for avenues of cooperation taking into account the position of the UK as a third country. Cooperation between the UK and Eurojust will continue in the form of the appointment of liaison officers (UK Liaison Prosecutor to Eurojust,[76] a Eurojust Liaison Magistrate in the UK[77]); in the form of the establishment of contact points;[78] and in the form of cooperation with a wide range of UK authorities. The UK competent authorities for cooperation with Eurojust are the International Justice and Organised Crime Division at the CPS, the Crown Office & Procurator Fiscal Service, the Public Prosecution Service Northern Ireland, and any other United Kingdom public body which is responsible for investigating and/or prosecuting criminal conduct or which acts as a central authority in any jurisdiction of the United Kingdom. The centrality of cooperation with the UK for Eurojust will lead to a broader re-think of Eurojust's internal legal framework with regard to the role and powers of liaison officers of third states and exchange of information with third states. It may lead to

[72] Art 642 TCA.
[73] Art 568 TCA.
[74] Art 568(1) and (2) TCA.
[75] Title VI TCA.
[76] Art 585 TCA.
[77] Art 586 TCA.
[78] Art 584 TCA.

the revision of internal EU law *acquis*—and in particular the Eurojust Regulation—in order to facilitate cooperation with third countries. In this manner, Brexit may act as a trigger for internal EU law reform.

(d) Benchmarks

A key question for the future of EU–UK relations in European criminal law involves the substance and the monitoring of the constitutional benchmarks underpinning such cooperation. Part III of the TCA contains a specific provision on the protection of human rights and fundamental freedoms in the field of law enforcement and judicial cooperation in criminal matters.[79] Cooperation is based on the parties' and member states' long-standing respect for democracy, the rule of law, and the protection of fundamental rights and freedoms of individuals, including as set out in the Universal Declaration of Human Rights and in the European Convention on Human Rights (ECHR), and on the importance of giving effect to the rights and freedoms in that Convention domestically.[80] Respect for and enforcement of the ECHR is thus key for cooperation under the TCA. The Court of Justice has already confirmed the importance of the UK being a party to the ECHR for post-Brexit cooperation.[81]

The European Union may terminate Part III if the UK denounces the ECHR.[82] Part III may also be suspended in the event of serious and systemic deficiencies within one party as regards the protection of fundamental rights or the principle of the rule of law.[83] It has been argued that the repeal of the Human Rights Act 1998 could, if not followed by a legislative substitute, be potentially considered as a deficiency big enough to trigger such suspension.[84] Part III may also be suspended in the event of serious and systemic deficiencies within one party as regards the protection of personal data, including where those deficiencies have led to a relevant adequacy decision ceasing to apply.[85] It includes detailed provisions on the data protection benchmarks applicable to cooperation.[86] The establishment by the Commission of data adequacy—that the UK offers an adequate level of data protection, interpreted by the ECJ as 'essentially equivalent' to EU data protection law, and entails regular and ongoing monitoring of the systems of third states[87]—is key in this context.

[79] Art 524 TCA.
[80] Art 524(1) TCA.
[81] Case C-327/18 PPU *Minister for Justice and Equality v RO* EU:C:2018:733.
[82] Art 692(2) TCA.
[83] Art 693(1) TCA.
[84] A Lazowski, 'Mind the Fog, Stand Clear of the Cliff! From the Political Declaration to the Post-Brexit EU–UK Legal Framework—Part I' (2020) 5 European Papers 1105, 1134.
[85] Art 693(2) TCA.
[86] Art 525 TCA.
[87] Case C-362/14 *Maximillian Schrems v Data Protection Commissioner* EU:C:2015:650, [75]–[76].

4 EU–UK Criminal Justice Cooperation Post-Brexit

(a) Domestic Legal and Operational Frameworks: Continuity and Modification

In the field of criminal justice cooperation, the TCA has resulted in limited legal change in the UK. This is in particular the case with regard to the Extradition Act and its interpretation by domestic courts after Brexit. Legislation has been adopted in 2020 in the form of the Extradition (Provisional Arrest) Act which changed rules on provisional arrest, introducing technical changes rather than major legislative changes. In the operation of the arrest warrant by UK courts there has largely been continuity and not change.[88] This may be explained by the fact that the TCA has introduced provisions which reflect changes in UK law before Brexit, in particular regarding taking proportionality into account when deciding to execute an arrest warrant.[89] It remains to be seen whether this approach will change following the development of the case law of the ECJ on arrest warrants under the TCA.[90]

On the other hand, a key manner of addressing the loss of operational cooperation capacity in the field of criminal law post-Brexit in the UK has been through the establishment of new domestic institutional and operational structures. A key example is the creation of the International Crime Coordination Centre (ICCC) in March 2019, which was intended to mitigate the impact of Brexit for policing in the United Kingdom (UK) by identifying those international policing tools to which the UK might lose access, together with a contingency or alternative system for each of them, and to raise awareness of and assist forces to access and use the tools that remained. The unit was staffed with a mix of seconded police officers, former officers with specialist experience, officers of the National Crime Agency (NCA), and contacts from Immigration Enforcement and the Crown Prosecution Service (CPS).[91] This move has been accompanied by the creation of the National Extradition Unit within the ICCC, which has since been absorbed into the Joint International Crime Centre (JICC), aiming at providing advice and support to forces, risk-assessing all incoming requests, liaising with foreign law enforcement, and undertaking removals from and collections to England and Wales.[92] On a practical level, a mutual legal assistance form was adopted in accordance with Article 635 of the TCA, and became

[88] P Arnell, 'Extradition/Surrender under the Trade and Cooperation Agreement – The Shifting Cooperative-Protective Balance' in G Davies and H Carrapico (eds), *UK-EU Police and Judicial Cooperation Post-Brexit* (Hart 2025); R Niblock, 'Post-Brexit Extradition Arrangements: The United Kingdom's Perspective on the TCA' (2024) 3 Transnational Criminal Law Review 86.

[89] On the evolution of the domestic proportionality case law see Niblock (n 88).

[90] Section 5.

[91] C Thomson, 'The Impact of Brexit on UK Policing—A Practitioner's View', in G Davies and H Carrapico (eds), *UK–EU Police and Judicial Cooperation Post-Brexit* (Hart 2025).

[92] ibid.

mandatory as of 1 September 2023 for all MLA requests to and from the UK, in relation to EU member states.[93]

(b) Domestic Legal and Operational Frameworks: Concerns

Notwithstanding these developments, concerns remain in view of the exclusion of the UK from SIS II in terms of the efficiency of the operation of the EAW system. As a consequence of losing access to SIS II, the UK is now reliant on EU member states uploading information and wanted notices to Interpol's database (known as 24/7) in addition to uploading the information to SIS II. If law enforcement in a member state does not take this additional step, the operational consequence is that a criminal wanted on an EAW could travel to the UK undetected.[94] Moreover, it has been noted that the time delays that emerged after the UK lost access to SIS II were of specific concern, since alerts and circulations generated in the UK must first be entered into the Police National Computer (PNC), followed by the completion of a secondary form, which is then forwarded to the NCA International Crime Bureau for uploading to the i24/7 system.[95] Concerns over the loss of operational capacity have also been linked to the need in the post-Brexit landscape for the UK to persuade EU member states to use Interpol for the purposes of cooperation. However, it has been reported that the number of red notices coming through Interpol is about 90 per cent of the number that were previously received through SIS II.[96]

As has been noted by Ben Jaffel, the UK has adopted a four-fold approach to address these operational challenges: persuading European police forces to duplicate data entry to maintain visibility of SIS II data as much as possible; mobilizing interpersonal relationships to query SIS II; multiplying bilateral police agreements to establish direct communication channels; and developing an International Law Enforcement Alerts Platform (I-LEAP).[97] Ben Jaffel notes that while I-LEAP has been primarily presented as a solution to make Interpol notices more swiftly accessible to frontline police officers, it is most significant due to the UK police's stated intention to formally

[93] Meeting on Mutual Legal Assistance Cooperation between the European Union and the United Kingdom | Eurojust | European Union Agency for Criminal Justice Cooperation; EU–UK Trade and Cooperation Agreement—Third Meeting of the Specialised Committee on Law Enforcement and Judicial Cooperation (LEJC) (Brussels, 19 June 2023) available at https://commission.europa.eu/document/download/9f935ebe-8986-4db2-b2a7-fd81854e4972_en?filename=Agenda%20-%20Third%20meeting%20of%20the%20Specialised%20Committee%20on%20Law%20Enforcement%20and%20Judicial%20Cooperation.pdf accessed 1 October 2025.

[94] G Davies and H Farrand Carrapico, *UK–EU Law Enforcement and Judicial Cooperation in Criminal Matters under Part Three of the Trade and Cooperation Agreement: The Impact on Scotland* (Scottish Parliament Academic Fellowship Report, September 2024).

[95] ibid.

[96] ibid.

[97] H Ben Jaffel, 'Security Practices Amid Politics: Data Replication, Transgression and Distanciation in Post-Brexit Police Cooperation' (*Political Anthropological Research on International Social Sciences* 2025, 1–55).

reconnect to SIS II at some point. I-LEAP's objective is to increase the connectivity of UK law enforcement to Interpol's data by enabling direct and real-time access to its network database system, allowing the I24/7 network where notices are circulated. Almost every UK police force can now access Interpol data through I-LEAP, the aim being to create real-time data exchange with international partners, especially in the EU. Ben Jaffel concludes that the subtlety of the objective is to rejoin SIS II without rejoining the EU.[98] In this manner, the UK has attempted to compensate for the legal barriers to cooperation inherent in its position as a third country after Brexit through the creative establishment of institutional and operational channels of cooperation.

5 TCA Criminal Justice Cooperation Framework: Interpretation by EU Institutions

(a) Impact on the UK Legal and Operational Framework

An important question in evaluating the post-Brexit UK framework in the field of criminal justice cooperation relates to the extent to which the development of the EU *acquis* in the field and the interpretation of the TCA provisions by EU institutions will have an impact on the development of the UK legal and operational framework. In the field of judicial cooperation in criminal matters, there have been limited legislative developments in the EU *acquis* after Brexit, with the bulk of developments emanating from the Court of Justice. The Court has also been active in case law on data protection in the field of security, where policy developments have been more vibrant in relation to criminal justice *stricto sensu*. Developments in EU criminal justice (such as the potential revision of the EAW or the EIO) will have an impact on the position of the UK in cooperation in criminal matters. However, at the time of writing, the key developments which may impact on the UK position are developments related not to the evolution of the internal EU legislative framework, but rather to the interpretation of the TCA by EU institutions. The present section will focus on two important aspects: on the role of the Commission in the adoption of data adequacy decisions vis-à-vis the UK; and on the role of the Court of Justice in interpreting the TCA in the context of judicial cooperation in criminal matters (the Arrest Warrant).

(b) The European Commission Adequacy Assessments

An important role for the European Commission in the implementation of the TCA is to assess the adequacy of the UK data protection framework. An adequacy finding has implications for a wide range of policy areas, and in the field of criminal law it is

[98] ibid.

relevant for both criminal justice cooperation and data transfers (such as PNR data) in the context of security and law enforcement. A key challenge for the UK in this context is the extent of regulatory alignment with EU data protection benchmarks as both UK and EU law evolve over time. The Commission is a powerful actor in shaping the post-TCA relationship in this context as a decision not to grant an adequacy assessment to the UK will have profoundly negative implications for EU–UK cooperation and data flows after Brexit.

Notwithstanding the existence of differences between EU and UK standards on personal data collection, processing, and transfer, thus far the Commission has decided not to rock the boat vis-à-vis post-Brexit data transfers. In June 2021, the Commission adopted two adequacy decisions enabling the ongoing flow of personal data between the UK and the EU.[99] In its adequacy assessment, the Commission examined the UK internal legal and institutional framework on data protection, placing emphasis on the UK's adherence to the ECHR and submission to the jurisdiction of the Strasbourg Court.[100] The Commission noted:[101]

> In its structure and main components, the UK legal framework applying to data transferred under this Decision is thus very similar to the one applying in the European Union. This includes the fact that such framework does not only rely on obligations laid down in domestic law, that have been shaped by EU law, but also on obligations enshrined in international law, in particular through the United Kingdom's adherence to the ECHR and Convention 108, as well as its submission to the jurisdiction of the European Court of Human Rights. These obligations arising from legally binding international instruments, concerning notably the protection of personal data, are therefore a particular important element of the legal framework assessed in this Decision.

Adherence to and compliance with the ECHR emerges as a key benchmark for EU–UK cooperation and suffices to establish trust even in cases of potential shortcomings in the UK system in specific cases. Adherence to the ECHR and to Council of Europe data protection instruments suffices to keep the UK as a member of what the Commission has called the 'European privacy family', but such adherence must be continued and is of particular importance for the stability and durability of the proposed adequacy findings.[102] Continuous monitoring by the Commission of the

[99] Commission Implementing Decision (EU) 2021/1772 of 28 June 2021 pursuant to Regulation (EU) 2016/679 on the adequate protection of personal data by the United Kingdom [2021] OJ L360/1; Commission Implementing Decision (EU) 2021/1773 of 28 June 2021 pursuant to Directive (EU) 2016/680 on the adequate protection of personal data by the United Kingdom (law enforcement) [2021] OJ L360/69.

[100] Recitals 120 and 161 respectively.

[101] Recitals 19 and 20 respectively.

[102] Data Protection: European Commission Launches Process on Personal Data Flows to UK, Commission press release (19 February 2021) https://ec.europa.eu/commission/presscorner/detail/en/IP_21_661 accessed 1 October 2025, cited in Lorna Woods, 'Data Protection, the UK and the EU: The Draft Adequacy Decisions (EU Law analysis blog, 24 February 2021) http://eulawanalysis.blogspot.com/2021/02/data-protection-uk-and-eu-draft.html accessed 1 October 2025.

application of the legal framework upon which the adequacy Decisions are based, as required by the ECJ in *Schrems*, is a key provision in both adequacy Decisions.[103] This emphasis on continuous monitoring of the UK data protection regime is crucial, but does not assuage concerns regarding the soundness of the Commission's adequacy assessment. A key concern is the compatibility of the UK regime on the bulk collection and retention of data with EU law, in particular following the development of the ECJ case law in *Tele2* and *Watson*,[104] and more recently in *Privacy International*[105] and *La Quadrature du Net and others*.[106] It has been demonstrated that subsequent legislative and judicial developments in the UK have not led to full compliance of the UK regime of bulk data collection and retention with EU law.[107] The European Data Protection Board has criticized the Law Enforcement draft adequacy decision including on the grounds of the inclusion of an 'immigration exemption' to data protection;[108] on the provisions on onward transfers of data to third countries; and on bulk interceptions.[109] The persistence of a large-scale surveillance regime in the UK casts doubts on the accuracy of the Commission's adequacy Decisions and may lead to these Decisions being challenged. The Commission proposed the renewal of this adequacy assessment in the summer of 2025.[110] However, compatibility of the UK data protection system with EU law will remain one of the key areas of contestation and evaluation in the years to come, with adequacy assessments also being contingent upon the development of the EU *acquis*, shaped decisively by the ECJ.

[103] Art 3(1) of both Decisions cited at (n 100). The Decisions have an extendable expiry date, 27 June 2025: Art 4 of both Decisions.

[104] Cases C-203 and 689/15 *Tele2 Sverige AB v Post -ochtelestyrelsen* (C-203/15) *and Secretary of State for the Home Department v Tom Watson* (C-689/15) EU:C:2016:970.

[105] Case C-623/17 *Privacy International v Secretary of State for Foreign and Commonwealth Affairs* EU:C:2020:790.

[106] Cases C-511, 512 and 520/18 *La Quadrature du Net v Premier Ministre* EU:C:2020:791. On the evolution of the CJEU case law, see V Mitsilegas, 'Data Retention and the Judicial Parameters of Mass Surveillance in EU Law' in E Kosta and I Kamara (eds), *Data Retention in Europe and Beyond: Law and Policy in the Aftermath of an Invalidated Directive* (Oxford University Press 2025) 26–44.

[107] M White, 'Is the Incompatibility of UK Data Retention Law with EU Law Really a Victory? (2021) 47 LS130. The Commission has been criticized for failing to consider the partial response of the UK authorities to the CJEU rulings, see Woods (n 103).

[108] According to Art 1(2) of the Law Enforcement Adequacy Decision, the decision does not cover personal data that is transferred for purposes of United Kingdom immigration control or that otherwise falls within the scope of the exemption from certain data subject rights for purposes of the maintenance of effective immigration control pursuant to paragraph 4(1) of Sched 2 to the DPA 2018.

[109] European Data Protection Board (EDPB), Opinion 14/2021 regarding the European Commission Draft Implementing Decision pursuant to Regulation (EU) 2016/679 on the adequate protection of personal data in the United Kingdom, adopted on 13 April 2021, points 12, 14, and 29.

[110] European Commission, 'Adequacy decisions' (webpage) https://commission.europa.eu/law/law-topic/data-protection/international-dimension-data-protection/adequacy-decisions_en#documents accessed 1 October 2025; European Commission, 'Draft renewal of EU adequacy decision for the UK under the GDPR' (PDF, 2025) https://commission.europa.eu/document/download/6f636fa0-30d4-4c05-a713-64484ad913fa_en?filename = Draft%20Renewal%20of%20EU%20adequacy%20decision%20for%20the%20UK%20under%20the%20GDPR.pdf accessed 1 October 2025.

(c) CJEU Case Law on Mutual Trust in Criminal Justice Cooperation

The Court of Justice has an important role in interpreting the TCA. In the field of criminal justice cooperation, of key significance will be the Court's interpretation of the parameters of mutual trust, including in the operation of the TCA Arrest Warrant mechanism. A key development in this context has been the Court's ruling in *Alchaster I*.[111] In this ruling, the ECJ held that the level of mutual trust between the UK and the EU is lower than intra-EU mutual trust, but also lower than the level of trust between the EU and third states such as Norway. The practical effect of this assessment is that the two-step *Aranyosi* test for examining whether a warrant will be executed in intra-EU EAW cases is not applicable in the context of UK–EU warrants, where a single test applies.[112]

In *Alchaster I*, the Court of Justice put forward a hierarchical taxonomy of mutual trust. The top tier includes EU member states. According to the Court, the principle of mutual 'trust specifically characterises relations between Member States',[113] which all share (and recognize that they share) a set of common values on which the European Union is founded, as stated in Article 2 TEU.[114] The Court further linked the principle of mutual trust with the creation and maintenance of a European area without internal frontiers.[115] The second tier of mutual trust consists of a high level of confidence, established via an international agreement, between EU member states and certain third countries.[116] Norway belongs to this tier.[117] What distinguishes Norway from other third states (such as the UK) is that[118]

> it has a special relationship with the European Union, going beyond economic and commercial cooperation, since it is a party to the Agreement on the European Economic Area, it participates in the Common European Asylum System, it implements and applies the Schengen *acquis* and it has concluded with the European Union the Agreement on the surrender procedure between the Member States of the European Union and Iceland and Norway, which entered into force on 1 November 2019.

[111] Case C-202/24 *MA Alchaster* EU:C:2024:649.

[112] ibid [55]: 'the requirement to carry out such a two-step examination cannot be transposed to the assessment, during the procedure for the execution of an arrest warrant issued on the basis of the TCA, of the risk of a breach of Art 49(1) of the Charter.'

[113] ibid [61], emphasis added.

[114] ibid [62].

[115] ibid [63], by reference to Opinion 2/13, EU:C:2014:2454, paragraph 191.

[116] ibid [65].

[117] ibid [66], referring to Case C-71/21 *Sofiyska gradska prokuratura (Successive arrest warrants)* EU:C:2023:668, [32] and [39].

[118] ibid [67], referring to Case C-488/19 *JR (Arrest warrant—Conviction in a third State, Member of the EEA)* EU:C:2021:206, [60].

The Court noted, first, that in the preamble to that agreement, the contracting parties expressed their mutual confidence in the structure and functioning of their legal systems and their ability to guarantee a fair trial and, second, that the provisions of that agreement are very similar to the corresponding provisions of Framework Decision 2002/584.[119] The special relationship between the EU and certain third states is based on specific relations between the European Union and certain EEA member states but cannot be extended to all third countries.[120] The UK does not belong to this special relationship. The Court noted in particular that the United Kingdom is not part of the European area without internal borders, the construction of which is permitted, inter alia, by the principle of mutual trust.[121] Although it is apparent from the wording of Article 524(1) of the TCA that cooperation between the United Kingdom and the member states is based on long-standing respect for the protection of the fundamental rights and freedoms of individuals, that cooperation is not presented as being based on the preservation of mutual trust between the states concerned that existed before the United Kingdom left the European Union on 31 January 2020.[122] The Court further based its finding that the UK does not have a 'special relationship' with the EU on the grounds of the existence of what it called 'the substantial differences' between the provisions of the TCA relating to the surrender mechanism established by that agreement and the corresponding provisions of Framework Decision 2002/584.[123]

In *Alchaster I*, the Court of Justice sent a political signal regarding the implications of leaving the EU. Through the use of the term 'special relationship', an overtly political rather than legal term, the Court downplayed the degree to which the UK, after Brexit, continues to share common values with EU member states, and declared that the UK is not, post-Brexit, worthy of a high level of trust. However, a number of the legal arguments put forward by the Court in support of this political stance can be contested. First, the Court relied on the linkage between mutual trust and Europe as an area without internal frontiers. While this argument partly reflects the justification behind the adoption of the EAW system (automaticity based on mutual trust is necessary to ensure speed in cooperation to compensate for the speed in the crossing of borders by suspects),[124] the fact remains that participation in the system of mutual recognition in criminal matters in the EU is not contingent upon full Schengen membership, and that the Schengen area continues to be marked by variable geometry and by uneven, and in certain cases limited, trust.

Second, the Court arguably overplayed the significance of the differences between the intra-EU EAW and the TCA Arrest Warrant systems. As demonstrated above, the two systems continue to have many similarities, especially as regards the form and aimed efficiency of cooperation. Yes, EU member states are allowed in the TCA to

[119] ibid [68], referring to Case C-897/19 PPU *Ruska Federacija* EU:C:2020:262, [73]–[74].
[120] ibid [69].
[121] ibid [70].
[122] ibid [71].
[123] ibid [72], [73]-[78].
[124] Mitsilegas (n 29) Ch 4.

deviate from certain EAW automaticity elements, but in the implementation of the TCA practice has shown that many member states have chosen not to avail themselves of these options. Moreover, the main examples of differences that the Court uses in *Alchaster I* concern provisions which aim to enhance, rather than undermine, the protection of fundamental rights.

This brings us to our third objection, which concerns the implicit assessment of the level of fundamental rights protection in the UK compared to EU member states and third states benefiting from a 'special relationship', such as Norway. The Court adopts a rather formalistic approach in referring to the Preamble to the EU–Norway agreement and the expression of the contracting parties' mutual confidence in the structure and functioning of their legal systems and their ability to guarantee a fair trial. Protection of fundamental rights commitments can be found in the TCA. Moreover, and importantly, in terms of substance, the current record of domestic protection of fundamental rights in the UK does not justify a difference in the approach by the ECJ compared to other European third states. The Court's underpinning assertion that the UK no longer shares the common values enshrined in Article 2 TEU is not based on a substantive evaluation of what has changed on the ground in a former EU member state after its decision to leave the EU. Many would argue that the level of fundamental rights protection in the UK remains higher than the level of fundamental rights protection in a number of EU member states, including, and in particular, in the field of criminal justice.

The irony of the Court's ruling in *Alchaster I* is that its outcome ensures a higher level of fundamental rights protection in the field of surrender under the TCA in comparison to the fundamental rights protection offered in the intra-EU EAW system under the cumbersome *Aranyosi* two-step test. The perceived lack of mutual trust focuses the mind on a single assessment of breaches of fundamental rights, a development which may not be optimal from a law enforcement perspective, and which may generate more refusals to execute arrest warrants. It remains to be seen whether *Alchaster I* will lead to a change in approach by the UK courts called to execute arrest warrants under the TCA, who have thus far continued their practice largely in line with the pre-Brexit era.

6 Conclusion

From an operational perspective, the UK's landing in the post-Brexit era of criminal justice cooperation with the EU and its member states has been a hard one. Notwithstanding political concerns regarding the impact of European integration in criminal matters on sovereignty, the UK has been during its membership of the EU an active participant, and on occasion a leader, in criminal justice cooperation at EU level. The UK has been a key user and promoter of EU mutual recognition instruments such as the Framework Decision on the EAW and EU criminal justice agencies such as Europol and Eurojust. Brexit has led to a manifest reduction of legal avenues for the UK to make full use of these instruments in its new position as a third state. The TCA reflects a willingness by both the EU and the UK to maintain the UK in a position as close as possible to key mechanisms of cooperation, in particular in the field of surrender, but the fact remains that the UK is a third state after Brexit, and this means that the UK can no longer make full use of the cooperation avenues available to UK judicial and law enforcement authorities before Brexit. Post-Brexit the UK has opted for legal continuity, with minimal legal or regulatory change, and has emphasized instead change at the operational and institutional levels, with the establishment of key networks and systems aimed at replicating, to the extent possible, pre-Brexit cooperation arrangements. Post-Brexit UK adjustment in the field of criminal justice has thus been operational rather than legal/regulatory.

In current discussions on the revision of the TCA, the appetite from executive authorities in the UK to ensure a closer relationship with the EU is evident. A position paper from the Scottish government advocates a mutual trust clause with the EU 'to illustrate the strong commitment on both sides to human rights and data protection standards'.[125] The intent would be to reduce the necessity for the giving of explanations, undertakings, and assurances during TCA surrender proceedings, thereby making proceedings more efficient and effective. The position paper further calls upon the UK government to seek to agree a mechanism for the real-time sharing of arrest warrants between the UK and EU in order to prevent those individuals subject to live proceedings slipping through the net and to seek an arrangement of alert-sharing whereby police forces across the UK and the EU can effectively, quickly, and efficiently create alerts and share information and intelligence. It also advocates for an arrangement on the transfer of prisoners, which is currently missing in the TCA.[126] The position paper is a clear reflection of where practitioners see gaps in EU–UK criminal justice cooperation. Its ambition will be tempered by the legal constraints underpinning the UK's position as a third state, including limits in participating in the SIS and the perception of the UK as worthy of a lower level of mutual trust.

In any discussions on the future of EU–UK criminal justice cooperation, one must always remember the centrality of respect of EU values, including fundamental rights, in order to secure a close(r) relationship with the EU. Withdrawing from the ECHR will mean the end of this relationship.

[125] Scottish Government, 'Law Enforcement and Criminal Justice Cooperation with the EU: Position Paper' (1 July 2025) available at https://www.gov.scot/publications/law-enforcement-and-criminal-justice-cooperation-with-the-eu-position-paper/ accessed 1 October 2025.

[126] ibid.

Postscript

The Supreme Court's Judgment in *Dillon*

*Christopher McCrudden**

1 Introduction

Several chapters in this book mention that some of the analysis presented in those chapters would likely be impacted by the Supreme Court's long-awaited judgment in the case of *In the matter of an application by Martina Dillon, John McEvoy, Brigid Hughes, and Lynda McManus for Judicial Review* ('*Dillon*'), which was a judicial review challenge to the controversial Northern Ireland Troubles (Legacy and Reconciliation) Act 2023 ('the Legacy Act'). The Court's unanimous judgment in *Dillon* overturning the Court of Appeal's judgment[1] which had largely upheld the High Court's judgment[2] disapplying sections of the Act was handed down on the 7 May 2026,[3] just before this book was finalized.

The purpose of this Postscript on the judgment of the Supreme Court is limited. That judgment in effect considers two separate legal issues: the appropriate interpretation of the ECHR as applied to the Legacy Act; and the application of Article 2(1) of the Windsor Framework to the Legacy Act. This Postscript considers only the latter issue, dealing as it does with the status of an important part of the Brexit settlement in Northern Ireland.

The judgment of the Supreme Court in *Dillon*, engaging with the various issues that arise in the context of Article 2 of the Windsor Framework, is complex and not entirely clear in its meaning.[4] There are, however, several elements of the judgment which are clear, at least in broad terms, although each requires further nuance. Part 1 of this Postscript sets out these broad-brush conclusions. Part 2 considers several of the issues that arise in greater detail and introduces some much-needed nuance into

* Nothing in this Postscript should be considered to reflect the views of the Equality Commission for Northern Ireland, which intervened in *Dillon*, and which I represented before the Supreme Court. The understanding of the case presented here reflects my views alone.

[1] [2024] NICA 59.

[2] [2024] NIKB 11.

[3] [2026] UKSC 15.

[4] This Postscript is an amended version of Christopher McCrudden, 'Reading *Dillon*,' *UK-EU Relations Law*, 7 May 2026, https://eurelationslaw.com/blog/reading-dillon.

the discussion. It is not unfair to the Supreme Court, I hope, to say that the judgment is not an easy read.

As well as not dealing with the ECHR parts of the judgment, a second limitation on the scope of this Postscript is of critical importance. My purpose is to provide as clear as possible a legal analysis of the judgment from the perspective of what it means for the purposes of domestic UK law. It does not seem productive in the immediate aftermath of the judgment to attempt to re-litigate the case, arguing that the judgment is legally 'wrong' for the purposes of domestic law. The Supreme Court's judgment is clearly binding authority throughout the United Kingdom.

A third limitation is that I do not consider whether the judgment of the Supreme Court on the Article 2(1) WF issues is consistent with the international law obligations of the United Kingdom under the Withdrawal Agreement. Before that issue can be satisfactorily addressed, the issue of what exactly the judgment means must be addressed.

Fourth, I do not consider the implications of the judgment for the cases that have been stayed in Northern Ireland courts, pending this judgment, which will likely now proceed,[5] and nothing in this Postscript should be interpreted as commenting directly or indirectly on these cases. As we shall see, there are several issues of critical importance that remain uncertain after the judgment, and much will depend on what subsequent courts make of it. This Postscript is in the nature of a provisional assessment, rather than a definitive analysis. In several respects, it is too early to judge what the effect of the *Dillon* judgment will be, until we have a clearer view of how these courts will interpret it. It would also be unsurprising if the Supreme Court is called on to clarify its judgment in the future.[6]

2 Broad-brush Conclusions

The first conclusion that can be drawn is that the Supreme Court did not disturb the interpretation of Article 2 WF concerning a significant number of issues that the Northern Ireland Court of Appeal had considered. Where the Supreme Court did not explicitly or by implication overrule the approach taken by the Court of Appeal, the judgment of that Court in *Dillon* remains good law.

[5] In particular, the Northern Ireland Court of Appeal will now consider the Northern Ireland Secretary of State's appeal in *The Northern Ireland Human Rights Commission and JR 295's Applications and In the matter of the Illegal Migration Act 2023* [2024] NIKB 44.

[6] So far as I am aware, at the time of writing (14 May 2026), no extended legal commentary has been published, apart from McCrudden in *EU-UK Relations Law*. Two short opinion pieces on the judgment by academic lawyers have been published: Colin Murray, 'Still Living in Boris Johnson's Brexit: The UK Supreme Court's Dillon Judgment ..., *Slugger O'Toole*, 13 May 2026, https://sluggerotoole.com/2026/05/13/still-living-in-boris-johnsons-brexit-the-uk-supreme-courts-dillon-judgment/; Richard Ekins, 'What this Supreme Court ruling means for Northern Ireland', *The Spectator*, 8 May 2026, https://spectator.com/article/what-this-supreme-court-ruling-means-for-northern-ireland/.

The second conclusion that can be drawn is that the Supreme Court did not accept the more wide-ranging elements of the Government's submissions. Although, we shall see that the Supreme Court did accept significant elements of the Government's submissions, the attempt to render Article 2 WF substantially non-justiciable in particular through the strategy of substantially denying it 'direct effect' was unsuccessful. This means, therefore, that Article 2 WF has been accepted as capable of being directly effective in domestic law in a wide set of circumstances, and where that is the case, fully justiciable. This issue is considered in more detail subsequently.

The third conclusion is that the provisions of Article 2 WF are to be interpreted as part of the Withdrawal Agreement, such that the general provisions of that Agreement apply, in particular Article 4 of the Withdrawal Agreement, which is accepted as specifying that the approach to be adopted in understanding the concept of 'direct effect' is that specified by the CJEU.

The fourth conclusion that can be drawn is that, although the judgment ranges widely, the Supreme Court's decision to uphold the Government's appeal against the Court of Appeal judgment was substantially based on the ground that the meaning and effect of the EU Victims Directive, which had been a central part of the applicants' argument as to why the Legacy Act fell foul of EU law, should not be interpreted as broadly as both the High Court and the Court of Appeal had done. This is a relatively narrow ground for allowing the appeal, and while it is important in the context of victims' rights and 'legacy', has relatively little effect beyond that.

The fifth conclusion is that the effect of section 7A of the 2018 Act, which is the provision of domestic law that incorporates the Withdrawal Agreement into domestic law, has been recognized as having the effect that a breach of Article 2 WF by primary legislation enacted after section 7A came into effect would be remediable in domestic law (although the specific remedy was left unaddressed by the Court).

The sixth conclusion is that the EU Charter of Fundamental Rights (CFR) continues to have effect in domestic law, primarily in the context of interpreting directly effective EU law that is relevant in the context of Article 2 WF. Whether the provisions of the CFR are themselves directly effective in domestic law through Article 2(1) remains to be determined. The role of the Charter is considered further subsequently.

The seventh conclusion is that the approach that should be adopted to the interpretation of Article 2(1) WF is accepted, at least in principle, as governed by customary international law, effectively the provisions of the Vienna Convention on the Law of Treaties (VCLT), and no distinction is drawn in this context in construing the reference in Article 2(1) WF to the Belfast-Good Friday Agreement, between the Multi-Party Agreement and the British-Irish Agreement.

The eighth conclusion is that the Explainer Document's interpretative authority is significantly weakened by it not being regarded as evidence of subsequent agreed practice for the purposes of the VCLT although whether it should nevertheless be accorded some authority as evidence of the intentions of the Government at the time that Article 2 WF was agreed (and the intention of Parliament when section 7A was adopted) is not considered. The use of such material is considered subsequently.

The ninth conclusion is that the rights specified in the relevant provisions of the Belfast-Good Friday Agreement ('RSEO') should be interpreted in light of the first sentence of paragraph 1, which specifies that the Parties adopted the listed rights '[a]gainst the background of the recent history of communal conflict', but how far this is a significant limiting factor on the interpretation of those rights is uncertain and is considered in more detail subsequently.

The tenth conclusion is that reliance on the 'civil rights' language of the relevant provisions of the RSEO is now problematic. This is not to say that reliance on that phrase is necessarily ruled out; rather, it means that applicants attempting to ground their reliance on Article 2(1) through 'civil rights' are likely to face an up-hill struggle to convince the court that the Supreme Court has not closed off that avenue of direct effect. This issue is considered subsequently.

3 Adding Nuance and Complexity

Having set out my reading of the Supreme Court's judgment in broad terms, it is now necessary to consider some of these issues in more detail, pointing to where those broad-brush conclusions require a degree of nuance before a fully accurate picture of the effects of the judgment emerges.

I will consider the issue of direct effect, the status of 'civil rights' in RSEO Paragraph 1, the scope and function of the 'bullet point' rights, litigation involving the Annex 1 Directives, the role of the Charter of Fundamental Rights, and the future use of non-statutory materials, including the Explainer Document.

(a) Direct Effect

Although Article 2 WF is capable of 'direct effect', the Court spends some time considering under what circumstances it can be used in UK domestic courts. Obviously, this is of critical significance for future litigation. There are several critical steps in the Court's reasoning at this point in the judgment.

The first step is what the test of direct effect is to be. The answer, in principle, is straightforward and clear: 'The justiciability of article 2(1) of the Windsor Framework depends on whether it meets the conditions for direct effect under EU law'.[7] The relevant test for 'direct effect' is seen by the Court[8] as being the test set out by the CJEU for the effect 'of an international agreement between the EU and non-Member States', namely whether, 'regard being had to its wording and to the purpose and nature of the agreement, the provision contains a clear and precise obligation which is not

[7] *Dillon* (n 4) [111].
[8] ibid [112].

subject, in its implementation or effects, to the adoption of any subsequent measure'.[9] Applying that test to Article 2(1) WF, the Court concluded that the relevant question was 'whether, having regard to the wording and to the purpose and nature of the RSEO chapter and of article 2(1) of the Windsor Framework, those provisions read together impose a clear and precise obligation which satisfies the test for direct effect.'[10]

The second step in the process involves the Court setting out its answer to that question. There are three elements in the Court's answer. The first is that certain provisions of the RSEO chapter are not themselves directly effective because they do not meet the CJEU's test. The Court identifies specifically[11] the 'commitment to "the civil rights … of everyone in the community" in paragraph 1 in that context, in addition to the provisions regarding victims in paragraphs 11 and 12 RSEO. 'These provisions,' says the Court, 'are expressed at a high level of generality. The reference to "civil rights" in paragraph 1 is accompanied by broad references to "mutual respect" and "religious liberties".' The language adopted in the victims' provisions 'is far too general to give rise to any directly enforceable rights in relation to inquests, civil proceedings or prosecutions.'

The third step in the process is for the Court to emphasize the need to pay attention to the language in Article 2(1) itself.[12] As the Court puts it, it is necessary 'to focus on "rights, safeguards or equality of opportunity, *as set out in [the RSEO chapter]*"'.[13] 'It is necessary,' says the Court, 'to identify a clear and precise obligation in EU law by reference to the RSEO chapter. It is only in this way that the obligation not to diminish rights, safeguards or equality of opportunity acquires any content.'[14] The Court considers it 'necessary to read article 2(1) of the Windsor Framework in conjunction with the RSEO chapter in order to identify a clear and precise obligation which satisfies the test for direct effect'.[15] Article 2(1), therefore, is capable of being directly effective, when taken in combination with at least some of provisions of the RSEO chapter.[16]

This conclusion is clearly supported by the other amendments made by the European Union (Withdrawal Agreement) Act 2020 to the Northern Ireland Act 1998. As the Commissions argued, the new section 78C empowers the Human Rights Commission and the Equality Commission to bring judicial review proceedings in respect of an alleged breach or potential future breach of Article 2(1) of the Windsor Framework or to intervene in such proceedings. The new section 78D empowers those Commissions to assist persons who have brought proceedings in respect of an

[9] Case 12/86 *Demirel v Stadt Schwabisch Gmund* [1987] ECR 3719 ('*Demirel*') [14], in terms which the CJEU reiterated in Case C-240/09 *Lesoochranárske zoskupenie VLK v Ministerstvo životného prostredia Slovenskej republiky* [2012] QB 606, [44].

[10] *Dillon* (n 3) [113].

[11] ibid [114].

[12] ibid [116].

[13] ibid [116], emphasis added.

[14] ibid [116].

[15] ibid [117].

[16] ibid [118].

alleged breach or potential future breach of article 2(1) of the Windsor Framework. The Court drew on these provisions as 'evidence of the view of Parliament that article 2(1) is capable of giving rise to a directly enforceable right in certain circumstances'.[17]

In what circumstances, exactly, is set out in the fourth step of the Court's reasoning. The Court holds that the test may be met in either of two situations. First, where the EU discrimination Directives, as set out in Annex 1, are in issue. The Court holds that 'article 2(1) might operate in conjunction with a directly effective provision of one of the Annex 1 Directives so as to give rise to a directly effective obligation not to diminish such a right.'[18] Technically, this holding is *obiter*, since the Directives in Annex 1 had no application in the present case and were not relied on by the applicants, but it is nevertheless a clear indication of what the Court would be minded to do were that situation to arise. A second situation where Article 2 is viewed as capable of having direct effect is 'in conjunction with other EU instruments falling within the ambit of the rights listed with bullet points in paragraph 1 of the RSEO chapter, or within the ambit of paragraphs 11 or 12, if the *Demirel* requirements are satisfied in respect of the obligation imposed.[19] Whether these two situations are to be considered as giving rise to a similar analysis is considered subsequently. The Court concluded the discussion of the direct effect of Article 2(1) with a brief paragraph that essentially constitutes the Court's ratio decidendi on the issue.[20]

> While the provisions of paragraphs 1, 11, and 12 of the RESO chapter do not themselves have direct effect, article 2(1) of the Windsor Framework may be capable of having direct effect in conjunction with other EU instruments falling within the ambit of the RSEO chapter if the *Demirel* requirements are satisfied in respect of the obligation imposed.

Two situations that the Court identifies which satisfy those requirements are those set out in paragraph 118 of the judgment. A question that arises, however, is whether the two situations are *examples* of where the *Demirel* requirements are satisfied, or whether they constitute the only circumstances in which the Court considers the *Demirel* requirements could possibly be satisfied.

(b) Future Role of 'Civil Rights'

Beyond the two situations identified in paragraph 118, it appears that the Court was unwilling to countenance an argument that Article 2(1) could be read more broadly, in particular by using the 'civil rights' provision in paragraph 1, operating in conjunction

17 ibid [120].
18 ibid [118].
19 ibid [118].
20 ibid [125].

with other EU instruments falling within the ambit of civil rights, to produce direct effect. However, the status of 'civil rights' as an RSEO right which might ground a justiciable claim in much the same way as the 'bullet point' rights that follow it is not entirely clear.

Ruling out this use of 'civil rights' is supported by the Court's subsequent analysis of the role of the Charter of Fundamental Rights.[21] We shall consider the Court's treatment of the CFR in more detail below. For the purpose of determining the extent of the direct effect of Article 2(1), it is important to bear in mind that when the Court is considering the argument that the Charter is directly enforceable in domestic law because of Article 2(1), the Court considers whether the Charter rights could be said to have been 'set out' in the RSEO chapter. The Court continues,[22]

> The only provision in the RSEO chapter which could arguably 'set out' Charter rights in this appeal is the reference to 'civil rights' in paragraph 1. As pointed out above, this is expressed at a high level of generality and is accompanied by broad references to 'mutual respect' and 'religious liberties'. This very generalized phrase is not apt to set out specific, enforceable legal rights, including such rights as are set out in the Charter.

That appears to be a clear rejection of 'civil rights' as having any role in a justiciable claim more generally. However, in another part of the judgment, in which the Court rejects the applicants' arguments concerning the Victims' Directive, the Court arguably takes a somewhat different approach. One of the applicants' arguments in that context[23] was that certain rights in the Directive fell within the ambit of the RSEO chapter because of the reference to 'the civil rights … of everyone in the community' in paragraph 1 of the RSEO chapter. One might have expected, in light of the approach adopted by the Court when dealing with the Charter,[24] for the Court to have simply dismissed this argument on the ground that 'civil rights' could never play that role, but the Court takes the different approach of apparently assuming that 'civil rights' might play such a role but failed to do so *in this case*. In paragraph 131, the Court states that 'the provisions of the Victims Directive relied upon are not concerned with civil rights in the sense in which that term is employed in the first sentence of paragraph 1, where it appears to refer at a general level to civil and political rights, of which the rights which are then listed ('in particular') are specific examples.' Why the Court would consider it necessary (or even possible) to interpret 'civil rights' in this context is unclear if the term is necessarily non-justiciable.

Where that leaves the status of 'civil rights' in future litigation is uncertain and will, no doubt be the subject of future litigation. We appear to have several uncertainties

21 ibid [148].
22 ibid [148].
23 ibid [130].
24 ibid [148].

that need to be addressed: (i) the apparent tension between the approaches taken by the Court in paragraphs 131 and 148 is to be resolved, and (ii) the apparent ambiguity in the critically important paragraphs 118 and 125.

(c) Scope and Function of the 'Bullet Point' rights

One significant effect of the Court's approach to the direct effect of Article 2(1) is to focus attention on the 'bullet point' rights in paragraph 1 of RSEO. As we have seen, in future cases it will be necessary to establish that the alleged breach of Article 2(1) concerned rights that were 'within the ambit of the RSEO chapter'.[25] There are several dimensions to this that require attention.

First, the Court cannot have been ignorant of the significance of the phrase 'within the ambit of', given the Court's intimate and sustained engagement with the jurisprudence of the European Court of Human Rights, which uses the phrase to describe the relationship that must be established between Article 14 ECHR and the other ECHR substantive rights, in order for Article 14 to be engaged.[26] The Court will also have been aware that the precise meaning of 'within the ambit' in that context is notoriously ambiguous and it is likely that, as a result, further litigation can be expected as to its meaning in the context of Article 2(1).

Second, that issue aside, there is also the further question as to how the 'bullet point' rights themselves are to be interpreted. In this regard, the Court's brief analysis of these rights in paragraph 119 is likely to be poured over by legal advisers and subsequent courts alike. There are several aspects of paragraph 119 that are striking: the analysis of the bullet point rights is set in the historical context of the Belfast-Good Friday Agreement, which is seen by the Court as 'aimed at establishing peace in Northern Ireland after decades of sectarianism and civil conflict.' Second, the bullet point rights are to be seen within the context of the text of the Paragraph 1 RSEO, which, according to the Court, 'speaks at a high level of generality of civil rights and religious liberties against the background of what, in 1998, was a recent history of communal conflict.' Building on these two points, the Court concludes that,[27]

> The rights listed with bullet points are all concerned with ending sectarian conflict. These include freedom of political thought, freedom of religion, the right to pursue national and political aspirations, the right to seek constitutional change by peaceful and legitimate means, equal opportunities and freedom from sectarian harassment.

[25] ibid [125].
[26] See, eg, Lady Black in *R (Stott) v Secretary of State for Justice* [2018] UKSC 59, [2020] AC 51.
[27] *Dillon* (n 3) [119].

Technically, these observations are all obiter dicta since the applicants did not rely on any provision of EU law falling within the scope of the bullet point rights listed in paragraph 1 of the RSEO chapter, and they are, therefore, as the Court observed, 'clearly inapplicable to the matters in issue in these proceedings'. Nevertheless, obiter dicta by the Supreme Court are likely to be highly influential and must be taken seriously. What then are we to make of the Court's analysis?

Taken at face value, they appear to limit the scope of the bullet point rights quite significantly if all the rights are to be viewed solely through the lens of 'ending sectarian conflict'. So, for example, the bullet point right to equal opportunities, seen through this lens, would appear to apply only to the types of discrimination that are usually associated with religious and political discrimination. And while this understanding has a logic to it, in the sense that it is conceivable that such an approach might have been adopted by those negotiating the Agreement, it appears to fly in the face of the text of the bullet point rights themselves. Thus, the 'equal opportunities' provision explicitly provides: 'the right to equal opportunity in all social and economic activity, regardless of *class, creed, disability, gender or ethnicity*'. It is not at all clear why such an extended list of protected grounds would be included if the intention was simply to 'end[] sectarian conflict'. It is perhaps telling (and unfortunate) that the Court did not actually quote this provision in full.

It is also noteworthy that, in listing the bullet point rights in paragraph 119, the Court failed to list all the rights, in particular the 'the right of women to full and equal political participation'. Again, it is unclear how that provision fits the neat, but ultimately unpersuasive, conclusion that 'all' the bullet point rights 'are concerned with ending sectarian conflict.' Subsequent courts will be called on to engage in a somewhat more sophisticated and historically-informed analysis than the Supreme Court engaged in. In defence of the Court, the issue did not actually arise for decision and therefore did not, perhaps, receive the attention it deserved.[28] In light of all these concerns, it is uncertain how far it can be said that the Court intended that in future cases it would be a prerequisite for reliance on the bullet points that there is also a link to the resolution of the troubles.

(d) Litigation using Annex 1 Directives

There is a third issue that arises which relates to the Court's analysis in paragraph 118 of when Article 2(1) has direct effect. As set out above, the Court holds that one of these situations arises where the EU discrimination Directives, as set out in Annex 1, are in issue. The issue that arises here is how holding this relates to the bullet point

[28] The Court's attention was drawn to the only historical analysis of these provisions so far undertaken, Christopher McCrudden, 'The origins of "civil rights and religious liberties" in the Belfast–Good Friday Agreement' (2024) 75 NILQ 443, but the Court does not appear to have engaged with this analysis.

rights in Paragraph 1. Addressing this issue requires a close analysis of the Court's approach in paragraph 118. The way in which the Court puts its decision is as follows.[29]

> The six EU Directives listed in Annex 1 all relate to the prohibition of discrimination. Before us, it was common ground between the Secretary of State and the applicants that article 2(1) might operate in conjunction with a directly effective provision of one of the Annex 1 Directives so as to give rise to a directly effective obligation not to diminish such a right.

The precise issue that arises is whether, when reliance is placed on the Annex 1 Directives, engagement with the bullet point rights is also necessary. This may seem to be a trivial point. After all, one of the bullet point rights relates to the right to equal opportunities, and so even if an engagement with a bullet point right is required, don't all the Directives listed in Annex 1 fall clearly 'within the ambit of' that right? Unfortunately, however, that approach does not fully take on board the approach which we have seen the Court adopts to the analysis of the bullet point rights. If, the Court's analysis that all the bullet point rights have to be interpreted through the lens of them aiming to address 'sectarian conflict' stands, then that would significantly limit how far the Directives could be seen to be engaged by Article 2(1). If, on the other hand, there is no requirement to engage a specific bullet point right for the rights in the Annex 1 Directives to be protected from diminution without further reference to a bullet point right, the Court's analysis of the lens through which the bullet point rights have to be viewed is not relevant where reliance is placed on the Annex 1 Directives.

Unfortunately, the answer appears to depend on two separate aspects of the text of paragraph 118. The first textual point relates to 'such a right' in the quotation set out above. Does that refer to a right that derives from the Directives, or does it relate to a right as set out in one of the bullet points? The second textual point relates to the word 'also'. This is because the Court follows its analysis of direct effect in the Annex 1 context with the following: 'We *also* consider that article 2(1) may be capable of having direct effect in conjunction with other EU instruments falling within the ambit of the rights listed with bullet points in paragraph 1 of the RSEO chapter ...' (emphasis added). Does the insertion of the word 'also' in this context mean that we should consider the two examples of where direct effect applies are to be taken as effectively two examples of the same principle (that EU instruments are required to fall within the 'ambit' of a bullet point right)? Or is 'also' to be read as identifying a different type of situation, with the reference to the ambit of the bullet point rights being restricted to the second situation and not applying to the first?

[29] *Dillon* (n 3) [118].

This is another issue that, in time, will require further judicial consideration. What I have termed as the 'ratio' of the Court in deciding the direct effect issue[30] appears to point to the former, rather than the latter, conclusion. We have seen that the Court concludes the discussion of the direct effect of Article 2(1) as follows: '[A]rticle 2(1) of the Windsor Framework may be capable of having direct effect *in conjunction with other EU instruments falling within the ambit of the RSEO chapter* (. . .)'.[31] No distinction between the two situations identified in paragraph 118 appears to be being made, but I consider that the issue is arguable either way.

(e) The Role of the Charter of Fundamental Rights

Turning now to the Court's consideration of the role of the EU Charter of Fundamental Rights, we are faced with some difficulty in determining how the Court's analysis should be applied in subsequent cases.

Some elements of the Court's analysis are clear. The first is that the Court's ultimate decision that the Charter does not apply in this case is on the basis that the requirement that the Charter provisions are engaged only when a member state is 'implementing' EU law, has not been established by the applicants,[32] on the ground that merely establishing that measures addressing victims was an EU competence was not sufficient. This finding is specific to the facts of this case and, while important for the legacy context, provides little guidance for how the CFR is to be applied in other cases.

Although I think it is clear that the Court's ratio in the context of the Charter is thus limited, the Court does engage in quite a detailed analysis of the status of the Charter, even though it is not strictly necessary, and therefore its observations are strictly obiter, if (of course) highly persuasive. One of the key points that is clarified is that the Charter appears to continue to be relevant in the interpretation of other provisions of EU law. This was the approach adopted in the Court of Appeal, and the Supreme Court does not take any exception to the Court of Appeal's analysis in this respect. The Supreme Court is solely concerned with whether the CFR rights are what it terms as 'freestanding', as a result of Article 2(1).[33]

Unfortunately, the Court's observations on this key question are far from crystal clear, and subsequent litigation will be required for some of the key issues in the future application of the Charter to be determined. The unsatisfactory nature of the Court's approach is due to the Janus-like quality of the Court's judgment on the issue, looking two ways at the same time. Unfortunately, this results in the Court arguably contradicting itself. The starting point must be paragraph 145. The Court states that,[34]

30 ibid [125].
31 ibid [125], emphasis added.
32 ibid [157].
33 ibid [141], [145], [148].
34 ibid [145].

> [T]he retention in domestic law of the Charter was specifically excluded by section 5(4) of the 2018 Act, subject to relevant separation agreement law. However, the effect of the applicants' argument that freestanding reliance on Charter rights is permitted would be to significantly expand the application of the Charter. As the Secretary of State pointed out, the applicants' case means that:
>
> > "The limited language of article 2(1) [of the Windsor Framework]'s reference to the diminution of rights has indirectly [led] via a reading into the RSEO chapter of the [Belfast Agreement] of the entirety of the [Charter] (which did not exist at the time), a general and free-standing source of civil, political, economic and social rights accompanied by the most powerful remedial consequences known to domestic law (namely the disapplication of primary legislation of the sovereign Parliament)."
>
> This would surely require the clearest possible statutory language.

The impression that may be gained from this paragraph, if close attention is not paid to the rest of the judgment, is that the Court is here ruling out any 'freestanding' role for the CFR in the context of Article 2(1), and it is likely that some will seek to argue that this is, in fact, the implication of the Supreme Court's judgment. This is largely due to the way in which section 5 of the 2018 Act is discussed. As we can see from the quotation from the judgment, there is explicit citation only of section 5(4), which provides that 'The Charter of Fundamental Rights is not part of domestic law on or after IP completion day.'

Section 5(7) is only obliquely referenced ('subject to relevant separation agreement law') but remains otherwise unaddressed explicitly. Yet section 5(7), to which the Court's attention was drawn, is surely of critical importance, providing as it does that section 5(4) is 'subject to relevant separation agreement law', specifically the Withdrawal Agreement (incorporating the provisions of the Windsor Framework). Section 5, taken as a whole, therefore, merely states the problem, that is, what does the Windsor Framework require vis a vis the CFR. It is misleading to consider that it states a principle that the CFR is not part of domestic law which requires further statutory language in order to override that principle. Section 5 simply leaves the issue to the courts as to what Article 2(1) requires and does not give any guidance as to what the position of the CFR should be, even in principle.

It would, in my view, be a mistaken interpretation, for the reasons that follow, to consider the paragraph as indicating an intention to rule out any role for the CFR in the context of Article 2. That is not to deny, however, that paragraph 145 is deeply problematic and somewhat ill-drafted. Were paragraph 145 to be seen as ruling out any use of the CFR in the context of Article 2(1), it would be entirely inconsistent with the approach adopted by the Court in the remainder of the judgment. That is most clearly the case regarding the interpretative role of the CFR, but also more broadly. Read with care, the approach in the paragraphs that follow paragraph 145 results in the conclusion that CFR rights *are* capable, not only as having an interpretative role, but also of being considered as having significant direct implications in the context of Article 2(1).

To justify that conclusion, we can turn initially to paragraph 148. The Court initially considers the issue that we have seen is the Court's principal interpretative starting point of Article 2(1) WF, namely that 'article 2(1) applies to rights "as set out" in the RSEO chapter.' The Court continues: 'For the Charter to apply on a freestanding basis it is therefore necessary to identify how the rights mentioned in the Charter are so "set out".' We can pause at this point to observe that if the Court's conclusion were to have been to deny the CFR any 'freestanding' status, it would not have framed the issue in this way; it would have been entirely unnecessary to do so.

We shall see that what the Court means by 'freestanding' in this context is ambiguous. This Court's next move is to examine what, if any provisions of the RSEO, might be interpreted as 'setting out' Charter rights, concluding that,[35]

> The only provision in the RSEO chapter which could arguably 'set out' Charter rights *in this appeal* is the reference to 'civil rights' in paragraph 1. As pointed out above, this is expressed at a high level of generality and is accompanied by broad references to 'mutual respect' and 'religious liberties'. This very generalised phrase is not apt to set out specific, enforceable legal rights, including such rights as are set out in the Charter.

Specifying that the only provision that might ground Charter rights '*in this case*', again leaves open (intentionally, I suggest) the possibility that other RSEO specified rights (notably those in the bullet point rights) could arguably 'set out' Charter rights, and therefore provide the basis for Charter rights to apply on a 'freestanding' basis.

This interpretation of the Court's judgment up to this point is, I suggest, further strengthened by paragraph 157, which in essence sets out the Court's ratio for the non-application of the Charter in this case. Two aspects of that paragraph stand out. First, the conclusion is framed in terms that indicate the narrowness of the Court's conclusions regarding the Charter.[36]

> *In the present case*, article 2(1) of the Windsor Framework would only give rise to a situation 'governed by EU law' in so far as the RSEO chapter 'set out' directly effective EU law rights. For reasons given above, paras 1, 11, and 12 of the RSEO chapter do not set out any *relevant* directly effective rights, nor do they set out Charter rights. There was no 'implementation' of EU law so as to allow for the application of the Charter. We agree with the Court of Appeal that it is not sufficient that an EU competence may be engaged and that the Charter has no application unless

[35] ibid [118], emphasis added.
[36] ibid [157], emphasis added.

it is 'anchored' in a provision of EU law which is being implemented. It is not so anchored *in this case*.

The second noteworthy aspect of paragraph 157 relates to the apparently broad statement that 'para[] 1 ... of the RSEO chapter do[es] not set out any relevant directly effective rights, nor do they set out Charter rights', which only makes sense in the context of the judgment as a whole if the reference to 'para 1' is restricted to the 'civil rights' provision in paragraph 1 and is not a reference to the bullet point rights in paragraph 1, given that we have seen that the Court earlier allowed the possibility for the bullet point rights to ground directly effective rights. So too, here, the better conclusion is that the bullet point rights could be seen as grounding Charter rights.

Where does that leave future courts as regards Charter rights in the context of Article 2(1)? What the Court has rejected explicitly is any submission that 'a breach of a Charter right could breach Article 2(1) of the Windsor Framework independently'.[37] In holding thus, the word 'independently' is doing a significant amount of work and must be interpreted in light of the paragraphs that precede it. Perhaps the best way of viewing the Supreme Court's approach is to view Charter rights as somewhat equivalent in legal status to the Annex 1 Directives, in the sense that neither has a continuing status in UK law *as EU law* (unlike, for example, the provisions of EU law listed in Annex 2 of the Windsor Framework which are incorporated into UK law *as EU law*).

Rather, the Charter enters the picture in a different way: either indirectly as a set of interpretative principles, or directly, with the latter situation being the one that the Supreme Court primarily focuses on. According to the logic of the Court's judgment, Charter rights become relevant directly in the context of Article 2(1) where all three of the following conditions are satisfied: (a) where the Charter right operates within the ambit of a specified right in the RSEO chapter; (b) where the Charter right is 'anchored' to other directly effective provisions of EU law that operated within the ambit of a specified right in the RSEO chapter; and (c) where the Charter right itself would be directly effective in EU law. (In numerous cases, the CJEU has held that provisions of the Charter do indeed meet the conditions for direct effect, and it would appear that this jurisprudence must now be applied where CFR rights are directly in issue in the context of Article 2(1).)

Where all three conditions are satisfied, that Charter right cannot be diminished as a result of the UK leaving the EU, meaning that the UK is required to produce the same *result* as would have been the case prior to Brexit. In that context, a breach of a Charter right is not a breach Article 2(1) of the Windsor Framework 'independently', but it is of very considerable legal significance, and in practice courts will have to pay considerable attention to the Charter in Article 2(1) litigation.

[37] ibid [158].

This interpretation is consistent with, and helps us to understand, what the Supreme Court states in paragraph 158, in which it discusses what the Government was proposing to the ECHR and the NIHRC in its proposals concerning the Dedicated Mechanism in 2018. The Court says,[38]

> Finally, the Equality Commission relied upon the background to the Explainer document as supporting the applicants' cross-appeal. They contended that this showed that the United Kingdom Government contemplated that a breach of a Charter right could breach article 2(1) of the Windsor Framework independently. (. . .) [W]e do not consider that it supports the applicants' case. The references to reliance on Charter rights there made were in the context of other EU law rights. So, for example, in a proposal by the UK Government dated 18 September 2018 concerning the proposed remit of the 'dedicated mechanism' referred to in article 2(1) of the Windsor Framework and discussed at para 120 above, it is stated that it is only where the 'rights and principles underpinning the Charter exist elsewhere in directly applicable EU law, or EU law which has been implemented in domestic law, or in retained EU case law' that Charter rights may be relied upon. Further, in a letter of 13 November 2018 to the equality Commission and the Human Rights Commission, the Northern Ireland Office of the United Kingdom Government stated that '[the Charter] will not form any part of the 'no diminution' commitment directly'.

The interpretation of the judgment as regards the role of the Charter derives further support, I suggest, when we see what follows the quotation from the 18 September 2018 proposal set out in paragraph 158. Immediately following that sentence, the Proposal continues: 'This means that, to the extent that a substantive Charter right is relevant to a right in the Rights, Safeguards and Equality of Opportunity chapter of the Belfast Agreement, that right cannot be diminished as a result of the UK leaving the EU.'

The issue that then arises is the relationship between Charter rights and ECHR rights. In paragraph 147, the Court points to paragraph 2 of the RSEO chapter which requires that the ECHR 'be incorporated in the law of Northern Ireland', and the Court points out that this was 'achieved through the enactment in 1998, and commencement in 2000, of the Human Rights Act and its application to Northern Ireland.' The Court then further observes that 'There has been no diminution of those (non-EU law) rights.' But what if there had been? Would that affect the application of the Charter? No answer is provided and we must await further judicial consideration. This would, perhaps, have been one of the issues that would have arisen for determination if the Court had reached the issue of remedies, which it did not.[39]

[38] ibid [158].
[39] ibid [138].

(f) Use of Non-Statutory Materials: Status of the Explainer Document

In the context of how to consider the scope of remedies under Article 2(1), one significant question will be when disapplication of the offending domestic law is required. Submissions to the Supreme Court on this issue were detailed and lengthy. One of the sources of the argument from the applicants and the Commission interveners was the Explainer Document, which appears to show the Government's commitment that disapplication should take place in the same way as when EU law is breached by member states. As we have seen the Court did not consider the issue of remedies. The Court did, however, consider what materials may legitimately be placed before the Court, including the Explainer Document itself, and so it is worth considering this more limited question since it is likely to feature in important ways in future litigation, not least in considering the remedies issue.

The issue of the use of what are sometimes termed 'extraneous' materials has proven a significant issue before the Supreme Court in recent years. In the *Dillon* case, the Court very largely considers the issue in a very limited way,[40] namely in the context of deciding whether materials that had been presented to the Court on the background to the negotiations over what became the Explainer Document could be used as evidence, under the VCLT of subsequent practice of the parties that casts light on the meaning that should be given to Article 2(1). The Court concluded that it could not. The Court went further in also rejecting the use of the Explainer Document for this purpose as well.

It will be important in subsequent cases not to overinterpret this rejection of these materials in this context. In particular, it is important not to confuse the use of extraneous materials in order to interpret the provisions of an international agreement under the VCLT, with the use of extraneous materials for the purpose of interpreting domestic statutory provisions, where the VCLT's does not apply. Nothing in the judgment of the Court indicates a refusal to use the Explainer Document, or other extraneous materials, as evidence that is relevant for understanding the purpose of section 7A of the 2018 Act. The detailed examination of the VCLT's issue does not touch on the issue of how the Court's explicitly purposive interpretative approach should be evidenced. Unless the Court explicitly rejects the use of the Explainer Document in the latter context, future courts should be presented with the Explainer Document as evidence as to the Government's understanding of what it was attempting to achieve in section 7A including in the area of remedies, and indeed what Parliament's intention was in passing section 7A.

[40] ibid [121]–[124], [158].

4 Conclusion

This Postscript has examined the Supreme Court's judgment in the *Dillon* case, focusing specifically on how Article 2 of the Windsor Framework interacts with domestic law. Several broad conclusions are identified, including, notably, that the Court rejected what appeared to many to be the Government's attempts to make this provision substantially non-justiciable, with the Supreme Court now confirming that Article 2(1) can, indeed, be directly effective in the United Kingdom, as all previous Northern Ireland courts have done. Ultimately, while the judgment marks a defeat for the actual applicants in the case, it constitutes the recognition by the highest court in the land of the binding legal framework for future challenges to the diminution of rights in Northern Ireland after Brexit.

However, the analysis highlights a degree of uncertainty as to the future role of 'civil rights' and a restrictive judicial approach regarding the 'bullet point' rights in the RSEO chapter of the Belfast-Good Friday Agreement, which the Court appears to have narrowly linked to the historical goal of ending sectarian conflict. In that context, the unresolved interpretative weight to be accorded to the Government's Explainer Document, and other materials, is likely to feature. The Postscript has also explored the complex status of the EU Charter of Fundamental Rights, arguing that it remains relevant when anchored to other specific EU law obligations. Over time, further litigation will be required to clarify these and other uncertainties and ambiguities in the judgment, and the critically important, but unaddressed issue of the scope of remedies where a breach of Article 2(1) has occurred, but the Supreme Court's judgment is a significant step in the process of making Article 2(1) effective.

Index

For the benefit of digital users, indexed terms that span two pages (e.g., 52–53) may, on occasion, appear on only one of those pages.